The Letters of Samuel Beckett offers for the first time a comprehensive range of letters of one of the greatest literary figures of the twentieth century. This volume includes letters written between 1929 and 1940. It provides a vivid and personal view of Western Europe in the 1930s, marked by the gradual emergence, against his own hesitations and the indifference or hostility of others, of Beckett's unique voice and sensibility. Even in the tentativeness of the early writing, the letters show his care for his work as well as what he must share or relinquish to allow it to have a life beyond himself. Detailed introductions, translations, explanatory notes, profiles of major correspondents, chronologies, and other contextual information accompany the letters. For anyone interested in twentieth-century literature and theatre this edition offers not only a record of achievements but a powerful literary experience in itself.

Samuel Beckett to Mary Manning Howe, 13 December 1936
Harry Ransom Humanities Research Center,
The University of Texas at Austin

THE LETTERS
OF
SAMUEL BECKETT
Volume I: 1929–1940

Editors:
Martha Dow Fehsenfeld, Lois More Overbeck

Associate Editors:
George Craig, Dan Gunn

CAMBRIDGE
UNIVERSITY PRESS

CAMBRIDGE UNIVERSITY PRESS
Cambridge, New York, Melbourne, Madrid, Cape Town, Singapore, São Paulo,
Delhi, Dubai, Tokyo

Cambridge University Press
The Edinburgh Building, Cambridge CB2 8RU, UK

Published in the United States of America by Cambridge University Press, New York

www.cambridge.org
Information on this title: www.cambridge.org/9780521867931

First published 2009
Sixth printing 2010

Printed in the United Kingdom at the University Press, Cambridge

A catalogue record for this publication is available from the British Library

Library of Congress Cataloguing in Publication data
Beckett, Samuel, 1906–1989.
[Correspondence. Polyglot. Selections]
The letters of Samuel Beckett / editors, Martha Dow Fehsenfeld, Lois More Overbeck;
associate editors, George Craig, Dan Gunn.
p. cm.
Includes bibliographical references and index.
ISBN 978-0-521-86793-1
1. Beckett, Samuel, 1906–1989 – Correspondence.   2. Authors, Irish – 20th century –
Correspondence.   3. Authors, French – 20th century – Correspondence.   I. Fehsenfeld,
Martha Dow.   II. Overbeck, Lois More.   III. Craig, George, 1931–   IV. Gunn, Dan.   V. Title.
PR6003.E282Z48   2009
848′.91409–dc22
[B]
2008025530

ISBN 978-0-521-86793-1 hardback

Major support from The National Endowment for the Humanities (1991–1997) has
facilitated the preparation of this Edition. Any views, findings, or conclusions
expressed in this publication do not necessarily reflect those of the National
Endowment for the Humanities.

To Samuel Beckett who began "it all."

MARTHA FEHSENFELD

To Kristen, Andrew, and Jonathan, whose years have been spent
with this edition, deep appreciation for their forbearance, humor,
and regard, and especially for the pleasure of their company in this
as in so much else. To James Overbeck, who endured, with gratitude
for his loving advice and constant support.

LOIS OVERBECK

To Kate Craig, for her unfailing support and sense of the appropriate.

GEORGE CRAIG

To George Craig, my teacher for thirty years, from whom I am learning
still; and in memory of Catharine Carver, the very best of editors.

DAN GUNN

CONTENTS

ILLUSTRATIONS

GENERAL INTRODUCTION

My unique relation with my work – and it is a tenuous one – is the making relation. I am with it a little in the dark and fumbling of making, as long as that lasts, then no more. I have no light to throw on it myself and it seems a stranger in the light that others throw.[1]

Samuel Beckett was one of the great literary correspondents of the twentieth century, perhaps of any century. His letters, which stretch over a period of sixty years from 1929 to 1989, are not only numerous (more than 15,000 have been found and transcribed by the editors) but of an extraordinary range and intensity. They demonstrate his numerous commitments: to reading in a systematic way the classics as well as the literatures of several cultures; to training himself in music and the visual arts; to learning languages, becoming fluent in at least five and familiar with many more; to keeping up with a broad range of acquaintances, friends, and professional associates; to answering in polite and timely fashion practically every letter that was addressed to him, even when he became famous and the inquiries grew in number; to *writing*, of course – criticism, fiction, poetry, drama; and perhaps more surprisingly, a commitment to getting published and to seeing his dramatic work realized on stage. The letters also show the author's endeavor to lead the life that would make all these commitments realizable.

In view of how abruptly and rapidly letter writing has declined in recent decades – a decline that makes it hard to predict a great twenty-first-century literary correspondence – it may be important to state that Beckett answered his own mail. There are a few exceptions to this general rule: in the late 1940s Suzanne Deschevaux-Dumesnil represented his interests in early negotiations with Les Editions de Minuit; Beckett's French publisher Jérôme Lindon drafted some letters concerning legal or business matters for his signature; for a short time in the late 1960s A. J. Leventhal assisted him; and later, when ill health and eye problems made writing difficult, he jotted notes for the replies that he wished Les Editions de Minuit to write on his behalf.

While Beckett complained of the onerousness of writing, he answered his "mountains of mail" in a scrupulous manner. His letters were composed on various typewriters but more often in a longhand that became notorious for its difficulty, though when he took pity on the postman it could be quite readable. Ink blotches are relatively few, but pens and pencils differ widely in their legibility. One manuscript specialist proffered what was for the editors the less-than-encouraging opinion that Beckett had the worst handwriting of any twentieth-century author. The letters themselves provide ironic commentary: "Don't suppose you can read this but can't face the machine."[2] Typed letters might promise to be a transcriber's boon, but in fact Beckett often wore a ribbon to shreds; in their amendments and corrections, typewritten letters often show more changes of mind and expression than do handwritten ones. Beckett also availed himself of any letterhead or paper at hand: tearing a page from a notebook, using the back of an invitation, writing out poems on an envelope or a match book.

The Letters of Samuel Beckett is a selected rather than a complete edition of the letters owing principally to three factors: the terms of Beckett's authorization; the impossibility, so near in time to his death in 1989, of fixing the corpus definitively; and the practical difficulties of publishing in print form what would require more than a score of volumes to present *in extenso*. The four volumes of selected letters will present about 2,500 letters with another 5,000 quoted in the annotations. Until now, Beckett enthusiasts have had only one volume dedicated to Samuel Beckett's correspondence, and, as in the other publications that include letters, the letters here were addressed to a single recipient.[3] *The Letters of Samuel Beckett* will, therefore, be the first to integrate letters to the full range of recipients and to sample them over sixty years of Beckett's life and work.

Beckett's letters are addressed to intimates over decades of friendship, to occasional collaborators, to scholars, critics, students, and readers. The balance varies considerably. In Volumes I and II, up to the point where Beckett achieves public recognition – which corresponds roughly to the success of *En attendant Godot (Warten auf Godot, Waiting for Godot)* – the letters are predominantly to close friends and associates (including publishers), among whom are Thomas McGreevy, George Reavey, Mary Manning Howe, Charles Prentice, Morris Sinclair, Georges Duthuit, Mania Péron, Jérôme Lindon, Barney Rosset, and Jacoba van Velde. In Volumes III and IV are letters from the last three decades of Beckett's life, a time when his writing achieves worldwide attention, marked by the award of the Nobel Prize for Literature in 1969. The long exchanges of letters with friends continue, and by now these include his publishers Siegfried Unseld, John Calder, and Charles Monteith, as well as translators, directors, actors, producers, and other colleagues (Alan Schneider, Donald McWhinnie, Jack MacGowran, Barbara Bray, Ruby Cohn, Walter Asmus, Christian Ludvigsen, and Antoni Libera, among them). There are numerous letters to writers and aspiring writers.

By the end of his life, Beckett's work had been translated into more than fifty languages. His enduring concern with translation is evident in correspondence with his translators. Whether explaining a local reference or advising them to find an equivalent in their own literature, Beckett worked closely with those whose languages he knew and willingly responded to the questions of translators whose languages were unfamiliar to him.

HISTORY OF THE EDITION

Those who, from their reading of his work or of the several biographies of him, have become used to thinking of Samuel Beckett as an exceptionally private man may be surprised at learning that in February 1985 Beckett authorized an edition of his letters, to be gathered during his lifetime and published following his death. Beckett's earlier antipathy toward publication of his letters, his general refusal to grant interviews, and his avowed "inability" to talk about his own writing, make it all the more welcome that he specifically wished to see published his letters bearing on the work.

The complexities of language, the dispersal of letters, and the complications of ownership, as well as negotiations with publishers and The Estate of Samuel Beckett have all contributed to delaying publication of the letters, as the history of the edition will make clear.

In February 1985 Beckett appointed his long-time friend and American publisher Barney Rosset (then President of Grove Press) as

General Editor of the letters, Martha Dow Fehsenfeld as Editor, and he confirmed Lois More Overbeck as Associate Editor. Beckett had first become acquainted with Fehsenfeld in 1976 while she was preparing *Beckett in the Theatre* (1988, co-authored with Dougald McMillan). Following his request that she take charge of editing his correspondence, he gave her his written authorization "to consult my letters and take copies, in view of eventual publication, of such passages as are relevant to her research." He added, "This permission applies to all my letters, to whomsoever addressed and wheresoever preserved."[4] Beckett made it clear that he himself had no wish to direct the edition, writing for example to Carlton Lake at the Harry Ransom Humanities Research Center, The University of Texas at Austin, that queries regarding the collecting and editing of his letters should not be addressed to him, since "I will not personally be responsible in any way for their selection and editing."[5]

Notwithstanding his reluctance to direct the enterprise of gathering and publishing his letters, Beckett did have many conversations with Fehsenfeld about the edition he envisaged. He enjoined the editors not merely to collect the letters but to establish their context.

Paris
18-3-85

Dear Martha,
    Thanks for yrs of Feb 20.
    I do have confidence in you & know that I can rely on you to edit my correspondence in the sense agreed on with Barney, i.e. its reduction to those passages only having bearing on my work.
    It would be a most difficult job and I am relieved at the thought of its being in such devoted and capable hands as yours.
    I hope we may meet in Paris before too long & talk it over.
    Yours ever,
        Sam[6]

Realizing the scale of the project, Beckett suggested to Martha Fehsenfeld that she enlist an assistant, whereupon she chose Lois More Overbeck, then Editor of *The Beckett Circle* and a scholar of modern drama whose studies of Beckett were based on manuscript research, and with whom she had previously worked on several extended projects. In 1989, in order to create a shorter document of authorization that could be shared with foundations, archives, and recipients of letters, a memorandum of agreement was signed by Samuel Beckett, Barney Rosset, and the editors. It stated: "The purpose of this project is to establish an authorized text of Mr. Beckett's correspondence, to be published internationally after the author's death, on terms and by publishers subject to Mr. Beckett's approval."[7] This agreement was countersigned by Beckett's nephew Edward Beckett after his uncle's death, with the addendum, "I fully support the edition of the correspondence of Samuel Beckett under the terms and conditions as agreed and signed to above by the author."[8]

Shortly after the contract was signed (along with that for Beckett's "production notebooks") in March 1985, Grove Press was sold to Weidenfeld and Getty; Barney Rosset was appointed Chief Executive Officer of Grove Press within the new company; it was a post he expected to hold for at least five years. However, in June 1986 Rosset was released from this position and began legal action against Weidenfeld and Getty for breach of contract. Although the editors continued their research, only when this matter was settled could they be confident that the newly constituted Grove Press "owned" the original contract and, therefore, that they could seek funding to permit the work on the edition to go forward. In 1993 Grove Press merged with Atlantic Monthly Press to become Grove/Atlantic Inc.

The corpus of the letters grew rapidly, far beyond initial expectations; by 1996 the editors realized that a four-volume edition was necessary. Grove/Atlantic affirmed that it would be willing to consider reassigning the rights for publication of a scholarly edition of the letters, upon approval of The Estate of Samuel Beckett. Cambridge University Press, long known for its publication of literary letters, expressed interest, and its Director of Humanities, Andrew Brown, entered into formal negotiations with The Estate of Samuel Beckett.

Negotiations between Cambridge University Press and The Estate of Samuel Beckett began in early 1999, chiefly through Beckett's Literary Executor, the owner and publisher of Les Editions de Minuit, Jérôme Lindon. Deliberations proved complex, not least because of radically differing interpretations of what Samuel Beckett, now dead ten years, would have wished from an edition "only having bearing on my work." The issue was whether this implied that the letters should be restricted to those in which there was specific mention of individual works or of his *oeuvre* (the Lindon view). The view of the editors was and remains that the letters themselves are important acts of writing, and signal Beckett's relation to other writers and artists. When Jérôme Lindon died, in April 2001, no contract had been agreed on, although Cambridge University Press had made clear its intention to publish only Beckett's *literary* correspondence. The position of Literary Executor passed to Edward Beckett, with whose support, in September 2003, the original contract which named Barney Rosset as General Editor was released by Rosset and reassigned by Grove/Atlantic to Cambridge University Press. Protracted discussion was still necessary before a formal contract was eventually signed among the various parties in November 2005.

During the years of these complex negotiations the editors continued to work on the task of preparing the corpus, and as they did so they expanded the editorial team. Both Richard Ellmann, Editor of the *Letters of James Joyce*, and John Kelly, General Editor of *The Collected Letters of W. B. Yeats*, urged the editors to seek the assistance of the distinguished editor Catharine Carver. She agreed to guide the editors in establishing the principles for the edition and offered creative editorial solutions to the many issues raised by the letters of Samuel Beckett. Knowing that her health would place limits on her participation, Catharine Carver introduced the editors to her friend Dan Gunn, Professor of Comparative Literature and English at The American University of Paris. In turn, he could think of no one better prepared to be French translator for the edition than George Craig, who had been his own mentor at the University of Sussex. As the French translator of the edition, Irish-born George Craig brings unusual qualifications to bear, having followed Beckett's own academic pathway, from Trinity College Dublin to the Ecole Normale Supérieure in Paris. Later, responsibility for German translations for the edition was taken on by Viola Westbrook of Emory University, a native German speaker and a specialist in linguistic pedagogy, who also had a serendipitous tie to Samuel Beckett in that her mother Ilse Schneider had known Beckett when he was in Hamburg in 1936.

As the project developed, it became evident that it would be best served by affiliation with a research university. At the urging of Irish literary scholar and editor Ann Saddlemyer, together with the support of

Ronald Schuchard and Alice Benston (both of Emory University), the Correspondence of Samuel Beckett found its academic home in the Graduate School of Emory University in 1990. Emory's generous support provided space and basic funding for research; its library and faculty (from Art History to Ophthalmology, from Physics to Classics) provided a rich intellectual base for what rapidly became a worldwide endeavor. The graduate fellows who worked with the editors at Emory and in libraries abroad contributed their scholarship, insight, and energy; Emory undergraduates helped marshal the books, paper, and electronic files of the edition. Emory University contributed in-kind support for successive grants from the National Endowment for the Humanities and the Florence Gould Foundation. The Gould Foundation award for research in French and American archives also made it possible for The American University of Paris (AUP) to serve as a Paris center for the edition. Students there collaborated in the French research as interns with the edition; they pursued queries in French libraries and, thanks to the international nature of the AUP student population, offered their further help in Germany, Greece, and England.

As the "Acknowledgments" indicate, the editors have received many grants for research in specific libraries and archives. What cannot be shown in a mere listing of names is how archivists and librarians from many institutions have become valued colleagues. Beckett scholars have been generous in sharing their work and papers with the edition. The small measure of acknowledgment afforded in print cannot begin to indicate the contribution in expertise and encouragement that the very large unofficial "team" has made to the edition.

Edward Beckett, as representative of The Estate of Samuel Beckett, has been a working partner in the preparation of this edition. He has joined editorial meetings and has been a ready negotiator at challenging junctures. Within the limitations placed on the edition by Samuel Beckett himself, he has responded generously where there was disagreement over what counts as "having bearing on the work."

LOCATING AND TRANSCRIBING
THE LETTERS

When Samuel Beckett met the editors during the summer of 1986, he said simply, "You will get round and see these people, won't you."

These people were, of course, his correspondents. For Beckett, letters first of all represented a means of staying in touch; they were part of a living and often a life-long relationship. In order to discover and comprehend the common ground that letters both indicated and cultivated, the editors took Beckett's advice to "get round," and wherever possible met the persons with whom he had corresponded. Beckett's family, friends, and colleagues have been helpful and supportive, and in this they reflect the respect and affection they felt for the man they knew as "Sam."

The editorial project is known as "The Correspondence of Samuel Beckett," even though its publication is entitled *The Letters of Samuel Beckett*. Both sides of the conversation between letter writers needed to be heard, although few recipients had kept either letters received or copies of letters sent during the early years of correspondence. In order to discern the context of relationships and issues in the correspondence, the editors interviewed recipients, their families, and their colleagues; they consulted many archival collections well beyond those containing Beckett's letters, together with biographies, bibliographies, editions of letters, newspapers, and journals. Beckett's letters bear upon current events as well as on the broader reaches of history, literature, art, music, philosophy, psychology, linguistics, medicine, economics, philology, sport, and even meteorology. These all became indispensable fields of reference.

Samuel Beckett suggested persons whom the editors should approach, wrote cards of introduction, and made contacts on behalf of the editors. Even when he wrote directly to affirm his permission, these personal missives were occasionally challenged: "That never is Sam Beckett's handwriting," said one correspondent, "I can read every word." Beckett's letters to Thomas McGreevy (which form the backbone of the first volume of the edition, as they do of the several biographies for the period of the 1930s) were in private hands in 1985, but Beckett agreed that the editors should consult them, saying: "I talk a lot about my work in them." These letters produced a core for further research, as other collections did for the post-war period, particularly the letters to Georges Duthuit, Mania Péron, Jacoba van Velde, and Jérôme Lindon. For Volumes III and IV, letters to publishers, translators, directors, and old friends offered comparable starting points from which paths of research emerged.

The editors first consulted Beckett collections in public archives such as the Harry Ransom Humanities Research Center in Austin, the Beckett International Foundation at Reading University in England, and the manuscript reading room above the Long Room of the Library of Trinity College Dublin. By reading widely in corollary collections as well, the editors established a growing list of persons known to have corresponded with Samuel Beckett. Next, the editors arranged to consult corporate collections, including a publisher's archive kept in boxes under the stairs and an agent's collection brought from a riverside warehouse. The editors also pursued private collections, where it was not uncommon to find Beckett's letters mingled with a lifetime's accumulation of papers and books; to sort through these materials took care and time. Increasingly over the years since the project began in 1985, collections have shifted from private ownership to archives – sometimes as gifts, sometimes through a series of sales via auction houses and dealers. Often, transition has delayed access.

Whenever possible, the editors met Beckett's correspondents; if the individuals had died, the editors contacted family members and associates, and examined archives that related to their lives and work. These conversations led to other individuals within a particular circle of friends or clarified the roles played by the staff members in a publishing house or illumined Beckett's work with a theatrical production team. This both widened an understanding of the context of the letters and provided awareness of relationships between people and of differences between cultures: Dublin was as unlike Paris in the 1930s as Berlin in 1936 was unlike Berlin in 1975.

"Reading" the letters was a process involving several steps. Whenever possible, the editors first consulted the letters on location, whether in an archive or at someone's dining-room table. Letters were transcribed, both on site and (with the help of photocopies) in the project's office; they were compared as necessary with letters and documents from further collections. Additional research was done to complete partial titles or confirm a date or verify a name. The final step was to verify transcriptions against the originals.

Because each recipient's letters from Beckett embody an evolving and sometimes decades-long relationship, the editors transcribed collections from beginning to end, consulting corollary correspondences and investigating related publications. This was hardly a neatly compartmentalized process since archives and people were seldom in a single locale, and research was done for several collections when these were held in a common archive. In the case of business archives, the editors were greatly helped by those familiar with the procedures of a publisher or theatrical agent or the artistic processes of a production group. Judith Schmidt Douw assisted with the Grove Press archives at the University of Syracuse; Leah Schmidt helped with the London archive of Curtis Brown (the agents representing Beckett's theatrical work in English), providing context for the history of the firm's work on behalf of Beckett's texts. Stefani Hunzinger and Connie Ricono, theatrical agents representing Beckett's work in Germany and Italy respectively, offered insight into theatre management in their countries; Reinhard Müller-Freienfels, cameraman Jim Lewis, and soundstage engineer Konrad Körte, who had collaborated with Beckett on the realization of his tele-vision plays at Süddeutscher Rundfunk, helped the editors understand that process.

When a critical mass of individual collections had been prepared, all the letters were organized into a single chronological file. The merged files filled in details and offered new associations. More importantly, this overview of the whole collection, together with the chronicle of the individual collections of letters, made it possible to adjudicate propor-tion and balance in the subsequent process of selecting letters for publication. While it had been assumed that the letters themselves would suggest narrative lines, what also emerged was a sense of the widely varying voices of the writer. Letters written on the same day to different persons might present similar information, but to very differ-ent effect. Sometimes the passage of time altered points of view, as when a new idea or a particular production problem led Beckett to reconsider how a play might be enacted.

Viewing the letters from beginning to end made clear the scale of the editorial task. This supposedly "withdrawn" and "taciturn" writer was engaged in voluminous correspondences: two hundred letters to one individual, three hundred to another, over six hundred to another.

PRINCIPLES OF SELECTION

The four volumes of *The Letters of Samuel Beckett* will publish approxi-mately 2,500 letters in full, with as many as 5,000 others cited in the annotations. As mentioned above, Beckett himself supplied the first principle of selection, when he gave permission to publish "those passages only having bearing on my work."

Selection is, inevitably, an act of interpretation. The explicit goal has been to strike a balance between the unique and the representative, while making available as many letters as possible that are pertinent to Beckett's writing. The editors' first step was to establish the corpus in order to draw from the largest possible sense of the whole. As letters continued to appear or to be discovered, these inevitably tested and altered the editors' frame and perspective. Certain letters presented themselves as obvious candidates for inclusion, no matter what the size or scope of the individual collection; others fluctuated in the context of surrounding letters. It was important that the scope and diversity of the letters be registered: simple acknowledgments, precise instructions to a publisher, rights negotiations, experiments with regard to production issues, hesitant venturings, extended aesthetic discussions, and thoughtful gestures of friendship. The selected edition needed to give space to letters that were remarkable in tone or content, and it needed to have breadth and nuance. The editors were concerned that their own interests should not dictate this scope; indeed, the diversity of their specialties helped ensure that the dialogue of selection was a lively and balanced one.

Principles of inclusion were formed and tested, then re-formed, re-tested, and re-applied. Among the central questions were: Does the letter record a signal event in Beckett's working life? Does the letter reveal Beckett as a writer? Does it represent the working relationships that he had with colleagues? Does it offer glimpses of Beckett's reading, thinking, and valuing? Does it show his responses to art and music? Subtending all these questions: Does the letter illuminate the *oeuvre*?

Everywhere there were choices to be made. A great many postcards were written when Beckett was away on holiday, and many letters confirm receipt of books or newspaper cuttings. Most of Beckett's correspondents in the later years received a small correspondence card written to arrange, say, an eleven o'clock coffee at the Petit Café Français de l'Hôtel PLM on the Boulevard St. Jacques; some correspondents received many such cards. A choice among similar letters and cards was determined, in part, by the contribution each could make to the overall narrative. Did the particular card or letter establish or show a continuing working relationship? Did it fill a gap in time or explain a change of location? Did it lead to further communication that became important to Beckett's work?

The line between the life and the work is not easy to distinguish. What may appear entirely personal in a particular letter may turn up, months or years later, practically unchanged, in a published work. What may appear as markedly literary has often emerged from an intimate, lived sense of connection or dislocation.

The editors wished to present letters in their entirety, annotated with portions of other letters Beckett wrote. They had to accept, however, that any edition that deals with living contemporaries and their imme-diate families must respect personal privacy and public reputation. The editors' views have not always coincided with those of The Estate of Samuel Beckett, particularly when the Literary Executor was Jérôme Lindon who understood Beckett's "work" to mean only the published *oeuvre*. When Edward Beckett became Literary Executor, he largely agreed with the editors' insistence that letters themselves are impor-tant acts of writing, that "work" included jettisoned as well as pub-lished writing, and that Beckett's reading, and his interests in art and music, as well as his relation to other writers, musicians, and artists, were all significant to the literary work.

The editors believe, especially because the several biographies of Beckett make liberal use of the letters in quotation or paraphrase, that there remains very little reason to exclude a letter, or part of a letter, because of what Beckett says about himself. To take one exam-ple, it is the editors' view that Beckett's frequent, at times almost obsessive, discussion of his health problems – his feet, his heart palpi-tations, his boils and cysts – is of direct relevance to the work; with this The Estate of Samuel Beckett has disagreed.

Rather than exclude a letter because it speaks of an individual's difficulties, or includes repetition of mere gossip (here considered the relaying of the comments of a third party), or touches on matters judged too intimate, the editors have followed a policy of *inclusion*, publishing letters relevant to Beckett the writer. Although doing so has required some ellipses, the editors have tried to limit these. Every letter included in the edition is cited with its current ownership, and those in archives can be consulted in full.

LANGUAGES

Beckett wrote letters primarily in English (65 percent), and also in French (30 percent), and German (5 percent). The choice of language may have been determined by the first language of his recipient or by a language they had in common, or sometimes by other factors, such as when he writes to McGreevy in French to safeguard the privacy of their exchanges, or when he wishes to play. The richness of his language and syntax, as well as Irish turns of phrase, occasional Gallicisms, and multilingual puns, his knowledge of several languages and his willingness to mix them, his etymological curiosity and his immense vocabulary – all these as well as many other features present challenges not faced by editors working on a writer more solidly anchored in a single tradition or time.

PRESENTATION

Beckett's letters themselves have guided the formation of the editorial principles. The editors' goal has been to let the letters speak for themselves wherever possible, their preference being for a minimum of intrusion. The letters are presented as written, preserving Beckett's habits and idiosyncrasies. Letters are presented as *clear copy*, reflecting the changes that Beckett made as or after he wrote them, that is to say, the letter as it was received by its recipient. If Beckett canceled a word and inserted a phrase, his insertion is included; if Beckett corrected his spelling, the corrected word is shown. Other than obvious typographical errors such as overtypes and extra spaces, there are no silent emendations. Editorial emendations made to clarify ambiguity are presented within square brackets (preceded by a question mark if a reading is doubtful) to signal that these are not Beckett's words. Letters are presented in their original language; translation into English follows; words or phrases from languages other than the dominant one of the letter are translated in the notes.

Each letter is prefaced by the name of the recipient and the place to which the letter was written (if known), since Beckett seldom includes the recipient's name and address in the body of his letters. The date and the place of writing are given as written. Beckett's signature is recorded as written. Postscripts are placed following the signature; their placement in the original is noted, if it differs from what appears.

A bibliographical note follows each letter, presenting a description of the document, indicating whether autograph or typed, whether signed or initialed, whether postcard or lettercard; this includes the number of leaves and sides of the letter. It also records any notations on the letter in another hand or damage to the document that affects legibility. This note indicates if the letter is written on letterhead or if a card bears the imprint of Beckett's name; it records the image in the case of a picture postcard. Also included are the details of sending and the envelope, if one exists: the addressee and address, the postmark, and any other notations, even in another hand, such as forwarding instructions. Finally, the note records the ownership or repository of the letter.

This information is followed, where required, by a discussion of dating. Beckett occasionally misdates letters, especially at the beginning of a new year. In a correspondence that follows a personal meeting or in which letters are exchanged with rapidity, as for example in that with Georges Duthuit, only the time of day or the day of the week may be given. Any dating supplied editorially is given within square brackets, with doubtful dating noted; occasionally the dating supplied can only suggest a date range.

ANNOTATION

During early conversations concerning the edition, Beckett told the editors, "Please, no commentary." The editors rejoined: "Not commentary, but there must be context." And to this he readily agreed.

The inevitable questions (Who? What? When? Where? Why?) led the editors into sometimes arcane areas of research, such as menus and timetables, playbills and weather reports, exchange rates and sports results. A recipient's letters to Beckett were of course the most helpful resource, when they were available. When they were not, the recipients and their associates were usually informative and ready to suggest further avenues of research. Often, other Beckett letters provided necessary information; whenever possible, these are used in the notes. When need arose to clarify an issue not addressed by published sources, specialists and scholars in many fields were consulted. In shaping the annotations, the editors wanted to open future research, not limit it, keeping in mind that future generations of readers and scholars would ask new questions of these letters.

There are several views which may be taken of notes in an edition of letters, ranging from what could be called the "maximalist" approach, employed for example in *The Collected Letters of W. B. Yeats* under the General Editorship of John Kelly, to the "minimalist" approach favored by Richard Ellmann in his edition of the *Letters of James Joyce*. Both approaches have their virtues. The former helps the inquiring reader to understand the context and the often obscure references, but risks distracting attention from the letters themselves. The latter keeps the focus on the principal object, but risks leaving the reader with many unanswered questions. This is a selected rather than a complete edition of the letters, annotated whenever possible by other letters written by Beckett. The editors have tended toward the "minimalist" approach to annotation, although, because of the very complex nature of the material, at times it may not seem so. The governing principle is that what is indispensable to the understanding of the letter be noted; however, with a writer as learned, as multi-lingual, and as well versed in the history of literature, art, and music as Beckett was, the quantity of what may be indispensable is often dauntingly extensive.

Any annotation makes assumptions about the level of general and specialized knowledge that readers might be expected to have, as well as about the research tools to which readers might reasonably be expected to have ready access. While the readers who may be familiar with the 1930s or even the 1950s have been decreasing in number, the quantity of readers has been growing who have almost instant access, through internet search engines, to a fund of sources, such as digitalized out-of-print texts, electronic catalogues of museum collections, and searchable text bases. The present edition seeks to be a scholarly edition of record, and it presumes levels of cultivation that this implies, while presuming this unevenly: given that readers of Beckett are more likely to be well versed in literature than in the visual arts, more is taken for granted in literary arenas than in the domains of art or music, or indeed those of chess or mathematics or television production, or the myriad other fields in which Beckett invested himself.

Annotations immediately follow the letter, its bibliographical note, and its translation; because the notes apply to both the letter and its translation, endnotes have been preferred to footnotes. The notes seek to identify the persons, places, events, and other references in letters. Often they point to sources for further detail, such as Beckett's own notebooks, various editions of his works, and his reading, but allusions to parallel passages or echoes in Beckett's works are not supplied because these would be too numerous. When possible, annotations draw upon other documents and letters to, from, and about Beckett. Sources of quotations are cited within the note, including location information for unpublished materials. At the end of each volume there is a bibliography of published works cited.

The initial identification of a person generally includes the full name, followed by any nickname or pseudonym, dates of birth and death, and a brief note on his or her career or activity at the time of first reference; any dubious information is preceded by a question mark. Subsequent reference will not repeat this information, but may expand on it as an individual changes name, role, or occupation; readers who do not read sequentially should use the index for the location of this information. Short biographies of recipients and other persons as well as brief accounts of publications and institutions referred to with some frequency in the letters can be found in the appendix, "Profiles." Fuller detail concerning editorial practice, including abbreviations, notations, idiosyncrasies of Beckett's usage, as well as a discussion of the editorial principles of translation, are presented later in the introductory matter. A chronology for each year provides an overview and precedes the letters for each year.

THE FOUR VOLUMES

The original contract for the edition called for three volumes of letters, but the quantity of the sixty years of correspondence quickly made four volumes more practical. The divisions between the volumes presented themselves rather naturally.

Volume I (1929–1940) begins with a letter written from Germany to James Joyce in Paris; it ends with a letter to Marthe Arnaud, the companion of Bram van Velde, written as the Nazis were about to occupy Paris. In the eleven years represented in Volume I, Beckett explores a world beyond Ireland: he is on the move, from his post at the Ecole Normale Supérieure to his lectureship at Trinity College Dublin, from his alternating periods of residence in London and Dublin between 1933 and 1937 to his travels through Germany in late 1936 and early 1937. Although Beckett has settled in Paris by the end of 1937, Ireland is never entirely left behind.

In the early years, Beckett is imagining a literary life even while he proclaims his disqualification from it. Thomas McGreevy is the principal sounding-board during this period, while others provide a more or less perceptive and responsive audience: George Reavey, Arland Ussher, Edward Titus, Samuel Putnam, Eugene and Maria Jolas, James Joyce, Jack B. Yeats, Charles Prentice, Nuala Costello, Mary Manning Howe, Brian Coffey, to name but the most significant figures. The writing of letters constitutes for Beckett both a warming-up exercise and an end in itself, an act of writing often as exciting as anything he is composing with a view to publication. Although some of his writing from this period remains unpublished, Beckett's *Proust, Echo's Bones and Other Precipitates, More Pricks than Kicks*, and the novel *Murphy* appear in print, as do poems, essays, and stories in Dublin, London, and Paris journals.

During the War years, Beckett served in the French Resistance and avoided capture by the Gestapo by escaping to Roussillon in Unoccupied France. While there were communications during this period, they were official telegrams transmissible only to and through the Irish Legation in Vichy – the barest lines telegraphed on behalf of Beckett to his family about health or money, with no mention of his work.

Volume II (1945–1956) opens in the aftermath of World War II, when Beckett is visiting Ireland before his return to France in 1945 as a member of an Irish Red Cross field hospital team. In the twelve years represented in this volume Beckett produces the work for which he is best known – a period, then, of unprecedentedly intense literary activity, but also a period of sometimes frenetic letter-writing. By the end of this time, *En attendant Godot* has been translated and performed in France and Germany (1953), England and Ireland (1955), as well as the United States (1956), and Beckett's reputation is secure. During this period, Beckett begins to write seriously in French, most notably the three novels, *Molloy, Malone meurt*, and *L'Innommable*, and the plays *Eleutheria* and *En attendant Godot*. This period also sees Beckett form his most explicit and fully articulate aesthetic, which grows in no small measure out of his long and impassioned correspondence with Georges Duthuit, art historian and Editor of the post-war version of the journal *Transition*. During this period, and not without difficulty, Beckett forges permanent ties with publishers and agents who will represent his work for the rest of his creative life: Les Editions de Minuit in France, Grove Press in New York, John Calder and Faber and Faber in London, Fischer Verlag and Suhrkamp in Germany.

Although Beckett resigned himself to being "written out" by 1957, the letters of Volume III record a period marked by experiment. During this time, Beckett writes for radio and film, creates new possibilities for drama in *Fin de partie*, *Krapp's Last Tape*, and *Happy Days*, and generates new and formidably challenging narrative forms with *Comment c'est* and other, shorter fictions. He also becomes personally engaged in the practical realization of his work on the stage and in radio, film, and television. Beckett decided, certainly by the time of the English translation of *En attendant Godot*, that he must himself take responsibility for translating his texts, whether conceived and written in French or English, into the other language, and, with very few exceptions, he did. Still, for him, moving a work from one language to another was next to impossible.

Letters from this period are often directed to specific issues: questions posed by translators, the problems of directors, or the sequencing of a series of short prose pieces for inclusion in a collection. Supporting materials for this volume include interviews with Beckett's friends, editors, directors, designers, performers, and "crrritics." The editors consulted scripts, photos, recordings, reviews, and letters to and from Beckett's production teams. While the research for this volume has been marked by a greater possibility of direct conversation with the recipients of Beckett's letters, it has also entailed working with papers that are primarily in private hands, or which are in the process of being transferred to archives.

At the end of 1969, Beckett was awarded the Nobel Prize, an honor which his wife Suzanne described as a "catastrophe." The unsought bounty of worldwide attention that follows is reflected in Volume IV, which stretches from 1970 to the author's death in 1989. The encumbrance of mail intensifies: there are replies to old friends, responses to new correspondents, meetings to arrange, and projects to authorize, guide, or deflect. Still, Beckett finds ways to retain the privacy necessary for his writing, for this is a period that sees the publication and production of many new works. The possibilities of television are more fully explored in *Ghost Trio,* ... *but the clouds* ..., *Nacht und Träume,* and *Quad.* In his stage plays, Beckett expands the presence of interiority often through recorded sound, in such works as *That Time, Footfalls, Rockaby, Ohio Impromptu, Catastrophe,* and *Quoi où.* As he has done from the start of his writing career, Beckett continues to write poetry during his final years, and the resulting works range from the brief and pithy *Mirlitonnades* to the open-ended musing of "Comment dire." This is the period of *Le Dépeupleur, Still, Company, Mal vu mal dit, Worstward Ho,* and *Stirrings Still.*

LACUNAE

There were times when Beckett and his correspondents were moving frequently between countries with little more than what a suitcase could hold; unnecessary papers were jettisoned as a result. Along with documents that have been lost, places have changed: certain buildings no longer exist where they once stood, streets have been renamed. Works of art are moveable properties: it is not surprising that some of the paintings which Beckett saw in one museum should be in a different collection now. Normal changes over time were multiplied by the havoc of World War II. Some works of art that Beckett viewed in private collections and museums during his German travels in 1936–1937 were confiscated, sold, or destroyed. The editors' research has necessitated identifying the location and ownership of such art works, both past and present.

All contemporary readers are removed in time and culture from the immediate contexts of Beckett's letters. The editors readily acknowledge that there are gaps in their knowledge, and have not hesitated to report the limits of what they have been able to discover, indicating when handwriting is illegible, when a reference is unclear, when evidence is insufficient, or when the relevant information has simply not been found. Whether in a reference to a once-common patent medicine or to a reel-to-reel tape recorder, the letters testify to how rapidly the quotidian reality has changed.

The fact that most of Samuel Beckett's letters open with some form of "Glad to have your letter" shows that letters were, for him, a welcome and real connection. In writing replies, Beckett acknowledges and often attempts to bridge the gaps of time, distance, and circumstance. Even though the instability of all the terms (the writer, his fictive voice, the occasion, *and* the reader) conspire against it, a letter purports to mitigate, if not to close, the gap between writer and reader.[9]

NOTES

1 Samuel Beckett to Arland Ussher, 6 November 1962, Harry Ransom Humanities Research Center, The University of Texas at Austin (hereafter "TxU"). Hereafter "SB" will be used in the notes to refer to Samuel Beckett.
2 SB to Mary Manning Howe, 25 December 1965, TxU.
3 Samuel Beckett, *No Author Better Served: The Correspondence of Samuel Beckett and Alan Schneider*, ed. Maurice Harmon (Cambridge, MA: Harvard University Press, 1998). Some of these letters were published in Samuel Beckett, "Beckett's Letters on 'Endgame': Extracts from His Correspondence with Director Alan Schneider," *The Village Voice* 19 March 1958: 8, 15; rpt. in *The Village Voice Reader: A Mixed Bag from the Greenwich Village Newspaper*, ed. Daniel Woolf and Edwin Fancher (New York: Doubleday, 1962) 182–186; 2nd edn. (New York: Grove Press, 1963) 166–169; rpt. as "On Endgame" in Samuel Beckett, *Disjecta: Miscellaneous Writings and a Dramatic Fragment*, ed. Ruby Cohn (New York: Grove Press, 1984) 106–110, and in translation.
  The following publish full letters to individuals: Samuel Beckett and Erich Franzen, "Correspondence on Translating MOLLOY," *Babel* 3 (Spring 1984) 21–35; Claire Stoullig and Nathalie Schoeller, eds., *Bram van Velde* [to Marthe Arnaud, Bram van Velde, Jacques Putman, some facsimile] (Paris: Musée National d'Art Moderne Centre Georges Pompidou, 1989) 160, 165, 172–175, 183, 185, 187–189; Maurice Nadeau, *Grâces leur soient rendues* (Paris: Albin Michel, 1990) 363–369; Vivienne Abbot, "How It Was: Egan and Beckett" in *Desmond Egan: The Poet and His Work*, ed. Hugh Kenner (Orono, ME: Northern Lights, 1990) 45–53; Samuel Beckett, "Letters to Barney Rosset," *The Review of Contemporary Fiction* 10.3 (Fall 1990) 64–71; Samuel Beckett and Barney Rosset, "The Godot Letters: A Lasting Effect" (Letters of Samuel Beckett and Barney Rosset), *The New Theatre Review* 12 (Spring 1995) 10–13; Marin Karmitz, *Comédie* [facsimile] (Paris: Les Editions du Regard, 2001) 14–25; and Anne Atik, *How It Was: A Memoir of Samuel Beckett* [to Avigdor Arikha and Anne Atik, facsimile] (London: Faber and Faber, 2003).
  Exhibition, library, and dealer catalogues in print and on the Web have reproduced Beckett's letters. Those that reproduce the widest range of letters are: Carlton Lake, with the assistance of Linda Eichhorn and Sally Leach, *No Symbols Where None Intended: A Catalogue of Books, Manuscripts, and Other Material Relating to Samuel Beckett in the Collections of the Humanities Research Center* (Austin: Humanities Research Center, The University of Texas at Austin, 1984); Marianne Alphant and Nathalie Léger, eds., *Objet: Beckett* (Paris: Centre Pompidou, IMEC-Editeur, 2007).
  Numerous publications have included individual letters. The letter to Axel Kaun and the letter to Sergei Eisenstein included in this volume have been the most frequently published. Previous publications of individual letters are indicated in the bibliographical notes for them in this and subsequent volumes.

4 SB to Martha Dow Fehsenfeld [summer 1986], private collection.
5 SB to Carlton Lake, 24 October 1987, John J. Burns Library of Rare Books and Special Collections, Boston College, Rosset Collection (hereafter "Burns Library").
6 SB to Martha Dow Fehsenfeld, 18 March 1985, private collection.
7 Signed by SB, 28 March 1989.
8 Signed by Edward Beckett, 24 April 1990.
9 "Three Dialogues with Georges Duthuit" in Beckett, *Disjecta*, 144.

FRENCH TRANSLATOR'S PREFACE

Translation is never simple, but it is normally, in at least one major respect, straightforward: the translator renders from the native language of the writer into the native language of the reader. With Beckett we have a different reality. In the first place, his native language is English; French is a language which he gradually acquires, in a learning process that runs from total ignorance in early childhood to near-total ease and competence in later years. When Beckett permanently settles in France from late 1937 and begins to make friends with, among others, monoglot French-speakers, some at least of the letters have to be written in French, whatever his level of competence. It is, of course, not a simple switch. In most cases, he does it for the obvious practical reasons: the addressee knows only French, or has only limited English. But Beckett sometimes chooses to write in French to friends or acquaintances whose native language is English – now playfully, now ostentatiously, now as part of a particular intimacy. Many of the English letters contain some French, from single words or short phrases to whole paragraphs.

The translator, then, must keep in mind two dimensions of Beckett's French: the historical-developmental and the tonal. In the first, the earliest step will be deciding where Beckett is, at the moment of writing, in what we have come to call the learning curve. Inevitably this will matter above all in the early letters, when he is only a little way on from his formal study of French, and less and less as time goes on, although it never disappears. In later volumes we shall see Beckett writing drafts of French-language letters, especially if the letter involves the essentially unfamiliar territory of legal or administrative language (as for instance in inquiries about rights, or negotiations with theatre managers and impresarios, as distinct from directors and actors, with whom communication is both easier and more natural). There is one extraordinary letter that illustrates the effects of such hesitation: Beckett's request to Sergei Eisenstein (dated 2 March 1936) to be allowed to work in Moscow under his guidance. The document that survives has a standard French beginning (the formal "Monsieur") and a comparably formal French ending ("Veuilliez agréer mes meilleurs hommages") although the first word is incorrectly spelled. The tone of the whole mixes English and French styles. The initial choice of French is of course sensible: it is highly probable that Eisenstein will be more at ease with French. The body of the letter, however, is in English, but here too there are unmistakable signs of haste: three not-quite-sentences, dotted with abbreviations, sketching in his CV, as well as other oddities. In short, it reads like a draft. It seems wholly unlikely that anybody with Beckett's respect for Eisenstein could have sent such a mishmash while asking, or at least hoping, for a favorable response from the great man. Beckett's letters to friends give evidence of the ease with which he moves between English and French, but this letter exemplifies hesitations that go beyond language. It is impossible to say what changes of thought or mood triggered the decision to send it, but send it he did.

The developmental dimension takes on greater importance once Beckett has decided to write some of his works for publication in French, a decision which means, among other things, that writing in French can never again be exclusively private. The letters allow us insight into the consequences of Beckett's decision, but remind us too that Beckett is still also an English-speaker, still also someone who writes for publication in English. This brings up a question of enduring importance. Responsible translators worry at times about whether they have or have not "got it right"; whether their man or woman "would have said that." They worry, in fact, that they may have betrayed the writer whose work they have rendered. Always, as if in mockery of their attempts, they can hear the dire finality of "traduttore traditore"; but they learn to live with that risk. With Beckett, the situation is more challenging. Of virtually any letter it could be said that he might have written part or all of it in English. But the body of English-language letters is there to remind the boldest as well as the most timorous of translators that English-Beckett, or indeed Beckett-English, cannot simply be presumed – or, without great risk, invented. What is to be done with his idiosyncratic wordplay? Will the translator's nonce-words give the flavor of Beckett's? And what of his disregard for French practice in capitalization (names of days or months, titles of books, names of institutions), or again, his erratic use of diacriticals (his address for some months, the "Hôtel Libéria," often appears without diacriticals; the cedilla needed on "ça" or "Ça" hardly ever appears, partly due to the limitations of his typewriter)? And so on.

Clearly, these questions cannot be left in the air. The decisions taken for this edition are as follows. The governing assumption is that we will at all points draw on the English-language letters of the time as indicative of what is idiomatically appropriate, particularly in the case of colloquialisms. This has often meant excluding what might well be neater or more forceful expressions if these were not in circulation at the time of writing. Thus World War II slang moved beyond "fed up" to "browned off" and on through variants like "cheesed (off)" to the near-universal "pissed (off)": all or any of these would have fitted the mood of Beckett faced with publishers' neglect or rejections, but none of them was available in the 1930s, when almost all of the letters in the first volume were written. Nor is this only a matter of choice of words. It was customary in the 1930s to write "I did not," "they were not," "it is," and so on; by the end of the 1940s the contractions "I didn't," "they weren't," "it's," etc., are much more frequently found. Not the least interesting feature of such changes is the wide variation in speed of acceptance: trend-conscious journalists in the fast lane, so to speak, elderly scholars stalling in the slow lane. Beckett's own practice is variable. It is worth noting, for example, that in the late 1930s, Beckett was still writing "to-day" and "to-morrow." In the case of his inventions (nonce-words, portmanteau-words, and the like), the aim is that of representing not just the semantic or tonal direction, but also the *charge* (the greater or lesser boldness). As for Beckett's "mistakes" (slips of the pen, misspelled or misremembered proper names, the occasional incoherence inevitable in unrevised writings), policy is not to repeat these in editorial matter, but rather to use the form regarded as correct now ("today," "Hôtel Libéria") and, in the case of capitalization in titles, to use current French practice for French words and English for English.

Dwarfing all these is a still more troubling, even frightening, worry. It is the obverse side of Beckett's decision to write for publication in French. What would he have said in the other language? A single example will make the point. If, when writing to a friend, he were to say of a man they both know: "Il y a longtemps que je ne l'ai pas vu," there are obvious translations: "I have not seen him for a long time," or "It is a long time since I saw him." But Beckett is an Irishman, and, if writing to a fellow Irishman, he might well have said (and often did say) "I have not seen him this long time," a phrase requiring an audible stress on "long," a usage not found in standard English. If the translator is aware of both possibilities, which one should he choose? In practice, our decision is to allow Irishisms only where it is clear that the addressee is familiar with them. This hypothetical example is relatively trivial, but it points up something that goes far beyond the usual preoccupations of translators: Beckett's relation to his native language – which is, let us be quite clear, English, not Irish, a language which he does not know. That relation is not something that can be dealt with in these few pages, but certain aspects of it are immediately relevant. For the relation is not symmetrical, in a pattern where, as it might be, the French gets better while the English gets worse. Then again, Beckett's case is quite unlike that of, say, Kafka, aware of a linguistic limbo in which, for external historico-political reasons, three languages press on him: German, Czech, and Yiddish. Nor is Beckett like Nabokov, whose eventual decision to go over to writing in English is linked to his rejection of Soviet Russia.

Beckett's case is in fact a familiar one – but not among writers. It is the case of all those who, for whatever reason, have freely chosen to immerse themselves in the life, language, and culture of another country. Not unlike the evolution of a love affair, the first phase is often marked by idealization of the new object, and a tendency to run down what went before. This is very much in evidence in the second and third volumes of the *Letters*, written in a period when he is working on translations of his own work into English. This task is for him both burdensome and irritating, in part at least because of his ambivalent relation with his native language (at one moment, "cette horrible langue"). He never loses his distaste for the chore of translation, but his acute concern with the translation of his own work indicates that the issues go well beyond likes and dislikes.

Once the fame of *Godot* has spread, translations follow, almost all into languages of which Beckett knows little or nothing, but there is at least one interesting intermediate case: German. His reading and his visits to Germany have given him some familiarity with the language: nothing comparable to his grasp of French, or indeed of Italian, but capable of prompting in him worries about aspects of his translator's work. As it happens, his primary German translator, Elmar Tophoven, is capable of responding appropriately, and there ensues a fascinating correspondence and an enduring friendship. More generally, Beckett's letters to his translators, as well as illustrating his moral generosity and his appreciation of their efforts, abound in acute and revealing reflections on writing and language.

There is one further area in which international difference matters: the representation of words, and above all proper names, from languages (Russian, Greek, Arabic mainly) that do not use the Roman alphabet. The case of Russian illustrates the difficulty perfectly. Transliteration is an attempt to represent as closely as possible the sounds of Russian, but the representations themselves vary according to the norms of the receiving language. Thus the Russian poet is Pushkin for English-speakers, but Pouchkine for the French, while the dramatist is respectively Chekhov and Tchekhov. But for anyone who knows no Russian, the local transliteration is the only one to matter. Exactly the same will be true, for example, for Arabic place-names: Marrakesh for the English, Marrakech for the French. Much of Beckett's writing life is in France, and what he sees will usually be French transliterations. As it happens, the issue of Russian names arises again, in a very different cultural and historical context. The world of dance is profoundly affected, first and foremost in France, by the innovations of Sergei Diaghilev, the founder of the Ballets Russes. The very name of the company hints at the long-established link between Russia and France (educated Russians in those days spoke French, some indeed as their first language), and it was to France that Diaghilev took his dancers. Many of these settled there – and took on French versions of their names. Massine and Fokine (like Lénine and Staline, in this respect if no other) have that final "e" in French in order to avoid what would otherwise be an unwarranted nasal sound in the second syllable. These are the names that Beckett is used to seeing on billboards, tickets, programs. The same holds for writers, musicians (whether composers or performers), and actors. Beckett, unsurprisingly, will tend to reach for the first name to hand, regardless of language, when he comes to write about any of them. Finally, there is Beckett's capricious handling, influenced by where he happens to be at the time of writing, of foreign names or terms. In the letters inspired by his tour of German art collections in the late 1930s, he often adopts the German spelling "barock" for what English, following French, refers to as "baroque"; or calls French towns by the German version of them: "Strassburg" for "Strasbourg," "Kolmar" for "Colmar." Against that, he also uses the English spellings of certain French place-names, for instance "Marseilles."

But it is the French/English divide and its consequences that matter above all. Within that, a new divide appears: before *Godot* and after. Fame brings its rewards, but exacts a price which Beckett finds heavy. The effect on the letters is immediate. His correspondents are no longer only friends, old or new. For the first time, wariness appears in the writing. Beckett's legendary courtesy ensures that letters will be answered, but many raise, directly or indirectly, questions that irritate or dismay him (letters to friends indicate how much). The division in time is accompanied by a division in kind: on the one hand, letters to intimates; on the other, letters to the rest.

To these questions specific to Beckett must be added other inescapable but more general issues. All letters written in French to anyone other than an intimate will normally have one of a set of formal openings, and one of a set of even more formal endings. With the openings, the very formal "Monsieur" or "Madame" and the rather less formal "Cher Monsieur" or "Chère Madame" must be adjusted in English to include the person's surname. But it is the writer who decides on the degree of formality. Decisions of this kind may well be difficult, which is why the much less formal and neatly non-committal "Cher ami" is such a boon to writers. But since there is no direct equivalent in English, the choice of degree of intimacy is pushed back on to the translator. Here another factor comes in. The habit among men of using surnames hung on much longer in France than in England, where the American preference for first names edges it out. "Cher ami" gives no clue whether it would be more appropriate to write "Dear Smith" or "Dear John"; and this is something which, like the "vous"/"tu" distinction, may have surprising importance. An example can be found in the ending of Beckett's letter to his agent George Reavey, with whom relations have gone from cool, even frosty, to trusting. The distance traveled can be seen, even in the jokiness, with "Vas-y" (go ahead) at the beginning and "A toi" (yours) at the end, both in the intimate form.[1]

Endings are less troubling, for although the battery of conventional formulas is much greater, the differences between them are, for Beckett, largely unimportant. Their ostentatious formality and apparent obsequiousness have no echo in English. The typical "Je vous prie de croire, Monsieur, à l'assurance de mes sentiments les meilleurs" would sound grotesque in English if rendered "literally." It, and its like, have virtually no emotional charge in French, however, and so must be represented by a neutral, comparably uncharged formula. English has in fact very few of these, so "Yours sincerely" will appear very often.

Then there is the matter of punctuation. Beckett's practice is unpredictable, but that merely compounds a difficulty: the difference between standard French and English usages. In French, for example, it is perfectly proper to connect two main clauses by a simple comma; English requires a semicolon (as in this sentence), or a new sentence. Here again, the only reliable guidance for the translator comes from the English-language letters.

More interesting, perhaps, is the question of "swearwords": the whole territory that French calls engagingly "la langue verte." The issue surfaces in the letters concerned with the Lord Chamberlain's refusal to allow performance in England of the text of *Fin de partie* unless certain cuts are made. The main point is that French and English "swearwords" do not overlap neatly. Some of the French ones are the etymological cousins of the English ones, but patterns of use are not at all the same. Several French words ("connerie" is an example) have been virtually emptied of their scabrous or vulgar content. The base-word "con" is close kin to the English word "cunt," but has long been used without any of the harsh or sexual associations of the English word. It is a very common way of saying "fool," "idiot," "nitwit," so that a "connerie" is what someone like that would do or say: something stupid. Similarly, years before well-brought-up young women would have said "shit" in public, "merde" and its cognates were in common use in France. Elderly ladies were saying "Mon Dieu" in French and meaning little more than "Goodness me" when their English equivalents would not have dreamed of saying "My God." The particular significance of "connerie" is that it is one of the words that the Lord Chamberlain objected to in the projected performances at the Royal Court Theatre of *Fin de partie*. Clearly, he or his adviser was unaware of the wide difference in practice between French and English, and assumed that the word was one of the words then forbidden (in 1957 there was still a long way to go to the lifting of restrictions that followed the verdict in the *Chatterley* trial and led eventually to the abolishing, in this connection, of the powers of the Lord Chamberlain).

But these orders of difficulty, concerned as they are with small differences of cultural practice, are as nothing compared with that raised by Beckett's wordplay. It is not just that at any moment he may spice his English with a word or a phrase in French: that much is expectable from an expatriate English-speaker writing to a friend in Ireland or England or the USA. Nor is French the only foreign language he draws on – we are also likely to be faced with words or passages in Italian, or German, or Latin – usually because the language chosen has a neater or more expressive rendering of what he wants to say. This, after all, is the currency that translators must expect to deal in. But Beckett's practice is often at the boundary of languages. There are Gallicisms: deliberate, as in "was for much in" ("était pour beaucoup dans" [was an important influence in or played a considerable part in]); unconsciously mimetic, as in "the script is function of its ... " ("le scénario est fonction de ses ...").[2] No single editorial formula can deal satisfactorily with all examples. Even single-word usages (such as "transatlantic," modeled on the French "transatlantique") cannot be definitively pigeon-holed, since it is not always possible to know whether Beckett's choice is deliberate or involuntary.[3] Then there is the difference between such calques and the cases where Beckett plays with both languages simultaneously, as when he writes "fucking the field," where he brings to life a dead French metaphor – the long-familiar colloquialism "foutre le camp" even then meant little more than "to leave suddenly," "to get away" – in a deliberately grotesque English version.[4] The painful mismatch – Beckett's brief verbal thrust as against the present labored explanation/commentary – is evidence enough: neat categories are not possible here.

There are inventions galore. And there are instances where the punning, telescoping, or other wordplay simply has no equivalent in English. Above all there are the wholly idiosyncratic, almost always breathtaking, representations of particular insights or ventures, as when, in a covering note to two poems he is sending to George Reavey, he writes "Voici deux Prépuscules d'un Gueux."[5] The combining of the very grand (in the echo of *Le Crépuscule des dieux* [*The Twilight of the Gods*]) with the grotesquely self-deprecating "prépuces" (foreskins) and the more ordinarily modest "opuscule" (small literary work) leads on to more playing at self-abasement in the nicely archaic "Gueux" (beggar). Some of this verbal play, dependent on French, is simply untranslatable, either because nothing in English corresponds to the play, or because the invention itself is so idiosyncratic as to be unrecoverable.

In my second suggested dimension, the tonal, interpretation of a different kind is required. Here what is at issue is the altogether more testing question of the relation of Beckett to the addressee at the time of writing, on a spectrum that runs from the exalted or desperate to the factual–businesslike. In this, the only indicator available to the translator is the "vous"/"tu" distinction, as in the Reavey example above, as compared with the "vous"-based letter to Eisenstein.

The letters are in this respect quite unlike the rest of his *oeuvre*, in which the notion of a particular addressee simply does not arise. The letters themselves bring all the illustration one could need. Whatever their purpose, they are always Beckett writing. For the translator, there is only ever the task of catching, as far as that is possible, the shading of this passage or that, this letter or that. There is no pre-existing method; translation is, after all, a reading differently articulated – but one that takes place in the shadow of what it was for Beckett, a writing differently articulated.

George Craig

NOTES

1 SB to George Reavey, 23 June 1934.
2 SB to Thomas McGreevy, 20 February [1935]; SB to Sergei Eisenstein, 2 March 1936.
3 SB to Thomas McGreevy, 4 August 1932.
4 SB to Thomas McGreevy, [after 15 August 1931]; SB to Thomas McGreevy, 16 January 1930.
5 SB to George Reavey, 6 November 1932.

GERMAN TRANSLATOR'S PREFACE

For the translator, the letters that Samuel Beckett wrote in German present an unusual problem. Even though he is writing in German, he is thinking in his native English. Beckett's thoughts become subsequently "verfremdet," estranged or distanced from their intent, when translated into a language still quite foreign to him. In order to put them back into English, the translator must therefore look behind the "Schleier," or veil, that the German language created for Beckett.[1] Although George Craig also alludes to this issue in his translator's preface with regard to Beckett's writings in French, Beckett's German letters clearly reflect the much greater distance between his native language and his acquired German. This comes as no surprise, as French was a language Beckett learned as a child and maintained all his life, whereas he did not begin his study of German until adulthood, a disadvantage never quite overcome. Nonetheless, Beckett is never less than sophisticated in his thinking and his awareness of language. A great deal of the challenge involved in Beckett's letters in German therefore lies in discerning and representing the difference between his lack of full linguistic competence and his intentional language play.

Since Beckett's German letters span a wide range of biographical contexts, they provide wonderfully clear examples of what George Craig defines as dimensions of SB's "historical-developmental" and "tonal" uses of the language.[2] In fact, Beckett's German letters were not written for purely practical reasons, namely, out of the necessity to make himself understood, but rather because he wanted to write in German. Thus, George Craig's analogy of a "love affair" seems all the more fitting in the case of Beckett's relationship to German.

Beckett's earliest German letter was written to his cousin Morris Sinclair in 1934 and is familiar in tone. Apparently Beckett trusted that his ventures into testing, in word and thought, the limits of his still quite rudimentary language abilities would not be faulted. In

December 1936 when Beckett writes to his new friend and contemporary Günter Albrecht, the letter is casual in tone and content, relating his travel experiences following his stay in Hamburg. Intended to practice his much-improved German, albeit still a little stilted at times, this letter shows only a few mistakes such as typographical errors, insignificant oversights, and some errors of syntax.

For many reasons the most problematic German letter in Volume I is the draft dated 9 July 1937 and addressed to Axel Kaun, to whom Beckett was introduced by Günter Albrecht. Not only was Kaun a somewhat distant acquaintance, but the occasion for the letter related to a commission of translation, and its content extends to a broader discussion of language itself. Hence it is a letter of greater tonal formality, as well as greater complexity and breadth of reference. In this letter Beckett perhaps most accurately reflects all three of the aspects that Matthew Feldman found revealed in Beckett's German Workbook: namely, the extent of Beckett's knowledge of German in 1936; his developing artistic outlook; and his temperament.[3]

The translation of this letter to Axel Kaun was further complicated by the fact that it exists only as a corrected draft which, to make matters worse, has had a history of over-correction. Therefore this letter remains very difficult to judge linguistically, and to a degree continues to raise interpretive issues about its intended message.[4]

After some deliberations we have decided not to mark grammatical or syntactical errors in Beckett's German letters, following the editorial principle to present Beckett's letters as written. Only where we had to make an interpretive decision have we indicated in a note the reading that we have used for our translation. For example, the sentence in a letter of 5 May 1934 to Morris Sinclair, "So bitte ich dich, ihm für mich vorzustellen, diese Versäumung sei mir zum Trotz" (So I ask you to get him, on my behalf, to imagine that this omission might be in spite of myself), not only contains several grammatical errors, but also various possibilities of interpretation based on the two understandings of the main verb "vorstellen" (imagine and introduce). Further complicating clear understanding was Beckett's use of syntax that is possible in English but not in German.[5]

As a language teacher with many years of experience, I am all too familiar with the types and patterns of mistakes that English-speaking students of the German language commonly make. This proved to be particularly helpful in translating Beckett's German letters. Many of the grammatical and syntactical problems encountered in these letters are neither uncommon nor surprising in learners of German and generally do not require undue guesswork. Near misses such as those that result from merging German and English syntax in, for example, the expression "lass es dir gut gefallen" were more difficult to sort out.[6]

Another aspect of discovering a foreign language involves creative wordplay, word inventions, and unusual word combinations. Students of foreign language and culture immensely enjoy combining, mixing and matching sounds, images, and words to create new word inventions. How much more would the mind of a Samuel Beckett find delight in such possibility? Rarely if ever does a teacher have the opportunity, and the privilege, of working with a "student text" composed by a future Nobel laureate, who is subjugating his creative images and rich thought-constructions to a language not his own. And so the translator struggles with intriguing word creations such as "Unwort," "Gegenstandsauger," "schweizzige Moralisten," and "verpersonifiziert."[7]

In addition, and not unlike many advanced language students, Beckett had a distinct affinity for that most cumbersome of German constructions: the extended adjective expression. Beckett confronts the challenge to stretch his German. The extended adjective construction allowed him to experiment creatively by testing sophisticated imagery and wrapping it in complex syntax. There are many illustrations to be found in Beckett's early German letters. For example, he writes "eine ganz andere Ruhe, als die zu dieser groben, englischen Landschaft gehörende" in a letter to Morris Sinclair,[8] and "auf jenem alten faulen von Musik und Malerei längst verlassenen Wege" in the letter to Axel Kaun.[9] In the same letter, Beckett chooses a similarly complicated construction when referring to Beethoven's Seventh Symphony: "die von grossen schwarzen Pausen gefressene Tonfläche in der siebten Symphonie von Beethoven, so dass wir sie ganze Seiten durch nicht anders wahrnehmen können als etwa einen schwindelnden unergründliche Schlünde von Stillschweigen verknüpfenden Pfad von Lauten?"[10] Such linguistic excursions do not translate literally into English because such constructions generally require added verbs or division into more than one clause to make them intelligible.

A different, perhaps more common problem presents itself in Beckett's unusual word combinations, such as "Biedermeier bathing suit," an image that we retained rather than distort because its unique emotional and cultural attachments have no equivalent in English.[11] Or the translator may be faced with a phrase such as "sächsischer Stützwechsel," mixing historical-cultural dimensions with multiple meanings of words, the whole concocted into sophisticated imagery shot through with irony – indeed a challenge.[12]

On the one hand, if we assume that, when composing his letters in German, Beckett would formulate his thoughts in his native English first, then the particular challenge for the translator in the case of the German letters was to return as closely as possible to that original English articulation. On the other hand, though, it also seemed important to reflect and retain in the English translation, particularly for the reader not familiar with German, some of the awkwardness of Beckett's German, especially in his early letters. One benefit that this provided was a way to demonstrate both Beckett's remarkable progress and his equally impressive linguistic courage in "massaging" the language and seeking German formulations appropriate to the complexity of his thoughts, even when the latter far outstripped the former. Beckett, quite like the ardent lover alluded to earlier, never ceased to push to the limits of his language abilities or to risk experimenting with innovative attempts to express himself in German, this language he so loved to embrace.

Viola Westbrook

NOTES

1 SB to Axel Kaun, 9 July 1937: "Und immer mehr wie ein Schleier kommt mir meine Sprache vor, den man zerreissen muss."
2 George Craig, "French translator's preface," this volume, p. xxxiii.
3 Matthew Feldman, *Beckett's Books: A Cultural History of Samuel Beckett's "Interwar Notes"* (New York: Continuum, 2006) 26.
4 When Beckett gave this draft to Lawrence Harvey in the early 1960s, it was already marked with corrections; possibly either Beckett himself, or Beckett and Harvey, went over the German and made further corrections. This is also a letter that has appeared in a transcription and translation by Martin Esslin in Ruby Cohn's edition of Beckett's writings, *Disjecta*; readers will find differences between Esslin's corrected edition and our transcription and translation (Samuel Beckett, "German Letter of 1937" tr. Martin Esslin in *Disjecta*, ed. Cohn, 51–54, 170–172).
5 SB to Morris Sinclair, 5 May 1934 n. 7: SB's German construction would have been correct had he used the word "erklären" (explain). By using "vorstellen" instead, he merged the two constructions possible with that verb and thereby the two meanings

(introduce and imagine), with the result that neither form is used correctly. Considering the contents and tone of the letter, we have settled on "imagine."

6 SB to Thomas McGreevy, 22 December 1936 n. 2.

7 SB to Axel Kaun, 9 July 1937; SB to Morris Sinclair, 5 May 1934.

8 SB to Morris Sinclair, 5 May 1934: "[Sometimes I long for those mountains and fields, which I know so well, and which create] a completely different calm from the one associated with this coarse English landscape."

9 SB to Axel Kaun, 9 July 1937: "[Or is literature alone left behind] on that old, foul road long ago abandoned by music and painting."

10 SB to Axel Kaun, 9 July 1937: "[Is there any reason why that terrifyingly arbitrary materiality of the word surface should not be dissolved, as for example] the sound surface of Beethoven's Seventh Symphony is devoured by huge black pauses, so that for pages on end we cannot perceive it as other than a dizzying path of sounds connecting unfathomable chasms of silence?"

11 SB to Axel Kaun, 9 July 1937.

12 SB to Günter Albrecht, 30 March 1937.

EDITORIAL PROCEDURES

Unlike a novel, letters to old friends are not checked carefully before they are sent, and inevitably eccentricities appear: slips of the pen, typos, accidental substitutions, oddities of spelling (particularly of proper names that SB had misheard or mis-remembered), and persistent confusions (sent and send). To signal each one with "sic" or "for" would interfere with reading, so we do so only when they might prevent or distort understanding. Letters are transcribed as written and presented as a clear text, that is, the final text as sent to the recipient.

Sequence Letters are presented chronologically. If more than one letter was written on the same day, the letters are ordered alphabetically by recipient's name, unless internal evidence suggests another sequence. When the editors supply dating, the letter appears in sequence according to the presumed date.

Recipient The full name of the recipient, with a corporate identification if relevant, and the city to which the letter was sent are indicated in a header in small capitals. These are editorial additions; Beckett himself seldom included a recipient's name and address in a letter; however, when he does, this is shown as written.

Date Dates are presented as written by Beckett, who most often follows European format (day, month, year), but placement is regularized. If the date, or any portion of it, is incomplete or incorrect, editorial emendation is given in square brackets; if a date, or any portion of it, is uncertain, this emendation is preceded by a question mark. The rationale for the dating is given, if needed, in the bibliographical note following the letter.

Place Place is presented as written, but placement is regularized. Where place is incomplete, editorial emendation is given in square brackets, preceded by a question mark if uncertain. Occasionally, the place of writing is not congruent with the place of mailing; for example, Beckett may write as if from Paris, but post the letter in La Ferté-sous-Jouarre. This is not corrected.

Orthography Beckett's idiosyncratic spelling, capitalization, and abbreviation are preserved: this includes abbreviations without punctuation (wd, cd, yrs), varying presentation of superscripts (M^r, Y^r, 14me), use of ampersands, contractions written without an apostrophe ("wont" *for* "won't"), and use of diacriticals. Beckett's practice of indicating the titles of works by underscoring is inconsistent: sometimes he does, sometimes he does not, sometimes he underscores partially. When grammatical or spelling variants interfere with sense, these are editorially expanded or corrected within square brackets in the text.

Beckett often uses words or phrases from other languages when writing in English or French, but he seldom underscores such words or phrases. If Beckett's shifts from one language to another produce what appears to be a variant spelling in the dominant language of the letter, this is marked or explained in a note.

Beckett frequently spells a name incorrectly, most often when he has only heard the name and not met the person or read the name. When a person's name, a title, or another reference is misspelled in the text of a letter, the corrected spelling is given in the notes and the index; if the misspelled name is likely to confuse, its first use is corrected within square brackets in the text: e.g. "Stevens [*for* Stephens]." When, as in a joke or pun made with a name, a misspelling is judged to be deliberate, it stands as written; correct spelling is given in the notes and the index.

In Volume I, there are two exceptions to this rule, and both are noted at their first occurrence. Thomas McGreevy changed the spelling of his family name toward the end of 1941 to *Mac*Greevy. Since all of the letters through 1940 are addressed to *Mc*Greevy, that spelling is retained through the present volume; in subsequent volumes his name will be spelled *Mac*Greevy. During the period covered by Volume I, Beckett almost always spelled the name of Gwynedd Reavey as "Gwyn*n*ed"; this is noted at the first occurrence and then silently emended. When Beckett does spell her name correctly, this change is also noted.

Beckett presents ellipses with spaced dots; however, these are variously two dots or three dots. Beckett occasionally punctuates with a dash instead of a period at the end of a sentence.

Authorial emendation The results of Beckett's cancelations, insertions, and inversions are presented as a clear text. When a reading of an emendation by Beckett is uncertain, it is given within square brackets in the text, preceded by a question mark.

Beckett often overwrites or overtypes to self-correct; when typing, he sometimes cancels a word or phrase if it does not fit the space on the page, and then rewrites it on the next line or page. Beckett changes his mind as he writes: sometimes omitting or inserting a word, phrase, or sentence; inverting word order; extending a thought in the margins. Typed letters contain both typed and handwritten corrections. Drafts of letters show many more changes.

When Beckett's changes are substantive – that is, not merely corrections of spelling or typos or false starts – these are presented in the notes: e.g., SB wrote "<the Aldingtons> Richard and Bridget." Scholars interested in the patterns of Beckett's changes will wish to consult the original manuscripts.

Editorial emendation Editorial emendations to the text are supplied only when necessary to understanding. Other than obvious typographical errors (overtypes, space slips, extra spacing, false starts), and other than what is stated above, there are no silent emendations.

Placement and indentation of date, address, closing and signature lines are regularized. Paragraph indentations are standardized. Line ends are marked only in poetry. Postscripts are presented following the signature; if their original placement differs, this is described in a note.

Editorial ellipses in letters and other unpublished manuscripts are shown by three unspaced dots within square brackets; editorial ellipses in published materials are shown with three spaced dots.

Illegibility Illegibility is noted in square brackets [illeg]. If a reading is uncertain, it is given within square brackets and preceded by a question mark. Damage to the original manuscript that obscures or obliterates the text is described in the bibliographical note and is indicated in the text as illegibility.

Signature The closing and signature lines are regularized. An autograph signature or initial can be assumed for an autograph letter; in a typed letter, the notation "s/" indicates a handwritten signature or initial. A typed letter may have both an autograph and a typed signature. When these are not identical, both are shown. When these are identical, rather than present the signature twice, the existence of an autograph signature is indicated only by "s/" and the typed signature is presented in the line that follows:

> With best wishes
> s/
> Samuel Beckett

An unsigned carbon copy presents only the typed signature, but spacing allows for an autograph signature in the original:

> With best wishes
>
> Samuel Beckett

Bibliographical note Following each letter is a bibliographical note which gives a description of the letter (e.g. ALS, autograph letter signed) followed by the number of leaves and sides (2 leaves, 4 sides). Description of the physical document may include its letterhead (if SB replaces or alters it), the image on a postcard, and enclosures. This note also includes the address on a postcard or envelope, the postmark, and any additional notation on the envelope, whether written by Beckett or in another hand (e.g. forwarding address, postal directives, or other notations). Postmarks are described by city (not by post office) and date. Editorial markers are given in italics: e.g. *env to* George Reavey; *pm* 16-5-35, Paris. The ownership of the physical property is given with the designated library abbreviation, collection name and accession information; private ownership is indicated according to the owner's preference, by name or simply as "private collection." Previous publication is noted when the letter has been published in full or in a substantial portion (more than half); facsimile reproductions are indicated in this note.

Notations used in the bibliographical description indicate whether the letter is handwritten or typed; whether a letter, postcard, telegram, or pneumatique; it indicates the number of leaves and sides, and whether it is signed, initialed, or unsigned. A leaf is a physical piece of paper; a side is a page written on, whether recto or verso. A postcard may bear an address on the recto (1 leaf, 1 side) or on the verso (1 leaf, 2 sides). Beckett sometimes folded a single piece of paper so that it had four sides (1 leaf, 4 sides). All editorial notations are detailed under "Abbreviations."

Discussion of dating When the date of a letter is corrected or derived from internal or external evidence, the rationale for the assigned date or date-range is given following the bibliographical note. Undated or partially dated letters are not unusual. Beckett may not date a letter when it is part of a frequent exchange or when it follows or anticipates a personal meeting; he often misdates letters at the beginning of a new year. If envelopes are clearly affiliated with the letter in question, the postmark may be helpful in dating. Some correspondence received by publishers and other businesses was routinely date stamped; this is noted in the bibliographical note and may inform incomplete dating. While Beckett occasionally delivers a note personally, it is also the case that some stamped letters are sent without cancellation. Telegrams are often difficult to date precisely and may bear only the date of receipt.

Translation Letters written entirely in a language other than English are translated immediately following the transcription of the original and its bibliographical note. Translators' initials are given when other than George Craig for French and Viola Westbrook for German. In the first volume, when published translations were not available, Adolf von Baden-Württemberg and George Craig have translated from Latin and Greek; Dan Gunn has translated from Italian.

Translations of words or phrases are provided in the notes to the letter. Translations are given with the following formulation: "Bon travail & bon sommeil" (work well & sleep well). The language of the original is not indicated in the translation unless there may be ambiguity; if required, these abbreviations are used: colloq., colloquial; Fr., French; Ger., German; Gk., Greek; Ir., Irish; It., Italian; Lat., Latin; Sp., Spanish. Published translations are used for literary quotations, if available, and are so noted (see below).

Beckett may write the name of a German city with German, French, or English spelling; however, translations and editorial material present the English spelling of city and place names. Translations do not repeat Beckett's mistakes (slips of the pen, misremembering or misspelling of proper names, and the occasional incoherence inevitable in unrevised writings). In the rare cases when spelling norms have changed (in the 1930s Beckett wrote "to-day" and "to-morrow"), current practice is followed. Although Beckett practiced English-style capitalization when writing the titles of books in other languages, translations and notes use the capitalization practice of the language in which the book was written. In the translation of letters, all titles of books are indicated by italics.

ANNOTATIONS

In the notes, Samuel Beckett is referred to as "SB." Translations follow British spelling and punctuation practice; all other editorial materials follow American English spelling and punctuation. Although all letters are presented as written, in line with standard French practice the edition does not put accents on initial capitals in editorial matter. All other accents are displayed, even where, as in editorial headers, the material is represented in small capitals. This affects *only editorial matter in French*; other languages have other conventions.

Identifications of persons The first reference gives a person's full name (including birth name, and/or acquired appellations including pseudonyms and nicknames), years of birth and death, and a brief statement of identification. Additional statements of identification may be given over the course of a volume, or over the four volumes, when a person's primary occupation, affiliation, or relationship to Samuel Beckett changes. Identifications are not given for well-known figures such as William Shakespeare, René Descartes, Dante Alighieri.

Names Names are not necessarily constant over time. Thomas McGreevy chose to change the spelling of his family name; after World War II, Georges Pelorson changed his name to Georges Belmont. Some women assume their husband's surname when they marry: Mary Manning became Mary Manning Howe and then Mary Manning Howe Adams, but she used her maiden name professionally. Editorial practice is to follow Beckett's spelling of the name at the time of writing (with the exception of misspelling), but also to refer to writers by the name given on the title page of their books.

Painters are often given a name that includes their parentage, their city of origin, or their association with a school of painting. Beckett's practice varies, so identifications in the annotations follow those given by *The Grove Dictionary of Art*, with variant names and spellings given only where confusion might otherwise arise.

Some persons become known by their initials, some by their nick-names, and some by both. Abraham Jacob Leventhal generally indi-cates his name in publications as A. J. Leventhal, but he is most often referred to in Beckett's letters by his nickname, "Con." Beckett's cousin Morris Sinclair may also be addressed as "Maurice," or by his family nickname "Sunny" which in German becomes "Sonny" (indeed he was the only son in the Sinclair family).

After first reference, editorial practice is to use the name that Beckett uses. When a name changes, a note will signal this change. Both/all names will be entered as one heading in the Index.

Dates Approximate dates are preceded by c. (circa), fl. (flourished), or a question mark; when dates are approximated as a range, the earliest birth year and the latest death year are given, preceded by c. to indicate approximation. If only the birth year or death year is known, it is given as, for example, (b. 1935) or (1852–?) or (d. 1956). Rarely, the only date known is a marriage date; this will be given as (m. 1933). When a date is unknown, it is indicated as (n.d.).

Titles In editorial material (translations, annotations, appendices), titles are presented with the capitalization and spelling conventions of the original language. The title of a work of art is presented in English since the language of the artist may not be the same as the language of the museum or collections that have owned it. Generally, a catalogue raisonné gives titles in several languages. Titles of musical works are often in the language of the composer and remain untranslated; however, lines from songs, recitatives, and arias are translated. Titles of books that are referred to in the text appear in the notes in their original language, followed by date of first publication and title in English if there is a published trans-lation, e.g. *Voyage au bout de la nuit* (1932; *Journey to the End of the Night*); if the English title is given in roman font, e.g. *Die notwendige Reise* (1932; The Necessary Journey), this indicates that an English trans-lation has not been published and that the translated title has been supplied by the editors.

Sources for names, titles, and dates To arbitrate varying names, spellings of names, and dates, editorial practice has relied upon *The Grove Dictionary of Music*; *The Grove Dictionary of Art*; *The Cambridge*

Biographical Encyclopedia, second edition; the catalogues of the Bibliothèque Nationale, the British Library, the National Library of Ireland, the Library of Congress, as well as other national libraries; and *The Oxford Dictionary for Writers and Editors*.

Glosses Unusual or archaic English words or foreign-language terms that have entered common English usage are not glossed if they can be found in the second electronic edition of *The Oxford English Dictionary*.

References References to unpublished materials give the archive and manuscript identification of the documents. References to published materials give a full bibliographical citation at the first mention, and a short-title reference thereafter. The Bibliography includes all published materials that are cited. Titles that are identified in the text but not cited do not appear in the Bibliography, but they are indexed.

Cross-reference Cross-reference that refers back to specific material within the edition is given by indicating the date of the letter and the number of the pertinent note, e.g. 9 January 1936, n. 5. References are rarely given forward. It is presumed that most readers will read sequentially; those who wish to pursue a single figure will be able to do so by use of the Index.

Choice of editions Although it is necessary to select standard editions for editorial reference, these choices are not governed by a single rule. For example, most often the Bibliothèque de la Pléiade edition of French text is used, or the more recent of these where two editions exist, because these editions take into account earlier editions. Exceptions have been made when a reference requires a first edition or an edition that Beckett refers to in a letter, or one he is known to have read, or the only one he could have read. The choice of standard editions is explained at the point of first reference. Volumes II, III, and IV of *The Letters* may present other issues in this respect. Where there is no standard edition, editions are selected for their accessibility, for example the Riverside edition of Shakespeare's works. Biblical references are taken from the King James Version. Although the publication information is given for all first and subsequent editions of Beckett's texts when this information is germane to the context of a letter, quotations are generally taken from the Grove Press editions.

Choice of translations English literary translations are provided for Beckett's foreign-language citations. Beckett nearly always read in the original language, and so choice of a translation is seldom directed by his reading.

Chronologies Chronologies precede each year of the letters to present an overview of the events mentioned by Beckett's letters; these include significant world events.

Profiles Biographical profiles of persons who have a continuing role in the narrative of *The Letters of Samuel Beckett* appear in the Appendix. Those who have a profile are indicated with an asterisk following their first reference. A profile presents a narrative of a person's life and work, with regard particularly to his or her association with Beckett. Profiles appear in the first volume of the letters in which the person becomes a figure of significance. The profiles cover the historical range of a person's association with Beckett because they will not be reprinted in subsequent volumes of the edition. Profiles are also given for certain institutions, publications, and organizations.

ACKNOWLEDGMENTS

The family of Samuel Beckett has been welcoming as well as generous in sharing memories and documents. The editors warmly thank Edward and Felicity Beckett, Caroline and Patrick Murphy, Diana Zambonelli, Jill Babcock, and remember with gratitude Ann Beckett (d.), John Beckett (d.), Sheila Page (d.), and Morris Sinclair (d.).

FUNDING AND CONTRIBUTIONS

The Graduate School of Emory University has generously supported the research for *The Letters of Samuel Beckett* since 1990. The editing project at Emory, known as "The Correspondence of Samuel Beckett," is a laboratory for humanities research in which graduate students in several disciplines of the humanities are engaged. Faculty and staff colleagues at Emory have unfailingly supported the edition with their knowledge and resources.

The extensive process of gathering, organizing, and preparing documents and oral histories fundamental to such an edition was facilitated by major support from The National Endowment for the Humanities from 1991 to 1997. The Graduate School of Emory University contributed both the overhead and cost-sharing for these grants.

The research for this edition is international and cross-cultural. The Florence Gould Foundation supported the French and American partnership of this research from 1995 through 2003. The Graduate School of Emory University and The American University of Paris contributed cost-sharing. The support of the Gould Foundation helped to establish a Paris center for the research at The American University of Paris, directed by Associate Editor Dan Gunn; students there served as interns, conducting research in French collections.

The Mellon Foundation supported research at the Harry Ransom Humanities Research Center of The University of Texas at Austin

(1993–1994); the Huntington Library / British Academy Exchange Fellowship (1994–1995) supported research at the Huntington Library; the Helm Fellowship supported research at the Lilly Library, Indiana University (1997–1998, 2002–2003). The Rockefeller Foundation enabled the editorial team to meet at its Bellagio Study Center, Italy (2004–2005), to work together on the first two of the edition's four volumes.

The Cultural Division of the Department of European Affairs of Ireland has undertaken the distribution of copies of each of the four volumes of *The Letters of Samuel Beckett* to universities and public libraries overseas and those operated through the Irish Diplomatic Missions abroad. We appreciate the support of Noel Treacy TD, former Minister for European Affairs, for making possible this tribute to Samuel Beckett's Irish legacy.

Without the continuing and substantial contributions of Emory Professors Alice N. Benston and George J. Benston (d.), the project to edit *The Letters of Samuel Beckett* would not have gone forward. Their belief in the centrality of literature and the arts in an educated life, their intellectual mentorship and, especially, their personal encourage- ment and friendship have been an immeasurable gift.

We are grateful for the efforts of Joseph Beck of Kilpatrick Stockton LLP, who has been a steadfast adviser providing *pro bono* assistance to the edition in the area of copyright law. His thoroughness, expertise, and capacious understanding guided the editors; his personal support has been unbounded. We also thank Pam Mallari of Kilpatrick Stockton LLP for her *pro bono* services.

The editors greatly appreciate the generous in-kind contributions of the following persons: Mimi Bean, Brenda Bynum, R. Cary Bynum, Carainn Childers, Maydelle and Sam Fason, Neil Garvin, Barbara Grüninger, David Hesla, Jacob Hovind, Nori Howard-Butôt, Alexandra Mettler, Breon Mitchell, Maria Chan Morgan, James Overbeck, Eduardo Paguaga, Lynn Todd-Crawford, Colette and Denis Weaire, and Gerald Weales.

The edition has been the beneficiary of gifts from individual donors, all of whom have additionally enriched this endeavor with their con- tinuing interest: Laura Barlament, Jean B. Bergmark, Brenda and R. Cary Bynum, Claydean Cameron, Hilary Pyle Carey, Brian Cliff, Mary Evans Comstock, Judith Schmidt Douw, Jennifer Jeffers, Louis LeBroquy and

Ann Madden, Victoria R. Orlowski, and Frances L. Padgett in honor of Brenda Bynum.

EMORY UNIVERSITY

The vision and support of the Deans of the Graduate School have brought the edition to fruition; the editors especially thank George Jones, Alice N. Benston, and Eleanor Main (d.), who made the edition's affiliation with Emory possible, and subsequent Deans Donald G. Stein, Robert Paul, and Lisa Tedesco, who continued this support. The editors also thank Vice Provost of International Affairs Holli Semetko for contributions to the international research for the edition.

The Advisory Board at Emory University includes Alice N. Benston, Ronald Schuchard, Maximilian Aue, Geoffrey Bennington, and Sandra Still. The editors wish to recognize them and the contributions of other Emory faculty colleagues: Matthew Bernstein, Philippe Bonnefis, Thomas Burns, Brenda Bynum, David A. Cook, Michael Evenden, Steve Everett, William Gruber, Josué Harari, David Hesla, Geraldine Higgins, Peter Höyng, Dalia Judovitz, Judith Miller, Clark V. Poling, Donald Verene, and J. Harvey Young (d.).

Emory University Libraries have been at the heart of the research for the edition: The Woodruff Library – Directors Joan Gotwals, Linda Matthews, and Richard Luce, and Librarians Rachel Borchardt, Lloyd Busch, Joyce Clinkscales, Margaret Ellingson, Erika Farr, Kristin Gager, Marie Hansen, Erin Mooney, Anne Nicolson, Eric Nitschke, Marie Nitschke, Elizabeth Patterson, Chuck Spornick, Sandra Still, Ann Vidor, Elaine Wagner, Sarah Ward, Erik Wendt, and Gayle Williams; The Manuscript and Rare Book Library (MARBL) – Director Stephen Enniss, Teresa Burk, Ginger Cain, David Faulds, Naomi Nelson, Ellen Nemhauser, Elizabeth Russey, Kathy Shoemaker, and Donna Bradley; the staff of The ECIT center; The Michael C. Carlos Museum – Catherine Howett Smith; Woodruff Health Sciences Center Library – Director Carol Burns, Barbara Abu-Leid, and Erin Busch.

The dedicated support team in the Beckett Project office over the years has managed the varied demands of the edition superbly: Amanda R. Baker, Daphne Demetry, Julia Getman, Courtney King, Suzanne Powell, Molly Stevens, and especially Lynn Todd-Crawford. The editors appreciate the assistance of Rosemary Hynes and Geri Thomas in the

Graduate School, as well as the services of members of the Emory technical support staff: Adolf von Baden-Württemberg, Mahbuba Ferdousi, Wei Ming Lu, and Laura Pokalsky.

Emory University Graduate Fellows have served the research of the project with diligence and creativity: Adrienne Angelo, Levin Arnsperger, Jeffrey Baggett, Laura Barlament, Jenny Davis Barnett, André Benhaïm, Patrick Bixby, Karen Brown-Wheeler, Brooke Campbell, Lauren Cardon, Miriam Chirico, Brian Cliff, Curtis Cordell, Kathryn Crowther, Brian Croxall, Anthony J. Cuda, Anna Engle, John Fitzgerald, Christian Paul Holland, Jacob Hovind, Jennifer Jeffers, Michael Johnson, Jason Jones, Margaret Koehler, Paul Linden, Dominic Mastroianni, Martha Henn McCormick, Michelle Miles, Jennifer Poulos Nesbitt, Eduardo Paguaga, John Peck, Ralph Schoolcraft, Petra Schweitzer, Jennifer Svienty, Melissa Thurmond, Derval Tubridy, Kerry Higgins Wendt, Patrick Wheeler, and Julia McElhattan Williams.

Emory University Undergraduate Assistants have been effective and energetic in their work with the project: Margaret Anello, Amanda Barnett, Maiben Beard, Jonah Bea-Taylor, Shantal Chan-Friday, Rebecca Conner, Daphne Demetry, Kirsten Dorsche, Natasha Farquharson, Neil Garvin, Jessica Gearing, Julia Hendricks, Lisa Hutchinson, Erin Igney, Danielle Kuczkowski, Josh Millard, Touré Neblett, Alina Opreanu, Victoria Orlowski, Sarah Osier, Jason Rayles, Amanda Robinson, Brian Serafin, Danielle Sered, Emily Shin, Hannah Shin, John Southnard, Shannon Weary, Amanda Wilburn, and Ashley Woo.

THE AMERICAN UNIVERSITY OF PARIS

Initiated with the award of a grant from the Florence Gould Foundation, the edition's partnership with The American University of Paris has included faculty, staff, and students. The editors appreciate the assistance and support of Presidents Lee Huebner, Michael Simpson, and Gerardo della Paolera; Deans William Cipolla, Andrea Leskes, Michael Vincent, and Celeste Schenck; faculty – Christine Baltay, Geoffrey Gilbert, Richard Pevear, Roy Rosenstein, and University Librarians Toby Stone and Jorge Sosa Ortega, as well as the assistance of William Gatsby, Beatrice Laplante, Brenda Torney, and Karen Wagner.

AUP student interns: Amy Christine Allen, Lauren Anderson, Isolde Barker-Mill, Maranda Barnes, Susan Bell, Mischa Benoit-Lavelle, David

Bornstein, Brian Brazeau, Chrislaine Brito-Medina, Zachary Brown, Sarah Champa, Christina Chua, Laura Cook, Alessandra Cortez, Lisa Damon, Lindsay Franta, Natalie Frederick, Mia Genoni, Delphine Henri, Eric Hess, Laura Kaiserman, Alkmini Karakosta, Jennifer Kerns, Anthony Kraus, Caroline Laurent, Jennifer Laurent, Eugene Manning, Caroline Markunas, Ivy Mills, Candace Montout, Disa Ohlsson, Caleb Pagliasotti, Marta Lee Perriard, David Pollack, Jennifer Scanlon, Pamela Schleimer, Nils Schott, Jonathan Scott, Avra Spector, Jan Steyn, Alix Strickland, Leigh Thomas, Geoffrey Thompson, Gina Tory, Ulrike Trux, Todd Tyree, Christian West, Eugenia Wilbrenninck, Alison M. Williams, and April Wuensch.

ADVISORY TEAM

A number of colleagues have served the edition in an informal but important advisory capacity. The editors convey warm appreciation for their scholarship, counsel, and wisdom: Walter Asmus, Alice N. Benston, George J. Benston (d.) Brenda Bynum, Ruby Cohn, David Hesla, James Knowlson, Gerard Lawless, Breon Mitchell, Mark Nixon, Catherine Putman, Hilary Pyle, Roswitha Quadflieg, Ann Saddlemyer, Susan Schreibman, Ronald Schuchard, Carolyn Swift (d.), James White (d.), Katherine Worth, and Barbara Wright.

For their insight and assistance with the research for Volume I of *The Letters of Samuel Beckett*, the editors wish to thank the following persons: H. Porter Abbott, Mary Manning Howe Adams (d.), Klaus Albrecht, Avigdor Arikha, Anne Atik, Günter Aust. Ellie Balson, Iain Banks, William H. Baskin, Marcus Beale, Jean-Paul Beau, Georges Belmont, Helmut Berthald, Mrs. Wilfred Ruprecht Bion, Therese Birkenhauer (d.), Uli Bohnen, Gerard Bourke SJ, Nicola Gordon Bowe, Patricia Boylan, Enoch Brater, Barbara Bray, Robert I. Brown (d.), Terence Brown, Christopher Buckland-Wright, G.H. Burrows (d.) Gottfried Büttner, Marie Renate Büttner. John Calder, William Camfield, David E. Cartwright, Mary Ann Caws, John Charlton (d.), Carainn Childers, Louise Cleveland, Lisa Bernadette Coen, Brian Coffey (d.), Bridget Coffey (d.), John Coffey, Ann Colcord, Sally Hone Cooke-Smith (d.), Anne Corbett, John Corcoran, Liam Costello, Jean Coulomb (d.), Nick Coulson, Thomas Cousinau, Sharon Cowling, Gareth Cox, Ann Cremin, Anthony Cronin, William Cunningham (d.).

Norris Davidson, Gerald Davis, Maria Davis-Obolensky, Émile Delavenay (d.), Morgan Dockrell, Philippe and Michelle Douay, Gerry Dukes. Valerie Eliot, Maude Ellmann, Richard Ellmann (d.). Margaret Farrington, Raymond Federman, Sally Fitzgerald (d.), John Fletcher, M. R. D. Foot, Pierre Fourcaud, Wallace Fowlie (d.), Patricia Frere-Reeves (d.), Erika Friedman, Everett Frost. Bridget Ganly (d.), Padraic Gilligan, Gilles Glacet, Stanley Gontarski, Michael Gorman, John Graham, Greene's Book Shop, Nicholas Grene, Margaret Grimm, William E. Groves, Barbara Grüninger, James H. Guilford (d.).

Michael Haerdter, Anthony Harding, Clive Hart, Lawrence Harvey (d.), Ada Haylor (d.), Odile Helier, Jocelyn Herbert (d.), Phillip Herring, John Herrington, Michael Hertslet, Ian Higgins, Arthur Hillis (d.), David Hone, Oliver Hone, Fanny Howe, Susan Howe, Tina Howe, Werner Hüber, Alice Hudgens, John Michael Hudtwalcker, Liza Hutchinson. Randall Ivy. Brendon Jacobs (d.), Michael Jacobs, Thomas Jenkins, Robert Joesting, Harry Johnson, Ann and Jeremy Johnston, Tina Johnston, Bettina Jonič, Stephen Joyce. Marek Kedzierski, Ernest Keegan (d.), Eileen Kelly, John Kelly, Ben Kiely, Naum Kleiman, Margret Klinge, Elizabeth Knowlson, Charles Krance. Nigel Leask, Pierre Leber, Alex Léon, Roger Little, Mark Littman, Carla Locatelli, Herbert Lottman, Cyril Lucas, John Luce, Vanda and Jeremy Lucke, Bridget Lunn.

Bill McBride, Brian McGing, Barry McGovern, Dougald McMillan (d.), Franz Michael Maier, Alain Malraux, John Manning (d.), James Mays, Daniel Medin, Winrich Meiszies, Vivian Mercier (d.), Günter Metken (d.), Anna-Louise Milne, Ruth Morse, Dame Iris Murdoch (d.). Maurice Nadeau, Robert Nicholson, Robert Niklaus, Kevin Nolan, Ian Norrie, Marian von Nostitz. Fergus O'Donoghue SJ, Patrick O'Dwyer, Annick O'Meara, Christine O'Neil, Cathal O'Shannon, Prince Alexis N. Obolensky (d.), Serge S. Obolensky, Hugh Oram. Marjorie Perloff, Alexis Péron, Michel Péron, Lino Pertile, Alastair Pringle. Jean-Michel Rabaté, Lord Rathdonnell, Claude Rawson, Yvonne Redmond, Christopher Ricks, Bob Ritchie, Philip Roberts, Rachel Roberts, Anthony Rota, Elizabeth Ryan (d.), Robert Ryan.

Claude and Zoubeida Salzman, Elliseva Sayers, Pierre Schneider, Natalie Sheehan, Andrée Sheehy-Skeffington (d.), Philip Shields, Marc Silver, Anne Simonin, Seymour Slive, Colin Smythe, Michael Solomons, G. P. Solomos, Elizabeth Curran Solterer (d.), Helen Solterer, Sandra Spanier, Dame Natasha Spender, Arvid Sponberg, Emily Stanton, Lady

Staples, James Steffen, Diana Childers Stewart, Gerald Pakenham Stewart (d.), Marion Stocking, Elisabeth Stockton (d.), John Stone III, Claire Stoullig, Francis Stuart (d.). Sheila Harvey Tanzer, Dan Thompson, Deborah Thompson, Jeremy Thompson, Piers Thompson, Toby Thompson, Ursula Thompson (d.), Erika Tophoven, C. H. Trench (d.), Michael Jay Tucker. Helen Vendler, John Vice, Srdjan Vujic. Joachim Heusinger von Waldegg, Mervyn Wall (d.), David Wheatley, Thomas Whitehead, Clara Wisdom, Anne Leventhal Woolfson (d.). Anne Yeats (d.), Michael Yeats (d.).

Contributions that pertain primarily to later volumes of the edition are accordingly acknowledged there.

LIBRARIES AND ARCHIVES

Scholars, librarians, and archivists have developed valuable collections and have broadened our access to them with electronic catalogues, on-line finding aids, databases, and textbases. In particular, we wish to thank James Knowlson for his vision in establishing the Beckett International Foundation at Reading University, a central archive of the papers of Samuel Beckett, and for fostering collaboration among Beckett scholars internationally; we also thank Mary Bryden, Ronan McDonald, Anna McMullan, Mark Nixon, John Pilling, and Julian Garforth for their valued collegial assistance.

The editors acknowledge with gratitude the knowledgeable colleagues in libraries, archives, museums, and other offices of record who have assisted them with queries.

Aargauer Kunsthaus: Corinne Sotzek. *The Admiralty*, Foreign and Commonwealth Office, London: Gervaise Cowell (d.). *Akademie der Bildenden Künste München*, Archiv und Sammlungen: Birgit Joos. *American Library Association*: Renée Prestegard. *Archives of American Art*: Susan Marcott, Judy Throm. *Art Gallery of Ontario*, E. P. Taylor Research Library and Archives: Kathleen McLean. *Art Institute of Chicago Library*: Susan Goldweski, Mary K. Woolever.

Bank of Ireland: Éamon MacThomas. *Eduard-Bargheer-Haus*, Hamburg: Dirk Justus, Peter Zilze. *Barnard College Archives*: Donald Glassman. *Bayerische Staatsgemäldesammlungen*, Munich: Helge Siefert. *BBC Sound Archives*: Gösta Johansson. *BBC Written Archives*: John Jordan, Jacqueline Kavanagh, Erin O'Neill, Julie Snelling, Tracy Weston. *Bibliothèque*

Acknowledgments

Publique d'Information Centre Georges Pompidou, Paris. *Bibliothèque Polonaise*, Paris. *Bibliothèque Sainte-Geneviève*, Paris. *La Biennale Di Venezia Archive*: Daniela Ducceschi. *Boston College*, John J. Burns Library of Rare Books and Special Collections Library: Director Robert O'Neill, John Atteberry, Shelley Barber, Amy Braitsch, David E. Horn, Susan Rainville. *Boston University*, Howard Gotlieb Archival Research Center: Director Howard Gotlieb, Margaret Goostray, Christopher Noble, Sean Noel, Alexander Rankin, Kim Sulik. *British Film Institute*: Janet Moat, Wilf Stevenson. *British Institute of Florence*, Harold Acton Library: Alyson Price. *British Library*: Nicholas Barker, John Barr, Sally Brown, Christopher Fletcher, Andrew Levett, Alice Prochaska, Rupert Ridgewell; Newspapers, Colindale – Stewart Gilles; Oriental and India Office Collections, APAC – Dorian Leveque. *The British Museum*: Christopher Denvir. *Galerie Jeanne-Bucher*, Paris.

  Cambridge University: University Library – Peter M. Meadows; Trinity College Library – Diana Chardin. *Campbell College*, Belfast: Keith Haines. *Columbia University*, Butler Library, Rare Books and Manuscripts: Director Jean Ashton, Director Bernard Crystal, Tara C. Craig, Jennifer Lee. *Cornell University*: John M. Olin Library, Department of Rare Books – David R. Block; Fiske Collections, Division of Rare and Manuscript Collections – Patrick J. Stevens. *Courtauld Institute of Art*: Julia Blanks, Barbara Hilton-Smith, Sue Price, Ernst Vegelin.

  Dartmouth College, Rauner Special Collections Library: Director Philip Cronenwett, Director Jay Satterfield, Joshua Berger, Stephanie Gibbs, Sarah I. Hartwell. *Department of Foreign Affairs*, Dublin: Bernadette Chambers. *DePaul University*, Richardson Library: Joan M. Mitchanis. *Deutsches Literatur Archiv, Schiller National Museum*, Marbach: Ute Doster, Gunther Nickel, Jutta Reusch. *The Dictionary of Irish Biography*: James McGuire. *Dresden Kunsthalle*: Martin Roth. *Dublin City Archives*: Mary Clark. *Dublin City Gallery The Hugh Lane*: Director Barbara Dawson, Patrick Casey, Liz Forster, Joanna Shepard. *Dublin Writers Museum*: Esther O'Hanlon.

  Eastman School of Music, Sibley Music Library: Jim Farrington. *Feis Ceoil*, Dublin: Ita Beausang, Maeve Madden. *Fondation Maeght*, St. Paul-de-Vence: Annette Pond. *Ford Foundation*: Alan Divack, Jonathan Green. *Association Les Amis de Jeanne et Otto Freundlich*: Edda Maillet. *Frick Museum Library*: Lydia Dufore, Sue Massen.

  Georgetown University Libraries: Nicholas B. Sheetz. *Germanisches Nationalmuseum Nürnberg*: Ulrike Heinrichs-Schreiber. *Global Village*:

John Reilly. *The Goethe Institut* (now *Goethe-Zentrum*), Atlanta: Michael Nentwich, Gusti Stewart. *Grolier Club Library*: J. Fernando Peña. *The Peggy Guggenheim Museum*, Florence: Phillip Rylands. *Hamburg University*: Hans Wilhelm Eckardt, Eckart Krause. *Hamburger Kunsthalle*: Director Helmut R. Leppien (d.), Ute Haug, Ulrich Luckhardt, Matthias Mühling, Uwe M. Schneed, Annemarie Stefes. *Händel-Haus Library*, Halle: Götz Traxdorf. *Harvard University*: Countaway Library of Medicine – Julia Whelan; Fogg Art Museum – Lizzy Bamhorst, Sarah Kianovsky; Harvard Theatre Collection – Annette Fern, Fredric Woodbridge Wilson; Houghton Library – Michael Dumas, Elizabeth Falsey, Susan Halpert. *Hiroshima Museum of Art*: Y. Furutani. *The Huntington Library*: Sara S. Hodson. *Leonard Hutton Galleries*: Shary Grossman.

Illustrated London News: Richard Pitkin. *Indiana University*, The Lilly Library: Director Lisa Browar, Director Breon Mitchell, William Cagle, Saundra Taylor. *Institut mémoires de l'édition contemporaine (IMEC)*, Paris-Caen: Director Olivier Corpet, André Derval, Albert Dichy, Nathalie Léger, Martine Ollion. *Internationales Musikinstitut Darmstadt*: Wilhelm Schlüter. *Inverclyde Libraries*, James Watt Library, Greenock, Scotland: Betty Hendry, Rebecca McKellar. *Irish Copyright Licensing Agency*: Jorid Lindberg. *Irish Jewish Genealogical Society and Family History Centre of the Irish Jewish Museum*, Dublin: Stuart Rosenblatt.

Kent State University Libraries: Kathleen Martin, Stephanie Wachalec. *Kingston University*: Anne Rowe, Jane Ruddell. *Kungliga Biblioteket*, Stockholm: Anders Burius. *Kunstmuseum Basel*: Christian Selz.

Law Society of Ireland: Linda Dolan. *Leeds University Library*: Christopher Sheppard. *Leibniz-Archiv*, Hanover: Herbert Breger. *Library of Congress*, Department of Manuscripts, Washington, DC: Alice Love Birney, Jeffrey M. Flannery. *Linen Hall Library*, Belfast: Gerry Healey. *London Transport Museum Library*: Helen Kent.

McMaster University, Mills Memorial Library: Jane Boyko, Eden Jenkins, Carl Spadoni, Charlotte A. Stewart-Murphy. *Middle Temple Library*, London: Stuart Adams. *Munch Museum*, Oslo: Gerd Woll. *Museum Ludwig*, Cologne: Ulrich Tillman. *The Museum of Modern Art*, New York. *The Museum of Modern Art*, Oxford: David Elliot, Pamela Ferris.

National Archives, Washington, DC: John E. Taylor. *National Archives of Ireland*: David Craig, Catriona Crowe, Aideen Ireland, Tom Quinlan. *National College of Art and Design*, Dublin: Alice Clarke. *National*

Acknowledgments

Gallery of Art, Washington, DC: Anne Halpern. *National Gallery of Ireland*: Leah Benson, Márie Burke, Niamh MacNally, Ann M. Stewart. *National Gallery* London, Libraries and Archive Department: Flavia Dietrich-England, Jacqueline McComish; New Media: Charlotte Sexton. *National Irish Visual Arts Library*: Ciara Healy, Donna Romano. *National Library of Ireland*: Director Patricia Donlon, Catherine Fahy, Patrick Hawes, Elizabeth M. Kirwan, Noel Kissane, Gerard Lyne. *New Directions Publications*: James Laughlin (d.). *New York Public Library*: Berg Collection – Director Isaac Gewirtz, Mimi Bowling, Philip Milito, John D. Stinson; Billy Rose Theatre Collection – Director Robert Taylor, Mary Ellen Rogan, Nina Schneider; Theatre on Film and Tape Archive – Betty Corwin. *New York University*: Fales Library and Special Collections – Ann E. Butler, William J. Levay; Tisch School of the Arts – Elaine Pinto Simon. *Northwestern University*, McCormick Library of Special Collections: Director R. Russell Maylone, Scott Krafft, Susan R. Lewis, Sigrid P. Perry, Allen Streicker.

The Office of Public Works, National Monuments Division, Dublin: William S. Cumming. *Ohio State University Libraries*, Department of Rare Books and Manuscripts: Director Geoffrey D. Smith, Director Robert A. Tibbetts, Elva Griffith, Keith Lazuka. *Operhaus Halle*: Iris Kruse. *Oxford University*: Bodleian Library – Colin Harris, Judith Priestman; McGowin Library, Pembroke College. *Princeton University Libraries*: Mudd Library, Rare Books and Special Collections – Tad Bennicoff; Rare Books and Special Collections – Annalee Pauls, Jean F. Preston, Margaret M. Sherry Rich, Don C. Skemmer. *Public Records Office of Northern Ireland*: Ian Maxwell.

Radio Telefís Éireann (RTE), Dublin: Brian Lynch. *Random House*: Jean Rose, Jo Watt. *Reading University Library*, Location Register of English Literary Manuscripts – David Sutton; Special Collections – Director Michael Bott, Director James A. Edwards, Verity Andrews, Rosemarie Jahans, Frances Miller, Brian Ryder. *Rotunda Hospital Library*, Dublin: Aoife O'Connor. *Royal Academy of Music Library*, Dublin: Philip Shields. *Royal College of Physicians*, Dublin: Robert Mills. *Royal College of Surgeons in Ireland*: Fiona Allen. *Royal Hibernian Academy*, Dublin: Aoife Corbett, Ella Wilkinson. *Royal Irish Academy*: Linde Lunney. *Royal National Theatre*: Nicola Scadding. *Royal Society of Literature*, London: Kathleen Cann.

Paul Sacher Stiftung, Basel: Robert Piencikowski. *St. Bride Foundation Library*: Rosalind Francis. *St. Mary's Cathedral Galway*: Noreen Ellecker.

Sotheby's, London: Peter Beal, Sarah Cooper, Anthony W. Laywood, Sarah Markham, Tessa Milne, Bruce W. Swan. *Southern Illinois University at Carbondale*: Center for Dewey Studies – JoAnn Boydston; Morris Library, Special Collections Research Center – Randy Bixby, David V. Koch. *Sprengel Museum*, Hanover: Martina Behnert. *Staatliche Galerie Moritzburg*, Halle: Wolfgang Büche. *Staatliche Museen zu Berlin, Kunstbibliothek*: Bernd Evers. *Staatsarchiv Aargau*: Marcel Giger. *Staatsbibliothek zu Berlin*: Roland Klein, Jutta Weber. *Stadtarchiv Halle*: Roland Kuhne. *Stanford University Libraries*, Special Collections: Sara Timby. *State University of New York at Buffalo*, The Poetry Collection: Director Michael Basinski, Director Robert J. Bertholf, Heike Jones, Sue Michael, Sam Slote. *Syracuse University Libraries*, The George Arents Research Center: Carolyn Davis, Kathleen Manwaring.

Tate Modern, Archive: Jane Ruddell. *Théâtre de l'Odéon*, Paris: Laure Benisti. *Trinity College Dublin*: Secretary to TCD, Michael Gleeson; Monica Alcock, Phyllis Graham, Jean O'Hara; Library – Charles Benson, John Goodwillie, Trevor Peare; Manuscripts Department – Director Bernard Meehan, Jane Maxwell, Linda Montgomery, Stuart Ó Seanóir.

Herzog Anton Ulrich Museum, Brunswick: Silke Gatenbröcker. *Ulster Museum*, Belfast: S. B. Kennedy. *UNESCO Library*, Paris: Jens Boel. *Universal Edition*: Elisabeth Knessl. *University of California Berkeley*, The Bancroft Library: Anthony Bliss, Bonnie Hardwick. *University of California Davis*, University Library, Department of Special Collections: Melissa Tyler. *University of California Los Angeles*, University Research Library: David Zeidberg. *University of California San Diego*, Mandeville Library: Linda Corey Claassen. *University of Chicago*, Regenstein Library, Special Collections Research Center: Director Alice Schreyer, Betsy Bishop, Stephen Duffy, Robert Kovitz, Daniel Meyer, Suzy Taraba, Jonathon Walters. *University of Delaware Libraries*, Special Collections: Director Timothy D. Murray, L. Rebecca Johnson Melvin, Jesse Rossa. *University College Dublin*, Special Collections: Seamus Helferty, Norma Jessop. *University of Glasgow*, Special Collections: Claire McKendrick, Lesley M. Richmond. *University of Manchester*, John Rylands Research Institute: Stella Halkyard, Peter McNiven. *University of Maryland* (College Park), Archives: Beth Alvarez, Naomi Van Loo. *University of New Hampshire*, Library: Roland Goodbody. *University of North Carolina at Chapel Hill*, Ackland Art Museum: Anita E. Heggli. *University of Notre Dame Library*, Department of Special Collections: Ben Panciera. *University of*

Acknowledgments

Rochester Library, Rare Books and Manuscripts: Mary M. Huth. *University of Sheffield Libraries*, Special Collections: J. D. Hodgson. *University of Sussex*, Archives: Michael Roberts. *The University of Texas*: Harry Ransom Humanities Research Center: Director Thomas Staley, Linda Ashton, Patrice Fox, Kathy Henderson, John Kirkpatrick, Carlton Lake (d.), Sally Leach, Richard Oram, Maria X. Wells, Richard Workman. *University of Toronto*: Fisher Library – Edna Hajnal, Kathleen McMorrow; Pratt Library – Robert Brandeis, Gabbi Zaldin. *University of Tulsa*, The McFarlin Library, Special Collections: Director Sidney Huttner, Melissa Burkart, Lori N. Curtis. *University of Western Ontario*, Library: Meville Thompson.

Victoria and Albert Museum: The National Art Library – Nina Appleby, Alison Baber, Mark Evans, Francis Keen; The Theatre Collections at the Victoria and Albert (formerly The London Theatre Museum Archives) – Janet Birkett.

Wake Forest University, Reynolds Library: Sharon Snow. *Washington University in St. Louis*: Olin Library, Department of Special Collections: – Director Holly Hall (d.), Director Anne Posega, Chatham Ewing, Sonya McDonald, Carole Prietto, Kevin Ray. *Walker Art Center*: Jill Veiter. *Waterford County Museum*: Martin Whelan.

Yale University: Beinecke Rare Book and Manuscript Library – Vincent Giroud, Kathryn James, Nancy Kuhl, Natalia Sciarini, Patricia Willis, Tim Young; Gilmore Music Library – Suzanne Eggleston Lovejoy; Sterling Memorial Library, Manuscript and Archives Department – Christine Weidemann.

Zurich James Joyce Foundation: Director Fritz Senn, Ruth Frehner, Ursula Zeller.

MANUSCRIPT DEALERS

The following manuscript dealers have been helpful to the research for the edition, especially for informing us of offerings and forwarding our inquiries: Antic Hay Books; Charles Apfelbaum; Blue Mountain Books and Manuscripts; Alan Clodd (d.); Seamus DeBúrca; R. A. Gekoski; Thomas A. Goldwasser; Glenn Horowitz; George J. Houle; Index Books; Joseph the Provider; Kennys; Kotte-Autographs; Maggs Bros. Ltd.; Bertram Rota Ltd.; Sotheby's; Swann Gallery; Steven Temple Books; Ulysses Books; Waiting for Godot Books.

PUBLISHERS

Barney Rosset was Samuel Beckett's American publisher at Grove Press. The editors are grateful for his important contributions to modern publishing and express appreciation for his efforts as the edition's original General Editor. The editors also thank all those at Grove Press who assisted with the research, with special mention of Judith Schmidt Douw, Fred Jordan, Richard Seaver, Astrid Myers, and John Oakes, as well as Morgan Entrekin and Eric Price at Grove/Atlantic, for their professional support of the edition in its publishing transition.

The late Jérôme Lindon, Director of Les Editions de Minuit and Samuel Beckett's French publisher, was a trusted adviser to Samuel Beckett who appointed him as his Literary Executor. The editors thank Irène Lindon, Director of Les Editions de Minuit, for her cooperation.

Cambridge University Press is committed to presenting *The Letters of Samuel Beckett* as an edition of the literary correspondence. The editors are grateful for the confidence and support of editors Andrew Brown and Linda Bree, the fine copyediting of Leigh Mueller, the care of proof-reader Anthony Hippisley, and the assistance of Caroline Murray, Alison Powell, Maartje Scheltens, and Kevin Taylor.

The editors express their gratitude for the assistance of many associates who have read all or portions of this manuscript and who have made helpful suggestions. Any errors remain the editors' responsibility. The editors would be pleased to receive corrections or additions for possible inclusion, with appropriate acknowledgment, in subsequent editions.

PERMISSIONS

The editors and publishers acknowledge the following sources of copyrighted documents and are grateful for the permission to reproduce these materials. While every effort has been made, it has not been possible to trace all copyright holders. If any omissions are brought to our notice, we will be pleased to include the appropriate acknowledgments in subsequent editions.

Letters, manuscripts, and other documents written by Samuel Beckett are reproduced in this volume by courtesy of The Estate of Samuel Beckett.

Other letters and documents are reproduced with the kind permission of the following copyright holders: Klaus Albrecht for Günter Albrecht; The Estate of Samuel Beckett for Frank Beckett; Lisa Jardine for Jacob Bronowski; The Random House Group Ltd. for letters written by Charles Prentice, Ian Parsons, and Harold Raymond on behalf of Chatto and Windus, and for the letter written by Charles Prentice to George Hill; Pollinger Limited and the proprietor of The Estate of Richard Church; John Coffey for The Estate of Brian Coffey; Gilbert Collins for Seward Collins and Dorothea Brande; Anthony R. A. Hobson on behalf of The Estate of Nancy Cunard; Penguin Books Ltd. for Hamish Hamilton; David Hone for Joseph Hone; Betsy Jolas for Eugene Jolas and Maria Jolas; Margaret Farrington and Robert Ryan for Thomas McGreevy; The Estate of Samuel Putnam; Susan Bullowa and Jane Bullowa for George Reavey; A. D. Roberts for Michael Roberts, and for his permission to consult The Michael Roberts Archive before its deposit in the National Library of Scotland; Routledge (an imprint of the Taylor and Francis Group) for T. M. Ragg; The Board of Trinity College Dublin for letters written by Thomas Brown Rudmose-Brown, Walter Starkie, and Robert W. Tate on behalf of Samuel Beckett; Daniel Hay for Jean Thomas; Lady Staples and other representatives of The Estate of Arland Ussher; John H. Willis; Gráinne Yeats on behalf of the copyright held by Michael Yeats for Jack B. Yeats.

Permission to publish has also been granted by the following owners of letters, manuscripts, and other documents: Klaus Albrecht; Archives nationales, Paris; The Beckett International Foundation, Reading University; Trustees of The British Museum; The Poetry Collection, State University of New York at Buffalo; University of Cape Town; The Chatto and Windus Archives at Reading University; Special Collections Research Center, University of Chicago Library; Rare Book and Manuscript Library, Columbia University; Private Collection of Nuala Costello; Dartmouth College Library; Special Collections, University of Delaware Library; Association Les Amis de Jeanne et Otto Freundlich; Peter Gidal, London; David Hone; The Lilly Library, Indiana University; Department of Special Collections, Kenneth Spencer Research Library, University of Kansas; Private Collection of Dr. Katarina Kautsky, née Sauerlandt; Northwestern University Library; Berg Collection of English and American Literature, The New York Public Library, Astor, Lenox and Tilden Foundations; Princeton University Library; Archives Jacques Putman, Paris; Tatiana Goryaeva, Director, Rossijsky Gosudarstvenny Arkhiv Literatury i Iskusstva (RGALI; Russian State Archive of Literature and Art); Morris Sinclair; Harry Ransom Humanities Research Center, The University of Texas at Austin; The Board of Trinity College Dublin; Zurich James Joyce Foundation, Hans E. Janke Bequest.

ABBREVIATIONS

LIBRARY, MUSEUM, AND INSTITUTIONAL
ABBREVIATIONS

AN	Archives nationales, Paris
AUP	The American University of Paris
BIF	Beckett International Foundation, University of Reading
BM	British Museum, London
Burns Library	John J. Burns Rare Book and Manuscript Library, Boston College
CtY	Beinecke Rare Book and Manuscript Library, Yale University
DeU	University of Delaware Library, Newark
ENS	Ecole Normale Supérieure, Paris
GN	Germanisches Nationalmuseum Nürnberg
HK	Hamburger Kunsthalle, Hamburg
ICSo	Southern Illinois University, Carbondale
ICU	Special Collections Research Center, Regenstein Library, University of Chicago
IEN	Charles Deering McCormick Library of Special Collections, Northwestern University
IMEC	Institut mémoires de l'édition contemporaine, Paris-Caen
InU	The Lilly Library, Indiana University
KF	Kaiser Friedrich Museum, Berlin
KU	Kenneth Spencer Research Library, University of Kansas
MBA	Musée des Beaux-Arts, Strasburg
MOMA	Museum of Modern Art, New York

NBuU	The Poetry Collection, State University of New York at Buffalo
NGB	Neue Nationalgalerie, Berlin
NGI	National Gallery of Ireland
NGL	National Gallery, London
NhD	Rauner Special Collections Library, Dartmouth College
NjP	Manuscripts Division, Department of Rare Books and Special Collections: Princeton University Library
NLI	National Library of Ireland
NNC, RBML	Rare Book and Manuscript Library, Columbia University
NPG	National Portrait Gallery, London
NYPL, Berg	New York Public Library, Berg Collection
OkTU	Department of Special Collections, McFarlin Library, University of Tulsa, Oklahoma
RHA	Royal Hibernian Academy, Dublin
RTE	Radio Telefís Éireann
TCD	Manuscript Room, Trinity College Dublin Library, when used with reference to manuscript identification; in other instances, a short form for Trinity College Dublin
TxU	Harry Ransom Humanities Research Center, The University of Texas at Austin
UoR	Department of Special Collections, University of Reading

PRIVATE COLLECTIONS

Albrecht	Private collection of Klaus Albrecht
Costello	Private collection of Nuala Costello
Gidal	Private collection of Peter Gidal, Index Books
Sinclair	Private collection of Morris Sinclair

ABBREVIATIONS FOR PUBLICATIONS, MANUSCRIPTS, AND TRANSLATORS

AvW	Adolf von Baden-Württemberg
GD	Samuel Beckett's German Diaries, Beckett International Foundation, University of Reading Library
NRF	*Nouvelle Revue Française*
OED	*Oxford English Dictionary*, second electronic edition
Pyle	Refers to numbers assigned to paintings by Jack B. Yeats in Hilary Pyle, *Jack B. Yeats: A Catalogue Raisonné of the Oil Paintings* (London: Andre Deutsch, 1992) 3 vols., and Hilary Pyle, *Jack B. Yeats: His Watercolours, Drawings and Pastels* (Dublin: Irish Academic Press, 1993)
SBT/A	*Samuel Beckett Today/Aujourd'hui*

EDITORIAL ABBREVIATIONS

b.	born	m.	with date of marriage
c.	circa		or to indicate
d.	died		married name
f.	folio	n.d.	no date
fl.	flourished	pseud.	pseudonym
[illeg]	illegible word, words	s/	signed
ins	inserted	?	uncertain
		<___>	cancelation

ABBREVIATIONS IN BIBLIOGRAPHICAL NOTES

ACI	autograph card initialed
ACS	autograph card signed
AH	another hand
AL draft	autograph letter draft
ALI	autograph letter initialed
ALS	autograph letter signed
AMS	autograph manuscript
AN	autograph note

ANI	autograph note initialed
ANS	autograph note signed
APCI	autograph postcard initialed
APCS	autograph postcard signed
APS	autograph postscript
env	envelope
illeg	illegible
imprinted	imprinted with SB's name
letterhead	imprinted letterhead
pm	postmark
Pneu	pneumatique
PS	postscript
TLC	typed letter copy
TLcc	typed letter carbon copy
TLdraft	typed letter draft
TLI	typed letter initialed
TLS	typed letter signed
TMS	typed manuscript
TPCI	typed postcard initialed
TPCS	typed postcard signed
TPS	typed postscript

INTRODUCTION TO VOLUME I

"I find it more & more difficult to write, even letters to my friends." So wrote Samuel Beckett in 1936 to Tom McGreevy, his chief correspondent for the period represented here, 1929 to 1940.[1] The difficulty of writing letters is not the only one of which the young Beckett complains, nor is it even the most acute. "I can't read, write, drink, think, feel, or move," he tells his friend Mary Manning Howe, while making his lonely tour round Germany's art treasures; "I seem impelled to address my friends when least in a condition to."[2] Immobility, impossibility, illness, and impasse: across a human landscape populated by negation, doubt, refusal, and retreat, the letters collected here cut their way, making connections, opening possibilities, courting half-chances, chastising indifference. During this period, letters matter inordinately to Beckett. They are often his sole means of connection: to places where he is not, to people with whom he cannot converse directly, to others with whom he would not wish to converse directly. Letters are a channel to possible selves, selves of which he is as yet only dimly aware, even to selves he would deny. Letters make possible a writing, a voice perhaps, which his more public work does not yet dare to deploy.

Although Beckett claims in various ways that he hates letters, his sixty years of letters, taken as a whole, number more than fifteen thousand, and form one of the great literary correspondences of the twentieth century. No special pleading need be made as to the importance of even perfunctory letters from the hand of a writer as important as Beckett. Yet what will strike the reader is the fact that Beckett seldom writes perfunctory letters. Even when responding in haste, even when

---

[1] SB to Thomas McGreevy, 28 November 193[6].
[2] SB to Mary Manning Howe, 14 November 1936.

penning a note on the back of a postcard, even when appealing from deep distress, Beckett is an extraordinarily painstaking and careful correspondent. In later years, especially after *Waiting for Godot* brings its author unexpected celebrity, the quantity of letters which his conscientiousness obliges him to write increases significantly – for him, alarmingly. And as the man becomes a public figure, however reluctantly, their nature changes too, becoming in large part reactive: responses to requests for information from academics, for permissions from directors, for interpretations from translators, for advice from producers, for schedules from publishers. Here, in the early years, the letters are fewer, but they matter all the more, sent as they are into an epistolary space about which little can be assumed. The early letters convey information nearly always as a secondary function, their primary role being that of establishing a relation – by requesting, stirring, provoking, even outraging if necessary. The interest of the recipient is not always assured, often has to be stimulated and then maintained – and this, when what Beckett has to offer is usually far from conventional or easily palatable.

Biography has an almost ineluctable tendency to make an individual's greatness seem predestined. The individual's letters, if that individual is as lucid in his hesitations and ambivalences as Beckett, serve to restore the uncertainty informing the choices, the dilemmas and daily doubt which might at any point have compelled desertion of the cause or defection to some camp of lesser achievement. Beckett's letters reveal the compromises as well as the bold refusals, the longing for recognition as well as the revulsion at publicity, the numerous false paths almost taken as well as the inner conviction that only one path – the literary – is truly worth following.

Before being one of communication, the job of a letter is, then, to establish common terms between the writer and the recipient (whom the French language helpfully names the *destinataire*): to create some complicity or solidarity between aspirant and respondent; and to do so beyond the immediate social, geographical, professional, even intellectual, environs which might otherwise have fostered less deferred or indirect verbal exchange. In doing so the letters permit – or permitted, since one of the things which adds to the value of this correspondence is that it is hard to imagine there ever arising a twenty-first-century equivalent – an intimacy which is both magnified and diminished, both accelerated and delayed, with respect to what could be expected or achieved in conversation. For Beckett, however, the complicity which he is seeking in his letters is also one of which he is acutely wary; he is strongly suspicious of the demand implicit in solidarity; and he is almost cripplingly aware of the extreme constraints forever placed upon intimacy, not least when that intimacy is formed or sustained by the self-consciousness and control which letters permit, with their possibilities of revision and self-censorship. It may be partly in this sense that his "hatred" of letters is to be understood. For Beckett, merely to write, and then release, a letter during this period implies a sort of self-overcoming, a provisional acceptance of community when, as he puts it, "all groups are horrible";[3] a climb down from the solitary self-sufficiency to which he aspires, whether he does so as self-laceration or as self-aggrandizement (nobody loves me / the world does not deserve me). More simply, letters take their author *out of himself*, they take him *elsewhere*. They do this, when the desire to be freed from self, to be elsewhere, is itself being critically appraised by Beckett as one of the primary ruses for evasion of truth and desertion of any putative literary vocation.

The restlessness which Beckett experiences during this period allows him to settle only briefly, and he is almost constantly on the move, between Dublin, London, and Paris, taking in Germany too on several occasions, opting finally for Paris in late 1937, just in time to move again in 1940, although by forces largely beyond his control. The danger in all such physical displacements is clear to him. Writing to Tom McGreevy from Germany in 1936, it is expressed as a question: "Was it then another journey from, like so many?"[4] Then, as a confession, he writes to Mary Manning Howe, from the tail-end of his German sojourn: "It has turned out indeed to be a journey from, and not to, as I knew it was, before I began it."[5] The journey *from*: when those journeys which are letters are equally haunted by the suspicion that they are serving as flight. They are haunted despite the fact that they are incontrovertibly *to*, letters *destined to* indeed – and not just to anyone. In their wonderful variety, Beckett's letters are written to appeal to the unique sensibilities and language-possibilities of their particular reader.

---

[3] SB to Thomas McGreevy, 6 June 1939.   [4] SB to Thomas McGreevy, 9 October 1936.
[5] SB to Mary Manning Howe, 13 December 1936.

The letters collected in this volume attest to a loneliness deriving from a lack of much more than mere companionship. But even as they attest to this lack, they also attenuate it. Wherever Beckett is, he can also be elsewhere, even when on the road. His letters trace out an alternative reality for their writer, and help him to sustain himself, almost as in a spider's web of his own weaving, wherever he is living – and failing fully to live. Of course, for the letter's journey to be successful, for the else-wheres to serve their function, these must be invested with affect, whether of desire, ambition, anger, or the longing for recognition. Every recipient must represent some alternative, if not of place or of feeling then of possibility, as in the numerous letters to agents and publishers, letters written reluctantly and with a sinking heart, but in the knowledge that without them his work will remain unknown and his options will only narrow further.

Feeling and possibility may yet meet, and when they do, as in the great letters to McGreevy, a writing emerges which is quite as exciting as anything Beckett is achieving with a view to publication. Even to McGreevy, Beckett can be reticent: he writes to him in French when he wishes to avoid the risk of being over-read; he scarcely discusses with him the details of his sexual life, barely mentioning, for example, that he has "seen quite a lot" of Peggy Guggenheim in 1938; and he tells him on occasion that he prefers to discuss certain private matters with him in person.[6] Yet to McGreevy, as to a few select others, he opens some-thing perhaps more important than any details of the life lived or the works completed. He opens a sense of the life not yet embarked upon, the life only dreamed of, when these will be immersed to saturation in the past and future that are art: music, painting, literature. Being already the Beckett which he perhaps will only later become in his published *oeuvre*, he must apologize, even when issuing insights of incalculable value, for a "miserable letter,"[7] for "this futile and not even melancholy letter,"[8] for "a very white kind of letter,"[9] for "this Jeremiad."[10] But being already, here in his letters, the Beckett who can allow a writing to emerge which is born of vulnerability and release, he

---

[6] SB to Thomas McGreevy, 5 January 1938.
[7] SB to Mary Manning Howe, 18 January 1937.
[8] SB to Thomas McGreevy, 24 February 1931.
[9] SB to Thomas McGreevy, 4 November [*for* 3 November 1932].
[10] SB to Thomas McGreevy, 4 August 1932.

can also admit that "I'm not ashamed to stutter like this with you who are used to my wild way of failing to say what I imagine I want to say and who understand that until the gag is chewed fit to swallow or spit out the mouth must stutter or rest. And it needs a more stoical mouth than mine to rest."[11]

The authorized biography of Samuel Beckett, by James Knowlson, bears the title, *Damned to Fame* (1996). Certainly, Beckett was amazed and often dismayed by the popularity his work gained during the last thirty years of his life. As we have suggested above, this popularity had a direct impact on Beckett the correspondent, dramatically increasing the number and considerably altering the nature of the letters he wrote. Yet what is striking about Beckett before the years of "fame," is how wary he was of the public dimension of the arts, even as he was attempting to gain this dimension for himself and his work. Nowhere is this more patent than in his dealings with publishers. Here, his wariness turns often into a disdain or hostility which is all the more notable in that his principal interlocutors at publishing houses or journals tend to be intelligent, patient, learned, supportive, and gentlemanly: men such as his publisher Charles Prentice at Chatto and Windus, a figure almost unimaginable in the cut and thrust of today's trade publishing world. "Truck direct with publishers," writes Beckett in 1936 when such "truck" is still largely a fantasy, "is one of the few avoidable degradations."[12] For Beckett, merely attempting to be published is cursed as "creeping and crawling and sollicitation [sic],"[13] tantamount to transporting "a load of manure or a ton of bricks"[14] to "literary garbage buckets."[15] A six-week delay in response from a certain Rupert Grayson sparks a rare paranoid reaction in which the usual self-deprecation turns into self-inflation, as Beckett worries that: "I have an idea he may try and do the dirty. He has no background and I have nothing to show that he has any of my property."[16] In rage, the same day, he writes to George Reavey, one of whose roles it was to mediate his relations with the presses: "Grayson has lost it or cleaned

---

[11] SB to Thomas McGreevy, 18 October 1932.
[12] SB to Thomas McGreevy, 7 August 1936.
[13] SB to Thomas McGreevy, 18 [August 1932].
[14] SB to Thomas McGreevy, 1 March 1930.
[15] SB to Thomas McGreevy, Friday [? summer 1929].
[16] SB to Thomas McGreevy, 8 October 1932.

himself with it. Kick his balls off."[17] Reavey, who fills the role of agent while helping Beckett in many other ways, is the object of the greatest swings of mood and judgment during these years, as Beckett goes from soliciting him to reviling him to needing him, from shunning him to recommending him to his friends. "I neither trust him nor like him," he writes in 1936, "but know no other agent."[18] Things deteriorate when Reavey publishes a Beckett text without its author's permission, to the point where Beckett writes to Reavey a letter so scathing that this perhaps explains why it no longer exists; though its content may be reconstructed from a letter Beckett writes to McGreevy, in which Reavey is described as: "(1) A liar (2) A clumsy Sophist (3) An illiterate."[19] Within a month, however, Beckett writes, "I extended the little finger of reconciliation to G.R.";[20] and some short time after that he is content once more to be "dumping the work on Reavey."[21]

The temptation is ever present, for Beckett, to abandon the effort to diffuse the work beyond the closest circle of friends. But this temptation is weak compared to the pressure coming from another source, which Beckett believes can be relieved only by its receiving public recognition. "I dread going home with nothing cut & dried to do," he writes to McGreevy from Germany in 1937: "Proofs & a publication would carry me over till I could get away again."[22] He writes of his mother, that she "supposes I am brimming over with material for books [...] anything rather than désoeuvrement."[23] Publishers and their acceptance become the propitiatory flag which he hopes to wave at his exasperated family members, who are in a state of incomprehension as to the choices he is making and refusing to make in his life. That the flag is never large enough or appropriately marked, that the public recognition does not arrive in time or from the appropriate quarters, remains one of the major disappointments of Beckett's life.

When approval does come, from as valued a reader as McGreevy, Beckett's joy, if short-lived, is unequivocal. When he learns of his

---

[17] SB to George Reavey, 8 October 1932.
[18] SB to Thomas McGreevy, 7 August 1936.
[19] SB to Thomas McGreevy, 27 June 1936.
[20] SB to Thomas McGreevy, 26 July [1936].
[21] SB to Thomas McGreevy, 7 August 1936.
[22] SB to Thomas McGreevy, 16 February 1937.
[23] SB to Thomas McGreevy, 20 February [1935]. "Désoeuvrement" (having nothing to do).

friend's favorable judgment of the manuscript of *Murphy*, he responds: "I need not tell you I was delighted with your letter. I was afraid you would not like it much at all. I find the people all so hateful myself, even Celia, that to have you find them lovable surprises and delights me."[24] Much more common than approval, however, are misprision and rejection, when the skin is never thick enough for these not to hurt. Beckett's brother asks him, "'Why can't you write the way people want'";[25] this question is repeated, in more euphemistic terms, by nearly every publisher he encounters. Rejection is accompanied by "the usual kind words,"[26] by "honeyed regrets,"[27] or by "the classical obeisance et l'obligeance prophétique."[28] Or it comes bluntly: "Heard from Frere-Reeves yesterday, a curt rejection. 'On commercial grounds we could not justify it in our list.' And of course what other grounds of justification could there be."[29] Some revenge can be wrought, through mockery of "Shatton & Windup" or "The Hogarth Private Lunatic Asylum,"[30] or through a limerick penned at the expense of Doubleday Doran.[31] But this revenge is slight when compared to the need: "The chief thing is to get the book OUT."[32]

The willingness of the young author to offer words of compromise in order to facilitate publication may surprise readers familiar only with the intransigence of an older Beckett. In response to a publisher's wish for cuts in *Murphy*, he writes to Reavey: "I should be willing to suppress such passages as are not essential to the whole and adjust such others as seem to them a confusion of the issue"; the admonishment to Reavey which follows is an agent's nightmare: "Be astonished, firm, & up to a point politely flexible, all at once, if you can."[33] Not surprisingly, the negotiation proves unfruitful, although, with a desperation almost as audible as the irony, Beckett would write: "The last I remember is my

---

[24] SB to Thomas McGreevy, 7 July 1936.
[25] SB to Thomas McGreevy, 7 August 1936.
[26] SB to Thomas McGreevy, 9 October 1936.
[27] SB to Thomas McGreevy, 17 July [1936].
[28] SB to George Reavey, 23 February 1937. "Obligeance prophétique" (prophetic obligingness).
[29] SB to Thomas McGreevy, 7 August 1936.
[30] SB to George Reavey, 8 October 1932. And again to Reavey, 27 December 1936.
[31] SB to George Reavey, 4 August 1937.
[32] SB to George Reavey, 27 December 1936.
[33] SB to George Reavey, 13 November 1936.

readiness to cut down the work to its title. I am now prepared to go further, and change the title if it gives offence, to Quigley, Trompetenschleim, Eliot, or any other name that the publishers fancy."[34] When finally, thanks in part to the intercession of McGreevy and the painter and writer Jack B. Yeats, Routledge makes an offer on *Murphy*, Beckett writes, "I would sign anything to get the book out";[35] a tractability which asks to be weighed alongside the apparently contradictory, but perhaps equally true, assertion: "I feel even less about its being taken than I did when it was rejected."[36]

Indifference on the part of the world, or rejection from the public realm, corresponds so closely – so much more closely than success – to what is being experienced internally, that it provokes instant recognition. Defeat before the act, before the writing, will become the very ground of Beckett's imaginative world. Here, already, it gives rise to a plethora of confessions. To McGreevy, of his essay on Marcel Proust's novel *A la recherche du temps perdu*, he writes, "I can't start the Proust."[37] This matures into "I have not put pen to paper on Proust";[38] which becomes "You know I can't write at all. The simplest sentence is a torture";[39] followed by "I can't write anything at all, can't imagine even the shape of a sentence";[40] leading to "I haven't tried to write. The idea itself of writing seems somehow ludicrous."[41] Yet somehow his *Proust* does get written, and he even feels some pride in it, before this is overtaken by distaste at what he judges to be "very grey & disgustingly juvenile,"[42] "a merely critical extension [. . .] blafard, gritty like the Civic Guard's anus."[43]

Having been relegated, in this period, to what he calls "slopemptying," critical writing comes in for very harsh censure:[44] "dishonest & surfait" is how he describes his review of Jack Yeats's novel *The*

---

[34] SB to George Reavey, 20 December 1936. "Trompetenschleim" (Ger., trumpetslime).
[35] SB to Mary Manning Howe, [after 10 December 1937].
[36] SB to Thomas McGreevy, 22 December 1937.
[37] SB to Thomas McGreevy, Thursday [? 17 July 1930].
[38] SB to Thomas McGreevy, [before 5 August 1930].
[39] SB to Thomas McGreevy, 25 January 1931.
[40] SB to Thomas McGreevy, 8 November 1931.
[41] SB to Thomas McGreevy, 4 August 1932.
[42] SB to Thomas McGreevy, 3 February 1931.
[43] SB to Thomas McGreevy, 11 March 1931. "Blafard" (wan).
[44] SB to Mary Manning Howe, [after 10 December 1937].

Amaranthers.[45] But the judgment meted out to his poetry and fiction is only slightly more generous. "Fake" is a word he uses freely of his own work,[46] "involontairement trivial";[47] or "really a most unsavoury & not very honest work," as he writes of the first draft of *Murphy*[48] – "It reads something horrid."[49] Nowhere does he express more eloquently what he feels to be lacking in his writing than in a letter to McGreevy from 1932, where he berates himself for its lack of necessity. "Homer & Dante & Racine & sometimes Rimbaud" – these become the whips with which to punish the literary self whose productions are never anything better than "trigged up" or "<u>facultatif</u>." His own writing lacks the urgency and inevitability which for him distinguish work that is true, which must be as instinctive and automatic as a physical reflex, and which he describes memorably, in an expression that will echo through his whole writing life: "I'm in mourning for the integrity of a pendu's emission of semen [...] the integrity of the eyelids coming down before the brain knows of grit in the wind."[50]

The gap between the self which writes and the self which reads can be as much of an affliction as a solace. Yet there is, despite asseverations to the contrary, no shortage of reading done during these years. It is tempting to invoke a notion like "apprenticeship" in this context, and certainly the later Beckett *oeuvre* is inconceivable without the mass of books consumed during this period. Yet, if apprentice Beckett is, not least to the writer who acts as his mentor and guide during much of the period, James Joyce, then he is one who feels he is not so much learning a trade as failing to gain initiation into a sect. He fears that the very knowledge he is accruing may itself be ruining his future chances, turning him into a "Sorbonagre," leading him to a spurious realm of knowingness.[51] "If I am not careful," he writes, after he has found in some German novels a new justification for a figure from *Murphy*,

---

[45] SB to Thomas McGreevy, 17 July [1936].
[46] See, for example, SB to Thomas McGreevy, Saturday [3 September 1932], quoted in SB to Thomas McGreevy, 13 [September 1932], n. 4.
[47] SB to Thomas McGreevy, 8 September 1935. "Involontairement" (involuntarily).
[48] SB to Thomas McGreevy, 23 May [1936].
[49] SB to Thomas McGreevy, 9 June 1936.
[50] SB to Thomas McGreevy, 18 October 1932. "Facultatif" (optional); "pendu" (hanged man).
[51] SB to Thomas McGreevy, 11 March 1931.

"I shall become clear as to what I have written."[52] It is not just that an ever-increased awareness of literary heritage furnishes the aspiring writer with a yardstick of personal unworthiness; it is that the particular sort of success which writing constitutes is already perceived to be achievable only in a sort of blind or spastic incomprehension. "Jenseit der Spekulation kommt erst der Mensch in sein Eden" (Only beyond speculation does man reach his Eden), he writes in 1934 to his cousin Morris Sinclair.[53] Though only later will he formulate this idea fully, in the letters to Georges Duthuit from after World War II, the awareness is already present here of the enticements and traps of knowledge. The remark he makes to Samuel Putnam, as early as 1932, concerning his indebtedness to James Joyce, that "I vow I will get over J. J. ere I die," is just the thin end of the writer's uncomfortable wedge.[54] Little wonder that he is delighted to report to McGreevy in 1935 a remark made to him by Nuala Costello: "'You haven't a good word to say for anyone but the failures.'"[55] For writing, if it is to matter, must constitute itself as a sort of shedding, a venturing out with no clear landmarks, not even when these are literary, and with no sure hope of return: "when to have ever left one's village ceases to seem a folly," he writes to Mary Manning Howe in 1937, "perhaps it is only then that the writing begins."[56]

Fortunately perhaps, not every writer's work which Beckett encounters during this period strikes him as being as necessary as that of Homer or Dante. "I have been reading wildly all over the place," he tells McGreevy in 1936, "Goethe's Iphigenia & then Racine's to remove the taste."[57] Beckett's reading may not be wild, but diverse it certainly is, as even a partial list of authors absorbed will make abundantly clear: Ariosto, Aristotle, Jane Austen, D'Annunzio, Darwin, Diderot, George Eliot, Fielding, Geulincx, Grillparzer, Guarini, Hölderlin, Samuel Johnson, Ben Jonson, Kant, Keats, Lawrence, Leibniz, Melville, Plato, T. F. Powys, Ramuz, Jules Renard, Rimbaud, Rousseau, Sade, Sainte-Beuve, Sartre, Schopenhauer, Stendhal, Sterne, Tasso, Vigny. Few invite quite the excoriation that Goethe's *Tasso* receives, yet the view which Beckett forms of

---

[52] SB to Mary Manning Howe, 18 January 1937.
[53] SB to Morris Sinclair, 5 May 1934.   [54] SB to Samuel Putnam, 28 June 1932.
[55] SB to Thomas McGreevy, 8 September 1935.
[56] SB to Mary Manning Howe, 18 January 1937.
[57] SB to Thomas McGreevy, 25 March 1936.

this work may stand for the many among the canonical greats – Darwin's *The Origin of Species* is "badly written catlap"[58] – which he dismisses: "He really invites one very patiently to think of him as a machine à mots, a cliché separator, & a bunker of the suffering that has not proved its merit in a thousand impressions, or a vademecum edition."[59] And the dead fare better than the living. It is for his contemporaries that Beckett reserves his most hostile fire, ignited as this is by a mix of genuine contempt and barely admissible envy. Beckett calls T. F. Powys's writing "a fabricated darkness & painfully organised unified tragic completeness."[60] D'Annunzio has a "dirty juicy squelchy mind, bleeding and bursting, like his celebrated pomegranates."[61] Aldous Huxley's latest offering does not even merit reiteration of its title, becoming "Cunt Pointercunt. A very painstalling work."[62] Lawrence trades in a "tedious kindling of damp."[63] T. S. Eliot's essay on Dante is "insufferably condescending, restrained & professorial."[64] And Proust too comes in for rough treatment, much rougher in the letters than in the essay on his work, his prose being deemed "more heavily symmetrical than Macaulay at his worst," and his loquacity being judged "certainly more interesting and cleverly done than Moore's, but no less profuse, a maudlin false teeth gobble-gobble discharge from a colic-afflicted belly."[65]

Little wonder that the prospect of having to read Proust, or of having, as Beckett puts it, "to contemplate him at stool for 16 volumes," is far from charming.[66] Yet for the *Proust* to be written, Proust must be read, and not once but twice, in an infuriatingly inadequate edition. More than the exasperation, louder than the condemnations, stronger than the disgust and the envy, what informs Beckett's reading, as it does his writing in his letters about his reading, is its *energy*. When he wishes to read the work of Arnold Geulincx, "without knowing why exactly,"[67]

---

[58] SB to Thomas McGreevy, 4 August 1932.
[59] SB to Thomas McGreevy, 5 March 1936. "Machine à mots" (word machine).
[60] SB to Thomas McGreevy, 8 November 1931.
[61] SB to Thomas McGreevy, 7 July 1930 [*for* 7 August 1930].
[62] SB to Thomas McGreevy, 4 August 1932.
[63] SB to Thomas McGreevy, Tuesday [7 August 1934].
[64] SB to Thomas McGreevy, 4 August 1937.
[65] SB to Thomas McGreevy, Friday [? summer 1929].
[66] SB to Thomas McGreevy, Friday [? summer 1929].
[67] SB to Thomas McGreevy, 5 March 1936.

he forces himself into the library at Trinity College in Dublin, which he has compelling reasons to wish to avoid, day after day. Kant's complete works have to be lugged, when they arrive in Paris, from Customs to his lodging. And as the few examples just given may indicate, to the physical efforts to gain access to the work he deems important there corresponds an irrepressible linguistic verve.

Beckett is rarely more inventive than when writing about other writers, especially when insulting them. Nor do the efforts in language stop there. Geulincx's work is unavailable in translation, and so the determined reader works his Latin up to a suitable level to tackle him in the original. He reads Kant and Goethe in German, Dante, Ariosto and D'Annunzio in Italian, Proust of course in French, and efforts are made in Spanish that will later permit him to translate an anthology of Mexican poetry. Of course, one might remark that even as he was fleeing his one surefire career path, as a university professor, the ingrained scholarly habits remained. But such a remark only begs the question, when his polymathic drives were anything but obvious to a man of his family background or cultural milieu. Certainly, there are local satisfactions to be drawn from reading, along with the whips for self-punishment and the squibs to throw at the feet of rivals. In Schopenhauer, Beckett finds "an intellectual justification of unhappiness – the greatest that has ever been attempted."[68] A French translation of *The Odyssey* offers "something of the old childish absorption with which I read Treasure Island & Oliver Twist and many others."[69] He is "enchanted with Joseph Andrews," which is "Jacques and the Vicar of W. in one."[70] Sainte-Beuve offers "the most interesting mind of the whole galère."[71] Somewhat surprisingly, "the divine Jane [...] has much to teach me."[72] And, less surprisingly, Sade's *Les cent-vingt journées de Sodome*, whose "composition is extraordinary, as rigorous as Dante's," inspires in him "a kind of metaphysical ecstasy."[73] Yet no amount of local satisfaction, even when it rises to enchantment or ecstasy, quite accounts for the sense one gathers from the letters, that Beckett is

---

[68] SB to Thomas McGreevy, Friday [c. 18 July 1930 to 25 July 1930].
[69] SB to Thomas McGreevy, Tuesday [c. 22 September 1931].
[70] SB to Thomas McGreevy, 8 October 1932.
[71] SB to Thomas McGreevy, 5 December [1932]. "Galère" (crew).
[72] SB to Thomas McGreevy, 14 February [1935].
[73] SB to Thomas McGreevy, 21 February 1938.

following a rigorously demanding linguistic and literary curriculum, devised by the writer he had not yet become – and in defiance of precisely this same writer.

It may be in the context of such a tension informing literary practice – be it writing or reading – that Beckett's dreams of an escape which would eradicate for ever any such problem should be understood. Yes! If he were to throw in the word-towel, give it all up, and become – what? Even as late as aged thirty, in 1936, he can be dreaming of a flight from the literary which is staggeringly literal: "I think the next little bit of excitement is flying," he writes to McGreevy; "I hope I am not too old to take it up seriously, nor too stupid about machines to qualify as a commercial pilot." The reasons for grasping at employment are never more clearly expressed than here: "I do not feel like spending the rest of my life writing books that no one will read. It is not as though I wanted to write them."[74] That Beckett never viewed his work in words as a lofty or romantic vocation leaps out from nearly every letter. That he viewed it not even as an honest career is only slightly less evident, perhaps because this view is overshadowed by his family's stronger, even outraged, conviction of the same. And so it is that the idea of a "real job" gives rise to: Beckett the trainee filmmaker laboring under Sergei Eisenstein in Moscow; Beckett the advertising agent at work in London; Beckett the assistant in the National Gallery, Trafalgar Square; Beckett the Harvard lecturer, the Cape Town lecturer, the Milan lecturer; Beckett the translator for an international organization in Geneva; Beckett the teacher of French in a technical school in Bulawayo, Southern Rhodesia; and even more fancifully, Beckett the instructor of Princess Elizabeth "in the Florentine positions."[75]

Letters are the vehicles for the requests and applications to these other lives, countries, cities, destinations. Hence they may be, for Beckett, the purveyors of deception, for who is he to pretend to expertise in anything, even in literature and languages – especially in literature and languages. Letters are, it gradually becomes clear, not just the means, but also the end, by which the blocked road of the present becomes, in writing, the uncluttered highway of a future. They permit their writer to imagine

[74] SB to Thomas McGreevy, 26 July [1936].
[75] SB to Thomas McGreevy, 4 August 1932.

himself in other roles and lives, and to describe these new characters and their plots to his friends. And they do so while permitting their absurdity to become transparent. Shortly after he has given up "this grotesque comedy of lecturing" at Trinity College Dublin, to his parents' everlasting dismay,[76] a job in Bulawayo tempts, "but a few minutes consideration equipoised so perfectly the pros & cons that as usual I found myself constrained to do nothing."[77] To the organization in Geneva he replies, "asking for particulars, but forgot to sign the letter." He does not fail to draw his conclusion: "a nice example of Verschreiben."[78]

Nowhere does the ambivalence informing that slip of the pen take firmer root than in the ground which Beckett treads throughout this period, the home turf. Behind the idea of joining the family business at Clare Street in Dublin lies a whole fantasy of fitting in, following in his father's footsteps, belonging. When his brother Frank enters the family business in 1930, the fantasy only quickens. "I wonder would my Father take me into his office," he writes to McGreevy in 1932, "That is what Frank did."[79] The endorsement of genealogy which settling in Dublin represents becomes only the more urgent when his father dies in 1933: "I can't write about him," he tells McGreevy shortly after, "I can only walk the fields and climb the ditches after him."[80] The fact that he can always undo his own idea – "There is no room for another clerk in the office, and even if there were I simply could not do the work" – does little to stanch the guilt felt before his family.[81] The fact that, if Frank were to welcome him into the office, "my present saliva would burn a hole in the envelope" – this counter-perception does little to slow regression toward the nostalgic idyll.[82] This last – because first – resort is pungent with premature resignation, with dejected posturing in cardigan and slippers, the bottle of stout by the fire; thick with a voluptuousness of self-pity at the *homme moyen sensuel* he suspects he is becoming, in an Ireland from which escape is no longer thinkable: "I feel now that I shall meet the most of my days from now on here and in tolerable content, not feeling much guilt at

---

[76] SB to Charles Prentice, 27 October 1930.
[77] SB to Thomas McGreevy, 3 November 1932.
[78] SB to Thomas McGreevy, 5 June 1936 [*for* 1937]. "Verschreiben" (Ger., slip of the pen).
[79] SB to Thomas McGreevy, 4 August 1932.
[80] SB to Thomas McGreevy, 2 July 1933.
[81] SB to Thomas McGreevy, 18 [August 1932].
[82] SB to Thomas McGreevy, 5 March 1936.

making the most of what ease there is to be had and not bothering very much about effort."[83]

When, in the winter of 1937 to 1938, escape from Ireland does happen, it is described as "like coming out of gaol in April."[84] On the wall of his room where he has taken temporary lodging, in the Hôtel Libéria in Paris, Beckett sees confirmation of the release achieved: "A sunlit surface yesterday," he writes to McGreevy, "brighter than the whole of Ireland's summer."[85] The terms are ones which he knows McGreevy will appreciate, so much of their correspondence being concerned with surfaces and light. Beckett's investment in the literary during this period is more than matched by his investment – of energy, of time, of language – in the visual arts, and in painting specifically. With McGreevy, who was already a connoisseur and who would go on to become Director of the National Gallery of Ireland, the investment bears fruit, as Beckett explores a world unbeset by any of the envy or ambivalence pervading the literary. The efforts he makes to study art, to visit galleries and museums, in Ireland, in London, in Paris, most of all in Germany, are unflagging. He spends entire days absorbing painting and learning the artists and traditions, mastering a visual language which he will himself never practice. And he does so with one eye ever on the possibilities of the present, possibilities clearer to him in this domain than in the literary. Since the primary appeal of Beckett's work is so often to the ear rather than to the eye, it might be easy to neglect what an exceptionally acute and well-trained eye he possessed. The letters reveal that eye as it roves, as it trains itself, as it probes, absorbs, quizzes, rejects, and is ravished. It is not until he corresponds with the art historian and critic Georges Duthuit, in letters which form the basis of the *Three Dialogues* published in 1948 (and which provide the backbone to Volume II of the present edition), that anything approaching a manifesto of the possible and significant in art of the present will be extracted from him. But these dialogues are dependent upon the prior exchanges with McGreevy, exchanges in which it is less the range of knowledge deployed which is remarkable than the immensity of the

[83] SB to Thomas McGreevy, 26 April 1937. "Homme moyen sensuel" (average man with average tastes and appetites).
[84] SB to Thomas McGreevy, 10 December 1937.
[85] SB to Thomas McGreevy, 27 January 1938.

curiosity displayed. Once again, Beckett is pursuing his own arduous curriculum, one which takes him away from the literary, but from which he is convinced the literary must learn.

Beckett's letters testify to an extraordinary visual memory, largely unassisted by the technical supports of photographs or reproductions. "I remember the Bassano in Hampton Court very well," he tells McGreevy; "In the second or third room, isn't it? The wild tormented colour."[86] His memory is such that he challenges established attributions – and several of his re-attributions have been vindicated by subsequent catalogues. "I had forgotten the little Fabritius," he writes to McGreevy after a further visit to the Louvre, "A very slapdash attribution. More like a Flinck."[87] He refuses to believe that a small portrait of a head in Ireland's National Gallery is a Velázquez (though he is much less certain about how to spell this painter's name). He advises his friend Arland Ussher, on the basis of a poor photograph, as to the possible attribution of a painting which Ussher has purchased: "As a decorative statement of weights & tensions," he writes, "it seems to me to lack only technique & bravura to pair up with the easel recreations of Gianbattista [*for* Giambattista] Tiepolo & Sons."[88] He compiles for McGreevy exhaustive lists of the works he views during his tour of Germany, and even as he claims that "there is really not much point writing like this about the pictures," he "can't stop without mentioning the Poussin Venus. Beyond praise & appraisement."[89] He reports to McGreevy on the career of George Furlong, who is appointed Director of Ireland's National Gallery in 1935, with a highly critical gaze, mocking his lapses of taste in acquisitions, and ending by condemning his entire aesthetic policy: "It is time someone put him in mind of the purpose of a picture gallery, to provide pictures worth looking at and the possibility of seeing them."[90] And he does this, characteristically, while all the time claiming that: "I'm afraid I couldn't write about pictures at all. I used never to be happy with a picture till it was literature, but now that need is gone."[91]

[86] SB to Thomas McGreevy, 7 March 1937.
[87] SB to Thomas McGreevy, 3 April 1938.
[88] SB to Arland Ussher, 14 June [1939].
[89] SB to Thomas McGreevy, 16 February 1937.
[90] SB to Thomas McGreevy, 14 May 1937.
[91] SB to Thomas McGreevy, 28 November 1936.

Though the previously published and by now famous 1937 "German Letter" to Axel Kaun uses Beethoven's Seventh Symphony to sketch a possibility for literature, and though the letters do contain some fascinating insights into music – and into ballet and film as well – it is in painting that Beckett most commonly intuits directions in which he believes writing should be heading.[92] In the work of Cézanne, first, Beckett sights – or sites – an all-important representation of the otherness of the world, "incommensurable with all human expressions whatsoever." The "deanthropomorphizations of the artist" are the more precious in Cézanne's portraits, where the individual subject becomes "incapable of loving or hating anyone but himself or of being loved or hated by anyone but himself"; a claim which Beckett immediately and doubly undermines, as if he had seen too much or reached too far, by signing off his letter in a firm rejection of solipsism – "God love thee" – and in a request to McGreevy that he "forgive the dégueulade."[93]

What is glimpsed in Cézanne is more fully grasped in the work of the artist who will elicit from Beckett something as close as he comes at this stage to a fully fledged theory. Perhaps it is the very excitement at locating the artistic horizon so nearby, in the work of an approachable compatriot, that leads him to find so many excuses not to accept Jack Yeats's repeated invitation to visit his studio during his "at-homes." "Set out on Saturday afternoon to see Jack Yeats," he tells McGreevy, "and then en route changed my mind."[94] Yeats stirs in Beckett a rare acquisitive instinct, until the young unemployed writer is able to scrape together the cash to put down a deposit on a painting, *Morning*. As with Cézanne, it is the "ultimate hard irreducible inorganic singleness" that fascinates Beckett, and the sense in Yeats's painting of "the convention & performance of love & hate, joy & pain, giving & being given, taking & being taken" having been "suddenly suspended." Yeats leads Beckett to a "perception & dispassion" which, in contrast to what he finds in Watteau (to whom he likens Yeats), is "beyond tragedy." Even as one resists the temptation to find countless adumbrations of Beckett's later work in the letters, it is hard not to hear harbingers of the tone and vision that will become "Beckettian," when he writes: "the way he puts down a man's head & a woman's head side by side, or face to face, is

---

[92] SB to Axel Kaun, 9 July 1937.
[93] SB to Thomas McGreevy, 8 September 1934. "Dégueulade" (throwing up).
[94] SB to Thomas McGreevy, 13 [September 1932].

terrifying, two irreducible singlenesses & the impassable immensity between."[95] In Yeats's work, nature itself, Ireland's nature, becomes the setting of "the ultimate inorganism of everything." And again the future looms, the theatrical work for which Beckett will be most celebrated, in the metaphor he uses to describe Ireland here: "a nature almost as inhumanly inorganic as a stage set."[96] When, in 1938, returning to Ireland after a prolonged absence, he visits Yeats's studio and sees his "magnificent new picture," entitled *Helen,* he rediscovers the "same extraordinary tenderness & distinction of handling," and beyond that, "depth and a courage more than of conviction, of certainty, absolutely natural & unrhetorical." He rediscovers the very sense of necessity that years previously he located in Homer and Dante, the sense of art as a physical extension of the self, an art which is as natural as breathing. Unable to produce his own art to match, Beckett the viewer none the less absorbs the impact: "I was really knocked all of a heap."[97]

If art hits, and must hit, the body, this is because it must emerge from the body to begin with, if it is to be necessary. For the greats, this may be as easy as breathing; for the remainder, which includes Beckett himself, whose writing emerges "above an abscess and not out of a cavity," the somatic impetus is less unambiguously life-sustaining or satisfying.[98] Commenting on Aldous Huxley's use of the term "mental masturbation," Beckett says, with a sideways glance at his own restricted productivity, that there are worse things, "mental aspermatism for example."[99] When finally two poems do arrive, they are blessed as "a double-yoked orgasm in months of aspermatic nights & days."[100] At its best, writing is evacuation of pus, or is ejaculation of sperm. Being very rarely at its best, it is more commonly – even obsessively – that less exalted convulsion, defecation. When, amidst the "dies diarrhoeae,"[101] some poems are taken by a journal, Beckett celebrates this acceptance of "three turds from my central lavatory." The toilet is not private, and the

---

[95] SB to Cissie Sinclair, 14 [August 1937].

[96] SB to Thomas McGreevy, 14 August 1937.

[97] SB to Thomas McGreevy, Thursday [4 August 1938].

[98] SB to Thomas McGreevy, 18 October 1932.

[99] SB to Thomas McGreevy, 28 November 1937 [*for* 1936].

[100] SB to Thomas McGreevy, Saturday [12 September 1931].

[101] SB to George Reavey, 8 October 1932. "Dies diarrhoeae" (Lat., literally, days of diarrhea, echoing the *Dies Irae* of the reguiem Mass).

"Proustian arse-hole"[102] needs to be contemplated, as we saw above, while the critic himself is "at stool."[103] To McGreevy, Beckett conveys his intention to return to writing as a determination to "take down the petites merdes de mon âme."[104] Beckett envisages writing a work which might finally please a publisher, in the following terms: "When I imagine I have a real 'twice round the pan & pointed at both ends' I'll offend you with its spiral on my soilman's shovel."[105] Of his poems which he calls "the Bones," his hope is that they will become a "bolus," which, on publication, will cause readerly discomfiture – "May it stick in their anus."[106] Even when the work is not itself fecal, it can still do cloacal duty. When an article is requested of him, he finds himself "looking through my essuie-cul de réserve."[107] The scatology may contain an undergraduate's jocularity, but that it is no mere joke, still less any mere trope, is clear even without recourse to Beckett's *oeuvre*. Writing and shitting: without recourse to Freud, either, these may be seen to share for Beckett an all-important intimacy, an urgency, a necessity even, just as they share a difficulty and delight in emission and transmission. They share, that is to say, both the requirement and the limits of *expression*. And so the irony is much fainter than might at first be imagined, when, after a publisher suggests substantial cutting of *Murphy*, what are envisaged next are "The Beckett Bowel Books." Such new work might at least have a rhythm, one which would tie it to the body and its necessary functions: "My next work shall be on rice paper wound about a spool, with a perforated line every six inches and on sale in Boots. The length of each chapter will be carefully calculated to suit with the average free motion."[108]

What writing and the rectal spasm share is that they take the subject, quite literally, *out of himself*. They are not the only spasms to do this, however, and there are others which take Beckett so far out of himself that he fears he may never return. "I always see the physical crisis just round the corner," he writes to Cissie Sinclair in 1937, confirming

---

[102] SB to Thomas McGreevy, 25 August [1930].

[103] SB to Thomas McGreevy, Friday [? summer 1929].

[104] SB to Thomas McGreevy, [? after 15 August 1931]. "Petites merdes de mon âme" (droppings from my soul).

[105] SB to Charles Prentice, 15 August 1931.

[106] SB to George Reavey, 9 January 1935 [*for* 1936].

[107] SB to George Reavey, 6 May 1936. "Essuie-cul de réserve" (spare bumf).

[108] SB to Mary Manning Howe, 14 November 1936.

that this crisis is far from merely dreaded: "It would solve perhaps the worst of what remains to be solved, clarify the proven anyway, which I suppose is the best solution we can hope for."[109] The "crisis" takes the form of boils, cysts, and especially heart palpitations, all of which, even while he tries to attribute to them purely organic origins, Beckett suspects are psychosomatically induced.

It is only when the crisis puts "the fear of death" into him,[110] that Beckett finally decides to move into a quite new word-setting, a highly alien one, yet one in which, as in writing, language must do the work of relation and creation: in 1934 he begins a psychoanalysis with W. R. Bion, then a junior analyst, whom he quickly re-christens "the covey." He counts the sessions: "On Monday I go for the 133rd time."[111] He fears that "the analysis is going to turn out a failure."[112] Yet he sees "no prospect of the analysis coming to an end." The somatic symptoms persist, but with a new force he realizes: "how lost I would be bereft of my incapacitation."[113] The shift in perception may appear slight, but what the letters make clear – clearer than Beckett ever intends – is how significant it is, to the point where he can write in 1935 to McGreevy: "The old heart pounces now & then, as though to console me for the intolerable symptoms of an improvement";[114] or write to him later, after the analysis has ended, that he has "overcome the need of returning to my vomit."[115]

The letters manifest the shift not just in what they say, but also in the way they say it. They present a change, achieved in part through words used in the highly specialized context of psychoanalysis, through those words used in the not-entirely-different context that is letter-writing: not just their information, now, but their increasingly undefended style that becomes a disarming directness. Certainly, there is still room for highly self-conscious Beckett parades, of the sort that make him say of his early work, "of course it stinks of Joyce in spite of most earnest endeavours to endow it with my own odours."[116] The letters do provide

---

[109] SB to Cissie Sinclair, 14 [August 1937].
[110] SB to Thomas McGreevy, 10 March [1935].
[111] SB to Thomas McGreevy, 8 February [1935].
[112] SB to Thomas McGreevy, 1 January 1935.
[113] SB to Thomas McGreevy, 14 February [1935].
[114] SB to Thomas McGreevy, 20 February [1935].
[115] SB to Thomas McGreevy, 14 May 1937.
[116] SB to Charles Prentice, 15 August 1931.

plentiful opportunities for the flexing of newly acquired linguistic muscles, as well as for old-fashioned showing-off. Those written to Nuala Costello, for example, are quite as narcissistically turned, as elliptical and excessive at once, as anything he ever wrote, an awareness of which he seems to catch even as he protracts it, telling her: "My velleities of self-diffusion in this stew of LETTERS have been repulsed with the traditional contumely, so now I'm sulking and won't play."[117] Here, as on occasion with Cissie Sinclair, the seductions of verbal play seem to take the place – as it were, synechdochally – of seduction more palpable. He even goes so far as to say, at one point, with tongue only half in cheek, that "Perhaps the literary value of this letter [. . .] would be promoted by a few lines of verse."[118]

Shortly after writing to McGreevy of "obstipation" and "tepid eviration,"[119] Beckett declares: "I find that eschewal of verbal sanies is one of my New Year resolutions."[120] Of course, this resolution is quite as hard to keep as any other. Yet the verbal play and display in the letters, which will yield a tone familiar from the published work of the 1930s, can indeed cede at any point to something less ostentatious or guarded. When Beckett's writing darts between languages or registers, at times he may be less demonstrating his cleverness than exploring the shortcomings in the words at his disposal. The distinction between this exploration and his Joycean play may seem slim, but it is none the less important, as he invites not so much his reader's admiration as an apprehension of a shared incapacity – shared with language, too, now. When Beckett writes that "the Irish Times accuses reception of his new prose work," he may not be merely forgetting he is writing in English.[121] When he writes to McGreevy, upon one more rejection of a work, "Anyhow tant piss," he may be offering more than a transnational pun; may be inviting his friend into a verbal space where no ready-made language can do justice to what he feels, when this includes a wish to shrug off the whole disappointment in the fewest words possible.[122] When he skips across registers and languages searching

[117] SB to Nuala Costello, 27 February 1934.
[118] SB to Cissie Sinclair, 14 [August 1937].
[119] SB to Thomas McGreevy, 4 November [*for* 3 November 1932].
[120] SB to Thomas McGreevy, 5 January [1933].
[121] SB to Arland Ussher, 25 March 1936.
[122] SB to Thomas McGreevy, 18 [August 1932]. "Tant piss" (pun on "tant pis" [too bad]).

for a word, he is not always just parading his learning. Sometimes, he is being as straightforward as possible. When he jots on the back of a picture postcard to McGreevy sent from Florence, "Che tu fossi meco," he is not only finding a fancy way of saying, "Wish you were here"; he is above all trusting in his friend to catch the compacted message, which includes their shared love of languages, of Italy and Italian, of Dante, and of the escape which all these together imply.[123] When he flashes between English and French – and Latin – in his letters to McGreevy, when he complains that "this vitaccia is terne beyond all belief," he is not only repudiating the "terne" in his very formulation.[124] He is coaxing his reader on to a fragile ground between languages, a ground that he will make ever more daringly his own in the years to come.

Beckett's letters reveal, they present, explain, harangue, occasionally theorize, more rarely justify. But as, from the moment he started to write – and not only because of the influence of Joyce – their author turned his back on any instrumentalist understanding of language, the letters do these things as acts of a writer, as acts of writing. What might appear a contradiction – between a highly self-conscious Beckett for whom the act of writing mattered even when it came to letters and the Beckett we have tried to sketch above, who always had his *destinataire* in mind, who wrote letters *to* – may, in fact, offer a key to what is distinctive in the tone and style of the letters, as compared to his more purposefully literary work of the period. For Beckett's writing in his letters is never so unadornedly itself as when it is moving out of itself, never so fresh and indicative of his future as when he feels confident of his *destinataire*. The letters presented here deploy their range of languages and idioms not merely for show; they do so in order to tickle, engage, challenge their intended reader, and they do so on the reader's linguistic home-ground. From the cod-bombast of his French to his cousin Morris Sinclair, to the super-formal English of his applications for jobs, to the slang of his back-slapping to Arland Ussher – and beyond: Beckett writes as he hopes, and increasingly trusts, he will be heard.

---

[123] SB to Thomas McGreevy, 2 February 1937.

[124] SB to Thomas McGreevy, 24 February 1931. "Vitaccia" (It., miserable life, wretched existence). "Terne" (colorless).

Beckett's letters, like his literary works of the period, are performances as much as they are communications; only, if they are performances, they are so for a very particular audience. And when his faith in
this audience grows, as it does with McGreevy, his language leaps,
explores the in-between spaces, achieves sudden condensations. So
too may it relax. Then, a freedom, an unselfconscious simplicity,
emerges which may not be found in the *oeuvre* until Beckett turns to
writing fiction in French at the end of World War II. This is what one
senses in the extraordinary letter of 10 March 1935, in which Beckett
explains to McGreevy his reasons for entering into and persisting with
his psychoanalysis; explains his attempt, compelled by his acute physical crises, to shed his "feeling of arrogant otherness," his "feeling that
I was too good for anything else," in favor of something for which he has
not yet found a name – unless its name is the extended one offered by
this marvelous letter.[125] "It is more than I can do to go on," he writes to
Arland Ussher in 1937 – having gone on at length in his letter.[126] "How
hard it is to reach a tolerable arrangement between working & living,"
he writes to McGreevy, when the letter is the indispensable link in just
such an "arrangement."[127]

---

[125] SB to Thomas McGreevy, 10 March 1935.
[126] SB to Arland Ussher, 26 March 1937.
[127] SB to Thomas McGreevy, 8 October 1935.

LETTERS
1929–1940

CHRONOLOGY 1906–1929

1906	13 April	Samuel Barclay Beckett born at Cooldrinagh on Good Friday.
1911		A pupil at the Elsner kindergarten.
1915		A pupil at Earlsfort House School.
1916	24 April	Sees flames and smoke rising from Dublin while walking in the Wicklow Mountains with his father: The Easter Rising.
1918	11 November	End of World War I.
1919	21 January	Start of the Anglo-Irish War.
1920	April	SB joins brother Frank Beckett as a pupil at Portora Royal School, Enniskillen, Co. Fermanagh.
	23 December	Partition of Ireland by Government of Ireland Act.
1921	6 December	Signing of Anglo-Irish Treaty.
1922	28 June	Start of the Irish Civil War.
	September	SB appointed Junior Prefect, Portora Royal School.
1923	May	Sits entrance exam for Trinity College Dublin.
	23 May	End of Irish Civil War.
	August	SB leaves Portora Royal School as Senior 6th Form Prefect.
	1 October	Enters Trinity College Dublin.
1924	March	Sees Sean O'Casey's *Juno and the Paycock* at the Abbey Theatre, Dublin.
1925	March	Takes part in Donnybrook motorcycle trial.
	April	Picked for Trinity College Dublin Cricket First XI.
	June	Becomes Senior Exhibitioner.

1926 January   Studies Italian with Bianca Esposito in Dublin.

8, 11 February   Attends premiere of Sean O'Casey's *The Plough and the Stars* at the Abbey Theatre with Geoffrey Thompson. Attends again on the night W. B. Yeats addresses the audience.

31 May   Places fourth in the Foundation Scholarship (Modern Languages), which entitles him to live free of charge in rooms in College.

August–September   Takes first trip to France; meets and travels with American student Charles Clarke.

Michaelmas Term (autumn)   Moves into rooms in Trinity College Dublin, 39 New Square. Meets Alfred Péron, French exchange Lecteur at TCD from the Ecole Normale Supérieure, Paris.

1927 22 March   Recommended to be exchange Lecteur to the Ecole Normale Supérieure by Trinity College Dublin Board.

20 April–August   Takes first trip to Italy. Lives in Florence, spends time with the Esposito family; reads Dante with Bianca Esposito. Is joined in Italy by Charles Clarke. Visits mountains near Lake Como with Mario Esposito.

6 July   Thomas McGreevy remains in the post of Lecteur at the Ecole Normale Supérieure for 1927–1928. SB is offered an alternative position at the University of Besançon, with assurance of appointment at the ENS in autumn 1928; on the advice of his Trinity College Dublin mentor, T. B. Rudmose-Brown, he turns this down.

October   Awarded First Class Moderatorship in Modern Literature at Trinity College Dublin with Large Gold Medal. Wins travel grant.

8 December   BA degree from Trinity College Dublin formally conferred.

1928 January–July   Teaches at Campbell College, Belfast, an interim post arranged by Rudmose-Brown.

July   Is visited in Dublin by cousin Margaret (Peggy) Sinclair and Charles Clarke.

September	Stays with Sinclair family in Kassel; visits Peggy Sinclair in Vienna.
By 1 November	Arrives at the Ecole Normale Supérieure in Paris. Thomas McGreevy still resident in Paris; he introduces SB to James Joyce, Jean Beaufret, Richard Aldington, and Eugene Jolas.
December	Joyce suggests a topic for SB's contribution to *Our Exagmination*. SB spends Christmas in Kassel.

1929	January	SB proposes French Doctorate on Proust and Joyce.
	23 March	Responds to Joyce's suggestions regarding his essay "Dante … Bruno. Vico .. Joyce."
	31 March	Visits the Sinclairs for Easter holiday.
	10 May	Formally requests renewal of appointment at the Ecole Normale Supérieure for 1929–1930.
	June	SB story "Assumption" and essay "Dante … Bruno. Vico .. Joyce" published in *transition*.
	27 June	Attends Déjeuner Ulysse at Hôtel Léopold, Fontainebleau.
	16 July	Censorship of Publications Act in Ireland.
	July or August	SB visits the Sinclairs in Kassel.
	October	Remains at Trinity College Dublin at start of the Michaelmas Term pending arrival of exchange Lecteur from the Ecole Normale Supérieure, delaying his return to the ENS.
	24 October	New York Stock Market crash.
	14 November	Essay "Che Sciagura," published in *T. C. D.: A College Miscellany*; written in response to the Censorship Act.
	28 November	SB returns to Paris to take up position as exchange Lecteur at Ecole Normale Supérieure.
	December	Begins French translation of Joyce's "Anna Livia Plurabelle" with Alfred Péron. Georges Pelorson arrives in early December to begin as the Ecole Normale Supérieure exchange Lecteur at Trinity College Dublin in the Hilary Term (January 1930).

25 December	SB in Dublin. Pelorson joins the Beckett family on Christmas Day.
26 December	SB leaves for Kassel.
31 December	Relationship between Peggy Sinclair and SB broken off.

JAMES JOYCE
PARIS

23/3/29   Landgrafenstr. 5
                                           Kassel

Dear Mr Joyce

Here is the latest insertion. I think it might follow the passage which treats of form as a concretion of content. I have succeeded in combining the three points in a more or less reasonable paragraph.[1]

I tried a bookshop to-day for Grimm, but found nothing that would please you.[2] However there are plenty more.

Will you remember me to Mrs Joyce and Giorgio & Lucia?[3]

Sincerely yours

Sam Beckett

ALS; 1 leaf, 1 side; NjP, Sylvia Beach Papers, C0108/138/1.

1 SB refers to "Dante ... Bruno. Vico .. Joyce," an essay commissioned by James Joyce* (1882–1941) on his *Work in Progress* (published in 1939 as *Finnegans Wake*); SB's essay was prepared for *Our Exagmination Round His Factification for Incamination of Work in Progress*, a collection of essays intended to suggest the fundamental design of *Work in Progress*, which was then appearing only in extracts ([Paris: Shakespeare and Company, 1929] 1–22; hereafter *Our Exagmination*).

Although SB's essay first appeared in *transition* (16–17 [June 1929] 242–253), it was set from proofs of the book. On 25 April 1929, Eugene Jolas* (1894–1952), founder and Editor of *transition** (April 1927–1938), wrote to Sylvia Beach* (née Nancy Woodbridge Beach, 1887–1962), the publisher of *Our Exagmination*, to request the proof of SB's essay: "Mr. Joyce would like to have it published in the next number of Transition. It is a very brilliant exegesis" (NjP, Sylvia Beach Papers, C0108/138/1; discussion of the dating: Maria Jolas to James Knowlson, BIF, UoR, MS 1277/1/2/28, and Records of Expenses for *Our Exagmination*, NjP, Sylvia Beach Papers, C0108/138/3).

No manuscript showing the additional paragraph has been found; this paragraph may well have been inserted before a proof copy was given to *transition*. Comparison between the essay as published by *transition* and by Shakespeare and Company shows additions and changes on pages 13-15 of the latter (John Pilling, *A Samuel Beckett Chronology* [Houndsmill, Basingstoke, Hampshire: Palgrave Macmillan, 2006] 19).

2 Although Joyce alludes to Grimm's Fairy Tales and Grimm's Law in *Finnegans Wake*, it is not known which of the works of the German mythologists and philologists Jakob Ludwig Carl Grimm (1785-1863) and his brother Wilhelm Carl Grimm (1786-1859) Joyce had requested.

3 James Joyce's wife Nora (née Barnacle, 1884-1951), son Giorgio* (1905-1976) and daughter Lucia* (1907-1982).

JAMES JOYCE

PARIS

[26 April 1929]   [Paris]

Dear Mr Joyce
    The text is:
ἐκπορεύομενον [*for* ἐκπορευόμενον]
παρα πατρος^1
    The infinitive:
ἐκπορεύεσθαι^2
    The substantive
το + Infinitive^3
            Sincerely yours
                Sam Beckett

ALS (pneu); 1 leaf, 2 sides; *to* James Joyce, Rue de Grenelle 19 (Square Robiac), Paris VII; *pm* 12:55, 26-4-29, Paris; *pm received* 13:00, 26-4-29, Paris; NBuU; *previous publication*: Patricia Hutchins, *James Joyce's World* (London: Methuen and Co., 1957) 169 (facsimile), and Hugh Kenner, *The Pound Era* (Berkeley: University of California Press, 1971; rpt. London: Pimlico, 1991) 102. *Dating*: from pm on pneumatique.

1 Beckett wrote to Patricia Hutchins Graecen (1911-1985) on 25 April 1954: "I fear I have no recollection of that note to Joyce and can shed no light on it" (TCD, MS 4098/11).
    The source of the text that SB sends to Joyce is not certain. The Greek phrase "ἐκπορευόμενον παρα πατρος" (ekporeuomenon para patros [proceeding from the Father]) alludes to John 15:26, and is central to the *Filioque* debate that divided

the Roman Catholic and the Eastern Orthodox churches. *Filioque* (and from the Son). For suggestions of how this passage may relate to *Finnegans Wake*: Roland McHugh, *Annotations to Finnegans Wake*, rev. edn. (Baltimore: Johns Hopkins University Press, 1991) 156, and a letter of 26 June 1975, from Danis Rose to Karl Gay, Curator, Lockwood Library Poetry Collection, State University of New York at Buffalo.

2 "ἐκπορεύεσθαι" (ekporeuesthai [to proceed]).

3 "το" (to: [the]).

ERNEST VESSIOT, ECOLE NORMALE SUPÉRIEURE
PARIS

10/5/29   Ecole Normale
                                                 [Paris]

Monsieur le Directeur[1]

Je vous écris dans l'espoir que vous voudrez bien ratifier mon désir de passer l'année scolaire prochaine à l'Ecole comme lecteur d'Anglais.[2]

Mon travail personnel sera la préparation d'une thèse pour le Doctorat de l'Université de Paris.[3]

Veuillez agréer, Monsieur le Directeur, l'expression de mes sentiments respectueux.

                 Samuel B. Beckett

ALS; 1 leaf, 1 side; AN 61AJ/202. Displayed in an exhibition at the Archives Nationales (1994).

10/5/29   Ecole Normale
                                                 [Paris]

Dear Sir[1]

I am writing to you in the hope that you will ratify my wish to spend the next academic year at the Ecole as Lecteur in English.[2]

My private work will be the preparation of a thesis for the Doctorate of the University of Paris.[3]

Yours respectfully

Samuel B. Beckett

1 Ernest Vessiot (1865–1952), Directeur, Ecole Normale Supérieure,* from 1927 to 1935.

2 SB was nominated to be the Lecteur d'anglais (English language assistant) for 1927–1928 in the exchange program between Trinity College Dublin and the Ecole Normale Supérieure in Paris by his mentor Thomas Brown Rudmose-Brown* (known as Ruddy, 1878–1942), Professor of Romance Languages at Trinity College Dublin. Without prejudice to SB's nomination, the administration of the ENS decided to renew the appointment of the current Lecteur, Thomas McGreevy* (1893–1967), who was also a graduate of TCD (Gustave Lanson, Directeur, Ecole Normale Supérieure [1919–1927] to Rudmose-Brown, 31 July 1927, AN: 61AJ/ 202). SB was offered the appointment for 1928–1929.

SB's request to be retained for a second year was subject to the approval of both institutions; Ernest Vessiot wrote to Alfred Blanche, Consul Général de France en Irlande, 14 May 1929, that he was inclined to grant this request (AN: 61AJ/ 202).

3 As the subject for his thesis, SB proposed Joyce and Marcel Proust (1871–1922), but he was discouraged from this by Professor Célestin Bouglé (1870–1940), Directeur-adjoint, Lettres (Assistant Director, Arts), Ecole Normale Supérieure (James Knowlson, *Damned to Fame: The Life of Samuel Beckett* [New York: Grove Press, 2004] 107, and notes of an interview with SB by Lawrence Harvey in the early 1960s [NhD, Lawrence Harvey Collection, MS 661, Notes for *Samuel Beckett: Poet and Critic*, 16]).

THOMAS McGREEVY

PARIS

Friday [? summer 1929]   Landgrafenstr. 5

                                          Kassel

My dear McGreevy[1]

The abominable old bap Russel[l] duly returned my MSS with an economic note in the 3rd person, the whole in a considerably understamped envelope. I feel slightly paralysed by the courtesy of this gesture. I would like to get rid of the damn thing anyhow, anywhere (with the notable exception of 'transition'), but I have no acquaintance with the less squeamish literary garbage buckets. I can't imagine Eliott [*for* Eliot] touching it – certainly not the verse. Perhaps Seumas O'Sullivan's rag would take it?[2] If you think of an address I would be grateful to know it.

To my astonishment I arrived in Kassel at the hour numerous officials assured me I would arrive, must arrive.[3] I had the carriage to myself all night, but did not succeed in getting any sleep. The aspirin was a snare and the coffee a delusion. So I was reduced to finishing Le Desert de l'Amour, which I most decidedly do not like. A patient tenuous snivel that one longs to see projected noisily into a handkerchief.[4]

We came back from Kragenhof yesterday.[5] I am scorched to ribbons by the sun, and am as uncomfortable in the bunk as Florence.

> 'Che non può trovar posa in su le piume
> ma con dar volta suo dolore scherma.'[6]

I have read the first volume of 'Du Côté de chez Swann', and find it strangely uneven. There are incomparable things – Bloch, Françoise, Tante Léonie, Legrandin, and then passages that are offensively fastidious, artificial and almost dishonest.[7] It is hard to know what to think about him. He is so absolutely the master of his form that he becomes its slave as often as not. Some of his metaphors light up a whole page like a bright explosion, and others seem ground out in the dullest desperation. He has every kind of subtle equilibrium, charming trembling equilibrium, and then suddenly a stasis, the arms of the balance wedged in a perfect horizontal line, more heavily symmetrical than Macaulay at his worst, with primos & secundos echoing to each complacently and reechoing. His loquacity is certainly more interesting and cleverly done than Moore's, but no less profuse, a maudlin false teeth gobble-gobble discharge from a colic-afflicted belly. I think he drank too much tilleul.[8] And to think that I have to contemplate him at stool for 16 volumes! Cissie is devouring Ulysses, and likes talking about it and Joyce, a delicate activity in the presence of Peggy, who has no interest in books and who cannot be persuaded that literacy is not a crime.[9] I have made up my mind to write to 'transition' for the money they owe me, but have lost their address.[10] If you are writing I would be grateful to have it.

Are you doing any work or are you infested by the aimable Thomas? How did Agrég. go? How is the position with regard to 'Les Enfants'... [11]

Write when you feel strong. You know how glad I would be to hear from you. Cissie remembers you well and sends her kindest. The Boss is in Ireland and the children conveniently dispersed, so there is a strange hot peace in the flat. I could'nt [*for* couldn't] sleep last night and read 'Sir Arthur Savile's Crime', 'The Something Ghost' & 'Poems in Prose', this last enormous I thought.[12]

    Leb wohl.[13]

        Yrs ever

        S. B.

ALI; 1 leaf, 4 sides; TCD, MS 10402/1. *Dating*: although James Knowlson assigns a probable date of June 1930 to this letter, summer 1929 is more likely (Knowlson, *Damned to Fame*, 639–641, n. 90, n. 118). The agrégation examinations took place in the early summer, and SB describes serious sunburn. The relatively formal greeting suggests this may be among the first of SB's letters to McGreevy with the issue of 12 April 1930, publication of *The Irish Statesman* ceased, and, given AE's definitive dismissal of SB's submission in early 1930 (see 1 March 1930), it is more likely that the understamped rejection described here is earlier than 1930.

  1 McGreevy remained in Paris after SB took up his appointment as Lecteur d'anglais at the Ecole Normale Supérieure; he introduced SB to Joyce and to English novelist and poet Richard Aldington* (1892–1962).

2 Irish poet, painter, and editor George William Russell (pseud. AE, 1867–1935) edited *The Irish Statesman* (15 September 1923 to 12 April 1930), a journal that advocated national ideals and liberal policy on divorce and censorship. On the suggestion of Thomas McGreevy, who had published poems in the journal under the pseudonym L. St. Senen, SB may have submitted a prose piece to *The Irish Statesman*; John Pilling suggests "Assumption" (Pilling, *A Samuel Beckett Chronology*, 19). SB's story "Assumption" was published in *transition*, 16–17 (June 1929), 268–271. Reference to an understamped envelope suggests that the submission was longer than one or two pages.

Thomas Stearns Eliot (1888–1965), poet and Editor of *The Criterion* (1923–1939). Poet and essayist Seumas O'Sullivan* (né James Sullivan Starkey, 1879–1958) edited *Dublin Magazine* (1923–1958).

3 SB writes from Kassel, Germany, from the home of his paternal aunt Frances Sinclair* (née Beckett, known as Fanny, and by family and friends as Cissie, 1880–1951) and her husband William Abraham Sinclair* (known as Boss, 1882–1937), an art dealer.

4 François Mauriac, *Le Désert de l'amour* (1925; *The Desert of Love*).

5 Between 1923 and 1925 the Sinclairs had lived in the Pension in Kragenhof on the Fulda River, near Kassel; they continued to go to Kragenhof to swim and take walks along the river or through the forests (Morris Sinclair, 20 October 1993).

6 The city of Florence is compared to a sick woman by Dante Alighieri (1265–1321): "Che non può trovar posa in su le piume, / ma con dar volta suo dolore scherma" ("that can find no rest on her bed of down but with turning seeks to ease her pain") (*La Divina Commedia*, with comment by Enrico Bianchi [Florence: Adriano Salani, 1927], *Purgatorio* Canto VI, lines 150–151; Dante Alighieri, *The Divine Comedy of Dante Alighieri*, Vol. II, *Purgatorio*, tr. and comment John D. Sinclair [London: John Lane The Bodley Head, 1939, rev. 1948] 89). All citations are from these editions.

SB used the 1926 Salani edition, although he did not think highly of it; the editors could only obtain a 1927 edition. For further discussion of the Salani edition, see Daniela Caselli, "The 'Florentia Edition in the Ignoble Salani Collection': A Textual Comparison," *Journal of Beckett Studies* 9.2 (2001) 1–20; Daniela Caselli, "The Promise of Dante in the Beckett Manuscripts," *Notes Diverse Holo*, Special issue *SBT/A* 16 (2006) 237–257.

SB read Dante in Italian, not in translation. The editors chose the prose translation of Sinclair with the Italian text, "the critical text of the Società Dantesca Italiana revised by Giuseppi Vandelli," on the facing page, so readers can consult both texts (*The Divine Comedy of Dante Alighieri*, I, *Inferno*, 9).

7 SB refers to characters in Du côté de chez Swann, the first part of Proust's novel *A la recherche du temps perdu* (1913–1927; *In Search of Lost Time*).

8 English writer and statesman Thomas Babington Macaulay (1800–1859); Irish novelist George Augustus Moore (1852–1933).

The narrator of Proust's *A la recherche du temps perdu* recovers memories of his childhood when drinking a cup of "tilleul" (lime-flower infusion) with a madeleine.

9 Ruth Margaret Sinclair* (known as Peggy, 1911–1933), daughter of Cissie and Boss Sinclair, had spent time with SB in Dublin in the summer of 1928, and in September 1928 in Kassel and Vienna, where she studied dance and movement at the Schule Hellerau-Laxenburg (Pilling, *A Samuel Beckett Chronology*, 17).
James Joyce, *Ulysses* (1922).

10 SB's essay "Dante … Bruno. Vico . . Joyce," and his story "Assumption," had just appeared in *transition*.

11 McGreevy continued to have a room at the Ecole Normale Supérieure. Jean Thomas* (1900–1983), Agrégé-répétiteur at the ENS (1926 to 1932), coached students preparing for the agrégation, the highest-level university examination. SB taught students taking the agrégation d'anglais.
McGreevy had been asked to consider translating *Les Enfants terribles* (1929) by Jean Cocteau (1889–1963) (McGreevy to George Yeats, 21 August 1929, NLI, MS 20,849; Susan Schreibman, 15 January 2007).

12 *Lord Arthur Savile's Crime, The Canterville Ghost, Poems in Prose* by Oscar Wilde (1854–1900) (London: James R. Osgood, McIlvaine, 1891).

13 "Leb wohl." (Ger., Be well.)

ROGER DION, ECOLE NORMALE SUPÉRIEURE
PARIS

25/II/29   Trinity College
                                                Dublin

Cher Monsieur Dion[1]

Je peux maintenant vous annoncer définitivement la date de mon retour à l'Ecole. Il m'est impossible de partir avant jeudi, le 28 de ce mois.[2] Je me présenterai à l'Ecole dans l'après[-]midi du vendredi suivant.

Veuillez agréer, Monsieur Dion, l'expression de mes sentiments les plus distingués,

s/ S. B. Beckett

TLS; 1 leaf, 1 side; AN, 61AJ/119. *Dating*: although written in Roman numerals, the date refers to November.

25/11/29   Trinity College
                                             Dublin

Dear Monsieur Dion[1]

I can now tell you definitively the date of my return to the Ecole. It is impossible for me to leave before Thursday the 28th of this month. I shall come to the Ecole in the afternoon of the following Friday.

Yours sincerely

S. B. Beckett

---

1 Roger Dion (1896–1981), a member of the Social Sciences faculty, was Surveillant, a senior administrator with responsibility for discipline, at the Ecole Normale Supérieure in 1929.

2 SB's return to the Ecole Normale Supérieure in the autumn of 1929 was delayed by Rudmose-Brown, who asked that SB remain at Trinity College Dublin in the absence of André Parreaux (1906–1979). Parreaux had been the ENS exchange Lecteur at TCD in 1928–1929 and had been expected to return for 1929–1930; however, he was detained in Paris to retake examinations in English and Philology (Rudmose-Brown to the Directeur, Ecole Normale Supérieure, 9 October 1929, AN, 61AJ/202). When it was determined that Parreaux would not be returning to TCD for 1929–1930, the ENS named Georges Pelorson* (after 1945 known as Georges Belmont, b. 1909) to take up the appointment at TCD beginning in the Hilary term (27 January 1930). Only when this decision was reached could SB return to his position at the ENS.

CHRONOLOGY 1930

1930	March	SB poem "For Future Reference" published in *transition*.
	14 May	SB submits English translations from Italian for a special issue of *This Quarter*.
	1 June	Richard Aldington proposes to Chatto and Windus that they publish what will become The Dolphin Books series.
	15 June	SB submits MS of *Whoroscope* to the Hours Press.
	16 June	Awarded Hours Press Prize for *Whoroscope*.
	After 1 July	Applies for Trinity College Dublin lectureship in Modern Languages.
	5 August	Sends two pages of French translation of Joyce's "Anna Livia Plurabelle" to Philippe Soupault.
	25 August	Has begun to write *Proust*. Jacob Bronowski selects three of the four poems by SB published in *The European Caravan*: "Hell Crane to Starling," "Casket of Pralinen for the Daughter of a Dissipated Mandarin," "Text," and "Yoke of Liberty."
	16 September	SB leaves Paris for London.
	17 September	Personally delivers the MS of *Proust* to Charles Prentice at Chatto and Windus in London.
	1 October	In Dublin for the beginning of the Michaelmas Term at Trinity College Dublin.
	10 October	Chatto and Windus accept *Proust*.
	14 October	SB proposes adding a conclusion to *Proust*.

15 October	*Bifur* issues printer's proofs of translation of "Anna Livia Plurabelle" by SB and Alfred Péron, but Joyce withdraws the translation.
17 October	Chatto and Windus sends contract for *Proust*.
By 14 November	SB presents "Le Concentrisme," a spoof study of an invented poet, Jean du Chas, to the Modern Languages Society, Trinity College Dublin.
25 November	Visits Jack B. Yeats for the first time.
By 12 December	Sends final typescript of *Proust* to Chatto and Windus.
December	Song lyric "From the Only Poet to a Shining Whore: for Henry Crowder to Sing" published in Henry Crowder's *Henry-Music*.

1/3/30   Paris

Cher Ami

I bearded the 2 salauds in den 40 [*for* 42] as instructed, and translated their titles. They gave me other things to do, notably an archaeological chronicle by Delaporte and two lists of illustrations – Maillol & Picasso.[1] It is all done and sent off. No letters for you at the hotel.

Russel[l] sent back the pome, with a note to the effect that I might save myself the trouble of sending him anything further, couched in the following terms: 'I have a copy box stuffed to the brim with poetry sufficient to supply the needs of the Statesman for a year to come without taking in a single MS. and it is no use in accepting new Mss to add to the pile waiting their turn for publication'!![2] Now I think that is about the best so far. As if I were trying to sell him a load of manure or a ton of bricks. And the nice little whimper I wrote specially for him! Dear dear dear. Worked with the Penman last night. He recited Verlaine and said that poetry ought to be rimed and that he couldn't imagine anyone writing a poem 'sinon à une petite femme.' He talked a lot about petites femmes.[3] His own did not appear. No news – except that to-day the Spring is here at last. Alan has had a dream – that he received a parcel of books including 2 new works by Shaw, a play and an analysis of a murder trial.[4] Repressed desires!

Amusez-vous bien[5]

Yours ever

Sam Beckett

ALS; 1 leaf, 2 sides; TCD, MS 10402/5.

1 SB stood in for Thomas McGreevy, who was Secretary for the English edition of *Formes: an International Review of Plastic Art*, a journal of art theory published in French and English (December 1929 – March 1933). *Formes* was directed by Shigetaro Fukushima (1895-1960) with Waldemar George (né Waldemar Jerzy Jarocinski, 1893-1970) as Art Director, and Marcel Zahar (1898-1989) as Secretary; its editorial office was at 42 Rue Pasquier, Paris 8. Normally, McGreevy translated and typed "between 25 and 30 thousand words every month" for *Formes* (Thomas McGreevy to James Pinker, Sunday [1930], NYPL, Berg: James B. Pinter and Sons Records 1893-1940). However, SB had only translated the titles of articles, a list of illustrations, and a "Chronicle of Archaeology" by Louis Delaporte (né Louis-Joseph Delaporte, 1874-1944) (*Formes*, 4 [April 1930] [2], 25). The illustrations by Pablo Picasso (1881-1973) and French sculptor Aristide Maillol (1861-1944) were related to articles on the artists: "Aristide Maillol" ([2], 5-7) by French novelist Jules Romains (né Louis Farigoule, 1885-1973) and "The Passion of Picasso" ([2], 8-9) by Waldemar George. SB's translations are unsigned.
"Salauds" (bastards).

2 *The Irish Statesman* published its final issue on 12 April 1930. SB probably submitted "Sonnet" ("At last I find . . .), which he thought would appeal to AE who was a theosophist (Lawrence E. Harvey, *Samuel Beckett: Poet and Critic* [Princeton: Princeton University Press, 1970] 283-285; Pilling, *A Samuel Beckett Chronology*, 23). "Sonnet" was later published as part of SB's story "Sedendo et Quiesciendo [*for* Quiescendo]", *transition* 21 (March 1932) 17, and in Samuel Beckett, *Dream of Fair to Middling Women*, ed. Eoin O'Brien and Edith Fournier (New York: Arcade Publishing, in association with Riverrun Press, 1993) 70; all citations are from this edition.

3 James Joyce was known as the Penman (after his character Shem the Penman in *Finnegans Wake*). French poet Paul Verlaine (1844-1896).
"Sinon à une petite femme" (except to a little woman).

4 Alan George Duncan* (1895-1943) lived in Paris from 1924; he and his wife Isabel Belinda Atkinson Duncan* (1893-1964) were frequently Beckett's café companions. Alan Duncan's "only subject" was Shaw (Brian Coffey, June 1993).
George Bernard Shaw (1856-1950) did have a new play, *The Apple Cart* (first published in German as *Der Kaiser von Amerika: Eine politische Komödie in drei Akten*, tr. Siegfried Trebitsch [Berlin: S. Fischer Verlag, 1929], and then in English with *Saint Joan* in George Bernard Shaw, *The Works of Bernard Shaw: Collected Edition*, XVII [London: Constable, 1930], as well as separately in December 1930 [London: Constable, 1930]). In Shaw's *Doctor's Delusion, Crude Criminology, and Sham Education* (1931), several essays were republished that offered analyses of criminal cases (see Dan H. Laurence, *Bernard Shaw: A Bibliography*, I [Oxford: Clarendon Press, 1983] 187-189).

5 "Amusez-vous bien" (enjoy yourself).

THOMAS McGREEVY
TARBERT, CO. KERRY

Sunday [c. 27 April to 11 May 1930]   E.N.S.
                                                        [Paris]

My dear Tom

I have just read your letter, and am glad you have found some peace & happiness with your Mother & sisters.[1] Here there is very little of either, except perhaps to-day, when this place is empty and silent. I have started vaguely to work. I saw Goll. Another slave. I am seeing Soupault to-morrow, to ask him to take on my part of the rivers & let me begin on the base translation.[2] Last night I drank with Alan, Belinda, Harry Clark [*for* Clarke] & the McKennas.[3] [...]

Harry C. left for London this morning. The McKs. arrived last night laden down with Poe & Goethe for him to sign.[4] Aren't people shits? Signed photographs, signed books, signed menus. I suppose the Gilberts & Carduccis would feel honoured if Joyce signed a piece of his used toilet paper.[5] I saw J.J. on Thursday night. Miss Weaver was there.[6] I like her very much. And just Lucia and Mrs. A pleasant evening. Sometimes I hear from Germany, but now with a very decent irregularity.[7] I have been doing a little tapirising & reading Keats, you'll be sorry to hear. I like that crouching brooding quality in Keats – squatting on the moss, crushing a petal, licking his lips & rubbing his hands, 'counting the last oozings, hours by hours.' I like him the best of them all, because he doesn't beat his fists on the table. I like that awful sweetness and thick soft damp green richness. And weariness. 'Take into the air my quiet breath.' But there's nobody here to talk to, & it[']s so rarely one is enthusiastic, or glad of something.[8]

I am afraid the Trinity – Ecole arrangement is doomed. I'm afraid I'm going to be embarrassed again – if they offer me anything. I only heard indirectly, Pelorson via Beaufret – so keep it close.[9] They are making a big mistake.

Don't worry about Formes. I have had practically nothing to do so far, and it[']s as good a way of creating [a] past as any other – & safer than most.[10]

Lucia is coming to tea. God bless.

Yrs ever

Sam

ALS; 1 leaf, 4 sides; TCD, MS 10402/6. *Dating*: Harry Clarke left Pau at the end of April 1930, stopping in Paris and London on the way to Dublin, where he arrived on 16 May (Nicola Gordon Bowe, *The Life and Work of Harry Clarke* [Dublin: Irish Academic Press, 1989] 223). The date for their evening together may have been 26 April, 3 or 10 May, with the first two most likely. Joyce was in Zurich c. 13 May to c. 17 June.

1 McGreevy's father Thomas McGreevy (1858–1930) died on 19 April; McGreevy had returned to Tarbert to be with his mother Margaret McGreevy (née Enright, 1855–1936) and his sisters.

2 When asked to undertake a French translation of the Anna Livia Plurabelle chapter of *Work in Progress*, SB was assisting Joyce by translating into French references to over a thousand names of rivers woven through that section of the manuscript later published as *Finnegans Wake* ([New York: Viking Press, 1959] 196–216; for a listing of the rivers see McHugh, *Annotations to Finnegans Wake*, 196–216).

Ivan Goll (né Isaac Lang, 1891–1950), born in St.-Dié-des-Vosges, Lorraine, wrote poetry, drama, and novels in both French and German. On behalf of the Basel publisher Rhein-Verlag, Goll approached Joyce about publishing German translations of his work. As a polyglot, Goll was helpful to Joyce as he wrote *Work in Progress*.

French surrealist poet, writer, and critic Philippe Soupault (1897–1990).

3 Alan and Belinda Duncan.

Dublin illustrator and stained-glass artist Harry Clarke (1889–1931). These McKennas have not been identified.

4 Harry Clarke illustrated editions of *Tales of Mystery and Imagination* (London: G. G. Harrap, 1919) by Edgar Allan Poe (1809–1849) and *Faust* (London: G. G. Harrap, 1925) by Johann Wolfgang von Goethe (1749–1832).

5 Stuart Gilbert (1883–1969) worked on the French translation of Joyce's *Ulysses* and helped to popularize Joyce's work with his book, *James Joyce's Ulysses: A Study* (1930). French poet and translator Auguste Morel (n.d.) translated *Ulysses* as *Ulysse* (1929), assisted by Gilbert; the translation was revised by French novelist, poet, critic, and translator Valery Larbaud (1881–1959). (For discussion of the process: Richard

14 May 1930, Putnam

Ellmann, *James Joyce: New and Revised Edition* [Oxford: Oxford University Press, paperback with corrections, 1983] 562–563, 601–602; James Joyce, *Letters of James Joyce*, I, ed. Stuart Gilbert [New York: Viking Press, 1957] 28).

The Italian composer and music critic Edgardo Carducci-Agustini (1898–?), set Joyce's poem "Alone" to music, and for some months "read to Joyce in Italian for two hours a day" (Ellmann, *James Joyce*, 648).

6 Harriet Shaw Weaver (1876–1961) published and promoted Joyce's work in England. She was a devoted friend and benefactor of Joyce.

7 SB's German correspondent is his cousin Peggy in Kassel, with whom he had been emotionally involved (see Knowlson, *Damned to Fame*, 113–114).

8 "Tapirising," from "tapir" (French academic slang, private pupil).

SB misquotes a line from "To Autumn" by John Keats (1795–1821): "Thou watchest the last oozings hours by hours"; the second quotation is from "Ode to a Nightingale" by Keats: "I have been half in love with easeful Death, / Call'd him soft names in many a mused rhyme, / To take into the air my quiet breath" (John Keats, *The Poems of John Keats*, ed. Jack Stillinger [Cambridge, MA: Belknap-Harvard University Press, 1978] 476–477; 369–372).

9 Rudmose-Brown expected SB to return to Trinity College Dublin as his assistant in the autumn of 1930. That year, TCD did not propose a candidate for the exchange program with the Ecole Normale Supérieure (William Kennedy, Trinity College Registrar, to Ernest Vessiot, Ecole Normale Supérieure [31 May 1930], AN, 61AJ/202). In the place of someone from TCD, Robert I. Brown (1907–1996) from the University of Glasgow was accepted as Lecteur d'anglais by the ENS. In a further complication, Georges Pelorson petitioned to remain at TCD for 1930–1931 rather than accept an assignment at the University of Glasgow (Pelorson to the Directeur, Ecole Normale Supérieure [21 June 1930], AN, 61 AJ 202).

Jean Beaufret* (known as Bowsprit, 1907–1982) was a Philosophy student and had been McGreevy's roommate at the ENS; "Bowsprit," based on the French, "beaupré" (bowsprit) (Knowlson, *Damned to Fame*, 150–151).

10 SB continued to stand in for McGreevy at *Formes*, so that McGreevy could retain his position while he was away from Paris (see 1 March 1930, n. 1).

SAMUEL PUTNAM

PARIS

14/5/30   Ecole Normale
                                                          Rue d'Ulm 45 [Paris]

Dear Mr Putnam

This was nearly finished when your pneu came, so I went on with it.[1] It is far and away the best of a bad lot. There are some good things in the Favola Gattesca – do you remember it? It is roughly four times as long as Paesaggio. Do you wish me to translate it – or would you prefer something shorter in the way of a pendant to this rather watery pastoral humility: Crepuscolo Mitologico, for example.[2] I will not start anything until I hear from you.

Very sincerely yours

s/ S. B. Beckett

TLS; 1 leaf, 1 side; enclosure not with letter; NjP, *New Review* Correspondence of Samuel Putnam, C0111/1/9.

1 As Associate Editor of *This Quarter*, Samuel Putnam* (1892–1950) compiled the "Miniature Anthology of Contemporary Italian Literature" for *This Quarter*, 2.4 (April–May–June, 1930). It included SB's translations: "Paesaggio" by the Italian writer Raffaello Franchi (1899–1949) translated by SB as "Landscape"; "Delta" by Eugenio Montale (1896–1981); and "The Home-Coming" by Giovanni Comisso (1895–1969) (672, 630, 675–683).

*The European Caravan: An Anthology of the New Spirit in European Literature** had been planned as a two-volume anthology; an Italian section was to appear in the second volume, but this was not published (ed. Samuel Putnam, Maida Castelhun Darnton, George Reavey, and J[acob] Bronowski [New York: Brewer, Warren, and Putnam, 1931]).

2 Franchi's *Favola Gattesca* was published in *Piazza natia* (Turin: Fratelli Buratti Editori, 1929) 97–106. "Crepuscolo mitologico" (120–122) is the third section of *Diorama* (107–124) in *Piazza natia*.

THOMAS McGREEVY

TARBERT, CO. KERRY

Thursday [? 17 July 1930]   Ecole Normale

                                             [Paris]

My dear Tom

Glad to get your letter & know that things had gone well in London. You do not say anything about the Connoisseur people.[1] Did you see them? Here nothing more interesting than the usual drink & futility. Alfy is here, and we saw Soupault together. We are working on the bloody thing together in a vague ineffectual kind of way.[2] Alfy has gone to repose himself at Boulogne sur Merde (or sur Seine, as you like) and then of course he must lie with his subtle Russian sweet. Indeed, I have seen very little of him. He is changed or I have or both. I guess at the old Alfy. The first evening he burst out in a fury about Ethna, and the 'salaud qui m'a fait rater ma vie'. Since then nothing, mockery & decompositions and dreadfully perfect. Shining agates of negation. How energetic they always are, these self-avowed cynics and désabusés, bristling with passionate estimates and beating their breasts in a jemenfoutiste & jusquauboutiste frenzy.[3] He will be here till the end of the month and then in Auvergne. How can we do any thing in that time, meeting tired in the evening and gal[l]oping through a page? I know there is nothing to be done and that nothing of any value will be done, but one goes on, driven by a wind, like the accidiosi.[4]

The 14th was all right, because I was drunker than either Nancy or Henry. There were other people there, God knows who, but they went off early for a little coucherie I suppose.[5] God knows also what I said & did, but I think it was all right. I was so tired at the end that I could hardly climb into a taxi. They liked the Rahab tomfoolery, God help them. Henry said several times that it was 'vey vey bootiful & vey vey fine in-deed.' He was very nice & behaved very well, and played the piano at the Cigogne, where I described arabesques of an original pattern.[6] I heard from Nancy from London. She has given me her Parallax that I asked her for, & lent me The Apes of God & some Pound Cantos. I read Parallax. I don't know what to say about it. There are some fine things:

> 'By the Embankment I counted the grey gulls
> Nailed to the wind above a distorted tide.'[7]

No . . ? And then a lot of padding I am afraid. I don't know. Perhaps it's very good.

Thursday [? 17 July 1930], McGreevy

I can't start the Proust. Curse this hurry any how.[8] Did they mention it in London? I know what will happen: that the German trip will be sacrificed to no purpose, and that I will creep away at the last moment without having done any thing – Joyce or Proust. At least I have finished reading the bastard.

I had a terrible 1½ h[our] with Alan & B. in the usual kip. I was sitting there with Alfy (whom they know) & Pelorson, and of course they had to be invited to our table. Then the noble captain & traducer turned on his salivary glands and his supply of Shaw texts, and was a camelot on the strength of the 14th's bunting. He went on & on & Alfy heaped fuel on the flame by disagreeing. Pelorson collapsed spontaneously on the banquette and I observed a terrible silence that will never be forgiven by Rathmines.[9] It is more impossible every time I see them. Fortunately Louis le Cardonnel was there & the exquisite Thérive. Pelorson was delighted. Thérive left without paying for his beer, and the fat Chestertonian individual refused angrily to pay for him.[10] Pelorson was in an extraordinary state of excitement & hilarity. Really he is charming – specially alone. Yesterday we were up all night. At last we bought a bottle of champagne à la Charlus, and brought it up here with his gramophone & played Tristan & Isolde & the Oiseau de Feu. Poor Pelorson! What an unhappy person. Il n'y a que cela he said.[11]

A long cheerless letter but very friendly from Ruddy. He can't find a publisher for a book he wants to write on Racine. Could anything be done with Chatto & Windus? I bought the Larousse edition & tried to read Esther. What is wrong with me? I find chevilles everywhere, and I never did before in Racine.[12]

I had a nice friendly card from Peggy from the North Sea, where she is with the Boche Hausfreund & Cissie & the youngest girl.[13] I was very glad. I sent the pome to the Boss.[14]

A letter from Lucia too. I don't know what to do. She is unhappy she says. Now that you are gone there is no one to talk to about that. I <u>dare</u> not go to Wales, and I promised I would if they were there on my way through.[15] But it is impossible. There is no solution. What terrible instinct prompts them to have the genius of beauty at the right – or the wrong – moment!

To-morrow I will get your book & send it along. I forwarded to Tarbert a bulky letter from Jack Yeats I think.[16] I have not seen Mario but will to-morrow evening. We are bring[ing] the Bowsprit out for a spree.

Yes, I was in time for Angelo. He was to have come this afternoon & I hurried back to find a note saying he had to go about his papers to the consulat.[17]

The light has collapsed again & they won't come & mend. The room is full of candles.

   Love

    Sam

Alfy dit que les Japonais aiment beaucoup à enculer des canards agonisants, à cause du duvet, parait-il.[18]

Gaudin is collé, poor creature, & he wanted to get married. Réclame pour moi![19]

ALS; 5 leaves; 10 sides; PS upper right margin, side 1; TCD, MS 10402/2. *Dating*: SB's reference to the strength of the 14th's bunting indicates Bastille Day. A letter from Jack B. Yeats to McGreevy in Paris on 14 July 1930 ("I expect Paris in the summer is rather stuffy," enclosing reviews of Yeats's show in London [TCD, MS 10381/111]) was forwarded by SB to Tarbert, Ireland. In July 1930, the Joyces were in Wales, but they returned to England on 28 July (see [before 5 August 1930], n. 3). *The Apes of God* had been published by June 1930. Nancy Cunard was in London from 15 July through at least 21 July 1930, when she attended a dinner party in honor of George Moore. Hence the date of this letter is probably Thursday 17 July 1930.

1 On his way from Paris to his family home in Tarbert, McGreevy passed through London. From November 1925 to February 1927, McGreevy had been Assistant Editor of *The Connoisseur, a Journal of the Arts* (1901–1992), London.

 SB canceled "<u>Criterion</u>" and inserted above it "Connoisseur."

2 Alfred Rémy Péron* (1904–1945) entered the Ecole Normale Supérieure in 1924 and was agrégé d'anglais by 1929; he first met SB when he was Lecteur in French at Trinity College Dublin (1926–1928), and they were together at the ENS in 1929. Péron was working with SB on the French translation of the "Anna Livia Plurabelle" chapter of Joyce's *Work in Progress*, which had been first published separately in English (James Joyce, *Anna Livia Plurabelle* [New York: Crosby Gaige, 1928]). Philippe Soupault was directing the translation originally intended for publication in the Paris journal *Bifur* (May 1929 – June 1931), edited by Georges Ribemont-Dessaignes (1887–1974).

3 Marie Lézine (known as Mania, 1900–1988); she married Péron in 1930.

Ethna Mary MacCarthy* (1903–1959), SB's contemporary in Modern Languages at Trinity College Dublin, figures as a beloved in SB's poem, "Alba," and in *Dream of Fair to Middling Women*. "'Salaud qui m'a fait rater ma vie'" (bastard who ruined my life).

"Désabusés" (disillusioned ones); "jemenfoutiste" (don't-give-a-damnish); "jusquauboutiste" (no-half-measures-ish).

4 SB alludes to the "accidiosi" (slothful) in Dante's *Divine Comedy*, but seems to confuse them with the "lussuriosi" (lustful). Those souls "driven by the wind" in the *Comedy* are the Lustful in *Inferno* Canto V, and more briefly the Incontinent in *Inferno* Canto XI (line 71). The "accidiosi" appear in Canto VII of *Inferno*, but as they are under slime, no wind can reach them: "'Tristi fummo / ne l'aere dolce che dal sol s'allegra, / portando dentro accidioso fummo: / or ci attristiam ne la belletta negra'" ("'We were sullen in the sweet air that is gladdened by the sun, bearing in our hearts a sluggish smoke; now we are sullen in the black-mire'") (Dante, *La Divina Commedia*, *Inferno* Canto VII, lines 121–124; Dante, *The Divine Comedy*, I, *Inferno*).

5 Bastille Day, the French national holiday celebrated on 14 July.

SB wrote *Whoroscope* on 15 June and submitted it that night to the competition of the Hours Press for the best poem on time. With Richard Aldington, Nancy Cunard* (1896–1965), English writer, journalist and publisher of the Hours Press (1928–1934), had selected SB's *Whoroscope* (Paris: Hours Press, 1930) as the winner. To Louise Morgan (1883–1964) Cunard wrote a letter dated only with the time, "3 a.m." (in AH June 1930):

> We found a poem, a beauty, by a poet – so much so that it must be printed by itself. Irishman of 23, Ecole Normale here, that's all I know, but am seeing him tomorrow. Richard says many of the allusions are to Descartes[.] I shouldn't have known. Much in it none of us will ever know, and the whole thing so good it proves again the rest doesn't matter.
>
> Will you announce please that the Hours Press prize for best Time poem is awarded to Samuel Beckett. Poem called "The Eighth Day"[...] (CtY, GEN MSS 80, series V, 36/861)

The exact date of publication is uncertain, probably between 1 and 8 July 1930. In a card to Morgan dated Mon. [30 June 1930], Cunard wrote "Beckett is very good (not a Honey!) Doing his poem tomorrow – will send – do insert note of Prize winning." Louise Morgan was an Editor of *Everyman*; an announcement of the award included notice that the poem would be published "almost immediately in an edition consisting of 100 signed and 300 unsigned copies at 5s. and 1s. respectively" ("Books and Authors," *Everyman* 75 [3 July 1930] 728). Writing on Saturday [6 July 1930], Cunard indicates:

"Will be sending you Beckett's Poem Tues" (CtY, GEN MSS 80, series V, 36/361). See also Knowlson, *Damned to Fame*, 116–118, and Nancy Cunard, *These Were the Hours: Memories of My Hours Press, Réanville and Paris, 1928–1931* [Carbondale: Southern Illinois University Press; London: Feffer and Simons, 1969] 109–111).

Nancy Cunard's companion and assistant at Hours Press was the American jazz pianist Henry Crowder* (1895–1954).

"Coucherie" (fun between the sheets).

6 SB wrote "From the Only Poet to a Shining Whore: for Henry Crowder to Sing" (Henry Crowder, *Henry-Music* [Paris: Hours Press, 1930] [6, 12–14]). The opening phrase of SB's poem is "Rahab of the holy battlements," an allusion to Rahab, the harlot of Jericho (Joshua 2; see Harvey, *Samuel Beckett*, 305). Henry Crowder played the piano at Les Cigognes, 187 Rue de la Croix-Nivert, Paris 15. In his memoir, Crowder writes of SB: "Nancy became very interested in this man and he did have a very charming personality" (Henry Crowder and Hugo Speck, *As Wonderful as All That?: Henry Crowder's Memoir of His Affair with Nancy Cunard 1928–1935*, ed. Robert L. Allen [Navarro, CA: Wild Trees Press, 1987] 76).

7 Nancy Cunard was in London from 15 July through at least 21 July 1930 (Nancy Cunard to Louise Morgan, Saturday [6 July 1930], CtY, GEN MSS 80, series V, 36/861; Evelyn Waugh, *The Diaries of Evelyn Waugh*, ed. Michael Davie [London: Weidenfeld and Nicolson, 1976] 323).

Nancy Cunard's letter to SB from London has not been found. Nancy Cunard, *Parallax* (London: Hogarth Press, 1925) 11.

The Apes of God (1930) by Wyndham Lewis (né Percy Wyndham Lewis, 1882–1957) was published in June.

The *Cantos* of Ezra Loomis Pound (1885–1972) were then an ongoing literary work of which two sections had been published in limited editions: *A Draft of XVI Cantos of Ezra Pound: For the Beginning of a Poem of Some Length*, initials by Henry Strater (Paris: Three Mountains Press, 1925), and *A Draft of the Cantos 17–27 of Ezra Pound*, initials by Gladys Hynes (London: J. Rodker, 1928).

8 Richard Aldington conveyed McGreevy's suggestion that SB prepare a monograph on Proust for The Dolphin Books series to his friend and publisher Charles Prentice* (c. 1892–1949) of Chatto and Windus; Prentice agreed that SB should submit his manuscript for consideration (Prentice to Richard Aldington, 20 June 1930, ICSo, Aldington 68/5/11). Although McGreevy intimated to SB that there was some urgency, the work was not a commission; perhaps, rather, it was incumbent on SB to complete some work of scholarship in lieu of a doctoral thesis before returning to teach at Trinity College Dublin in the autumn.

9 Alan Duncan (a pensioned veteran of World War I), Belinda Duncan (who was from Rathmines, Co. Dublin), Alfred Péron, Georges Pelorson. George Bernard Shaw's texts were published in a *Collected Edition* (London: Constable, 1930). "Camelot" (hawker).

10 French symbolist poet Louis le Cardonnel (1862–1936) became a priest in 1896 and is primarily known for religious poetry. "The Fat Chestertonian" may refer to le Cardonnel.

André Thérive (né Roger Puthoste [other pseuds: Candidus d'Isaurie, Romain Motier, Zadoc Monteil], 1891–1967) was a conservative and influential critic for the French newspaper *Le Temps* (1861–1942); he wrote on the crisis of the postwar novel, criticizing the tendency toward aestheticism, hermeticism, and snobbery (Benoît Le Roux, *André Thérive et ses amis en 14–18* [Saint-Brieuc: B. Le Roux, 1987] 18).

11 Le Baron de Charlus is a major character in Proust's *A la recherche du temps perdu.* The opera of Wilhelm Richard Wagner (1813–1883), *Tristan und Isolde* (1865; *Tristan and Isolde*), and *L'Oiseau de Feu* (1910; *The Firebird*) by Igor Stravinsky (1882–1971).
"Il n'y a que cela" (There is nothing else).

12 Rudmose-Brown had published a critical edition of Racine's *Andromaque* (Oxford: Clarendon Press, 1917), but he did not publish a book-length critical study of Jean Racine (1639–1699). Racine's tragedy *Esther* (1689).
"Chevilles" (padding, superfluous words).

13 Peggy Sinclair, her mother Cissie, and her youngest sister, Deirdre (b. 1920, m. Hamilton), were with the "Boche Hausfreund." "Boche" (French soldiers' epithet for a German), "Hausfreund" (Ger., friend of the family).

14 SB may have sent Boss Sinclair a copy of his first book publication, *Whoroscope*, or his poem "Casket of Pralinen for a Daughter of a Dissipated Mandarin"; the latter has many allusions to SB's experiences in Kassel. (See discussion by Harvey, *Samuel Beckett*, 273–274, 277–296.)

15 In May 1930 SB had informed Lucia Joyce that he was not romantically interested in her (Knowlson, *Damned to Fame*, 111). SB's uneasiness with Lucia Joyce is evident in Georges Pelorson's account of an awkward lunch he attended with SB and Lucia (Georges Belmont, *Souvenirs d'outre-monde: Histoire d'une naissance* [Paris: Calmann-Lévy, 2001] 170–173). In July, Lucia Joyce was with her family in Wales at the Grand Hotel, Llandudno, until they returned to England on 28 July 1930 (letter from Joyce to Valery Larbaud in James Joyce, *Letters of James Joyce*, III, ed. Richard Ellmann [New York: Viking Press, 1966] 201).

16 Irish painter and writer Jack Butler Yeats* (1871–1957) wrote to McGreevy in Paris on 14 July 1930, enclosing reviews of his London exhibition (TCD, MS 10381/111).

17 Mario and Angelo were waiters at the Cochon de Lait, 7 Rue Corneille, Paris 6 (interview with SB, November 1989); McGreevy was tutoring Mario.

18 "Alfy dit que les Japonais aiment beaucoup à enculer des canards agonisants, à cause du duvet, paraît-il." (Alfy says the Japanese love to bugger dying ducks, on account of the down, it appears.)

19 Augustin Gaudin (1905–1987) entered the Ecole Normale Supérieure in 1926 to study English, but spent 1926–1927 and 1928–1929 at King's College, London. Gaudin completed the Diplôme d'études supérieures in June 1929, and was in residence at the ENS in 1929–1930, taking the agrégation examination in 1930. "Gaudin is collé" (Gaudin has failed). "Réclame pour moi!" (Publicity for me!) refers to SB's role in tutoring Gaudin for the exam. In 1932 Gaudin married Elsie Shillito (n.d.), who graduated from King's College in 1927. After a long and successful career in France, Gaudin became Proviseur (Head) of the Lycée Français de Londres.

THOMAS McGREEVY
TARBERT, CO. KERRY

Friday [c. 18 to 25 July 1930]   Ecole ...
                                                  [Paris]

My dear Tom

Your letter came this morning and this evening I saw Mario and he gave me the 200 fr. Shall I send them to you as they are or change them & send or keep them for your return? Alas! I cannot avail myself of your invitation. I saw Laugier this afternoon and arranged about the caffeine.[1] The Proust spreads more & more, and it seems more & more unlikely that I can finish it before I leave. Perhaps so, when Péron & Pelorson have gone. We (Péron) are galloping through A. L. P. It has become comic now. I suppose that is the only attitude.[2]

I wish you were here that I could talk to you. A rather di[s]pleasing thing has happened – but I cannot write about it. It must keep. And when I see you it will be decided, one way or another.[3]

Harry Sinclair turned in the other morning. He was very hospitable & stood me dinner twice at the Hotel Bristol, where I tasted the best wine – Chablis Moutonne 1926 – that I have ever tasted, and alas also suffered the 5 acts of Louise at the Opéra Comique.[4] He has gone away now. He was asking for you.

In this particular aspect of Ruddy's case, I am not confusing human affection with literary appreciation. I think he can write the book on Racine that nobody else can write, – a book that you would never like (even if the author was anonymous), but that for me would represent at last the truth, no, not the truth, but a courageous appreciation (how rare).[5] I had a letter from Pinker (who is he) expressing the usual eyewash and giving a list of his clients – a list that I am afraid did not impress me.[6]

I saw Alan & Belinda the other night with Pelorson. He is applying for Assistant Curatorship of some museum in Belfast – backed by O'Brien & God knows whom. Oh, he is all of a do-da! And Belinda too, with the possibility of a car and back to the land. Don't spread it, because it might have been a confidence, although I don't think so.[7] Angelo is gone, and Mario and the other are all smiles and willingness. The Bowsprit comes & talks abstractions every second day, and déniche books for me in the library.[8] The Scotsman is here, though I have not seen him, with 80 kilos weight of Burns Carlyle Scott und so weiter.[9]

I won't forget your offer. I haven't the courage to accept it – nor the courage to flee to Italy, as I could, and let Trinity go to hell & all its works. The acceptance of this thing makes flight & escape more & more complicated, because if I chuck Dublin after a year, I am not merely chucking Dublin – definitely – but my family, and causing them pain. I suppose I may as well make up my mind to be a vegetable.[10]

A letter from Lucia .. calm. I sent the Penman Whoroscope.[11] I am glad you are happy at home, & can understand why. I fear there is no equivalent waiting for me in Trinity. Perhaps I may prepare something – but do something ... no.

Apes of God is truly pitiful. If that is satire a child's petulance is satire. But the more I think about the gulls the more I disagree with your 'visual mechanics.' Better than that. Yes, the didacticism is regrettable.[12]

I sent Frank 'La Beauté sur la Terre' of Ramuz for his birthday. Have you read it? I will send it to you, Ruddy can't stand him, so perhaps you will like it. It is the best novel I have read modernly after the shell-shocked triangle![13] I am reading

Schopenhauer. Everyone laughs at that. Beaufret & Alfy etc. But I am not reading philosophy, nor caring whether he is right or wrong or a good or worthless metaphysician. An intellectual justification of unhappiness – the greatest that has ever been attempted – is worth the examination of one who is interested in Leopardi & Proust rather than in Carducci & Barrès.[14]

Let me know about the 200 & bon travail & bon sommeil & tante belle cose.[15]

Sam

ALS; 4 leaves, 8 sides; TCD, MS 10402/3. *Dating*: the Fridays after 17 July 1930 and before Frank Beckett's birthday on 26 July are 18 July and 25 July. This letter follows SB to McGreevy [?17 July 1930]: *The Apes of God* was received from Nancy Cunard; a letter was received from Rudmose-Brown seeking a publisher for a book on Racine; Robert I. Brown arrived in Paris in July and oversaw delivery of his books (see n. 9 below); Charpentier's opera *Louise* was performed on 10 and 22 July 1930; Alan Duncan had applied for a position in Belfast and by 8 August 1930 was among four final candidates (J. C. Nolan, Director, Ulster Museum, 4 August 1993).

That SB and Péron are "galloping through A. L. P." suggests that this letter precedes that to Soupault dated 5 July 1930 [*for* 5 August 1930] when two pages of translation were sent to Soupault.

1 McGreevy had invited SB to join him later in the summer when he traveled to see Richard Aldington at Aiguebelle near Le Lavandou on the Côte d'Azur, France.

Henri Laugier* (1888–1973) was Professor of Physiology at the Conservatoire National des Arts et Métiers (1929–1936) and a physician. A prescription was necessary to purchase caffeine.

2 SB stayed on through the summer at the Ecole Normale Supérieure to work on his study of Proust and the translation of "Anna Livia Plurabelle" with Péron.

3 The circumstance is not known.

4 Henry Morris Sinclair (known as Harry, 1882–?1938) was the twin brother of William Sinclair and the proprietor of Harris and Sinclair, Antique Plate, Jewellery and Works of Art, 47 Nassau Street, Dublin.

The Hôtel Bristol, 112 Rue du Faubourg St.-Honoré, Paris 8. The opera *Louise* by Gustave Charpentier (1860–1956) was performed at the Opéra Comique on 10 July and 22 July; *Louise* has four, not five acts, but Act II has two parts.

5 "Racine pleases me more than any other dramatist," wrote Rudmose-Brown in his memoirs: "I have never ... really cared for what ought to be, or what might be. Mine has been the scientific (or artistic) turn of mind, interested in what is, and why it is ... I have never been deceived by the cant and slogans and shibboleths of politicians and moralists: but I have never been indignant at the folly and corruption of the world"

(A. J. Leventhal, ed., "Extracts from the Unpublished Memoirs of the Late T. B. Rudmose-Brown," *Dublin Magazine* 31.1 [January–March 1956] 32).

6 James Ralph Seabrooke Pinker (fl. 1900–1950), of Messrs James B. Pinker and Sons, London, literary agents for Richard Aldington and Thomas McGreevy.

7 Duncan applied for the position of Assistant in the Ulster Art Gallery and Museum in Belfast in June 1930; by 8 August 1930, of the thirty-six applicants who had been considered, four, including an Irishman living in Paris, were selected for interviews (Nolan, 4 August 1993).

The Irish portrait painter Dermod O'Brien (1865–1945) was President of the Royal Hibernian Academy (1910–1945) and President of the United Arts Club, Dublin.

8 Jean Beaufret.
"Déniche" (digs out).

9 When Robert I. Brown arrived in Paris in July 1930, he oversaw delivery of his books to the Ecole Normale Supériéure, but he did not reside at the ENS until October. His books did not include volumes of Scottish writers Robert Burns (1759–1796), Walter Scott (1771–1832), or Thomas Carlyle (1795–1881) (Robert I. Brown, 5 August 1994).
"Und so weiter" (and so forth).

10 McGreevy, who was now in Ireland, planned to spend late August and the first weeks of September in Aiguebelle.

11 SB may have sent *Whoroscope* to Joyce in Llandudno, Wales, or to his home in Paris, 2 Square Robiac. *Whoroscope* was announced as forthcoming on 30 June 1930 and was probably published between 1 and 8 July 1930 ("Our London Letter," *The Irish Independent*: 8; SB to McGreevy Thursday [? 17 July 1930], n. 5; Cunard, *These Were the Hours*, 210).

12 In *The Apes of God* by Wyndham Lewis, the character Horace Zagreus speaks about satire with Julius Ratner, saying: "To be a true satirist Ratner you must remain upon the surface of existence … You must never go underneath it" ([London: Arthur Press, 1930; rpt. Santa Barbara, CA: Black Sparrow Press, 1981] 451).

Although "gulls" are mentioned in *The Apes of God*, it is probable that SB is responding to McGreevy's comment on the image of "gulls" in Nancy Cunard's poem, *Parallax*, a passage that SB had praised in his previous letter to McGreevy [?17 July 1930].

13 The birthday of SB's brother Frank Edward Beckett* (1902–1954) was 26 July. *La Beauté sur la terre* (1927; *Beauty on Earth*) was written by Swiss-born novelist Charles-Ferdinand Ramuz (1878–1947). The "shell-shocked triangle" probably refers to the following novels of World War I: Henri Barbusse (1874–1935), *Le Feu, journal d'une escouade* (1916; *Under Fire*); Georges Duhamel (né Denis Thévenin, 1884–1966), *La Vie des martyrs* (1917; *The New Book of Martyrs*); Roland Dorgelès (né Roland Lecavelé, 1885–1973), *Les Croix de bois* (1919; *Wooden Crosses*); the first two were awarded the Prix Goncourt in 1917 and 1918 respectively.

14 German philosopher Arthur Schopenhauer (1788–1869) discusses happiness as "mere abolition of a desire and extinction of a pain" in his essay "On the Suffering of the World"; he adds that, if one's fellow man is seen as a "fellow sufferer," it "reminds us of what are the most necessary of all things; tolerance, patience, forbearance and

charity, which each of us needs and which each of us therefore owes" (*Essays and Aphorisms*, ed. and tr. R. J. Hollingdale [London: Penguin, 1970] 42, 50).

Jean Beaufret and Alfred Péron.

Italian poet Giacomo Leopardi (1798–1837); for SB's student notes on Leopardi: TCD, MS 10971/9. For further discussion of Leopardi's influence on SB, see C. J. Ackerley and S. E. Gontarski, *The Grove Companion to Samuel Beckett: A Reader's Guide to His Works, Life, and Thought* (New York: Grove Press, 2004) 316–317.

SB refers to Italian poet and Professor in Classics at the University of Bologna (1860–1904) Giosuè Carducci (1835–1907); for SB's student reading notes: TCD, MS 10965 and MS 10965a.

Maurice Barrès (1863–1923), French novelist, journalist, politician, fervent and anti-semitic Nationalist, was author of two trilogies of novels, *Le Culte du moi* (1888–1891; The Cult of Ego) and *Le Roman de l'énergie nationale* (1897–1902; The Novel of National Energy).

15 "Bon travail & bon sommeil" (work well & sleep well); "tante belle cose" (It., all good wishes).

THOMAS McGREEVY
TARBERT, CO. KERRY

[before 5 August 1930]   Ecole Normale
                                          [Paris]

Dear Tom

I cannot find the phrase you want, but may yet. I thought I knew where it was, but was wrong as usual. Have you no idea. I thought it was amongst the negligent, but it was not.[1] What poem do you mean? Every second poem of Laforgue is about jeunes filles & couvents. I will send you my volume of Laforgue. I will look in Corbière and send it along.[2] Anything I can do I am only too glad to do. But you may be sure I will do it all wrong & badly.

I have not put pen to paper on Proust. But I will, & then I hope it will go quickly. I am reading him all again before starting & it tires me a lot. I am supposed to be going on with the Joyce too, alone now that Alfy has gone, God help & save me. I can't do the bloody thing. It's betrayal as well as everything else.

[...]

I heard from Lucia. I never think of her now. I think they have left Llandudno for Oxford.[3] I saw Bronowski. A talkative shit. I think I like Putnam & Reavey.[4] But possibly not much. Reavey bought a new ribbon for my typewriter & that works very well now. When are you coming back? Hurry up in the name of God. Sorry to hear about the Bibesco. Surely he'll pay all the same?[5] I had a card from Angelo from Piedmont, and was very glad. I saw your doctor & he gave me some bloody stuff that isn't bad, but I'd rather have caffeine.[6] They never do what you ask them. I am looking forward to pulling the balls off the critical & poetical Proustian cock. He adored Ruskin & the Comtesse de Noailles and thought Amiel was a forerunner! I am going to write a poem about him too, with Charlus's lavender trousers in a Gothic pissotière.[7] I will write again to-morrow and give all information I can. Have you heard from Aldington?[8] You sent on an offer of a complimentary photographical séance from one Miss Vaughan! It'd be better for a man to be dead! When you come we will drink 2 bottles of Chambertin & half a bottle of cochon fine & find a ciné cochon.[9] You are unwise to leave me your 200. You know I will spend it. I brought my shoes to a shop and they refused to mend them, but I can still wear them on very dry days. Another pair too I had they refused to mend.

Schopenhauer says <u>defunctus</u> is a beautiful word – as long as one does not suicide.[10] He might be right.

Love

Sam

ALS; 1 leaf, 4 sides; TCD, MS 10402/4. *Dating:* Jacob Bronowski was editing the English and Irish sections of *The European Caravan* for Samuel Putnam; Bronowski was in Paris 31 July to 3 August 1930, and again, overnight, on 16 August as he returned to London (Bronowski to Putnam, 28 July 1930; Bronowski to Putnam, 14 August 1930 [NjP, *New Review* Correspondence of Samuel Putnam, C0111/1/23]). SB may have met Bronowski at either of these times, but early August 1930 is more likely. The Joyces were in Llandudno during late June and much of July; Joyce wrote to Valery Larbaud from England on 28 July 1930 and to Stanislaus Joyce from Oxford on 3 August 1930 (Joyce, *Letters of James Joyce*, III, 512, 201). SB's surmise that the Joyces are back in Oxford would confirm a date toward the end of July or early August.

1 The Princes who have been negligent of salvation are found in Canto VII of Dante's *Purgatory*. McGreevy does not cite Dante in his *Thomas Stearns Eliot: A Study*, The Dolphin Books (London: Chatto and Windus, 1931); he does quote from Dante in his poem "Fragments" (1931) (Thomas MacGreevy, *Collected Poems of Thomas MacGreevy: An Annotated Edition*, ed. Susan Schreibman [Dublin: Anna Livia Press; Washington DC: The Catholic University of America Press, 1991] 38, 140–142).

2 Several poems by French poet Jules Laforgue (1860–1887) are quoted in McGreevy's *Thomas Stearns Eliot*, 30–33: "Figurez-vous un peu" (*Derniers vers*), "Pétition," "Petite prière sans prétentions," and "Le bon apôtre" (a section that is also part of "Le Concile Féerique"). McGreevy seeks a poem with allusion to a convent; the untitled twelfth poem of the *Derniers vers* takes as its headnote (in English) a portion of Hamlet's speech to Ophelia, beginning: "Get thee to a nunn'ry" (Shakespeare, *Hamlet*, in *The Riverside Shakespeare: The Complete Works*, General and Textual ed. G. Blakemore Evans, assisted by J. J. M. Tobin, 2nd edn. [Boston: Houghton Mifflin, 1997] III.i.120–129; all subsequent Shakespeare citations are from this text). McGreevy discusses the influence on Eliot of French poet Tristan Corbière (né Edouard-Joachim Corbière, 1845–1875), quoting from Corbière's poem "Vésuves et Cie," published in *Les Amours jaunes* (1873) (McGreevy, *Thomas Stearns Eliot*, 25–26).

3 The Joyce family left the Grand Hotel, Llandudno, for the Randolph Hotel, Oxford, about 1 August 1930 (Danis Rose, *The Textual Diaries of James Joyce* [Dublin: Lilliput Press, 1995] 188).

4 Polish-born mathematician and scientist Jacob Bronowski* (1908–1974) was an Editor of the Cambridge University undergraduate journal *Experiment* (1928–1931), begun by William Empson (1906–1984), William Hare (né William Francis Hare, Lord Ennismore; from 1931, the 5th Earl of Listowel; 1906–1997), and Humphrey Jennings (1907–1950); in 1929 Hugh Sykes [Davies] (1909–1984) replaced Empson as Editor. George Reavey* (1907–1976), also at Cambridge, published in the journal.
With George Reavey, Maida Castelhun Darnton (1872–1940), and Samuel Putnam, Bronowski was compiling and editing *The European Caravan*.

5 Prince Antoine Bibesco (1878–1951) was the Romanian envoy in London, a life-long friend of Marcel Proust, and a dramatist. It is not known what McGreevy had begun to translate for Bibesco, but possibly it was his play *Laquelle . . . ?* (1930). Although unacknowledged as such, McGreevy was translator of *Le Destin de Lord Thomson of Cardington* (*Lord Thomson of Cardington, a Memoir and Some Letters* [London: Jonathan Cape, 1932]) by Princesse Marthe Lucie Bibesco (née Lahovary, also pseud. Lucile Decaux, 1886–1973), Romanian-born novelist, biographer, and travel writer, a cousin by marriage to Antoine Bibesco.

6 McGreevy's doctor was Henri Laugier.

7 Proust spent several years translating and annotating the works of the English art critic and writer John Ruskin (1819–1900): *Sesame and Lilies* (1865–1869) as *Sésame et les*

lys (1906) and *The Bible of Amiens* (1885) as *La Bible d'Amiens* (1904). Poet and woman of letters, Anna de Brancovan, Comtesse Mathieu de Noailles (1876–1933). *Journal Intime* (1883–1884) by Henri-Frédéric Amiel (1821–1881), Swiss poet and philosopher, Professor of Aesthetics and Moral Philosophy at the University of Geneva.

In Proust's *A la recherche du temps perdu* the Baron de Charlus frequents pissotières (street urinals) for the purpose of soliciting.

8   Richard Aldington.

9   Reference to a circular from a photographer Miss Kay Vaughan (n.d.), 44A Dover Street, London W1.

"Cochon fine" (house brandy); "ciné cochon" (blue film).

10   In his "Doctrine of Suffering of the World," Schopenhauer writes: "Life is a task to be worked off; in this sense *defunctus* is a fine expression" (*Studies in Pessimism* in *Parerga and Paralipomena: Short Philosophical Essays*, tr. E. F. J. Payne, II [Oxford: Clarendon Press, 1974] 300). SB uses "defunctus" as the final word in *Proust*, The Dolphin Books ([London: Chatto and Windus, 1931] 72; pagination is identical in *Proust* [New York: Grove Press, 1957]).

PHILIPPE SOUPAULT

PARIS

5/7/30 [*for* 5 August 1930]   Ecole Normale

Rue d'Ulm 45

Paris 5e

Cher Monsieur Soupault

Voici enfin. Deux copies, dans le cas que Bifur en voudrait une.[1] Mais je ne voudrais pas publier cela, pas même un fragment, sans l'au[t]orisation de Monsieur Joyce lui-même, qui pourrait très bien trouver cela vraiment trop mal fait et trop éloigné de l'original.[2] Plus j'y pense plus je trouve tout cela bien pauvre. Enfin, tel quel, je vous l'envoie.

Cordialement

s/ Samuel Beckett

TLS; 1 leaf, 1 side; enclosure: TMS with AN; 2 leaves, 2 sides of preliminary translation into French of Joyce's "Anna Livia Plurabelle"; CtY, James Joyce collection, GEN MSS 112, Series II, 5/102; photocopy OkTU, Ellmann collection.

The typescript enclosure ends: "Patain de foudre! En voilà du pourpraupérisme!" It is possible: (1) that more pages were originally enclosed; (2) that the translation was continued by SB, with or without Péron (an argument that might be made for maintaining the date as 5 July 1930); or (3) that the translation was completed by others to whom it was not attributed. Proof pages from *Bifur*, date stamped 16 October 1930, incorporate the few AN corrections on the original typescript; the proof pages are themselves heavily corrected (GEN MSS 112, Series II, 5/103; http://beinecke/library. yale.edu/dl_crosscollex/default.htm, and Folder 641, Broadside case). This proof indicates that the translation was done by "M. Perron and S. Beckett," but this is changed to read "A. R. Peron."

A further, though unsigned, typescript reflects the changes made on the *Bifur* proof (GEN MSS 112, Series II/5/104; this is ten pages long, although paginated to 9 because two pages are marked "7").

Dating: the editors have dated this letter as 5 August 1930, based on the contextual sequence of undated letters from [? 17 July 1930] to [7 August 1930].

5/7/30 [*for* 5 August 1930] Ecole Normale
Rue d'Ulm 45
Paris 5e

Dear Monsieur Soupault

Here at last. Two copies, in case Bifur wanted one.[1] But I would not wish to publish this, not even a fragment, without permission from Mr Joyce himself, who might very well find it all really too badly done and too far from the original.[2] The more I think of it, the more I find it all very poor stuff. Anyhow, such as it is, I send it to you.

Best wishes
Samuel Beckett

1 SB and Alfred Péron prepared the preliminary French translation of the "Anna Livia Plurabelle" section of Joyce's *Work in Progress* for publication in *Bifur* (TM; 2 Leaves, 2 sides; CtY, James Joyce collection, GEN MSS 112, Series II, 5/102); photocopy, OkTU, Ellmann collection).

2 Adrienne Monnier (1892–1955), proprietor of La Maison des Amis des Livres, the Paris bookshop, wrote: "This translation … went to the stage of being set in type … but it did not go to the stage of being approved for printing, for while Joyce was very satisfied with the result when he was consulted, he got it into his head to team seven persons together under his guidance … That was to have the

pleasure of saying my 'Septuagint'" (*The Very Rich Hours of Adrienne Monnier* [New York: Scribner-, 1976] 167).

Revision began with regular weekly sessions in November 1930 and continued into the spring, with Soupault as the "driving force behind the translation" (Paul Léopoldovitch Léon [1893–1942] to Roger Vitrac [1899–1953], 30 December 1932 in James Joyce and Paul Léon, *The James Joyce – Paul Léon Papers in The National Library of Ireland: A Catalogue*, compiled by Catherine Fahy [Dublin: National Library of Ireland, 1992] 120).

Philippe Soupault described the process in "A Propos de la traduction d'Anna Livia [*for* Livie] Plurabelle" (*La Nouvelle Revue Française*, 36.212 [1 May 1931] 633–636); although written as "Livia" in the title of this essay, throughout the essay, and as the heading for the translation itself, the title is given as "Anna Livie Plurabelle." The translation is attributed to Samuel Beckett, Alfred Perron (*for* Péron), Ivan Goll, Eugène (*for* Eugene) Jolas, Paul L. Léon, Adrienne Monnier, and Philippe Soupault, in collaboration with the author (*La Nouvelle Revue Française*, 36.212 [1 May 1931] 637–646). For more detail about the translation process: "Traduttore ... Traditore?" in Maria Jolas, ed., *A James Joyce Yearbook* (Paris: Transition Press, 1949) 171–178; this reprints Soupault's memoir from his *Souvenirs de James Joyce* (Algiers: Editions Fontaine, 1943), and Eugene Jolas's account of the translation process from the manuscript of his then unpublished autobiography, *Man from Babel*, ed. Andreas Kramer and Rainer Rumod, Henry McBride Series in Modernism and Modernity (New Haven: Yale University Press, 1998).

THOMAS McGREEVY

TARBERT, CO. KERRY

7/7/30 [*for* 7 August 1930]   E.N.S.

[Paris]

Dear Tom

Here is the Corbière and the baronial nausea. You see I exaggerated as usual. Vinegar not cowpiss. I hope you will not be too disappointed. Alas I cannot find the words of Dante, and I have been all through it. I am sorry but it is hopeless when I don't know where to look. I am sending you my copy of Laforgue.[1]

The Proust is crawling along though I have not started to write anything. 17000 words is the hell of a lot, and I can't see myself doing so much.[2] Alfy is gone. I am going to write to him now that I cannot go on with the translation alone. I can't do it. And then to that bastard Soupault that I will sign no contract.

I sent him two copies of what we had already done, one for Joyce and one for Bifur if Joyce is not too disgusted by the chasm of feeling and technique between his hieroglyphics and our bastard French.[3] But I will not go on alone. It can't be done, and I am tired enough and have enough to do without that. I was reading d'Annunzio on Giorgione again and I think it is all balls and mean nasty balls. I was thinking of Keats and Giorg[i]one's two young men – the Concert and the Tempest – for a discussion of Proust's floral obsessions. D'A. seems to think that they are <u>merely</u> pausing between fucks. Horrible. He has a dirty juicy squelchy mind, bleeding and bursting, like his celebrated pomegranates.[4] My head was a torrent of ideas and phrases last night or rather this morning in bed, but it did me no good as I could neither go to sleep nor get up and put them down. My shoe exploded this afternoon in the Boul Mich so I had to go in and buy a pair. I left them in the shop and felt relieved when I got away without them. Saw A. and B. last night. Napoleon Danton and Louis quatorze[']s red heels![5] Dining with Nancy tomorrow. She says Little Red Riddensnood is selling, but I don't believe her.[6]

God bless, hurry up back.

s/ <u>Sam</u>

TLS; 1 leaf, 2 sides; TCD, MS 10402/7. *Dating*: Nancy Cunard was in Paris through the middle of August; she wrote to Louise Morgan on 13 August 1930: "These are the last days here thank God. Then off [...] into the car and so down Pyreneenwards [...] If Beckett goes to London on his way to Dublin I'll make so bold as to send him you. He's a grand person" (CtY, Beinecke, GEN MSS 80, series v, 36/361).

1 SB sent his copy of Corbière's *Les Amours jaunes* and of the poems of Laforgue. Although it is not known which edition of Laforgue he sent to McGreevy, or whether McGreevy returned the book, according to James Knowlson SB owned the 1903 edition of Laforgue's *Poésies* (Paris: Mercure de France) at the time of his death.

2 SB's essay turned out to be about the same length as other books in the Chatto and Windus Dolphin Books series.

3 Neither SB's letter to Péron, nor a further letter to Soupault has been found.

4 *Il fuoco* (1900) by the Italian writer Gabriele D'Annunzio (1863–1938) includes a discussion of the three figures in *The Concert* (Palazzo Pitti, Florence), then attributed to Italian painter Giorgione (né Zorzi da Castelfranco, also known as Zorzon, c. 1477–1510), but now attributed to Titian (né Tiziano Vecellio, c. 1485–1576). D'Annunzio's character Stelio Effrena lectures on the painting, describing the gaze exchanged between the musician at the harpsichord and the older man on the right, who gently touches his shoulder; the other figure in the painting, a man on the left in a plumed hat, is described by D'Annunzio as an apparently detached onlooker. Stelio says that "Giorgione seems to have created [him] under the influence of a ray reflected from the stupendous Hellenic myth whence the ideal form of Hermaphrodite arose" (*Il fuoco: I romanzi del Melagrano* in *Prose di romanzi*, II, ed. Ezio Raimondi, Annamaria Andreoli, and Niva Lorenzini [Milan: Arnoldo Mondadori Editore, 1989] 247; *The Flame of Life: The Romances of the Pomegranate*, tr. Kassandra Vivaria [Boston: L. C. Page and Company, 1900] 62–63). In *Proust*, SB quotes a passage from *Il fuoco* that captures the sensuous nature of the supposed onlooker, and compares him with another onlooker in Giorgione's painting, *The Tempest* (Venice: Accademia) (see *Il fuoco*, 248; *The Flame of Life*, 63; Beckett, *Proust*, 70). D'Annunzio does not discuss *The Tempest* in this context, although the painting is mentioned in passing in his essay on Giorgione ("Dell'arte di Giorgio Barbarelli," *Prose scelte* [Milan: Fratelli Treves, Editori, 1924] 17–22).

SB alludes to the gushing red juice of the crushed pomegranate in *Il fuoco* (311; *The Flame of Life*, 142). Stelio Effrena takes the pomegranate as his personal emblem; suggesting the "idea of things rich and hidden," it is an image of sexuality throughout the novel (*Il fuoco*, 207, 209–211; *The Flame of Life*, 13).

In his essay, SB contrasts Proust's "floral obsessions" with those of D'Annunzio and Keats; SB concludes that "there is no collapse of the will in Proust, as there is for example in Spenser and Keats and Giorgione" (*Proust*, 68–70).

5 Alan and Belinda Duncan. SB refers to Napoleon Bonaparte (1769–1821), the beheaded Jacobin leader Georges Jacques Danton (1759–1794), and Louis XIV (1628–1715), but his suggestion is unclear.

6 SB refers to *Whoroscope* as "Little Red Riddensnood."

THOMAS McGREEVY
LE LAVANDOU, VAR

25ᵗʰ August [1930]   E.N.S.
                                                                                  [Paris]

My dear Tom

Bronowski wrote me asking for your address. Said he wanted more poems. I sent it to him. Was that all right? He says he is using three turds from my central lavatory. But alas not the twice round & pointed ones.[1] I started writing this morning, worked like one inspired for $2\frac{1}{2}$ hours, then tore everything up and made a present of it to the panier. Since I have been moistening the Schöne Lippen, having first taken the precaution to provoke salivary hyper-secretion by the grace of Black & White.[2] I can't do the <u>fucking</u> thing. I don't know whether to start at the end or the beginning – in a word should the Proustian arse-hole be considered as entrée or sortie – libre in either case. Anyhow I don't know what to [sic] or where I am, but I'll write 17000 words before I leave, even though my observations may have as little variety and none of the sincerity of Orlando's wood carvings.[3] Schopenhauer has a nice explanation of the temptation to write one[']s nominative letters across the frieze-fesses. Stimulation of the will. Since the fesses as fesses as Platonic Idea – have no action on the Thing in Itself (God help it!), they will bloody well have a reaction. I am going now to try his 'Aphorismes sur la Sagesse de la Vie', that Proust admired so much for its originality and guarantee of wide reading – transformed. His chapter in Will & Representation on music is amusing & applies to P., who certainly read it. [([It is alluded to incidentally in A. La R.) A noble bitch observes to the Duchesse de Guermantes: 'Relisez ce que S. dit sur la Musique.' Duchesse snarls & sneers: 'Relisez! Relisez! Ça alors, c'est trop fort!', because she had the snobism of ignorance.[4]

[. . .] Cards from Nancy & Henry from Albi and Moissac. Henry says: dear priest says this is fine church. Well I don't like the <u>dam</u> thing, I like a church as a building. When has he been reading the cohesion theory of Arthur, or spittle by spittle.[5] I said in my condemned preamble that the philosopher considered the public as a convenient spit[t]oon for his syllogisms, &

that M͟r George Shaw might be considered as called rather than chosen.[6] But I haven't got the heart to jeer any more.

Bronowski rejected Ruddy's poems, who immediately wrote to know who was M͟r Buggeroffski or Buggerin-Andoffski, and if he had the intelligence of an ivory testicle.[7]

Well, amuse-toi bien, and write soon, because if Ruddy is depressed I am suppressed.

> Much Love
>
> Sam
>
> Meilleures amitiés au ménage.[8]

ALS; 1 leaf, 4 sides; TCD, 10402/8. *Dating*: McGreevy left Paris for London before 14 July 1930 and was in London on 14 July 1930 on his way to Dublin (Prentice to Aldington, 15 July 1930, ICSo, Aldington 68/5/12); by 16 August 1930 he was back in Paris (Pilling, *A Samuel Beckett Chronology*, 26), and afterwards was expected to visit Aldington in Le Lavandou (Aldington to Derek Patmore, 9 August 1930, indicates his route and that he was expected; ICSo, VFM 9). SB gave the manuscript of *Proust* to Prentice on 17 September 1930 (Prentice to Aldington, 17 September 1930, ICSo, 68/5/12).

1 SB wrote "<laboratory> lavatory."

Jacob Bronowski included four poems by Thomas McGreevy in *The European Caravan*: "Aodh Ruadh Ó Domhnaill," "Homage to Marcel Proust," "Homage to Jack Yeats," and "Golders Green" (493–496). Poems by SB in *The European Caravan* are: "Hell Crane to Starling," "Casket of Pralinen for the Daughter of a Dissipated Mandarin," "Text," and "Yoke of Liberty" (475–480); Pilling surmises that "Yoke of Liberty" was not yet selected (*A Samuel Beckett Chronology*, 26).

SB uses words from an untitled ode on the public lavatory that he wrote as a student at Trinity College:

> There is an expert there who can
> Encircle twice the glittering pan
> In flawless symmetry to extend
> Neatly pointed at each end.
> (Gerald Pakenham Stewart, *The Rough and the Smooth:
> An Autobiography* [Walkanae: Heritage, 1994] 22)

2 "Panier" (the bin). "Schöne Lippen" (beautiful lips). Black & White, a brand of Scotch whisky.

3 "Sortie" (exit); "libre" (free): the reference to a standard shop sign, "entrée libre" (in effect, feel free to enter without buying).

Orlando's verses to Rosalind are hung on trees in Shakespeare's *As You Like It*.

4 "Frieze" refers to the decorative architectural element between the architrave and cornice of a building, and "fesses" refers to the horizontal line marking the center of an escutcheon; in the sense suggested by Schopenhauer's example below, SB refers to a need to leave one's initials as a mark of visitation on an architectural feature of a monument.

In *Die Welt als Wille und Vorstellung*, Schopenhauer distinguishes those who are capable of taking pleasure in the beautiful from those "wholly incapable of the pleasure to be found in pure knowledge" who are "entirely given over to willing." As an example of the latter's need to "in some way excite their will," he observes that they write their names at places that they visit in order "to affect the place, since it does not affect them" (*The World as Will and Representation*, I, tr. E. F. J. Payne [Indian Hills, CO: The Falcon's Wing Press, 1958] 314; with appreciation to Michael Maier for his assistance with this allusion).

Schopenhauer "viewed the will as the thing in itself" ("Ding an Sich"), a notion that SB abbreviates in his later Philosophy Notes as "TII" (David E. Cartwright, *Historical Dictionary of Schopenhauer's Philosophy* [Lanham, MD: The Scarecrow Press, 2005] 171, 181; see also reference to TCD, MS 10967/252, by Matthew Feldman, *Beckett's Books: A Cultural History of Samuel Beckett's 'Interwar Notes'* [New York: Continuum, 2006] 49). Schopenhauer wrote that "aesthetic satisfaction everywhere rests on the apprehension of a (Platonic) idea" (*The World as Will and Representation*, II, tr. E. F. J. Payne [Indian Hills, CO: The Falcon's Wing Press, 1958] 414).

While SB may have borrowed a copy from Jean Beaufret, the library of the Ecole Normale Supérieure had a copy of Schopenhauer's *Aphorismes sur la sagesse dans la vie* in *Parerga et Paralipomena*, tr. J.-A. Cantacuzène (Paris: Félix Alcan, 1914).

Schopenhauer's chapter on music is "On the Metaphysics of Music" in *The World as Will and Representation*, II, 447–457; music is also discussed in I, 256–266.

In Proust's *Le Temps retrouvé*, the Marquise de Cambremer says: "'Relisez ce que Schopenhauer dit de la musique'" ("You must re-read what Schopenhauer says about music"); the remark made by the Duchesse de Guermantes is: "'*Relisez* est un chef-d'oeuvre! Ah! non, ça, par exemple, il ne faut pas nous la faire'" ("Re-read is pretty rich, I must say. Who does she think she's fooling?"(*A la recherche du temps perdu*, IV, ed. Jean-Yves Tadié, Bibliothèque de la Pléiade [Paris: Gallimard, 1989] 569; *Time Regained* in *In Search of Lost Time*, VI, tr. Andreas Mayor and Terence Kilmartin, rev. D. J. Enright [New York: Modern Library, 1993] 444–445). SB mis-remembers the response by the Duchess de Guermantes as "'Relisez! Relisez! Ça alors, c'est trop fort!'" ("Re-read! Re-read! Really, that's a bit much!").

5 Nancy Cunard and Henry Crowder wrote to SB from the Midi-Pyrénées, northeast of Toulouse. Albi is known for the thirteenth-century Cathedral of Ste. Cécile; the mass of the exterior contrasts with the lavish interior decorations by Italian painters and a mural of the Last Judgment painted by unknown Flemish artists (1474–1484).

Moissac is known for its Romanesque abbey church of St. Pierre, with seventy-six well-preserved capitals and four cloister-walks, as well as a depiction of St. John's vision of the Apocalypse on the south portal.

In the first volume of *The World as Will and Representation*, Arthur Schopenhauer discusses cohesion as a universal force of nature, along with gravitation and impenetrability (125, 214, 533). In the second volume, Schopenhauer writes: "For architecture, considered only as *fine* art, the Ideas of the lowest grades of nature, that is gravity, rigidity, and cohesion, are the proper theme, but not ... merely regular form, proportion, and symmetry. These are ... properties of space, not Ideas; therefore they cannot be the theme of fine art" (*The World as Will and Representation*, 414).

"Arthur, or spittle by spittle" makes play with the rhythm of a famous title, *Eric, or Little by Little* (Frederic William Farrar, *Eric, or Little by Little: The Story of Roslyn School* [Edinburgh: Adam and Charles Black, 1858]). An edifying tale of school life, the book was popular in its day, but later became a by-word for virtuous claptrap.

6   SB refers to his discarded false start to *Proust*.

SB cites Matthew 20:16 and 22:14, with reference to Shaw's habit of prefacing his plays with extended discussions of his political and philosophical positions. Shaw himself explained: "'When the subject of a play is a large one, there is a great deal about it that cannot be put on the stage though it can be said in an essay'" (Bernard Shaw, *The Complete Prefaces, Bernard Shaw*, I, *1889–1913*, ed. Dan H. Laurence and Daniel J. Leary [London: The Penguin Press, 1993] vii).

7   Although Bronowski rejected Rudmose-Brown's poems for inclusion in *The European Caravan*, he wrote a mollifying preface to Rudmose-Brown's essay, "Grace Withheld from Jean Racine" which was published (558–564): "He is a scholarly critic whose work should influence the younger Irish critics: and, although of a pre-war generation, stands out as having anticipated the direction of much contemporary French and English criticism" (558).

8   "Amuse-toi bien" (enjoy yourself).

"Meilleures amitiés au ménage" (Love to the whole houseful of you); McGreevy is with an Aldington house party in Le Lavandou.

SAMUEL PUTNAM

FRANCE

[? before 9 September 1930]   45 Rue d'Ulm

[Paris]

Dear Putnam

I pneued Léon and rang him up again. No reply and out again. The best thing for Bronowski to do is to write to M. Paul Léon, 27 rue Casimir[-]Périer, Paris, & <u>make an offer</u> specifying the passage he wants to use.[1] If you want to get into communication with Léon, his tel. is Littré 88.89. But he never seems to be at home. I would go and see him if I had a second. I am working all day & most of the night to get this <u>fucking</u> Proust finished.[2]

How are things? Must try & arrange a proper booze before I return – like a constipated Eurydice to the shades of shit.
> Yours ever
>> Sam Beckett

ALS; 1 leaf, 1 side; NjP, *New Review* Correspondence of Samuel Putnam, C0111/1/9. Enclosed with undated letter [before 9 September 1930] from Putnam to Bronowski. *Dating*: see n. 1. SB completed the MS of *Proust* before 15 September 1930, when he wrote to Charles Prentice to make an appointment to deliver the manuscript in London on 17 September 1930.

1 Jacob Bronowski sought permission to publish an excerpt from Joyce's *Ulysses* for the English and Irish section of *The European Caravan* that he was editing. Athough he had written to Sylvia Beach to ask about the "copyright position of Ulysses" in the United States, Bronowski reported to Putnam that he was "still at sea with Joyce's material" and asked Putnam to "go to the Shakespeare shop and find out [. . .] precisely how we would stand" (30 August [1930], NjP, *New Review* Correspondence of Samuel Putnam, C0111/1/23). Bronowski wrote again to Putnam on 9 September 1930 about the matter, but this letter crossed in the mail with Putnam's reply to the first: "I have done my utmost about Joyce, without avail. Beckett likewise has tried. We simply have been unable to get into touch with J.'s agent, a chap by the name of Leon [*for* Léon]. I enclose a letter from B.[eckett] with regard to this" (undated letter [before 9 September 1930], NjP, *New Review* Correspondence of Samuel Putnam, C0111/1/23). The present letter from Beckett was that enclosure.

The American rights were at issue because *The European Caravan* was to be published in New York. The Joyce extract in *The European Caravan* (from the "Proteus" chapter of *Ulysses*) was drawn from, but is not identical to, the text as published in *The Little Review* (James Joyce, "Ulysses: Episode III," *The Little Review*, 5.1 [May 1918] 31–45); *The Little Review* was published from 1914 to 1929 by Margaret Anderson (1886–1973) and Jane Heap (1887–1964), and so a request for permission would have required contacting them. Paul Léon was Joyce's assistant.

2 SB planned to leave for Ireland a few days later, to assume duties at Trinity College Dublin.

CHARLES PRENTICE, CHATTO AND WINDUS
LONDON

15/9/30
> Ecole Normale
> 45 Rue d'Ulm
> Paris V^e

Dear Mr Prentice

Could I see you for a moment Wednesday morning or after-noon, and hand you over my 'Proust' for your Dolphin Series? Thomas McGreevy assures me that you will not consider this suggestion as an impertinence.[1]

I will be staying at Garlands hotel for two nights on my way to Dublin – arriving Tuesday evening.[2] Could you leave word for me there?

Sincerely yours

Samuel Beckett

ALS; 1 leaf, 1 side; *date stamped* received 16-9-30; UoR, MS 2444, CW 24/9.

1 SB wrote to McGreevy: "I saw Prentice this morning and handed over Proust. He was charming, but I have a feeling he won't touch it for Chatto & Windus, that it isn't scholarly & primo secundo enough. However there it is and off my hands at last" (Weds. evening [17 September 1930], TCD, MS 10402/9).

2 Garland's Hotel, 15–17 Suffolk Street, London. It was destroyed by bombs in 1943.

THOMAS McGREEVY

PARIS

5/10/30   Cooldrinagh

                                                          [Co. Dublin]

My dear Tom,

Delighted to get your letter. Do write again. This life is terrible and I dont understand how it can be endured. Quip – that most foul malady – Scandal & KINDNESS. The eternally invariable formulae of cheap quip and semi-obscene entirely contemptible potin chez Ruddy & in the Common Room Club, and Kindness here at home, pumped into me at high pressure. I am getting my rooms (Fry's) ready at the top of 39.[1] Perhaps things will be better when I get in there. But the Ruddy vico seems to be a dead end. If I could merely listen to him talking philosophy or Motin & the Précieux, things would be easy. But all his old anti-isms are flourishing and I am tired of them: you know what they are – priests and soldiers & the Romantics – mainly. And then the enduring & unendurable QUIP, far worse than the Giraudoux astuce.[2] I like Ruddy toujours and very much as you know, but how am I to give him that impression when he quiptificates in the midst of his adorers. – And live? I know it means a row, sooner than later, if one can make a row. A rowdiness I suppose you might call it. Looking vaguely round college I know there is nothing but loneliness, and perhaps that is the most satisfactory conclusion I have reached since coming back to Ireland – although God knows it was sufficiently clear & necessary in abstracto in Paris. I have done nothing so far except a little examining – and am on again this afternoon & to-morrow & Friday. It is really something to lean up against, this sense that j'en aurai pour un an au maximum.[3] I can only hope to read a few books in that time. How can one write here, when every day vulgarises one's hostility and turns anger into irritation & petulance? [. . .]

Thanks for the Prentice revelations. I have not heard a word from him, although he promised to write and let me have his opinion. Looking at the thing again, the end is terribly hurried, but I can't do anything to it now.[4] [. . .]

Won't you let me know about your Eliot. I wish I could have read it before leaving. Did you get in the Nobiscum peregrinator?[5] Have you any further plans or are you sticking to Formes for the winter?[6] I suppose there is no chance of your coming to Dublin? I saw a lone 'poetic comedy' by Austin Clarke, the 'Hunger Demon', at the Gate. Truly pernicious. And a revival of Dervorgilla by the old poisse Gregory. A gutter snippet. Vulgarly conceived & vulgarly written and of course reinforced by the ineffable bitch Crowe, playing the regal lover like Frau Lot petrified into a symbolic condemnation of Free Trade.[7]

I want to inflict myself on Lennox Robinson & Jack Yeats, for a moment, but so far la main m'en manque.[8]

I wrote to the Bowsprit, but have had no reply. Please God he has had enough of a miserable sinner whose interest in the conditions of the artistic experience is fragmentary & intermittent.

Do write again. I needn't tell you I will miss you too, and all that life in Paris that was an approximation to something reasonable.

Much love

<u>Sam</u>

ALS; 2 leaves, 3 sides; TCD, MS 10402/11.

1 SB speaks of "potin chez Ruddy" (gossip at Ruddy's) and gatherings in the Common Room at Trinity College Dublin. SB's rooms were at 39 New Square, Trinity College; they had been occupied previously by Professor of Natural Philosophy Matthew Wyatt Joseph Fry (1864–1943), who was appointed Senior Lecturer of TCD in 1927, the highest academic officer in the college after the Provost.

2 The Ruddy "vico" (It., way). SB enjoyed hearing Rudmose-Brown discoursing on the French poet Pierre Motin (1566–1610) and the Précieux, a seventeenth-century "movement" originating with Catherine de Vivonne, Marquise de Rambouillet (1588–1665) and her salon.

Rudmose-Brown's "anti-isms" are evident in his memoirs: "I accept no dogma and deny none" (31); "the greatest good is, for me, the greatest possible degree of individual liberty. That is why I am neither Fascist, nor Communist, Imperialist nor Socialist" (Leventhal, ed., "Extracts from the Unpublished Memoirs of the Late T. B. Rudmose-Brown," 33).

"Astuce" (clever-clever). Jean Giraudoux (né Hippolyte-Jean Giraudoux, 1882–1944), French novelist and playwright.

3 "Toujours" (still). "J'en aurai pour un an au maximum" (I'll only have a year of it to do at most).

4 McGreevy had been in correspondence with Prentice in early October 1930 about the terms of publication of his book on Eliot in the Chatto and Windus The Dolphin Books series.

5 McGreevy did include "Nobiscum peregrinatur" (Lat., comes along with us), a quotation that SB may have suggested to him: "Schopenhauer remarked that

Americans might say of their own vulgarity what Cicero said of science, 'Nobiscum peregrinatur'" (McGreevy, *Thomas Stearns Eliot*, 4). Marcus Tullius Cicero (106–43 BC).

6 See 1 March 1930, n. 1. In a letter received by Charles Prentice on 2 December 1930, McGreevy wrote: "Formes has busted, is all over. There was a row over policy and the Editor resigned and the proprietor thought it was a good opportunity to cut the losses he's been talking so much about. I'm undecided yet what to do" (UoR, MS 2444, CW 41/2); later, funding was found to permit *Formes* to continue for a further three months (Charles Prentice to Richard Aldington, 18 December 1930, ICSo, Aldington 68/5/13).

7 Irish poet and dramatist Austin Clarke* (né Augustine Joseph Clarke, 1896–1974). His play, *The Hunger Demon*, was produced by the Gate Theatre from 27 September to 4 October 1930; the play had been published under the title *The Son of Learning* (1927).

The Abbey Theatre revived *Dervorgilla* (1907), an Irish folkplay by Lady Gregory (née Isabella Augusta Persse, 1852–1932); presented with *The Courting of Mary Doyle* by Irish playwright Edward McNulty (1856–1943), it was performed from 29 September to 4 October 1930. Irish actress Eileen Crowe (1899–1978).

The author of over forty plays, Lady Gregory was a founder of the Irish Literary Theatre (1899–1901) and the Abbey Theatre (1904).

"Poisse" (slang, bad luck, punning on "Persse").

8 Lennox Robinson* (né Esmé Stuart Lennox Robinson, 1886–1958), producer-director at the Abbey Theatre. "La main m'en manque" (I haven't the hand for it), SB's variation on the familiar "le coeur m'en manque" (I haven't the heart for it).

CHARLES PRENTICE, CHATTO AND WINDUS

LONDON

14/10/30   Cooldrinagh

                                              Foxrock

                                              Co Dublin

Dear Mr Prentice

Thank you very much for your letter and the trouble you have taken over my essay. I am perfectly satisfied with the terms of your contract and would be glad to sign it at your earliest convenience. I find it necessary to avail myself of your very generous offer to pay me an advance of 20 pounds on the signing of the agreement.[1]

No, of course the library rats wouldn't buy a swagger edition stained by such an attribution. But wouldn't the drawing-room rattesses love to expose a more declamatory testimonial than a 2/- pamphlet? Or is the race of undershot Proustian lèche-fesses extinct? Don't take any notice of this bad-tempered irrelevancy.[2]

I am afraid the U.S.A. would insist on a more copious revelation. It might go there if I stuck on a scandalous biography.[3] I know the Professor of French at Yale. I might try him.[4]

I was greatly encouraged and reassured by the nice things you said about the book, because I really had no idea at all what kind of impression it would make. I wrote the conclusion in a hurry.[5] Would you let me add 5 or 6 pages to the last 9? Or would that make it too long? I would like to develop the parallel with Dostoievski and separate Proust's intuitivism from Bergson's.[6]

Yours very sincerely

s/ Sam Beckett

TLS; 1 leaf, 1 side; *date stamped* received 15-10-30; UoR, MS 2444 CW 24/9.

1 On behalf of Chatto and Windus, Prentice had written to SB on 10 October 1930 accepting *Proust* for publication and giving the terms; the advance of £20 covered the sale of "about 2000 copies" (UoR, MS 2444 CW letterbook 130/193).

2 Prentice had explained that certain of The Dolphin Books were printed in two editions, the "cheap one at 2/-, bound in paper boards" and the "Large-Paper edition" published for collectors; he noted, however, that such special editions were not selling well, and as SB's name was "not yet before the collecting and bibliophilic public," he advised publishing *Proust* only in the 2/- edition (10 October 1930, UoR, MS 2444 CW letterbook 130/193).
"Lèche-fesses" (arse-lickers).

3 Prentice's letter had indicated that SB would retain US and translation rights, but added that Chatto and Windus would be happy to represent the book in the United States and in serial publication for an agent's fee of 10 percent; Prentice suggested that it not be serialized in England (10 October 1930, UoR, MS 2444 CW letterbook 130/194).

4 Charles Cameron Clarke (1861–1935), Professor of French in the Sheffield Scientific School (associated with Yale University), was the father of Charles Lemaieur Clarke (1900–1979), whom SB had met in Tours in the summer of 1926 when both were making a cycling tour of the Loire valley. In 1927, Charles L. Clarke met SB in Italy and visited the Becketts in Foxrock.

5 Prentice wrote to SB: "I found it most interesting, and passages, I think, are excellent. It seems to me an extraordinarily able piece of work" (10 October 1930, UoR, MS 2444 CW letterbook 130/194).

6 SB discusses Proust's intuitivism as "instinctive perception." "Instinct ... is also a reflex, from the Proustian point of view ideally remote and indirect, a chain-reflex"; SB translates and quotes Proust: "'An impression is for the writer what an experiment is for the scientist - with this difference, that in the case of the scientist the action of the intelligence precedes the event and in the case of the writer follows it'" (*Proust*, 63–64). SB compares Proust and Fyodor Mikhailovich Dostoevsky (1821–1881) in terms of Proust's "non-logical statement of phenomena in the order and exactitude of their perception"; SB continues, "in this connection Proust can be related to Dostoievsky, who states his characters without explaining them" (66).

French philosopher Henri Bergson (1859–1941) distinguishes between "analysis" and "intuition." The former stays on the outside of an object; the latter enters into it (see Bergson, "Introduction à la métaphysique," *Revue de Métaphysique et de Morale* 11 (1903) 1–36; *Introduction to Metaphysics*).

CHARLES PRENTICE, CHATTO AND WINDUS
LONDON

27/10/30   39 TRINITY COLLEGE,

                                                              DUBLIN

Dear Mʳ Prentice

Many thanks for cheque & contract. It is unfortunate about Snowden. Perhaps I will be able to recover part of it.[1]

Thanks also for saying that there is no hurry about poor Proust.[2] I would get it done in a couple of days I[f] only I were free of this grotesque comedy of lecturing.

How is Tom McGreevy? He wont write.[3]

Very sincerely yours
Samuel Beckett

ALS; 1 leaf, 1 side; *letterhead* <COMMON ROOM> A *ins* "39" TRINITY COLLEGE, DUBLIN; *date stamped* received 28-10-30; UoR, MS 2444 CW 24/9.

1 Prentice had sent the Chatto and Windus contract for *Proust* on 17 October 1930. A check for the advance and a copy of the countersigned contract were sent to SB by Chatto and Windus on 22 October 1930. Prentice explained that Mr. Snowden of the accountancy department of Chatto and Windus indicated that authors in Southern Ireland were considered to be "resident 'abroad' for Income Tax purposes"; this meant that Chatto and Windus had to deduct tax from SB's advance. However, Prentice enclosed a form so that SB might reclaim a portion of this deduction.

2 With his letter of 15 October 1930, Prentice had returned the manuscript of *Proust*, saying: "Do by all means add five or six pages at the end, if you would like to" (UoR, MS 2444 CW letterbook 130/238). In his letter of 22 October 1930, Prentice had told SB that he had "heaps of time" to send the addition to his manuscript of *Proust* (UoR, MS 2444 CW letterbook 130/322).

3 McGreevy arrived in Italy on 28 October 1930 to meet Richard Aldington, and Charles Prentice, who joined them there on 31 October; McGreevy returned before 11 November (Richard Aldington to Derek Patmore, 25 October 1930, ICSo, VFM 9; Charles Prentice to Thomas McGreevy, 11 November 1930, UoR, MS 2444 CW letterbook 130/541).

THOMAS McGREEVY

PARIS

14/11/[30]   39 TRINITY COLLEGE

                                                    DUBLIN

My dear Tom

Glad to get your card. Did you stumble in Saint Mark[']s?[1] Here negation & negation to feed a sterile will-less phallus of black fire. Armistice Day & letters to the Irish Times and Luce & Ruddy and all the other means of the Spermopauleatic paroxysm.[2] Fruitless retreat from Monday to Friday and then the degrading cotton wool interpolation of the week end, breaking the continuity of what is vacuous & uniform & pure in a kind of dark Satanic fashion. I don't get on well with my classes and that flatters me and exasperates my pride and makes me feel that the

Sorbonne comedy was a statement of some kind of reality. How long it will drag on, my dear Tom, I have no idea. The Ruddy adhesion is fast enough and our intersections are cleaner and simpler than I ever thought they could be. The room is full of bastards talking about war films and the National Anthem – having ideas – et quelles idées – à toute vitesse.[3] And making little jokes – the kind that dribble into a subtle smile.

I read a paper to M.L.S. on a non[-]existent French poet – Jean du Chas – and wrote his poetry myself and that amused me for a couple of days.[4] I've done nothing more to the Proust and am thinking of sending it back untouched. I 'used to enjoy Felix' (Rowe). I talked with Broderick one evening, and liked him. But he is defeated. I haven't gone to see either L. R. or Jack Yeats.[5] Simply can't work up to it. Indeed I see nobody. Suddenly, out of nowhere, unless it was from a vision of his shoulders in Jammet's, a reaction against S. O'Sullivan & Whitechurch.[6] Harry Sinclair is slowly taking the form of a garrulous turd! That's too strong but near enough with the reservation. I wish to God I were in Paris again, even Germany, Nuremberg, annulled in beer.

No news from Rue de Grenelle.[7]

I wonder could I work a job in London?

This tired abstract anger – inarticulate passive opposition – always the same thing in Dublin. Do write Tom, and forgive all this gossip from the only source I have, the only source of reference, my own bloody self.

Much love

ever

Sam

ALS; 2 leaves, 4 sides; *letterhead* <COMMON ROOM> A *ins* "39" TRINITY COLLEGE, DUBLIN; TCD, MS 10402/22.

1 McGreevy had been with Richard Aldington in Venice at the end of October. SB alludes to Proust's narrator who stumbles on the cobblestones in the courtyard of the Princesse de Guermantes, which suddenly restores to him the memory of a time in Venice when he stumbled in the baptistery of St. Mark's (*A la recherche du temps perdu*, IV, 446–451; see also Beckett, *Proust*, 52).

2 Having served in World War I, McGreevy was sensitive to how service in the British army was perceived in Republican Ireland. Letters to the editor of *The Irish Times* regarding the twelfth anniversary of Armistice Day included one signed "Rosna," expressing pride in having fought "in solidarity" with the British in the Great War, although he respected those who had not, adding that he considered himself to be a Republican in contemporary Ireland (10 November 1930: 8). Another letter, signed "Jellicoe" and written from London, called for support of the sale of poppies to help the British Legion to raise funds to care for needy veterans (11 November 1930: 5).

Arthur Aston Luce (1882–1977), Professor of Mental and Moral Science at Trinity College Dublin and a specialist in the study of Irish philosopher George Berkeley (1685–1753), was SB's tutor (a counseling, not a teaching, function).

3 The Irish National Anthem, "Amhrán na bhFiann" (The Soldier's Song), was written in 1907 and first published in 1912; its chorus was formally adopted as the National Anthem in 1926, replacing the earlier Fenian anthem, "God Save Ireland."
"Et quelles idées – à toute vitesse" (and what ideas – at full speed).

4 SB's academic parody in French of the life and work of an invented French poet Jean du Chas "and the poetic movement allegedly founded by him, 'Le Concentrisme,'" was delivered to the … Modern Language[s] Society"; it begins with "a letter describing how his papers came to light" (Mary Bryden, Julian Garforth, and Peter Mills, eds., *Beckett at Reading: Catalogue of the Beckett Manuscript Collection at the University of Reading* [Reading: Whiteknights Press and the Beckett International Foundation, 1998] 144); BIF, UoR, MS 1396/4/15; Beckett, "Le Concentrisme" in *Disjecta*, 35–42 (all citations from this edition); for discussion of the manuscript of "Le Concentrisme," see Ruby Cohn, *A Beckett Canon*, Theater: Theory/Text/Performance (Ann Arbor: University of Michigan Press, 2001) 21–22.

5 Charles Henry Rowe (1894–1943), Professor of Mathematics at Trinity College Dublin, had a keen interest in music and was an accomplished pianist, although "all that interested him in a piece of music was its bone structure" (Walter Starkie, *Scholars and Gypsies: An Autobiography* [London: John Murray, 1963] 112). SB's quotation of Rowe alludes to German composer Felix Mendelssohn (1809–1847).

Timothy Stanislaus Broderick (1893–1962) graduated from TCD in 1918, lectured occasionally in the College in the 1920s, and was elected Fellow in 1930 in Mathematics; he was a "shy retiring man who rarely spoke in company" (John Luce, 20 July 1991).
L. R. is Lennox Robinson.

6 Jammet's French restaurant, 46 Nassau Street, Dublin. Seumas O'Sullivan lived in Grangehouse, Whitechurch, an area that is now Rathfarnham, Co. Dublin.

7 James Joyce lived at 2 Square Robiac, just off the Rue de Grenelle, Paris.

CHARLES PRENTICE, CHATTO AND WINDUS,
LONDON

3/12/30   39 Trinity College
                                           Dublin

Dear Mr Prentice

It was very kind of you to send me Alcestis.[1] Thank you very much indeed. I have added nothing to Proust. I can't do anything here – neither read nor think nor write. So I am posting it back to you within the next day or two with practically no changes made.[2] I must apologise for the absurdity of the entire proceeding. I expected more generous rifts in the paralysis.

Tom wrote from Venice, out of a lush of Giorgiones.[3] Here nothing but fog and submission – one rebus from dawn to dark.

Yours very Sincerely

Sam Beckett

ACS; 1 leaf; 2 sides; *date stamped* received 4-12-30; UoR, MS 2444 CW 24/9.

1 Euripides, *Alcestis*, tr. Richard Aldington, The Dolphin Books (London: Chatto and Windus, 1930). It was sent to SB "in order that you may see what the Dolphin books are like" (Prentice to SB, 29 November 1930, UoR, MS 2444 CW 130/740).

2 Also in his letter of 29 November, Prentice wrote: "I don't want to hurry you about Proust, but if you could let me have the MS. soon, I would get it set-up, and we would be able to publish in March or April." See 27 October 1930, n. 2.

3 McGreevy had also visited Castelfranco, the hometown of Giorgione, before his return to Paris (Prentice to McGreevy, 11 November 1930, UoR, MS 2444 CW 130/541).

CHRONOLOGY 1931

1931 24 January   SB visits Jack B. Yeats with Georges Pelorson.

By 25 January   Sends manuscript of *Proust* to literary agent J. R. Pinker who refuses to represent it in the United States, saying there is not enough time before March publication by Chatto and Windus

By 18 February   Sends TMS of *Proust* requested by *The Bookman*.

19–21 February   Performance of "Le Kid," parody of Corneille's *Le Cid* written by Georges Pelorson with SB, at the Peacock Theatre, as the French contribution to the annual theatrical event of the Modern Languages Society.

5 March   Chatto and Windus publishes *Proust*.

By 11 March   *Dublin Magazine* asks SB to review McGreevy's *Thomas Stearns Eliot* and Eliot's translation of St.-John Perse's *Anabase*.

12 March   *T.C.D.: A College Miscellany* publishes, anonymously, SB's "The Possessed," written in reaction to a critical review of "Le Kid."

25 March   In London en route to Paris.

26 March   In Paris for Adrienne Monnier's Joyce evening.

5 April   Visits Kassel for Easter.

1 May   *Nouvelle Revue Française* publishes French translation of "Anna Livia Plurabelle," reflecting the first draft by SB and Péron that was revised by Joyce and others.

By 29 May   Begins writing the "German Comedy" which will become part of *Dream of Fair to Middling Women*.

29 June	Leaves Dublin with brother Frank to travel in France.
30 June	In Rouen.
6 July	In Toulon.
8–12 July	In Le Lavandou, where McGreevy has been staying with Aldington.
12–20 July	To Paris via Digne, Grenoble, Annecy, Dijon, and Troyes.
21–27 July	In Paris.
27 July	In London.
28 July	Meets Prentice, proposes a book on Dostoevsky.
August	*New Review* publishes "Return to the Vestry."
2 August	SB travels from London to Dublin; stays in rooms at Trinity College Dublin.
8 August	Submits two "Albas" to *Dublin Magazine*.
By 15 August	Sends story "Walking Out" to Pinker. Sends story "Sedendo et Quiescendo" to Prentice.
By 31 August	Pinker returns "Walking Out." SB sends it to McGreevy. Prentice returns "Sedendo et Quiescendo" with his personal reactions.
By 22 September	*Dublin Magazine* accepts poem "Alba" ("the sheet poem"). *Dublin Magazine* rejects "Yoke of Liberty" ("lips of her desire").
By 8 October	SB sends "Yoke of Liberty" to *Everyman*. Translates René Crevel's "Négresse du Bordel" and plans to do more translations for Nancy Cunard's *Negro, Anthology Made by Nancy Cunard, 1931–1933*.
13 November	Publication of *The European Caravan*.
By 27 November	Sends "Enueg 1" to *Dublin Magazine*.
8 December	MA from Trinity College Dublin conferred.
By 20 December	*Dublin Magazine* returns "Enueg." SB sends it to McGreevy.
26 December	Leaves for Germany.

25/1/31

39 Trinity College
[Dublin]

My dear Tom

I am very sorry to hear that you are laid up again: at the Corneille, n'est-ce pas? Write soon and say that you are up again & well. – Does no one but Thomas come and see you? I heard about Sophie J. and that her sister had gone over to Paris; I think S. O'S. en profite, from what I am told.[1]

I am looking forward to reading your Eliot. In a fit of energy – exasperation – I retyped the Proust and posted it to Pinker. He says that he might have been able to place it in America if he had received it a month ago, but that it is too late to do anything now, since C. & W. are publishing it in March. A short cold note without any sign of bonne volonté.[2]

Rue de Grenelle sounds all very terrible & complicated and my scepticism can't find the necessary ascriptions for beauty & light & honour. I had a very calm letter from Lucia, advising me to accept the world and go to parties.[3] I also received the 'Henry Music' and then a letter from Henry from London when I wrote to thank him.[4]

Term starts next Thursday, and I will have less work, now that Pelorson is here. I see something of him, and nothing of anybody else (not even Ruddy) except a fortnightly collapse upon the disquieted bosom of my family.[5] Wilful seclusion is the natural measure of protection and it is only an inadequate compromise. Yesterday afternoon P.[elorson] & I went round to Jack Yeats, but he was not receiving so we went for a long walk through Ringsend and out towards the Pigeon house.[6] Very beautiful and nervous & melancholy & windy, with that livid Dublin evening light on the shallows. To[-]day I am alone until 1 or 2 to-morrow morning, phrase-hunting in St Augustine and ekeing out the last of my coal, assoupi.[7] The thought of teaching again paralyses me. I think I will go to Hamburg as soon as I get my Easter cheque, by boat & stay there & waste my substance for a month and perhaps hope for the courage to break away. Frank is rather down on his luck, aware of a kind of suspended futility, & permanent, absolutely incapable of rejection or acceptance & talks about growing old in the shadow of a compromise.

Have you read Malraux: 'Les Conquérants' and 'La Voie Royale'. I had a peer at the opening of the latter, & it looked promising. Pelorson has much admiration for 'Les Conquérants'.[8]

You don't say if there is any chance of your coming to Ireland – I mean for me. You know I have a spare bed and could put you up fairly comfortably. My skip is discreet and attached to me and Fry never comes near the place.[9]

I saw L.R[.]'s Critic. Raté and positively lamentable at the end. I liked Miss Travers-Smith's back-cloth.[10]

You know I can't write at all. The simplest sentence is a torture. I wish we could meet & talk – before I become inarticulate or eloquently suave. God bless and look after yourself. I suppose The Workhouse Ward is off.[11] Have you seen Alan since Harry Clarke's death?[12]

    Much love

       Yours ever

        Sam.

ALS; 2 leaves, 4 sides; TCD, MS 10402/15.

1 McGreevy stayed at the Hôtel Corneille, 5 Rue Corneille, across from the Théâtre de l'Odéon. He had been ill with flu (Charles Prentice to McGreevy, 15 January 1931, TCD, MS 8092/23). "N'est-ce pas?" (isn't that right?).

Jean Thomas.

Sophie Jacobs (née Solomons, 1887–1972) studied opera in France and sang with the Beecham and Quinlan opera companies before her marriage to Bethel Jacobs (1881–1955) (Bethel Solomons, *One Doctor in His Time* [London: C. Johnson, 1956] 20, 67). Sophie Jacobs's personal circumstances at this time are not known. Her sister was the Irish painter Estella Solomons (1882–1968), who was known by her maiden name although married to James Starkey (known as Seumas O'Sullivan).

"En profite" (is making the most of the opportunity).

2 McGreevy's *Thomas Stearns Eliot* was published by Chatto and Windus on 22 January 1931 (Charles Prentice to Richard Aldington, 23 January 1931, ICSo, Aldington 68/6/1). In his letter offering to publish *Proust*, Prentice had indicated that SB would retain "the U.S.A. and translation rights" (15 September 1930, UoR, MS 2444 CW letterbook 129/858). McGreevy may have suggested that SB send a copy of *Proust* to his literary agent, James Ralph Pinker, to place it in the United States.

"Bonne volonté" (goodwill).

3 The Joyce family; Lucia Joyce.

4 SB's poem "From the Only Poet to a Shining Whore: for Henry Crowder to Sing" was set to music by Henry Crowder (*Henry-Music*, 12–14); the copy dedicated to SB by Henry Crowder is at Ohio State University. SB's letter to Henry Crowder has not been found.

5 Pelorson had returned to his duties as Lecteur at Trinity College Dublin after Christmas holidays in France.

6 SB and Pelorson walked along the area known as Ringsend, extending east into Dublin Bay, from the canal at its junction with the River Liffey. A mile and a quarter from Ringsend, on the south wall of Dublin Bay, was Pidgeon House (also spelled Pigeon House), named after John Pidgeon (n.d.) who was once caretaker of the building (Bruce Bidwell and Linda Heffer, *The Joycean Way* [Baltimore: Johns Hopkins University Press, 1981] 59, 139; Éamonn MacThomáis, *Me Jewel and Darlin' Dublin* [Dublin: O'Brien Press, 1974] 97).

7 SB's phrase-hunting in the *Confessions* of St. Augustine, Bishop of Hippo (354–430), is evident in his notebook for *Dream of Fair to Middling Women* (BIF, UoR, MS 1227/1–3). In *Beckett's Dream Notebook*, John Pilling indicates that SB read from the edition of *Confessions* translated by E. B. Pusey in the Everyman's Library (London: Dent, 1907); although there are some references in SB's notebook to a Latin text, the edition is not known (Pilling, ed., *Beckett's Dream Notebook* [Reading: Beckett International Foundation, 1999] 11–30). SB's notes on Augustine's life and work can be found in TCD, MS 10968; see Everett Frost and Jane Maxwell, "TCD, MS 10968: Augustine of Hippo and Porphyry on Plotinus," *Notes Diverse Holo*, Special issue *SBT/A* 16 (2006) 91–93.

"Assoupi" (drowsy).

8 *Les Conquérants* (1928; *The Conquerors*) and *La Voie royale* (1930; *The Royal Way*) by French writer André Malraux (1901–1976).

9 SB's skip (college servant) was J. Power (SB to A. J. Leventhal, 6 August 1953, TxU; TCD, MS 3717d–e [also TCD MUN/V/75/62]). As a Fellow of Trinity College Dublin, Matthew Joseph Fry had a room in 39 Trinity College where he could give tutorials, but he would have had no need of it as accommodation, since he was married and had a home in Dublin (John Luce, 4 August 1993).

10 Lennox Robinson directed *The Critic, or, a Tragedy Rehears'd* by Irish playwright Richard Brinsley Sheridan (1751–1816); the play opened at the Abbey Theatre in Dublin on 6 January 1931; Robinson adapted the burlesque of eighteenth-century London to contemporary Dublin. Dublin theatre critic Joseph Holloway (1861-1944) called it a "mutilation" (Joseph Holloway, *Joseph Holloway's Irish Theatre*, I, *1926–1931*, ed. Robert Hogan and Michael J. O'Neill [Dixon, CA: Proscenium Press, 1969] 71).

"Raté" (no good).

Dublin artist and set-designer Dorothy Travers-Smith (known as Dolly, 1901–1977) married Lennox Robinson in London on 8 September 1931.

11 *The Workhouse Ward* (1908) by Lady Gregory was on a double bill with *The Critic* at the Abbey Theatre (6 to 17 January 1931).

12 Alan Duncan.

Harry Clarke died in Coire, Switzerland, on 6 January 1931.

THOMAS McGREEVY

PARIS

3/2/31   39 Trinity College
                                                         [Dublin]

My dear Tom

Forgive me for having taken so long to acknowledge & thank you for your letter and T.S.E.[1] My teeth have been afflicting me and some have to come out and some have to be filled and I am feeling very sorry for myself.

The Eliot left me with an impression of enviable looseness & ease. You know what I mean by looseness – something supple & well hung. I couldn't help feeling that you were doing your best to be nice about it. Your lateral slaughter – Shaw, Bennett & the Galère, did my heart good, my 'petit coeur de neige', and it almost achieved liquefaction with the fesses turned to the commonroom cap-&-gownness.[2] The phrase-bombs are there too, something better than that – phrase voltage. The God Almighty – Marion de Lorme was strong & shining and delighted me altogether.[3] Altogether I envy you an essay that has so much unity of atmosphere & tension & sincerity, and your long arms that fetched so much colour. My Proust seems very grey & disgustingly juvenile – pompous almost – angry at the best. Tant pis. As for the critics – I don't know. I don't think I care very much. I feel dissociated from my Proust – as though it did not belong to me, ready of course to get any credit thats going but – genuinely, I think – more interested than irritated at the prospect of the nose-pickers' disgust. I may be altogether wrong. What you quoted of R. W.'s criticism reduces, it seems to me, to almost unqualified approval. Perhaps the fatuous enthusiasms are more painful than anything.[4]

Last Saturday I went with Pelorson to see Jack Yeats.[5] He was alone and we had two entirely delightful hours looking at a lot of pictures we had not seen and talking. He wanted a definition of cruelty, declaring that you could work back from cruelty to original sin. No doubt. But I don't think it is possible to define cruelty, because somehow or other it would have to be separated from all the concomitant pointers in order to be apprehended. Can one imagine a pure act of cruelty? The old question!

Léon wrote for Joyce's Gazetteer which I had stolen and a list of the rivers used by Péron & myself in our fragment of translation. I think Joyce & Soupault are going to work on it together. Poor Soupault![6]

Do you mean you would come home if you got those translations?[7] I expect to leave here about end of March & stay away a month. I am still on Hamburg –

      Love ever

      <u>Sam</u>

ALS; 1 leaf, 4 sides; TCD, MS 10402/16.

1 McGreevy, *Thomas Stearns Eliot*.

2 In his monograph, McGreevy establishes a context for Eliot's work in American, British, and Continental literary movements. British novelist and critic Enoch Arnold Bennett (1867–1931) is described as "a fivepenny English master" in the course of discussion of American vulgarity (*Thomas Stearns Eliot*, 3). McGreevy dismisses George Bernard Shaw, whose satire and indignation he judges to lack universality: "Did a soldier ever read Bernard Shaw with pleasure before an attack?" (17). McGreevy dismisses Tristan Corbière as a poet and as an influence on Eliot (26).

"Galère" (crew); "petit coeur de neige" (little heart of snow); "fesses" (buttocks).

3 SB refers to a passage in McGreevy's *Thomas Stearns Eliot*: "One can imagine how outraged Victor Hugo and Rossetti would be if they knew that forty years after they died there would be writers of genius who found the Lord God a greater source of inspiration than Marion de Lorme or Jenny" (37). *Marion de Lorme* (1829) by Victor Hugo (1802–1885) is a play about a seventeenth-century French courtesan of that name (c. 1613–1650). "Jenny" may refer to the poem of that name by Dante Gabriel Rossetti (né Gabriel Charles Dante Rossetti 1828–1882).

4 Spurred by a request from Richard Aldington, Rebecca West (1892–1983) mentioned McGreevy's *Thomas Stearns Eliot* in her column in the *Daily Telegraph*; she compared McGreevy to St. Augustine, saying that he "makes every sentence with the imprint of his personality, and a very delightful personality it is ... This book is crammed full of profitable arguments" ("New Books," 23 January 1931: 15). While McGreevy appreciated her friendly intention, he had no admiration for West (McGreevy to Prentice, Sunday [25 January 1931], UoR, MS 2444 CW 41/2).

"Tant pis" (too bad).

5 Jack Yeats had his "at home" day on Saturdays.

6 "Joyce's Gazetteer" may refer to an atlas owned by James Joyce or to one of the books by Irish geographer Patrick Weston Joyce (1827–1914): *Irish Names of Places* (1913), *Atlas and Cyclopedia of Ireland* (1900), *Philips' Atlas and Geography of Ireland* (1883).

Paul Léon was working with Philippe Soupault, Joyce, and others to continue the translation of "Anna Livia Plurabelle" begun by SB with Alfred Péron; see SB to Soupault, 5 July 1930 [*for* 5 August 1930], n. 1.

7 McGreevy sought commissions for translation from the London publisher Victor Gollancz (1893–1967) and from Charles Prentice, Chatto and Windus, to whom he had proposed to translate one of two monographs by Louis Bertrand (1866–1941): *Philippe II à l'Escorial* (1929) or *Philippe II contre Antonio Pérez* (1929) (McGreevy to Prentice, Monday [1 December 1930], UoR, MS 2444 CW 41/2; Prentice to McGreevy, 6 February 1931, TCD, MS 8092/29). As McGreevy explained to Prentice after the proposal was turned down: "For me it was only a question of being assured of sufficient money (for work that I should not be ashamed to put my name to) to enable me to go home for a couple of months or three and translate and work on my own at the same time" (Saturday [7 February 1931], UoR, MS 2444 CW 41/2).

Richard Aldington sent money to McGreevy, who, so assisted, chose to go to Florence rather than to stay in Paris (Aldington to Brigit Patmore, 9 February 1931, TxU).

CHARLES PRENTICE, CHATTO AND WINDUS
LONDON

16/2/31   39 TRINITY COLLEGE,
                                           DUBLIN.

Dear Mr Prentice

Thank you for your letter. I am glad to know that the date of publication is fixed. Yes – of course March 5th suits me perfectly. I did not expect it would be ready so soon.[1]

After your kindness and the trouble you have taken I am anxious that the Proust should not prove a washout.[2] I hope sometime to send you something more genuine & direct.

How did the Eliot go?[3] I read it & liked it.

Very sincerely yours
Sam Beckett

ALS; 1 leaf, 2 sides; *letterhead*: <COMMON ROOM,> *A ins* "39" TRINITY COLLEGE, DUBLIN; *date stamped* received 18-2-31; UoR, MS 2444 CW 24/9.

1 Prentice wrote on 12 February 1931: "We are publishing 'Proust' on March 5th; I hope this will be O.K. Your presentation copies will arrive a few days before that date" (UoR, MS 2444 CW letterbook 31/576).

2 Prentice assured SB in his reply: "Your Proust, I think, will do very well; Proust himself has not a great many readers, but many people have asked me most curiously about your book, and the subscription sales in the country are promising" (18 February 1931, UoR, MS 2444 CW letterbook 31/647).

3 In the same letter, Prentice wrote: "The Eliot is doing very well. I do not mean that it is a best-seller; the sales, however, are developing very steadily, and, being in a series, the essay will have a good run to look forward to."

THOMAS McGREEVY
FLORENCE

24/2/31   39 TRINITY COLLEGE,
                                           DUBLIN.

My dear Tom

What kind of pieces are you going to master là-bas. I wonder why you are off Italy.[1]

Anyhow your Eliot is making some noise.[2] I know that Proust wont even squelch if stood on. I had a cable from American Bookman asking for a copy – after that bastard Pinker choking me off. I sent it along – without any enthusiasm.[3]

This vitaccia is terne beyond all belief. Thursday, Friday & Sat. we gave 3 plays at the Peacock – La Quema, Souriante Mme. Beudet & Le Kid (Corneille & Bergson). They might have gone worse. The inevitable vulgarisation leaves one exhausted & disgusted. We had a nice Cartesian Infanta in the Kid, inarticulate & stupefied, crossing the stage to Ravel's Pavane. Trench was delighted.[4]

I scramble through lectures & chafe for the end of term when I hope to go away to Hamburg. That will be about 20th March. Does that mean I will miss you on your way through Dublin? Il ne manquait que cela.[5]

To-night I have to go & eat with the Provost & his hostile brats. Cela me fait chier, wear a gown & say 'Yes sir' 'no sir'.[6] When I've posted this I'll go & have a Turkish bath & stupefy my nerves in sweaty duration. My person is developing dirty habits.[7] At the R.D.S. yesterday afternoon the music was so tepid that I was conscious of my neck. Impossible to hear any music here. Yesterday they played one of Beethoven's last string quartets, a Mendels[s]ohn Quintette & a Schubert Quintette.[8] I feel that Beethoven's Quartets are a waste of time. His pigheaded refusal to make the best of a rather pettyfogging [*for* pettifogging] convention annoys me. He needed a piano or an orchestra. And why do they go on playing that bloody Mendels[s]ohn! Verbalism & not very competent – Leventhal's conversation[.][9] The Schubert had plenty of nobility and one understood the need of relating his chamber music to his song settings. I don't know any chamber music that <u>works</u> so skilfully. A waste in conception – you know that lamentable pebble in the pond effect – but rigid economy of application. Alas! Why can't I tell you what I feel without getting on a platform.

I went to a doctor because my bitch of a heart was keeping me awake. He smothered my sense of importance with a contemptuous '<u>Smoke less</u>'. So I try to smoke less.

Ruddy is always polite but drifting to a conveniently remote accessibility. Pelorson is a mystery. Charming sometimes & dreadfully rich in hopeful gestures. He has shown me a lot of interesting verse. I have written nothing since leaving Paris. I am reading '<u>Journal Intime de Jules Renard</u>' ... Odd things.[10]

Forgive this futile and not even melancholy letter. In 20 years I may be fit to have friends.

If you look up the Esposito say I often think of them (actually true, though rather of myself evolving before them.) I don't think you would have anything to say to Mario, but am sure you would like Bianca – & the mother. Remember me to the Aldingtons if you think they would care for that.[11] I'll sent [sic] you a Proust as soon as I get one. I think it is due for March 5. Won't you keep me au courant.[12]

      Love ever

      Sam

ALS; 3 leaves, 6 sides; *letterhead:* <COMMON ROOM> *A ins* "39" TRINITY COLLEGE, DUBLIN; TCD, MS 10402/17.

1 McGreevy had decided to join Richard Aldington in Florence for a driving tour in Italy (Aldington to Brigit Patmore, 13 February 1931, TxU); Aldington encouraged McGreevy to choose their itinerary, which included Tuscany, and even plans to go as far south as Brindisi (Aldington to Charles Prentice, 5 March 1931 and 6 March 1931; UoR, MS 2444 CW 48/6). Prentice, who had backed the trip, hoped it would allow McGreevy to work on his novel (12 February 1931, ICSo, Aldington collection 68/6/1). James Joyce wrote to Harriet Weaver on 11 March 1931: "McGreevy has also left Paris. Some person or persons gave him an annuity of 300 £ a year to do original work, and

he has gone to Ireland via Italy" (Joyce, *Letters of James Joyce*, I, 303). "Là-bas" (down there).

2 Besides the review by Rebecca West, McGreevy's *Thomas Stearns Eliot* had been announced by Chatto and Windus in an advertisement that mentioned it as "a short but pointed and distinguished study of a writer who has for some years been regarded by intelligent people as of paramount influence in modern letters" (*Times Literary Supplement* 22 January 1931: 54); it had been reviewed by H. F. in "T. S. Eliot," *Time and Tide* (12.6 [7 February 1931] 165).

3 Seward Collins (1899-1952), Editor of *The Bookman: A Review of Books and Life* (New York, 1895 - March 1933), cabled SB on 17 February 1931: "COULD I SEE COPY YOUR FORTHCOMING STUDY MARCEL PROUST FOR POSSIBLE PUBLICATION IN AMERICAN BOOKMAN ADDRESS THREE EIGHTY SIX FOURTH AVENUE NEWYORK" (CtY, YCAL MSS 12, Series I, 2/42). SB did not hear from *The Bookman* until August 1933 (when it had become *The American Review*): "When it came we had rather an embarrassment of riches, so far as articles on Proust were concerned. Mr. Collins liked it, however, and hoped to use it, but now feels that he cannot afford the space" (Dorothea Brande [1893-1948], Associate Editor of *The American Review*, to SB, 7 August 1933, CtY, YCAL, MSS 12, Series I, 2/42).

Pinker had not pursued publication in America.

4 "Vitaccia" (It., miserable life, wretched existence); "terne" (dull, colorless).

SB wrote "<Gat[e]> Peacock."

The Modern Languages Society production of a French play at the Peacock Theatre was an annual event at Trinity College Dublin; Georges Pelorson was in charge of the program of three plays. A comedy in Spanish, *La Quema* (1922), by the brothers Serafín (1871-1938) and Joaquín Álvarez Quintero (1873-1944), was directed by Walter Starkie (1894-1976), Professor of Spanish and Italian at Trinity College Dublin. SB suggested *La Souriante Mme. Beudet* (1921; *The Smiling Mrs. Beudet*), by Denys Amiel (né Guillaume Roche, 1884-1977) and André Obey (1892-1975). *Le Kid*, a burlesque of *Le Cid* (1637; *The Cid*) by Pierre Corneille (1606-1684), was devised by Pelorson with advice from SB and influenced by Henri Bergson (for discussion: Knowlson, *Damned to Fame*, 125-128; Dougald McMillan and Martha Fehsenfeld, *Beckett in the Theatre: The Author as Practical Playwright and Director, From "Waiting for Godot" to "Krapp's Last Tape"* [London: John Calder; New York: Riverrun Press, 1988] 17-23).

Maurice Ravel (1875-1937), *Pavane pour une infante défunte*, for piano (1889; *Pavane for a Dead Princess*). SB generally refers to this piece as the "Infanta."

Wilbraham Fitzjohn Trench (1873-1939), Professor of English at Trinity College Dublin.

5 McGreevy planned to pass through Dublin on his way to Tarbert, Co. Kerry, in the spring. "Il ne manquait que cela." (That's the last straw.)

6 Edward John Gwynn (1868-1941), an eminent scholar of Old Irish, was Provost of Trinity College Dublin (1927-1937).

"Cela me fait chier" (It really gets me down, literally, makes me shit).

7 At this time, Trinity College Dublin did not have bathing facilities; the Turkish bath on Lincoln Place and another on Leinster Street were the two nearest to TCD.

8 The Royal Dublin Society's chamber music concert on 23 February 1931 was played by the Unity String Quartet, with the addition of a second viola and cello. The

program included the String Quartet in E-flat major, op. 127 by Ludwig van Beethoven (1770–1827); an unspecified Mendelssohn String Quintet (either no. 1 in A major, op. 18, or no. 2 in B-flat major, op. 87); the String Quintet in C, D 956 by Franz Schubert (1797–1828); *Souvenir de Florence*, String Sextet in D major, op. 70 by Pyotr Ilich Tchaikovsky (1840–1893); and the String Quartet in D major, op. 33 by Italian-born Dublin composer, Michele Esposito (1855–1929).

9   Abraham Jacob Leventhal* (known as Con, 1896–1979).

10   SB read from the four-volume, posthumously published *Le Journal, 1887–1910* of French writer Jules Renard (1864–1910) (Paris, F. Bernouard, 1927). See SB's notes taken from this edition in Pilling, ed., *Beckett's Dream Notebook*, 30–34 (BIF, UoR, MS 5000).

11   The family of Michele Esposito included his wife Natalia (née Klebnikoff, 1857–1944), their daughters Bianca Esposito (1879–1961), Vera Dockrell (née Esposito, 1883–1967), and Nina Porcelli (née Esposito, 1890–1970), and son, Mario Esposito (1887–1975) (Knowlson, *Damned to Fame*, 84; J. Bowyer Bell, "Waiting for Mario: The Espositos, Joyce, and Beckett," *Éire-Ireland* 30.2 [1995] 7–26; Michael M. Gorman, "Mario Esposito (1887–1975) and the Study of the Latin Literature of Medieval Ireland" in Mario Esposito, *Studies in Hiberno-Latin Literature*, ed. Michael M. Gorman, Variorum Collected Studies Series [Aldershot, UK: Ashgate/Variorum, 2006] 300–309). SB took private Italian classes with Bianca Esposito at a school of languages and music at 21 Ely Place, Dublin; she "nurtured his love for Dante" (Knowlson, *Damned to Fame*, 67–68, 630). SB had visited Italy in the late spring through the summer of 1927 to prepare for his final examinations in Italian and had stayed some time in Florence where the Espositos then lived (NhD: Lawrence Harvey, Interviews with SB, 92; Knowlson, *Damned to Fame*, 83–84).

12   "Au courant" (up to date).

THOMAS McGREEVY

FLORENCE

11/3/31   39 T.C.D.

[Dublin]

My dear Tom

A thousand thanks for all you say about my Proust. You would have had your copy before now were it not for what Charlus would call an unhappy 'enchaînement de circonstances'. My parcel was sent to Foxrock & I only got it a couple of days ago. And I have been paralysed with a most atrocious cold that shackled me to the fire. The wind for 3 days was terrifying, Siberian vitriol, and I got so nervous listening to it hoisting itself to the one note behind my bedroom that I got ready to retreat to the anthracite bosom of my family. Then it dropped and I felt as though I had had a tooth out after long fumigations.[1]

After reading your appreciation of that essay I know that it is worth more than I thought. I read the book through quickly and really wondered what I was talking about. It seemed like pale grey sandpaper, stab stab stab without any enchantment. It's too abstract because my head comes breaking every now & then through the epidermis for a breath of merely verbal enthusiasm. It has the plausibility of a pattern, a kind of flat syllogistic drift, like the fan of the long division sum in 'Portrait of the Artist': at its best a distorted steam-rolled equivalent of some aspect or confusion of aspects of myself.[2] That is what you see & what pleases you, because I have the good-fortune to have your affection. I mean you see your intuition as a formula. That is the only stimulus that I can find for your pleasure. As a merely critical extension, what could be more <u>blafard</u>, gritty like the Civic Guard's anus.[3] No sinewy membrane between it & its official motive – the only motive that the most easy going public will give me any credit for – Proust. I feel it tied somehow on to Proust, on to his tail board, with odds & ends of words, like bundles of grass[,] jack in the boxing under a kite. Not that I care. I don't want to be a professor (it[']s almost a pleasure to contemplate the mess of this job). And what the hell do I care for the sneers of the Faguets & the Lansons & the Gwynns & the Brunetières and all the Sorbonagres when you write pleased with even the mutilated statement of an identification & a participation effected a summer's day of fathoms deeper than the little cormorant plunge of voracious curiosity.[4] I won't forget your letter. I read it on the railings, just as the sun took it into its head to bare its bottom over censored Dublin. – Douceurs.[5]

Seumas O'Sullivan asked me to review your Eliot for his next number – after the one that is just coming out. I would like to. I may? He sent me Eliot's translation of Anabase for review. I don't like Anabase – I think it[']s bad Claudel, with abominable colour. The translation is very uneven. Good when he drops the text altogether.[6] I've been reading nothing but Rimbaud – tired out by Renard. Oh a good name – foxy foxy. I'll come back to him. But I can't talk about Rimbaud, though I had to try & explain the mystery to my foul Senior Sophisters. I told them about the eye suicide – <u>pour des visions</u> – you remember. (Poètes de 7 ans).[7] Guffaw. As they guffawed when I quoted:

'Noire bise, averse glapissante
Fleuve noir et maisons closes'.

So I repeated. Titter. I, in my innocence, couldn't understand, and wondered could 'maisons closes' have tickled their repressions. I told Pelorson who kindly explained that the joke resided in the 'pissante' of 'glapissante'.[8] Oh the bitches & the stallions. Pelorson s'éloigne, toujours très pris, très mélancolique, mal aux yeux, au coeur, aux bronches, hallucinations, rêves, seuil de la folie & the usual.[9] Always alone except when he or Frank comes in. Ruddy s'efface. Had a rather terrible letter from Beaufret from Berlin. He had a beautiful phrase: 'le diamant du pessimisme'.[10]

I long to be away and of course can't bear the idea of going & can't understand why Hamburg, where it won't be warm & where I will be probably frightened. That's the latest cardiac feather. Fear – followed by no genitive.

O'Sullivan said Alan was in Dublin. Pas vu. Stella said that Cissie was asking for me & wishing to see me. Tonic or balm?[11]

God bless now. Keep me in the current. And again – all that is good.

Sam

Kindest regards to the Aldingtons.
No reply from Bookman.[12]

ALS; 2 leaves, 7 sides; TCD, MS 10402/18.

1 In Proust's *Le Côté de Guermantes* M. de Charlus says: "'Et je ne parle pas seulement des événements accomplis, mais de l'enchaînement de circonstances'" ("'And I do not speak only of events that have already occurred, but of the chain of circumstances'"); the narrator comments: "une des expressions favorites de M. de Charlus'" (a favourite expression of M. de Charlus's) (*Le Côté de Guermantes* in *A la recherche du temps perdu*, II, ed. Jean-Yves Tadié, Bibliothèque de la Pléiade [Paris: Gallimard, 1987–1989] 583; *The Guermantes Way*, in *In Search of Lost Time*, III, tr. C.K. Scott Moncrieff and Terence Kilmartin, rev. D. J. Enright [New York: Modern Library, 1992–1993] 389).

SB's copies of *Proust* had been sent to him at his family home rather than to 39 Trinity College, Dublin.

From 6 to 8 March 1931 Dublin experienced easterly winds that changed to northeasterly winds on 9 March.

2 See James Joyce's *A Portrait of the Artist as a Young Man*, ed. Chester G. Anderson (New York: Viking Press, 1964) 102–103:

> The equation on the page of his scribbler began to spread out a widening tail, eyed and starred like a peacock's; and, when the eyes and stars of its indices had been eliminated, began slowly to fold itself together again ...
>
> It was his own soul going forth to experience, unfolding itself sin by sin, spreading abroad the balefire of its burning stars and folding back upon itself, fading slowly, quenching its own lights and fires.

3 "Blafard" (wan).

The Civic Guard was formed in August 1922, in preparation for the transfer of political power from the British to the Provisional Irish Government.

4 SB dubs as "Sorbonagres" a group of influential academic figures who were associated with the Ecole Normale Supérieure, the University of Paris-Sorbonne, and Trinity College Dublin. The term was coined by François Rabelais (?1494–?1553) in *Gargantua et Pantagruel* (1532–1533).

Emile Faguet (1847–1916), Professor of French Poetry at the Sorbonne, defended the classical ideal and interpreted literary history with an evolutionary model (*Maîtres et élèves, célébrités et savants: l'Ecole Normale Supérieure, 1794–1994* [Paris: Archives Nationales, 1994] 158); his five-volume *Etudes littéraires* (1885–1891) surveyed sixteenth- to early twentieth-century literature.

Gustave Lanson (1857–1934), Professor at the Sorbonne from 1897 to 1900, and Directeur, Ecole Normale Supérieure, from 1902 to 1927. Among his writings is *Histoire de la littérature française* (1894) and *Manuel bibliographique de la littérature française moderne, depuis 1500 jusqu'à nos jours* (1909–1912, 4 vols.).

Edward John Gwynn, Provost of Trinity College Dublin (see 24 February 1931, n. 6).

Ferdinand Brunetière (1849–1906), Professor of French Literature at the Ecole Normale Supérieure from 1886 to 1904, advocated that art should have a moral purpose and that literature was governed by evolution; he edited the *Revue des Deux*

Mondes from 1893 to 1906, and wrote, among other works, *Histoire et littérature* (1884–1886), *L'Evolution des genres dans l'histoire de la littérature* (1890), *L'Evolution de la poésie lyrique au dix-neuvième siècle* (1894), *Manuel de l'histoire de la littérature française* (1897), and *L'Art et la morale* (1898).

5 The Nassau Street boundary of Trinity College Dublin was called "the railings." "Douceurs" (soft sweetness).

6 SB did not write a review of McGreevy's *Thomas Stearns Eliot* for *Dublin Magazine*, nor one of T. S. Eliot's translation of *Anabase*, a poem by St.-John Perse (né Alexis Saint-Léger, 1887–1975) which was published as *Anabasis* by Faber and Faber in 1930. Nonetheless, SB had closely read Eliot's translation which presents the French and English texts on facing pages.

SB compares the poem to the work of Paul Claudel (1868–1955), a prominent figure in the French Catholic literary renaissance of the early twentieth century.

7 Jules Renard, *Le Journal*; "renard" (fox).

A Senior Sophister is in the fourth and final year of study for an undergraduate degree at Trinity College Dublin.

In 1871, Arthur Rimbaud (1854–1891) wrote "Les Poètes de sept ans" ("Seven-Year-Old Poets"); the poem follows Rimbaud's two "Les Lettres du voyant" ("The Letters of the Seer") which set forth his program to explore poetic vision through a deliberate derangement of his senses. In this poem, the image of a child who "dans ses yeux fermés voyait des points" (shut his eyes to see spots) leads to what SB calls the "eye suicide," the image of a child deliberately grinding his fists into his eyes: "Et pour des visions écrasant son oeil darne" (Squeezing his dazzled eyes to make visions come) (Arthur Rimbaud, *Oeuvres complètes*, ed. Antoine Adam, Bibliothèque de la Pléiade [Paris: Gallimard, 1972] 43–44; Arthur Rimbaud, *Complete Works*, tr. Paul Schmidt [New York: Harper and Row, 1975] 77–78).

8 Jules Laforgue, "XII," *Derniers Vers*: "Noire bise, averse glapissante / Et fleuve noir, et maisons closes" (Black wind, downpour yelping, / Black river, and houses closed), (*Poésies complètes*, II, ed. Pascal Pia [Paris: Gallimard, 1979] 215; *Poems of Jules Laforgue*, tr. Patricia Terry [Berkeley: University of California Press, 1958] 183).

"Maisons closes" (brothels); "pissante" (pissing); "glapissante" (yelping). The guffawing students found "pissante" irresistible.

9 "Pelorson s'éloigne, toujours très pris, très mélancolique, mal aux yeux, au coeur, aux bronches, hallucinations, rêves, seuil de la folie" (Pelorson is drifting away, always very busy, very melancholic, eye trouble, heart trouble, bronchial trouble, hallucinations, dreams, edge of madness).

10 "S'efface" (keeps out of the way).

Jean Beaufret was in Germany studying the work of Martin Heidegger (1889–1976); the phrase "'le diamant du pessimisme'" (the diamond of pessimism) appears in a letter from him to SB.

11 Seumas O'Sullivan, speaking of Alan Duncan.

"Pas vu" (not seen).

Estella Solomons was a close friend of SB's paternal aunt Cissie Beckett Sinclair.

12 McGreevy is in Italy with Richard Aldington and Brigit Patmore (née Morrison-Scott, 1882–1965), Aldington's companion from 1928 to 1936.

SB wrote to Charles Prentice on 18 February 1931: "Many thanks for forwarding a promising communication from the editor of the American Bookman. I have sent him the Proust" (UoR, MS 2444 CW 24/9).

CHARLES PRENTICE, CHATTO AND WINDUS
LONDON

13/3/31   39 Trinity College,
                                               Dublin.

Dear M[r] Prentice

Glad to hear that Proust has got off with so many of the few.[1] Tom wrote me a most charming letter about the book.[2] It is very good of him to think that I am worth labelling with a flag. I had not noticed whether the Dolphin was green or brown.[3]

Could I have another half dozen? I am enclosing cheque for 13/-. Is 1/- enough for postage?

Very sincerely yours
Sam Beckett

ALS; 1 leaf, 1 side; *letterhead:* <COMMON ROOM,> *A ins* "39" TRINITY COLLEGE, DUBLIN; *date stamped* received 16-3-31; UoR, MS 2444 CW 24/9. In another hand, figures to the left of the signature, related to the cost of six additional copies (see Prentice to SB, 16 March 1931: "The six copies of 'Proust' will be sent to you today, and the balance of your cheque returned. I do not know yet how the sum will work out, but you are of course charged at trade terms, i.e., at 1/4d. instead of 2/- a copy" [UoR, MS 2444 CW letterbook 31/985]).

1 Prentice wrote to SB on 12 March 1931: "The book has made a very decent start. It was published last Thursday, and we have already sold 639 copies. When the reviews begin to appear, I hope there will be more exciting news to report" (UoR, MS 2444 CW letterbook 31/948). Rebecca West's review in the *Daily Telegraph* calls *Proust* "an excellent work, for Mr. Beckett is a very brilliant young man," but warns that "his metaphysics and his habit of allusiveness" pose an intellectual challenge (6 March 1931: 18).

2 McGreevy's letter to SB has not been found, but SB's appreciation of his warm comments about *Proust* is evident in his reply of 11 March 1931, above.

3 Prentice mentioned receiving a note from McGreevy about the cover of *Proust*: "Tom tells me I have done wrong in giving you a brown Dolphin. It should, he says,

have been green; clearly I have been trying to steal you from Ireland. Will you please forgive?" (Prentice to SB, 12 March 1931, UoR, MS 2444 CW letterbook 31/948).

SAMUEL PUTNAM, THE NEW REVIEW

PARIS

Monday [? 30 March to 13 April 1931]   Hotel Corneille

                                              Rue Corneille

                                              Paris 6ᵉ

Dear Putnam

Do you ever come up to town? I'd like very much to see you before taking myself off, Wednesday afternoon or Thursday evening? Will you drop me a line?[1]

Congratulations on your Review. Greavy gave me a copy. It's full of good stuff.[2]

A bientôt n'est-ce pas?[3]

Sam Beckett

ALS; 1 leaf, 1 side; NjP, *New Review* Correspondence of Samuel Putnam, C0111/1/9. *Dating*: SB arrived in Paris on 26 March; Pilling notes that SB went to Kassel for the Easter holiday on 5 April (*A Samuel Beckett Chronology*, 7); SB details his travel from Paris via Nürnberg to Kassel in April 1931 (BIF, UoR, GD 5/f. 55, 1 March 1937). He may have returned to Paris immediately afterwards, for Wambly Bald (1902–1990) mentions SB in his column "La Vie de Bohème (As Lived on the Left Bank)" on 7 April: "Another Irish poet now among us is Samuel Beckett," which suggests that SB was in Paris at that time and possibly into the following week (*Chicago Daily Tribune, European Edition* [Paris] 7 April 1931: 4; rpt. in Wambly Bald, *On the Left Bank, 1929–1933*, ed. Benjamin Franklin, V [Athens: Ohio University Press, 1987] 57). SB returned to Dublin for the Trinity Term that began on 20 April 1931.

1 SB arrived in Paris on 26 March 1931, the day of a "Séance consacrée à James Joyce" (session devoted to James Joyce) organized by Adrienne Monnier at La Maison des Amis des Livres (see Ellmann, *James Joyce*, 636–637, and Knowlson, *Damned to Fame*, 129–131). The offices of *The New Review* (1930–1932) were situated in Fontenay-aux-Roses, near Paris.

2 George Reavey had given SB the first issue of *The New Review* (January–February 1931), edited by Putnam. Although the second issue and its contents were announced for March–April 1931, it was published as May–June–July 1931. SB had submitted

"Return to the Vestry," but the poem was not published until the third issue, August–September–October 1931 (98–99); there was also a mention of *Proust* in this issue.

  3 "A bientôt n'est-ce pas?" (Till soon, am I right?).

THOMAS McGREEVY
TARBERT, CO. KERRY

29/5/31   Cooldrinagh,
                                               Foxrock,
                                               Co. Dublin.

Dear Tom

Very glad to get your letter. Yes I got the box of dolls that morning and left them round at the Abbey for L. R.[1] Joyce sent me H. C. E. & N. R. F. both autographed. I'm afraid I let too many days pass before answering to thank him, which I did finally via Sylvia, rushing in foolishly to say that it was impossible to read his text without understanding the futility of the translation. I can't believe that he doesn't see through the translation himself, its horrible quip atmosphere & vulgarity, necessarily because you can't translate a motive; I had a Whitsun card from the three of them with an address in London.[2]

I have been in bed for the last week with a dry pleurisy, & God knows when I'll be let out of the room though I feel all right except for a reluctance to sneeze & belch. Poor Ruddy & Pelorson have been sharing my work.[3]

Glad to hear that the Aldington is finished & away. Thanks for using a phrase out of my book. T.C.D. honoured you with an éreintement last week. I hear they have done mine this week but I have not seen it. I am thinking now of my review of your T.S.E. for Seumas O'S. together with the translation of Anabase.[4] I am writing the German Comedy in a ragged kind of way, on & off, and would like to show you a page or two when you come up. I'll never believe that the intoxicated dentist was an artist though I don't know anything about him except a few shocking lines here & there.[5]

> Was ich weiss kann jeder wissen,
> mein Herz hab['] ich allein!!

Herz![6] Always the break down & the flabby word & the more than menstrual effusion of credulity. If I could only get you to sleep in Dostoievski's bed somewhere! I'm reading the 'Possédés' in a foul translation. Even so it must be very carelessly & badly written in the Russian, full of clichés & journalese: but the movement, the transitions![7] No one moves about like Dostoievski. No one ever caught the insanity of dialogue like he did.

Do you know a decent French life of Marie Stuart?[8]

Yes a temperance hotel is like a celibate brothel.

If you arrive after 1 o'clock Monday 8th I could meet you at station with car. Try and keep an evening for me if you can.

> Love ever
> Sam

ALS; 1 leaf, 4 sides; letterhead; TCD, MS 10402/19.

1 Abbey Theatre, Lennox Robinson.

2 James Joyce, *Haveth Childers Everywhere: Fragment from Work in Progress* (Paris: Henry Babou and Jack Kahane, 1930; Paris: Fountain Press, 1930; Criterion Miscellany [London: Faber and Faber, 1931]); it is likely that Joyce sent the Faber edition which was published on 2 April 1931.

James Joyce, "Anna Livie Plurabelle," tr. Samuel Beckett *et al.*, *La Nouvelle Revue Française*, 637–646.

SB wrote to Joyce care of Sylvia Beach. At this time, the Joyces and Lucia were at 28B Campden Grove, Kensington W8, London. Whitsun (Whitsunday, the celebration of Pentecost) follows fifty days after Easter; in 1931 it fell on 24 May.

3 SB's classes were taught by Rudmose-Brown and Pelorson.

4 As an epigraph for his book, *Richard Aldington: An Englishman*, The Dolphin Books (London: Chatto and Windus, 1931), McGreevy quoted SB: "Yesterday is not a milestone

that has been passed, but a daystone on the beaten track of the years, and irremediably part of us, within us, heavy and dangerous. We are not merely more weary because of yesterday, we are other, no longer what we were before the calamity of yesterday" (*Proust*, 3).

McGreevy's *Thomas Stearns Eliot* received an unfavorable review in *T.C.D: A College Miscellany*, a weekly journal of Trinity College Dublin (D. H. V., "Reviews" [21 May 1931] 162). SB's *Proust* was reviewed in the following issue: "His critical integrity and close comprehension of his subject make this essay a valuable piece of penetrating criticism" (W. J. K. M., "Reviews" [28 May 1931] 177).

"Ereintement" (slating, harsh review).

No review of McGreevy's *Thomas Stearns Eliot* or of Eliot's translation of St.-John Perse's *Anabase* was published in *Dublin Magazine* (see 11 March 1931, n. 6).

5 "The German Comedy" may refer to the first of the Belacqua stories, "Sedendo et Quiescendo," as Ruby Cohn suggests, but more probably to its expanded form as part of *Dream of Fair to Middling Women* (*A Beckett Canon*, 28; John Pilling, *Beckett Before Godot* [Cambridge: Cambridge University Press, 1997], 56–57). Belshazzar is a "fat dentist of a chess-player" in *Dream of Fair to Middling Women*. When he invites Smeraldina to his table she rebuffs him; when he invites Belacqua to the table, he accepts. This causes Smeraldina to insist that she and Belacqua leave at once (Beckett, *Dream of Fair to Middling Women*, 89–91).

6 "Ach, was ich weiß kann jeder wissen – mein Herz habe ich allein!!" (Ah, the knowledge I possess anyone can acquire, but my heart is all my own) (Johann Wolfgang [von] Goethe, *Die Leiden des jungen Werthers, Synoptischer Druck der beiden Fassungen 1774 und 1787*, ed. Annika Lorenz und Helmut Schmiedt [Paderborn: Igel Verlag Literatur, 1997] 123; Johann Wolfgang von Goethe, *The Sorrows of Young Werther*, *Goethe's Collected Works*, XI, ed. David E. Wellbery, tr. Victor Lange and Judith Ryan [New York: Suhrkamp Publishers, 1988] 52).

7 At this time the only French translation of Dostoevsky's novel was *Les Possédés*, 2 vols, tr. Victor Derély (Paris: Editions Plon, 1886).

8 There were no contemporary French biographies of Mary Stuart, Queen of Scotland (1542–1587).

SEUMAS O'SULLIVAN, DUBLIN MAGAZINE
DUBLIN

7/8/31   39 T.C.D.

[Dublin]

Dear Seumas

May I propose these samples of embarrassed respiration to you in the first instance and to your magazine in the second instance?[1]

Beautiful greetings to Stella and to yourself[2]

s/ Sam Beckett

TLS; 1 leaf, 1 side; *poems not enclosed*; KU, James Starkey collection.

1 SB called the two poems he sent to O'Sullivan "the Albas," as is clear from the letter written by SB to McGreevy, Saturday [12 September 1931]. And, later, SB to McGreevy, Tuesday [c. 22 September 1931]: "Seumas O'Sullivan condescends to publish the 'sheet' Alba, but he wouldn't touch the other. He didn't like 'give us a wipe' & he didn't like the anthrax" (TCD, MS 10402/13).

The "Alba" that was published included the lines "whose beauty shall be a sheet before me" and "only I and then the sheet / and bulk dead" (*Dublin Magazine* 6.4 [October–December 1931] 4). The "second" "Alba" poem, that included the lines "give us a wipe for the love of Jesus" and "shining round the corner like an anthrax," was published later under the new title "Enueg 2" in Samuel Beckett, *Echo's Bones and Other Precipitates*, Europa Poets 3 (Paris: Europa Press, 1935; Samuel Beckett, *Poems 1930–1989* [London: Calder Publications, 2002] 16).

2 Estella Solomons.

CHARLES PRENTICE, CHATTO AND WINDUS

LONDON

15/8/31   39 Trinity College

                                           Dublin

Dear Prentice

For your more than charming letter gratias tibi. You're right about my top heavy <u>Sedendo et Quiescendo</u>, though the title's meant to embrace the following section also: <u>They Go Out for the Evening</u>.[1] And of course it stinks of Joyce in spite of most earnest endeavours to endow it with my own odours. Unfortunately for myself that's the only way I'm interested in writing. The next is a clumsy exercise, ribs false & floating & unbreakable (?) glass. Believe me I am grateful for your interest & the trouble you have taken and touched by your letter. I meant what I said to you in London. I wasn't showing it to Chatto & Windus. I was showing it to you.[2] When I imagine I have a real 'twice round the pan & pointed at both ends' I'll offend you with its spiral on my soilman's shovel. I'm glad to have the thing back again in the dentist's chair. I still believe there's something to be done with it.

I have just finished what I might describe as a whore's get version of Walking Out, the story I spoke to you of in London, & sent it to Pinker who won't be able to place it but will be annoyed I hope.[3] That old dada is narrowing down at last to an apex and then I hope it will develop seven spectral petals.[4]

Forgive me for keeping Apocalypse so long.[5] It yielded so much on the first reading that I put it aside relying on your indulgence. But the sponge will soon be dry again.

Dublin is bloody. But it's almost a pleasure to be paralysed after the French daymare and the rain is lovely.

> Yours ever
>
> Sam Beckett

ALS; 1 leaf, 2 sides; *date stamped* received 18-8-31; UoR, MS 2444 CW 24/9.

1 "Gratias tibi" (my thanks to you).

"Sedendo et Quiescendo" (It., Sitting and Reposing) was published in *transition* 21 (March 1932) 13–20, with a typo as "Sedendo et Quiesciendo"; it was later reworked in SB's novel, *Dream of Fair to Middling Women* (64–73). Prentice's letter to SB responding to the story has not been found, but Prentice did write in some detail to McGreevy, and from this letter it is clear that the story as given to Prentice began with "The Smeraldina's Billet Doux" (*Dream of Fair to Middling Women*, 55–61); this story, with some variants, is also part of *More Pricks Than Kicks* ([New York: Grove Press, 1972] 152–157); all citations are from this edition.

Prentice wrote to McGreevy: "The love letters at the beginning of the story are devastating, as rendingly good as anything I have ever read in this vein. But the Joyce bit that comes next seems to be more suitable for a long work than a short one, & anyhow it's not his own style, & the best parts, though there are some supreme times in them, dribble through one's hands in a way that cannot be wholly intentional" (3 August 1931, TCD, MS 8092/50). The story that SB calls "They Go Out for the Evening" became the next section of *Dream of Fair to Middling Women* (74–99).

2 SB met Prentice in London on 28 July 1931 as he traveled from France to Dublin. As SB explained to McGreevy: "A very pleasant evening with Charles Prentice. His voice slows down your heart and tires your eyes. I brought him round the ? next day though I hadn't meant to. Haven't heard anything since. Proposed a Dostoievski for the sake of something to say more than anything else & knowing bloody well I would (could) never do it. Fortunately the partner refrained from being interested" ([? after

2 August to 8 August 1931], TCD, MS 10402/12). Prentice wrote to McGreevy: "He didn't formally submit the story, but he allowed me personally to see it – yet I fear that the firm won't do it, if it were offered to them" (3 August 1931, TCD, MS 8092/50).

3 "Walking Out" was published as a story in *More Pricks Than Kicks* (London: Chatto and Windus, 1934). "Whore's get" (Ir. slang, lowest of the low).

4 "Dada" (colloq., hobbyhorse).
The seven spectral petals suggest the women in the amphitheatre of Paradise, who sit at Mary's feet; Rachel with Beatrice, Sarah, Rebecca, Judith, and Ruth are enthroned on the rose, dividing those who believe in the Christ yet to come from those who held their eyes on the Christ already come (Dante, *The Divine Comedy*, III, *Paradiso*, tr. John D. Sinclair [London: John Lane The Bodley Head, 1946, rev. 1948] Canto XXXII, lines 7–18, 463).

5 Charles Prentice had sent SB his copy of D. H. Lawrence's *Apocalypse*, edited by Richard Aldington (Florence: G. Orioli, 1931); Lawrence's commentary on the Book of Revelation had been published in this limited edition on 3 June 1931; trade editions did not follow until November 1931 (New York: Knopf) and May 1932 (London: Secker). Prentice replied to SB: "By all means, keep 'Apocalypse' until you have properly finished with it. There is no hurry, but when you have finished with it I shall be glad to have it back again" (18 August 1931, UoR, MS 2444 CW letterbook 133/708).

THOMAS McGREEVY
LE CANADEL, VAR

[? after 15 August 1931]   T.C.D.
                                            [Dublin]

Dear Tom

May all things come right somehow and you be happy some-how[.][1]

No news from outside or inside. Charles Prentice sent my thing back with a covering letter putting charming and gracious relations before me. He is very nice. Pinker sent back a short story with a rejection slip.[2] I don't know whether he is very nice or not. I'm very tired, tired – enough to slip back into the embarrassed respirations. Herewith. I can't write like Boccaccio and I don't want to write like Boccaccio.[3] I'll stay in town and take down the petites merdes de mon âme. No I never did the T.S.E. Télégraphie sans éther.[4] Nothing more about Leipzig. Cissie may be coming to settle in Ireland with the two youngest children. Boss won't leave the sinking ship – because of the virgins on board.[5] I was reading your cab poem. Went up in a spasm is a great phrase.[6] Yes, Night of the Rabblement is good. Silence Exile and Cunning isn't quite H.C.E. However I don't feel there's anything wrong anywhere. He's getting a great name for himself in Dublin by the way. The cute thing to do now would be to write the Prolegomena of W.I.P. Do you feel like collelaborating? And what about making a book on the title?[7] I have not yet said anything to Ruddy about fucking the field. He wanted me to apply for a job, oh a very good job, in Capetown or for a job, oh quite a good job, in Cardiff, where I could lie with Rikky. Starkie will probably be appointed at Oxford – he was first man out last time, and then my dear Sam of course they'll appoint you Professor of Italian Literature juxta Dublin juxta Dublin.[8] That'll be the real pig's back. I'll feel like a fricatrix on her bicycle, the sabreflat fricatrix, for dear death pedalling faster and faster, her mouth ajar and her nostrils dilated. Daddy says come off it for the love of God, come out and dine, I'll give you a drink, kiss and make friends. God bless dear Daddy Mummy Frank Bibby and all that I love and make me a good boy for Jesus Christ's sake armen.[9] So I said something quiet and flat and blank but I won't. No sir. Nothing would induce me to. Pelorson was glad to hear about Grasset. He is very mou and I don't see enough of him. Like one of his own policepigeons – mous et lourds sur les toits du monde.[10]

Dear Tom forgive and forget this pestilential letter. I feel hollow.

Beautiful greetings to Richard and Bridget [*for* Brigit][11]

and love ever

TL; 1 leaf, 1 side; TCD, MS 10402/25. *Dating*: follows SB to Charles Prentice 15 August 1931 which indicates that Pinker had returned the story.

1   Richard Aldington, with whom McGreevy was staying in Le Canadel, was unwell, as was McGreevy's mother. Of further concern to McGreevy was where he would go when Aldington left the south of France; he confided to Prentice that staying with Hester Dowden* (1868–1949) in London would be impossible because the forthcoming marriage of her daughter Dolly Travers-Smith to Lennox Robinson "has been rather a knock out" (29 July 1931, UoR, MS 2444 CW 41/2).

2   Prentice's letter to SB has not been found in the Chatto and Windus files (UoR), which suggests that it was a personal letter covering the return of the stories.

3   SB sent "Walking Out" to McGreevy. Giovanni Boccaccio (1313–1375), Italian author best known for the *Decameron* (1349–1351).

4   "Petites merdes de mon âme" (droppings from my soul).
SB did not write the review of McGreevy's *Thomas Stearns Eliot*, nor of Eliot's translation of *Anabase* by St.-John Perse.
SB spins T.S.E. (Eliot's initials) into "Télégraphie sans éther" (literally, telegraphy without ether), playing on "Télégraphie Sans Fil" (wireless), commonly referred to in France as TSF.

5   SB had been thinking of going to Leipzig (see [12 September 1931]). Cissie Sinclair considered leaving Germany and returning to Ireland with her two youngest children, Deirdre and Morris (1918–2007); however, her husband, Boss, was unwilling to leave Kassel because their older daughters Annabel Lilian (known as Nancy, 1916–1969), Sara Estella (known as Sally, 1910–1976), and Peggy wanted to remain in Germany where they had boyfriends (Morris Sinclair, 10 August 2004).

6   McGreevy's "cab poem" is "Crón Tráth Na nDéithe" (Twilight of the Gods); the phrase is from part III: "When the Custom House took fire / Hope slipped off her green petticoat / The Four Courts went up in a spasm / Moses felt for Hope" (MacGreevy, *Collected Poems of Thomas MacGreevy*, 19, 107–122; the translation of the Irish title is supplied by Susan Schreibman with an explanation of its context, 109).

7   "Night of the Rabblement" plays on the title of an indignant essay by James Joyce about the parochialism of the Irish Literary Theatre, "The Day of the Rabblement" (15 October 1901); Joyce's essay was rejected by *St. Stephen's*, a magazine published by students of University College. Joyce protested to the President of the University, and, in the end, the essay was privately printed (F. J. C. Skeffington and James Joyce, *Two Essays: A Forgotten Aspect of the University Question, and The Day of the Rabblement* [Dublin: Gerrard Brothers, 1901] 7–8; rpt. in *The Critical Writings of James Joyce*, ed. Ellsworth Mason and Richard Ellmann [Ithaca, NY: Cornell University Press, 1959] 68–72).
Near the end of Joyce's *A Portrait of the Artist as a Young Man*, the character Stephen Dedalus avows: "I will try to express myself in some mode of life or art as freely as I can and as wholly as I can, using for my defence the only arms I allow myself to use – silence, exile, and cunning" (247).
Padraic Colum (1881–1972) reviewed Joyce's *Haveth Childers Everywhere* ("From a Work in Progress," *Dublin Magazine* 6.3 [July–September 1931] 33–37); a review of Stuart Gilbert's study *James Joyce's "Ulysses"* had appeared in the previous issue of *Dublin Magazine* (6.2 [April–June 1931] 64–65). The London wedding of James and Nora Joyce received mention in *The Irish Times* (4 July 1931: 6; 11 July 1931: 6). SB proposes that he and McGreevy write a preface or introduction to *Work in Progress*, or a book on the (as yet unannounced) title of the novel.

8 "Fucking the field": SB's grotesque English-literal adaptation of the dead French metaphor "foutre le camp" (get away quickly). Rudmose-Brown encouraged SB to seek academic positions in Cape Town, South Africa, and at the University of Cardiff, Wales. Leopold John Dixon Richardson (known as Reeky, called by SB "Rikky," 1893–1979), who had won highest honors in Classics at Trinity College Dublin; he was lecturer in Latin at the University of Cardiff.

Walter Starkie had been a Visiting Professor at the University of Madrid (1928–1929) and may have been considered for a position at Oxford, but he remained at TCD until 1940, when he became Director of the British Institute in Madrid.

9 The image of the sabreflat fricatrix appears in *Dream of Fair to Middling Women* as "the hard breastless Greek Slave or huntress" (83); the phrase "his mouth ajar and his nostrils dilated" appears in the opening of this novel (1). The prayer beginning "God bless" is found in *Dream of Fair to Middling Women* (8); Bibby was SB's nanny (Bridget Bray, n.d.) (Knowlson, *Damned to Fame*, 35–36, 134–135).

10 SB had written to thank McGreevy for sending on the manuscript of Georges Pelorson's novel "Claudiurnales" to Henri Muller (1902–1980); Muller, a friend of Pelorson, worked directly with Bernard Grasset (1881–1955), the founder and editor of Les Editions Grasset, Paris. SB commented to McGreevy: "Neither do I think Grasset will take it" ([after 2 August – before 8 August 1931] TCD, MS 10402/12). Pelorson had typed the novel on SB's typewriter, and sent it to McGreevy at SB's insistence; the manuscript was indeed refused (Belmont, *Souvenirs d'outre-monde*, 415–416).

"Mou" (soft); "mous et lourds sur les toits du monde" (soft and heavy on the roofs of the world). Pelorson said he saw a similarity between the walk of an Irish policeman and the strutting of pigeons (interview 2 November 1990).

11 Richard Aldington, Brigit Patmore. SB wrote "<the Aldingtons> Richard and Bridget."

SAMUEL PUTNAM

PARIS

[before 7 September 1931]   [Dublin]

[no greeting]

Many thanks for N.R. and for including my lovely lovely poem and for somebody's obliging observations on my Proust turd.[1] Hoping to send you sometime something very nice.

Tanti saluti to the thousands of them that love me.[2]

Yrs ever

Samuel Beckett

Saturday [12 September 1931], McGreevy

ACS; 1 leaf, 1 side; NjP, *New Review* Correspondence of Samuel Putnam, C0111/1/9. *Dating*: before 7 September 1931, when Prentice sent SB a copy of Richard Thoma's "Island Without Serpents," a review of McGreevy's *Thomas Stearns Eliot* (*The New Review* 1.3 [August–September–October 1931] 119–121; UoR, MS 2444 CW letterbook 133/944).

1 *The New Review* 1.3 (August–September–October 1931) included SB's poem "Return to the Vestry," as well as a note by Samuel Putnam announcing that SB's *Proust* would be reviewed in the following issue, "along with Ernest Seillière's new *Proust*. Need we say that we prefer Beckett?" (98–99, 124).

2 "Tanti saluti" (many greetings). SB echoes Exodus 20:6.

THOMAS McGREEVY

LE LAVANDOU, VAR

Saturday [12 September 1931]   39 T.C.D.

[Dublin]

Dear Tom

Many thanks for your letter and then for Thoma's article in the New Review that Prentice sent along and that I had already read, Putnam having sent me a copy of the New Review, and that I don't thing [*for* think] need detain us.[1] I was very pleased to know that you liked the Albas. No, nothing either very new or very beautiful, when I come to think of it. They came together one on top of the other, a double-yoked orgasm in months of aspermatic nights & days. I sent them 3 weeks ago to Seumas O'Sullivan. So far he has not acknowledged their receipt. I'm afraid the 'Give us a wipe' class of guttersnippet continues to please me, or at least to recommend itself to me in as much as 'true.'[2] One has to buckle the wheel of one's poem somehow, nicht wahr? Or run the risk of Nordau's tolerance.[3]

And most affectionate gratias tibi for offering to mitigate my distress à paraître with a share of your substance. You're the kindest of friends and if I knew you were in Paris I would be very much less concerned about going to Leipzig. But Paris (as such) gives me the chinks at the moment and it's about the last place in the world I want to go. Too many Frenchmen in the wrong streets. Anyhow I've no idea when I'll get away or if I ever shall. Said nothing to Ruddy – the old cowardice of keeping one[']s hand off the future.[4] And I'm too tired and too poor in guts or spunk or whatever the stuff is to endow the old corpse with a destination & buy a ticket & pack up here. The 'pottamus waits for his angels.[5] And really I can't seriously suppose that there's anything I want to rid myself of or acquire, no growth of freedom or property that can't be shed or assumed with as absurd a coefficient of plausibility here in the miasma as anywhere else. Nothing is so attractive anyhow as abstention. A nice quiet life punctuated with involuntary exonerations (Albas). And isn't my navel worth 10 of anyone else's, even though I can't get a very good view of it.

Pelorson has some good stuff in his new book that I think I spoke to you of and that he has just finished. He'll be off very soon, not that I see much of him now anymore (the only reason I hope being that he is not as free as he used to be.)[6] I am fond of Leventhal for no reason good bad or indifferent which is surely the only possible way of being fond of anybody, and I see a little of him. I had an invitation from J[.] B. Yeats to go round some Saturday but I haven't had the courage to go so far. Frank emerges now & then from the fading fact of my family. Then there are sometimes the green tulips and always the quiet life (after the pubs close.)[7]

Do write and tell me how yourself goes & how yr. work goes. Schöne grüsse to R. & B.[8] And love ever

Sam

ALS; 1 leaf, 4 sides; TCD, MS 10402/24. *Dating*: after 7 September 1931, when Charles Prentice forwarded Thoma's review of McGreevy's *Thomas Stearns Eliot* to SB. On 7 August 1931, the "Albas" were submitted to Seumas O'Sullivan. At the time of this letter to McGreevy, SB did not yet know that one of the poems would be published by Seumas O'Sullivan in *Dublin Magazine*.

1 American writer Richard Thoma (1902–1974), along with Samuel Putnam and Harold J. Salemson (1910–1988), wrote the "Direction" manifesto (1930) in response to *transition*'s call for a revolution in writing; it formed the editorial basis for *The New Review*, edited by Putnam with Thoma as an Associate Editor. Thoma's review was critical of McGreevy's parochialism, his preoccupation with Catholicism, and his "rambling, pedantic, speculative, dilettantish" style ("Island Without Serpents," 119–121). George Reavey wrote a riposte ("Letter to Richard Thoma," *The New Review* 1.4 [Winter 1931–1932] 397).

2 SB sent "the Albas" to Seumas O'Sullivan on 7 August 1931 as well as to McGreevy. There is no manuscript of either poem in the archives of *Dublin Magazine* (TCD). SB's reference to the phrase "'give us a wipe guttersnippet'" in the rejected "Alba" indicates that it is the poem later retitled "Enueg 2."

3 Max Simon Nordau (1849–1923), Hungarian-born philosopher, literary critic, and Zionist. His two-volume study *Entartung* (1892; *Degeneration*) tried to demonstrate that many artists and authors share mental features with the criminal and the insane. SB read and made notes from Nordau's *Degeneration* (translator not indicated [London: William Heinemann, 1895]; see Pilling, ed., *Beckett's Dream Notebook*, 89–97).
"Nicht wahr?" (isn't that so?).
SB is presumably referring to the twist or surprise of the poem (John Pilling, March 2005).

4 SB originally wrote "if I" and changed it to "when I'll get away."
"Gratias tibi" (thanks to you).
"A paraître" (that lies ahead).
SB had mentioned Leipzig as a destination in previous letters to McGreevy; he had not yet spoken to Rudmose-Brown about his thought of leaving Trinity College Dublin (see [after 15 August 1931], n. 8).

5 SB refers to T. S. Eliot's poem "The Hippopotamus" (T. S. Eliot, *Complete Poems and Plays: 1909–1950* [New York: Harcourt, Brace, and World, 1952] 30–31).

6 Before leaving Dublin in the autumn of 1931, according to what he later wrote, Pelorson had been trying feverishly to finish his third manuscript, which he called "l'espèce de truc sans dénomination" (the sort of nameless something-or-another); he had "un demi-cahier de poèmes, un roman achevé" (half a notebook of poems, a finished novel) as well as the new work. At the same time, he was preoccupied with his then secret marriage to Marcelle Graham (1900–?), the complications of resigning from the Ecole Normale Supérieure, and the need to support himself in France or elsewhere (Belmont, *Souvenirs d'outre-monde*, 324, 333–334).

7 Frank Beckett. SB evokes "the tulips of the evening / the green tulips" in his poem "Enueg 2" (*Echo's Bones*, [16–17]; rpt. Beckett, *Poems 1930–1989*, 16). SB explained to scholar and biographer Lawrence Harvey (1925–1988), who had asked him about the color: "Those sky tulips I called green because I saw them that colour & the flower" (8 March 1965, NhD, MSS 661, Lawrence Harvey collection).

8 "Schöne Grüsse" (warm greetings) to Richard Aldington and Brigit Patmore.

89

THOMAS McGREEVY
PARIS

Tuesday [c. 22 September 1931]   Trinity College
                                       [Dublin]

My dear Tom

Many thanks for your envoi. Frankly I much prefer your Eliot, which simply means I suppose, that I am more in sympathy with one subject than with the other.[1] The poetry you quote is for me really the most lamentable stuff.[2] What I did enjoy was the rhythm of your phrase that always charms me and the lassoo [sic] leaps of your mind capturing analogies all round you. The carelessly disposed of parallel between Aldington & Lurçat as the adepts of Natures Vivantes I found very effective. But d'une façon générale I find the book less dense and rapid than the Eliot.[3] Don't mind this from me – I'm suffering from literary caries.

I was glad to know what your plans were, even in vague outline. Here is the address of the people in Florence.

> Signorina Ottolenghi
>   via Campanella 14

They charged me 30 lire a day (3 meals) and are cultured decent people – and it['}s a quiet part of Florence, off the Piazza Oberdamm [*for* Oberdan] & not far from the Campo di Marte. You would probably find something near for L 30 or L 35. I'll ask my Father next time I see him. I see him very seldom.[4]

I have done nothing at all except booze my heart quiet and gal[l]op through Bérard's Odyssey. He certainly makes it easy to read, and I really recovered something of the old childish absorbtion [sic] with which I read Treasure Island & Oliver Twist and many others – free of all pilfering velleities. But I dislike very much his Alexandrine diction, and if that kind of hemistich neuralgia exasperates me what would it be like for a Frenchman? He has some most wonderful glittering phrases: La quenouille[,] chargée de laine purpurine - ! Et tout le jour le joug tressauta sur les cous.[5]

Seumas O'Sullivan condescends to publish the 'sheet' Alba, but he wouldn't touch the other. He didn't like 'Give us a wipe' & he didn't like the anthrax.[6]

Georges leaves early next week and I see so little of him that only a few adhesions will be ruptured. I see something of Leventhal and like him, though I'm aware & frightened of the sterile formulae of his attitude. I've done nothing further about getting away.[7] Ruddy loads me with the invigilations that he can't find time to accomplish in person, and those of his fucking master and advocate Goligher.[8] I am very angry but must take it all smiling as long as I'm 'assisting' and paralysed by shilly-shally. I probably won't afford Germany at Xmas. Do write & love ever and don't think me too splenetic.

Sam

Amitiés à Beaufret et Thomas si tu les vois.[9]

ALS; 2 leaves, 2 sides; PS, upper left margin side 1; TCD, MS 10402/13. *Dating*: McGreevy's book, *Richard Aldington: An Englishman*, was published by Chatto and Windus on 17 September 1931, and the Tuesday following was 22 September 1931 (Charles Prentice to McGreevy, 23 August 1931, TCD 8092/53). SB's poem "Alba" was published in *Dublin Magazine* 6.4 (October–December 1931) 4.

1 SB has received his copy of McGreevy's *Richard Aldington: An Englishman*.

2 McGreevy quotes numerous passages from Aldington's poetry, but without always indicating their titles; the first pagination given in what follows refers to the texts as published in *The Complete Poems of Richard Aldington* (London: Allan Wingate, 1948), and the second, to the pagination of the passages in McGreevy's book. From *Images*: "In the Old Garden" (34; 12–13); "Choricos" (21–23; 14–15); "Lesbia" (28; 18); "After Two Years" (44; 18); "Amalfi" (35; 19); "At Mitylene" (26; 19); "In the Tube" (49; 23–24); "Inarticulate Grief" (64; 25–26); "Captive" (68; 26–27); "Sunsets" (68; 26–27); "The Faun Captive" (69–70; 27–28).

Tuesday [c. 22 September 1931], McGreevy

From *Images of War*: "Taintignies" (108; 28); "Bombardment" (105; 29); "A Village" (90–91; 29–30); "Machine Guns" (93; 33–34); "Epitaph (2)" (106–107; 34); "Insouciance" (80; 35). From "A Fool i' the Forest" (193–239), McGreevy uses several passages: (194; 42); (198; 420); (202; 43); and two sections (206; 43).

From "Short Poems" (numbered with both arabic and roman numerals): 4 (295–296; 65); IV (297; 65).

3 McGreevy notes that Aldington and French artist Jean Lurçat (1892–1966), both of whom were marked by their experiences in World War I, share a commitment to depicting what he calls "*natures vivantes*," whereas T. S. Eliot "was painting verbal *natures mortes*" (31). McGreevy argues that the War caused Aldington and Lurçat to "bring their work closer to objective reality," but without the danger of nineteenth-century realism, both because "their technical point of departure is not realistic" and because "the principal reality that has been impelling them to expression is so vast and so terrible to look back on" (32).

"D'une façon générale" (in a general way).

4 SB locates the *pensione* in which he stayed when he was in Florence in 1927, the summer prior to his undergraduate examinations in French and Italian (see Knowlson, *Damned to Fame*, 83–86). The Campo di Marte is near the Piazza Oberdan in Florence. SB's father, William Beckett* (1871–1933), a quantity surveyor, would have paid the bill.

5 Victor Bérard (1864–1931) presents his French translation of *The Odyssey*, attributed to Homer (eighth century BC), as "poésie homérique" (Homer, *L'Odyssée*, tr. Victor Bérard [Paris: Société d'édition "Les Belles lettres," 1924]). Bérard's introduction explains: "Que l'on supprime la rime qui jalonne de douze en douze syllabes cette 'diction alexandrine' et l'on aura, je crois, un modèle de la prose que l'on peut concevoir pour obtenir en français un rythme équivalent à celui du texte homérique" (xxxii) (If we take away the rhyme which marks, in the succession of twelve syllables, this 'alexandrine diction,' we shall have, I think, a model of the prose that can be imagined in order to obtain in French a rhythm equivalent to that of the Homeric text).

A hemistich is the half, or section, of a line of verse as divided by the caesura.

"La quenouille, chargée de laine purpurine" (The distaff, laden with crimson wool) (I, 82). The second line, "Et tout le jour le joug tressauta sur les cous" (And all day long the yoke rose and fell on the necks), is not an exact quotation of the phrase which appears three times in the translation: "Le joug, sur leurs deux cous, tressauta tout le jour" (The yoke, on their two necks, rose and fell all day long) (I, 75; I, 116; II, 205).

McGreevy had recommended Bérard's translation, saying that it read like a novel, one that he could read and read again (*Richard Aldington: An Englishman*, 17). *Treasure Island* (1883) by Robert Louis Stevenson (1850–1894). *Oliver Twist* (1837–1839) by Charles Dickens (1812–1870). For SB's reading notes from Bérard's translation: Pilling, ed., *Beckett's Dream Notebook*, 102–103.

6 "Alba," *Dublin Magazine* 4. For discussion of the two Alba poems: 7 August 1931, n. 1.

7 SB wrote "<terrifying>" and inserted above it "sterile."

Georges Pelorson's arrangements following his marriage to Marcelle Graham may have delayed his departure plans; in his memoir he writes that he did not leave Dublin until shortly before mid-October 1931 (*Souvenirs d'outre-monde*, 332–334).

8 SB assisted Rudmose-Brown with teaching, which included invigilating examinations for him as well as for William Alexander Goligher (1870–1941), Registrar from 1930 to 1937; Goligher is described as one who "commanded respect" and enjoyed the

"substance of power," but whose remarks were often "caustic or cynical" (R. B. McDowell and D. A. Webb, *Trinity College Dublin, 1592–1952: An Academic History* [Cambridge: Cambridge University Press, 1982] 442).

9 "Amitiés à Beaufret et Thomas si tu les vois." (Greetings to Beaufret and Thomas if you see them.)

THOMAS McGREEVY

PARIS

8/11/31   39 Trinity College
                                                              Dublin

My dear Tom

One letter – yours – last week and none more welcome. It is a more than usually implacable Dublin Sunday. Mist & rain & chimes & teetotal. Last Sunday I took myself for a walk – from Rathfarnham to Enniskerry, through the Pine Forest. All beautiful and lancinant, and the limp down the hill in the dark to Enniskerry & flat stout in the Powerscourt Arms.[1] Pelorson says he understands Rimbaud who used to compose poems walking. But for me, walking, the mind has a most pleasant & melancholy limpness, is a carrefour of memories, memories of childhood mostly, moulin à larmes.[2] But to-day everything is dripping & there is nothing at all to be done and nobody at all to go and see.

You seem to be installed quite comfortably at the Trianon. I'll be surprised if Chatto & Windus rise to it & publish your verse. I hope they do. Don't be so vague about your book. Où en es-tu?[3] I'll send you an Irish Press.[4] Delighted to rescue your dishes if I can. Where do I go?

I'm right in a dead spot, one of the knots in my life teak but I suppose I'll get clear sooner or later. I can't write anything at all, can't imagine even the shape of a sentence, nor take notes (though God knows I have enough 'butin verbal' to strangle anything I'm likely to want to say), nor read with understanding, goût or dégoût.[5] I was presented with a lovely polyglot edition of Horace, and I haven't the guts to start into it.[6] I read two books of Powys: Mark Only and Mr Tasker's Gods, not knowing his work at all, & was very disappointed. Such a fabricated darkness & painfully organised unified tragic completeness. The Hardy vice caricatured. Everybody had been telling me what a great writer he was. And what a style![7] Everything is very grey & identical, specially ton serviteur. I was hoping to get away at Xmas – even to Paris if not to Germany – but what with the pound & an overdraft & petty debts & the remoteness of my cheque, I don't think it can be done. I don't think I'll ever get away now. I'll be renominated (sauf scandale) this time 2 years & settle down to professorial incompetence. I really believe so. Without very much regret.[8]

They are giving Ruddy a D. Litt. Stip. Cond. at next commencement. Together with Curtis & Allison [*for* Alison] Phillips. Gracious & nugatory.[9] [...]

[...]

I suppose you have no news of the new Transition. They have stuff of mine – carmina quae legunt cacantes.[10]

Dear Tom, I wish I could write you a cheerful easy newsy letter like yours to me. I'm inextricably morveux and I beg your pardon. I underestimated this terrible Dublin.

Pourvu que cela ne t'empêche pas de ré[é]crire.[11]

God bless. Is there no chance of seeing you here soon?

Love ever
Sam

ALS; 1 leaf, 4 sides; TCD, MS 10402/21.

1 SB walked from Rathfarnham, south of central Dublin, to the Powerscourt Arms Hotel in Enniskerry in Co. Wicklow, a distance of about 10 miles. The forest, Tibradden, is approximately 2½ miles south of Rathfarnham, Co. Dublin.
"Lancinant" (poignant).

2 "Carrefour" (crossroads); moulin à larmes (tearmill, adapted from "moulin à vent" [windmill]).

3 McGreevy was living at the Trianon-Palace Hotel, 1 bis – 3 Rue de Vaugirard, Paris 6. He had been encouraged by Charles Prentice to send his poems to Chatto and Windus, and he did so; however, as Prentice wrote to Richard Aldington, Chatto and Windus was unlikely to publish them (3 November 1931, ICSo, Aldington 68/6/5). McGreevy continued to work on his novel (see TCD, MS 8039–55).
"Où en es-tu?" (How far have you got?)

4 *The Irish Press* commenced publication in Dublin on 5 September 1931, proposing to represent "an Irish Ireland, an Ireland aware of its own greatness, sure of itself, conscious of the spiritual forces which have formed it into a distinct people having its own language and customs and a traditionally Christian philosophy of life"; its motto was: "Truth in news" (5 September 1931: 5). McGreevy's first contribution was "A Great Christian Drama for Irish Players" (*The Irish Press* 28 December 1932: 6, 11).

5 "Butin verbal" (verbal booty), a reference to SB's "note-snatching" (see Pilling, ed., *Beckett's Dream Notebook*, xvi–xviii).
"Goût or dégoût" (taste or distaste).

6 Horace, *Oeuvres complètes d'Horace* ... French tr. Jean-Baptiste Monfalcon, Spanish tr. Javier de Burgos, Italian tr. Tommaso Gargallo, English tr. Philip Francis; German tr. Christoph Martin Wieland and Johann Henrich Voss, Polyglotte edn. [Latin text with translations into French, Spanish, Italian, English, and German] (Paris and Lyon: Cormon et Blanc, 1834).

7 Theodore Francis Powys (1875–1953) wrote *Mark Only* (1924) and *Mr. Tasker's Gods* (1924); both were published by Chatto and Windus.
Thomas Hardy (1840–1928).

8 "Ton serviteur" (your servant); "sauf scandale" (barring a scandal). The British pound went off the gold standard on 21 September 1931, and then the pound fell by 25 percent; the Saorstát pound was set against the British pound.

9 Trinity College Dublin conferred the title of Doctor of Letters on Rudmose-Brown, Edmund Curtis (1881–1943), Professor of Irish History, and Walter Alison Phillips (1864–1950), Lecky Professor of Modern History and Chief Assistant Editor, *Encyclopaedia Britannica*, 11th edn.

10 There was a hiatus in the publication of *transition*: numbers 19–20 were published as a single issue in June 1930 and number 21 in March 1932; the latter published SB's story "Sedendo and Quiesciendo" [for Quiesciendo] (13–20).
SB quotes from an epigram by Martial (né Marcus Valerius Martialis, first century AD): "carmina quae legunt cacantes" (poems which people read at stool) (Martial, *Epigrams*, II, tr. Walter C. A. Ker [Cambridge, MA: Harvard University Press; London: Heinemann, 1968] XII.61: line 10, 362–363). It is cited by SB from *The Anatomy of Melancholy* (1621) by Robert Burton (1577–1640) (see Pilling, ed., *Beckett's Dream Notebook*, 104).

11 "Morveux" (snotty-nosed). "Pourvu que cela ne t'empêche pas de ré[é]crire." (Just so long as that doesn't stop you writing back.)

SEUMAS O'SULLIVAN, DUBLIN MAGAZINE
DUBLIN

[27 November 1931]   39 T.C.D.
                                                          [Dublin]

Dear Seumas
        Darf ich …?[1]
                SBB

                ENUEG[2]

Exeo in a spasm,
tired of my darling's red sputum,
from the Portobello Private Nursing Home,
its secret things,
and toil to the crest of the surge of the steep perilous bridge,
and lapse down blankly under the scream of the hoarding,
the stiff bright banner of the hoarding,
into a black west
throttled with clouds.

Above the mansions, the algum-trees,
the mountains,
my head sullenly,
clot of anger,
skewered aloft, strangled in the cangue of the wind,
bites like a dog against its chastisement.

I trundle along rapidly now on my ruined feet,
flush with the livid canal;
at Parnell Bridge a dying barge
carrying a cargo of nails and timber

rocks itself softly in the foaming cloister of the lock;
on the far bank a gang of down-and-outs would seem to be
    mending a beam.

Then for miles only wind
and the weals creeping alongside on the water
and the world opening up to the south
across a lamentable parody of champaign land to the
    mountains
and the stillborn evening turning a filthy green
manuring the night-fungus
and the mind annulled
wrecked in wind.

I splashed past a little wearish old man,
Democritus,
scuttling along between a crutch and a stick,
his stump caught up, horribly, like a claw, under his breech,
smoking.
Then because a field on the left suddenly went up in a blaze
of shouting and urgent whistling and scarlet and blue ganzies
I stopped and climbed a bank to see the game.
A child fidgeting at the gate called up:
"Would we be let in, Mister?"
"Certainly" I said "you would."
But, afraid, he set off down the road.
"Well" I called after him "why wouldn't you go on in?"
"Oh" he said, knowingly,
"I was in that ground before and I got put out."
Then on,
derelict,
as from a bush of gorse on fire in the mountain after dark,

or, in my dream of Sumatra, the jungle hymen,
the still, flagrant rafflesia.

Next:
a pitiful family of grey verminous hens
perished out in the sunk field,
trembling, half asleep, against the closed door of a shed,
with no visible means of roosting.

The great mushy toadstool,
green black,
oozing up after me,
soaking up the tattered sky like an ink of pestilence,
in my skull the wind going fetid,
the water .....

Next:
on the hill down from the Fox and Geese into Chapelizod,
a small malevolent goat, exiled on the road,
remotely pucking the gate of his field.
The Isolde Stores a great perturbation of sweaty heroes,
endimanchés,
come hurrying down in time for a pint of nepenthe or half-
    and-half
from watching the hurlers in Kilmainham.

Blotches of drowned yellow in the pit of the Liffey;
the finger of the ladders hooked over the parapet,
solliciting;
a slush of vigilant gulls in the grey spew of the sewer.

Ah! the banner,
the banner of meat bleeding

on the silk of the seas and the arctic flowers!
(they do not exist) . . . .

ACI; 1 leaf, 1 side; TMS, 2 leaves, 2 sides; *env to* Seumas O'Sullivan Esq., Editor, Dublin Magazine, 2 Crow Street [Dublin]; *pm* 27-11-31, Dublin; TCD, MS 4630–49/3332/1–4. *Dating*: from pm and SB to McGreevy, 20 December 1931: "Herewith a pome that S. O'S. wouldn't have on account of the <u>red sputum</u>!"

1 "Darf ich . . . ?" (May I . . . ?)

2 "Enueg" was rejected by *Dublin Magazine*; it was published in *Echo's Bones* (1935) as "Enueg 1," and the second "Alba" poem was retitled "Enueg 2.""Enueg" (Provençal, complaint).

THOMAS McGREEVY
PARIS

20/12/31   COOLDRINAGH,

                                                   FOXROCK,

                                                   CO. DUBLIN.

Dear Tom

Forgive me for not having replied to you before this. All kinds of imaginary melancholy circumstances to excuse me. I have had to reintegrate my father's roof for a few days but am off, malgré tout et malgré tous, immediately after Noel, via Ostend, somewhere into Germany, as far as Cologne anyway, next Saturday night from North Wall, not to return I hope (& entre nous) for many months, though I have not resigned from Trinity.[1] If I have to let them down, tant pis. Some charming little cunt of a gold medallist will be nominated deputy for a term until they can get some really <u>responsible</u> person, & wont that be a happy surprise for the New Year.[2] (And by the way all the usual voeux et que tous les tiens soient exaucés.)[3] Of course I'll probably crawl back with my tail coiled round my ruined poenis. And maybe I wont. Is there no

99

chance of seeing you at all. I dont know whether you are still in
Paris. It would be grand to spend Xmas with you, but I dont want
France – above all not the comic Marseilles – & I know you don't
want Germania, unless maybe Weimar! It's madness really to go
away now with the exchange u.s.w. but it really is now or never.[4]
And as usual I'm not burning any boats! I'm hoping to be able to
spit fire at them from a distance.

I've been several times to look at the new Perugino Pietà in
the National Gallery here. It's buried behind a formidable bar-
rage of shining glass, so that one is obliged to take cognisance of
it progressively, square inch by square inch. It's all messed up by
restorers, but the Xist and the women are lovely. A clean shaven,
potent Xist, and a passion of tears for the waste. The most
mystical constituent is the ointment pot that was probably
added by Raffael[l]o. Rottenly hung in rotten light behind this
thick shop window, so that a total view of it is impossible, and
full of grotesque amendments. But a lovely cheery Xist full of
sperm, & the woman touching his thighs and mourning his
jewels.[5] I thought Orpen's Ptarmigan & Wash House nearly as
bad as Keating.[6]

How is the novel going?[7] I started yet again & soon saw no
reason to continue.[8] I have just reread the Rouge et Noir. Such an
obsession with heights & ladders & gothic pillars & terraces
and grottos in the Juras & the dungeon up in the air at the end.
And the same thing again all through the Chartreuse. Nimrod of
novelists[.][9]

Herewith a pome that S. O'S. wouldn't have on account of
the red sputum! I haven't tried to place it elsewhere, & thought
I'd send it to you à tout hasard.[10]

No news from Pelorson since I applied for a slight service.
Again so much piss.

20 December 1931, McGreevy

Writing to the Penman for Xmas about statues, Professor
Webb & Chapelizod c/o Pinker. I've no idea where he is.[11]
Do write home (here) & they'll send it on wherever I am.

Love ever

Sam

ALS; 1 leaf, 4 sides; *letterhead*; *enclosure not extant*; TCD, MS 10402/23.

1 SB had not resigned his post at Trinity College Dublin, but, in anticipation of
leaving for Germany on 26 December, he removed his belongings from 39 Trinity
College to the family home in Foxrock. "Reintegrate" (Gallicism for "return to").
"Entre nous" (between ourselves). The repercussions anticipated, "malgré tout et
malgré tous" (in spite of everything and everyone), were complicated by SB's automobile accident injuring Ethna MacCarthy before Christmas. For a full discussion of SB's
circumstances of departure: Knowlson, *Damned to Fame*, 141–142.

2 SB's resignation letter or telegram has not been found, but the information
record of the Board Minutes for 20 January 1932, kept by Registrar W. A. Goligher,
indicates that: "B. has just sent in his resignation"; A. J. Leventhal was appointed
Lecturer in French on 20 January 1932 (Jane Maxwell, Manuscripts Department,
TCD, 19 August 2004; Jean O'Hara, Alumni Office TCD, 6 August 2004).

3 "Voeux et que tous les tiens soient exaucés" (wishes and may all yours be granted).

4 McGreevy is in Paris.
For the year ending 31 December 1931, the rate of exchange between the German
mark and the British pound had dropped from 20 to 14 (M. Epstein, ed., *The Annual
Register: A Review of Public Events at Home and Abroad for the Year 1931* [London: Longmans,
Green and Co., 1932] 66; for further information see 8 November 1931, n. 8).
"U.s.w." is the abbreviation of "und so weiter" (and so on).

5 Perugino's *Pietà* (NGI 942) was purchased on 12 June 1931 by Thomas Bodkin
(1887–1961), Director of the National Gallery of Ireland (1927–1935). The Umbrian
artist and architect Perugino (né Pietro di Cristoforo Vannucci Perugino, c. 1450–1523)
taught Raphael (né Raffaello Sanzio or Santi or Sanzi, 1483–1520), who may have
added the ointment pot below the feet of Christ; a similar painting by Perugino in
the Uffizi Gallery in Florence lacks the ointment pot (Ernst T. Dewald, *Italian Painting
1200–1600* [New York: Holt, Rinehart and Winston, 1961] 397–399).

6 Sir William Orpen (1878–1931), Irish-born painter who lived in London, was
official painter of the 1919 Paris Peace Conference and was elected to the Royal
Academy in 1921; SB refers to Orpen's self-portrait *The Dead Ptarmigan* (NGI 945)
which had been bequeathed to the National Gallery of Ireland in 1930, and *The Wash
House* (NGI 946). Orpen had been a teacher of Cissie Sinclair at the Dublin Metropolitan
School of Art (see Knowlson, *Damned to Fame*, 140).
Seán Keating (also Seán Céitinn, 1889–1977), Irish artist, a student of Orpen who
painted in the Aran Islands for four years, was a traditionalist known for fine draughts-
manship; he was elected to the Royal Hibernian Academy (Dublin) in 1923, but
resigned in 1962 as a protest against contemporary art.

101

7 McGreevy's unpublished novel was provisionally entitled "Neither Will I" (TCD, MS 8039/55).

8 SB is writing stories which become portions of *Dream of Fair to Middling Women* and *More Pricks Than Kicks*.

9 SB refers to *Le Rouge et le noir* (1830; *The Red and the Black*) and *La Chartreuse de Parme* (1839; *The Charterhouse of Parma*) by Stendhal (né Marie-Henri Beyle, 1783–1842).

10 SB encloses "Enueg" (later entitled "Enueg 1") which opens with "Exeo in a spasm / tired of my darling's red sputum."
"A tout hasard" (on the off-chance that it will interest you).

11 SB's letter sent to James Joyce care of Joyce's agent, Ralph Pinker, has not been found; Joyce may have been in Paris, at 2 Avenue S. Philibert, Passy, at this time (Rose, *The Textual Diaries of James Joyce*, 190).
Thomas Ebenezer Webb (1821–1903), Professor of Moral Philosophy and later Regius Professor of Laws, and Public Orator of Trinity College Dublin. Webb translated Goethe's *Faust* (1880), and his last work promoted Sir Francis Bacon (1561–1623) as author of Shakespeare's works.
The village of Chapelizod is situated on the northern bank of the River Liffey, between Island Bridge and Palmerston; by legend it is associated with Isould (Isolde), daughter of Anguisshe, King of Ireland. In *Finnegans Wake*, Humphrey Chimpden Earwicker, husband of Anna Livia Plurabelle, owns a tavern in Chapelizod.

CHRONOLOGY 1932

1932	January	SB is in Kassel. Sends two poems to Samuel Putnam for *The New Review*.
	20 January	Resigns from Trinity College Dublin as recorded in Minutes of the Board of TCD.
	2 February	In Paris. Attends Joyce's fiftieth birthday party.
	By 8 February	Proposes an essay on Gide for the Chatto and Windus Dolphin Books series, which Prentice declines.
	16 February	Éamon De Valera becomes Prime Minister of Ireland.
	20 February	SB lunches with Prentice and McGreevy in Paris.
	March	SB's story "Sedendo et Quiescendo" and the manifesto "Poetry is Vertical," to which SB's name is appended, are published in *transition*.
	April	*The New Review* publishes the poem "Text."
	7 May	Assassination of Paul Doumer results in scrutiny of travel papers of all foreigners in France; lacking valid papers, SB stays with the artist Jean Lurçat, until his *carte de séjour* is in order.
	After 7 May	Edward Titus purchases SB's translation of Arthur Rimbaud's poem "Le Bateau ivre."
	June	SB writes poem "Home Olga."
	By 28 June	Sends additional poems and/or portion of the MS of his novel *Dream of Fair to Middling Women* to Samuel Putnam.
	29 June	Sends *Dream of Fair to Middling Women* to Prentice.
	5 July	Prentice sends his comments on *Dream of Fair to Middling Women*.

12–13 July	SB leaves Paris on overnight boat to London.
Mid-July	Gathers testimonials for teaching applications.
20 July	Dines with Charles Prentice. Gives, or has given, poems to Prentice.
22 July	Applies for reader's ticket for the British Museum.
27 July	Prentice returns SB's poems.
29 July	Takes McGreevy's letter of introduction, *Dream of Fair to Middling Women*, and poems to Hogarth Press. Sees Desmond MacCarthy. Files application with teaching agency, Truman and Knightley.
August	*This Quarter* publishes SB's translations of work by Paul Eluard, André Breton, and René Crevel.
17 August	SB meets Ellis Roberts of the *New Statesman*, who encourages him to submit an article on Gide.
By 18 August	Hogarth Press returns *Dream of Fair to Middling Women* and poems. Cape returns *Dream of Fair to Middling Women*. SB gives it to Grayson and Grayson. Gives poems to Derek Verschoyle of *The Spectator*; they are returned.
c. 25 August	SB returns to Dublin.
30 August	Sends poems to Wishart.
By 13 September	Writes draft of "Serena 1." Rudmose-Brown assists SB in finding "grinds."
By 8 October	Joins brother Frank on a trip to Galway, Achill, and Connemara, SB's first visit to this area. *Contempo* accepts "Home Olga." Titus accepts story "Dante and the Lobster" for *This Quarter*. SB sends McGreevy the poem "Serena I."
By 18 October	Grayson returns *Dream of Fair to Middling Women*. SB sends it to Edward Titus.
By 4 November	Sends McGreevy "Serena 2."
By 6 November	Sends two poems to George Reavey, "Serena 1" and what is later entitled "Sanies 2."

December	*This Quarter* publishes "Dante and the Lobster."
1 December	SB has surgery on neck cyst and a hammer toe; in nursing home until nearly Christmas.
26 December	Walks near Donabate and Portrane Asylum.
31 December	Dines with Joe Hone, Killiney.

SAMUEL PUTNAM

FRANCE

April 3 [1932]   Trianon-Palace Hotel
                                         Rue de Vaugirard
                                         Paris 6ᵉ

Dear Putnam

Thanks for proof which ecco.[1]

Curious to know did you ever get 2 poems I sent you from Germany about middle January. One long & one short.[2] May I have them if you are not using them?

Hoping to see you one of these days. Why don't you look in a day you're in town.[3] Always here afternoon.

Kindest regards to M̲̲ͬͩ Putnam [.]

    Yrs

        Sam Beckett

ALS; 1 leaf, 1 side; NjP, *New Review* Correspondence of Samuel Putnam, C0111/1/9. *Dating*: SB was at the Trianon-Palace Hotel, Paris, from early February 1932.

1 SB's prose fragment "Text," was published in *The New Review* 2.5 (April 1932) 57. "Ecco" (here).

2 The poems sent by SB to Putnam from Germany in January 1932 have not been identified with certainty. The long poem may have been the unpublished "Spring Song," and the short poem may have been "Dortmunder" (14 lines, written in Kassel), "The Vulture" (6 lines, based on Goethe's *Harzreise im Winter*), or "Gnome" (based on Goethe's *Xenien*) ("Spring Song," TxU, Leventhal, and TxU, Belmont).

3 Putnam and his wife Riva (1893–1979) lived in Fontenay-aux-Roses.

28 June 1932, Putnam

SAMUEL PUTNAM
PARIS

28/6/32   Trianon Palace Hotel
                                         1 Bis -3, Rue De Vaugirard
                                         Paris

Dear Putnam

Herewith the latest, positively the latest hallucinations[.][1]

I take one fleet pace to the rere and submit them with the chiroplatonic flourish that it has taken me years to master.

Thanks for nice things in preface to Reevey [*for* Reavey]. But I vow I will get over J. J. ere I die. Yessir.[2]

Wont you let me know if you get 'em how you like 'em.

Mr T. McG. would love to know did you get his desquamation of Mr Tate.[3]

When do we rencounter?

Tanti saluti[4]

   s/ <u>Sam Beckett</u>

TLS; 1 leaf, 1 side; *letterhead*; NjP, *New Review* Correspondence of Samuel Putnam, C0111/1/9.

1 SB may have sent poems or a portion of his manuscript of *Dream of Fair to Middling Women*. The final issue of *The New Review* was that published in April 1932. However, Putnam fully intended to continue publication. He wrote to George Reavey on 22 August 1932: "As to when the NR is coming out again, I cannot say now. I can only say that it will come out"; and again, on 13 September 1932: "The NR is going on, a triple number this autumn" (TxU, uncatalogued Reavey, 15).

2 Samuel Putnam, to whom the book is dedicated, wrote the introduction to George Reavey's *Faust's Metamorphoses: Poems* (Fontenay-aux[-]Roses, Seine, France: The New Review Editions, 1932). He said of Reavey:

> One of the three or four young after-Joyce Irishmen who have some significance and some promise to offer. There is Samuel Beckett, there is Thomas McGreevy ... Each ... is going very much his own way, choosing his own climate. Beckett is the closest, perhaps as yet too close, to Joyce; but then, he

sees a task for himself in poetry which Joyce has left untouched, – the task perhaps of expressing, as Rimbaud expressed, passionate nihilism, and transcendental vision at one and the same time. (7–8)

Jacob Bronowski's introduction to the English and Irish selections of *The European Caravan* links SB's poetry to Joyce: "In Irish poetry there is a direction given by Joyce, for example in the later work of Beckett" (436). In his preface to SB's poems, Bronowski wrote that Beckett "has adapted the Joyce method to his poetry with original results. His impulse is lyric, but has been deepened through this influence and the influence of Proust and of the historic method" (475).

3 Although McGreevy wrote a review of *Poems: 1928–1931* (1932) by American poet Allen Tate (1899–1979), it was not published in *The New Review* (TCD, MSS 8009/4).

4 "Tanti saluti" (many greetings).

THE DIRECTOR [SIR GEORGE HILL], THE BRITISH MUSEUM

LONDON

22/7/32   4 Ampton St
                        off Gray's Inn Rd
                        [London] W.C. 1

Dear Sir

I wish to apply for permission to use the Reading Room of the British Museum. I have read in the Library of Trinity College Dublin, the National Library, Dublin, the Library of the Ecole Normale Supérieure, Paris, Ste-Geneviève, and the Bibliothèque Nationale.[1]

Generally speaking, I have need of original texts in French and Italian in greater detail than is available in other collections. My immediate concern is with the minor pre-Revolutionary writers of the 18th century. I have been obliged to interrupt a study of Giambattista Vico and Vittorio Alfieri, on which I have been engaged in Paris for some months past, in the absence of various original texts: notably, Vico's Misogallo and Diritto Universale, and Alfieri's Autobiography.[2]

I enclose a letter of introduction from my publishers, Messrs Chatto and Windus.[3]

I trust you may be pleased to approve this application.[4]

Yours faithfully

s/

(Samuel Beckett)

The Director
British Museum
W.C.1
Enc.

TLS; 1 leaf; 1 side, and enclosed TLS from Charles Prentice, Chatto and Windus, 21 July 1932; Archives, British Museum; copy UoR, MS 5047.

1 The Bibliothèque Sainte-Geneviève is the library of the Sorbonne, University of Paris.

2 Italian philosopher of history and social theorist Giambattista Vico (1668–1744) addressed the subject of universal law in his *Diritto universale* (*Universal Right*) in 1720–1722. The Italian poet and dramatist Vittorio Alfieri (1749–1803) was the author of *Il Misogallo* (1799; The Francophobe), a satire in verse and prose, and *Vita di Vittorio Alfieri scritta da esso* (1804; *The Autobiography of Vittorio Alfieri*). SB misidentifies Vico as the author of *Il Misogallo*.

3 Charles Prentice wrote to the Director of the British Museum: "We warmly recommend Mr. Samuel Beckett for the issue of a reader's ticket at the British Museum Reading Room. We have known him personally for the last two years or so and have published a book by him on Proust; we consider that he would be a very fit recipient. He has taught at Trinity College Dublin, where he also took his degree, and at the Ecole Normale Supérieure in Paris. He wishes to study XVIIIth century literature" (22 July 1932, British Museum Archives).

SB's Professor of Italian at TCD, Walter Starkie, later wrote on Alfieri in *The Waveless Plain: An Italian Autobiography* ([New York: E. P. Dutton and Co., 1938] 16).

4 On 23 July 1932 British Museum communication no. 3398 informed SB that he would be issued a reader's ticket for six months; at the top of this communication is noted the number: B 51078, dated 28 July 1932 (British Museum Archives); this was renewed in September 1934, and again in October 1937.

THOMAS McGREEVY
TARBERT, CO. KERRY

4ᵗʰ August [1932]

4 Ampton St
[London] WC. 1

My dear Tom

Glad things went so well between here and Tarbert. That was nice of Jack Yeats. But they are not. Still, if Father was impressed – I don't know what has become of Frank. I write him for his birthday send him papers and hear nothing. Got a friendly letter from Mother, day after you left I think, written in Switzers: 'Come home.'[1] And here I am, perfecting my methodol[og]y of sleep, and little else. No courage for galleries or palaces. I went into St Paul's and thought it was hideous. And circumambulated the enceinte of the tower, and kept my 6$^{\underline{d}}$.[2] I sat on the wharf and watched the little steamers dipping their funnels to get under the bridge, and it opening for a big boat to go under. Très émouvant.[3] That's all I do now – go out about 2 and find some place to sit till the pubs open and get back here about 7 and cook liver and read the Evening News.[4] I couldn't stand the British Museum any more. Plato & Aristotle & the Gnostics finished me.[5] I bought the Origin of Species yesterday for 6$^{\underline{d}}$ and never read such badly written catlap. I only remember one thing: blue-eyed cats are always deaf (correlation of variations).[6] I finished Vanity Fair and Cunt Pointercunt. A very painstalling work. The only thing I won't have forgotten by this day week is Spandrell flogging the foxgloves.[7] I bought Moby Dick to-day for 6$^{\underline{d}}$. That's more like the real stuff. White whales & natural piety.[8] I sleep more and more – 10 hours at a stretch. I wish it were 20. I haven't opened my mouth except in bars & groceries since you left this day week: to haughty barpersons and black-souled grocers. About going where I don't know. I suppose I must go home. I haven't tried to write. The idea itself of writing seems somehow ludicrous. I spilt a bottle of ink instead over the poor Lady with Fan.[9] I went round last Friday to Tavistock Square to the Hogarth Press with letter, Dream, poems and your letter of introduction. But Mr Woolf was away in the country, not expected back till September. The Secretary said she would forward the whole caboodle. She may have for all I know. I have heard nothing since.[10] I rang up the foul fucker MacCarthy about 50 times before getting him at last. He appears to have done nothing. That was last Friday also. I asked him would he write me a chit for Grayson and send it. Yes, he would dictate it that very morning. He would propose Alfieri, he would propose Vico, he would propose me with my book, he would do all that first thing and send it. Since when nothing at all.[11] I left copies of three testimonials chez Truman & Knightley & filled in an enormous form, in which I was asked if I was musical. My qualifications looked really remarkable when I had thought of them all and got them all down. I walked out of the place expecting to be offered the Provostship of Johannesberg [*for* Johannesburg] or somewhere by the first post next morning.[12] Since when (last Friday: all these démarches were taken in a kind of fever last Friday) nothing. I wonder would my Father take me into his office. That is what Frank did. He went home after 3 years in India and went into the office.[13] And now look at him. With a car and a bowler-hat. I see by the Evening News this evening that Nancy is back in Harlem after 3 weeks in the West Indies, where, in Jamaica, she was welcomed by the King of Kingston and fêted by the Marcus Garvey negro Association.[14] Nothing from Titus, nothing from Gilbert, nothing from Jolas.[15] Your letter this evening is the first for a week.

If I could work up some pretext for writing a poem, short-story, or anything at all, I would be all right. I suppose I am all right. But I get frightened sometimes at the idea that the itch to write is cured. I suppose it[']s the fornicating place & its fornicating weather. Lethal thunder and torrents of rain.

This afternoon I sat in St James's Park in a 2$^\text{d}$ transatlantic and was appropriately moved almost to eyedew by a little boy playing at 'empty buses' with a nurse that had exactly the same quality of ruined granite expression as mine had before she married her gardener and became polypara, and calling her Nanny. I had to run away for a piss to the Circus Underground and when I came back to the same chair they were gone.[16] I wanted to get off with Nanny. Soon I will be cabling for my Mother to come and kiss me to sleep. Fall in love to write a lot of poems: have a child to engage a Nanny. She must have a strawberry nose and suck cloves, or at least peppermints. She carried his big ball in a net bag and they shared a green apple.

Perhaps I will screw a free drink from Charles when I bring him back his book. A note accompanied the poems . . 'A new & strange experience . . if only he would escort me on longer flights: so sorry, very very sorry.'[17] Perhaps I will get proofs of poems & Dream from Woolf to-morrow morning, or an offer to instruct the Princess Elizabeth in the Florentine positions. To-day is her mother's birthday. I hope the Duke got back from 'under canvas' all right. I'm well up in Social news. Britannia's truck is 171 feet above her water-line & carries £3000 worth of canvas: only 8 ft lower than the Underground offices! Grandi is here. The pound is at 89.[18]

Well, dear Tom, forgive this Jeremiad. I'm depressed the way a slug-ridden cabbage might be expected to be. I hope something turns up for you in Dublin. And that you get going with Talky.[19] And all the best always. And write soon again. Love Sam

ALS; 3 leaves, 3 sides; year added by AH in ink; TCD, MS 10402/28. *Dating*: year confirmed by *Evening News* of 4 August 1932.

1 McGreevy traveled from Paris to his family home in Tarbert, at the end of July, stopping in London, and then in Dublin, where he saw Jack Yeats. McGreevy's letter to SB has not been found, and so what McGreevy relayed about the Beckett family is not known.

Frank Beckett's birthday was 26 July. Maria Jones Roe Beckett* (known as May, 1871-1950), SB's mother.

Switzer's department store was located at 92 Grafton Street, Dublin.

2 The upper portions of St. Paul's cathedral in London could be reached by stairs; admission to the Whispering Gallery within the lower dome, the exterior Stone Gallery around the base of the dome, and to the Library, cost 6d (Findlay Muirhead, ed., *Short Guide to London* [London: Ernest Benn, 1933] 119).

3 "Très émouvant." (Very moving.)

4 *Evening News* [London] (1881-1980, 1987).

5 Plato (c. 428 - c. 348 BC) and Aristotle (384-322 BC), and the Gnostics (Middle-Eastern thinkers, 2nd century BC - 4th century AD). For SB's reading notes on pre-Socratic philosophy: TCD, MS 10967; Everett Frost and Jane Maxwell, "TCD MS 10967: History of Western Philosophy," *Notes Diverse Holo*, Special issue *SBT/A* 16 (2006) 67-89; Ackerley and Gontarski, *The Grove Companion to Samuel Beckett*, 18, 229-230, 442-443.

6 Charles Darwin (1809-1882) wrote: "Some instances of correlation are quite whimsical: thus cats with blue eyes are invariably deaf; colour and constitutional peculiarities go together" (*On the Origin of Species: A Facsimile of the First Edition* [1859], [Cambridge, MA: Harvard University Press, 1964] 11-12).

7 *Vanity Fair* (1847-1848) by English novelist William Makepeace Thackeray (1811-1865). In *Point Counter Point* (1928) by English novelist and essayist Aldous Leonard Huxley (1894-1963), the character Maurice Spandrell flogs foxgloves in a reaction of outrage against a conventional assumption about God and nature (*Point Counter Point* [Garden City, NJ: Doubleday, Doran and Co., 1928] 343-344).

8 *Moby Dick* (1851) by Herman Melville (1819-1891).

9 SB may refer to a reproduction of *Lady with Fan* (c. 1640-1642) by the Spanish painter Velázquez (né Diego Rodriguez de Silva y Velázquez, 1599-1660) from the Wallace Collection, London.

10 Neither SB's covering letter nor the letter of introduction from McGreevy has been found. The Hogarth Press, located at 52 Tavistock Square, was directed by English writer and publisher Leonard Sidney Woolf (1880-1969) and Virginia Woolf (née Adeline Virginia Stephen, 1882-1941).

SB sent *Dream of Fair to Middling Women* to Chatto and Windus on 29 June 1932 (Charles Prentice to Richard Aldington, 1 July 1932, ICSo Aldington 68/6/7). On 5 July 1932 Prentice sent SB his personal response to the novel:

> It has been some experience reading the "Dream". But it's a strange thing, and I don't know how to react to it from a publishing point of view; we shall have to sit on it in conclave. [...] The party, the P.B. and the shipboard bit out from Caxhaven [*for* Cuxhaven] are entrancing. You're at your best there, right away from Joyce, and on your own, and the beauty and precision of the language moved me from the feet up. (UoR MS 2444 CW letterbook 39/478)

SB reported further on his conversation with Prentice, while the novel was with a second reader: "Charles seemed somehow embarrassed in speaking of it, though he said all the nice things he could lay his tongue to. I think it is as good as rejected" (SB to McGreevy, 14 July [1932], TCD, MS 10402/27). On 19 July 1932, Chatto's response was negative (UoR, MS 2444 CW letterbook 140/164). SB next took the novel and his poems to the Hogarth Press.

SB's timing in respect of the poems was not propitious. John Lehmann (1907-1987) abruptly left his position with the Hogarth Press during August 1932; it was he who had proposed the Hogarth Press modern poetry collection, *New Signatures*, published in February 1932, ed. Michael Roberts (né William Edward Roberts, 1902-1948). In addition, Leonard Woolf and Dorothy Violet Wellesley (née Ashton, 1889-1956), the latter the patron of The Hogarth Living Poets series, had serious differences. As a result, the Hogarth Press published no poetry from July 1932 to March 1933 (John Lehmann, *Autobiography*, I, *The Whispering Gallery* [London: Longmans, Green and Co., 1955] 194-206, 260-261; Leonard Woolf, *Downhill All the Way: An Autobiography of the Years 1919-1939* [London: Hogarth Press, 1967] 176-177).

Normally, fiction submitted to the Hogarth Press was screened by Leonard Woolf or John Lehmann before being given to Virginia Woolf for final approval; from the fact that she was very ill that summer, and in the absence of any record of submission or rejection, John H. Willis (*Leonard and Virginia Woolf as Publishers: The Hogarth Press, 1917-1941*, 1992) conjectures that SB's novel and poetry were rejected by Lehmann "without involving the Woolfs or Wellesley" (John H. Willis, 16 November 1993).

11 English journalist Desmond MacCarthy (1877-1952) was Literary Editor (1921-1927) of *New Statesman*; Editor (1928-1933) of *Life and Letters* (1928-1935); and senior literary critic (from 1928) of *The Sunday Times*. Charles Prentice had sent a copy of *Proust* to MacCarthy following his meeting with SB on the previous evening (Prentice to SB, 21 July 1932, UoR, MS 2444 CW letterbook 140/181).

Cyril Connolly wrote of Desmond MacCarthy: "He was, in every sense, the most generous of men. When he helped young writers, he really did help them, he found them work, lent them money and studied the particular originality through which each could best distinguish himself … His laziness, however, like his unpunctuality, was proverbial" (Desmond MacCarthy, *Memories*, foreword by Cyril Connolly [London: MacGibbon and Kee, 1953] 10).

Grayson and Grayson Publishing Company, 66 Curzon Street, Mayfair, London W1, had just established itself as a family firm; prior to 1932, the firm had been Eveleigh Nash and Grayson.

12 The testimonials were from William Duff Gibbon (1890-1955), Headmaster of Campbell College (1922-1943), Rudmose-Brown, and Jean Thomas (the latter two were enclosed with 29 July 1937; Archives of The University of Cape Town). Truman and Knightley Ltd., Scholastic Agents, 61 Conduit Street, London W1, published *Schools* and the *Journal of Careers*.

SB refers to the University of Witwatersrand, founded in 1922 in Johannesburg, South Africa.

13 "Démarches" (steps).

Frank Beckett was in India from 1927 to 1930, and then entered the firm of Beckett and Medcalf, Quantity Surveyors.

14 The paper announced Nancy Cunard's return to New York following a three-week journey to the West Indies: "In Jamaica last month she was welcomed by the chief magistrate of Kingston and feted by the Marcus Negro Association ... When Miss Cunard was last in New York she lived for a time in a hotel in Harlem to collect material for a book she is writing about Negroes" ("Miss Nancy Cunard: In New York after Another 'Colour Question' Trip," *Evening News* 4 August 1932: 7). Alamont E. DeCosta, OBE, Custos of Kingston, greeted Cunard at the reception given by the Universal Negro Improvement Association at Edelweiss Park ("Miss Nancy Cunard Welcomed at Colourful Function," *The Daily Gleaner* 29 July 1932: 18, 23; Anne Chisholm, *Nancy Cunard: A Biography* [New York: Alfred A. Knopf, 1979] 203).

Marcus Garvey (né Moziah, 1887–1940) founded this group as the Universal Negro Improvement and Conservation Association and African Communities League in 1914; Garvey was deported in November 1927 from the United States, and tried to carry on his mission from Jamaica (E. David Cronon, ed., *Marcus Garvey*, Great Lives Observed [Englewood Cliffs, NJ: Prentice-Hall, 1973] 17, 24).

15 SB had submitted "Dante and the Lobster" (later the opening story in *More Pricks Than Kicks*) to Edward William Titus* (1870–1952), an American publisher then living in Paris, and Editor of *This Quarter*. SB had submitted "Home Olga," an acrostic poem on James Joyce, to Stuart Gilbert, editor of *Contempo* (1931–1934). SB may have expected payment from Eugene Jolas for the publication of his story "Sedendo and Quiescendo." Although SB may have given Jolas something further from the manuscript of *Dream of Fair to Middling Women, transition* did not publish anything more by SB until number 24 (June 1936).

16 "Transatlantic" (Gallicism for "deckchair"). The nanny seen in St. James's Park, London, is compared to SB's nanny, Bibby. By "Circus Underground," SB refers to Piccadilly Circus station.

17 Charles Prentice wrote to SB: "I wish I could follow you for longer flights." He admired "the beauty and terror of 'Spring Song', and the horror of 'There is a Happy Land'." Prentice praised 'Alba 2' as "superb," but felt it was not "so important or significant as these two other poems." Finally, he wrote with regret, "I don't see that Chatto's could do anything with the poems," although for him they meant "the beginning of a rare and strange experience." Prentice apologized: "I am worried at being a disappointment to you again; I am very, very sorry" (27 July 1932, UoR, MS 2444 CW letterbook 140/274). "Spring Song" remains unpublished. "There was a Happy Land" is the first line, and probably the working title, of the poem published as "Sanies 2"; "Alba 2" is the early title of "Enueg 1" (Knowlson, *Damned to Fame*, 648, n. 80; John Pilling, 21 April 1995; see 7 August 1931, n. 1).

18 The 32nd birthday of Elizabeth, Duchess of York (née Elizabeth Bowes-Lyon, 1900–2002), consort of Prince Albert, Duke of York (1895–1952) was 4 August 1932; their daughter Princess Elizabeth (b. 1926, later Queen Elizabeth II) was then six years old. The Royal racing cutter *Britannia* concluded a week of racing at Cowes, The Royal London Yacht Club regatta, on Saturday 6 August 1932 (*The Times* 8 August 1932: 6).

Dino Grandi (1895–1988) was Italy's Minister of Foreign Affairs from 1929 to 1932 and Italy's Ambassador to England from 1932 to 1939; Grandi arrived in London on the

evening of 3 August 1932 to present his credentials to the King (*The Times* 4 August 1932: 10; *The Times* 10 August 1932: 13).
The French franc was 89 to the pound on 4 August 1932 (*The Times* 5 August 1932: 16).

19   McGreevy hoped to interest Lennox Robinson, producer at the Abbey Theatre, in his translation of Alexander Pushkin's "Boris Godunov" (Lennox Robinson, 11 September 1932; TCD, MS 8026).
McGreevy's "Talky" is not identified; SB mentions it again, as "talkie," in his letter to McGreevy, 30 August 1932 (TCD, MS 10402/30).

THOMAS McGREEVY
TARBERT, CO. KERRY

18th [August 1932]   4 Ampton St
                                                                [London] W.C.1

Dear Tom

Glad to hear the book is on the move again, and hope to have good news of it in your next.[1] What you write about an undercurrent of communism is surprising.[2] Or I suppose one ought to be surprised. I think the only thing that would surprise me about Ireland, or any other land, would be to have it established as a more unpleasant site wherein to serve one's life than this core of all faex. And the heat ...[3] I wrote home this evening for my fare home. Write to Cooldrinagh. There is no use my insisting further here. This month of creeping and crawling and sollicitation has yielded nothing but glib Cockney regrets. The book came back from the Hogarth Press, and the poems, with merely the formal rejection slip. Nothing from L.W. He was out of London as I told you when I brought it round. I have good reason to believe that the MS never left London and that in all probability he never saw it. But he must have got my letter. Or perhaps it is his turn for the asylum. Anyhow tant piss.[4] I then brought it to Grayson and Cape. It came back yesterday from Cape. Their reader's report "did not encourage them to make me an offer for publication rights". It would be interesting to see some of these readers' reports.[5] So far no reply from Grayson. I saw Rupert Grayson when I went round, the "author son of Sir Henry". And a proper pudding he appeared. He assured me at least that if they did not take the thing they would tell me the reason why.[6] That will make pleasant reading. I went round to see Derek Verschoyle, Literary Editor of Spectator, he was disguised as a student in T.C.D. while I was still functioning, and gave him the three last poems. Got them back this evening.[7] He had no books for review. But he received me very kindly and gave me a cigarette. I went round yesterday to see Mr Ellis Roberts, gaga in chief of New Statesman. He had no books for review. He thought he might possibly be interested [in] a statement of [for on] Gide, covering all that artists's [sic] vicissitudes from André Walter to Oedipe in the space of not more than 1800 words, or one of similar length of [for on] the modernity of Vico.[8] I promised to do my best. But of course it can't be done. I don't believe I could put a dozen words together on any subject whatsoever. But Mr Roberts received me kindly too, and gave me a cup of tea. My Father very generously sent me a five pound note which I received last Saturday morning. I put it in my drawer, and went yesterday to get it. It was gone. And a temporary lodger was gone also. Whether he took it or whether Mrs Southon or the cretinous Heep it is impossible to know. Mr. S. produced a really superb condition of Cockney distress yesterday evening. Such a thing had never happened before, never in all these years, as the lodger who appears to have his being in the kitchen could testify. Mr S would rather have lost his lower testicle than have such a catastrophe occur. That finishes this villeggiatura. I think I may stay in bed till more comes from the "blue eyes of home".[9] I have not been to see Prentice. I will bring him back his book to-morrow, and start clearing the scuppers.[10] T. & K. sent me notices of jobs in Cornwall, Devon, Derbyshire, here, Sussex, and Basel: this last as English instructor in Berlitz School, 275 francs monthly, 40 hours per week! Stiil [sic], if I were not so tired and eviscerate at the moment, I would apply. Better Basel where love is not than D. D. D. with sentimental salmagundis and other on the mat.[11] [...] I really dread going back to Dublin and all that, but there is nothing else for it at this stage. I was not serious when I said about going into the office. There is no room for another clerk in the office, and even if there were I simply could not do the work.[12] It will have to be private school or training college or else unhandy Andy in the garage and back garden at home. If I could even mend a puncture.

The heat is frightful, culminating to-day in 92 in the shade. I met Arty Hillis, you remember the big-hearted musical morpion at the Ecole, and he lent me a quid and offered to put me up free at Hampstead as from next Monday.[13] But it won't be worth my while changing now. If they don't reimburse me here I won't pay any more rent and I'll clear out as soon as I get my fare. Is there a chance of my seeing you soon in Dublin? I thought of making a dash for Paris, but I am too unbelievably gutless to do anything and my Mother would throw a fit.

So. Write to Cooldrinagh. Love ever

s/ Sam

TLS; 2 leaves; 2 sides; TCD, MS 10402/29. *Dating*: month and year added, possibly in AH, confirmed by description of the weather, and SB's move from London to Dublin (see SB to McGreevy, 30 August 1932, TCD, MS 10402/30); Prentice wrote to Richard Aldington, 5 September 1932, that SB had left for Ireland about ten days before (ICSo, Aldington 68/6/8).

1 McGreevy had resumed work on his novel (Charles Prentice to Richard Aldington, 1 July 1932, ICSo, Aldington 68/6/9; see also 20 December 1931, n. 7).

2 Anti-Communist articles appeared in the Dublin press at this time, for example: "To Check Communism," *The Irish Times* 16 August 1932: 7; "Mr. Cosgrove and

'Communism,'" *The Irish Press* 5 August 1932: 1–2; and a report on the effect of Communist propaganda on theatre ("Before the Footlights," *The Irish Times* 11 August 1932: 4).

3 London was experiencing a heat wave, with a high of 90° on 18 August.
"Faex" (Lat., the dregs).

4 Leonard Woolf had made no comment on *Dream of Fair to Middling Women*, or on the poems, nor did he respond to SB's letter (for further information, see 4 August 1932, n. 10).
"Tant piss" (SB's adaptation of "tant pis" [too bad]).

5 The letter to SB from London publishing house Jonathan Cape has not been found, but a reader's report is in the Cape archives. On 13 August 1932, Edward Garnett (1868–1937) wrote of *Dream of Fair to Middling Women*: "I wouldn't touch this with a barge pole. Beckett probably is a clever fellow, but here he has elaborated a slavish, & rather incoherent imitation of Joyce, most eccentric in language & full of disgustingly affected passages – also *indecent*; this school is damned – & you wouldn't sell the book even on its title. Chatto was right to turn it down" (UoR, Cape; published in edited form in Michael Howard, *Jonathan Cape, Publisher: Herbert Jonathan Cape, G. Wren Howard* [London: Jonathan Cape, 1971] 137).

6 Sir Henry Grayson, Bt., KBE (1865–1951), and his son Brian Grayson (1900–1989) were Directors of Grayson and Grayson; another son, novelist Rupert Stanley Harrison Grayson (1897–1991), was Literary Advisor.

7 Derek Hugo Verschoyle (1911–1973) was Literary Editor of *The Spectator* from 1932 to 1940; he matriculated at Trinity College Dublin in 1929, but did not take a degree. It is not known which poems SB submitted.

8 Richard Ellis Roberts (1879–1953) was Literary Editor of the *New Statesman* from 1930 to 1932; he continued as a regular contributor when he became Literary Editor of *Time and Tide* (1933 to 1934) and *Life and Letters* (November 1934 to 1935).
André-Paul-Guillaume Gide (1869–1951) wrote *Les Cahiers d'André Walter* (1891; *The Notebooks of André Walter*); among his later works was the prose play *Oedipe* (1931; *Oedipus*).
Giambattista Vico.

9 Mrs. Southon was SB's landlady. The person to whom SB refers has not been identified, although "Heep" alludes to Uriah Heep in Dickens's *David Copperfield* (1849–1850). Mr. S. is Mr. Southon.
"Villeggiatura" (holiday).
For possible sources of the "blue eyes of home," see John Pilling, *A Companion to "Dream of Fair to Middling Women"* (Tallahassee, FL: Journal of Beckett Studies Books, 2004) 78.

10 Prentice had lent D. H. Lawrence's *Apocalypse* to SB (15 August 1931, n.5), but SB may be referring to another book.

11 Truman and Knightley (see 4 August 1932, n. 12). "D.D.D." (Dear Dirty Dublin).

12 Frank Beckett worked in their father's quantity surveying firm, Beckett and Medcalf.

13 Arthur Henry Macnamara Hillis* (1905–1997), lawyer and international economist, had been in SB's year at Trinity College Dublin. He may have visited SB at the Ecole Normale Supérieure in Paris.
"Morpion" (literally a crab louse, but here a mild form of student abuse).

THOMAS McGREEVY
TARBERT, CO. KERRY

13th [September 1932]   Cooldrinagh
                                         Foxrock, [Co. Dublin]

My dear Tom

I will do all I can to raise the two quid when I go into town this morning on my father's bicycle. I don't think Frank would refuse me. Anyhow I owe you about 25/- for transition, and I wish I could have paid you before, but I have found no work here and depend on my father for everything. There is a prospect of a few grinds turning up at the end of the month. Ruddy has been very good recommending me and I wish there were no P.B. in Dream.[1] No news from Grayson, and I hesitate to write them a stinger. But now it is a good three weeks since they promised me their decision immediately. Rickword never acknowledged the poems.[2] Nothing seems to come off. I made a desperate effort to get something started on Gide but failed again.[3] I began a poem yesterday, the first since Home Olga, a blank unsighted kind of thing, but looking at it it is clear that it can never turn out to be more than mildly entertaining at the best. The old story – ardour and fervour absent or faked so that what happens may be slick enough verse but not a poem at all.[4] I seem to spend a lot of time in the National Gallery, looking at the Poussin Entombment and coming stealthily down the stairs into the charming toy brightness of the German room to the Brueghels and the Masters of Tired Eyes and Silver Windows. The young woman of Rembrandt is splendid.[5] I hope we may meander through sometime together. Cissie lucky woman has gone back to Germany with Deirdre leaving Sally here on the job. We managed a good afternoon together before she left, in the gallery and then the Moira and then pubs.[6] I met R. N. D. Wilson last Sunday chez Percy Ussher, and he was full of enthusiasm about your Eliot. I thought there was not much to him and felt vaguely uneasy with him. He read or declaimed acres of his verse, and to be sure there were odds and ends of agreeablenesses here and there. He has nice thick shining black hair and his little prose-poem diapason seems to be keyed to A. E.'s. A. E. & W. B. play a lot of croquet together at Riversdale, Rathfarnham, and the former always wins by a mile. I suppose James Starkey holds the stakes. Austin Clarke and Monk Gibbon seek on the bank a definition of obscenity.[7] I wish I had seen "Things that are Caesar's"[.] "Temporal Powers" seems to be the usual rubbish.[8] I set out on Saturday afternoon to see Jack Yeats, and then en route changed my mind and went for a ride along the coast instead. Pretending to like fresh air and salt water I got the old intercostal rheumatism back, this time on the left side. But it is going away and I am denied even the excitement of a little dry pleurisy in safe surroundings. For me also the alternative seems to be here or Paris, and not having heard anything from Titus, though there are a number of counts on which he might write, I have no idea how I stand with him. Won't the Copulation Intellectuelle be functioning?[9] Anyhow be sure and let me know if you are passing thorugh [sic] and in the meantime alles gut and the quiet unfurling of your book that I know you want.[10]

>Love ever
>s/ Sam

TLS; 1 leaf, 1 side; TCD, MS 10402/32. *Dating*: SB's meeting with Grayson is reported in his letter to McGreevy 18 [August 1932]; this meeting "a fortnight ago" is recounted in SB's letter to McGreevy of [3 September 1932] (TCD, MS 10842/31). The present letter indicates that it has been over three weeks since SB has seen Grayson about *Dream of Fair to Middling Women*, and SB's letter to McGreevy of 8 October 1932 mentions that it has been "over 6 weeks."

1 "Grinds" (colloq., tutoring jobs). SB had represented Rudmose-Brown as the Polar Bear in *Dream of Fair to Middling Women*.

2 SB wrote on Saturday [3 September 1932] to McGreevy: "I saw the Brothers G. a fortnight ago now in London and they promised me a speedy decision. I don't know whether to think the delay good or bad." In the same letter, SB said of the poems: "I don't expect them to be taken on by Wishart, but I wish I had sent them earlier and that I had seen Rickword in London. It was Grayson put me on to them" (TCD, MS 10402/31).

London publisher Ernest Edward Wishart (1902–1987). In 1932, the English poet and critic Edgell Rickword (1898–1982) worked occasionally for Wishart, and had not yet joined the firm full-time; he had just translated Marcel Coulon, *Poet under Saturn: The Tragedy of Verlaine* (1932).

3 In February 1932, SB had proposed a monograph on Gide to Charles Prentice; Prentice responded: "Your idea of a short study of Gide is a most attractive one, but we don't see how we could be of any use to you about it just now," suggesting that SB write "the essay as a long article to appear in two or more parts" (8 February 1932, UoR, MS 2444 CW letterbook 136/513). SB pursued the matter with Ellis Roberts at the *New Statesman* (SB to McGreevy, 18 [August 1932], n. 8). SB wrote to McGreevy: "I'm afraid to start anything on Gide, though I have all the notes & quotations I want without opening a text"; he added: "How would 'paralysed in ubiquity' do for Gide?" (SB to McGreevy, Saturday [3 September 1932], TCD, MS 10402/31).

4 SB wrote to McGreevy: "Typing out the poems yet again and fiddling about with them I felt more than ever that all the early ones – all the Caravan ones – were fake and that nothing could be done with them and that it was only à partir de Whoroscope that they began to be worth anything. I know you are good enough to disagree with me, but I felt it more & more" (Saturday [3 September 1932], TCD, MS 10402/31). "A partir de Whoroscope" (from *Whoroscope* on). "Home Olga" was written for Joyce and submitted to Stuart Gilbert, Editor of *Contempo*. The new poem is a draft of "Serena 1" (Beckett, *Echo's Bones* [15–27]).

5 For SB, *The Entombment* (NGI 214) by Nicolas Poussin (1594–1665) was "extraordinary. I never saw such blue & purple, such lyrical colour" (Saturday [3 September 1932], TCD, MS 10402/31). In the German room were *A Peasant Wedding* (NGI 911) by Pieter Brueghel the younger (c. 1564 – c. 1638), and *Christ in the House of Martha and Mary* (NGI 513) by Peter Paul Rubens (1577–1640) with Jan Brueghel (1568–1625). SB also mentions *Portrait of an Old Lady* (NGI 903) by the early Flemish painter known as the Master of the Tired Eyes (fl. c. 1540) and *A Portrait of a Young Lady* (NGI 808) by Harmensz Rembrandt van Rijn (1606–1669). The painter of *Scenes from the Life of St. Augustine* (NGI 823) is identified in the 1945 catalogue of the National Gallery of Ireland as the Master of the Silver Windows (c. 1550); later catalogues identify him as the Master of St. Augustine (c. 1500) (Thomas MacGreevy, *Pictures in the Irish National Gallery* [London: B. T. Batsford, 1945] 11–12; James White, ed., *National Gallery of Ireland: Catalogue of the Paintings* [Dublin: National Gallery of Ireland, 1971] 197; *National Gallery of Ireland: Illustrated Summary Catalogue of Paintings*, intro. Homan Potterton [Dublin: Gill and Macmillan, 1981] 107).

6 Cissie Sinclair returned to Kassel with her youngest daughter Deirdre; her daughter Sally remained in Dublin. The Moira Hotel and Restaurant, 15 Trinity Street, Dublin.

7 The first collection of Northern Irish poet R. N. D. Wilson (né Robert Noble Denison Wilson 1899-1953) was *The Holy Wells of Orris and other Poems* (1927); John Hewitt's obituary describes Wilson as a "small dark man with something of the appearance of a little bird full chested with its song" (*Dublin Magazine* 28.2 [April-June 1952] 54-55). SB compares Wilson's poetry to that of AE. SB met Wilson at the Dublin home of Percival Arland Ussher* (known as Percy to mid-1937, then as Arland, 1899-1980), Irish writer and philosopher.

The home of William Butler Yeats (1865-1939), "Riversdale," Willbrook, Rathfarnham, Co. Dublin, had a croquet lawn where Yeats played with enthusiasm that AE, among other regular guests, "rearranged their visiting hours to avoid a game" (Ann Saddlemyer, *Becoming George: The Life of Mrs. W. B. Yeats* [Oxford: Oxford University Press, 2002] 453-454). SB also refers to poets Austin Clarke and William Monk Gibbon (1896-1987).

8 *Things That are Caesar's* by Irish playwright Paul Vincent Carroll (1900-1968) opened on 15 August and won the Abbey Theatre Prize in 1932. *Temporal Powers* by Teresa Deevy (1894-1963) opened at the Abbey Theatre on 12 September; Joseph Holloway said that none of the characters "became real on the stage" (Holloway, *Joseph Holloway's Irish Theatre*, II: *1932-1937*, ed. Hogan and O'Neill, 216).

9 In May 1932 SB had undertaken the translation of Arthur Rimbaud's "Le Bateau ivre" ("The Drunken Boat") for Edward Titus; SB had received payment, but no word of publication (for further background see Samuel Beckett, *Drunken Boat*, ed. James Knowlson and Felix Leakey [Reading: Whiteknights Press, 1976] 7-10).

More recently, SB had translated poems and essays for the surrealist number of *This Quarter* 5.1 [September 1932]), guest-edited by André Breton (1896-1966) (for a list of SB's translations: Raymond Federman and John Fletcher, *Samuel Beckett: His Works and His Critics, An Essay in Bibliography* [Berkeley: University of California Press, 1970] 92-93).

SB had also submitted his story "Dante and the Lobster" to Titus.

10 "Alles gut" (all the best).

GEORGE REAVEY

LONDON

8/10/32
Cooldrinagh
Foxrock
Co Dublin

Dear Reavey

Thank you for your letter. I'll excavate for a poem for you one of these dies diarrhoeae. I suppose it's the usual case of honour and glory. So much piss. I have an idea I enshrined

Primrose Hill and Crystal Palace seen thence, as though I were Marcel Schwob peering through incipient cataract at a red moutier, in a long sad one that does me great credit. Très émouvant. There is also a drill's arse and Daniel Defoe.[1] They coexist very amiably. All Uebersetzungen gratefully received & done in the eye into Dublin stutter.[2]

The novel doesn't go. Shatton & Windup thought it was wonderful but they couldn't they simply could not. The Hogarth Private Lunatic Asylum rejected it the way Punch would. Cape was écoeuré in pipe & cardigan and his Aberdeen terrier agreed with him. Grayson has lost it or cleaned himself with it. Kick his balls off, they are all over 66 Curzon St, W.1.[3]

I'll be here till I die, creeping along genteel roads on a stranger's bike.

Beautiful greetings to Bronowski when and if and tell him I had a simply wonderful time in Ampton St till a coinmate poor fellow whose need was quicker than mine happened to come across a five pun note tossing and turning in my Milner valise and – what do you think – took it unto himself. Ergo ... [4]

Things to see: Desmond Savage Hazlitt Lamb Wodehouse Milton Makepeace MacCarthy and the sparrows at the Spaniards.[5]

    Salut

      s/ Sam Beckett

TLS; 1 leaf; 1 side; TxU.

1 "Dies diarrhoeae" (literally, days of diarrhea, echoing the *Dies Irae* of the requiem Mass).

   SB refers to his poem "Serena 1" in which he mentions London's Primrose Hill (London NW, north of Regent's Park Zoo) and the Crystal Palace (built for The Great Exhibition of 1851, and in 1854 moved to Sydenham Hill in London SW).

   Mayer-André-Marcel Schwob (1867–1905), French medievalist, critic, short-story writer, and translator. In his journal, *Premières Esquisses*, Schwob writes: "Je connais deux espèces de gens; des hommes-microscopes et des hommes[-]télescopes" (I know two types of people: microscope-men and telescope-men); according to Schwob, microscope men could drown in a glass of water, telescope men find outlines in every-thing (Pierre Champion, *Marcel Schwob et son temps* [Paris: Bernard Grasset, 1927] 26–27). Schwob's story "L'Etoile de bois" describes a village in minute detail, including a mon-astery seen in a vision of rosy mist: "un moutier, semblable à une brume vermeille ébarbée, où Saint-Georges, armé de sang, plongeait sa lance dans la gueule d'un dragon de grès rouge" (a monastery, like a neatly trimmed rosy mist where St. George, armed with blood, was plunging his lance into the mouth of a red sandstone dragon) (*Cosmopolis* 8 [22 October 1897] 104; rpt. *L'Etoile de bois* [Paris: Editions du Boucher, 2003] 13).

"Serena 1" ends with "peering," a close-up image of a housefly on a window.

"Très émouvant" (very moving). The poem mentions "the burning b.t.m. of George the drill" (a West African species of baboon) as well as British novelist and essayist Daniel Defoe (né Foe, 1660–1731). "B.t.m." (children's language, bottom).

2 "Uebersetzungen" (translations).

3 Chatto and Windus, the Hogarth Press, Jonathan Cape, and Grayson and Grayson had turned down or failed to respond to SB's *Dream of Fair to Middling Women*. Jonathan Cape was "écoeuré" (disgusted). Rupert Grayson had not yet replied.

The London weekly satirical magazine *Punch* was published from 1841 to 1992 and from 1996 to 2002.

4 Bronowski had suggested that SB stay with Mrs. Southon in Ampton Street. A manufacturer of safes by the name of Milner has been identified, but not of valises or briefcases.

"Pun" (Ir. colloq., pound).

5 Reavey had begun his Bureau Littéraire Européen in Paris and was developing an office in London for his several publishing ventures (18 April 1986: notes of Emile Delavenay). Delavenay (1905–2000) was French Lecteur from the Ecole Normale Supérieure at Gonville and Caius College Cambridge (1927–1929) where he met Reavey who was then a student. When Reavey went to France, Delavenay introduced Reavey to Thomas McGreevy (Emile Delavenay, *Témoignage: d'un village savoyard au village mondial [1905–1991]* [La Calade: Diffusion EDISUD, 1992] 117). In his draft memoirs, Reavey says, however, that he met McGreevy through Alan Duncan (TxU).

SB facetiously gives to Desmond MacCarthy the names of English writers: Richard Savage (1697–1743), William Hazlitt (1778–1830), Charles Lamb (1775–1834), P. G. Wodehouse (né Pelham Grenville Wodehouse, 1881–1973), John Milton (1608–1674), William Makepeace Thackeray (1811–1863).

The Spaniards Inn on Hampstead Heath was built in 1585 as a residence for the Spanish Ambassador; it was opened as an inn in the middle of the eighteenth century by two Spanish brothers and later became well known as a pub. Nearby streets are named for it.

6 "Salut" (greetings).

THOMAS McGREEVY

TARBERT, CO. KERRY

8/10/32
                                            Cooldrinagh
                                            Foxrock [Co. Dublin]

Dear Tom

Forgive me for not answering the first of your last two letters. I did write, but it turned out such a jeremiad that I refrained from posting it. Don't for God's sake bother your head about the 2 quid. Frank is not in that hurry. Wait for a flusher time. I got a few grinds and am doing a few at the moment and will get paid one of these fine days, early next week probably, and can let you have then what I owe you, which is about one quid ten as well as I remember. It is rotten to hear things are so difficult and that the book has slowed down again. I don't think you would have stuck the Irish Press very long, but it would have been something to be going on with.[1] Dublin stagnates as usual. I occasionally go in on the bike for the ride and the wayside pubs, but seldom, and on the surface at least she seems unmoved by all the goingson.

Frank had to go down to Galway on a job and he very decently stood me the trip with him and so I saw Galway at last. A grand little magic grey town full of sensitive stone and bridges and water. We went on to Mallaranny and spent a day walking on Achill right out over the Atlantic. We came back all along L. Mask and right through the mountainous Joyce's country and between L.s [sic] Mask and Corrib. Everywhere we went Croagh Patrick was standing up over everything, with an Arrarat [*for* Ararat] cloud always somewhere near the chapel on the summit. Altogether it was an unforgettable trip and much too short, through bog and mountain scenery that was somehow far more innocent and easy and obvious than the stealthy secret variety we have here. I would like to go back to Galway and spend a little time there. There was some damn retreat on the Saturday morning we were there so we couldn't get into the Dominican and Franciscan churches where there are supposed to be some remarkable mosaics. But we saw

St Nicholas's which is charming and where they say Cristoforo C. had a dish of mass before committing his indiscretion.[2]

Yes, I had that letter from Reavey. He also condescended to mention that he had heard "rumours" of my novel when speaking to publishers and that he would have some translations for me in the near future if I was wise enough to keep in touch with him.[3] Did I tell you Gilbert acknowledged Home Olga at last with assurance of its inclusion among the suceculeries of Contempo? Hope ev[e]ry-one may be pleased.[4] And that Titus wrote about Dante and the L. which he says pleased him and which he proposes to run in his next number?[5] Nothing at all from Grayson. It is now well over 6 weeks since he viva voce assured me a speedy decision. I wrote him a polite note a fortnight and more ago which he did not acknowl-edge. So by this same post he is getting a stinger and may the devil look after his own and take the hindmost and in fact do all the parlour tricks that may be necessary. I have an idea he may try and do the dirty. He has no background and I have nothing to show that he has any of my property. Titus enquired after the book and suggested my sending it to him. Better that than gar nix. But I'd rather send him the poems. Rickword never acknowledged them.[6] To hell with them all. Titus has benn [sic] a monument of courtesy compared with the most of them.

[...] Cissie has gone back to her Mann, bringing the big Ibach with her. It had all that salt air for nothing. They have found a new flat now, with twice the sun and half the rent. She says there is a chaise longue there for me. But I don't know what that means. Peggy read the transition sublimen and said for God's sake to spell pfennig with two enns next time! I had a letter from Nancy from Lot, on her way back to Paris, wanting to get in touch. Perhaps she has some work. Titus's quick little blurb in his preface to his surréaliste number might get me some clients.[7]

This obstinate sobriety in all modes here is beginning to hurt seriously, but I haven't the guts to make a dash for it again out into the cold cold world. You must manage at least one evening in Dublin if you are going through. I want very much to see you and talk over the prospects in Paris.

[...]

I'm enclosing the only bit of writing that has happened to me since Paris and that does me no particular credit as far as I can judge.[8] I'm enchanted with Joseph Andrews, Jacques and the Vicar of W. in one.[9] The reminiscences of Diderot interest me very much, the ironical replis and giving away of the show pari passu with the show, as when he executes a purely professional apostrophe to Vanity and then observes that something had to be done to spin out a chapter that otherwise would have been too short. And the hero is suggested admirably, almost a physical weight on the page, all thighs and sex, palpitant, like Aminta or a Marivaux prétendant, nothing of the volupté pensée and pensante of Diderot. Such a thing never to have read! I think the very short chapters are an idea.[10]

Can you recommend me an informative book on Dutch painting?[11]

Love ever
s/ Sam

I put pen to this
vague carmen that
is so much pleasanter easier
more'n my line nor prose
and my kakoethes or as they say evil propensity
ain't got Gott sei dank no butt
what I mean is I don't love her

nor scape of land sea or sky
nor our Saviour particularly
I haven't signed any contract either I couldn't quite bring it off
no my algos is puss in the corner I just feel fervent
ardent in a vague general way
and my lil erectile brain God help her
thuds like a butcher's sex

    without the grand old British Museum
    Thales and the Aretino
    on the bosom of the Regent's Park the phlox
    crackles under the thunder
    scarlet beauty in our world dead fish adrift
    all things full of gods
    pressed down and bleeding a weaver bird is tangerine
      the harpy is past caring
    the condor likewise in his mangy boa
    they stare out across monkey-hill the elephants
    Ireland
    the light creeps down their old home canyon
    sucks me aloof to that old reliable
    the burning b.t.m. of George the drill
    ah across the way an adder
    broaches her rat
    white as snow
    in her dazzling oven strom of peristalsis
    limae labor

    ah father father that art in heaven

    I find me taking the Crystal Palace
    for the Isles of the Blest from Primrose Hill
    alas I must be that kind of person

hence in Ken Wood who shall find me
my quiet breath in the midst of thickets
none but the most quarried lovers

I surprise me moved by the many a funnel hinged
for the obeisance to Tower Bridge
the viper's curtsey to and from the City
until at dusk a lighter
blind with pride
tosses aside the scarf of the bascules
then in the grey hold of the ambulance
throbbing on the brink ebb of sighs
then I hug me below among the people
until a guttersnipe blast his cerned eyes
demanding have I done with the Mirror
I stump off in a fearful rage under Married Men's Quarters
Bloody Tower
and afar off at all speed screw me up Wren's giant bully
and wish to Christ caged panting on the platform
the urn beacon aloft
that I were Daniel Defoe no less

but then again as I say
who is likely to run across me in Ken Wood

my brother the fly
common house-fly
creeping out of darkness into light
fastens on his place in the sun
whets his six legs
revels in his planes his poisers
it is the autumn of his life
he could not serve typhoid and mammon

TLS; 4 leaves, 4 sides; includes untitled poem, later published as "Serena 1" (with the omission of the first stanza; there are variants with respect to published version); TCD, MS 10402/33.

1 McGreevy was working on his novel; he had hoped to do some writing for *The Irish Press*, but had not yet begun (SB to McGreevy, 8 November 1931, n. 4).

2 Connemara is a district in the west of County Galway. Mallaranny is the town to the east of Achill Island, the largest island off the Irish coast, west of the Curraun Peninsula. The Joyce country is to the north and west of Galway, a desolate land of rock, bog, and mountain that includes Lough Mask and Lough Corrib; it is named for the Joyce family of this region, not for James Joyce. Croagh Patrick (2,510 feet), known as the "holy mountain" because of the associations with St. Patrick; a church at its summit is a place of pilgrimage. Ararat alludes to the mountain on which Noah's ark is said to have come to rest.

The Franciscan Friary and the Dominican church (St. Mary's on the Hill) in Galway are not notable for mosaics, but the Dominican church in nearby Claddagh has a mosaic depicting a church on a hill, a boat, and a young man and woman. Galway's St. Nicholas-of-Myra church, founded in 1320, is the largest medieval church in Ireland; while myth has it that Christopher Columbus (1451–1506) prayed there before sailing to America, it is more likely he stopped in Galway during a voyage to Iceland in 1477 (Gianni Granzotto, *Christopher Columbus*, tr. Stephen Sartarelli [Norman: University of Oklahoma Press, 1985] 36–37).

3 Reavey had moved to London. Reavey's letter to SB has not been found.

4 Stuart Gilbert edited *Contempo* (1931–1934) in Chapel Hill, North Carolina; "Home Olga," written for James Joyce's birthday in 1932, was published in the last issue of *Contempo* (3.13 [February 1934] 3).

"Suceculeries" (bumsuckings).

5 Edward Titus published "Dante and the Lobster" in *This Quarter* 5.2 (December 1932) 222–236.

6 SB's stinger to Grayson is not extant. At the very least, SB wanted his manuscript returned so that he could send it to Titus. "Gar nix" (Ger. colloq., from "gar nichts" [nothing at all]); see also Pilling, *A Companion to "Dream of Fair to Middling Women*," 37.

Rickword still had the manuscript of the poems sent on 30 August 1932.

7 The Sinclairs' piano was an Ibach.

Peggy Sinclair's comment refers to SB's story "Sedendo et Quiescendo," which describes Smeraldina approaching Belacqua's train; SB writes that her platform ticket had cost "ten Pfenigs" (*for* "Pfennige" [pennies]) (*transition* 21 [March 1932] 13).

The texts that Nancy Cunard wanted SB to translate were related to Nancy Cunard, ed., *Negro, Anthology Made by Nancy Cunard, 1931–1933* (London: Published by Nancy Cunard at Wishart and Co., 1934).

In his introduction to the surrealist number of *This Quarter*, Edward Titus wrote: "We shall not speak of the difficulties experienced in putting the material placed at our disposal into English, but we cannot refrain from singling out Mr. Samuel Beckett's work for special acknowledgement. His rendering of the Eluard and Breton poems in particular is characterizable only in superlatives" ("Editorially: By the Way of Introducing This Surrealist Number," 5.1 [September 1932] 6).

8 Most of the poem enclosed was published as "Serena 1."

9 *The Adventures of Joseph Andrews and his Friend, Mr Abraham Adams* (1742) by English novelist Henry Fielding (1701–1754) is compared by SB to *Jacques le fataliste et son maître* (1796; *Jacques, the Fatalist*), a novel by French writer Denis Diderot (1713–1784) and *The Vicar of Wakefield* (1766), a novel by Irish writer Oliver Goldsmith (1728–1774).

10 SB refers to *Joseph Andrews*. Fielding's novel is divided into four books, each with short chapters; the self-referential narrator weighs his narrative choices as well as his readers' possible responses. "Replis" (foldings, meanderings). Both chapter headings and narrative interruptions point to the events before they unfold.

In the apostrophe "O Vanity!" introduced at the end of Book I, chapter 15, the narrator writes: "Nor will it give me any Pain, if thou [Vanity] should'st prevail on the Reader to censure this Digression as errant Nonsense: for know to thy Confusion, that I have introduced thee for no other Purpose than to lengthen out a short Chapter; and so I return to my History" (Henry Fielding, *Joseph Andrews*, ed. Martin C. Battestin [Middletown, CT: Wesleyan University Press, 1967] 69–70).

SB's comparison of Joseph Andrews with the character of Aminta may refer to the pastoral play, *L'Aminta* (1581), by Italian author Torquato Tasso (1544–1595), or to a "prétendant" (suitor) of French dramatist Pierre Carlet de Chamblaine de Marivaux (1688–1763).

"Palpitant" (quivering). "Volupté pensée and pensante" (voluptuousness as thought, voluptuousness as thinking).

11 It is not known if McGreevy made a suggestion.

THOMAS McGREEVY
TARBERT, CO. KERRY

18ᵗʰ Oct. 32   Cooldrinagh
                                              Foxrock [Co. Dublin]

My dear Tom

To know you like the poem cheers me up.¹ Genuinely my impression was that it was of little worth because it did not represent a necessity. I mean that in some way it was 'facultatif' and that I would have been no worse off for not having written it. Is that a very hairless way of thinking of poetry? Quoi qu'il en soit I find it impossible to abandon that view of the matter.² Genuinely again my feeling is, more and more, that the greater part of my poetry, though it may be reasonably felicitous in its choice of terms, fails precisely because it is facultatif. Whereas the 3 or 4 I like, and that seem to have been drawn down against the really dirty weather of one of these fine days into the burrow of the 'private life', Alba & the long Enueg & Dortmunder & even Moly, do not and never did give me that impression of being construits.[3] I cannot explain very well to myself what they have that distinguishes them from the others, but it is something arborescent or of the sky, not Wagner, not clouds on wheels; written above an abscess and not out of a cavity, a statement and not a description of heat in the spirit to compensate for pus in the spirit. Is not that what Eluard means?

> Quel est le rôle de la racine?
> Le désespoir a rompu tous ses liens.[4]

I'm not ashamed to stutter like this with you who are used to my wild way of failing to say what I imagine I want to say and who understand that until the gag is chewed fit to swallow or spit out the mouth must stutter or rest. And it needs a more stoical mouth than mine to rest.

There is a kind of writing corresponding with acts of fraud & debauchery on the part of the writing-shed. The moan I have more & more to make with mine is there – that it is nearly all trigged up, in terrain, faute d'orifice, heat of friction and not the spontaneous combustion of the spirit to compensate the pus & the pain that threaten its economy, fraudulent manoeuvres to make the cavity do what it can't do – the work of the abscess.[5] I don't know why the Jesuitical poem that is an end in itself and justifies all the means should disgust me so much. But it does – again – more & more. I was trying to like Mallarmé again the other day, & couldn't, because it's Jesuitical poetry, even the Swan & Hérodiade.[6] I suppose I'm a dirty low-church P. even in poetry, concerned with integrity in a surplice. I'm in mourning for the integrity of a pendu's emission of semen, what I find in Homer &

Dante & Racine & sometimes Rimbaud, the integrity of the eyelids coming down before the brain knows of grit in the wind.[7]

Forgive all this? Why is the spirit so pus-proof and the wind so avaricious of its grit?

I never see nor write to nor hear from nor am seen by Ethna MacC. now. 'Tis better thus!' I incline to the opinion that when it is not possible to see people simply it is more satisfactory to wait till they turn up in the memory. I can't see her and I can't imagine her. Occasionally it happens that I remember her and then, presto! I had nothing up my sleeve nor she in her amethyst bodice.[8]

The Grayson Bros. were stimulated by my multicuspid stinker to return my MS. 'circumscribed appeal . . Gratuitous "strength"'! What is that? I replied soliciting favour of readers['] reports. Reply to the effect that there was no written record of condemnation, that my book, an unusual, he might say, privilege, had been read by 3 most distinguished readers and discussed verbally with the Fratellacci; that their advice to me frankly and without the least desire to wound was to lay aside Dream altogether, forget it ever happened, be a good boy in future and compose what I was well-fitted to compose – a best-seller.[9] When I had done that they would be interested to hear from me again. So I dried my eyes and sent it off to Titus, who has not acknowledged it yet. I tremble lest I should push him too far.[10]

Another scribble from Nancy from the Cunégonde on subject of touch. She has some Breton & Eluard MSS. I wrote saying it was always a pleasure to translate Eluard & Breton.[11]

I'm sorry I can't enclose what I would like to in this letter, because I have not yet touché the filthy commodity.[12] As soon as I do I will.

Talking with a French woman here, Mme. Redmond, married to a Doctor, I was advised to address myself to Mr Blumenfeld, editor of Daily Express, who is a bussom friend of hers and to whom she would be most happy to give me a letter of introduction overflowing with boniments of all kinds. Acting on same I composed last night an irresistible document. I may post it to-day – and I may not.[13] My cuticle urges me to hibernate here, but the weight of minuses is beginning to bow me down. I walk immeasurably & unrestrainedly, hills and dales, all day, and back with a couple of pints from the Powerscourt Arms under my Montparnasse belt through the Homer dusk. Often very moving and it helps to swamp the usual palpitations. But I disagree with you about the gardenish landscape. The lowest mountains here terrify me far more than anything I saw in Connemara or Achill. Or is it that a garden is more frightening than a waste? I walked across Prince William's Seat, a low mountain between the Glencullen & Glencree rivers, and was reduced almost to incontinence by the calm secret hostility. I ran down into Enniskerry.[14]

They are doing Romeo & Juliet at the Gate when they have finished idealizing Wilde's husband. I lacked the spunk to go to Peer Gynt. Such wonderful lighting, my dear, all coming from behind instead of in front. Imagine that! And Grieg without mercy.[15]

Donagh Bryan is dead.[16] Love ever.

Sam

ALS; 2 leaves, 4 sides; McGreevy, TCD, MS 10402/34.

1 With his letter of 8 October 1932, SB had sent McGreevy an untitled poem, later published (without the first stanza) as "Serena 1."

2 "Facultatif" (optional).
"Quoi qu'il en soit" (Whatever the case).

3 The poems "Alba," "Enueg 1," and "Dortmunder" were published in *Echo's Bones* ([18], [12–15], and [19]). "Moly" was published under the title "Yoke of Liberty" (Harvey, *Samuel Beckett*, 314; as "Moly," this poem is in the archives of *Poetry Magazine* (ICU) and in the A. J. Leventhal collection (TxU)).
"Construits" (deliberately constructed).

4 SB alludes to the work of Richard Wagner.

These lines are from a poem by French surrealist poet Paul Eluard (1895-1952), "L'Invention" (Paul Eluard, *Capitale de la douleur* [Paris: Gallimard, 1964] 12-13); they are translated by SB as "What is the role of the root? / Despair has broken all his bonds" (Paul Eluard, *Thorns of Thunder: Selected Poems*, tr. Samuel Beckett, Denis Devlin, David Gascoyne *et al.*, ed. George Reavey [London: Europa Press and Stanley Nott, 1936] 8).

5 "Terrain" (soil or ground); "faute d'orifice" (for want of an orifice).

6 Poems of Stéphane Mallarmé (1842-1898). "Swan" refers to the sonnet, "Le vierge, le vivace et le bel aujourd'hui" (The Virgin, Beautiful and Lively Day) (*Oeuvres complètes*, I, ed. Bertrand Marchal, Bibliothèque de la Pléiade [Paris: Gallimard, 1998] 36-37; "Sonnet" in Stéphane Mallarmé, *New and Collected Poems*, tr. Roger Fry, with commentaries by Charles Mauron, The New Classics Series [New York: New Directions Books, 1951] 67). Mallarmé's "Hérodiade" exists in several forms (*Oeuvres complètes*, I, 17-22, 85-89, 135-152).

7 P. is Protestant. "Pendu" (hanged man).

8 Ethna MacCarthy. "Tis better thus" may allude to the play *All for Love* by John Dryden (1631-1700); referring to Antony, who is dead, Cleopatra says: "And, oh! 'tis better far to have him thus, / Than see him in her arms" (John Dryden, *All for Love* and *The Spanish Fryar*, ed. William Strunk, Jr. [Boston, D. C. Heath and Company, 1911] 144).

9 Although Charles Prentice wrote to Richard Aldington that he had heard Grayson and Grayson were going to publish *Dream of Fair to Middling Women*, they did not (5 September 1932, ICSo, Aldington 68/6/8). SB's letters to Grayson and Grayson are not extant. "Fratellacci" (wretched brothers).

10 SB sent *Dream of Fair to Middling Women* to Edward Titus, who was Editor of *This Quarter* from 1929 through 1932, and Editor of the Black Manikin Press from mid-1926 to spring 1932.

11 Cunard wrote to SB from Cunèges, in the Dordogne, conflated by SB with Cunégonde, a character in *Candide ou l'optimisme* (1759) by Voltaire (né François-Marie Arouet, 1694-1778). SB translated "Murderous Humanitarianism" by the "Surrealist Group" in Paris, a group which included André Breton and Paul Eluard (Cunard, ed., *Negro, Anthology*, 574-575). Although SB writes to McGreevy that Cunard plans to send him "Eluard & Breton," as she does in December 1932 (21 November 1932, TCD, MS 10402/38), there is no indication that SB translated other work by either writer for Cunard. He had translated their writing for the surrealist number of *This Quarter* (see 13 [September 1932], n. 9).

12 "Touché" (got my hands on).

13 Mme. Marie Redmond (née Robinson, known as Elsie, 1885-1976), married to Dr. H. E. Redmond (1882-1951), was born in Paris of English parents and had grown up there. In Dublin she was the "go to" person for French lessons and taught SB. In later years, she would say, "That Beckett fellow has done quite well, it seems" (Annick O'Meara, 17 October 2007).

Ralph D. Blumenfeld (1864-1948), the American-born Editor of the *Daily Express* (London) from 1902 to 1932, was a family friend of Mme. Redmond's parents. "Boniments" (sales talk or puffs).

14 Prince William's Seat is a promontory south of Dublin on the Wicklow Way; the town of Enniskerry lies north of it in the direction of Foxrock.

15 *Romeo and Juliet* by William Shakespeare (1564–1616) opened at Dublin's Gate Theatre on 1 November 1932. Oscar Wilde's *An Ideal Husband* had played there from 18 October; prior to that, from 27 September to 15 October, the Gate produced a revival of *Peer Gynt* by Henrik Ibsen (1828–1906). Hilton Robert Edwards (1903–1982), a founder of the Gate Theatre, had directed the original production in October 1928; his revival was "improved" with the scenic concept of light coming from the back of the stage (*The Irish Times* 29 September 1932: 4).

Incidental Music to *Peer Gynt* for Solo Voices, Orchestra and Chorus, op. 23, by Norwegian composer Edvard Hagerup Grieg (1843–1907).

16 J.D.O. Bryan (known as Donagh, 1903–1932), a gold medalist and Research Prizeman in History at Trinity College Dublin, was appointed as Assistant Lecturer in History there in January 1931; he died on 9 October 1932.

THOMAS McGREEVY
TARBERT, CO. KERRY

4th Nov. [*for* 3 November 1932]   Cooldrinagh,
                                          Foxrock,
                                          Co. Dublin.

My dear Tom

Because the morning is balmy and the wind in the southwest I can come out of the grate and sit at the table and write a letter. Though there is little news. The work I did for Ruddy has not yet been paid. I was waiting to write till it would be, but I see no signs of any money forthcoming, and I can't bring myself to write & ask him for it. I sent my <u>Dream</u> to Titus about 3 weeks ago, but have had no acknowledgment.[1] There is nothing at all to be done here, in this house. Sitting about all day from one room to another & moving cautiously about the parish, regretting that my old friend obstipation excludes me from more frequent enjoyment of the seats in rosewood. I tried once or twice to get something started, but as soon as a word goes down out it must come. So I gave it up. I got a letter of introduction to Blumenfeld of the Daily Express and wrote him a begging letter. He regretted rather coarsely to be unable -- I nearly applied for an [sic] job as teacher of French in Technical School in Bulawayo, S. Rhodesia, but a few minutes consideration equipoised so perfectly the pros & cons that as usual I found myself constrained to do nothing.[2] But nearly anything would be a grateful change after these slow months of tepid eviration, with the mind in slush.

I had a letter from George Reavey with a poem out of his new Quixote Series. Better than his usual, at least more amusing. He is full of plans & Editors & publishers & literary agencies. He might prove useful before he dies. Nothing further from Nancy Cunard.[3]

And yourself? You were sad when you wrote last. I was glad to hear the Lurçat deal concluded. I have heard nothing about it, but then I do not have the occasion.[4] The Gallery is closed for re-hanging. I have not seen J.B.Y. Those Sat. afternoons chez lui are rather dreadful. To-morrow afternoon I am having 3/- worth of Gods to hear Horowitz at the Royal. The programme is interesting.[5]

The Income Tax bastards have been after me, sending up the local sergeant to see what I am at and spying in the office in Clare St. So far no formal demand. Anyhow I cant pay them anything.[6]

I push the bike up into the mountains in the late afternoon to the Lamb Doyle's or Glencullen or Enniskerry and have a pint and then free wheel home to Tom Jones. Yes, as you say, as far as he goes. But he's the best of them. I like the short chapters more & more and the ironical chapter-titles. His burlesque is rather clumsy but his serious mood is very distinguished. Somehow I expected more from Tom Jones.[7]

Dear Tom this is a very white kind of letter but I cant do any better. I'm enclosing a photo that I thought you would like and another poem.[8]

God love you

Sam

this seps of a world

see-saw she is blurred in sleep
she is fat she is half dead the rest is freewheeling
part the black shag the pelt
is ashen woad
snarl and howl in the wood wake all the birds
hound the whores out of the ferns
this damfool twilight threshing in the brake
bleating to be bloodied
this crapulent hush
tear its heart out

in her dreams she leaps again[9]
way back in the good old dark old days
in the womb of her dam panting
in the claws of the Pins in the stress of her hour
the womb writhes bagful of ferrets
first come first served no queuing up in the womb
the light fails it is time to lie down
Clew Bay vat of xanthic flowers
Croagh Patrick waned Hindu to spite the pilgrims
she is ready to lie down above all the islands of glory
straining now this Sabbath evening of garlands
with a yo-heave-ho of able-bodied swans
out from the doomed land their reefs of tresses
whales in Blacksod Bay dancing
as to the sound of a trumpet
in a hag she drops her young
the asphodels come running the flags after
cloppety-clop all night she drops them
till dawn the trollop fillips the clots of love
from her infamous finger

she wakes whining

she was deep in heat when Pavlov came
with a cauter and a metronome he came
toiling on bottom gear through the celtic mizzle
to where stiff with nits
blotch and pearly ticks she lay
her hot snout pointing south
vermifuge quotha from this time forth
and donnerwetter she'll wet on my tomb

she took me up on to a high watershed
whence like the rubrics of a childhood
lo Meath shining through a chink in the mountains
posses of larches there is no going back on
a rout of tracks and streams fleeing to the sea
kindergartens of steeples and then the harbour
like a woman making to cover her breasts
and left me

with whatever trust of panic we went out
with so much shall we return
there shall be no loss of panic between a man and his dog
bitch though he be

sodden packet of Players
it is only a dream
muzzling the cairn
the light randy slut can't be easy
this clonic world
all these phantoms shuddering out of focus
it is better to close the eyes
all the chords of the earth broken like a bad pianist's

the toads abroad again on their rounds
sidling up to their snares
the fairy-tale of Meath ended
say your prayers now and go to bed
your prayers before the lamps start to sing behind the larches
here at these knees of stone
then to bye-bye on the bones

ALS; 3 leaves, 5 sides; *letterhead*; *enclosure* TMS 2 leaves, 2 sides ("this seps of a world"); the photo is not extant with this letter; *env to* Thomas McGreevy Esq., Tarbert, Kerry; *pm* 3-11-32, Dublin; TCD, MS 10402/35. *Dating*: SB misdates the letter a day later than the postmark.

1 Rudmose-Brown. SB sent *Dream of Fair to Middling Women* to Edward Titus before 18 October 1932.

2 Neither SB's letter to Ralph Blumenfeld nor Blumenfeld's reply has been found. Bulawayo, S. Rhodesia, is now Bulawayo (alt. Buluwayo), Zimbabwe.

3 Reavey sent one of the following poems, written in 1932 for the Quixotic series: "Adios Prolovitch," "Hic Jacet," "Squirearchy," or "Perquisition" (George Reavey, *Quixotic Perquisitions: First Series* [London: Europa Press, 1939] 11–12, 17–23).

4 McGreevy had made the arrangements for the Society of Friends of the National Collections of Ireland to acquire *Decorative Landscape* (1932) by Jean Lurçat (see McGreevy to Dermod O'Brien, TCD, McGreevy, MSS 8126/47–48). Sarah Purser (1848–1943), Chairman of the Society, expressed reservations: "'I am a little nervous about its acceptance and reception by our rather *arriéré* public'" (letter to McGreevy quoted in Patricia Boylan, *All Cultivated People: A History of the United Arts Club, Dublin* [Gerrards Cross, Bucks., UK: Colin Smythe, 1988] 187–188). The painting (no. 709) was kept in storage until the new Municipal Gallery of Modern Art opened in Charlemont House on 19 June 1933 (now known as the Dublin City Gallery The Hugh Lane; see Elizabeth Mayes and Paula Murphy, eds., *Images and Insights* [Dublin: Hugh Lane Gallery of Modern Art, 1993] 258–259).
"I do not have the occasion" (Gallicism for "I do not have the opportunity").

5 The National Gallery of Ireland.
"Chez lui" (at-homes); SB often lamented that other people were present.
The gods: cheap seats in top gallery.
On 5 November 1932, Russian-born American pianist Vladimir Horowitz (1903–1989) gave a recital in Dublin's Theatre Royal. The program included the Organ Toccata in C, BWV 564, by Johann Sebastian Bach (1685–1750), arranged for piano by German-born Italian composer Ferruccio Benvenuto Busoni (1866–1924); "Flight of the Bumble Bee" from the opera *The Tale of Tzar Saltan* by Russian composer Nikolai Andreyevich Rimsky-Korsakov (1844–1908); a fantasia based on the opera *Carmen* by

French composer Georges Bizet (1838–1875) (possibly Horowitz's own "Variations on a Theme from *Carmen*"); a Sonata in E-flat major by Franz Joseph Haydn (1732–1809); "Funérailles" from *Harmonies poétiques et religieuses*, second version (S173, no. 7), by Franz Liszt (1811–1886); "Variations on a Theme by Paganini," op. 35, and two of the three Intermezzos for Piano, op. 117, by Johannes Brahms (1833–1897); the Pastorale and "Toccata" from *Trois pièces*, op. 48, by Francis Poulenc (1899–1963); Stravinsky's "Danse Russe" from the ballet *Petrouchka*; and Etude in F major, op. 10, no. 8, and Barcarolle in F-sharp major, op. 60, by Frédéric Chopin (1810–1849).

SB wrote to McGreevy:

> The Horowitz concert was very remarkable and yet somehow unsatisfactory. The Haydn Sonata was unspeakable and coming so early on put me in a bad temper for the rest of the programme. He played with great intelligence, especially the Brahms Intermezzi, affecting to feel his way through them. The Poulenc Pastorale & Toccata were charming. Still & all I was glad to get away before the torrent of encores and into the Scotch House. (11 November 1932, TCD, MS 10402/37)

6 Beckett and Medcalf, 6 Clare Street.

7 Lamb Doyles, an inn on the Hill of Stepaside near the base of the Three Rock Mountains, Co. Wicklow. Glencullen and Enniskerry are towns at the southern edge of Co. Dublin in the Wicklow hills.

Henry Fielding's novel *The History of Tom Jones, a Foundling* (1748).

8 A "white kind of letter" (Gallicism for a "blank, colorless" letter). This poem, untitled here, is an early draft of "Serena 2" (*Echo's Bones*, [28–30]). The photo has not been identified.

9 SB wrote "<wakes again> leaps."

GEORGE REAVEY

LONDON

6/11/32 Cooldrinagh,
Foxrock
Co. Dublin.

Dear Reavey

Herewith 2 Prépuscules d'un Gueux.[1]

I dont know yet how things are with my book. If you think you could place a truss of poems for me you are very welcome to see them.[2] Let me know. Perhaps I may get to Paris myself sometime. But I don't think that is likely.

Best of luck in your new venture.

Yours

Sam Beckett

Thanks for the Quix poem. I liked it very much.[3]

ALS; 1 leaf, 2 sides; *letterhead*; *env to* Monsieur George Reavey, Bureau Littéraire Européen, 13 Rue Bonaparte, Paris 6ᵐ, *pm* 7-11-32, Dublin; enclosure not extant with letter; TxU.

1 SB's enclosure is not extant. However, SB's letters to McGreevy indicate that he had sent two poems to Reavey, one of which was "[There was a] Happy Land," published in *Echo's Bones* as "Sanies 2" (21 November 1932 and 11 November 1932, TCD, MS 10402/ 38 and 37), which was also given to Charles Prentice (see 4 August 1932, n. 17). Pilling indicates the poems as "Serena I" and "Sanies II" (*A Samuel Beckett Chronology*, 40).

SB puns on *Crépuscule des dieux* (Twilight of the Gods), French form of the title of Wagner's opera, *Götterdämmerung* (1876).

"Prépuce" (foreskin); "gueux" (beggar, wretch, knave).

2 Edward Titus had received *Dream of Fair to Middling Women*, "but has not read it" (SB to McGreevy, 11 November 1932, TCD, MS 10402/37). Rickword had not acknowledged the poems sent by SB in August; SB tries Reavey's interest in placing them.

3 Following signature, in pencil in AH: "P.T.O."; PS on verso.

One of the four poems written in 1932 for *Quixotic Perquisitions*: SB to Reavey, 4 November [*for* 3 November 1932], n. 3.

THOMAS McGREEVY

TARBERT, CO. KERRY

5ᵗʰ December [1932]　　　　Merrion Nursing Home

28 Upper Merrion St

Dublin

My dear Tom

At last I worked myself up to seeing a doctor about my neck, which he described as a deep-seated septic cystic system!! And advised me to have the whole thing cleaned up une fois pour toutes.[1] So I came in here last Wednesday & was operated on Thursday morning. I had a joint off a hammer toe at the same time. Everything went well and I am much better now & able to get up & hobble round, but do not expect to be allowed out for another week at least. I have an agreeable room full of sun all morning, and it is pleasant enough lying in bed sleeping & reading & feeling vaguely spoilt & victimised and comic all at the same time. [...]

I was re-reading the first volume of Le Temps Retrouvé – Paris during the war & the pleasures & opinions of Charlus. I disliked it before and thought it mere bourrage & badly out of control – so obviously ajouté & hors d'oeuvre. But this time I simply couldn't get on with it at all. Balzac gush – and the allusion to Morel's physical terror of Charlus & Charlus's letter when he confesses to having planned to murder Morel seem to me pure Balzac.[2] Then the second volume – the last of the book – surely the first 100 pages are as great a piece of sustained writing as anything to be found anywhere. I find it more satisfactory at every reading.[3]

I have a great admiration for Sainte-Beuve & I think his was the most interesting mind of the whole galère but I can't help regretting that it was applied to criticism. I think if you read the Causeries chronologically [? you'd] notice a rather horrible process of crystallisation into a plausible efficiency of method, the only thing added material – pièce de [for à] conviction – dossier souplesse becoming clockwork.[4] But if you have not read his novel Volupté I have it & would like to send it to you when I get out & can delve for it. It's very beautifully written and I never could see why it is usually rated as rather dark & sinister. The images are so well framed and the colours so numerous, like a faded kaleidoscope. It's more like Rousseau's Rêverie[s] that [for than] the Confessions d'un Enfant du Siècle, but without the madness & the distortion. In a way I suppose he had a lot in common with Rousseau. I wish he had done something more than work out a critical method and préciser an attitude. Aren't there plenty of Taines for that?[5]

Nothing from Titus or Nancy.[6] I came independently to the same conclusions concerning Kruschen.[7]

> Do write her & God love you
>
> ever
>
> Sam

ALS; 2 leaves, 4 sides; *env to* Thomas McGreevy Esq, Tarbert, Co. Kerry; *pm* 6-12-32; Dublin; TCD, MS 10402/39. *Dating*: from pm.

1 "Une fois pour toutes" (once and for all).

2 Proust's *Le Temps retrouvé* (*Time Regained*) is the final part of *A la recherche du temps perdu*.
"Bourrage" (padding); "ajouté & hors d'oeuvre" (added on & extraneous). SB compares Proust here to Honoré de Balzac (1799–1850). M. de Charlus's letter of confession is from *Le Temps retrouvé* in *A la recherche du temps perdu*, IV, 384–385); *Time Regained* in *In Search of Lost Time*, VI, 167–168).

3 In the edition that SB used, the second book of the final volume of *Le Temps retrouvé* begins within what is entitled "Chapter III," as M. de Charlus enters the courtyard of the Guermantes mansion ("En roulant les tristes pensées [...]" in Marcel Proust, *A la recherche du temps perdu*, VIII, Book 2, [Paris: Librairie Gallimard, Editions de la Nouvelle Revue Française 1927] 7; *Le Temps retrouvé* in *A la recherche du temps perdu*, IV, 445; "Revolving the gloomy thoughts ..." in *Time Regained* in *In Search of Lost Time*, VI, 255).

4 Charles-Augustin Sainte-Beuve (1804–1869) wrote *Causeries du lundi* (1858–1872), a collection of weekly articles on literary subjects.
"Galère" (crew).
"Material – pièce à conviction – dossier souplesse" (Material Exhibit A, file under versatility).

5 Sainte-Beuve, *Volupté* (1834; *Volupté: The Sensual Man*).
Les Rêveries du promeneur solitaire (1776–1778, published 1782; *The Reveries of the Solitary Walker*) by Jean-Jacques Rousseau (1712–1778). It is probable that SB, writing from memory, has conflated Rousseau's *Les Confessions* (1782) with the autobiographical novel *Confessions d'un enfant du siècle* (1836) by French poet, dramatist, and novelist Alfred de Musset (1810–1857).
"Préciser" (set out in detail).
French critic, historian, and philosopher, Hippolyte-Adolphe Taine (1828–1893), author of *Les Origines de la France contemporaine* (1874–1894; *The Origins of Contemporary France*).

6 Edward Titus had not sent the December issue of *This Quarter* which included SB's "Dante and the Lobster," nor any word about *Dream of Fair to Middling Women*. Nancy Cunard had proposed translations of Eluard and Breton to SB, but still had not sent their books; SB reflected on the prospect: "I think I'll have real pleasure transposing them" (SB to McGreevy, 12 [December 1932], TCD, MS 10402/40).

7 Kruschen, mineral salts, taken dissolved in warm water; a mild diuretic, it was advertised as a weight-loss product in 1932, said to be good for the kidneys and restorative of vigor.

146

CHRONOLOGY 1933

1933	January	SB continues translation for Cunard's *Negro, Anthology*.
	1 January	Hitler appointed German Chancellor.
	By 5 January	SB applies for teaching position in Milan.
	26 January	Considers applying for teaching position in Manchester.
	c. 2 February	Completes translations for Cunard. Resolves not to teach again. Works on Mozart with piano teacher.
	By 20 March	Sends a short story, possibly "Ding-Dong," to *Dublin Magazine*.
	15 April	Cycles through Malahide, around the Portrane estuary, and through Swords.
	By 23 April	*Dublin Magazine* returns story. SB writes another poem, "Sanies 1," and another story, possibly "Fingal." Takes countryside walk with his father.
	3 May	Has second operation on his neck. Peggy Sinclair dies in Germany.
	Before 13 May	SB introduced to an editor from Methuen. Sends McGreevy draft of "Sanies 1."
	13 May	Sends McGreevy draft of "Sanies 1."
	By 22 June	Titus returns *Dream of Fair to Middling Women*. SB sends it to Methuen.
	22 June	SB's father William Beckett suffers a heart attack.
	26 June	William Beckett dies.

By 25 July	SB sets up an "office" at 6 Clare Street in which to receive students for "grinds." Cissie Sinclair returns to Dublin.
c. July–August	SB augments story collection by taking material from *Dream of Fair to Middling Women* ("A Wet Night" and "The Smeraldina's Billet Doux") and by incorporating passages into "What a Misfortune" and "Draff."
By 6 September	Sends ten stories to Chatto and Windus. All the members of the Sinclair family now in Dublin. SB meets Nuala Costello in Dublin.
By 25 September	Chatto and Windus accepts the stories, with provisos, including change of title.
3 October	SB accepts contract from Chatto and Windus and supplies a new title: *More Pricks Than Kicks*.
By 9 October	Beckett family moves to Dalkey for a month. SB sends poem "Serena 3" to McGreevy. Applies for a position with The National Gallery (London).
By 1 November	Tries to write a final story for *More Pricks Than Kicks*, for which Belacqua must be "revived." The National Gallery rejects SB's application.
8 November	Beckett family returns to Foxrock.
By 10 November	SB sends "Echo's Bones," the final story for *More Pricks Than Kicks*, to Prentice.
12 November	Prentice returns "Echo's Bones": Chatto and Windus will publish *More Pricks Than Kicks* without it.
By 6 December	SB writes poem "Echo's Bones" following rejection of the story of the same name. Corrects part of the proofs of *More Pricks Than Kicks*.
By 18 December	Prentice sends proofs with McGreevy's notes on them, which SB approves.
25 December	SB is in Dublin.

5ᵗʰ Jan [1933]   Cooldrinagh
                                  [Foxrock, Co. Dublin]

Dear Tom

Forgive this long silence. Noel & Silvester were big hurdles, and I only got out of the clinique just in time to take them.[1] My neck is still a bit troublesome about cleaning & healing, but I am really much better than I was. And quieter every way.

Your intricate observations on the subject of absolute & relative nearly strangled me. Or should I say seriousness & irony. Why not both, a little seriousness in the stress of irony. But I find that eschewal of verbal sanies is one of my New Year resolutions. So you can sit back.[2]

Cissie writes; they are quite down now, piano, pictures and everything gone.[3] Even Percy Ussher felt sick when he went to visit them.

I am doing stuff for Nancy at present – some interesting (Congo Sculpture) some balls (Madagascar). There's one there waiting about the usual assassin signed by the whole surrealiste guild. And a long one by Péret.[4]

I applied for a job in Milan, but nothing doing. But I am being borne in mind.

No more news from Titus.[5]

[...]

I dined (I write dined, but nothing of the kind happened) at Joe Hone's of Killiney last Saturday, & his wife [...] Do you know them? Now he is collaborating with one Rossi (the Berkeley better half) in a book on poor Swift. A boring moribund creature.[6] I stole away to Jesus and did the bonafide in Loughlinstown, and thence home on 9 toes between the years.[7]

I was down at Donabate on Boxing Day and walked all about Portrane lunatic asylum in the rain. Outside the gate I was talking to a native of Lambay, and asked him about an old tower I saw in a field nearby. 'That's where Dane Swift came to his motte' he said. 'What motte?' I said. 'Stella.' What with that, and the legend about the negress that his valet picked up for him, and the Portrane lunatics and round tower built as relief work in the Famine, poem scum is fermenting, the first flicker in the wash-tub since the bitch & bones.[8]

I dribble malgré moi and knowing I do & oughtn't to is no help.[9] There may be Gods, but what ice do they cut?

I'll look up Volupté forthwith and send it. I've been reading nothing but a little history (Greene! [*for* Green]), his libel on poor Charles 2.[10] The royal mumper!

   God bless & love ever

    Sam

ALS; l leaf, 2 sides; *env to* Thomas McGreevy Esq, Tarbert, Kerry, *pm* 5-1-33, Dublin; TCD, MS 10402/43. *Dating*: from pm and context.

1 Sylvester: New Year's Eve, Saint Sylvester's day.

2 "Sanie" (Lat., morbid discharge). SB gave two poems this name.

3 Cissie Sinclair had returned to Kassel and had written of the effect that the Depression was having on her family's circumstances.
Boss Sinclair was a dealer in modern art and owned many paintings; one known to be in his collection at this time was *Abendmahl* by the German artist Ewald Dülberg (1888–1933); James Knowlson indicates that it had been in the collection of the Hamburger Kunsthalle, but was "destroyed in 1939, two years after its confiscation in the 'Entartete Kunst' (Degenerate Art) action" (James Knowlson, "Beckett in Kassel: Erste Begegnungen mit dem deutschen Expressionismus," in *Der unbekannte Beckett: Samuel Beckett und die deutsche Kultur*, ed. Therese Fischer-Seidel and Marion Fries-Dieckmann, tr. Marion Fries-Dieckmann [Frankfurt: Suhrkamp, 2005] 76–78, 94).

The Sinclairs also owned a painting by the American artist Lyonel Feininger (1871–1956): *Bathers I*, an oil on canvas (current ownership unknown, possibly lost) (see no. 109, in Hans Hess, *Lyonel Feininger* [New York: Harry N. Abrams, 1961] 66, 257; also Knowlson, "Beckett in Kassel," 76).

4 SB is translating French essays selected for Nancy Cunard's *Negro, Anthology*. Although he translated others for the book, here SB refers to: "Essay on Styles in the Statuary of the Congo" by Henri Lavachery (1852–1934) (687–693); "A Short Historical Survey of Madagascar" by Jean-Jacques Rabéarivelo (1903–1937) (618–622); "French Imperialism at Work in Madagascar" by Georges Citerne (1906–1944) and Francis Jourdain (1876–1958) (801–802).

Still to do were "Murderous Humanitarianism" by "The Surrealist Group in Paris," a collective statement signed by André Breton, Roger Caillois (1913–1978), René Char (1907–1988), René Crevel (1900–1935), Paul Eluard, Jules Monnerot (1909–1995), Benjamin Péret, Yves Tanguy (1900–1955), André Thirion (1907–2001), Pierre Unik (1909–1945), Pierre Yoyotte (? d. 1941) (574–575); and "Black and White in Brazil" by Benjamin Péret (1899–1959) (510–514).

5 No response had been received from Edward Titus about *Dream of Fair to Middling Women*.

6 Irish biographer and critic Joseph Maunsel Hone* (1882–1959) founded the Dublin publishing house Maunsel and Company. His wife Vera (née Brewster, 1886–1971) was described in Hone's obituary as "an American of great beauty, and famous both for her caustic wit and for her tireless devotion" ("Mr. Joseph Hone; Biographer and Critic," *The Times* 28 March 1959: 19). With Mario Manlio Rossi (1895–1978), Hone wrote *Bishop Berkeley: His Life, Writings, and Philosophy* (1932) and *Swift; or, the Egoist* (1934).

7 SB alludes to the African-American spiritual "Steal Away." It was possible to drink legally outside drinking hours "providing one had accomplished the business of covering the three miles that was the statutory 'journey' establishing your claim as a traveller" (John Ryan, *Remembering How We Stood: Bohemian Dublin at the Mid-Century* [Dublin: Gill and Macmillan, 1975] 25). In popular usage "bona fide," pronounced in three syllables rather than the required four, was taken to refer to the pub, rather than the traveler. Loughlinstown, a small village near Killiney, about 8 miles southeast of Dublin.

8 Boxing Day (26 December).
Donabate, Co. Dublin, is inland from Lambay Island, north of Dublin. The Portrane Lunatic Asylum (now St. Ita's Hospital) once housed 1,640 inmates in a cluster of buildings and facilities on 600 acres; it is 2 miles from the Donabate Station.
Jonathan Swift (1667–1745) was guardian for Esther Johnson (known as Stella to Swift, 1681–1728), the natural child of Sir William Temple; Swift was Temple's secretary and half-brother. After Temple's death in 1699, Swift left England and returned to Ireland; Stella followed him. Although they remained close and rumors suggested they had secretly married, Swift would see Stella only when a third party was present. "Motte" (Ir. colloq., young woman). Portrane had once been Stella's country home. The Stella Tower is a Martello tower built during the famine (Eoin O'Brien, *The Beckett Country: Samuel Beckett's Ireland* [Dublin: The Black Cat Press in association with Faber and Faber, 1986] 373, 232–233; see also Victoria Glendinning, *Jonathan Swift: A Portrait* [New York: Henry Holt and Co., 1999] 215–228).

In Ireland, Swift (Dean of St. Patrick's Cathedral) was commonly referred to by the uneducated as the "Dane." Among traditional Irish stories about Swift is that he would ask his servant to "find him a woman for the night"; various tellings make the woman old and ugly, or crippled, or black (Mackie L. Jarrell, "'Jack and the Dane': Swift Traditions in Ireland," *Journal of American Folklore* 77.304 [April–June 1964] 101–102). SB would have been aware of this legend through mention of it by W. B. Yeats in "The Words Upon The Window Pane: A Commentary," *Dublin Magazine* 6.4 (October–December 1931) 17; SB's poem "Alba" immediately preceded this essay (Ian Higgins and Claude Rawson pointed to these sources for the Swift "legends").

The area of SB's walk figures in the poem "Sanies 1" in *Echo's Bones*, and also in the story "Fingal" in *More Pricks Than Kicks*.

9   "Malgré moi" (in spite of myself).

10 *Volupté*: 5 December [1932], n. 5.

John Richard Green, *A Short History of the English People* [New York and London: Harper and Brothers Publishers, 1898] 620–664. King Charles II of England (1630–1685).

THOMAS McGREEVY
TARBERT, CO. KERRY

Lundi [20 March 1933]   [Dublin]

Cher Ami

Merci de ta lettre. Quand aurai-je le plaisir de te revoir? Je sais que tu as de la peine à lire mon Ogham, et c'est seulement pour t'assurer que je t'aurais répondu plus tôt si je n'avais été tellement pris par un conte que je gâte cette bonne carte et que je m'y mettrai dès ce soir[.]¹

A toi S.

APCI; 1 leaf, 2 sides; *to* Thomas McGreevy Esq., Tarbert, KERRY; *pm* 20-3-33, Dublin; TCD, MS 1040/47. *Dating*: from pm.

Monday [20 March 1933]   [Dublin]

Dear Tom

Thank you for your letter. When shall I have the pleasure of seeing you again? I know that you have trouble reading my

Ogham, and it is only to assure you that I would have answered you earlier if I had not been so caught up with a short story that I am spoiling this good card, and will set about doing so no later than this evening.[1]

Your S.

1 Ogham, a system of writing, with an alphabet of twenty characters, used by ancient British and Irish people as secret writing.

SB sent this story to Seumas O'Sullivan for *Dublin Magazine*, as he wrote the next day in a letter to McGreevy: "I sent a short story to Seumas O'Solomon [sic] last night, which I think you'd like, but few others" (21 [March 1933], TCD, MS 10402/48). The story has not been identified, although Pilling suggests that it might be "Ding-Dong," which later became part of *More Pricks Than Kicks* (*A Samuel Beckett Chronology*, 42).

O'Sullivan's wife was Estella Solomons and SB conflates her name with his.

THOMAS McGREEVY

PARIS

23ʳᵈ [April 1933]   Cooldrinagh

Foxrock [Co. Dublin]

My dear Tom

I'm so tired belting away at the old typewriter that I venture to address you thus. I hope you'll be able to read it.

I am sure you were right to go to Paris. I wish I had the courage to go as you did, with only your fare and vague copulation à l'arrivée. But I don't know any Junyers or Lurçats.[1] Of course your letter made me wish very much to be there. The sensation of taking root, like a polypus, in a place, is horrible, living on a kind of mucous [*for* mucus] of conformity. And in this of all places. The mind is in league with one's nature, or family's nature, it pops up and says 'égal'. I'd love to see Beaufret en militaire, looking something between the drummer and the mascot. Thomas in his testimonial credited me with 'très précieuses amitiés.'[2] I seem to have squandered them all. Sean O'Sullivan asked me would I like a ticket for Academy vernissage for a friend. And then: 'Oh I forgot, you don't go in for that luxury.'[3] Luxury is the word. Gide seems to be making a whirl of gaiety out of his last days. Perhaps he hopes to end where Dostoievski began, with a 'Pauvres Gens'. I had heard of Voyage au bout de la nuit and admired the title. Are you sure it isn't Pelorson's![4] It's like his phrase.

Seumas O'S. returned the short story at last – [? remarking] that he was behind the times, which was the only place where he could be 'reasonably happy' and that was his 'great secret'! Not so secret. I thought of sending it to the Adelphi.[5] Is that entirely ridiculous? I don't know. I wrote another (zig zag acquis!) and a poem having passed the Alba in the street, on which occasion my salute was function of Leventhal's. It requires care not to take a serious view of these accidents. Easter was endless, Father and Frank away in Wales. On Saturday I went off for the day on the bike, through Malahide & round the estuary to Portrane and back by Swords.[6] The penny pleasure of homing in the gloaming. On Monday with Mother to the Botanic Gardens. All very deliberately agreeable & faute de mieux.[7]

[...]

Lovely walk this morning with Father, who grows old with a very graceful philosophy. Comparing bees & butterflies to elephants & parrots & speaking of indentures with the leveller. Barging through hedges and over the walls with the help of my shoulder, blaspheming and stopping to rest under colour of admiring the view. I'll never have any one like him.

Mindful of Alfieri I tried to read Plutarch, but in vain. Mindful of Alfieri! And Berkeley's Commonplace Book, which Hone recommended as a beginning, and which is full of profound things, and at the same time of a foul (& false) intellectual canaillerie, enough to put you against reading anything more. I wish I could go into the library and work at Heraclitus & Co., but I never go into town except to buy coffee.[8] I understand Boss Sinclair, & others, who won't go out unless praised or accompanied. I send Dream . . to Gollancz. He will be 'most delighted to have it read.'!![9] Frank's all right. Rien ne presse et lui pelote.[10] Love to Angelo. Eat a Parmentier to my health.[11] Write again soon.

Love ever
Sam   no likely quarters we might share?

ALS; 1 leaf, 2 sides; TCD, MS 10402/42. *Dating*: McGreevy in Paris; Seumas O'Sullivan has returned the short story.

1 McGreevy was in Paris, staying at the Ecole Normale Supérieure (McGreevy to Charles Prentice, Tuesday [11 April 1933], from 45 Rue d'Ulm, Paris 5). Among friends of McGreevy in Paris were Jean Lurçat and the Catalonian painter Joan Junyer (né Junyer y Pascual, 1904–1994).

"A l'arrivée" (on arrival).

2 "Egal" (all square); "en militaire" (in uniform); "très précieuses amitiés" (very valuable friendships).

The testimonial from Jean Thomas was written on 22 July 1932 and is included below as an enclosure with SB's letter of 29 July 1937 to the University of Cape Town.

3 Seán O'Sullivan* (1906–1964), Irish portrait artist. The Royal Hibernian Academy has no record of the date of the "vernissage" (private view) of their exhibition in 1933 (Ella Wilkinson, Royal Hibernian Academy and Library, Dublin).

4 In December 1932, Gallimard began publication of *Oeuvres complètes d'André Gide* and, by April 1933, the first three volumes had appeared (Jean Prévost, "Les oeuvres d'André Gide (Tomes I, II, et III)," *Notre Temps* (16 April 1933) 121; Claude Martin, *Gide* [Paris: Editions du Seuil, 1963 and 1995] 211).

SB's suggested connection between Gide and the Dostoevsky of *Pauvres Gens* (1846; *Poor Folks*) may well be based on Gide's recent reflections on poverty in Africa (*Voyage au Congo*, 1927, and *Retour du Tchad*, 1928; translated together as *Travels in the Congo*).

Voyage au bout de la nuit (1932; *Journey to the End of the Night*) by French writer Louis-Ferdinand Céline (né Louis-Ferdinand Destouches, 1894–1961).

5 *The Adelphi* (1923–1955) was founded by John Middleton Murry (1889–1957) who was Editor until August 1930 and thereafter remained a regular contributor. *The Adelphi* published work by D. H. Lawrence (né David Herbert Richards Lawrence, 1885–1930), whom McGreevy knew through Aldington.

6 "Zig zag acquis" (zig-zag momentum).

In *More Pricks Than Kicks* the character of Alba (associated with Ethna MacCarthy) appears in "What a Misfortune" as well as in "A Wet Night," an episode that was written for *Dream of Fair to Middling Women*; Alba also figures in "Draff"; however, this was written later in 1933.

The poem is "Sanies I." Malahide is south of Portrane, and the town of Swords lies to the west of Malahide (for discussion and images: O'Brien, *The Beckett Country*, 239–240). Pilling suggests that the story may be "Fingal," in which Portrane also figures (*A Samuel Beckett Chronology*, 42).

In 1933 Easter fell on 16 April.

7 The National Botanic Gardens, Glasnevin.

"Faute de mieux" (for want of anything better).

8 Plutarch (c.46 – c.120). George Berkeley, *Berkeley's Commonplace Book*, ed. G. A. Johnston (London: Faber and Faber, 1931). The philosophical notes of George Berkeley (1685–1753) towards his "New Principle," or idealism, were made as an undergraduate at Trinity College Dublin in the early 18th century and contain many local Dublin references.

"Canaillerie" (cheap rubbish).

The work of Heraclitus of Ephesus (c.535 – c.475 BC) and other Greek pre-Socratics interested SB. SB's systematic study of philosophy may have begun in 1930; he continued it by reading philosophy at the British Museum in the summer of 1932 (see 4 August 1932) and later. His notes and sources are recorded in TCD, MS 10967; for description: Frost and Maxwell, "TCD, MS 10967: History of Western Philosophy," *Notes Diverse Holo*, Special issue *SBT/A* 16 (2006) 67–89.

9 The letter to SB from the London publishers Victor Gollancz Ltd. has not been found.

10 "Rien ne presse et lui pelote" (No hurry, and he is womanizing).

11 "Parmentier" is a dish made from mashed potatoes and minced meat, more formally "un hachis parmentier."

THOMAS McGREEVY
PARIS

May 13 [1933]

Cooldrinagh
[Co. Dublin]

My dear Tom

I am delighted to hear that you have started something again. Is it the old novel again or another?[1] You seem to be working under difficulties. Could you not find somewhere better than the Mahieu. Down in the far corner of the Cluny would be better and the coffee is better there too and there are no Alans, populistes or Serbs. I remember one Sunday afternoon you were out at Ville d'Avray trying to write a bit of the Belacqua there and failing to find a word and then going back to the hotel and doing no better there.[2] This writing is a bloody awful grind. I did two more 'short stories', bottled climates, comme ça, sans conviction, because one has to do something or perish with ennui. Now I have five.[3] But I don't think I could possibly invite a publisher to wipe his arse with less than a dozen. Hone rang up one day to introduce a young man from Methuen, Mr Colin Summerford, whose peace of mind apparently depended on his standing me lunch at the Shelbourne.[4] He wanted the book, but it was not available, not having come back from Titus, nor yet from Gollancz. Methuen![5] They publish Wilhelmina Stitch so I suppose they can afford to take a chance, at least in the summer when Lucas is too busy at Lord[']s to bother. I gave him the poems and a couple of stories and he bowed me away hoping that good would come.[6] I think he came over with Stevens [*for* Stephens] who it appears is on to an Academy anthology. That ought to be lovely. He says Stevens is a great poet, Strict Joy hot stuff by heaven, and a great philosopher. He seemed to have seen the whole bordel over here from Gogarty to frog-hopping Curtis.[7] He was very pale, elegant and graceful, knew Brigit, Richard, Douglas, Pino, Derek, Michael, Charles, Eliot (nice man but bad poet) et en était très évidemment. I'll get no more than I've got, viz., lobster and Capsule Chablis, from Mr Summerford.[8]

I had the neck done with a local anaesthetic last Wednesday week in town and then came home. It was all right till next day and the next and the next and the next, which I spent in bed with pus pouring out into foments through the stitches. The stitches are out now and the cut is healing and the discharges are nearly over but I have no confidence that it wont come back again. The doctor says he hopes it[']s all right.

Last Wednesday week also, in the early morning, Peggy died at Wildungen near Kassel, quite peacefully after a fit of coughing in a sleeping-draught sleep. I did not hear from Cissie but from Sally here in Dublin. Her German fiancé was with her to the last and is reported to be inconsolable.[9] She had just been up to Kassel to see the doctor and had been told that she was better and that she could lie out in the sun, so they all had great hopes of her getting quite well. It appears that she and her fiancé had lately been indulging in regular paroxysms of plans of what they would do when they were married. She has been cremated.

Mr Sean Cagney threatens me with distrainment if I don't fork up 5 guineas in a week. But how can he distrain when I have no effects? And what would be the good of his taking me to court when he would have to pay the costs himself? So that is the next little bit of excitement, a visit to Mr Cagney to beg for a respite. He can't make my father responsible and the bumtraps can't enter my father's house. And as far as I know he can't have me put in prison for debt.[10]

Two queer dreams the same night: flying down hill on the bike with Rudmose-Brown in a panic on the step, and trying desperately and in vain, missing trains etc., to begin a long walk by the sea with Jack Yeats.[11]

I owe you something out of the 50 fs., but I'm so broke that I'm going to hold on to it till I see you! I'm so terrified of getting sick away and everything seems so dead against being abroad that even if I succeeded in placing something and getting some money I don't think I would bother my arse to move. Here at home they encourage my endeavours to build myself up on stout, and I feel that for stout my world is better lost than for Lib., Egal., and Frat., and quarts de Vittel.[12] They don't say anything about my getting a job and I begin to be impervious to their inquiétude. It's an ill cyst blows nobody any good. I find it more and more difficult to write and I think I write worse and worse in consequence. But I have still hopes of its all coming in a gush like a bloody flux. Here's a poem. I showed it to Leventhal. One long spittle, he said pleasantly. But I had to laught [sic] all the same. He thought <u>funds ways home</u> had something to do with paying her tram fare! I think I like Leventhal better and better. He bought me a yellow shirt for my birthday.[13] Sometimes I ride to Enniskerry on Sunday afternoon and meet him in the Enniskerry Arms and do the bona fide till it's Mahlzeit time with pa and ma. And it[']s quite pleasant, the ride to Enniskerry and the booze and the ride home through the Scalp, and it's quite pleasant to reach home half screwed and eat a little and go to sleep[.] Everything quite pleasant and pleasantly null.[14]

Glad to hear the Churches are back. Have you not begun your translations for him?[15]

I went to the Academy. Literally nothing there. The best is a Leo* Whelan clock that Sir Neville Wilkinson took for a warming-pan.[16]

Tocher's play is on and seems to be a sad affair by all accounts.[17]

Frank pelote and plays golf and develops his capacity for holding whisky which is already quite remarkable.[18]

Herzlichste Grüsse to the Bowsprit if you see him.[19]

Love ever and write soon again[.]

s/ Sam

* Or maybe an Atty one.

WEG DU EINZIGE!

all the livelong way this day of sweet showers from Portrane
  on the seashore

Donabate sad swans of Turvey Swords
pounding along in three ratios like a sonata
like a reiter [*for* ritter] with pommeled scrotum atra cura on
  the step
Botticelli from the fork down pestling the transmission
tires bleeding voiding zeep the high road
all heaven in my sphincter

müüüüüüde now
potwalloping now through the promenaders
this trusty all-steel this super-real
bound for home like a good boy
where I was born with a clunk with the green of the larches
oh to be back in the caul now with no trusts
no fingers no spoilt loves
belting along in the meantime clutching the bike
the billows of the nubile the cere wrack
pot valiant grotesque waisted in rags hatless
for mama and papa chicken and ham
luke Grave too say the word
happy days snap the stem shed a tear
this day Spy Wedinsday [*for* Wednesday] seven pentades past
oh the larches the pain pulled like a cork
the penis took the day off up hill and down dale
with a ponderous fawn from the Liverpool London and Globe
back the shadows lengthen the sycomores are sobbing
to roly-poly oh to me a spanking boy

buckets of fizz childbed is thirsty work
for the midwife he is gory
for the proud parent he washes down a gob of gladness
for footsore Achates also he pants his pleasure
sparkling beestings for me
tired now hair gums ebbing ebbing home
good as gold now in the thirties the husks forgotten
oh yes and suave
suave urbane beyond good and evil
biding my time without rancour you may take your oath
distraught merry courting the sneers of these fauns these smart
   nymphs
clipped as to one trouser-end like a pederast
sucking in my bloated lantern behind a Wild Woodbine
cinched to death in a filthy slicker
flinging the proud Swift forward breasting the sea of Stürmers

I see main verb at last
her whom alone in the accusative
I have ever dismounted to love
moving towards me dauntless alma on the face of the waters
dauntless daughter of desires in the old black and flamingo
get along with you now take the six the seven the eight or the
   little single-decker
home to your prison your parlour in Sandymount
or take the Blue Line for all I care home to the cob of your web in
   Sandymount
your ma expects you anny minute
I know her she is still then she gets up
then too the tiger in our hearts is smiling
that funds ways home

TLS; 4 leaves, 4 sides; AN side 2; T *env to* Monsieur Thomas McGreevy, Ecole Normale Supérieure, 45 Rue d'Ulm, Paris 5e; *pm* 13-5-33, Dublin; TCD, MS 10402/49. *Dating:* see n. 17.

1 McGreevy had put aside his novel in January; he wrote to his agent James Pinker from Tarbert on 24 January 1933: "I have finally abandoned effort to write a novel now. It may be that I will come back to it but I must start out and try to make money some other way for the time being [. . .] am going to try and get back to Paris and see if there are any small pickings to be had there" (IEN, Pinker collection).

2 Café Mahieu (more commonly known as Café le Mahieu) situated on the Boulevard St.-Michel at Rue Soufflot, near the Place Edmond Rostand. The Café de Cluny was at the corner of Boulevard St.-Germain and Boulevard St.-Michel. SB refers to Alan Duncan and others whose conversation was often political. SB wrote part of *Dream of Fair to Middling Women* in the Café de Cluny.

American writer Henry Church (1880-1947) and his German-born wife, Barbara (n.d.), lived at 1, Avenue Halphen, Ville d'Avray, in a neoclassical home ("Villa Church") which was augmented and renovated by Swiss architect Le Corbusier (né Charles-Edouard Jeanneret, 1887-1965). Richard Aldington had introduced McGreevy to the Churches (Thomas McGreevy, "Richard Aldington as Friend," TCD, MS 10402/7996/1, 8-11).

3 Five of the stories for *More Pricks Than Kicks* had been written: "Dante and the Lobster," "Fingal," "Ding-Dong," "Walking Out," and possibly "Yellow," "What a Misfortune," or "Love and Lethe" (Pilling, *A Samuel Beckett Chronology*, 43; Pilling, *Beckett before Godot*, 96). The newest were "Ding-Dong" and "Fingal."

"Comme ça, sans conviction" (just like that, without conviction).

4 Colin Summerford (1908-1989) represented London publisher Methuen; SB met him with Joseph Hone at the Shelbourne Hotel, 27 St. Stephen's Green. Summerford was described by Peter Wait as a "'clever, amusing rather feckless character'" (Maureen Duffy, *A Thousand Capricious Chances: A History of the Methuen List, 1889-1989* [London: Methuen, 1989] 95).

5 Manuscripts of *Dream of Fair to Middling Women* were still with Edward Titus and Gollancz.

6 Methuen published the verse of Wilhelmina Stitch (née Ruth Collie, 1889-1936), often two or three books a year: e.g. *Tapestries* (1931), *Through Sunny Windows* (1931). E. V. Lucas (né Edward Verrall Lucas, 1868-1938) was a director of Methuen and Company. Lord's is a cricket ground in central London, and headquarters of the MCC, then the governing body of English cricket.

7 Summerford had come to Dublin with Irish poet James Stephens (1880-1950) who had written *Strict Joy: Poems* (1931). Stephens had proposed to Methuen an anthology of writing by the members of the Irish Academy of Letters. "The project was not completed, partially due to the difficulty in obtaining material from all the writers involved" (*Letters of James Stephens*, ed. Richard J. Finneran [London: Macmillan, 1974] 274-275).

SB refers to the members of the Irish Academy of Letters, including Oliver St. John Gogarty (1878-1957) and Edmund Curtis, as the "bordel" (literally, brothel). Denis Devlin* (1908-1959) wrote to McGreevy, 10 November 1933: "Won't Stephen[s]'s

Irish anthology be absurd without us four?" (SB, McGreevy, Devlin, and Brian Coffey*
[1905–1995]; TCD, MS 8112/2).

8 Brigit Patmore, Richard Aldington, English writer Norman Douglas (1868–1952),
Italian publisher and writer Pino Orioli (1884–1942), Brigit's sons Derek Patmore
(1908–1972) and Michael Patmore (1911–?), Charles Prentice, T. S. Eliot.
"Et en était très évidemment" (and very clearly was one of them).

9 Peggy Sinclair died of tuberculosis on 3 May 1933; although not formally engaged,
her "fiancé" was Heiner Starcke.

10 Sean Cagney, Collector of income tax, 41 Kildare Street, Dublin.
Bumtrap (or bum-trap, slang for bailiff) (see C. J. Ackerley, *Demented Particulars: The
Annotated Murphy*, 2nd rev. edn. [Tallahassee, FL: Journal of Beckett Studies Books,
2004] 59).

11 "On the step" (slang, in a hurry).

12 "Liberté, Egalité, and Fraternité" (Liberty, Equality and Fraternity), motto of the
French Republic. "Quarts de Vittel" (quarter-liter bottles of Vittel, a French mineral
water).

13 "Inquiétude" (worry).
"Weg du Einzige!" was published, with many changes, in *Echo's Bones* as "Sanies 1." "Weg
du Einzige" (Away you one and only). The closing lines of the poem ("and let the tiger go on
smiling / in our hearts that funds ways home") are linked by Lawrence Harvey to a limerick
which suggests closure on a love affair (Harvey, *Samuel Beckett*, 148–149).

14 The Scalp, a rocky gap, is about 2 miles north of Enniskerry, south of Dublin. The
Enniskerry Arms (known also as the Enniskerry, Powerscourt, and Leinster Arms
Hotel) is a public house there.
SB wrote "<time> Mahlzeit time"; "Mahlzeit" (meal).

15 Henry Church's plays were published in French: *Les Clowns* (1922), *Vasthi* (1929),
Barnum (1934), and *L'Indifférente* (1934; *Indifference*); McGreevy translated *Clowns* in 1929,
Barnum in the autumn of 1932, and worked on the translations of the others through
1933 (see letters from Henry Church to Thomas McGreevy, TCD, MS 8119/3–5; TCD, MS
8021–8023, 8189; Susan Schriebman, 5 January 2007).

16 In the annual exhibition at the Royal Hibernian Academy, Dublin painter
Michael Leo Whelan (1892–1956) had several portraits and three interior scenes –
The Letter, *Adagio Cantabile*, and a drawing entitled *Aida* – but none with a clock. SB
uses an asterisk after Whelan's name to point to his autograph P.S., also marked with
an asterisk: the words "or maybe an Atty one." The reference to "Atty" is unclear.
Sir Neville Wilkinson (1869–1940) was Ulster King of Arms, Dublin Castle, from
1908 to 1940.

17 *A Bride for the Unicorn* by E. W. Tocher (pseud. of William Denis Johnston,
1901–1984), which opened on 9 May 1933 at the Gate Theatre, broke with realistic
staging and was called a "courageous experiment" (*The Irish Times* 10 May 1933: 6).
Johnston used the pseudonym through 1934, after which time the early plays
(*Rhapsody in Green* [1928; retitled and performed as *The Old Lady Says No*, 1929], *The
Moon in the Yellow River* [1931], and *A Bride for the Unicorn* [1933]) appeared under his given
name.

18 "Pelote" (is womanizing).

19 "Herzlichste Grüsse" (most cordial greetings).

THOMAS McGREEVY
PARIS

2/7/33   Cooldrinagh
                                            Foxrock [Co. Dublin]

My dear Tom

Father died last Monday afternoon after an illness lasting just under a week, and was buried the following Wednesday morning in a little cemetery on the Greystones side of Bray Head, between the mountains and the sea.[1] Mother and I nursed him while he was ill. The doctor saw him the morning he died and told us that he was much better. I was so delighted that I got into the brightest clothes I could find. The doctor was scarcely out of the house before he collapsed. I fear he suffered a great deal before he died about 4 o'clock in the afternoon. We were all with him. He was very beautiful when it was all over. I thought Mother would go to pieces, but she was and is wonderful. It is a very blank silent house now.

It is too soon to know how things will work out. We would all like to remain on here, but it may not be possible. Frank will carry on the office.[2] My position of course is vaguer than ever. For the moment I answer the endless letters on her behalf and look after her as well as I can. Frank is up to his eyes in matters connected with the office and the estate, and it appears that I can be of no help to him. A brother of my Mother, living in England, of whom she is very fond, came over for the funeral and is staying with us until Tuesday next.[3]

He was in his sixty first year, but how much younger he seemed and was. Joking and swearing at the doctors as long as he had breath. He lay in the bed with sweet pea all over his face, making great oaths that when he got better he would never do a stroke of work. He would drive to the top of Howth and lie in the bracken and fart. His last words were "Fight fight fight" and "What a morning". All the little things come back – mémoire de l'escalier.[4]

I can't write about him, I can only walk the fields and climb the ditches after him.

> God love thee.
> s/ Sam

TLS; 1 leaf,1 side; TCD, MS 10402/52.

1 William Beckett died on 26 June 1933; he was buried in Redford Protestant Cemetery, south of Bray, Co. Wicklow (see Knowlson, *Damned to Fame*, 166–167).

2 Frank Beckett had already been working at Beckett and Medcalf.

3 Edward Price Roe (known to SB as Uncle Ned, 1869 – c.1952); he was now living in Nottinghamshire, having returned to England from Africa where he had been "an accountant with the British Central Africa Company in Blantyre in Nyasaland (now Malawi)" (Knowlson, *Damned to Fame*, 44, 621).

4 Howth, the hill above the district of Howth on the north side of Dublin Bay.
   SB substitutes "mémoire" (memory) for "esprit" in the expression "esprit de l'escalier" (an inspired afterthought that comes to one only after leaving, that is, on the stairs).

THOMAS McGREEVY
FLORENCE

9/10/33   6 Clare Street
                                          Dublin

My dear Tom

Many thanks for Beatrice, Giotto & then Lungarno news. Indeed I wish to God I could join you there, but for this year at least I need not think of getting away.[1] [...] Sometimes I'm just fit society for the family noose & sometimes I'm like this poem.[2] Chatto's took a short book of short stories called More Pricks Than Kicks, and paid me 25 pounds less 25% advance on royalties, which cheered me up for a time.[3]

I'm afraid I didn't get much kick out of Coffey & Devlin, their pockets full of calm precious poems. It was pleasant to hear the Paris news, what films were on and the latest 10% of Surréalisme. I gave them the Enueg and we went to the Gallery (grosse erreur) and we had a drink and I haven't seen them since. Coffey seemed to find the Enueg highly delighting amusing delighting. Devlin didn't know what an algum tree was and I couldn't enlighten him. They also had pockets full of French jeunes [*for* jaunes], "lac des mains" and all the usual.[4] I'm a kranky man & I don't like anyone.

The Income Tax sow-gelders are dunning me for enormous sums, notices in scarlet ink and threats to distrain & proceed regardless of costs. I go and see Mr Cagney, cagne cagneuse, and say that the whole thing is a tissue of misrepresentation, that I never earned so much in my life, that anyhow I can't pay and have no chattels and no costs and that if they proceed they must do so without me; Mr Cagney scowls, sneers at my unemployed condition & makes a note of it.[5] I met Michael Farrell and he destroyed me with an endless disparaging hyperbole on his own bland suspension between the vulgarities of great talent and the roots in the anus of genius now & then. The little tubercular tot in the cot buttons across its double-brested pilche [*for* double-breasted pilch], the little cheeks meet on the inside, the accumulated wisdom of the world unites the little lips like a zip fastener, and Mr Farrell is glad he is a doctor.[6]

In a moment of gush I applied for a job of assistant at the National Gallery, Trafalgar Square, and got Charles Prentice &

Jack Yeats to act as referees. I think I'd be happy there for a time among the pigeons and not too far from the French charmers in the Garrick. Apart from my conoysership that can just separate Uccello from a handsaw I could cork the post as well [as] another.[7] Also if I took up residence in England between now & April I would recover my 6 pounds 10 from Chattos.[8] But it won't come off & I don't expect it to.

Glad to hear the novel grows. Are you going down to Tarbert to finish it or have you found a room in Dublin?[9] Do let me know your plans. I have to do another story for More Pricks, Belacqua redivivus, and I'm as stupid as a goat. If only I could get the poems off now I'd be crowned. Nissssscht mööööööglich! Ce qu'il est sentimentique![10]

Tante belle cose. Give my love to San Miniato.[11]

    Yours ever

    s/ Sam

gape at this pothook of beauty on this palate
it is final if you like

come down her she is paradise and then
plush hymens on your eyeballs

on Butt Bridge take thought for yer buzzum
the mixed declension of those mammae
cock up thine arse there is no other word for it
cock her up well to the tulips that droop in the west
swoon on the arch-gasometer
on Misery Hill brand-new pale livid
oh a most ferocious West African baboon's
swoon on the lil puce
house of prayer

something Heart of Mary
the Bull and Pool Beg that will never meet
not in this world

whereas dart away through the cavorting scapes
bucket o'er Victoria Bridge that's the idea
slow down slink down the Ringsend Road
Irishtown Sandymount puzzle find the Hell Fire
the Merrion Flats scored with a thrillion sigmas
Jesus Christ Son of God Saviour His Finger
girls taken strippin that's the idea
on the Bootersgrad breakwind and water
the tide making the dun gulls in a panic
the sands quicken in your old heart
hide yourself not in the Rock keep on the move
keep on the move

TLS; 2 leaves, 3 sides; enclosed draft of poem published as "Serena 3" in *Echo's Bones*; *T env to* Thomas McGreevy Esq, c/o Messrs. Thomas Cook & Son, Via Tornabuoni, Florence, Italy; *pm* 9-10-33, Dublin [on verso, *pm* 12-XI, Florence]; TCD, MS 10402/55.

1 Having traveled there from Austria on 28 September to meet Henry Church and his wife Barbara, McGreevy was now with them in Florence (McGreevy to his mother, 23 September 1933, TCD MS 10381/59). In Florence, Lungarno is the name given to the road along the Arno River. Giotto (né Giotto di Bondone, c.1267–1337) designed the Campanile (bell tower) of the Duomo; his frescos are in Santa Croce Church in Florence. It is likely that McGreevy sent SB picture postcards with related images, and that one depicted Dante's Beatrice.

2 The poem is a draft of "Serena 3."

3 SB wrote to McGreevy: "I had been working at the short stories and had done about half or two thirds enough when it suddenly dried up and I had to leave it there. Perhaps I may get it going again now. But it is all jigsaw and I am not interested" (22 June 1933, TCD, MS 10402/51). Also in this letter, SB reported that Edward Titus had finally replied and returned *Dream of Fair to Middling Women*: "A most soothing letter from Titus at last, who finds himself forced to slide with the dollar, and abandon his Quarter and Mannekins" [*for* Manikin]. By the end of July, SB wrote to McGreevy from the "top room, 6 Clare St, where I've rigged up a rudimentary appartment [sic] where I pretend to work" (25 [July 1933], TCD, MS 10402/52); before 6 September, he submitted his stories to Charles Prentice: "I sent 10 contes, about 60,000 words, to Charles" (SB to McGreevy, 7 September 1933, TCD, MS 10402/54). "Contes" (stories).

Having had no positive response to *Dream of Fair to Middling Women*, SB may have decided to use selections from it to fill out the stories written for the new collection, initially called *Draff*. He sent it to Charles Prentice by 6 September; on 25 September Prentice wrote that "Chatto's would be delighted to publish the stories," although he asked for a livelier title for the book, "something tripping and conversational" (Prentice to SB, 6 September 1933, UoR, MS 2444 CW letterbook 149/420, and 25 September 1933, UoR, MS 2444 CW letterbook 150/134–135).

SB offered *More Pricks Than Kicks* as a new title and held out the possibility of adding another story or two to the book, according to Prentice's response of 29 September 1933: "Another 10,000 words, or even 5,000 for that matter, would, I am certain, help the book, and it would be lovely if you could manage to reel them out" (UoR, MS 2444 CW letterbook 150/196–197).

4   Denis Devlin wrote to McGreevy about their meetings with SB:
> We have seen Sam Beckett twice in the last few days. He has been charming to us and we talked for hours about Paris and poetry; I was delighted to hear his account of the meeting with Breton and Eluard; Breton impressed him and Eluard inspires affection; which is proper; I think I shall like him. I am discovering him slowly; and according to his movement of course, which is hesitating like a shy horse. He likes using only the essential phrase which makes conversation between him and Brian very amusing. ([23 September 1933], TCD, MS 8112/1)

Coffey and Devlin had proposed to publish poems by McGreevy, SB, and themselves as Christmas cards. SB had written to McGreevy: "About your poem scheme, I suppose I could cast before them the canal Enueg, they might know where Parnell Bridge was and the Fox & Geese, but to tell you the truth I'm not very keen" (7 September [1933], TCD, MS 10402/54). Devlin reported to McGreevy that SB "did promise us his quietest piece and gave it with an air of (and phrase of) 'There; I understand perfectly your difficulties. Commercial, Christmas, Holy Ireland'. What must the others be like! However I like it and we can publish it in perfect safety for its surprise is not sexual nor theological" (23 September 1933, TCD, MS 8112/1). The series did not materialize. The poem "Enueg 1" is the one rejected by *Dublin Magazine* (see [27 November 1931], n. 2).

An algum tree: *Juniperus excelsa* or Grecian juniper.

"Jaunes" (a kind of cigarette); "lac des mains," reference obscure.

5   "Cagne cagneuse," a play on "cagne" (literally, knock-kneed, worn-out horse); the English equivalent of the phrase might be "Cag the nag," with reference to Mr. Cagney the tax collector.

6   Irish novelist and journalist Michael Farrell (1899–1962) studied Medicine at the National University and Trinity College Dublin. His five-volume novel *Thy Tears Might Cease* was Farrell's life's work; he could not bear to cut the novel, which was posthumously edited by Monk Gibbon to 100,000 words and published in 1963.

7   SB's application to the National Gallery (London) for the position of Assistant has not been found; the advertisement called for "a special knowledge of Art History and Study" with preference given "to those with proficiency in Foreign Languages" (*The Times* 8 and 11 September 1933: 3d). Prentice wrote to SB on 4 October: "I do hope that your application to the Nat. Gall. will come off with a bang. [. . .] They

haven't written to me yet in my capacity of 'referee'" (UoR, MS 2444 CW letterbook 150/245). The Garrick Theatre on Charing Cross Road was situated behind the National Gallery.

Florentine painter Paolo Uccello (né Paolo di Dono, 1397–1475); a play on Hamlet's line where he claims to know a "hawk from a hand-saw" (*Hamlet*, II.ii.379); "uccello" (bird).

8 Along with the countersigned contract for *More Pricks Than Kicks*, Prentice sent SB the advance on royalties with the income tax deducted, as he was required to do for non-resident writers; he post-dated the cheque, to "fall within the next six-months report. If you come to live in England before April 5th, we shall pay you the balance of £6.5.0., but if you don't I'll send you the usual voucher regarding the deduction of Income Tax" (4 October 1933, UoR, MS 2444 CW letterbook 150/245). Prentice's calculation is not correct.

9 McGreevy returned to Paris briefly, staying "long enough to verify various matters concerned with work," and then he went on to London. His plan was to settle in Dublin by mid-November: "I must not bury myself in Tarbert at first, shall have to make Dublin my headquarters for some time, but will get home when I can, at Christmas if not before" (McGreevy to his mother, 23 September 1933, TCD, MS 10381/59). He was still in London in mid-November: "I must stay on in London till I make sure of having plenty of work to keep me going when I go to Ireland" (McGreevy to his mother, 19 November 1933, TCD, MS 10381/62).

10 The story became "Echo's Bones" (NhD, Harvey collection). Prentice wrote to SB: "From the tone of your postcard, I infer that the 10,000 yelps will soon be parcelled up and on their way to Holyhead. Good for Belacqua" (2 November 1933, UoR, MS 2444 CW letterbook 151/138; SB's postcard to Prentice has not been found).

"Redivivus" (brought back to life). Belacqua has to be brought back to life because he dies in the final story of the collection, "Draff."

Before 22 June, SB had sent *Dream* to Methuen, but had had no response.

"Nissssscht mööööööglich" (from "nicht möglich" [not possible]) was part of the comic routine of the Swiss clown, Grock (né Charles Adrien Wettach, 1880–1959).

"Ce qu'il est sentimentique!" (How sentimantic he is!); "sentimentique" is a portmanteau word combining "sentimental" and "romantique."

11 "Tante belle cose" (all good things).

Although SB may refer to the town of San Miniato, which is approximately 25 miles from Florence, more probably he refers to the Florentine church of San Miniato al Monte.

THOMAS McGREEVY

LONDON

6/12/33 [*for* 5 December 1933]   6 Clare Street

Dublin

My dear Tom

I haven't been up to anything let alone taper à la, why I couldn't tell you.[1] Perhaps it was the weather which has been fiendish, irresistible cold and damp. I was rejoiced to hear from you though sad also at the impression I got that you were very sad. However a letter from Charles this morning stating you in good form and with the prospects of work.[2] That is good news. Indeed I wish to God I were in London – for a change or en passant – and that we could serve some of this time together again. I thought of apprenticing myself to some advertising firm in London. At least it would get me out of here for a bit and it might be entertaining. Or perhaps there is a faculty of advertising in London by this time. I don't know a damn about it but it has been in my mind for a long time and I had often been on the point of putting it up to father. Now I can put it up to mother. There is always someone to whom one can put it up. If there were only always someone in whom ...

I haven't been doing anything. Charles's fouting à la porte of Echo's Bones, the last story, into which I put all I knew and plenty that I was better still aware of, discouraged me profoundly, au point même de provoquer ce qui suit:

> Asylum under my tread all this day
> Their muffled revels as the flesh rots
> Breaking without fear or favour wind
> The gantelope of sense and nonsense run
> Taken by the worms for what they are.

But no doubt he was right. I tell him so, therefore all that entre nous.[3] The proofs have begun to come in, and I returned a consignment, corrigées si on peut dire, to them to-day.[4] If you have blank hours you would be kind to run your eye over them.

But if not it doesn't matter. They've been corrected so often, long before they got near Charles, that it's beyond further mitigation. Only compositor's errors. I hate the sight of them.

[...]

Shem toujours froissé dans la perfection, c'est dégueulasse.[5]

Read Jeremy Taylor & Leibniz. Why two books, Holy Living & Holy Dying, when one would have done the trick.[6] Surely the classical example of literary tautology. Leibniz a great cod, but full of splendid little pictures.

Horowitz gave a recital at the Royal, but the programme was dull and he out of form. I see the local band is going to give Prokoviev's [for Prokofiev's] Symphony and a Mozart concerto with the Fachiri, so I suppose one must go and take one's medicine. I caught catarrh from their last performance, all the strings distressed ladies and all the rest poilus off for the day.[7]

God love thee.

s/ Sam

TLS; 1 leaf, 2 sides; *T env to* Thomas McGreevy Esq, c/o Mrs Dowden, 15 Cheyne Gardens, London; *pm* 5-12-33, Dublin; TCD, MS 10402/57. *Dating*: from pm.

1 "Taper à la [machine]" (to type).

2 On 28 November 1933, Prentice returned McGreevy's translations of three plays by Henry Church, *Barnum, Indifference,* and *Vasthi,* with regret that Chatto and Windus could not publish them (UoR, MS 2444 CW letterbook 151/497; see also 13 May [1933], n. 15). McGreevy wrote to his mother: "Still stuck in London and still uncertain as to when I'll get home. The bigger schemes mature only slowly though prospects of bringing them off are not discouraging and as for smaller ones I am already reviewing for some of the weeklies here" (30 November 1933, TCD, MS 10381/63/1).

3 Prentice acknowledged receipt of "Echo's Bones" on 10 November, 1933 (UoR, MS 2444 CW letterbook 151/241). He wrote to SB on 13 November 1933: "Do you mind if we leave it out of the book – that is, publish 'More Pricks Than Kicks' in the original form in which you sent it in? Though it's on the short side, we'll still be able to price it at 7/6d. 'Echo's Bones' would, I am sure, lose the book a great many readers." Prentice detailed his own reactions: "It is a nightmare. Just too terribly persuasive. It gives me the jim-jams. The same horrible and immediate switches of the focus, and the same wild unfathomable energy of the population. There are chunks I don't connect with. I am so sorry to feel like this. Perhaps it is only over the details, and

I may have a correct inkling of the main impression. I am sorry, for I hate to be dense, but I hope I am not altogether insensitive. 'Echo's Bones' certainly did land on me with a wallop." However, Prentice took responsibility for what he called "a dreadful débâcle – on my part, not on yours. [...] Yet the only plea for mercy I can make is that the icy touch of those revenant fingers was too much for me. I am sitting on the ground, and ashes are on my head. Please write kindly" (UoR, MS 2444 CW letterbook 151/277).

"Fouting à la porte" (kicking out; a joke anglicizing of a French expression). "Au point même de provoquer ce qui suit" (to the point indeed of provoking the following). This is a draft of the poem, "Echo's Bones." SB wrote to Prentice before 17 November 1933, for Prentice replied: "Your forgiveness is like oil of absolution – but I cannot absolve myself for my failure. Thank you very much. If I may, I'd like to keep 'Echo's Bones' [the story] a little longer, but we'll go ahead with the setting up of the book" (17 November 1933, UoR, MS 2444 CW letterbook 151/325). *More Pricks Than Kicks* was given over to the printer on 20 November.

4 "Corrigées si on peut dire" (corrected, if you can call it that).

5 "Shem toujours froissé dans la perfection, c'est dégueulasse" (Shem still all crinkled up in perfection, it is enough to make you throw up).

6 *The Rule and Exercises of Holy Living* (1650) and *The Rule and Exercises of Holy Dying* (1651) written by Jeremy Taylor (1613–1667), Bishop of Down and Connor in Ireland after the Restoration. German philosopher, mathematician, and logician Gottfried Wilhelm Leibniz (1646–1716).

7 Vladimir Horowitz's concert at the Theatre Royal took place on 18 November 1933; the program included four chorale preludes by Bach arranged for piano by Busoni; Beethoven's Piano Sonata no. 26 in E-flat major, op. 81a ("Das Lebewohl, Abwesenheit, und Wiedersehn" [more commonly known as "Les Adieux"]); *Arabeske* in C major, op. 18, by Robert Schumann (1810–1856); Liszt's "Après une lecture du Dante, fantasia quasi sonata," *Années de pèlerinage, deuxième année, Italie, 2 versions*, no. 7; two études, a mazurka, and the Scherzo in B minor, op. 20, by Chopin; the études "Pour les arpèges composés" and "Pour les cinq doigts," by Claude-Achille Debussy (1862–1918); and Horowitz's own "Variations on a Theme from Bizet's Opera *Carmen*" (*The Irish Times* 17 November 1933: 6; 20 November 1933: 4).

Rather than the program indicated by SB (a Mozart concerto and a symphony by Russian composer Sergei Prokofiev [1891–1953]), the Dublin Philharmonic Orchestra presented a program featuring Hungarian-born violinist Adila Fachiri (1886–1962) on 3 March 1934. She played the Beethoven Violin Concerto in D major, op. 61, and the "Introduction and Rondo Capriccioso" for Orchestra and Solo Violin, op. 28, by French composer Camille Saint-Saëns (1835–1921). The Dublin Philharmonic Orchestra played two pieces by Wagner: the Overture and Bacchanal from the opera *Tannhäuser* and the "Forest Murmurs" from his opera *Siegfried*; it also played *The Wand of Youth*, op. 1, no. 2, by British composer Edward Elgar (1857–1934) ("Dublin Philharmonic Society: Last Concert in Theatre Royal," *The Irish Times* 5 March 1934: 5).

"Poilus" (Other Ranks).

CHRONOLOGY 1934

1934 By 23 January   SB moves to London, living at 48 Paultons Square. Recommends A. J. Leventhal's thesis to Chatto and Windus; it is rejected.

By 27 January   Begins psychotherapy with W. R. Bion, going three times a week.

By 1 February   Sends proofs of *More Pricks Than Kicks* to Rinehart, who forwards them to US partner, Farrar.

15 February   *Contempo* publishes "Home Olga."

16 February   Publication of *Negro, Anthology Made by Nancy Cunard, 1931–1933.*

By 4 April   Chatto and Windus offers *More Pricks Than Kicks* to Harrison Smith and Haas in New York.

By 7 May   SB writes what he calls "a couple of Quatschrains."

By 9 May   McGreevy submits SB's review of J[ames] B[lair] Leishman's translation of Rilke's *Poems* to *The Criterion.*

23 May   *The Spectator* publishes "Schwabenstreich," SB's review of the English translation, *Mozart on the Journey to Prague*, written by Eduard Mörike.

24 May   Publication of *More Pricks Than Kicks.*

22 June   *The Spectator* publishes "Proust in Pieces," SB's review of Albert Feuillerat's *Comment Proust a composé son roman.*

23 June   SB accepts Reavey's offer to represent *More Pricks Than Kicks* abroad.

July	*Dublin Magazine* publishes poem "Gnome" and SB's review of McGreevy's *Poems*, "Humanistic Quietism."
13 July	*The Criterion* publishes SB's review of Leishman's translation of Rilke's *Poems*.
August	*The Bookman* publishes SB's story "A Case in a Thousand" and, under the pseudonym of Andrew Belis, his critical essay "Recent Irish Poetry."
2 August	SB leaves London for Dublin.
By 7 August	*The Bookman* asks for an article on censorship in Ireland.
By 16 August	SB sends "Enueg" (later "Enueg 1") to *The Bookman*.
By 27 August	*The Bookman* rejects "Enueg" SB sends "Censorship in the Saorstat" to *The Bookman*.
2/3 September	Returns to London; moves to 34 Gertrude Street. Resumes psychotherapy.
23 October	*More Pricks Than Kicks* is placed on the "Index of Forbidden Books in Ireland."
1 November	SB sends poems to *Poetry Magazine*: "Dortmunder," "Echo's Bones," "Enueg," and "Moly" (later "Yoke of Liberty").
December	Reviews published in Christmas issue of *The Bookman*: "Ex Cathezra" (of Ezra Pound's *Make It New*), "Papini's Dante" (of Giovanni Papini's *Dante Vivo*), and "The Essential and the Incidental" (of Sean O'Casey's *Windfalls*).
c. 20 December	SB in Dublin for the holidays.
31 December	Charles Prentice resigns as Partner of Chatto and Windus.

27/1/24 [*for* 1934]   48 Paulton's Square
                                        [London] S.W. 3

Cher ami[1]

Ta lettre, reçue ce matin, m'a fait beaucoup de plaisir et
j'espère que tu m'en adresseras beaucoup de semblables. Je n'ai
eu aucune peine à la déchiffrer. Aussi tes communications,
exprimées, j'ose [le] dire, avec une lucidité peu inférieure à
celle des frères Grimm, n'ont-elles nullement embarrassé la
connaissance très imparfaite que j'ai de la langue allemande.[2]
Vas-y donc de bon coeur – hebdomadairement, au moins.

Enchanté d'apprendre que la vie te sourit, nonobstant le
climat plutôt vert de tes humanités, et que l'étrange quadrupède
aux bosses inverties garde sa sérénité. Cet animal-là, il m'a
toujours inspiré d'une [*for* une] certaine inquiétude à son égard,
c'est que la vie très quiétiste qu'il mène ne le pousse un de ces
jours à se précipiter, à la façon d'un porc biblique, dans la mer. Ce
serait à regretter. Tu ferais peut-être bien de l'entretenir à ce sujet.
Explique-lui que l'ennui est le plus supportable de tous les maux,
étant le plus fréquent, et que mieux vaut avoir le cafard que le
ventre plein de homards. Si d'abord il a l'air de ne pas vouloir
se laisser convaincre, tu n'as qu'à le prendre par son côté faible,
à savoir sa vanité (car tout cheval est excessivement vain), en
lui représentant que la courbe de son échine aurait fait venir la
salive aux lèvres de Botticelli, et que ce serait vraiment dommage,
voire criminel, de priver les yeux des Howthiens d'un tel triomphe

de sinuosité.[3] Et enfin si, en manière de conclusion, tu lui dis: "Que m'importe que tu sois sage, Sois beau et sois triste", ce sera fini, n'en doute pas, de sa résistance. Il se rendra. Il condescendra à être beau, il est même possible que sa tristesse, absorbée dans la conscience de sa rhapsodie dorsale que grâce à toi il vient d'acquérir, s'évanouisse complètement. Mais puisque la tristesse ajoute toujours à la beauté, puisqu'elle est comme l'élément éternel, invariable, de ce que Baudelaire appelle le "divin gâteau", du moins à mon avis, j'aimerais mieux que notre cheval reste fidèle aux attitudes, boudeuses et mélancoliques, que je lui ai toujours connues.[4] Quoi qu'il en soit, et en relisant ce que je viens si péniblement d'énoncer, je constate que je m'en fous royalement, du cheval, de son sort, de ses bosses inverties et des esthètes de Howth. Qu'il se noie s'il veut. Qu'il agonise lentement, [en] proie aux plus affreuses douleurs, dans son champ, renversé sur le dos, les quatre jambes levées au ciel. Je m'en désintéresse totalement. N'en parlons plus.

Cissie m'a dit que tu fais du Bach. Malheureux! Toi, je veux dire, pas lui, qui ne l'a jamais été. J'ai dû essuyer une énorme composition de lui, humoristiquement intitulée: Suite pour Orchestre, dirigée par l'ignoble Furtwängler, qui, parait'il, s'est récemment fait couvrir le meilleur de sa nudité de Hackenkreuze [*for* Hakenkreuze] entrelacés.[5] Il a la charmante modestie de se laisser diriger par ses cuivres (qui soufflent comme seuls les buveurs de bière savent le faire), tout en faisant de sa petite main gauche des gestes très osés à l'intention de ses premiers violons, qui n'y ont fait heureusement pas la moindre attention, et en agitant ses tendres chairs postérieures comme s'il avait une grosse envie de visiter le[s] lavabos. A peine m'étais-je remis de cet assaut qu'il a eu l'incroyable impertinence d'attaquer la 4me Symphonie de Schumann, qui ressemble moins à une symphonie qu'à une ouverture commencée par Lehar, terminée par Goering et revue par Johnny Doyle (sinon par son chien), et qui ne vaut vraiment pas la peine d'être considérée, sans parler d'être attaquée.[6] Il va de soi que Furtwängler l'assassin, avec la connivance de ses âmes damnées, a remporté la victoire, si le fait de massacrer une partition qui n'a certainement jamais vécu peut constituer une victoire. Réduire rien à rien, et y mettre trois quarts d'heure, voilà du beau! Puis enfin il a pu aller au[x] lavabos. Mais, au lieu d'y passer le reste de sa vie, il est revenu, suivi de ses bourreaux adjoints, afin de nous déchirer la 7me de Beethoven en tout petits morceaux. Monsieur Furtwängler, bon Nazi, il ne tolère point les mystères, et c'est assez comme un oeuf au plat ou, si tu préfères, comme un pied là-dedans, qu'il a bien voulu nous pré[s]enter cette musique. Il a joué le dernier mouvement comme un Ständchen des plus élégants. Il a remporté un succès fou. Non content de boutonner cette pauvre symphonie jusqu'à l'étranglement, il s'est permis d'en garnir la boutonnière. ET [sic] de quoi, bon sang de bon Dieu? D'un Würstchen.[7]

Trois fois par semaine je me livre aux fouilles chez mon psychiâtre, ce qui m'a déjà fait, je crois, du bien, dans le sens que je peux me tenir un peu plus tranquille et que les coups de panique la nuit deviennent moins fréquents et moins aigus. Mais le traitement sera nécessairement long, et j'en aurai peut-être pour des mois encore. Je ne m'en plains pas, je me considère très fortuné d'avoir pu l'entreprendre, c'est l'unique chose qui m'intéresse actuellement, et comme ça c'est bien, car ces sortes de chose-là exigent qu'on s'y consacre à l'exclusion presque de tout autre intérêt.[8] Par conséquent, je n'ai pas le loisir, même si j'en avais l'envie, de faire quoi que ce soit en fait de littérature. Et comme ça c'est peut-être bien aussi. J'en ai déjà fait beaucoup trop, peu et pourtant trop, n'ayant jamais rien compris à rien. A part les tâtonnements dont je parle et de nombreux station-nements devant des tableaux, je reste chez moi, où je suis assez confortablement logé, vautré dans un fauteuil devant mon radiateur, en attendant qu'il soit temps d'aller me coucher, mouvement que maintenant je peux faire avec un peu plus de confiance qu'il y avait un mois. Et voilà tout. Phase comme les autres.

Salue la famille, très familièrement. Fais-les écrire, j'aimerais bien une lettre de Boss, et écris toi-même.

      A toi

         s/ Sam

TLS; 2 leaves, 4 sides; Sinclair. *Dating*: SB lived at this address in 1934.

27/1/24 [*for* 1934]   48 Paulton's Square

                                    S.W. 3

Dear Sonny,[1]

Your letter, received this morning, gave me a great deal of pleasure, and I hope that you will send me many more like that. I had no difficulty in making it out. So you see your missives, expressed, I make so bold as to say, with a lucidity little short of that of the Grimm brothers, in no way troubled the very imperfect understanding that I have of the German language.[2] So set to, without stint – weekly, at the least.

Delighted to hear that life is looking kindly on you, notwith-standing the rather green climate of your humanities, and that that strange quadruped with the inverted humps is keeping up his serenity. That animal has always inspired in me a certain anxiety, which is that the very quietistic life that he leads might drive him one of these days to throw himself, like the Biblical swine, into the sea. That would be a matter for regret. You might perhaps do well to engage him on this subject. Explain to him that ennui is the most bearable of all ills, being the commonest, and that it is better to be down in the dumps than to have a bellyful of lobsters. If at first he looks unwilling to let himself be persuaded, all you have to do is to get hold of him by his weak side, that is his vanity (for every horse is exceedingly vain), by making out to him that the curve of his spine would have made Botticelli's mouth water, and that it would be a great pity, nay it would be criminal, if he deprived the Howthians of such a triumph of sinuousness.[3] And if, by way of conclusion, you say to him: 'What matter whether you are good, / Be beautiful and be sad', that will be, make no doubt of it, the end of his resistance. He will give in. He will condescend to be beautiful. It is even possible that his sadness, absorbed into the awareness of his dorsal rhapsody, which thanks to you he has just acquired, will vanish altogether. But since sadness always adds to beauty, since it is the eternal, invariable element of what Baudelaire calls the 'divine cake', in my view at least, I would prefer our horse to remain faithful to the pouting, melancholic attitudes that I have always known him to have.[4] However all that may be, and on re-reading what I have just, with such difficulty, put into words, I note that I do not give a tuppenny damn for the horse, his destiny, his inverted humps, or the aesthetes of Howth. Let him drown if he wants to. May he have a slow death, with the most frightful pains, in his field, on his back, with his four legs up in the air. I have no further interest in him whatsoever. No more of him.

Cissie tells me that that you are on to Bach. Poor wretch! You, I mean, not Bach, who never was that. I have had to put up with a huge composition by him, humorously entitled: Suite for Orchestra, conducted by the ignoble Furtwängler, who, it appears, has had the better part of his nudity covered with interwoven swastikas.[5] He has the charming modesty of letting himself be led by his brass-players, who blow as only beer-drinkers can, while making with his little left hand very daring gestures towards his first violins, who fortunately paid not the least attention to them, and swinging the soft fleshiness of his posterior as if he longed to go the lavatory. Hardly had I recovered from this assault when he had the impertinence to launch into Schumann's Fourth Symphony, which is less like a symphony than like an overture begun by Lehar, completed by Goering, and revised by Johnny Doyle (if not his dog), and which is not really worth thinking about, let alone launching into.[6] Needless to say that the murderous Furtwängler, with the connivance of his damned souls, was victorious, if massacring a score that has certainly never been alive can count as a victory. To make nothing out of nothing, and take three-quarters of an hour over it, now there is an achievement! Then finally he was able to go to the lavatory. But instead of staying there for the rest of his life, he came back, followed by his assistant executioners, in order to tear into tatters, in front of us, Beethoven's 7th. Mr Furtwängler, like the good Nazi he is, cannot tolerate mysteries, and it was rather like a fried egg, or, if you prefer, like a foot put in it, that he presented this music. He played the last movement like the most elegant of Ständchen. He had a rapturous reception. Not only did he button up that poor symphony to the point of strangulation, but he took the liberty of giving it a colourful buttonhole. And with what, in God's name? A Würstchen.[7]

Three times a week I give myself over to probing the depths with my psychiatrist, which has already, I think, done me some good, in the sense that I can keep a little calmer, and that the panic attacks in the night are less frequent and less acute. But the treatment will necessarily be long, and I may have months more of it yet. I am not complaining, I regard myself as very fortunate to have been able to embark on it, it is the only thing that interests me at the moment, and that is how it should be, for these sorts of things require one to attend to them to the exclusion of virtually anything else.[8] As a result, I have not the leisure, even if I had the desire, to do anything whatever in the way of literature. And perhaps that too is as it should be. I've already done far too much, little and yet too much, never having had any idea about anything. Apart from the gropings that I've spoken of, and a great number of moments spent standing in front of pictures, I stay at home, where I am quite comfortable, draped in an armchair in front of my radiator, passing the time until I can go to bed, which is an operation I can carry out a little more confidently than a month ago. And that is all. A phase like any other.

Regards, fond regards to the family. Get them to write, I would like a letter from Boss, and write yourself.

> Yours
>
> Sam

1 SB's cousin Morris Sinclair was known in the family as "Sunny," although SB often used "Sonny," alluding to "Sonne" (sun).

2 Jakob and Wilhelm Grimm (see 23 March 1929, n. 2). Morris Sinclair observed, "the Grimm brothers [. . .] collected many of their folk tales from an old woman who lived in a hamlet just south of Kassel" (Morris Sinclair, 28 November 1993).

3 In his letter to SB, Morris Sinclair had described this horse in a field on Howth. Botticelli (né Allesandro di Mariano di Felipepi, c. 1444–1510).

4 "Madrigal triste," a poem by Charles Baudelaire (1821–1867), opens with the lines: "Que m'importe que tu sois sage? / Sois belle! et sois triste!" ("What does it matter to me that you are wise? / Be lovely – and be sad!") (Charles Baudelaire, *Oeuvres complètes*, I, ed. Claude Pichois and Jean Ziegler, Bibliothèque de la Pléiade [Paris:

Gallimard, 1975–1976] 137–138; Charles Baudelaire, *Les Fleurs du Mal, The Flowers of Evil*, tr. Richard Howard [Boston: David R. Godine, 1982] 170–171).

SB also refers to Baudelaire's prose poem, "Le Gâteau," in which a shared piece of bread becomes "gâteau" to two brothers who fight over it, until it disappears (Baudelaire, *Le Spleen de Paris* in *Oeuvres complètes*, I, 297–299).

5 On 22 January 1934, Wilhelm Furtwängler (1886–1954) conducted the Berlin Philharmonic Orchestra at Queen's Hall, London; the concert comprised Bach's Suite for Orchestra no. 2 in B minor, BWV 1067, Schumann's Symphony no. 4 in D minor, op. 120, and Beethoven's Symphony no. 7 in A major, op. 92.

SB alludes to Furtwängler's decision to remain in Germany and to his continuing dealings with the Nazi regime (for full discussion of the latter: Hans-Hubert Schönzeler, *Furtwängler* [London: Gerald Duckworth, 1990] 48–90).

"Hakenkreuze" (swastikas).

6 Schumann's Symphony no. 4 was recorded by Furtwängler with the Berlin Philharmonic (Deutsche Grammophon, LPE 17 170). Franz Lehar (1870–1948), Hungarian-born Viennese composer and conductor, was best known for his operettas, especially *The Merry Widow*, and his military marches.

Hermann Goering (1893–1946), President of the Reichstag (1932) and later Commander of the Luftwaffe.

SB's reference to Johnny Doyle is not certain and may be generic. He may refer to J. C. Doyle (n.d.), a vocalist famous for his renditions of Irish songs ("Well-Known Dublin Singer," *Irish Times* 10 November 1930: 4); or, as Morris Sinclair has suggested, he may refer to J. M. Doyle, a postman in the Baily postal district (Howth, Co. Dublin) where the Sinclairs lived when they returned from Germany to Dublin (Morris Sinclair, 5 November 1994).

7 "Ständchen" (serenade),"Würstchen" (sausage).

8 SB had recently begun psychotherapy with Wilfred Ruprecht Bion* (1897–1979). Although SB consistently uses the term "analysis," as Lois Oppenheim has observed, Bion was not yet qualified as a psychoanalyst (Lois Oppenheim, "A Preoccupation with Object-Representation: the Beckett–Bion Case Revisited," *International Journal of Psycho-Analysis* 82.4 [2001] 768).

NUALA COSTELLO

LONDON

27/2/34   48 Paulton's Sq.

[London] S.W. 3

Dear Nuala[1]

It's a great handicap to me in all my anabases and stases that I can't express myself in a straightforward manner, and that I cannot behave in a way that has the most tenuous propriety of relationship to circumstance. A great handicap. I regret it very much, more than I can ever hope to be able to tell. But there it is. One is not what one is not. Not for doing, I find in my Dante, but for not doing, is Virgil in Limbo, though honoured above the deadborn that are there, and above the throngs of men and women who exercised all the virtues at top pressure save only the theological group with which they were not familiar that are there also, with a roving commission as far as the purgatorial Eden, where he withdraws and the ladies take over.[2] Well I might do worse than find myself as it were polarised between Democritus and Heraclitus for all eternity, in a place where sighing is out of melancholy and not out of torment. I would be familiar with the position. There seems to be contradiction inherent in the idea of Democritus doing anything so romantic, and indeed of Heraclitus doing anything so restrained, as sighing, but one must not mind that.[3] There is really nothing that one should mind, or if there is I should be interested to know what for example. Perhaps Curtis would know.[4] I have asked Percy and found his divulgations always somehow unsatisfactory.[5] Perhaps the author of the Coloured Dome would know, he might look it up for me in his Saint Teresa; or perhaps Mr R. B. Barry would know, he might find it in one of the Inns of Court, the Middle Temple Library say, which possesses some curious works on witchcraft; or if none of those know, perhaps the petrified asp at the junction of d'Olier, College, Pearse and Townsend Streets, if I have not forgotten my Dublin, might be persuaded to pronounce on the question, or the wild waves of the outfall at the Pigeon House, or even the noble étron which on the night of my departure I remarked in College Green and which is still there no doubt.[6] But if none of these or cognate authoritie[s] know, or knowing decline to tell, then I must just stay as I am, and console myself as best I can with the thought that I have been saved the trouble of moving. For the essence of all anabasis, I mean of all anabasis of good quality, is to be sought in its purity from destination and hence from schedule. That follows on most naturally, does it not, from what I have been saying, while from it again in its turn, if indeed the word turn has any sense in the context, I mean from this delicious conception of movement as gress, pure and mere gress, one arrives like a bird to its nest, though nest scarcely seems to be the right word in such a passage, at an elucidation of the crime immotivé that never occurred and never could to Gide or to any of his kidney, or indeed to any person within earshot of the ringing grooves save only to myself, who I assure you could not be induced to part with it for love or money or any other incitement whatever, on account of its inestimable antiphlogistic properties that exceed anything of the kind I ever tried, and I have tried everything, from cold water to reduce blushing to Guinness as an anterotic.[7]

I did not call on you after all, the weather made it impossible. Also I would like to correct now while I think of it an error that occurred I seem to remember in my last letter to you, where I spoke of changing for Harley Street and the Zoological Gardens.[8] Of course one does not change, one alights. Alight for Monkey Hill, alight for the Wild Asses House, Small Rodents House, Small Cats House, Fellows Tea Pavilion, for the Adders, the Brush Turkies [*for* Turkeys], the Prairie Dogs and Waders, alight for the Gnus Paddock, the Goat Hills, the Gazellez [*for* Gazelles] Sheds and the Racoons [*for* Raccoons] Cages, for the Swine, the Lemurs, the Civets and the Birds of Prey, alight for Karin Stephen, Melanie Klein, Creighton Miller [*for* Crichton-Miller] and Burt White, alight to them that sprawl in darkness and in the shadow of – resurrection.[9] Or go on to Hampstead and have a drink at the Spaniards, and look at your brother the fly, oh the Spanish fly, moving out of darkness into light, et sqq. Where do the cantharides go in the winter time? Amn't I after telling you, some go to Hampstead and the rest do like the swallows do, rush into a coagulum and drown themselves in a dewpond. Mass suicide, Percy knows all about it.[10] Hence we arrive at the couplet that deserves the Croix de Guerre, or perhaps better the Dunmow Flitch:

> Light and sweetness, sweetness and light,
> Obliterate gloom, engender delight.[11]

Yes, I wrote two little poems, one after a brief interview with the Author of the Strange Necessity (positively surprising my dear), and the other after profound and prolonged communion with the strange (not to be believed my dear) flora and fauna of my sunken garden, and ut infra respectively they gallop along:

> There once was a woman called West
> Whose distinction it was to be blest
> > With so unremitting
> > A sense of the fitting
> That she seldom, if ever, undressed.

(Until she met Wells, and then I supposed she had to.)[12] This poemetto has been well received in certain quarters. This other, which I now propose to you but only after some hesitation, and in a regular little storm of scraping and bowing and moping and mowing believe me, less well:

> Mammon's bottoms,
> La Goulue's, mine, a cob's,
> Whipt, caressed,
> My mother's breast.
>
> But God's
> A goat's, an ass's,

Alien beauty,
The Divine Comedy.[13]

You don't care for it. I don't care for it much myself. But that it is a poem and not verse, that it is a prayer and not a collect, I have not the slightest doubt, not the slightest.

It is hard to believe what you say of Dublin, that the youth, the talent and harmosity are flown. I bought yesterday a bottle of ink

> (Said the elephant to the owl:
> "Oh what'll you have to drink?"
> Said the elephant to the owl:
> "Oh what'll you have to drink?"
> Said the elephant to the owl:
> "Oh what'll you have to drink?"
> "Oh thank you kindly, sir", he said,
> "I'll have a bottle of ink.")

from a lady of Clonmel extraction and who dared not cook herself up with the vain hope of ever setting foot again in Fishguard.[14] But then in the next breath you quote Percy, and indeed the passage was so real to me as I read it that I had to take out my handkerchief. Now I think you will be put to the pin o[f] your collarette to make Percy drinking coffee and saying things like that consist with Dublin bereft. I am thinking that I might well employ these long, sober (Kia-ora and the wildest scenes of virtue) evenings in writing a True-born Jackeen on the model of Defoe's True-born Englishman, though of course infinitely more amusing and competent.[15] He shall have it then hot from the vinegar.

My velleities of self-diffusion in this stew of LETTERS have been repulsed with the traditional contumely, so now I'm sulking and won't play. The book won't be out for a month at least. Can't get it taken in U.S.A.[16] So I read the last word in obscenities in the British Museum, to whose incredible central sanctum I have gained admittance on the strength of an irrepressible anxiety to "consult the lesser know[n] French and Italian texts that are not available elsewhere", and then walk home across the string of Parks beginning with the Horse Guards, shivering and my feet in marmalade, past the celebrated pelicans that really have a most charitable expression and whose inward eye they deign to extra-vert and bliss of solitude interrupt readily at any time to feed (for who knows when they may have to disembowel themselves at a moment's notice?), and eat the most expensive egg that money can buy, though it is surely a strange thing that a rich man would be in and out of heaven twenty times over while you would be looking for a duck's egg in Old Chelsea, and perhaps this is the moment to mention that I am a Bigendian, not instinctively but by education. Instinctively I am a Smallendian, with the result that when I am tired or my mind clouded these two wretched affinities, the civilised for the large, and the primitive for the small, end of the egg, come into conflict and the egg is not eaten.[17]

No, I think I am all set now to give Liffey's stinking tide a long long miss, and indeed for the moment I have no choice in the matter, but must remain on here as long as this treatment lasts, and God knows how long that will be, probably more months than I like to contemplate. Anyhow I can't stop now, and dare not if I could, for if I did the second state of this man ... So my life is the complete Comédie à tiroirs-vides.[18]

My obeisances where obeisances are due, and thee I embrace, as Sordello Virgil, là 've il minor s'appiglia, and if you write me a very nice letter I'll give you the reference.[19]

      A toi

        s/ Sam

TLS; 2 leaves, 4 sides; Costello.

1 Nuala Costello* (1907–1984) began postgraduate study at the Sorbonne in 1929; in Paris, she met Lucia Joyce, and, through Giorgio and Helen Joyce, met SB (Patrick

O'Dwyer, "Letters from Paris," *The Great Tuam Annual* [1991] 73, 75). Of her, SB had written to McGreevy: "I met a Miss Cóstéllo (where is the accent?) once met chez Giorgio's flitch, when Shem was there and Colum and all the galère, affiancée then but now disponible, and she frightened me back into my âme des glaces. Who is she?" (7 September [1933], TCD, MS 10402/54). "Galère" (crew); "affiancée" (SB's conflation of "affianced" and "fiancée"); "disponible" (available); "âme des glaces" (soul of ice).

Helen Fleischman (née Kastor, 1894–1963) married Giorgio Joyce in December 1930; Padraic Colum (1881–1972), Irish-American writer and critic.

2   In Dante's *Inferno*, Virgil is among the honored in Limbo, the first Circle of Hell, because as a pagan he could not ascend to Paradise. Virgil is allowed to lead Dante on his journey through the Circles of Hell and through Purgatory; when he withdraws, he says to Dante: "'per ch' io te sovra te corono e mitrio'" ("therefore over thyself I crown and mitre thee") (Dante, *La Divina Commedia, Purgatorio*, Canto XXVII, line 142; Dante, *The Divine Comedy*, II, *Purgatorio*, tr. Sinclair, 357).

Dante is led farther by the fair lady culling flowers, Matilda, and by Beatrice; these two lead him into Paradise. In keeping with his statement that "I can't express myself in a straightforward manner," SB refers directly not to the *locus classicus* in which Limbo is depicted, *Inferno* Canto IV, but to Virgil's account of himself delivered to Sordello in *Purgatorio* Canto VII, line 25: "'Non per far, ma per non fare'" ("Not for doing, but for not doing") (Dante, *La Divina Commedia*; Dante, *The Divine Comedy*, II, *Purgatorio*, tr. Sinclair, 95).

3   SB wrote "Democritus <sighing> doing."

In *Inferno* IV, lines 136–138, the pre-Socratic philosophers Democritus (c.460–c.370 BC) and Heraclitus are presented. Democritus is reputed to have laughed at human folly, and Heraclitus is reputed to have wept at it; SB imagines himself "polarized between" the two extremes. SB cites from *Purgatorio* VII, lines 29–30: "ove i lamenti / non suonan come guai, ma son sospiri" (where the laments have no sound of wailing but are sighs) (Dante, *La Divina Commedia*; Dante,*The Divine Comedy*, II, *Purgatorio*, tr. Sinclair, 95, 97).

4   Edmund Curtis, Professor of Modern History at Trinity College Dublin from 1914 to 1943, was author of *The Normans in Lower Italy* (1912), *A History of Mediaeval Ireland from 1110 to 1513* (1923), and, at that time, was writing *A History of Ireland* (1936).

5   SB may have asked this question in conversation.

6   Francis Stuart* (né Henry Francis Montgomery Stuart, 1902–2000), Australian-born Irish writer, author of *The Coloured Dome* (1932) and *Women and God* (1931). Stuart was influenced by his reading of Evelyn Underhill's *Mysticism* (1912) and studied the lives of the saints. The "most important of all, to him, [was] St. Thérèse of Lisieux," according to his biographer Geoffrey Elborn: "Stuart speculated that if St. Thérèse 'had not been a nun what a lover she would have made.' This interpretation formed part of the foundation for Stuart's belief that the search for fulfilment through women was part of the same longing for a passionate relationship with God" (Geoffrey Elborn, *Francis Stuart: A Life* [Dublin: Raven Arts Press, 1990] 73–74).

Ralph Brereton-Barry (1899–1943) graduated from Trinity College Dublin and was called to the Irish Bar in 1922, and to the English Bar (Gray's Inn) in 1933. As a member of one of the four Inns of Court, he would have had access to the library of the Middle Temple, whose Rare and Antiquarian historical collections include some books and tracts on witchcraft; however, there is no current collection as such (Stuart Adams, Library, Middle Temple, London, 1 April 2005).

The junction of D'Olier, College, Pearse, and Townsend streets is on the west side of TCD.
Pigeon House: 25 January 1931, n. 6.
"Etron" (turd).

7 "Gress" (movement; a noun derived from "gressus," supine of Lat. verb "gradior,
gradi, gressus" [to walk, to step]).

"Crime immotivé" (unmotivated crime). André Gide's novel, *Les Caves du Vatican*
(1914; *The Caves of the Vatican*), explores an "acte gratuit" (a gratuitous act) which
takes the form of a crime.

SB quotes from the poem "Locksley Hall" by Alfred Tennyson (1809–1892):
"Forward, forward let us range, / Let the great world spin for ever down the ringing
grooves of change" (*Tennyson: A Selected Edition, Incorporating the Trinity College
Manuscripts*, ed. Christopher Ricks [Berkeley: University of California Press, 1989] 192).
Guinness stout.

8 SB's previous letter to Nuala Costello has not been found. Harley Street, London
W1, has a concentration of physicians' consulting rooms; it is off Marylebone Road,
near Regent's Park station at the southeast side of Regent's Park; the Zoological
Gardens, off Prince Albert Road, near Primrose Hill, were on the northeast side of
Regent's Park.

9 Within SB's list of animal houses in Regent's Park Zoo, he includes practitioners
whose rooms might be found in the vicinity of nearby Harley Street: psychiatrist Karin
Costelloe Stephen (1889–1953); psychoanalysts Melanie Klein (1882–1960) and Hugh
Crichton-Miller (1877–1959); and surgeon and gynaecologist Harold J. Burt-White
(1901–1952) who was much in the news on account of reckless driving and a divorce case.

10 The Spaniards Inn, Hampstead Heath (see 8 October 1932, n. 5).
An aphrodisiac, "Spanish fly," also known as cantharides. The dried bodies of the
Lytta vesicatoria (also *Cantharis vesicatoria*) beetle, or blister beetle, are a natural inflam-
matory agent. Most cantharides pass the winter as coarctate larvae.
"Et sqq." (Lat., and the following [abbreviation for *et sequentes*]).
In conversation with SB, Arland Ussher may have observed a similarity between the
mass deaths of beetles and swallows, or this may be SB's invention. There was a
contemporary occasion for such comparison, for in 1931, swallows died in massive
numbers when their migration patterns were severely disrupted by storms in the Alps
(see *The Times* 5, 7, 25, and 28 September 1931).

11 The Dunmow Flitch award was given to the "Happiest Couple." The expression
"eating Dunmow bacon" was used of happily married couples, who had lived long
together and never quarreled. It alludes to the custom begun in 1104: "Any person
going to Dunmow, in Essex, and humbly kneeling on two sharp stones at the church
door, might claim a flitch of bacon if he could swear that for 12 months and a day he
had never had a household brawl or wished himself unmarried" (Ebenezer Cobham
Brewer, *Brewer's Dictionary of Phrase and Fable*, rev. Adrian Room,16th edn. [New York,
HarperResource-HarperCollins, 1999] 373). The Flitch Trials still are held in Little
Dunmow before a jury of six spinsters and six bachelors.

12 Rebecca West, *Strange Necessity* (1928). West had an affair in the autumn of 1913
with H[erbert] G[eorge] Wells (1866–1946), and a child by him, the writer Anthony
West (1914–1987). SB's "interview" with Rebecca West is not documented.
"Ut infra" (as below).

13 "La Goulue" (greedy woman), the Moulin Rouge performer Louise Weber (1870–1929), whose nickname came from out-drinking anyone in the bar; she and her performing partner, Jacques Renaudin (nicknamed Valentin le Désossé, 1843–1907), were depicted by Henri de Toulouse-Lautrec (1864–1901) in his poster *Moulin Rouge – La Goulue*.

14 Clonmel, Co. Tipperary, Ireland, 30 miles northwest of Waterford. Fishguard, Wales, on the Irish Sea, the ferryport to Rosslare, County Wexford, Ireland.

15 Kia-Ora is an orange fruit drink, originally lemon, created in Australia and marketed in Britain since 1913; "Kia-Ora" (Maori, good health).

Whether SB's proposal of a "Trueborn Jackeen" was in jest, or, as John Pilling asserts, a fictional project using Irish materials later abandoned, James Knowlson indicates that SB did make notes on Irish history for Joyce ("'For Interpolation': Beckett and English Literature," *Notes Diverse Holo*, Special issue *SBT/A* 16 [2006] 223]; Knowlson, *Damned to Fame*, 638, n. 49; Everett Frost and Jane Maxwell, "TCD MS 10971/2: Irish History," *Notes Diverse Holo*, Special issue *SBT/A* 16 [2006] 126).

"Jackeen" (Anglo-Irish, a self-assertive, worthless fellow). Defoe's satirical poem was "The True-Born Englishman" (1701).

16 *More Pricks Than Kicks* was published by Chatto and Windus on 24 May 1934, held up while Charles Prentice attempted to find a publisher in the United States. He first contacted the publisher of Joyce at Viking Press, Benjamin W. Huebsch (1876–1964), who declined (Prentice to Huebsch, 23 January 1934 [UoR, MS 2444 CW letterbook 153/175]; Prentice to SB, 23 January 1934 [UoR, MS 2444 CW letterbook 153/177]; Huebsch to Prentice, 31 January 1934 [UoR, MS 2444 CW 57/2]). Prentice then sent uncorrected proofs to Stanley Marshall Rinehart (1897–1969), who offered to forward them to his publishing partner John Farrar (1896–1974) (Prentice to Rinehart, 1 February 1934; Prentice to Rinehart, 7 February 1934; UoR, MS 2444 CW letterbook 153/307 and 1378).

Having had no final word from Rinehart/Farrar, Prentice sent *More Pricks Than Kicks* to New York publishers, Harrison Smith and Robert Haas (1932–1936), as he wrote to SB on 4 April 1934:

> So, unless we click with Smith & Haas, or unless you would like us to try another Yank, I am rather inclined to think that the manufacture of the book should be put in hand when we hear from Smith & Haas, whatever their decision is. But just as you like. I don't want to hurry you a bit. The object of this letter is simply to find out what your own opinion is. (UoR, MS2444. CW letterbook 155/91)

17 SB's reading in the British Museum: 22 July 1932.

SB describes his walk across London parks from Trafalgar Square in the direction of Chelsea: the Horse Guards' Parade, St. James's Park, Green Park, Buckingham Palace Gardens, Hyde Park, Kensington Gardens. The lake in St. James's Park is a sanctuary for ducks and pelicans.

Marmalade (anything soft, squishy). Reference to Matthew 19:24: "it is easier for a camel to go through the eye of a needle than for a rich man to enter the kingdom of God." SB refers to Jonathan Swift's "A Voyage to Lilliput" in *Gulliver's Travels* (1726), in which Catholics are caricatured as Big-Endians and Protestants as Small-Endians, according to which end of a boiled egg should be broken first.

18 SB refers to his therapy with Bion. SB may allude to Matthew 12:45 and Luke 11:26, which both write: "the last state of that man is worse than the first." Or he may allude to the

"second state of man" discussed by Emanuel Swedenborg (1688–1772) in *Heaven and Its Wonders and Hell: Drawn from Things Heard and Seen*, in which "Our Second State of Man After Death" is one in which "we are given access to the deeper reaches of our minds, or our intentions and thoughts" (tr. George F. Dole, with notes by George F. Dole, Robert H. Kirven, and Jonathan Rose, The New Century Edition of the Works of Emanuel Swedenborg, series ed. Jonathan Rose [West Chester, PA: Swedenborg Foundation, 2000] 380).

"Comédie à tiroirs-vides" (a play with lots of sub-plots, more commonly, a "roman à tiroirs" [a novel with lots of sub-plots]; SB catches up the literal meaning of "tiroirs" [drawers of a chest] and adds "vides" [empty]).

19 Sordello embraces Virgil twice. With the first embrace, Sordello recognizes Virgil as a fellow Mantuan: "'O Mantovano, io son Sordello / de la tua terra!' e l'un l'altro abbracciava" ("O Mantuan, I am Sordello of thy city." And the one embraced the other) (Dante, *La Divina Commedia, Purgatorio*, Canto VI, lines 74–75; Dante, *The Divine Comedy*, II, *Purgatorio*, tr. Sinclair, 85). With the second, Sordello recognizes Virgil in humility: "là 've 'l minor s'appiglia" (clasping where the inferior does) (Dante, *La Divina Commedia, Purgatorio*, Canto VII, line 15 [SB writes "il" for "'l"]; Dante, *The Divine Comedy*, II, *Purgatorio*, tr. Sinclair, 95). SB quotes the reference from Canto VII.

MORRIS SINCLAIR
DUBLIN

4/3/34   48 Paulson's Square
                                              [London]

Cher Ami

Sois rassuré. Les peccadilles d'omission n'ont pas d'emprise sur moi. Je veux dire que j'y suis tellement sujet moi-même que leur manifestation chez autrui ne peut que me chauffer le coeur, chose dont j'ai assez besoin en ce moment. Merci donc de ta lettre qui, pour s'être fait attendre, ne m'a pas moins charmé l'esprit et égayé la solitude, et merci aussi de la coupure, où je trouve que ce vieux chameau paranoïaque n'est pas suffisam[m]ent maltraité. Mais c'est tout de même un commencement --

Tu as de la chance de pouvoir jouer dans un orchestre, quelque moche qu'il puisse être. C'est une occasion nonpareille pour te familiariser avec les détails d'une partition-- Je n'ai jamais pu me réconcilier avec la Symphonie Pastorale où j'ai l'impression que Beethoven a versé tout ce qu'il avait de vulgaire, de facile et d'enfantin (et c'était beaucoup), pour en finir avec une fois pour toutes.[1] J'ai entendu un superbe concert donné par le Quatuor Pro Arte, dont j'ai déjà parlé à Cissie et sur lequel partant je ne reviendrai maintenant pas-- Mais un autre, donné par le Quatuor Busch, qui présente actuellement dans une série de cinq concerts tous les quatuors pour cordes de Beethoven, vaut la peine qu'on y fasse allusion.[2] Le programme se composait de trois quatuors, le premier ("Harfen") de 1809, c'est à dire je crois, entre la Pastorale et la Septième; le second de 1800; et le troisième de 1825.[3] C'est pour celui-ci que je suis allé et je peux dire que je n'ai été nullement déçu-- Bien que ce ne soit que l'avant-dernier de ses quatuors il a pour Finale la dernière composition qui soit venue de sa main, un Allegro incomparablement beau. Mais c'est la Cavatina qui précède immédiatement cet Allegro qui m'a le plus frappé – mouvement qui en calme finalité et intensité dépasse tout ce que j'ai jamais entendu du vénérable Ludwig et dont je ne l'aurais pas cru capable – vraiment si tu ne connais pas ce Quatuor déjà (B Mol Mineur, op. 130) [*for* (si bémol majeur, op. 130)], tu ferais bien de te le procurer.[4] Le dernier concert de la série est pour samedi le dixsept, fête de notre infecte Patrice, et je viens de me garantir en quelque degré contre le souvenir de ses cochonneries zoologiques et botaniques en achetant un billet. Il y aura le dernier Quatuor en F (op. 135) avec le célèbre "Schwer Gefasste Entschluss":

Puis quelques jours plus tard, le 20 je crois, il y a Jacques Thibaud avec un programme formidable – embrassant la Chaconne de Vitali, le concerto en A du kleiner Wolferl, et une galaxie d'Espagnols.[6] Mais même en commençant déjà à faire des économies, je ne sais si je vais pouvoir me le payer. C'est vraiment une tempête de musique à Londres en ce moment, un tel embarras de richesses que si l'on pouvait se les payer tous on aurait de la peine à choisir entre les concerts qui ont lieu le même jour. Mais voilà par exemple une [*for* un] dilemme qui ne me trouble pas! Hélas!

Il n'est pas possible d'exprimer les étranges douceurs que je ressens à l'approche du printemps, et si c'est là une phrase qui invite le ridicule tant pis pour moi. Positivement je ne l'ai jamais regardé venir avec tant d'impatience et tant de soulagement. Et j'y pense comme à une victoire emportée sur la nuit, les cauchemars, les sueurs, la panique et la folie, et aux crocus et aux narcisses comme aux gages d'une vie au moins tolérable, déjà goûtée mais dans un passé si lointain que toute trace, et jusqu'au souvenir, en était presque perdus. Que les puissances veuillent que je ne m'y trompe pas – la péninsule doit être radieuse. Et le cheval s'est-il un peu renouvelé parmi les Zéphyrs? Ne manque pas de me rappeler à son souvenir.

Et le travail, cela avance? Cette anthologie Ruddiesque est en effet comme tu dis, une chose puante, et du reste pleine de pièges. Je te conseille d'étudier cela avec une carte de la France sous la main. Comme cela il y a au moins un intérêt géographique à en extraire. Autrement c'est une corvée intolérable. D'ailleurs je ne l'ai jamais lu. Fais surtout attention à la région provençale (Maurras, etc.), car c'est le pays d'élection du noble professeur. Et ce n'est pas la peine de te dire que l'étude des textes qu'on donne à étudier est beaucoup moins importante que celle de celui qui les donne. Autrement dit, mets-toi dans la peau de Ruddy (il y a de la place) et fous-toi plus ou moins de ses anthologies.[7]

J'ai sur la conscience de ne pas avoir encore répondu à la lettre de ton auguste père. Mais à mesure que les heures de

lumière [se] développent et que s'y absorbent celles des ténèbres, il se forme dans l'immense creuset de mon esprit les seules
combinaisons verbales dignes de lui et de moi par rapport à lui.
[Ré]conforte-le donc, quand par hasard il aurait besoin d'un tel
soin, au moyen de cet avant-goût de la chose qui se prépare.

Devant ta magnifique mère, de la part de qui une accusation
de réception de la divine lettre que je lui ai récemment adressée
est vivement et instamment à souhaiter, je me prosterne et
me remplis la bouche avidement de poussière. Représente-lui
cette attitude.

Et à toi, mon cher ami, je souhaite, maintenant et à l'avenir,
tout ce qu'il y a de plus bienfaisant et propice dans un monde où
de telles vertus ont l'air de devenir de plus en plus rares.

> Affectueusement
>
> Sam

ALS; 3 leaves, 3 sides; Sinclair.

4/3/34 48 Paulson's Square
[London]

Dear Sunny,

Let me reassure you. Peccadillos of omission have no hold on
me. I mean that I am myself so subject to them that the fact of
their appearing in someone else can only warm my heart, something I am rather in need of at the moment. So thank you for
your letter, which, for all that it was long in coming, has none
the less charmed my mind and enlivened my solitude, and thank
you too for the cutting, in which I think that that paranoic old
brute is not treated badly enough. But still it is a start.

How lucky you are to be able to play in an orchestra, however
third-rate it is. It is a matchless opportunity to get to know the

details of a score. I have never made my peace with the Pastoral Symphony into which I have the impression Beethoven poured everything that was vulgar, facile, and childish in him (and that was a great deal), so as to have done with it once and for all.[1] I heard a superb concert by the Pro Arte Quartet that I have already spoken of to Cissie, and to which I shall therefore not return now. But another one, given by the Busch Quartet, which is at the moment putting on a series of five concerts in which they are performing all of Beethoven's string quartets, is worth a mention.[2] The programme was made up of three quartets, the first one ('Harfen') from 1809, that is I think between the Pastoral and the Seventh; the second from 1800; and the third from 1825.[3] This is the one that I went to, and I can say that I was in no way disappointed. Although it is only his penultimate quartet it has as its finale the last composition we have from his hand, an incomparably beautiful Allegro. But it is the Cavatina that immediately precedes that Allegro that made the greatest impression on me. A movement which in calm finality and intensity goes beyond anything I have ever heard by the venerable Ludwig, and which I would not have believed him capable of – really, if you are not already familiar with this quartet (B Flat minor, op. 130), you would do well to get hold of it.[4] The last concert in the series is on Saturday the 17th, feast of the unspeakable Patrick, and I have just gone some way to protecting myself against the memory of his vulgar zoological and botanical nonsense by buying a ticket. There will be the last Quartet in F (opus 135) with the famous 'Schwer Gefasste Entschluss':

grave   allegro

Muss es sein?   Es muss sein!   Es muss sein![5]

Then a few days later, on the 20th I think, there is Jacques Thibaud with a tremendous programme – including the Vitali Chaconne, the Concerto in A by kleiner Wolferl, and a galaxy of Spaniards.[6] But even starting already to save up for it, I do not know whether I shall be able to afford it. There is a positive storm of music in London just now, such a wealth of splendid things that even if one could afford them all it would be hard to choose between concerts happening on the same day. Now there is a dilemma that costs me no sleep! Alas!

The strange, gentle pleasures that I feel at the approach of spring are impossible of expression, and if that is a sentence inviting ridicule, so much the worse for me. I have positively never watched it coming with so much impatience and so much relief. And I think of it as a victory over darkness, nightmares, sweats, panic and madness, and of the crocuses and daffodils as the promise of a life at least bearable, once enjoyed but in a past so remote that all trace, even remembrance of it, had been almost lost. May the powers will it that I am not wrong – the peninsula must be radiant. And has the horse revived a little among the Zephyrs? Do remember me to him.

And how is the work going? This Ruddiesque anthology is indeed, as you say, a stinking affair, and moreover full of traps. My advice to you is to study it with a map of France to hand. That way there is at least a geographical interest to be got out of it. Otherwise it is an intolerable chore. Incidentally, I have never read it. Pay particular attention to the Provençal part (Maurras, etc.), for that is the domain beloved of the noble Professor. And I need hardly tell you that the study of the texts that are being proposed for study is far less important than that of the person proposing them. In other words, put yourself in Ruddy's skin (there is room), and to hell more or less with his anthologies.[7]

On my conscience is the fact that I have not replied to your august father's letter. But as the hours of light grow, and those of darkness are absorbed into them, there are forming in the immense crucible of my mind the only verbal combinations worthy of him, and of me in relation to him. Comfort him, then, if perchance he had need of such care, with this foretaste of what is in preparation.

Before your magnificent mother, from whom an acknowledgement of the divine letter which I recently dispatched to her is most urgently and insistently to be wished, I prostrate myself and eagerly fill my mouth with dust. Go through these movements for me.

And to you, my dear friend, I wish, now and for the future, all that is most beneficent and propitious in a world where such virtues seem to be growing more and more scarce.

      Love

      Sam

1 Beethoven's Symphony no. 6 in F major, op. 68 ("Pastoral").

2 The concert given by the Pro Arte Quartet at the BBC Broadcasting House on 16 February 1934 comprised Beethoven's String Quartet no. 14 in C-sharp minor, op. 131; String Quartet no. 4 in C major, op. 91 by Béla Bartók (1881–1945); and Debussy's String Quartet in G minor, op. 10 ("Music This Week," *The Times* 12 February 1934: 8).
The Busch Quartet played a series of ten concerts at Wigmore Hall between 24 February and 17 March 1934; they actually played the Beethoven string quartets in six concerts (26 February, and 2, 3, 9, 15, and 17 March).

3 On 2 March the Busch Quartet played Beethoven's String Quartet no. 10 in E-flat major, op. 74 ("Harp"); String Quartet no. 3 in D major, op. 18; and String Quartet no. 13 in B-flat major, op. 130. "Harp" was indeed written between Beethoven's Symphony no. 6 and Symphony no. 7 in A major, op. 92.

4 SB speaks of the Cavatina and Allegro of String Quartet no. 13 in B-flat major, op. 130. Beethoven originally composed the *Grosse Fuge* as a finale for this quartet; persuaded that it was too long, he published it separately (*Grosse Fuge* in B-flat major, op. 133) and composed the Allegro as a second ending (Philip Radcliffe, *Beethoven's String Quartets*, 2nd edn. [Cambridge: Cambridge University Press, 1978] 135–137).

5 Beethoven's String Quartet no. 16 in F major, op. 135, was performed in the last Busch concert of the series on 17 March 1934, St. Patrick's Day. SB quotes the epigraph

of the final movement as well as its musical motif: "Der schwer gefasste Entschluss / Muss es sein? Es muss sein! Es muss sein!" (The heart-wrenching decision / Must it be? It must be! It must be!) (John Briggs, *The Collector's Beethoven* [Westport, CT: Greenwood Press, 1978] 41–42; Radcliffe, *Beethoven's String Quartets*, 170–174).

6 From 1905 to 1935, French violinist Jacques Thibaud (1880–1953) often performed as a member of a trio with French pianist and conductor Alfred Cortot (1877–1962) and Catalan cellist and composer Pablo Casals (1876–1973). The program of Thibaud's recital at Wigmore Hall, 20 March 1934, included the Chaconne in G minor, then attributed to Italian composer Tomaso Battista Vitali (1663–1745); Violin Concerto in A major, K. 219, by Wolfgang Amadeus Mozart (1756–1791); the Violin Sonata in G major, by Belgian composer Guillaume Lekeu (1870–1894); "Fountain of Arethusa" from *Myths*, op. 30, no. 1, by Polish composer Karol Szymanowski (1882–1937); the malagueña "Rumores de la Caleta," from *Recuerdos de viaje*, op. 71, no. 6, by Isaac Albéniz (1860–1909), arranged for violin by Austrian-born American violinist and composer Fritz Kreisler (1875–1962); "Danse originale," dedicated to Thibaud, by Enrique Granados y Campiña (1867–1916); and the Suite from the lyric drama *La vida breve* by Spanish composer Manuel de Falla (1876–1946). (For the current attribution of the Chaconne: Wolfgang Reich, "Die Chaconne g-Moll – von Vitali?" *Beiträge zur Musikwissenschaft* 2 [1965] 149–152.)

With the phrase, "kleiner Wolferl" (little Wolfie), SB refers to Wolfgang Amadeus Mozart.

7 In the 1933–1934 *Calendar* of Trinity College Dublin, *Nouvelle Anthologie des troubadours*, ed. Jean Audiau (Paris: Delagrave, 1928), is listed for the Michaelmas examinations, although the editor's name is incorrectly given as Audian (127). Rudmose-Brown was very interested in the Provençal literary renaissance and was a member of the Société des Félibriges.

Charles Maurras (1868–1952) was a member of the Ecole romane, founded by Jean Moréas (1856–1910), Ernest Raynaud (1864–1936), Maurice du Plessys (1864–1924), and Raymond de la Tailhède (1867–1938); the group sought a return to the classical tradition in reaction against the Symbolists, the Parnassians, and the Romantics. See also Roger Little, "Beckett's Mentor, Rudmose-Brown: Sketch for a Portrait," *Irish University Review* 14 (spring 1984) 34–41.

MORRIS SINCLAIR

DUBLIN

SB's errors of German in this letter have not been corrected.

5/5/34   48 Paulton's Square

London S.W. 3

Lieber Sonny

Wer einst Rosen pflücken will, der soll die Zeit, die ihm auferlegt ist, dann und wann ermuntern. Verzeihe mir also, wenn ich mich benötigt finde, meinen französischen Quatsch augenblicklich fallen zu lassen. Zwar aus dieser unentbehrlichen Veränderung wird uns keine Vorteil entstehen, doch vielleicht ein bischen Spass. Vorteil! Was wollen sie eigentlich sagen, unsre [?schweizzige] Moralisten,[1] mit ihrem Schreien von Vorteil! Sie fürchten sie so schrecklich vor dem Leben, das wenn sie aus irgendeinem Gegenstand keinen gewissen Gewinn ziehen können, so fühlen sie sich wie geschlagen, wo nicht fast ermordet. Für diesen Leute werden Spass und Vorteil allmählich so durchaus unverträglich, dass alle Handlung nur zum Spass gemacht ihnen wie eine Selbstverstümmelung scheinen muss. Wenn ich den Glaube hätte, ohne den niemand hassen kann, würde ich sicher diesen Gegenstandsauger hassen.[2]

Ich wünsche dir allen möglichen Erfolg im Feis.[3] Ich habe lange keine Musik gehört. Ausser Horowitz, der ein Paar Konzerten gibt, und dem Ring, d. h. die Saison, schon in vollem Gange und Klange, hat es nichts gegeben.[4] Jedenfalls ist es mir, aus Gründen die mir Gott sei dank unbekannt sind, als wäre ich von der Musik ausgeschlossen, und dazu habe ich keinen geringsten Appetit....

Ich wollt' ich wär' noch älter,
und runziger und kälter....

Mit meiner Manie für alles, das mit der Frage nur die mindeste Beziehung hat, wirst du hoffentlich Nachsicht haben.

Ich habe gern diese Sommerzeit, weil dadurch werden die Finsternis und alle seine schlechte Dinge wenigstens aufgeschoben. Da ich Manichäer bin, in was die Dunkelheit betrifft.[5]

Hier spreize ich mich, kann und will nicht anders, und habe keine Ahnung, ob Gott mir hilft, oder nicht. Es gibt doch eine fast nie versagende Freude, nämlich, das Denken an jenen Millionen, die weniger glücklich als ich sind, oder sein sollten. Was für ein Schmaus ist das! Da es aber klar wird, sobald man die

Sache ein bischen überlegt, dass zwischen Leiden und Fühlen gar keine Verhaltnis festzustellen ist, so fängt auch jene Freude an, trügerisch auszusehen. Wenn ich, zum Beispiel, in der Zeitung lese, der arme Herr Dings solle morgen früh, ehe ich aus meinem Bette sein werde, hinrichten werden, und mich sofort zu gratulieren beginn, dass ich keine solche Nacht zuzubringen habe, so täusche ich mich, insofern ich zwei Umstände, anstatt zweier Gemütsbewegungen, vergleiche. Und es ist höchstwahrscheinlich, dass der zum Tode Verurteilte wenigere Angst als ich hat. Wenigstens weiss er genau um was es sich handelt und genau um was er sich zu kümmern hat, und das ist nun ein grösserer Trost als man im allgemeinen zu glauben pflegt. So gross, dass viele Kranken Verbrecher werden, nur damit sie ihre Angst begrenzen und jenen Trost bekommen mögen. Jenseit der Spekulation kommt erst der Mensch in sein Eden, in jeden [for ?jenen] Schutzort wo keine Gefahr mehr ist, oder vielmehr eine, die bestimmt ist und die man zum Fokus bringen kann.

Neuerdings habe ich an den Lehrer der englischen Sprache viel gedacht, und mich gefragt, wie es ihm geht. Freilich muss ich mich bei ihm entschuldigen, dass ich seinen sehr vortrefflichen Brief noch nicht beantwortet habe.[6] So bitte ich dich, ihm für mich vorzustellen, diese Versäumung sei mir zum Trotz.[7] Kaum nehme ich die Feder in der Hand, um irgendetwas auf englisch zusammenzusetzen, als ich die Empfindung habe, verpersonifiziert zu sein, wenn man einen solchen herrlichen Ausdruck gebrauchen darf.[8] Deshalb würde alles, was ich damals schreiben könnte, meinem Vorhaben, dessen Wirkung sozusagen momentanisch gelämt ist, am fernsten liegen. So lohnt es sich kaum. Es ist ein fremdes Gefühl, unwillkürlich weit von sich zurückzutreten und sich wie durch ein Schlüsselloch zu beobachten. Fremd ja, und zum Briefschreiben überhaupt unpassend.

Ich weiss nicht, wann ich nach Hause zurückgehen können werde. Der Aufenthalt in dieser Stadt gefällt mir nur wenig. Ausser den Bildern, die meistenteils, ihres Fensterladenglases wegen, nur tropfenweise in die Augen kommen, gibt es nichts, das man ansehen darf.[9] Manchmal verlange ich nach jenen Bergen und Feldern, den ich so gut kenne, und die eine ganz andere Ruhe, als die zu dieser groben, englischen Landschaft gehörende, bilden. Wenn nur Dublin ungewohnt wäre, so wär' es angenehm, sich irgendwo in seiner Nähe niederzulassen.

Was für ein Schlusszierat gehört zu diesem Klagelied? Man atmet, also...? Oder: Was Hänschen nicht lernt...? Die Symphonie unvollendet zu lassen, das ist jedenfalls die Hauptsache. Dabei kann alles in Ordnung aussehen.

Herzlich
Sam

ALS; 3 leaves, 3 sides; Sinclair.

5/5/34   48 Paulton's Square
                                                    London S.W. 3

Dear Sunny,

Whoever wants to pick roses some day should now and then cheer up the time imposed on him. Forgive me therefore when I feel the urge to drop my French nonsense right away. It is true that out of this indispensable change no gain will accrue to us, but perhaps a bit of fun. Gain! What actually do they want to say, our [? Swiss] moralists, with their cries about gain![1] They are so terribly afraid of life that if there is any object from which they can draw no sure profit, they feel beaten, if not nearly murdered. For these people fun and gain slowly become so completely irreconcilable that any action done just for fun must seem to them like self-mutilation. If I had the faith without which no one can hate, I would surely hate this object-gobbler.[2]

I wish you every conceivable success in the Feis.[3] I have not heard any music for a long time. Besides Horowitz, who is giving a few concerts, and the 'Ring' (i.e. the season) already in full swing and sound, there has been nothing.[4] At any rate, it seems to me, for reasons unknown to me thank God, as if I were cut off from music, and I have not the least bit of appetite for that.

I wish I were even older
And wrinklier and colder . . . .

I hope you will make allowances for my obsession with everything that is even the least bit related to that question.

I am fond of this summertime because darkness and all its bad things are at least being postponed thereby. Since I am a Manichaean as far as darkness is concerned.[5]

Here I strut about, I cannot and will not do otherwise, and have no idea if God helps me or not. There is after all an almost never-failing joy, namely the thought of those millions who are less fortunate than I, or ought to be. What a feast that is! But as it becomes clear as soon as one reflects a bit on the matter that no relationship between suffering and feeling is to be found, then even that joy begins to look deceptive. If, for example, I read in the paper that poor Mr. So-and-so is to be executed early in the morning, before I get out of bed, and immediately start to congratulate myself that I do not have to spend such a night, I deceive myself in as much as I compare two circumstances instead of two emotions. And it is highly probable that the man condemned to death is less afraid than I. At least he knows exactly what is at stake and exactly what he has to attend to, and that is a greater comfort than one is generally inclined to believe. So great that many sick people become criminals solely in order to limit their fear and gain that comfort. Only beyond speculation does man reach his Eden, that refuge where there is no more danger, or rather one which is determined and which one can bring into focus.

Lately I have thought a good deal about the teacher of the English language and have wondered how he is getting on. Of course, I must apologize to him for not yet having answered his excellent letter.[6] So I ask you to get him, on my behalf, to imagine that this omission might be in spite of myself.[7] No sooner do I take up my pen to compose something in English than I get the feeling of being "de-personified", if one may use such a marvellous expression.[8] Therefore, everything that I might have written at that time would lie furthest away from my intention, the effect of which would be, so to say, momentarily paralysed. Thus it is hardly worth doing. It is a strange feeling to step back instinctively, well away from oneself, and observe oneself as through a keyhole. Strange, yes, and altogether unsuitable for letter writing.

I do not know when I shall be able to come home. Staying in this town gives me little pleasure. Except for the pictures, which because of their shop-window glass meet the eye for the most part only drop by drop, there is nothing that one is allowed to look at.[9] Sometimes I long for those mountains and fields, which I know so well, and which create a completely different calm from the one associated with this coarse English landscape. If only Dublin were unfamiliar, then it would be pleasant to settle somewhere nearby.

What kind of final embellishment might go with this lamentation? One breathes therefore...? Or: What little Johnny does not learn...? To leave the symphony unfinished, that at any rate is the main thing. With that everything can appear to be in order.

Love,

Sam

1 SB writes "schweizzige" but it is unclear what he meant to signify here: possibly "schweizer" (Swiss) or "schweissige" (sweaty) or even "geschwätzige" (chattering).

2 "Gegenstandsauger" (object-gobbler), possibly a play on the German word "Staubsauger" (vacuum cleaner, literally dust sucker).

3 Morris Sinclair was a violinist and competed in the Feis Ceóil, a Dublin music festival and competition, which began on 8 May 1934.

4 Vladimir Horowitz played three concerts in London during the following week: a charity concert at Queen's Hall on 8 May, a BBC concert at Queen's Hall on 9 May, and a recital at Queen's Hall on 28 May 1934.

Two complete cycles of Wagner's opera festival *Der Ring des Nibelungen* (*Das Rheingold*, *Die Walküre*, *Siegfried*, *Götterdämmerung*) were performed at the Royal Opera House, Covent Garden, from 1 to 18 May 1934. On 2 May, the third act of *Die Walküre* was broadcast over the London Regional radio station.

5 As it stands, SB's statement of identification with Manichaeism is a grammatical and logical fragment.

6 SB refers to Morris Sinclair's father Boss Sinclair who gave English lessons in Kassel (Morris Sinclair, 1 May 2003; Knowlson, *Damned to Fame*, 153).

7 SB's German construction would have been correct had he used the word "erklären" (explain). By using "vorstellen" instead, he merges the two constructions possible with that verb and thereby the two meanings ("introduce" and "imagine"), with the result that neither form is used correctly. Considering the contents and tone of the letter, we have settled on "imagine."

8 SB is playing with German, as it were undoing the word "*per*sonifiziert" (personified) with "*ver*personifiziert" (de-personified).

9 In German, use of the expression "tropfenweise" with reference to painting is as startling as "drop by drop" is in English.

NUALA COSTELLO

DUBLIN

10/5 [1934]   48 Paulton's Sq.

[London] S.W. 3

Dear Nuala

You seem to be having a wunnerful time, with your new nastorquemada nyles.[1] This is very deep. I am reading Amelia.[2] I saw Man of Aran and felt I am afraid irretrievably glued to the seat. Very smart no doubt as far as it goes, sea, rocks, air and granite gobs very fine, but a sensationalisation of Aran wouldn't you be inclined to say, as Synge's embroidery a sentimentalisation. Also I felt the trucs of montage and photography, very keenly, very keenly indeed. The boy fishing is pure Harold Lloyd. The tempest au ralenti is Eve's Revue. Komrade King caulking his curragh was very nice. The odd glimpse of the Pins also.[3] Very depressing film, caricature of what we all do, struggling to ensure our dying every second, except that we acquire our 27 foot sharks in a less amusing manner. But so much mere nature all at once, is it not very dumpling. I was forgetting the rock flowers, they were a relief, like a preterite in Corneille at last. And no poteen?[4] Surely a little poteen would not have been inessential. Didn't the wild waves make a strange noise, not specially marine I thought. There are better waves in Epstein's Finis Terrae.[5] Smaller and better. In fact the whole thing was very Hugo, Hugo at his most Asti. Not Lautréamont, Lautréaval. Pauvres Gens oxygenated.[6] I now find that the only possible development of this denigration is in indecency. And I scarcely know you well enough for that. But haven't I been very amusing. Ochone ochone I seem to have been most amusing.[7] No doubt it[']s good exercise.

How can you [? be] so little equitable, when I obviously suffer from the acutest paraesthesia to all that is said and written to and of me. When I hear a small boy giggle two liberties off I redden to the rotten roots of my white hair. The slightest unkindly cut is a dagger stuck in my heart, another dagger. So please never say anything to me that you <u>know</u> I couldn't care to hear. "Bloody cheek" was an awful thing to have said to me, a positive dumdum.

As I cannot give you the glittering account of my health that we all would wish, so I shall content myself with remarking, that the various eviscerations characteristic of my distemper are at the very top of their form. Can you imagine a quarry in ebullition. I have now ceased to wish to amuse you. Forgive me. Now whereas this interesting neolithic effervescence had hitherto been so forgiving as to confine itself roughly to my centre of inertia & environs, it has lately begun to embrace me without fear or favour from sinciput to planta. It takes my mind off my corns, no small favour I assure you. No ordinary somersault will take place one of these days, something tells me in the late autumn, if such generosity of recul is any indication, and I am given to understand that it is an index of a prime order.

> "And Autumn LIFE for him did choose
> A season damp/dank with mists and rain,
> And took him, as the ev[e]ning dews
> Were settling o'er the fields again."

Pardon our emotion. Unseasonable with Commonwealth day so nigh.[8]

Was the blurb in the Observer sufficiently imbecile? Is it necessary to say that I have never read either Leprechaun or Télégraphie Sans Egal, that my More Pricks are as free from Joycean portmanteaux as from allusion, and that I NEVER contract, can't do it my dear, I only bid.[9] The major influences are Grock, Dante, Chaucer, Bernard de Mandeville and Uccello.[10] Publication on Commonwealth Day fills my mind with a thousand tender fancies.

I postcarded you that I was sending Tom McGreevy's poems just released, with the fond hope that you would do the best you could for them. Is this an age of aesthetic integrity? I think not.

I have not yet sent them, but shall, to-day or to-morrow, which is also a day. Heap abuse on hardhearted Hanna when he has not got hundreds of copies in his window. Ceci me tient, je ne dis pas au coeur, organe qui n'offre plus de prise, mais enfin à une andouille quelconque.[11]

Are you connected, how remotely soever, with The Maid Of The Cyprus Isle, Miss Louisa Stuart Costello?[12]

I hear Percy has withdrawn definitively to Cappagh.[13] But I have no doubt I am misinformed.

If you haven't read Green's Adrienne Mesurat, my advice to you is, don't. I paid a flying visit to The Country Boneyard. Never do this.

> Up he went & in he passed
> & down he came with such endeavour
> As he shall rue until at last
> He rematriculate for ever.[14]

I grow gnomic. It is the last phase.

Beautiful Greetings
s/ Sam

TLS; 1 leaf, 2 sides; Costello. *Dating*: from the publication of *More Pricks Than Kicks*, 24 May 1934.

1 "Nastorquemada nyles" has not been identified with certainty. The segment "Torquemada" may refer either to the Inquisitor General of the Spanish Holy Office, Tomás de Torquemada (1420–1498), or to the deviser of the cryptic crossword in *The Observer* from 1926 to 1939, Edward Powys Mathers (pseud. Torquemada, 1892–1939).

2 Henry Fielding, *Amelia* (1751).

3 American filmmaker Robert Flaherty (1884–1951) directed the documentary film *Man of Aran* (1934), which was shot on location in the Aran Islands, west of Galway Bay. Depicting a struggle of man against nature, the film was reviewed by Ivor Montagu as having turned "reality to romance" ("Romance and Reality," *New Statesman and Nation* [28 April 1934] 638). SB compares Flaherty to John Millington Synge (1871–1909), who lived among the Aran islanders for periods from 1898 to 1902; this is reflected in his play *Riders to the Sea* (1904) and recorded in his observations in *Aran Islands* (1907).

Flaherty used montage. SB compares the routines of the boy, played by Mickleen Dillane, to silent film comedian Harold Lloyd (1893–1971).

"Trucs" (tricks); the "truca" used footage from two cameras to create special effects (Roger Boussinot, ed., *L'Encylopédie du cinéma* [Paris: Bordas, 1967] 1437–1438; Maurice Bessy and Jean-Louis Chardans, *Dictionnaire du cinéma et de la télévision*, IV [Paris: Pauvert, 1971] 431–446). "Au ralenti" (in slow motion).

A blacksmith named Coleman "Tiger" King (n.d.) played Komrade King in *Man of Aran*. "The Twelve Pins," the mountain range northeast of Galway Bay.

4   The preterite is rarely used in Corneille's plays.
"Poteen" (Irish, illicitly distilled whiskey).

5   French filmmaker Jean Epstein (1897–1953) directed *Finis terrae* (1929), the first of his cycle of films made on the coast of Brittany.

6   SB refers to Asti Spumante, an Italian sparkling wine.
Victor Hugo's *Les Pauvres gens* (*The Poor People*), collected in *La Légende des siècles* (1859).
Comte de Lautréamont (né Isidore Ducasse, 1846–1870), author of *Les Chants de Maldoror* (1868). SB plays with the last two syllables of Lautréamont's name: "amont" (upstream) is replaced with its opposite, "aval" (downstream): "Lautréaval."

7   "Ochone" (an Irish exclamation of lament, heard in keening).

8   "From sinciput to planta" (frontal part of the skull to the sole of the foot). "Recul" (withdrawal or retreat).
SB quotes Synge's poem "Epitaph," but he substitutes "LIFE," for "Death" and "damp/dank" for "dank" (J. M. Synge, *Collected Works*, I, *Poems*, ed. Robin Skelton [London: Oxford University Press, 1962] 31).
In 1934 the Labour Party proposed that Empire Day should be renamed "Commonwealth Day" (*The Times* 28 April 1934: 14); *More Pricks Than Kicks* was to be published on that day, 24 May 1932. Commonwealth Day is now celebrated on the second Monday in March.

9   The advance notice about *More Pricks Than Kicks* in *The Observer* read:
> One of the few English books on Marcel Proust was the work of Mr. Samuel Beckett. Mr. Beckett now reveals himself as a writer of short stories. They are not conventional stories. The same young Dubliner appears in each of them. Together they form an epitome of his life. Imagine Mr. T. S. Eliot influenced by "The Crock of Gold," and not unmindful of Mr. Joyce's vocabulary, and you will have a notion of Mr. Beckett. Events in "More Pricks than Kicks," due on the 24th from Chatto, are ordinary; their narration is oblique. Mr. Beckett's mixture of mock heroic and low comedy surprises. When you expect him to expand, he contracts. The Dubliner in hospital is a triumph. Elsewhere, minor brilliancies abound. Mr. Beckett is allusive, and a future editor may have to provide notes. (Anon., "Books and Authors," 6 May 1934: 6)

SB refers to the story of the leprechauns of Gort na Cloca in *The Crock of Gold* by James Stephens and spins T. S. E. (Eliot's initials) into "Télégraphie Sans Egal" (telegraphy without equal) playing on "Télégraphie Sans Fil" (wireless), commonly referred to in France as TSF.
Playing on the notion of "contract" in the announcement, SB uses it in the sense found in the game of bridge.

10 Grock, the Swiss clown, see 9 October 1933, n. 10; for his influence: Pilling, *A Companion to "Dream of Fair to Middling Women,"* 33.
Geoffrey Chaucer (c.1342/1343–1400).
Bernard de Mandeville (1670–1733) was a Dutch doctor and pamphleteer who settled in London after being implicated in a popular uprising in Rotterdam; his *Fable of the Bees, or: Private Vices, Publick Benefits* (1714) was influential on eighteenth-century social philosophy.
The Florentine painter, Uccello.

11 Thomas McGreevy, *Poems* (1934).
SB plays on the name of Dublin bookseller Fred Hanna, 29 Nassau Street, by reference to a popular song, "Hard-Hearted Hannah ... the vamp of Savannah," composed by Charles Bates, Robert Bigelow, and Jack Yellin (New York: Ager, Yellen and Bornstein, 1924/1950).
"Ceci me tient, je ne dis pas au coeur, organe qui n'offre plus de prise, mais enfin à une andouille quelconque." (This is close, I shall not say to my heart, an organ that no longer offers grip, but to some entrail or other.)

12 Irish-born miniature painter, poet, and novelist Louisa Stuart Costello (1799–1870) lived in Paris; her first poems were published as *The Maid of the Cyprus Isle* (1815).

13 Arland Ussher had moved from Dublin to the family home, Cappagh, Co. Waterford.

14 French-American writer Julien Green (1900–1998) wrote *Adrienne Mesurat* (1927; *The Closed Garden*).
In this title, SB alludes to "Elegy Written in a Country Churchyard" by Thomas Gray (1716–1771). The lines of verse are SB's own.

GEORGE REAVEY

LONDON

23/6/34   48 Paulton's, not Portland,
                            Square, [London] S.W. 3 right enough.

Cher ami

Vas-y et que toutes les putains de l'Olympe nous soient favorables. Shatupon & Windup t'enverront probablement te promener Rue des Bâtards sans nombre de Ponsieur Doumerde.[1] Au besoin je peux te gratifier des épreuves, non pas en placards Dieu soit loué mais en pages, oui positivement en pages, et dont je me réservais le plaisir de me torcher les lèvres auxilia[i]res au plus triste de cet hiver de fécontent que j'entends venir avec un boucan de pétard et de mâts sous la tempête, plaisir auquel je veux bien renoncer aux intérêts de l'ars longa, et d'autant plus facilement que j'ai Zarathustra sous la main.[2] Love & Lethe se traduit Mort Plus Précieuse.[3]

    A toi

        s/ Sam Beckett

TLS; 1 leaf, 1 side; *pencil signature*; TxU.

23/6/34   48 Paulton's, not Portland,

                Square, [London] S.W. 3 right enough.

Dear George,

    Off you go, and may all the whores on Olympus look favourably on us. Shatupon & Windup will probably throw you out, down the Street of the Bastards (unnumbered) of Pister Doomerd.[1] I can if necessary favour you with proofs, not in galleys God be praised but in pages, yes positively pages, which I had set aside for the pleasure of wiping my secondary lips with at the darkest moment of this winter of fecontent that I can hear coming with a terrible din of banger and masts before the storm, a pleasure which I am happy to renounce in the interests of ars longa, especially as I have Zarathustra to hand.[2] Love & Lethe should be translated as Mort plus précieuse.[3]

    Yours

    Sam Beckett

1 Chatto and Windus had actively sought an American publisher for *More Pricks Than Kicks* prior to publication on 24 May 1934, and they responded to a request to represent the German rights on 12 June 1934 (Chatto and Windus to Mrs. G. M. Griffiths, London; UoR, MS 2444 CW letterbook 156/479). That SB had proofs to offer makes it likely that Reavey had asked to be allowed to represent the stories to French or American publishers; even with SB's permission, Reavey would need to clear this with Chatto and Windus.

    John Pilling asserts that Reavey offered to publish SB's poems on a self-paying basis (*A Samuel Beckett Chronology*, 48). However, Chatto and Windus had already refused the poems, so there would be no question of Reavey needing their permission.

"Ponsieur Doumerde" is SB's corruption of Monsieur [Gaston] Doumergue (1863–1937), twelfth President of the Republic of France (1924–1931), retired but recalled to act as Premier Ministre during the Serge Alexandre Stavisky scandal (February through November 1934).

2 "Cet hiver de fécontent" alludes to Richard of Gloucester's opening line in Shakespeare's *Richard III* (I.i.1): "Now is the winter of our discontent"; SB conflates "fécond" (fecund, fruitful) with "discontent."

"Ars longa" (art is long). The phrase, though used by Latin writers, is a translation of the Greek physician Hippocrates (460–370 BC), speaking of medical practice: "Life is short, the Art long, opportunity fleeting, experience treacherous, judgment difficult" (Hippocrates, "Aphorisms" in *Hippocrates, Heraclitus*, ed. T. E. Page, E. Capps, and W. H. D. Rouse, tr. W. H. S. Jones, The Loeb Classical Library, IV [London: William Heinemann; New York: G. P. Putnam's Sons, 1931] 99).

Zarathustra (in Greek, Zoroaster, n.d.), legendary teacher of ancient Persia, warned of corruption and the impending destruction of the world; Friedrich Nietzsche (1844–1900) fictionalized him as a returning visionary in *Also sprach Zarathustra* (1883–1885; *Thus Spoke Zarathustra*).

3 "Mort Plus Précieuse" (Death More Precious).

In SB's story "Love and Lethe," the suicide pact between Belacqua and Ruby Tough ends in passion, a turn that SB marked with a line from a "Sonnet for Hélène, LXXVII" by Pierre de Ronsard (1524–1585): "Car l'Amour et la Mort n'est qu'une mesme chose" (For Love and Death are but one thing) (Ronsard, *Le Second Livre des sonnets pour Hélène*, LXXVII, in *Oeuvres complètes*, I, ed. Jean Céard, Daniel Ménager, and Michel Simonin, Bibliothèque de la Pléiade [Paris: Gallimard, 1993] 423; "Love and Lethe" in *More Pricks Than Kicks* [New York: Grove Press, 1972] 100).

MORRIS SINCLAIR

DUBLIN

[after 13 July – before 2 August 1934]   48 Paulton's Square
                                            [London] S W 3

Cher Ami

Ravi de te savoir reçu, et si éminemment[.]¹ L'avenir t'appartient, à condition que tu ne prenne [*for* prennes] jamais au sérieux ce que je te dis. Car je suis comédien.

Ne crois pas que le ballet soit de la musique. C'est précisément parce que la musique y joue un rôle subordonné que le ballet m'irrite.² Car la musique sérieuse ne peut pas <u>servir</u>. Représenter une musique d'une manière particulière, par [*for* au] moyen de danse, gestes, décors, costumes, etc., c'est la dégrader, en en réduisant la valeur à une simple anecdote. Il y a des gens qui ne savent se satisfaire que visuellement. Quant à moi, et pour mon malheur sans doute, je ne peux partir que les paupières fermées.

Content de savoir que Boss ne m'en veut pas. Mais je le savais d'avance.[3]

Jus est une jolie expression. Ça graisse le siège de la vie, organe dont je n'ai jamais pu déterminer la position.

Je suppose que tu vas t'installer dans Trinity. Penses-tu étudier le droit? Façon de gagner la vie évidemment. Sonst ...[4]

Malgré ce que je t'ai écrit touchant l'impossibilité de travailler, je viens de me livrer à des efforts d'enragé pour écrire ce que personne ne veut entendre.[5] N'est-ce pas qu'on a des idées insensées, rien moins que des abérrations [sic].

Le soir je me promène pendant des heures, dans l'espoir de me faire un sommeil d'épuisé. Et avec d'autant plus de satisfaction que le mouvement tout seul constitue une espèce d'anesthésie.

La douce lumière d'un Velásquez dans ma chambre ce matin.[6] Mais dans l'après midi ce sera un four.

Tout à toi, et, encore une fois félicitations.

Sam

ALS; 2 leaves, 2 sides; Sinclair. *Dating*: examination results were not yet announced when SB wrote to Morris Sinclair on 13 July 1934, for he asks "Is Sizarship result out yet?" SB left London on 2 August, and he wrote to McGreevy on 3 August from Cooldrinagh (TCD, MS 10402/59).

[after 13 July – before 2 August 1934]   48 Paulton's Square
[London] S W 3

Dear Sunny,

Delighted that you have got it, and so splendidly.[1] The future belongs to you, provided that you never take seriously what I tell you. For I am a player.

Do not believe that ballet is music. It is precisely because music has a subordinate part in it that ballet annoys me.[2] For serious music cannot be of use. To represent a piece of music in a particular way, by means of dancing, gestures, settings, costumes, etc., is to degrade it by reducing its value to mere anecdote. There are people who cannot achieve satisfaction unless they can see. As for me, to my misfortune no doubt, I cannot go off unless my eyes are closed.

Glad to hear that Boss bears me no ill-will. But that I knew beforehand.[3]

Juice is a pretty expression. It lubricates the seat of life, an organ whose exact position I have never been able to determine.

I suppose that you are going to take rooms in Trinity. Do you think you will read Law? A way of making a living obviously. Sonst ... [4]

In spite of what I wrote to you concerning the impossibility of working, I have just been making the most outlandish efforts to write what nobody wants to hear.[5] We do have mad ideas, don't we, nothing short of aberrations.

In the evenings I walk for hours, in the hope of tiring myself out in order to sleep. And enjoying it all the more since motion itself is a kind of anaesthesia.

A soft Velázquez light in my room this morning. But in the afternoon it will be an oven.

Ever and all yours, and, again, congratulations.

Sam

1 Morris Sinclair was awarded the Sizarship in 1934; he is identified in the 1934–1935 *Calendar* as a Rising Junior Freshman Sizar. Sizarships awarded by Trinity College Dublin are scholarships that exempt students from tuition and commons fees, based upon the results of a competitive examination; sizarships are tenable for four years.

2 On 13 July 1934, SB had written to Morris Sinclair: "Also saw a few ballets, among which de Falla's <u>Tricorne</u>, with Picasso décor & costumes. You would have loved it." *Le Tricorne* (1919; *The Three-cornered Hat*), with set and costumes by Picasso and choreography by Léonide Massine (né Leonid Fyodorovich Myasin, 1896–1979), and with Massine in his original role as the Miller. The ballet was in repertory at Covent Garden Theatre beginning on 19 June 1934, with a performance that night and on 13 July 1934.

3 The publication of "The Smeraldina's Billet Doux" in *More Pricks Than Kicks* upset Peggy Sinclair's parents Cissie and Boss Sinclair (see Knowlson, *Damned to Fame*, 176–177).

4 Sinclair did not take up the study of law.
"Sonst" (otherwise).

5 SB had written to Morris Sinclair on 13 July 1934: "I can't do any work, no more than a man can pick his snout and thread a needle at the same time. So I've nearly given up trying" (Sinclair).

THOMAS McGREEVY
LONDON

Tuesday [7 August 1934]

Beckett & Medcalf,
Quantity Surveyors
Frank E. Beckett, B.A.I.
6, Clare Street,
Dublin

My dear Tom

Your letter this morning. Somehow things at home seem to be simpler, I seem to have grown indifferent to the atmosphere of coffee-stall emotions [...] But people's feelings don't seem to matter, one is nice ad lib. to all & sundry, offender & offended, with a basso profundo of privacy that never deserts one. It is only now that I begin to realize what the analysis has done for me.

[...] And now I am obliged to accept the whole panic as psychoneurotic – which leaves me in a hurry to get back & get on. Had a long walk with Geoffrey Sunday to Enniskerry & got soaked.[1] He likes you very much & hopes to be writing to you soon.

[...]

I suppose it is always gratifying to know that one is missed. I seem to be sailing dangerously near Gide's BANAL. All that you see fit to Hester. Beef on the Tiles is cowardly composition, like all the painting & writing in this place.[2] The terror of outline. I have it myself, but at least I know that I have.

I hear some creature called Kirwan (if that is how he spells it) has been abusing me right, left & centre all over London, but with particular emphasis in the Café Royal. A translator. I never heard of him.[3]

I saw Yeats's two latest – Resurrection & the King of the Ould Clock Tower at the Abbey Saturday. The ancient Hemolater at play. Balbus building his wall would be more dramatic. And the Valois rolling her uterine areas with conviction. And Dolan chanting what Yeats, greatly daring, can compose in the way of blasphemy, making the Christ controvert the Plato.[4]

A/The difference between the cities: Dublin consumes one's impatience, London one's patience. Which is the worse incendie?[5]

With no papers, and all the journalists creeping about miserably, or filing mountains of copy that will never become public, Dublin is at her humanest.[6]

I think what you find cold in Milton I find final, for himself at least, conflagrations of conviction cooled down to a finality of literary emission. With Laurence [*for* Lawrence] it is the conflagration transmitted telle quelle, which could never mean anything, even if the conflagration were a less tedious kindling of damp to begin with.[7] But I know that very often what I like to call the signs of enthusiasm you call the wreck of enthusiasm.

The Bookman writes, postponing all articles on Gide, Rimbaud & kindred dangers, in favour of one on the wicked Censorship in Ireland. By all means. I tried to get the Criminal Law Amendment Act, but it has not yet been issued in the form of a bill, or even taken shape as such according to Eason's expert.[8]

Love ever. Write soon

Sam

Frank & Geoffrey send salutations.

ALS; 2 leaves, 4 sides; *letterhead*, A date by SB; *env to* Thomas McGreevy Esq, 15 Cheyne Gardens, Chelsea, London S. W. 3; *pm* 8-8-34, Dublin; TCD, MS 10402/60. *Dating*: pm 8 August 1934 was a Wednesday, and so the previous Tuesday was 7 August 1934.

1 Arthur Geoffrey Thompson* (known as Geoffrey, 1905–1976) was a pupil with SB at Portora Royal School in Enniskillen, Ulster, and later at Trinity College Dublin where he qualified in Medicine in 1928. From 1930 he was a Physician at Baggot Street Hospital in Dublin, and then in 1934 he went to London to study psychoanalysis.

2 In his essay "De l'influence en littérature," André Gide wrote: "Un grand homme n'a qu'un souci: devenir le plus humain possible, – disons mieux: DEVENIR BANAL" ("A great man has only one care: to become as human as possible, – I would rather say: TO BECOME BANAL") (André Gide, *Oeuvres complètes d'André Gide*, III, ed. Louis Martin-Chauffier [Paris: Nouvelle Revue Française, 1933] 262; in H[agop] J. Nersoyan, *André Gide: The Theism of an Atheist* [Syracuse: Syracuse University Press, 1969] 193).

Hester Dowden, with whom McGreevy stayed in London.

SB's reference to *Beef on the Tiles* in the context of Irish painting and writing is not clear, although his mention of an outline suggests Jean Cocteau's scenario *Le Boeuf sur le toit ou The Nothing Doing Bar* (1920; *The Ox on the Roof*) for the ballet composed by Darius Milhaud (1892–1974) as *Le Boeuf sur le toit*, op. 58.

3 Patrick Kirwan (n.d.), a friend of Rupert Grayson, translator, and author of *Black Exchange* (1934), published by Grayson and Grayson. The Café Royal, 68 Regent Street, London.

4 The Abbey Theatre production of *The Resurrection* and *The King of the Great Clock Tower* by W. B. Yeats opened on 30 July 1934. The "ancient Hemolater" refers to Christ; astonished characters, who have been discussing the Resurrection, observe of the ghostly figure of Christ in the play: "the heart of a phantom is beating" (W. B. Yeats, *The Collected Plays of W. B. Yeats*, 2nd edn. [New York: Macmillan and Co.,

1952] 372; see also Holloway, *Joseph Holloway's Irish Theatre*, II *1932-1937*, ed. Hogan and O'Neill, 35).

The historical Lucius Cornelius Balbus (first century BC), a Phoenician who became a Roman consul and member of the first triumvirate, was a chief of engineers. In *Portrait of the Artist as a Young Man*, Joyce describes a drawing on the door of a water closet "of a bearded man in a Roman dress with a brick in each hand and underneath was the name of the drawing: *Balbus was building a wall* " (Joyce, *A Portrait of the Artist as a Young Man*, 43–44); this sentence was a common example in Latin textbooks (Mary Colum, *Life and the Dream* [Garden City, NY: Doubleday and Co., 1947] 357).

Irish-born dancer, teacher, and choreographer Ninette de Valois (née Edris Stannus, 1898-2001), who had been a soloist with the Ballets Russes (1923-1926) of Sergei Pavlovich Diaghilev (1872-1929), was Principal of the Abbey Theatre School of Ballet. Yeats dedicated *The King of the Great Clock Tower* to her ("Asking pardon for covering her expressive face with a mask"); she performed the role of the Queen who dances with the severed head of the Stroller (*The Collected Plays of W. B. Yeats*, 397, 400).

Actor and Manager of the Abbey Theatre Michael J. Dolan (1884-1954) played the role of Musician in *The Resurrection* . At the close of the play, the Musican sings, "Odour of blood when Christ was slain / Made all Platonic tolerance vain / And vain all Doric discipline" (*The Collected Plays of W. B. Yeats*, 373).

5 SB wrote "A" over "The" and joined them with a bracket. "Incendie" (fire).

6 A newspaper strike began in Dublin on 26 July and ended on 29 September 1934 (*The Times* 27 July 1934: 16; *The Times* 29 September 1934: 12).

7 SB compares John Milton (1608-1674) and D. H. Lawrence. "Telle quelle" (just as it is).

8 *The Bookman* (London, 1891-1934).
Although the Criminal Law Amendment Act, which sought to protect young girls and suppress brothels and prostitution, was introduced in the Dáil Éireann on 21 June 1934, it was not enacted until 28 February 1935. The proposed Act did not affect the censorship laws except to close a "loophole in the Censorship of Publications Act (1929), which outlawed the advertisement of contraceptives while not legally proscribing their importation or sale" (James M. Smith, "The Politics of Sexual Knowledge: The Origins of Ireland's Containment Culture and 'The Carrigan Report' (1931)," *Journal of the History of Sexuality* 13.2 [April 2004] 213).

Eason and Sons, bookseller, manufacturing stationer, and publisher, 70 and 80–82 Middle Abbey Street, Dublin.

THOMAS McGREEVY
TARBERT, CO. KERRY

8/9/34   34 Gertrude Street
                          [London] S.W. 10

My dear Tom

Glad to hear from you & that all is well. My kindest respects to your Mother & sister. I hope you have the quiet time & rest that I know you are in need of & that your botherations will leave you quite alone.[1] [...] Glad to hear Higgins hasn't got his prop of song in pickle for me, the Olympic mistletoe one doesn't mind.[2]

I think I like this place, Mrs Frost (née Queeney from dear old Athlone among the bushes) & Mr Frost, retired chauffeur & maid to some of the extinct nobility, know all about pipes of port & China tea, Fred Frost Jr. dentist's mechanic & person of incredible handiness about a house, installing baths & closets without the least aid or assistance, has just fixed up a reading lamp for me with which I can visit the remotest corners of the room, & Queeney Frost, the midinette complete with weak eyes that I had given up all hope of.[3] A larval piano in front drawing room with the first note of Jeune Fille Aux Cheveux alas in abeyance.[4] Mrs F. is a kind of mother on draught, you pull the pull & she appears with tea, Sanatogen, hot water to stupe a stye, every variety of abstract succour & a heavy sane willing presence altogether.[5] I am made free of the kitchen regions, which is better than a million golden gas-rings, & my collapses into an atmosphere of home-made jam & the Weekly Telegraph are encouraged without being solicited. A plaster for panic at all times, if it's only Mr F.'s snoring next door in the small hours or the young married couple upstairs (waiter at the Cadogan & maid to one of the somnolent furies at the Hans Crescent) waking up for a quick one.[6] Big big room with plenty of space to pace the masterpieces up & down & linoleum like Braque seen from a great distance. Rent same as at P.S., extras haply very much less.[7] I take nearly all my meals downstairs in the kitchen & she didn't flinch when I produced my Lapsang in favour of her Lipton's. For the moment at least all is well.

I got your letter this afternoon when I called round to 15. I looked in on Thursday for a tune but found the Steinway comme un prêtre mis en morceaux & a man with a green baize cache-sexe-à-peine combing the wreck for moths. It was reassembled this morning but N. wouldn't hear of it being touched till the tuner came on Mon.[8] I protested there would be no harm trying but she swelled & perspired visibly on the right side of the threshold & I went off to the gallery in a pet. However I had already collected books & coat.

I rang up Bookman with my larynx quivering with sneers & girds, but Ross Williamson the Younger poured such ecstasies down the wire that I couldn't place one. The article on the Censorship had doubled him up with Hodder & Stoughton satisfactions, his brother was at that very moment en train de baver là-dessus (meaning that they were very doubtful about its propriety), they were living in the hope of luring (who has been getting at them?) me out to Hammersmith, Norah Maguinness [*for* McGuinness] was on the verge of return, goodbye.[9] Since when no proofs bad cess to them & no invite thank God. Then I went to see Goldsmith. La gueule rose et grave à en mourir. He had no news of the verges, i.e. bad news, so I didn't apply for particulars. Richard was back at the gears en route for the Loire.[10] I said that when a man had got into the habit, as I would have seemed to, of estimating his life in terms of apprehending (the eyes closed at this first sign of danger & the wary wobble of the jowls) & the motive for living as the impulse to understand perhaps a little improvement on self-justification in the sphere of welfare-working, the only calamity was suspension of the faculty or, worse still, the need, to apprehend & understand. He stood up:

Some people apprehend too much, goodbye, know there's no good asking you for dinner, lunch some day, goodbye.

The covey seemed nice after the rest from him & we got going again. I had an appointment yesterday, but had to put him off on account of my eye which has been rather bad but which is all right to-day more or less, thanks to stuping, eye-shade & optrex.[11] Also one of the more endearing derivatives of impetigo on my lip, where there is quite a little colony of erectile tissue as I discovered during my holiday. I have hopes of analysis going a bit faster now. If I could get it over by Xmas I'd be crowned.

What a relief the Mont Ste. Victoire after all the anthropomorphised landscape – van Goyen, Avercamp, the Ruysdaels, Hobbema, even Claude, Wilson & Crome Yellow Esq., or paranthropomorphised by Watteau so that the Débarquement seems an illustration of "poursuivre ta pente pourvu qu'elle soit en montant", or hyperanthropomorphized by Rubens – Tellus in record travail, or castrated by Corot; after all the landscape "promoted" to the emotions of the hiker, postulated as <u>concerned</u> with the hiker (what an impertinence, worse than Aesop & the animals), alive the way a lap or a <u>fist</u> (Rosa) is alive.[12] Cézanne seems to have been the first to see landscape & state it as material of a strictly peculiar order, incommensurable with all human expressions whatsoever. Atomistic landscape with no velleities of vitalism, landscape with personality à la rigueur, but personality in its own terms, not in Pelman's, <u>landscapality</u>.[13] Ruysdael's [for Ruisdael's] <u>Entrance to the Forest</u> – there is no entrance anymore nor any commerce with the forest, its dimensions are its secret & it has no communications to make.[14] Cézanne leaves landscape maison d'aliénés & a better understanding of the term "natural" for idiot.[15]

So the problem (as it would seem to preoccupy perhaps the least stultified of the younger Dublin decorators, viz.

McGonigail [*for* MacGonigal]) of how to state the emotion of Ruysdael in terms of post-impressionist painting must disappear as a problem as soon as it is realised that the Ruysdael emotion is no longer authentic & Cuyp's cows as irrelevant as Salomon's urinator in Merrion Square except as a contrivance to stress the discrepancy between that which cannot stay still for its phases & that which can. I felt that discrepancy acutely this last time in Dublin, myself as exhausted of meaning by the mountains, my sadness at being chained to the oar of my fidgets.[16] And the Impressionists darting about & whining that the scene wouldn't rest easy! How far Cézanne had moved from the snapshot puerilities of Manet & Cie when he could understand the dynamic intrusion to be himself & so landscape to be something by definition unapproachably alien, unintelligible arrangement of atoms, not so much as ruffled by the kind attentions of the Reliability Joneses.[17]

Could there be any more ludicrous rationalisation of the itch to animise than the état d'âme balls, banquets & parties. Or – after Xerxes beating the sea, the Lexicographer kicking the stone & the Penman under the bed during the thunder – any irritation more mièvre than that of Sade at the impossibilité d'outrager la nature. A. E.'s Gully would have thrilled him.[18]

Perhaps it is the one bright spot in a mechanistic age – the deanthropomorphizations of the artist. Even the portrait beginning to be dehumanised as the individual feels himself more & more hermetic & alone & his neighbour a coagulum as alien as a protoplast or God, incapable of loving or hating anyone but himself or of being loved or hated by anyone but himself.

God love thee & forgive the dégueulade.[19]

 Ever

  s/ Sam

The Folies Bergères [*for* Bergère] was looking unspeakable but the Umbrellas lovely.[20]

TLS; 2 leaves, 3 sides; *A env to* Thomas McGreevy Esq, Tarbert, Limerick, Irish Free State; *pm* 10-9-34, London; TCD, MS 10402/63.

1 McGreevy is in Tarbert with his mother and one of his sisters. McGreevy had deferred his holiday due to work in London; he was also worried about his mother's and his own health (McGreevy to his mother, 29 August 1934 and 23 September 1934, TCD, MS 10381/70 and /71).

2 Irish critic and poet Frederick Robert Higgins (1896–1941) advocated that Irish poets write from folk materials. In his "Recent Irish Poetry," published in *The Bookman* under the pseudonym of Andrew Belis, SB admired the "good smell of dung" in Higgins's poetry but placed him among the "antiquarians"; in this essay SB quoted the poem that Higgins addresses "To my blackthorn stick": "'And here, as in green days you were the perch, / You're now the prop of song'" (*The Bookman* 86. 515 [August 1934] 235–236); F. R. Higgins, *Arable Holdings: Poems* [Dublin: The Cuala Press, 1933] 7–8).

SB's essay had "raised a storm" in Dublin; according to a letter from Denis Devlin to McGreevy: "It appears Yeats was furious; it appears that Austin Clarke [. . .] will pursue Sam to his grave; it appears Seamas [*for* Seumas] O'Sullivan thought he might have been mentioned at least"; while Higgins was "glad 'he got off so lightly'" (31 August 1934, TCD, MS 8112/5).

3 SB had just moved from Paultons Square to 34 Gertrude Street, Chelsea, two blocks north of the World's End pub on King's Road. Mrs. Frost was from Athlone, Co. Westmeath, Ireland.

"Pipes of port" refers to a measure for 550 litres of port; "midinette" (shopgirl).

4 A "larval" piano is one with woodworm in the sounding board (Edward Beckett). The first note of Debussy's "Jeune Fille aux cheveux de lin" is D-flat.

5 Sanatogen was the trade name of glycerophosphated casein, a protein supplement advertised as a nerve tonic to increase appetite and red blood corpuscles if taken daily.

6 *The Weekly Telegraph* (1862–1951), a Saturday newspaper with national circulation produced by *The Sheffield Telegraph*, with offices in London and Sheffield.

The Cadogan Hotel, 75 Sloane Street, London SW1; The Hans Crescent Hotel and Service Flats, 1 Hans Crescent, Belgravia, London SW1.

7 Georges Braque (1882–1963), French fauvist/cubist painter.

P[aultons] S[quare].

8 15 Cheyne Gardens, Chelsea, home of Mrs. Hester Dowden. N. is Mrs. Neighbour (n.d.), her housekeeper (Edmund Bentley, *Far Horizon: A Biography of Hester Dowden, Medium and Psychic Investigator* [London: Rider and Company, 1951] 44).

"Comme un prêtre mis en morceaux" (like a priest torn to pieces); "cache-sexe-à-peine" (a string that couldn't even be called G).

9 In response to the request of *Bookman*, as SB reported to McGreevy, "I ground out miserably 1800 words on Censorship for Bookman, which they will surely reject" (28 [*for* 27] August 1934, TCD, MS 10402/62).

The Editor of *The Bookman* from 1930 to spring 1934 was Hugh Ross Williamson (1901–1978); he was succeeded by his younger brother Reginald Pole Ross Williamson (1907–1966). The journal was in financial difficulty, so the publishers Hodder and Stoughton decided to halt publication; although the Williamson brothers then tried to buy the journal, the final issue of *The Bookman* was that of December 1934.

"En train de baver là-dessus" (slobbering over it). Reginald Ross Williamson lived in Hammersmith.

Irish-born painter, book illustrator, and designer Norah McGuinness (1901–1980) had studied in Paris and lived in London at this time.

10   Goldsmith has not been identified.

"La gueule rose et grave à en mourir" (all pink faced and desperately solemn). "Verges" (penises, i.e. pricks [*More Pricks Than Kicks*]).

Richard Aldington had spent June through early September in Austria recovering from an automobile accident, and now was driving to France.

11   "Covey," SB's usual nickname for W. R. Bion, is a variant on the slang "cove" (bloke).

Optrex was a commercial eye drop.

12   SB's reference to *Mont. Sainte-Victoire* by Paul Cézanne (1839–1906) is to *La Montagne Sainte-Victoire au Grand Pin* (Venturi 454) from the collection of Samuel Courtauld (1876–1947); it was on loan to the National Gallery, London, from March 1934 and would have been on public display through that year (Jacqueline McComish, The National Gallery, 26 April 1994).

Dutch artists Jan van Goyen (1596–1656), Hendrik Avercamp (1585–1634), Salomon van Ruysdael (c. 1600–1670), Meindert Hobbema (1638–1709); French artist Claude (le) Lorrain (né Claude Gelée or Gellée, c. 1604–1682); Welsh painter Richard Wilson (c. 1713–1782) SB may refer to English artist John Crome (1768–1821) as "Crome Yellow Esq."

The landscape by Jean-Antoine Watteau (1684–1721), *Pèlerinage à l'île de Cythère* (1717; known as *Embarkation for the Island of Cythera*, Louvre 8525); since 1961 it has been suggested that the theme of the painting is actually *departure from* the island of Cythera (Michael Levey, "The Real Theme of Watteau's *Embarkation for Cythera*," *Burlington Magazine* 103.698 [May 1961] 180–185; Margaret Morgan Grasselli and Pierre Rosenberg, *Watteau, 1684–1721* [Washington, DC: National Gallery of Art, 1984] 399–401).

"Poursuivre ta pente pourvu qu'elle soit en montant" (follow your incline so long as it is uphill), possibly from André Gide, *Les Faux-Monnayeurs*: "Il est bon de suivre sa pente, pourvu que ce soit en montant" (It's a good thing to follow one's inclination, provided it leads upward) (*Romans: récits et soties, oeuvres lyriques*, ed. Yvonne Davet and Jean-Jacques Thierry, Bibliothèque de la Pléiade [Paris: Gallimard, 1958] 1215; *The Counterfeiters*, tr. Dorothy Bussy [New York: Alfred A. Knopf, 1927] 327).

SB characterizes the landcapes of Rubens in terms of Tellus, the Roman goddess of nature, in "travail" (labor). French realist painter Jean-Baptiste-Camille Corot (1796–1875). In the fables attributed to Aesop (629–560 BC), animals have human attributes. Italian baroque painter, Salvator Rosa (1615–1673).

13   "A la rigueur" (just about, perhaps).

W. J. Ennever (1869–1947) founded the Pelman Institute for the Scientific Development of Mind, Memory, and Personality in 1989 in London; Pelmanism was a memory theory based on association which was applied specifically to language learning; the method was widely advertised as a means to develop the mind's latent powers.

14 SB refers to a painting, not by Salomon van Ruysdael but by Jacob van Ruisdael (1628/1629–1682), *Entrance to the Forest* (National Gallery, London, 2563). Although identified as such in the *National Gallery Illustrations: Continental Schools (excluding Italian)* ([London: Printed for the Trustees, 1937] 326), the attribution to Jacob van Ruisdael is now considered dubious; the painting appears as *Ford in a Wood near a Church* in Seymour Slive, *Jacob van Ruisdael: A Complete Catalogue of His Paintings, Drawings and Etchings* (New Haven: Yale University Press, 2001) 638.

15 "Maison d'aliénés" (lunatic asylum).

16 Irish landscape painter Maurice J. MacGonigal (1900–1979). Dutch landscape painter Aelbert Cuyp (1620–1691). *The Halt* (1667, NGI 507) by Salomon van Ruysdael includes a figure urinating against a wall on the far right side of the painting.

The National Gallery of Ireland is on Merrion Square.

17 "Manet & Cie" refers to Edouard Manet (1832–1883) and his fellow impressionists.

SB substitutes "Reliability" for "Capability" and conflates the name of English landscape architect Capability Brown (né Lancelot Brown, 1716–1783) with that of English architect Inigo Jones (1573–1652).

18 "Etat d'âme" (mood).

Xerxes the Great (519–465 BC), King of Persia from 486 to 465 BC, built a bridge across the Strymon and two bridges of ships across the Hellespont; when these were destroyed by a storm, he had the sea whipped.

Samuel Johnson (1709–1784) refuted Bishop Berkeley's argument "to prove the non-existence of matter, and that every thing in the universe is merely ideal" by "striking his foot with mighty force against a large stone" (James Boswell, *Boswell's Life of Johnson, Together with Boswell's Journal of a Tour to the Hebrides and Johnson's Diary of a Journey into North Wales*, ed. George Birkbeck Hill, rev. and enlarged L. F. Powell, I, *The Life (1709–1765)* [Oxford: Clarendon Press, 1934] 471).

The "Penman" James Joyce feared thunderstorms: "The thunderstorm as a vehicle of divine power and wrath moved Joyce's imagination so profoundly that to the end of his life he trembled at the sound" (Ellmann, *James Joyce*, 25).

"Mièvre" (childishly vapid).

The Marquis de Sade (né Donatien-Alphonse-François, Comte de Sade, 1740–1814), wrote, for example, in *La Nouvelle Justine ou, Les Malheurs de la vertu* (1797): "l'impossibilité d'outrager la nature est, selon moi, le plus grand supplice de l'homme" (the impossibility of an outrage against nature is, for me, man's greatest torment) (Marquis de Sade, *Oeuvres complètes du Marquis de Sade*, VI, ed. Annie Le Brun and Jean-Jacques Pauvert [Paris: Pauvert, 1987] 281).

AE's *Seascape: The Gully* (Municipal Gallery of Modern Art, now the Dublin City Gallery The Hugh Lane, no. 243) shows two female figures upon a rock, surrounded by the rush and eddy of the surf.

19 "Dégueulade" (long puke).

20 Manet's *Un Bar aux Folies-Bergère* was on exhibit at the National Gallery from the collection of Samuel Courtauld from 1 March 1934. The painting had been in such poor condition that, when shown in the Manet Exhibition in Paris (1932), it was placed in a specially designed box that controlled conditions; after two years of restoration by Kennedy North, it was lent to the National Gallery (Frank Rutter, "Manet's 'Bar aux Folies-Bergère,'" *Apollo* 19.113 [May 1934] 244–247).

Les Parapluies (*The Umbrellas*; National Gallery 3268) by Pierre-Auguste Renoir (1841–1919) was part of the Hugh Lane bequest to the National Gallery that was disputed because of an unwitnessed codicil that altered his bequest to the National Gallery of London in favor of the Municipal Gallery of Modern Art in Dublin.

THOMAS McGREEVY

TARBERT, CO. KERRY

Sunday [16 September 1934]   34 Gertrude Street
                                                            London S.W. 10

My dear Tom

Glad you had such a pleasant time at Dunquin & that your Mother is happy. I feel your holiday has been a great success so far & may it end with the beam in your mind that will make such a difference to you.[1]

Geoffrey is crossing Friday next & I am seeing him Saturday morning. Unfortunately he is only staying the week-end. But he will be telling you his plans himself. It seems on the cards that you will cross together -- [2]

I am all right, belting along with the covey with great freedom of indecency & conviction. No work for myself –

I do not see any possibility of relationship, friendly or unfriendly, with the unintelligible, and what I feel in Cézanne is precisely the absence of a rapport that was all right for Rosa or Ruysdael for whom the animising mode was valid, but would have been false for him, because he had the sense of his incommensurability not only with life of such a different order as landscape but even with life of his own order, even with the life – one feels looking at the self-portrait in the Tate, not the Cézanne chauve but with the big hat – operative in himself.[3] I can understand the humility in terms of "there but for the grace of G."

or "there but for the disgrace of this old bastard", humility before the doomed & the assumed, but before the panoplies of blankness ... comprends pas. No doubt I exaggerate the improbability of turning into landscape one very fine day, is that why the Ghirlandaio Dafne means so much to me?[4] But from one's own ragbag of dissociations to the pantheistic monism of the Metamorphoses is a saut too périlleux altogether.[5] Alas that Stendhal's thesis that the world had lost its energy when it substituted the devoir de discrétion for the folie pour rien should be so true now: "La vie d'un homme était une suite de hasards. Maintenant la civilisation a chassé le hasard, plus d'imprévu."[6]

I must think of Rousseau as a champion of the right to be alone and as an authentically tragic figure in so far as he was denied enjoyment of the right, not only by a society that considered solitude as a vice (il n'y a que le méchant qui soit seul) but by the infantile aspect, afraid of the dark, of his own constitution. And he knew it himself, that he would always fall for a show of tenderness as being more like the genuine uterine article than the face of even the Ile de St. Pierre: "Mon plus grand malheur fut toujours de ne pouvoir résister aux 'caresses'".[7] If he had known how to trim his sails between the two positions he would have suffered less. And why not whimper under the bougie?[8] I haven't read the Contrat, but I suppose Emile at least is an attempt to resolve the dichotomy or make the passage between its terms less of a gauntlet & more of a right-of-way.[9] But always the back ground of promeneur solitaire, micturating without fear or favour in a décor that does not demand to be entertained, & I think the freedom ample enough to allow of that would not object to Diderot's unbuttoning himself in a select public. A society that can be induced to put up with the "douceur du désoeuvrement" will put up with anything.[10]

Herewith divil the much better than nothing. Shall send a quid to-morrow or next day to await you chez Geoffrey.[11]

Love ever Sam –

Haven't yet been round to see Hester.[12]

ALS; 2 leaves, 4 sides; PS, upper left top margin of side 1, written perpendicularly to the page; *env to* Thomas McGreevy Esq., Tarbert, Limerick, Irish Free State; *pm* 16-9-34, London; TCD, MS 10402/64. *Dating:* pm; 16 September 1934 was Sunday.

1 Dunquin, Co. Kerry, is a cliff-top village overlooking the Blasket Islands, near the Dingle Peninsula.

2 McGreevy returned to London from Dublin by 22 September (McGreevy to his mother, 23 September 1934, TCD, MS 10381/71). Geoffrey Thompson.

3 SB refers to a *Portrait of Cézanne* (1879–1882, Venturi 366, in the collection of Lord Ivor Spencer Churchill), on loan to the Tate Gallery from February 1934 to February 1935 (Jane Ruddell, Tate Gallery Archive, 23 March 1994). Cézanne's *Self-Portrait with Olive Wallpaper* (sometimes called *Cézanne chauve*, 1880–1881, Venturi 365) was acquired by the Tate in 1926 through the Courtauld Fund, but is now in the National Gallery, London (NGL 4135).

4 SB wrote "<his> in terms of."
"Comprends pas" ([I] don't understand).
Florentine painter Domenico Ghirlandaio (c.1448–1494) did no painting of Daphne. SB may be referring to *Apollo and Daphne* (1470–1480, NGL 928), painted by Antonio Pollaiuolo (c.1432–1498), which depicts the dynamics of the chase just as Apollo has seized Daphne, whose arms have turned to tree branches so that she cannot be carried off by him. "Dafne" is the Italian spelling of "Daphne."

5 The *Metamorphoses* of Ovid (né Publius Ovidius Naso, 43 BC – AD ?17). "Pantheistic monism" is a term used by Baruch Spinoza (also Benedict de Spinoza, 1632–1677).
"Saut" (leap); "périlleux" (dangerous); SB separates the constituents of "saut périlleux" (acrobat's leap).

6 Before he seduces Mathilde (Mlle. de la Mole), Julien considers: "Son premier devoir était la discrétion" (His first duty was to be discreet) (Stendhal, *Le Rouge et le noir: chronique du XIXe siècle* [Paris: Librairie Garnier Frères, 1925; rpt. 1928] 360; *Red and Black*, ed. and tr. Robert M. Adams, Norton Critical Editions [New York: W. W. Norton & Co., 1969] 290). In the margin of his edition of *Le Rouge et le noir*, SB noted: "Beyle's [']Folie pour rien' … isme" ([Paris: Librairie Garnier Frères, 1925] 360; see also Pilling, ed., *Beckett's Dream Notebook*, 127–130; with appreciation to Mark Nixon). "Folie pour rien" (madness for its own sake).
"La vie d'un homme était une suite de hasards. Maintenant la civilisation a chassé le hasard, plus d'imprévu" ("The life of a man was one continual train of dangers. Nowadays civilization … [has] eliminated danger, and the unexpected never happens") (*Le Rouge et le noir* [1928] 329; *Red and Black*, 265–266). SB adds the underscore of "était."

7 SB cites Denis Diderot's *Le Fils naturel* (1757), where Constance says, "J'en appelle à votre coeur, interrogez-le, et il vous dira que l'homme de bien est dans la société, et

qu'il n'y a que le méchant qui soit seul" (I appeal to your heart; that oracle will answer, "The virtuous man reveres society; [only] the wicked ... avoids it") (*Le Fils naturel et les Entretiens sur "Le Fils naturel,"* ed. Jean-Pol Caput [Paris: Librairie Larousse, 1970] 82; *Dorval, or the Test of Virtue: A Comedy,* tr. unattributed [London: privately printed, 1767] 47).

In the fifth promenade of *Les Rêveries du promeneur solitaire* (1782; *The Reveries of the Solitary Walker*), Rousseau wrote of his visit to the island of St.-Pierre in Lac de Bienne, north of Neuchâtel, Switzerland, where he took a walking tour from 12 September to 25 October 1765.

In *Confessions,* Book 8, Jean-Jacques Rousseau wrote: "Mon plus grand malheur fut toujours de ne pouvoir résister aux caresses" (It has always been my greatest misfortune not to be able to resist flattery) (Jean-Jacques Rousseau, *Oeuvres complètes,* I, ed. Bernard Gagnebin and Marcel Raymond, Bibliothèque de la Pléiade [Paris: Gallimard, 1959] 371; *Confessions,* tr. Angela Scholar [Oxford: Oxford University Press, 2000] 362). SB adds the single quotation marks around "caresses."

8   SB refers to the "bougie" or catheter with which Rousseau was treated to relieve the painful effects of intermittent urine retention. The treatment itself was far from painless.

9   Rousseau's *Du Contrat social, ou Principes du droit politique* (1762; *The Social Contract or Principles of Political Right*) and his novel *Emile ou de l'éducation* (1762; *Emile or On Education*). SB wrote "<reconcile the> resolve." He wrote "<it possible for a man to> the passage."

10   Rousseau's meditations, *Les Rêveries du promeneur solitaire.* "Douceur du désoeuvrement" (sweet pleasures of idleness).

11   "Divil" (Ir. colloq., devil, e.g. "divil the bit" [nothing at all]). SB enclosed a "quid" with his letter of 18 September [1934] to McGreevy, "Chez Geoffrey" (at Geoffrey Thompson's home), 36 Lower Baggot Street, Dublin (TCD, MS 10402/65).

12   Hester Dowden.

THE EDITOR, POETRY MAGAZINE
CHICAGO

[1 November 1934]

DORTMUNDER[1]

In the magic the Homer dusk
past the red spire of sanctuary
I null and she royal hulk
hasten to the violet lamp to the thin K'in music of the bawd.

She stands before me in the bright stall
sustaining the jade splinters
the scarred signaculum of purity quiet
the eyes the eyes black till the plagal east
shall resolve the long night phrase.
Then as a scroll, folded,
and the glory of her dissolution enlarged
in me, Habbakuk, mard of all sinners.
Schopenhauer is dead and the bawd
puts her lute away.

MOLY[2]

The lips of her desire are grey
and parted like a silk loop
threatening
a slight wanton wound.
She preys wearily
on sensitive wild things
proud to be torn
by the grave crouch of her beauty.
But she will die and her snare
tendered so patiently
to my vigilant sorrow
will break and hang
in a pitiful crescent.

ECHO'S BONES[3]

asylum under my tread all this day
their muffled revels as the flesh breaks
breaking without fear or favour wind

the gantelope of sense and nonsense run
taken by the worms for what they are

ENUEG[4]

Exeo in a spasm
tired of my darling's red sputum
from the Portobello Private Nursing Home
its secret things
and toil to the crest of the surge of the steep perilous bridge
and lapse down blankly under the scream of the hoarding
into a black west
throttled with clouds.

Above the mansions the algum-trees
the mountains
my head sullenly
clot of anger
skewered aloft strangled in the cang of the wind
bites like a dog against its chastisement.

I trundle along rapidly now on my ruined feet
flush with the livid canal;
at Parnell Bridge a dying barge
carrying a cargo of nails and timber
rocks itself softly in the foaming cloister of the lock;
on the far bank a gang of down and outs would seem
   to be mending a beam.

Then for miles only wind
and the weals creeping alongside on the water
and the world opening up to the south
across a lamentable parody of champaign land to the
   mountains

and the stillborn evening turning a filthy green
manuring the night fungus
and the mind annulled
wrecked in wind.

I splashed past a little wearish old man,
Democritus,
scuttling along between a crutch and a stick,
his stump caught up horribly, like a claw, under his breech,
smoking.
Then because a field on the left suddenly went up in a blaze
of shouting and urgent whistling and scarlet and blue ganzies
I stopped and climbed a bank to look at the game.
A child fidgeting at the gate called up:
"Would we be let in Mister?"
"Certainly" I said "you would."
But, afraid, he set off down the road.
"Well" I called after him "why wouldn't you go on in?"
"Oh" he said, knowingly,
"I was in that field before and I got put out."
So on,
derelict,
as from a bush of gorse on fire in the mountain after dark,
or, in Sumatra, the jungle hymen,
the still flagrant rafflesia.

Next:
a pitiful family of grey verminous hens
perished out in the sunk field
trembling, half asleep, against the closed door of a shed,
with no visible means of roosting.

The great mushy toadstool
green-black,
oozing up after me,
soaking up the tattered sky like an ink of pestilence,
in my skull the wind going fetid,
the water . . .

Next:
on the hill down from the Fox and Geese into Chapelizod
a small malevolent goat, exiled on the road,
remotely pucking the gate of his field;
the Isolde Stores a great perturbation of sweaty heroes,
endimanchés,
come hastening down for a pint of nepenthe or moly or
    half and half
from watching the hurlers above in Kilmainham.

Blotches of drowned yellow in the pit of the Liffey;
the fingers of the ladders hooked over the parapet,
soliciting;
a slush of vigilant gulls in the grey spew of the sewer.

Ah! the banner
the banner of meat bleeding
on the silk of the seas and the arctic flowers!
(they do not exist)

TMSS; 2 leaves, 3 sides; enclosing letter not extant; *env to* The Editor, "POETRY," 232 East Erie Street, Chicago, ILL., U.S.A.; *pm* 1-11-34, London; SB's name and address at lower right margin side 1 and side 3 (only that on side 3 shown here); date stamped received Nov 8, 1934; AN on env, by other hands: *(1)* Efflusia; *(2)* The long one seems pure Joycean, but might be worth taking; *(3)* [*in Harriet Monroe's hand*] Maybe I feel lukewarmish; ICU, Zabel Papers, Box 1/F 5. *Dating:* from pm.

1 Variants in this text of "Dortmunder" with respect to the version published in *Echo's Bones* [19]: l.3 "null and" replaced by "null she"; l.10 "Then" replaced by "then"; l.13 "dead and" replaced by "dead, the."

2 "Moly" was published in *The European Caravan* (480) as "Yoke of Liberty"; variants between the 1931 version and this text: line 5, "she" corrected to "She"; line 11, "tamed and watchful sorrow" replaced by "vigilant sorrow."

3 Variants between this text of "Echo's Bones" and the version published in *Echo's Bones and Other Precipitates* [36]: line 2, "breaks" replaced by "falls"; line 5, "worms" replaced by "maggots."

4 "Enueg" was first published as "Enueg 1" in *Echo's Bones* (1935) [12–15]. It had been submitted to Seumas O'Sullivan for *Dublin Magazine* by 27 November 1931 (TCD, MS 4644) and rejected before 20 December 1931. A carbon copy of the poem was found among the papers of Richard Aldington, together with the poem then called "Enueg 2"; the poems came to Aldington before SB renamed "Enueg 2" as "Serena 1," that is before 4 November 1932 (ICSo, Collection 74/1/2; SB to McGreevy, TCD, MS 10402/35).

SB sent a group of his poems to Chatto and Windus (rejected 27 July 1932), to the Hogarth Press (rejected mid-August 1932), then to Rickword (mid-August 1932, with no reply), and possibly to *The Bookman* (16 August 1934, which rejected a poem by 27 August 1934): no manuscript versions of these submissions have been found. Then SB submitted this version of the poem to *Poetry Magazine*, on 1 November 1934.

CHRONOLOGY 1935

1935	19/20 January	SB returns to London, traveling with Frank Beckett.
	By 29 January	Sends story "Lightning Calculation" to *Lovat Dickson's Magazine*; it is returned immediately.
	3 February	Geoffrey Thompson arrives in London to assume position at Bethlem Royal Hospital.
	8 February	SB sends "Lightning Calculation" to *Life and Letters*.
	14 February	Lucia Joyce in London until 16 March.
	26 February	SB attends the opening of an exhibition of paintings by Estella Solomons, Mary Duncan, and Louise Jacobs at Arlington Gallery, London.
	15 March	Modifies the title of his collection of poems to *Echo's Bones and Other Precipitates*.
	20 April	Easter holiday in Dublin.
	4 May	SB visits Jack B. Yeats.
	20 May	Returns to London.
	23–31 July	SB's mother visits England: together they tour Porlock Weir, Stratford, Wells, Lynmouth, Winchester, Bath, Gloucester, and Rugby.
	1 August	On his own, SB visits Samuel Johnson's birthplace, Lichfield.
	By 7 August	Sends his poem "Da Tagte Es" to *Dublin Magazine*.
	20 August	Begins *Murphy*.
	By 8 September	Sees Nuala Costello in London.
	18 September	Visits Geoffrey Thompson and goes "round" the ward with him.

October	Receives proofs of *Echo's Bones and Other Precipitates*.
2 October	Dines with Bion and attends C. G. Jung's third Tavistock Institute lecture.
13 October	Receives Reavey's prospectus for *Echo's Bones*.
2 November	Acts as best man at wedding of Geoffrey and Ursula Thompson, West Lulworth.
December	Publication of *Echo's Bones*.
By 25 December	SB returns to Dublin. Ill with pleurisy.

1/1/35
Cooldrinagh
[Co. Dublin]

My dear Tom

Thanks for your letter, & for sending papers. Hope the 10/-
got through all right. Sorry to hear about Dilly. Have you had to
move to Miss Dawkins?[1]

The best days have been these spent walking with the dogs.
One was specially lovely, over the fields from here across the
3 Rock & 2 Rock & back by Glencullen & the Lead Mines. It was so
still that from the top of 2 Rock I could hear a solitary accordeon
[sic] played down near the Glencullen river, miles away. I thought
of a Xmas morning not long ago standing at the back of the
Scalp with Father, hearing singing coming from the Glencullen
Chapel.[2] Then the white air you can see so far through, giving the
outlines without the stippling. Then the pink & green sunset that
I never find anywhere else and when it was quite dark a little pub
to rest & drink gin in.

[...]

Jack Yeats rang up on Saturday, but I was already on my way
to Howth. Apparently he was exquis to Mother on the phone.
I must call round. Boss is working in Harry's shop, while Harry
still vacates the fort in the Langham. It seems a miracle is
required, & Boss awaits it confidently.[3]

Yesterday evening I received an astonishing letter from one
John Coghlan, Berkeley Road, Dublin, forwarded from Chattos,

in praise of the Proust which he had been reading, and inquiring if I had written anything else. M.P.T.K. will change his tune. I was highly gratified, especially as it cheered up Mother. I had things out with her, mildly & cautiously, & now things are much more satisfactory. [...] I fear the analysis is going to turn out a failure. The heart has not been very good since coming over, & I had one paralyzing attack at Cissie's, the worst ever. Bion is now a dream habitué.[4]

I found Con & Ethna in such romantic chiaroscuro over a dying fire that I could not decently do more than make a bow & depart. Heureuse Jeunesse.[5] Sean O'Sullivan rang up, but I was not in, or at least that was the impression he received. I must look him up however, if only to pump him on the subject of the gallery. Nobody seems to know anything about it.[6]

I suppose you saw Francis Stuart's noble quadruped in the Irish Times. Why doesn't he go to bed with them & get rid of it that way. He looks more & more like Percy Ussher.[7]

I have been reading The Mill on the Floss. It is at least superior to Shakespeare's Histories. She seems to have understood infancy after her fashion. The humour is seedy. What a lot Dickens took from her. The facetious columnist especially.[8]

Dublin is as ever only more so. You ask for a fish & they give you a piece of bog oak. The form & features of the Gaelic bureaucrat are already highly stylised. I have justified my visit by stealing back my little Larousse.[9]

Nancy Sinclair showed me a very nice Campendonk in the Junge Kunst series. Do you know his work? I only did from one picture the Boss had in Germany.[10] I find it very interesting. But I think you would jib at the German canister.

Apologise to Hester for my stupid note. I was laid out that day. I shall look forward to playing the Ravel. Schöne Grüsse to Hester & Dilly & Raven.[11]

Love ever

Sam

ALS; 2 leaves, 3 sides; [*black edged env, does not match stationery*] *to* Thomas McGreevy Esq, 15 Cheyne Gardens, Chelsea, London; *pm* 1-1-35, Dublin; TCD, MS 10402/67.

1 Hester Dowden's friend, Irish playwright and novelist Geraldine Dorothy Cummins (known as Dilly, 1890–1969), had come to stay in Hester Dowden's home, 15 Cheyne Gardens, Chelsea, London SW3, so that McGreevy was obliged to move to another house, that of George Henry Dawkins who lived at 22 Cheyne Walk.

2 SB describes landmarks of County Dublin: the mountains Three Rock and Two Rock, which are named for their outcroppings. The town of Glencullen (1.75 miles northwest of Two Rock, 4.5 miles west of Bray) and the Lead Mines in Carrickgollogan, which are marked by an abandoned rock chimney (3.75 miles west-northwest of Two Rock, and 2.5 miles west of Bray), were on the return route to Foxrock. A description of the Scalp: 13 May [1933], n. 14.

3 "Exquis" (delightful).
Boss and Cissie Sinclair lived in Howth. Boss was working at Harris & Sinclair, dealers in works of art, 47 South Nassau Street; the firm was managed by Harry Sinclair. When he was in London, Harry Sinclair lived at the Langham Hotel, Portland Place, London W1 (Morris Sinclair, 13 March 1991).

4 John Coghlan has not been identified. *More Pricks Than Kicks*.
"Habitué" (turns up regularly).

5 A. J. Leventhal and Ethna MacCarthy. "Heureuse jeunesse" (happy youth).

6 Thomas Bodkin resigned as Director of The National Gallery of Ireland, effective 1 March 1935, at a special meeting of the Board on 28 December 1934 ("National Gallery of Ireland, Resignation of Dr. Bodkin," *The Irish Times* 29 December 1934: 4).

7 Francis Stuart's poem, "A Racehorse at the Curragh" (*The Irish Times* 29 December 1934: 5).

8 *The Mill on the Floss* (1860) by George Eliot (pseud. of Mary Ann Evans, 1819–1880). SB may refer to the character Jefferson Brick, a war correspondent for the *New York Rowdy Journal* in *Martin Chuzzlewit* (1843–1844) by Dickens.

9 The *Petit Larousse*, a French dictionary and encyclopedia.

10 The book on German expressionist Heinrich Campendonk (1889–1957) was by Georg Biermann, *Heinrich Campendonk*, Junge Kunst (Leipzig: Verlag von Klinkhardt und Biermann, 1921). The Sinclairs owned Campendonk's painting *A Dream* (Morris Sinclair, 20 September 1990; private collection, on long-term loan to the Courtauld Institute of Art Gallery, London, LP.2002.xx.16).

11   SB's note to Hester Dowden has not been found.

For Ravel's "Pavane," see 24 February 1931, n. 4.

"Schöne Grüsse" (warm greetings).

Thomas Holmes Ravenhill (known as Raven, 1881–1952) studied medicine at the University of Birmingham; he conducted pioneering research in high-altitude medicine as a medical officer in Chile and served in the Royal Army Medical Corps from 1914 to 1918. After the war, he left medicine and became a painter, lodging in Hester Dowden's house in Chelsea for over twenty years (Bentley, *Far Horizon: A Biography of Hester Dowden*, 58; J. B. West, "T. H. Ravenhill and His Contributions to Mountain Sickness", *Journal of Applied Physiology* 80.3 [March 1996] 715–724).

THOMAS McGREEVY

TARBERT, CO. KERRY

29/1 [1935]   34 Gertrude St

                                                                      [London] S.W. 10

My dear Tom

I have your news from Hester whom I saw last Sunday. I know how awful it must be for you to have it drag on and on. There is nothing to say. I can only hope you have found some means of patience & comfort.[1]

I came back with Frank last Sunday week. He returned, & Geoffrey arrived, on the Tuesday morning. Geoffrey went back on the Wednesday night. He has secured a post at an asylum near Beckenham, & will be coming over at the end of this week to stay three months at least, for which I am very grateful, as you can imagine. I have resumed with Bion and am feeling better, in spite of all the symptoms, which left me more or less alone during the holiday, having come flocking back. It is a kind of confirmation of the analysis.[2]

I had tea & a long conversation with Raven Sunday afternoon in his studio. But he is impossible to talk with. He has obviously been through it. He does not seem to have emerged altogether.

Hester looks very well and apparently her concert was a great success. I am invited to dine there this evening and try the Infanta.[3]

I have sent a new short story to Lovat Dickson. It is very short & very tenuous. I think it would probably stand a better chance with the Evening Standard. I mean to try & see Muir. Perhaps he could put me in the way of some translations.[4] The National Gallery after the "5th in Christendom" ("Amateur" in Irish Times) is like the 15 acres after a cabbage allotment.[5]

[...]

It is an enormous relief being back in London. I miss you acutely. I had to go with a party of Frank's to "Young England," and so was obliged to sit it out, an exasperation beyond all description. I should look up MacCarthy, but dread the trend of conscientious solicitude it sets up inside me.[6]

I have read Jonson's two Everyman & Poetaster & begun Volpone, which opens superbly. The longueurs of culture are at least an improvement on the longueurs of facility. What a pity the lexicographical *f* keeps creeping in so often.[7]

God love thee

Yours ever

Sam

ALS; 1 leaf, 2 sides; *env to* Thomas McGreevy Esq, Tarbert, Limerick, Co. Kerry, Irish Free State; *pm* 29-1-35, London; TCD, MS 10402/69.

1 McGreevy's mother was ill.

2 SB and Frank Beckett arrived in London on 20 January.
Geoffrey Thompson came to London on 22 January to be interviewed for a position at the Bethlem Royal Hospital near Beckenham; he began there on 4 February 1935. Study of psychiatric medicine was not possible in Dublin, as SB wrote to McGreevy: "Geoffrey says a psychoanalyst would be run out of the town. Is that really possible? By the doctors themselves in the first place, he says" (18 January 1935, TCD, MS 10402/68).

3 Hester Dowden was a concert pianist; this concert has not been identified. "Infanta": see 24 February 1931, n. 4.

4   Horatio Henry Lovat Dickson (1902–1987), Australian-born London publisher and biographer, was Associate Editor of *Fortnightly Review* (1929–1932), Editor of *Review of Reviews* (1930–1932), Editor of *Lovat Dickson's Magazine* (1934–1937), a journal devoted to short stories, and Managing Editor of Lovat Dickson Ltd. (1932–1938). SB submitted "Lightning Calculation" to Lovat Dickson (Pilling, *A Samuel Beckett Chronology*, 50–51; Cohn, *A Beckett Canon*, 70–71; unpublished manuscript of "Lightning Calculation," BIF, UoR, MS 2902).

The *Evening Standard*, London newspaper (1827 to present, under various titles).

The translations of Scottish-born poet and literary critic Edwin Muir (1887–1959), done with his wife Willa Muir (née Anderson, 1890–1970), included books by Lion Feuchtwanger (1889–1958), Gerhart Hauptmann (1862–1946), Franz Kafka (1883–1924), and Heinrich Mann (1871–1950), published by the London publishers Martin Secker, Routledge, and Gollancz. Muir had reviewed SB's *More Pricks Than Kicks* in "New Short Stories," *The Listener* 12.268 (4 July 1934) 42.

5   In response to the news of Thomas Bodkin's resignation as Director of the National Gallery of Ireland, a letter to *The Irish Times* signed "Amateur" pays tribute to his leadership, indicating that "Our Gallery ranks fifth in the world," and wonders whether Bodkin might stay if offered "an adequate emolument" ("Dr. Bodkin," *The Irish Times* 12 January 1935: 6).

"The fifteen acres" refers to the broad open space in Dublin's Phoenix Park, by contrast to the small plots of land leased to non-landowners so that they could grow their own produce (MacThomáis, *Me Jewel and Darlin' Dublin*, 111; Declan Kiberd, 12 September 2006).

6   *Young England*, a patriotic melodrama by Walter Reynolds (1851–1941), proprietor of the Theatre Royal (Leeds), was voted by critics as "the worst show that had opened in London in 20 years"; it rapidly developed a cult following and "a quarter of a million people saw the play," including a person who "boasted of 150 visits" ("'Wrong Door, Wrong Door,'" *Time* [25 December 1939] 24–25; "Daly's Theatre: 'Young England,'" *The Times* 22 January 1935: 10; "The Victoria Palace: Shows," www.victoriapalacetheatre.co.uk [History], 24 July 2005).

Desmond MacCarthy.

7   *Everyman in his Humour* (1598), *Everyman out of his Humour* (1599), *Poetaster* (1601), *Volpone* (1606): plays of Ben Jonson (1572–1637).

The long "s" ("ſ") was the standard representation of the letter "s" in roman fonts until the late 1700s in English.

THOMAS McGREEVY
TARBERT, CO. KERRY

8/2 [1935]
34 Gertrude St
[London] S.W. 10

My dear Tom

It is good news that you have the translation, even of a little sensationalist like M. Also that you are keeping well. You ought to get out a bit more. Have you only your married sister with you now?[1]

Of myself there is nothing to tell, except that the feeling of relief & vitality of the first week after my return has quite gone, & now I feel beyond description worthless, sordid & incapacitated. Basta.[2]

I heard Maryjo Prado play at Hester's last Sunday week. The Footner turned up. I don't like her. Hester says she is intelligent. I feel her Jansenist précieuse. The Prado played some things well, a Rameau gavotte & variations that I did not know, Scriabin, the Vie de Brevet, Prokoviev's [*for* Prokofiev's] Tentations Diaboliques [*for* "Suggestion Diabolique"], & some flashy Dohnyani [*for* Dohnanyi]. But her Chopin & Debussy were dragged out by the scruff of the neck, very disagreeable. She sits perched up above the keyboard like Mme. Mahieu at the seat of custom. Her left hand in the Scriabin was extremely scrupulous & good. I suppose now I must go to her concert at the Aeolian Hall next Thursday. Mr Prado was sehr sympathisch.[3] I had lunch with Hester & Raven last Sunday afternoon, & played duets with her afterwards. The Infanta could go quite well. She offered me a latch+key to come in & practise whenever I liked, but I contrived to parry this kindness. Since then I have not been round. I get terribly tired of all the psychic evidence, wonder what it has to do with the psyche as I experience that old bastard. Also the dogs & cats.[4]

Am reading the Cousine Bette. The bathos of style & thought is so enormous that I wonder is he writing seriously or in parody. And yet I go on reading it. I have finished with Adler. Another one track mind. Only the dogmatist seems able to put it across.[5] I wish you were to talk pictures, though I know you don't like talking much of the Dutchmen. I thought Teniers was the last word in Netherland drawing till I looked into the Brouwers, alas so scarce. I found a lovely one in the Victoria & Albert, a man playing a lute. The one in the National, with the woman pulling the man's hair, is invisible. Their only other is in what the attendant calls the "reference section".[6] Do they employ some journalist, I wonder, to invent these expressions. Also in the V. & A. an adorable tiny Terborch, portrait of a man in black, tucked away behind a screen in the Forster Collection. I have been promising myself a long look at the Dulwich Cuyps, but every morning finds me shirking the cold journey.[7]

Geoffrey arrived last Sunday & is now sumptuously installed at the Bethlem Royal Hospital near Beckenham. I have seen him only once. Perhaps it will be somewhere to go in the spring.[8]

[...]

I ran into Mr Arthur Hillis, & de fil en aiguille to his Cheyne Walk first floor flat, very nice, with Paul Henry at first hand & Peter de Hooch at an infinite remove, reconciled somehow. He is really very decent, is a Hispanophile, with Spanish Petit Larousse, a Bechstein piano & a good gramophone, & records of Cortot playing Seguidillas, Malaguena, etc. His background is the classics, and he dilated learnedly extempore on the influence of that minor author Theophrastus on the English Renaissance in general & John Earle in particular.[9]

To-morrow afternoon I have the Lener, but alas one cannot book a seat for a mood.[10] A sad little letter from Maurice Sinclair from Ronda, drinking a lot of wine & frileux playing his fiddle in olive-groves on the rock, & reading Maupassant. He is going on to Seville, sometime. It does not sound as though he were doing much good. Cissie has left the Adelaide & gone home, very little the better.[11]

Nothing more from Lucia Gottlob. Helen has got Giorgio where she wants him now. The Costello seems to have cast me off & kein Wunder.[12] Lovat Dickson sent back the story by return. I sent it on to Life & Letters. I have neither seen nor sought to see Charles.[13] The thought of venturing forth into the cold world in the evening is intolerable. I feel I must squabble with Bion, & so I do. On Monday I go for the 133rd time.[14]

God love thee & write again soon.

s/ Sam

TLS; 2 leaves, 2 sides; *env to* Thomas McGreevy Esq, Tarbert, Limerick, Co. Kerry, I.F.S.; *pm* 8-2-35, London; TCD, MS 10402/70.

1 McGreevy translated *Les Célibataires* (1934), by French writer Henry Millon de Montherlant (1895-1972), as *Lament for the Death of an Upper Class* (London: John Miles, 1935). McGreevy's unmarried sister Margaret McGreevy (known as Ciss, 1887-1952) was at home during this time; his sister Honora Phelan (née McGreevy, known as Nora, 1891-1974) also lived in Tarbert.

2 "Basta" (enough).

3 Mary Jo Prado (née Turner, n.d.) was married to Flavio Prado Uchoa (n.d.), resident of London and São Paulo, Brazil, whom SB found "sehr sympathisch" (very pleasant).

Mary Jo Prado played: "Gavotte" from *Nouvelles suites de pièces de clavecin ... avec des remarques sur les différens genres de musique*, by French composer Jean-Philippe Rameau (1683-1764); music by Russian composer Aleksandr Scriabin (1872-1915); "Two Dances" from Manuel de Falla's lyric drama *La vida breve*; Prokofiev's "Navazhdeniye" ("Suggestion diabolique") from *Four Pieces* (rev. of *Four Pieces*, 1908), op. 4, no. 4; and music by Hungarian composer Erno Dohnanyi (né Ernst von Dohnanyi, 1877-1960).

Amica de Biden Footner (1874-1961), British portrait painter, whose subjects included many prominent persons; her sister recalled the "directness and naivety of her conversation" (*The Times*, 20 October 1961: 15).

Mme. Mahieu (n.d.), proprietor of Café le Mahieu.

There is no indication of a concert by Mary Jo Prado on 14 February 1935 at Aeolian Hall; however, a piano recital was given there that evening by Elena Cavalcanti (n.d.) ("Music this Week," *The Times* 11 February 1935: 8).

4 Hester Dowden, known for her experiments in automatic writing as a professional medium, had built "a clientèle second to none throughout the country" (Bentley, *Far Horizon: A Biography of Hester Dowden*, 44). Hester Dowden's pets included Siamese cats and Pekinese dogs. "Infanta": see 24 February 1931, n. 4.

5 Balzac, *La Cousine Bette* (1846; *Cousin Bette*).

Alfred Adler (1870–1937), Austrian-born psychologist. SB's notes on psychology include those taken on Adler's *The Neurotic Constitution: Outlines of a Comparative Individualistic Psychology and Psychotherapy*, tr. Bernard Glueck and John E. Lind (New York: Moffat, 1916; rpt. London: Kegan Paul, 1921); these notes are undated, and SB may have read other works by Adler (TCD, MS 10971/8/f 24r–33r).

6 Flemish painter David Teniers the younger (1610–1690), who was influenced by Brouwer.

Adriaen Brouwer (c.1605–1638) was a Flemish painter who spent much of his working life in Holland. *Interior of a Room with Figures: A Man Playing a Lute and a Woman* (c.1635, Victoria and Albert Museum, CAI/80).

The Brouwer painting in the National Gallery described by SB is *Tavern Scene* (NGL 6591), on loan from Sir Edmund Bacon "from July 1907 until at least 1971"; it was acquired by the National Gallery in July 2002 (Alan Crookham and Flavia Dietrich-England, 1 July 2005). The painting in the "reference section" (or lower galleries) then attributed to Brouwer was entitled *Three Boors Drinking* (NGL 2569) (*National Gallery Illustrations, Continental Schools [excluding Italian]*, 36); it is now attributed to "style of [Adriaen] Brouwer" and is entitled *Four Peasants in a Cellar* (Gregory Martin, *The Flemish School, circa 1600 – circa 1900* [London: National Gallery, 1970] 12).

7 Gerard Ter Borch the younger (also Terborch, 1617–1681), *Man in Black Dress*, measures 19 × 21.6 cm (Forster Bequest, F. 35, V&A); the Collection was a bequest of John Forster (1812–1876). The collection of the Dulwich College Picture Gallery contains Flemish, Italian, and Dutch art, including many paintings by Dutch artist Aelbert Cuyp (1620–1691).

8 Geoffrey Thompson was Senior House Physician at Bethlem Royal Hospital from 4 February to 31 October 1935 and extended his service there to January 1936.

9 "De fil en aiguille" (by easy stages). Arthur Hillis lived at 131 Cheyne Walk in Chelsea. Hillis's Bechstein piano was his father's wedding gift to his mother. Hillis owned a painting by Paul Henry (1876–1958), Irish portrait and landscape artist, and an interior scene painted by Pieter de Hooch (1629–1684), who was associated with the School of Delft.

Alfred Cortot recorded Albéniz's "Seguidillas" from *Suite española*, op. 232, no. 5, and the malagueña "Rumores de la Caleta" from *Recuerdos de viaje*, op. 71, no. 6, also by Albéniz (see "Alfred Cortot plays Short Works," Biddulph Recordings, LHW 020, 1994, and "Alfred Cortot: Rare 78 rpm Recordings & Rare Pressings 1919–1947," Music & Arts, CD-615, 1989).

Arthur Hillis read Classics and Law at Trinity College Dublin. Greek philosopher Theophrastus (c.372–287 BC), head of the Peripatetic School after Aristotle, is known for his study of "Characters," human types related to the humour theory of personality dominant through the English Renaissance. John Earle (1601–1665) wrote a collection of character sketches, *Microcosmographie* (1628), based on the model of Theophrastus.

10 SB's ticket for the Léner Quartet, playing a Beethoven program at Queen's Hall, was not for 9 February, but for 3 pm on 9 March 1935 (see below, 20 February 1935 and 10 March 1935).

11 Ronda is a city built on a high plateau in the Andalusia region of Spain. "Frileux" (sensitive to cold).
French writer Guy de Maupassant (1850–1893).
Cissie Sinclair had been treated at the Adelaide Hospital in Dublin.

12 Lucia Joyce. "Gottlob" (God be praised).
Giorgio Joyce and his wife Helen were in New York, where he was pursuing a musical career (Ellmann, *James Joyce*, 678, 683).
Nuala Costello. "Kein Wunder" (no wonder).

13 SB's story "Lightning Calculation" was sent on to *Life and Letters* which, from November 1934, was edited by Richard Ellis Roberts (Pilling, *A Samuel Beckett Chronology*, 51).
Charles Prentice.

14 SB had been in therapy with Bion for a little more than a year.

THOMAS McGREEVY
TARBERT, CO. KERRY

14/2 [1935]   34 Gertrude Street
                                              [London] S.W. 10

My dear Tom

Delighted at the prospect of seeing you soon. Will you be going to Cheyne Gardens?[1]

There is nothing in the Criterion.[2]

Frank's friend Guilford arrived yesterday, & I have to be with him rather more than I would if he were not Frank's friend.[3] I know Hester will be froissée if I do not turn up at the Aeolian this evening & hear the Prado, but I do not think I will be able. I have not been round to 15 for a long time now, so the Infanta is no further.[4]

I have seen very little of Geoffrey. He has no time to spare, between the detainees at Bethlem, Hadfield & Miss What is her name, and I have seen nothing of him.[5]

By the way did you ever receive Sorel's Chute de la Royauté that I sent you from Dublin. It was very scantily parcelled & I felt doubtful about it at the time.[6]

I see no prospect of the analysis coming to an end. But I realize how lost I would be bereft of my incapacitation. When will the old sub renounce?[7]

Stella is giving a show at the Arlington Galleries. Here is a photo of her looking like Holofernes Leyster. She promised in Dublin that she would send me a card, but she has not.[8]

I finished Cousine Bette – incomprehensibly. A Stock Exchange Hugo. Now I am reading the divine Jane. I think she has much to teach me.[9] It is curious how English literature has never freed itself from the old morality typifications & simplifications. I suppose the cult of the horse has something to do with it. But writing infect[ed] with selective breeding of the vices & virtues becomes tiresome, whether resulting in humours à la Jonson or Coglioni Lorenziani. Isn't Aldington straight out of the Chester cycle?[10]

The two Rests on the Flight School of Patinir are lovely. If the little Flemish annexe contained a chair it would be perfect. The Master from Delft Crucifixion triptych is inexhaustible. There are passages straight out of Bosch apparently.[11] If only one could afford the choices in the Classiker der Kunst [for Klassiker]. Zwemmer's have a number at reduced prices. I nearly bought a Brouwer in the K[ü]nstlermappen series, but withheld my hand like Michelangelo from Brutus. 6/- with 6 coloured plates, including an astonishing landscape.[12]

> Love
>
> Sam

ALS; 1 leaf, 2 sides; enclosure, cutting from the *Daily Sketch* 12 February 1935: n.p., featuring a photo of Estella Solomons with the caption "Irish Art" (AN added to portion of headline above the pictures, wavy underscoring, addition of double exclamation points: FUNDS HEAVY); *env to* Thomas McGreevy Esq, Tarbert, Limerick, Co. Kerry, I.F.S.; *pm* 14-2-35, London; TCD, MS 10402/71. *Dating*: from pm and enclosure.

1 When he was in London, McGreevy usually stayed at Hester Dowden's home, 15 Cheyne Gardens, Chelsea, London SW3.

2 McGreevy anticipated a review in *The Criterion* of his *Poems* which had been published in May 1934 by William Heinemann Ltd. in London, and in November 1934 by Viking in New York; none appeared.

3 James H. Guilford (1903-1997) lived in Foxrock, near the Beckett family home.

4 "Froissée" (offended). The concert on 14 February was not by Mary Jo Prado (see 8 February 1935, n. 3). SB had been invited to use Hester Dowden's piano when he liked (see 29 January [1935], n. 3.

5 Geoffrey Thompson joined the Tavistock Clinic in 1935. James Arthur Hadfield (1882-1967) was Director of Studies and a consultant of the Tavistock Clinic from 1928 to 1951. Thompson was courting Ursula Stenhouse (1911-2001), who taught at Crohamhurst School in Croydon (1933-1935), and then Croydon High School for Girls, south of London (Deborah Thompson, 13 June 1994).

6 Albert Sorel (1842-1906), *La Chute de la royauté 1789-1795*, the second of the eight-volume *L'Europe et la révolution française* (1885-1904); rpt. Paris: Plon, Nourrit: 1914-1922.

7 Sub: subconscious.

8 "Pictures of Cornwall, Yorkshire, Donegal, Portraits, Etchings," the group exhibition by Estella Solomons, Mary Duncan (1885-1967), and Louise R. Jacobs (1880-1946), was held at The Arlington Gallery, from 26 February to 8 March 1935.
A notice of the show appeared in the *Daily Sketch*, 12 February 1935, with Estella Solomons's picture (n.p.). SB compares her photograph to *Judith Holding the Head of Holofernes* (NGI 186) by Lucas Cranach (1472-1553), probably alluding to what McGreevy later describes as Judith's "purposeful expression" (*Pictures in the Irish National Gallery*, 47). SB conflates this image with Judith Leyster (1609-1660), Dutch artist, whose *An Interior: Woman Sewing by Candlelight* is also in the collection of the National Gallery of Ireland (NGI 468).

9 Balzac's *La Cousine Bette* is compared to the writings of Victor Hugo.
English novelist Jane Austen (1775-1817).

10 In the medieval morality play characters often exemplified virtues and vices.
The humour theory of human types and behaviors was exemplified by Ben Jonson's *Everyman in His Humour* (1598) and *Everyman Out of His Humour* (1599).
"Coglioni Lorenziani" (Lawrentian balls) is an allusion to D. H. Lawrence.
SB places Richard Aldington and/or the characters in his novels in the context of the Chester cycle plays which enacted biblical narratives to illuminate themes of sin and redemption; Aldington's *Death of a Hero* (1929), *The Colonel's Daughter* (1931), *All Men are Enemies* (1933).

11 Joachim Patinir (also Patenir, Patenier, c.1480-1524), early Flemish landscapist. SB refers to two paintings ascribed to the School of Patinir: *Rest on the Flight into Egypt* (NGL 3115) and *The Flight into Egypt* (NGL 1084). The Master from Delft (fl. 1490-1520) triptych *Scenes from the Passion of Christ* (NGL 2922) depicts the Crucifixion in the central panel, with scenes of the Procession to Calvary, Judas hanging from a withered tree, the Virgin swooning with Saint John and three Holy Women, and the Agony and preparation for the Capture. Netherlandish painter Hieronymus Bosch (1450-1516).

In the National Gallery, London, the little Flemish annex, room XIII, was off a corridor between rooms XII and XIV; these rooms were rearranged and remodeled in 1935.

12 The Klassiker der Kunst in Gesamtausgaben (1904–1937) was a series of comprehensive studies with illustrations that included works by painters such as Rembrandt, Titian, Dürer, and Rubens. The London bookstore A. Zwemmer, 76–78 Charing Cross Road, specialized in fine art books. The volume on Adriaen Brouwer in the Künstlermappen series (no. 83) was written by Kurt Zoege von Marteuffel, *Adriaen Brouwer: acht farbige Wiedergaben seiner Werke* (Leipzig: E. A. Seemann, 1936).

Michelangelo (né Michelangelo Buonarroti, 1475–1564) began sculpting a bust of Brutus (1540, Museo Nazionale del Bargello, Florence) "as a tribute to the republican spirit of Florence," but abandoned the project when "reminded of the crime" of Brutus' murder of Caesar (Howard Hibbard, *Michelangelo*, 2nd edn. [Cambridge, MA: Harper and Row, 1985] 264).

THOMAS McGREEVY

TARBERT, CO. KERRY

20/2 [1935]   34 Gertrude Street

London S.W[.] 10

My dear Tom

It is good news that I may look forward to seeing you in a fortnight. Herewith the spinsterian pound. I have seen nothing at all of Hester. I feel no inclination to ring up & ask may I go in & play, even if I felt like playing, and I don't. She took my address carefully on two occasions & she can write & invite me if she wants me, which I believe & frankly hope she does not. It is a strain there always and the animals like Renard's hedgehog – a decaying pudenda with nowhere to go, how castrated soever.[1]

I went to my concert a month too soon. It is not till the 9th of March.[2]

Frank's pal has been liquidated without casualty. It was only about a ptosis belt that he came, so he is as far from the sights of it as ever.[3]

I like Jane's manner, in the sense that there is material that can be treated most conveniently in the crochet mode, and somehow Elinor Dashwood is realised as concubine no less desirable than Fielding's Sophie. I suppose the Baron Hulot was for much in the elaboration of Charlus.[4] Brouwer ran away from Hals & Haarlem, & Rubens & Rembrandt owned pictures by him, & so I think did Teniers.[5] It is very hard to see the Elsheimers in the German room, but the Tobias & the Angel seems exquisite. Rubens let off a lot of obituary steam for him, deplored his "indolence"![6] The Geertgen Adoration must be one of the earliest spotlight paintings. Surely it is only half the story to date them from Raphael's Liberation of St. Peter. I never saw the Oxford Uccello mentioned in this connection either.[7]

Miss B. O'Brien is in Florence "studying the Old Masters". Perhaps Dermot [*for* Dermod] is working her up for the Gallery.[8] Mary Manning is now Mrs Mark De Wolf[e] Howe & on her honeymoon to New York & the ... Bermudas![9] Do you know the story of the chaste centipede, who said to her suitor, crossing her thousand legs: "No, a thousand times no."

Lucia is in Grosvenor Place with her aunt, who.. "is on her way to Ireland", whatever that means.[10] She wrote wanting to see me. I have done nothing – except make détours.

I have seen nothing of Geoffrey, but have planned to go down & see him at the hospital next Sunday.[11] It may help to solve the destination of the day. I inspected the plaster caricatures of Vischer & Kraft in the V. & A. Nothing. The Great Hall was full of whores. The Raphael Room is closed.[12]

The MacCarthy has taken her picture.[13]

I go on with Bion ... histoire d'élan acquis. I see no reason why it should ever come to an end. The old heart pounces now & then, as though to console me for the intolerable symptoms of an improvement. Mother writes, she supposes I am brimming over with material for books…anything rather than désoeuvrement.[14]

Estella S. sent me a card for vernissage (et comment) next Tuesday. She is with Mary Duncan & Louise Jacobs at the Arlington. Landscapes from Donegal & Yorkshire.[15]

Last night I dropped my glasses from balcony of this room into the area.[16] I found the lenses this morning, unbroken. I was wanting to scrap the frame anyway.

  Love Sam

ALS; 1 leaf, 2 sides; *env* to Thomas McGreevy Esq, Tarbert, Limerick, Co. Kerry, *in lower left corner* Irish Free State; *pm* 20-2-35, London; TCD, MS 10402/72. *Dating*: pm and opening of the Arlington Gallery before exhibition March 1935.

1 McGreevy did not arrive in London as he had planned (see 10 March 1935).

Hester Dowden had offered SB the use of her piano. SB compares the cats and dogs of her household to Renard's "Le Hérisson," in *Histoires naturelles*, a series of humorous vignettes written first for newspaper publication and then collected:

"Le Hérisson"

Essuyez votre… S. V. P.
II
Il faut me prendre comme je suis et ne pas trop serrer.

"The Hedgehog"

Please wipe your …
II
You have to take me as I am and not squeeze too tightly.

(Jules Renard, *Oeuvres*, II, ed. Léon Guichard, Bibliothèque de la Pléiade [Paris: Gallimard, 1971] 126)

2 The Léner Quartet at Queen's Hall on 9 March 1935 (see 8 February 1935, n. 10).

3 James Guilford was in London to consult specialists; a ptosis belt is used to alleviate the symptoms of a hernia.

4 SB compares Elinor Dashwood in Jane Austen's *Sense and Sensibility* (1811) with Joseph Fielding's character, Sophia Weston, in *Tom Jones* (1749). He also sees Baron Hulot, a character from Balzac's *La Cousine Bette*, as a forerunner of the Baron de Charlus in Proust's *A la recherche du temps perdu*. SB uses a Gallicism, "être pour beaucoup dans" for "to count for a good deal in."

5 Adriaen Brouwer served an apprenticeship in Haarlem under Frans Hals (c.1581–1666); he left for Amsterdam, later returned to Haarlem from c.1625 to 1631, and then spent the remainder of his life in Antwerp (Gerard Knuttel, *Adriaen Brouwer: The Master and His Work*, tr. J. G. Talma-Schilthuis and Robert Wheaton [The Hague: L. J. C.

Bancher, 1962] 109). Rubens owned seventeen Brouwers (179); Rembrandt's collection of Brouwer included seven paintings, another "after Brouwer," and a book of drawings (Kenneth Clark, *Rembrandt and the Italian Renaissance* [London: John Murray, 1966] 193–202). Brouwer influenced Teniers the younger, but the only evidence that Teniers owned a painting by Brouwer is Teniers's painting *The Artist in His Studio* (1635, private collection) which depicts Teniers painting a self-portrait in his studio which is hung with thirty-three paintings by himself and contemporaries, including Brouwer's *Drinker Asleep* (*The Sleeping Toper*, AH:64:05, Fisher Gallery, University of Southern California; Margret Klinge, *David Teniers the Younger: Paintings – Drawings*, Antwerp: Koninklijk Museum Voor Schoene Kunsten, 11 May–1 September 1991 [Ghent: Snoeck-Ducaju and Zoon, 1991] 50, 52–53; Margret Klinge, 14 February 2007).

6   The paintings of Adam Elsheimer (1578–1610) in the German room (XIX) of the National Gallery in London included *St. Paul on Malta* (c.1600, NGL 3535, also known as *The Shipwreck of St. Paul*), *St. Lawrence Being Prepared for Martyrdom* (c.1600–1601, NGL 1014), *The Baptism of Christ* (c.1599, NGL 3904), and *Tobias and the Archangel Raphael* (c.1650, NGL 1424, then attributed to Elsheimer, now considered to be after Elsheimer). On 14 January 1611, Rubens wrote to a biologist and collector living in Rome, Dr. Johann Faber (fl. early seventeenth century), who had informed him of Elsheimer's death: Elsheimer "had no equal in small figures, in Landscapes, and in many other subjects. He has died in the flower of his studies." Rubens deplored Elsheimer's "sin of sloth, by which he has deprived the world of the most beautiful things" (Keith Andrews, *Adam Elsheimer: Paintings – Drawings – Prints* [New York: Rizzoli, 1977] 51).

7   SB refers to *The Nativity* (late fifteenth century, NGL 4081) by Geertgen tot Sint Jans (1460/1465–1495), noting that it was earlier than the *Liberation of St. Peter from Prison* (1513–1514) by Raphael, which was painted over a window-opening in the Vatican (Frederick Hartt, *History of Italian Renaissance Art: Painting, Sculpture, Architecture*, 3rd edn. [New York: Harry N. Abrams, 1987] 513–514). Also earlier is Uccello's *Hunt in the Forest* (c.1470, Ashmolean Museum A79).

8   Irish artist, Rose Brigid O'Brien (m. Ganly, 1909–2002) was the daughter of Dermod O'Brien, who was on the Board of Governors and Guardians of the National Gallery of Ireland; the museum was seeking a new Director.

9   Irish writer Mary Manning* (1905–1999) married the American historian and biographer Mark de Wolfe Howe (1906–1967) on 28 February 1935.

10   Lucia Joyce arrived in London on 14 February 1935 with her aunt, Mrs. Eileen Schaurek (née Eileen Isabel Mary Xavier Brigid Joyce, 1889–1963), with whom she stayed at the Mascot Hotel in York Street, not Grosvenor Place. While Mrs. Schaurek was in Dublin (24 February to 1 March), Lucia Joyce stayed with Harriet Weaver at 74 Gloucester Place. However, from 26 to 27 February, she stayed on her own in a hotel on Gloucester Street, returning afterwards to stay again with Harriet Weaver. Lucia left for Ireland with her aunt on 16 March 1935 (Ellmann, *James Joyce*, 681; Carol Loeb Shloss, *Lucia Joyce: To Dance in the Wake* [New York: Farrar, Straus and Giroux, 2003] 308–312, 509; Brenda Maddox, *Nora: The Real Life of Molly Bloom* [Boston: Houghton Mifflin Co., 1988] 305–309). According to Joyce's letter to Giorgio and Helen Joyce, 19 February 1935, during this period Lucia met SB "a few times and they had dinner together" (Joyce, *Letters of James Joyce*, III, 344).

11   Geoffrey Thompson was in Beckenham.

12 Nineteenth-century plaster casts in the Victoria and Albert collection (room 46A) included the highly ornamented Gothic canopy and enclosure of the *Tomb of St. Sebaldus* (1508–1519, St. Sebalduskirche, Nuremberg; V&A repro. 1869–14) by Peter Vischer the elder (c.1460–1529) that was decorated with statuettes and reliefs; other works by Peter Vischer in the collection were casts of the *Monument of Count Otto IV of Henneberg* (1488, Städtkirche, Römhild; V&A repro. 1873–580:1) and of *A Bronze Monument* (1497, Magdeburg Cathedral; V&A repro. 1904–55:0). Also among the collection of casts in this room was the *Schreyer-Landauer Monument* (1490–1492, St. Sebalduskirche, Nuremberg; V&A repro. 1872–53) by German sculptor Adam Kraft (also Krafft, fl.1490–1509).

The Raphael Room (48), with cartoons for tapestries commissioned by Pope Leo X (1515) for the Sistine Chapel, was closed intermittently between April 1934 and August 1935, as paintings were removed in stages for repair. The records of the Victoria and Albert Museum indicate that the cartoon then known as "Peter and John at the Beautiful Gate" (now "The Healing of the Lame Man," 1515–1516) was removed in early February 1935, treated, and replaced in its frame on 6 March 1935 (Alison Baber, National Art Library, Victoria and Albert Museum, 1 June 1994, from the Museum's registered papers). The "Great Hall" may have been the main entrance to the Museum or the Octagon Court which displayed loan exhibitions; there are no records to confirm what was exhibited there in 1935 (Alison Baber, 13 June 1994).

13 Ethna MacCarthy's painting, *Portrait of a Lady* (inscribed 1599 "age 61") by the School of Pourbus, had been offered at auction (Sotheby's, 13 June 1934, no. 85) but had not met the reserve price. The Pourbus family of Flemish painters included Pieter Pourbus (1523/1524–1584), his son Frans Pourbus (1545/1546–1581), and Frans Pourbus II (1569–1622). SB had been asked to pick up the painting and keep it for MacCarthy.

14 "Histoire d'élan acquis" (just a matter of momentum).
"Désoeuvrement" (having nothing to do, idleness).

15 "Vernissage (et comment)" (private view [and how]). The exhibition opened for private view on 26 February 1935. Mary Duncan's landscapes were largely of Cornwall, those by Louise Jacobs were of Yorkshire, and those by Estella Solomons were of Donegal.

16 SB wrote "<this> balcony of this room ..."

THOMAS McGREEVY

TARBERT, LIMERICK, CO. KERRY

10/3 [1935]   34 Gertrude Street

London SW10

My dear Tom

Very glad to have your letter & touched at your bothering your head about my old Grillen.[1] All I ever got from the

Imitation went to confirm & reinforce my own way of living, a way of living that tried to be a solution & failed. I found quantities of phrases like qui melius scit pati majorem tenebit pacem, or, Nolle consolari ab aliqua creatura magnae puritatis signum est, or the lovely per viam pacis ad patriam perpetuae claritatis, that seemed to be made for me and which I have never forgotten.[2] Amg many others. But they all conduced to the isolationism that was not to prove very splendid. What is one to make of "seldom we come home without hurting of conscience" and "the glad going out & sorrowful coming home" and "be ye sorry in your chambers" but a quietism of the sparrow alone upon the housetop & the solitary bird under the eaves? An abject self-referring quietism indeed, beside the alert quiet of one who always had Jesus for his darling, but the only kind that I, who seem never to have had the least faculty or disposition for the supernatural, could elicit from the text, and then only by means of a substitution of terms very different from the one you propose.[3] I mean that I replaced the plenitude that he calls "God", not by "goodness", but by a pleroma only to be sought among my own feathers or entrails, a principle of self the possession of which was to provide a rationale & the communion with which a sense of Grace. Thus the Imitation could be made [to] subserve the "Sin" of Luciferian concentration. And I know that now I would be no more capable of approaching its hypostatics & analogies "meekly, simply & truly", than I was when I first twisted them into a programme of self-sufficiency. I would still find it, so far from being a compendium of Christian behaviour, with oeuvres pies, humility, utility, self-effacement, etc. etc., in all probability conceived & composed on the rebound from the fiasco of just such an effort in behaviour, your "long, long experience of unhappiness"; and that if certain forms of contact are commended by the way, it is very much by the way, and incidental & secondary to the fundamental contact – for him, with "God". So that to read "goodness & disinterestedness" every time for "God", would seem the accidental for the essential with a vengeance & a mining of the text; whereas to allow the sceptical position (which I hope is not complacent in my case, however it may be a tyranny), & replace a principle of faith, absolute & infinite, by one personal & finite of fact, would be to preserve its magnificent basis of distinction between primary & secondary, in the interests of a very baroque solipsism if you like.[4] I cannot see how "goodness" is to be made a foundation or a beginning of anything. Am I to set my teeth & be disinterested? When I cannot answer for myself, and do not dispose of myself, how can I serve? Will the demon – pretiosa margarita! – disable me any the less with sweats & shudders & panics & rages & rigors & heart burstings because my motives are unselfish & the welfare of others my concern? Macché![5] Or is there some way of devoting pain & monstrosity & incapacitation to the service of a deserving cause? Is one to insist on a crucifixion for which there is no demand?

For me the position is really a simple & straightforward one, or was until complicated by the analysis, obviously necessarily. For years I was unhappy, consciously & deliberately ever since I left school & went into T.C.D., so that I isolated myself more & more, undertook less & less & lent myself to a crescendo of disparagement of others & myself. But in all that there was nothing that struck me as morbid. The misery & solitude & apathy & the sneers were the elements of an index of superiority & guaranteed the feeling of arrogant "otherness", which seemed as right & natural & as little morbid as the ways in which it was not so much expressed as implied & reserved &

kept available for a possible utterance in the future. It was not until that way of living, or rather negation of living, developed such terrifying physical symptoms that it could no longer be pursued, that I became aware of anything morbid in myself. In short, if the heart had not put the fear of death into me I would be still boozing & sneering & lounging around & feeling that I was too good for anything else. It was with a specific fear & a specific complaint that I went to Geoffrey, then to Bion, to learn that the "specific fear & complaint" was the least important symptom of a diseased condition that began in a time which I could not remember, in my "pre-history", a bubble on the puddle; and that the fatuous torments which I had treasured as denoting the superior man were all part of the same pathology. That was the picture as I was obliged to accept it, and that is still largely the picture, and I cannot see that it allows of any philosophical or ethical or Christlike imitative pentimenti, or in what way they could redeem a composition that was invalid from the word "go" & has to be broken up altogether.[6] If the heart still bubbles it is because the puddle has not been drained, and the fact of its bubbling more fiercely than ever is perhaps open to receive consolation from the waste that splutters most, when the bath is nearly empty.

If I cod myself with all this I cod myself & that is all. It will have been an expensive canular.[7] I have tried to face the possibility of its failing to render the business of remaining alive tolerable, & I have not been able to. It claims to do more, but if it does as much the year of two fears or three fears will seem to me better spent than any others I can point to up till now.

—— ———— —— ——— ——— —

Reavey has been active, founding a branch of his International Bureau over here, or something equally interesting. Your defection at the 6 Bells was still present in his mind. I was wishing I had his precious Anthologie Surréaliste to return to him. But he will be back in a fortnight. He is full of translations, anthologies, adaptations & centos & transactions of every kind. He showed me a poem that surprised me it was so much better than anything I had seen of his hitherto.[8]

The Lucia ember flared up & fizzled out. But more of that viva voce.

I do not see much of Hester, but it always goes very well when I go round, and we play the Pavane with special reference to the obeisances in the dance.[9]

The news from home is good. I sent Mother Morton's In the Steps of the Master for her birthday & she was delighted.[10] Frank never writes.

I spent an evening with Geoffrey and to-day I am going down to Eden Park to spend afternoon & evening. He is in excellent form and is now attached to the outpatients psychological department at Bart's, so that he can proceed to little analyses on his own![11]

I went to the Lener playing the Rasumovsky Quartets at Queen's Hall yesterday & was very disappointed. Their playing seemed dry & finickety to the point of Old Maidishness & Ludvig never so Rembrandtesque.[12]

Stella's exhibition with Louise Jacobs & Mary Duncan was really lamentable. She had a 10 year old portrait of Jack Yeats priced at £100! The place was packed with the chosen & faithful for the opening day. I was talking to Louise Jacobs, on whose work alone the eye could rest, & who personally seems an agreeable woman.[13] Seumas says he will publish my four wan lines about the surrogate goodbyes in his April number. But that means nothing.[14]

I have been reading Wahrheit und Dichtung in Hester's copy and have got to the Strassberg [for Strasburg] period & contact with Herder. I find parts of it absorbing, for example the literary picture during his Leipzig phase. The early years in Frankfurt, long description of crowning of King of Hesse etc., are dull. What an awful shit of a Father he had.[15] They are doing The Alchemist at the Embassy next week & I hope to go. What an admirable dramatic unity of place the besieged house provides & how much he makes of it. The feverish, obsidional atmosphere of Nourri dans le sérail etc–[16]

I spend most of my time, when not with Bion or walking, reading on top of the fire. Snow yesterday. I occasionally see MacCarthy. Ethna has had her picture taken away for removal to Dublin.[17]

Do hurry up & come over.

My best wishes for comfort & contentment to your mother. The Spring should make things a bit gayer for her.

>Love ever

>Sam

ALS; 3 leaves, 6 sides; env to Thomas McGreevy Esq, Tarbert, Limerick, Co Kerry, Irish Free State; pm 11-3-35, London; TCD, MS 10402/73. Dating: from pm; concert by Léner Quartet at Queen's Hall, 9 March 1935.

1 SB may use the term "Grillen," as Goethe frequently did, "to denote his moodiness and troubles" (Mark Nixon, "'Scraps of German': Samuel Beckett reading German Literature," Notes Diverse Holo, Special issue SBT/A 16 [2006] 265).

2 German-born theologian Thomas à Kempis (né Thomas Haemmerlein, 1380–1471) wrote what is known in English as The Imitation of Christ in 1441; it was first published in 1471. Latin citations that follow in this and related notes are from Thomas à Kempis, De imitatione Christi libri quatuor: sacrae scripturae textuum adnotatione et variis rerum indicibus locupletata, new edn. (Mechliniae, Belgium: H. Dessain, 1921); sections and subsections of the text are given in roman numerals followed by the page reference in arabic numerals. Modern English translations are taken from Thomas à Kempis, The Imitation of Christ, ed. Ernest Rhys, Everyman's Library (London: J. M. Dent; New York: E. P. Dutton, 1910), which is widely available. Rhys's translation is based on the first English translation, De imitatione Christi, ed. J. K. Ingram, Early English Text Society Extra Series (London: Kegan Paul, Trench, Turner and Co., 1893). For the convenience of readers as well as scholors of the classical text, page references are given to both English translations. SB's notes are in his Notebook for

Dream of Fair to Middling Women, BIF, UoR, MS 5000; see Pilling (ed.), *Beckett's Dream Notebook*, 80–87.

"Qui melius scit pati, majorem tenebit pacem" (II.iii, 87) ("He that can well suffer shall find most peace") (Rhys, 66; Ingram, 43).

"Nolle consolari ab aliqua creatura, magnae puritatis, et internae fiduciae signum est" (II.vi, 93) ("For a man not to wish to be comforted by any creature is a token of great purity") (Rhys, 72; Ingram, 47).

"Per viam pacis, ad patriam perpetuae claritatis" (III.lxiv, 296) ("Direct him by the way of peace to the country of everlasting clearness") (Rhys, 228; Ingram, 150).

3 In "Of Eschewing Superfluity of Words" (I.x), Thomas à Kempis asks why we do not simply avoid conversation, since "seldom we come home without hurting of conscience"; he suggests that "we seek comfort each from the other and to relieve the heart that is made weary with divers thoughts," but concludes that "such outward comfort is a great hindering of inward and heavenly consolation" (Rhys, 16; Ingram, 11).

From I.xx, "Of Love of Silence and to Be Alone," Thomas à Kempis cites: "Be ye sorry in your chambers" (from Isaiah 26:20) (Rhys, 37; Ingram, 25). He advises withdrawal from the world: "Laetus exitus tristem saepe reditum parit: et laeta vigilia serotina triste mane facit" ("glad going out ofttimes bringeth forth a sorrowful coming home and a glad watching over evening bringeth forth a sorry morning") (Rhys, 38; Ingram, 25).

From IV.xii, "With how great Diligence he ought to prepare himself that should receive the Sacrament of Christ." Thomas à Kempis's advice is to shut oneself in as "passer solitarius in tecto" ("a solitary bird under the evesings [eaves]") (Rhys, 268; Ingram, 276).

4 "Pleroma" (Gk., fullness, abundance), related to Gnosticism.

From Kempis, I.v, "Of Reading of the Scriptures": "If thou wilt draw profit in reading read meekly simply and truly, not desiring to have a name of knowledge" (Rhys, 10; Ingram, 107).

"Oeuvres pies" (works of piety).

SB seems to be quoting from McGreevy's letter to him which has not been found.

5 "Pretiosa margarita" (precious pearl), an analogy to the Kingdom of Heaven (see Matthew 13:45–46).

Thomas à Kempis wrote: "Quam multi ore tenus praedicant, sed vita longe dissentiunt: ipsa tamen est pretiosa margaríta, a multis abscóndita" (III.xxxvii, 213) ("Many preach with the mouth but in living they depart far therefrom. Nevertheless it is a precious margaret (pearl) and hid from many") (Rhys, 167; Ingram, 108).

SB wrote "<terrors> shudders." "Macché" (It. colloq., Come off it!).

6 "Pentimenti" (acts of contrition).

7 "Canular" (Ecole Normale Supérieure slang, practical joke).

8 With Marc Lvovich Slonim (1894–1976), George Reavey had founded the Bureau Littéraire Européen, 4, Square Léon Guillot, Paris XV; for several years, following work on *The European Caravan*, he had been interested in establishing a London base for his agency as the European Literary Bureau.

The Six Bells was a pub on King's Road near Glebe Place, Chelsea. *Petite Anthologie poétique du surréalisme*, ed. Georges Hugnet (Paris: Editions Jeanne Bucher, 1934).

With Slonim, Reavey edited and translated from the Russian *Soviet Literature: An Anthology* (London: Wishart and Co., 1933; tr. into French as *Anthologie de la littérature soviétique, 1918-1934* [Paris: Gallimard, 1935]). His edition of Paul Eluard's poems, *Thorns of Thunder*, included many translated by SB; it was released in conjunction with The International Surrealist Exhibition in London (11 June to 4 July 1936).

Reavey had embarked on the first of his translations of the works of Nikolai Aleksandrovich Berdyaev (1874-1948), *Smysl istorii* (1923; *The Meaning of History*, 1936).

Reavey's current poetry was based on centos: e.g. the two collections he published in 1935: *Faust's Metamorphoses: Poems; Nostradam: A Sequence of Poems*, Europa Poets 1 (Paris: Europa Press, 1935); *Signes d'adieu (Frailty of Love)*, tr. Pierre Charnay, Europa Poets (Paris: Editions Europa, 1935). It is not known which poem Reavey had shown SB.

9 Lucia Joyce in London: see 20 February [1935], n. 10.

SB and Hester Dowden were playing Ravel's *Pavane pour une Infante défunte* for piano, four hands (24 February 1931, n.4).

10 *In the Steps of the Master* (1934) by H[enry] V[ollam] Morton (1892-1979). May Beckett's birthday was 1 March.

11 Eden Park, an area of southeast London, near Beckenham. St. Bartholomew's Hospital (Barts), Westsmithfield, London, EC 1.

12 The Léner String Quartet played all of Beethoven's *Rasumovsky Quartets*, op. 59, at Queen's Hall on 9 March 1935.

13 The exhibition Landscapes from Donegal to Yorkshire: 20 February [1935], n. 15.

Estella Solomons's portrait of Jack Yeats, painted in 1922, is now in the collection of the Sligo County Library and Museum; she had included her portraits in the exhibition at the urging of Louise Jacobs (Louise Jacobs to Stella Solomons Starkey, 10 October 1934, TCD, MS 4644/1208). Jacobs's paintings included landscapes (*The Café Montmartre, A Tournament in Toyland, Red Roofs of Whitby*) as well as portraits (TCD, MS 4644/3521; Michael Jacobs).

14 SB was disappointed: "The Dublin Magazine is out, but my poem not in" (SB to McGreevy, 26 April 1935, TCD, MS 10402/74). In a letter to Leventhal, SB wrote: "[O'Sullivan] has a quatrain of mine, due in the last awful issue, but perhaps he has smoked its indiscriminate application to death-bed & whoral turns"; SB enclosed the poem "Da Tagte Es" (7 August [1935], TxU).

15 Goethe's autobiography *Aus meinem Leben: Dichtung und Wahrheit* (1811-1833; *Memoirs of Goethe: Written by Himself*). SB may have read an edition that presented the title in "inverted word order," namely *Aus meinem Leben: Wahrheit und Dichtung*, of which there are several. Notes on his reading of Goethe can be found in TCD, MS 10971/1; for a description: Everett Frost and Jane Maxwell, "TCD, MS 10971/1: German Literature," *Notes Diverse Holo*, Special issue *SBT/A* 16 (2006) 115-116, 120-123.

SB had read as far as Goethe's meeting with the German philosopher, Johann Gottfried von Herder (1744-1803) (Book X). Goethe himself depicts his father as imperious, yet respected.

16 The action of Ben Jonson's *The Alchemist* (1610) is set in a single house of a doctor. SB quotes from Racine's *Bajazet* (1672): "Nourri dans le sérail, j'en connais les détours"

("In the Seraglio reared, I know its ways") (Jean Racine, *Bajazet* [Paris: Editions du Seuil, 1947] 124; Jean Racine, *Complete Plays*, II, tr. Samuel Solomon, [New York: Modern Library, 1969] 64).

17   MacCarthy's painting: see 20 February [1935], n. 13.

GEORGE REAVEY

PARIS

[15 March 1935]   34 Gertrude St
                                                            London S.W.19.

[no greeting]

Not <u>Poems</u> after all, but: <u>Echo's Bones, and Other Precipitates.</u>[1]
C'est plus modeste.[2]
S.B.

TPCI; 1 leaf, 2 sides; *to* Monsieur George Reavey, Bureau Littéraire Européen, Rue Bonaparte 13, Paris 6me; *pm* 15-3-35, London, *pm* 16-3-35, Paris; *AN recto, in another hand* Giacometti, 46 Rue Hippolyte, XIV Maindron Rue d'Alesia; *AN verso, in another hand* 6 March 1935; TxU. *Dating*: from pm.

1   For the title of the book, SB chose the title of the final poem in the collection.

2   "C'est plus modeste." (It is more modest.)

THOMAS McGREEVY

LONDON

5/5/35   Cooldrinagh
                                                            [Co. Dublin]

My dear Tom

    Glad to hear that Devlin's visit was a success. Did you see his poem in Saturday's Irish Times? An agreeable change from all the Hymns Ancient & Modern.[1]

Except for the heart bad a couple of nights, things have been pretty well with me. I have been a lot with Mother, & note with pleasure that she forgets to be wretched more often than formerly. Also walking enormously. Quando il piede cammina il cuore gode.[2]

Yesterday afternoon I had Jack Yeats all to myself, not even Madame, from 3 to past 6, and saw some quite new pictures. He seems to be having a freer period. The one in the Academy – Low Tide – bought by Meredith for the Municipal is overwhelming.[3] He can only recall my watercolour very vaguely, as being probably the fish market in Sligo.[4] He was asking for you, and stressed the advisability of your not failing to apply for the Gallery, though saying nothing to make it appear that he was in the know.[5] He had some story from Miss Purser of the Lurçat, now exposed in the Municipal, having been attacked with spits & sticks. In the end we went out, down to Charlemont House to find out about Sunday opening, & then to Jury's for a drink. He parted as usual with an offer to buy me a Herald. I hope to see him again before I leave, but do not expect ever to have him like that again.[6]

[...]

I went one evening with Leventhal to see Ethna. She has some kind of a job in the Castle. The Pourbus seems held up indefinitely in the Customs.[7] She lent me two volumes of Albéniz. I have found some charming and playable de Falla of my own.[8]

I am getting on well with the Torre. It is a pity that he can't keep off the flowers of speech. The precedent hunting seems very brilliant, though I imagine a historian would cavil at the Revolution as merely an episode in a national tradition of anti-feudalism, and at the sequitur from the rejection of the Reform to the convocation of the States General. But for me the simplification & easy going dogmatism is good enough.[9]

[...]

I suppose you remember the little Del Mazo <u>Musicians</u> in the Gallery. I seem to remember your having spoken of it as a pet of yours. It is charming, with something of Watteau in it. The Wilson Tivoli views are good, one is almost a replica of the one in Dulwich.[10]

Second lesson at church this evening was the passage of Christ's commission to Peter. "Care my lambs, care my sheep, care my sheep", & the "Peter, lovest thou me" thrice. Poor Peter, he was always getting it in threes. Anyway I remembered the Raphael Cartoon of the Commission, & the rest of the service was easy, even a sermon all about demes & $1/120^{th}$ part of a [? lav] per caput (si on peut dire).[11]

Dublin is lovely with no trams & buses, the hills & sea seem to have crept nearer.[12]

I expect to stay the month, which means I would be back in London to-morrow fortnight. I don't want to accept this life quite yet, but I loathe the thought of returning to London. However, it must be.

I wonder did you remember to take the books I left at Gertrude St. to the library?

No news from Geoffrey. C'est l'amour.

Schöne Grüsse to Hester & Dilly.[13]

> Love ever
>
> Sam

ALS; 3 leaves, 6 sides; *env to* Thomas McGreevy Esq, 15 Cheyne Gardens, London S.W. 3; *pm* 6-5-35, Dublin; TCD, MS 10402/75.

1 Denis Devlin had joined the Department of External Affairs and was traveling in connection with his work. Devlin's poem "Moments" was in three parts, each beginning from a specific observation; whereas earlier poems had been drawn principally from religious or historical contexts ("Moments," *The Irish Times* 4 May 1935: 7; see Denis Devlin, *Collected Poems of Denis Devlin*, ed. J. C. C. Mays [Dublin: Dedalus Press, 1989] 93–99, 107–108).

2 "Quando il piede cammina il cuore gode" (When the foot walks, the heart gladdens). Source unknown, probably proverbial.

3 Yeats was aware of SB's preference, as he wrote to McGreevy on 13 February 1935: "I tried to get Beckett on the phone one day but he was away. I wanted to arrange a day for him to come here – when there wouldn't be other visitors as he doesn't so much like having them about" (TCD, MS 10381/125). His wife was artist Mary Cottenham Yeats (née White, known as Cottie, 1867–1947).

Low Tide (1935, Dublin City Gallery The Hugh Lane, no. 727; Pyle 454) was shown in the 1935 Royal Hibernian Academy Exhibition; it was sold to Justice James Creed Meredith (1875–1942), who in 1937 presented it to the Municipal Gallery of Modern Art (Pyle, *Jack B. Yeats: A Catalogue Raisonné of the Oil Paintings*, I, 312; III, 196).

4 The watercolor is *Corner Boys* (private collection, Pyle 701) (Pyle, *Jack B. Yeats: His Watercolours, Drawings and Pastels* [Dublin: Irish Academic Press, 1993] 165).

5 The position of Director of the National Gallery of Ireland was advertised for two weeks from 9 April 1935; the advertisement announced a closing date for applications of 21 May 1935 and stated that "Personal canvassing of members of the Board is prohibited" (*The Irish Times* 9 April 1935: 6). Jack Yeats counseled McGreevy: "I wish you were certain to get the directorship of the National Gallery here. I am sure you have a good chance" (13 February 1935, TCD, MS 10381/125); later he sent a copy of the advertisement, and wrote: "I daresay that the field will be so overwhelming on each other that, if you came ghost up along, determinedly, you might, just, get it" (15 April 1935, TCD MS 10381/126). Brian Coffey, whose father Dr. Denis Coffey (1865–1945) was President of University College Dublin and a member of the Board, also encouraged McGreevy (16 May 1935, TCD MS 8110/19). McGreevy applied for the position on 18 May, but he was not invited to interview.

6 The attack on Lurçat's *Decorative Landscape* (Dublin City Gallery The Hugh Lane, no. 709) was reported to the City Manager by the Curator, John J. Reynolds (n.d., Curator from 14 April 1924 to 30 September 1935) (26, 27 April 1935, Records of the Municipal Gallery of Modern Art). SB reported to McGreevy: "A large hole was clean through the middle sky, with scratches extending left to the 'magic' ledgy passage, & what looked like spit marks" (15 May 1935, TCD, MS MS 10402/76). Sarah Purser, Dublin artist and art patron, had accepted the Lurçat painting on behalf of the Society of Friends of the National Collections of Ireland: 4 November [*for* 3 November 1932], n. 4. SB writes about the damage in "La Peinture des van Velde ou le Monde et le Pantalon," *Cahiers d'Art*, 20–21 (1945–1946) 349; rpt. in Samuel Beckett, *Disjecta*, 119.

Jury's Hotel was then located at 6–8 College Green; Yeats was a regular reader of the *Evening Herald* (1891–).

7 Ethna MacCarthy's painting by Pourbus: see 20 February [1935], n. 13. Her position in Dublin Castle is not known.

8 It is not known which of the piano scores of Isaac Albéniz had been lent to SB by Ethna MacCarthy. Manuel de Falla's compositions for piano are numerous and include piano adaptations of music from his ballet scores.

9 Guillermo de Torre (1900–1971), Spanish critic, was a member of an experimental poetic movement, "ultraism" (fl. 1919–1923); in South America it included such poets as Argentinian writer Jorge Luis Borges (1899–1986) and Chilean poet and diplomat

Pablo Neruda (né Neftalí Ricardo Reyes Basoalto, 1904–1973). SB may have been reading Torre's *Literaturas europeas de vanguardia* (1925); Torre was a founder of *La Gaceta Literaria* (Madrid) and had contributed to *The New Review* 1,4 (Winter 1931–1932).

10 *The Musicians* (NGI 659) by Spanish painter Juan Bautista Martínez del Mazo (c.1613–1667) is compared to paintings by Antoine Watteau. Of the two paintings by Richard Wilson in the collection of the National Gallery of Ireland, *A View of Tivoli over the Campagna* (NGI 746) and *A View of Tivoli* (NGI 747), the first is more similar in composition to Dulwich's *Tivoli, the Cascatelle and the "Villa of Maecenas"* (DPG 171).

11 Christ's commission to Peter (John 21:15–17) was one of the lessons in the lectionary appointed for the evening service on the second Sunday after Easter (5 May 1935).

SB refers to *Christ's Charge to Peter*, one of the seven Raphael cartoons in the collection of the Victoria and Albert Museum (see 20 February [1935], n. 12; www.vam.ac.uk/).

SB's reference to "Demes" is unclear. A legal term of minimum repayment is 1/120th part of the remains of a debt. The second lesson for the evening service was Philippians 3:7–21; verse 9 speaks of the difference between worldly possession and faith: "not having mine own righteousness, which is of the law, but … the righteousness which is of God by Faith" (*The Book of Common Prayer … The Church of Ireland* [Dublin: Association for Promoting Christian Knowledge, Church of Ireland, 1927] xxxvii).

"Si on peut dire" (to put it that way).

12 Tram and bus drivers were on strike in Dublin; service resumed only on 18 May 1935 ("Sixty Days of Tramway Strike," *The Irish Times* 1 May 1935: 8; "Trams and Buses To-Day," *The Irish Times* 18 May 1935: 9).

13 SB refers to Thompson's courtship of Ursula Stenhouse; "c'est l'amour" (it's love). "Schöne Grüsse" (warm greetings). Hester Dowden, Geraldine Cummins (Dilly).

GEORGE REAVEY
LONDON

23/5/35

34 Gertrude Street
London S.W.10

Cher ami

Nostradamus et Michel de l'Hospital en collaboration, astres et cadastres, vraie cellule de l'histoire.[1] Tes poèmes en retirent la membrane. Pôles et principes mâle et femelle, castagnettes de même si tu veux, c'est plutôt à celui-ci que je me surprends à songer par tous les secteurs de ton cycle, ce qui est dans ton dessein sans doute.[2] Mais félicitations avant tout de cette menace ou promesse grandissant comme orgasme à échéance imprévisible, celle du très Saint-Barthélemy, qui n'est après tout qu'une façon de .. gémir, et dont le firmament n'est guère plus consolé que d'un pet en combustion.[3]

Tous les signes sont d'adieu.[4] Lâche-moi en [*for* Lâche-m'en] un tout de même.

Amitiés

s/ Sam

ALS; 1 leaf, 1 side; TxU.

23/5/35   34 Gertrude Street
                                          London S.W.10

Dear George,

Nostradamus and Michel de l'Hospital in collaboration, celestial bodies and terrestrial plots, a true cell of history.[1] Your poems pull the membrane from it. Male and female poles and principles, ditto castanets if you like, this is the one I catch myself musing over through all the sectors of your cycle, which is no doubt part of your design.[2] But congratulations above all on that threat or promise, swelling like some orgasm whose term is unpredictable, of the very Saintly Bartholomew, which is after all only a manner of ... moaning, something no more consoling to the firmament than a fart on fire.[3]

All signs are of farewell.[4] Let me have one all the same.

All the best

Sam

1 For the sequence of poems *Nostradam*, Reavey cites as an epigraph lines from D. H. Lawrence's poem "The Ship of Death":

"Build then the ship of death, for you must take
The longest journey[,] to oblivion.
And die the death, the long and painful death
That lies between the old self and the new." ([3])

The poems in the first section of *Nostradam*, "A Word for Nostradamus" (9–22), explore political and religious upheaval following the death of Henry II (1519–1559), as predicted by French physician and astrologer Nostradamus (Latin name of Michel de Notredame, 1503–1566). Michel de l'Hospital (c.1505–1573) represented Henry II at the Council of Trent (1545–1563), and, after the King's death, became Chancellor of France from 1560 to 1568; he advocated policy reform and religious toleration, but as the Wars of Religion (Catholics vs. Huguenots) resumed in 1567, L'Hospital and the moderates were discredited.

Reavey's epigraph for this section is drawn from Nostradamus, I, 53, although it modernizes some words:

"Lorsqu'on [*for* Las qu'on] verra grand peuple tourmenté
Et la loy sainte [*for* Loy Saincte] en totale ruine
Par autres fois [*for* loix] toute la Chrestienté
Quand d'or d'argent trouve nouvelle mine."

("Alas, how a great people shall be tormented
And the Holy Laws in total ruin,
By other laws, all Christianity troubled,
When new mines of gold and silver will be found.")

(*The Complete Prophecies of Nostradamus*, ed. and tr. Henry C. Roberts, [New York: Crown, 1947] 26)

Reavey dedicated the poem "Tell me that Dream" to SB; it considers Nostradamus's dream of death (*Nostradam*, 13).

2   The second sequence of six poems in Reavey's *Nostradam* is entitled "A La Belle Dame Sans Merci" (21–28). SB alludes to the contrasts between the two sections of *Nostradam*.

3   On the feast day of St. Bartholomew in 1572, a massacre of French Huguenots began in Paris and continued in the countryside for a month.
"Façon de . . gémir" (manner of . . moaning, adapted from "façon de parler" [manner of speaking])

4   SB alludes to Reavey's *Signes d'adieu*.

GEORGE REAVEY

LONDON

23/6/35

34 Gertrude St
London SW 10

Cher ami

Oui, elle et lui foyers de la vie ellipse de solitudes. On finira bien par ne plus se donner la peine de vérifier les distances.

Je suis bien aise de pouvoir te dire que tes Signes me plaisent plus que tout ce que j'ai lu de toi jusqu'ici.[1] Comme articulation – lyrisme succinct, pensée qui n'insiste pas, litote sans sécheresse – ils ne risquent guère de se perdre. (Femmes si réelles et quatre derniers vers de Souci Tristesse).[2] Mais c'est avant tout comme tempérament que j'en admire la qualité, tempérament que je ne me souviens pas d'avoir trouvé ailleurs sinon dans les Tragiques de Jouve, qui l'a toutefois beaucoup plus indiqué.[3]

Je n'ai pas besoin de l'original pour comprendre que la traduction est excellente.[4]

Merci infiniment.

A toi   Sam

ALS; 1 leaf, 1 side; TxU.

Dear George

Yes, he and she sources of life ellipsis of solitudes. We shall end up not troubling to check the distances.

I am very pleased to be able to tell you that I like your *Signes* more than anything I've read of yours up till now.[1] As articulation – succinct lyricism, unobtrusive thought, litotes without dryness – they are in no danger of losing their way. ("Femmes si réelles" and last four lines of "Souci tristesse").[2] But it is above all for their temperament that I admire the quality of them, a temperament that I cannot remember finding anywhere except in Jouve's *Tragiques*, where in any case it is much more insistent.[3]

I do not need the original to understand that the translation is excellent.[4]

Very many thanks

Yours

Sam

1 Reavey, *Signes d'adieu.*

2 Reavey's poem:

> Femmes si réelles votre réalité n'est pas sûre
> quant à ce qui est des caresses
> signes d'adieu d'étoiles mourantes
> apposition des mains mésintelligence
> des lèvres et des yeux
> l'enchaînement de certains moments
> et l'inconséquence de la plupart.

(21)

SB discusses the four last lines of:

> Souci tristesse
> ainsi parle cette musique
> mais le coeur s'y laisserait prendre?
> Jamais! c'est une ravine où l'on s'affaisse
> ô destin plus fort que l'acier
> et plus puissant que tout vouloir
> il est là tapi dans cette musique
> et le désir vous effleure
> mais dans les failles des montagnes
> la neige s'écoule en torrents.

(16)

3 *Tragiques* (1923), a collection of poems by Pierre-Jean Jouve (1887–1976).

4 *Signes d'adieu*, the French translation of Reavey's poems: 10 March [1935], n. 8; an English edition, *Frailty of Love*, was announced, but it was not published.

THOMAS McGREEVY

TARBERT, IRELAND

8 Sep [1935]

34 Gertrude St
[London]

My dear Tom

The discrepancy between mind and body is terrible. It is something that the four of you are together.[1] And that you have been able to feel close to her if only briefly. May it all be over soon, for her and for you all.

I have been as you know me. I miss you greatly. I had a card from Hester announcing remove to Sorrento.[2] Geoffrey was round, less Cytherean. We had a lovely walk in Battersea Park.[3] I would like to live in a perpetual September. One does one's best to prefer Spring, in vain. I had a letter from Simon & Schuster, asking to see all available material. I told Chatto's to send Proust & Pricks. Parsons expressed himself overcome by the sound of my voice after so long. Were he not just on the point of going on holiday, etc. When could Chatto's look forward to hearing from me in my hack's capacity. So long now since. No news of Charles if not a card from the midlands, where wonderful dinners are being had by him. No inquiries for you.[4]

I have been working over the poems, in the expectation of proofs which have not come. The Undertaker's Man is the hardest to mitigate. It never was a poem and the best I can do now is to cut my losses. Yet it has something that will not let me leave it out altogether. They will provoke the irritated guffaw & heehaw all right. Déjà quelquechose. I have also been working at other stuff, I fear involontairement trivial.[5] Well if it is so and I am so, amen. Really anything at all is better than the perpetual blankness and obliteration before the fact. I hope to keep at it.

Miss Costello turned up from Las Palmas, but Poggioli was the best I could put up. Their spaghetti alla B. are very aphrodisiac, pace Geoffrey and the courting extremists. We went to a brief Spanish colour film in Tottenham Court Rd., La Cucaracha.[6] That cooled me off. And a good thing, with such an unclitoridian companion.

[...]

I begin to think I have gerontophilia on top of the rest. The little shabby respectable old men you see on Saturday afternoon and Sunday, pottering about doing odd jobs in the garden, or flying kites immense distances at the Round Pond, Kensington. Yesterday there was a regular club of the latter, with a sprinkling of grandchildren, sitting in a crescent waiting for a wind. The kites lying in the grass with their long tails beautifully cared for, all assembled and ready. For they bring them in separate pieces, the sticks and tail rolled up in the canvas and a huge spool of string. Some have boats as well, but not the real enthusiasts. Then great perturbation to get them off at the first breath of wind. They fly them almost out of sight, yesterday it was over the trees to the south, into an absolutely cloudless viridescent evening sky. Then when the string is run out they simply sit there watching them, chucking at the string, the way coachmen do at a reins, presumably to keep them from losing height. There seems to be no competition at all involved. Then after about an hour they wind them gently in and go home. I was really rooted to the spot yesterday, unable to go away and wondering what was keeping me. Extraordinary effect too of birds flying close to the kites but beneath them. My next old man, or old young man, not of the big world but of the little world, must be a kite-flyer. So absolutely disinterested, like a poem, or useful in the depths where demand and supply coincide, and the prayer is the god. Yes, prayer rather than poem, in order to be quite clear, because poems are prayers, of Dives and Lazarus one flesh.[7]

Then there is the "old boy" of the house opposite, whose seizure of course remains the felony that was first described to me, and whose cup is still on the sill where he left it, though the crusts have been taken away. I suppose they keep hens in the back. Well, I suppose the less dirty clouds of dirty glory people trail about with them, the more likeable they are, and so the clean old man takes the eye. The doctrine of reminiscence may hold for turds. And even they cool quickly.[8]

Miss Costello said to me: "You haven't a good word to say for anyone but the failures". I thought that was quite the nicest thing anyone had said to me for a long time.

You know all I wish for you. That the hope of your <u>Arrangement</u> be not much longer deferred, to begin with.[9] Then the rest.

Love ever

s/ Sam

TLS; 1 leaf, 2 sides; TCD, MS 10402/80. *Dating*: in a letter of 31 August 1935 (TCD), SB writes to McGreevy that his brother Frank is in Donegal for a fortnight, and on 22 September 1935 that Frank and May Beckett have moved to Killiney. *Previous publication*: The paragraph beginning "I begin to think ..." is published in Deirdre Bair, *Samuel Beckett: A Biography* (New York: Harcourt Brace Jovanovich, 1978) 207.

1 McGreevy wrote to Richard Aldington: "My mother has been very bad but is easier now, her mind as clear as ever" (10 September 1935, TxU: Derek Patmore). Two of McGreevy's six sisters were with him in Tarbert – Honora Phelan and Margaret McGreevy.

2 Hester Dowden was on holiday in Ireland; having stayed in Bray with her friend Geraldine Cummins, she was now visiting her daughter Dolly Robinson at her home, "Sorrento," in Dalkey (Cummins to Thomas McGreevy, 14 August 1935, TCD MS 8111).

3 Geoffrey Thompson. Battersea Park, London SW 11, on the Thames.

4 The New York publishers, Simon and Schuster.
Ian Parsons (1906–1980) was an Editor at Chatto and Windus. By "hack work" SB refers to his critical writing. In 1932, he had proposed a study of Gide to Chatto and Windus (see 13 [September 1932], n. 3).
Charles Prentice had retired as a Director at Chatto and Windus at the end of 1934 (Prentice to Harold Raymond [1887–1975], a Partner in Chatto and Windus, 3 January 1935, enclosing a copy of the "Deed of Release, duly signed & witnessed" [UoR, MS 2444 CW 54/13]). SB reports Parsons's latest news of Prentice; unsurprisingly,

McGreevy misunderstood this to mean that Prentice had stayed in contact with SB, though not with him: "Sam gets an odd postcard with no mention of me ever" (McGreevy to Richard Aldington, 11 September 1935, TxU, Derek Patmore collection).

5 SB was expecting to receive proofs of his first collection of poems, *Echo's Bones*, published by The Europa Press in November 1935. By "The Undertaker's Man," he refers to "Malacoda" [33–34].

"Déjà quelquechose" [*for* quelque chose] (better than nothing); "involontairement" (involuntarily).

6 Nuala Costello. Las Palmas, Gran Canaria. Poggioli was an Italian restaurant, 5 Charlotte Street, Soho. *La Cucaracha* (1934), directed by Lloyd Corrigan (1900–1969).

7 "Gerontophilia" is a term included in SB's notes taken on Ernest Jones's *Papers in Psycho-Analysis* (1923) (TCD, MS 10971/8/18).

SB wrote "<prayers> poems are prayers."

"Dives and Lazarus" refers to the parable of the rich man, Dives, whose petition was not granted, whereas that of Lazarus was (Luke 16:19–31).

8 The "old boy" and his felony are described in Bair, *Samuel Beckett*, 207, where no source is given.

9 McGreevy's novel *Arrangement*, also entitled *Neither will I*, was never published (see TCD, MS 8039/55).

THOMAS McGREEVY

TARBERT, CO. KERRY

Sunday [22 September 1935]   34 Gertrude St.,

[London]

Dear Tom

I lunched to-day with Hester & Raven. She looks a new woman after her holiday. Result I suppose of having fixed things with Dolly. She seems to have got about a lot & seen all the Jonsons, from O'Casey up or down. She was overjoyed at my being able to identify Longford from her description of eunuch seen at first night of Higgins, who she calls O'Higgins.[1] She appears to know of your name in connexion with Municipal Gallery, but says she heard of nothing but highest praise of

Reynolds. Funny you heard nothing more from Stewart. Perhaps the Münden in is coming a cropper.[2]

I had no application for a poem, & proofs of mine have not yet come. Had a card from Reavey from Toledo – Count Orgel [*for* Orgaz]. Nothing more from S. & S. Chatto's may not have bothered sending the books. Should not think anything is likely to come of it, unless they want to have me under contract for a possible some thing some day.[3]

I have been forcing myself to keep at the book, & it crawls forward. I have done about 9000 words. It is poor stuff & I have no interest in it.[4]

The intestinal pains are worse than they have been so far. Bion is not interested. Geoffrey checks a smile. I feel absolutely certain that I will get no further with analysis than I have done, that from now on it is money thrown away. Yet I have not the courage to call it off. I also feel certain that there is something wrong with my guts, yet have not the courage to consult a doctor on my own. Where one is as devoid of courage as I am there seems to be nothing more to be said or done.

Geoffrey is getting married on Nov. 2nd down at Lulworth Cove, Dorset, in church. I had long ago promised to be his witness in registry office, so now find myself booked for the misfortunes of Hairy. I was down at Bedlam this day week & went round the wards for the first time, with scarcely any sense of horror, though I saw everything, from mild depression to profound dementia.[5]

I went to Woizikovski [*for* Woizikovsky] ballet Thursday & saw <u>Sylphides</u>, which I find positively ugly, <u>Amour Sorcier</u> & <u>Petrouchka</u>. Tarakanova danced the Widow & the Doll extremely well. I went with Hillis whom I ran into again in King's Road. I dined with him one evening in Cheyne Walk, & he played the Debussy Quartet for me & some songs (si on peut dire) from Pelléas. Very pleasant. He is very pleasant, knows a lot of music. Woizikovski does not dance so subtly as Massine, yet the Petrouchka as philosophy was elucidated without any attempt to do so having appeared, the man of low humanity worshipping the earthball, & the man of high execrating his creator.[6]

News from home satisfactory. They have reached Killiney at last.[7] Frank never writes, but Mother seems happier. All the visitors have left, which means strain intensified for both of them.

Raven was very gay (for him) & breathed forth guarantees concerning your books. I have the Boissier down for renewal on Wednesday & shall not forget.[8] It is no trouble. I am glad you have your catalogue. I have not been to a gallery for weeks. Preoccupation with the writing sucks all the attention I have out of me. If one could even look forward to going to bed!

Montchrétien I don't know at all. Hester was saying very nice things of the Montherlant, & of Guy de Pourtalès' Chopin, which I must say I should not care to face.[9] I have got stuck in the Rabelais again, on the voyage round the world to consult the oracle of the Bottle.[10]

The weather had been so exquisite that it was impossible to stay in, especially at dusk, but since the monstrous moon of last Thursday week it has gone to bits. The kites at the Round Pond yesterday were plunging & writhing all over the sky. The book closes with an old man flying his kite, if such occasions ever arise.[11]

Cissie has moved from Howth & is now in Moyne Road, Rathgar. She has hired a piano & writes very happy at having a sanctuary, except that Boss refuses to leave Newcastle.[12]

Hilliard is still about. I walked out of the door one morning and there he was playing cricket with the street-urchins. No doubt he is staying with Paddy Trench whom I see flying about on an old motor-bike.[13]

Your mother's powers of recovery are amazing & hope they bring her to something worth having. It is certainly very awkward about Delia, though I am sure you are blessing the extra presence in the house.[16]

Love ever

Sam

ALS; 3 leaves, 3 sides; *env to* Thomas McGreevy Esq, Tarbert, Co Kerry, Irish Free State; *pm* 23-9-35, London; TCD, MS 10402/81. *Dating*: pm; Thursday 19 September 1935 was the only evening that the Woizikovsky ballet included *Les Sylphides*, *L'Amour Sorcier*, and *Petrouchka* on the same program at the Coliseum.

1 Hester Dowden and Thomas Holmes Ravenhill. Hester Dowden had just returned from Ireland and a visit with her daughter Dolly Robinson; the allusion to Ben Jonson suggests that she had seen all of the playwrights connected with the Abbey Theatre, of which her son-in-law Lennox Robinson was Director.

Edward Arthur Henry Pakenham, sixth Earl of Longford (1902–1961), theatrical producer and dramatist, supported the fledgling Gate Theatre from 1931 to 1936, at which time it divided into the Gate Company and the Longford Players, each group playing six months in residence in Dublin and six months touring.

F. R. Higgins became a Director of the Abbey Theatre in 1935; the opening of his verse play *The Deuce of Jacks*, on 16 September 1935, was attended by Lord Longford and Irish playwright Sean O'Casey (1880–1964) (Holloway, *Joseph Holloway's Irish Theatre*, II, *1932–1937*, 48).

2 John J. Reynolds (n.d.) was Curator of the Municipal Gallery of Modern Art from 1924 until 30 September 1935; he was replaced by John F. Kelly (n.d.) on 1 October 1935.

William McCausland Stewart (1900–1989), then Professor of French at the University of St. Andrews, Scotland, had mentioned the Directorship of the Municipal Gallery of Modern Art to McGreevy and indicated that if McGreevy were interested he should be in touch with W. B. Yeats and Dermod O'Brien to support his application (Stewart to McGreevy, 19 August 1935 [TCD, MS 8136/76]; Susan Schriebman, 15 January 2007).

"Münden in" (Ger., flowing out, as at the mouth of a river).

3 Proofs of *Echo's Bones* were awaited from George Reavey, Europa Press. Reavey had sent a card from Spain depicting *The Burial of Count Orgaz* (1586, Church of Santo

Tomé, Toledo) by Crete-born artist El Greco (né Domenikos Theotokopoulos, 1541–1614); SB was familiar with the painting, having referred to it in *Dream of Fair to Middling Women*: "Her great eyes [...] went as big and black as El Greco painted, with a couple of good wet slaps from his laden brush, in the Burial of the Count of Orgaz the debauched eyes of his son or was it his mistress?" (174).

The request of Simon and Schuster: 8 September 1935.

4 The manuscript of *Murphy*.

5 SB was best man for Geoffrey and Ursula Thompson on 2 November 1935 in Lulworth, England (Cynthia Frazier, 18 July 1994). SB's character Capper Quin, "known to his admirers as Hairy," was best man for Belacqua's marriage to Thelma bboggs (*More Pricks Than Kicks*, 124).

Thompson was Senior House Physician at Bethlem Royal Hospital (popularly known as Bedlam), although by 1914 it was described as a "charitable institution for the better-class insane, especially for curable cases (over 50% are dismissed as cured)" (Findlay Muirhead, *London and Its Environs*, 2nd edn., The Blue Guides [London: Macmillan, 1922] 319.

6 The company of Polish dancer and choreographer Léon Woizikovsky (1899–1975) performed on Thursday 19 September 1935 at the London Coliseum. The ballet *Les Sylphides* (1909; previously entitled *Chopiniana*) was choreographed by Michel Fokine (1880–1942) and orchestrated by Aleksandr Konstantinovich Glazunov (1865–1936), Igor Stravinsky, and Sergei Ivanovich Taneyev (1856–1915), from music by Frédéric Chopin.

In the ballet *L'Amour sorcier* (1935; *Love the Magician*), Woizikovsky created new choreography for Manuel de Falla's one-act ballet *El amor brujo* (1916–1917); in this production, the Widow was danced by Nina Tarakanova (1915–1994); she also performed the role of the Ballerina/Doll choreographed by Michel Fokine in Stravinsky's ballet *Petrouchka* (also *Petrushka*).

Arthur Hillis recalled SB's enthusiasm for *Petrushka*, and also that SB was particularly interested in the structure of Debussy's String Quartet in G minor, op. 10: how the piece builds in the first three movements and then "blows it to bits in the fourth" (Arthur Hillis, 3 July 1992). Selections from Debussy's opera in four acts, *Pelléas et Mélisande*, were recorded as "A Collector's Pelléas" (Paris Recordings, VAIA 1083, 1927–1928).

"Si on peut dire" (if I may call them that).

Léonide Massine played leading roles in Diaghilev's ballets between 1914 and 1928. Woizikovsky was a member of the Diaghilev Ballets Russes from 1915 to 1929, where he and Massine alternated in major roles.

In *Petrushka*, the Blackamoor infers that the coconut contains a powerful god and salutes it, and the Old Wizard defuses the dismay of onlookers by showing that Petrushka is merely a puppet.

7 May and Frank Beckett had moved temporarily to a house in Killiney.

8 Ravenhill reacted positively to McGreevy's recent publications: *Poems* (1934), and his translation, *Lament for the Death of an Upper Class*.

While McGreevy was away from London, SB renewed the loan of a library book by Gaston Boissier (né Marie-Louis-Antoine-Gaston Boissier, 1823–1908), French classical scholar.

9 Antoine de Montchrétien (c.1575–1621), French dramatist and economist.
  Guy de Pourtalès (1881–1941), *Chopin; ou, le Poète* (Paris: Gallimard, 1926), which was translated as *Frederick Chopin: A Man of Solitude*, tr. Charles Bayly Jr. (London: T. Butterworth, 1927).

10 SB had purchased Rabelais's *Gargantua et Pantagruel* (1532–1533) in the Génie de la France edition (Paris: R. Hilsum, 1932; Paris: Gallimard, 1932) in four volumes (SB to McGreevy, 25 [July 1935], TCD, MS 10402/77). Rabelais relates a quest around the world to reach the "oracle of the Holy Bottle" (Books III–V). Although notes taken from this edition are included in TCD, MS 10969, there are none from books IV or V (Everett Frost and Jane Maxwell, "TCD, MS 10969: Germany, Europe, and the French Revolution. Rabelais," *Notes Diverse Holo*, Special issue *SBT/A* 16 [2006] 96–97, 102–103).

11 The ending of *Murphy*: see 8 September 1935.

12 With her children Nancy, Deirdre, and Morris, Cissie Sinclair had moved to 85 Moyne Road, Rathgar, Co. Dublin; the house belonged to the Beckett family estate. Boss Sinclair was being treated at the National Hospital for Consumption in Ireland, known as Newcastle Sanatorium, in Newtownmountkennedy, near Greystones, Co. Wicklow.

13 Robert Martin Hilliard (1904–1937) studied at Trinity College Dublin, represented Ireland as a featherweight boxer in the 1928 Olympic Games, was ordained and took a parish in the Church of Ireland in Belfast (1933-1934); he moved to London where he worked as a journalist (1935) (Chalmers [Terry] Trench, 27 August 1993, and 13 September 1993; Rev. Barr to Terry Trench, 28 September 1993; John Corcoran, "The Rev. Robert Martin Hilliard (1904–1937)," *Kerry Archaeological and Historical Society Journal*, 2nd series, 5 [2005] 207–219).
  Patrick Trench (1896–1939), the elder son of the TCD English Professor Wilbraham Fitzjohn Trench, lived at 351 King's Road in September 1935.

16 Bridget McGreevy (known as Delia, 1896–1977) had not found a teaching position, and thus remained in Tarbert at the McGreevy family home.

THOMAS McGREEVY

TARBERT, CO. KERRY

Oct. 8th '35   34 Gertrude St

                                                  [London] S.W. 10

Dear Tom

  I did not find your letter in <u>Observer</u> but expect it will be in next Sunday. What a paper – tout de même! The pompous trimming of that pisspot Garvin. Next week you will have it starched & unfurled.[1]

It is good news that your sister has found even temporary work, I supposed [*for* suppose] it has saved the situation vis-à-vis your mother.

I think I saw Hester last Saturday night week. I went round & found her with the niece & husband.[2] I have not been round since.

I dined one evening with Bion, a hurried but good sole at the Etoile in Charlotte St., & went on to hear Jung at the Institute of Psychological Medicine. He struck me as a kind of super AE, the mind infinitely more ample, provocative & penetrating, but the same cuttle-fish's discharge & escapes from the issue in the end.[3] He let fall some remarkable things nevertheless. He protests so vehemently that he is not a mystic that he must be one of the very most nebulous kind. Certainly he cannot keep the terminology out of his speech, but I suppose that is a difficulty for everyone. His lecture the night I went consisted mainly in the so called synthetic (versus Freudian analytic) interpretation of three dreams of a patient who finally went to the dogs because he insisted on taking a certain element in the dreams as the Oedipus position when Jung told him it was nothing of the kind! However he lost his neurosis among the dogs – again according to Jung.[4] The mind is I suppose the best Swiss, Lavater & Rousseau, mixture of enthusiasm & Euclid, a methodical rhapsode.[5] Jolas's pigeon all right, but I should think in the end less than the dirt under Freud's nails.[6] I can't imagine his curing a fly of neurosis, & yet he is said to have actually cured cases of schizophrenia. If this is true he is the first to do it. He insists on patients having their horoscopes cast![7]

Bion off the job is pleasant, but against a background of tooth & yank camps that makes me tremble.[8] I hope he hasn't done us both a disservice by inviting me to meet him in that way.

I don't think I shall go on with the analysis after Xmas. I don't expect the troubles I hoped first & foremost to get rid of via analysis will be gone then any more than they are now. Tant pis. I must use me to them.[9]

As to going away even to Spain, I fear that is unlikely for some time. Mother will be feeling there is a lot of me due to her, & perhaps after all I may find myself immune to Dublin now, & able to work there. She writes from Killiney more happily I think than since it happened, & with a new sense of how she must accept what is left behind. She went to see Count of Montecristo film with Frank! Miracle.[10]

I expect the proofs of the poems this week. All this business of sending be done. The Undertaker's Man is well changed, the rest more or less as you know them. It will be a relief to have them out & abused.[11]

I have been working hard at the book & it goes very slowly, but I do not think there is any doubt now that it will be finished sooner or later. The feeling that I must jettison the whole thing has passed, only the labour of writing the remainder is left.[12] There is little excitement attached to it, each chapter loses its colour & interest as soon as the next is begun. I have done about 20 000 words. Perhaps I will send you a chapter & chance its getting through, but I think I would rather wait till you can have it all together.

I never see Geoffrey. He is leaving Bethlem at the end of this month, & so far as I know his plan to get married on Nov. 2nd still holds good, with me holding the hat. What a bloody nuisance.[13]

I went one day to the Gallery & saw a lot in the Segers that I had not seen before & in the Fabritius musician.[14] There are various shows one might go to, but I have not been to any. Hillis wants me to go to Boris on Thursday, but even purified of Rimsky that strikes me as too large & too hot a potato altogether. I think there is a quartet at Wigmore Hall that evening playing Brahms, Wolf & Sibelius, & we might go to that. Hillis – ça va. There is Otway's Soldier's Fortune, T.S.E.'s Sweeney & the Ballets Jooss and a new Garbo Karenina. Perhaps the last might be managed.[15]

Ervine broke all his records in the Ob. I sent you. "Yes, my dear"! But MacCarthy on Mr 'Awkins wasn't far behind. Thank God one can write without an eye on these pukes.[16]

I trust Devlin was kind to us. I fear he has hooked on to Dev a little late in the day.[17]

Did I tell you I had a letter from Jack Yeats with news of the picture which he has traced? He had been to Tobias & Angel at Abbey. What is that?[18]

Mrs Frost has had a row with the pair of Lieblings above, over their wireless which never stops, & they are going. Next Saturday. God be praised. Now perhaps I shall be able to keep some stamps. She wonders would Geoffrey & wife take it over! Then the bed would creak to a purpose.[19]

Your Boissier falls due again this week & I shall not forget to renew it.[20] I have been reading nothing at all. The Evening Standard & Baedeker's Paris before starting to lie awake.[21] Sleeping very badly, I suppose because of the book. How hard it is to reach a tolerable arrangement between working & living.

Cissie owes me a letter this long time. I do not think Boss is strong enough to write. He will not leave Newcastle. No news from Simon & Schuster. I wonder did Chatto's let me down.[22] Haven't the interest to inquire.

God love thee

Sam

ALS; 2 leaves, 4 sides; *env to* Thomas McGreevy Esq, Tarbert, Co Kerry, Irish Free State; *pm* 9-10-35, London; TCD, MS 10402/83.

1 McGreevy's letter, "Italian Art Problem," discussed the nude figures in the background of Michelangelo's *Holy Family with the Infant St. John the Baptist* (c.1506/1508, painted for the Doni family, Uffizi Gallery, Florence) as representing the Law of Nature while the foregrounded Holy Family represented the Law of Grace (*The Observer* 13 October 1935: 15).

"Tout de même" (all the same).

James Louis Garvin (1868–1947) was Editor of *The Observer* from 1908 to 1942 and of the *Encyclopaedia Britannica* (13th and 14th edns.). His editorial, "Keep Out This Time," claimed that the attack of the Italian army on Adowa, Abyssinia, confirmed his view that Mussolini and Hitler posed a genuine threat, that Britain's policy of sanctions was fallacious and inept, and that the Letter of Covenant of the League of Nations was invalid after the withdrawal of the United States, Japan, and Germany (*The Observer* 6 October 1935: 18).

2 SB refers to McGreevy's sister Delia.

Hester Dowden's niece has not been identified; her sister Hilda Mary Dowden (1875–1936) did not marry.

3 L'Etoile, 30 Charlotte Street, Soho.

Carl Gustav Jung (1875–1961) was invited by the Institute of Medical Psychology (Tavistock Clinic) to give a series of five lectures from 30 September to 4 October 1935. Bion was a discussant for lectures two and four; he took SB to the third lecture (Wednesday, 2 October 1935).

AE was interested in theosophy, ancient Irish myth, and mysticism.

4 Following his lecture, Jung was asked how he would fit mysticism into his scheme of psychology and the psyche. He responded: "Mystics are people who have a particularly vivid experience of the processes of the collective unconscious. Mystical experience is experience of archetypes." He added that he made no distinction between archetypal forms and mystical forms (C. G. Jung, *Analytical Psychology: Its Theory and Practice, The Tavistock Lectures* [London: Routledge and Kegan Paul, 1968] 110–111). Jung discussed the "anima figure" in dreams in his lecture (99–100). He also told of a patient who wanted to be a professor although his dreams indicated this goal to be beyond his ability; the patient, however, thought his dreams represented an unrealized incestuous wish that could be overcome. Jung reported: "it took him just about three months to lose his position and go to the dogs" (96–105).

5 SB wrote "<He is very> The mind."

Johann Kaspar Lavater (1741–1801), Swiss poet, physiognomist, and theologian, a close friend of Herder and Goethe. Jean-Jacques Rousseau, citizen of Geneva. Euclid, (third century BC).

6 "In Jung's writings Jolas found the metaphysics he had sought in vain in Freud's work" (Eugene Jolas, *Man from Babel*, xxi–xxii).

7 In discussion following the third Tavistock lecture, Jung concluded, "I cannot cure schizophrenia in principle. Occasionally by great good chance I can synthesize the fragments" (Jung, *Analytical Psychology*, 113).

Jung wrote on 6 September 1947 to B. V. Raman, *Astrological Magazine* (India): "In cases of difficult psychological diagnosis I usually get a horoscope in order to have a further point of view from an entirely different angle" (C. G. Jung, *C. G. Jung: Letters*, I, ed. Gerhard Adler and Aniela Jaffé, tr. R. F. C. Hull [Princeton: Princeton University Press, 1973] 475; see also Aniela Jaffé, *From the Life and Work of C. G. Jung*, tr. R. F. C. Hull and Murray Stein [Einsiedeln, Switzerland: Daimon Verlag, 1989] 17–45).

8 "Tooth and yank camps," an allusion to the proponents of rival psychoanalytic theories.

9 "Tant pis" (too bad). "Use me to them" (Gallicism for "get used to them").

10 *The Count of Monte Cristo* (1934), directed by American-born Rowland V. Lee (1891–1975), featuring Robert Donat (1905–1958) and Elissa Landi (née Elizabeth Marie Christine Kühnelt, 1904–1948), was shown at the Metropole in Dublin during the week of 23 September 1935.

11 Europa Press, publisher of SB's *Echo's Bones*, depended upon subscriptions to underwrite the costs of printing a book. SB refers to his poem "Malacoda."

12 SB was working on the draft of *Murphy*.

13 The Thompsons' wedding: see 22 September 1935, n. 5.

14 *A Mountainous Landscape* (NGL 4383), then ascribed to Hercules Segers (also Seghers, c.1589–c.1638) is now ascribed to an imitator of Segers (Neil MacLaren, *The Dutch School, 1600–1900*, I, rev. Christopher Brown [London: National Gallery, 1991] 420). Dutch painter Carel Fabritius (1622–1654), *A View of Delft with Musical Instrument Seller's Stall* (1652, NGL 3714).

15 Hillis proposed that they attend the opera *Boris Godunov* by Modest Petrovich Mussorgsky (1839–1881), which opened the Sadler's Wells 1935–1936 season on 29 September 1935. The production was billed as the first English production of the original 1869 version of the opera; Mussorgsky revised it in 1872, and his musical executor Nikolai Rimsky-Korsakov also reorchestrated the opera in 1896 and 1908.

SB conflates two concerts. On Saturday, 12 October in Wigmore Hall, the Isolde Menges Quartet played String Quartet in D minor, op. 56 ("Voces Intimae"), by Finnish composer Jean Sibelius (1865–1957); the string quartet *Serenade* in G major ("Italian Serenade") by Austrian composer Hugo Wolf (1860–1903); and String Quartet in D major, op. 9, by Belgian-born French composer César Franck (1822–1890). On Thursday 17 October in Wigmore Hall, the Isolde Menges Quartet led by violinist Isolde Menges (1893–1976), with the addition of Helen Just (1903–1989) and Alfred De Reygher[e] (fl. 1930s–1940s), played Tchaikovsky's string sextet *Souvenir de Florence* in D major, op. 70; Brahms's String Sextet no. 2 in G major, op. 36; and the String Sextet by English composer Frank Bridge (1879–1941).

"Ça va" (is all right).

The Soldier's Fortune (1680) by English playwright Thomas Otway (1652–1685) was playing at the Ambassadors Theatre. T. S. Eliot's *Sweeney Agonistes* (1926) was at the Westminster Theatre; the Ballets Jooss, the company of German dancer and choreographer Kurt Jooss (1901–1979), was performing *The Green Table* and *The Mirror* in repertoire with *Ballade*, *The Big City*, and *Ball in Vienna* at the Gaiety Theatre. The film of *Anna Karenina* (1935) with Greta Garbo (1905–1990) was playing at the Empire Theatre in Leicester Square.

16 St. John Ervine (né John Greer Ervine, 1883–1971), Irish-born playwright and novelist, wrote a column, "At the Play," for *The Observer*; a young reader had written that a sector of theatre audiences wished merely to be entertained by plays "that have nothing to do with their everyday life ... Do you see what I mean?" Ervine's retort was "Yes, my dear, I see" ("The Generations Disagree," 6 October 1935: 17).

As Book Editor of *The Sunday Times*, Desmond MacCarthy reviewed *Anthony Hope and His Books* (1935) by Sir Charles Mallet (1863–1947) ("Anthony Hope: Achievements and Disappointments," 6 October 1935: 6). *Anthony Hope and His Books* was a biography of Anthony Hope (né Anthony Hope Hawkins, 1863–1933), author of *The Prisoner of Zenda* (1894).

17 Denis Devlin broadcast readings and comments on literature on Irish radio; he wrote to McGreevy: "I don't know whether you may have listened to 2RN last night (i.e. the 4th instant) and heard my marvellous recital of your Nocturne of the Self-Evident Presence. It ran 'Mr. Thomas McGreevy, an Irishman, who has been most incomprehensibly neglected.' [...] Are you pleased? I am glad to have got the chance." Apparently McGreevy had not heard the broadcast, because Devlin continued this letter on 22 October: "I am chagrined that you did not hear me" (5 October 1935 continued 22 October 1935, TCD, MS 8112/7). The Dublin radio station was 2RN. "Nocturne of the Self-Evident Presence" was originally published by MacGreevy under the pseudonym L. St. Senan in *The Irish Statesman* 7.3 (25 September 1926) 57; rpt. MacGreevy, *Collected Poems of Thomas MacGreevy*, ed. Schreibman, 42–43.

Devlin worked in the Department of External Affairs; as Secretary to the legation, he accompanied Éamon De Valera (popularly known as Dev, 1882–1975), then Taoiseach (Prime Minister) of the Irish Free State and Head of Council of the League of Nations, to the League of Nations in Geneva (3 September to 2 October 1935) (Devlin, *Collected Poems of Denis Devlin*, 19; "Back from Geneva," *The Irish Times* 2 October 1933: 7).

18 Yeats may have traced the provenance of *Corner Boys*, which had had an owner previous to SB (see 5 May 1935, n. 4).

Tobias and the Angel by Scottish playwright James Bridie (né Osborne Henry Mavor, 1888–1951) was performed at the Gaiety Theatre (not the Abbey Theatre) as part of the Dublin Summer School of Acting on Sunday, 22 September 1935 (*The Irish Times* 23 September 1935: 8).

19 Mrs. Frost, SB's landlady at 34 Gertrude Street. The "Lieblings" (lovers), presumably the couple described in 8 September 1934.

Geoffrey Thompson and Ursula Stenhouse were shortly to be married.

20 Boissier: see 22 September 1935, n. 8.

21 German publisher Karl Baedeker (1801–1859) published travel guides for various regions of Europe; updated versions continue to be published.

22 Simon and Schuster and SB's request to Chatto and Windus: 8 September 1935.

GEORGE REAVEY
LONDON

13/10/35   34 Gertrude Street
                                  London SW10

Dear George

Thanks for letter & prospectus. Further victims:

Charles Rowe, Esq., F.T.C.D., Trinity College, Dublin.

Miss Frances Steen, Carrickmines, Co. Dublin.[1]

It is better for you to diffuse them, but let me have a dozen in case I think of someone else.

The American publishers I have in mind are Messrs. Simon & Schuster, 386 Fourth Avenue, New York. They wrote to me about a month & a half ago, asking to see whatever material I had available for publication in USA. I sent them Proust & Pricks & have not yet had their decision. They seem well disposed. This being the position, it occurs to me that they ought to be offered the first refusal of Bones, also that it might be advisable to wait for their decision as to prose before submitting the verse. However I leave you to deal with the matter as you think best. I am quite satisfied with 20% for EP [for EB].[2]

I hope the Bones are not covered in the canary of the prospectus. If this is your dastardly intention and the covers have not yet been put in hand, be an angel and change it to PUTTY.[3]

Yours ever

s/ Sam

TLS; 1 leaf, 1 side; AN in another hand: checkmarks, and underscoring; TxU.

1   Charles Henry Rowe, Professor of Mathematics at Trinity College Dublin.

Frances Steen (n.d.), schoolmate of SB's at Earlsfort House School, Dublin; her brother, Robert Ellsworth Steen (1902–1981) was a friend of SB's at TCD, and they golfed together at Carrickmines, Co. Dublin.

2 *Echo's Bones.*

3 The color of the prospectus was warm gold; the color of the final cover for *Echo's Bones* was putty.

GEORGE REAVEY
LONDON

Saturday [after 13 October 1935]   34 Gertrude St
                                          [London] SW10

Cher ami

It might be a good idea to send a copy to Observer, "for favour of etc.", & if so to Humbert Wolfe, lest it should fall into black claws of Austin Clarke.[1]

For distribution in Dublin I know:

Mr PEMBRY [*for* Pembrey] Green's [*for* Greene's] Library, Clare St. & both Tom & Brian know

Mr NAIRN, Combridge's, Grafton Street

Hodges & Figgis also might take a few copies.[2]

Looking over it at leisure I am very pleased with layout. I only find one mistake: there should be a space in Enueg 2 between "doch I assure thee" & "lying on O'Connell Bridge." Pas sérieux-[3]

I have sent out 5 more prospectuses this morning that may bring a few more bob.

A mardi

Sam

I have found MS of Serena III which you can have [4]

ALS; 1 leaf folded, 2 sides; from "Looking over it …", text appears upside down because SB has turned the folded page; PS written to left of signature; TxU. *Dating*: in 15 March 1935, SB gives his choice of title for the volume of poems; in 8 October 1935, SB anticipates proofs that week; in SB's letter to Reavey of 13 October 1935, SB discusses the color of the cover. The imprint of *Echo's Bones* gives the publication date as November 1935. "Enueg 2" was published in *Echo's Bones* without the correction SB requested in this letter, and with "Serena III" (published as "Serena 3," *Echo's Bones* [31–32]). The date, therefore, is after 13 October, but before 30 November 1935, probably early to mid-November.

1 Humbert Wolfe (1885–1940), English poet, satirist, and civil servant. Austin Clarke reviewed for the *Times Literary Supplement* and *The Spectator*; SB was wary of retaliation (see 8 September 1934, n. 2).

2 Herbert S. Pembrey (1909–2000), sub-postmaster and proprietor with his father, Herbert H. Pembrey, of Greene's Library, 16 Clare Street.

Thomas McGreevy; Brian Coffey.

Ernest Nairn (d. 1970), a book expert who worked for about fifty years at Combridges, at 18–20 Grafton Street in 1935. Hodges & Figgis, bookstore, was then at 20 Nassau Street.

3 See discussion of *dating* above.

"Pas sérieux" (anglicism for "pas grave" [no great matter]). Reavey may have misunderstood SB's comment, as the page layout was not altered in this or in subsequent editions.

4 "A mardi" (till Tuesday).

CHRONOLOGY 1936

1936	January	SB pursues interest in film theory and methods.
	18 January	Visits Jack B. Yeats.
	24 January	T. S. Eliot speaks at University College Dublin.
	1 February	SB visits Jack B. Yeats with Morris Sinclair.
	2 March	Applies to study with Eisenstein.
	7 March	Germans occupy the Rhineland.
	By 25 March	SB travels with Frank Beckett to Galway. Visits Clonmacnoise.
	By 9 April	Tells Reavey that *transition* can choose any poems to publish from *Echo's Bones*.
	2 May	Declines to undertake more translations of Eluard's poems for Reavey.
	6 May	Offers *transition* the unpublished "Censorship in the Saorstat," updating it with the censorship registry number for *More Pricks Than Kicks*.
	By 7 May	Buys Jack B. Yeats's painting *Morning*.
	By 9 June	Finishes a first draft of *Murphy*.
	11 June	Opening of the International Surrealist Exhibition, New Burlington Galleries, London. Publication of Eluard's *Thorns of Thunder* with SB's translations.
	27 June	*Murphy* typescript finished.
	29 June	SB sends *Murphy* to Ian Parsons at Chatto and Windus, to Charles Prentice, and to McGreevy.

July	*Dublin Magazine* publishes "An Imaginative Work!" SB's review of *The Amaranthers* by Jack B. Yeats.
By 7 July	SB sends *Murphy* to Simon and Schuster in New York.
15 July	Chatto and Windus rejects *Murphy*.
Mid-July	SB sends poem "Cascando" to *Dublin Magazine*.
By 17 July	Sends *Murphy* to Frere-Reeves at Heinemann. Receives author's copy of *Thorns of Thunder*.
17 July	Spanish Civil War begins.
By 6 August	Heinemann rejects *Murphy*.
12 August	SB translates Samuel Johnson's Letter to Lord Chesterfield into German in his notebook.
18 August	Drafts German translation of "Cascando."
By 19 August	Sends *Murphy* to Reavey so that he can act as agent.
c. 31 August	Visits Arland Ussher at Cappagh with Joe Hone; sees Ardmore and Cashel.
6 September	Reavey visits Dublin from Belfast.
29 September	SB leaves for Germany.
30 September	Arrives in Le Havre.
2 October	Arrives in Hamburg.
By 5 October	Simon and Schuster rejects *Murphy*. *Dublin Magazine* publishes poem "Cascando."
7 October	SB settles in the Pension Hoppe, Hamburg.
3 November	Visits Lübeck.
5 November	German museums ordered to remove "decadent art."
13 November	SB refuses to accept cuts in *Murphy* requested by Houghton Mifflin, Boston. Asks Reavey how to acquire permission to use "apes at chess" for frontispiece of *Murphy*.
4 December	Leaves Hamburg; visits Lüneburg.

5 December	In Hanover; visits home of Leibniz.
6 December	In Brunswick.
7 December	In Riddagshausen.
8 December	In Wolfenbüttel; visits Lessing Museum.
10 December	In Hildesheim.
11 December	Arrives in Berlin.
c. 16–17 December	Settles in Pension Kempt, Berlin.

9/1/35 [*for* 1936]   6 Clare Street
                                                        Dublin

Dear George

Thanks for your card. I am more or less all right again now.
Coffey left here I think last Friday, for a lecture at Sorbonne
Sat. morning, so I suppose you didn't see him in London. He said
he had sent you some more Bones.[1] Yes, let me have as many
more as I am due. I think he got my copy of the This Quarter in
question. I said i [sic] was not keen on doing more translations,
but would if necessary.[2] He appears to want to make the philosophical series very serious & Fach. But my Geulincx could only
be a literary fantasia.[3]

I am glad to hear of the European Quarterly. I suppose I have
odd poems, or perhaps I might let you have an excerpt from the
prose work I mentioned. But there doesn't seem to be much,
among my papers or in my mind.[4] I have not seen Devlin. He
works in an office, you know. Then in the evening the ballroom.
Codpiece Bordel de Danse, Gipsy Scrotum and his Band. Ne suis
pas à la hauteur.[5]

My friends here esquivent the Bones for the more part, which
means the bolus has gone home. What shall they say, my not even
enemies. May it stick in their anus. "I am sure you were not born
with a pop." But am I not sparkling? Then how should the birth
be still? Sois calme, ô mon soûleur . .[6] Andersen was the byblow of
a Frenchman from the Marne. Ca explique Dieu.[7]

How much longer London? As I broached the stairs to your party, as to observatory platform at uranal distance from the young lady whose name escapes me altogether don't you know, the garçon tirebouchon (ce qui m'intéresse, c'est le tirebouchon, non pas le Chandon – Gide) smirked his inadequacy. His heart was not pure. Non pas le condom.[8]

Hommages to Miss Cordon non pas bas bleu.[9]

Your obedient servant

s/ Sam

Ce n'est pas au pélican

Pas si pitoyable

Ni à Marie

Pas si pure

Mais à Lucie

Egyptienne oui et peaussière aussi

Qui ne m'a pas guéri mais qui aurait pu

Et à Jude

Dont j'ai adororé la dépouille

Que j'adresse la cause désespérée

Qu'on dirait la mienne.[10]

TLS; 1 leaf, 1 side; TxU. *Dating: Echo's Bones* was published in November 1935, and so the year must be 1936.

1 SB had been ill with pleurisy (SB to McGreevy 31 December [1935], TCD, MS 10402/84).

Brian Coffey left Dublin for Paris on Friday, 3 January 1936. Before he had left Paris for the Christmas holidays in Dublin, he had sent George Reavey copies of *Echo's Bones*, which had been published by Europa Press in Paris (Brian Coffey to George Reavey, 17 December 1935; TxU).

2 SB wrote "<He came down here to see me, as I was not yet promenable,> I think."

Coffey had taken SB's copy of *This Quarter* 5.1 (September 1932) in which SB's translations of Paul Eluard's poems ("Lady Love," "Out of Sight in the Direction of My Body," "Scarcely Disfigured," "The Invention," "Definition," "A Life Uncovered or The Human Pyramid," "The Queen of Diamonds," "Do Thou Sleep," "Second Nature," "Scene," "All-Proof: Universe-Solitude," and "Confections") had appeared (86–98). Reavey was preparing *Thorns of Thunder*, a collection of Eluard's poems in translation, which included SB's translations already published in *This Quarter*; Reavey had apparently asked, through Coffey, if SB would prepare more.

3   Brian Coffey had in mind a monograph series on philosophers; he was studying the philosophy of science with Catholic thinker Jacques Maritain (1882–1973) at the Institut Catholique de Paris.

"Fach" (professional).

Despite his disclaimer, SB pursued study of Flemish metaphysican Arnold Geulincx (1624–1669) in the library of Trinity College Dublin, as he wrote to McGreevy: "I put my foot within the abhorred gates [of TCD] for the first time since the escape, on a commission from Ruddy. And I fear I shall have to penetrate more deeply, in search of Geulincx, who does not exist in the National, but does in TCD" (9 January 1935 [*for* 1936], TCD, MS 10402/85). SB read and took extensive notes in Latin from the *Ethica* of Arnold Geulincx, in the edition *Arnoldi Geulincx antverpiensis Opera Philosophica. Sumptibus providerunt Sortis spinozianae curatores*, 3 vols., ed. Jan Pieter Nicolaas Land (The Hague: apud Martinum Nijhoff, 1891–1893). For SB's notes on his reading of Geulincx, see TCD, MS 10971/6; Everett Frost and Jane Maxwell, "TCD MS 10971/6 Latin excerpts from Arnoldus Geulincx and R. P. Gredt," *Notes Diverse Holo*, Special issue *SBT/A* 16 (2006) 141–155.

4   As SB wrote to McGreevy, "A card from Reavey, decided to launch European Quarterly . . What would I like to give him for nothing?" (9 January 1935 [*for* 1936]). It is not known what poems or prose SB had in mind, although a poem appears at the end of the present letter. Reavey did not establish a quarterly journal.

5   Denis Devlin (see 5 May 1935, n. 1).

"Bordel de Danse" (Dance Brothel). "Ne suis pas à la hauteur" ([I'm] not up to it).

6   *Echo's Bones* was mentioned as forthcoming in the "Irishman's Diary: Irish Writers," *The Irish Times* 7 December 1935: 6. "Esquivent" (are dodging); "the more part" (Gallicism for "the most part"). SB wrote to McGreevy: "No professional reactions to the poems in any quarter that I know of. Con & Ethna were able to get out of the awkward position by remarking that they were already familiar with most of them. Ruddy had only feuilleté" (9 January 1935 [*for* 1936], TCD, MS 10402/85). "Feuilleté" (leafed through).

SB imagines a response to the line from "Sanies I": "I was born with a pop with the green of the larches" (*Echo's Bones*, [19]). He mentally prepares a retort with wordplay based on sparkling wine/water and still, birth, and stillbirth.

In "Sois calme, ô mon soûleur" (Be calm, oh my intoxicator), SB makes play with the opening line of Baudelaire's poem "Recueillement": "Sois sage, ô ma Douleur" (Behave, my sorrow) (Baudelaire, *Oeuvres complètes*, I, 140; Baudelaire, *Les Fleurs du Mal, The Flowers of Evil*, 173).

7   Hans Christian Andersen (1805–1875) was born *in* wedlock, his parents having married two months before his birth (1805); his father, Hans Andersen, was a journeyman shoemaker from Odense (Elias Bredsdorff, *Hans Christian Andersen: The Story of His Life and Work, 1805–75* [London: Phaidon Press, 1975] 15–16).

"Ça explique Dieu" (That explains God).

8   The young woman, as far distant as the planet Uranus, has not been identified.

"Garçon tirebouchon (ce qui m'intéresse, c'est le tirebouchon, non pas le Chandon – Gide)" (The waiter with the corkscrew [what interests me is the corkscrew, not the Chandon – Gide]). Reference unclear.

"Non pas le condom" (Not the condom).

9 "Hommages to Miss Cordon non pas bas bleu" (Respects to Miss Cordon not bleu); "bas bleu" (bluestocking). Punning combines this with "Cordon bleu." The subject of SB's reference is not known.

10 This version of the poem varies from that published in French in SB's *Dream of Fair to Middling Women*, 21. For a discussion of sources and nuances, see also Pilling, *A Companion to "Dream of Fair to Middling Women,"* 54–55. SB did not translate this poem.

> It is not to the pelican
> Not so pitiable
> Nor to Marie
> Not so pure
> But to Lucie
> Yes, the Egyptian (and in the leather trade)
> Who did not cure me but who might have
> And to Jude
> Whose hide I adorored
> That I put the desperate case
> That might look like mine.

THOMAS McGREEVY

LONDON

16/1 [1936]   Foxrock

[Co. Dublin]

Dear Tom

Very glad to have your letter & poems. The verdict of Oxford is final & excellent. I do not care so much for its preparation. Davies matters as little as the jelly. J'irai dans le désert I liked also. But is it not rather from the desert. Call it camp foutu.[1]

Rutter turns out to be of some service at last – in his indication of Vollard's new book.[2]

I found Devlin the other day among his external affairs & am lunching with him to-morrow. His poems are in hand & he has a new prose-cum-verse romance. But he said he had written to you himself. He wondered were you böse with him. I said: Macché![3]

The weather is dreadful & I cannot get warm. I trailed down to Newcastle one day with Cissie to see Boss. Always when I get there I am glummer than the whole institution put together. On the way back a hard hit publican in Bray quoted Daniel O'Connell to prove there was no hope remaining for this country. A cow, a cow, my Free State for a cow. In the train from Bray, vainly unrecognized, the pestiferous Michael Farrell fresh from Kilmacanogue & next doordom to All Forlorn (whose elucubration on Coriolanus at the Abbey I trust you read in the Chelsea Library). He is finishing a work, really very beautiful, & admired by All Forlorn, himself naively 5 minutes later extolled by Farrell as a critic![4]

No news from Coffey since I saw him here. I shall have to go into TCD after Geulincx, as he does not exist in National Library. I suddenly see that <u>Murphy</u> is break down between his <u>ubi nihil vales ibi nihil velis</u> (positive) & Malraux's <u>Il est difficile à celui qui vit hors du monde de ne pas rechercher les siens</u> (negation). I have not done a tap since I saw you. Shelves are going up slowly in the room where I hope to dig in, and books slowly from Clare Street.[5]

The X-Ray shows nothing. Je m'en doutais.

I was hoping to see JBY last Saturday but went to the Gallery instead. Not a picture touched, only two "British" rooms closed.[6]

Bion in his last acknowledgment of the filthy "trusted I had by now taken up my work with pleasure and satisfaction", as he was sure I must "even though not entirely freed from neuroses"! Mother's whole idea of course is to get me committed to life here. And my travel-courage is so gone that the collapse is more than likely. I find myself more than ever frightened by the prospect of effort, initiative & even the little self-assertion of getting about from one place to another. Solitude here, perhaps more sober than before, seems the upshot of the London Torture. Indeed I do not see what difference the analysis has made. Relations with M. as thorny as ever and the nights no better.[7] A heart attack last night that would have done credit to three years ago. The only plane on which I feel my defeat not proven is the literary. Warte nur ... [8] Frank I feel censorious as not before. He is so successful.[9] To-day gone to Galway, not to return till Saturday.

I have not seen Ruddy since. It is very difficult to get across from here, and when one does ... But I hear he gets on well.[10] I have seen all the Jew faithful, Con etc., but really feel I do not want to see them any more. If nothing has survived but the habit, to insist is like doffing to the Cenotaph.[11] Now, just as I seem to have committed myself to some months here, London & you & Geoffrey seem the sanctuary & reality. Perhaps the flight will be sooner than I expect, but no more Bion. As I write, think, move, speak, praise & blame, I see myself living up to the specimen that these 2 years have taught me I am. The word is not out before I am blushing for my automatism.

Geoffrey seems to be working too hard at the Maudsley. He has applied for a demonstratorship in physiology, 4 hours a week well paid & work that would give him no trouble. Then he could give up the Maudsley. I should say he has a very good chance of getting in. He will be upset by the death of Andy Frank Dixon announced in to-day's paper. One of the few good minds left in the place.[12]

Poor Dilly, in the running for Lynd's good opinion. Surely your gaffe will save her. Greetings to her & Hester & Raven.[13] Write very soon again.

Love
Sam

Sean O'Sullivan was over taking plan & elevation of Shem.
He asked did I dive with my glasses on. Sean liked Leon [for Léon].
They all got jolly together, chez Fourquet [for Fouquet]. Paraît
que Lucia est à Londres.[14]

ALS; 2 leaves, 3 sides; *env to* Thomas McGreevy Esq, 15 Cheyne Gardens, Chelsea,
London S W 3; *pm* 20-1-36, Dublin; TCD, MS 10402/86. *Dating*: from pm.

1 McGreevy's letter to SB has not been found; it is not known which of the poems
he enclosed.

W. B. Yeats selected and introduced the poems included in *The Oxford Book of Modern
Verse: 1892–1935* (Oxford: Oxford University Press, 1936).

McGreevy was aware that his poems "Aodh Ruadh Ó Domhnaill" and "Homage to
Jack Yeats" would be included (333–335). Since his friend George Yeats (née Bertha
Georgie Hyde-Lee, 1892–1968) was handling permissions and compiling the index for
the anthology in early January 1936, McGreevy is likely to have seen the other poems
selected (Ann Saddlemyer, *Becoming George*, 495–496).

Welsh-born poet William Henry Davies (1870–1940) was represented in the anthology by seven poems (128–133).

The poem referred to as "J'irai dans le désert" (I will go into the desert) has not been
identified.

"Camp foutu" (off duly buggered); SB deliberately inverts "foutre le camp" (to get
away or to bugger off).

2 Frank Rutter (1876–1937), Art Critic for *The Sunday Times*, wrote an appreciative
review of *Recollections of a Picture Dealer* (1936), the memoirs of the Paris art dealer
Ambroise Vollard (1867–1939), saying that it was "full of absorbingly interesting
subject-matter and good stories" ("Oddest Art Dealer, Ambroise Vollard: Memories of
Famous Painters," 12 January 1936: 5).

3 Devlin's collection of poems, *Intercessions*, was not actually published until August
1937. SB's reference to Devlin's "prose-cum-verse romance" is not clear. Although
there is an undated TMS draft entitled "Prose" in the Devlin archives, the "prose-
cum-verse romance" may refer to a group of poems called *Adventure*, "the generic
title of a number of MS poems dating from the early thirties, which D[enis] D[evlin]
never published as a group or sequence"; the first of these, "The Statue and the
Perturbed Burghers," appeared in a second draft as "Romance sentimentale"
(National Library of Ireland, The Literary Papers of Denis Devlin, MS 38, Box 5;
Devlin, *Collected Poems of Denis Devlin*, 334).

"Böse" (angry); "Macché" (Come off it).

4 Bray, on the coast road, at the southern end of Killiney Bay, was the terminus of the
rail line from Dublin. Daniel O'Connell (1775–1847), the "Liberator" who led the campaign for Catholic emancipation of Ireland (April 1829) advocating political rather than
violent means; as Mayor of Dublin (1843), he led the failed movement to repeal the Act of
Union in order to secure an Irish parliament. "A cow, a cow, my Free State for a cow"
parodies "A horse, a horse! my kingdom for a horse!" (Shakespeare, *Richard III*, V.iv.7).

Michael Farrell wrote for *The Bell* and Radio Éireann: see 9 October 1933, n. 6. Kilmacanogue, Co. Wicklow, on the slopes of Sugarloaf.

"All Forlorn" is SB's rendering of Irish writer Sean O'Faolain (né John Whelan, 1900–1991), who lived in Kilmacanogue. O'Faolain wrote a letter to the Editor that condemned the *Irish Times* drama critic for only "watery approval" of the Abbey Theatre production of Shakespeare's *Coriolanus*, directed by Hugh Hunt (1911–1993), which he felt was a "dashing" and "vigorous" performance (*The Irish Times* 15 January 1936: 3; see also Holloway, *Joseph Holloway's Irish Theatre*, II, *1932–1937*, 50–51).

SB wrote "<Gate>" and inserted above "Abbey." The Chelsea Library in Manresa Road, near McGreevy's residence in Cheyne Gardens.

5 Brian Coffey was in Paris.

Geulincx: see 9 January 1936, n. 3.

In *Ethica*, Tract I, Cap. II, S. II., Paragraph 3 (p. 37), Geulincx discusses "Sui Despectio" (Contempt of Self); his note to this term includes the phrase "Ubi nihil vales, ibi nihil etiam velis" (*Opera philosophica*, III, 222; Where you are worth nothing, may you also wish for nothing [tr. GC]).

André Malraux writes in *La Condition humaine* (1933): "Solitude dernière, car il est difficile à celui qui vit hors du monde de ne pas rechercher les siens" ("The ultimate solitude, for it is difficult for one who lives isolated from the everyday world not to seek others like himself") (Malraux, *Romans*, Bibliothèque de la Pléiade [Paris: Gallimard, 1947] 353; Malraux, *Man's Fate*, tr. Stuart Gilbert [New York: Random House, 1961] 246). See SB's *Murphy*, 178–179.

SB wrote to McGreevy on 9 January 1935 [*for* 1936]: "I feel I shall finish it all right, and begin it again, somehow after all" (TCD, MS 10402/85). He was setting up a work space at the family home, moving back the books from the study he had had at the office of Beckett and Medcalf, 6 Clare Street, prior to his move to London in 1934.

6 "Je m'en doutais." (I thought as much.)

Jack B. Yeats.

Shortly after his appointment as Director of the National Gallery of Ireland in October 1935, George Furlong (1898–1987) undertook a refurbishment of the museum and restoration of the collection. The re-hanging took place later in 1936, when the museum was closed from the end of September to the end of November.

7 SB notes Bion's response to the final payment which marked closure of SB's therapy with him. "M." refers to Mother.

8 "Warte nur ... " (just wait). From Goethe's "Ein Gleiches" ("Another Night Song") (Christopher Middleton, ed., *Johann Wolfgang von Goethe Selected Poems* [Boston: Suhrkamp/Insel, 1983] 58–59).

9 Frank Beckett was running Beckett and Medcalf, Quantity Surveyors.

10 Rudmose-Brown had been ill and was recovering at his home, 8 Shanganagh Terrace, on the road from Ballybrack to Killiney.

11 A. J. Leventhal.

George Atkinson (1880–1941), Headmaster of the Metropolitan School of Art from 1918 to 1936 and Director of the National College of Art from 1936 to 1941, designed the *Cenotaph* or *Celtic Cross Memorial*. It was installed on Leinster Lawn in 1923 as a temporary monument; in 1950 the *Cenotaph* was replaced by a granite obelisk (Frederick O'Dwyer, *Lost Dublin* [Dublin: Gill and Macmillan, 1981] 50, 56).

12 Geoffrey Thompson was then working at the Maudsley Hospital, London. Andrew Francis Dixon (1868–1936), Professor of Anatomy and Chirurgery and Dean of the Faculty of Physic at Trinity College Dublin, died on 15 January; Geoffrey Thompson had been his student.

13 Geraldine Cummins hoped for a good review of her novel *Fires of Beltane* (1936) from Robert Lynd (1879–1949), Literary Editor of the *News Chronicle* and contributor to the *New Statesman*. McGreevy reviewed it for *Time and Tide* 17.37 (12 September 1936) 1260.
Hester Dowden and Thomas Holmes Ravenhill.

14 Seán O'Sullivan had been in Paris to sketch James Joyce for a portrait commissioned by Joyce's friend Constantine Curran (1880–1975) (James Joyce to Constantine Curran, 18 September 1935, in Joyce, *Letters of James Joyce*, I, 384). See a drawing from this sitting dated 1935 (NGI, 2027).
Paul Léon.
Fouquet's was Joyce's favorite restaurant, 99 Avenue des Champs-Elysées. "Paraît que Lucia est à Londres" (Appears that Lucia is in London). Actually Lucia Joyce was in St. Andrew's Hospital, Northampton, for ten weeks from mid-December 1935 through February 1936 (Shloss, *Lucia Joyce*, 373–374; Jane Lidderdale and Mary Nicholson, *Dear Miss Weaver: Harriet Shaw Weaver 1876–1961* [London: Faber and Faber, 1970] 355–356).

THOMAS McGREEVY

LONDON

29/1/35 [for 1936]   Cooldrinagh
                                                     [Co. Dublin]

Dear Tom

Thanks for your letter. Galley & page of home counties sound last two straws. Hope they are paying you pro rata.[1]

[...]

I went round to JBY last Sat. week, found him all alone & Mrs invisible with a 'acking corf. He has painted a lot of new small pictures for exhibition in London in March, I forget where but not at Alpine, some gallery in Vigo St. I think.[2] The new stuff, some of it, is superb. One small picture especially, <u>Morning</u>, almost a skyscape, wide street leading into Sligo looking west as usual, with boy on a horse 30 pounds. If I had ten I would beard him with an easy payments proposition. But I have not.

I let fall hints here that were understood but not implemented. But I have not given up hope of raising it. Do you think he would be amenable to instalments. It's a long time since I saw a picture I wanted so much. I ran into him again yesterday in the library, but he was uneasy & looked ill and wouldn't have a drink. I hope to bring young Sinclair round to see him next Sunday.[3]

I was at the Gate to see <u>Berkeley Square</u>, ragged adaptation of the ragged <u>Sense of the Past</u>, last Tuesday. Quite well played in parts by MacC. [*for* MacL], to whom in the comp[an]y of Mme. & M. Jammet I was presented earlier in the afternnoon. Of course it is not a play at all, but a very interesting psychological situation with all kinds of unuttered obiters that are scarcely developed in the book either as well as I remember.[4] The whole of dirty Dublin was there, from Longfords & bloodshot blue eyed fourth estaters to Séumas [*for* Seamus] McCall & Skeffington mit Frau. McCall now highly successful journalist, novelist & biographer, with as many publishers as he has faculties. He has done 25,000 on T. Moore and is commissioned to do a large work on Mitchel, by what London firm I forget, as [has] he that he owes me best part of a pound. He is so morally self-righteous, living in "Fort of the Oak", Dalkey, & at the same time so widely read, that I sent him a copy of the <u>Bones</u>.[5]

Last night I went across to the Jammet's in Blackrock. Good coffee & fine. But it didn't go. They are the enemy & one shouldn't go near them. The commercial attaché, M. Lyord (?), deaf, bald & obesely wizened, complete with Gaeltacht fiancée, Miss Larkin ("c'est une Titiane!"), was there, walking up & down sopping up oeufs sur le plat with sandwiches of saumon fumé.[6]

TSE has been all over the place, speaking at National to a motion affirmed by Rev. Burke-Savage, S.J., who savaged what he didn't burke, & then alone next day on Relation of Literatures, tralalala. Shem "an unconscious tribute to a Catholic education acquired at a time when few people were educated at all." The old fall back on pedagogics. His murder was played by the National Dramatic. I think he was staying with Curran.[7] I haven't seen anything more of Devlin, who was reading his poems at [2]RN last night. He thinks of calling his poems with Reavey Intercessions, which I think is an excellent title.[8] I borrowed a lot of works on cinema from young Montgomery, who is certainly a curious little card: Pudovkin, Arnheim & back numbers of Close Up with stuff by Eisenstein. How I would like to go to Moscow and work under Eisenstein for a year. Then one would be beautifully qualified for the execrations on another plane.[9] Nothing by the way from Reavey, not a word about the poems & no sign of the oustanding copies that are due to me. Nor from Coffey, who promised me Geulincx & Eluard informations. And no reactions here to the poems of any kind whatsoever.[10]

It is good of you to be willing to see Bion, but I think the less that scab is scratched the better. As you say, he has been as probe as he could, with the probities respectively homologous to mother & me.[11] But there is one thing you might do for me if you will. Of the two coats I sent to myself here before leaving London, identically addressed & declared, one came through without demand, the other with demand for 3/6 which I refused to pay & sent the parcel away from the door, thinking I could go into the offices in town after Xmas & explain about it. When I went in the other day they said they had sent it back to the sender according to the regulations, which means that it ought now to be with Mrs. Frost, though I have no intimation from her. Would you go round & see? If [it] is there you might address it to me marked: old leather coat, bought in Dublin, personal belongings. It appears the personal is the keyword. Mother is most anxious that the gardener should enjoy it before the Spring sets in. Forgive me for bothering you. If it is not there don't bother about it any further. And love to Mrs Frost et famille.[12]

I have not been able to get over to see Ruddy again, & I hear he has been complaining about me. It is very hard to get from here. He is so much better now that he is up but will not be lecturing this term. Ethna MacCarthy has got the job of doing his Provençal lectures and I have been helping her out of the Tresor du Felibrige. Aubanel seems the best of them. They have Mistral's <u>Mireio</u> & <u>Memori et Raconte</u>. She is doing medicine in TCD now and the two are too much for her.[13]

Cissie pushed up some Italian books that had been left behind by outgoing tenant, Machiavelli's plays including the <u>Mandragora</u>, nice editions of Manzoni and that old bumsucking pedant Varchi (cinquecento) and the Gerusalemme. Also Giusti's poetry. All bought at Florence by Maud Joynt, at the end of last century. She might have been nice to know.[14]

I have got all my stuff together in this little room at last, and shelves up. I wish you could see my four old men over the mantelpiece, the Chartres Aristotle & Père Eternel, the Buonarotti Crepusocolo [for Buonarroti Crepuscolo] & the Tête du Christ du Calvaire from the Puits de Moïse at Dijon. If you can't get a woman ...[15] I have done next to no work on <u>Murphy</u>, all the sense & impulse seem to have collapsed. There are three, four, chapters to write, only about 12000, but I don't think they will be. Yes, sometime I hope I may get away, perhaps to Bavaria in the early summer. Then it would be too late for Spain. Or better still to Lüneburg & Hanover, from Cove to Hamburg etc.[16]

I met one Fitzgerald, cinematography expert, I think the father of Jelly. He was very nice and showed a little film on a pillow cover. He has a good 16mm. camera & projector and seems to know a lot about the actual tricks of phot[o]graphy. Mais pauvre en génie. And no interest in montage. How should one set about getting into a decent studio, or even a bad one, simply to pick up the trade? Se munir d'un scenario?[17]

Mother keeps well, having added a family of measles to her good works. Yesterday she actually took herself to the pictures. Frank blooms. Yesterday he walked from Rathfarnham to here via Glendoo, Featherbed, Glencree, Enniskerry, Scalp, Kilternan, Carrickmines. Only the best part of 20 miles. T[h]en brought his girl to see the Bergner at the Royal in Escape me Never.[18]

I wonder did you notice about a months [sic] ago in Irish Times a short letter from Vera Esposito, soft soaping Smyl[l]ie for his tolerance of colonial expansion in the case of Japan and making Italy a parallel case.[19]

God love thee & write very soon.

s/ S

TLI; 2 leaves, 3 sides; TCD, MS 10402/87. *Dating:* TCD, MS 10402/87 includes a T env to Thomas McGreevy Esq, 15, Cheyne Gardens, Chelsea, London S.W.3.; pm 8-2-36, Dublin; however, for reasons given below, this envelope is incorrectly linked to 29 January 1935 [*for* 1936].

Although the letter is typed with a blue ribbon, and the envelope is typed with a black ribbon, it is possible that the ribbon was changed or that two different type-writers were used; furthermore, because the envelope differs in quality of paper and in size from others that SB used at this time, it is possible that SB prepared the envelope from a location other than his home. However, internal evidence makes the 8 February 1936 postmark impossible for this letter: SB gives McGreevy instructions for sending his coat in this letter, and his letter to McGreevy of 6 February [1936], postmarked 7 February 1936 (TCD, MS 10402/88), acknowledges receipt of the coat. The year 1936 is confirmed by the context of the letter.

1 It is not known what McGreevy had been asked to do.

2 Jack Yeats received visitors on Saturday afternoons.

Yeats's exhibition was at the Dunthorne Gallery, 5 Vigo Street, London ("Jack B. Yeats: Recent Paintings," opening 19 March 1936); it included a number of small (9 in. × 14 in.) paintings that were exhibited for the first time in this show: *The Eye of Affection* (Pyle 475, Warren S. Halbourne, Bermuda); *Boy and Horse* (Pyle 476, private collection); *Below the Golden Falls* (Pyle 478, private collection); *The Falls of Sheen* (Pyle 479, Waddington Galleries, London) (Pyle, *Jack B. Yeats: A Catalogue Raisonné of the Oil Paintings*, I, 431, 433; II, 1098; III, 203, 204).

3 SB refers to Jack Yeats's painting *A Morning*, now in the National Gallery of Ireland (NGI 4628, Pyle 482) (Pyle, *Jack B. Yeats: A Catalogue Raisonné of the Oil Paintings*, I, 436).

Morris Sinclair.

4 *Berkeley Square* (1931) was revived at the Gate Theatre from Tuesday, 28 January 1936; John Lloyd Balderston (1889–1954) and John Collings Squire (1884–1958) adapted for the stage the fragment of a novel by Henry James (1843–1916) that was posthumously edited by Percy Lubbock (1879–1965), "The Sense of the Past" (1917). Mícheál MacLiammóir (né Alfred Willmore, 1899–1978), actor and founder of the Gate Theatre, played Peter Standish in this production.

Having taken it over from his father, Louis Jammet (1894–1985) was owner of Jammet's Restaurant from 1927 to 1967; his wife was the artist, Yvonne Jammet (née Auger, 1900–1967).

5 Lord Longford, patron of the Gate Theatre (1931–1936), was Director of The Longford Players from 1936.

Seamus MacCall (1892–1964) had written a biography, *Thomas Moore* (1935), and was writing another, *Irish Mitchel: A Biography* (1938); he had also recently published a novel, *Gods in Motley* (1935). McCall lived at "Dun Daire" (Ir., Fort Oak), Mount Salus, Dalkey. SB wrote "<anthologist> biographer."

Owen Sheehy Skeffington (1909–1970) was then Lecturer in French at Trinity College Dublin; his wife was the French-born writer Andrée Sheehy Skeffington (née Denis, 1910–1998). "Mit Frau" (with wife).

6 The home of Louis and Yvonne Jammet was "Clonmore," 8 Queen's Park, Blackrock. Although he assumed the title of commercial attaché only in February 1939, Eugène Lestocquoy (1895–?) had been a French commercial agent in Ireland from 1932; Miss Larkin has not been identified.

"Fine" (old brandy). "Gaeltacht" (Ir., one of the Gaelic-speaking regions of Ireland). "C'est une Titiane!" (She is a Titian!). "Oeufs sur le plat" (fried eggs). "Saumon fumé" (smoked salmon).

7 T. S. Eliot spoke in Dublin as a guest of the University College Dublin Historical, Literary, and Aesthetical Society in the Council Chamber, Earlsfort Terrace, on 23 January 1936. Reverend Roland Burke-Savage SJ (1913–1998) read an address, "Literature at the Irish Crossroads," to which T. S. Eliot was one of the respondents. Burke-Savage called for an Irish literature that would parallel the revival of the Irish language. He claimed that Anglo-Irish literature "had run the whole gamut of paganism" from "romanticism" to "cynicism," "nihilism," "materialism," and "despair," and proposed that a true Irish literature lay in acceptance of the Catholic tradition. In his response, Eliot agreed that the new generation of Irish writers could not simply take its direction from the current mainstream, and he paid tribute to Yeats and

claimed that Joyce was "the most Irish" and "most Catholic writer in English of his generation" ("Literature at the Cross-Roads," *The Irish Times* 24 January 1936: 8; SB's quotation also comes from this article). Texts of both address and response can be found at Harvard, Houghton Library, T. S. Eliot, 1888–1965 Papers, bMS Am 1791/28–30.

On 24 January, Eliot lectured at University College Dublin on a literary tradition that developed from broad reading and fertilization from older or foreign cultures, rather than one formed merely on the patterns of the previous generation, claiming that "poetry could not flourish in an intellectual vacuum" ("Originality in Poetry: Fertilisation of Literature," *The Irish Times* 25 January 1936: 6). A production of *Murder in the Cathedral* (1935) was performed by the College Dramatic Society, with Eliot in the audience ("Irishman's Diary," *The Irish Times* 25 January 1936: 6). It is not known if Eliot stayed with Constantine Curran.

8 Denis Devlin read his poems on Radio Athlone on 29 January 1936 ("A Poet Reads," no. 3, Denis Devlin, *The Independent* 28 January 1936: 6). Devlin's poems were to be published by Reavey in the Europa Poets series; in a letter to Reavey, Devlin indicated that the title for his collection was *Intercessions* (18 January 1936, TxU).

9 Niall Montgomery (1914–1987), Dublin poet and architect, son of Film Censor James Montgomery (1866–1948). *Film Technique* (1930, rev. 1933) by Vsevolod Pudovkin (1893–1953), *Film* (1933) by Rudolf Arnheim (1904–2007), and issues of *Close Up* (July 1927 – December 1933) in which Russian film director Sergei Eisenstein (1898–1948) had published essays about his approach to cinema, including: Eisenstein, W. I. Pudowkin, and G. V. Alexandroff (also Grigory Aleksandrov, 1903–1983), "The Sound Film: A Statement from the U.S.S.R.," 3 (October 1928) 10–13; Eisenstein, "The New Language of Cinematography," 4 (May 1929) 10–13; "The Fourth Dimension in the Kino," 6 (March 1930) 184–194; "Filmic Art and Training (in an interview with Mark Segal)," 6 (March 1930) 195–197; "The Fourth Dimension in the Kino II," 6 (April 1930) 253–268; "The Dinamic Square," 8 (March 1931) 2–16 and (June 1931) 91–95; "The Principles of Film Form," 8 (September 1931) 167–181; "Detective Work in the GIK," 9 (December 1932) 287–294; and "Cinematography with Tears!: The Way of Learning," 10 (March 1933) 3–17.

10 Copies of *Echo's Bones*: see 9 January 1935 [for 1936], n. 1.
Brian Coffey returned to Paris early in January; he had proposed that SB prepare a monograph on Geulincx. Coffey had SB's copy of *This Quarter* with his translations of poems by Eluard (see 9 January 1935, [for 1936], n. 2).

11 It is not known why McGreevy offered to see W. R. Bion.

12 The customs duty on overcoats was 60 percent of value unless personally owned and substantially worn. SB had lodged in London with Mrs. Frost at 34 Gertrude Street. "Et famille" (and family).

13 Although Rudmose-Brown's health was reported as improving, it was announced that his Trinity College Dublin lectures during the term would be given by other members of the staff (*The Irish Times* 25 January 1936: 6). Ethna MacCarthy was responsible for his lectures on the Provençal poets; she was a Scholar and Senior Moderator in Modern Languages (1926), although by this time she had begun medical studies at TCD.

The "Félibrige" was a literary movement for the restoration of the "langue d'oc" (a language of southern France), begun in 1864 by Frédéric Mistral (1830–1914), Théodore Aubanel (1829–1886), and Joseph Roumanille (1818–1891). Mistral edited *Lou Tresor dóu félibrige ou Dictionnaire provençal-français embrassant les divers dialectes de la langue d'oc moderne . . .* (1878–1886). Readings for the course included *Mirèio* (1859) and *Memòri et raconte* (1901) by Mistral, a Nobel laureate in 1904. SB's notes on Mistral and the Félibrige Poets can be found in TCD MS 10971/4; see Everett Frost and Jane Maxwell, "TCD, MS 10971/4: Frédéric Mistral and the Félibrige Poets," *Notes Diverse Holo*, Special issue, *SBT/A* 16 (2006) 133–136.

14 Cissie Sinclair gave SB books left behind at 85 Moyne Road by the former tenant Maud Joynt (1869–1940). Joynt, who had a wide knowledge of languages, translated and/or edited from Latin, French, and Gaelic, and was an Editor of the Royal Irish Academy's *Irish Dictionary* (1939).

La Mandragola (1518), a play by the Italian politician and writer Niccolò Machiavelli (1469–1527). The collected works of Italian writer Alessandro Manzoni (1785–1873) run to ten volumes; SB is mostly likely to have acquired *I promessi sposi* (1827; *The Betrothed*). It is not known which of the works by Florentine historian and writer Benedetto Varchi (1503–1565) SB received. He refers to Torquato Tasso's epic poem *Gerusalemme liberata* (1575; *Jerusalem Delivered*) 6th edn. (Milan: Ulrico Hoepli 1923). It is not known which edition of the works of Italian satirical poet Giuseppe Giusti (1809–1850) SB was given.

15 SB refers to a reproduction of *Aristotle*, a twelfth-century sculpture on the Royal Portal, Chartres Cathedral (Etienne Houvet, *An Illustrated Monograph of Chartres Cathedral* [Chartres Cathedral: E. Houvet, 1938] 29). "Père Eternel" may refer to any of several sculptures of God the Father in Chartres Cathedral, but none is known by this name: *God Creating Day and Night* (thirteenth century, North Portal), *God Creating the Birds* (thirteenth century, North Portal), *God Creating the Moon and the Sun* (n.d., North Portal), *God Creating Adam* (thirteenth century, North Portal), *God Creating the Earthly Paradise* (n.d., North Portal), or *God Beyond Time* (twelfth century, Royal Portal) (Houvet, *An Illustrated Monograph of Chartres Cathedral*, 44–48, 50).

SB refers to Michelangelo's *Il crepuscolo* (Dusk), a sculpted figure on the Tomb of Lorenzo dei Medici in the Medici Chapel, Florence.

Tête du Christ du Calvaire from Puits de Moïse (10 miles from Dijon), possibly by Netherlandish artist Claus Sluter (c. 1360–1406), is now in the Musée Archéologique in Dijon (see Cor Engelen, *Le Mythe du Moyen Age: premiers éléments d'une remise en question du style moyenâgeux*, tr. Benoît Boëlens van Waesberghe [Leuven: C. Engelen, 1999] 214).

"If you can't get a woman . . . "; reference not traced.

16 Cove (now Cobh), Co. Cork; Lüneburg, Hanover, Hamburg, in northern Germany.

17 Neither Fitzgerald nor "Jelly" has been identified.
"Mais pauvre en génie" (But no genius).
"Se munir d'un scénario?" (Equip oneself with a scenario?)

18 Frank Beckett's walk circled from the Dublin suburb of Rathfarnham to the southeast in Co. Dublin, into Co. Wicklow, returning north to Foxrock.

German actress Elisabeth Bergner (née Ettel, 1897–1986) starred in the film *Escape Me Never* (1935) which opened in Dublin on Sunday, 26 January 1936 at the Theatre Royal.

19 In a letter from Florence dated 2 January 1936, Vera Esposito complimented R. M. Smyllie (né Robert Maire Smyllie, also known as Bertie, 1894–1954), Editor of *The Irish Times* from 1934 to 1954, on his article entitled "Japan's Millions" in which he had argued that Japan needed opportunities for expansion, as did Italy (*The Irish Times* 30 December 1935: 6). She concurred with Smyllie, citing from his conclusion that "'real peace never will come until the world finds some way to recognize such facts, and to provide for them without recourse to violence'" (*The Irish Times* 7 January 1936: 4).

THOMAS McGREEVY
LONDON

6/2 [36]   Cooldrinagh
                                              Foxrock,
                                              [Co. Dublin]

Dear Tom

The coat arrived safely this morning. It was very good of you to look after it for me so promptly and I hope it did not mean too much of a corvée.[1] Thanks also for letter. Newman did his best to be nice about Will Summer, and with only the Rio Grande to set it against he was able to carry it off.[2]

[...] No news at all lately from Geoffrey. I came across all the "Surrealism & Madness" texts I translated for Titus and sent them to him with the Eluard & Breton Essais de Simulation .. Perhaps these were too much for him.[3]

What I would learn under a person like Pudovkin is how to handle a camera, the higher trucs of the editing bench, & so on, of which I know as little as of quantity surveying.[4] The most liberal government imaginable, in effect & disposition, would not make me a bit wiser in that respect. It is interesting that Becky Sharp in colour, which I think had a long run in Lc ˙

3⌐

was a complete flop here and was taken off at the Savoy after three days & not transferred to any other house. That does not encourage my hope that the industrial film will become so completely naturalistic, in stereoscopic colour & gramophonic sound, that a back water may be created for the two-dimensional silent film that had barely emerged from its rudiments when it was swamped. Then there would be two separate things and no question of a fight between them or rather of a rout.[5]

I brought Maurice Sinclair to see J.B.Y. last Saturday. He did not seem at all perturbed about his brother. There was only himself and all went very well. I can't ask him to let me have the picture for nothing & I can't raise the amount of even a modest first instalment.[6] The policy being to keep me tight so that I may be goaded into salaried employment. Which reads more bitterly than it is intended.

I lunched with Denis Devlin last Monday. He was meeting a girl that night at Brinsley MacNamara's première. He has called his poems Intercessions. What the hell is Reavey doing? Not a word from him & still the outstanding copies in abeyance. Not that I have need of them.[7]

A letter from Charles who is giving up Athens & coming slowly home by Provence & Paris. He asks for news of Murphy. There is none. There only remain three chapters of mechanical writing, which I haven't the courage to begin, choking myself off with assistance to young Sinclair, who is up for Schol, & to Ethna MacCarthy, who is doing Ruddy's Provençal in T.C.D. Parallel by the way between Felibres & Gaels very exact.[8] I wonder what is the present state of "notre beau parler de Saint-Remi". I heard that Ruddy had been complaining of my neglect, so walked over one afternoon to see him, to find him in a thick TCD atmosphere, O'Toole & Liddell (the new German man from Manchester – pernicious – German-Scottish). Ruddy himself is apparently quite well again – but of course liable to another fulmination any time.[9] Have been walking feverishly, with Frank & alone. Quando il piede cammina, il cuore gode. "Gode" is rather strong. "Posa" would be better. For hours last Sunday along the ridge between Glendalough & Glenmalure. And alone anything from 5 to 10 miles locally daily. It saves cafard & masturbation.[10]

I like the title of Huxley's new novel announced in Chatto's Spring List: Eyeless in Gaza (Samson Agonistes). Footless in Dublin. What about a new series of yarns: Less Kicks than Pricks or More More Pricks.[11]

Longford lost God knows how many thousands in the Gate's last season. It appears they are unlikely to return. He is running a company in their absence and the Drama League is once more in full Fragonard.[12] And Denis Johnson [*for* Johnston] talks to the Old Dublin Society of Swift & Stella in Capel Street.[13] Beecham is coming with London Philharmonic next Saturday & Sunday week, but no programme announced. I am taking Mother à tout hasard.[14]

Have just read the Mandragola & started Clizia. He apologises as uom saggio e grave, for writing so frivolously, in what de Sanctis calls "cattivi versi ma strazianti". I quote them because I think they will please you:

> Scusatelo con questo, che s'ingegna
> Con questi van pensieri
> Fare il suo tristo tempo più soave:
> Perchè altrove non ave
> Dove voltare il viso:
> Chè gli è stato interciso

Monstrar con altre imprese altra virtue,
Non sendo premio alle fatiche sue.[15]

I want to get hold of Folengo & Berni and the Cardinal of
Bibbiena (La Calandra) and the theatre of Bruno & much else
besides. I picked up Reid's complete works in good condition in
18th century edition at Green's [*for* Greene's] for sixpence.
Translate Fracastoro's Sifilide e poi mori.[16]

> Love ever
> Sam

ALS; 2 leaves, 3 sides; *env to* Thomas McGreevy Esq, 15 Cheyne Gardens, Chelsea,
London S W 3; *pm* 7-2-36, Dublin; TCD, MS 10402/88. *Dating*: from pm; response to
letter 29 January 1935 [*for* 1936] re: coat and Pudovkin.

1 The coat that McGreevy re-sent to SB: see 29 January 1935 [*for* 1936]. "Corvée" (chore).

2 Ernest Newman (né William Roberts, 1868–1959), Music Critic of *The Sunday
Times*, reviewed new work by Constant Lambert (1905–1951). Newman wrote that
Lambert's masque for baritone, chorus, and orchestra, "Summer's Last Will and
Testament," was "not likely to prove a serious rival to the splendid 'Rio Grande'" (for
piano, chorus, and orchestra, 1927) ("This Week's Music: Chamber Music," *The Sunday
Times* 2 February 1937: 7). McGreevy was a friend of Lambert and had written the
libretto for the work that became the ballet *Pomona*.

3 SB had translated many of the texts in the surrealist number of *This Quarter*
(5.1 [September 1932]); for a list of the texts by Breton, Eluard, and René Crevel
translated by SB, see Federman and Fletcher, *Samuel Beckett: His Works and His Critics*,
92–93. SB also refers to essays written by both Breton and Eluard that he translated for
this issue: "The Possessions," "Simulation of Mental Debility Essayed," "Simulation of
General Paralysis Essayed" (119–125); SB also translated Crevel's "Simulation of the
Delirium of Interpretation Essayed" (126–128).

4 Pudovkin understood the art of filmmaking as a process of selection of scene,
angle, balance of light and shadow; in *Film Technique* he emphasizes the development of
the scenario, cinematographic analysis in the shooting-script, and the close relationship between technical knowledge and the creative faculty.
    "Trucs" with reference to "truquage" (special effects): 10 May [1934], n.3.

5 By applying the technicolor processing employed in cartoons by the Disney
Studios (founded by Walt Disney, 1901–1966), *Becky Sharp* (1935) marked a turning
point in the cinema industry. However, the unnamed Cinema Correspondent for
The Irish Times called it a "rather poor film," noting that the novelty of color could
reduce the demand for quality, as did the introduction of sound with the "Talkies"

("Film Notes," 28 January 1936: 4). The film did not run at the Savoy, but at the Capitol Theatre, Dublin, from 24 to 30 January 1936 to record audiences.

6 W. B. Yeats had suffered a heart attack on 29 January 1936 in Palma, Majorca ("Illness of Mr. W. B. Yeats: Improvement Reported," *The Irish Times* 1 February 1936: 9). SB wrote to Morris Sinclair on 31 January 1936 to arrange to go with him to see Jack Yeats the following day: "Bring £30 (thirty pounds) & we'll buy the Morning" (Sinclair).

7 *The Grand House in the City* by Brinsley MacNamara (1890–1963) opened on Monday, 3 February 1936, at the Abbey Theatre.

Denis Devlin's collection of poems, *Intercessions*, was to be published in the Europa Poets series by George Reavey, but Reavey deferred publication until August 1937 (Devlin to Reavey, 4 March 1936, TxU). *Echo's Bones*, published in November 1935, had not been reviewed or distributed in Ireland; Devlin had reported to Reavey that Combridge's order had not been filled (18 January 1936, TxU), and Brian Coffey had advised Reavey to approach Dublin booksellers directly himself (14 January 1936, TxU).

8 Charles Prentice, having retired as a Director of Chatto and Windus, had been pursuing archeological interests in Greece.

Morris Sinclair was preparing for the Foundation Scholarship examination in Trinity College Dublin.

Ethna MacCarthy was teaching Rudmose-Brown's course in the Provençal Poets during his illness. Both the Félibres (modern Provençal poets) and the Gaels (the Gaelic poets of the Irish renaissance) sought to recover the past through language.

9 By "notre beau parler de Saint-Remi" (Saint-Rémy speech), SB refers to the Occitan language of Southern France, here associated with the town and region of Saint-Rémy-de-Provence. In his notes taken from Gaston Paris, *Penseurs et poètes*, ed. Calmann Lévy (Paris: Ancienne Maison, Michel Lévy Frères, 1896), SB cites Paris's observation of a similarity: "how the spoken language of San-Remi (Mistral's center for Félibriges) became a new literary language ... [and] how the Florentine dialect did the same for Tuscany" (Everett Frost and Jane Maxwell, "TCD, MS 10971/4: Frédéric Mistral and the Félibrige Poets," *Notes Diverse Holo*, Special issue *SBT/A* 16 [2006] 135).

Rudmose-Brown was confined to his home (8 Shanganagh Terrace, Killiney) while recovering from illness. Éamonn O'Toole (1883–1956) was Professor of Irish at Trinity College Dublin from 1929 to 1954. Maximilian Friedrich Liddell (1887–1968) was Professor of German and Lecturer in Anglo-Saxon at Trinity College Dublin from 1933 to 1968; Liddell was not at Manchester earlier in his career, but he taught at the University of Birmingham from 1920 to 1932.

10 "Quando il piede cammina, il cuore gode": see 5 May 1935, n. 2. "Posa" (rests).

From Laragh, the walk from Glendalough (site of St. Kevin's churches) south along a ridge to Glenmalure follows the upper reaches of the Avonbeg River, Co. Wicklow.

"Cafard" (low spirits, gloom).

11 Aldous Huxley's *Eyeless in Gaza* (1936) takes its title from John Milton's dramatic poem *Samson Agonistes* (1671) in which the blind Samson is held captive in Gaza by the Philistines.

12 Lord Longford began a new company, the Longford Players, that planned to present modern plays at the Gate Theatre while the Gate company, led by Hilton

Edwards, was on tour (*The Irish Times* 4 February 1936: 4). In addition, Lennox Robinson, Lord Longford, Mrs. W. B. Yeats [George], and Olive Craig (Mrs. Frank Craig, n.d.) revived the Dublin Drama League to produce "uncommercial" plays on Sundays and Mondays; their first performances in the new series included *Orpheus* (*Orphée*, 1925) by Jean Cocteau, *His Widow's Husband* (*El marido de su viuda*, 1908) by Jacinto Benavente (1866–1954), *Hotel Universe* (1930) by Philip Barry (1896–1949), and *Murder in the Cathedral* (1935) by T. S. Eliot (*The Irish Times* 14 January 1936: 4).

"Full Fragonard" invokes the French court painter Jean-Honoré Fragonard (1732–1806), probably an allusion to opulent color and display.

13 Denis Johnston's talk to the Old Dublin Society on 3 February 1936, "Some Dublin Relics of the Late Doctor Swift" (*The Irish Times* 4 February 1936: 8). Stella lived in Capel Street.

14 Thomas Beecham (1879–1961) conducted the London Philharmonic Orchestra at the Theatre Royal, Dublin on 15 and 16 February; the programs were announced in *The Irish Times* 14 February 1936: 6.

"A tout hasard" (on spec.).

15 *La Mandragola* and *Clizia* (1525), plays by Machiavelli. "Uom saggio e grave" (a man wise and serious) is taken from the line "D'un uom che voglia parer saggio e grave" ("For one who likes to be thought wise and serious") (*Mandragola* in *Tutte le opere di Niccolò Machiavelli*, II, ed. Francesco Flora and Carlo Cordiè [Milan and Verona: Arnoldo Mondadori, 1950] 561; *Mandragola* in *The Literary Works of Machiavelli*, tr. J. R. Hale [London: Oxford University Press, 1961] 6).

Italian literary historian Francesco de Sanctis (1817–1883) wrote of the passage that SB quotes from the prologue to *La Mandragola*: "Cattivi versi, ma strazianti" (bad verses, but heart-rending) (*Storia della letteratura italiana*, ed. Niccolò Gallo, II [Turin: Giulio Einaudi Editore, 1958] 598).

> Forgive him: for he tries with idle dreams
> To make the hour less bitter than it seems.
> Bitter, for he can turn no other way
> To show a higher worth, do what he may;
> For graver themes
> He sees no chance of patronage or pay.
> (*Mandragola* in *The Literary Works of Machiavelli*, 6)

16 SB expresses the wish to read three Italian writers of the Cinquecento, whose work is characterized by robust humor and earthy satire: Teofilo Folengo (né Girolamo, pseud. Merlin Coccalo or Cocai, 1491–1544), the most important of the "macaronic poets" whose best-known work is *Baldus* (1517); Francesco Berni (c. 1497–1535); Bernardo Bibbiena (né Bernardo Dovizi, 1470–1520), whose most celebrated work was *La Calandra* (1513; *Calandra*), perhaps the most scurrilous play of the 1400s; and the philosopher Giordano Bruno (1548–1600) whose only play was *Il Candelaio* (c. 1582; *The Candle-Bearer*).

Thomas Reid (1710–1796), Professor of Moral Philosophy at the University of Glasgow. There were many eighteenth-century three-volume editions of Reid's *Essays on the Intellectual and Active Powers of Man*, collecting essays published in 1785 and 1788; however, the earliest collected edition was *The Works of Thomas Reid* (Edinburgh: Bell and Bradfute, 1803).

2 March 1936, Eisenstein

Italian physician Girolamo Fracastoro (1478–1553) wrote the epic poem *Syphilis sive de morbo gallico* (1530: *Syphilis or the French Disease*), whose central figure Syphilis suffers from the disease that now bears his name.
SB adapts the famous line about Naples, "Vedi Napoli e poi muori" (See Naples and die).

SERGEI EISENSTEIN

MOSCOW

2/3/36   6 Clare Street
                                       Dublin
                                 Irish Free State

Monsieur

I write to you on the advice of Mr Jack Isaacs of London, to ask to be considered for admission to the Moscow State School of Cinematography.[1]

Born 1906 in Dublin and "educated" there. 1928–1930 lecteur d'anglais at Ecole Normale, Paris. Worked with Joyce, collaborated in French translation of part of his Work in Progress (N.R.F., May 1931) and in critical symposium concerning same (Our Exagmination, etc.).[2] Published Proust (essay, Chatto & Windus, London 1931), More Pricks Than Kicks (short stories, do., 1934), Echo's Bones (poems, Europa Press, Paris 1935).

I have no experience of studio work and it is naturally in the scenario and editing end of the subject that I am most interested. It is because I realise that the script is function of its means of realisation that I am anxious to make contact with your mastery of these, and beg you to consider me a serious cinéaste worthy of admission to your school.[3] I could stay a year at least.

Veuilliez [*for* Veuillez] agréer mes meilleurs hommages.[4]

s/

(Samuel Beckett)

317

TLS; 1 leaf, 1 side; Russian State Archive of Literature and Art, Eisenstein archive 1923-I-1642; copy, Museum of Modern Art, Oxford; *previous publication* (transcription with variants): Jay Leyda, ed., *Eisenstein 2: A Premature Celebration of Eisenstein's Centenary*, tr. Alan Y. Upchurch, *et al.* (Calcutta: Seagull Books, 1985; rpt. London: Methuen, 1988) 59, and transcription in "Scripted by Beckett," *Rolling Stock* 7 (1984), 4.

1 Jack Isaacs (1896–1973), Professor of English Language and Literature at Queen Mary College (London), was a founding member of the Film Society (1925–1938). He performed in Eisenstein's film, *Lost*, and when Eisenstein came to London, Isaacs was his guide.

2 For James Joyce, "Anna Livia Plurabelle," see 29 May 1931, n. 2. Beckett, "Dante ... Bruno. Vico. . Joyce," *Our Exagmination*.

3 Describing the curriculum at the GIK (Gosudarstvenni institut kinematografii [State Institute of Cinematography]) in Moscow, Eisenstein wrote: "To realize how it is done and actually participate in the process seems to me most advantageous and instructive for students" ("Cinematography *with* Tears!" 9). The scenario was the phase between narrative treatment and its cinematographic analysis, the "shooting script" (Vsevolod Pudovkin, *On Film Technique*, tr. Ivor Montagu [London: V. Gollancz, 1929] 176–177).

4 "Veuillez agréer mes meilleurs hommages" (Yours respectfully).

THOMAS McGREEVY

LONDON

5/3/36   Cooldrinagh

[Co. Dublin]

Dear Tom

I hope you are feeling better & with perhaps some birds in a bush somewhere.

It is difficult to write from the appalling sameness, blankness, apathy, stupidity, pusillanimity, day after day, herE [sic]. Molly the cousin from Wales is over till the Grand National, an epidemic having released her from her dummy pianos.[1] She is held to be company for mother. Thus she is not an evil communication.

I have been reading Geulincx in T.C.D., without knowing why exactly. Perhaps because the text is so hard to come by. But that is rationalisation & my instinct is right & the work worth doing, because of its saturation in the conviction that the sub specie aeternitatis vision is the only excuse for remaining alive. He does not put out his eyes on that account, as Heraclites did & Rimbaud began to, nor like the terrified Berkeley repudiate them.[2] One feels them very patiently turned outward, & without Schwärmerei turned in-ward, Janus or Telephus eyes, like those of Frenhofer in the Chef d'Oeuvre Inconnu, when he shall have forgotten Mabuse & ceased to barbouiller.[3]

Tasso again also with boredom, & Ariosto, feeling him to be the greatest literary artist (as distinct from poet) of them all perhaps & Goethe's Tasso, than which, except for some good rhetoric, anything more disgusting would be hard to devise. If he wants to state a personal position, as seems the case here, why can't he do so directly, even if only with the directness of the Wahlverwandtschaften, without soliciting precedents from among the installed, whereby he is condoned & they falsified? He really invites one very patiently to think of him as a machine à mots, a cliché separator, & a bunker of the suffering that has not proved its merit in a thousand impressions, or a vademecum edition.[4]

Dermod O'Brien, to come down to heaven, addressing Cork or rather Limerick, freedom of which had just been conferred on him, would rather be a good Irishman than a great painter! Brigit [for Brigid] is marrying a dentist [...][5]

I haven't seen JBY for a fortnight. Last time I was there with a crowd including Fearon grinding out mots and Miss Purser scuttling along the treetops; and Miss MacCardle [for Macardle], smelling of Castle Cromer.[6] HE is I think OFF to the Alpine next week, before when I hope to see him.[7] I perceived Miss Purser again at the R.D.S. the following Monday at Cortot's recital which was a disappointment. I think he was very ill. He played all the Preludes, Children[']s Corner & Liszt's 2nd Rhapsodie.[8]

A letter from Brian this morning, furious with Reavey for having dragged in Herbert Reid [*for* Read] to the Eluard party. I have not had a word from him for months, & no news of the Bones from any quarter.[9]

Murphy will not budge. I am thinking of asking Frank does he want stamps licked in Clare Street. Though I fear my present saliva would burn a hole in the envelope.

> Love
>
> Sam

ALS; 2 leaves, 2 sides; *env to* Thomas McGreevy Esq, 15 Cheyne Gardens, Chelsea, London; *pm* 6-3-36, Dublin; TCD, MS 10402/91.

1 Maria Belis Roe (known as Molly, 1903–1986), SB's cousin, daughter of Edward Price Roe, May Beckett's brother. Molly taught music at Howell's School in Denbigh, Wales, which at that time was closed on account of an outbreak of measles. The Irish Grand National steeplechase was run on 13 April in 1936, but Molly left on 2 April 1936 ("The cousin left this day week," SB to McGreevy, 9 April [1936], TCD, MS 10402/93).

2 In *Ethica* (*Opera philosophica*, III), Arnold Geulincx advocates total submission to God, "sub specie aeternitatis" (in the perspective of eternity). See also 16 January [1936], n. 5.

SB mentions philosophers and a poet who repudiated literal reality (as perceived through the eyes). According to Dante's account, "Heraclitus wept," see 27 February 1934, n. 3. For Rimbaud's "eye-suicide," see 11 March 1931, n. 7. The "immaterialist hypothesis" of George Berkeley denied the existence of matter, and claimed that material objects have no existence outside of the mind; see 8 September 1934, n. 18).

3 "Schwärmerei" (effusiveness). The Roman god Janus was symbolized by a double-faced head looking in opposite directions. When Telephus, the son of Hercules, was wounded in battle by Achilles, the Delphic Oracle said that only rust from the spear that wounded him would cure his wounds.

In Balzac's "Chef d'Oeuvre Inconnu" (1837; "The Unknown Masterpiece"), the character of the aging artist Frenhofer, who is the only pupil of the Flemish painter Mabuse (né Jan Gossart, c. 1478–1532), has been working on a secret painting for years; when, after his disappearance, it is revealed, all that can be seen is a mass of lines and layers of paint. "Barbouiller" (to daub, or slap on paint).

4 Torquato Tasso: see 29 January 1935 [*for* 1936], n. 14.

It is probable that SB was reading *Orlando furioso* (1532) by Italian poet Lodovico Ariosto (1474-1533), which he had read earlier for his Trinity Moderatorship Examination; see TCD, MS 10962 for SB's notes on Ariosto (Everett Frost and Jane Maxwell, "TCD, MS 10962: Machiavelli and Ariosto," *Notes Diverse Holo*, Special issue, *SBT/A* 16 [2006] 31-32). SB refers to Goethe's verse play *Torquato Tasso* (1788-1790) and his *Die Wahlverwandtschaften* (1809; *Elective Affinities*).

"Machine à mots" (word machine).

5 Dermod O'Brien, who was born in Co. Limerick, received the "Freedom of the City" award in Limerick (*The Irish Times* 29 February 1936: 11). Brigid O'Brien married dental surgeon and writer Andrew Ganly (1908-1982) on 19 May 1936.

6 William Robert Fearon (1892-1959) was a Professor of Biochemistry (1934-1959) at Trinity College Dublin as well as a playwright, author of *Parnell of Avondale* (1934).

"Mots" (witticisms).

Sarah Purser.

Dorothy Macardle (1899-1958), historian, playwright, novelist, and drama critic; she was active in the Irish War of Independence and the Irish Civil War and as a journalist with the League of Nations in Geneva. At this time she was writing *The Irish Republic* (1937), a history commissioned by Éamon De Valera, founder and President of Fianna Fáil, and later President of Ireland (1959-1963). Castlecromer is a coal mining town in Co. Kilkenny.

7 Jack B. Yeats's exhibition was not at the Alpine Club Gallery in London, but at the Rembrandt Gallery (also known as the Robert Dunthorne Gallery), 5 Vigo Street, London, opening 19 March 1936 (*The Times* 24 March 1936: 21; Pyle, *Jack B. Yeats: A Catalogue Raisonné of the Oil Paintings*, II, 1098; see 29 January 1935 [*for* 1936], n. 2).

8 Pianist Alfred Cortot performed at the Royal Dublin Society in two programs on 24 February 1936. SB refers to the evening program: Chopin's Twenty-four Preludes, op. 28, and his *Andante Spianato* in G major, op. 22; Debussy's suite *Children's Corner*; and Liszt's *Hungarian Rhapsody* no. 2 in C-sharp minor ("Royal Dublin Society Recital: Cortot Plays to Large Audiences," *The Irish Times* 25 February 1936: 5).

9 Brian Coffey.

British poet, art critic, and essayist Herbert Edward Read (1893-1968) edited *Burlington Magazine* from 1933 to 1939, wrote regularly on art for *The Listener*, and published *The Meaning of Art* (1933) and *Art Now* (1933). He was one of the organizers of the 1936 Surrealist Exhibition in London.

Paul Eluard chose Herbert Read to write the preface for the English translations of his selected poems, *Thorns of Thunder*. Eluard wrote to Reavey on 5 May 1936: "'J'avais pensé à Herbert Read parce que je crois qu'il a une assez large audience en Angleterre. Mais je serais très heureux que vous l'écriviez'" ("I thought of Herbert Read because I think that he has quite a wide audience in England. But I would be very pleased if you would write it") (Paul Eluard, *Oeuvres complètes*, I, ed. Marcelle Dumas and Lucien Scheler, Bibliothèque de la Pléiade [Paris: Gallimard, 1968] 1459).

That Read wrote the introduction troubled more than one of Eluard's translators; Denis Devlin wrote to Thomas McGreevy on 15 March 1936: "I demurred at Read, then I found R.[eavey] had not told Br.[ian] and Sam about Read. Anyhow Br.[ian] & Sam refuse to appear with Read and I too" (TCD MS 8112/9).

GEORGE REAVEY

LONDON

12/3 [1936]   6 Clare St

[Dublin]

Dear George

Geheimrat Roberts is sublime.[1] Would he care to appoint a
time do you think for me to bend over. Poets' bottoms are so very
much the same.

Fail to see the point of holding up Denis's poems. The Fall
will not sell them any more than the Rise.[2]

If I succeed in getting away from here it will not be to London.

Several people, including Mrs Salkeld, asked for my poems in
Combridges, in vain. They told her they had written to you, in vain.[3]

Yours

Sam

ALS; 1 leaf, 1 side; *letterhead* <Royal Hibernian Hotel Co. Ltd., Dublin>; TxU. *Dating*: AN
AH *1935 and ?12/5/36 (pencil)* are incorrect dates; Denis Devlin's collection *Intercessions* was
not published until October 1937, after much delay by Reavey; although SB's *Echo's Bones*
was published in November 1935, in 5 March 1936, SB complains that he has not heard
from Reavey nor anything of *Bones* in months. In 25 March 1936 to McGreevy, SB also
mentions Roberts, which confirms 1936 as the year of this letter.

1 Michael Roberts had written to George Reavey on 12 February 1936 with his
response to *Echo's Bones*. While it is not clear that Reavey sent the letter to SB, he did
send a copy to McGreevy on 8 March 1936, with the note: "Dear Tom. Enclosed critique
of pure reason."

> My dear George,
>   It was most kind of you to send me Samuel Beckett's new book.
>   The poems mostly leave me without any definite impression: I mean, they
> dont impinge poetically. I get some sort of idea of the kind of person S.B. is,
> I learn that he knows Dublin, has read Joyce, and gets a lyrical experience
> from things which used to be thought not to give it. But does he discover new
> and exciting collisions of words, do his rhythms seem dead accurate, does he
> create myth, like [C]oleridge in Christabel, does he make a marmoreal
> moment like Wordsworth in some of the Lucy poems, does he see more in
> things than most people, like Shakespeare, or do some new thing?

I dunno. His [s]ensibility to language (if he claims to do these things) isnt mine. Who is, or will be, his audience? Obviously you see something important in the poems or you wouldn't print 'em. What is their virtue apart from the negative one of not expressing any opinion or moral judgment, and therefore not laying themselves open to irrelevant attacks (c.f. attacks on Eliot & Auden)[.] Is he afraid that he might be silly or sentimental if he talked? Or does he say: there is so little I can be certain of, I will say only that which I know – i.e. the things I see & touch.

Has he a theory of verbal rhetoric?

How, in short, is he to be read, and what is the advantage of reading him?

Yours,

Michael [Roberts]

(TLcc, 1 leaf, 1 side; A. D. Roberts; TLS copy, TCD, MS 8117/9)

"Geheimrat" (Privy Counselor).

2 SB had written to Reavey about the delayed publication of Denis Devlin's poems in the Europa Poets series. Devlin's letter of 15 March 1936 to McGreevy clarifies SB's concern:

My book [...] was to be out last November! Reavey left me without any information whatever for months, then wrote about a fortnight ago saying he had transferred his business to London and that he would not publish me till about the Summer. It makes me mad. Sam advised me to take the affair from him but I can't afford to lose the £20 I have paid him – he would certainly not give that back. He wants just to publish his book of translations of Eluard in time for the Surréaliste exhibition in May next [...] I am bitterly disappointed that my book should be delayed again & again. (TCD, MS 8112/9)

3 Irish poet Blanaid Salkeld (1880–1958) acted with the Abbey Theatre company under the stage name of Nell Byrne and was known in Dublin for her literary salon.

THOMAS McGREEVY

LONDON

25/3/36   Cooldrinagh

[Co. Dublin]

Dear Tom

Thank you for your letter & enclosure, which I greatly liked and appreciated.[1]

It is a long time since I was in the country at this time of year. I have to sleep with my window closed so that the birds wont wake me at 6 in the morning. The days pass pearly, mild and tolerable. I seldom go to town, unless to read Geulincx in Trinity or do a pressing tot or square for Frank when hard beset.[2] I could go into the office any time at a small salary, or so I imagine, though nothing has been said, but shall not. Mary née Manning, touting for Houghton Mifflin, writes for more copies of my works, and urges me to put in for lectures at Harvard, where her father-in-law is a mugwump. Je n'en ferai rien.[3] Murphy goes from bad to worse. I have written to Eisenstein asking him would he take me on at the Moscow State Institute of Cinematography if I went over. I have had no reply. Shall probably go soon whether or no. I read Pudovkin's new book and disliked it.[4]

Maurice Sinclair up for Schol. comes out perhaps once a week for a lesson. I expect him to get in with ease.[5] He has dug out some more Italian books for me, including the Storie Fiorentine, which pleases me greatly; and I found some for myself at Webb's, left in by some little Jez called Boyle or Doyle, lepping fresh from Florence, including the accounts of Dante by the Villani, Boccaccio, Aretino & Manetti brought together in one volume.[6] I have been reading wildly all over the place, Goethe's Iphigenia & then Racine's to remove the taste, Chesterfield, Boccaccio, Fischart, Ariosto & Pope! "Is there no bright reversion in the sky" is lovely. Pope says bright or white, Goethe golden and Hugo vermeil.[7]

Frank had to go down to Galway so I went with him, just two nights & a day there, a pick day, the Corrib shining & foaming, and the light coming through the Connaught walls like filigree. On the way back we stopped at Clonmacnoise, which is indescribably beautiful, as site & monument.[8]

Poor Ruddy is in a bad way again, inextricably worried in countless ways. If things do not improve I fear he will not last long. He lent me a rather dull work by one Greene [*for* Green] called Minuet on 18th century in France & England. Some interesting information about Rétif however. I have asked Brian to get me his Paysan-Paysanne & Monsieur Nicolas, but nothing so far.[9] Devlin I see has gone to Zurich. I lunched with him one day and he was upset by the postponement of his poems, which I think is very bad of Reavey, & wrote & told him as much. I wont appear after a preface by Herbert Reid [*for* Read]. The roubles of Geheimrat Roberts don't interest me. But I was at the Salkeld's last night, when Blanaid told me she had been in 5 or 6 times to Combridge for my poems, & that they had written for them to Reavey as often in vain. He says he has sent out copies for review.[10] I don't believe him. I saw Cecil's poems for the first time and was immensely impressed. He was dithering in bed with a triple concerto and slap up full length verse play.[11]

Was it my old room you occupied at Mrs Frost's? I do not think of it with nostalgia.[12] No news at all from Geoffrey, except indirectly that he is "idyllically" happy. The bewitching Eileen Hennessey has married Ganly the brother of the Ganly who is engaged to Bridget [*for* Brigid] O'Brien. And she also is idyllically happy.[13]

My anus has been giving me a good deal of trouble and I still come to the boil out of my sleep, but otherwise am all right, and nothing matters very much. Frank is going to Llandudno for Easter and I shall try to arrange excursions for mother, to get her away from the house while it is being springcleaned.[14] She keeps well, while her friends and friends' friends die off all round.

    Love

    s/ Sam

TLS; 1 leaf, 1 side; *A env to* Thomas McGreevy Esq, 15 Cheyne Gardens, London S W 3; *pm* 25-3-36, Dublin; TCD, MS 10402/92.

1 McGreevy's enclosure has not been identified.

2 Frank Beckett, Beckett and Medcalf.

3 Mary Manning Howe was neither an agent for SB nor a reader for the Boston company Houghton Mifflin who were her own publishers.

Mary Manning Howe's father-in-law was Mark Anthony DeWolfe Howe (1864–1960), Harvard graduate and Editor of the Alumni publication to 1913, a writer of biography and an Editor of *The Atlantic Monthly*; his wife Fanny Huntington Quincy Howe (1879–1933) was a descendant of Josiah Quincy (1772–1864), President of Harvard from 1829 to 1845 (*The New York Times* 1 March 1967: 43). SB did not apply to Harvard: "Je n'en ferai rien" (I shall do no such thing). In his next letter to McGreevy, 9 April [1936], SB says: "I shall certainly suggest you for Harvard. All one needs apparently is a chit from Joyce, whom the proudest in Mass. adore" (TCD, MS 10402/93).

4 *Murphy* was still incomplete.

SB did not receive a reply to his letter of 2 March 1936 to Eisenstein.

Vsevolod Pudovkin's *Film Acting: A Course of Lectures delivered at the State Institute of Cinematography, Moscow*, tr. Ivor Montagu (London: G. Newnes, 1935).

5 Morris Sinclair met SB to study for the Scholarship examination, among the most valued of awards open to students of Trinity College Dublin. Scholars are members of the Corporation of the College, receive commons and reduced room and tuition fees, and hold their Scholarships through the end of the June quarter of the fifth year following their election or until the awarding of a Master of Arts degree (*Thom's Directory of Ireland for the Year 1936* [Dublin: Alex. Thom and Co., 1936] 482).

6 As well as the books given to him by Cissie Sinclair (see 29 January 1935 [*for* 1936], n. 14), SB had bought others at George Webb's, Dublin booksellers, 5 & 6 Crampton Quay. Francesco Guicciardini (1483–1540) wrote *Storie fiorentine dal 1378 al 1509* (1509; *Florentine Histories*); there was a 1931 edition of this book (Bari: G. Laterza & Figli).

"Jez" (Dublin slang, Jesuit). The former owner of the books may have been Fr. Francis Boyle (20 September 2005, Fergus O'Donoghue SJ, Archivist, The Society of Jesus, Ireland). "Lepping fresh" (Dublin slang, describing freshly caught fish).

Giovanni Villani, Filippo Villani, Giovanni Boccaccio, Leonardo Aretino, and Giannozzo Manetti, *Le vite di Dante*, intro. and notes by G[iuseppe] L[ando] Passerini (Florence: G. C. Sansoni, 1917).

7 Goethe, *Iphigenie auf Tauris* (written as prose in 1779, and reshaped as blank verse, 1786–1787; *Iphigenia in Tauris*); Racine *Iphigénie* (1674). Lord Chesterfield (Philip Dormer Stanhope, 4th Earl of Chesterfield, 1694–1773), noted for his *Letters to his Son*, *Letters to Lord Huntingdon* (1774). SB's specific reading in Boccaccio at this time is not known. German satirist and literary opponent of the counter-reformation Johann Fischart (called Mentzer, 1547–1590) adapted *Gargantua* (as *Geschichtklitterung*, 1575) by Rabelais. For Ariosto: see 5 March 1936, n. 4.

SB cites from "Elegy on an Unfortunate Lady" by Alexander Pope (1688–1744).

8 Lough Corrib, the second largest lake in Ireland, is 24 miles northwest of Galway; the province of Connaught includes Connemara, Lough Corrib, and Clonmacnoise. Stone walls form the boundary of many fields. Clonmacnoise, a monastery founded by St. Ciaran in 548, is one of the most celebrated of Ireland's holy places and was a center of learning in the Middle Ages; the site, on a plain south of Athlone beside the Shannon River, includes a cathedral, eight church ruins, two round towers and three sculpted high crosses.

9 Rudmose-Brown had been recovering from illness, and was not teaching in Trinity College that term.

F[rederick] C[harles] Green, *Minuet: A Critical Survey of French and English Literary Ideas in the Eighteenth Century* (London: J. M. Dent, 1935); the chapter on Nicolas-Edmé Rétif (known as Rétif de la Bretonne, 1734–1806) is entitled "The Leopard's Spots." Rétif wrote *Le Paysan perverti* (1775), *La Paysanne pervertie* (1784), and *Monsieur Nicolas* (1794–1797). Brian Coffey was then in Paris.

10 Denis Devlin was in Zurich with the Irish Department of External Affairs; when he wrote to George Reavey on 19 April 1936 from the Hotel Eden au Lac, Zurich, he noted that he had been abroad a month (TxU).
Devlin's impatience with the postponed publication of *Intercessions* and SB's letter to Reavey: 12 March [1936], n. 2. For SB's distress that Herbert Read had been invited to write the preface for *Thorns of Thunder*: 5 March 1936, n. 9.
The negative response of Michael Roberts to *Echo's Bones*: 12 March 1936, n. 1.
Reavey had sent review copies of *Echo's Bones* to the *Times Literary Supplement, Time and Tide, New Statesman & Nation, English Review, The Criterion, Scrutiny, Life and Letters Today, The Spectator, Dublin Magazine, The Dublin Review, Cambridge Review, The Observer, The Sunday Times* (see Lake, ed., *No Symbols Where None Intended*, 30).

11 Although better known as a painter and engraver, Irish artist Cecil ffrench Salkeld (1904–1969) was also a poet, playwright, and publisher of Gayfield Press; in 1921 he studied art in Kassel under Ewald Dülburg, and worked in Germany through late 1925 (see S. B. Kennedy, "An Incisive Aesthetic," *Irish Arts Review* 21.2 [Summer 2004] 90–95). None of the writing mentioned by SB has been published or identified.

12 Mrs. Frost, SB's landlady in London at 34 Gertrude Street, S.W. 10.

13 Geoffrey Thompson had recently married. In 1936 Eileen Patricia Margaret Hennessey (1904–1983) married William Percy Ganly (1910–1974), a brother of Andrew Ganly, the fiancé of Brigid O'Brien.

14 From 8 to 15 April 1936, Frank Beckett was in Llandudno, Wales (SB to McGreevy, 9 April [1936]; SB to McGreevy, 15 April [1936]; TCD, MS 10402/93 and 94).

ARLAND USSHER

CAPPAGH, CO. WATERFORD

25/3/36   Cooldrinagh

[Co. Dublin]

Alter Freund und Ego

I thank you for your letter, & Heaven that Cappa[gh] has not strained your quality.[1]

Faces set steadfastly towards the Kildare Street Club, Joe & his Old Dutch, Old London, Salvation Army & Sherry Party. He looks as I remember him, Il Traviato, in a world not worth the whetting.[2] All the family had had colds.

Kah[a]n, having found Seville provincial, has now left Gib.[raltar].[3]

Con you know.[4]

Bei Blanaid Salkeld last night. Cecil was vibrating in bed, with triple concerto, full length verse play, from which he read me an extract, in which the phrase occurs: "Love is a gift refused. This is perversion." His mother shewed me his poems, which I liked immensely on rapid perusal, and advised him to submit to TSE. I do not remember ever having seen any of them before.[5] One in which the rime mouth-drouth occurs repeatedly is most remarkable, like the bull let loose among the cows in Eisenstein's General Line, a reference which I confess only occurs to me this moment, in the calm light of March winds caught up like sleeping daffodils.[6] I understand that one evening at the Sinclairs' you paved the way for one of your explosions of reality, I allude of course to your laugh, whereby you are separated not only from the lower but also from the higher forms of natura naturata,[7] with a remark to the effect that the mutual dislike of Cecil & me was the mutual jealousy of two drunks. Now I did not dislike Cecil nor grudge him his dipsos, any more than I liked him or approved it. And I cannot do him the injury of imagining that his feeling for me was any more precise. Now that he has noted on his music paper my address in town and my telephone number in the country, I do not say that an affective tissue is out of the question. But my jealousy and dislike could only be of his talent.[8]

Sean I do not see. Not only is he a veronicist, but he reads Mauriac with relish.[9]

Jack Yeats created in a very short time some magnificent works for his exhibition, now in full Fragonard, at the Rembrandt Galleries, Vigo Street. And the Irish Times accuses reception of his new prose work, The Amaranthers.[10] Walking along Stephen's Green, N., I quoted to him L.D.'s quatrain beginning: "What wonder if the poet . . " It made him feel that death would only change charades into dumbcrambo.[11]

Since my double dry pleurisy at Xmas time I cannot point to any precise affliction, unless it be a sebaceous cyst in my anus, which happily a fart swept away before it became operable.

I am obliged to read in Trinity College Library, as Arnoldus Geulincx is not available elsewhere. I recommend him to you most heartily, especially his <u>Ethica</u>, and above all the second section of the second chapter of the first tractate, where he disquires on <u>his</u> fourth cardinal virtue, Humility, <u>contemptus negativus sui ipsius</u>.[12]

Humiliter, Simpliciter, Fideliter,[13]

s/ Sam

TLS; 1 leaf, 1 side; TxU.

1 "Alter Freund und Ego" (Ger., old friend and; Lat., self). SB plays with "alter" (Ger., old; Lat., other).

Arland Ussher's family home, Cappagh, was 5 miles from Dungarvan and Cappoquin, thirty miles from Waterford, in Co. Waterford.

2 Joe Hone and friends are invoked in SB's allusion to the Kildare Street Club, 1–3 Kildare Street, Dublin. In *Parnell and His Island* (1886), George Moore wrote that the Kildare Street Club represented "all that is respectable" and described it as "a sort of oyster-bed into which all the eldest sons of the landed gentry fall as a matter of course. There they remain spending their days, drinking sherry and cursing Gladstone" (Thomas Pakenham and Valerie Pakenham, eds., *Dublin: A Travellers' Companion* [New York: Atheneum, 1988] 219).

SB uses "Il Traviato" (man misled) to describe Joe Hone. SB's joke is based on the title of the opera *La traviata* by Italian composer Giuseppe Verdi (1813–1901).

3 Robert Isaac Kahan (1895–1951), who was described by Arland Ussher as a "Dublin literary friend" (Arland Ussher to Stanley Cooke-Smith, 15 January 1957, private collection).

4 A. J. ["Con"] Leventhal.

5 "Bei" (Ger., at the home of).

Cecil Salkeld's triple concerto, verse play, and poems have not been identified; T. S. Eliot edited *The Criterion* and was on the staff of Faber and Faber.

6 Eisenstein's film *General Line* used the technique of simultaneous montage to create the "vision of a gigantic stud bull [that] suddenly appears over the cows"

(Rudolf Arnheim, *Film*, tr. L. M. Sieveking and Ian F. D. Morrow [London: Faber and Faber, 1933] 125).

7 "Natura naturata" (created nature, in this case, humanity); see SB's Philosophy Notes taken on Spinoza (TCD, MS 10967/188; quoted by Feldman, *Beckett's Books*, 51).

8 "Town" refers to SB's room at Beckett and Medcalf, 6 Clare Street; "country" to the family home in Foxrock.

9 Seán O'Sullivan was known for his portraits. SB may refer to the image of Christ's face purportedly retained on the cloth offered him by St. Veronica on the journey to Calvary. French Catholic writer François Mauriac (1885–1970).

10 Jack B. Yeats's exhibition: see 5 March 1936, n. 7.
"Accuses reception" (Gallicism for "acknowledges receipt").
Jack B. Yeats's *The Amaranthers* (London: Heinemann, 1936) was announced under "Publications Received" (*The Irish Times* 21 March 1936: 7).

11 "A Thought of Suicide" by John Lyle Donaghy (1902–1942): "What wonder if a poet grow tired / Of a charade unendingly conspired, / If weary mid a mental whoredom / He seek at length a change of boredom" (*Into the Light, and Other Poems* [Dublin: The Cuala Press, 1934] 82).
Dumbcrambo is a game in which one set of players has to guess a word proposed by the other set; after being told what it rhymes with, a designated player acts out the word in dumb show until teammates guess it correctly.

12 Geulincx, *Ethica* (1665), in his *Opera Philosophica*, III, ed. Land (1–271). In the first tractate, the second section of chapter two addresses humility: "Requiritur ergo ad Humilitatem contemptus *negativus* sui ipsius, quo quis de se non laboret, se non curet, nullam sui, prae Amore Rationis, rationem ducat" (29) (Therefore, in the search for humility one must deny oneself, not work for oneself, not care for oneself, [desire] nothing for oneself except the love of reason which leads to reason [tr. AvW]).
See also the analysis of "contemptus negativus sui ipsius" by McMillan and Fehsenfeld, *Beckett in the Theatre*, 53–54.

13 "Humiliter, simpliciter, fideliter" (meekly, simply, truly), from Thomas à Kempis (*De imitatione Christi*, I: v, 10; *The Imitation of Christ*, ed. Rhys, 10, Ingram, 7).

GEORGE REAVEY

LONDON

2/5 [1936]   [Dublin]

[no greeting]

    Afraid I can't manage the Eluard at the moment, as I am up to my eyes in other work.[1]

With regard to translations of mine you are using: will you please insert a note to the effect that they have already appeared in This Quarter of such a date.[2]

What did you do about Transition? Have you heard anything from them since? When is it expected to appear?[3]

Thanks for 2 further Bones. 5 lines of faint damn in Dublin Mag. Sonst nix.[4]

    Sorry I can't oblige.

        Yours

        S.

APCI; 1 leaf, 2 sides; *env to* George Reavey Esq, European Literary Bureau, 30 Red Lion Square, London W.C. 1; *pm* 4-5-36, Dublin; AN AH *pencil*, 2 May '36; TxU. *Dating*: from pm. *Place*: from pm.

1 Reavey had asked SB to translate Paul Eluard's poem from *La Rose publique* (1934), "La Personnalité toujours neuve" (A Personality Always New) for publication in *Thorns of Thunder*, but as Reavey reported to Eluard on 12 May 1936: "J'ai demand[é] Beckett mais il n'a pas eu le temps de la faire si vite non plus" (I asked for Beckett but he did not have the time to do it so quickly either [TxU]). The translation of "La Personnalité toujours neuve" had been begun by British poet David Gascoyne (1916–2001), but neither he nor Reavey was satisfied with it (Lake, *No Symbols Where None Intended*, 32–34). In *Thorns of Thunder* only a fragment, the last 13 of the 126 lines of the poem, was published; Gascoyne was indicated as translator (55).

SB's "other work" is *Murphy*; as he wrote to McGreevy, 9 April [1936]: "Murphy wont move for me at all. I get held up over the absurdest difficulties of detail. But I sit before it most day of most days" (TCD, MS 10402/93).

2 In *Thorns of Thunder*, Reavey reprinted some of SB's translations of Eluard's poems that were first published in *This Quarter* 5.1 (September 1932) 86–98: "Lady Love," "The Invention," "Scarcely Disfigured," "Scene," "All-Proof: Universe-Solitude," and "Out of Sight in the Direction of My Body" (1, 8, 36, 37–38, 40–41, 42). Reavey's editorial foreword acknowledges *This Quarter*, and SB's translations are initialed in *Thorns of Thunder*.

3 Three poems from *Echo's Bones*, "Malacoda," "Enueg 2," and "Dortmunder," were reprinted in *transition* 24 (June 1936) 8–10.

4 *Echo's Bones* was reviewed with other books of poetry by D. C. S.-T., *Dublin Magazine* 11.2 (April–June 1936) 77–80: "I am somewhat bewildered by Samuel Beckett. Bewildered, but impressed." The reviewer quotes from SB's poem "The Vulture," and writes:

> That poem and "Enueg I" and "Enueg II" are real to me. The flight from emotion in "Enueg I" is a very real thing. Mr. Beckett finds himself, I think, in those poems. And perhaps in "Alba." Others, because of his idiom, - a

very private, personal idiom – I am not at all sure of. There is a confusion of accidental phenomena that leaves me adrift. Adrift; but, in spite of myself, impressed. (78)

"Sonst nix" (Ger. colloq., nothing else).

GEORGE REAVEY

LONDON

6/5/36 6 Clare Street

Dublin

Dear George

In your first communication re Jolas you did not say anything about their wanting "from 6 to 10" pages in addition to the poems.[1] Looking through my essuie-cul de réserve I find an article of about 2000 words on the censorship in Ireland, commissioned about this time 2 years ago by the Bookman & still inédit. They can have that, always on the same understanding, that they pay me for it. I shall forward it to you in a day or two, mis au jour.[2]

I regret very much about the Eluard. It would take a lot of time, & if I do not finish what I am doing within the next few days, I never shall.[3]

Thank you very much for your proffer of sanctuary. I look forward to availing myself of it.

I trust you have no objection to noting after my Eluard translations their provenance & date. I would be gratified.[4]

Yours

[no signature]

TL; 1 leaf, 1 side; TxU.

1 With regard to the poems: see 2 May 1936, n. 3. On 9 April 1936, SB wrote to McGreevy that he had told Reavey that *transition* could publish any of the poems from *Echo's Bones* (TCD, MS 10402/93).

Although the letter from Maria Jolas* (1895–1987) to Reavey has not been found, it is clear from other correspondence between Eugene and Maria Jolas during March 1936 that the short prose piece solicited from Beckett through Reavey for *transition* was a "prose sketch" to appear among the collection of "paramyths," this being the theme of the next issue of *transition* (Lois More Overbeck and Martha Dow Fehsenfeld, "In Defense of the Integral Text," *Notes Diverse Holo*, Special issue, *SBT/A* 16 [2006] 354–355).

2 In August 1934, *The Bookman* had commissioned SB to write an article on censorship in Ireland. SB wrote "Censorship in the Saorstat," but it was not published by *The Bookman* (see 8 September 1934, n. 9).

Although SB refers to the "inédit" (unpublished) essay as an "essuie-cul de réserve" (spare bumf), he revised it, "mis au jour" (brought up to date), to include mention of the Irish censorship list of 30 September 1935, on which his *More Pricks Than Kicks* appeared as number 465.

3 The Eluard translation: see 2 May 1936, n. 1.
SB was trying to finish the manuscript of *Murphy*.

4 Reavey republished some of SB's Eluard translations from *This Quarter* (see 2 May 1936, n. 2), and acknowledged their previous publication in his editorial foreword (Eluard, *Thorns of Thunder*, vii).

THOMAS McGREEVY
LONDON

7/5/36   Cooldrinagh
                                          Foxrock
                                          Co. Dublin.

Dear Tom

I had a line from Mary Manning this morning in which she says that she is writing to you and will speak to Howe père. With a little management the job should come off. Would you object to asking Joyce for a chit? It appears they adore him at Harvard.[1]

Jack Yeats brought up the subject of the picture, & though I was too broke even to make an offer at the time, I since borrowed £10 which he accepted as a first instalment, the remaining £20 to follow God knows when, & have now got the picture. Mother & Frank can't resist it much after the Sligo watercolour.

It is nice to have Morning on one's wall that is always morning, and a setting out without the coming home.[2]

Transition have guaranteed payment for the poems & want "6 pages" in addition. I put the old censorship article au jour & sent it. The difficulty of my own book having been banned since I wrote the article I got over by giving my registered number, with all becoming modesty.[3]

All Forlorn is now giving his appreciation of indigenous furniture at the Spring Show, in the Irish Times.[4]

I read The Amaranthers which he gave me & would like to review it for the Dublin Mag. except that I don't like asking favours of Seumas. I agree it is a lovely book, its latebra all bright. L'Ile des Paradisiers.[5]

Reavey asked me to translate another poem for his Eluard sacrifice, but I declined. I have been & am very busy with Murphy, which gets near its first end at least at last.[6] It will be very short, thanks be to God.

I had a long letter from Coffey some time ago, most of which I could not see, let alone read.[7]

So far as I can see I shall be here till the autumn at least, & indeed have no inclination to leave the light & the sea for a city.[8] We seem to have settled down at home to a kind of reciprocal gentleness & reserve that is the best we can do. [...]

I was talking to a custodian in the Gallery, who said they would all die for Furlong with the greatest of pleasure. His diligence does not yet appear in the public rooms, but it appears he has gone through the cellar with a fine comb, painted under the roof somewhere, acquired a large Correggio (David & Goliath), itches to rehang the Dutch rooms, & intends to remove the Jordaens altogether. A new landscape by de Vries is up, very correct & dull.[9]

The Academy opening seems to have been wonderful, with Higgins behind the scenes debating with someone before the microphone & Montgomery comparing the beautiful pictures there to the ugly ones he has to look at in Molesworth St.[10]

I have seen absolutely no one for the past fortnight, unless Maurice Sinclair came out. He is laid out after Schol. but seems to have done well.[11] A Paris gallery wrote to Harry Sinclair about the painting of Salvado, enclosing photographs. Perhaps they would like to present one to the Municipal. Sinclair says he has found a Boucher, in the voice of one who hears a cuckoo on Xmas Eve.[12]

Love ever

Sam

ALS; 1 leaf, 4 sides; *letterhead*; *env to* Thomas McGreevy Esq, 15 Cheyne Gardens, London S. W. 3; *pm* 9-5-36, Dublin; TCD, MS 10402/94.

1 SB had written to Mary Manning Howe on behalf of McGreevy: "asking her to substitute you for me in her Harvard scheme & giving her your address. I know she will do all she can & that you will hear from her soon" (15 April [1936], TCD, MS 10402/94). Mary Manning's father-in-law, Mark Anthony DeWolfe Howe: see 25 March 1936, n. 3.

From 1933 to 1935 there were three senior honors theses on Joyce written by Harvard students. Among attributes of "The Harvard Man" was that he "knows his James Joyce" ("Genus Harvardiensis," *Harvard Crimson* 29 January 1930: 2).

2 SB refers to *A Morning* by Jack B. Yeats (Pyle 482; NGI 4628). On Yeats's Sligo watercolor *Corner Boys*: 5 May 1935, n. 4. The allusion to Thomas à Kempis: 10 March [1935], n. 3.

3 For information about the poems and *transition*'s request for additional material from SB: SB to Reavey, 6 May 1936, n. 1 and n. 3.

"Censorship in the Saorstat" was augmented with a paragraph about the "618 books and 11 periodicals" listed as banned by the Register "as on 30th September 1935"; SB closes the essay by writing: "My own registered number is 465, number four hundred and sixty-five, if I may presume to say so. / We now feed our pigs on sugarbeet pulp. It is all the same to them" (Beckett, *Disjecta*, 87–88).

4 Sean O'Faolain wrote "Irish Modes in Furniture: Novel Development of Folk-Motif," *The Irish Times* 7 May 1936: 6.

5 SB did ask Seumas O'Sullivan if he could review Yeats's novel *The Amaranthers* for *Dublin Magazine* (see 13 May [1936]).

L'Île des Paradisiers (The Isle of Birds of Paradise); reference not found.

6 Eluard, *Thorns of Thunder*.

7 Brian Coffey's handwriting was unusually small. His letter to SB has not been found.

8 SB had mentioned the possibility of travel to Germany in early summer in his letter to McGreevy of 29 January [1936].

9 George Furlong had been Director of the National Gallery of Ireland since 1 October 1935.

SB refers to *David Slaying Goliath* (NGI 980) by Italian artist Orazio Gentileschi (1563–1639), not Antonio Allegri Correggio (c. 1494–1534), which had been purchased for the National Gallery of Ireland in 1936. The paintings in the collection of the National Gallery of Ireland by Flemish artist Jacob Jordaens (1593–1678) were *St. Peter Finding the Tribute Money* (NGI 38), *The Church Triumphant* (NGI 46), and *The Supper at Emmaus* (NGI 57). In 1934 the National Gallery of Ireland acquired *Landscape with Figures* (NGI 972) by Dutch painter Roelof Jansz de Vries (1631–1681).

10 The Royal Academy of Arts opened its 168th exhibition on 4 May 1936. James Montgomery, whose law offices were at 13 South Molesworth Street and whose office as Official Film Censor was at 34 South Molesworth Street, probably compared the pictures in the exhibition to those at the Leinster Studio at 3 South Molesworth Street.

11 Morris Sinclair and the Scholarship examination: 25 March 1936, n. 5.

12 Catalan painter, ceramicist, and stained-glass artist Jacinto Salvado (1892–1983) studied in Barcelona, Marseille, and Paris, and was active in Paris in the 1920s; a friend of Derain and Picasso, he was depicted by Picasso in *Portrait of Jacinto Salvado as Harlequin* (Basel Künstmuseum, G 1967.9).

Harry Sinclair: Friday [c. 18 to 25 July 1930], n. 4. SB mentions the Municipal Gallery of Modern Art (now the Dublin City Gallery The Hugh Lane), perhaps remembering that McGreevy had arranged for Lurçat to make such a gift.

French painter François Boucher (1703–1770).

SEUMAS O'SULLIVAN

DUBLIN

13/5/[1936]   [Dublin]

[no greeting]

Many thanks for book. It is good of you to let me do it.[1]

Fear I have no poems at the moment, but if anything turns up between now & then I shall send it to you.

Next Sunday I am not free but perhaps that day week.

  Yours

  SB

APCI; 1 leaf, 2 sides; *env to* Editor, DUBLIN MAGAZINE, 2 Crow Street, DUBLIN; *pm* 14-5-36, Dublin; TCD, MS 4630–49/1346. *Dating and place*: from pm and Beckett to McGreevy, 23 May 1936.

  1 O'Sullivan sent SB a copy of *The Amaranthers* by Jack Yeats for review in *Dublin Magazine* (see 7 May 1936).

THOMAS McGREEVY

LONDON

23/5 [1936]   Cooldrinagh [Co. Dublin]

Dear Tom

  I was very glad to hear from JBY of the proposed work.[1] He showed me some photographs of his pictures. They do not lose so much as I expected, not even the later ones. I feel the book will give you little trouble & much pleasure. And to have something specific in hand will make you feel better. Tell me more about it in your next letter.

  Did I tell you I got the Amaranthers from S.' OS. [*for* S. O'S.] by return of post, with an exceedingly amiable note asking for poems & why I did not go & see them. He allows me only 500 words. How can one be anything but dense with so little space?[2]

  I have set Murphy on fire at last & 2000 words should polish it off. It is really a most unsavoury & not very honest work. I am not sure that Chatto's are so unlikely to take it. I shall send copies to Charles & Parsons simultaneously. I would be glad to be saved the trouble of hawking it round.[3]

I met Bobby Childers, younger son of Erskine, married to Christabel, younger daughter of Mrs Manning, for the first time the other night. He looks after the Irish Press machinery. Talks in a high urgent English voice about [? volts, amts], & the political arena. Attends turf-cutting competitions & lives in Bushy Park Rd. next to Luce.[4] We shall never be in Delphi together.

No news at all from Geoffrey, & his brother Alan has had none for a long time. A friend called Stewart, who shared rooms with me for a time in Trinity, just home with wife from a Cisindian province, writes from Putney. Will he be seeing me at the Scholars' Dinner! Leventhal, a decade behind, or in front, is also looking forward to getting drunk gratis. I prefer to stay sober at my own expense.[5]

I bathed twice at 40 Foot this week, in spite of the east wind. The only other was a reverend Father McGrath, red all over with ingrowing semen & exposure, whom I used to meet with father in the Turkish Baths. The last time I saw him was nearly three years ago, at our front door, calling to console.[6]

Charles writes he is going to London to see doctors. He does not say what is wrong.[7]

I keep seeing the water & woods of Elsheimer & the round backs of the sheep of Geertgen. Bryan's Dictionary of Painters, published at £7.17.6, is going in Green's for £4.17.6. If I had the money I would buy it.[8]

Write soon
    Love ever
        Sam

ALS; 1 leaf, 2 sides; *env to* Thomas McGreevy Esq, 15 Cheyne Gardens, London S.W. 3; *pm* 23 May 1936, Dublin; TCD, MS 10402/96.

1 McGreevy had proposed to do a study of the painting of Jack B. Yeats.

2 SB's review was published as "An Imaginative Work!" *Dublin Magazine* 11.3 (July–September 1936) 80–81.

3 Charles Prentice, who had proved such a sympathetic reader of Beckett's work, was no longer with Chatto and Windus (see 8 September 1935, n. 4); Ian Parsons was in Prentice's position with the firm.

4 Robert Alden Childers (known as Bobby, 1911–1996), whose wife was Christabel Manning (1910–1988), the daughter of Susan Manning (c. 1874–1960); Bobby was the son of Irish nationalist Robert Erskine Childers (known as Erskine, 1870–1922), and his older brother was Erskine Hamilton Childers (also known as Erskine, 1905–1974), President of Ireland (1973–1974).

Bobby and Christabel Childers lived at 12 Bushy Park Road; they were immediate neighbors of A. A. Luce, 13 Bushy Park Road, Rathgar. SB wrote "<voice> English voice."

5 Geoffrey and his brother, Alan H. Thompson (1906–1974), were both friends of SB's from school days at Portora Royal School in Enniskillen, and from Trinity College Dublin. Alan Thompson was appointed Assistant Physician and Pathologist to the Richmond Hospital in 1932.

Gerald Pakenham Stewart (1906–1998) shared rooms with SB at TCD in 1926 when they were both Scholars of the House; Stewart became an Assistant Commissioner in the Indian Civil Service, Assam, where he met and married his wife Elisabeth Scott (1912–1971). Putney is in southwest London.

Con Leventhal (TCD BA Mod. in French and German, 1920) was elected to Schol. in 1916.

6 The 40 Foot is the name given to the nude bathing place, at that time for men only, in Sandycove, Co. Dublin; it was named for the 40th Regiment of Foot.

It is not known to which Father McGrath SB refers. William Beckett died on 26 June 1933.

7 Charles Prentice.

8 SB recalls paintings by Elsheimer and Geertgen in the National Gallery, London (see 20 February 1935, n. 6 and n. 7). Michael Bryan (1757–1821) prepared *Bryan's Dictionary of Painters and Engravers*, 1816; it was revised and enlarged in five volumes by George C. Williamson (London: G. Bell, 1903–1905; 4th edn., 1926–1934).

THOMAS McGREEVY

LONDON

9/6/36   Foxrock

[Co. Dublin]

Dear Tom

It's a long time since I heard from you. I hope you had no serious trouble with the bronchitis. Write very soon & tell me how you are.

I have finished <u>Murphy</u>, meaning I have put down last words of first version. Now I have to go through it again. It reads something horrid. One should have a continuity-girl, like régisseurs.[1]

I wrote review of <u>Amaranthers</u> for Seumas. Only 500 words. I was tired & it is bad. I compared him with Ariosto.[2]

Maurice Sinclair failed Schol. by a few marks. First man out.[3] And about 5 times as intelligent as the best of them that got it.

I wrote a fierce stinger to Reavey last night. I was really furious. He wrote saying my censorship article had arrived too late for <u>transition</u>, & that mention was made of it in the first of Mrs Jolas's letters that he sent me. He did no such thing. He quoted an extract from her letter, in which there was no request for a prose contribution but only for permission to use some poems from <u>Echo's Bones</u>. He sent me her second letter, reiterating request for prose contribution, whereupon I sent the article by return of post.[4] Then he sends me prospectus of the Eluard poems. <u>Thorns of Thunder</u> !!! I object to my name appearing near such an abomination. I object to Mr Read's bloody preface. I object to the suggestion conveyed by the blurb that I am performing at the new Burlington BAVE. I was not consulted on any of these matters. Blast his little Antrim Road Soul.[5]

There must be something the matter with Charles.[6] I have written two letters without reply. The last I heard from him he spoke of London & doctors.

I was at Seumas O'Sullivan's about 3 weeks ago. He mentioned he had heard from you, & that he would very much like to publish some of your criticism. Curtis was there, organising the review of his new history book. Bethel & Sophy were there, he slugger than ever, she very nice. I went with Cissie.[7]

Susan Manning says that Mary says that her pa-in-law says that he has not heard from you.[8] Did you not write? I hope you are not letting it slide.

I have been bathing & am frightfully tired this evening. The fellow I shared rooms with in College, & was in school with, & who now runs some Garden of Oriss[a] in Assam for the I.C.S., came out for lunch to-day, with his wife, cat-eyed, New Zealand & d'accent.[9] They all became horribly hearty. "I am not sure" he said, "but I think I am a pragmatist."

While I was bathing a filthy little mongrel got into a profound coït with our old bitch, now in the height of heat. I, & the act, were surrounded by a ring of guffawing boys, naked, urging me not to interfere, nor spoil sport, etc. I had to carry the two of them, without assistance, into the sea, & hold them under till the glans contracted. Then I had to bring her down to a dog abortionist on the upper Dargle Road, & pay 7/6 to have her washed out.[10] And still she may drop a litter of monsters. And she is ten, fat & decrepit.

Furlong has weeded out the Italian room & improved. The Pordenone has been cleaned & brought down to a visible height & is excellent, as I always suspected. The new Gentileschi (£ 600) is awful. There is an excellent Guercino Joseph & Child that I had not seen before.[11]

I met a man from the I.T. I knew, one day by chance in the street, & he said no copy of the Bones had reached them for review. Though I gave Reavey the name of who to send it to. I sent him a copy, but no review so far. Same man told me that Hillis was married, had been for months. Now perhaps he can return my Princesse de Clèves.[12]

Have you done anything at the Yeats book? [? Rute] Tierney: "Difference between Eliot & Yeats; one says something beautifully, the other nothing very beautifully."[13]

I owe Coffey a letter for months. Haven't the energy to go & find out in the library what he wants to know.[14]

Not a word from Geoffrey, for about 3 months.[15]

Went down one day to Newcastle to see Boss Sinclair. Fear there is no improvement. Hackett called on him.[16]

Did you see a copy of "Ireland To-day", the latest rag. O'Faolain & Co. Dentist John Dowling on JBY is exquisite. Says his plumbing is execrable.[17]

Love ever

Sam

ALS; 2 leaves, 4 sides; *env to* Thomas McGreevy Esq, 15 Cheyne Gardens, LONDON S.W. 3.; *pm* 10 June 1936, Dublin; TCD, MS 10402/98.

1 "Régisseurs" (assistants to film or theatre director).

2 In his review of *The Amaranthers* by Jack B. Yeats, SB writes: "The irony is Ariostesque [...] The discontinuity is Ariostesque" ("An Imaginative Work!" 80).

3 Morris Sinclair was top of the list of those whose marks fell below the cut-off point in this competitive examination for Scholarship (Schol.).

4 Although Reavey had communicated *transition*'s interest in SB's poems, there is no evidence that Reavey had conveyed *transition*'s initial request for a prose piece, specifically for a "paramyth" (see 6 May 1936, n. 1); SB responded immediately to the "reiterated" request by sending his piece on censorship.

5 The prospectus for *Thorns of Thunder* has not been found, but may have included Herbert Read's preface to the book which was published in conjunction with the International Surrealist Exhibition at the New Burlington Galleries, London (11 June – 4 July 1936). Read delivered a lecture, "Art and the Unconscious," on 19 June 1936 as part of the events of the exhibition; he also led a discussion organized by the Artists' International Association on 23 June 1936 (*International Surrealist Bulletin* 4 [September 1936] 2, 7–13).

Paul Eluard gave a lecture on 24 June 1936, "La Poésie surréaliste," and on 26 June he read poems by himself and other French surrealists. The announcement for the latter indicated: "English versions by Samuel Beckett, Denis Devlin, David Gascoyne, George Reavey." SB may have been expected to read his translations at this time, as Gateau writes of the "séance de lecture de poèmes avec traduction immédiate, dont certaines par le jeune Samuel Beckett" (a program of readings of poems with immediate translation, some by the young Samuel Beckett) (Jean-Charles Gateau, *Paul Eluard, ou, le Frère voyant, 1895–1952* [Paris: Editions Robert Laffont, 1988] 235).

"Bave" (slobber).

George Reavey's office was in Red Lion Square, London WC 1; while he had grown up in Russia and in Western Europe, the Reavey family home in Belfast was "Stramore" in Chichester Park, off the Antrim Road, a middle-class professional and largely Protestant part of Belfast ("George Reavey – Preliminary Draft of *Memoirs*," 2, and SB to Reavey, 21 August [1936], TxU). SB angrily associates the Antrim Road with smugness and self-interest.

6 Charles Prentice. Ian Parsons wrote to Richard Aldington, 2 June 1936: "I dined with Charles last week and he told me he was still far from cured of his Greek bug" (UoR, MS 2444 CW letterbook 174/282).

7 Seumas O'Sullivan and Estella Solomons lived at "The Grange," in Rathfarnham, Co. Dublin.

Edmund Curtis, Professor of Modern Irish at the University of Dublin, published *A History of Ireland* (1936), which was reviewed by P. S. O'H., *Dublin Magazine* 11.3 (July–September 1936), 60–62.

Bethel Jacobs and his wife Sophy (or Sophie) were visiting Dublin from England. SB's aunt, Cissie Sinclair Beckett, was a close friend of Estella Solomons.

8 A possible position at Harvard through Mary Manning Howe's family: 25 March 1936, n. 3.

9 Gerald Pakenham Stewart (see 23 May [1936], n. 5). SB's notion of "some Garden of Oriss[a] in Assam" is groundless, according to Stewart (22 March 1993). "D'accent" (in her accent).

10 The one vet listed on Dargle Road, Bray, is Miss Hilda Bisset, MRCVS (*Thom's Directory of Ireland for the year 1936*, 1543).

11 George Furlong, Director of the National Gallery of Ireland. SB refers to: *A Count of Ferrara* (NGI 88) by Giovanni Antonio de' Sacchis Pordenone (c. 1483–1539); *David Slaying Goliath* by Gentileschi; and *St. Joseph with the Christ Child* (NGI 192) by Guercino (né Giovanni Francesco Barbieri, 1591–1666).

12 SB refers to Lionel Fleming (1904–1974) who wrote for *The Irish Times* from 1935 through 1936 (see 27 June 1936). Fleming later worked for the BBC in London and abroad; when he returned to Dublin, he wrote on foreign affairs for *The Irish Times*. W. Alec Newman (1905–1972), then Asssistant Editor for *The Irish Times*, was "in charge of the book page" (Lionel Fleming, *Head or Harp* [London: Barrie and Rockliff, 1965] 168). Newman later became Editor of the paper from 1954 to 1961. Both Fleming and Newman had been at Trinity College Dublin with SB.

If indeed SB sent Reavey a letter with the name of the person to whom a review copy should be sent, this letter has not been found; *The Irish Times* was not among those newspapers to which Reavey initially sent review copies of *Echo's Bones* (TxU, George Reavey, Europa Press).

Arthur Hillis married Lillian Mary Francis (1907–1990) in 1936; from 1942 to 1951 she was a Programme Assistant and later Assistant in the Spanish Section, South European Service of the BBC.

La Princesse de Clèves (1678; *The Princess of Cleves*) by Mme de La Fayette (Marie-Madeleine Pioche de La Vergne, Comtesse de La Fayette, 1634–1693).

13 Michael Tierney (1894–1975), Professor of Greek from 1932 to 1947 at University College Dublin, and its President from 1947 to 1964. It is not known whether Tierney said or wrote this.

14 Brian Coffey's research request is not known.

15 Geoffrey Thompson.

16 Boss Sinclair's treatment for tuberculosis: see 22 September 1935, n. 12. Francis Hackett (1883–1962), Irish-born American author and journalist.

17 *Ireland To-day* (June 1936 – March 1938) was edited by Frank O'Connor (pseud. of Michael O'Donovan, 1909–1966); contributors included Sean O'Faolain. The review of the Royal Hibernian Academy exhibition said of Jack B. Yeats: "Now we demand of a painter, or of a plumber, that when he begins a work he should have some idea of what the result will be. Jack Yeats' method does not allow of this" (John Dowling, "Art: The Academy," *Ireland To-Day* 1.1 [June 1936] 61); Dowling was a dentist.

GEORGE REAVEY

LONDON

20 June 36   [Dublin]

George Reavey[1] ELEMENT COMBUSTIBLE REVOLTANT[2]

The verb is S'EMMERDER[3]
lu et approuvé s/ Man Ray[4]
et Comment! s/ Jocelyn Herbert[5]
Pardit [*for* Pardi][6]
Humphrey Jennings[7]

TPC with ANS; 1 leaf, 2 sides; T *address, to* George Reavey Esq., 30 Red Lion Square, London W.C.1; *pm* 20-6-36, Dun Laoghaire; TxU. *Dating:* from pm. *Place:* from pm. All names are signatures in black ink except as otherwise indicated.

1 SB had sent an unsigned typed card to Reavey to correct his spelling (the shaded portions of the card above). Reavey, as well as other members of a group, gathered at one of the events related to the 1936 Surrealist Exhibition in London, then added their comments and signatures.

2 "ELEMENT COMBUSTIBLE REVOLTANT" (Revolting combustible element), written in black ink around the postmark.

3 "S'EMMERDER" (get bored). SB typed this on the original card to correct an error in Reavey's letter to him (not found) that responded to SB's "stinger" of 9 June 1936 (see also SB to McGreevy, 27 June 1936).

4 "Lu et approuvé" (read and approved), written in blue ink. Man Ray (né Emmanuel Radnitzky, 1890–1976), American painter, photographer, film-maker, and graphic artist; Ray was a participant in the Surrealist Exhibition.

5 "Et comment" (and how). Jocelyn Herbert (1917–2003), at this time a student at the London Studio Theatre.

6 "Pardi" (of course), in another hand.

7 British documentary film-maker, poet, and painter Humphrey Jennings (1907–1950) was an organizer of the Surrealist Exhibition; he signed his name across the bottom of the card.

THOMAS McGREEVY
LONDON

27/6/36   Foxrock
                                                     [Co. Dublin]

Dear Tom

Murphy is finished & I shall send off three copies on Monday. One to you, one to Parsons & one to Charles.[1] I could do more work on it but do not intend to. All the more grievous losses have been cut. It has been hard work the past month & I am very tired, of it & words generally. I don't want you to bother with it. Just throw your eye over & let me have it back. Write in say a fortnight. I want to send a copy to Simon [&] Schuster.[2]

I suppose you know about Charles being operated on for appendicitis. He seemed to get well in record time & went back to Greenock last Friday.[3]

Reavey wrote angrily in reply to my angry letter. He is (1) A liar (2) A Clumsy Sophist (3) An illiterate. He spells emmerder en merder. Another abscess burst, & none too soon.[4]

Last time at JBY's, fortnight ago, Dermod O'Brien was there with Tonks. Said O'Brien, pointing to a plane of light: "That's a lovely waterfall". Yeats had the answer pat: "If waterfalls looked like nothing but waterfalls & planes of light like nothing but planes of light – , etc." Tonks was beautiful, decrepit & pleasant, very willowy & Honeish, full of George Moore, Rowlandson & Sickert.[5]

I was in the Gallery the following Monday & found a surprisingly good Suffolk landscape by Gainsborough, rather Booth [*for* Both] in quality, & the tree formula less prominent. Also a pleasant Wilsonish landscape by a contemporary Smith, of whom I knew nothing. The usual exertion before Poussin[']s Peleus & Thetis. Ran into Yeats, who explained the Poussin blue, & wondered what colour Géricault's horse had once been. He was very James Joyceish before the appalling new Gentileschi: "First nude I ever saw with dirt in his toenails."[6]

Young Sinclair is off to Paris on Monday, with return ticket, £8 & an address in the Place de la Bastille (100 fr. per month!) & introduction to Hughes sculptor.[7] I met Shephard [*for* Sheppard] for the first time one day at Howth. He said Sleator was his model for the G.P.O. Cuchulain, & that he fainted with his head so sunken.[8]

I have been bathing at 40 Foot every day, sometimes twice, & am in very much better health than a year ago. No news at all from Geoffrey. Mary née Manning arrives here from Boston to-morrow. Did you have any reply from Harvard?[9]

I find it impossible to correspond with Coffey. Have seen nothing at all of Devlin. Fleming of the Irish Times, when he asked for Echo's Bones, said: "A good review or none." That was 3 weeks ago. No review has appeared.[10]

I see by to-day[']s Irish Times that "Dublin is reading" Fires of Beltane according to one bookseller. I saw a dull review in last Sunday Times. Hope it sells well.[11]

Had a statement of accounts from Chattos. 2 <u>More Pricks</u> sold during the past year, & 20 odd <u>Prousts</u>.[12]

Mother is up & down, mainly the latter round about now, 3<u>rd</u> anniversary. The Roes were always very strong on anniversaries. See little of Frank. He has gone to Treard[d]ur Bay, near Holyhead, for the weekend.[13]

The next move is to get away. It is not going to be easy. I owe £36. And now that the book is finished I shall be very surprised if Chattos do not turn it down.

    Love

    Sam

ALS; 2 leaves, 3 sides; *env to* Thomas McGreevy Esq, 15 Cheyne Gardens, Chelsea, London S W 3; *pm* 27-6-36, Dublin; TCD, MS 10402/99.

1 SB sent *Murphy* to Ian Parsons, Editor of Chatto and Windus, on 29 June 1936 (UoR, MS 2444 CW 59/9). Charles Prentice had retired from Chatto and Windus, and SB would have sent it to him personally.

2 Simon and Schuster had shown interest in SB's work in 1935; see 8 September 1935 and 13 October 1935.

3 Charles Prentice underwent surgery in a London clinic on 19 June and recovered sufficiently to leave for his home in Greenock, Scotland, on 25 June (Ian Parsons to Richard Aldington, 17 June 1936, UoR MS 2444 letterbook 174/466;) Ian Parsons to Richard Aldington, 25 June 1936, UoR MS 2444 letterbook 175/56-57).

4 Neither SB's angry letter nor Reavey's angry response has been found. "Emmerder" (bore).

5 Dermod O'Brien, President of the Royal Hibernian Academy.
British physician and artist Henry Tonks (1862-1937) taught drawing at the Slade School London from 1892 to 1930, and was an official War artist in World War I. SB compares him to Joseph Hone, both in demeanor and for his friendship with George Moore, whose biography Hone was then completing. Tonks was in Ireland on holiday, staying, at Hone's suggestion, in Co. Mayo, and visiting Dublin (see Hone, *The Life of Henry Tonks* [London: William Heinemann, 1939] 291, 303-305).
British artist Thomas Rowlandson (c. 1756-1827), best known for his drawings and cartoons. German-born British artist Walter Richard Sickert (1860-1942), who was associated with the Fitzroy Group and the Camden Town Group (1905-1913).

6 SB compares *A View of Suffolk* (NGI 191) by Thomas Gainsborough (1727-1788) to the painting by Jan Both (c. 1618-1652) that was then in the National Gallery of Ireland, *An Italian Landscape* (NGI 179). At this time, the National Gallery of Ireland

had two paintings called *A Landscape* (NGI 383 and NGI 740) attributed to British painter George Smith (c. 1714–1776), although now only NGI 383 retains that attribution; in the early 1980s, NGI 740 was attributed to Irish painter William Ashford (c. 1746–1824). SB compares Smith's painting to the style of landscapist Richard Wilson.

The Wedding of Peleus & Thetis (NGI 814) was the title given to the painting of Nicolas Poussin up to "about 1960" when the title was changed to *Acis and Galatea* (see also Thomas MacGreevy, *Nicolas Poussin* [Dublin: The Dolmen Press, 1960] 14–16; Sylvain Laveissière, *Le Classicisme français: Masterpieces of Seventeenth Century Painting, a loan exhibition from the Louvre and French regional museums at the National Gallery of Ireland, 30 April – 9 June 1985*, tr. Kim-Mai Mooney and Raymond Keaveney [Dublin: The Gallery, 1985] 61).

In his study *Nicolas Poussin*, McGreevy discusses the "luminous blue" in this painting (14).

A Horse (NGI 828) by French painter Jean-Louis-André-Théodore Géricault (1791–1824) is described as a grey stallion (*National Gallery of Ireland: Catalogue of Oil Pictures in the General Collection* [Dublin: The Stationery Office, 1932] 41); it is now referred to as "after Géricault."

Acquisition of Gentileschi's *David Slaying Goliath*: 7 May 1936, n. 9.

7   Morris Sinclair was going to Paris with an introduction to Irish-born sculptor John Hughes (1865–1941), who had lived and worked abroad for many years.

8   The best-known piece by Irish sculptor Oliver Sheppard (1865–1941) was *The Death of Cuchulain* (c. 1911–1912), chosen as a memorial to the 1916 Rising, and placed in the General Post Office, Dublin. Irish painter James Sleator (1889–1950) was the model for the head.

9   Geoffrey Thompson.
Harvard position in relation to Mary Manning Howe: 25 March 1936, n. 3, and 7 May 1936, n. 1.

10   Brian Coffey. Denis Devlin.
Lionel Fleming: 9 June 1936, n. 12. A mention of SB's *Echo's Bones* occurs in the column signed by M. C., "Transition, A Very Modern Magazine, The Artistic Left Wing" (*The Irish Times* 25 July 1936: 7): "Incidentally, the present issue has a local interest. Mr. Samuel Beckett reproduces three poems from his latest book, 'Echo's Bones.' They are 'difficult,' but not more so than the poems of many modern authors, and in no way to be compared with the extravagances of some of the other contributors."

11   Geraldine Cummins's novel *Fires of Beltane* (1936) was reviewed by Doreen Wallace: "Ireland in Fiction: More Stories about 'The Troubles'" (*Sunday Times* 21 June 1936: 9). Her novel was also listed as a best-selling book in the 20 and 27 June 1936 column, "What Ireland is Reading" (*The Irish Times*: 7).

12   Chatto and Windus sent a statement of accounts dated 1 April 1935 to 31 March 1936 showing sales of thirty copies of *Proust* (twenty-eight in Britain, two as export) and two copies of *More Pricks Than Kicks* (InU, John Calder, Ltd., Authors' Correspondence, Box 1/52).

13   The third anniversary of William Beckett's death was 26 June.
Trearddur Bay, Anglesey, Wales.

1. William Beckett, Samuel Beckett's father

2. Samuel Beckett's uncle Edward Price Roe with his mother Maria Jones
Roe Beckett (known as May)

3. William Abraham Sinclair
(known as Boss)

4. Frances Beckett Sinclair (known
as Fanny, and as Cissie)

5. Ruth Margaret Sinclair
(known as Peggy)

6. Morris Sinclair (known in the
family as Sunny)

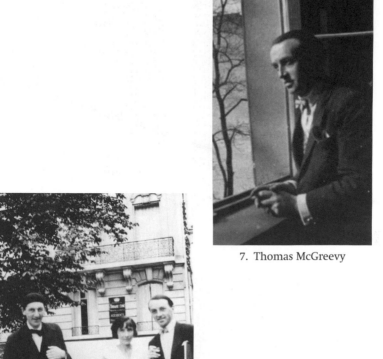

7. Thomas McGreevy

8. Alan and Belinda Atkinson Duncan,
   with Thomas McGreevy

9. Geoffrey Thompson

10. Samuel Beckett

11. Abraham Jacob Leventhal
(known as Con)

12. Percival Arland Ussher

13. Ethna MacCarthy
by Seán O'Sullivan

14. Mary Manning Howe

15. Nuala Costello

16. Ilse Lynn Schneider

17. Geer and Lisl van Velde, Gwynedd Reavey, and, lower right,
George Reavey

IAN PARSONS

CHATTO AND WINDUS, LONDON

June 29th 1936   6 Clare Street

                                          DUBLIN

Dear Parsons

Just a scribble to cover Ms. I am sending you by this post. Not short stories this time, I am glad to say.[1]

Will you let me have Chatto's decision as soon as conveniently possible? I need not say how glad I would be to be published again by you.[2]

I hope you keep well.

Very Sincerely

Sam. Beckett

ALS; 1 leaf, 1 side; notations in AH; UoR, MS 2444 CW 59/9.

1 Submission of SB's novel *Murphy*.

2 Chatto and Windus had published *Proust* (1931) and *More Pricks Than Kicks* (1934).

THOMAS McGREEVY

LONDON

July 7th 1936   Foxrock

                                          [Co. Dublin]

Dear Tom

I need not tell you I was delighted with your letter. I was afraid you would not like it much at all. I find the people all so hateful myself, even Celia, that to have you find them lovable surprises and delights me.[1]

The point you raise is one that I have given a good deal of thought to. Very early on, when the mortuary and Round Pond scenes were in my mind as the necessary end, I saw the difficulty and danger of so much following Murphy's own "end".[2] There seemed 2 ways out. One was to let the death have its head in a frank climax and the rest be definitely epilogue (by some such means as you suggest. I thought for example of putting the game of chess there in a section by itself.) And the other, which I chose and tried to act on, was to keep the death subdued and go on as coolly and finish as briefly as possible. I chose this because it seemed to me to consist better with the treatment of Murphy throughout, with the mixture of compassion, patience, mockery and "tat twam asi" that I seemed to have directed on him throughout, with the sympathy going so far and no further (then losing patience) as in the short statement of his mind's fantasy of itself.[3] There seemed to me always the risk of taking him too seriously and separating him too sharply from the others. As it is I do not think the mistake (Aliosha mistake) has been altogether avoided.[4] A rapturous recapitulation of his experience following its "end" would seem to me exactly the sort of promotion that I want to avoid; and an ironical one is I hope superfluous. I find the mistake in the mortuary scene, which I meant to make more rapid but which got out of hand in the dialogue. Perhaps it is saved from anticlimax by presence of M. all through. I felt myself he was liable to recur in his grotesque person until he was literally one with the dust. And if the reader feels something similar it is what I want. The last section is just the length and speed I hoped, but the actual end doesn't satisfy me very well.

Thanks a thousand times for reading it and writing[.] I value your opinion more than anybody's.

I had a curt acknowledgement of MS. from Parsons and so far nothing further.[5] It would save trouble if they took it on, but in many ways I would be glad if they did not. I sent my own copy to Simon & Schuster. Charles, back in Greenock now and due in London soon again, wrote very amiably about it, suggesting Frere Reeves if Chattos turned it down.[6]

Mary Manning Mark de Wolfe Howe is here now and sad about your not getting Harvard job. She knows nothing of Farmer except that his application arrived before yours. She has a play going on at St. Martins in September.[7] I meet [for met] Eileen Hennessey Ganly last night with her bull and found her unpleasant.[8] I went out to Lachan (Glencree valley) to see Lilian Donaghy who is living in a cottage (Joe Campbell's) with Charlie Gilmore, brother of George. She has Donaghy's 2 sons there and a daughter by Gilmore. He is sehr simpatisch [for sympathisch], a gipsy, on the dole.[9] Lyle is in Merrion Avenue the last I heard, with one of Leventhal's single beds. I was looking through his Into the Light, full of good things in what he believes to be the Celtic-Aristocratic-Classical channel, and an absurd preface, with words like puissant and affiliations with Higgins.[10] I was down at the mailboat last Monday week meeting Frank returning from Anglesea and WB stalked off with his bodyguard, Lennox, Dolly, Gogarty, Walter Starkie, O'Connor, Hayes, Higgins, all twined together. I went last Sunday to see Ruddy and met Hackett and his Danish wife, colour of urine and a devout gardener. Her Hans Christian Andersen I have not had the pleasure of, but understand she makes him burst into sobs every third page. Ruddy's mother was a Dane – Ru[d]mose – and Andersen read his fairy tales to her. Hackett was dressed from head to foot in white twill and was amusing. He is now at work on a historical novel about Anne Boleyn from the Butler end. His Green Line [for Green Lion] was banned.[11]

Had a letter from Geoffrey at last. He seems worked to death at the Maudsley and Bunty has chicken pox. He wonders at me, for having stayed here so long.[12] Mother's brother from Notts (big game, angling[,] Wimbledon, arthritis, tobacco plantations, Mombassa [*for* Mombasa] and no money) arrives with his second wife (styles of furniture and the historical sense) in a fortnight's time, to stay a fortnight, and until that is over I can't get away, even if I had the money.[13]

I am reading Grillparzer, but not the best of him (Hero & Leander), only the Jason-Medea trilogy, of which third part at least is magnificent.[14] Do you know Barry's portrait of Dr Johnson or where it is? Looked at in reproduction beside the various Reynoldses it is very impressive, the mad terrified face that I feel was the truth a very little below the adipose.[15]

I am very glad Fires of Beltane seems to go well. I saw it favourably reviewed by O[']Faolain I think in that new rag Ireland Today.[16]

Frank doesn't seem in very good form and Mother remains alertly bereaved, which is not meant to be an unkind description of a behaviour she cannot help. She read Esther Waters with loathing.[17]

I wrote to Brian, with none of the information he wanted.[18] Reavey has not send [sic] me my copy of the Eluard. I presume he avails himself of the words that passed to enjoy an extra free copy. I am glad you liked my translations. I have not seen them for years. Does the one you mention begin "She is standing on my lids"? I have not even got copies of them.[19]

I saw a cautious review by Denis of O'Connor's poems, in I. Today, accomplished & noncommittal.[20] Himself I have not seen for a long time.

God love thee, write again very soon and all my thanks for writing what is so nice to read, pace Mr Church, to hell with Mr Church.[21]

> Yours ever
> s/ Sam

TLS; 2 leaves, 3 sides; *A env* to Thomas McGreevy Esq, 15 Cheyne Gardens, London S. W. 3; *pm* 7-7-36, Dublin; TCD, MS 10402/100. *Previous publication*: the paragraph that begins "The point you raise [...]" is published in Bair, *Samuel Beckett*, 228–229, and Beckett, *Disjecta*, 102 (however, both give the date as 17 July 1936).

1 McGreevy's letter responding to the manuscript of *Murphy* has not been found. Celia is the heroine of *Murphy*.

2 After Murphy's death, the scene in the mortuary (*Murphy*, 254–276) is followed by a scene at the Round Pond (*Murphy*, 276–282) (see 8 September 1935 and 22 September 1935).

3 Murphy's chess game with Mr. Endon is part of chapter 11 (*Murphy*, 240–248).
"Tat twam asi" (Sanskrit, that thou art) is a phrase drawn from the *Chandogya Upanishad* (c. 600 BC) and taken up by Arthur Schopenhauer in the essay "Character"; Schopenhauer differentiates between two ways of "regarding the world": the first understands all others as "not ourselves," and the second, which he calls the "*Tat-twam-asi – this-is-thyself* principle," understands all others as "identical with ourselves" (*On Human Nature: Essays (partly Posthumous) in Ethics and Politics*, selected and tr. by Thomas Bailey Saunders [London: George Allen and Unwin, 1897; rpt. 1926] 95).
SB refers to chapter 6 of *Murphy* in which "Murphy's mind pictured itself as a large hollow sphere" (107–113).

4 SB refers to Alyosha in Dostoevsky's *The Brothers Karamazov*.

5 *Murphy* was acknowledged by Ian Parsons, Chatto and Windus, on 1 July 1936 (UoR, MS 2444 CW letterbook 175/114).

6 Simon and Schuster, New York publishers.
Charles Prentice's letter to SB has not been found. However, on 8 January 1937, Harold Raymond wrote to English poet and critic Richard Thomas Church (1893–1972):
> As I thought, Samuel Beckett's novel was very carefully read both by Ian Parsons and by my old partner, Charles Prentice, both of whom had always been especially interested in his work. They both felt full of respect for this novel but came to the conclusion that because of Beckett's frequent abstruse allusions and his generally somewhat recondite manner of writing, we might not fare any better with it than we did with his short stories. (UoR, MS 2444 CW letterbook 178/689)

Alexander Stuart Frere-Reeves (known to some as Frere, 1892–1984) was with the London publisher William Heinemann from 1923 to 1961, serving as its Chairman from 1945 to 1961.

7 Mary Manning de Wolfe Howe and the position at Harvard: see 25 March 1936, n. 3. Albert John Farmer (1894–1976) of the University of Bordeaux taught at Harvard during the first half of the academic year 1936–1937 on a French exchange program; from 1945 to 1964 he was Professor of English at the Sorbonne, University of Paris (Patrice Donoghue, Harvard University Archives, 7 November 1991).
Mary Manning did not have a play produced at the St. Martin's Theatre in London in the 1936–1937 season. However, her play *Youth's the Season ...?* opened in London at the Westminster Theatre on 5 October 1937 as part of the Longford Players Irish Season.

8 William and Eileen Hennessey Ganly.

9 Lilian Donaghy (also Lilyan, née Roberts, n.d.) had been married to Irish poet, John Lyle Donaghy. She and Charlie Gilmore (1905–1987), who, like his brother George Gilmore (1898–1985), was an Irish Nationalist, lived in Lachan, in the Glencree Valley near Enniskerry, Co. Wicklow; their cottage belonged to Irish poet and scholar, Joseph Campbell (1879–1944).
"Sehr sympathisch" (very nice).

10 John Lyle Donaghy was staying in Dublin with A. J. Leventhal, whose address at this time is not known. SB writes Merrion Avenue, but there was none in Dublin (only Merrion Lane, Place, Square, Road, Row, and Street, and, near Blackrock, Mt. Merrion Avenue).

Donaghy discusses the "poetic tradition in Ireland" in his preface to *Into the Light*, saying that poets who had studied the classics created an Irish poetry that had affinities with Latin and Greek poetry: "By pure scholarship, the Irish tradition became essentially Gaelic classical" and "characteristically aristocratic" [i–ii]. Donaghy concludes:

> F. R. Higgins is the most important of these poets who have in mind, once more, Irish poetry, integrally classical and aristocratic; national because they are national; imaginative, achieving the universal through the particular; individual, concrete, humanly rich, learned in craft and proudly licensed, strict, puissant. My own work is also in this tradition. ([iii])

11 Both Frank Beckett and W. B. Yeats returned to Ireland on the *Hibernia*. Associates from the Abbey Theatre who greeted Yeats on arrival were Lennox and Dolly Robinson, Oliver St. John Gogarty, Walter Starkie, Frank O'Connor, Dr. Richard Hayes (1882–1958), F. R. Higgins, and Ernest Blythe (1889–1975) ("Mr. W. B. Yeats at Home Again: Welcomed at Dun Laoghaire," *The Irish Times* 30 June 1936: 9; this article identifies Dr. Richard Hayes as Liam Hayes).

On 4 July SB met Francis Hackett and his wife Signe Toksvig (1891–1983) at the home of Rudmose-Brown. Toksvig, who wrote *The Life of Hans Christian Andersen* (1934), had edited his *Fairy Tales and Stories* (1928). Toksvig's garden at Killadreenan House is often a subject in *Signe Toksvig's Irish Diaries 1926–1937*, ed. Lis Pihl (1994).

Hackett wrote historical fiction, *Henry the Eighth* (1928) and *Francis the First* (1934); he began his novel on Anne Boleyn (1507–1536) from the perspective of one of her cousins, James Butler, later 9th Earl of Ormond (c. 1496–1546), whom Anne had declined to marry (see *Queen Anne Boleyn, a novel* [New York: Doubleday Doran, 1939] 44–45, 478, 485). Hackett's novel *The Green Lion* (1936) considers the last campaign of Irish Nationalist leader Charles Stewart Parnell (1846–1891) to regain popular support after he was deposed by his party over issues of adultery and divorce.

12 Geoffrey Thompson's wife, Ursula (known as Bunty), had contracted chickenpox.

13 May Beckett's brother, Edward Roe, married his second wife, Florence Bentley (n.d.), in 1917. Having lived in the British protectorate Nyasaland (from independence in 1964 known as Malawi) in East Africa, Roe would have been familiar with the Indian Ocean city of Mombasa, Kenya.

14 Austrian writer Franz Grillparzer (1791–1872) wrote *Des Meeres und der Liebe Wellen* (1831; *The Waves of the Sea and of Love*, also translated as *Hero and Leander*) and *Das Goldene Vliess* (1821; *The Golden Fleece*), a dramatic trilogy of the Jason-Medea story, the third part of which was *Medea*.

15 The unfinished sketch in oils of a portrait, *Dr. Samuel Johnson* (NPG 1185), was made by James Barry (1741-1806) for *The Distribution of Premiums*, a mural in the series "The Progress of Human Culture" (The Royal Society of Arts, London). Joshua Reynolds (1723-1792) painted several portraits of Johnson: National Portrait Gallery (1597); Knole, Sevenoaks, Kent (258); Tate Britain (887); Harvard University (HNA50).

16 Geraldine Cummins's novel *Fires of Beltane* was reviewed by Sean O'Faolain ("Fiction," *Ireland To-Day* 1.2 [July 1936] 70-72).

17 George Moore, *Esther Waters* (1894).

18 Brian Coffey (see 9 June 1936, n. 14).

19 Eluard, *Thorns of Thunder*. With regard to the words that passed: 9 June 1936, 20 June 1936, and 27 June 1936; for SB's translations see 2 May 1936, n. 2. "She is standing on my lids" is the first line of SB's translation of Eluard's "L'Amoureuse" (*Thorns of Thunder*, 1).

20 Frank O'Connor's collection of poems *Three Old Brothers* (1936) was reviewed by Denis Devlin, "Another Irish Poet," *Ireland To-Day* 1.2 (July 1936) 77-79.

21 SB may be referring to Henry Church, a patron of McGreevy's, who had not cared for SB's *More Pricks Than Kicks*, which he had read on McGreevy's advice; Church had commented, "when a friend recommends a friend, je me méfie. I mean we are always inclined to magnify a friend's talent, to bask in the sun of his genius; that we are all apt to practice nepotism" (Henry Church to Thomas McGreevy, 16 December 1935, TCD, MS 8119/19). "Je me méfie" (I am on my guard).

SEUMAS O'SULLIVAN

DUBLIN

[c. mid-July 1936]   [Dublin]

Two Poems by Samuel Beckett[1]

1.

why were you not simply what I despaired for
an occasion of wordshed[2]
is it better to abort than be barren

The hours after you are gone are so leaden
they will always start dragging too soon
the grapples clawing blindly the bed of want

355

bringing up the bones the old loves
sockets once filled with eyes like yours
all always better too soon than never [3]
the black want splashing their faces
saying again nine days never floated the loved
nor nine months
nor nine lives

2.

saying again
if you do not teach me I shall not learn
saying again there is a last
even of last times
last times of begging
last times of loving
of knowing not knowing pretending
a last even of last times of saying
if you do not love me I shall not be loved
if I do not love you I shall not love

the churn of old words in the heart again
love love love thud of the old plunger
pestling the unalterable
whey of words

terrified again of not loving
of loving and not you
of being unloved and not by you
of knowing not knowing pretending
pretending

I and all the others that will love you
if they love you[4]

[OS]

TMS; 2 leaves, 2 sides; initialed by Seumas O'Sullivan and on each page <Sam. Beckett>; TCD, MS 4630–49/3333. *Dating*: mid-July 1936; a copy of poems was sent to McGreevy [15 July 1936]; SB writes in his letter to McGreevy, 17 July [1936]: "Forgive the poems [...] I send [sic] poems to Seumas O'S."

1 The Trinity College Dublin catalogue for the Seumas O'Sullivan collection indicates the heading for this MS to be: "2 poems, 'title added by S. O'Sullivan; printed as one poem Cascando.'" The manuscript was published as one poem under the title "Cascando" in *Dublin Magazine*, 11.4 (October–December 1936) 3–4.

2 In the poem as published in *Dublin Magazine*, these first two lines are omitted.

3 In the poem as published in *Dublin Magazine*, this line was printed as "all always is it better too soon than never." It is unknown if SB made this change.

4 SB wrote to McGreevy on 26 July 1936 that he had added another line to the end of this poem: "Unless they love you." This line appears in the poem as published in *Dublin Magazine*, in a separate section, numbered 3:

3.

unless they love you.

IAN PARSONS

CHATTO AND WINDUS, LONDON

17/7/36 6 Clare Street
Dublin

My dear Parsons

Thank you for your letter, also MS. Believe me, I understand your position very well.[1]

Yours very sincerely
Sam. Beckett

ALS; 1 leaf, 1 side; UoR, MS 2444 CW 59/9.

1 Ian Parsons wrote to SB on 15 July 1936:

Dear Beckett,
We have read "Murphy" with very great pleasure and I wish I could write and say that we felt able to publish it. But truth to tell the novel racket has reached such a pass today that a book, such as yours, which makes real demands on the reader's intelligence and general knowledge has less chance than ever of gaining a hearing, and I'm afraid we've reluctantly had to decide that times aren't good enough generally to allow us to take it on despite the state of the market.

I hope I need not say how extremely sorry I am to have to give you this decision. We should so very much have liked to have another work of yours on our list. But you will, I'm sure, understand our position and I hope not think too hardly of us. And no doubt you'll be able to find another publisher who thinks as highly of "Murphy" as we do, but who takes a less gloomy view of the outlook for books of this kind. At any rate I sincerely hope so.

With kindest regards, and renewed regrets,

Yours sincerely,

[Ian Parsons]

P.S. I am posting the MS. back to you under separate registered cover.

(UoR, MS 2444 CW letterbook 175/318)

THOMAS McGREEVY

LONDON

17/7 [1936]   Foxrock [Co. Dublin]

Dear Tom

Forgive the poems.[1]

Just heard from Parsons. Honeyed regrets. So am sending M. to Frere-Reeves to-day. No news at all from Simon & Schuster, not even acknowledgement of receipt.[2]

——— ————— ——— —— —— ——— ———

Ran into Devlin one evening in town. Noticed no change. He has I think a bad poem in Dublin Mag. My own review of JBY seems dishonest & surfait. However it pleased him & that is all that matters.[3]

Brian Coffey has just rung up. I shall be very glad to see him again –[4]

The new acquisitions in the Gallery, on view on screen in the mortuary department, 2 Bazzani & a Jan Lys, are really appalling. Not quite so bad perhaps as the Gentileschi, but sublime waste of money.[5] As though it were not precisely an excess of that dreary third rate that spoils the Gallery & swamps the Treasures. The Perugino has gone to London to be cleaned (the big one). It was overcleaned long ago I thought.[6] The last time I was there I couldn't rest before anything. It was fuller than I ever saw it, Americans mostly, & a sprinkling of the surprised without coats or umbrellas. I send [*for* sent] the poems to Seumas O'S.[7]

I was at Yeats's Saturday. He had just finished a new picture, a man sitting reading in a fuchsia hedge, with storm clearing over sea. Lovely passages but unsatisfactory I found generally. Something almost like artificial excitement. How is the book going. He told me you were getting on with it.[8]

Maurice Sinclair got back from Paris yesterday. I think he saw Joyce but I was only talking to him for a second.[9]

My copy of the Eluard came, duly signed by author & all available translators. He does come through after a fashion, the frailty & nervousness. But no attempt seems to have been made to translate the pauses. Like Beethoven played strictly to time.[10] God love thee. Write soon

EVER

Sam

ALS; 1 leaf, 2 sides; *env to* Thomas McGreevy Esq, 15 Cheyne Gardens, London SW 3; *pm* 17-7-36, Dublin; TCD, MS 10402/102. *Dating:* from pm.

1 SB had sent the two poems, later made one as "Cascando," to McGreevy on 15 July 1936 (TCD MS 10402/101).

2 SB refers to Ian Parsons's letter of 15 July 1936 rejecting *Murphy*. It was Charles Prentice's suggestion to try Frere-Reeves, if Chatto and Windus refused *Murphy* (see 7 July 1936). Beckett sent *Murphy* to Simon and Schuster before 7 July 1936 (see 27 June and 7 July 1936).

3 Denis Devlin's poem "The Investiture of D'Artagnan" appeared in *Dublin Magazine* 11.3 (July–September 1936) 4.

SB's review of Jack B. Yeats's novel *The Amaranthers:* "An Imaginative Work!" 80–81. SB refers disparagingly to his own review in an Anglicism, as if "surfait" (overrated) meant "overdone."

4 Brian Coffey was in Dublin on summer holidays.

5 In 1936, the National Gallery of Ireland purchased *Our Lord Meets His Mother* (NGI 982) and *The Descent from the Cross* (NGI 983) by Giuseppe Bazzani (1690–1769) and *The Vision of St. Jerome* (NGI 981) by Johann Liss (also Lys. c. 1595–1631). Gentileschi, *David and Goliath:* see 7 May 1936, n. 9.

6 Perugino's *Pietà* (NGI 942) had been purchased for the National Gallery in 1931 (see 20 December 1931, n. 5). Sebastian Ysepp (n.d.), Restorer to the Künsthistorische

Museum in Vienna, submitted his evaluation on 6 June 1936; it indicated that the Perugino had been "spoiled through early restoration – particularly through unnecessary overpainting, darkened retouching, cracks in the paint and dangerous blisters" (NGI Archives). The painting was sent to Vienna for reconditioning, via London for X-ray photo, in July 1936 (Homan Potterton, "Introduction," *National Gallery of Ireland: Illustrated Summary Catalogue of Paintings* xxxv–xxxvi; the 23 June 1936 Agenda for the Board of Governors and Guardians meeting on 1 July 1936 [NGI Archives]).

7 See SB to Seumas O'Sullivan, [mid-July 1936].

8 Jack B. Yeats, *In Tír na nÓg* (Gaelic, The Land of the Young) (private collection, Pyle 491), pictures a young man reading beneath a hedge (Pyle, *Jack B. Yeats: A Catalogue Raisonné of the Oil Paintings*, I, 446; III, 209).

McGreevy had begun work on the essay published (under MacGreevy) as *Jack B. Yeats: An Appreciation and an Interpretation* (Dublin: Victor Waddington Publications, 1945).

9 Morris Sinclair's meeting with Joyce: 26 July [1936] and n. 9.

10 Eluard's poems in *Thorns of Thunder* were translated by SB, Denis Devlin, David Gascoyne, Eugene Jolas, Man Ray, George Reavey, and Ruthven Todd. It is not known who had signed SB's copy.

THOMAS McGREEVY

LONDON

July 26th [1936]   Foxrock

[Co. Dublin]

Dear Tom

Many thanks for your letter & remarks on the poems. I think you are probably right about the opening. I was afraid you would find the second half sloppy & am relieved that you did not. I have added a line to the end: "Unless they love you."[1]

Had a note from Frere acknowledging MS. He was good enough to remember our brief meeting Place du Panthéon, & to regret we had not met in London. They won't touch it. What disquiets me is absence of news from Simon and Schuster. Not even an acknowledgement of MS though they have had plenty of time to do so.[2]

About meeting Dolly & Lennox, I feel it would probably go quite well with her, but not at all with him –[3]

Frank left yesterday for a motoring holiday in Northern Ireland, & will be away 10 days. He is 34 to-day. Mother is the picture of misery, one of her periodical attacks. I brought her last Tuesday to a donkey show at Goff's Stables, & found Jack Yeats there, making sketches for a picture.[4] Mother had not met him before. She remarked how sad & ill he looked.

Was in the Gallery yesterday. Another new work, vaguely Austrian primitive, a panel painted both sides, on one Veronica's Sudarium, on the other the 12 in a strange scene.[5] The magnificent glass case in which it is exposed in centre of floor of Brouwer's room, cost £50. Good old Furlong. He hopes to take all the Dutch pictures down to the print room, & extend the Italians into the Dutch rooms, in single line hanging.[6] Yesterday I was looking at the drawings & found an Elsheimer, to my joy. And a Mantegna sketch for the Triumph of Caesar.[7]

The walk with Brian was ambling and incoherent. He takes refuge, or perhaps seeks clarity for himself, in Thomist terms that I do not follow. Perhaps the problem is common, the problems, but stated so differently that no headway is possible. He talked attractively of Spinoza.[8]

Boss Sinclair is being turned out of Newcastle, where they say they can do nothing more to help him. He is perhaps better than when he went in 14 months ago. He returns to his family next Tuesday week. Sonny saw Joyce for about 5 minutes only. He was very pris & rather cold from what I can make out. His face lit up at your name, but not at mine. What can only have been Léon arrived while Sonny was there.[9]

Had a sad friendly note from Hester.[10] I can imagine her bewildered & resentful.

Am reading Guarini's Pastor Fido again. Lancret to Tasso's Watteau except that the technique is magnificent. Then I hope to settle down to Faust.[11]

Newman has been very plausible on the symphonic ballet. Is he a bad logician on purpose, because he knows how much more persuasive sophistry is? And how appallingly English the sense of humour. Surely a Wagnerite must admire <u>Choreartium</u> for all the wrong reasons. And to extend a protest against symphony for balletic purposes to a protest against lyric for Lieder purposes surely is nonsense.[12]

Leventhal is reviewing <u>Thorns of Thunder</u> for Seumas, so I may get a kind word at last. I got my copy & wince at my translations. I extended the little finger of reconciliation to G.R. & had it cordially wrung. Transition has appeared with 3 Bones, but no payment.[13]

The news of Geoffrey is good, & he hopes soon to escape from hospital psychiatry to psychoanalysis. Ursula has been considerably ill but is well again now.[14]

I can't get away till September at earliest, as Mother's brother & his wife are coming in the middle of August to stay a fortnight.[15] I think the next little bit of excitement is flying. I hope I am not too old to take it up seriously, nor too stupid about machines to qualify as a commercial pilot. I do not feel like spending the rest of my life writing books that no one will read. It is not as though I wanted to write them.

Charles is in London again & expects to have to stay there for about two months for post-operative treatment. He still has some bug in his gut.[16]

God love thee & write very soon

    Ever

      Sam

Schöne Grüsse to Hester[17]

ALS; 2 leaves, 4 sides; *env to* Thomas McGreevy Esq, 15 Cheyne Gardens, London SW 3; *pm* 26-7-36, Dublin; TCD, MS 10402/103.

1 The opening lines, "why were you not simply what I despaired for / an occasion of wordshed" were omitted when published as "Cascando," in *Dublin Magazine*, 3–4, but restored in subsequent publications. For the added line: [c. mid-July 1936], n. 4.

2 SB had sent *Murphy* to A. S. Frere-Reeves on 17 July 1936. Simon and Schuster: 7 July 1936, n. 6.

3 Dolly and Lennox Robinson.

4 Frank Beckett.
Goff's Stables, dealing in bloodstock sales, celebrated their fiftieth anniversary in 1936. The donkey show was on 21 July. Jack Yeats wrote to McGreevy on 23 July also mentioning his meeting with SB and May Beckett (TCD, MS 8105/138).

5 The two Austrian primitives purchased in 1936 were on separate, and not necessarily associated, panels: *The Apostles Bidding Farewell* (NGI 978) ascribed to the Styrian School (fifteenth century) may have been a central panel; *The Crucifixion* (NGI 979) by the Salzburg School (c. 1425) may have been a side panel. The National Gallery of Ireland purchased both from the Gallerie St. Lucas in Vienna in February 1936. A case for the Austrian primitives was authorized at the 29 June 1936 meeting of the Board of Governors and Guardians of the National Gallery of Ireland, where it was suggested that they be displayed together; no cost is noted (NGI Archives). The case was placed in the room where the paintings by Adriaen Brouwer were hung.

6 George Furlong refurbished the galleries, moved Dutch paintings to Room I, and expanded the Italian Gallery for single-line hanging (for images of this change, see Fionnuala Croke, "Introduction to the Exhibition: Part I," in Fionnuala Croke, ed., *Samuel Beckett: A Passion for Paintings* [Dublin: National Gallery of Ireland, 2006] 12–13, 16; for a discussion of the completed rehanging, see Elizabeth Curran, "The National Gallery Revisited," *The Bell* 2.5 [August 1941] 65–72).

7 In 1936 the gouache was attributed to Adam Elsheimer as *Wooded Landscape at Dusk*, and later to the Dutch draughtsman, etcher, and painter Gerrit van Battem (1636–1684) as *A Wooded Landscape at Night*. Now it is attributed to Dutch draughtsman and etcher Pieter de With (fl. 1650–1660) as *A Wooded Landscape after Sunset* (NGI 2101) (Hans Möhle, "Eine bisher unbekannte Landschaftsgouache von Adam Elsheimer," *Zeitschrift des Deutschen Vereins für Kunstwissenschaft* 19.34 (1965) 192–196; Adriaan Waiboer, *Northern Nocturnes: Nightscapes in the Age of Rembrandt* [Dublin: National Gallery of Ireland, 2005] 82).
The ink drawing, "The Corselet Bearers" (from *The Triumph of Julius Caesar*, NGI 2187) is now considered to be after, not by, Andrea Mantegna (c. 1430–1506).

8 Brian Coffey was studying the work of French philosopher Jacques Maritain who was a Thomist (advocating the revival of the ideas of the Dominican theologian Thomas Aquinas [1225–1274]).

9 Boss Sinclair did not leave the sanatorium.
Morris Sinclair had a letter of introduction from his uncle Harry Sinclair to Joyce; Joyce was unable to read the handwriting and asked Morris to do so: "It proved highly

embarrassing telling him what a charming fellow I was. Standing, we chatted about this and that, whereupon, having asked me where I was staying (the Catholic hostelry visibly irked him), he said he would be in touch and that I must come to the apartment one evening. I left, and there was no further communication" (Morris Sinclair, 9 May 1991).

"Pris" (preoccupied).

10 Hester Dowden's sister, Hilda Dowden, died 17 July 1936.

11 Giovanni Battista Guarini (1538–1612) was the author of *Il pastor fido* (1589; *Pastor Fido*), which emulates Tasso's *L' Aminta* (see 8 October 1932 SB to McGreevy, n. 10). SB compares Guarini to Tasso by analogy to a comparison of the French painter Nicolas Lancret (1690–1743) to Jean-Antoine Watteau.

SB intended to read Goethe's *Faust* in the German, *Der Tragödie erster Teil* (1808) and *Der Tragödie zweiter Teil* (1832).

12 In his column "The World of Music" in *The Sunday Times*, Ernest Newman wrote a series of articles (5 July to 26 July 1936) on "Symphonies and Ballets" in which he takes issue with the argument raised against symphonic ballet by Richard Capell (1885–1954) in "Symphonic Ballets: Massine's Little Miscalculation of the Eloquence of Legs," *Daily Telegraph* 17 June 1936: 9; the first of Newman's articles was answered by J. A. Westrup, "'Choreartium' Again: A Footnote to Controversy," *Daily Telegraph* 18 July 1936: 7.

Choreartium is a symphonic ballet in four parts choreographed by Massine to Johannes Brahms's Symphony no. 4 in E minor, op. 98. In his first essay, Newman addressed the argument that, by attempting to combine poetry and music, Richard Wagner violated the essential nature of both ("Symphonies and Ballets: I. Clearing the Ground" 5 July 1936: 7). Enthusiasts of Wagner held the opposite view, which extends, in SB's discussion, to *Choreartium*. In his third article in the series, Newman argued against the proposition that "nothing that is complete should be, can be, added to ... ," saying that this "seems to wipe off the slate ... all the great song writers from Schubert to Wolf; for if poems such as those of Goethe and Heine are not complete in themselves, and would have been [in]complete to the end of time had no composer ever added music to them, words seem to me to have no meaning." ("III. A Further Clearing of the Ground" 19 July 1936: 7).

13 A. J. Leventhal wrote an article, not a review, to introduce surrealism as a movement ("Surrealism or Literary Psycho-Therapy," *Dublin Magazine* 11.4 [October–December 1936] 66–73). In this essay he reprinted with admiration SB's translation of Eluard's poem, "Lady Love" (Eluard, *Thorns of Thunder*, 1; rpt. 72).

No letter to or from George Reavey regarding a reconciliation has been found.

"Malacoda," "Enueg 2," and "Dortmunder" were reprinted from *Echo's Bones* in *transition* 24 (June 1936) 8–10.

14 The Thompsons moved to 71 Harley Street in 1936, where Geoffrey had a consulting room on the ground floor. Ursula Thompson had been ill with chickenpox.

15 Edward and Florence Roe.

16 Charles Prentice.

17 "Schöne Grüsse" (warm greetings). Hester Dowden.

THOMAS McGREEVY
LONDON

Aug 7<u>th</u> 1936   Cooldrinagh.
                                        Foxrock.
                                        Co. Dublin.

Dear Tom

Heard from Frere-Reeves yesterday, a curt rejection. "On commercial grounds we could not justify it in our list." And of course what other grounds of justification could there be. I think now of dumping the work on Reavey.[1] I neither trust him nor like him, but know no other agent. Truck direct with publishers is one of the few avoidable degradations.

I have not seen the <u>transition</u> in which my poems appeared, nor heard what poems they used, nor received the payment guaranteed by Mme. Jolas.[2]

Seumas O'Sullivan has accepted the poem for Dublin Mag.[3]

I had a pleasant bathe & conversation with Brian last Sunday. I brought him back here for lunch, showed him the Yeats picture & lent him some Minotaures.

Geoffrey's mother died suddenly last Monday and he is over for the funeral. I have not seen him yet but shall do so to-day. His brother Alan is also ill, I think rather seriously.[4]

I was with Jack Yeats Saturday afternoon. I saw the man in the fuchsia picture again & liked it much better than the first time. He has an excellent new small picture also, shelling peas (green) in Moore St. It was one of my instantive afternoons and one can't peer in 18 without all kinds of perturbations to make sure the coast is clear. He inquired was there anything wrong with me, and advised 5 miles walking daily, whether it was mental or physical. I thought, the ice is breaking at last. He was very pleased with Read's very favourable review in the Spectator of Amaranthers, and even though it was Read, so was I.[5]

[...]

Read Cecil's life of Cowper, The Stricken Deer. Very bad. But what a life![6] It depressed & terrified me. How did he ever manage to write such bad poetry?

Am stuck in Hughes's High Wind in Jamaica, A. A. Milne & Rum.[7]

Am half way through Faust Part 1. There seems to be a surprising amount of irrelevance for the work of a lifetime. In Auerbach's Cellar & the Witches' Kitchen for example.[8] But perhaps it justifies itself later. I think he was the kind that couldn't bear to shorten anything.

I hope you saw W. B.'s advise [*for* advice] to young Indian poets quoted in the Irishman's Diary.[9]

Frank came back from his 10 days in Donegal last Tuesday, apparently not relishing the prospect of another long spell in what he now calls the "Turmoil". When he heard Heinemann had turned down the book he said, "Why can't you write the way people want", when I replied that I could only write the one way, i.e. as best I could (not the right answer, by the way, not at all the right answer), he said it was a good thing for him he did not feel obliged to implement such a spirit in 6 Clare St. Even mother begins to look askance at me. My departure from here is long overdue. But complicated by my owing them £10 apiece. The Yeats picture is paid off at last.[10]

How is your own work going and how are you yourself?

I hope Dilly's sales keep good. I saw Joe Hone one day, copper in the face from correcting Moore proofs. He was crying out for a book to translate in the long winter evenings. I suggested Breton's <u>Nadja</u>.[11]

Leventhal says Faust Part 2 is very surréaliste & that all good old men go surréaliste. Haven't observed it myself. Tuohy apparently said also when asked by Sean O'Sullivan why he did not promote his income with contributions to Punch, that only old men had a sense of humour. Sean looks forward to getting a teaching job in the reorganized School of Art, at £6 a week, that will relieve him from the necessity of painting at all.[12]

Write very soon.

Love ever

Sam

"Schöne Grüsse" to Hester[13]

ALS; 2 leaves, 8 sides; *letterhead*; *env to* Thomas McGreevy Esq, 15 Cheyne Gardens, LONDON SW 3; *pm illeg*, Dublin; TCD, MS 10402/104.

1 SB had sent *Murphy* to Frere-Reeves (see 7 July 1936, n. 6).

SB sent *Murphy* to George Reavey's European Literary Bureau, asking him to act as agent; he wrote to McGreevy: "As you say, they are all the same, & with Reavey I will be spared the labour & embarrassment of introducing myself. I had also thought of Wishart & suggested it to Reavey. They have rejected work of mine before" (Wednesday [19 August 1936], TCD, MS 10402/105).

2 SB was aware that his three poems from *Echo's Bones* had been published in *transition* in June (26 July 1936, n. 13; the request for these poems: 7 July 1936). Maria Jolas served as Managing Editor of *transition*.

3 "Cascando," *Dublin Magazine*, 3–4.

4 Brian Coffey. *Morning* by Jack B. Yeats.

Presumably SB lent Coffey some issues of *Minotaure*, a lavishly illustrated art journal published in Paris from June 1933 to May 1939.

Geoffrey and Alan Thompson's mother, Lillian Thompson (née Bourne).

5 Jack Yeats lived at 18 Fitzwilliam Square.

SB describes *In Tír na nÓg*: 17 July 1936, n. 8. *Shelling Green Peas, Moore Street* (Allied Irish Bank Collection, Dublin, Pyle 461) (Pyle, *Jack B. Yeats: A Catalogue Raisonné of the Oil Paintings*, I, 420; III, 199).

Herbert Read compares Yeats to Joyce, Soupault, and Sterne, writing "The book is a magnificent satire, an irrational and hilarious farce written with the greatest verve and wit" ("A Surrealist Novel," *The Spectator* 31 July 1936: 211).

6 Lord David Cecil, *The Stricken Deer; or, The Life of Cowper* (1930). English poet William Cowper (1731–1800) suffered from periods of melancholia, and attempted suicide several times.

7 Richard Hughes, *High Wind in Jamaica: The Innocent Voyage* (1929). Alan Alexander Milne (1882–1566).

8 For SB's notes on Goethe's *Faust*, in an edition by Robert Petsch (Leipzig: Bibliographisches Institut, [1925]), see BIF, UoR, MS 5004 and MS 5005; for a description, see Dirk van Hulle, "Samuel Beckett's *Faust* Notes," *Notes Diverse Holo*, Special issue *SBT/A* 16 (2006) 283–297. SB elaborated on his reading in his next letter to McGreevy:

> I have been working at German & reading Faust. Finished Part I last night. It leaves me with an impression of something very fragmentary, often irrelevant & too concrete, that perhaps Part 2 will correct. Auerbach's Cellar, the Witches Kitchen & Walpurgisnacht, for example, - little more than sites & atmospheres, swamping the corresponding mental conditions. All the <u>on & up</u> is so tiresome also, the determined optimism à la Beethoven, the unconscionable time a-coming. The vinegar & nitre of Kant & Heraclitus. It takes a German to apotheose the busybody. I can understand the "keep on keeping on" as a social prophylactic, but not at all as a light in the autological darkness, or the theological. And the "pure doing" affects me like the "cordial fornication" of DHL, the "Sentimentique" of a fidgeter, fit for the D.-J. Reddins. (SB to McGreevy, Wednesday [19 August 1936], TCD, MS 10402/105)

"Vinegar & nitre" refers to Proverbs 25:20: "As he that taketh away a garment in cold weather, and as *vinegar* upon *nitre*, so is he that singeth *songs* to an heavy heart," In this context, SB suggests opposition between German philosopher Immanuel Kant (1724–1804) and Heraclitus.

SB refers to D. H. Lawrence; he mentions reading *D. H. Lawrence: A Personal Record by E. T.* [Jessie Chambers] (1935), "his mining district, on & off fiancée" (SB to McGreevy, Wednesday [19 August 1936], TCD, MS 10402/105).

"Sentimentique" (a French portmanteau word, combining the ideas of "sentimental" and "romantic": sentimantic).

D[istrict]-J[ustice] Kenneth Sheils Reddin (1895–1967), from 1922 to 1957 and from 1958 to 1964 Principal Justice, and his wife; he was a playwright, having had two productions at the Abbey Theatre in 1924, *The Passing* and *Old Mag*.

For SB's further notes on Goethe's *Faust*, BIF, UoR, MS 5004/33, see Dirk van Hulle, "Samuel Beckett's *Faust* Notes," 295; Nixon, "'Scraps of German,'" *Notes Diverse Holo*, Special issue *SBT/A* 16 (2006) 272. SB's German-language study notes can be found in BIF, UoR, MS 5002 and MS 5003; the cover of the first notebook is dated 13/7/36.

9 A message from W. B. Yeats to young Indian poets: "Write in your mother tongues. Choose that smaller audience. You cannot have style and vigour in English … When you write, speak, think in English, you are a musical instrument without a sounding board" (*The Madras Chronicle* 17 June 1936: n.p.; rpt. "The Irishman's Diary: Yeats and India," *The Irish Times* 6 August 1936: 6).

10 Frank Beckett is referring to Beckett and Medcalf, 6 Clare St. Jack B. Yeats's *Morning*.

11 Geraldine Cummins's novel, *Fires of Beltane*; see 27 June 1936, n. 11. Joseph Hone, *The Life of George Moore* (1936). André Breton, *Nadja* (1928).

12   A. J. Leventhal. The classical witches' sabbath is in part II of *Faust.*
Irish artist Patrick Tuohy (1894–1930).

The Dublin Metropolitan School of Art was reorganized by the National Board of Education as the National College of Art in September 1936, and invited applications for professorships at £500 per year (John Dowling, "The National College of Art," *Ireland To-Day* 1.4 [September 1936] 54–55).

13   "Schöne Grüsse" (warm greetings). Hester Dowden

THOMAS McGREEVY
LONDON

19/9/36   Foxrock

Dear Tom

No I have heard nothing of the Exagmination. I have no copy, but think it was published by SylviA. No doubt we are being roulé, but I am too tired to do anything about it. When I think of that 10 year stale push, I would willingly withhold it & forgo the 1%, if any. And if I protested it would have to be in that sense.[1]

I have booked passage in the Washington sailing from Cove 29th inst., calling at Le Havre and reaching Hamburg Oct. 1st. Frank may have to go to Waterford about a job, in which case I would drive that far with him. Otherwise I shall go down by train next Monday week. The prospect of getting away is a great relief. My plans are none. Simply to get to Germany, & then selon le vent.[2] I hope to be away a loong, loong time. I was promising myself return by Holland, but by all accounts things there are frightfully expensive, so I don't expect it will come off.

Frank has had an awful month with neuritis in his shoulder & it is only now that it begins slowly to improve. At the same time he is up to his eyes in the office, working till 8 every evening, with the feeling all the time in the not so remote background that he is strangling his life. But who does not.

Only a question of the hold employed. I think it is perhaps a little easier for him when I am not here, though I think also he misses me.

[...]

I think I told you about S. O'S.'s request for an inch off the poem. Circumcised accordingly, it now begins with the abortion dilemma.[3]

I don't know exactly what Mrs Howe said to Dev. I know she mentioned absurdity of not having reproductions available.[4]

I saw J. B. last Saturday. He had extended his rose picture 2 stages further 1. Tyranny of the Rose. 2. Rose dying. 3. Dusty Rose. The first two are exquisite. The third less so. The refusal of the rose to crumble, its embalming of itself instead, compelled him to take it off the mantelpiece & on to a table with the room all round. So that 3 is less of a flower than of an interior. I had him alone, Cotty spared us.[5]

The Klassische Walpurgisnacht was too much for me & I feel no inclination to go on, though I am told it improves in Acts 3 & 5.[6] I have just read Viaggio in Irlanda by Mario Rossi (Hone's collaborator in Berkeley & Swift books). Lady Gregory he apostrophises at length with opulent curves as coextensive with the "spirit" of Ireland. Glendalough is a "luogo dolce". Walter Starkie is the finest product of Trinity humanism "homo singolarment vivace ed umano . ." [for "uomo singolarmente vivace, umano"] & Gogarty is the all round man of the Quattrocento. And a chapter is entitled: "Serenità Protestante." In fact the work of a professor. He wrote a "Saggio sul rimorso" full of false teeth, as soft as the old man's mentula.[7]

I do not know if Brian is back. I want to see him before I leave. He lent me Brunchwiff's Spinoza et ses Contemporains, the Ethica in the Classiques Garnier with Latin en regard, of which I have had time only for enough to give me a glimpse of Spinoza as a solution & a salvation (impossible in English translation), and Maritain's nauseating Docteur Angélique, which I soon lay down. Feeling what a pity the tetragonal Peripatetic did not fall for the whore proposed by his brother.[8]

A letter from Charles. Still lingering on in London, having treatment.[9]

Reavey still in Belfast, whence he sent a first chapter of a translation of yet another Berdaiev [for Berdyaev] for the kindness of suggestions. He promises to let me know about Murphy next week. Nothing from New York.[10]

Now I have to go to Cabinteely Barracks & fill up application for a new passport. I am wondering will it be put through in time.[11]

Love ever. If I don't hear before I leave, write Postlagernd, Hauptpostamt, Hamburg.[12]

Sam

ALS; 3 leaves, 3 sides; TCD, MS 10402/108.

1 SB refers to the reprint edition of Sylvia Beach, ed., *Our Exagmination Round His Factification for Incamination of Work in Progress* (London: Faber and Faber, 1936).

"Roulé" (done, cheated), with reference to royalties for their essays.

SB probably refers to publication and promotion of Joyce's *Work in Progress*, which had been published in sections, the first fragment appearing as "From Work in Progress," *Transatlantic Review* 1.4 (April 1924) 215–223.

2 SB left from Cove (now Cobh).

SB had written to McGreevy on Wednesday [19 August 1936]: "I still live in hopes of getting away in September, but shall probably go direct from Cove to Hamburg. And perhaps this time next month I'll be on the Brocken" (TCD, MS 10402/105). The Brocken, also called Blocksberg, is the highest mountain in the Harz region of northern Germany, and the site of rites enacted on Walpurgis Night (30 April), the setting for Walpurgisnacht in Goethe's *Faust*.

On 9 September [1936], SB had written to McGreevy: "If I had the price of it I'd fly to Amsterdam" (TCD, MS 10402/107).

"Selon le vent" (as the wind takes me).

3 SB cut the first two lines of his poem "Cascando," for publication in *Dublin Magazine*; he wrote to McGreevy: "Seumas O'S. sent another proof with request to make one line of two somewhere, anywhere, in the interests of his pagination"

(9 September [1936], TCD, MS 10402/107). In the same letter SB mentioned that O'Sullivan had proposed "that I should take over the editorship of the D. M., he paying for the printing for 3 years. This <u>entre nous</u>. What I said at length was: Merci."
"Entre nous" (between ourselves). "Merci." (Thank you, no.)

4   In his letter of 9 September [1936], SB reported that "Mary Manning Howe interviewed DEV on eve of her departure. I told her to tackle him on the Gallery. She did & he promised to see about it" (TCD, MS 10402/107). Mary Manning Howe had spent the summer in Dublin, and, within her role as a freelance writer, arranged to interview Éamon De Valera, then Taoiseach of the Irish Free State. It was during this time that she later claimed to have had an affair with SB (Knowlson, *Damned to Fame*, 215).

5   Jack Yeats "always painted with a rose pinned to his easel, or placed on the table beside him" (Hilary Pyle, *Jack B. Yeats: A Biography* [London: Routledge and Kegan Paul, 1970] 133). The first painting, a "close up of a red rose," here called "Tyranny of the Rose," now is known as *A Rose* (private collection, Pyle, 484).
Yeats's series of paintings "showing a cut rose at various stages of its blooming until it finally withers" includes *The Rose Dying* (private collection, Pyle 486) and *A Dusty Rose* (private collection, Pyle 485) (Pyle, *Jack B. Yeats: A Catalogue Raisonné of the Oil Paintings*, I, 438–442; III, 207, 294).
Cottie Yeats.

6   The "Klassische Walpurgisnacht" (Classical Walpurgis Night) is the first scene of *Faust* II, Act 2.

7   M[ario] M. Rossi's *Viaggio in Irlanda* (Milan: Doxa Editrice, 1932) was translated by Joseph Hone in a much abridged version, *Pilgrimage in the West* (Dublin: Cuala Press, 1933); Rossi, a Professor of Italian at the University of Edinburgh, collaborated with Hone on two other books (see 5 January 1933, n. 6).
In *Viaggio in Irlanda*, Rossi addresses a four-page apostrophe to Lady Gregory: "Sarà necessario, Lady Gregory, che qui parli di Voi? Non ho parlato di Voi finchè ho parlato dell'Irlanda – e dovunque ho scritto il nome sacro della poesia?" ("Is it necessary, Lady Gregory, that I should speak of you here? Have I not spoken of you since I spoke of Ireland – and wherever I have written the sacred name of poetry?" (*Viaggio*, 182–185; *Pilgrimage*, 46–50). Lady Gregory died on 22 May 1931, the same day that Rossi sent his book to his Italian publisher: "the book which she had encouraged me to write – this book written for her" (*Pilgrimage*, 3).
Glendalough, Co. Wicklow, the site of seven churches founded by St. Kevin, is called "Un luogo dolce, disteso" ("a gentle open place") (*Viaggio*, 54; *Pilgrimage*, 26).
Walter Starkie is described by Rossi as "uomo singolarmente vivace, umano" (a man of exceptional liveliness and humanity) (*Viaggio*, 125; excluded from *Pilgrimage*).
Rossi enumerates Gogarty's roles as "chirurgo, 'causeur', uomo politico, aviatore, poeta" ("surgeon, conversationalist, politician, airman, poet"). He claims that Gogarty "ricorda i grandi italiani del '400" ("recalls the great Italians of the Quattrocento") (*Viaggio*, 177; *Pilgrimage*, 43–44).
Chapter 24 is called "Serenità Protestante" (Protestant Serenity) (*Viaggio*, 126–128; excluded from *Pilgrimage*).
Mario Rossi's *Saggio sul rimorso* (Turin: Fratelli Bocca, 1933) is a study of ethics and emotions.

8 Brian Coffey had been in Kerry with his father.

Spinoza et ses contemporains (1923) by French philosopher Léon Brunschvicg (1869–1944), who studied at the Ecole Normale Supérieure and taught at the Sorbonne. SB's spelling of Brunschvicg's name presumably reflects a private joke with McGreevy.

Benedictus de Spinoza, *Ethique, démontrée suivant l'ordre géométrique et divisée en cinq parties, Texte latin soigneusement revu*, tr. Ch[arles] Appuhn, Classiques Garnier (Paris: Garnier frères, 1908; rpt. 1934). "Latin en regard" (Latin on facing page).

Jacques Maritain's *Docteur Angélique* (1930) is based on the life of Thomas Aquinas, whose brother Raynald tempted him with a prostitute to persuade him to break his vows to the church; but Thomas drove the girl from his room with a log from the fire, burning the sign of the cross on his door with the ember.

Maritain argued that theology should be peripatetic, moving out among the world and among other disciplines, following the example of Aquinas. "Tetragonal peripatetic" refers to Aquinas's "peripatetic axiom."

9 Charles Prentice.

10 George Reavey's family home was in Belfast. Having translated *Smysl Istorii* (1923; *The Meaning of History*, 1936) by Nikolai Berdyaev, Reavey was preparing a translation of *Ya i Mir Ob'ektov* (1934; *Solitude and Society*, 1938).

Murphy was being read by the London publisher, Stanley Nott (1887–1978), co-publisher with Europa Press of Eluard, *Thorns of Thunder*; Reavey had said he "would have Knott's [*for* Nott's] verdict by the middle of the month" (SB to McGreevy, 9 September [1936], TCD, MS 10402/107). SB had also sent a typescript of *Murphy* to Simon and Schuster, New York.

11 The Dublin Passport Office was at 16 Upper Merrion Street, but paperwork and validation of identification were carried out at the Cabinteely Barracks Garda Station, on the Old Bray Road, Dublin 18, and forwarded to the Passport Office.

12 "Postlagernd, Hauptpostamt" (General delivery, Main Post Office).

THOMAS McGREEVY

TOPPESFIELD, ESSEX

30/9/36 <u>Le Havre</u>

Here for the day. On to Hamburg this evening. Wish I could stay where I am. The place is charming & the people ... French. There's an old Peter Brueghel at the end of the street, but it won't see me.[1]

Love.

Sam

APCS; 1 leaf, 1 side; "Le Havre. Bassin du Commerce et Place Gambetta"; *to* Thomas McGreevy Esq, 15 Cheyne Gardens, London SW 3, Angleterre, *forwarded, AH, to* The Block Hse, Toppesfield, Essx; *pm* 30-9-36, Le Havre, 1-10-36, Chelsea; TCD, MS 10402/109.

1 The names of the two generations of this family of Flemish painters are usually spelled differently: the elder Pieter Bruegel (c. 1525–1569) had two sons, Pieter Brueghel the younger and Jan Brueghel.

At the far end of the Rue de Paris from the Quai was the Musée des Beaux-Arts; it was destroyed in World War II. In the new Musée Malraux there are two paintings now ascribed to Pieter Brueghel the younger: *Consultation at the Procurer's* (77.24) and *Interior of a Peasant Kitchen* (77.14), but there is no record of one by the elder Pieter Bruegel.

THOMAS McGREEVY

TOPPESFIELD, ESSEX

9/10/36   bei Hoppe

Schlüterstrasse 44

Hamburg 13

Dear Tom

I collected your card all right at the Poste Restante. The above, which I have tried to write clearly, is my address now & will be I expect for a fortnight at least. On n'est pas mal, au sein du chauffage central. Il fait un froid à faire sauter les couilles. Le pain est noir, l'horizon aussi. What in the world are you doing among the thatches. Was it then another journey from, like so many? I can't believe you'd go to Tappesfield [*for* Toppesfield] of your own free will.[1]

I got here last Friday, 24 hours late. The town is superb, nothing older than middle 19th century. One exquisite green steeple (truly a guglia), that of the Petrikirche. And the Alster pièces d'eau are masterpieces.[2] I got a lovely vision of T. C. D. & its terra infirma reclaimed from the land, the Liffey lying calm over Nassau Street, as no doubt once it did, washing the fringes of Leinster Lawn, Lecky & the Kook of Bells submerged, & Frank going to his lunch in a canoe.[3] That would be the only town planning – away with the town! Manning Robertson would agree I am sure.[4]

I found Klopstock, buried with his cockpecked wife & son, right at the end of Altona's most charming promenade, under the inevitable snivelling lime, in the grip of ivy. "He who then liveth & believeth in me shall never perish." Then I had a Bauernfrühstück in the Hauptbahnhof.[5]

The Gallery here was something of a disappointment, but may improve. The building is magnificent and the pictures admirably presented (one line hanging against matt white throughout), but there is an appalling quantity of rubbish, worse than unimportant locals. Meisters BERTRAM & FRANKE don't say much to me either.[6] There are a lot of lovely Van Goyens, a Van Uden – Teniers not as good as the one in Dublin, a so called Brouwer landscape that might conceivably be a pot boiler, a couple of Everdingens and a characteristic landscape of that German-Roman that you don't like & whose name I can never remember.[7] Then roomfuls of Tischbein, Menzel & God knows who else. There is a lovely Dégas Portrait de Femme, another hardly up to standard by Lautrec, and a sentimental Picasso Femme à l'Absinthe.[8] The modern Germans are more interesting, Leibl, Corinth, Nolde etc. There is a lot of Munch also, & I found an excellent portrait of a woman by one Jaeckel, of whom I know nothing. He has nothing else in the Gallery. Marc's <u>Mandrill</u> is amusing, but I think not so good as the Boccioni that Boss Sinclair had in Kassel.[9]

It is nice to be away, but when I have seen the pictures & struggled into the language I don't think I'll be sorry to go. I begin to think that Germany's charm is perhaps after all mainly for me a matter of associations. I feel sad enough & often enough for that to be so. Now that Holland & France have come off the truce, I hope to return that way.[10] Holland in the early spring & Paris in the late, if Europe has not been obliterated before then.

Simon & Schuster turned down <u>Murphy</u>, with the usual kind words, brilliance, 5 % appeal & ruisselant avenir.[11] Houghton & Mifflin now have it. Nott has not yet made up his mind. Perhaps he must get in touch with Mme. Beeton before he can reach a decision.[12]

My truncated poem is in this number [of] <u>Dublin Magazine</u>. To judge by quantity of spare space that follows it, the circumcision was uncalled for. I see in the same number a harmless paragraph on Dilly's book from the com[p]te-gouttes of Norah Hoult.[13]

A letter from the physical jerking Charles, still in London, but hoping soon to 'Take his leave' (!!) Richard mit vache is back "big, red & jovial".[14]

Frank drove me to Waterford. Very sad parting from him. It felt like a desertion. He was tearfully & continuously depressed for weeks before I left. Overwork, neuritis, sex worries, home gloom, etc.

God love thee & write incontinent. I don't seem to have had a proper letter from you for ages.

Ever
Sam

<u>Elsheimer</u> is the man.

ALS; 2 leaves, 4 sides; TCD, MS 10402/110.

1 "On n'est pas mal, au sein du chauffage central. Il fait un froid à faire sauter les couilles. Le pain est noir, l'horizon aussi" (Comfortable enough, with the central heating all round one. It is brass monkey weather. The bread is black, so is the horizon). For further description, see Knowlson, *Damned to Fame*, 217.

McGreevy had the loan of a cottage (Black House) in the tiny village of Toppesfield, Essex (Jack B. Yeats to McGreevy, 30 November 1936, TCD, MS 8105/138).

2 SB arrived in Hamburg on 2 October. For images and detailed information about his stay in Hamburg, consult the website by Roswitha Quadflieg, Fritz-Renzo Heinze, and Clements-Tobias Lange: "Beckett in Hamburg 1936," 11 November 2007, www.beckett-in-hamburg-1936.de/.

Nearly a quarter of Hamburg was destroyed by fire in May 1842, which necessitated massive rebuilding in the mid 19th century. The tower of St. Peter's Church had burned at this time and was reconstructed in Gothic style with a 436-foot tower. "Guglia" (obelisk, hence spire).

The inner and outer Alster lakes are formed by locks on the Alster river; these sheets of water are bounded by tree-lined streets and promenades. "Pièces d'eau" (ponds).

3 SB imagines the River Liffey overspreading its banks to cover the land occupied by Trinity College Dublin and Nassau Street, with the water lapping the edges of the lawn that extends from Leinster House (the Parliament Building of Ireland) to Merrion Square.

The statue of historian William Edward Hartpole Lecky (1838–1903) is on the library green of TCD. In his wordplay, SB alludes to the *Book of Kells*, the illuminated manuscript of the Gospels, created in Ireland c. AD 800, kept in the TCD Library. Frank Beckett's office was at 6 Clare Street, an extension of Nassau and Leinster Streets.

4 Irish urban planner Manning Robertson (1888–1945) wrote *Dun Laoghaire: The History, Scenery and Development of the District* (1936) in which he advocated preservation of open spaces.

5 German poet Friedrich Gottlieb Klopstock (1724–1803) was buried in the Christiankirche cemetery, at the end of the Palmaille in Ottensen, in the Altona section of Hamburg. Also buried there is his first wife Margareta Möller (Meta, 1728–1758), their stillborn son, his second wife Joanna Elisabeth Dimpfel von Winthem (1747–1821), and his brother Victor Ludwig Klopstock (1744–1811); the verse, John 11:26, is SB's translation (Samuel Beckett, *Alles kommt auf so viel an: Das Hamburg-Kapitel aus den "German Diaries"* 2.Oktober–4.Dezember 1936, transcribed by Erika Tophoven [Schenefeld: Raamin-Press, 2003] 13. For SB's note about the cemetery, see BIF, UoR, MS 4848, and, in Facsimile with a photo, in Roswitha Quadflieg, *Beckett was here: Hamburg in Tagebuch, Samuel Becketts von 1936* [Hamburg: Hoffman und Campe, 2006] 31–32).

"Bauernfrühstück" (country breakfast); "Hauptbahnhof" (central train station).

6 The Hamburger Kunsthalle was constructed in 1867–1869 in an Italian Renaissance style.

The chief work of Master Bertram von Minden (fl. 1367–c. 1415) is the *Altarpiece of St. Peter's* (also known as the *Grabow Altarpiece* or *The Creation of the Animals*, HK 500). Among works by Master Franke (fl. 1400–1425) in Hamburg is the *Altarpiece of the Traders with England* (also known as the *St. Thomas Altarpiece*, HK 490–498).

7 Dutch landscape painter and draughtsman Jan van Goyen.

Peasants Merrymaking (NGI 41) in the collection of the National Gallery of Ireland was painted by David Teniers with Flemish painter Lucas van Uden (1595–1672); SB compares this with paintings by Teniers in the Hamburger Kunsthalle: *The News* (HK 125), *Peasants by the Fireside* (HK 175), *Moonlit Landscape* (HK 176), and *The Bleachery* (HK 337).

Adriaen Brouwer *Landscape* (HK 339) is now entitled *Hilly Landscape with Herd* and reattributed as "Anonymous of South Nederland" (c. 1640/1650).

Paintings by Allart van Everdingen (1621–1675) in the collection were *Northern Landscape with Waterfall* (HK 55), *Hilly Landscape* (HK 56), *Norwegian Fjord* (HK 312), *Northern Waterfall* (HK 313). In his diary entry for 8 October 1936, SB mentions two Everdingens, but the museum cannot confirm which paintings were on display (Beckett, *Alles kommt auf so viel an*, 14; Dr. Ute Haug, 8 February 2006).
SB recalls the name of Adam Elsheimer as a postscript to this letter.

8 There is a family of painters by this name: Johann Henrich Tischbein (1722–1789), Johann Jacob Tischbein (1725–1791), Johann Friedrich August Tischbein (1750–1812), and Johann Heinrich Wilhelm Tischbein (1751–1829), who as a friend of Goethe was known as the "Goethe Tischbein" (*Goethe in the Roman Campagna*, Städelsches Kunstinstitut and Städtische Galerie [no. 1157]). Of the Tischbein family, SB specifically mentions Johann Jacob and Johann Heinrich Wilhelm Tischbein (Beckett, *Alles kommt auf so viel an*, 20).
Hamburg also had many works by genre painter Adolf Friedrich Erdmann von Menzel (1815–1905).
The painting by French impressionist painter Hilaire-Germain-Edgar Degas (1834–1917) is now known as *Mme. Joséphine Gaujelin* (formerly known as *Portrait of a Woman*, HK 2417). SB refers to the *Female Portrait: The Daughter of the Village Sergeant* (HK 1253) by Henri de Toulouse-Lautrec.
The Absinthe Drinker (HK 2353) by Picasso was confiscated by the Nazis, and hung in the 1937 Munich exhibition of "Entartete Kunst" (Degenerate Art); it is now in the Doris Im Obersteg collection, on loan to the Kunstmuseum Basel (Im 1411) (Stephanie Barron, ed., "*Degenerate Art*": *The Fate of the Avant-Garde in Nazi Germany* [Los Angeles: Los Angeles County Museum of Art, 1991] 168; Charlotte Guzwiller, Registrar, Kunstmuseum Basel, 7 June 2006).

9 Wilhelm Leibl (1844–1900), Lovis Corinth (1858–1925), and Emil Nolde (1867–1956). The 1927 *Katalog der neueren Meister* of the Hamburger Kunsthalle shows only two works by Norwegian expressionist painter Edvard Munch (1863–1944): *Male Portrait* (Director Brünings) (HK 2309; confiscated in 1937 and now in a private collection) and *Woman in Blue* (HK 2310).
The only painting by Willy Jaeckel (1888–1944) in the Hamburger Kunsthalle at this time was *St. Sebastian I* (HK 1679). On 19 November, SB recorded that a portrait he had seen on 8 October 1936 had "gone from its place" (Beckett, *Alles kommt auf so viel an*, 14, 44).
The Mandrill (HK 1688, confiscated in 1937; since 1964, in the Pinakothek der Moderne in Munich, 13467) by Franz Marc (1880–1916) is compared to *The Laugh* (once owned by William Sinclair, now MOMA 656.1959) by Italian painter Umberto Boccioni (1882–1916).

10 It is likely that the truce to which SB refers is the economic shift of 26 September: France (in agreement with Britain and the United States) devalued its currency to reduce barriers to trade, followed by Holland and Switzerland in early October 1936 ("Valuing the Franc," *The Times* 28 September 1936: 12; "A New Beginning," *The Times* 28 September 1936: 13; "Fetters to Trade," *The Times* 6 October 1936: 13).

11 The rejection letter from Simon and Schuster has not been found; "ruisselant avenir" (dazzling future).

12 Boston publishers Houghton Mifflin.

Stanley Nott had been considering *Murphy* (see 19 September 1936, n. 10). SB's facetious reference is to Isabella Mary Beeton (née Mayson, 1836–1865), whose *Mrs. Beeton's Book of Household Management* (1861) was the influential cookbook for over one hundred years.

13 "Cascando," *Dublin Magazine* 3–4. The cut in the poem: 19 September 1936, n. 3.

Norah Hoult's review of *The Fires of Beltane* by Geraldine Cummins called the novel "a detailed and unsentimental story with a touch of genuine poetic imagination" ("New Fiction," *Dublin Magazine* 11.4 [October–December 1936] 96).

"Compte-gouttes" (literally, drop-by-drop).

14 Charles Prentice.

Richard Aldington and his companion Brigit Patmore had returned to London from Austria; also at about this time, Aldington had begun an affair with Netta Patmore (1911–1977), Brigit's daughter-in law (Charles Doyle, *Richard Aldington: A Biography* [Carbondale: Southern Illinois University Press, 1989] 176). SB quotes from Prentice's letter which is not extant.

"Mit" (Ger., with), "vache" (Fr. slang, bitch).

IAN PARSONS

CHATTO AND WINDUS, LONDON

7/11/36   Hamburg 13
                       Schlüterstrasse 44 bei Hoppe
                       Germany

My dear Parsons

Will you be so kind as to have three More Pricks Than Kicks and three Prousts sent to me at above address. I enclose cheque for one pound, and trust my arithmetic is correct.[1]

With best wishes.

Yours very sincerely,

s/

(Samuel Beckett)

TLS; 1 leaf, 1 side; *date stamped* received 9-11-36; UoR, MS 2444 CW 59/9.

1 SB had promised a copy of his *Proust* to Günter Albrecht* (1916–1941), an apprentice in the bookshop of Kurt Saucke (1895–1970) in Hamburg (Beckett, *Alles kommt auf so viel an*, 33, 26).

GEORGE REAVEY
LONDON

13/11/36   Schlüterstrasse 44 bei Hoppe
                           Hamburg 13

Dear George

Thank you for letter with Greenslet's enclosed.[1]

Let me say at once that I do not see <u>how</u> the book can be cut without being disorganised. Especially if the beginning is cut (& God knows the first half is plain sailing enough) the later part will lose such resonance as it has. I can't imagine what they want me to take out. I refuse to touch the section entitled <u>Amor Intellectualis quo M. se ipsum amat</u>. And I refuse also to touch the game of chess. The Horoscope chapter is also essential.[2] But I am anxious for the book to be published and therefore cannot afford to reply with a blank refusal to cut anything. Will you therefore communicate to Mr Greenslet my extreme aversion to removing one third of my work, proceeding from my extreme inability to understand how this can be done and leave a remainder. But add that if they would indicate precisely what they have in mind, and the passages that cause them pain, I should be willing to suppress such passages as are not essential to the whole and adjust such others as seem to them a confusion of the issue. Be astonished, firm, & up to a point politely flexible, all at once, if you can. Do they not understand that if the book is slightly obscure, it is so because it is a compression, and that to compress it further can only result in making it more obscure? The wild & unreal dialogues cannot, it seems to be [*for* me], be removed without darkening & dulling the whole thing. They are the comic expression of what elsewhere is expressed in elegy, namely if you like the hermetism of the spirit. Is it here that they find the "skyrockets"? There is no time and no space in such a book for mere relief. The relief has also to do work and reinforce that from which it relieves. And of course the narrative is hard to follow, & of course deliberately so. Am I then Berdaev [for Berdyaev]? That I should adorn with historical amnions & placentae a non-historical uterus? And sink grapples in a womb ceaselessly pregnated & never delivered? And crowd the last chapter with oyster kisses & Murillo brats? But this is all dans le vide, & must remain so, until I know in detail what it is that upsets them.[3]

Perhaps if Nott were to express willingness in event of USA collaboration to publish the book as it stands, or totters, and furthermore to give out as his opinion that cuts are not desirable, the Mifflin Zerstörungswut might be pacified.[4]

I am also very anxious to obtain permission to use enclosed photograph, without subscript, as frontispiece. I came across it first in a Daily Sketch months ago, & found it again here in an Illustrierte. I have somewhere the date of issue of D.S. in question.[5] I presume I cannot use it without permission, & am not sure how I should set about getting permission. Anyway keep it it [sic] carefully.

I shall be here a little time still, & until I can let you have another address, write me here.

Amicalement[6]

s/ Sam

TLS; 1 leaf, 1 side; T env to George Reavey Esq, European Literary Bureau, 30 Red Lion Square, London W.C. 1, ENGLAND; pm 13-11-36, Hamburg; TxU. Previous publication: Bair, Samuel Beckett, 243; rpt. Beckett, Disjecta, 103.

1 The letter from Ferris Greenslet (1875–1959), Editor of Houghton Mifflin, with regard to Murphy, has not been found.

2 In *Murphy*: "Amor Intellectualis quo M. se ipsum amat" (Intellectual Love with which M. loves himself) (ch. 6, 107–113); the game of chess (ch. 11, 242–246); the Horoscope chapter (ch. 3, 26–41).

3 Reavey had translated the work of Nikolai Berdyaev.
Although there are "oyster kisses" between Miss Counihan and Wylie (*Murphy*, 117), there are none in the last chapter. The secular paintings of Spanish painter Bartolomé Esteban Murillo (1617–1682) were composed almost entirely of scenes of young children.
"Dans le vide" (guesswork).

4 SB makes this suggestion since Stanley Nott was unwilling to undertake publication of *Murphy* alone.
"Zerstörungswut" (destructive mania).

5 The caption for the image is "But he's done it! Mate!" It appeared with four other photos of apes playing chess: "Chess is a Shouting Match the Way these Two Play It," *Daily Sketch* [London] 11 July 1936: 10. The reproduction in a German *Illustrierte* has not been located. "Illustrierte" (glossy magazine).

6 "Amicalement" (All the best).

MARY MANNING HOWE
CAMBRIDGE, MASSACHUSETTS

14/11/36   Hamburg

Dear Mary

Congratulations.[1]

Praised be the day before evening. Or not at all.

Send your poem. I know. It has the colour of lead and the texture of worn plush, and is rich in place-names. And Mons Venerillae?[2] Now you must be very careful, what you write, think, say, wish and fear. The appendix pain has gone, and will not return. The first communion glow steals over you from time to time. And impertinence you pity rather than pardon.

Reavey wrote enclosing a letter from Greensletandhindrance. I am exhorted to ablate 33.3 recurring to all eternity of my work. I have thought of a better plan. Take every 500th word, punctuate carefully and publish a poem in prose in the Paris Daily Mail.

Then the rest separately and privately, with a forewarning from Geoffrey, as the ravings of a schizoid, or serially, in translation, in the Zeitschrift für Kitsch.[3] My next work shall be on rice paper wound about a spool, with a perforated line every six inches and on sale in Boots. The length of each chapter will be carefully calculated to suit with the average free motion. And with every copy a free sample of some laxative to promote sales. The Beckett Bowel Books, Jesus in farto. Issued in imperishable tissue. Thistledown end papers. All edges disinfected. 1000 wipes of clean fun. Also in Braille for anal pruritics. All Sturm and no Drang.[4]

I replied, dear agente provocatrice, that I would not have a finger laid on the section entitled Amor intellectualis etc., nor on the Thema Coeli, nor on Endon's Affence, nor on the last will and fundament, but that so far as the rest was concerned I would willingly remove all ties and supports, dripstones, keystones, cornerstones, buttresses, and, with especial pleasure, the entire foundations, and accept full and entire responsibility for the ensuing detritus.[5] The owls, cats, foxes and toads of the higher criticism could be relied on to complete the picture, a romantic one.

After all one is always flattered. It is only from the highest unities that a third can be negligently carved away and the remainder live. The amoeba's neck is not easily broken. Nor his countenance put out.

I dream, with the help of black coffee, of a lap the size of the fifteen acres, with all appurtenances strictly to scale, all to myself in my present deformity. Beauty is a blank wall with Paste No Bills. I am tired dashing my skull against it. I run the gauntlets of galleries, up and down the highly waxed calvaries, a cockshy and an Auunt [*for* Aunt] Sally of art. I go to an old woman this evening, whose house is a shrine to Schmidt-Rottluff, a painter on Picasso's level, and it is like going to be keel-hauled.[6] I should have been away from here this long time, there are so many other hoops to be gone through, and not another ball in sight. Ireland? I feel nothing but the dread at having to return.

I can't read, write, drink, think, feel, or move.

I seem impelled to address my friends when least in a condition to.

People like me – for a little.

Mother was all set to join Susan in London & then of course cried off. Frank still works every evening till 8.[7]

That is worse than being disliked from the beginning. I hope I am not obscure. Where it hurts? No aim need be taken. It doesn't hurt anywhere. And is worked up into a hurt everywhere. I feel like an anaesthetised Sebastian affecting to choke back his cries.

They will give the Nobel prize to Kurt Götz next.[8]

Love

s/ S

Through the wall come female Danish voices, two Jutland tarts in colloquy. Pure chirping. They should be on a funeral urn, in the Genesiacal period. Now I know how Ophelia should speak the flower speech. And that Hamlet <u>was</u> mad. He is buried in no fewer than 54 Jutlandish localities.[9] All the lavatory men say Heil Hitler. The best pictures are in the cellar.[10]

TLI; 1 leaf, 2 sides (ANS PS on verso); TxU.

1 SB's reference is not known. Mary Manning Howe was pregnant with her first child.

2 The poem by Mary Manning Howe is not identified.
Mary Manning Howe was writing a novel, *Mount Venus* (1938); SB's use of the term Mons Venerillae in *More Pricks Than Kicks* is drawn from Burton, *The Anatomy of*

Melancholy (see Pilling, ed., *Beckett's Dream Notebook*, 123; Pilling, *A Companion to "Dream of Fair to Middling Women,"* 263).

3 The letter of Ferris Greenslet: 13 November 1936, n. 1.
The *Paris Daily Mail* was the title of the continental edition of the *Daily Mail* (London) published in Paris from 1905 to 1946.
As a trained psychiatrist, Geoffrey Thompson was competent to treat schizophrenia.
"Zeitschrift für Kitsch" (Magazine for Kitsch), Beckett's invention.

4 SB wrote "<trimmed> disinfected." Boots, chemists.
SB's pun refers to the "Sturm und Drang" (Storm and Stress) movement in the arts in Germany in the late eighteenth century.

5 "Thema Coeli" refers to the horoscope section of *Murphy* (32–33), "Endon's Affence" to the chess game (243–245), and Murphy's "last will and fundament" to the reading of his will (268–269).

6 The fifteen acres: 29 January [1935], n. 5.
On 15 November 1936, SB was invited for a second visit to the home of the art historian Rosa Schapire (1874–1954). He knew that the intensity of her opinions was heightened by the fact that, as a Jew, she had been forbidden to publish or lecture (Beckett, *Alles kommt auf so viel an*, 39–41).
Karl Schmidt-Rottluff (né Karl Schmidt, 1884–1976, who added the place of his birth to his name in 1905) was a member of the Brücke painters who formed a group from 1905 to 1913: Erich Heckel (1883–1970), Fritz Bleyl (1880–1966), Ernst Ludwig Kirchner (1880–1938), Otto Mueller (1874–1930), Max Pechstein (1881–1955), and Emil Nolde. For photos of Schapire's home with Schmidt-Rottluff's portraits of her, as well as furniture and functional objects decorated by him, together with Schapire's extensive bibliography of his work, see Gerhard Wietek, "Rosa Schapire" in *Jahrbuch der Hamburger Kunstsammlungen*, IX (Hamburg: Dr. Ernst Hauswedell and Co. Verlag, 1964) 114–160.
The term "Aunt Sally," derived from fairground games, signifies an easy target.

7 Susan Manning, mother of Mary Manning Howe.

8 The 1936 Nobel Prize for Literature had just been awarded to American play-wright Eugene O'Neill (1888–1953). German actor, director, novelist, and dramatist Kurt Götz (1888–1960) never received it.

9 The entire PS is handwritten in ink on the verso of the typed page.
Danish tour groups resided in the Pension Hoppe in October and November 1936 (Beckett, *Alles kommt auf so viel an*, 19, 40).
SB's allusion to a funeral urn may be related to a lecture that he heard on 12 November 1936 by Dr. Eugen von Mercklin, Curator of Ancient Art, Museum für Kunst und Gewerbe (Arts and Crafts Museum), Hamburg, who spoke on the "Geometrische Periode," which he defined as 800 to 600 BC (Beckett, *Alles kommt auf so viel an*, 37); SB imagines a vase from the "Genesiacal period" (the time of Genesis), which, according to the Jewish Calendar, is c. 3761 BC.
SB alludes to Ophelia's flower speech (Shakespeare, *Hamlet*, IV.v.175–177, 180–186).

10 Having bought the 1927 Hamburger Kunsthalle *Katalog der neueren Meister*, SB noted that many pictures were no longer on view, and that many were not described (Beckett, *Alles kommt auf so viel an*, 28).

THOMAS McGREEVY
LONDON

28/11/37 [*for* 1936]   Hamburg

Dear Tom

Forgive my too long silence. I find it more & more difficult to write, even letters to my friends.

The weather is appalling, a leaden yellow all day, and the first drizzles of snow beginning. It will be colder in Berlin, but brighter. I leave here next Thursday or Friday.[1] I expect to spend a night in Luneburg, perhaps a couple in Hanover, & then for a week sit down in Brunswick, from where excursions to Hildesheim, Goslar, Wolfenbüttel, Halberstadt, Quedlinburg, Riddagshausen, & Königslutter.[2]

The whole north Harz region is the richest in early Roman of all Germany.[3] If only I felt more up to looking at things, but for the past week I am in rotten form, grippé I think, with the old herpes & a slowly festering finger. I wanted to go to Bremen before leaving Hamburg, but the light is so frightful, and the constitution of the gallery there now so doubtful (I mean what pictures have they left hanging), & my apathy so enormous, that I have not made the trip.[4] From Brunswick I expect to go straight to Berlin, arriving there about a week or 10 days before Xmas. There I will remain at least a month.[5]

I have met a lot of friendly people here, mostly painters. Kluth, Ballmer, Grimm, Bargheer, Hartmann – perhaps a name is familiar to you. It is an interesting group, especially Ballmer (a Swiss) & Grimm, for me.[6] They are all more or less suppressed, i.e. cannot exhibit publicly and dare sell only with precaution. The group was broken up in 1933, their library confiscated, etc. The influences are in every imaginable dosage Munch, Nolde and the "Bridge" (Schmidt-Rottluff, Kirchner, Heckel, etc.).[7] I have seen several excellent private collections (where alone living art is to be seen in Germany at present. The Kronprinzenpalais in Berlin is closed, & that is typical for the whole country, and the campaign against "Art-Bolschevism" is only just beginning[8]), those of Fräulein Dr. Rosa Schapire, art historian, exclusively Schmidt-Rottluff;[9] of Frau Sauerlandt, widow of Professor Sauerlandt of the Art & Crafts Museum here, whose banned book on the painting of the past 30 years I succeeded in obtaining, mostly Nolde;[10] and of a merchant prince called Hudtwalcker, mostly Munch.[11] I also got permission to view the Cellar of the Gallery, or rather one of the cellars, & saw there in the twilight some excellent pictures of the "Bridge" Group; in another cellar are some 60 pictures of the German impressionist Liebermann.[12] I was refused permission in the Art & Crafts Museum to inspect a carpet after design by Schmidt-Rottluff.[13] I have introductions to Schmidt-Rottluff, Nolde & Heckel in Berlin.[14] The fundamental antithesis, & the two poles of influence, is Schmidt–Rottluff–Nolde. Spend [for spent] a very interesting evening with Grimm & Ballmer, then Grimm alone. Their enthusiasm for early Christian miniature painting, especially the Irish Celtic.[15] Ballmer's painting is like nothing I have seen, except some moods of the later Picasso (do you remember the tremendous figure on a shore that I liked so much in the big Paris Exhibition?), metaphysical concrete.[16] Grimm draws like Lautrec, & then frail lyrical tempera colours. Bargheer is very violent & intelligent & anatomical. Pollaiuolo, whom I mentioned, he analyzed with admiral [for admirable] justness & sensitiveness.[17] They are all profoundly serious and therefore only a very little disturbed by the official attitude towards them. I shall be surprised & lucky if I find such energetic underground of painting in other parts of Germany. I hear on all sides that Hamburg is an island.[18] I meant to go home by Paris, but think now of going home the way I came. By April I expect to be far too tired for Paris. Perhaps I shall get off the boat at Southhampton or Plymouth or wherever it calls and have a short time in London & see you & Geoffrey. I suppose that will partly depend on what happens with Murphy. I hear from Reavey that Nott would take it if an American mug could be found, & furthermore that Houghton Mifflin are "on", but screaming for a cut of one third![19] So the matter still pends, I not having refused blankly to change a syllable, but having replied with a polite request to be told how I was to remove more than I had already removed & leave a remainded [*for* remainder].

Drunken Boat was to have been published in New Poetry; but I hear this has been deferred, to make room for an article by Ezra Pound.[20]

I am glad you have got a translation from Heinemann, but sorry you have had to lay the Yeats aside. I'm afraid I couldn't write about pictures at all. I used never to be happy with a picture till it was literature, but now that need is gone.[21]

I heard a lovely concert with the Berlin Philharmonic under Sabata (pupil of Toscanini) from Milan: Strauss's Don Quixote, which belongs to same period as Heldenleben & which therefore I expected would be awful but which was exquisite; Bolero, mistimed as usual, ejaculatio praecox as usual; & Brahms' 2$\underline{^{nd}}$ Symphony superbly played, so that I understand Brahms (the Brahms of the symphonies) a little for the first time & why I had almost [*for* ? always] found him so difficult to understand. Sabata was more conducted than conducting.[22]

I was invited one evening to a Hausmusik. Wolf sung by a Kraft durch Freude spinster from Altona. But Hindemith's

Matthias der Maler symphony on gramophone.[23] I so want to see the Isenheimer Altar in Colmar, but don't see how it is to be managed. There is something also in Aschaffenburg & I think in Munich, but apparently trivial beside the Isenheimer.[24]

News from home is good. Frank seems to be in magnificent form. Mother has had no holiday & wont take one. Young Sinclair has a job waiting in South Africa (I think thanks to Dorothy Elvery), but is not well enough to travel. He is spending a few days at Cooldrinagh! Boss has been moved to Rathdrum & fallen in love with a nun. Cissie is beyond writing to me, & I have this news from home.[25]

We have an Icelander in the Pension now, fresh from Edinburgh, which he found appalling. And there is an Irishman called Power, who has not been in Ireland, who was born in Gibraltar, whose home is in Peru, whose interests are in Spain & family in Marburg, whose family left Waterford, while the going was good, in the 18th century. He stood me lunch in a vegetarian restaurant.[26]

I am tired of this Pension. I wonder is there a whore left in Brunswick would take me in. Only in ports does the new Germany tolerate brothels.[27]

I met a Proust fiend in the University, a Flamant [for Flamand] called Brulez, professor of French here, & gave him my book, which released his compliments.[28] And through him a real little German pedant Fräulein Tied[t]ke, whose thesis on the Proustian Symbol I am at present skimming. She wrote me a long letter in crabbed French about the shortcomings of my book, & I must meet here [for her] Monday before a flowershop & render an account. But there is something magnificent in doing a doctorate in 1936 with a work on not merely an "exquisite", but a non-Aryan.[29] Brulez quoted with scorn Huxley's "mental masturbation". I said there were worst things, mental aspermatism for example. My <u>Proust</u> is apparently not positive & intellectual enough for the disciples of Curtius, I mean my presentation of Proust. They want to make his "solution" a little moral triumph, the reward of endeavour & the crown of a life of striving à la Goethe.[30]

Forgive this dry letter. It is all I can do to-day & to-morrow would be more than I could do.

Perhaps you would write in about a week to Poste Restante, Braunschweig. I expect to be there from about 8th to 15th December.

Love ever

Sam

I hear Fearon has been put on Censorship Committee.[31]

ALS; 2 leaves, 4 sides; TCD, MS 10402/145. *Dating*: the letter is dated 193[7], the 7 added by AH; however, the year should be 1936, when SB was in Hamburg and Professor W. R. Fearon was appointed to the Irish Censorship of Publications Board (see n. 31 below).

1 SB left Hamburg for Lüneburg on 4 December (Beckett, *Alles kommt auf so viel an*, 57).

2 Riddagshausen is a small town east of Brunswick with a church from 1278, part of a Cistercian monastery; Königslutter, a small town on the river Lutter, has a Romanesque church dating from 1150. In the end, SB did not visit Goslar (Lower Saxony), Halberstadt, or Quedlinburg (see 31 December 1936 below).

3 SB refers to early Romanesque architecture.

4 "Grippé" (with flu). The collections of the Bremen Kunsthalle had become diminished by circumspection in view of increasing government pressure (see Andreas Kreul, *Oskar Kokoschka: Pariser Oper*, Kunsthalle Bremen 30 June–30 August 1992 [Berlin: KulturStiftung der Länder and Kunstverein Bremen, 1992]; for the directive of 5 November 1936 to German gallery directors instructing them to remove decadent modern art, see Knowlson, *Damned to Fame*, 223).

5 SB made side trips from Brunswick and then made his way to Berlin, arriving on 11 December 1936 (Knowlson, *Damned to Fame*, 226).

6 German painters Karl Kluth (1898–1972), Willem Grimm (1904–1986), Eduard Bargheer (1901–1979), Erich Hartmann (1886–1974), and Swiss painter Karl Ballmer (1891–1958).

SB met Kluth and Hartmann at a dinner on 23 November at the home of Margaritha (née Hoffmann, 1883–1955) and Theodor Durrieu (1875–1967); SB met Kluth again on 25 November and also on that day he visited Grimm (Beckett, *Alles kommt auf so viel an*, 27, 48–49, 50). As he wrote in his diary: "Grimm's painting most interesting I have yet seen of Hamburg group ... Munch influence seems worked out ... Exquisite colour & composition" (Beckett, *Alles kommt auf so viel an*, 50). For Ballmer, see n. 16 below.

7 These artists were members of the Hamburg Secession group which "saw itself as the successor to Die Brücke"; it was established in 1919 and "disbanded itself on 16 May 1933 in response to the Nazi demand to expel its Jewish members" (Struan Robertson, "A History of the Jews in Hamburg: Three Jewish Women Hamburg Secessionists" [www1.uni-hamburg.de/rz3a035//secession.html], 27 October 2006). The Bibliothek der Anthroposophischen Gesellschaft had been closed on 16 November 1935 (Quadflieg, *Beckett was here*, 171).

8 The Kronprinzenpalais was the department for modern art of the Berlin National Gallery, Unter den Linden, 3; the upper rooms on its first floor "were closed on 30 October 1936" because works by "Barlach, Beckmann, Dix, Hofer, Nolde and other contemporary artists" were exhibited there (Professor Dr. Bernd Evers, Kunstbibliothek, Staatliche Museen zu Berlin, 3 June 1993). Ernst Barlach (1870–1938), Max Beckmann (1884–1950), Otto Dix (1891–1969), Karl Hofer (also Carl, 1878–1955).

The Nazi campaign against "Art-Bolshevism" ("Kulturbolschewismus") perniciously linked Communists, Jews, and contemporary artists, attacking them as degenerate influences on Aryan culture.

SB adopts the German spelling of the root word (Bolsche-) and adds an English ending (-vism).

9 Dr. Rosa Schapire: 14 November 1936, n. 6.

10 SB visited Frau Alice Sauerlandt (née Schmidt, 1880–1972), the widow of Max Sauerlandt, who had been Director of the Museum für Kunst und Gewerbe until 1933. SB's notes on his visits on 21 and 26 November mention work by Nolde, Schmidt-Rottluff, Kirchner, and Ballmer (Beckett, *Alles kommt auf so viel an*, 46, 52). Aware that Sauerlandt's catalogue, *Die Kunst der Letzten 30 Jahre* (1935) had been banned, SB asked Frau Sauerlandt if he could buy a copy from her (Beckett, *Alles kommt auf so viel an*, 46).

11 Through Rosa Schapire, SB met Dr. Heinrich C. Hudtwalcker (1880–1952), industrialist and art patron in Hamburg, whose collection he visited on 22 November. SB admired Munch's *Girls on the Bridge* (1900; now HK 5052) and a painting of a man and a woman by Otto Müller; he noted works by the German-born Norwegian painter Rolf Nesch (1893–1975) and Munch's portraits of Hudtwalcker (1925, Oslo, Munch Museum 116) and *Maria Agatha Hudtwalcker* (1927; Oslo, Munch Museum 124) (Beckett, *Alles kommt auf so viel an*, 47; Quadflieg, *Beckett was here*, 145–146; Maike Bruhns, *Kunst in der Krise: Hamburger Kunst im "Dritten Reich"* [Hamburg: Dölling und Galitz Verlag, 2001] 244; Arne Eggum, *Edvard Munch: Portretter* [Oslo: Munch-Musette / Labyrinth Press, 1994] 23, 244).

12 SB went to the Hamburger Kunsthalle on 19 November to view Schmidt-Rottluff and Kirchner drawings in its Kupferstichkabinett or Print Gallery. Rosa Schapire was

there, and, through her intervention, SB was allowed to visit the storage area. SB's spontaneous visit broke with restrictions, and there were repercussions for the museum staff (see Matthias Mühling, *Mit Samuel Beckett in der Hamburger Kunsthalle* [Hamburg: Hamburger Kunsthalle, 2003], frontispiece and 29–30).

Here SB saw works by Schmidt-Rottluff, Kirchner, Pechstein; he specifically mentioned *Windbride* by Oskar Kokoschka (1886–1980) (HK 2256, confiscated as degenerate art in 1937; now in the Basel Kunstmuseum, 1745) and Nolde's *Christ Among the Children* (also known as *Christ and the Children*, HK 1683, confiscated as degenerate art in 1937; now in MOMA 341.55). The last of these moved SB to say: "Feel at once on terms with the picture, & that I want to spend a long time before it, & play it over & over much like the record of a quartet" (Beckett, *Alles kommt auf so viel an*, 44; with appreciation to Mark Nixon and James Knowlson for their assistance with this transcription).

The Hamburg museum listed sixty-four paintings or studies by Max Liebermann (1847–1935). Liebermann's work was banned for its depiction of laborers and because he was Jewish; he was pressured to resign as President of the Prussian Academy of Art in 1932.

13 SB went to the Museum für Kunst und Gewerbe on 17 November 1936 (Beckett, *Alles kommt auf so viel an*, 42).

14 Frau Sauerlandt gave SB addresses for Nolde, Schmidt-Rottluff, and Heckel, and permission to use her name in contacting them; she also encouraged SB to visit the collection of Gustav Schiefler (1857–1935) in Hamburg (Beckett, *Alles kommt auf so viel an*, 52).

15 At the studio of Willem Grimm on 25 November, SB met the painter and graphic artist Gretchen Wohlwill (1878–1962), and artist Hans Martin Ruwoldt (1891–1969) (Quadflieg, *Beckett was here*, 155). Grimm and Ruwoldt were especially interested in the Celtic motifs found in the Book of Kells (Beckett, *Alles kommt auf so viel an*, 51).

16 SB visited Ballmer in his studio on 26 November 1936. He described Ballmer's paintings: "Transparent figures before landscapes … Wonderful red *Frauenkopf*, skull earth sea & sky." He continued: "Would not occur to me to call this painting abstract. A metaphysical concrete. Nor nature convention, but its source, fountain of Erscheinung. Fully a posteriori painting. Object not exploited to illustrate an idea … The communication exhausted by the optical experience that is its motive & content" (Beckett, *Alles kommt auf so viel an*, 51–52; Quadflieg, *Beckett was here*, 168–169; Ballmer's *Head in Red* [Aargauer Kunsthaus, Aargau, Switzerland, 2847]). "Erscheinung" (manifestation).

SB likens Ballmer's work to Picasso's *Figure au bord de la mer* (1929; MOMA, on loan, no. 187 in the Exposition Picasso at the Galeries Georges Petit, Paris, 16 June–30 July 1932 (Charles Vrancken, ed., *Exposition Picasso: 16 juin–30 juillet 1932* [Paris: Galeries Georges Petit, 1932] 62, illus. follows 70).

17 SB was especially drawn to Grimm's "Rummelpott" series; he preferred "the stillness & unsaid of Grimm & Ballmer" to the preoccupation with the "dynamics of movement" in the work of Eduard Bargheer, which he called "the bull of painting by the horns" (Beckett, *Alles kommt auf so viel an*, 50, 53; Quadflieg, *Beckett was here*, 175–176). SB met Eduard Bargheer at his studio on 27 November; as Bargheer had recently returned from Italy, SB asked him about the painting of Piero Pollaiuolo (1441–1496) (for their discussion see Beckett, *Alles kommt auf so viel an*, 53).

18 Ballmer had not been able to exhibit since 1933, and Bargheer had experienced similar difficulties (Beckett, *Alles kommt auf so viel an*, 52–53; Quadflieg, *Beckett was here*, 170).

19 Both Geoffrey Thompson and McGreevy were in London. Attempts to publish *Murphy*: see SB to George Reavey, 13 November 1936, and to Mary Manning Howe, 14 November 1936.

20 Commissioned by Edward Titus, SB had translated Rimbaud's poem "Le Bateau ivre" as "The Drunken Boat" in 1932 (see 13 September 1932, n. 9). It was to be published not in *New Poetry*, but in *Contemporary Poetry and Prose*. However, SB's translation was displaced by a letter that Ezra Pound had written against surrealism, "The Coward Surrealists," to which the editor Roger Roughton (1916–1941) replied ("Eyewash, Do You?," *Contemporary Poetry and Prose* 7 [November 1936] 137–138). The following number of *Contemporary Poetry and Prose* (8 [December 1936]) was a short-story issue. The journal's final two numbers were issued as a quarterly in 1937.

21 McGreevy was translating *Oasis interdites: de Pékin au Cachemire* (1937) by Ella K. Maillart (1903–1997) for Heinemann; the translation was entitled *Forbidden Journey: From Peking to Kashmir*. Prior to this, he had been working on his study of Jack B. Yeats.

22 On 20 November at the Conventgarten Theatre, SB heard the Berlin Philharmonic conducted by Victor de Sabata (1892–1967), pupil of Italian-born conductor Arturo Toscanini (1867–1957). *Don Quixote*, op. 35 ("Fantasy with Variations on a Theme of Knightly Character, for cello and orchestra"), and *Ein Heldenleben* (*A Hero's Life*), op. 40, by Richard Strauss are both tone poems. SB refers to *Boléro* by Maurice Ravel and Brahms's Symphony no. 2 in D major, op. 73 (see Beckett, *Alles kommt auf so viel an*, 45–46).

23 SB went to a "Hausmusik" (home concert) at the home of Drs. Maria and Paul Rümker (n.d.) on 24 November; the singer from Altona has not been identified. "Kraft durch Freude" (Strength through Joy) was a Nazi slogan and the name of a Nazi organization created in 1933 to sponsor "appropriate" recreation and leisure activities for the working population.

Austrian composer Hugo Wolf is known for his musical settings of poetry. The symphony *Mathis der Maler* (1934) was the first musical response by Paul Hindemith (1895–1963) to his interest in the north German painter Grünewald (né Mathis Gothart, also called Nithart or Neithardt, c. 1475–1528), on whose life and work he later (1938) based his opera of the same name.

24 Grünewald's *Isenheim Altarpiece* (Museum Unterlinden, Colmar). SB also refers to the altar by Grünewald for the Mariaschnee Chapel in the Church of St. Peter and St. Alexander in Aschaffenburg and paintings in the collection of the Alte Pinakothek in Munich.

25 Morris Sinclair went to South Africa as a tutor to two boys on a sheep farm near Graaff Reinet; Dorothy Kay (née Elvery, 1886–1964), Irish-born South African artist, a girlhood friend of Morris's mother Cissie Beckett Sinclair, arranged this post for him (Morris Sinclair, 9 May 1991).

Boss Sinclair had been moved from the National Hospital for Consumption in Ireland (Newcastle Sanatorium) in Newtownmountkennedy in Co. Wicklow to St. Colman's Hospital, Rathdrum, Co. Wicklow, which was run by The Sisters of the Poor Servants of the Mother of God.

26 The Icelander is mentioned in SB's diary entry for 24 November 1936, but not named (Beckett, *Alles kommt auf so viel an*, 50). Power's full name is not known; he and SB had lunch together on 17 November (Beckett, *Alles kommt auf so viel an*, 26, 41).

27 Brothel regulation was an element in Nazi policy from 1933 up until the War (see Julia Roose, "Backlash against Prostitutes' Rights: Origins and Dynamics of Nazi Prostitution Policy," *Journal of the History of Sexuality* 11.1–2 [2002] 67–94).

28 Dr. Lucien Brulez (1891–1982) was a Lektor (Lecturer) in French at the University of Hamburg from 1920 to 1956; he taught nineteenth- and twentieth-century French literature, although his publications were primarily in philosophy (Eckart Krause, 27 July 1993). SB met Brulez through Frau Durrieu, and attended his lecture on Diderot on 12 November 1936; SB noted that Brulez was interested in Proust "as philosopher & symbolist" (Beckett, *Alles kommt auf so viel an*, 38).
    Flamand (Fleming).

29 Irma Tiedtke (1910–? 1943) took her dissertation oral examinations in June 1935; Dr. Brulez directed her thesis, which was published as *Symbole und Bilder im Werke Marcel Prousts* (1936) (Quadflieg, *Beckett was here*, 120). SB arranged on 28 November to meet her on Monday, 1 December; she was also present on 16 November when SB met Brulez again.

30 On 16 November, Brulez discussed "Proust, Bergson, Plato & Kant" (Beckett, *Alles kommt auf so viel an*, 44). Brulez apparently quoted from Aldous Huxley's *Eyeless in Gaza* a passage in which the narrator discusses meditation as one of many "bolt-holes" from unpleasant reality: "Charismata like masturbations. Masturbations, however, that are dignified, by the amateur mystics who practise them, with all the most sacred names of religion and philosophy. 'The contemplative life'" ([London: Chatto and Windus, 1936] 503).
    Ernst Robert Curtius (1886–1956), German literary historian and Professor of French at the universities of Bonn, Marburg, and Heidelberg.

31 W. R. Fearon was named to the Censorship of Publications Board in Ireland on 23 November 1936 ("Censorship Board: Resignation of Mr. Thrift, Dr. Fearon Appointed as Successor," *The Irish Times* 24 November 1936: 7).

BRIAN COFFEY

DUBLIN

5/12/36

[no greeting]

C'est ici que pendant 50 ans il se faisait des idées distinctes, ou, pire, s'en laissait faire. C'est maintenant musée des arts et des métiers.[1] Solidement assis dans une lumière nord il barrait à tombeau ouvert. Je viens de subir une petite amende (1RM) pour m'être promené d'une façon dangereuse. Par conséquent je pars, pour Braunschweig, en silence doré, d'où je t'écrirais.

Sam

APCS; 1 leaf, 1 side; "Hannover: Leibniz-Haus"; *to* Brian Coffey Esq, 41 Fitzwilliam Square, Dublin C 19, Irland; *pm* 5-12-36, Hannover, 7-12-36, Dublin; DeU, Coffey.

5/12/36

[no greeting]

This is where, for fifty years, he formed distinct ideas, or, worse, let them form in him. Now it is a museum of arts and crafts.[1] Solidly seated in a north light he did his deleting and striking out over an open tomb. I have just had a small fine (1 RM) imposed on me for walking in a dangerous fashion. As a result, I am leaving for Braunschweig, in golden silence. I would write to you from there.

Sam

1 The Leibnizhaus in Hanover was restored in 1891–1892 and at this time housed the Kunstgewerbe-Museum (Arts and Crafts Museum). The building was destroyed in World War II and subsequently rebuilt.

Leibniz administered the library that was moved from the Herrenhausen Palace into Hanover in 1679; from 1698, the library had its own building, and included living quarters for the librarian. From 1690, Leibniz was also librarian for the more important Herzog August Bibliothek in Wolfenbüttel.

MARY MANNING HOWE
CAMBRIDGE, MASSACHUSETTS

13/12/36   Hotel Deutsche Traube
                               Berlin n 4,
                               Invalidenstraße 32

dear Mary

I'm writing this to you in a pub, because my room in the picture gives me the chinks. I was very glad to have your long letter, which reached me here, where I have been for 2 days, having come slowly from Hamburg by Hannover & Brunswick.[1] In a few weeks I shall go on to Dresden & from there to Munich & from there I suppose slowly home, probably the same way I came. For by April I expect to be far too tired for Paris. I am tired already.

I did not know I wrote you any unkind cryptograms, and am heartily sorry if so. I shall now try and be clear & pleasant. Even an improvement in the script perhaps you may notice.[2]

I do not know Grene.[3] If he is the person that was once pointed out to me in Dublin, he looks like a semicircumcised bugger.

I am not on the lookout for a lap.[4]

The last I heard about the book from Reavey, as I thought I wrote to you, was that Mifflin were suggesting that 1/3 should be ablated, & enclosing a letter that I have forgotten. I replied to Reavey, saying that I did not understand how more could be taken away from the unfortunate book than I had already taken away myself, & leave a remainder; but that I only asked to be in this matter enlightened, by some critic more alive to the economy of the work than I was myself. To this humble obeisance I have received no reply. Nott was apparently prepared to take on the book if an American mug could be found; & Mifflin if an English mug.[5] It seemed to me, unfamiliar with the niceties, that my agent had merely to bring the mugs together & the abuse would begin to pour in. It seems I was wrong again.

I also am very interested in the Johnson-Thrale-Piozzi arrangement, and often thought what a good subject was there, perhaps only one long act.[6] What interested me especially was the breakdown of Johnson as soon as Thrale disappeared. I do not think Piozzi enters Johnson's psychological situation at all. I think that his abuse of Piozzi is a blind. Piozzi was the pretext that he needed, to get away with an appearance of justification.[7] What interests me above all is the condition of the Platonic gigolo or housefriend, with not a testicle, auricle or ventricle to stand on when the bluff is called. His impotence was mollified by Mrs Thrale so long as Thrale was there, then suddenly exasperated when the licensed mentula was in the connubial position for the first time for years, thanks to rigor mortis.[8] Think of a film opening with Johnson dancing home to his den in Fleet Street after the last visit to Mrs Thrale, forgetting a lamppost & hurrying back. Can't think why there hasn't been a film of Johnson, with Laughton. But I think one act, with something like the psychology above, in an outburst to Mrs Thrale, or in his house in confidence to the mysterious servant, would be worth doing. There are 50 plays in his life.[9]

The trip is being a failure. Germany is horrible. Money is scarce. I am tired all the time. All the modern pictures are in the cellars. I keep a pillar to post account, but have written nothing connected since I left home, nor disconnected.[10] And not the fhart of a book beginning. The physical mess is trivial, beside the intellectual mess. I do not care, & don't know, whether they are connected or not. It is enough that I can't imagine anything worse than the mental marasmus, in which I totter & sweat for months. It has turned out indeed to be a journey from, and not to, as I knew it was, before I began it. I can't begin to make it clear to you, I haven't the energy to make it clear to myself. An instinctive respect, at least, for what is real, & therefore has not in its nature, to be clear. Then when somehow this goes over into words, one is called an obscurantist. The classifiers are the obscurantists.

Write to Leperstown.[11]

Love

Sam

ALS; 1 leaf, 2 sides; *letterhead*, A date by SB; TxU.

1 The letterhead shows an image of the Hotel Deutsche Traube (see frontispiece). Having taken the train from Hamburg to Lüneburg and on to Hanover via Celle on 4 December 1936, SB was in Hanover on 5 December and traveled on to Brunswick that afternoon (Beckett, *Alles kommt auf so viel an*, 57; see also 5 December 1936 above).

2 Mary Manning Howe had responded to SB's letter to her of 14 November 1936.

3 Grene has not been identified.

4 See SB's letter of 14 November 1936 to Mary Manning Howe.

5 Houghton Mifflin's request for cuts to *Murphy* apparently threatened Reavey's arrangement with Stanley Nott (see 28 November 1937 [*for* 1936]).

6 Mary Manning Howe's letter to SB has not been found, but must have included a reference to the "Johnson-Thrale-Piozzi arrangement." In 1936 there was considerable interest in Johnson's life; in March new Boswell manuscripts were found ("Yet More of Boswell," *The Times* 9 March 1936: 15). In April C[olwayn] E[dward] Vulliamy published *Mrs. Thrale of Streatham, Her Place in the Life of Dr. Samuel Johnson and in the Society of her Time, her Character and Family Affairs* (London: Heinemann). In November a new edition of James Boswell, *Boswell's Journal of a Tour to the Hebrides with Samuel Johnson, LL.D.*, ed. Frederick A. Pottle and Charles H. Bennet, based on recently discovered manuscripts, was published. Also in November the play *Dr. Johnson's Mrs. Thrale* by Winifred Carter (1884–1949) was produced in London; a review of Carter's play noted of Johnson: "Twice he is on the point of declaring his illicit passion, and twice he is saved by a trivial interruption" ("Strand Theatre, 'Dr. Johnson's Mrs. Thrale,'" *The Times* 25 November 1936: 12).

In 1765 Johnson was introduced to Henry Thrale (c. 1728–1781), brewery owner and Member of Parliament for Southwark from 1765 to 1780, and to his wife Hester Lynch (née Salusbury, 1741–1821). From 1766 until Thrale's death in 1781, Johnson was an intimate of the Thrales, such a frequent guest that he had his own room in their various houses in Streatham, Southwark, Brighton, and Grosvenor Square; he also traveled with them to Wales and France.

Thrale's death was, as SB put it to McGreevy, "the causa irritans"; it changed the relationship between Mrs. Thrale and Johnson as well as their material situation ([before 23 July 1937], TCD, MS 10402/129). Mrs. Thrale, at forty, looked forward to a less encumbered life, whereas Johnson, at seventy-one, confronted physical and emotional displacement from the Thrales' comfortable household and suffered a "breakdown" (W. Jackson Bate, *Samuel Johnson* [New York: Harcourt Brace Jovanovich, 1975] 560, 568, 572, 575–579).

After her husband's death, Mrs. Thrale fixed her attentions on Gabriel Mario Piozzi (1740–1809); despite objections by Johnson, family, and friends, she married him in 1784 (Bate, *Samuel Johnson*, 572).

7 SB may refer to Johnson's antagonism to Piozzi on grounds that he was Catholic, Italian, and a social inferior to Mrs. Thrale; Johnson's stated objection to their marriage was that it would cause Mrs. Thrale to desert "country, religion, and family" (Leslie Stephen, *Samuel Johnson*, English Men of Letters [New York: Harper and Brothers, 1879] 153).

8 In *Mrs. Thrale of Streatham*, Vulliamy wrote that "no serious attempt has ever been made to examine the sexual character of Dr. Johnson," raising the issue if not the question that SB asks himself (243). Johnson's testicular hydrocele was eventually diagnosed as a tumor (Bate, *Samuel Johnson*, 577, 581-583). SB writes "<member> mentula."

9 One of Johnson's compulsive habits was "touching the posts as he passed, and going back if he missed one" (Bate, *Samuel Johnson*, 382).

American film actor Charles Laughton (1899–1962) starred in *The Private Life of Henry VIII* (1934), *The Barretts of Wimpole Street* (1934), *Les Misérables* (1935), *Mutiny on the Bounty* (1935), and *Rembrandt* (1936).

SB refers to Francis Barber (known as Frank, 1735–1801), a freed slave from Jamaica placed in Johnson's care from the age of ten; Johnson educated him, and Barber was later Johnson's "man-servant" (Bate, *Samuel Johnson*, 325–327, 503–504).

10 SB refers to his German Diaries (BIF, UoR).

11 Leopardstown, once known as Leperstown, was near Foxrock station, Co. Dublin.

GEORGE REAVEY

LONDON

20/12/36   Berlin W. 50

                                 bei Kempt

                                 Budapesterstrasse 45

dear Georg

This pigeonhole will find me for a fortnight or three weeks, so make a sign, before I leave for Dresden. I came on slowly from Hamburg last week, by Lüneburg, Hannover, Brunswick, Hildesheim, etc.

Is there no further news about Quigley, I mean Murphy? Have you not contrived to join the hands of the two philanthropists across the pond? I know finding the terms is child[']s play to bringing them together. The last I remember is my readiness to cut down the work to its title. I am now prepared to go further, and change the title, if it gives offence, to Quigley, Trompetenschleim, Eliot, or any other name that the publishers fancy.[1]

I don't even know if you got the apes at chess. Lighten my darkness.[2]

Heil, Sieg, fette Beute and a Merry Xmas¡[3]

Sam

APCS; 1 leaf, 2 sides; *to* George Reavey Esq, 1 Parton Street, London, WC 1, England; *pm* 20-12-36, Berlin-Charlottenburg; TxU.

1 Quigley is the name of the person supporting Murphy in SB's novel.

Reavey's efforts to find an American publisher to join forces with Stanley Nott: 13 November 1936, n. 4, and 13 December 1936, n. 5.

"Trompetenschleim" (trumpet slime); this suggestion derives from a conversation on the evening of 13 October 1936 in SB's pension in Hamburg, during which amusing names were discussed (Beckett, *Alles kommt auf so viel an*, 16).

2 The "apes at chess": see 13 November 1936, n. 5.

3 "Heil, Sieg, fette Beute" (Hail, victory, rich spoils).

THOMAS McGREEVY
[LONDON]

22/12/36

Berlin 10–50
bei Kempt
Budapesterstr. 45

Dear Tom

I do not like sending this to you c/o Hester, but have no alternative, as I have lost your [? Lad] Lane address, & cannot remember Heinemann[']s.[1]

I do not know if the grotesque Dossi attribution is old or recent. As hung it is given to Giorgione, and I do not know who else could have painted it. It is infinitely more interesting for me at least than the very early lyrical Giorgione of the Kaiser Friedrich, also herewith. No doubt you know them both in reproduction. I felt as soon as I saw the Brunswick picture, and each time I went back to it, that it was made for you, and that you should have this faint echo at least. Lass es dir gut gefallen.[2]

I had a week in Brunswick on the way here, and made various excursions to the incredibly beautiful Hildesheim, and to Wolfenbüttel, where I would not have been surprised to see Lessing come limping out of the August Bibliothek and across the square, to take up the thread of the "happiest year of his life."[3] I wanted to visit Halberstadt & Quedlinburg on the way to Berlin, but was tired & broke and feel anyway that they would be only shadows of Hildesheim, so came on straight here. The first week I spent in a sinister hotel in the North, a German North Star as opposite Amiens St. Station; then found this place, beside the Zoo & the Kurfürstendamm. Museum Island is au diable, but the tube is child's play. The collections are stupendous; the town itself a monstrous comic, but rapidly sympathetic, with skies nearly as good as Dublin[']s, one wonderful park and an excellent brim to the hat, lakes, plain & forest. The weather is lovely, ciel quintessencié, but desperately cold. I expect to stay till middle of January, & then go on to the Porcelaine Madonna.[4]

News from home good. Frank is in Mürren, playing in the snow. So Mother is alone. But writes in excellent spirits. Young Sinclair is on his way to South Africa, Boss still alive in Rathdrum. Cissie got a bad turn when out visiting, I don't know exactly what, but seems to be well over it.[5]

No further news of the book. The last was my willingness to cut the work down to its title and to change that, if it gave offence.[6]

I sent Bion a card for Xmas, the Subarair earth goddess in the Tell Halaf museum, complete with chalice for the fertilising rain and archaic smile.[7]

Geoffrey is well dug in in Harley Street, with more patients than he can manage. Bion is his "supervisor" in the clinic, does me the honour to remember me, deprecates my untimely departure, just when I was all set to become the <u>uomo universale</u>, & looks forward to getting his hooks into me again. Quien sabe![8]

The modern rooms of the Kronprinzenpalais are closed, i.e. modern German painting from Nolde on. I got a permit in Hamburg to visit the various works no longer accessible to German public, and shall try it on director of Kronprinzenpalais here, though it is only valid for Hamburg. On the ground floor are wonderful Munchs & Van Goghs.[9]

I hope you have got the translation behind you & are getting on with the Yeats, or work of your own. I seem not to have heard from you for ages. I have almost decided to cut out Paris on way home (Devisen complications) & take boat from Hamburg to Southhampton, & thence to London, where I shall hope to find you. That will probably be in May.[10]

In the meantime drop me a line to this address. I don't know anyone here and though I am often lonely don't feel like picking up anyone. Expect to spend Xmas alone with a bottle of wine & the Kaiser Friedrich catalogue, full of impayable quotations from Bode. Do you know Friedländer[']s <u>Niederländische Malerei</u> or <u>Dehio</u>'s colossal work?[11]

> Love ever
>
> Sam

ALS; 2 leaves, 2 sides; TCD, MS 10402/111.

1 SB addressed this letter to McGreevy care of Hester Dowden. There was a Lad Lane in Dublin, but, at this time, none in London; McGreevy wrote to Lennox Robinson on 29 December 1936 from 49 Harrington Road, London SW (TCD, MS 8103/259).

Heinemann published McGreevy's *Poems* (1934) and had commissioned the translation of Maillart's *Oasis interdites: de Pékin au Cachemire*.

2 SB had sent McGreevy a reproduction of the Giorgione painting in Brunswick, *Self-portrait as David* (Herzog Anton Ulrich Museum, GG 454). In 1900 the Italian

art historian Adolfo Venturi (1856–1941) attributed the painting to Dosso Dossi (né Giovanni di Niccolò di Luteri, c. 1486 – c. 1542); in 1908, Ludwig Justi (1876–1957), Director of the Berlin Nationalgalerie from 1909 to 1933, "recognized the connection of [this] painting with a print by Wenzel Hollar, which bears an inscription saying that the depiction is a self portrait by Giorgione" (Dr. Silke Gatenbröcker, 9 December 2005; see also Sabine Jacob and Susanne König-Lein, *Herzog Anton Ulrich-Museum Braunschweig: Die Italienischen Gemälde des 16. bis 18. Jahrhunderts* [Munich: Hirmer, 2004] 60–62; Wenceslaus [Wenzel, Vaclav] Hollar, 1607–1677).

By comparison, SB refers to Giorgione's *Portrait of a Young Man* (KF 12A; now in the Gemäldegalerie, Berlin).

"Lass es dir gut gefallen" (May it please you).

3   The town of Hildesheim had retained much of its early character, including the Romanesque architecture of St. Michael's Church, St. Godehard's Church, the Cathedral, and the late-Gothic Rathaus.

The German poet, dramatist, philosopher, and critic Gotthold Ephraim Lessing (1729–1781) was Librarian of the Herzog August Bibliothek in Wolfenbüttel from 1770 to 1781. On 8 October 1776, Lessing married Eva Catharina König (née von Hahn, 1736–1778). Lessing referred to the time of his marriage as "'mein glücklichstes Jahr'" ("my happiest year"); his wife and a child died in January 1778. (Dieter Hildebrandt, *Lessing: Biographie einer Emanzipation* [Munich: Carl Hanser Verlag, 1979] 403; Kurt Wölfel, ed., *Lessings Leben und Werk in Daten und Bildern* [Frankfurt: Insel Verlag, 1967] 220).

4   The North Star Hotel, 26–30 Amiens Street, Dublin, was across from what was then called Amiens Street Station and is now called Connolly Station.

SB stayed in the Pension Kempt, near the Berlin Zoological Garden at the intersection of the Kurfürstendamm and Kurfürstendammstrasse, in a house that had been the setting for Theodor Fontane's novel *Irrungen, Wirrungen* (1888; *Delusions, Confusions*) (Erika Tophoven, *Becketts Berlin* [Berlin: Nicolai Verlag, 2005] 14–19).

Museumsinsel is located between the River Spree and the Kupfergraben, a channel of the Spree. The five museums of Museumsinsel were built between 1824 and 1930, each structure designed to reflect the nature of its collection: the Altes Museum (1830), the Neues Museum (1859), the Alte Nationalgalerie (1876), the Kaiser-Friedrich-Museum (1904, renamed the Bode Museum in 1956), and the Pergamon Museum (1930). All of these museums were heavily damaged in World War II.

"Au diable" (miles out).

SB refers to the Tiergarten, west of the Brandenburg Gate, bounded on the North by the River Spree, a park that spreads over 600 acres. "Ciel quintessencié" (sky of the most utterly refined blue).

SB mentions Dresden's most famous work of art, Raphael's *Sistine Madonna* (Dresden Gemäldegalerie, no. 90).

5   Frank Beckett was on a skiing holiday in Mürren, Switzerland. Morris Sinclair and Boss Sinclair: 28 November 1936, n. 25.

6   *Murphy*: see 20 December 1936.

7   SB's card to Bion has not been found.

Die grosse thronende Göttin des Tell Halaf (2850 BC; The Large Enthroned Goddess of Tell Halaf) held a chalice in her right hand to capture rain and is described as having an "archaisches Lächeln" (archaic smile); this image was on the cover of the catalogue of the Tell Halaf Museum in Berlin (*Führer durch das Tell Halaf-Museum, Berlin* [Berlin: Max Freiherr von Oppenheim-Stiftung, 1934] 29–30). The sculpture is pictured and described under the title *Grosse Grabfigur einer thronenden Frau* (Large Grave Monument of a Woman Enthroned) in Max Freiherr von Oppenheim, *Tell Halaf*, III, *Die Bildwerke*, ed. Dietrich Opitz and Anton Moortgat (Berlin: Walter de Gruyter and Co., 1955) 35–36. The Tell Halaf Museum was badly damaged during the war, and this sculpture was destroyed; from the rubble, fragments of the Tell Halaf collection were rescued and stored in the Pergamon Museum, where they will be displayed when the restoration of the Museumsinsel is complete.

8 Geoffrey Thompson's offices were at 71 Harley Street; SB had received a letter from him on 8 December 1936 (BIF, UoR, GD 2/f. 47).

W. R. Bion.

"Uomo universale" (It., universal man). "Quién sabe!" (Sp., Who knows!)

9 The closed rooms in the Kronprinzenpalais: 28 November 1936, n. 8.

On 26 November 1936, Roland Adolphi of the Akademische Auslandsstelle Hamburg (Academy for Foreign Visitors) wrote to Dr. Freiherr von Kleinschmit, Director, Hamburger Kunsthalle, to request permission for SB to see the collections in the cellars in Hamburg; this is reproduced in Matthias Mühling, *Mit Samuel Beckett in Der Hamburger Kunsthalle*, 41.

Paintings by Munch then in the collection of the Kronprizenpalais were: *The Snow Shoveler* (destroyed in 1945); *Embrace* (also known as *Summer Day*, from the "Linde-Frieze"; now in a private collection); *Music on the Karl-Johan Street in Oslo* (gift of Curt Glaser in 1932, withdrawn in 1941; now in the Kunsthaus Zurich, 2534); two paintings from the twelve panels of the "Reinhardt-Frieze" (1907): *Summernight: The Lonely People* (Museum Folkwang, G 368, Hagen) and *Melancholy* (NGB 2/97); and a set design for Ibsen's *Ghosts* (current location unknown) (Bernd Evers, 2 June 1993; Gerd Woll, 20 April 2006; Manfred Tschirner, 16 August 2006).

The paintings by Vincent van Gogh (1853–1890) that were still exhibited on the ground floor were: *Garden of Daubigny* (Hiroshima Museum of Art, B025), *Le Moulin de la Galette* (NGB A II 687), *The Lovers* (confiscated 1937; present owner unknown), and *Painter in Cornfield* (disappeared in World War II).

10 McGreevy's translation: see 28 November 1936, n. 21. McGreevy had begun to work on his study of Jack B. Yeats during August 1935.

"Devisen" (foreign currencies).

11 Wilhelm von Bode (1845–1929) had been Director of the Kaiser Friedrich Museum from 1890 to 1929. SB may have purchased all five volumes of Staatliche Museen Berlin, *Die Gemäldegalerie* (Berlin: Paul Cassirer Verlag, 1929–1933), for he owned Staatliche Museen Berlin, *Die Gemäldegalerie*, I, *Die Deutschen und altniederländischen Meister* (Berlin: Paul Cassirer Verlag, 1929).

Max J. Friedländer (1867–1958), Bode's successor as Director of the Kaiser Friedrich Museum from 1929 to 1933, had written several books on Dutch painting, culminating in *Die altniederländische Malerei*, 14 vols. (Leiden: A. W. Sijthoff, 1924–1937).

Georg Dehio (1850–1932) edited several monumental art histories, including *Geschichte der Deutschen Kunst*, 4 vols. (Berlin: Walter de Gruyter and Co., 1919–1934). Dehio had initiated the Handbuch der deutschen Kunstdenkmäler series in 1900, as a work of many hands; by World War I the series had completed volumes on all German regions. The series was further revised by Ernst Gall (1888–1958) between the wars.

GEORGE REAVEY
LONDON

27/12/36   Budapesterstrasse 45
                            bei Kempt
                            Berlin W. 50

Dear George

Thanks for your card, letter & enclosure. Congratulations on the Duhamel.[1] Best wishes for the new year.

I would prefer of course to be done by Dent, or even the Hogarth Private Lunatic Asylum, that [*for* than] by Stanley N., whom I can't say I relished when I met him in Harrington Road. But if all else fails I would prefer to be done by Nott than not at all. The chief thing is to get the book OUT. Better a bougie than a burst bladder. As to the question of an advance, if Mifflin offers one, as they certainly would, I think it is up to the English publisher to do so also. But similarly, if it is impossible to get the book out without foregoing [*for* forgoing] an advance, I shall forego [*for* forgo] an advance. The main thing is to get the book OUT.[2]

I was very pleased to hear you were trying Dent. As I think I mentioned to you before, my Boston Hetzerin suggested to me some time ago that you should try Dent, as Mifflin were in parley with Dent with especial reference to Irish authors. The sheep in wolfs' [*for* wolf's] clothing turned down the Dream of Fair to Middling Women some years ago, but they of course are unaware of this.[3]

I am not clear as to the American attitude. Have you had any direct communication with Mifflin? I think they wrote to you screaming for cuts. But are they definitely on if an English firm can be found to share the shame? Or are they shuffling out? I take it Dents know that Mifflins have seen the book and are interested. If the two safety-match heads could be rubbed together we might get the titther [*for* tither] of fire that is all we want. I leave it to your discretion to lever Dent with Nott's conditional acceptance. And by all means keep Nott waiting to the extent of his patience. He has the hopeless feet of a good waiter.[4]

All suggestions as to delenda & addenda grovellingly received.

The chimpanzees are more or less than a good joke, I want if possible to use them as a frontispiece, or better still on the jacket.[5]

I shall be here till 14th January at least. If I don't hear before then I shall let you have an address in Dresden as soon as I can.[6] Expect to be in London on the way home late in April or early in May.

Sorry to say I have nothing at all to send you, not a line. Is the Rimbaud translation sidestepped or merely deferred?[7]

All the best.

   Yours
    s/ Sam

TLS; 1 leaf, 1 side; TxU.

1 Georges Duhamel gave Reavey the option for cinematographic and theatrical adaptation of his five-volume sequence, *Vie et aventures de Salavin* (Georges Duhamel to George Reavey, 11 December 1936, TxU). The novels, except for the second volume *Deux hommes*, had been published in English as *Salavin*, tr. Gladys Billings (1936).

2 Having reached a stalemate about the publication of *Murphy* with the British publisher Stanley Nott, Reavey considered trying to interest another English publisher in partnering with the American publisher Houghton Mifflin, namely Dent or the Hogarth Press.

Thomas McGreevy lived for a time at Harrington Road, London.

"Bougie" (an old term for an early form of catheter); see [16 September 1934], n. 8.

3 SB's Boston "Hetzerin" (rabble-rouser) is Mary Manning Howe.

There is no evidence that Houghton Mifflin and Dent published together.

There is no record that Dent were among publishers who considered *Dream of Fair to Middling Women*.

4 These questions reflect SB's lack of clarity about an American–British publication partnership (see 13 December 1936, n. 5).

5 "Apes at chess": 13 November 1936, n. 5.

6 SB arrived in Dresden on 29 January 1937, later than he had expected.

7 *Le Bateau ivre*: 28 November 1937 [*for* 1936] n. 20.

GÜNTER ALBRECHT

HAMBURG

SB's errors of German in this letter have not been corrected.

31/12/36   Berlin W. 50
                           bei Kempt
                           Budapesterstrasse 45

Lieber Herr Albrecht!

Es ist einsam gewesen, seit ich fort von Hamburg bin, aber auf eine so freundliche Weise, dass es mir nicht einmal eingefallen ist, nach dem zu suchen, was man "Anschluss" nennt. Freilich denke ich öfter an diejenigen in Hamburg, die einem Fremden und Unbekannten so viele Freundlichkeit erwiesen haben. Ein anderes Vergnügen ist es, bloss (!) mit Dingen zu verkehren, doch wohl ein Vergnügen, wenn auch endlich ein sehr gefähr-liches. Weiter ist es auch sehr die Frage, ob man sich jede Abreise und jene letzte vom Lande überhaupt mit erst entstehenden Sympathien immer schwieriger machen sollte.[1] In Deutschland gibt es schon einen Ueberfluss von dem, was ich werde verlassen müssen, ja habe verlassen müssen, ohne es kennenlerner [*for* kennenlernen] zu können. Z. B., den Giorgione in Braunschweig, obgleich ich ihn jeden Tag für eine Woche besucht habe.[2]

Von den verschiedenen Ausflügen, die ich von Braunschweig aus machen wollte, habe ich mich mit den nach Königslutter,

407

Riddagshausen, Wolfenbüttel und Hildesheim begnügen müssen. Hildesheim bleibt Hildesheim. In den 8 oder 9 sehr kurzen, kalten, feuchten und trüben Stunden, die mir ein Hundeswetter gegönnt hat, ist es mir vielleicht gelungen, wenn ich mich nicht schmeichle, das Zwanzigstel, von dem anzusehen, was ich sehen wollte, d.h., das Fünfzigstel von dem, was es zu sehen gibt.[3] In der Heiterkeit von Wolfenbüttel hätte ich nicht gebraucht, das erste Fragment in der August-Bibliothek zu lesen, um mir Lessing gegenwärting zu machen. Es liegt nämlich in dieser kleinen Stadt jene französische Kühle, die ich so oft bei Lessing selbst zu fühlen geglaubt habe. Ich habe nie verstehen können, wie ein so cartesischer Geist den Geist von Descartes so ganz und gar habe misverstehen können.[4]

Fachwerkhäuser und Sandsteingiebel habe ich in unheimlichem Masse gesehen. Ich freue mich, dass es keine hier gibt.

Es herrschte in Hannover eine kulturelle Begeisterung von solcher Allgemeinheit, das man sie bis in dem Café Kröpcke wahrnehmen konnte. Man hatte nämlich gerade die Echtheit des in der Neustädten Kirche liegenden Skeletts von Leibniz durch eine eingehende Untersuchung der rechten grossen Zehl [for Zehe] festgestellt.[5]

Der Braunschweiger Dom war geschlossen, einer Wiederherstellung des Inneren wegen. Wir wissen, was das heisst. Während der Mittagspause habe ich mich durch die Baustelle, die die ganze südliche Seite der Kirche verbirgt, bis zu einem Eingang gedrängt, um da einem unerbittlichen Schupi zu begegnen. Der Hauptgiebel des Gewandhauses ist gleichfalls verschwunden, hinter dem schönsten Gerüst, das ich gesehen habe.[6]

Ich wollte natürlich nach Goslar, Halberstadt und Quedlinburg, habe mich aber plötzlich am Notwendigen – Geld, Laune und Energie – so arm gefunden, dass ich nicht konnte. Die bösen Finger habe ich selbst in Braunschweig aufgeschnitten, mit gutem Erfolg.[7]

Berlin kommt mir etwas wie eine geschwätzige Sphinx vor, die ausser der Inkonsequenz ihrer Erscheinung kein Rätsel aufzugeben hat. Eine männliche, ja eine bärtige Sphinx, wie man sie im Tell Halaf Museum bewundern kann. Dem löwen gehört Unter den Linden, dem Menschen Museum Insel, die Flügel aber bildet der Himmel, dessen Todeskämpfe, die freilich vielmehr wie Umarmungen aussehen, beinahe so schön sind, wie jene allerdings mehr schleichende, die man auch nach den finstersten Tagen von O'Connell Bridge in Dublin anschauen kann.[8] So lassen sich die Eindrücke nicht bestimmen, es sei denn, dass man ihnen das Wesentlichste abzieht. Ich verstehe z.B. schon sehr gut, wie leicht es wäre, sich von Berlin begeistern zu lassen; und weiss doch schon vorher, mit welchem Befriedigungsgefühl, als ob es sich um eine Flucht handelte, ich die Reise nach Dresden in ungefähr 14 Tagen antreten werde.

Der Obergeschoss der Kronprinzen Palais ist "heute geschlossen." Ein Diener hat es sogar gewagt, mir sein Bedauern darüber mitzuteilen. Es gibt aber eine ausgezeichnete Sammlung von Zeichnungen, wo man die Giftmischer im Intimsten ihres Schaffens geniessen darf. Ich habe weiter die sehr angenehme Ueberraschung erlebt, 6 Bilder von Liebermann in der Nationalgalerie zu finden.[9]

Die 22 Bücher, die Sie als Paket geschickt haben, sind noch nicht da. Ich nehme es an, wenn sie verloren gegangen sind, wie es hier der Fall zu sein scheint, es sei nichts daraus zu machen, da das Paket nicht eingeschrieben war. Es ist natürlich auch möglich, dass es sich bloss um eine zwar unverständliche

Verspätung handelt. Dagegen ist das Buch von Keyserling richtig erhalten worden, wie alles, was ich als Briefpaket habe schicken lassen.[10]

Ich lese sehr wenig, vor allen Dingen keine Zeitung. Ich habe den Grünen Heinrich begonnen und werde aus verschieden Gründen an Manzoni erinnert, eine Analogie, die sich ohne Zweifel würde dokumentieren lassen. Die Geschichte des Meretleins, die die mindeste Uebertönung ins Lächerliche hätte ziehen müssen, habe ich erschütternd gefunden.[11]

Grüssen Sie bitte von mir Ihre Familie, Herrn Saucke, den Maler und seinen Freund, deren Namen ich nie richtig vernommen habe, und lassen Sie es Ihnen gut gehen.[12]

Mit besten Wünschen für das neue Jahr,
    Ihr
        s/ Samuel Beckett

TLS; 1 leaf, 2 sides; BIF, UoR, MS 5037.

31/12/36   Berlin W. 50
                                   c/o Kempt
                              Budapesterstrasse 45

Dear Mr. Albrecht,

It has been lonely since I have been gone from Hamburg, but in such a pleasant manner that it hasn't even occurred to me to look for any so-called connections. Of course, I frequently think about those in Hamburg who extended so much hospitality to a foreigner and stranger. It is a different pleasure to be dealing solely with things, however a pleasure nevertheless, even if in the end a very dangerous one. Furthermore, it is also very much a question whether one should make every departure more and more difficult for oneself – with friendships that are only just beginning to form – and especially that last departure, when leaving the country altogether.[1] In Germany there is already an abundance of what I will have to leave behind, yes, had to leave, without being able to get to know it. For example, Giorgione in Braunschweig, even though I visited him every day for a week.[2]

Of the various excursions which I wanted to go on from Braunschweig, I had to make do with those to Königslutter, Riddagshausen, Wolfenbüttel and Hildesheim. Hildesheim remains Hildesheim. In the 8 or 9 very short, cold, damp, and dreary hours which foul weather allowed me, I succeeded in seeing perhaps a twentieth, if I don't flatter myself, of what I wanted to see, that is a fiftieth of what there is to see.[3] In the serenity of Wolfenbüttel I could have done without reading the first fragment in the August Library to bring Lessing to life for me. There is in this small town that kind of French reserve which I so often thought I sensed in Lessing himself. I have never been able to understand how such a Cartesian mind could so thoroughly misunderstand the mind of Descartes.[4]

Half-timbered houses and sandstone gables I have seen in uncanny numbers. I am glad there are none round here.

In Hanover there was such a pervasive sense of cultural euphoria that one could detect it all the way to Cafe Kröpcke. The authenticity of the skeleton of Leibniz buried in the Neustädten church had been confirmed through lengthy examination of his right big toe.[5]

The Braunschweig cathedral was closed because of renovations of the interior. We know what that means. During the lunch break I forced my way past the building site, which is covering up the entire southern side of the church, all the way to the entrance, only to run into an unforgiving policeman. The main gable of the 'Gewandhaus' has disappeared likewise, behind the most beautiful scaffolding I have ever seen.[6]

Of course, I wanted to visit Goslar, Halberstadt, and Quedlinburg but suddenly found myself so wanting in necessities – money, enthusiasm, and energy – that I was quite unable. In Braunschweig, I myself cut open my bad fingers with good results.[7]

Berlin appears to me a bit like a gossipy sphinx that has no other riddle to offer than the insignificance of her own appearance. A male, yes a bearded Sphinx, like the one you can admire in the Tell Halaf Museum. The lion owns Unter den Linden, man owns the Museum Island, however the skies shape the wings; the skies, whose death throes look rather more like embraces, are almost as beautiful as those admittedly more creeping ones that one can observe also from O'Connell Bridge in Dublin even after the darkest days.[8] Thus impressions defy definition unless one strips them of the essential. For example, I do understand quite well how easy it would be to let yourself be taken with Berlin; and yet I already know, in advance, the feeling of satisfaction with which I will embark on the journey to Dresden in about a fortnight, as if it were a matter of escaping.

The upper level of the Kronprinzen Palais is 'closed today'. A servant even dared to communicate to me his regrets about that. There is however an excellent collection of drawings where one may savour the poison peddlers in the most intimate moment of their creativity. In addition, I experienced the very pleasant surprise of finding 6 pictures by Liebermann in the Nationalgalerie.[9]

The 22 books which you sent in a parcel are not here yet. I assume that if they got lost, as seems to be the case here, there is probably nothing to be done about it since the parcel was not registered. It is of course also possible that it is only a matter of delay, however inexplicable. On the other hand, the book by Keyserling was received without difficulty as was everything I sent by letterpost.[10]

I read very little, above all no newspapers. I have started *Der Grüne Heinrich* and for various reasons am reminded of Manzoni, an analogy that undoubtedly could be documented. I found myself deeply moved by the story of Meretlein, the slightest over-doing of which would have inevitably rendered it ridiculous.[11]

Please, give my regards to your family, Herr Saucke, the painter and his friend whose name I never properly heard, and be well yourself.[12]

With best wishes for the New Year,

Yours,

s/ Samuel Beckett

1 The host of SB's pension in Hamburg was Kurt Hoppe (b. 1891), who introduced SB to many people in Hamburg, who in turn introduced him to others.

2 Giorgione's *Self-portrait as David* in Brunswick: see 22 December 1936, n. 2.

3 SB was in Riddagshausen on 7 December, where he visited the Frauenkapelle, and the Klosterkirche that was consecrated in 1278 and once belonged to a Cistercian monastery. He was in Hildesheim on 10 December 1936 (see Mark Nixon, "Chronik der Deutschlandreise Samuel Becketts 1936/37," *Der unbekannte Beckett: Samuel Becket und die deutsche Kultur*, ed. Therese Fischer-Seidel and Marion Fries-Dieckmann [Frankfurt: Suhrkamp, 2005] 34–63).
Königslutter: see n. 7 below.

4 SB visited the August Bibliothek in Wolfenbüttel on 8 December 1936. The "Wolfenbüttel Fragments" were published by Lessing as *Fragmente eines Ungenannten* (1774–1777; *Fragments of an Unnamed*) from a manuscript by the German philosopher Hermann Samuel Reimarus (1694–1768) entitled "Apology for the Rational Worshippers of God"; this essay challenged evidence for the Resurrection of Christ and thus provoked controversy (Nixon, "Chronik der Deutschlandreise Samuel Becketts 1936/37," 36).
René Descartes (1596–1650).

5 The Café Kröpcke, although destroyed during World War II, was rebuilt at the same location, Georgstrasse 35 in Hanover; it is a central meeting point (Walter Asmus, 16 June 2005).

SB wrote "Zehl" which is not a German word, so we have presumed that he intended to write "Zehe" (toe). The authenticity of Leibniz's remains was not at issue in 1936, having been confirmed in 1902 (Professor Dr. Herbert Breger, Leibniz-Archiv, 27 June 2005).

6   In Brunswick, the romanesque Cathedral of St. Blasius dates from the twelfth century. The Gewandhaus, the Cloth Merchants' Hall, from the Renaissance, is located in the Altstadtmarkt.

"Schupi" for "Schupo" (slang for policeman).

7   Goslar, Halberstadt, and Quedlinburg are all towns south of Wolfenbüttel; on the evening of 10 December, SB had considered stopping in Königslutter the next morning and Halberstadt in the afternoon, but on 11 December he decided to go directly to Berlin by an afternoon train (BIF, UoR, GD 2/f. 53).

On the subject of SB's infected finger and thumb, see Knowlson, *Damned to Fame*, 225.

8   The bearded sphinx in the Berlin Tell Halaf Museum was known as "Erster Skorpionenvogelmann" (First Scorpion-bird-man) (Max Freiherr von Oppenheim, *Tell Halaf*, III, *Die Bildwerke*, 118–119; it was destroyed in 1943).

The broad avenue of Unter den Linden stretches from the Brandenburg Gate at the Pariser Platz eastward to the Schlossbrücke on the River Spree. SB refers to an equestrian statue of Kaiser Wilhelm I (the National Memorial to Kaiser Wilhelm I) that once dominated the square of the Stadtschloss of the Hohenzollern, the Schlossfreiheit, at the eastern end of Unter den Linden; a lion at each corner of the monument looks outward, including one with a gaze directed westward down Unter den Linden. Designed from 1892 to 1897 by Reinhold Begas (1831–1911) and Gustaf Halmhuber (1862–1936), the statue was dismantled after World War II by the East German government. O'Connell Bridge spans the Liffey in Dublin.

The Museumsinsel, a man-made island, is the site of the Kaiser Friedrich and other museums: 22 December 1936, n. 4.

9   The closed sections of the Kronprinzenpalais: 28 November 1937 [*for* 1936], n. 8. The drawings by the artists who had been attacked by the Nazis as "entartet" (degenerate) have not been identified.

The paintings by Liebermann in the Kaiser Friedrich Museum (now in the Nationalgalerie, Berlin) were *Women Plucking Geese* (A I 524), *Shoemaker's Workshop* (A I 644), *Flax Barn in Laren* [Holland] (A I 431), *Self Portrait with Sportscap at an Easel* (A II 466), *Portrait of Dr. Wilhelm Bode* (A III 533), and *Portrait of Otto Braun* (NGB 10/60; these were confiscated in 1937, shown in the "Entartete Kunst" exhibition in Munich in 1937, and reacquired by the Berlin Nationalgalerie in 1960).

10   SB had been asked by Arland Ussher to send him a copy of *Reisetagebuch eines Philosophen* (1919; *The Travel Diary of a Philosopher*) by Hermann Graf von Keyserling (1880–1946); although Keyserling had been banned from speaking in public, SB was able to order a copy of this book, which he received in Berlin (Beckett, *Alles kommt auf so viel an*, 54, 56).

The list of books purchased in Hamburg and sent to Dublin, as well as of those purchased in Hamburg and forwarded to SB in Berlin, is given in the *Whoroscope* notebook (BIF, UoR, MS 3000/34 and 36; see Nixon, "'Scraps of German,'" 278).

11   *Der grüne Heinrich* (1908; *Green Henry*) by Gottfried Keller (1819–1890). The story of Meretlein (Part I, ch. 5) is that of a child punished and shunned to control her behavior, told largely from the viewpoint of the abuser; the child seems to die, but comes to life

from her coffin, only to die again. SB compares Keller's book to the writing of Alessandro Manzoni, whose best-known work is *I promessi sposi* (1827; *The Betrothed*).

12   Herr Saucke was the bookdealer for whom Albrecht worked in Hamburg (see 7 November 1936, n. 1); on 29 November 1936, SB had met the painter ("child painter, name forgotten") and his friend, identified only as a painter doing posters for Hapag (Hamburg-Amerikanische-Packetfahrt-Actien-Gesellschaft, a shipping firm based in Hamburg), and Albrecht's family, on 29 November 1936 (Beckett, *Alles kommt auf so viel an*, 54; Mark Nixon).

CHRONOLOGY 1937

1937	8 January	SB attends production of Schiller's *Maria Stuart* at Schauspielhaus in Berlin.
	12 January	Visits Potsdam and Sanssouci. Attends production of Hebbel's *Gyges und sein Ring* in Berlin.
	By 18 January	Learns that Richard Church, a reader for Dent, has written positively about *Murphy* to Reavey. Meets Axel Kaun and film comedian Josef Eichheim.
	22–23 January	Leaves Berlin. In Halle.
	24–25 January	In Erfurt.
	25–26 January	In Naumburg.
	26–28 January	In Leipzig.
	29 January	In Dresden, Pension Höfer, until 18 February.
	4 February	Learns that Dent and Cobden-Sanderson have both rejected *Murphy*.
	16 February	Visits Pillnitz.
	18 February	Attends Fedor Stepun's lecture on Andrei Bely in Dresden.
	19 February	In Freiberg; travels to Bamberg.
	20–23 February	In Bamberg.
	24–25 February	In Würzburg; travels to Nuremberg.
	26 February	In Nuremberg; travels to Regensburg.
	3–4 March	In Regensburg; travels to Munich.
	5 March–2 April	In Munich. From 6 March, at the Pension Romana.
	By 20 March	Tells Reavey to reclaim *Murphy* from Houghton-Mifflin.

31 March	Meets Karl Valentin.
2 April	First airplane flight, from Munich to London. Stays at 34 Gertrude Street.
By 12 April	Returns to Dublin.
17 April	Visits Jack Yeats. Beckett family dog, Wolf, destroyed.
By 26 April	SB working on play about Samuel Johnson. Learns from Reavey of another rejection of *Murphy*.
4 May	Death of Boss Sinclair. SB writes tribute for *The Irish Times* that is not published.
By 14 May	Jack Yeats, his wife, and Joe Hone have tea at Cooldrinagh. Harry Sinclair initiates libel action against Oliver St. John Gogarty; SB is a witness.
14–18 May	Whitsunday holiday with Frank Beckett to Cahir, Galtee Mountains and Knockmealdowns, Cashel, and Limerick.
By 5 June	Constable rejects *Murphy*. Lovat Dickson reading *Murphy*. On behalf of Rowohlt Verlag, Axel Kaun invites SB to select and to translate poems of Joachim Ringelnatz.
By 15 June	SB gathers testimonials to apply for a position teaching Italian at the University of Cape Town. Frank Beckett is engaged to be married.
By 3 July	SB responds to Cunard's request for a contribution to *Authors Take Sides on the Spanish Civil War*.
4–6 July	Visits Arland Ussher's home, Cappagh.
9 July	Declines Ringelnatz commission; advances his views on "logoclasm" to Axel Kaun.
By 27 July	Mary Manning Howe sends *Murphy* to Covici-Friede in New York.
29 July	SB applies to the University of Cape Town.
14 August	Sends poem "Whiting" (later entitled "Ooftish") to Cissie Sinclair and Thomas McGreevy.
25 August	Marriage of Frank and Jean Beckett.
By 2 September	Doubleday Doran rejects *Murphy*.

18 September	SB involved in an automobile accident.
27–29 September	In Waterford with Frank. Does not plan to return to Cooldrinagh after quarrel with his mother.
1 October	May Beckett leaves Cooldrinagh, giving SB time to prepare to leave for Paris.
4 October	SB appears before Shankill Court for dangerous driving. Dines with Francis Stuart.
16/17 October	Leaves Dublin for London and Paris.
27 October	Writes from Chez Sarrazin, Paris.
10 November	Back in London, there awaiting word about when the Sinclair vs Gogarty libel action will begin in Dublin.
22 November	Jack B. Yeats recommends *Murphy* to Routledge.
By 23 November	SB in Dublin for Sinclair libel action against Gogarty (23–27 November).
3 December	In Paris at Hôtel Libéria.
7–10 December	Works with Giorgio Joyce on galleys of Joyce's *Work in Progress*.
9 December	Receives telegram announcing that *Murphy* has been accepted by Routledge.
10 December	Decides not to write essay on Joyce for homage issue of *La Nouvelle Revue Française*.
22 December	Encourages McGreevy to come to Paris; urges him to apply for a subvention to write articles about France for British publication.
25 December	Christmas with the Joyces.
31 December	New Year's Eve with Giorgio and Helen Joyce.

THOMAS McGREEVY

LONDON

9/1/37   [Berlin]

[no greeting]
Very glad to have yr. letter to-day, as I have been wanting to write
you & respire keeping putting it off. I leave for Dresden next week
& may pause in Leipzig on the way. I am very tired & often feel like
turning back, but back where? I saw Maria Stuart in the
Schauspielhaus last night.[1] Very creamy. T. Eliot is toilet spelt
backwards. Writing.
    Dein[2]
      Sam

APCS; 1 leaf, 1 side; Adriaen Brouwer, *Der Hirt am Wege*; *to* Thomas McGreevy, 49
Harrington Rd., London S.W. 7, ENGLAND; *pm* 9-1-37, Berlin; TCD, MS 10402/112.

1 *Maria Stuart* by Friedrich Schiller (1759–1805) was performed at the Schauspielhaus
in Berlin on 8 January 1937, directed by Lothar Müthel (1896–1964), with Hermine
Körner (c. 1882–1960) as Queen Elizabeth, Hilde Weissner (1909–1987) as Maria
Stuart, Paul Hartmann (1889–1977) as Leicester, and Walter Franck (1896–1961)
as Burleigh (Herbert A. Frenzel, "Umbesetzte 'Maria Stuart' im Staatlichen
Schauspielhaus," *Der Angriff* [Berlin] 20 December 1936: 4).

2 "Dein" (your).

MARY MANNING HOWE

BOSTON, MASSACHUSETTS

18/1/37   Berlin

Dear Mary
    You are very good to me, you are, sending me embalmed
ananas. The format is striking, like the delights that can be

knuckled out of the eyeballs. It followed me on from Hamburg, in a tempest of fiscal excitement. Thank you. Also for your long letter, with enclosed legs, one more beautiful than the other. Tetragono ai colpi di . . Do you happen to know does she bite?[1]

I am not in love with George Reavey, but Stanley Knott [*for* Nott] is directly unpleasant. From the dim dribbles that come to me from London, I gather that the book is now under consideration by Dent, for whom it has been read by Richard Church, who at the point of one of Reavey's carp lunches represented himself as "greatly impressed"[.][2] Wax without the works.

Provoked by belated romantic German novels I find new planes of justification for the bondage in the chair that were not present to me at the time. Or rather for the figure of the bondage in the chair. If I am not careful I shall become clear as to what I have written.[3]

I would not be still here, but in Naumburg, Weimar, Leipzig or Dresden, if a large lump had not suddenly come between wind & water, where the soil was so fertile that any [*for* only] two endurable positions remained, both fully recumbent. So most of the past week, with unforgettable intervals of obligations discharged in sweat & torture, has been spent in bed, by one who I now begin gradually to realise was I. All I ask, all!, is that it may spare me for two more months, so that I can see Dresden & Munich & Frankfurt, because I don't think I shall be in Germany again. The sicker I am when I get home the better, it will postpone the playacting. I shall lock up my ischial hemispheres for the surgeon's trowel like a bridegroom taking off his braces, I shall lie in a large bed all alone in slight pain receiving attention.

The creature in all the world most to be envied is Patricia Maguire of Chicago. She sleeps since 1931, her stupor lightens briefly at meal times, she is massaged daily, her fanmail is composed mostly of proposals of marriage.[4]

Not a word to anyone about me. All roads & boreens of communication lead to your mother, and from her to mine, who if she heard I had such a splendid brand new excres[c]ence would come flying with Parishes [*for* Parrish's] Food & antiphlogistine.[5]

No, I have written nothing at all, and have no plans. Mother writes why don't I contribute to the papers, I write at least as well as the Irishman Diarist. Frank writes what about the Lafcadio Hernia I was so full of before I left. Reavey applies for contributions of what kind or form soever for the review he is starting in the Spring. I have nothing.[6]

When the problem has quite vanished in the data, or better the trovata; when to have ever left one's village ceases to seem a folly; perhaps it is only then that the writing begins.[7] If I were less tired I should be in no hurry.

I saw Schiller's Mary Stuart in the Schauspielhaus. It stays alive for 4 acts without betraying how it continues to do so. Then Werner Krauss in Hebbel's Gyges, which is such good poetry that it never comes alive at all. Krauss is a great actor, the best I have seen. I had only seen him in films before. The new Ufa & Tobis films are indescribably bad. But if one with Krauss called Burg Theater comes to Boston, see it.[8] Though it would lose practically everything in synchronisation.

Shortly after I got to Germany I had a letter from Yodaiken saying he had prepared a place for me at the Court of Eisenstein in Moscow through his friend Malraux's brother who moves floats there or swings the suttle or God knows what. I did not answer.[9] Moscow is another journey.

I brushed a lot of people in Hamburg but have seen nobody here, except a bookseller's improver and a film comedian.[10]

The Yeats joke is excellent. Publish it before he dies.[11]

The Toller-Johns[t]on mixture sounds terrible.[12] Iced beestings.

Thomas Mann, after 3 years at the brink of complete proscription, has had his citizenship taken away. Heinrich is down the drain long ago.[13]

This is a miserable letter but I can't do any better. Shall write you again from Dresden, if I ever get there. Write to Foxrock yourself. You must have plenty of leisure now, or are you crocheting?[14]

I know the smell you describe. The decay ingredient you omit, what you get in a cemetery. You like it because it is associated with your years of innocence. I dislike it for the same reason. It is part of the home poison. A swamp smell.

     Love

     Sam

ALS; 2 leaves, 2 sides; *env to* Mrs Mark Howe, 136 Myrtle Street, Boston, Mass. USA; *pm* 21-1-37, Berlin; TxU.

1 "Ananas" (pineapple). Neither Mary Manning Howe's letter nor its enclosure has been found.

SB quotes Dante's *Paradiso* XVII, line 24: "'tetragono ai colpi di ventura'" ("foursquare against the blows of chance") (*La Divina Commedia*; *The Divine Comedy*, III, *Paradiso*, 243).

2 Discovering whether Stanley Nott really did want to publish *Murphy* was proving so difficult that SB's misspelling of the name here is probably deliberate.

Richard Church, a reader for J. M. Dent and Sons, wrote to George Reavey on 12 January 1937:

> I have now read Samuel Beckett's novel and I think this man is a most remarkable and highly equipped writer. The humour, the sophistication, the sense of structure, and the queer originality make me agree with you that he is a man fully worth while fostering. I have been on the telephone with Harold Raymond of Chatto & Windus and said what I think about the book and also that I believe they are making a mistake if they let him go. Raymond has accordingly asked to see the manuscript again [...] but he does not want Beckett to know this in case he has to come to the same conclusion as the other directors and again disappoint the author.

For our part, we can only take on a limited amount of immediately unremunerative work [...] Otherwise I should not hesitate about urging my directors to accept Beckett's book. (TxU)

Harold Raymond to Church of 8 January 1937: UoR, MS 2444 CW letterbook 178/689; Raymond to Reavey of 19 January 1937: UoR, MS 2690.

3 SB was reading Hermann Hesse, *Demian: die Geschichte einer Jugend* (1919; *Demian: The Story of Emil Sinclair's Youth*), and Walter Bauer, *Die notwendige Reise* (1932; The Necessary Journey). For SB's reflection on *Murphy* in the light of this reading: Knowlson, *Damned to Fame*, 230, and BIF, UoR, GD 4/f. 15.

4 Patricia Maguire (1905–1937) had been ill with a sleeping sickness for five years and seven months when she died in Chicago on 28 September 1937 ("Patricia Maguire Dies in Hospital," *The New York Times* 29 September 1937: 14).

5 "Boreens" (Ir., lanes).
Parrish's Chemical Food, an iron tonic invented by the Philadelphia pharmacist Edward Parrish (d. 1872).

6 "An Irishman's Diary" in *The Irish Times* was a daily column of anecdote and commentary on the leader page begun in 1927 by R. M. Smyllie, sometimes appearing under his pseudonym, "Nichevo"; in the early 1930s Smyllie wrote most of the columns, "with paragraphs from ... freelance sources," and he continued to write it on Saturdays "even after he became editor" (Hugh Oram, 18 July 2005; Hugh Oram, *The Newspaper Book: A History of Newspapers in Ireland, 1649–1983* [Dublin: MO Books, 1983] 162–163).
SB's pun is based on the name of writer and teacher Patrick Lafcadio Hearn (also known as Koizumi Yakumo, 1850–1904) with its echo of the name of the character Wluiki Lafcadio in Gide's *Les Caves du Vatican*.
George Reavey's plans for a review did not materialize.

7 "Trovata" (serendipitous find).

8 The performance of *Maria Stuart*: 9 January 1937, n. 1.
Gyges und sein Ring (1856) by dramatist Friedrich Hebbel (1813–1863) was performed at the Schauspielhaus in Berlin on 12 and 13 January, with Werner Krauss (1884–1954) in the role of Candaules, King of Lydia. Krauss had starred in *The Cabinet of Dr. Caligari* (1919), *The Brothers Karamazov* (1920), *Danton* (1921), *Othello* (1922), and *Tartuffe* (1926). *Burg Theater* (1936) with Krauss as Friedrich Mitterer, a once brilliant but now aging actor, was produced by Tobis-Europe films.
Although Ufa (Universum Film Aktiengesellschaft) was created in 1917 to promote German culture, its purpose subsequently changed; by 1933 Ufa was producing both entertainments and Nazi propaganda films (Anthony Slide, *The International Film Industry* [New York: Greenwood, 1989] 357–358). The Tobis sound film production company was created in 1927, and by 1933, with Ufa, it dominated the German film industry.

9 The letter to SB from Leslie Daiken (né Leslie Yodaiken, 1912–1964), Irish-born writer who was active in the British Film Society, has not been found. Knowing of SB's interest in studying with Eisenstein (see 2 March 1936), Daiken offered to contact the half-brother of André Malraux, Roland Malraux (1912–1945),

who had known Eisenstein in the early 1930s when he had been working in Moscow for the Paris newspaper, *Ce Soir*.

The terms "float" and "suttle," relative to their use in the film industry of the 1930s, have not been defined.

10 Axel Kaun* (1912–1983) had just begun to work for Rowohlt-Verlag; SB was introduced to Kaun by Günter Albrecht, whom he had met in Hamburg. The film comedian Josef Eichheim (1888–1945) was also staying at the Pension Kempt with SB; the owner of the Pension, Willy Kempt (n.d.), and SB went with Eichheim to see two films in which Eichheim had major roles: *Der lachende Dritte* (1936; *The Chuckling Third*) and *Der Jäger von Fall* (1936; *The Hunter of Fall*) (Knowlson, *Damned to Fame*, 232).

11 Mary Manning Howe's joke about W. B. Yeats is not known.

12 *The Blind Goddess*, a play by German expressionist Ernst Toller (1893–1939), was freely adapted by Denis Johnston as *Blind Man's Bluff*; it opened on 26 December 1936 at the Abbey Theatre, Dublin. The reviewer in *The Irish Times* noted: "Only a very little of the original remains; little more than the theme, something of the plot, and a little of the dialogue" ("Blind Man's Bluff," 28 December 1936: 8).

13 Thomas Mann (1875–1955) emigrated to Switzerland in 1933, and to the United States in 1938; his brother Heinrich Mann emigrated to France in 1933 and to the United States in 1940. Thomas Mann, his wife, and his children, were stripped of their German citizenship on 3 December 1936 ("93 Germans Deprived of Nationality: Thomas Mann and His Family Penalized," *The Times* 4 December 1936: 15; for further details: Nigel Hamilton, *The Brothers Mann: The Lives of Heinrich and Thomas Mann, 1871–1950 and 1875–1955* [London: Secker and Warburg, 1978] 263–269).

14 "Write to Foxrock yourself," i.e. to May Beckett.
Mary Manning Howe was pregnant.

THOMAS McGREEVY

LONDON

18/1/37

Berlin W. 50
bei Kempt
Budapesterstrasse 45

Dear Tom

Sorry to hear the reproduction arrived in such bad order. The hunched pose troubled me too the first time I saw, but soon it begins to belong with the face.[1] I talked to the elderly

Jewish art-historian whose acquaintance I made in Hamburg, who schwärms madly for Schmidt-Rottluff, she was here for Xmas, about the picture. She poohpoohed & much preferred the Giorgione here, "an early lyrical work – but then it was an essentially lyrical talent." If she went in for spit[t]oons in her Hamburg home, they would be designed by Schmidt-Rottluff. The metaphysical alone can claim her interest, and the metaphysical is always soulful.² All she cares for in Brunswick is the Rembrandt family-picture. Signorelli is 2nd class – beside Piero della Francesca. To talk of a tragic in Brouwer is to talk nonsense, he was a talented Taugenichts & no more.³ We disagreed with each other all evening, in a room with Heckels, Kirchners, wretched Kolbes and frail faces traced by Rottluff on pebbles polished by the sea, her voice crackling as a whole group of German voices crackles, raining down curses on the government.⁴ I could have visited them all here. Nolde, Rottluff, Heckel, etc., de la part de Frau Sauerlandt, widow of the late director of the Museum in Hamburg, who wrote a poor book on Nolde and called it Art of the past 30 Years, to whom Fry dedicated his Art Now, mais je n'en ai rien fait.⁵ They are all great proud angry poor putupons in their fastnesses, and I can't say yessir and nosir any more. So I have lived all the time alone, except for the acquaintance in the last few days of a young bookseller's improver who has just been taken on by the publisher Ruhwoldt [*for* Rowohlt], who does Hackett, Fleming, Wolf[e] and Romains. Fleming is here with a large propaganda aeroplane at his disposal, & Wolf[e] comes to Berlin as others to the peace of the countryside.⁶ Sometimes in the evening I go out and drink beer with my host and a film comdedian [*for* comedian] at the height of his popularity. Strangers pause at our table and say to him, where have we seen your face, which pleases him & Kempt also.[7]

The last week has been the worst for a long time. I meant to leave Berlin for Dresden last Wednesday but a lump came between wind & water. They often come there and go away soon with a little discharge, but this one got bigger and bigger till only two endurable positions remained, both fully recumbent. But I had appointments with the bookseller, on the eve of his departure for the Riesengebirge, and then finally day before yesterday, when the thing was at its worst, with the bookseller from Hamburg, on his way through to join the other.[8] He was to have left here at 8, but missed the train by half a minute, so I had him from 4 in the afternoon till after midnight. May it be a long time before I have another 12 such hours. [...] I am very tired and only want to go home and lie down, but I feel I shan't be in Germany again after this trip. Travelling as I do, with the living wage of charity coming through regular every month, and the aversion to human beings hardening with every outing, I shall never learn what to do with my tither of life. But not a word, all roads of comminucation [*for* communication], the boreens also, lead to Mrs. Susan Manning, and from her to mother.[9]

I am glad you liked Cascando, the last echo of feeling.[10]

The Pergamum altar is impressive barock, not at all beautiful.[11]

The Kaiser Friedrich is terrific. An exquisite Masaccio predella to the London Madonna, and a separate picture of a woman lying in receiving visitors.[12] Wonderful Signorellis especially the big Pan as God of Nature and Master of Music, with a shepherd very like the El Greco son of Laocoon in London.[13] The two del Sartos are the best I have seen, one a portrait of the del Fede.[14] Practically a repetition of the Savoldo Magdalene in London, the same lovely pearl-yellow cloak and hastening figure, only called here Venetian Woman.[15] Roomfuls of Botticellis and Bellinis, including a wonderful Pietà given to old Jacopo, very Paduan.[16] A Butinone Pietà that bears out the little picture in London, Turas, Crivellis, Vivarinis, Ercole de' Robertis, rather unassuming Mantegnas and a prodigious Carpaccio Entombment.[17] The usual acres of Titain [*for* Titian] at his best, if you like that kind of thing, I haven't been able to look at him for very long this trip. The Rembrandts and Halses must be the best outside Holland, if you like that kind of thing.[18] 6 or 7 Brouwers in the dark corner that is always reserved for him, with the first landscapes that have seemed to me to belong to his spirit. The famous Moon Landscape, that belonged to Rubens, is of course denied me, having been sent to Paris for the Rembrandt & Contemporaries exhibition.[19] Very good Terborchs, including a surprising loose bright free courtyard scene, say the Terborch Kupplerin.[20] The two Vermeers and De Hooch looking very trivial & Ma[e]s beside them. And Elsheimers, "pictures" and miniatures and a lovely drawing on loan from the Louvre, water, night, wood, glades, moon and a tiny fire being kindled on the shore.[21] Of the 2 Velasquez the Musicians do not matter very much, and the Countess Olivares doesn't seem to belong to him at all. It was formerly given to del Mazo, and doesn't seem good enough for del Mazo.[22] The Flemish collection is amazing, a roomful of Van Eyck, 3 Flémalle, 3 Hugo van der Goes, 6 van der Weyden, a lovely Geertgen John Baptist sitting very gloomy in a landscape. They are all there, except Campin, unless Flémalle is Campin, or Roger v. d. W.[23] There is a Provost adoration that you would like, & Marmion, Foucquet & Daret. The Mabuses are sublime, there is one big bevelled penis,

I forget whether Adam's or Neptune's, like the lady in Tamburlaine naked in a net of gold, soigné like a glass or curl of lemon–rind by Kalf or Heda.[24] The Brueghel [*for* Bruegel] Proverbs are worthy to be sent to Sir Robert Tate, with key. What happy hours he would spend. But a gallery is not the names in its catalogue and perhaps it would have been better simply to say that I shall leave Berlin clearer in my impatience with the immensely competent bullies and browbeaters and highwaymen and naggers, the Rembrandts & Halses and Titians and Rubenses, the Tarquins of art.[25] Or is it a pettiness to move away from the art that takes me by the scruff of the neck?

Talking about the Tarquins, I was at a Beethoven concert of the Berlin Symphonic under Eugen Jochum, Leonore, a late middle piano concerto and the Pastoral. Jochum is the kind of conductor that one feels must have begun on a bus or a tram. Furtwängler has spent the whole season in retirement. The horn passage in the Leonore was as I have always imagined and never heard it, innaccessibly [sic] distant, sylvan and autumn dusk, and also as I have never heard it the churn passage for strings, love's epilepsy. The concerto was pretty and tiresome, rather like the Frühlings violin sonata, played by the soloist with a perspiring stiff-wristed powerlessness that was terrible. And the Pastorale more irrefragably than ever an insult to the ear and understanding.[26]

I had a long letter from Frank. He couldn't stand Mürren and what he calls the "skating, skiing and skiting" and left after a few days. He saw Alan & Belinda in Paris on the way back, Alan as usual half tight which seems to be the best he can do.[27] As soon as he got home he went to bed with flu and is only just up again. He went straight through London, otherwise would have looked you up.

I am glad you are more easy in Harrington Road. I did not feel Black Cottage or whatever it was called was the place for you. Are you still on the Heinemann translation? Or have you been able to take up the Yeats again?[28] I had a very nice letter from him for Xmas, with a gay sad pen & crayon drawing of the west from O'Connell Bridge and fantasies about skating on the rollers of the brain. Charles wrote from Greenock just setting out for Florence.[29]

I also find it difficult to keep up with Murphy. From time to time I get nebulosities from Reavey. The book seems to be now under consideration by Dent for whom it was read by Richard Church who at the point of one of Reavey's lunches declared himself "greatly impressed" . . Reavey invites me to contribute to the review he is starting, but presumably he does not pay.[30] And I have nothing I like well enough to give away.

I managed to get in Potsdam just before this plague came on me, in a bright cold weather. Sanssouci is exquisite. It has nothing at all to do with Versailles, it is a big summerhouse and truly an architecture without care.[31] The terraces are rather too heavy for the palace and one is disconcerted at first by the facing all the way up and along of vine frames, but only at first.[32] The shallow green dome not so much rising from the gently bayed centre as resting on it is to a hair the mock heroic that is fitting and with the long low yellow front the chord of just the right interval. And the caryatids are all laughing, pretending to be bowed down.[33] I could not keep away from it, keep [sic] coming back to look at it again from all over the gardens, and was very sad to leave it, feeling that I would not see it again. I went through the rooms, which are very beautiful, but it was painful to be allowed only a glimpse of the countless Watteaus that are there. Voltaire's room is altogether charming and comic, complete

Princesse de Babylone, with fantastic birds and flowers all over the walls and ceiling and La Fontaine on the chair covers, and yet somehow full of exile and loneliness.[34] The picture gallery was an eyeopener; school of Rubens and van der Werff! Practically nothing else. Nowhere else in the world can there be so many van der Werffs gathered together in one place. Real pornography, that would make Fragonard look like Fra Angelico.[35]

I saw Maria Stuart and Hebbel's Gyges with Werner Krauss in the Schauspielhaus. The Schiller remains alive till the last act without betraying the secret of how it contrives to do so. The Hebbel is superbly written, full of tense intellectual poetry, but even Krauss could only put it across here and there. He is a very great actor. Hebbel is [in] the dramatist pigeonhole, but it is as a poet that he counts.[36] I had booked for Martha (!) in the Opera but was not well enough to go. I gave the ticket to the film-actor who came back highly delighted.[37]

I still hope to have a look at Weimar, Naumburg & Leipzig on the way to Dresden, but if this thing holds me up much longer I shan't be able to. I don't know when I shall be in London, hardly before May, unless my remaining strength gives out earlier than I have calculated. I shall try and save up to fly home, I can't bear the thought of trains and boats and customs and the case extirpating my arms.

All being well I shall be able to give you an address in Dresden within a fortnight.

Love ever

s/ Sam

TLS; 4 leaves, 4 sides; TCD, MS 10402/113.

1 SB sent McGreevy a reproduction of Giorgione's *Self-portrait as David* from the Herzog Anton Ulrich Museum in Brunswick; see 22 December 1936, n. 2.

2 SB talked about the Giorgione painting in Brunswick with Dr. Rosa Schapire, having met her in Berlin on 21 December 1936; her collection is described in 14 November 1936, n. 6. She preferred Giorgione's *Portrait of Young Man* (Gemäldegalerie, Berlin, 12A).

3 Rembrandt, *Family Group* (1638, Anton Ulrich Herzog Museum, Brunswick, GG 238).
Italian painters Luca Signorelli (c. 1450–1523) and Piero della Francesca (1420–1492).
"Taugenichts" (good-for-nothing).

4 The works by Erich Heckel, Ernst Kirchner, and German sculptor Georg Kolbe (1877–1947), as well as the stones etched by Karl Schmidt-Ruttloff, were in Schmidt-Rottluff's flat in Berlin, which Rosa Schapire used while the painter and his wife were out of town (Mark Nixon, 7 May 2006).

5 "De la part de" (literally, on behalf of; here, thanks to). Alice Sauerlandt's introductions: 28 November 1936, n. 14; Sauerlandt and his work: 28 November 1936, n. 10.
Herbert Read, not the English art critic Roger Fry (1866–1934), was the author of *Art Now*; Read's dedication: "To Max Sauerlandt in admiration of his knowledge of the art of all ages and in recognition of his devotion to the cause of modern art" (*Art Now: An Introduction to the Theory of Modern Painting and Sculpture* [New York: Harcourt, Brace and Co., 1933] n.p.).
"Mais je n'en ai rien fait" (but I did nothing about it).

6 SB's first meeting with Axel Kaun was on 11 January (Tophoven, *Becketts Berlin*, 119–120; BIF, UoR, GD 4/f. 1).
Rowohlt published German translations of *Henry the Eighth* (1929; *Heinrich der Achte*) and *Francis the First* (1935; *Franz der Erste*) by Irish writer Francis Hackett, and *Brazilian Adventure* (1933; *Brasilianisches Abenteuer*), *One's Company* (1934; *Mit mir allein*), and *News from Tartary* (1936; *Tataren Nachrichten*) by English writer Peter Fleming (1907–1971). The last was published serially in the *Frankfurter Zeitung*, and Fleming was on "a ten-day lecture tour...hopping from place to place by air" in early 1937 (Duff Hart-Davis, *Peter Fleming: A Biography* [London: Jonathan Cape, 1974] 198).
Rowohlt also published translations of *Look Homeward, Angel* (1929; *Schau heimwärts, Engel!*) and *Of Time and the River* (1935; *Von Zeit und Strom*) by American author Thomas Wolfe (1900–1938). Wolfe frequently visited Germany (Thomas Wolfe, *The Letters of Thomas Wolfe*, ed. Elizabeth Nowell [New York: C. Scribner's Sons, 1961] 442; Elizabeth Nowell, *Thomas Wolfe: A Biography* [Garden City, NY: Doubleday and Co., 1960] 271–277, 325; David Herbert Donald, *Look Homeward: A Life of Thomas Wolfe* [Boston: Little, Brown and Co., 1987] 319–326).
Rowohlt was also the publisher of a translation of *Le Dieu des corps* (1928; *Der Gott des Fleisches*) and the first six volumes in the novel cycle by Jules Romains, *Les Hommes de bonne volonté* (from 1932; *Die guten Willens sind*).

7 Kempt and the actor Josef Eichheim: 18 January 1937 to Mary Manning Howe, n. 10.

8 SB refers to Axel Kaun, who was on his way to the Riesengebirge, a sub-Alpine mountain range on the border of Poland and Czechoslovakia, and to Kaun's friend Günter Albrecht.

9 Susan Manning, mother of Mary Manning Howe and close friend of May Beckett.

10 SB refers to his poem "Cascando," *Dublin Magazine*, 3–4.

11 The Pergamon altar of Zeus and Athena (c. 175 BC), a 40-foot-tall white marble Hellenistic temple, was taken from its original location in Pergamon (now Turkey) and installed in the Pergamon Museum in Berlin in 1871. Around its base are relief sculptures of battles between the Gods and the Titans; their dramatic gestures and high degree of contour led scholars to describe them as "baroque."

12 Issues of provenance are complicated by the circumstances of political doctrine, war, and occupation. Nearly 400 works in the collections of the Kaiser Friedrich Museum in 1936 were destroyed during World War II. Further, in the post-war division of the city, the remaining collection was divided between the Berlin-Dahlem Museum in the West and the Bode Museum in the East. In 1997 these collections were reunited in the Gemäldegalerie in the Kulturforum, Potsdamer Platz, and, from autumn 2006, the Bode Museum reopened with European art from late classical antiquity to 1800.

The Virgin and Child (NGL 3043) by Florentine painter Masaccio (né Tommaso di Ser Giovanni di Mone Cassai, 1401–1428) in the National Gallery (London) was painted as the center of an altarpiece for the chapel of Saint Julian in Santa Maria del Carmine, Pisa. Several panels of the predella of this altarpiece are in the Kaiser Friedrich Museum: *The Adoration of the King* (58A); *The Crucifixion of St. Peter* / *The Decollation of the Baptist* (58B); *St. Julian Killing his Parents* / *St. Nicholas Dowering the Three Daughters* (58E) (Henning Bock, Irene Geismeier, Rainald Grosshans, *et al.*, eds., *Gemäldegalerie Berlin: Gesamtverzeichnis* [Berlin: Staatliche Museen zu Berlin Preussischer Kulturbesitz, 1996] 463).

The Lying-in of a Noble Florentine Woman (also known as *Birth Scene*, 58C) is now thought to be by the younger brother of Masaccio, Giovanni di Ser (1406–1486) (Keith Christiansen, "Some Observations on the Brancacci Frescoes after their Cleaning," *Burlington Magazine* 133.1054 [January 1991] 15; Bock, Geismeier, Grosshans, *et al.*, eds., *Gemäldegalerie Berlin: Gesamtverzeichnis*, 464).

13 Signorelli's *Pan as God of Nature and as Master of Music* (also known as *Court of Pan* and *The Education of Pan*, KF 79A) was destroyed in 1945; it is reproduced in Tom Henry and Laurence Kanter, *Luca Signorelli: The Complete Paintings* (New York: Rizzoli, 2002) 172–173.

El Greco's *Laocoön and His Sons* was on loan to the National Gallery, London, from May 1934 to December 1935; it is now in the collection of the National Gallery, Washington, DC (NGW 1946.18.1) (Jonathan Brown and Richard G. Mann, *Spanish Paintings of the Fifteenth through Nineteenth Centuries*, The Collections of the National Gallery of Art Systematic Catalogue [Washington, DC: National Gallery of Art; Cambridge: Cambridge University Press, 1990] 64).

14 The paintings by Andrea del Sarto (also Andrea d'Agnolo, 1486–1530) are *Portrait of a Young Woman* (KF 240, considered to be a portrait of del Sarto's wife Lucrezia del Fede) and *Mary with the Child* (KF 246).

15 The painting in the Kaiser Friedrich collection by Giovanni Girolamo Savoldo (also Giovan Gerolamo, fl. 1506–1548) is *Venetian Woman* (also known as *St. Mary Magdalene*, KF 307); it lacks the iconic alabaster vase of ointment that is in his painting *Mary Magdalene* (NGL 1031) in London's National Gallery. The Berlin painting presents a

three-quarter figure, whereas the London painting depicts a one-half figure; the dates ascribed to the paintings range from 1527 to 1540.

16 There were eight paintings in the Kaiser Friedrich Museum by Botticelli and his school; there were seventeen by Giovanni Bellini (c. 1431–1516), his school and work-shop, his brother Gentile Bellini (1429–1507), and his father Jacopo Bellini (1400–c. 1471). The *Lamentation of Christ* (KF 1678) ascribed to Jacopo Bellini was destroyed in 1945.

17 SB compares the *Lamentation of Christ* (KF 1144) by Bernardino Butinone (c. 1450–1510) to Butinone's *Nativity* (NGL 3336) in the National Gallery, London; the latter is an attribution that had been disputed prior to 1929 (Jacqueline McComish, 24 May 1995).

SB mentions Cosimo Tura (c. 1430–1495), of the Ferrarese School; Venetian painter Carlo Crivelli (1430–1495); the Venetian family of painters Antonio Vivarini (1418–1476), Bartolomeo Vivarini (c. 1440 – after 1500), and Antonio's son, Alvise Vivarini (c. 1442 – c. 1505; and Ercole de Roberti (c. 1455–1496), who was active in Ferrara and Bologna.

The Mantegna paintings in the collection were *Portrait of Ludovico Cardinal Mezzarota* (KF 9), *The Presentation of Christ in the Temple* (KF 29), and *Madonna with Sleeping Child* (KF S.5).

SB refers to the *Burial of Christ* (KF 23A) by Italian artist Vittore Carpaccio (c. 1460–1525).

18 For paintings in the Kaiser Friedrich collection by Titian, Rembrandt, and Franz and Dirck Hals: Bock, Geismeier, Grosshans, *et al.*, eds., *Gemäldegalerie Berlin: Gesamtverzeichnis*, 120; 101–102; 58–59.

19 Adriaen Brouwer's *Dune Landscape in Moonlight* (KF 853B), once owned by Rembrandt, was on loan for the Paris exhibition La Peinture flamande: Rubens et son temps at the Musée de l'Orangerie (November–December 1936) (Charles Sterling, *La Peinture flamande: Rubens et son temps* [Paris: Librairie des Arts Décoratifs, 1936] n.p.).

20 There were eleven paintings by Gerard ter Borch the younger in the collection of the Kaiser Friedrich Museum; SB mentions *The Knife Grinder's Family* (KF 793), which depicts a brightly lit workman's yard. SB compares it to the painting by Jan Vermeer van Delft (1632–1675), *The Procuress* (also *Die Kupplerin*, RPG 1335).

21 Vermeer's two paintings in the Berlin collection are *The Pearl Necklace* (KF 912B) and *The Glass of Wine* (KF 912C). There were five paintings by Pieter de Hooch in the collection (see Bock, Geismeier, Grosshans, *et al.*, eds., *Gemäldegalerie Berlin: Gesamtverzeichnis*, 62). Two paintings by Dutch genre painter Nicolaes Maes (1634–1693) were in the collection: *An Old Woman Peeling Apples* (KF 819C) and *Repudiation of Hagar* (KF 819D, destroyed in 1945).

The gouache that SB describes by Adam Elsheimer was on loan from the Louvre from November 1936: *Evening Landscape* (Louvre 18,658).

22 SB refers to *The Three Musicians* (KF 413F) and *Portrait of a Woman* (KF 413E) by Diego Velázquez; the subject of the portrait was debated, and in 1936 the Condesa de Olivares was given as one possibility; it is now identifed as Doña Leonora da Guzmán, Condesa de Monterrey (Bock, Geismeier, Grosshans, *et al.*, eds.,

Gemäldegalerie Berlin: Gesamtverzeichnis, 123). Spanish painter Juan Bautista del Mazo (c. 1613–1667) was the son-in-law of Diego Velázquez, and worked with him; this "has led to the attribution to him of several pictures not considered good enough for Velázquez" (Peter Murray and Linda Murray, eds., *Penguin Dictionary of Art and Artists* [London: Penguin, 1993] 266).

23   The Flemish collection at the Kaiser Friedrich Museum included eleven paintings by or after Jan van Eyck (1390–1441). The South Netherlandish painter Robert Campin (c. 1375–1444) is now accepted as the Master of Flémalle; the three paintings by him in the Berlin collection are: *Portrait of a Man* (KF 537), *Portrait of Robert de Masmines* (KF 537A), and *Madonna on a Bank of Roses* (KF 1835); from his school, *Christ on the Cross* (KF 538A) and *The Adoration of the King* (KF 538).

The three paintings by Hugo van der Goes (1440–1482) are *Lamentation of Christ* (KF 1622), *Adoration of the King* (KF 1718), and *Adoration of the Herdsmen* (KF 1622A).

Those by Rogier van der Weyden (c. 1400–1464) were the *Bladelin Altar* (also known as the *Mittelburger Altar*, KF 535), the *Altar of Mary* (also known as the *Miraflores-Altar*, KF 534A), the *Altar of John the Baptist* (KF 534B), *Portrait of a Woman with Wimple* (KF 545D), *Saints Margaret and Apollonia* (534C), and *Charles the Bold, Duke of Burgundy* (KF 545, now given to the Workshop of Rogier van der Weyden).

John the Baptist in the Wilderness (KF 1631) by Geertgen Tot Sint Jans depicts a meadow landscape.

24   SB refers to *Adoration of the Magi* (HK 551B) by South Netherlandish painter Jan Provost (1465–1529). In Berlin, the work of illuminator and painter Simon Marmion (c. 1425–1489) consists of wings from the *Altarpiece of St. Omer* showing the life of St. Bertin (KF 1645 and KF 1645A). French painter Jean Fouquet (c. 1425 – c. 1478) was represented in the Berlin collection by *Etienne Chevalier with Holy St. Stephen* (KF 1617). Works by South Netherlandish painter Jacques Daret (c. 1400–1466) in Berlin are two panels from the Altarpiece from the St. Vast Abbey in Arras: *The Adoration of the Magi* (KF 527) and *The Visitation* (KF 542).

SB refers to *Neptune and Amphitrite* (KF 648) by Mabuse. Zenocrate, consort of Tamburlaine, was wrapped in a sheet of gold when she died, but was not interred until the death of Tamburlaine (Christopher Marlowe, *Tamburlaine II*). "Soigné" (carefully worked) in the manner of the still life paintings of Dutch artists Willem Kalf (c. 1619–1693) and Willem Claesz Heda (1594–1680), which often included glass objects and a spiral of lemon peel.

25   SB refers to Pieter Bruegel the elder's painting *The Dutch Proverbs* (KF 1720) which illustrated 100 proverbs; a key to the proverbs was exhibited with the painting. Professor Robert William Tate (1872–1952) was Public Orator of Trinity College Dublin from 1914 to 1952 and Junior Dean from 1919 to 1931 (a frank portrait of him can be found in McDowell and Webb, *Trinity College Dublin 1592–1952: An Academic History*, 400).

Tarquin refers, figuratively, to two legendary kings of the early Romans, Lucius Tarquinius Pricus (616–578 BC) and Lucius Tarquinius Superbus (534–510 BC).

26   The 13 January 1937 concert of the Berlin Philharmonic Orchestra, with Eugen Jochum (1902–1987) as guest conductor and Eduard Erdmann (1896–1958) as piano soloist, was a Beethoven program that included the *Leonora Overture* no. 3, op.72a; Piano Concerto no. 5 in E-flat major, op. 73 ("Emperor"); and Symphony no. 6 in F major, op. 68 ("Pastoral"; SB uses the German spelling, "Pastorale"). SB refers to the

trumpet calls in the second section of the *Leonore Overture* as the "horn passage." In SB's German diary, he describes a passage that opens with the first violins joined in turn by the second violins, violas, and cellos; it may be this opening of the Presto movement that he calls the "churn passage" (see BIF, UoR, GD 4/f. 9). SB compares the Piano Concerto to Beethoven's Violin Sonata in F major, op. 24, no. 5 ("Frühlings sonata").

Following the Wagner festival at Bayreuth in the summer of 1936, Furtwängler went into retirement until March 1937 (Schönzeler, *Furtwängler*, 79–80); see also SB to Morris Sinclair, 27 January 1924 [*for* 1934], n. 5.

27 Frank Beckett had gone to Mürren, Switzerland, for his Christmas holiday. Alan and Belinda Duncan.

28 McGreevy returned to London in December 1936, and was staying at 49 Harrington Road; in the autumn of 1936, he had lived in a cottage in Toppesfield, Essex (see 9 October 1936, n. 1). McGreevy translated Maillart, *Oasis interdites: de Pékin au Cachemire* (1937; *Forbidden Journey: From Peking to Kashmir*) for Heinemann. Prior to this, he had been working on his study of Jack B. Yeats.

29 The letter from Jack Yeats to SB has not been found. The letter from Charles Prentice to SB has not been found.

30 Richard Church's response to *Murphy*: 18 January 1937 to Mary Manning Howe, n. 2. Reavey's review did not materialize.

31 Sanssouci in Potsdam, west of Berlin, was the summer house of King Friedrich II (later known as Frederick the Great, 1712–1786), who commissioned Prussian architect Georg Wenzeslaus von Knobelsdorff (1699–1753) to design it in 1744, based on his own sketches. Intended as a retreat, Sanssouci has only twelve rooms; SB compares the proportions and decorations with the massive scale of the Palais de Versailles.

32 The palace is at the top of a terraced hillside, called the "Weinberg"; each terrace is faced with grape arbors that can be enclosed by glass doors. SB's winter visit might have contributed to his first impression since the foliage did not then cover the architecture of the cascading terraces.

33 The single-story rococo palace is topped in the center by a shallow dome. The caryatids are decorative rather than structural.

34 The interior of Sanssouci was accessible only on a guided tour. Watteau's paintings in Sanssouci itself were *Village Wedding* (GK I 5603), *Italian Recreation* (GK I 5599), and *Fair with Comedians* (GK I 5602) in the Little Gallery; Watteau's *Concert* (GK I 5623) was hung in the Audience Room (Gerd Bartoscheck, Curator Bildergalerie, Park Sanssouci, 22 March 2006; Ettore Camesasca, *The Complete Paintings of Watteau* [New York: Harry N. Abrams, 1968] 90, 119, 108, 123, 126–127; Petra Wesch, with Rosemarie Heise-Schirdewan and Bärbel Stranka, *Sanssouci: The Summer Residence of Frederick the Great* [Munich: Prestel, 2003] 36–37).

Voltaire had his own room at Sanssouci, with lacquered wood furniture upholstered with embroidered scenes from the Fables of the French writer Jean de la Fontaine (1621–1695); the delicate bird and flower decorations on the walls and ceilings were by Johann Michael Hoppenhaupt (1709–1769) and his brother, Johann Christian Hoppenhaupt (1719–1785). SB refers to Voltaire's *La Princesse de*

Babylone (1768; *The Princess of Babylon*), a fantasy which takes place in the fortified city of Babylon ruled by King Bélus.

35 The Gallery is a separate building at Sanssouci that houses the extensive collection of Friedrich II. For images of the paintings in the Gallery by Rubens and by Dutch artist Adriaen van der Werff (1659–1722): Götz Eckardt, *Die Gemälde in der Bildergalerie von Sanssouci* [Potsdam: Sanssouci, 1975]).

In SB's sally, van der Werff's painting is pornographic enough to make Fragonard's work (often regarded as mildly pornographic) seem as innocent and pure as that of Florentine painter and illuminator Fra Angelico (Fra Giovanni di Fiesole, fl. 1417–1455).

36 *Maria Stuart*: 9 January 1937, n. 1; Hebbel's *Gyges*: SB to Mary Manning Howe, 18 January 1937, n. 8.

37 *Martha, oder Der Markt zu Richmond* (*Martha, or the Fair at Richmond*), an opera by Friedrich von Flotow (1812–1883), was performed at the Staatsoper on 15 January 1937. SB gave his ticket to his landlord Kempt, who gave it to SB's fellow boarder, actor Josef Eichheim (BIF, UoR, GD 4/f. 11, 14 January 1937).

THOMAS McGREEVY
LONDON

25/1/37   Naumburg

[no greeting]

They call these from his own hand but I don't see it. 3 heads are shanghaied in Windsor.[1] I was in Weimar for the week-end, in a pub in the Frauenplan. Only a short pause here to see the Dom, which is stupendous.[2] Going on to Leipzig this afternoon. Very good modern pictures in Halle and Erfurt.[3] Deep snow everywhere & a sterilizing cold. Met a grand stage decorator in love with Mexico, Traven & Darius Milhaud.[4] Shall write early next week from Dresden.

Love

S

APCI; 1 leaf, 1 side; heads of Judas and Peter on one panel and John on the other, "Residenzschloss Weimar; Grossherzog, Wohnräume"; to Thomas McGreevy Esq, 49 Harrington Road, London S.W.7; *pm illeg.*, Naumburg; TCD, MS 10402/114.

1 In the ducal apartment of the Residenzschloss Weimar were drawings after the heads of the Apostles in *The Last Supper* by Leonardo da Vinci (1452–1519); SB compares the heads of Judas, Peter, and John on this postcard to similar drawings in the large da Vinci collection in Windsor Castle.

According to records of the Residenzschloss, the drawings were copies made by Giuseppe Bossi (1777–1815) in 1807; they were not described in the 1913 catalogue of the Ducal collection (Viola Geyersback, Klassik Stiftung, Weimar; Kate Trauman Steinitz, "The Leonardo Drawings at Weimar," *Raccolta Vinciana* 20 [1964] 342–344). The drawing of Peter and Judas (as well as that of Thomas and James the Greater from the series) is now in the Ackland Art Museum, University of North Carolina at Chapel Hill (77.53.1; 77.53.2); the drawing of John that belongs to this series is in a private collection (Pietro C. Marani, *Il Genio e le passioni, Leonardo da Vinci e il Cenacolo: precedenti, innovazioni, riflessi di un capolavoro* [Milan: Skira, 2001] 196–197, fig. 60).

2 The Cathedral of St. Peter and St. Paul, the Naumburg Dom, dates from the twelfth and thirteenth centuries. Goethe lived at 1 Frauenplan for fifty years; the Goethe museum is located there today. SB stayed in the Weisser Schwan in Weimar on Frauentorstrasse, next to the Goethe Haus.

3 SB refers to the modern collection at the Moritzburg Museum in Halle, where he had to sign what was called the "'extra' visitor's book" on 23 January 1937, in order to view the "Schreckenskammer" (chamber of horrors), paintings that had been segregated from the collection (Wolfgang Bücke, Curator of Painting, Staatliche Galerie Morizburg, Halle, 22 February 1993). In his diary SB lists details of the paintings by Heckel, Paul Klee (1879–1940), Müller, Schmidt-Rottloff, Marc, Kokoschka, Nolde, Kirchner, the Russian-born Wassily Kandinsky (1866–1944), and Lyonel Feininger, including a series of views of Halle (BIF, UoR, GD 4/f. 23, 23 January 1937; for images and provenance: Andreas Hüneke, *Die faschistische Aktion "Entartete Kunst" 1937 in Halle*, Schriftenreihe zur Geschichte der Staatlichen Galerie Moritzburg Halle [Halle: Staatliche Galerie Moritzburg, 1987]; also Hess, *Lyonel Feininger*, 263, 278–280).

SB also visited the private collection of Marie Weise (née Herold, 1879–1971) and Felix Weise (1876–1961) in Halle, with works by Kirchner, Munch, Heckel, Schmidt-Rottluff, Lehmbruck, and Müller (for SB's conversation with Frau Weise and details of the collection: BIF, UoR GD 4/f. 36–37, 23 January 1937).

On 24 January 1937 SB visited the Anger Museum in Erfurt where the modern collection was still on display on the first floor; he notes works by Kirchner, Gerhard Marck (1889–1981), Kokoschka, Mueller, Feininger, Kandinsky, Nolde, Wilhelm Lehmbruck (1881–1919), Heckel, Dix, Schmidt-Rottluff, Barlach, Renée Sintenis (1888–1965), and Christian Rohlf (1849–1938) (BIF, UoR, GD 4/f.27, 24 January 1937).

4 Heinz Porep (1888–c. 1956) studied painting in Munich and Weimar as a painter; he designed the sets for the 1935 Halle production of *Ottone* by George Frideric Handel (1685–1759) (Götz Traxdorf, Library of the Handel-Haus of Halle; BIF, UoR GD 4/f. 22).

Prussian-born actor Hermann Albert Otto Max Feige (1882–1969) had written anarchist propaganda under the pseudonym of Ret Marut (1917–1923); later he adopted the pseudonym of B. Traven under which he wrote *The Treasure of the Sierra Madre* (1927).

Porep had visited Traven in Mexico; he was a friend of the French composer Darius Milhaud (1892–1974).

THOMAS McGREEVY

LONDON

30/1 [1937]   Dresden
                                                                  bei Höfer
                                                                  Bürgerwiese 15

[no greeting]
Arrived here yesterday from Leipzig, to stay 3 weeks at the most & probably less. The little I have seen is lovely. The cold is dreadful. Leipzig was apotheosis of Max Klinger and ignominis [*for* ignominious] in the Gewandhaus.[1] Write a long letter at once
        Love
          S

APCI; 1 leaf, 1 side; "Der Dom Zu Naumburg, Klagender Johannes am Westlettner"; *pm* 31-1-37, Dresden; *to* Thomas McGreevy Esq, 49 Harrington Road, London S.W. 7; TCD, MS 10402/115. *Dating*: pm and from 9 January 1937, above.

1 In 1937 Leipzig's Museum der Bildenden Künste and the Leipziger Kunstverein held a retrospective exhibition of the work of Max Klinger (1857–1920) displaying nearly 400 works (*Gedächtnis-Ausstellung Max Klinger* [Leipzig: Museum der Bildenden Künste, Leipziger Kunstverein, 1937] 3).

SB attended the Gewandhaus concert on 28 January 1937 which is discussed in greater detail in his letter to McGreevy of 16 February 1937 and in its n. 13.

GEORGE REAVEY

LONDON

30/1/37   Dresden
                                                                  bei Höfer
                                                                  Bürgerwiese 15

[no greeting]

Above my address here. There may be news from you lying in Berlin waiting to be forwarded. But whether or no tip us a wink to Florence on the Elbe, which will be too cold to hold me for more than a fortnight or 3 weeks.[1]

[no signature]

Heil und Sieg u fette Beute.[2]

APC; 1 leaf, 1 side; "Schlossmuseum Weimar, A. Dürer: *Bildnis der Felicitas Tucher*, 1499"; *to* George Reavey Esq, 1 Parton Street, London W.C.; *pm* 31-1-37, Dresden; tear, center bottom; TxU.

1 Dresden, on the Elbe River.

2 "Heil und Sieg und fette Beute" (Hail and victory and rich pickings).

THOMAS McGREEVY

LONDON

[2 February 1937]   [Dresden]

[no greeting]

Che tu fossi meco.[1]

S

APCI; 1 leaf, 1 side; "Antonello da Messine's [sic] *Der H.L Sebastian (Martyrdom of St. Sebastian)*, Amtliche Ausgabe des Ministeriums für Volksbildung zu Dresden"; *pm* 2-2-37, Dresden; *to* Thomas McGreevy, 49 Harrington Road, London S. W. 7; TCD, MS 10402/116. *Dating, Place:* from pm.

[2 February 1937]   [Dresden]

That you were here with me.[1]

S.

1 "Che tu fossi meco" is not idiomatic in Italian and presumably is SB's invention on the model of the English "Wish you were here," but in Trecento style ("meco" being archaic for "con me" [with me]).

GEORGE REAVEY

LONDON

15/2/37   Dresden

Cher ami

Je m'en doutais, comme disait Poil de Carott[e], quand on lui donna à boire [d]u déjà bu.[1]

> C'est une Dent
> Par conséquent
> Qui ne mord
> Aucunement.[2]

Murphy né ton serviteur, t'écrira sous peu et plus so[uv]ent de Bièreville-sur-Isar[3]

S

APCI; 1 leaf, 1 side; "Dom zu Meissen, *Schutzpatron Evangelist Johannes*"; to George Reavey Esq, 1 Parton Street, London W.C. 1, England; *pm* 15-2-37, Dresden; surface delaminated, having been pasted in a scrapbook and removed; TxU.

15/2/37   Dresden

Dear George

I thought as much, as Poil de Carotte used to say when what he was given to drink had already been drunk.[1]

> This Dent
> I meant
> Won't quite
> Bite.[2]

Murphy born your servant, will write to you shortly and more often from Beerville-on-Isar[3]

S

1 SB may be referring to a scene in Jules Renard's *Poil de Carotte* (1894; *Carrots*) in which the child, Poil de Carotte, is force-fed a soup which he is led to believe is made from his own excretion, as punishment for his having soiled his bed; thereafter he refuses to drink, saying he is not thirsty (Renard, *Oeuvres*, I, *Poil de Carotte*, 666–667).

2 SB puns on the name of the London publisher Dent, with "dent" (tooth). Despite Richard Church's positive response to the novel, Dent turned it down (see 18 January 1937 to Mary Manning Howe, n. 2).

3 "So[uv]ent" (often): text illegible due to delamination. SB refers to Munich, on the Isar River.

THOMAS McGREEVY
LONDON

16/2/37   Dresden
                                          bei Höfer
                                          Bürgerwiese 15

Dear Tom

It was a great disappointment that you could not make the trip, though I hardly expected you would be able.[1] You would like Dresden. It was a great 70 years under August the Strong & his son and Pöppelmann was a great architect. The Zwinger is very much restored, but well restored. It is altogether lovely, with sudden sad passages (arcades), far more Watteauesque tho' only a little earlier than Potsdam. The gallery wing, heavy dark 19th century Renaissance, does its best to spoil the other three, which should have been left as they were, open to the river.[2]

I don't know what to say about the Gallery. I suppose to us even the most discriminating royal collection of the 18th century, which it remains essentially, must have more defects than merits. There is a terrible lot of late Italian rubbish, no primitives, practically no Flemish of the great period, and rooms and rooms full of Mengs & Rosalba pastels and Bellotto views of Dresden. And it is badly lit and hung. I should not think for a moment of comparing it with the Kaiser Friedrich.[3]

The Giorgione is in a mess. The putto with the armour and the bright bird sitting at her feet (by Giorgione or Titian?) was painted over with senseless landscape in the 19th century and the whole line of the left leg destroyed. I haven't much of an eye for that kind of thing, but it entered it like Joyce's Parnell spit at the first look. I mean the wrongness from the knee down, before I was in possession of the information that explains it. The head and arm, all ascent, is miraculous, but sweet, for me at least, as the Hampton Court Shepherd is sweet, though I know he is not for you.[4] I looked forward to leaving Dresden with a more definite attitude towards Giorgione, but it is the other way round. He must remain to be seen in Castelfranco, as exclusively as Grünewald in Kolmar.[5] And God knows when that may be, though there is just the possibility of my making the latter excursion from Stuttgart on the way home.

The Raphael is very good indeed, though one doesn't want to look at her twice, the best Raphael I have seen after the South Ken[sington].[6]

The Antonello that I sent you is stupendous – the tiny figures of the quick in the background gossiping & making appointments, under a paradisal sky. It was not an 18th century acquisition.[7]

The Vermeer Kupplerin is also indescribably lovely, and already essentially Vermeer. If Giorgione[']s Venus is the sister of the young man in Berlin, the dark figure on the left here, with the crazy smile, is the brother of the girl in Brunswick.[8]

But dreadfully hung, in a dark room with dark dirty green patterned paper full of dark Rembrandts, between a Rembrandt old man and a Salomon Koninck Astronomer and cowering under a huge dark heavy Ferdinand Bol Jacob before Pharoah [for Pharaoh].[9]

There is really not much point writing like this about the pictures. But I can't stop without mentioning the Poussin Venus. Beyond praise & appraisement. There is no postcard and the big reproduction, that I wanted to send you, is very unfair to the original. Beside it is a Narcissus, not in the same class as the Louvre one, but with Echo turned to stone![10]

I bearded Director Posse (then why doesn't he!) and got him to show me the Röntgen photograph of the Giorgione, which wasn't much help. He asked who got the Dublin Gallery, but I could only remember the name of the man who should have.[11] He was seedy & dull, perhaps a beer débauché like myself, only not so intelligent or honest.

The journey from Berlin was an amusing and often lovely adventure. Halle (lovely modern pictures still actually on view to the public in the Moritzburg, a private collection mostly Kirchner and a charming stage decorator & Händel expert in love with Mexico and friend of Traven & Darius Milhaud, who was of a friendliness that bewilders me still),[12] Erfurt, Weimar, Naumburg with marvellous 13th century sculpture in the Dom, & Leipzig where I froze and was miserable & heard a Gewandhaus concert that was an insult to the senses & the understanding.[13]

Here I have met all kinds of friends & interesting people, especially an art historian called Grohmann who knows them all, from Picasso to Salkeld, and has done big catalogues of Klee, Kandinsky, Kirchner & Baumeister, and whose name perhaps you may remember having come across in Cahiers d'Art. He has Picassos & Klees & Kandinskys & Modrians [*for* Mondrians] and a lot of Germans. He was removed from his post in the Real Gymnasium here at the Gallery in 1933, like all the others of his kidney.[14] Through him I was able to visit one of the best private collections of modern art in Germany, the Ida Bienert collection, reaching from a marvellous Cézanne to Léger & Chagall & Archipenko & Marc & Munch & splendid examples from all the names I have written & a lot more besides. Including a Kokoschka portrait of Nancy Cunard!!! painted in Paris 1924. I went twice, for lunch the second time, and have the catalogue to show you, I hope in London in May.[15] Then a lot of amusing Russians (Obolensky), blue with blood and revolutionary privations, with whom I am so agreeably entangled that I cannot get away till Friday, though I had meant to go to-day.[16]

I heard (here of course) a marvellous performance of the Marriage of Figaro, with a Cherubin[o] like a red haired version of the Antonello boy? girl? in London.[17] The first opera that I was sorry to have over.

I expect to be in Munich a little before the end of the month, pausing on the way in Bamberg, Nürnberg, Regensburg & perhaps Würzburg, though I rather baulk at Nürnberg, of which I have the gloomiest memories.[18] Write in about a week poste restante, Munich.

I am delighted to hear you are in better form since being in London, which must seem a different place now that you are shut of Cheyne Gardens. Is Geoffrey organizing a ruelle in Harley Street? It is the kind of thing that I wouldn't put past him. He has not written. His wife is too <u>molle</u>.[19] Wisdom I know. He is the man who when he met me in Harley St. on my way to Bion asked me was I going to an alienist. He himself is being put on the spot by Ernest Jones. My first experience of him was in a day school in Dublin when he was famous for the joy he took in making the wheels for his own toy engines. He is a pedagogue.[20]

I had a dark letter from Bryan [*for* Brian], full of some mysterious "trouble" in Dublin, and of a "melo" timed for the end of this week. After my experiences of him in the Dolphin I can imagine what is wrong. If I am right I hope it is not as serious as it might be. He seems to be in a completely obsidianal condition, physically also.[21]

The anus is better, it was really awful for fully 10 days in Berlin – consternating. It was on the mend as I left Berlin, or rather I left Berlin as soon as it was on the mend, and now it has more or less settled down, though it is only a question of how often and how badly it will light up again before I finish this journey and can get home & have it cleared up. The damm old pruritis is just about as bad as ever, no doubt part of the same thing. But I am used to it. Otherwise I am as well as I ever am.

I suppose you have heard of the death of Charles Prentice's father, when Charles himself was in Florence. I had a calm letter from Greenock, and replied with paternal necrologies of a despairing kind that I regret.[22] One should simply say "deepest sympathy" & begin a new sentence.

I have neither written anything nor wanted to, except for a short hour, when the frail sense of beginning life behind the eyes, that is the best of all experiences, came again for the first time since Cascando, and produced 2 lines and a half.[23]

Perhaps you have heard also that Dent turned down Murphy, as I knew they would, in spite of Church's affabilities. So also, since, have Cobden Sanderson. So will have, soon, Faber, Secker & Hogarth. By which time if Nott does not renegue I shall be surprised. I dread going home with nothing cut & dried to do.[24] Proofs & a publication would carry me over till I could get away again. They will expect me to cash in on this journey at once & all at once, and that cannot be, it will have been a better journey than that. But mother will want Morton or Doyle.[25]

Love ever

Sam

ALS; 2 leaves, 4 sides; TCD, MS 10402/117.

1 On 4 February, SB had received McGreevy's letter indicating that he would not come to Dresden (BIF, UoR GD 4/f. 67).

2 August the Strong (known in Poland as Augustus II, and in Germany as Frederick Augustus I, Elector of Saxony, 1670–1733) and his son, Prince Augustus III (also known as Frederick Augustus II, Elector of Saxony, 1696–1763), established Dresden as a major center for the arts.

The Zwinger Museum in Dresden was built from 1709 to 1732 to house the Royal Collections. It was designed by Matthäus Daniel Pöppelmann (1662–1736); in 1936 a restoration had been completed under Dresden architect Hubert Ermische (1883–1951) (Dr. Angel Walter, Chief Curator, Staatliche Kunstsammlungen, Dresden, 12 March 1993). Sanssouci in Potsdam was built later, from 1745 to 1747.

In Pöppelmann's plan, the Zwinger was composed of seven halls and gatehouses connected by one-story galleries. In 1847–1854 a large gallery wing was added, designed in the style of the late Italian Renaissance by Gottfried Semper (1803–1879). It enclosed the square, closing off the north vista toward the Elbe River that had been integral to Pöppelmann's original vision of two long palaces connected by galleries, with steps down to the Elbe.

3 The Royal Collection housed in the Zwinger was greatly enhanced during the reign of Augustus III (1733–1763) (for details of the acquisitions of this period: K. Woermann, *Catalogue of the Pictures in the Royal Gallery at Dresden*, 7th edn. [Dresden: Kunstanstalt Wilhelm Hoffmann, 1908] 1–7). The collection includes paintings on German historical and biblical subjects, portraits and pastels by Anton Raphael Mengs (1728–1779), court painter to August III, as well as plaster casts. The collection held 157 pastels by Venetian artist Rosalba Carriera. SB refers to Bernardo Bellotto (who signed his name as Canaletto outside of Italy, 1721–1780). Augustus III invited Bellotto to be an official court painter from 1747 to 1758, and the collection includes fifteen views of Dresden by him.

4 Giorgione's *Venus* (RPG, 185) had been partially repainted after 1837 in order to repair damage; this eliminated the Cupid seated at her feet, holding a bird that can be recognized through X-rays and infrared light (see Hans Posse, "Die Rekonstruktion der Venus mit dem Cupido von Giorgione," *Jahrbuch der Preuszischen Kunstsammlungen*, LII

[Berlin: G. Grote, 1931] 29–35; this article prints the Röntgen photographs of the painting). According to Posse's analysis, the line of the left leg was not altered, although Martin Conway calls the foot "inelegant" (*Giorgione: A New Study of His Art as a Landscape Painter* [London: Ernest Benn, 1929] 55). The landscape of the background was formerly ascribed to Titian, but now is thought to have been begun by Giorgione and completed by Titian.

In James Joyce's *A Portrait of the Artist as a Young Man*, Mr. Casey tells the story of being with Parnell in Arklow, when the crowd was hostile; when Mr. Casey had had enough from a woman who was heckling Parnell, he spat his tobacco into her eye (36–37).

SB compares *Venus* with Giorgione's *Bust of Shepherd with Pipe* (Hampton Court, 111).

5 Giorgione was from Castelfranco, where many of his major works are kept. Matthias Grünewald's masterwork, the *Isenheim Altarpiece*, was painted for the Antonite monastery and hospital in Isenheim (Unterlinden Museum, Colmar); for images and description: Georg Scheja, *The Isenheim Altarpiece*, tr. Robert Erich Wolf (New York: H. N. Abrams, 1969).

SB uses the German spelling, Kolmar.

6 Raphael's *Madonna Sistina* (RPG 93), painted as an altarpiece, depicts the Virgin standing on clouds between Pope Sixtus II and St. Barbara. SB compares it with the Raphael Cartoons for tapestries hung in the Sistine Chapel; the Cartoons were in the collection of the Victoria and Albert Museum, South Kensington, London (see 20 February [1935], n. 12).

7 *The Martyrdom of St. Sebastian* (RPG 52) by Antonello da Messina (1430–1479) was acquired by the Zwinger in 1873 (Henner Menz, *The Dresden Gallery* [New York: Harry N. Abrams, 1962] 67).

8 SB compares Vermeer's *The Procuress* (RPG 1335) in the Zwinger collection to his painting *The Girl with a Wine Glass* in the Brunswick Herzog-Anton-Ulrich Museum (316). He finds similarity between Giorgione's "Venus" (n. 4 above) and his *Portrait of a Young Man* in Berlin (18 January 1937 to Thomas McGreevy, n. 2), and further notes the resemblance between the dark figure on the left in *The Procuress* in Dresden and the woman in the *The Girl with a Wine Glass* in Brunswick.

9 Vermeer's *The Procuress* was hung near *Portrait of an Old Man* (RPG 1567) by Rembrandt, *Jacob, Presented by Joseph to Pharaoh* (RPG 1605) by Ferdinand Bol (1616–1680), and *Astronomer* (RPG 1589A) by Salomon Koninck (1609–1656).

10 Poussin's *Venus with Amor* (RPG 721) was hung next to a painting of *Narcissus and Echo* (RPG 722), then ascribed to Poussin (see Christopher Wright, who suggests that it was painted by a competent follower: *Poussin Paintings: A Catalogue Raisonné* [London: Jupiter Books, 1984] 241; Menz claims that *Narcissus and Echo* is an early, not fully accomplished work by Poussin in his *The Dresden Gallery*, 304). SB compares the treatment of Echo, who is outlined on a block of stone, to Poussin's *Echo and Narcissus* (Louvre 7297) in Paris.

11 Hans Posse (1879–1942), Director of the Zwinger from 1910 until the gallery closed in 1939. From 26 June 1938 to 1942, Posse became Director of the Special Mission Linz, acquiring art works on behalf of Hitler's proposed museum in Linz, Austria (Barron, ed., *"Degenerate Art": The Fate of the Avant-Garde in Nazi Germany*, 399).

"Posse" (Lat., to be able).
George Furlong was appointed as Director of the National Gallery of Ireland in October 1935; McGreevy had applied for the position.

12   The collection of the Moritzburg in Halle and the collection of Felix Weise in Halle: 25 January 1937, n. 3. Porep, the stage decorator and Handel expert, friend of Traven and Darius Milhaud: 25 January 1937, n. 4.

13   The statues in the west choir of Naumburg's thirteenth-century Gothic Dom commemorate the family of Bishop Dietrich von Wettin (also known as Theodoric, 1243–1272) under whom the building was completed. There are four couples and four single men represented.

The concert on 28 January in the Gewandhaus in Leipzig was entitled "Heitere Musik" (Jovial Music). It presented a number of short pieces: "Fröhliche Musik für kleines Orchester" by Hermann Grabner (1886–1969); the recitative and aria of Zerbinetta "Grossmächtige Prinzessin, wer verstünde nicht" from Strauss's opera *Ariadne auf Naxos*, sung by Erna Berger (1900–1990) of the Berlin Staatsoper; "Gestern Abend war Vetter Michel da," a humoresque in variations, op. 74, composed and conducted by Prussian pianist Georg Alfred Schumann (1866–1952); the rondo "Aufforderung zum Tanze" in D-flat major, originally for piano, op. 65, by Carl Maria von Weber (1786–1826), orchestrated by Louis-Hector Berlioz (1803–1869) as "L'Invitation à la valse"; two arias by Weber sung by Erna Berger: the scena and aria "Non paventar, mia vita" for soprano and orchestra, op. 51, and the recitative and rondo "Il momento s'avvincia" for soprano and orchestra, op. 16; and *Kaiserwalzer*, op. 437, by Johann Strauss, II (1825–1899).

14   German art historian Will Grohmann (1887–1968). Dublin artist Cecil Salkeld; German expressionist Willi Baumeister (1889–1955); Dutch artist Piet Mondrian (1872–1944).

For a complete bibliography of Grohmann's studies of Paul Klee, Wassily Kandinsky, and Ernst Kirchner: Dina Sonntag, "Bibliographie Will Grohmann" in *In Memoriam Will Grohmann, 1887–1968: Wegbereiter der Moderne* (Stuttgart: Staatsgalerie Stuttgart, 1987) 58–64; for Grohmann's contributions to the Paris journal *Cahiers d'art*: *Index Général de la revue "Cahiers d'art," 1926–1960* (Paris: Editions Cahiers d'art, 1981) 58. After his death, some of Grohmann's collection was given to the Staatsgalerie in Stuttgart.

On 7 April 1933, "Jews and those deemed 'politically unreliable' were purged from government bureaucracies by the Professional Civil Service Restoration Act, an early milestone in Nazi persecution" (Barron, ed., *"Degenerate Art": The Fate of the Avant-Garde in Nazi Germany*, 396). Although Grohmann was dismissed from the Pädagogisches Institut der Technischen Hochschule, Dresden, he continued to write under the pseudonym Olaf Rydberg.

15   Ida Bienert (née Suckert, 1870–1965) was associated with the women's movement for social and educational reform in Saxony. She was a woman with "einem freien, unkonventionellen, geradezu revolutionären Geist" (free, unconventional, virtually revolutionary spirit) (Heinrike Junge, "Vom Neuen begeistert – Die Sammlerin Ida Bienert," in Heinrike Junge, ed., *Avantgarde und Publikum: zur Rezeption avantgardistischer Kunst in Deutschland 1905–1933* [Cologne: Böhlau, 1992] 29). Bienert developed her collection of modern art from 1905 to 1932 (Will Grohmann, ed., *Die Sammlung Ida Bienert, Dresden*, Privatsammlungen neuer Kunst, 1 [Potsdam: Müller & I. Kiepenheuer, 1933]). Bienert's collection survived the war, moving with her to Munich

in 1948; before her death, the collection was dispersed among German museums and private collections.

Artists represented in the collection included Paul Cézanne; French painter Fernand Léger (1881–1955); Marc Chagall (1889–1985); Ukrainian-born artist Alexander Archipenko (1880–1964); Franz Marc; Edvard Munch. For details of SB's visit to Bienert's collection: Knowlson, *Damned to Fame*, 233–235, and BIF, UoR, GD 5/f. 1.

Oskar Kokoschka's painting of Nancy Cunard, *Engländerin*, is now in the Sprengel-Museum, Hanover (Sammlung Sprengel, 1/146). Nancy Cunard recalls sitting for the portrait in 1924, according to her letter to Walter John Strachan, 21 June 1947 (ICSo, Strachan 58/1/5).

16 Anna von Gersdorff (née Obolensky, 1898–1973) was the daughter of Prince Alexis Dimitrievitch Obolensky (1855–1933), who had been Chief Procurator of the Holy Synod, a member of the Counsel of the Empire, Privy Counselor, Senator, and Equerry to His Majesty the Tsar. Writing later to Arland Ussher, SB described her as "intelligent and amusing" and told him to: "tell her I never think of Dresden without thinking of her but often think of her without thinking of Dresden" (SB to Arland Ussher, 11 July 1937, TxU). SB also met her husband Nicholas von Gersdorff (1882–1953) who taught Russian at a German school for officers, and her brothers, Dimitri Obolensky (1894–1945), who had been a cavalry officer in the Russian Imperial army, and Nicolas Obolensky (1896–1978), who was then a tour guide in Florence (RUL, GD 4/f. 69, 5 February 1937; see also Knowlson, *Damned to Fame*, 233–234).

17 Mozart's opera *The Marriage of Figaro*, K 492, was performed at the Dresden Opera House on 3 February 1937. The role of Cherubino was played by mezzo-soprano Martha Rohs (1909–1963), whom SB compares to the figure in *Portrait of a Boy* (NGL 2509), then attributed to Antonello but now attributed to Jacometto Veneziano (fl. 1472–1498) (Martin Davies, *National Gallery Catalogues: The Earlier Italian Schools* [London: National Gallery, 1986] 258).

18 SB refers to his overnight wait in the train station in Nuremberg in April 1931, as he traveled from Paris to Kassel (see BIF, UoR GD 5/f. 55, 1 March 1937).

19 McGreevy was no longer staying with Hester Dowden in Cheyne Gardens when he was in London.

Geoffrey Thompson and his wife Ursula lived above his offices in Harley Street. "Ruelle" (a bedroom salon); "molle" (soft, ineffectual).

20 John Oulton Wisdom (1908–1993) was educated with SB at Earlsfort House school in Dublin and Trinity College Dublin, where he was a Foundation Scholar in Mathematics, and graduated with First Class Honours in Philosophy in 1931 and a Ph.D. in Philosophy in 1933; from 1948 to 1965 he taught at the London School of Economics, and from 1969 to 1979 was Professor of Philosophy and Social Sciences at the York University, Toronto. Wisdom wrote many books on the history of philosophy and psychoanalysis; during the early 1930s, he was in analysis with psychoanalyst Alfred Ernest Jones (1879–1958), who had brought Freud to England, edited Freud's *Collected Papers* (1922–1924), and edited the *International Journal of Psychoanalysis* from 1920 to 1939.

21 Brian Coffey's trouble is not clear; "melo" is short for melodrama.

22 Charles Prentice's father Alexander Reid Prentice (1859–1937) died on 15 January 1937. Although SB's letter to Charles Prentice has not been found, Prentice wrote about it to McGreevy on 18 February 1937: "I've just received a letter from him from Dresden, a most touching & beautiful letter; but it's about my affairs & doesn't allude to his at all. A letter no one else could have written" (TCD, MS 8092/108).

23 SB's diary for 7 February 1937 records these lines: "Always elsewhere / In body also / The dew falls & the rain from" [incomplete line] (BIF, UoR GD 4/f. 77).

24 Richard Church's response to *Murphy*: SB to Mary Manning Howe, 18 January 1937, n. 2.
SB lists other London publishers that Reavey intended to try before going back to the offer of Stanley Nott to publish *Murphy* if a co-publisher could be found. SB had approved of Reavey's attempt to hold Nott's interest in reserve while he tried Dent (see 27 December 1936, n. 4).

25 SB had given his mother Morton's *In the Footsteps of the Master* (see 10 March 1935, n. 10). Lynn Doyle (né Leslie Alexander Montgomery, 1873–1961) was an Irish humorist known for his series of stories about the fictional Northern Irish village of Ballygullion.

ALICE SAUERLANDT

HAMBURG

19/2/37   Freiberg

Geehrte Frau Sauerlandt
    Grüssen Sie bitte Ihre Familie u. seien Sie selbst desgleichen begrüsst.
            Sam. Beckett

APCS; 1 leaf, 1 side; Freiberg, Tympanon der Goldenen pforte (Golden Portal); *to* Frau Sauerlandt, Hamburg, Loogestrasse 26; *pm* 19[-2-37], Freiberg; Katarina Kautzky. *Previous publication* (facsimile): Quadflieg, *Beckett was here*, 142.

19/2/37   Freiberg

Dear Mrs. Sauerlandt
    Please greet your family and be greeted yourself, likewise.
            Sam. Beckett

THOMAS McGREEVY
LONDON

20/2/37   Bamberg

[no greeting]
Got your card just before I left Dresden yesterday. Spent a few
hours in Freiberg in torrents, watery snow looking at this.
The Bathsheba 3rd from left is lovely.[1] Arrived hear [for
here] late last night. Going out now to have gawk – shall prob-
ably stay till Tuesday, then direct to Nürnberg or via Würzburg.
All well.
        Love
            Sam
John Ev/ David/ Bathsheba/ Aaron[2]

APCS; 1 leaf, 1 side; "Freiberg I.S. Dom, Die goldene Pforte, 2. Viertel des 13. Jahrh., Die
Gestalten des rechten Gewandes, <darunter, Aaron, Ecclesia, David.>"; pm 20-2-37,
Bamberg; to Thomas McGreevy, 49 Harrington Rd., London SW 7, ENGLAND; TCD, MS
10402/118.

1 SB refers to the photographic image of "Die goldene Pforte" (the Golden Gate)
of the Dom St. Marien, Freiberg, Saxony. The gate survives from the original
Romanesque church, Die Liebfrauenkirche (The Church of our Beloved Lady), with
sculptures that date from the 1230s. SB corrects the printed identification of the
figures on the right of the portal (image on the card) from left to right: John the
Evangelist, David, Bathsheba, Aaron. For several images of the door, and particularly
of Bathsheba: Rainer Budde, Deutsche romanische Skulptur, 1050–1250 (Munich:
Hirmer Verlag, 1979) 112–113 and figs. 299 and 302.

2 SB canceled printed identifications of the sculptures and wrote in his corrections.

GEORGE REAVEY
LONDON

23/2/37   Hotel Drei Kronen
                                            Bamberg

Dear George

Your letter dated 17th reached me in Dresden the morning I left. I suppose Murphy is now in the hands of Nott. I think there is another MS copy lying at home, that you could have had. Another is in Boston. And what is the position of Houghton Mifflin? Have you been in touch with them? Didn't Nott make it a condition that an American publisher should take sheets? Also it is possible that Dent's rejection may work on H.M. I understand the two firms are hand in gauntlet. You never mention the American end. Please do in your next.

The kind lady in Boston is doing it all for love, so far as I know.[1] But no sooner do I see this sentence written than it occurs to me she may expect a rake off from H.M. She calls herself their "literary scout". But she would certainly waive all her rights and expectations if to do so were to make things any easier for me. Perhaps you would write to her. Mrs Mark Howe, 136 Myrtle Street, Boston, Mass. Her brother-in-law is director or something in a big New York firm of publishers whose name I forget. They turned down Murphy with the classical obeisance et l'obligeance prophétique. She is perhaps known to you in her maiden style of Mary Manning, author of plays that have been performed at the Gate Theatre, Dublin. I think she expects to have something on in London soon. Pinker is her agent God help her. She ran for a time in Dublin in connexion with the Gate a periodical called Motley. She is writing a novel called Mount Venus. She is up to her eyes in the family way. So now is the time if ever to prey on her feelings. I should be happy to have you act for me in America as well as in England.[2]

With Chatto & Windus I am bound in no way whatever.[3] But I should not agree to an option on my next two books without a struggle. It is too general. Say on my next book of poems and prose work exceeding 60000 words.

Wollman can have whatever he wants. I take it he doesn't pay. I am glad you liked Cascando.[4] There has been nothing since.

I leave here to-morrow for Würzburg and expect to be in Munich about a week later. In Munich I shall stay at least a month. If you have not already written again to Dresden (in which case I shall not have the letter till the end of next week), or indeed whether you have or not, perhaps you would write Poste Restante, Munich, rather than wait till I can let you have a definite address.

I met a lot of Russians in Dresden, Obolenskys and Gersdorffs, very friendly, and heard an interesting lecture the evening before I leave [*for* left] by one Prof. Fedor Stepun on Belji. Why don't you translate the Silver Dove, or has it been done?[5]

> Ever
>
> s/ Sam

It was kind of Miss Vernon to mention me to Laughton. Please thank her. I am trying to think of something.[6]

TLS with APS; 1 leaf, 2 sides; *letterhead*; TxU.

1 SB left Dresden on 19 February.

In Boston, Mary Manning Howe had contacted Houghton Mifflin as a possible American co-publisher, with Nott in London, of *Murphy*. SB repeats what Howe has told him about a joint venture between Dent and Houghton Mifflin, but no evidence has been found that they were formally associated.

2 The brother-in-law of Mary Manning Howe was Quincy Howe (1900–1977), then Chief Book Editor with New York publishers Simon and Schuster, who had turned down *Murphy* in October 1936 (see 9 October 1936, n. 11).

"Et l'obligeance prophétique" (and prophetic obligingness).

Mary Manning Howe had been Publicity Manager for the Gate Theatre, Dublin, and Editor of *Motley*, its magazine (March 1932 – May 1934). Her plays for the Gate Theatre in Dublin were *Youth's the Season . . . ?* (1931), *Storm over Wicklow* (1933), and *Happy Family*

(1934). *Youth's the Season* . . . ? opened in London on 5 October 1937 (see 7 July 1936, n. 7). James Pinker was her agent. Her novel *Mount Venus* was published in 1938 by Houghton Mifflin.

Reavey represented SB's work in the United States.

3 SB had published *Proust* and *More Pricks Than Kicks* with Chatto and Windus. The contract for *More Pricks Than Kicks* (then entitled *Draff*), signed on 3 October 1933 and acknowledged by Prentice on 4 October 1933, stipulated that Chatto and Windus be given the first option on SB's next prose work of 60,000 words. SB offered them the manuscript of *Murphy*, which they declined (UoR, MS 2444 CW letterbook 150/245).

4 Maurice Wollman (n.d.), editor of *Poems of Twenty Years: An Anthology, 1918-1938* (London: Macmillan and Co., 1938) had asked Reavey to suggest younger writers whose poetry might be included in this collection. On 1 February 1937, Reavey suggested SB, Brian Coffey, Thomas McGreevy, and Denis Devlin; on 12 February Reavey sent Wollman a copy of Beckett's poem "Cascando" as well as *Echo's Bones* (TxU, Reavey). Wollman did not include any work by these poets in his anthology.

5 On 18 February, with Ida Bienert and the von Gersdorffs, SB attended a lecture by Dr. Fedor Stepun (1884-1965), who had studied at the University of Heidelberg and taught at the Technische Hochschule Dresden. He spoke on the Russian writer Andrei Belji (or Belyii, now transliterated in English as Andrei or Andrey, Bely or Biely, né Boris Nikolaevich Bugaev, 1880-1934). For SB's response to his lecture: BIF, UoR, GD 5/f. 9).

George Reavey did eventually translate *Serebryany Golub* (1909; *The Silver Dove*, 1974).

6 Autograph P.S., underscored by double looped line, similiar to an infinity sign.

Reavey's fiancée Clodine Gwynedd Cade* (née Vernon Jones, 1901-?) had told the American actor Charles Laughton about Beckett's interest in film and his idea of a film of Samuel Johnson starring Laughton (see 13 December 1936, n. 9). As SB reported to Mary Manning Howe: "Reavey wants me to write stories for Laughton, bursting with big programmes. Irish and decently indecent. On no account scenarios. He has his own scenarists. You ought to do something about this. I can't" (21 March 1937, TxU).

THOMAS McGREEVY

LONDON

4/3/37   [Regensburg]

[no greeting]

I wanted your help badly with this door, built by Irish (not Scottish) monks in 12th century. Does the name Rydan say anything to you? He was the architect.[1] It is one of the big "problems". Perhaps it means: "Heaven & Earth shall pass away, but. ." From Keltic motif one should arrive at something, but I am not competent.[2] Würzburg began Irish also: Kilian, Kolonat [for Colman] & Totnan, all martyred.[3] Going on this afternoon to Munich, where perhaps there is a letter from you waiting.

Love.

S

APCI; 1 leaf, 1 side; "Schottenportal, Regensburg"; to Thomas McGreevy Esq, 49 Harrington Road, London SW 7; pm 4-3-37, Regensburg; TCD, MS 10402/120.

1 The door is the north portal of St. Jakob Kirche (also known as the Schottenkirche); it was built by twelfth-century Irish monks who were replaced in 1577 by Scottish monks. The portal is "fitted into a showpiece wall covered with reliefs" (Uwe Geese, "Romanesque Sculpture," in Romanesque: Architecture, Sculpture, Painting, ed. Rolf Toman [Cologne: Könemann, 1997] 316). Inside the north portal is a relief of Friar Rydan (c. twelfth century), who is depicted with door bolt and key. His role in the intricate design is unclear; he may have been architect, master of the portal, or one who transmitted wisdom through the symbolic cycles depicted on the portal (Mona Stocker, Die Schottenkirche St. Jakob in Regensburg: Skulptur und stilistisches Umfeld, Regensburger Studien und Quellen zur Kulturgeschichte [Regensburg: Universitätsverlag Regensburg, 2001] 31, 54, 98, 106–107).

2 For a detailed study of the iconography of the portal of the Schottenkirche: Lore Conrad, Die romanische Schottenkirche in Regensburg und ihre Bildsymbolsprache: Darstellung einer systematischen Deutung sakraler Kunst aus dem Europa des 12. Jahrhunderts, 5th edn. (Regensburg: Lore Conrad, 1987). The symbols depict conflict between good and evil, Christ and Antichrist, East and West; Celtic motifs adorn the pillars of the portal and are evoked in the animal allegories (Budde, Deutsche romanische Skulptur, 1050–1250, 52–54, figs. 83–85).

SB refers to Luke 21:33: "Heaven and earth shall pass away: but my words shall not pass away."

3 Kilian (c. 640–689), a Bishop of Ireland, was commissioned in 686 by Pope Conon to evangelize in Franconia (now Baden-Württemberg, Thuringia, and Bavaria in Germany). With the priest Colman (d. 689) and a deacon Totnan (d. 689), Kilian converted Gosbert (n.d.), the Duke of Würzburg. According to legend, Kilian's preaching convinced Gosbert that he had been wrong to marry his brother's widow, Geilana (n.d.), provoking her to have Kilian and his cohorts killed (John J. Delaney, Dictionary of Saints, 2nd edn. [New York: Image-Doubleday, 2004] 358; the Martyrdom of St. Kilian and his Disciples is depicted by the Nuremberg Master [Mainfränkisches Museum, Würzburg: www.mainfraenkisches-museum.de]).

GEORGE REAVEY
LONDON

7/3/37   Pension Romana
                                                Akademiestrasse 7
                                                München

[no greeting]
I was hoping to find a letter from you Poste Restante. Here is my
address for 3 weeks or a month. I suggest you give the book to
the one & only Yess [sic] and have done with it.[1]

    Yours ever
    Sam

APCS; 1 leaf, 1 side; "Nürnberg, Selbstbildnis von Adam Kraft am Sakramentshäuschen in der Lorenzkirche," [fiber/glue residue obscures description]; *to* George
Reavey, 1 Parton Street, LONDON W.C.1; *pm* 7-3-37, Munich; TxU.

  1 Stanley Nott was the only publisher who had accepted *Murphy*, but on the condition of an American co-publisher being found.

THOMAS McGREEVY
LONDON

7/3/37   Pension Romana
                                                Akademiestrasse 7
                                                München

Dear Tom
    It was a great pleasure to find your letter waiting for me in
Munich. I arrived here last Friday evening from Regensburg &
rushed straight to the P.O., just in time to collect a large bundle
of letters. Yesterday I found this place, which is no worse than

another. My horizon is blotted out by the Counsel Academy, overpoweringly "lapidaire" as Thomas would say, with Castor & Pollux very black and Minerva against the sky looking like a quantity surveyer [*for* surveyor] taking a level.[1]

The impression so far, to me wandering blindly among the monuments of its classicism, is not very agreeable. The evening I arrived was lovely, almost a summer warmth, with the blue trams and a thrush singing in Maximiliansplatz and the sense of relief at having reached a resting point again. But now it is snowing again. The Isar is a poor kind of a piddle after the lyrical Main in Würzburg & the heroic Danube in Regensburg, taking the Regen without a ripple, and the reinforced concrete of Museum Island doesn't help it.[2] How does one scuttle an island?

I remember the Bassano in Hampton Court very well. In the second or third room, isn't it? The wild tormented colour. Weren't the season allegories mostly by the son Francesco? There is a good Good Samaritan by Jacopo in Berlin and 5 or 6 in Dresden, skied & dirty, looking like not very good early El Grecos.[3]

I haven't been to the Alte Pinakothek yet. I meant to go to-day, because of the nothing to pay & in spite of the mob, but discovered as I was setting out very late in the morning that it closes on Sunday at 1. A mark a time is a bit thick. Only 10 pf. for the Kaiser Friedrich and 20 pf. for the Zwinger.

The Tiepolo frescos in the Würzburger Residenz were wonderful, crown to the spacelessness set up by Neumann, or better a firmament. Otherwise Würzburg is Riemenschneider, whom one likes or doesn't. There are good things, a lovely Adam & Eve from the first period, but from 1510 on he seems to crumple up in the immature voulu Renaissance irresolutions plus spurious severity that one finds then again in Nürnberg in such painful abundance.[4] And he is always sentimental.

The great Nürnberg period is for me now a conspiracy. I mean the Pleydenwurff-Wohlgemut [*for* Wolgemut]-Dürer and the Stoss-Kraft-Vischer turnover from say 20 years before the century end to 20 years after.[5] It is all so terribly guildy and complacent jealous zealous artisan. What remains after the technique is the vision of the sturdy burgher full of the sense of his worth and the mysteries of his trade & the sweat of his brow & a determination to stand up to all princes & potencies sacred & profane. It is Hans Sachsism. Not only Meistersinger, but Meistermaler & Meisterbildhauer & Meistererzgiesser. Stairpainting & draperies.[6] The famous Kraft Ciborium Altar in the Lorenzkirche is a frightful machine, more gothic than the gothic, a miracle of laborious statics, a skyscrapery in dingy limestone with the pinnacle bent to follow the curve of the vaulting, showing that he could have gone on had not space forbidden. And the famous Vischer Sebaldus Altar in the Sebalduskirche is just a good black solid heavy job of work with no labour spared & no expense.[7] It was a democracy without historical context, over excited & over irritable. They drove out the Jews in 1499 and kept them out for 3 and a half centuries.[8] And the catastrophe of 1517 was right into their barrow. Stoss is the best of them, but seems to have been very much influenced by Riemenschneider & to have gone the way of Riemenschneider. In his last period crucifixes that are big & bare because bigness & bareness are the thing. Some of his earlier house Madonnas are lovely.[9] The Dürer room in the Germanisches Museum is a scandal. They have so little by him that any old rag dirty enough to have possibly come from his workshop is made to serve. The only unquestionable

Dürer in the whole of Nürnberg is the small portrait of Wohlgemut.[10]

And now it is the industrial centre of Bavaria and with Munich & Berlin the third centre of Nazidiffusion and the seat of Jewbaiting Streicher & his rag.[11]

I think I was at school with Mr Davidson. He writes facetious period novels, did you know? And enjoys I think £500 a year. Has Flaherty finished with his elephantboy?[12]

I had a letter from Brian who mentioned he had heard from you. He remains very mysteriously under some wooden sword of Damocles, says he told his father he was dead & so on.[13] How fortunate to have a father to say that one is dead to.

An amusing letter also from Jack Yeats, wanting to know the players' advice to Hamlet and very pleased with the Duchess of Malfi at the Gate.[14]

I met yesterday at breakfast a pleasant Californian student of art writing a thesis on the influence of 19th century Munich painting on the American primitives! I felt this to be an undertaking about as fruitful as say a study of the influence of Plato on Mrs Neighbour.[15]

I was hoping to find a word from Reavey in the P.O. here, but no. I really forget who was the last to scent the rejection slip. No doubt there have been several more since.[16]

I am very tired travelling and often feeling like making a bolt back. It is the same thing over & over again & I do no work. Stuttgart & Frankfurt remain after I am finished here, but unless the mood, which has been developing for weeks, changes, I shall give up the idea, move into digs here at half the price & save up for the price of an aeroplane to London, if I can find some not too particular travel agency to take Registermarks for the whole journey, and not merely to the frontier, as is the law.[17]

I have a couple of introductions to notabilities here and shall utter them I suppose in due course.[18]

Mary Manning writes from Boston that her belly is enormous. Doors open in May. She wants me to give one May Sarton an introduction to you. I don't know the lady, but apparently shall be obliged to. She is American, belle à peindre, intelligente à gémir, has published a slim volume & said adieu to all her amies. She will be in Jeake's house, Rye, Kent in April & May and invites me! I tink I prefer Mrs Frost.[19]

Why don't you try Mary Manning, who acts as intermediary for Houghton Mifflin, with your Eliot & Aldington and the suggestion that you do a third essay of the same length on Yeats (W. B.)? She would be flattered & I should say the chances of there [for their] being taken on are at least even. Something of the same kind was in the wind for me, i.e. a Gide & a Céline or Malraux to eke out the Proust, when they turned down the latter as too short to be worth separate publication. I really think you should try this & wonder how it did not occur to me long ago.[20] Her address: Mrs Mark Howe, 136 Myrtle Street, Boston, Mass.

> Love ever. Write soon
>
> Sam

ALS; 2 leaves, 6 sides; *letterhead* <HOTEL LEINFELDER MÜNCHEN>; TCD, MS 10402/121.

1 SB arrived in Munich on evening of 4 March. The Pension Romana faced the Akademie der Bildenden Künste München, Akademiestrasse 2, which SB calls the Counsel Academy. "Lapidaire" (lapidary) refers to the cut stone frieze that runs around the front façade and at the roofline of the center section of the building.
Jean Thomas.
Sculptures of Castor and Pollux flank the stairs at the center entrance of the Akademie. The huge statue of Minerva crowns the top of the building over this entrance; Minerva holds a rod (for images, see Winfried Nerdinger, *Gottfried von Neureuther, Architekt der Neorenaissance in Bayern, 1811–1887* [Munich: K. M. Lipp, 1978] 118, 126–127; Dr Birgit Jooss, Archiv und Sammlungen, Akademie der Bildenden Künste München, 22 March 2006).

2   Many of Munich's public buildings were designed by Leo von Klenze (1784–1864), court architect to the Kings of Bavaria, Maximilian I (1756–1825) and Ludwig I (1786–1868).

The Isar River, which flows through Munich and joins the Danube downstream from Regensburg, is too shallow for navigation over most of its length; at Regensburg the Regen River flows into the Danube. The Deutsches Museum is on an island in the Isar between the Ludwigsbrücke and the Corneliusbrücke, called the Museumsinsel (Museum Island).

3   In Hampton Court there are many paintings by Jacopo Bassano (c. 1510–1592), and several that are indicated in SB's notebook on Dutch painting (BIF, UoR, MS 5001/ 37); the specific painting to which SB refers is uncertain. The paintings of the "season series" belong to the period of collaboration (1575–1577) between Jacopo Bassano and his son, Francesco Bassano (1549–1592), but they are generally attributed to Francesco.

The Good Samaritan by Jacopo Bassano in Berlin (listed in the 1930 catalogue as 314) was destroyed in 1945 (Staatliche Museen Berlin, I, *Die Gemäldegalerie, Die Italienischen Meister 16. bis 18. Jahrhundert* [Berlin: Paul Cassirer Verlag, 1930] 9; Beverly Louise Brown and Paola Marini, *Jacopo Bassano, c. 1510–1592* [Fort Worth, TX: Kimbell Art Museum, 1993] 104). The paintings by Jacopo Bassano in the collection in Dresden are: *Samson Fighting with the Philistines* (254A), *The Israelites Journeying through the Wilderness* (253), *Young Tobias Returning Home* (254), *Moses and the Israelites at the Rock from which Water Flowed* (256), and *The Conversion of Saul* (258) (K. Woermann, *Catalogue of the Pictures in the Royal Gallery at Dresden*, 44).

4   The frescos on the ceiling and walls of the Kaisersaal of the Würzburger Residenz by Giovanni Battista Tiepolo (1696–1770) were designed by the architect of the Residenz, Balthasar Neumann (1687–1753). On the ceiling was *Apollo Conducting Beatrice of Burgundy to the "Genius" of the German Nation*, and on the walls were the *Investiture of Bishop Harold* and *Wedding of Frederick Barbarossa and Beatrice of Burgundy*. In addition to altarpieces for the Residenz chapel, Tiepolo painted the fresco on the stairwell of the Residenz, which SB called the "liquidation of architectural limits" (BIF, UoR, GD 5/f. 29). It depicts Prince-Bishop Karl Philipp von Greiffenclau-Vollraths (1690–1754, Prince-Bishop from 1749 to 1754) borne by Fame through the skies; at the lower edges of the fresco are depictions of the four continents; the turning of the stairs draws the eye toward the Kaisersaal which depicts Europe: the crown and firmament suggested by SB.

The late-Gothic German sculptor Tilman Riemenschneider (c. 1460–1531) was commissioned by the town council of Würzburg to create the stone figures of *Adam and Eve* for the Marienkapelle where they were installed in 1492; they were removed in 1894 to the Mainfranken Museum in Würzburg, but since the 1970s have been re-installed in the Marienkapelle (www.groveart.com).

"Voulu" (insistently deliberate).

5   Those painters and sculptors active during what SB names the "great Nürnberg period" were: Hans Pleydenwurff (c. 1420–1472); Michael Wolgemut (1434–1519), who took over Pleydenwurff's studio, and to whom Albrecht Dürer (1471–1528) was apprenticed from 1486 to 1489; and wood carver Veit Stoss (c. 1445–1533) and his workshop, stone mason Adam Kraft, and brassfounder and sculptor Peter Vischer.

6 Hans Sachs (1494-1576) was a master cobbler, author of moral fables and contributor of over 6,000 works to the art of the Meistergesang (Mastersong, song form of the Guilds). He is depicted as the central figure in Wagner's opera *Die Meistersinger von Nürnberg*.

"Meistersinger" (Master singer, or lyrical poet, one who invented new subjects and new forms), "Meistermaler" (Master painter), Meisterbildhauer (Master sculptor), "Meistererzgiesser" (Master metal caster).

7 Adam Kraft's *Sakramentshäuschen* in the Lorenzkirche in Nuremberg is a receptacle for the Host, rather than an altar, in the form of a 65-foot limestone spire that turns slightly at its peak, at its base are bronze figures of Kraft and his assistants with their aprons and tools.

Peter Vischer's Sebaldus Altar in the Sebalduskirche is an eight-ton shrine in cast bronze (1507-1519). Enclosing the silver shrine of St. Sebaldus, it is supported by snails and dolphins, and incorporates many statuettes.

8 Jewish persecution had a long history in Nuremberg: the Black Death massacres (1249), the Rindfleisch persecutions (1298), and the expulsion of Jews in 1499 (Geoffrey Wigoder, ed., *The New Standard Jewish Encyclopedia*, 7th edn. [New York: Facts on File, 1992] 716-717).

9 SB refers to Martin Luther (1483-1546), who in 1517 nailed his theses to the door of the castle church in Wittenberg; for SB, his reforms shut off the possibility of a Renaissance in German art (BIF, UoR, GD 5/f. 48, 28 February 1937).

Although they were contemporaries and he painted and gilded the figures in Riemenschneider's altar for the church at Münnerstadt (1503-1504), Veit Stoss is not thought to have been directly influenced by Riemenschneider, even though both artists incorporated the natural textures of wood and stone into their work. Within the large Stoss collection of the Germanisches Nationalmuseum in Nuremberg there are several of Stoss's earlier and smaller Madonnas; an example from 1520 is "Hausmadonna" (Pl.O 217) (G. Ulrich Grossmann und die Sammlungsleiter, eds., *Germanisches Nationalmuseum: Führer durch die Sammlungen* [Nuremberg: Verlag des Germanischen Nationalmuseums, 2001] 74). SB greatly admired Stoss's crucifix for the church of the Heiliggeist-Spital (Hospital of the Holy Spirit), c. 1501-1510; now in the Germanisches Nationalmuseum (Pl.O.62) (BIF, UoR GD 5/f57; Rainer Kahsnitz, ed., *Veit Stoss in Nürnberg: Werke des Meisters und seiner Schule in Nürnberg und Umgebung* [Munich: Deutscher Kunstverlag, 1983] 122-127).

10 The 1937 catalogue of the Germanisches Nationalmuseum indicates that Dürer's *Portrait of Michael Wolgemut* (1516, GN 885) and *Hercules Battling the Stymphalean Birds* (1500, GN 166) are initialed and dated; it claims that his unsigned *Portrait of Emperor Kaiser Maximilian I* (1518, GN 169) is authentic. Other unsigned works attributed to Dürer are: *The Lamentation of Christ* (GN 165), *Portrait of Emperor Charlemagne in Coronation Robes* (GN 167), *Portrait of Emperor Sigismund in Coronation Robes* (GN 168) (Germanisches Nationalmuseum, *Die Gemälde des 13. bis 16. Jahrhunderts*, I, ed. Eberhard Lutze and Eberhard Wiegand [Leipzig: K. F. Koehlers Antiquarium, 1937] 50-54).

11 From 1919, Julius Streicher (1885-1946) was active in anti-Semitic political groups. He founded the virulently anti-Semitic journal *Der Stürmer* which was published from 1923 to 1945. From 1925, he was *Gauleiter* of the Franconia region, which included Nuremberg. As a member of the Reichstag, he advocated the boycott of the Jews and helped prepare the Nuremberg Laws (1935). He was executed after condemnation at the International Military Tribunal in Nuremberg.

12 James Norris Goddard Davidson (1908–1998) was educated at Portora Royal School and the University of Cambridge; he became a leader in Irish documentary film-making, wrote two novels, *Galore Park* (1934) and *The Soft Impeachment* (1936), and after the War became a producer with Radio Éireann.

Davidson assisted American film-maker Robert Flaherty in the making of *Man of Aran* (see 10 May 1934, n. 3); *Elephant Boy* (1937) was an adaptation of "Toomai of the Elephants" by Rudyard Kipling (1865–1936). Shot on location in India, the film required script changes which in turn required prolonged refilming in London studios.

13 Brian Coffey's father, Denis Coffey.

14 Hamlet gives advice to the Players in *Hamlet*, III.ii. 1–14, 16–36, 38–45.

The Duchess of Malfi (c. 1614) by John Webster (c. 1580–1634) played at the Gate Theatre from 9 to 20 February 1937, directed by Peter Powell (1908–1985) ("This Week in Dublin," *The Irish Times* 8 February 1937: 5).

15 The research of Californian Robert Neuhaus (1909–1995) for his 1938 Ph.D. at the University of Marburg concerned American artists Frank Duveneck (né Francis Decker, 1848–1919), William Merritt Chase (1849–1916), and Joseph Frank Currier (1843–1909), who were part of the Leiblkreis (Leibl circle) in Germany, artists influenced by Wilhelm Leibl and Hans von Marées (1837–1887); Neuhaus published his study as *Bildnismalerei des Leibl-Kreises: Untersuchungen zur Geschichte und Technik der Malerei der zweiten Hälfte des 19. Jahrhunderts* (Marburg: Verlag des Kunstgeschichtlichen Seminars, 1953); see also Robert Neuhaus, *Unsuspected Genius: The Art and Life of Frank Duveneck* (San Francisco: Bedford, 1987) 7–27, 35–59.

Mrs. Neighbour was the housekeeper of Hester Dowden (Bentley, *Far Horizon: A Biography of Hester Dowden*, 44).

16 The effort to publish *Murphy*: 20 March 1937 to Reavey and 25 March 1937 to McGreevy.

17 Foreign currency controls were enforced to keep German money in the country, so that only travel to the border could be purchased with German marks.

18 Heinz Porep had given SB introductions to Karl Kluth and Dr. Richard Zarnitz (n.d.) (BIF, UoR, GD 4/f. 23–25).

19 Belgian-born American poet and novelist May Sarton (1912–1995) had been offered the use of Jeake's House on Mermaid Street in Rye, Sussex, by American writer Conrad Aiken (1889–1973); Sarton enlisted two friends to "share the house and the expenses" and took pleasure in inviting "friends to stay on weekends" (May Sarton, *A World of Light: Portraits and Celebrations* [New York: W. W. Norton, 1976] 194). Sarton's first volume of poetry was *Encounter in April* (1937).

"Belle à peindre" (lovely enough to deserve a painting); "intelligente à gémir" (painfully intelligent); "adieu to all her amies" (good-bye to all her women friends).

SB had lived in London at 34 Gertrude Street, in the house of Mrs. Frost.

20 Mary Manning Howe was a reader for Houghton Mifflin and had acted as an intermediary on behalf of SB's *Murphy*. SB refers to McGreevy's two studies, *Thomas Stearns Eliot* and *Richard Aldington: An Englishman*, published by Chatto and Windus. Although SB had proposed to write a study of Gide in 1932, there is no documentation

of a proposal, either by Houghton Mifflin to SB or by SB to Houghton Mifflin regarding publication of SB's *Proust* or studies by SB of Gide, Céline, or Malraux.

THOMAS McGREEVY
LONDON

20/3/37

Pension Romana
Akademiestr. 7
[Munich]

[no greeting]
I am hoping to hear from you soon, that you are all right again. This is perhaps not the best of the 3 Poussins here but it is very good. The best for me is the Bacchus & Midas, with superb female nude very like the Venus in Dresden.[1] Also alas not to be had as postcard. Expect to be here another fortnight.
> Love.
> S.

APCI; 1 leaf, 1 side; "Apollo und Daphne," Nicolas Poussin (1594–1665), Alte Pinakothek; *to* Thomas McGreevy Esq, 49 Harrington Road, London S.W. 7, England; *pm* 20-3-37, Munich; TCD, MS 10402/122.

1 SB refers to the image on the postcard, *Apollo and Daphne* by Nicolas Poussin (2334) in the Alte Pinakothek, Munich. SB compares Poussin's *Bacchus and Midas* (528) to Giorgione's *Venus* in Dresden. The third painting by Poussin in the collection is *The Lamentation over dead Christ* (625).

GEORGE REAVEY
LONDON

20/3/37

Pension Romana
Akademiestr. 7
München

Dear George

Many thanks for your letter.

By all means take the MS from Houghton Mifflin. You have a free hand to do what you like with the book in England and America.[1]

It is kind of you to suggest the possibility of backing the book yourself. I am afraid you would lose money.[2]

Yes, as I think I mentioned before, the book, before it went to Houghton Mifflin, was turned down by some gorgeous New York publishers with a Jewish name that I can't remember and have no note of with me.[3]

I stay here for a fortnight more & then I think return straight to London. I am tired cangiando loco and shall abandon the rest of the programme.[4] So I look forward to seeing you next month in London – Yours ever

Sam

ALS; 1 leaf, 1 side; *letterhead* <HOTEL LEINFELDER, MÜNCHEN>; TxU.

1 Houghton Mifflin had asked for cuts in *Murphy*. The idea of finding an American publisher to share costs with Nott in England had been languishing, as SB wrote to Mary Manning Howe: "The latest is that Houghton Mifflin, stimulated by a cable from Reavey quoting Nott's price for sheets, regret now to be unable, which has let Nott out also" (21 March 1937, TxU).

SB had already suggested that Mary Manning Howe's representation of the novel in the United States was undertaken as a friend, not as an agent: 23 February 1937.

2 SB received Reavey's letter in Munich on 20 March. It reported that *Murphy* had been given to Boris Wood in London, but if that failed Reavey would consider financing the book himself. Reavey's letter has not been found, but it is quoted by SB in his diary (BIF, UoR, GD 6/f. 25).

3 Before 7 July 1936, SB had sent *Murphy* to Simon and Schuster, a New York firm founded in 1924 by Richard L. Simon (1899–1960) and Max Lincoln Schuster (1897–1970) (see 27 June and 7 July 1936).

4 "Cangiando loco" (changing abode), a song by Italian painter and poet Salvator Rosa (also set by Giovanni Bononcini [1670–1747]): "Vado ben spesso cangiando loco" (I frequently go from place to place) (Luigi Dallapiccola, *Italian Songs of the 17th and 18th*

Centuries, for Voice and Piano, II [New York: International Music, 1961] 30–33; Ottilie G. Boetzkes, *Salvator Rosa: Seventeenth-Century Painter, Poet and Patriot* [New York: Vantage Press, 1960] 88).

SB wrote to Mary Manning Howe: "But have now decided I am tired and have had enough and can see nothing more but only look" (21 March 1937, TxU).

THOMAS McGREEVY

LONDON

25/iii/37   Pension Romana

Akademiestrasse 7

[Munich]

Dear Tom

You seem to have had a horrible time. I hope you will be repaid by an improvement in your general health. Raven is very kind. Remember me to him. And congratulate him from me. If he were here he would be too good a painter to sell anything, he would be in the darkness & the indigence with the 5%.[1]

I am very miserable to-day because I hear from home that our old Kerry bitch that I was so fond of & comes into one of the Pricks that I forget the title of is very sick, had to be tapped and was found to have growths. Mother did not say they had arranged to destroy her, but I take it that is the position. I shall have to go back to 1925 now and start killing myself again.[2]

The journey is over, mentally as usual long before physically, and from now on I shall simply be hanging around waiting to get into the air. I fly direct from here to London, changing machines in Frankfurt & Amsterdam. Departure from here 9.55, arrival in Croydon 3.35 p.m. It will probably be next Wednesday or this day week. By flying I can buy my ticket the whole way with registered marks, whereas overland or by sea from Hamburg I could only buy to the frontier.[3] So it is practically as cheap to fly & God how much more pleasant. I shall be glad to get out. Though I don't know what I shall do when I get home. To sit for hours & hours alone in a room that I haven't to pay for & no Sehenswürdigkeiten round the corner – that will be pleasant for a time. I was hoping to have the proofs of Murphy to screen me and break the shock of my aimless presence in the house again, but that is down the drain. I wrote a card to Reavey suggesting that he give the book to Nott & have done with it. And the last news as a result is that he cabled Nott's price for sheets to Houghton Mifflin who called back "Regret unable", which lets Nott out also, as his condition for English publication was American publication.[4]

I am delighted to hear about the play. Shouldn't you get paid a retainer between acceptance & performance?[5]

I have pre-vented an invitation from Geoffrey by writing a card to Mrs Frost, asking her to put me up for a week, for I don't expect to stay longer in London. If Geoffrey were alone I would be glad to stay with him, but not as it is. Charles is in Greenock or Galloway but may be in London early in April.[6]

I don't like Munich. I don't like to think of the places I am missing by not going on, Augsburg, Ulm, Stuttgart, Karlsruhe, Freiburg, Colmar, Strassburg, Frankfurt – but shall be very glad to get out of here. Of course the pictures are wonderful. Did you not see the Van Goghs, including the self-portrait, and the Cézannes, including the railway cutting that I think you sent me a postcard of once, when you were here?[7] They are scattered all over the place now, as a result of the burning of the Glaspalast some years ago and the transferring of the big exhibition that was there to the Neue Pinakothek, and again the brand new "House of German Art", looking like a Pompeian railway terminus, will be ready.[8]

I think the Paul in the 4 Apostels is Dürer's last & best word, better than any thing in the Paumgärtner altar.[9] The painter that interested you was probably Engelbrechtsen. He was the teacher of Lucas v. Leyden. The picture is a big lamentation, with rows of kneeling nuns & demons. I don't find it interesting.[10] The Dirk Bouts are wonderful & the Davids. The Rubens I haven't looked at. I take him for granted, like the wonders of modern science. Then there are the 17 Brouwers.[11]

I have met a few pleasant people; an actor, with some good pictures, including one by my dear Hamburg Ballmer; a private gallery man, who still dares to exhibit Marc & Nolde; a conservator in the Bavarian National Museum, who filled me up with Rhine wine & brandy & showed me his Klee, his translation of Sappho with drawings by Sintenis, his sister-in-law & his wife. Another friend of Rilke, who he declared resembled Proust in his "decentralisation of the soul", which did not pass without a loud protest from the ex-expert.[12] And a few painters, including the one & only German surréaliste, one Ende. He knew a daughter of Con Curran & disparaged Ernst, Picasso & Dali for their "want of integrity" (!) and schwärmed for Shem the Penman.[13]

There is absolutely nothing to go to in the evening, neither film, play, opera nor concert. I did attend, full of pious expectation, a concert of violin sonatas with Furtwängler at the piano looking like an invertebrate trying to sprain its back assisted by the first fiddle of the Berlin Philharmonic. It was fearful. They played the earliest Mozart & Beethoven they could find, nothing like as well as Paddy Delaney & Lennox Braid would have done, & then the brand new <u>GROSSE SONATE</u> that Furtwängler has been moulting over all winter. It was unspeakable & lasted over an hour. The maximum determination (to get it all off his chest in a modern manner) & the minimum ability, a frenzy of impotence, with reverberations from everyone from Berlioz to Bartok. My musical susceptibility seems all concentrated in my arse, which ached diabolically. And the whole thing in a Wesleyan chapel half inclined to be rococo.[14]

Everyone urges me vehemently to go to the mountains, & the valleys, but I have not been outside half a mile's radius from the Marienplatz in any direction. A typesetter in the Hofbräuhaus, pale with the need to stay sober for the morning edition, demonstrated to me that there were as many Masters of the Death of the Virgin as there were Masters and Dead Virgins, but only one Zugspitz[e].[15]

Please God you won't be gone when I am in London. I can't tell you for certain the day of my arrival but probably the afternoon of this day week. If money comes in time to let me buy my ticket & let you know for certain in advance, I shall do so.

God love thee,

    Ever

      Sam

ALS; 2 leaves; 6 sides; *letterhead* <HOTEL LEINFELDER, MUNICH>; TCD, MS 10402/124.

1 McGreevy was having teeth pulled; as SB wrote to Mary Manning Howe: "His last teeth have been macbethed" (21 March 1937, TxU).

An exhibition, "Recent Paintings by Holmes Ravenhill," opened on 25 February at the Cooling Galleries, London.

2 The Beckett family had several Kerry Blue terriers. Gerald Pakenham Stewart, who shared rooms with SB at Trinity College Dublin, recalls that when SB "ran over and killed his own Kerry Blue terrier, he was heart-broken" (19 January 1992; Knowlson, *Damned to Fame*, 80). The dog SB mentions here was called Wolf.

3 Croydon was then London's main airport.

4 "Sehenswürdigkeiten" (sights worth seeing).

Neither Houghton Mifflin's letter to Reavey nor Reavey's letter to SB has been found; in his diary SB notes that Reavey's letter indicated that Houghton Mifflin and Nott had backed down, that *Murphy* was being read by Boris Wood, and that Reavey was considering doing the book himself (BIF, UoR, GD 6/f. 22, 20 March 1937).

5 McGreevy's work on a play, whether his own, or an adaptation or translation, is not known.

6 Geoffrey Thompson. Mrs. Frost, 34 Gertrude Street. Charles Prentice.

7 At this time, the Van Gogh paintings in the collection of the Neue Pinakothek in Munich were *Still Life: Vase with Twelve Sunflowers* (8672), *View of Arles* (8671), and *The Plain at Auvers* (9584).

SB observed that the Vincent van Gogh *Self Portrait* was inscribed to Paul Gauguin (BIF, UoR, GD 5/f. 95). The painting was in the collection of the Neue Staatsgalerie from 1919 until 1938 when it was removed and exhibited as "Entartete Kunst" (Degenerate art), then sold to a private collector in 1939 by the Galerie Fischer in Lucerne, Switzerland, and finally given to the Fogg Museum, Harvard University, in 1951 (no. 1951.65; Sarah Kianovsky, Assistant Director of Painting, Sculpture, and Decorative Arts, The Fogg Gallery, 2 March 2006).

Paintings by Paul Cézanne were *The Railway Cutting* (8646), *Still Life with Commode* (8647), and *Self-Portrait* (c. 1878 to 1880, 8648).

8   The Munich Glaspalast was built in 1854 and destroyed by fire in June 1931; as a result, much of its collection was initially placed in the Neue Pinakothek. From February to April 1937 an extensive exhibition of German art, "Figur und Komposition im Bild und an der Wand" (Figure and Composition in Painting and on the Wall), was held at the Neue Pinakothek. This exhibition displaced a portion of the Museum's modern collection which was hung temporarily in the Library of the Deutsches Museum on Museum Island.

When the Museum of German Art designed by Paul Ludwig Troost was opened by Hitler on 18 July 1937, the German collections were shifted to the new building; this, together with the confiscation of those works declared "entartet," again reconfigured the collection of the Neue Pinakothek.

9   "Apostels," Anglicizing of German spelling.

Dürer's diptych *St. John and St. Peter* (545) and *St. Paul and St. Mark* (540) is known as the *Four Apostles*, also called *Four Holy Men* (since Paul was not one of the Apostles). The *Paumgartner Altar* consisted of the centerpiece, *Birth of Christ* (706); the left panel, *Stephan Paumgartner as St. George*, and, on the back, *The Virgin of the Annunciation* (701); and the right panel, *Lukas Paumgartner as St. Eustachius* (702).

10   The North Netherlandish painter Cornelis Engelbrechtsen (also Engelbrechtsz, c. 1460–1527) was the teacher of Lucas van Leyden; SB refers to *Lamentation over Christ* (H.G. 245).

11   Works by Dutch painter Dieric Bouts (also Dierick, Dirk, c. 1415–1475) in the Alte Pinakothek: *The Arrest of Christ* (990), *St. John the Evangelist* (H.G. 75), and *Christ Rising from the Dead* (H.G. 74). Paintings by Netherlandish artist Gerard David (c. 1460–1523) in the Alte Pinakothek: *The Adoration of the Magi* (715), *Mary with Children* (L. 684), and *Christ Bidding Mary Farewell* (L. 685).

In his diary, SB lists the seventeen paintings by Adriaen Brouwer in the collection of the Alte Pinokethek in Munich (BIF, UoR, GD 6/f. 5, 7). There were sixty-four paintings by Rubens in the collection.

12   Kluth had given SB an introduction to actor and director Kurt Eggers-Kestner (1891–1967); Ballmer had painted a portrait of his children (BIF, UoR, GD 6/f. 19). SB also spent some time with Joseph Eichheim, the actor he had met in Berlin.

Günter Francke (1900–1967) exhibited work by Marc and Nolde in his gallery in 1937 (Hilmar Hoffmann, *Ohne Auftrag: zur Geschichte des Kunsthandels*, I: *München, Sonderschau der Kunstmesse "Art Frankfurt," Frankfurt am Main vom 21–26 April 1989*, ed. Rupert Walser and Bernhard Wittenbrink [Munich: Walser and Wittenbrink, 1989] 266–268). See also Knowlson, *Damned to Fame*, 239.

Hans Rupé (1886–1947), a conservator in the Bavarian National Museum, translated a selection of the poems of the Greek poet Sappho (c. 612 – c. 557 BC), illustrated by the

German sculptor Renée Sintenis: *Sappho* (Berlin: Holle, n.d.). Rupé had been a friend of the German poet Rainer Maria von Rilke (1875–1926). See also Knowlson, *Damned to Fame*, 238–239.

13 SB met German painters Josef Scharl (1896–1954), Edgar Ende (1901–1965), and Joseph Mader (1905–1982); the work of Scharl and Ende was declared "degenerate," and Scharl emigrated to the United States at the end of 1938.
SB met Ende on 19 March 1937 and was shown "avalanches" of his pictures (BIF, UoR, GD 6/f. 17). Ende knew the Irish student of art history Elizabeth Curran (m. Solterer, 1915–2004). Her parents were Helen Laird Curran (1875–1957), a founding member of the Abbey Theatre, and Constantine Peter Curran (1883–1972), a lawyer active in the Irish freedom movement and a friend of James Joyce. Ende talked of Max Ernst (1891–1976), Pablo Picasso, and Salvador Dali (1904–1989), as well as James Joyce.
"Schwärmte" (was effusive, written with an English ending as "schwärmed").

14 On 16 March, Wilhelm Furtwängler and Hugo Kolberg (1899–1979), first violinist with the Berlin Philharmonic Orchestra, performed in an evening of chamber music at the Bayerischer Hof, Munich. They played sonatas for violin and piano: Mozart's Sonata in G major, K 379; Beethoven's Sonata in A major, op. 30, no. 1; and Furtwängler's *Grosse Sonate* in D minor, no. 1 (*Münchner Neueste Nachrichten* 10 March 1937: 4). SB refers to Hector Berlioz and Béla Bartók (1881–1945) (BIF, UoR, GD 5/f. 91).
Patrick Delaney (n.d.) was Professor of Violin at the Royal Irish Academy of Music from 1896 to 1946 (Richard Pine and Charles Acton, eds., *To Talent Alone: The Royal Irish Academy of Music, 1848–1998* [Dublin: Gill and Macmillan, 1998] 523). B. Lennox Braid (1878–1944) was a Dublin-area choral director, organist, and accompanist.

15 The Marienplatz in central Munich was between SB's hotel and the museums.
The typesetter has not been identified. The Hofbräuhaus is a Munich beer hall founded in 1579.
Among many unnamed artists known only by the titles of their paintings, there is the Master of the Death of the Virgin (fl. 1440–1450), a German engraver; prominent in the collection of the Alte Pinakothek is the work of the Master of the Life of the Virgin (fl. 1460–1480), with seven panels of an altarpiece (H.G. 618–624 /22–28).
The Zugspitze is the highest peak (9,718 feet) in Germany, located in the Garmisch-Partenkirchen area of Bavaria, on the border with Austria.

ARLAND USSHER
DUBLIN OR CAPPAGH, CO. WATERFORD

26/3/37   München

Süsser Arland

A song? Good God. Feldeinsamkeit without the warmth, if that is a Begriff; or One man went to mow, without the dog, since music is not one of your tumbles.[1] My poor old blue bitch is very sick, she has what Fielding died of without the belief in tarwater.[2]

I found a portrait of your Keyserling that would have pleased you; by Slevogt or Corinth I forget which, but there was no reproduction to be had. A whiskers like Tom [*for* Roger] Casement, no chin and a red wet lip showing the lining.[3]

Why Karg freitag? Because of the so stingy redemption? What a pity it did not coincide with the Feast of the Annunciation, instead of merely very nearly.[4]

There is a lovely picture in Berlin by Konrad Witz, called the Ratschluss der Erlösung. The Ayes have it, but only just. And are 3 in 1 a quorum? Surely rather a caucus. And on the right hand on the earth beneath and as it were in the margin a visitation, i.e. the first station. Witz indeed. He was born in Nantes.[5]

My memoirs begin under the table, on the eve of my birth, when my father gave a dinner party & my mother presided.

The journey is over. I am tired. I have bitten off more that [*for* than] I can spit out. I had meant to go on, Augsburg, Ulm, Stuttgart, Karlsruhe, Freiburg, Strassburg, Colmar, but it is aus.[6] I shall be in London at the end of next week and stay there a few days. Then back to the whispering gallery, or rather crypt. I only want to sit for aeons alone in a room that I haven't to pay for, & no Sehenswürdigkeiten. You might write a few kind words to 34 Gertrude St., S. W. 10, to break the shock.[7] All the policemen with [? ____] have anus guards.[8]

Things are so bad that I am reading Hans Carossa. Peach Kirkwood Hackett & sacred wafers. "Verlerne die Zeit, dass nicht dein Antlitz verkümmere, und mit dem Antlitz das Herz."[9] Can you beat it.

What anthology?[10]

26 March 1937, Ussher

I hear Cecil has ceased to inspect. I met an art historian in Dresden who had seen his picture.[11]

It is more than I can do to go on.

My kindest regards to your wife, to your father, to your daughter.

Gehorsamst[12]

Sam

ALS; 1 leaves; 2 sides; *letterhead* <HOTEL LEINFELDER, MUNCHEN>; TxU.

1 "Süsser" (sweet; my dear).
SB refers to a song by Brahms, "Feldeinsamkeit" (In Summer Fields), op. 86, no. 2. "Begriff" (concept).
"One man went to mow" refers to a popular children's song: "One man went to mow / Went to mow a meadow / One man and his dog / Went to mow a meadow / Two men went to mow ... "

2 The Beckett family dog, Wolf. Joseph Fielding suffered from dropsy, edema, jaundice, and gout, but probably died from "peritoneal cancer or cirrhosis of the liver" (Donald Thomas, *Henry Fielding* [London: Weidenfeld and Nicolson, 1990] 391). Fielding took an infusion of tar in water, a remedy for dropsy recommended by Bishop Berkeley in *Siris* (1744) (Pat Rogers, *Henry Fielding: A Biography* [London: Paul Elk, 1979] 213.

3 SB refers to a painting not by German artist Max Slevogt (1868–1932), but by Lovis Corinth, *Eduard, Count von Keyserling* (no. 8986) in the Neue Pinakothek, Munich: it depicts the German writer Keyserling (1855–1918), with a full upturned mustache; Sarah Purser's portrait *Roger Casement, Patriot and Revolutionary* (NGI 938) depicts Sir Roger Casement (1864–1916) with a similar mustache as well as a full beard. Inadvertently, SB writes the name of Roger Casement's brother Thomas Hugh Jephson Casement (1863–1939), who established the Coast Life Saving Service in Ireland. SB also conflates Eduard Graf von Keyserling with his cousin Hermann Graf von Keyserling whose book Ussher had requested that SB find for him (see 31 December 1936, n. 10).

4 "Karg Freitag" (meager Friday) rather than "Karfreitag" (Good Friday).
The date of the Feast of the Annunciation is 25 March; in 1937, Good Friday was celebrated on 26 March.

5 *Der Ratschluss der Erlösung* (The Decree of Redemption) by German-born Swiss painter Konrad Witz (c. 1400 – c. 1446), seen by SB in the Kaiser Friedrich Museum, is now in the Gemäldegalerie in Berlin (KF 1673). The painting depicts the Trinity with iconography of the Incarnation: God the Father on his throne designating an obedient Christ as redeemer, with a dove between them to represent the Holy Spirit hovering over the open book; a lamb just behind them, and a key suspended between them to signify the sacrifice and key of the house of David; Mary and Elizabeth, both pregnant,

475

are depicted in the right foreground. The painting is considered the "Visitation" or first station of the life of Christ; it is one panel from the *Altarpiece of the Mirror of Salvation* (also known as *The Heilsspiegel Altarpiece*) which was painted c. 1435 for the Leonhardskirche in Basel; its panels were dispersed in 1529. One double-sided panel is in the Musée des Beaux-Arts, Dijon (see 15 June 1938, n. 2).

"Witz" (joke).

Konrad Witz's birthplace is now known to be Rotweill, Germany; he was admitted to the Basel Guild of Painters as "Master Konrad of Rottweil" in 1434. Several times SB notes in his German diary that Witz's birth place was Nantes, and he reports that he had annoyed Günter Francke in Munich by mentioning that Witz was French (BIF, UoR: GD 3/f. 1, 18 December 1936; GD 4/f. 18, 21 January 1936; GD 6/f. 45, 25 March 1937; and GD 6/f. 71, 31 March 1937; Mark Nixon).

Konrad Witz was the son of the painter Hans Witz (n.d.) whose identity has historically been confused with other painters, one of whom worked in Nantes at the beginning of the fifteenth century (Josef Hecht, Konstanz, "Der Aufenthalt des Konrad Witz in Konstanz: Ein Problem und seine Lösung Neue Forschungen zur Lebensgeschichte des Meisters," *Zeitschrift für Kunstgeschichte* 6.5/6 [1937], 353–370; Emmanuel Bénézit, ed., *Dictionnaire critique et documentaire des peintres, sculpteurs, dessinateurs et graveurs de tous les temps et de tous les pays*, 3rd edn. [Paris: Gründ, 1976] 774).

6 SB uses the German spelling of these towns, with the exception of Colmar which, in German, is Kolmar. "Aus" (over).

7 Although St. Paul's Cathedral in London has a "whispering gallery," SB here refers to Dublin.

SB planned to spend a week with Mrs. Frost, 34 Gertrude Street, London.

8 SB omits a word here.

9 German poet and novelist Hans Carossa (1878–1956). "Peach Kirkwood Hackett" may refer to Mme. Eva Kirkwood Hackett (1877–1968), theatre producer in Dublin in the 1930s and later a film actress.

"O verlerne die Zeit, / Dass nicht dein Antlitz verkümmre / Und mit dem Antlitz das Herz!" (Learn to disregard time so that your countenance may not wither away, and with your countenance your heart) is from Hans Carossa's poem "Ein Stern Singt" (A Star Sings), first published in *Gedichte* (1923) and reprinted in Hans Carossa and Eva Kampmann-Carossa, *Gedichte: Die Veröffentlichungen zu Lebzeiten und Gedichte aus dem Nachlass* (Frankfurt: Insel, 1995) 64–65. SB writes the standard form, "verkümmere," whereas the poem uses the contracted form, "verkümmre."

10 It is not known which anthology Ussher had – presumably – mentioned in his letter.

11 While Cecil Salkeld may have had a position as an Inspector, this has not been confirmed. Will Grohmann was familiar with Salkeld's work (see 16 February 1937, n. 14).

12 Arland Ussher's first wife was Emily (née Whitehead, c. 1898–1974), his father was Beverley Grant Ussher (1867–1956), and his daughter is Henrietta Owen Ussher Staples (b. 1926).

"Gehorsamst" (most obediently).

GÜNTER ALBRECHT
HAMBURG

30/3/37   München
                                         Pension Romana
                                         Akademiestrasse

Dear Günter Albrecht
    Very many thanks indeed for your letters and the Fontane,
which I neither possess nor have read. I am sorry you have had
such trouble in getting in touch with me. Three weeks ago I left
instructions with the Postlagernd to send on everything here.
Perhaps it is their duty to get tired after a fortnight, when the
instructions are not renewed.[1]
    I write to you almost on the eve of my departure from
Germany. I am tired and can see nothing more, all the surfaces
remain surfaces and that is terrible. I had meant to go on by
Augsburg, Ulm, Stuttgart, Freiburg, Strassburg, Kolmar, Karslruhe
[*for* Karlsruhe], Frankfurt, Berlin again and home from there, and
as I write the names I curse the small capacity that excludes the
possibility, temporarily at least, of their being anything more than
names. I fly from here next Friday morning, straight to London,
where I shall stay probably a week before going on to Dublin.
    It was a strange zigzag from Berlin: Halle (to see the
Moritzburg pictures), a Bühnenbildner in love with Mexico
where he met Traven and the Weise Collection, (mostly
Kirchners), Erfurt (chiefly to see the Heckel frescos which are
not particularly good), Weimar, Naumburg, Leipzig (where even
the colossal Klinger Exhibition and a concert in the Gewandhaus
could not console me), and from there with relief straight to
Dresden.[2] I was content there for three weeks. I met a lot of

friendly and intelligent people, including a whole colony of Russians, blue with blood and privations taken good-humouredly. Biely and vodka go well together I found. Also the dancer Palucca and a charming art historian now duly in deep disgrace but also good-humoured, too interested in the phenomenon to think of exile, Will Grohmann, with to his credit books on and catalogues of Klee and Kandinsky and Baumeister and others.[3] Through him I was enabled to visit the Ida Bienert collection, which must be one of the best modern collections in Germany, practically everything from Cézanne to Mo[n]drian except the Brücke, which is not represented at all: the best Kandinsky I have seen, quantities of Klee and three lovely Picassos. And a portrait by Kokoschka of a woman I used to know in Paris years ago![4]

As you say the pictures in the Zwinger are vilely hung and lit. The Rembrandt room, Director Posse's pride and joy, is a scandal. The Vermeer Kupplerin, cowering between a Rembrandt old man and a Bol philosopher and beneath something enormous and dirty by I think Eeckhout, was literally invisible. I saw it for the first time the day I left in the full light of one of the end rooms, where a copyist had contrived to have it temporarily transferred.[5] The Giorgione is in a mess, the whole left leg destroyed by some damn 19th century restorer in the service of a taste offended by the putto with the bird, now painted over with senseless landscape. I saw the X-Ray photograph, which however doesn't show very much.[6]

But in spite of the wretched presentation and the gaps (no Flemish or Italian primitives) it remains a splendid collection. I never saw a better Antonello than the St. Sebastian.[7]

The Zwinger itself, in spite of the here and there very irresolute restoration, has still enough of what Pöppelmann meant it to have to give one the essence and the melancholy of barock. There are sad passages, the arcades leading up to the entrance on the garden side. I felt the Kronentor was wrong, too high and florid, an over-statement. But it was so from the beginning, according to Bellotto, whom I refuse to call Canaletto.[8]

I made a few halfhearted excursions, in spite of the weather, to Meissen, where some of the Dome [*for* Dom] statues are probably by the Naumburg Master, and to Pillnitz, where the core on the water is lovely.[9]

I saw more whores in Dresden, whores of the old school, any evening I felt so inclined, than in all the months since October and all the places since Hamburg put together. Sächsischer Stützwechsel![10]

From Dresden it went on by Freiberg, Bamberg, Würzburg, Nürnberg, and Regensburg. Nürnberg was so horrible, as I more or less expected, that I extended my resentments even to the Great Period and found good reasons, mostly connected with the expulsion of the Jews in 1499 (they didn't get back for nearly 4 centuries) and the Wittenberg catastrophe of 1517, for impugning the value of Stoss and Kraft and Pleydenwurff and Vischer and Wohlgemut [*for* Wolgemut] and even the great AD himself. The Dürer room in the Germanisches Museum is another scandal, the portrait of Wohlgemut eked out with the dreariest of workshop Kitsch and a copy of the Apostles![11]

I am too close to München to say anything more definite than that I infinitely prefer Hamburg or Berlin. Perhaps it is the Föhn! I spend most of my time needless to say in the Alte Pinakothek, which I now know so well that I can walk through the entire collection without having to pass a Rubens![12] I haven't made any of the prescribed excursions, Garmisch, Mittenwald,

Königsschlösser, etc., and shall not, in spite of an Alpine sportive compositor picked up in the Hofbräuhaus who assured me that there were as many Masters of the Death of the Virgin as there were Masters and Dead Virgins, but only one Zugspitz[e].[13]

I exchanged a few politenesses with a girl in Severing's bookshop who knew you and Kaun in Leipzig. You were "der grosse Schwarze" in her phraseology. I shall have the pleasure there in an hour's time of being introduced to Alverdes, whose Kleine Reise I began but did not go on with.[14] I have been reading a lot of Carossa, Geheimnisse, Gion and Führung, kindly lent by Kaun, and find it, to ne [for be] quite frank, bloody awful in the end, the complete flight into style. I met yet another friend of Rilke, every second person of a certain degree of culture in German seems to have been a friend of Rilke, a conservator in the Bavarian Nat. Museum, who assured me that Rilke linked up with Proust in his "decentralisation of the soul".[15] I also met the actor Eggers-Kestner, whom you may remember from the time he was in Hamburg. He has a lovely picture by Ballmer, Kluths and Ruhwohlds [for Ruwoldts] and the politest of polite Hartmann watercolours. He gave me Ballmer's Aber Herr Heidigger [for Heidegger]! to read and a MS Deutschtum u. Christentum in the same direction but too Steinerisch for the non-initiate.[16] I have just rung up Piper to try and get the Barlach drawings but the reply, in a very terrified tone, was "Ich will nicht, ich will nicht".[17]

I saw that Munich legend Valentin and found him a comedian of the very first order but perhaps just beginning his decline.[18]

The rest I leave over for another letter. My home address I think you have already: 6 Clare Street, Dublin, I.F.S. Let us keep in touch with one another. In the very throes of labour camp and military service you will have plenty to get off your chest and – I hope – leisure to do it. I was very glad to hear your painter friend had had some success. Remember me to him. I hear Grimm is married.[19]

Kindest regards to your family.

Yours ever

s/ Sam Beckett

TLS; 1 leaf, 2 sides; BIF, UoR, MS 5037.

1 On 28 March, SB received *Effi Briest* (1894) by German poet and novelist Theodor Fontane (1819–1898) (BIF, UoR, GD 6/f. 55).

"Postlagernd" (poste restante).

2 In this letter SB summarizes his experiences in Germany since leaving Berlin; rather than repeat information, the notes supply cross-references.

"Lebensstufen" ("Stages of Life"), Erich Heckel's fresco on the four walls of a room in the Anger Museum, Erfurt, was painted in 1922–1924. SB admired the figure of the German poet Stefan George (1868–1933) surrounded by members of his circle, but observed that the fresco was crowded with iconography and was not in good repair (BIF, UoR, GD 4/f. 27, 24 January 1937; see also Mechthild Lucke, Erich Heckel, and Andreas Hüneke, *Erich Heckel, Lebensstufen: die Wandbilder im Angermuseum zu Erfurt* [Dresden: Verlag der Kunst, 1992]). Later in 1937, and through the war, the entrance to the Heckel room was blocked off to hide it from the Nazis; as a result, the fresco suffered damage from prolonged damp and cold, but it is now on view in the Anger Museum, having undergone restoration.

The Max Klinger Exhibition in Leipzig: SB to Thomas McGreevy, 30 January 1937, n. 1; the concert in the Gewandhaus on 28 January in Leipzig: SB to Thomas McGreevy, 16 February 1937, n. 13.

3 The colony of Russians in Dresden, especially the Obolensky and von Gersdorff families: 16 February 1937; for the lecture on Bely: 23 February 1937.

Through Heinz Porep, SB met the German dancer and choreographer Gret Palucca (1902–1993), formerly married to Ida Bienert's son Fritz Bienert (1891–1969). Palucca introduced SB to the art historian Will Grohmann. Grohmann's writings: 16 February 1937, n. 14.

4 SB's visit to Ida Bienert's collection is discussed in 16 February 1937. Bienert purchased many of Kandinsky's works directly from the artist (Grohmann's catalogue of her collection is comprehensive only through 1933: *Die Sammlung Ida Bienert, Dresden*, 21, fig. 36, 36–42; later acquisitions as well as the current ownership of Kandinsky works in her collection can be found in Hans K. Roethel and Jean K. Benjamin, *Kandinsky, Catalogue Raisonné of the Oil Paintings*, 2 vols. [Ithaca, NY: Cornell University Press, 1982–1984] I, 346, 476; II, 672, 851; and watercolors can be found in Vivian Endicott Barnett, *Kandinsky Watercolours: Catalogue Raisonné*, II [Ithaca, NY: Cornell University Press, 1994] 150, 156, 280, 337, 373).

There were thirty-nine paintings by Paul Klee in the Bienert Collection (Grohmann, ed., *Die Sammlung Ida Bienert, Dresden*, 21–22, figs. 43–59). Picasso paintings in her collection were *Woman with Hat, Waltz,* and the gouache on paper *The Seamstress* (23–24, figs. 7–9).

Bienert also then owned the portrait of Nancy Cunard, *Engländerin,* painted by Kokoschka in 1924: see 16 February 1937, n. 15.

5 The Zwinger Museum in Dresden and its Director Hans Posse: 16 February 1937, n. 2 and n. 11.

Vermeer's *Kupplerin (The Procuress)* and its hanging in the Rembrandt Hall of the Zwinger are described in 16 February 1937, n. 8 and n. 9; it was hung between paintings by Rembrandt and Salomon Koninck and under a painting by Ferdinand Bol, not Gerbrand van den Eeckhout (1621–1674).

SB's last visit to the museum was on 17 February:

> See it, in the good light, really for first time, the man on left clearly, and the lurid evening sky through space between him & [? woman], that does not function in the Rembrandt room, & that flattens & defines the key of the whole picture, gives it substance & immediacy, an immediacy of the everlasting transitory, situates it in eternity. Without it the picture was [...] adrift, overcrowded, overheated, only excellent genre. With it it is Vermeer. (BIF, UoR, GD 5/f. 5, 17 February 1937, Nixon and Knowlson transcription)

6 Giorgione's *Venus* in the Zwinger collection: 16 February 1937, n. 4.

7 SB refers to Antonello da Messina's painting *The Martyrdom of St. Sebastian*; a card of this image was sent to McGreevy on 2 February 1937, and SB describes it further in 16 February 1937 (see also n. 7 to that letter).

8 SB's discussion of the architecture and restoration of the Zwinger: 16 February 1937, n. 2. The Kronentor, the tower that crowns the main entrance of the Zwinger Palace, is depicted in *The Zwinger Palace in Dresden* by Italian painter Bernardo Bellotto (NPG, 629; see bildarchiv.skd-dresden.de/). Bellotto adopted Canaletto as his name outside of Italy, but SB recognizes this as the name of his uncle and master Canaletto (né Giovanni Antonio Canal, 1697–1768).

9 On 12 February, SB went to Meissen. The sculptures in the choir and corners of the mid-Gothic Dom in Meissen (c. 1260–1280) are ascribed to the thirteenth-century Naumburg Master; they are larger than life-size, but less naturalistic than his sculptures in Naumburg (Hans-Joachim Mrusek, *Drei sächsische Kathedralen: Merseburg, Naumburg, Meissen* [Dresden: Verlag der Kunst, 1976] 370).

On 16 February, SB went to Pillnitz; he describes the town which is dominated by the Schloss Pillnitz designed by Matthäus Pöppelmann with steps down to terraces, and from there to the edge of the Elbe River.

10 "Sächsischer Stützwechsel" (Saxon support system); SB compares the prostitutes lined up along the street to "Stützenwechsel," a pattern typical of Romanesque architecture in Saxony that alternates styles of piers or columns; he has noted this term in his German diary when describing the Dom in Hildesheim.

11 Freiberg in Saxony. SB's discussion of Nuremberg: 7 March 1937.

12 The "Föhn" (warm, dry wind from the Alps) is often thought to be a cause of illness or nervousness, called Föhnkrankheit (Föhn-sickness).

The sixty-four paintings by Rubens in the collection of the Alte Pinakothek in Munich in 1936 were hung in Rooms V and VI, and in Cabinets XII and XIV; the rooms were located off a loggia, and the Cabinets were entered through the rooms (Karl Baedeker, *Das Deutsche Reich und einige Grenzgebiete, Reisehandbuch für Bahn und Auto* [Leipzig: Karl Baedeker, 1936] 472).

13 SB did not take typical excursions from Munich: Garmisch-Partenkirchen (where the 1936 winter Olympics had been held) and Mittenwald in the Bavarian Alps, and Königsschlösser, the castle of King Ludwig II (1845–1886) near Neuschwanstein in Bavaria. SB mentions the Hofbräuhaus, the compositor, the Masters of Dead Virgins, and the Zugspitze in his letter of 25 March 1937.

14 SB visited Severing's bookshop in Munich at the suggestion of Porep's friend, the dentist Dr. Richard Zarnitz. Axel Kaun: 18 January 1937 to Mary Manning Howe, n. 10.

"Der grosse Schwarze" (the big dark one).

SB met German writer and editor Paul Alverdes (1897–1979) at the bookstore on this day; SB began *Kleine Reise: Aus einem Tagebuch* (1933; Small Journey: From a Journal). Alverdes is best known for his novel *Die Pfeiferstube* (1929; *The Whistler*) which he discussed with SB (BIF, UoR, GD 6/f. 63).

15 Axel Kaun had lent SB Hans Carossa's *Geheimnisse des reifen Lebens: aus den Aufzeichungen Angermanns* (1936; Secrets of the Mature Life: From the Notations of Angermann), *Der Arzt Gion* (1931; *Doctor Gion*), and *Führung und Geleit, ein Lebensgedenkbuch* (1933; Guidance and Companionship: A Life Memoir).

SB refers to Hans Rupé (see 25 March 1937, n. 12). In his diary, SB recorded his discussion with Rupé about Rilke and Proust (BIF, UoR, GD 6/f. 77).

16 The art collection of Kurt Eggers-Kestner included a painting of the children of Eggers-Kestner by Ballmer (see 25 March 1937, n.12), several works by Kluth including a portrait of Barlach, and unidentified watercolors by Hartmann. SB had met artist Hans Martin Ruwoldt through Grimm (see 28 November 1937 [*for* 1936], n. 15, and Beckett, *Alles kommt auf so viel an*, 50–51).

Karl Ballmer, *Aber Herr Heidegger! Zur Freiburger Rektoratsrede Martin Heideggers* (Basel: Verlag von Rudolf Geering, 1933; But Mr. Heidegger! Concerning Martin Heidegger's Freiburg Inaugural Address as Rector). Ballmer was influenced by the theories of the Austrian-born founder of Anthroposophy, Rudolf Steiner (1861–1925). Ballmer's manuscript was of a book published much later, and perhaps by then revised, as *Deutschtum und Christentum in der Theosophie des Goetheanismus* (Besazio: Verlag Fomasella, 1966; Germanness and Christianity in the Theosophy of Goetheanism).

17 On SB's behalf, Eggers-Kestner contacted Munich publisher Reinhard Piper (1879–1953) to see if SB could acquire a volume of Ernst Barlach's drawings, *Zeichnungen* (1935), published by Piper Verlag. Piper was very reluctant, anxious that a copy might be discovered in customs, but he said he would think it over.

The collection of drawings by Barlach had been planned in 1934 when Barlach's work was still allowed; publication proceeded even though by 1935 Barlach's work had been withdrawn from public view. But on 24 March 1936, "The Bavarian Political Police forbade the further sale of the volume of Barlach's drawings and confiscated the 3,419 bound and unbound copies in the publisher's warehouse, on the grounds that the work's 'content is likely to endanger public safety and order'" (Peter Paret, *An Artist*

30 March 1937, Albrecht

Against the Third Reich: Ernst Barlach, 1933–1938 [Cambridge: Cambridge University Press, 2003] 96). Both Piper and Barlach took steps to fight this ban (Paret, 77–107).
"Ich will nicht, ich will nicht" (I don't want to, I don't want to).

18 SB saw a performance by the German cabaret and film comic Karl Valentin (1882–1948) at the Benz Cabaret in Munich, and soon after, on the day before he left Germany, SB went with the actor Eichheim to meet Valentin (Knowlson, *Damned to Fame*, 241; BIF, UoR, GD 6/f. 71 and f. 73).

19 In fulfillment of his Reichsarbeitsdienst (National Service), Albrecht served in a Labor camp in early 1937. Albrecht's painter friend has not been identified.
Willem Grimm married Käthe Franck (1910–1992) in March 1937.

GEORGE REAVEY

LONDON

13/4/37   6 Clare Street
                                                     Dublin

Dear George

Thanks for your note.

I hear that Nelson are trying to do a line in Irish authors. Perhaps you might send Murphy next to them.[1]

But the best chance seems now the USA & then Nott.[2] If you want a third MS I can let you have it. I trust you received the second safely.

Any time you feel like throwing your hat at the whole thing I shall stand you a new one.

Pomposo continues to occupy me.[3]

Kindest regards to Miss Vernon[4]

Yours ever

Sam

ALS; 1 leaf, 1 side; TxU.

1 The publishers Thomas Nelson and Sons, Edinburgh, London, and New York, published the novel *Somewhere to the Sea* (1936) by Irish writer Kenneth Sarr (né Kenneth Shiels Reddin), but there is no evidence of a new publishing direction for this firm.

2 SB refers to seeking a publisher for *Murphy*. Writing to Reavey on 23 February 1937, SB had indicated that a second manuscript was with Mary Manning Howe in the United States, and a third in Dublin.

3 SB refers to his research and writing on Samuel Johnson, who was nicknamed "Pomposo" by Charles Churchill (1731–1764) in his satirical poem *The Ghost* (London: William Flexney, 1762).

4 Clodine Gwynedd Cade (née Vernon Jones), Reavey's fiancée.

GEORGE REAVEY

LONDON

14/4/37   6 Clare St.

                                                    Dublin

dear George

Was it <u>Nelson</u> that I suggested in my note yesterday? Please note that was my intention.[1]

I hear from my friend Mrs Howe of Boston that she is showing <u>Murphy</u> to one Harrison Smith of Doubleday Doran & then if necessary to someone she knows in the Viking Press.[2] Don't you think you should get in touch with her if you intend to handle the MS in USA? In case you have lost her address it is: 136 Myrtle Street, Boston, Mass.

Gehorsamst[3]

Sam

APCS; 1 leaf, 1 side; TxU.

1 Publishers Thomas Nelson and Sons.

2 Oliver Harrison Smith (1888–1971) was an Editor with Doubleday Doran from 1936 to 1938, following the merger of his firm Haas and Smith with Random House in 1936 (Alden Whitman, "Harrison Smith of the Saturday Review is Dead," *The New York Times* 9 January 1971: 30; "Harrison Smith (1888–1971)," *Saturday Review* 54.4 [23 January 1971] 30).

Mary Manning Howe's contact at Viking Press in New York has not been identified.

3 "Gehorsamst" (most obediently).

THOMAS McGREEVY
LONDON

26/4/37   Foxrock [Co. Dublin]

Dear Tom

Many thanks for your letter. Your descriptions of O'Faolain &
Frere Reeves were reassuring.[1]

I have been in a daze since returning, very stupid & fairly
comfortable. The afternoon with JBY was as pleasant as it always
is when one has him to oneself. He had a lovely new swamp – &
sea piece called the Little Waves of Breffni [*for* Breffny]. He has
five pictures in the Academy, including the boy & horse that I
had the reproduction of and I think 2 quite new ones that I have
not seen. I have not been to the Academy.[2] Gogarty said publicly
he had never seen such a collection of pictures anywhere. Cottie
came in later from the Hone watercolours in Waddington's
Gallery in Anne Street, very rueful that she couldn't go with
Jack to the Academy dinner. I saw the Hones with Frank the
following Monday. There was a nice misprint in Crampton
Walker's blurb, Daubingy for Daubigny.[3]

You don't mention having received the Dublin Magazine
with my tortuous puff of the Amaranthers. I sent it to you.[4]

The Lurçat is back on the wall in Charlemont House, very
well repaired as far as I can see, but abominably hung, low down
in the long overlit room with the awful J. E. Blanches, in a
corner. I hear Kelly or whatever the curator is called confessed
sadly to Stella Solomons Starkey – of all people! – to not knowing
a great deal about it. But he was reading it up, he said.[5] The Jack
Yeats Low Tide, in the Academy I think 2 years ago, and presented by Justice Meredith, was being derided by three ladies the

day I was there. There seem to be a number of new AEs, including 2 girls in their nighties astride a roof ridge in the moonlight.[6]

The old bitch I was so fond of was destroyed (chloroformed) last Saturday week, unbeknown to me, while I was at Jack Yeats'. I was very upset, as I had wanted to be with her at the end, to try & make it perhaps a little easier.[7] Mother was prostrated, in bed for 2 days after it, and it was very hard work indeed getting her to take a reasonable view of what oneself could not take a reasonable view of. Apart from that she is much the same, with as few really good days as really bad. Frank spends most of his spare time with his girl. He has bought Joyce's Irish Place Names in 3 volumes, knows a lot already about Celtic etymologies & has cleaned his paint box. We are going to-morrow to the Exhibition of the Water-Colour Society![8]

I went one day with Cissie to see Boss. He has been moved, to the new place perched above Rathdrum attached to the county home, mainly the creation of my good uncle Gerald, run by some Sisters of mercy.[9] There he is more comfortable, and quite simply seven months worse than when I saw him last. I think he knows now he is dying & has given up the idea of ever coming home. I of course can't stimulate him, but when the Liam O'Briens & Seumas O'Sullivans go down he keeps them amused in the old way. Cissie is also a little worse than she was & less than ever able to move about. [...] The son is still in the veldt, chafing to get home.[10]

I had half a card from George, announcing another rejection. I sent him another copy & he has the two out now, I think one with Nelson. He also mentioned Brian had been over.[11] I have not looked him up, nor Dennis [*for* Denis] either. I hear Dennis asked Edward Sheehy, the only paid member of staff on Dublin To-Day [*for Ireland To-Day*] to get me to review his poems.

It is not a job that I would much relish, though of course I wd. have to execute myself.[12] So far I have heard nothing about it.

I had lunch with Leventhal but do not expect to see much of him. He seems to have made great friends with S. O'Sullivan & Austin Clarke, who has settled over here (Kimmage) now [...] & was seen at the Academy with even more than his melancholy expression.[13]

I called once on Ethna MacCarthy but she was not in. The young Pourbus Old Woman was leaning against the wall.[14]

I met Joe Hone in the library & he invited me to dine one Saturday evening, which I accepted. Then at the last moment he rang me up and said that his wife said that the Lennox Robinsons, also invited, were enemies of mine & that it would not go! I said I was stupid about such things, cd. never remember who loved me & who hated me & who tolerated me & who did not, and that by all means let it be called up. A couple of nights later I dined, the only guest, and was given a bottle of stout[15] [...]

Some of the Poussins have gone on loan to Paris, the Cranach to the Kaiser Friedrich and the awful Franz Hals somewhere else.[16]

Nancy Cunard sent me from France <u>Dos Poemas</u>, one by herself & the other by a Spaniard, the usual indignations.[17]

Ruddy making a fool of himself in Dublin Mag., dragging in the memory of his dead wife, the footsteps that do not come, no peace till he rests beside her, etc., all apropos of Lord de Talby's [*for* Tabley's] verse. A foul article by Lwellyn [*for* Llewelyn] Powys on Dr Johnson, making him out a John Bull, the orthodox balls in fact. By the way, I mentioned the Vincent O'Sullivan thing to Joe Hone, who had heard nothing of it & said he wd. very gladly subscribe if he knew to what quarter.[18]

I like walking more & more, & the less aim the better. I was on the Big Sugarloaf on Saturday and yesterday found in a field near Enniskerry a lovely small Celtic cross with still the dim low relief of a Christ crucified with head duly inclined to the north. Frank wants me to go with him at Whit to Clonmel & walk the Galtees & the Blackstairs & so I will. I should love to see Cashel again.[19]

I have been working, in so far as I have been working at all, at the Johnson thing, to find my petition of principle, after many disappointments, more strikingly confirmed than I had dared hope. It seems now quite certain that he was rather absurdly in love with her, all the 15 years he was at Streatham, though there is no text for the impotence. It becomes more interesting – the fake rage to cover his retreat from her, then the real rage when he realises that no retreat was necessary, and beneath both the despair of the lover with nothing to love with – and much more difficult.[20] It explains what has never been explained, i.e. his esteem for the imbecile Mr Thrale.[21] The last meeting in 1783, about 6 months before her marriage to Piozzi, a year before his death, has always remained nebulous. He has a brief reference to it in his Meditations. I think that is an interview that must be written, though I should have wished either to keep it all in 1784 or spread it to catch the scene where the Thrales find him on his knees before Dr Delap, praying for a continuance of his reason. Arthur Murphy is important, the only one, not excluding Fanny Burney, of the Streatham Circle who stuck to Mrs Thrale through the scandal. I think we will have a very quiet Dr Johnson. Perhaps his nigger Frank Barber was the only person he never bellowed at.[22]

I read Dujardin's Lauriers... and realised how extremely charitable it was in Joyce to invoke him to Larbaud & how very modest his proposal that his conception of the monologue was not identical with the model's. Or perhaps it was neither charity nor modesty, but simply <u>astuce</u> again.[23]

Alan Thompson's wife bore him a son yesterday.[24]

Your account of the evening with Charles was not very cheerful, but I think you are hypersensitive in that connexion. I have not written to him and must do so.[25]

I have had the old internal combustion heart & head a couple of nights, in the bed where I had it the first time almost exactly 11 years ago, but as little anxiety as then. Perhaps it is that the phase of impatience with one's own limitations has nearly exhausted itself. I feel now that I shall meet the most of my days from now on here and in tolerable content, not feeling much guilt at making the most of what ease there is to be had and not bothering very much about effort. After all there has been an effort. But perhaps I am wrong. Perhaps, it is Dr Johnson's dream of happiness, driving rapidly to & from nowhere in a postchaise with a pretty woman.[26]

Cissie met O'Malley at Grange House & liked him.[27]

Write again soon.

> Love ever
>
> Sam

ALS; 5 leaves, 5 sides; TCD, MS 10402/126.

1 McGreevy's comments about Sean O'Faolain and London publishers Frere-Reeves are not known.

2 Jack Yeats wrote to McGreevy on 20 April 1937 that SB had visited the previous Saturday, 17 April (TCD, MS 10381/143).

Yeats's new painting was *The Little Waves of Breffny* (private collection, Pyle 495). His paintings in the 108th Annual Exhibition of the Royal Hibernian Academy of Arts were: *Boy and Horse* (see 29 January 1936, n. 2), *While Grass Grows* (Waterford Municipal Art Gallery 76, Pyle 492), *A Morning in a City* (NGI 1050, Pyle 493), *An Evening in Spring* (private collection, Pyle 494), and *Dancing on the Deck* (Waddington Gallery, London, Pyle 443).

3   On 17 April, Cottie Yeats had seen an exhibition of oils and watercolors by Irish landscape painter Nathaniel Hone (1831–1917) at the Victor Waddington Gallery, 28 South Anne Street, that ran from 13 to 20 April. SB and Frank Beckett saw it on Monday, 19 April. Irish artist John Crampton Walker (1890–1942) prepared the *Catalogue of Exhibition of Pictures by the Late Nathaniel Hone R.H.A. at Victor Waddington Gallery*; in the one-page biographical essay the name of French landscape painter Charles-François Daubigny (1817–1878) is misspelled.

4   SB's review of *The Amaranthers*: "An Imaginative Work!" 80–81.

5   The damage to Lurçat's *Decorative Landscape* (a hole near the center and several small ones at the side) had been repaired by J.J. Gory's, Picture Restorer, 51 Grafton Street (invoice for repair, 13 August 1935, Dublin City Gallery the Hugh Lane; see also 5 May 1935, n. 6, and Sunday [22 September 1935], n. 2). John F. Kelly was Curator of the Municipal Gallery of Modern Art from 1 October 1935 to 1954. Stella Solomons Starkey was a good friend of Sarah Purser; Purser, as the leader of the Friends of the National Collections, had been responsible for bringing the painting into the collection.
The paintings by Jacques-Emile Blanche (1861–1942) in the collection at this time included *Jeanne* and *Mischief* (Dublin City Gallery The Hugh Lane, no. 294 and no. 293).

6   *Low Tide* by Jack B. Yeats had been shown in the 1935 Royal Hibernian Academy Exhibition; it was bought by Justice James Creed Meredith and presented in 1937 to the Municipal Gallery of Modern Art: 5 May 1935, n. 3.
There were thirteen paintings by AE in the collection at this time, many of which were part of the 1904 gift of Hugh Lane; the museum opened in Charlemont House in 1933, and may have rotated the paintings on exhibition, which would explain why the painting to which SB refers, *On the Roof Top, Moonlight* (Dublin City Museum The Hugh Lane, no. 32), may have been "new" to SB (Patrick Casey, Dublin City Museum The Hugh Lane, 2 June 2006).

7   SB refers to his dog Wolf.

8   Frank's girl, Jean Violet Wright (1906–1966).
Frank Beckett bought Patrick Weston Joyce, *The Origin and History of Irish Names of Places*, 3 vols. (Dublin: Educational Company of Ireland; London: Longmans, Green, n.d. [after 1913]).
The 83rd Exhibition of The Water Colour Society of Ireland was held at Mills's Hall, Merrion Row, Dublin, April–May 1937.

9   Gerald Paul Gordon Beckett (1888–1950), SB's uncle, was the County Medical Officer for Wicklow. Boss Sinclair had been moved in November 1936 (see 28 November 1937 [*for* 1936], n. 25).

10   Liam O'Brien (Ó Briaine, 1888–1974), Irish Nationalist and Professor of French, University College Galway. The Sinclairs' son, Morris Sinclair, was in South Africa.

11   George Reavey's letter to SB, to which SB's of 13 April is a reply, has not been found; however, Hamish Hamilton wrote to Reavey on 9 April 1937 rejecting *Murphy*: "Alas, Beckett's book is as obscure as I feared! I don't feel that I can make an offer" (TxU). SB had suggested Nelson as a possible publisher for *Murphy*, but no

evidence has been found of the manuscript being submitted to them. Brian Coffey had been in London.

12 SB refers to Denis Devlin's collection of poems *Intercessions*, not yet published by Reavey's Europa Press. Irish writer Edward Sheehy (c. 1910–1956) was on the staff of *Ireland To-Day*, a journal published from June 1936 to March 1938, edited by Frank O'Connor. SB did not write this review.
"Execute myself" (Gallicism for "do it as asked").

13 Kimmage is a Dublin suburb. The annual Royal Hibernian Academy Exhibition was at this time.

14 Ethna MacCarthy's painting by the School of Pourbus: 20 February 1935, n. 13.

15 Vera Hone; Lennox and Dolly Robinson.
"Would not go" (Gallicism for "wouldn't work").

16 Three works by Poussin were lent for the Chefs d'Oeuvre de l'Art Français Exhibition at the Palais National des Arts in Paris from June to October 1937: *The Entombment of Christ* (NGI 214), *Acis and Galatea* (NGI 814), and an ink and wash on paper, *The Marriage of Acis and Galatea* (NGI 2842). Lucas Cranach's painting *Christ on the Cross* (NGI 471) was lent to the Kaiser Friedrich Museum in Berlin (from 24 April 1937); *A Young Fisherman of Scheveningen* (also known as *The Fisher Boy*, NGI 193) by Franz Hals was lent for the Franz Hals Exhibition in Haarlem (July to September 1937) ("National Gallery of Ireland: Loans and Purchases," *The Irish Times* 8 April 1937: 8).

17 When in Spain during the summer and autumn of 1936, Nancy Cunard met Pablo Neruda, who introduced her to Spanish poets, and encouraged her to create a series to print poetry inspired by the Spanish Civil War. Six pamphlets were published in 1937, hand-printed by Cunard and Neruda on her press at Réanville: *Les Poètes du monde défendent le peuple espagnol* (Poets of the World Defend the Spanish People). The first number, *Dos Poemas*, consisted of a poem by Neruda, "Canto sobre unas ruinas", and another by Cunard, "Para hacerse amar", tr. Vicente Aleixandre (La Chapelle-Réanville, 1937; Chisholm, *Nancy Cunard: A Biography*, 235–238; Rafael Osuna, *Pablo Neruda y Nancy Cunard: les poètes du monde défendent le peuple espagnol* [Madrid: Editorial Orígenes, 1987] 21–30).

18 Thomas Rudmose-Brown published a review of the thesis of Erna Low, "Beitrage zur De Tabley Forschung" (University of Vienna, 1935) in *Dublin Magazine* 12.2 (April–June 1937) 72–74. In the review, Rudmose-Brown writes of how the poetry of John Byrne Leicester Warren, Baron de Tabley (1835–1895) influenced him while a student in Aberdeen; Rudmose-Brown alludes to his wife's death through quotation of de Tabley's lines ("How lonely all the years will run / Until I rest by thee" and "To listen for a step that will not come!").
Llewelyn Powys, "Dr. Johnson – Idler, Rambler and Straggler," *Dublin Magazine* 12.2 (April–June 1937) 9–15.
American-born British writer Vincent O'Sullivan (né Sean O'Suilleabhain, 1872–1940) had financial and US citizenship difficulties at this time (letter 6 March 1937 to Seumas O'Sullivan, TCD, MSS 4630–49/1439; letter to A.J.A. Symons 1 March [1937], in Vincent O'Sullivan, *Selected Letters*, ed. Alan Anderson [Loanhead, Scotland: Tragara Press, 1993] 43–45). Vincent O'Sullivan had done some paid research for

Joseph Hone's book on George Moore in 1934–1935 (Vincent O'Sullivan, *Fifteen Letters to Seumas O'Sullivan* [Edinburgh: Tragara Press, 1979] 20–24, 28).

19 Big Sugarloaf (1,659 feet) is southwest of Bray, Co. Wicklow. SB refers to the Fassaroe cross, 1 mile northeast of Enniskerry and 2 miles west-southwest of Bray, in a niche on the north side of a narrow by-road (road SN 337); a primitive crucifixion is on one side and two human heads on the other (Anthony Weir, *Early Ireland: A Field Guide* [Belfast: Blackstaff Press, 1980] 231; William Cumming, Architect, National Monuments Division, The Office of Public Works, Dublin, 1 November 1994).
Whitsunday fell on 16 May in 1937. Clonmel is the largest town in Co. Tipperary. The Galtee Mountains, the highest inland range in Ireland, extend westward for about 16 miles from Cahir, Co. Tipperary. Blackstairs Mountain (2,411 feet) is in Co. Carlow, near Cashel, Co. Tipperary.

20 SB's reading notes about Samuel Johnson, especially his relationship with Hester Thrale, can be found in his notebooks for *Human Wishes* (BIF, UoR, MS 3461/1–3). Johnson and the Thrales: 13 December 1936 and n. 6 and n. 8.
After his stroke, Johnson wrote to Hester Thrale on 19 June 1785: "I have loved you with virtuous affection, I have honoured You with sincere Esteem. Let not all our endearment be forgotten" (Samuel Johnson, *Letters of Samuel Johnson LL.D.*, II, *Jan 15, 1777 – Dec. 18, 1784*, col. and ed. George Birkbeck Hill [New York: Harper and Brothers, 1892] 303).
When Johnson suspected Mrs. Thrale had already married Piozzi, he berated her in what is known as his "rough letter" of 2 July 1784: "If you have abandoned your children and your religion, God forgive your wickedness." Then, thinking that he might still prevent the marriage, he added: "I who have loved you, esteemed you, reverenced you, & served you, I who long thought you the first of womankind, entreat that before your fate is irrevocable, I may once more see you" (Johnson, *Letters of Samuel Johnson, LL.D*, II, 405–406; BIF, UoR, MS 3461/1, f. 10–11R, f. 12 R).

21 Vulliamy wrote that Mr. Thrale "could never emerge from his constitutional torpidity, and all that we know of him proves him to have been a man whose intelligence was less than mediocre." Yet Johnson supported Thrale in domestic disputes and "expressed a high regard for Mr. Thrale, in which it was difficult to avoid seeing a trace of hypocrisy or of obstinacy" (*Mrs. Thrale of Streatham*, 68–69, 72).

22 Hester Thrale married Piozzi in London on 23 July 1784. Her last meeting with Johnson was on 5 April 1783, when Johnson wrote in his *Diary* (rather than his *Meditations*): "I took leave of Mrs. Thrale. I was much moved. I had some expostulations with her. She said that she was likewise affected" (Samuel Johnson, *Diaries, Prayers, and Annals*, ed. E. L. McAdam, Jr. with Donald Hyde and Mary Hyde, The Yale Edition of the Works of Samuel Johnson, I [New Haven: Yale University Press, 1958] 358–359).
When Mr. and Mrs. Thrale had discovered Johnson on his knees before Dr. John Delap (1725–1812) in June 1766, "Beseeching God to continue to him the use of his understanding," they resolved to take him into their country home, Streatham, where he stayed from late June until October, and where he later became a regular visitor (Bate, *Samuel Johnson*, 412; BIF, UoR, MS 3461/1, f. 41R).
Irish writer Arthur Murphy (né Charles Ranger, 1727–1805), Henry Thrale's oldest friend, had introduced Johnson to the Thrales; Murphy supported Mrs. Thrale in her decision to marry Piozzi, when even her friend Frances Burney (known as Fanny, 1752–1840), among others, sought to prevent it (Bate, *Samuel Johnson*, 572; BIF, UoR, MS 3461/1, f. 14R and f. 35 R).

When Frank Barber was interviewed by "Our Ingenious Meteorological Journalist" for *Gentleman's Magazine*, he reported that Johnson had never cursed at him, saying that the worst word he had had from Johnson was: "You dunghill dog" ("A Meteorologist's Tour from Walton to London," *Gentleman's Magazine and Historical* 63.1 [July 1793] 620).

23 *Les Lauriers sont coupés* (1887) by Edouard Dujardin (1861–1949). Joyce read the novel between 1902 and 1903, tried without success to be in touch with Dujardin in 1917, and acknowledged the impact of Dujardin on *Ulysses* (Ellmann, *James Joyce*, 126, 411, 520; Elizabeth van der Staay, *Le Monologue intérieur dans l'oeuvre de Valéry Larbaud* [Paris: Champion-Slatkine, 1987], 84–85; Mary Colum disputes this influence, *Life and the Dream*, 394–395). Joyce mentioned Dujardin's novel to Larbaud in 1921 and secured a copy for Larbaud, who became an admirer, writing the preface for *Les Lauriers sont coupés* when it was reissued (Paris: Messein, 1925) (Ellmann, *James Joyce*, 519–520).
"Astuce" (shrewdness).

24 Jeremy Thompson, son of Alan Thompson and Frances Sylvia Thompson (née Reeves, 1904–1982), was born on 25 April 1937.

25 Charles Prentice. If SB wrote to him, the letter has not been found.

26 On 19 September 1777 Boswell noted of Johnson: "'If (said he) I had no duties, and no reference to futurity, I would spend my life in driving briskly in a post-chaise with a pretty woman; but she should be one who could understand me, and would add something to the conversation'" (Boswell, *Boswell's Life of Johnson*, III, *The Life [1776–1780]*, 162). SB commented in his notebook for *Human Wishes* that this was a symptom of impotence (BIF, UoR, MS 3461/1, f. 90V).

27 At Seumas O'Sullivan's home, Grange House, Beckett's aunt, Cissie Sinclair, met Ernest O'Malley (1898–1957), a Republican, journalist, and advocate of Irish artists.

THOMAS McGREEVY
LONDON

14/5/37   Cooldrinagh Foxrock

Dear Tom

I was very sorry to hear about Raven. I can well imagine the kind of performance. He will probably feel much better for it, for a time. I wish you did not come in for all these dramas. Dont be persuaded to go back to 15.[1]

I have done very little for the past fortnight. Boss Sinclair died in Rathdrum Sanatorium last Tuesday week and was buried in the Jewish cemetery the following Thursday. The week before I was down with Cissie I don't know how many times. His last words to me were an apology for his poor company. Harry was with him at the end. Cissie takes it quite calmly, her affective apparatus is worn out. He is not missed from the house in Moyne Road because he was never there. Harry & Cissie asked me to write something for the Irish Times, which I did, with only an hour to do it. Harry put it into Smyllie's hand, I standing visible but aloof, and did not say whose it was. Smyllie promised to put it in, had in fact asked Harry for something, but it did not appear. Harry had to write something himself in the end.[2]

I suppose you have read about the action for libel that Harry is taking against Gogarty. I am in it up to the neck. And gladly in so far as Boss wanted it done, having seen the offending passage some weeks before his death. Gogarty has been evading service of writ for the past 3 or 4 days & I do not think they have got him even now. Dodging out of his back door, sleeping in Howth, etc. What good does he think that will do him. All kinds of dirt will be raked up & I suppose they will try & discredit me as author of the Pricks. That is if Gogarty faces the court, which I fancy he will do lepping, unless Cowan & Rich [*for* Rich & Cowan] insist on settling outside. Apparently he & they took advice at every point of the book, but from some London lawyer incompetent to appreciate the references! I think most people here disapprove of the action, however little sympathy they may have with the defendant, perhaps just on that account. But there are limits to scurrility, & to cynical laissez-faire. It is not pleasant for me and wont do me any good. But it will amuse me. And Boss wanted it. Assez.[3]

I met Furlong one evening at Hones and left him to it very shortly after dinner, left him talking about the dear Rajah who was so anxious to obtain his services and the exquisite Lady

Fingal[l], in his voice where the Nancy, Mayfair & Tipperary elements meet without mixing. Ineffable shoulders. His sole aesthetic remark was that Vermeer built up his pictures in a contrast of blue & yellow. I very nearly asked him which Vermeer he meant.[4] He talked all the stock sentimental bunk about the Nazi persecutions. He asked were you in Paris. I said, on the contrary. He doesn't smoke & he doesn't drink & tea parties are his passion -

I was really shocked to see what he had done with the Gallery. He has taken all the Dutch pictures down to the print room & the prints are in the cellars. The print room is done up a cold dark scientific laboratory or public lavatory green. There is no top light & the pictures, all boldly hung in a single line, are worse than invisible. As there is not room for them all on the walls he is experimenting with movable screens. He looks forward to treating the sculpture hall in the same way, i.e. removing the casts & putting pictures there. There is no top lighting there either. No matter how one addresses oneself to a picture one has the light in one's eyes. And they are all hung on about a level with the pubic bone.[5]

The mania for single line hanging, which is all very well when there is plenty of room & the line set at the right height, is carried on upstairs, where the Italian pictures begin now in the Dutch rooms (& Irish room) & finish with the awful Gentileschi & Piazzetta in the big room where they all were previously. The wallpaper has been done up an indescribable shade of anchovy which Furlong asserts "goes well" with "Italian pictures", as a man might have a prejudice in favour of stout with oysters. It has a pleasant effect on the blues of Canaletto & Bellotto. The result of the single line is acres of this heavy angry colour weighing down on the pictures and on the spectator. The rail he has removed altogether.[6] Views of Rosalba correspond across

the stairs. The big Perugino has gone to Vienna "for examination." The Barry Adam & Eve has gone down to the cellars.
Where he got the money from I don't know. Or how he got
even that Board of Guardians to consent. Now he wants artificial
lighting and evening opening.[7] It is time someone put him in
mind of the purpose of a picture gallery, to provide pictures
worth looking at and the possibility of seeing them.

Jack Yeats & Cottie came out to Foxrock for tea & got on well
with Mother. He has sold £280 worth in the last fortnight. A 30
pounder (the boy & horse) to Brian [*for* Bryan] Guinness; the £100
"Where Grass Grows" [*for* "While Grass Grows"] in the Academy
to the Haverty Trust & the big new Waves of Breffni [*for* Breffny]
that I think I mentioned to you to someone from London who
saw it in his studio, I think Talbot Davis was the name -[8]

The Academy was incredibly awful. Bridget [*for* Brigid]
O'Brien stands now in a fair way to take the place of papa -[9]

I had lunch one day with Brian.[10] He didn't admit me into
his confidence. Talked most of the time about Saint[e]-Beuve and
the critical function. And mentioned he was looking for a part
time teaching job in London. Saw him again yesterday in the
Library, looking really ill.

Mother went off on the mailboat this morning, with Mrs
Manning, who sails to-morrow from Liverpool to America, to
help deliver Mary. Then mother will go on to her brother near
Newark for a short stay. This afternoon Frank & I are going down
to Cahir for 3 or 4 days. I am looking forward to seeing Cashel
again on the way down -[11]

The George II they blew up yesterday in the Green was one
of the best statues in Dublin. If it had been Victoria or the
Cenotaph no one would have minded.[12]

I met the hearty (?) Mr Skeffington at the Academy (with
wife) & congratulated him on having resumed his cricket.[13] "Oh

I am sure" he said "you would love to be playing too, if you analysed yourself." The right answer was that I had overcome the need of returning to my vomit.

I am sorry that you mentioned anything to the Robinsons. Hone thought Vera's manoeuvre as gratuitous as I did. Why should he like my book? Or me? The Hones are off to Switzerland next week, with the wretched little David, who is to be left there. Vera has ordained that he is ill & half the doctors in town have had a whack at him.[14]

Leventhal's remark, a propos of the libel: "I appreciate the publicity value of your démarche."[15]

God love thee. Write very soon

Ever

Sam

ALS; 3 leaves, 6 sides; [*water damage and torn at lower left margin (recto), lower right (verso)*]; TCD, MS 10402/127.

1 Thomas Ravenhill, McGreevy's friend, who was resident at 15 Cheyne Gardens, Chelsea; the incident to which SB refers is unknown.

2 William "Boss" Sinclair died on 4 May 1937 and was buried in the Jewish Cemetery at Dolphin's Barn, Dublin, on 6 May. Harry Sinclair and Boss were twin brothers. Cissie Sinclair had moved the family to a house on Moyne Road, Rathgar, during Boss's illness and hospitalization. Although SB wrote "some 100 lines hurriedly on Boss Sinclair for the Irish Times," R. M. Smyllie, Editor of *The Irish Times*, published an unsigned obituary (SB to Mary Manning Howe, 22 May 1937, TxU); From a Correspondent, "William Abraham Sinclair," 8 May 1937: 10).

3 As reported in *The Irish Times* ("Alleged Libel in Novel: Summons against Dr. Gogarty: London Publishers to be Sued," 14 May 1937: 2), Harry Sinclair initiated legal action against Oliver St. John Gogarty, and his London publishers Rich and Cowan, for libelous passages in his novel *As I Was Going Down Sackville Street: A Phantasy in Fact* (London: Rich and Cowan, 1937). The plaintiff cited passages that maligned himself and his late brother, as well as his grandfather Morris Harris (1823–1909), who were in business as Harris and Sinclair, Antique Plate, Jewellery and Works of Art, 47 Nassau Street, until the shop was moved to 4 Grafton Street, Dublin.

SB was named as a witness, and the article cites from his affidavit:

> Mr. Wood read an affidavit by Mr. Samuel Beckett, author, of Cooldrinagh, Foxrock, who stated that he purchased a copy of "As I Was Going Down Sackville Street," his attention having been called to it by many advertisements that he had read, and, he said, the notoriety of its author.

On reading paragraphs at pages 65, 70 and 71 he instantly inferred that the lines commencing 'Two Jews in Sackville Street" referred to Mr. Henry Morris Sinclair and the late Mr. William Abraham Sinclair, and the words "old usurer" and "grandsons" referred to the late Mr. Morris Harris and his two grandsons. He considered that the words constituted a very grave charge against Mr. Henry Morris Sinclair and his late brother. (2)

SB thought that his authorship of *More Pricks Than Kicks* would be used to discredit him; *Proust* and *Whoroscope* also served that purpose in the trial (Ulick O'Connor, *Oliver St. John Gogarty: A Poet and His Times* [London: Jonathan Cape, 1964], 280–281).

"Assez" (Enough).

4   George Furlong, Director of the National Gallery.

It is not known to what Rajah Furlong refers. SB mentions a Maharajah of Chittagong (then in East Bengal, now in Bangladesh) in his letter to Mary Manning Howe (22 May 1937; TxU), but Chittagong had not been a regal colony since it was ceded to the East-India Company in 1760, and did not have a Maharajah (Dorian Leveque, Oriental and India Office Collections, British Library, 21 June 2006; Edward Thornton, *A Gazetteer of the Territories under the Government of the East-India Company and of the Native States on the Continent of India* [London: William H. Allen, 1857] 206.)

Furlong refers to Elizabeth Mary Margaret Plunkett (née Burke, 1866–1944), then Dowager Countess of Fingall (following the death of her husband Horace Plunkett, 11th Earl of Fingall in 1929). To SB, Furlong's voice contained tones of Nancy [? Cunard], Mayfair (smart London), and Tipperary (rural Ireland).

There was no Vermeer in the collection of the National Gallery of Ireland.

5   The Dutch collection of the National Gallery was rehung in a ground floor room that had been the print room, with the only light from side windows, darkened with frosted glass (John Dowling, "Art: Advice and Estimates Free," *Ireland To-Day* 2.10 [October 1937] 63, 77).

6   The Italian collection was rehung and distributed across the first floor rooms (formerly the Dutch, Irish and Italian rooms). SB refers to *David Slaying Goliath* (NGI 980) by Gentileschi and *A Decorative Group* (NGI 656, now attributed to the Studio of Giovanni Battista Piazzetta [1682-1754]).

Paintings by Canaletto: *A View of the Piazza San Marco* (NGI 286), *The Grand Canal with the Church of Salute* (NGI 705), and *The Grand Canal with the Church of the Carità* (NGI 1043). Those by Bellotto were *A View of Dresden Looking Down the Elbe* (NGI 181) and *A View of Dresden Looking Up the Elbe* (NGI 182).

7   The four pastels by Rosalba Carriera (1675–1757) were: *Spring* (NGI 3846), another called *Spring* (previously called *Summer*, NGI 3847), *Autumn* (NGI 3848), and *Winter* (NGI 3849).

The Perugino *Pietà* (942) was sent to Vienna for evaluation and cleaning (see 17 July [1936], n. 6).

Adam and Eve (NGI 762) by Irish artist James Barry (1741-1806) had been put into storage, awaiting refurbishment of the new Irish room.

Electric lighting was added to the offices and work rooms of the Gallery, which had had only natural light (Director [Furlong] to the Secretary, Department of Public Works, 4 December 1936; Director to The Secretary, Department of Education, 13 December 1937; NGI Archives). The government had suggested evening openings and the Board of

Governors and Guardians authorized this change on 3 February 1937 (S. O'Neill, Board of Education to the Director, National Gallery, 19 December 1936; Director to The Secretary, Department of Education, 3 February 1937; S. O'N[eill], Board of Education to Secretary, Department of Finance, 6 December 1937; NGI Archives).

8 Jack B. Yeats had five paintings in the Royal Hibernian Academy Exhibition in April 1937. Yeats's painting *Boy and Horse* (Pyle no. 476; private collection) was sold to Bryan Guinness (1905–1992), and *While Grass Grows* was sold to the Haverty Trust (now in the Waterford Museum of Art, no. 76). *The Little Waves of Breffny* (Pyle no. 495; private collection) was not in the Exhibition, but was sold directly to Henry Talbot de Vere Clifton (1907–1979), to whom W. B. Yeats dedicated his poem "Lapis Lazuli" (Pyle, *Jack B. Yeats: A Catalogue Raisonné of the Oil Paintings*, I, 450).

9 The 1937 Royal Hibernian Academy Exhibition.
Rose Brigid O'Brien Ganly, a member of the RHA since 1935, was the daughter of Dermod O'Brien who was then President of the RHA.

10 Brian Coffey.

11 After accompanying Susan Manning as far as Liverpool, May Beckett traveled on to visit her brother, Edward Price Roe, in Newark, Nottinghamshire.

12 The bronze equestrian statue of George II, sculpted by John van Nost the younger (d. 1780) and erected in St. Stephen's Green, was blown up in an act of protest in response to the coronation of King George VI (1895–1952) on 12 May 1937. W. B. Yeats in a letter to *The Irish Times* mourned it as the "only Dublin statue that has delighted me by beauty and elegance. Had they blown up any other statue in St. Stephen's Green I would have rejoiced" ("George II," 14 May 1937: 4).
Dublin's *Cenotaph*: 16 January [1936], n. 11. The statue of Queen Victoria, sculpted by John Hughes (1865–1941), was placed in front of Leinster House in 1903 (it was removed in 1947 and given in 1987 to the city of Sydney, Australia).

13 Owen and Andrée Sheehy-Skeffington.

14 SB refers to Vera Hone's withdrawn dinner invitation (see 26 April 1937). David Hone (b. 1928).

15 "Your démarche" (the step you have taken).

THOMAS McGREEVY
LONDON

5/6/36 [*for* 37]   Foxrock
                                                         [Co. Dublin]

Dear Tom

    Since coming back from Cahir there hasn't been any continuity. Mother was away for a week, seeing Mrs Manning

off at Liverpool, then staying with her brother in Notts.,
and came back rested but refusing to admit it. Frank and I
came back by Limerick, where he had some work, and I saw
St. Mary's. Appallingly restored and a lovely west door. I suppose
you know it. I happened to mention it to Sean O'Sullivan who
said, "It would take more than a west door to excite me". En
effet.[1]

The hearing for the injunction was on yesterday. Very
dull performance on both sides. Judgment reserved till
Monday. It doesn't seem to matter much whether we win
this round or not. The hearing proper with jury will probably
not be before October. God knows where I shall be then. I
suppose I must come back for it wherever I am. It is going
to be a very dirty fight and I wish I wasn't in it. It won't do me
any good, in spite of AJL's appreciation of its publicity value.
But even if there was a way out I wouldn't take it. The only
possible defence was indicated yesterday, that the cap was
not made to fit anyone. A bloody lie, but it may be hard to
prove the obvious. And even with a verdict for the plaintiff
here, it is only the beginning. Cowan & Rich have not filed an
appearance and so do not come within the jurisdiction. And the
American edition is much worse, 16 extra lines of doggerel to
the effect that whatever you bought there you were genuinely
sold.[2]

Constable turned down Murphy, with the customary sweep
of the hat. Now it is with Lovat Dickson.[3] I had a letter from a
firm of Berlin publishers (Rohwohlt) [*for* Rowohlt] suggesting
that I should make a selection from the poems of Joachim
Ringelnatz (ob. 1934, well known to the Sinclairs in Kassel)
and translate them. I wrote replying that I was on en principe,
which covers everything. They suggested a Faber & Faber

Miscellany. The Hogarth Press strikes me as more likely, but they can look after that end of it themselves.[4]

Geoffrey sent me an advertisement for post of translator from the French at Geneva for a "non-commercial organisation" cut out of the Listener. I replied asking for particulars, but forgot to sign the letter. A nice example of Verschreiben. And Ruddy sent me an advertisement for post of lecturer in Italian at Cape Town. They had written to him directly. I am not thinking of applying.[5]

The Sinclairs, all three, are going out to S. Africa in August to prevent the son coming home before the winter. I suppose also they want to be away when this thing is on. Cissie loathes the thought of it.[6]

I went round to the Currans for the first time and met Gorman there. He is doing a big biography of Joyce and was looking for the gates of night-town. I went rather expecting spits all round but it was no worse than tedious. I had a message for the daughter from a painter in Munich. She had brought back from Germany an exquisite little picture by a man called Scharl.[7] 50 RM. Constantine bumbled like a beetle on an exclusive residential cowpad and hadn't a bad word to say for anyone.

I saw Gorman again a few days later at Yeats's. He carried felicitations from Joyce to Harry Sinclair, which I must say rather surprised me. He talked about their group in Paris, Jolas, L. P. Fargue, Pelorson, and of their search for a Stammtisch with the booze cheap and the Stimmung transitional; and with tentative contempt of the rats who left the ship when the franc went kaputt.[8]

I drove Jack and Cotty and Joe Hone out one day to see mother and the donkey. I think it went quite well. Mother was as completely natural and at her ease as the donkey was and didn't allow Joe's remote mumblings to disturb her. Cotty had a penetrating basin hat and everything was jolly. Jack admired his pictures. He has been doing well by the way, did I tell you. 380 pounds worth sold within a week. Two out of the Academy, the small boy and horse to Brian [*for* Bryan] Guinness and the big Where Grass Grows [*for While Grass Grows*] to the Haverty and a lovely big new landscape from his studio to a London dealer, I think Langton Davis.[9] He has changed his day to Thursday.

I had lunch one Sunday with the Coffeys. The President discoursed on ecclesiastical architecture and Bri[a]n showed me his article on Sainte-Beuve. Apparently Denis Devlin wants me to give Ria Mooney a poem to read on the wireless. I think that is almost sufficient incentive to write a new one. Bri[a]n didn't tell me what his trouble was. We got on better than before I felt. He was amusingly disturbed by his desire to eat the tulips in Stephens Green refusing to wrap up into a notion. I had an anonymous communication from London the other day with envelope addressed in capitals, just the label from Barclay's beer bottle with Dr. J. as trademark stuck on to a blank sheet. I suppose it was from him. Also by same post El Greco's Munich Mater Dolorosa with just "Bonjour" and an illegible monogram.[10]

Austin Clarke was at Cissie's one evening I was there, together with Salkeld and ffffffffrench-Mullen, who has been staying with the Sinclairs for the past month, pending the building of a cottage near Mt. Venus. Clarke was full of hate but didn't seem to bear me any ill will for the Bookman article, if he ever saw it.[11] He is really pathetic and sympathetic. Or is it that one clutches at any kind of literary contact? He was asking for you. So of course was Gorman.

I heard from Charles and wrote him at length in reply.[12] His silence since makes me fear he is bad again and not able to make the trip to Florence. If you have any news of him pass it on.

The only thing resembling work has been in the library on Johnson. I know the whole thing pretty well now and could start anytime. But my married cousin is staying with us with her husband for a week and there is no possibility of settling down to writing till they are gone. We are all going to the Abbey this evening to see the Hunt-O'Connor thriller.[13] I haven't been there for years and years.

Have linked up in a kind of way again with my uncle Gerald who went about so much with Father. I suppose that is the reason. He is inspector of health for Wicklow and lives in Greystones. We bathe and play duets together and he tells me about coral reefs, Torquemada and how telepathy pisses in the eye of the rule about inversely as the square of the distance.[14]

How are the translations going? Do write very soon and tell me how it goes with you.[15]

> Love ever
> s/ Sam

TLS; 1 leaf, 2 sides; TCD, MS 10402/97. *Dating*: follows SB to McGreevy, 18 May 1937 (TCD, MS 10402/132) which anticipates SB's trip to Cahir and Cashel; preliminary hearing for Gogarty libel trial was reported in *The Irish Times*, 5 June 1937; advertisement for French translator appeared in *The Listener*, 5 and 12 May 1937.

1 St. Mary's Cathedral in Limerick, on King's Island in the River Shannon, has a Romanesque west door (restored in the nineteenth century) and for a 120-foot tower with four step turrets. The original church was founded in 1168 by the King of Munster, Donal Mór O'Brien, and the King's palace was incorporated into it. The west doorway may have been the palace entrance (Noreen Ellecker, St. Mary's Cathedral).

"En effet" (Indeed).

2 An injunction to restrain further publication of *As I Was Going Down Sackville Street* by Oliver St. John Gogarty was sought in a hearing on 4 June 1937. The defense, represented by Ralph Brereton-Barry, claimed that the description was not intended to identify the plaintiffs ("Gogarty Libel Action: New Injunction Sought: Court Reserves Judgment," *The Irish Times* 5 June 1937: 13).
A. J. Leventhal.
The London publishers of the book, Rich and Cowan.
The American editions included two additional verses and the beginning of a third:

> They kept a shop for objects wrought
> By masters famed of old
> Where you, no matter what you bought
> Were *genuinely* sold.

> But Willie spent the sesterces
> And brought on strange disasters
> Because he sought new mistresses
> More keenly than old masters.

> The other ...

(Gogarty, *As I Was Going Down Sackville Street, A Phantasy in Fact* [New York: Reynal and Hitchcock, 1937] 68–69; O'Connor, *Oliver St. John Gogarty*, 277–278)

3 London publishers: Constable and Company; Lovat Dickson.

4 Axel Kaun worked with Rowohlt, the publisher of German poet Joachim Ringelnatz (né Hans Boetticher, 1883–1934). Rowohlt's letter to SB suggesting that a selection of Ringelnatz's poems in English might be of interest to Faber and Faber's Criterion Miscellany (a monograph series published from 1919 to 1936) has not been found; nor has SB's reply. The Hogarth Press had published several poets in translation, including Rilke.

5 The advertisement sent by Geoffrey Thompson appeared in *The Listener* 17.434 (5 May 1937) 895 and 17.435 (12 May) 950. "Verschreiben" (a slip of the pen).
Rudmose Brown; University of Cape Town: 29 July 1937, below.

6 Cissie Sinclair and two of her daughters, Nancy and Deirdre, planned to visit Morris Sinclair in South Africa.

7 Constantine Curran was host to Herbert Sherman Gorman (1893–1954), who was writing his biography, *James Joyce* (1939); in Joyce's *Ulysses*, "Circe" (chapter 15) opens with set directions describing "The Mabbot street entrance of nighttown" (James Joyce, *Ulysses* [Paris: Shakespeare and Company, 1922] 408).
Elizabeth Curran had met Edgar Ende in Munich, whom SB also met there (see 25 March 1937, n. 13). SB refers to a painting by Josef Scharl entitled *Bauernhochzeit* owned by Elizabeth Curran.

8 It is not certain whether SB met Gorman again at the home of W. B. Yeats or Jack B. Yeats. Harry Sinclair, the brother of Boss Sinclair. Eugene Jolas, Léon-Paul Fargue, Georges Pelorson. "Stammtisch" (table for regulars, in a pub or simple restaurant). "Stimmung" (mood, atmosphere). Devaluation of the dollar against the franc

had made it more expensive to live in France, and many American expatriates who had lived there in the 1920s and early 1930s had left.

9 Jack and Cottie Yeats, Joseph Hone. SB owned *Corner Boys* and *Morning* by Yeats (see 7 May 1936, n. 2, and 5 May 1935, n. 4). For the pictures sold: 26 April 1937, n. 8; as indicated here, the picture may have been *The Little Waves of Breffny* which was sold not to Langton Davis but to Henry Talbot de Vere Clifton.

10 Brian Coffey's family; his father Denis Coffey was President of University College Dublin. Brian Coffey published his review: "*Sainte-Beuve, Les Meilleurs Textes*, intro. André Thérive," *The Criterion* 16.64 (April 1937) 716–721.

Denis Devlin's involvement in broadcasts of readings and comments on literature on Irish radio: 8 October 1935, n. 17. Ria Mooney (1904–1973), Irish actress and producer, often did readings for radio.

SB assumes that Coffey had sent the beer label anonymously. Barclay beer was produced by Barclay, Perkins, and Co. (the company formed to buy out Hester Thrale's interest in the Anchor Brewery on 31 May 1781). Samuel Johnson's image as "the stout academic clutching a pint pot became the brewery's emblem" (www.thrale.com/history/english/hester_and_henry/brewery/index.php, 15 June 2006).

El Greco's painting in Munich was *The Stripping of Christ* (Alte Pinakothek 8573), not *Mater Dolorosa* (The Virgin Mary), which is in the collection of the Musée des Beaux-Arts, Strasburg (MBA 276); hence both the identification of the image on the card and its sender are uncertain. SB wrote "monogram. <It might be Lucia>."

11 SB's article in *The Bookman* (1934), "Recent Irish Poetry," was not appreciative of Austin Clarke's writing.

Cecil Salkeld.

It may have been Douglas ffrench-Mullen (1893–1943) who was boarding with Cissie Beckett in Moyne Road, Rathgar; Mt. Venus, near Woodtown, Co. Dublin, is a cromlech.

12 Neither the letter from Charles Prentice nor SB's reply has been found.

13 Robina Sheila Page (née Roe, known as Sheila, and by SB as Eli, 1905–1993) and Donald Temple Page (1901–1989) were visiting Cooldrinagh. *In the Train*, adapted by Hugh Hunt from a short story by Frank O'Connor, had opened at the Abbey Theatre on 31 May 1937.

14 Gerald Beckett, younger brother of William Beckett, lived at Drummany (Burnaby Estate), Portland Road, Greystones, Co. Wicklow.

Tomás de Torquemada: 10 May [1934], n. 1.

Telepathy, the apparently direct transfer of impressions from one mind to another, runs counter to the cause–effect relationship described by the "inverse-square" law of physics.

15 McGreevy's translations were Maillart's *Forbidden Journey: From Peking to Kashmir* for Heinemann (see 22 December 1936, n.1), and *Young Girls* (London: George Routledge, 1937), the first volume of Henry de Montherlant's *Les Jeunes filles* (4 vols., 1936–1939; *Pity for Women*).

JOSEPH HONE
LAUSANNE, SWITZERLAND

July 3rd 1937   Dolphin Hotel
                                      Essex Street,
                                      (Parliament Street)
                                      Dublin

dear Joe

The passage I think you want is the following:

"One's prejudices guide one's judgments, & I confess that I like to think that my father went to the House of Commons like Empedocles to Etna, & flung himself over the edge because he wished to know what the interior of a crater was like. I am afraid that this explanation of my father's reasons for going to the House of Commons will appear whimsical to those who, like my brother, take a normal view of our national assembly; all the same my brother does not seem to have escaped altogether the prevalent belief that the House of Commons is an anachronism like the House of Lords. He does not chronicle the debates with the same untiring industry as Lord Morley & Mr. Winston Churchill. He is impressed by the importance of the division bell, but not to the same extent that they are, & he would have been still less impressed if he were acquainted with their works – excellent works, full of information, thoughtfulness & literary quality, lacking little, perfect works one would say were they not unreadable."[1]

———

I trust this is neither too little nor too much – –

I was delighted to have your letter. Arland (on se fait à tout) sent me your Lausanne address & I was meaning to write to you, but the days pass over me & I do nothing.[2]

To-morrow morning I leave with Kahn [*for* Kahan] for Cappagh in the old car. Wasn't it about this time last year that you & I went down? I look forward to Beverl[e]y not being there. Jack Yeats describes his voice at its most dulcet (i.e. cajoling young ladies in the club) as a sack of coal being delivered. The clack of a mill hopper occurs to me rather. It is Nash or Greene.[3] Which alas is the difference, part of the difference.

I was offered a job as agent to an estate (Lord Rathdowne's?) near Carlow. £300 per. an. & a free house. I passed it on to Percy but he turned it down, on the ground that Beverley would whip in a young wife the moment his back was turned. I thought it would have suited him exactly.[4]

Rudmose-Brown wants me to apply for a lectureship in Italian at Cape Town University, & perhaps I shall.[5] He says the fruit makes up for the Kaffirs. I should have reversed this proposition myself.

I heard from Nancy Cunard. She is collecting the opinions of writers on the Spanish business. I replied "Uptherepublic". Then she wrote again, to demand amplifications.[6]

A firm of Berlin publishers wrote asking me to make a selection of Joachim Ringelnatz & translate it for a Faber & Faber

[*page missing*][7]

Still there is a mass of marginalia that would be useful, e.g. in the Annals his recollection of the first time that the Heaven-Hell dichotomy was brought to his notice, when he was in bed with his mother aged 18 months. Heaven she described as the happy place where some people went, Hell as the <u>sad</u> place where the lost went. She does not seem to have been at all High Church. The following morning, so that he might impress the information on his mind, she required him to repeat it to Thomas Jackson, their serving man. But he would not.[8] All this would come in quite naturally in the last act, i.e. the fear of his death, when he was being reproached by his clerical friend Taylor for holding the opinion that an eternity of torment was preferable to annihilation. He must have had the notion of <u>positive</u> annihilation. Of how many can as much be said.[9]

I have been insulting myself with Belloc on Milton & diverting the surviving attention with Schopenhauer on women.[10]

My brother has got himself engaged to be married. So has my agent George Reavey.[11] Devlin's poems come out shortly in the same series as mine did. I recommend them to you. My book is with Allen & Unwin.[12]

Seumas gave me McNeice's [*for* MacNeice's] <u>Out of the Picture</u> to review. I passed it on to Mrs. Salkeld.[13]

Come back soon. I miss you. Remember me to Vera Sally David.[14]

> Yrs ever
>
> Sam

ALS; 3 leaves, 6 sides; *letterhead*; TxU.

1 The citation is from the preface to Maurice George Moore, *An Irish Gentleman, George Henry Moore: His Travel, His Racing, His Politics* (London: T. W. Laurie, 1913) xv–xvi. Joseph Hone writes in his memoir of SB: "I had asked him to look up for me a passage in George Moore's preface to his (Moore's) biography of their father, George Hay [*for* Henry] Moore, the Irish politician" ("A Note on my Acquaintance with Sam Beckett"; TxU, J. M. Hone / Works).

John Morley, 1st Viscount Morley of Blackburn (1838–1923); Winston Churchill (1874–1965).

2 Ussher's given names were Percival Arland; although he was previously called "Percy," he now preferred "Arland." "On se fait à tout" (one can get used to anything).

3 SB called Robert Kahan, who was with the Board of Works, "another frustrated intellectual" (SB to McGreevy, 7 July 1937, TCD, MS 10402/128); Kahan pursued the interests of a scholar, linguist, and literary critic and was the Irish correspondent of the *Jewish Chronicle* (A[rland] U[ssher], "Mr. Robert Kahan: An Appreciation," *The Irish Times* 12 December 1951: 5). Cappagh, the Ussher family home in Co. Waterford, was owned by Arland Ussher's father, Beverley.

SB refers to English dramatist and satirist Thomas Nash (1567–1601) and English poet, playwright, and novelist Robert Greene (1558–1592); a specific allusion has not been found. At the end of SB's "*Whoroscope*" Notebook (BIF, UoR, MS 3000) are twelve pages headed 'For Interpolation' that include citations from Robert Greene's *Menaphon* (1589), in *Groatsworth of witte, bought with a million of repentance; The repentance of Robert Greene, 1592*, ed. G. B. Harrison (London: Bodley Head, 1923), and *Plays and Poems of Robert Greene*, ed. J. Churton Collins, 2 vols. (Oxford: Clarendon Press, 1905) (Pilling, "'For Interpolation': Beckett and English Literature," 218–219).

4 SB is not certain of the owner of the estate. The Rathdowne estate was in County Dublin. It belonged to Godfrey John Boyle Chetwynd (1863–1936), Viscount Chetwynd, who was also Baron of Rathdowne; he was succeeded by his son Adam Duncan Chetwynd (1904–1965). The Rathdonnell estate in Country Carlow comes closer to the description SB gives. Thomas Leopold McClintock-Bunbury, Lord Rathdonnell (1880–1937), resided in England. His estate, Lisnavagh, had the same manager from 1930 to 1951, but it is possible that a smaller family property nearby, Oak Park, "could have required a manager in 1937" (Lord Rathdonnell [b. 1938], 30 November 1992; records of this estate are not extant).

SB described the position to Arland Ussher in his letter [before 15 June 1937]: "Most of your truck would be with the auditors and proprietor (who seems to spend most of his time in England and is somewhere over here at present, fishing. Alas I do not know his name") (TxU). SB wrote to McGreevy, 7 July 1937, that he had encouraged both Arland Ussher and Joe Hone to apply:

> I pushed Ussher for the job, but he would not go up for it, being apparently convinced that immediately he left the house at Cappagh his father would marry again & jeopardise the succession. I had mentioned all this writing to Joe Hone, now in Lausanne, & had a wire from him when in Cappagh entreating me to get the job for him! I wish I could, but fear it is now too late. (TCD, MS 10402/128)

5 SB wrote to Arland Ussher on 15 June 1937: "Now that I have assembled testimonials for the Cape Town Gehenna I am in a position to abstain from applying."

6 Neither Cunard's letters nor SB's replies have been found, but SB wrote to McGreevy on 7 July 1937: "Nancy Cunard circularised me for my opinion of the Spanish business. I replied Up the republic. She wrote again, for amplifications … I replied again, that I could not make myself any clearer, unless she insisted that I should. Since when nothing" (TCD, MS 10402/128).

The Cunard collection at the Harry Ransom Humanities Research Center holds documents related to Cunard's project, including some original letters in reply to the questionnaire sent from Paris in June 1937; "These replies are the only survivors of the 150 to 200 received by Cunard. The remainder 'disappeared during World War II, in my house at Réanville in Normandy'" (Lake, *No Symbols Where None Intended*, 36).

Nancy Cunard initiated the project in June 1937 from Paris, with "The Question" addressed to "Writers and Poets of England, Scotland, Ireland and Wales: ... Are you for, or against, the legal Government and the People of Republican Spain? Are you for, or against, France and Fascism?" SB's response ("¡UPTHEREPUBLIC!") was published in Nancy Cunard, ed., *Authors Take Sides on the Spanish War* (London: Left Review, [1937]) [6]. Writers were asked to limit their contributions to six lines: SB's was the briefest.

7   The proposed English translation of a selection of poems by Ringelnatz: 5 June 1936 [*for* 1937], n. 4. SB wrote to Arland Ussher on 15 June 1937: "I shall also back out of the Ringelnatz translation." SB's letter to McGreevy of 7 July 1937 offers greater detail: "The people in Berlin sent me three volumes of Ringelnatz. He is even worse than I thought and I do not think of undertaking the job of translating a selection from him. I had a letter from them again the other day asking for specimen translations to submit to T.S.E.!!!" (TCD, MS 10402/128).

At this point a page is missing from the letter; as Hone describes in his memoir of SB: "The attached letter, of which unfortunately a page is missing was written to me while I was in Switzerland in the summer of 1937" ("A Note on my Acquaintance with Sam Beckett"; TxU, J. M. Hone / Works). The letter continues with SB's discussion of his preparations for writing a play on Samuel Johnson.

8   SB refers to Samuel Johnson's entry in his *Annals* during Lent 1712 (*Diaries, Prayers, and Annals*, 10; BIF, UoR, MS 3461/3, f. 1R).

9   SB refers to John Taylor's *A Letter to Samuel Johnson, L.L.D. on the Subject of a Future State [With some letters of Dr. Johnson and possibly in part written by him]* (London: T. Cadell, 1787; BIF, UoR, MS 3461/2, f. 101V).

In a conversation with Anna Seward (1742–1809) who claimed that fear of annihilation "was groundless," Johnson reportedly said: "'Mere existence is so much better than nothing, that one would rather exist even in pain'" (Bate, *Samuel Johnson*, 452). In response to this conversation, SB notes: "Much as he dreaded the next world he dreaded annihilation still more" (BIF, UoR, MS 3461/2, f. 81R).

10   Hilaire Belloc, *Milton* (London: Cassell, 1935).
Arthur Schopenhauer, "Essay on Women," in *Essays and Aphorisms*, 80–88.

11   Frank Beckett was engaged to Jean Wright; SB wrote to McGreevy on 7 July 1937: "Frank hopes to get married about the middle of August. Another gone. From me I mean of course. He is house hunting. Do write & congratulate him" (TCD, MS 10402/128).
George Reavey was engaged to Clodine Gwynedd Cade. SB wrote to McGreevy on 7 July 1937: "I sent George a Meissen wine cup before I left [for Cappagh] but have had no acknowledgment. I suppose he knows what he is doing, but it is hard not to feel sorry for him. I don't think he'll write much more poetry" (TCD, MS 10402/128); a certificate of authentication dated 1 July 1937 from Harris & Sinclair, Dublin, is in Reavey's papers (TxU; Reavey collection, miscellaneous).

12   Denis Devlin, *Intercessions*, Europa Poets (London: Europa Press, 1937). SB's collection of poems *Echo's Bones* was the third in this series.
Murphy was being read by London publisher Allen and Unwin.

13 Seumas O'Sullivan asked SB to review *Out of the Picture* (1937) by Louis MacNeice (né Frederick Louis MacNeice 1907–1963); it was reviewed by Blanaid Salkeld in *Dublin Magazine* 12.4 (October–December 1937) 67–68.

14 Joe Hone's wife Vera, and their children Sally (m. Cooke-Smith, 1914–2003) and David (b. 1928).

AXEL KAUN

BERLIN

[*SB's Letter to Axel Kaun below exists only as a draft, corrected by various hands over time; it is presented here without editorial corrections.*]

9/7/37   6 Clare Street

Dublin

IFS

Lieber Axel Kaun!

Besten Dank für Ihren Brief. Ich war gerade im Begriff, Ihnen zu schreiben, als er kam. Dann habe ich verreisen müssen, wie Ringelnatz' männlicher Briefmark, obgleich unter weniger leidenschaftlichen Umständen.[1]

Das Beste ist, ich sage Ihnen sofort und ohne Umschweife, Ringelnatz ist meiner Ansicht nach nicht der Mühe wert. Sie werden sicherlich nicht mehr enttäuscht sein, dies von mir zu hören, als ich es gewesen bin, es feststellen zu müssen.

Ich habe die 3 Bände durchgelesen, 23 Gedichte ausgewählt und 2 von diesen als Probestücke übersetzt.[2] Das wenige, was sie notwendigerweise dabei verloren haben, ist natürlich nur im Verhältnis mit dem zu schätzen, was sie eigentlich zu verlieren haben, und ich muss [__]en,[3] dass ich diesen Verschlecterungskoeffizient, auch da, wo er am meisten Dichter ist, und am wenigsten Reimkuli, ganz gering gefunden habe.

Daraus ist gar nicht zu schliessen, dass ein übersetzter Ringelnatz weder Interesse noch Erfolg beim englischen

Publikum finden würde. In dieser Beziehung aber bin ich vollkommen unfähig, ein Urteil zu fällen, da mir die Reaktionen des kleinen wie des grossen Publikums immer rätselhafter werden, und, was noch schlimmer ist, unbedeutender. Denn ich komme vom naiven Gegensatz nicht los, zumindesten was die Literatur betrifft, dass eine Sache sich lohnt oder sich nicht lohnt. Und wenn wir unbedingt Geld verdienen müssen, machen wir es anderswo.

Ich zweifle nicht, dass Ringelnatz als Mensch von ganz ausserordentlichem Interesse war. Als Dichter aber scheint er Goethes Meinung gewesen zu sein: Lieber NICHTS zu schreiben, als nicht zu schreiben. Dem Uebersetzer aber hätte der Geheimrat selbst vielleicht gegönnt, sich dieses hohen Kakoethes unwürdig zu fühlen.[4]

Ich würde mich freuen, Ihnen meinen Abscheu vor der Verswut Ringelnatz' genauer zu erklären, wenn Sie Lust haben, ihn zu verstehen. Vorläufig aber will ich Sie schonen. Vielleicht mögen Sie die Leichenrede ebensowenig wie ich.

Gleicherweise könnte ich Ihnen eventuell die ausgewählten Gedichte anzeigen und die Probeübersetzungen schicken.

————————————————————

Es freut mich immer, einen Brief von Ihnen zu bekommen. Schreiben Sie also möglichst häufig und ausführlich. Wollen Sie unbedingt, dass ich Ihnen auf englisch das gleiche tue? Werden Sie beim Lesen meiner deutschen Briefe ebenso gelangweilt, wie ich beim Verfassen eines englischen? Es täte mir Leid, wenn Sie das Gefühl hätten, es handele sich etwa um einen Kontrakt, dem ich nicht nachkomme. Um Antwort wird gebeten.

Es wird mir tatsächlich immer schwieriger, ja sinnloser, ein offizielles Englisch zu schreiben. Und immer mehr wie ein Schleier kommt mir meine Sprache vor, den man zerreissen

muss, um an die hinterliegenden Dinge (oder das hinterliegende
Nichts) zu kommen. Grammatik und Stil! Mir scheinen sie ebenso
hinfällig geworden zu sein wie ein Biedermeier Badeanzug oder
die Unerschüttlichkeit eines Gentlemans.[5] Eine Larve. Hoffentlich
kommt die Zeit, sie ist ja Gott sei Dank in gewissen Kreisen
schon da, wo die Sprache da am besten gebraucht wird, wo sie
am tüchtigsten missgebraucht wird. Da wir sie so mit einem Male
nicht ausschalten können, wollen wir wenigstens nichts versäu-
men, was zu deren Verruf beitragen mag. Ein Loch nach dem
andern in ihr zu bohren, bis das Dahinterkauernde, sei es etwas
oder nichts, durchzusickern anfängt – ich kann mir für den heu-
tigen Schriftsteller kein höheres Ziel vorstellen.

Oder soll die Literatur auf jenem alten faulen von Musik
und Malerei längst verlassenen Wege allein hinterbleiben?
Steckt etwas lähmend heiliges in der Unnatur des Wortes, was
zu den Elementen der anderen Künste nicht gehört? Gibt es
irgendeinen Grund, warum jene fürchterlich willkürliche
Materialität der Wortfläche nicht aufgelöst werden sollte, wie
z.B. die von grossen schwarzen Pausen gefressene Tonfläche in
der siebten Symphonie von Beethoven, so dass wir sie ganze
Seiten durch nicht anders wahrnehmen können als etwa einen
schwindelnden unergründliche Schlünde von Stillschweigen
verknüpfenden Pfad von Lauten?[6] Um Antwort wird gebeten.

Ich weiss, es gibt Leute, empfindsame und intelligente
Leute, für die es an Stillschweigen gar nicht fehlt. Ich kann
nicht umhin, anzunehmen, dass sie schwerhörig sind. Denn
im Walde der Symbole, die keine sind, schweigen die Vögelein
der Deutung, die keine ist, nie.

Selbstverständlich muss man sich vorläufig mit Wenigem
begnügen. Zuerst kann es nur darauf ankommen, irgenwie
eine Methode zu erfinden, um diese höhnische Haltung dem

Worte gegenüber wörtlich darzustellen. In dieser Dissonanz von Mitteln und Gebrauch wird man schon vielleicht ein Geflüster der Endmusik oder des Allem zu Grunde liegenden Schweigens spüren können.

Mit einem solchen Programme hat meiner Ansicht nach die allerletzte Arbeit von Joyce gar nichts zu tun.[7] Dort scheint es sich vielmehr um eine Apotheose des Wortes zu handeln. Es sei denn, Himmelfahrt und Höllensturz sind eins und dasselbe. Wie schön es wäre, glauben zu können, es sei in der Tat so! Wir wollen uns aber vorläufing auf die Absicht beschränken.

Vielleicht liegen die Logographen von Gertrude Stein dem näher, was ich im Sinne habe. Das Sprachgewebe ist wenigstens porös geworden, wenn nur leider ganz zufälligerweise, und zwar als Folge eines etwa der Technik von Feininger ähnlichen Vorfahrens.[8] Die unglückliche Dame (lebt sie noch?) ist ja ohne Zweifel immer noch in ihr Vehikel verliebt, wenn freilich nur wie in seine Ziffern ein Mathematiker, für den die Lösung des Problems von ganz sekundärem Interesse ist, ja ihm als Tod der Ziffern direkt schrecklich vorschweben muss. Diese Methode mit der von Joyce in Zusammenhang zu bringen, wie es die Mode ist, kommt mir genau so sinnlos vor wie der mir noch nicht bekannte Versuch den Nominalismus (im Sinne der Scholastiker) mit dem Realismus zu vergleichen.[9] Auf dem Wege nach dieser für mich sehr wünschenswerten Literatur des Unworts hin, kann freilich irgendeine Form der nominalistischen Ironie ein notwendiges Stadium sein. Es genügt aber nicht, wenn das Spiel etwas von seinem heiligen Ernst verliert. Aufhören soll es. Machen wir also wie jener verrückte (?) Mathematiker, der auf jeder einzelnen Stufe des Kalkuls ein neues Messprinzip anzuwenden pflegte. Eine Wörterstürmerei im Namen der Schönheit.

Inzwischen mache ich gar nichts. Nur von Zeit zu Zeit habe ich wie jetzt den Trost, mich so gegen eine fremde Sprache unwillkürlich vergehen zu dürfen, wie ich es mit Wissen und Willen gegen meine eigene machen möchte und – Deo juvante – werde.[10]

> Mit herzlichem Gruss
>
> Ihr
>
> Soll ich Ihnen die Ringelnatz Bände zurückschicken?
>
> Gibt es eine englische Uebersetzung von Trakl?[11]

TL; 2 leaves, 2 sides; ink and pencil AN, possibly AH or several; Lawrence Harvey collection, Dartmouth, MS 661; *previous publication*: Beckett, "German Letter of 1937," *Disjecta*, tr. Martin Esslin; German text, 51–54; English text, 170–173; rpt. in Oliver Sturm, *Der letzte Satz der letzten Seite ein letztes Mal: Der alte Beckett* (Hamburg: Europäische Verlagsanstalt, 1994) 210–213; rpt. in Dutch, "Duitse brief uit 1937" (German letter of 1937), tr. Translators Collective of the Historische Uitgeverij Groningen, *Bulletin: Literair Magazine* 21.193 (February 1992) 35–36; rpt. in Spanish as "Samuel Beckett: carta alemana de 1937," tr. Ana Maria Carolano, *Beckettiana: Cuadernos del Seminario de Beckett* 5 (February 1997) 89–91.

The text presented here is a draft; that SB probably did send the letter is indicated by the fact that he sent a copy of a portion of it to Arland Ussher on 11 July 1937: "My affection for you leaves me with no alternative but to let you have the benefit of the enclosed, which is an extract from a letter addressed to the Ringelnatz League in Berlin"; this letter closes with: "Your thoughts on Logoclasm, will you please put them in order and bestow them on me" (TxU).

This text is based on a ribbon copy, not a carbon copy, and it may represent SB's typed draft, with ink corrections made by SB at the time the letter was written. This document was given by SB to Lawrence Harvey between 1960 and 1966; Philip N. Cronenwett, formerly Curator of Manuscripts, Dartmouth College Library, concurs with the editors that the pencil corrections and notations may have been made at that time by SB and/or by Lawrence Harvey.

Martin Esslin's transcription of this letter incorporates a wide variety of silent corrections (Beckett, *Disjecta*, 51–54).

9/7/37

6 Clare Street

Dublin

IFS

Dear Axel Kaun,

Many thanks for your letter. I was just about to write to you when it came. Then I had to go travelling rather like

Ringelnatz's male postage stamp, although under less passionate circumstances.[1]

It is best I tell you right away and without further ado that in my opinion Ringelnatz is not worth the effort. You probably will not be more disappointed to hear this from me than I was in having to determine it.

I read through the 3 volumes, chose 23 poems and translated 2 of these as samples.[2] The little that of necessity they lost in the process is of course only to be evaluated in relation to what they have to lose in the first place, and I must say[3] that I found this co-efficient of deterioration quite insignificant even where he is most poet and least rhymester.

From this it is not to be assumed at all that a translated Ringelnatz would not find interest or success with the English public. In this respect, however, I am totally unable to make a judgement since responses of small as well as large audiences are becoming more and more mysterious to me and, what is worse, less significant. For I cannot get away from the naive antithesis that, at least where literature is concerned, a thing is either worth it or not worth it. And if we absolutely must earn money, we do it elsewhere.

I do not doubt that Ringelnatz as a person was of rather exceptional interest. As poet, however, he seemed to have been of Goethe's opinion: *better to write NOTHING than not to write*. However, perhaps even the Geheimrat might have allowed the translator to feel himself unworthy of such high kakoethes.[4]

I would be happy to explain to you in more detail my disdain for Ringelnatz's verse-obsession if you feel like going into it. However, for the time being I will spare you. Perhaps you like funeral orations as little as I do.

Likewise, I could perhaps indicate to you the chosen poems and send you the sample translations.

————————————————————————

I am always delighted to receive a letter from you. Therefore do write as often and as extensively as possible. Do you absolutely want me to do the same for you in English? Do you get as bored reading my German letters as I composing one in English? I would be sorry if you had the feeling that perhaps this was a matter of a contract which I am not fulfilling. An answer is requested.

It is indeed getting more and more difficult, even pointless, for me to write in formal English. And more and more my language appears to me like a veil which one has to tear apart in order to get to those things (or the nothingness) lying behind it. Grammar and style! To me they seem to have become as irrelevant as a Biedermeier bathing suit or the imperturbability of a gentleman.[5] A mask. It is to be hoped the time will come, thank God, in some circles it already has, when language is best used where it is most efficiently abused. Since we cannot dismiss it all at once, at least we do not want to leave anything undone that may contribute to its disrepute. To drill one hole after another into it until that which lurks behind, be it something or nothing, starts seeping through – I cannot imagine a higher goal for today's writer.

Or is literature alone to be left behind on that old, foul road long ago abandoned by music and painting? Is there something paralysingly sacred contained within the unnature of the word that does not belong to the elements of the other arts? Is there any reason why that terrifyingly arbitrary materiality of the word surface should not be dissolved, as for example the sound surface of Beethoven's Seventh Symphony is devoured

by huge black pauses, so that for pages on end we cannot perceive it as other than a dizzying path of sounds connecting
unfathomable chasms of silence?[6] An answer is requested.

I know there are people, sensitive and intelligent people,
for whom there is no lack of silence. I cannot help but assume
that they are hard of hearing. For in the forest of symbols that
are no symbols, the birds of interpretation, that is no interpretation, are never silent.

Of course, for the time being, one makes do with little. At
first, it can only be a matter of somehow inventing a method of
verbally demonstrating this scornful attitude vis-a-vis the word.
In this dissonance of instrument and usage perhaps one will
already be able to sense a whispering of the end-music or of
the silence underlying all.

In my opinion, the most recent work of Joyce had nothing at
all to do with such a programme.[7] There it seems much more a
matter of an apotheosis of the word. Unless Ascent into Heaven
and Descent into Hell are one and the same. How nice it would
be to be able to believe that in fact it were so. For the moment,
however, we will limit ourselves to the intention.

Perhaps, Gertrude Stein's Logographs come closer to what I
mean. The fabric of the language has at least become porous, if
regrettably only quite by accident and, as it were, as a consequence of a procedure somewhat akin to the technique of
Feininger.[8] The unhappy lady (is she still alive?) is undoubtedly
still in love with her vehicle, if only, however, as a mathematician is with his numbers; for him the solution of the problem is
of very secondary interest, yes, as the death of numbers, it must
seem to him indeed dreadful. To connect this method with that
of Joyce, as is fashionable, appears to me as ludicrous as the
attempt, as yet unknown to me, to compare Nominalism (in the

sense of the Scholastics) with Realism.[9] On the road toward this, for me, very desirable literature of the non-word, some form of nominalistic irony can of course be a necessary phase. However, it does not suffice if the game loses some of its sacred solemnity. Let it cease altogether! Let's do as that crazy mathematician who used to apply a new principle of measurement at each individual step of the calculation. Word-storming in the name of beauty.

In the meantime I am doing nothing. Only from time to time do I have the consolation, as now, of being allowed to violate a foreign language as involuntarily as, with knowledge and intention, I would like to do against my own language, and – Deo juvante – shall do.[10]

Cordially yours,

Shall I send you back the Ringelnatz volumes?

Is there an English translation of Trakl?[11]

1 SB evokes Ringelnatz's poem "Ein männlicher Briefmark erlebt" (Hans Bötticher and Richard J.M. Seewald, eds., *Die Schnupftabaksdose: Stumpfsinn in Versen und Bildern* [Munich: R. Piper, 1912] 4; see text and translation by Ernest A. Seemann, www. beilharz.com/poetas/ringelnatz/, 25 May 2006). The poem personifies a male postage stamp that experienced arousal when licked by a princess; he wished to kiss her back, but had to go traveling, thus his love was unavailing.

2 SB had been sent three volumes of the poems by Ringelnatz's publisher Rowohlt, for whom Kaun worked, but it is not clear which books these were, nor which two poems SB had translated. He quotes "Die Ameisen" in his letter to Arland Ussher, 15 June 1937 (TxU).

3 SB wrote "<will Ihnen nicht verleugnen>" and then inserted "muss" to replace "will" and also added "-en" (the infinitive ending in German) without adding a verb stem. In order to have a translatable sentence, we have inserted (as did Esslin) the verb stem of "to say" to render "sagen."

4 SB cites Goethe's final sentence of the first chapter of *Die Wahlverwandtschaften*, in *Die Leiden des jungen Werthers, Die Wahlverwandtschaften, Kleine Prosa, Epen*, ed. Waltraud Wiethölter and Christoph Brecht, in *Sämtliche Werke*, VIII, ed. Friedmar Apel, Henrik Bines, and Dieter Borchmeyer (Frankfurt: Deutscher Klassiker Verlag, 1994) 278; Johann Wolfgang Goethe, *Elective Affinities*, tr. David Constantine, The World's Classics (Oxford: Oxford University Press, 1994) 9.

"Geheimrat" (Privy counselor), in reference to Goethe.

"Kakoethes" (Gk., wickedness, malignity); in SB's "Serena I": "or as they say evil propensity" (see 8 October 1932).

5 Influenced by the French Empire style, "Biedermeier" (1815–1848) is usually applied to furnishings and fashion of the German bourgeoisie; later it took on a derogatory connotation of conventional narrow-mindedness.

6 Beethoven's Symphony no. 7 in A major, op. 92.

7 Joyce's *Work in Progress*, published already in fragments, was published in full as *Finnegans Wake* in 1939.

8 "Logograph" is not a term used by American writer Gertrude Stein (1874–1946), although her writing emphasized sound and rhythm over sense, which SB compares to Lyonel Feininger's cubist technique, which layered prismatic planes of color.

SB wrote to Mary Manning Howe on 11 July 1937: "I am starting a Logoclasts' League. [...] I am the only member at present. The idea is ruptured writing, so that the void may protude, like a hernia" (TxU).

9 The philosophical tradition known as Realism holds that words such as "truth," "beauty," and "justice" are concepts that are general or universal, but also that they name extramental, actually existing entities. Nominalism holds that these words are merely names (Lat., *nomen*) for which there are no corresponding entities. A survey of the medieval controversy is given in Frederick Copleston, *A History of Philosophy*, II (Westminster, MD: The Newman Press, 1955) 136–155.

10 "Deo juvante" (with God's help).

11 The writing of Austrian poet Georg Trakl (1887–1914) had not yet been translated into English in 1937.

GEORGE REAVEY

LONDON

27/7/37   6 Clare St
                                     Dublin

dear George

I quote from a letter from Mrs Howe: "Please let Reavey know I've sent your MS. to Covici-Firede (?) Inc. [*for* Covici-Friede] in New York. If they turn it down it[']s to be sent to Hal Smith of Doubleday Doran. Let the New York offices of Reavey of which there is no address that I can find be notified & they can deal with matters after that."[1]

My efforts to document my Johnson fantasy have not ceased. The evidence for it is overwhelming. It explains what has never been explained (e.g. his grotesque attitute [*for* attitude] towards his wife & Mr Thrale). It is hard to put across, he being so old at the crisis, i.e. she could hardly have expected much from him.[2] We will make him younger & madder even than he was.[3]

Remember me to Miss Vernon.[4]

A toi[5]

Sam

ALS; 1 leaf, 1 side; TxU.

1 Mary Manning Howe's letter to SB has not been found. Pascal Covici (1888–1964), Romanian-born Chicago publisher, joined forces with Donald Friede (1901–1965) to form Covici-Friede (1928–1937) in New York.

There was no New York office for the European Literary Bureau.

2 In 1736, Samuel Johnson married the widow Elizabeth Porter (née Jervis, known as Hetty, 1689–1752) when she was forty-six and he was twenty-five (Bate, *Samuel Johnson*, 147). Bate notes that "between December 1737 and May 1739 Johnson and his wife 'began to live apart,' although Johnson visited her occasionally" (177–178, 187–188; Boswell, *Boswell's Life of Johnson*, I, 192). Yet Boswell disputed the observation of Sir John Hawkins that Johnson's fondness for his wife "was dissembled," writing: "we find very remarkable evidence that his regard and fondness for her never ceased, even after her death" (Boswell, *Boswell's Life of Johnson*, I, 192, 96, 234).

If, as it appears, SB's text reads "towards his wife and Mr Thrale," then the "grotesque attitude" that SB ascribes to Johnson bears upon his apparently incongruous admiration of them. If the slightly effaced page reads "M$^{r[s]}$" Thrale, then SB draws a parallel between Elizabeth Porter and Hester Thrale, who were romantically and sexually somewhat unlikely partners with their husbands.

Johnson was seventy-one years old when Henry Thrale died.

3 SB recorded in his notebook some details of Johnson's singular behavior in spring 1764 from *Boswell's Life of Johnson*: Johnson's symptoms of depression, his withdrawal from society and his "sighing, groaning, talking to himself, and restlessly walking from room to room." Boswell describes Johnson's obsessive-compulsive behavior as "superstitious habit" (e.g. arranging his steps so that the same foot always crossed the threshold), and notes Johnson's involuntary "sounds with his mouth ... chewing the cud, ... giving a half whistle ... clucking like a hen ... blowing out his breath like a whale" (*Boswell's Life of Johnson*, I, 483–486; BIF, UoR, MS 3461/1, f. 42R).

4 George Reavey married Clodine Gwynedd Cade on 16 July 1937.

5 "A toi" (your).

UNIVERSITY OF CAPE TOWN
SOUTH AFRICA

July 29th 1937   6 Clare Street
                                                 Dublin
                                                 Irish Free State

Dear Sir

I beg to apply for the post of Lecturer in Italian in the University of Cape Town.

I enclose copies of testimonials and a brief curriculum vitae.[1]

The following will act as referees:

Mr Thomas C. Ross, Solicitor, 31 South Frederic[k] Street, Dublin.

Captain the Reverend Arthur Aston Luce, D.D., F.T.C.D., Ryslaw, Bushey Park Road, Rathgar, Dublin.

Dr Geoffrey Thompson, 71 Harley Street, London W.1.

> Yours faithfully
> s/ Samuel Beckett
> (Samuel Beckett, M.A., T.C.D.)

Samuel Barclay Beckett
Church of Ireland
Single

April 1906.	Born in Dublin.
1916–19.	Earlsfort House Preparatory School, Dublin.
1919–23.	Portora Royal School, Enniskillen, Co. Fermanagh, Northern Ireland.
1923–27.	Trinity College, Dublin. Specialise in French and Italian. 1925 Senior Exhibitioner. 1926 Scholar of the House. April–August 1927 travelling in Italy.

	October 1927 graduate first of first class Moderators with large gold medal in French and Italian.
1928–30.	Lecturer in English at the Ecole Normale Supérieure Paris.
1930–32.	Lecturer in French at Trinity College, Dublin.
1932–37.	Private study and composition. Travel in France and Germany.
Publications.	Proust (Chatto and Windus, London, 1932.) Short Stories (Chatto and Windus, London, 1934.) Poems (Europa Press, Paris, 1935.) as well as various occasional translations, reviews, poems, short stories, etc.

PROFESSOR RUDMOSE BROWN TO UNIVERSITY
OF CAPE TOWN, SOUTH AFRICA

5 June 1937   Trinity College
                                                                          Dublin

I have great pleasure in supporting the application of Mr S. B. Beckett for the Lectureship in Italian in the University of Cape Town. Mr Beckett graduated in 1927 with the very highest distinction in French and Italian. He knows both languages thoroughly and in a scholarly way, as well as German. He has resided in Italy, France and Germany and has an intimate knowledge of the three countries as well as of their literatures. Mr Beckett spent two years as Lecturer in English in the Ecole Normale Supérieure in Paris (1928–1930) and has written a most illuminating book on Proust, as well as many articles on literary subjects and some prose fiction and verse. I may say without exaggeration that as well as possessing a sound academic knowledge of the Italian, French and German languages, he has remarkable creative faculty.

Signed: T. B. Rudmose-Brown, Professor of the Romance Languages in the University of Dublin, Secretary of the University Council, M.A., Litt.D., Docteur d'Université, Soci dou Felibrige.[2]

P.S. I may add that Mr Beckett has an adequate knowledge of Provençal, ancient and modern.

Copy

PROFESSOR WALTER STARKIE TO THE UNIVERSITY
OF CAPE TOWN, SOUTH AFRICA

11th June, 1937   University Club
                                                   Dublin

Mr. Samuel Beckett has asked me to testify to his knowledge of Italian language and literature. During the four years of his course at Dublin University he attended my lectures in Italian Literature, and he obtained an Honors Degree, first-class, in 1927, in Modern Literature (Italian and French). Mr Beckett was an excellent student and possesses a good knowledge of Italian history and literature. In the final examination the candidates are required to display special knowledge of the great classical authors, in particular, of Dante. Mr Beckett's answering showed distinction and literary gifts of no mean order. I wish to recommend him for a lectureship in Italian.

Signed: Walter Starkie, M.A., Litt.D., Professor in the University of Dublin, Fellow of Trinity College, Dublin.

Copy

PROFESSOR ROBERT W. TATE TO THE UNIVERSITY
OF CAPE TOWN, SOUTH AFRICA

June 12th 1937   40 Trinity College
                                                  Dublin

    Mr Samuel B. Beckett graduated in 1927 with a First Class
Moderatorship with large gold medal in French and Italian. In
his Italian studies I was closely associated with him both as
lecturer and examiner throughout his course. It is my conviction
that very few foreigners have a practical knowledge of that
language as sound as his, or as great a mastery of its grammar
and constructions.

    Signed: R. W. Tate, Fellow and Tutor T.C.D.

Copy

PROFESSOR RUDMOSE BROWN, GENERAL
TESTIMONIAL

7 July 1932   Trinity College
                                                  Dublin

    Mr S. B. Beckett had a most distinguished University career
at Trinity College, Dublin. He was the best student of his year
in French, a Scholar of the House in French and Italian, and a
1st Class Moderator (1st Class Honour Degree) in French and
Italian. I chose him to spend two years at the Ecole Normale
Supérieure as the nominee of Trinity College, and then picked
him out of all my graduates to become Lecturer in French at

Trinity College. He speaks and writes French like a Frenchman of the highest education. He has a most remarkable knowledge of French literature, and has written a very competent and interesting book on Marcel Proust. I found him an excellent Lecturer, far above the average standard of young lecturers, and regretted very much when he resigned his post in order to take up further residence in Paris. His knowledge of Italian is very little less than his knowledge of French. He also knows German.

I can most thoroughly recommend Mr Beckett for a University post.

Signed: T. B. Rudmose-Brown, Professor of Romance Languages in the University of Dublin, M.A., Litt. D., Docteur d'Univ., Soci dou Felibrige.

Copy

JEAN THOMAS, GENERAL TESTIMONIAL

le 22 Juillet 1932   Ecole Normale Supérieure, Université
                                 de Paris,
                                 45 Rue d'Ulm
                                 Paris 5me.

M. Samuel Beckett a été, pendant deux années consécutives, de Novembre 1928 à la fin de l'année scolaire 1930, Lecteur d'anglais à l'Ecole Normale Supérieure. Par sa connaissance à la fois de la littérature anglaise et de la littérature française, par sa culture aussi précise que riche, il a rendu à nos élèves les plus grands services. J'ajoute qu'il a noué avec certains Normaliens de précieuses amitiés et qu'il a laissé le meilleur souvenir dans l'esprit de tous ceux qui l'ont connu.

Signed: Jean Thomas, Agrégé de l'Université,
  Secrétaire de l'Ecole Normale Supérieure.

Copy

22 July 1932   Ecole Normale Supérieure, Université
                de Paris,
                45 Rue d'Ulm
                Paris 5

Mr. Samuel Beckett was, for two consecutive years, from November 1928 to the end of the academic year 1930, Lecteur in English at the Ecole Normale Supérieure. By his knowledge of both English and French literature, by his general culture, as exact as it was rich, he was exceptionally helpful to our students. I may add that he struck up close friendships with a number of Normaliens, and that he is fondly remembered by all who knew him.

Signed: Jean Thomas, Agrégé de l'Université,
  Secrétaire de l'Ecole Normale Supérieure.

TLS; 2 leaves, 2 sides; *enclosures*: T. B. Rudmose-Brown to University of Cape Town, 5 June 1937 (TLC; 1 leaf, 1 side); Walter Starkie to University of Cape Town, 11 June 1937 (TLC; 1 leaf, 1 side); R. W. Tate to University of Cape Town, 12 June 1937 (TLC; 1 leaf, 1 side); *general testimonial*: T. B. Rudmose-Brown 7 July 1932 (TLC; 1 leaf, 1 side) and Jean Thomas 22 July 1932 (TLC; 1 leaf, 1 side); University of Cape Town.

1 Testimonials were open documents, made available to the candidate; references were sent directly to the institution requesting them. The University of Cape Town does not hold letters from Thomas Conland Ross, a solicitor from 1896 to 1946 (d. 1947), Arthur Aston Luce, or Geoffrey Thompson, which suggests that they were not contacted as referees.

2 "Soci dou Felibrige" (Provençal, Fellow of the Society of the Felibrige).

THOMAS McGREEVY

4th Aug. 1937   Foxrock

Dear Tom

Very pleased with your lively letter.[1]

Dr J.'s dogmatisme was the facade of consternation. The 18th century was full of ahuris – perhaps that is why it looked like the age of "reason" – but there can hardly have been many so completely at sea in their solitude as he was or so horrifiedly aware of it – not even Cowper. Read the Prayers & Meditations if you don't believe me.[2]

Mrs Thrale was née Salusbury – Hester (!) Lynch (!!) Salusbury.[3] There is no question of being partisan in the matter one way or another. He made her Salon & she made him comfortable. When he wrote her the famous rough letter he didn't know what he was doing. Probably it was the only overt cruelty in the "friendship never infringed by one harsh expression during 20 years of familiar talk", as she herself expressed it in her admirably dignified last letter to him. And of the covert she certainly had no more to suffer than he, indeed certainly a great deal less, because she had none of that need to suffer, or necessity of suffering, that he had, and never found in him the peg to hang her pain on that he did in her. His horror at loving her I take it was a mode or paradigm of his horror at ultimate annihilation, to which he declared in the fear of his death that he would prefer an eternity of torment.[4] And if the play is about him and not about her, it does not mean that he was in the right, or any nonsense like that, but simply that he being spiritually self conscious was a tragic figure, i.e. worth putting down as part of the whole of which oneself is a part, & that she, being merely physically self conscious is less interesting to me personally. She of course didn't get what she wanted either, Piozzi being a poor performer. "<u>Human Wishes</u>".[5]

[...]

I would much rather you did the <u>Intercessions</u> for <u>Ireland To-day</u> than that I did. I can always get it from Seumas. I shall make it right with Denis.[6] I am so broke with weddings, & with the whole of August to go before the next cheque, that I haven't even been able to send Reavey a cheque for the 3 copies I had meant to order.[7] But I suppose he won't mind adding that to what no doubt I owe him already.

I applied last week for the Lectureship in Italian at Cape Town. It would be an excuse for taking up the subject again & people say Cape Town has its advantages. I am really indifferent about where I go or what I do, since I don't seem able or to want to write any more, or let us be modest and say for the moment. I suppose the prospect of Mother being left alone should have restrained me, but it hasn't.

The brute from Buffalo hasn't turned up yet. If he says there is anything going there I shall probably apply for it also.[8]

I haven't seen JBY for a fortnight. I am truly delighted to hear that you are doing something about him again. Was it the Constable that started you? I remember asking you had you ever seen the affinity, but you said no. I meant nothing more than occasional passages with resemblances of handling.[9]

I go very little away from the house, having no money to go with, except to Sandycove for a bathe. I must having [sic] been getting too much sea & sun lately, to judge by the limpness. Cissie & family are off to Port Elizabeth to-morrow week. That will be a loss.[10]

I enclose a photo of a section of the west wall at Ardmore with the kneeling figure that means something important to me. I think I mentioned it to you before. "Portant leur fatigue, etc."[11]

I read Eliot's <u>Dante</u>. How insufferably condescending, restrained & professorial. Then again Boccaccio's <u>Life</u> & Leonardo Bruni's, with the mention of Taddeo Gaddi's fresco portrait that used to be in Santa Croce.[12]

It seems ages since I heard from or wrote to Charles.[13] I wonder is there not something shut off there that even his dinners do not dissipate. Of course there is in us all, but I mean a whole habit of life that I certainly always felt a lonely one. I would like to know about his sexualities.

Love ever. Don't leave me long without a letter.

Sam

ALS; 4 leaves, 7 sides; TCD, MS 10402/130.

1 McGreevy's letter to SB has not been found.

2 "Ahuris" (bewildered people).
SB's comparison of English poet William Cowper (1731–1800) to Samuel Johnson is not reflected in his notes on Cowper's wish that he "'had never been.'" SB observes, "Into such a wish J. cd. never have entered" (BIF, UoR, 3461/2, f. 80R, Nixon transcription).

SB refers to Samuel Johnson's writings published posthumously as *Prayers & Meditations* (1785); they were edited by George Strahan (1744–1824) at Johnson's request.

3 SB's exclamation point following "Hester" may allude to Hester Dowden. SB knows that McGreevy will share his amusement at the sudden appearance of the very Irish "Lynch" among such very English names.

4 Johnson's "rough letter" to Hester Thrale: 26 April 1937, n. 20. SB refers as well to Hester Thrale's reply of 4 July 1784:

> I have this morning received from you so rough a letter in reply to one which was both tenderly and respectfully written, that I am forced to desire the conclusion of a correspondence which I can bear to continue no longer ... You have always commanded my esteem, and long enjoyed the fruits of a friendship never infringed by one harsh expression on my part during twenty years of familiar talk. Never did I oppose your will, or control your wish; nor can your unmerited severity itself lessen my regard; but till you have changed your opinion of Mr. Piozzi let us converse no more. God bless you. (Johnson, *Letters of Samuel Johnson LL.D*, II, 406; RUL MS 3641/1, f. 12R)

In this letter Mrs. Thrale uses the term "husband" of Piozzi, although they were not yet married.

5 Contemporaries of Mrs. Thrale advanced speculation about Piozzi's vitality (Vulliamy, *Mrs. Thrale of Streatham*, 234, 260).

Beckett's title for the Johnson play was "Human Wishes," playing on the title of Johnson's poem "The Vanity of Human Wishes" (1749) to suggest the disappointment of his desire for Mrs. Thrale (Boswell, *Boswell's Life of Johnson*, I, 192; Samuel Beckett, "Human Wishes," in *Disjecta*, 155–166).

6 Denis Devlin had asked SB to review his collection of poems *Intercessions* for *Ireland To-Day*. It was McGreevy who wrote the review; in it, he took the opportunity to sketch the similarities and differences between SB and Devlin as poets ("New Dublin Poetry," *Ireland To-Day* 2.10 [October 1937] 81–82). SB did not review *Intercessions* for *Dublin Magazine*; his review appeared as "Denis Devlin," *transition* 27 [April–May 1938] 289–294).

7 George Reavey had married on 16 July 1937 and Frank Beckett's wedding was imminent.

SB ordered three copies of *Intercessions* in the limited edition from Reavey's Europa Press on 3 August 1937 (see 14 August 1937) (InU, Mitchell/ Beckett Mss.).

8 Mary Manning Howe, whose husband had recently taken a faculty position at the University of Buffalo (now SUNY, Buffalo), had mentioned the possibility of a position there for Beckett. The person whom SB describes as "Buffalo Bill" in his letter to Howe of 30 August 1937 was probably Henry Ten Eyck Perry, Chairman of the English department, then on leave in Europe.

9 The centenary of the death of John Constable (1776–1837) was marked by exhibitions at the British Museum, the Tate Gallery, and the Wildenstein Gallery in London, from April to the end of August 1937.

Although in his *Jack B. Yeats*, McGreevy discusses the possibility of Constable's influence on Yeats's work, he underlines the differences between them: "Jack Yeats was concerned with human values. Constable was not" (11).

10 The 40 Foot: 23 May [1936], n. 6.

Cissie Beckett and family had left for Southampton, from there to travel to Port Elizabeth, South Africa, where they would visit Morris Sinclair.

11 SB had written about this figure in the west gable of the ruins of Ardmore Cathedral, Co. Waterford, reportedly the burial place of St. Declan (fl. fifth century), in his letter to McGreevy of 9 September 1936: "I spent a few days last week with Joe Hone at the Usshers in Cappagh (Dungarvan) and saw Ardmore & Cashel. On the west door at Ardmore there is an exquisite tiny carved stooping figure under a spear (Pelorson's Lance Grave), representing I suppose conversion of Declan. The loveliest six inches of stone I ever saw" (TCD, MS 10402/107; for photo see www.waterford-countymuseum.org).

The relief figure in the arcades on the west gable represents an ecclesiastic blessing a kneeling warrior, armed with a long spear; this reminds SB of a line from a poem, "Plans," written by Georges Pelorson: "portant la fatigue comme une lance grave" (Bearing weariness like a serious spear) (*transition* 21 [March 1932] 182–183).

12 T. S. Eliot, *Dante* (London: Faber and Faber, 1929).

Giovanni Boccaccio, *La Vita di Dante* (c. 1348 – 1373).

Although Florentine artist Taddeo Gaddi (1290-1366), a pupil of Giotto, created many of the frescos in Santa Croce in Florence, Leonardo Bruni (1369-1444) does not name him as the artist in his *La vita di Dante* (c. 1436): "La effigie sua propria si vede nella chiesa di Santa Croce, quasi a mezzo della chiesa, dalla mano sinistra andando verso l'altar maggiore, ed è ritratta al naturale ottimamente per dipintore perfetto del tempo suo." ("His portrait may be seen in Santa Croce, near the centre of the church, on the left hand as you approach the high altar, a most faithful painting by an excellent artist of that time") (Leonardo Bruni, *Le vite di Dante e del Petrarca*, ed. Antonio Lanza [Rome: Archivio Guido Izzi, 1987] 45; James Robinson Smith, tr. *The Earliest Lives of Dante: Translated from the Italian of Giovanni Boccaccio and Leonardo Bruni Aretino*, Yale Studies in English [New York: Holt, 1901; rpt. New York: Russell and Russell, 1968] 90).

A fifteenth-century copy of the lost fresco portrait of Dante can be found in the Biblioteca Nazionale, Florence, Banco Rari 215, Ms. Palantino 320/ f. II recto (Bernhard Degenhart and Annegrit Schmitt, *Corpus der Italienischen Zeichnungen, 1300–1450* [Berlin: Gebr. Mann Verlag, 1968], II, 282–284, n. 186, and IV, 205c; Frank Jewett Mather, Jr., *The Portraits of Dante: Compared with the Measurements of his Skull and Reclassified* [Princeton: Princeton University Press, 1921] frontispiece, 11–18).

13 Charles Prentice.

GEORGE REAVEY
LONDON

Aug 4ᵗʰ 1937   6 Clare St
                                               Dublin

dear George

> O Doubleday Doran
> Less OXY than moron
> You've a mind like a whore on
> A trip to Bundoran[1]

———————————

The Johnson thing has gone away to be dyed. I mean the idea of it. For nothing had been degraded to paper. I have been too tired.

Hope you enjoyed every moment of your trip. And that I shall see you both soon. Denis very pleased with his advance copy.[2] Herewith a last flicker. Place it if you can. Seldom in a woman. Never in a man.[3]

4 August 1937, Reavey

Love to Gwynedd[4]
Ever
Sam –

ALS; 1 leaf, 1 side; *no enclosure is extant*; TxU.

1 *Murphy* was to be sent to Doubleday Doran (see 14 April 1937, n. 2; 27 July 1937).
Bundoran, a seaside resort in Co. Donegal.
This verse appears, with variations, in SB's letter to Mary Manning Howe after
10 December 1937; it is cited as from a letter of 6 August 1937 in Bair, *Samuel Beckett*,
262 with variations from the text as written; the verse as found in Bair is reprinted in
Eoin O'Brien, *The Beckett Country*, 308.

2 George and Gwynedd Reavey had been on their honeymoon.
Denis Devlin's collection of poetry *Intercessions* was published on 15 October by
Reavey's Europa Press.

3 Although a verse is at the head of the letter, it is probable that the "last flicker"
refers to another piece of writing, possibly "Whiting," which was enclosed (there is a
slight rust mark from a paper clip at the upper right margin of the letter).
Beckett plays upon, among other things, a popular verse of the time:

> Patience is a virtue
> Possess it if you can
> Found seldom in a woman
> Never in a man.

4 SB habitually writes Gwynedd Reavey's name as "Gwynned." This mispelling of
her name will be silently corrected throughout. When SB correctly spells her name,
this is noted.

CISSIE SINCLAIR
SOUTHAMPTON, EN ROUTE TO SOUTH AFRICA

14th [August 1937]   Gresham Hotel
                                         Dublin

dearest Cissie
   [...]
   I was glad to get your letter this morning. I wanted you to
think of me sometimes when you had a drink. How else would I
render it likely? Have many.

At least I am escaped from Cooldrinagh, the Liebespaar & Molly. All the presents pouring in, a gong this morning so terrible, the impediments of detached domesticities, the circle closing round. How much freer & liebesfähiger (wenn es darauf [an]kommt!), furnished lodgings & no possessions.[1] To be welded together with gongs and tea-trolleys, the bars against the sky, how hopeless. Is that what "home" means for all women, solid furniture & not to be overlooked, or is there another sense of home in some of them, or are there some who don't want a home, who have had enough of that?

I saw Ilse again but she was "körperlich nicht ganz auf der Höhe". We all know what that means. So we conversed, yes really conversed. Hans had rung up inviting her to dine. She declined. Motze [*for* Motz] had been out.[2] It is something very close to disgust, nausea, & of course she feels it. Soon it will be over.

I can't work. I have not made a pretence of working for a month. Given up even the preoccupied look & the de quoi écrire.[3] If I got the job in Cape Town I don't think I'd hold it for a fortnight. It would be a degradation if the terms of reference had not shrivelled up. I always see the physical crisis just round the corner. It would solve perhaps the worst of what remains to be solved, clarify the problem anyway, which I suppose is the best solution we can hope for.

I had a letter from Tom by the same post as yours. He is writing about Jack Yeats, inspired apparently by some Constable exhibition & a chance remark of mine about the Watteauishness of what he has been doing lately. Every Thursday there seems to be something to prevent me going in to see him.[4] I suppose I don't want to see him. Watteau put in busts and urns, I suppose to suggest the inorganism of the organic – all his people are mineral in the end, without possibility of being added to or taken from, pure inorganic juxtapositions – but Jack Yeats

does not even need to do that. The way he puts down a
man's head & a woman's head side by side, or face to face, is
terrifying, two irreducible singlenesses & the impassable
immensity between. I suppose that is what gives the stillness
to his pictures, as though the convention were suddenly suspended, the convention & performance of love & hate, joy &
pain, giving & being given, taking & being taken. A kind of
petrified insight into one's ultimate hard irreducible inorganic
singleness. All handled with the dispassionate acceptance that is
beyond tragedy. I always feel Watteau to be a tragic genius, i.e.
there is pity in him for the world as he sees it. But I find no pity, i.
e. no tragedy in Yeats. Not even sympathy. Simply perception &
dispassion. Even personally he is rather inhuman, or haven't
you felt it?

Perhaps the literary value of this letter & so if the worst
comes to the worst (don't misunderstand me) its marketable
interest would be promoted by a few lines of verse. You may
find them trivial & unpleasant; there seemed no point to me in
beautifying them, or making them less direct in the fashionable
manner. They came just as they are here.

WHITING

Offer it up plank it down
Golgotha was only the potegg
cancer angina it is all one to us
cough up your T. B. don't be stingy
no trifle is too trifling not even a thrombus
anything venereal is especially welcome
that old toga virilis in the mothballs
don't be sentimental you won't be wanting it again
send it along we'll put it in the pot with the rest
with your love requited & unrequited

536

the things taken too late the things taken too soon
the spirit aching bullock's scrotum
you won't cure it if you can't endure it
it is you it equals you any fool has to pity you
so parcel up the whole issue & send it along
the whole misery diagnosed undiagnosed misdiagnosed
get your friends to do the same we'll make use of it
we'll make sense of it we'll put it in the pot with the rest
it all boils down to blood of lamb[5]

————————————

[...]

    Love ever Write often

      dein Sam[6]

ALS; 4 leaves, 8 sides; *letterhead*; Sinclair. *Dating*: SB's letter to Thomas McGreevy, 14 August 1937, encloses TMS of the same poem (with two minor variants); WHITING was published as "Ooftish" (see n. 6 below). SB's letter to McGreevy refers to the poem in similar words: "The enclosed you will probably find merely disagreeably trivial" and "I see no point in making it less direct or fiddling about with it. It came straight the way it is."

1 SB's cousin Molly Roe was visiting Cooldrinagh where preparations were being made for Frank Beckett's marriage; a reception and viewing of gifts took place at Cooldrinagh on 23 August, and the wedding on 25 August.

"Liebespaar" (lovers). "Liebesfähiger (wenn es darauf [an]kommt!")" (more capable of loving [when it matters]).

SB expands in this vein to Thomas McGreevy, 23 August 1937:

> Watching the presents come along has been painful. The awful unconscious social [c]ynicism that knows that what the relationship comes down to in the end is Gongs & tea-trolleys, that without them there is no "together". Till it seems almost a law of marriage that the human personal element should be smothered out of existence from the word go, reduced to a mere occasion for good housekeeping & home chat. The egg cup in the pie of domestic solidity. How much freer one would be to develop the spiritual thing, or even the physical thing, or to keep them alive, or to bring them together into one, that wd. be neither cordial fucking nor fucking cordiality, in the meanest of bed sitting rooms, where at least one owned nothing, i.e. was owned by nothing, than among the gongs & tea-trolleys, booming & trundling you out of

a relation into a condition. Or is it that when you grow up you stop talking about relationships – the bare unmitigated undeserved spiritual & physical commerce between 2 human beings & thank God if you can achieve the egg cup in the pie? Quoi qu'il en soit, it is horrible to see how society takes over at the least hint of a fresh social node of growth. Neither of them wants all this hullabaloo with presents & a reception, they would both have really preferred to do without the presents if they could have been spared the fuss, & yet they submit to it. (TCD, MS 10402/133)

"Quoi qu'il en soit" (whatever may be the case).

2 Ilse Starcke (n.d.) was the sister of Heiner Starcke; Heiner had been unofficially engaged to Peggy Sinclair when Peggy died of tuberculosis in the Starcke family apartment in Bad Wildungen in 1933 (24 July 1996, Morris Sinclair). Heiner and Ilse were visiting Dublin.

"Körperlich nicht ganz auf der Höhe" (physically not up to it).

Austrian-born Jewish physicist Hans Motz (1909–1987) earned a Master of Science in 1935 from Trinity College Dublin.

3 "De quoi écrire" (the wherewithal to write).

4 In a letter to McGreevy, a fragment [before 23 July 1937], SB wrote: "JBY gets Watteauer & Watteauer. The latest is entitled Boucicault & Bianconi, separated by a waterfall, in a glade by moonlight" (In Memory of Boucicault and Bianconi; Pyle 498; NGI 4206; TCD MS 10402/129). In his study Jack B. Yeats, McGreevy took up this statement by SB:

> A few months ago Samuel Beckett wrote me that he had been looking at some recent works by Jack Yeats. "He grows Watteauer and Watteauer," [...] the association held its own in my mind and when I had got over the surprise of having to co-relate the actual images which the works of the two painters had left in my memory, I found myself establishing points of similarity, not in their techniques but in their human approach. (MacGreevy, Jack B. Yeats, 14–15)

Thursday was Jack Yeats's "at-home" evening.

5 SB's poem "Whiting" was also enclosed in 14 August 1937 to McGreevy, with only slight variations: line 1 in this letter reads "Offer" whereas when enclosed to McGreevy it reads "offer"; line 10 in this letter reads "requited & unrequited," whereas, when enclosed to McGreevy it reads "requited and unrequited." The changes in the poem sent to McGreevy were retained in the poem when published as "Ooftish" in transition 27 (April–May 1938) 33.

6 "Dein" (your).

THOMAS McGREEVY
LONDON

14ᵗʰ August 37   Foxrock
                                                 [Co. Dublin]

Dear Tom

I used to pretend to be working at something, going about with the preoccupied look & de quoi écrire, but I really don't any more. I had the Johnson thing fairly clear in my mind, but with not thinking about it it has gone obscure again.[1] Perhaps it gets clearer elsewhere.

Frank came out of the home this day week and bathing him, driving him about, dressing him & so on has filled some of my time. He is almost quite well again & will not, as he feared he might, have to postpone his wedding on 25th inst. The honeymoon stands also, motoring in Scotland. I think they are thinking also of crossing to the Hebrides. Which reminds me I must give him the Dr's <u>Western Isles</u>. He seems very happy & serene about it all. Your <u>Leonardo</u> came & he was very pleased.[2]

Cissie & family left Wednesday morning. I drove them to the boat. I had a letter this morning from Southampton, all having gone well. In about another month I shall realize they are gone.

The last 3 mornings I have been in the Gallery. They have a big ugly new Giovanni Benedetto Castiglione, the <u>Finding of Cyrus</u>, very bad Rubens indeed, whereas the <u>Elijah invoking fire</u> (do you remember it?) seems to me fairly good Rubens. Furlong seems to have a passion for the considered enormities of the Settecento.[3] The big Perugino is back again, overcleaned. The Paris Bordone Portrait is really superb, nearly as good as the lovely one in Munich – more reticent – but I don't understand how they saddle him with the St. George. The big Oliverio has disappeared. The 2 big Moretto Saints were looking marvellous also. I think he must have looked hard at the Dürer Apostles.[4] How I wish we could have a few hours together in the newly hung Italian rooms. You would get a shock & here & there the pleasure of something for the first time. Of course the Dutch pictures are to all intents & purposes lost to the Gallery.[5] But that wd. not trouble you the way it does me.

There always seems something on Thursday to prevent me from going to see JBY.[6] What I feel he gets so well, dispassionately, not tragically like Watteau, is the heterogeneity of nature & the human denizens, the unalterable alienness of the 2 phenomena, the 2 solitudes, or the solitude & the loneliness, the loneliness in solitude, the impassable immensity between the solitude that cannot quicken to loneliness & the loneliness that cannot lapse into solitude. There is nothing of the kind in Constable, the landscape shelters or threatens or serves or destroys, his nature is really infected with "spirit", ultimately as humanised & romantic as Turner's was & Claude's was not & Cézanne's was not.[7] God knows it doesn't take much sensitiveness to feel that in Ireland, a nature almost as inhumanly inorganic as a stage set. And perhaps that is the final quale of Jack Yeats's painting, a sense of the ultimate <u>inorganism</u> of everything. Watteau stressed it with busts & urns, his people are <u>mineral</u> in the end. A painting of pure inorganic juxtapositions, where nothing can be taken or given & there is no possibility of change or exchange. I find something terrifying for example in the way Yeats puts down a man's head & a woman's head side by side, or face to face, the awful acceptance of 2 entities that will never mingle. And do you remember the picture of a man sitting under a fuchsia hedge, reading, with his back turned to the sea & the thunder clouds?[8] One does not realize how still his pictures are till one looks at others, almost petrified, a sudden suspension of the performance, of the convention of sympathy & antipathy, meeting & parting, joy & sorrow.

I am so glad it went well with Geoffrey. He owes me I don't know how many letters. I had a card from George & Gwynedd from Florence.

Are they back yet?[9]

I see little of Brian & nothing of Denis. I ran into Brian one day on his way to meet the assistant state prosecutor of Washington. Yes, he send [*for* sent] me the poem you mention. I liked it all but the Elizabethan beginning, appallingly "Ye olde". He said it was a transcription from Florio's Montaigne. I urged him to change it. I want to see Denis to arrange about the reviews of his poems. I raised the wind & sent George the price of 3 copies. Nothing so far.[10]

The enclosed you will probably find merely disagreeably trivial.[11]I see no point in making it less direct or fiddling about with it. It came straight the way it is.

God love thee. Write again soon.

Can you not cut out the Swiss trip & come over.

Ever

Sam

If you see Charles give him my love & tell him I'm writing-[12]

ALS; 3 leaves, 5 sides; TMS enclosure of "Whiting," 1 leaf, 1 side (see n. 11, below); TCD, MS 10402/131. Although ruled out by internal evidence, this enclosure is placed with TCD, MS 10402/113.

1 "De quoi écrire" (the wherewithal to write).

2 Frank Beckett had injured his hand; his wedding was planned for 25 August 1937. Samuel Johnson, *A Journey to the Western Islands of Scotland* (1775).
Paul Valéry, *Introduction to the Method of Leonardo da Vinci*, tr. Thomas McGreevy (London: J. Rodker, 1929).

3 Giovanni Benedetto Castiglione (1609–1664), *Shepherdess Finding the Infant Cyrus* (NGI 994). *Elijah Invoking, by Prayer, the Sacred Fire from Heaven* (NGI 357) was attributed to Castiglione in the 1932 catalogue of the National Gallery of Ireland, but later was given to Giacinto Diano (1731–1804); it was identified from 1956 as *The Dedication of the Temple at Jerusalem* (*National Gallery of Ireland: Catalogue of the Oil Pictures in the General Collection* [1932] 18; Dr. Marie Bourke, Keeper, National Gallery of Ireland, 16 October 1998).

4 Perugino's *Pietà* (NGI 942) had been cleaned and restored in Vienna (see 17 July [1936], n. 6).

SB compares *Portrait of a Man* (NGI 779) by Paris Bordone (1500–1571) to his *Portrait of a Man* in Munich (Alte Pinakothek 512). *St. George and the Dragon* (NGI 779) is attributed to Bordone by the National Gallery of Ireland.

The Virgin and Child Enthroned between Angels (NGI 480) is the larger of the two paintings in the National Gallery of Ireland by Venetian painter Alessandro Oliverio (fl. 1532–1544), it appears under his name in *National Gallery of Ireland: Catalogue of the Oil Pictures in the General Collection* (1932), but thereafter is entitled *Madonna and Child, Enthroned between Angels* and given to the Venetian School (*National Gallery of Ireland: Catalogue of Pictures of the Italian Schools* [Dublin: Stationery Office, (1956)] 75–76).

Saint Bartholomew (NGI 80) and *Saint John the Evangelist* (NGI 78) were attributed to Alessandro Bonvicino Moretto (né c. 1498–1554) in *National Gallery of Ireland: Catalogue of the Oil Pictures in the General Collection* (1932); however, these paintings were later reattributed to Il Talpino (né Enea Salmeggia, c. 1565-1626), School of Bergamo. SB invokes Albrecht Dürer's *St. John and St. Peter* and *St. Paul and St. Mark* in the Alte Pinakothek, Munich (545 and 540).

5 Prior to Furlong's rehanging of the collection, the Dutch paintings had been hung along one wall and the Italian along another in the large hall in the gallery; afterwards, the Italian pictures were shown with greater space, and the Dutch pictures were moved from a suite of well-lit rooms to a section of the basement (Curran, "The National Gallery Revisited," 66).

6 JBY is Jack B. Yeats.

7 SB refers to John Constable, Joseph Turner (1775–1851), Claude Lorrain, and Paul Cézanne.

8 *A Storm / Gallshíon* (Pyle 477, private collection; see Pyle, *Jack B. Yeats: A Catalogue Raisonné of the Oil Paintings*, I, 432).

9 Geoffrey Thompson.

George and Gwynedd Reavey were on their honeymoon on the Continent.

10 In his letter of 7 July [1937] to McGreevy, SB mentioned that he often saw Brian Coffey in the library: "I take him out for a drink or a cup of coffee & he educates me" (TCD, MS 10402/128).

Denis Devlin.

The Assistant State Prosecutor of Washington has not been identified, nor has the poem that Coffey had written that was based on Michel de Montaigne, *The Essays of Montaigne Done into English*, tr. John Florio, 3 vols. (1693). Michel Eyquem de Montaigne (1533–1592); John Florio (1553–1625).

Denis Devlin's collection of poems *Intercessions*: SB to McGreevy, 4 August 1937, n. 6 and n. 7.

11 SB's poem "Whiting" was enclosed but is not reprinted here as it was also enclosed with 14 [August 1937] to Cissie Sinclair (see n. 5 of that letter for the two slight variations between the enclosed texts).

SB told Lawrence Harvey that the poem was stimulated by a sermon given by Canon Henry C. Dobbs, All Saints' Church, Blackrock, which also argues for its composition in August 1937 when SB was in Dublin (Harvey, *Samuel Beckett*, 156).

12 McGreevy planned to leave on 21 August to travel with Hester Dowden by car to Vienna; SB wrote to him on 25 August 1937: "Sat. evening I thought of you setting out

on your journey & wished a different journey for you – A short one, into the west from where you were" (TCD, MS 10402/134).
    Charles Prentice. Placement of postscript: on three lines to right of closing and signature.

THOMAS McGREEVY
EN ROUTE TO MUNICH

19th Aug. [1937]   Foxrock
                                                       [Co. Dublin]

Dear Tom

    The modern pictures are divided between the Neue Staatsgalerie (Königsplatz, opposite the Glyptothek) & the Library of the Deutsches Museum on the Museumsinsel.[1] The former would hardly repay you a visit, being altogether 19th century German, though there are excellent Böcklin's, Hans v. Marées, Leibl's, Trübner's and Schuch's, especially of the last named[,] 3 wonderful still-lifes – Apples, Peonies & Asparagus.[2] But the Deutsches Museum is well worth a visit for the Van Gogh Self-Portrait, the Cézannes & Lautrecs. Also there are Renoirs, Courbets, I think a Matisse still life, & 4 rather dull Maillols.[3] When you enter the Courtyard of the Museum you turn to the left for the library. The pictures, very provisionally hung[,] are on the second floor. To get to the French pictures you walk straight through from the entrance door as far as you can go. They begin on the back wall with I think the Van Goghs. Then you recede back through them towards the entrance door again. Then I think if you are wise you go out, though elsewhere there are (or were, before the latest purge) Münch's [*for* Munch's], Marc's, Kokoschka's, two good Lehmbruck's, Barlach's, & Hodler's including the famous & I think very bad Lebensmüde, really a sentimental version of Dürer's Apostles.[4] So altogether well worth a quick look round, though it is au diable, but not for a moment I think to be preferred to a morning in the Alte Pinakothek.[5]

I had a card from Percy Ussher from Budapest, the Peasant Brueghel <u>Altes Ehepaar</u>.[6] I think he is now in Vienna. I hope the trip rests you. I fear you will be on the strain with Hester & bored with all the driving.

It is a great relief to me that you liked the poem. I had an afternoon with Brian yesterday, & he liked it too. All I knew was that it did not violate my goût as it went down. Of course I can't ventilate it anywhere, except perhaps in <u>Transition</u>.[7]

No more now. Shall write you again to Vienna.

Gute Reise & Viel Vergnügen. Love to Hester.[8]

> Ever
>
> Sam

ALS; 1 leaf, 2 sides; TCD, MS 10402/106. *Dating*: Thomas McGreevy went with Hester Dowden to Vienna: Charles Prentice to McGreevy, 24 August 1937 (TCD, MS 8092/110), and Prentice to McGreevy, 3 September 1937, addressed to Brussels acknowledging McGreevy's letter from Vienna and the news that Hester made the journey without tiring (TCD, MS 8092/111).

1 The configuration of museums in Munich: SB to Thomas McGreevy, 7 March 1937, n. 2.

The collection that SB describes in the Library of the Deutsches Museum on Museum Island was a temporary display since the Deutsches Museum primarily held exhibits of science and technology (see 25 March 1937, n. 7 and n. 8).

2 SB's usage here varies, sometimes showing a painter's pictures with an apostrophe (Leibl's), sometimes without (Cézannes).

Of paintings in the Neue Staatsgalerie by Swiss-German painter Arnold Böcklin (1827–1901), Hans von Marées, Wilhelm Leibl, German painter Wilhelm Trübner (1851–1917), and Viennese painter Carl Schuch (1846–1903), SB specifically mentions Schuch's *Still Life with Apples, Wine Glass, and Pewter Jug* (8563), *Peonies* (8599), and *Still Life with Asparagus* (8907).

3 SB's notes on the paintings that interested him in the Library of the Deutsches Museum (at that time provisionally hung on the second floor) are in his travel diary (BIF, UoR, GD 5/f. 93, 95).

The Cézannes, particularly *The Railway Cutting*, as well as Van Gogh's self-portrait and his other paintings in the collection: 25 March 1937, n. 7.

Of the paintings by French artists Renoir, Jean-Désiré-Gustave Courbet (1819–1877), and Henri Matisse (1869–1954) in the collection, SB specifically mentions Matisse's *Still Life with Geranium* (8669) (BIF, UoR, GD 5/f. 93).

In his diary, SB mentions *Youth* (B. 53), *Flora* (B. 154), *Bust of Madame Maurice Denis* (B. 54), and *Auguste Renoir* (B. 59) by Aristide Maillol, and *Portrait of Georges de Villechenon* (8667) and *In the Loge* (8666) by Toulouse-Lautrec (BIF, UoR, GD 5/f. 95).

4 In his diary, SB mentions Munch's *Peasant with Horse* (9037, removed as "entartet" in 1937; now, private collection) and *Young Woman on the Veranda* (9267; now in private collection); he notes Marc's *Deer in the Reeds* (9598) and *Red Deer II* (8923, removed as "entartet" in 1937; returned to the collection in 1940 and "ordered to be kept under 'lock and key'") (Annegret Hoberg and Isabelle Jansen, *Franz Marc: The Complete Works*, I, *The Oil Paintings* [London: Philip Wilson, 2004] 213; BIF, UoR, GD 5/f. 93).

Paintings by Kokoschka mentioned by SB in his diary were *Venice* (9328) and *Landscape in the Dolomites* (8985; now Leopold Museum, Vienna, no. 624). SB mentions two sculptures by Wilhelm Lehmbruck (1881–1919): *Female Torso* (B 87) and *Large Kneeling Woman* (on loan from Frau Lehmbruck) (Barron, ed., *"Degenerate Art": The Fate of the Avant-Garde in Nazi Germany*, 114, 292).

In his diary, SB refers to an unidentified sculpture of a shepherd, one of many by Ernst Barlach, and Barlach's sculpture *The Death* (B 155) (BIF, UoR, GD 5/f. 93; Carl Dietrich Carls, *Ernst Barlach* [New York: Frederick A. Praeger, 1969] 81, 212).

Of paintings by Ferdinand Hodler (1853–1918), SB writes in his diary particularly about *Die Lebensmüden* (9446) which he compares to Dürer's *Apostles* (see 25 March 1937, n. 9).

5 "Au diable" (miles out).

6 Arland Ussher, who was in Budapest, sent SB a card of *An Old Couple* (now *Peasants with a Pitcher*, Galerie Alter Meister, Budapest, 559); it was originally thought to be by Pieter Bruegel (here called not "the elder," but "the Peasant" to distinguish him from his sons), whose name is inscribed on the painting ("Petrvs Brvegel F."), but it is now attributed to "a Flemish or German Master, second half of the 16th century" (Ildikó Ember, Zsuzsa Urbach, and Annamária Gosztola, *Old Masters' Gallery: Summary Catalogue, Museum of Fine Arts, Budapest*, II, *Early Netherlandish, Dutch and Flemish Paintings* [Budapest: Szépművészeti Múzeum, 2000] 69).

7 SB showed Brian Coffey the poem then called "Whiting."
"Goût" (taste).

8 "Gute Reise & viel Vergnügen" (Have a good trip and much fun).

MARY MANNING HOWE

BUFFALO, NEW YORK

30th Aug. 1937   Cooldrinagh,
                                        Foxrock,
                                        Co. Dublin

Dear Mary

500 thanks for your note. And photographs. You look pétillante. And Susan beyond good & evil.[1]

No I have heard nothing from Doubledeal Doran. Reavey has been treacle mooning all over the Mediterranean with his new Welsch vase.[2] Supremely happy. They are all supremely happy. Can it be the free coition, do you think?

It gave me great pleasure to hear that I had a German girl. Do you think you could get me her name & address? Their conduct of the fore-period is unique.

I have no news at all likely to interest you. Percy is in Vienna. McGreevy in Buda Pest. The Sinclairs on their way to South Africa. Leventhal not seen (by me) for months. (He has been made editor of Hermathena!). Jack Yeats do [*for* ditto].[3] I do nothing, with as little shame as satisfaction. It is the state that suits me best. I write the odd poem when it is there, that is the only thing worth doing. There is an ecstasy of accidia – willless in a grey tumult of idées obscures.[4] There is an end to the temptation of light, its polite scorchings & consolations. It is good for children & insects. There is an end of making up one[']s mind, like a pound of tea, an end of patting the butter of consciousness into opinions. The real consciousness is the chaos, a grey commotion of mind, with no premises or conclusions or problems or solutions or cases or judgments. I lie for days on the floor, or in the woods, accompanied & unaccompanied, in a coenaesthesia of mind, a fullness of mental self-aesthesia that is entirely useless. The monad without the conflict, lightless & darkless. I used to pretend to work, I do so no longer. I used to dig about in the mental sand for the lugworms of likes & dislikes, I do so no longer. The lugworms of understanding.

Do not envy me, do not pity me.

I saw the Gilmores twice. Was at a party there one night. Arrived with Sean O'Sullivan, full of whiskey. All the usual, general bathe in pool towards morning. Then went one afternoon alone and drove them into town. The Reddins were invited to the party but Kenneth wouldn't go & wouldn't let Norah go.[5]

The Gilmores are on the right track. After a bit one wouldn't mind the filth & discomfort. One would want less & less. That is the right direction.

Had a couple of mildly amusing evenings with Sean & 2 American women from N.Y. City, foreskin hats, cellophane slickers & hard heads.[6] Nothing had even been there. American girls are irresistible, the charm of the inorganic.

I applied for the job at Cape Town & won't hear I suppose till late Autumn. I hear your Buffalo Bill has been & gone.[7]

Many pains are better than one.

    Love

      Sam

ALS; 2 leaves, 3 sides; *letterhead*; TxU.

1 Mary Manning Howe and her infant daughter Susan. "Pétillante" (sparkling).

2 SB refers to New York publishers Doubleday Doran, who had been considering the manuscript of *Murphy*.
George and Gwynedd Reavey were on their honeymoon.

3 A. J. Leventhal was not appointed Assistant Editor of the Trinity College Dublin review *Hermathena: A Series of Papers on Literature, Science and Philosophy by Members of Trinity College, Dublin* until 1957; in June 1937, William Alexander Goligher was named Editor of *Hermathena* (Eileen Kelly, TCD, 17 August 2005).

4 "Accidia" (It., torpor, sloth). "Idées obscures" (obscure ideas).

5 Charlie Gilmore and Lilian Donaghy lived together in the cottage of Joe Campbell in Co. Wicklow (see 7 July 1936, n. 9). SB described the evening in a letter to Thomas McGreevy, 23 August 1937: "I borrow & go on the blind. The last was last Saturday at a party in the Glencree valley. The Gilmores – Charlie & Lilian once Donaghy. I lost my lovely hat, my watch & half a bottle [of] J.J. And cut my head bathing in [4]0 foot at 2 a.m." (TCD, MS 10402/133; left side of page torn).
Kenneth Reddin (see 7 August 1936, n. 8, and 13 April 1937, n. 1) and Norah Reddin (née Ringwood, n.d.).

6 Seán O'Sullivan; the two women from New York have not been identified.

7 In his letter to Thomas McGreevy, 25 August 1937, SB had written: "I had a brief &
formal acknowledgement of application from Cape Town. How I dread getting that
job" (TCD, MS 10402/134).

   SB's allusion to the showman of the Wild West, William F. Cody (known as Buffalo
Bill, 1846–1917), probably points to the Chairman of the English department of the
University of Buffalo: SB to Thomas McGreevy, 4 August 1937, n. 8.

THOMAS McGREEVY

LONDON

Sep. 21st [1937]   Cooldrinagh

[Foxrock, Co. Dublin]

Dear Tom

   Thanks for your letter. I was laid up for about 10 days with
gastric flu (so called) and it is only in these last few days that I
feel up to even my poor normal level of energy again. The first
day I went out in the car I collided with a lorry. My car is finished
but I myself was not hurt. As I have only the compulsory minimum 3rd party insurance my only chance of compensation is to
claim off the other people, where I think my chance of succeed-
ing is very small. I was tired of the car anyway & meant to give it
up & buy a bike.

   Frank & wife got back from honeymoon last week. He
seems to have stood the course very well. At present they are
living at Cooldrinagh, as the house in Killiney will not be
evacuated till Oct. 1st. I was glad to hear he had sent you a card
from Scotland.[1] There is something rueful about him and a never-
to-be-spoken, but if it only depends on him it will work out. He
has plenty of practice in the matter of humouring the woman.

   I ran into Raven yesterday in Leinster Street.[2] I had not
known he was over. We had a quick cup of coffee. I wanted
him to lunch with me to-day but he rang up this morning to

say he couldn't manage it. He was very nice and I think sorry that we had not a little more time together. Someone had told him I was away or inaccessible...

Denis's poems came. There are lovely fragments, like the last stanza of the Statue & Perturbed Burghers, & here & there in the Eiffel Tower one, but I feel them adventitious and am on the whole rather disappointed. The few lines that I quoted in the Bookman article remain I think as good as anything in the book. The Bacchanal I find very very bad, the worst kind of Whitman-Kipling-aling piétinement sur place. As for the images, they seem to be not so much uncontrolled as cut adrift from the imaged altogether, doing a kind of Gymkana [*for* Gymkhana] all on their own. If it was deliberate it wouldn't matter. But the process is obviously one of working up the perceived, when it is not a screen for the failure to perceive, according to the usual mechanism. Because it seems an altogether perceptive, sensuous, instinctive & immediate talent, not at all conceptive or even meditative. When he gets metaphysical it is awful. Brian says he can't observe accurately & perhaps he can't. I don't think it matters. Perception is one thing & observation another. The stanza I mention is material exquisitely perceived, and I think the only image is in the first line, & it a mild one. I got the book for review from S. O'S. and shall not bother very much about the aspects of it that I can't commend. But I would rather not have to write about it at all. When I last saw Sheehy it was understood that you were doing it for Ireland ToDay.[3]

Higgins, because he is going to USA with the Abbey, gave his evidence for St. J. G. on commission. I have not yet seen the verbatim report but by all accounts it was sublime, the high point being reached when he described the verses complained of and others not yet complained of as <u>Folklore</u>! Pokornography! The hearing proper is not expected to come on before November.[4] If I get the job in Cape Town, & having got it accept it, two conditions unlikely to be satisfied, I shall go straight to Italy, and could if necessary give my evidence for Harry on commission also. But I hope it will not come to this. Bad witness & all as no doubt I am, I think I could be of more use to him in the box.

Brian is in Sligo with father & sister, returns on Thursday for a day or two, & then goes to Antrim with his sister. I had a long letter from him yesterday, with all the pros & cons for Denis alphaed betaed gammaed & deltaed. To-day a letter from Charles, saying your trip had done you good.[5] He keeps remarkably cheerful.

When I was ill I found the only thing I could read was Schopenhauer.[6] Everything else I tried only confirmed the feeling of sickness. It was very curious. Like suddenly a window opened on a fug. I always knew he was one of the ones that mattered most to me, and it is a pleasure more real than any pleasure for a long time to begin to understand now why it is so. And it is a pleasure also to find a philosopher that can be read like a poet, with an entire indifference to the apriori forms of verification. Although it is a fact that judged by them his generalisation shows fewer cracks than most generalisations.

Mother's plan of letting Cooldrinagh for a long period is temporarily off. She discovered that one of the tenants was tubercular. But I think we shall persuade her simply to go away for a holiday, perhaps to friends in London. I would probably remain on in Cooldrinagh with the cook & the dog.

No news from Cissie Sinclair since the P.C. from Cape Town. No sign from Reavey either. I was pleased that Denis & Brian liked Murphy.[7] I think it was perfectly genuine in each case. I still feel absurdly easy in my mind about its being published sooner or later, and to my surprise still anxious that it should be.

God love thee. Write soon again.

Ever

Sam

ALS; 2 leaves; 8 sides; TCD, MS 10402/136. *Dating*: A "37" is added in AH; Frank Beckett back from his honeymoon; F. R. Higgins's "verbatim" taken on 13 and 14 September 1937.

1 Frank and Jean Beckett had bought a house in Killiney.

2 Thomas Holmes Ravenhill.

3 In his review of Denis Devlin's *Intercessions*, SB makes particular reference to the final stanza of "The Statue & Perturbed Burghers," "Communication from the Eiffel Tower," and "Bacchanal" (*Intercessions*, 13-14, 32-47, 26).
   Walt Whitman (1819-1892) and Rudyard Kipling.
   "Piétinement sur place" (marking time).
   Brian Coffey.
   SB had quoted the third stanza of Devlin's poem "Est Prodest" (lines 51-57) in his essay "Recent Irish Poetry," 236; its first line is "Phrases twisted through other" (Devlin, *Intercessions*, 52).
   Edward Sheehy was on the staff of *Ireland To-Day* (see 26 April 1937, n. 12).

4 F. R. Higgins, Director of the Abbey Theatre, gave his testimony in the Sinclair vs. Gogarty and Cowan Rich suit on commission of Henry J. Moloney at the offices of Arthur Cox, Solicitor, 42 St. Stephen's Green, Dublin, on 13 and 14 September 1937. Portions of this testimony were presented at the trial, including reference to the verses that Higgins regarded "simply as folklore" ("£900 Damages Awarded in Libel Action," *The Irish Times* 24 November 1937: 5).

5 Charles Prentice.

6 It is not known what work(s) by Arthur Schopenhauer SB read at this time.

7 SB had received a postcard from Cissie Sinclair from Cape Town.
   The last communication from Reavey was before 4 September 1937; SB wrote to McGreevy on 4 September 1937, that "Doubledeal Doran had turned down the book . . 'the long metaphysical disquisitions, plainly of the Joycean school, hardly well enough done to justify the obvious objections, etc. etc.' whatever that means! The book is now with Faber" (TCD, MS 10402/135).
   Brian Coffey and SB had had "lunch the day before he left [for Sligo]. I had given him Murphy to read and he was I think quite genuinely enthusiastic" (SB to McGreevy, 4 September 1937 (TCD, MS 10402/135). SB had also given the book to Denis Devlin.

THOMAS McGREEVY
LONDON

Oct. 6th 1937   Cooldrinagh

Dear Tom

Thanks for your letter this morning. Frank will have his to-day also.

I have been sleeping here since Mother left. I do not know where she is or how long she will be away and Frank either has no definite news either or instructions to keep it to himself. I have been going through my papers & trying to get my books into some kind of order. At first I had intended to move every-thing to neutral territory but have now the kind permission to lock my study door & give Frank the key. So I am saved a lot of trouble.

Instead of creeping about with the agenbite, as I suppose I ought, I am marvelling at the pleasantness of Cooldrinagh with-out her. And I could not wish her anything better than to feel the same when I am away. But I don't wish her anything at all, neither good nor ill. I am what her savage loving has made me, and it is good that one of us should accept that finally. As it has been all this time, she wanting me to behave in a way agreeable to her in her October of analphabetic gentility, or to her friends ditto, or to the business code of father idealised – dehumanised – ("When ever in doubt what [to] do, ask yourself what would darling Bill have done") – the grotesque can go no further. It is like after a long forenoon of the thumb screws being com-manded by the bourreau to play his favourite song without words with feeling.[1] I simply don't want to see her or write to her or hear from her. And as for the peace in the heart and all the other milk puddings that the sun is said to set on so much better, they will never be there anyway, least of all as the fruit of formal reconciliation. There are the grey hairs that will go down in sorrow, that want to go down in sorrow, as they came up in sorrow, because they are that kind. And if a telegram came now to say she was dead, I would not do the Furies the favour of regarding myself even as indirectly responsible.

Which I suppose all boils down to saying what a bad son I am. Then Amen. It is a title for me of as little honour as infamy. Like describing a tree as a bad shadow.

If she does not return home before, I shall leave for London probably next Monday. I cannot make up my mind what to do about a room. G. R. has written inviting me to stay for a few days with him until I find somewhere. I might do that & go on then to Paris. Money will be very knapp. No more charity of supererogation. God knows I don't want to stay with anyone. Least of all with the Welchess.[2]

I like your review in Ireland Today very much, and was very pleased with what you quoted. I had the last son banging the door marked myself. I should think Denis wont be too delighted with the Fioretti, but haven't seen him to hear what he says. Brian was indignant that you weren't given more space.[3] Sheehy is clamouring for something, so I shall send him Whiting![4]

I spent most of last Monday at Shankhill Courthouse, waiting for my case to come on. I defended myself, to Mr D-J Reddin, and was fined £1 and 5/- costs, which makes it almost certain that I won't get any compensation from the other insurance company. Reddin delivered a homily to the assembly of Guards and felons in much the following terms: "Mr B. is one of the most distinguished of Irish writers. It would be a pity if his services were ended prematurely. Hum. Literature has also its corners. These he has tamed so far with – er – finesse. Of his driving I am not so sure. Etc."[5] Brian came down & stayed with me throughout, with a Raymond Roussel under his oxter. We are walking over the mountains this afternoon. I suppose you saw about the appointment of his father to the Censorship Committee.[6]

Francis Stewart [for Stuart], staying at the Dolphin, invited me to dine last Monday. He is researching in the Library for a novel about 18th century Ireland. He is a dull man. Goes about with Lady Glenavy, in the room of the Swedish Consul Erickssen [for Eriksson], now departed.[7]

The Gogarty thing cant come on before November, & I shall have to come back for that. I hear he is negotiating with the R.H.A. who want to buy his house & garden for their new premises. Harry is in difficulties.[8]

I had a letter from Cissie from S. A., telling me nothing of what I wanted to hear, i.e. how she was & how Sonny was.[9] Her description of Cape Town, with the University up in the hills surrounded by woods, was more encouraging than not.

I hear Leventhal has got some newly created job in TCD as "General Secretary" and has left Mary Street & is a new man. I have not had the good fortune to see him for some months.[10]

I shall let you know when I arrive in good time if I can. Though it may turn out to be a sudden last minute departure, in which case I would ring you up at Harrington Road on arrival. I am not sure if I have a note of your number. Would you drop me a card and let me have it?[11]

A bientôt.

Sam

ALS; 2 leaves, 4 sides; AN AH: *top margin of leaf 2, side 3*: <third, fourth & fifth coats, 5 3/4 lbs white lead @ 5d.>; TCD, MS 10402/139.

1 "Bourreau" (torturer).

2 The following Monday was 11 October. The "Welchess" is Gwynedd, wife of George Reavey.
"Knapp" (tight, short).

3 In his review of Denis Devlin's *Intercessions*, McGreevy quoted from Devlin's poem, "Communication from the Eiffel Tower": " . . . uncertain / Like a mother covering her ears / When the last son slams the door and she cowers from its echoes / I am made to speak " (*Intercessions*, 47).
McGreevy compared Devlin's poetry to *Fioretti di San Francesco d'Assisi*, (*Little Flowers of St. Francis Assisi*), a popular collection of legends regarding the life of St. Francis of Assisi, gathered anonymously before the end of the fourteenth century (Thomas McGreevy, "New Dublin Poetry," *Ireland To-Day* 2.10 [October 1937] 81–82).

4 It is not known if SB did indeed submit "Whiting" to Edward Sheehy for *Ireland To-Day*; it was not published there.

5 District Justice Kenneth Reddin. SB wrote to McGreevy on 28 September 1937:

> I am being persecuted by the Civic Guards for dangerous driving, in connection with the accident last Saturday week [18 September], & in my opinion so unjustifiably that I intend to go to the court next Monday [4 October] and fight them every inch of the way. I know this will mean my being fined twice as much as I would be if I went down on my knees & apologised. Tant pis. There is no animal I loathe more profoundly than a Civic Guard, a symbol of Ireland with his official Gaelic loutish complacency & pot-walloping Schreinlichkeit, & if I can insert even a fraction of this feeling into the gloved skull of Mr D.-J. Reddin before leaving this whoreless kip of a country I shall gladly pay an extra pound for the pleasure. If it were not for this next Monday I should probably be in London before the end of the week. (TCD, MS 10402/137)

"Tant pis" (too bad).
"Schreinlichkeit" (a neologism based on Ger., chest-ishness).

6 Brian Coffey was carrying a book by French writer Raymond Roussel (1877–1933). His father Dr. Denis J. Coffey was appointed to the Censorship of Publications Board at the end of September 1937 ("University Notes, Dr. Coffey's New Appointment, New Medical Societies Association," *The Irish Times* 4 October 1937: 4).

7 Francis Stuart was doing research for his novel *The Great Squire* (1939).
Beatrice Campbell (Mrs. Gordon), Lady Glenavy (née Elvery, 1881–1970). Harry Eriksson (1892–1957), Swedish Consul in Dublin from 1930 to 1 July 1937; his rooms were at 17 Fitzwilliam Square (Gören Rydebert, Head of Archives of the Foreign Ministry, Stockholm).

8 The trial regarding libel charges against Oliver St. John Gogarty's *As I Was Going Down Sackville Street* did not take place until the end of November.
In 1939 the Royal Hibernian Association purchased Gogarty's house, 15 Ely Place, and what was once George Moore's garden.
Harry Sinclair, plaintiff in the proceedings pending against Gogarty.

9 Cissie Sinclair was visiting her son Morris, who was tutoring for the Watermeyer family in Graaff Reinet, South Africa.

10   A. J. Leventhal had left Atlas Furnishing Company at 56–58 Mary Street, Dublin, a firm owned by his father-in-law, Joseph Zlotover (also known as Goldman, c. 1858–1938), and taken up an appointment as Secretary to the Registrar and Secretary to the Appointments Committee at Trinity College Dublin.

11   "Thomas McGreevy was living at 49 Harrington Rd., London SW7.

THOMAS McGREEVY

LONDON

Wednesday evg. [27 October 1937]   Chez Sarrazin

12 Rue de la Gde.

Chaumière

Paris VI$^{\underline{me}}$

[no greeting]

A room at 16 francs here seems the best I can do. I don't see myself lasting a week at the prices. Just had entrecôte & cheese & 1/2 carafe rosé at the Ste. Cécile – 19.75![1]

Excellent journey, very few travelling & brilliant sunshine soon after leaving the drizzle at Newhaven. No sign of Brian at the train.[2] Perhaps he is not here at all. Shall ring up his hotel tomorrow.

God love thee

Sam.

APCS; 1 leaf, 1 side; *to* Thomas McGreevy Esq, 49 Harrington Road, London S.W. 7; *pm* 27-10-37, Paris; TCD, MS 10402/141. *Dating*: from pm; 27 October 1937 fell on Wednesday.

1   SB had traveled from Dublin on Saturday night of 16 October arriving in London mid-day on 17 October (SB to McGreevy, [14 October 1937], TCD, MS 10402/140). SB wrote from Paris on 27 October 1937 to Reavey: "I tried Raspail, de la Paix & Libéria, and then collapsed into a 16 francs cabinet de malaisance here" (TxU). The Sarrazin was across the street from the Libéria, 9 Rue de la Grande Chaumière.

"Cabinet de malaisance" (conflation of a French term for lavatory, "cabinet d'aisance" [ease] with "malaise" [un-ease]).

The café or restaurant Ste. Cécile has not been identified.

2 Brian Coffey.
SB took the ferry from Newhaven to Dieppe, France, then traveled by train to Paris.

THOMAS McGREEVY
DUBLIN

[? 3 November 1937]   Chez Sarrazin
                             12 Rue de la Gde. Chaumière
                             Paris VI$^{\underline{me}}$

Dear Tom

Your letter this morning. Whenever it is you come, I hope we do not cross. I had a wire from Harry yesterday: "Case likely heard next week", which is horribly unsatisfactory. I have written to him now that I shall not leave for Dublin, whether from here or from London, until I get a definite summons from him. Surely he will know the precise date of hearing at least 3 or 4 days in advance, which would enable me to arrive in time.[1]

It is very kind of you to suggest my occupying your room in your absence & I may be very glad to do so. My cousin in Surrey (where my mother stayed when in London) wrote inviting me for a few days, and I would rather accept this than have you pay for me at 49. Then there is also the Reaveys.[2] Certainly it will be a question of living for next to nothing until the end of this month.

I ran into Thomas yesterday outside the Dome. He is now Maître de Conférences à la Faculté des Lettres de l'Université de Poitiers, but seems to live at least half the time in Paris. He asked about you very affectionately and for your address. As he said he was writing I shall not bother giving you his Paris address now. He is not to be back until next Tuesday so I shall hardly seem [*for* see] him again this trip. He was looking just the same, rather healthier than I remember him.³ He told me Péron had been appointed to a lycée here and that I would get his address from Baillou, the new secretary to the Ecole. Which I did, and called on him yesterday. It went very well. He has taken Pelorson's job at the Jolas's school in Neuilly. It was a real pleasure to be with him again. I dine with him Friday.

This morning I rang up Pelorson at Paris Midi and am meeting him this afternoon.⁴ I have decided also to try & get in touch with Joyce.

This evening I am invited with Brian & the Duncans to dine with Nick & Nina.⁵

I was at the Louvre yesterday, par un temps radieux, looking at the French primitives & the Fontainebleauistes. I had forgotten how lovely the Pietà d'Avignon was.⁶

At the very latest, & assuming I hear nothing from Harry in the meantime, I shall be back in London Wednesday morning, but more probably Tuesday morning. Please God you will be still there then.

        Love ever

        Sam

ALS; 1 leaf, 2 sides; *date added in AH,* 3-11-37; TCD, MS 10402/144. *Dating:* SB sent McGreevy a postcard from Paris on 30 October 1937; SB was in London on 10 November 1937 (card from SB to Harry Sinclair, postmarked from London 10 November 1937 [Gidal]). Even when in London SB was without definite plans for travel to Dublin.

SB stayed at the Sarrazin in Paris before returning to Dublin for the trial, and at the Hotel Libéria when he returned to Paris after the trial (see SB to George Reavey, 3 November 1937 [*for* 3 December 1937]).

1 The wire from Harry Sinclair, which has not been found, was sent after 30 October and by Sunday, 7 November 1937. In an undated letter [c. 3 November 1937] to Harry Sinclair, SB wrote from Paris:

    Received your wire yesterday. [...] I shall not leave till Monday evening unless I get a definite summons from you before then. That would not get me to Dublin till the Wednesday morning, as I should have to stop in London to collect the price of my ticket the rest of the way.

At the very latest, suppposing I hear nothing from you in the meantime, I shall be back in London next Wednesday. So it is better that you should address any letter or wire that cannot reach Paris before Monday evening to 49 Harrington Rd., S. W. 7, as before, where even if I do not stay I shall call & collect post. (NNC, RBML, Sighle Kennedy Papers)

On that Wednesday, SB wrote to Harry Sinclair from London (see 10 November 1937).

2 McGreevy had plans to be in Paris and had offered SB his room at 49 Harrington Road, London.

SB's cousin, Sheila Page.

3 Jean Thomas, having been Chargé d'enseignement complémentaire de langue et littérature françaises à la Sorbonne, 1934–1936, now had a new position at the universities of Poitiers and Lyon (1936–1944). The Café du Dôme, 108, Boulevard Montparnasse.

4 Jean Baillou (1905–1990) was Surveillant général of the Ecole Normale Supérieure in 1936, when the title of that position was changed to Secrétaire général (Pierre Jeannin, *Deux siècles à Normale Sup: petite histoire d'une Grande Ecole* [Paris: Larousse, 1994] 213).

Péron was appointed to the Lycée Buffon, Boulevard Pasteur, in 1936; while he may have taught as a substitute for a time at the Ecole bilingue de Neuilly begun by Maria Jolas, there is no documentation of this (Betsy Jolas, Alexis Péron). Georges Pelorson was Directeur des Etudes from 1936 until 1939; he also worked for *Paris-Midi* (1932–1940).

5 Brian Coffey; Alan and Belinda Duncan. The Russian friends of the Duncans, Nick (d. 1939) and Nina Balachef, have not been identified.

6 "Par un temps radieux" (in glorious weather).

By "French primitives," SB refers to artists who were active in France during the fourteenth and fifteenth centuries: Netherlandish painter Henri Bellechose (fl. 1415, d. c. 1445); the North Netherlandish illuminators, Pol de Limbourg (c. 1375 – c. 1415), Herman de Limbourg (c. 1385 – c. 1416), and Jean de Limbourg (d. before 1439), who were known for their work on the "Belles Heures" and the "Très Riches Heures" for Jean, Duc de Berry; French painter and illuminator Jean Fouquet; and the Avignon painter Enguerrand Quarton (c. 1420–1466). For their styles: Léon-Honoré Labande, *Les Primitifs français: Peintres et peintres-verriers de la Provence occidentale* [Marseille: Librairie Tacussel, 1932]).

SB comments on Quarton's painting *La Pietà de Villeneuve-lès-Avignon* (Louvre R. F. 156).

SB probably refers to the painters of the first School of Fontainebleau (1530s to early 1600s in France), which included the director of the workshops of Fontainebleau (c. 1533-1540), Italian fresco and decorative stucco artist Rosso Fiorentino (1494-1540); his successor Francesco Primaticcio (c. 1504-1570); Nicolò dell'Abate (c. 1509 – c. 1571); Antonio Fantuzzi (c. 1508 – c. 1550); Jean Cousin the elder (c. 1500 – c. 1560) and his son Jean Cousin the younger (c. 1525 – c. 1595); François Clouet (c. 1516-1572); Antoine Caron (1521-1599).

HENRY M. SINCLAIR

DUBLIN

[10 November 1937]   49 Harrington Rd
                                                London SW 7

[no greeting]

Got your letter on arrival this morning. Shall not leave till I get a definite summons from you. In case you want to phone you can get me at Kensington 7325 any morning up to 11 a.m. Glad you are pleased with the way things are going[.][1]

A bientôt

Sam

APCS; 1 leaf, 1 side; "Blackfriars Bridge"; *to* Henry M. Sinclair Esq, c/o Jammet's Restaurant, Nassau Street, Dublin, I.F.S.; *pm* 10-11-37, London; Gidal. *Dating*: from pm. *Previous publication*: Index Books, catalogue no. 6 (September 2003), facsimile on back cover.

1 SB was waiting to learn when the libel trial against Gogarty would begin. A subpoena to those giving testimony, among them SB, was issued on 12 November 1937; the trial was held from 22 to 24 November.

GEORGE REAVEY

LONDON

3/11/37 [*for* 3 December 1937]   Hotel Libéria
                                   Rue de la Gde. Chaumière
                                   [Paris] 6$^{\underline{me}}$

Dear George

I expect to be here for at least 10 days or a fortnight & possibly till after Xmas. So will you forward any thing that comes for me to here.[1]

I have not seen Jolas but learn that he is putting the Denis review in the coming number. I shall ask him has he any objection to your reprinting it when I see him. I gave it to Brian to read & told him to send it on to you.[2]

Expect to see V. Velde to-morrow morning when I shall give him the colours.[3]

Love to Gwynedd & again thanks.

    Yrs

      Sam

Hope your cold is better.[4]

APCS; 1 leaf, 2 sides; *to* George Reavey Esq, 7 Great Ormond Street, London W.C. 1; *pm* 3-12-37, Paris; TxU. *Dating:* SB dates 3/11/37, but pm is 3-12-37.

1 SB stayed with the Reaveys in London on his way back to Paris following the Gogarty libel trial in Dublin.

2 Eugene Jolas.
SB refers to his review, "Denis Devlin," forthcoming in *transition*, which he had given to Brian Coffey.

3 Writing from Paris on 2 November 1937 to Gwynedd, George Reavey reported that "Poor Van Velde has not got any paints at the moment, and is feeling rather miserable" (TxU). The Reaveys had asked SB to take a gift of paints to the Dutch painter Gerardus van Velde (known as Geer, 1898–1977).

4 Added, to the right of the greeting.

THOMAS McGREEVY

LONDON

3/11/37 [*for* 3 December 1937]   Hotel Liberia

                                Rue de la Gde. Chaumière

                                [Paris] 6$^{\underline{me}}$

Dear Tom

The crossing was very bad until 3/4 of the way across. I had to stay out in the wind, rain & spray in order not to be sick. Alan Belinda & Brian met me at the station. Brian had been able to get your room at the Libéria. It is certainly luxury after Sarrazin. We dined together at the Franco Italien. Brian miserable with incipient quinsy & the bordel international and vaguely cooing with Belinda & Alan doing the poor putupon and having visions of the Flore. I felt sadly remote, as I so often have before in the same company. And felt that whatever else Paris might be it was not that & will not be that. There is something in Belinda especially that fills me with scoram, the false calm & the tiny wisdoms, Olympian rabbit at burrow-mouth. Especially when Brian is there adoring from the midst of his torments.[1]

I rang up Shem now and was engaged by Norah [*for* Nora] while he finished his shave. She said she found you changed, but not how. Also that Jolas was putting in the Denis review. It suddenly occurs to me that it will damage him in Ireland, to be reviewed by me in Transition. But can anything damage him to the same extent as not to be damaged in Ireland? I dine with them this evening.[2]

I have been thinking a lot about you and practically made up my mind to go & see Laugier.[3] If he sends me off with a flea in my ear it won't be the first time. Even if you have your big toe in in [sic] London, what is it into? However I shall leave it to next week in case you have anything to say about it.

Belinda had no suggestions about a room. But perhaps Pelorson or Péron will. In the meantime I enquired the monthly price at the Libéria, & for 16 it is 480 fr. which is only a reduction of 2 fr per diem, and 10% service là-dessus. Already I have spent over 100 fr. So I shall go on from day to day at the Libéria jusqu'à nouvel ordre.[4] I think it would be better for you to forward post to there rather than to Brian. He is going home for Xmas -

Would you send your street map of Paris also? Mine is packed with my books waiting to be sent on, & God knows when that will be. I feel I could work but the unsettledness makes it difficult.

A carte d'identité valid for 3 years cost 200 fr. plus papier timbré plus 5 photographs.[5] Perhaps by the spring I shall be in a place of my own & clear of debt & with my papers in order.

The sense for the first time for months of no more forced moves, of the streets & houses & air not impregnated with farewell – But I suppose one never knows.

      Ever affectionately

        Sam

Grüsse to Hester & Raven[6]

ALS; 1 leaf, 4 sides; TCD, MS 10402/143. *Dating*: the date as written is orthographically similar to the card sent to George Reavey that is postmarked 3 December 1937. TM was in Paris in mid or late November.

1 Brian Coffey and Alan and Belinda Duncan. Coffey had booked the room at the Hôtel Libéria for McGreevy's November visit to Paris. There were several restaurants named the Franco-Italien (151 Rue Montmartre, Passage Panoramas, and 5 Avenue Matignon).

Coffey was living in the Collège Franco-Britannique, of the Cité Internationale Universitaire de Paris, a residential complex for foreign students, 9 Boulevard Jourdan, Paris 14.

"Bordel" (literally, brothel; here, awful mess).

Café de Flore, 172 Boulevard St. Germain, Paris.

In his autobiography, Georges [Pelorson] Belmont describes Belinda Duncan as having "beauté minuscule, d'une fragilité dissimulant une armature d'acier,... une douceur et un silence de velours d'où pouvaient jaillir sans crier gare, selon l'interlocuteur, soit les griffes de vérités redoutables, soit les énormités de la plus onctueuse obscénité" (tiny beauty, with a fragility that masks a steel-hard frame... a velvety sweetness and silence out of which, with no warning, might spring, depending on who was being addressed, either the claws of redoubtable truths, or the enormities of the smoothest obscenity) (Belmont, *Souvenirs d'outre-monde*, 367).

"Scoram" (It., from "scoramento," downheartedness).

2 James and Nora Joyce. Denis Devlin: see 3 November 1937 [for 3 December 1937] to George Reavey, n. 2. SB regularly writes "Norah" for Nora Joyce.

3 McGreevy's friend Henri Laugier was a member of the Cabinet of the Foreign Affairs Ministry, under Yvon Delbos (1885–1956), Minister of Foreign Affairs from 1936 to 1938. In this capacity Laugier was aware of government subventions for foreigners in France who would promote awareness abroad of French cultural affairs. SB thought of approaching Laugier to arrange such an opportunity for McGreevy.

4 "Là-dessus" (on top). "Jusqu'à nouvel ordre" (until further notice).

5 Foreigners wishing to remain in France longer than four months were required to obtain a "carte d'identité" (identity card); "papier timbré" (stamped paper).

6 "Grüsse" (greetings).

GEORGE REAVEY
LONDON

[10 December 1937]   Hôtel Libéria
                                                      [Paris]

Mes enfants!
Que le Dieu des blasphémateurs vous bénisse, en attendant que le blasphémateur des Dieux vous régale.[1]
     S.

APCI; 1 leaf, 2 sides; *to* Mr & Mrs George Reavey, 7 Great Ormond Street, LONDON WC1; *pm* 10-12-37, Paris; TxU. *Dating and place*: from pm.

                                                      Hôtel Libéria
                                                      [Paris]

My children!
May the God of blasphemers bless you, until such time as the blasphemer of the Gods can treat you royally![1]

1 SB responds to Reavey's telegram of 9 December 1937, which has not been found, announcing that the London publisher Routledge have accepted *Murphy*.

THOMAS McGREEVY
LONDON

10/12/37   H[ô]tel Libéria
                                                      Rue de la Gde Chaumière
                                                      [Paris] 6me

Dear Tom

Thanks for your long letter. I haven't seen any of the people so far. Do you mean that you definitely turn down Laugier's suggestion that you should write articles on French subjects for English consumption? Even if the "probationary" period were extended to say 3 months? I can't help thinking you would be wrong. At least it would get you here & enable you to look round for a gallery job. If I did go to see Laugier I would have to be in a position to say whether or not you were prepared to accept the kind of work he suggests.[1]

So far I have found nothing, after a lot of wearisome traipsing in the quarter. I finally abonnéd myself to P.O.P. (Public Offices Parisiens), 35 fr., and went through some of their addresses to-day. As far as I can see it is quite impossible to find even a single room of the kind I want, that is with heating and running water, for less than 4500 per an. unfurnished. At least so it appears from the POP lists.[2] This is just twice what I expected. I see myself stuck here till the middle of January at least.

For the past 3 days I have been working with Giorgio at his place in Villa Scheffer on the galleys of Parts I & III of Work in P. I shall be paid, how much I don't know. It is stupefying work & there remains a great deal to be done. When Shem suggested my doing it on the phone he was very tentative, as though very well aware of the attitude. I had already told Helen & Giorgio that the NRF article was my parting kick to criticism.[3] It goes slowly. I met Petitjean again and was confirmed in my impression of him as a rather tedious young man.[4]

I saw the Jolases one evening at the Grande Taverne. The proof of Denis Devlin arrived this morning, every second word a mistake.[5]

Haven't seen Alan or Belinda since the night I arrived. Si, Alan alone once. Apparently Nick is ill with gastric ulcers – and that, as Brian says.[6] He seems quite miserable, drifts in here sometimes and we eat or play billiards. He is very nice alone.

Harry Sinclair wrote that as I was subpoenaed in Dublin and got my 5/- there, there would be no claim for expenses off costs, but that he personally would see, when he cashed in, if he ever did, that I was not out of pocket. I replied saying I would not take anything under these circumstances. Roture oblige. He also asked would Joyce give evidence for him in London![7]

Péron quite miserable too. Pelorson too busy to think. I dined one night with him & Marcelle Chez Pierre. He collapses into blankness after an hour or so, unless the conversation remains concrete: Volonté[s] may be out Wednesday.[8]

No news at all from home. I wrote to Frank apologising for having caused him distress in Dublin & repeating my readiness to write to mother whenever he wanted, but he did not reply.[9]

I have been paralysed in listlessness & done nothing. There is a Picabia exhibition & a Lhote, but I haven't looked at a picture except my own, which stood the journey successfully. Van Velde was enthusiastic about the Yeats. He is very sympathetic to me, but you would not care for him I think.[10]

Passed Thomas one night coming out of Nègre de Toulouse. I was with Georges & Marcelle. He snatched off his hat, said "Tiens! Bonsoir" & hastened on.[11]

Used the Ecole Library once. Meuvray [for Meuvret] extended the top joint of his little finger. Etard was off for the day.[12]

When I got back late last night found a wire from George that Murphy has been taken by Routledge. Haven't heard any details yet. No jubilation, but bien content quand même. It is you I have to thank, & then JBY.[13]

This room would be better if a little remoter from the W. C.
Nothing changes the relief at being back here. Like coming
out of gaol in April.

God love thee. I feel this letter is crossing with one from you.

Ever Sam

Please send the little red map-guide I had with me before.

ALS; 2 leaves, 4 sides; PS upper left margin on side 1; TCD, MS 10402/146.

1 The terms of Laugier's proposal are indicated in 22 December 1937.

2 "Abonné" (subscribed), to which SB adds an English verb ending.
Public Offices Parisiens, Service Vente Appartements, 44 bis Rue Pasquier, Paris 8
(*Annuaire officiel des abonnés au téléphone*, Région de Paris, avril 1937).

3 At this time Giorgio and Helen Joyce lived on the short street, Villa Scheffer, in the
16th arrondissement. On 18 December 1937, Paul Léon wrote to Harriet Shaw Weaver
about corrections and enlargements for Part II of Work in Progress (working title of
Finnegans Wake): "My part of it seems to be done but it takes some five or six other
people to check the corrections, verify the additions and read the proofs" (Joyce, *Letters
of James Joyce*, III, 409).
Although asked by Joyce to write an essay on the yet-to-be-published *Finnegans
Wake* for the *Nouvelle Revue Française*, SB gave up the task shortly before Christmas
1937 (Bair, *Samuel Beckett*, 272). Only an essay by Jacques Mercanton appeared
("Finnegans Wake," *La Nouvelle Revue Française* 52.308 [May 1939] 858–864);
however, Joyce's card to Mercanton of 8 September 1939 says that he expects a
second essay by Mercanton to appear in this review (Joyce, *Letters of James Joyce*, III,
454–455).

4 French critic Armand Petitjean (1913–2003), a Normalien, regularly wrote for the
Nouvelle Revue Française; Petitjean had translated and written on Joyce for *transition* and
for the journal *Mesures* (1935–1940, 1948), edited by Henry Church.

5 Maria and Eugene Jolas; the Grande Taverne, 16 Rue du Faubourg-Montmartre. SB
refers to proofs for "Denis Devlin," SB's review of Devlin's *Intercessions* in *transition*.

6 Alan and Belinda Duncan; Nick Balachef; Brian Coffey. "Si" (Yes I have).

7 Harry Sinclair, the plaintiff in the Gogarty libel case, had won damages of £900
and costs, but had not yet received payment ("Libel Action Findings, £5 Damages
for Dr. Gogarty, Plaintiff to Receive Award of £900," *The Irish Times* 25 November
1937: 2).
SB plays with the familiar notion "Noblesse oblige" (nobility carries obligations),
replacing "noblesse" by "roture" (membership of the common people).
Rich and Cowan, the London publishers of Gogarty's *As I Was Going Down Sackville
Street: A Phantasy in Fact*, did not fall within the jurisdiction of the Irish courts, and so
Sinclair was considering bringing suit against them in London.

8 Alfred Péron.

Georges Pelorson was preparing the first issue of the journal *Volontés* (December 1937 – August 1939, Spring 1940), while also working at *Paris-Midi* and at the Ecole bilingue de Neuilly. Marcelle was Pelorson's wife. Chez Pierre, 4 Rue de Valois.

9 SB had apologized to Frank for the negative attention created by his testimony at the Sinclair vs. Gogarty trial (see Knowlson, *Damned to Fame*, 254–259).

10 The exhibition by French painter Francis Picabia (1878–1953), "Francis Picabia: peintures Dada, paysages récents," was held at La Galerie de Beaune, 19 November to 2 December 1937. French cubist André Lhote (1885–1962) had work in several exhibitions in Paris in 1937, and a solo show at the Galerie Poyet in December 1937 (*André Lhote, 1885–1962: Cubism* [New York: Leonard Hutton Galleries, 1976] 26; Musée de Valence, *André Lhote, 1885–1962* [Paris: Réunion des musées nationaux, 2003] 249).

Geer van Velde liked the painting *A Morning*, by Jack B. Yeats, owned by SB: see 29 January 1936, n. 3.

11 Jean Thomas. The café Au Nègre de Toulouse was at 157–159 Boulevard du Montparnasse at this time. "Tiens! Bonsoir" (Well, well! Good night).

12 Library staff at the Ecole Normale Supérieure at this time included Jean Meuvret (1901–1971), who was Sous-bibliothécaire (Assistant Librarian) from 1926 to 1943; Paul Etard (1905–1963) was the Librarian from 1936 to 1950 (*Association amicale des anciens élèves de l'Ecole normale supérieure* [Paris: Hachette-Université, 1973] and *Supplément historique* [Paris: Hachette-Université, 1990]).

13 George Reavey's telegram has not been found. "Bien content quand même" (very glad all the same).

At McGreevy's urging, Jack Yeats wrote to T. M. Ragg (1897–1953), who was Yeats's editor at Routledge, on 22 November 1937:

> A friend of mine, Sam Beckett, has the manuscript of a novel "Murphy" which is to be submitted to your firm. I have not seen it, but his other novel I read and I thought it the real thing. There was inspiration in it. [...] I write to ask you, if you cannot read Beckett[']s MS yourself just now, to give it to some very open minded reader. (UoR, Routledge, 1715)

Ragg wrote to Reavey on 6 December 1937: "I shall look forward [...] to discussing with you Sam Beckett's book MURPHY the reading of which I have enjoyed more than anything else for a very long time – though I confess always with the feeling that it is going to be a very difficult book to sell" (UoR, Routledge, 1733). Ragg also wrote to thank Jack Yeats on 8 December 1937:

> I enjoyed it immensely. I want to publish it, and I am seeing Reavey tomorrow to talk the matter over with him. I am afraid there is no doubt that it is far too good to be a big popular or commercial success. On the other hand it, like your own book [*The Charmed Life*], will bring great joy to the few. Thank you very much for introducing it to me. (UoR, Routledge, 1715)

MARY MANNING HOWE

BUFFALO, NEW YORK

[after 10 December 1937]   [Paris]

[Fragment]

Agate's notice of YTS in Sunday Times. At least the intention was friendly.[1] I have not written a word of the Johnson
blasphemy. I trust that acts of intellection are going on about
it somewhere. Which will enable me eventually to see how it
coincides with the Pricks, Bones and Murphy, fundamentally,
and fundamentally with all I shall ever write or want to write.[2]

I know you will be glad to hear that Murphy has been taken
at last, after 18 months, by Routledge. Jack Yeats wrote a letter
recommending me to the director, behind my back at Tom
McGreevy's instance.[3] They are paying me twelve ten on signing
of contract and the same on publication on a/c of 10% on first
1000. And want option on next 2 works of fiction. I don't know
much about the firm except that they have only come lately to
publishing fiction and are working up a French side with
Montherlant and Malraux. Anyway I would sign anything to
get the book out. I suppose as a result of this something may
be done in USA. They want to set it up straight away and get it
out in Feb.[4]

I have had no reply from Cape Town but of course would
back out now in the event of my being appointed. I wouldn't
mind going to Buffalo for a few months in the summer if I got
some work there and my fare paid. Otherwise I couldn't afford
it.[5] I fear Tom McG. has queered his pitch in USA with the Eliot
book. He is too absolute and Ireland-haunted and an almost
impossible person to help, like most of the people one wants

to help. He is quite miserable in London, doing art notes at starvation rate for the Studio.[6]

I saw Geoffrey & Ursula each time I was in London, coming & going, and found them much easier and better than so far. She has improved in appearance, got more definition, and in certain combinations of mood, light, ebriety and seminal intoxication has a very beautiful exterior.[7]

Please pass on the following:

> "Oh Doubleday Doran
> Less oxy than moron,
> You've a mind like a whore on
> A trip to Bundoran."[8]

Calomniez! calomniez! Il en restera toujours quelquechose.[9]

I am giving my critical career the long awaited kick in the arse with an article on Joyce for the homage number of the Nouvelle Revue Française in Feb. Or March. Then no more slopemptying. Work in P. is due out alsoe [*for* also] Feb. Or March. I am so hard up that I have had to allow myself to be employed by him as proof corrector in chief.[10] Keep this to yourself. The association will be hard enough to break down without insisting on the mere appearance of further adhesions.

Love

s/ Sam[11]

I converted the dollar you sent for Lilian to my own purposes, when in London. Then in Dublin I ran into Charlie, looking for a job as a fireman, and gave him 4/- and the P.O., which I think he was needing even more than usual.[12] I couldn't get out to see them. Donaghy is in Enniskerry, living in sin with his beard.[13]

There are pretty things in the Sarton poems, but rococo- let it go is the worst even I have seen for a long time.[14]

TLS; 1 leaf, fragment (opening page[s] missing): TxU. *Dating*: on or after 10 December 1937 (see SB to McGreevy, 10 December 1937) and before 7 January 1938 (when SB was stabbed in Paris).

1 Mary Manning Howe's play *Youth's the Season* ...? (1931) was produced by Lord Longford's Players at the Westminster Theatre in London, opening on 5 October 1937. James Agate (1877–1947), Drama Critic for *The Sunday Times*, wrote, "This is a little play of considerable quality written with considerable skill [...] I found to my astonishment that very rare thing, a stage full of living people" ("'Youth's the Season ...?,' A Play. By Mary Manning," 10 October 1937: 4).

2 SB refers to his research toward a play on the relationship between Samuel Johnson and Mrs. Thrale. *More Pricks than Kicks, Echo's Bones*, and *Murphy*.

3 Jack B. Yeats's recommendation of *Murphy* to Routledge: 10 December 1937 to McGreevy, n. 13.

4 "Twelve ten" (£12 10s) was the advance paid to SB by Routledge. SB's signed contract was returned by Reavey to T. M. Ragg on 16 December 1937; the advance was sent to George Reavey on 17 December 1937 (UoR, Routledge, 1716).

Routledge published Malraux's *L'Espoir* (1937), translated by Stuart Gilbert and Alastair MacDonald as *Days of Hope* (1938). Montherlant's *Les Jeunes filles* (4 vols., 1936–1939) was published in English as *Pity for Women* (Part I: *Young Girls* [1937], tr. Thomas McGreevy; Part II: *Pity for Women* [1937], tr. John Rodker).

5 In July SB had applied for a position as Lecturer in Italian at the University of Cape Town; Mary Manning Howe had earlier suggested that SB apply for a teaching position at the University of Buffalo, New York.

6 McGreevy's *Thomas Stearns Eliot* was published by Chatto and Windus in its Dolphin series (1931); in it he inveighed against American vulgarity (see 3 February 1931, n. 2) as well as Eliot's New England Protestantism:

> Mr. Eliot's verse has purified itself of merely social elements as he has moved towards Catholicism, even the bastard, schismatic and provincial if genteel kind of Catholicism that, for the time being, at any rate, he has, somewhat New Englishly, stopped at. (To be an Anglo-Catholic, to try to compromise between John Bullishness, or Uncle Sammishness, and Catholicism is almost to try to reconcile Mammon and God). (McGreevy, *Thomas Stearns Eliot*, 16)

McGreevy was chief Art Critic for *The Studio*.

7 Geoffrey and Ursula Thompson. SB traveled between Paris and Dublin via London when he had to return to Dublin for the Gogarty trial, 22–23 November 1927.

8 Doubleday Doran had read *Murphy* at the instigation of Mary Manning Howe, but rejected it (see 27 July 1937). SB sent his joke to several people, with minute textual differences (see 4 August 1937 to George Reavey).

9 "Calomniez! Calomniez! Il en restera toujours quelque chose." (Keep on slandering! Something will always stick.)

10 Joyce wanted a collection of critical essays on *Work in Progress* to appear in the *Nouvelle Revue Française* prior to its publication as *Finnegans Wake* (see 10 December 1937

to McGreevy). Joyce intended to have *Work in Progress* ready to be published on his birthday, 2 February 1938, then by his father's birthday on 4 July, but it was not published until 2 February 1939.

11 Signature written over the final two typed paragraphs.

12 Lilian Donaghy and Charlie Gilmore.
4/- (4 shillings). P.O. (Postal Order).

13 John Lyle Donaghy had been married to Lilian.

14 Mary Manning Howe had attempted to arrange a meeting between SB and May Sarton and had sent her poems to him. SB is referring to her "Sonnet 15" which repeats the phrase "let it" six times (May Sarton, *Encounter in April* [Boston: Houghton Mifflin, 1937] 81).

THOMAS McGREEVY
LONDON

22/12/37   Hotel Liberia
                                 9 Rue de la Gde Chaumière
                                 Paris 6

Dear Tom

Many thanks for plan.[1]

As you see I have found nothing yet.[2] I never shall. Someone will have to do it for me.

I have just written to my mother, suggesting that we at least correspond. I hope it may make Xmas a little less sad for her.[3]

I wrote to Bérard about a week ago but have had no reply.[4] I then wrote to Laugier & had a note from him yesterday, written from bed where he is for the 3rd time this month with flu, asking me to call on him the same day, which I did. He was very friendly & this is the upshot of our conversation.

It is almost certain that you would be granted a subvention of 10000 (ten thousand) francs for 3 months if the application were made in a suitable form. Laugier cannot do that directly, on his own initiative. Some third person (in this case it would be I) has to apply formally on your behalf to M. le chef de cabinet, setting forth the circumstances and specifying sum required. Laugier writes d'accord on the application, it goes through & the sum is deposited with me. There seems to be no question of your doing any specific work of any kind in return for this. The phrase "rapprochement-franco-britannique" is no more than a phrase and does not commit you to any form of partisan journalism whatever. I suggested to Laugier that as you were anxious to hold on to the job in the Studio it would not be desirable for you to be committed to spending the whole 3 months in Paris. He agreed that the application would be in no way prejudiced or jeopardised by its being made in such terms as would only commit you to visits to France, & not to uninterrupted residence for the whole of the 3 months. I explained your anxiety to obtain something permanent over here, such as the job that Miss Heywood (?) enjoys (?) at the Louvre. He said that of course that lay rather outside his sphere of influence, but that he would be very glad to support any démarche you might make in that direction. He spoke of you with great sympathy & affection, tapped his head and said profoundly "Très riche".[5]

Now my dear Tom I know you will immediately begin to see all kinds of difficulties & dangers in your accepting this proposition, the inconvenience of your dividing your time between London & Paris, the possibility in spite of my conviction to the contrary of your being involved in the rôle of political agent, & a lot more than would not occur [to] me, and I beseech you not to give them more weight than they deserve. Even if no permanent work in Paris emerges from the three months, you are no worse off than you are at present, & you will have been refreshed & stimulated. Also I should think it almost quite certain that with the Exhibition opening in the Spring and new exhibitions or pictures being organised in connexion with it, you would find work of a kind agreeable to you.[6] As to your having to have something to show for the money spent on you, that remains as far as I understand the position a matter entirely for yourself and your own choice of terms. There is no question of your being a political person. It is thoroughly understood that it is as a cultural intelligence that you are being recommended and on a cultural basis that the whole arrangement would rest. Laugier is anxious to do you as a friend a good turn, cannot do it directly and so the rules of the game have to be observed in order that he may do it all. He would I am sure be the last person to involve you in a situation hateful to you.

I know a number of points will occur to you on which you will feel you must have more definite information before you can make up your mind. If you let me know them I will put them before Laugier. But I personally feel it would perhaps be better, & more satisfactory for yourself, if you communicated them directly to Laugier yourself. I after all feel restraint with him that you who know him fairly well would not feel.

I would of course, in the event of your agreeing en principe, submit my letter to you before sending it in.

You know how much I wish you would say yes.

I have a filthy cold, do not feel so grand, drift around, drink too much & do not work. Joyce paid me 250 fr. for about 15 hrs. work on his proofs. That is needless to say only for your ear. He then supplemented it with an old overcoat and 5 ties! I did not refuse. It is so much simpler to be hurt than to hurt. I am invited to dine with them Xmas night. With the Leons & the Giorgios! And no doubt the Jolases if they were not going away. Helen has bad news of her father & will be leaving soon for the States. She nearly left yesterday. She wants G.[iorgio] to go & he doesn't want. I think ça marche assez mal.[7] I have done nothing more with the NRF article and feel like dropping it. Certainly there will be no question of prolegomena or epilegomena when the work comes out in book form. And if that means a break, then let there be a break. At least this time it wont be about their daughter, who by the way as far as I can learn gets deeper & deeper into the misery & less & less likely ever to emerge.[8]

No more news from George. I sent back the contract without having signed it (a pure omission & no doubt very significant) which probably annoyed him.[9]

You will have seen Brian. I gave him a book for you. I glanced through it after buying it & fear you will not find much in it to interest you. Charles wrote with delight about <u>Murphy</u>.[10] I feel even less about its being taken than I did when it was rejected.

God love thee, & Hester & Raven.[11] Write very soon & say "carry on".

Ever

Sam

ALS; 2 leaves, 4 sides; TCD, MS 10402/148. *Dating*: two types of paper were used for this letter: leaf 1 r/v is on stationery; leaf 2 r/v on graphed paper, torn from a notebook (side 3 ragged left margin, side 4 ragged right margin). Content continues from side 2 to side 3 ["your being / involved in the rôle"], hence a single letter can be assumed, the date for which is given on side 1 by SB.

1 SB had asked McGreevy to send him his Paris map book, *Plan de Paris* (10 December 1937).

2 SB was seeking an apartment in Paris.

3 SB's break with his mother is discussed by Knowlson in *Damned to Fame*, 253–254.

4 Armand-Max-Jean Bérard (1904–1998), a Normalien, had been Chef de cabinet du Sous-secrétaire d'Etat aux Affaires étrangères from June 1936, then Chef-adjoint du cabinet du Ministre in July 1937 (*Annuaire diplomatique et consulaire de la République Française*, nouvelle série 49 [Paris: Imprimerie Nationale, 1938] 223).

5 Laugier's position: SB to Thomas McGreevy, 3 November 1937 [*for* 3 December 1937], n. 3.
McGreevy's position with *The Studio*: [after 10 December 1937], n. 6.

No one by the name of Heywood was working at the Louvre in 1937 (Mme. Besson, Bibliothèque des Musées Nationaux Palais du Louvre, 14 March 1995).

"D'accord" (agreed); "démarche" (move); "très riche" (very rich).

6 Under the patronage of King George VI, the President of the French Republic and the French National Museums Council, an exhibition of British painting, La Peinture anglaise: XVIIIe & XIXe siècles, was opened at the Louvre on 4 March 1938 and was extended to 22 July 1938 to allow King George to visit it ("Art et curiosité: commiss-aires-priseurs," *Le Temps* 22 July 1938: 5).

7 Paul Léon and his wife Elisabeth Lucie Léon (pseud. Lucie Noël, 1900–1972), Giorgio, Helen, and Stephen Joyce (b. 1932), Eugene and Maria Jolas.

Helen Joyce's father was American businessman Adolf Kastor (1856–1947). "Ça marche assez mal" (Things are not going all that well).

8 The proposed *NRF* article about Joyce's *Finnegans Wake*: [after 10 December 1937], n. 10.

9 George Reavey.

10 The book sent via Brian Coffey for McGreevy has not been identified. Charles Prentice's letter of congratulations has not been found.

11 Hester Dowden, Thomas Holmes Ravenhill.

CHRONOLOGY 1938

1938	By 5 January	SB sees Peggy Guggenheim, Laz Aaronson, Adrienne Bethell, Brian Coffey, and Gwynedd Reavey. Meets Hemingway.
	6 January	Stabbed on the Avenue d'Orléans. Hospitalized at the Hôpital Broussais.
	9 January	May, Frank, and Jean Beckett arrive in Paris.
	17 January	SB receives proofs of *Murphy*.
	22 January	Released from hospital.
	25 January	Returns proofs of *Murphy*. Writes the poem "they come."
	31 January	Responds to McGreevy's essay on Jack B. Yeats.
	2 February	Attends Joyce's birthday party with Peggy Guggenheim.
	By 11 February	Sends "they come" to *Ireland To-day*. Jack Kahane proposes that SB translate Sade's *Les 120 journées de Sodome*.
	14 February	SB attends arraignment of his assailant, Prudent.
	28 February	Attends trial of Prudent.
	7 March	Publication of *Murphy*.
	8 March	Accepts Kahane's offer for Sade translation, but Kahane postpones for several months.
	April	Péron's French translation of "Alba" published in *Soutes*.
	By 3 April	SB writes first of several poems in French.
	By 14 April	Moves to apartment, 6 Rue des Favorites, Paris 15.

May	"Ooftish" and SB's review "Denis Devlin" of Devlin's *Intercessions* published in *transition*.
3 May	In London for the opening of Geer van Velde's exhibition at Guggenheim Jeune, private view 5 May.
12 May	In Paris.
By 15 June	His books arrive from Dublin. Attends an exhibition of Otto Freundlich's work.
15 June	Sends French poems to McGreevy.
By 20 June	Travels to Chartres with Geer and Lisl van Velde and Peggy Guggenheim.
28–30 June	Drives with Peggy Guggenheim to take Geer and Lisl van Velde to Cagnes-sur-Mer; SB and Guggenheim stop in Dijon on return trip to Paris.
19 July	In London for some days en route to Dublin.
30–31 July	Weekend with Frank and Jean Beckett in South Donegal.
10 August	Attends premiere of W. B. Yeats's play *Purgatory* at the Abbey Theatre.
By 19 August	Longman Green in New York reject *Murphy*.
Late August	SB and Suzanne Deschevaux-Dumesnil visit Arland Ussher in Normandy and Péron in Brittany.
29 September	The Munich Agreement is signed.
c. 24 October or later	Writes ten poems in French and half-finishes a French version of "Love and Lethe." Writes "Les Deux Besoins" which he gives to Freundlich.
9–10 November	Kristallnacht.
December	SB in Dublin for Christmas; writes from Greystones where his mother temporarily resides.

5/1/38   Hotel Liberia
                                        [Paris]

Dear Tom

                  Epître à Ronsard

Ton esprit est, Ronsard, plus gaillard que le mien;
Mais mon corps est plus jeune et plus fort que le tien;
Par ainsi je conclus qu'en savoir tu me passes
D'autant que mon printemps tes cheveux gris efface.

L'art de faire des vers, dût-on s'en indigner,
Doit être à plus haut prix que celui de régner.
Tous deux également nous portons des couronnes:
Mais, roi, je les reçus; poète, tu les donnes.
Ton esprit enflammé d'une céleste ardeur
Eclate par soi-même, et moi par ma grandeur.
Si du côté des dieux je cherche l'avantage,
Ronsard est leur mignon, et je suis leur image.
Ta lyre, qui ravit par de si doux accords,
Te soumet les esprits, dont je n'ai que les corps.
Elle t'en rend le maître[,] et te fait introduire
Où le plus fier tyran n'a jamais eu d'empire.[1]

————————————————

    Forgive the delay. I have been completely affolé for the past
fortnight, with people going and people coming. There has been

even more than the usual drama with the Joyces, mostly about Helen and Giorgio suddenly deciding to go to New York, where her father is very ill. I was the buffer. They departed this morning. Norah [*for* Nora] was in a frightful state, would not go out at all New Year's Eve, after I had sat listening for 2 hours to Shem trying to persuade her, with result that he would not go out either and I spent the last hour of the old year alone with Helen & Giorgio. I hope to get the parents out to see Modern Times this evening.[2]

I am delighted that you are willing to accept the Laugier thing en principe. As soon as you want me to write the letter, let me know, though obviously it might come better from someone better known and of more standing in Paris.[3]

Peggy Guggenheim has been here and I have seen quite a lot of her. She is starting a gallery in Cork Street, opens on 22nd inst. with Cocteau drawings and furniture. Then there will be Kandinsky, Arp, Brancusi, Benno, etc., and in May a Geer van Velde one man. George will have told you about it.[4] I gave Guggenheim your address and she is anxious to get in touch with you at earliest op. She returns to London probably to-morrow. I hope something may come out of it for you.

Aaronson was here too. I like him more and more. Also a Mrs Bethell from Dublin whom I know quite well. Brian got back Monday.[5] Letters from Harry but no money.[6] Haven't done a tap of work or looked for a room. Arranged with Shem to write the homage in NRF without mentioning his name.[7] The idea seemed to please him. No proofs yet from Routladge [*for* Routledge].[8] George says they should be along any day. I thought Gwynedd was looking frightful, about 75. She was quite sick leaving. I hope it didn't develop into anything serious.[9]

The Beach introduced me to Hemingway in her shop. Exactly like Alan's Packard. McAlmon is staggering about also.[10]

A very affectionate letter from mother. A tie that came anon. was from her and she was toasting me in champagne Xmas night before my letter came. It is a relief. I shall not go back to Ireland but we can meet in London. George wants me to go over when Murphy comes out and I shall certainly be there in May for the van Velde exhibition. He wants me to go to Holland with him and his wife in the spring. Qui sait.[11] I see coming also, when WIP is finished, an invitation to go to Zurich. He offered me 100 fr if I guessed the title.[12] He was sublime last night, deprecating with the utmost conviction his lack of talent. I don't feel the danger of the association any more. He is just a very lovable human being.

The entire works of Kant arrived from Munich. I had to go away beyond the Gare de l'Est to collect them. I haven't had time to open them, two immense parcels that I could hardly carry from customs to taxi. [13]

The pound wasn't a mistake.

Hester's card was charming and I shall write to her. I have seen nothing at all of A. & B., nor L.R. I am glad Dolly's visit was a success.[14]

I look forward to seeing the full text of the JBY. Everyone's delighted with his Morning.[15]

God love thee.

Ever

s/ Sam

TLS; 2 leaves, 2 sides; TCD, MS 10402/150.

1 McGreevy had requested the text of this poem written by King Charles IX (1550-1574); he quotes two lines from the poem in his study of Jack B. Yeats: "Ta lyre, qui ravit par de si doux accords, / Te soumet les esprits, dont je n'ai que les corps" (Your lyre, which delights by such sweet chords, makes subjects of men's minds; I have only their bodies) (*Jack B. Yeats*, 32). The text recorded in the letter varies slightly from the published text, and lacks the final two lines of the poem as published in *Parnasse Royal: Poèmes choisis des monarques françois et autres personnages royaux*, ed. Gauthier

Ferrières (Paris: Chez Sansot, Libraire, 1909) 105–106: "Elle amollit les coeurs et soumet la beauté: / Je puis donner la mort, toi l'immortalité."

2 "Affolé" (driven mad). The film *Modern Times* (1936) by Charlie Chaplin (né Charles Spencer Chaplin, 1889–1977) was released in France as *Les Temps modernes* in spring 1936; it played in Paris at the Delambre-Cinéma, 11 Rue Delambre, from 29 December 1937 to 5 January 1938 (*Cinémonde* 479 [29 December 1937 – 5 January 1938]).

3 The subvention suggested by Henri Laugier: 3 November 1937 [*for* 3 December 1937], n. 3, and 22 December 1937.

4 Heiress and American art collector Marguerite Guggenheim* (known as Peggy, 1898–1979) opened a gallery at 30 Cork Street, London, on 22 January 1938.

Guggenheim Jeune's first exhibition; it ran from 24 January to 12 February 1938. Following were exhibitions of the work of Kandinsky (18 February to 12 March) and "Contemporary Sculpture" (8 April to 2 May) which included work by Romanian-born sculptor Constantin Brancusi (1876–1957) and German-born artist Hans Arp (1887–1966). Arp's work was also included in the "Collages" exhibition (3 November to 26 November 1938). The paintings of American artist Benjamin Benno (1901–1980) and Danish artist Rita Kernn-Larsen (1904–1998) were exhibited from 31 May to 18 June. Geer van Velde's exhibition was held from 5 May to 26 May.

George Reavey.

5 English poet Lazarus Aaronson (1894–1965), a friend of Con Leventhal, taught Economics at the City of London College.

Adrienne James Bethell (née Hope, n.d.; m. John Lionel Bethell, 1933) stayed in Paris in late 1937; later, as owner of an antique shop in Dun Laoghaire, Co. Dublin, she indicated that she had corresponded with SB (see "Beckett, 1937," *Evening Press* 10 November 1969: n.p.). SB mentions her Paris visit in 1937–1938 in his letter to Harry Sinclair: "I saw something of Adrienne when she was over and brought her one evening to dine with the Joyces" (2 February 1938, NNC, RBML, Sighle Kennedy Papers).

Brian Coffey had returned to Paris from holidays with his family in Dublin.

6 Harry Sinclair, the plaintiff in the Gogarty trial, was awarded damages, but had not yet reimbursed SB for the expenses he had incurred in returning to Ireland to testify (see SB to Thomas McGreevy, 10 December 1937, n. 7).

7 The *Nouvelle Revue Française* essay to introduce Joyce's *Finnegans Wake*: SB to Thomas McGreevy, 10 December 1937, n. 4; SB to Mary Manning Howe [after 10 December 1937]; and SB to Thomas McGreevy, 22 December 1937, n. 9.

8 Routledge was preparing to publish *Murphy*; the text was sent to the printer on 17 December 1937, and a specimen page was sent to Routledge for approval on 23 December 1937 (UoR, Routledge).

9 Gwynedd Reavey was suffering from pleurisy.

10 Sylvia Beach's bookshop Shakespeare & Company was a gathering place for authors. SB compares Ernest Hemingway (1899–1961) to Alan Duncan's large American car, a Packard. The American writer and publisher Robert Menzies McAlmon (1896–1956) was a friend of Brian Coffey.

11   According to a letter from George Reavey to Virginia Dorazio, 15 April 1975: "Both of us and especially Sam persuaded Peggy to show [Geer van Velde's] work in London" (TxU, Reavey collection).
"Qui sait" (who knows).

12   James Joyce encouraged people to guess what would be the title for his "Work in Progress" when it was finally published; Eugene Jolas guessed correctly (Ellmann, *James Joyce*, 543, 708).

13   SB had ordered *Immanuel Kants Werke*, ed. Ernst Cassirer, Hermann Cohen, Arthur Buchenau, *et al.* (Berlin: Bruno Cassirer, 1921–1923), in eleven volumes.

14   Hester Dowden's card to SB has not been found.
Alan and Belinda Duncan.
Lennox Robinson was in Paris, while his wife Dolly Robinson visited her mother Hester Dowden in London.

15   SB refers to the painting he owned by Jack B. Yeats: *A Morning*.

THOMAS McGREEVY
LONDON

12/1/38   Hôpital Broussais
                                                Rue Didot
                                                Paris 14 ^me

Dear Tom

I shall be all right, as far as I can see. The pleura were wounded but apparently not the lung. First I was in a ward, then Joyce had me moved into a private room. Everyone has been incredibly kind. Mother Frank & Jean came. From the very beginning I begged everyone to stop them. But it seems to have been all over Dublin at once & horribly exaggerated. Mother looks poorly, Frank can't give the time & of course doesn't want to leave her here alone. She says she will stay until I am quite well again. Enfin - -[1]

I hope the Charles was what you wanted.[2]

I have to stay on my back to breathe & the nights are pretty bad, i.e. from 9 pm - 5 am - For the rest, ça va.

Nancy Cunard bounced in the other evening from Spain. I was very glad to see her.[3]

Poor Alan & Belinda have had a frightful time, dealing with police & keeping reporters away. I suppose you saw they got the chap M. Prudent.[4]

I wonder did you hear from Laugier, & if anything has been decided.

Write soon & give me your news. Love to George & Gwynned. Thanks for telegram & letter. Ask him has he found the Apes. Shall try & think of some names for Routledge.[5]

> Love
>
> Sam

ALS; 1 leaf, 1 side; TCD, MS 10402/151.

1 On the night of 6 January, SB was stabbed while walking with Alan and Belinda Duncan from the Café Zeyer, 234 Avenue du Maine at Avenue d'Orléans (now Avenue du Général Leclerc), to their apartment on the Villa Coeur de Vey. A man, later identified as Robert-Jules Prudent (n.d.), importuned SB, and SB reacted: "I pushed him. He had a knife" (Samuel Beckett, July 1989). When SB and the Duncans realized the seriousness of the wound, SB was taken to the Hôpital Broussais (see also Knowlson, *Damned to Fame*, 259–262).

The following day *The Irish Times* reported this version of the event: "Mr. Beckett received a wound near the heart and was taken to the hospital in serious condition." It continued: "Mr. Beckett was seeing some friends home when he was pestered by a tramp. Told to go away the tramp is alleged to have kicked Mr. Beckett and there was a scuffle. When Mr. Beckett entered his friend's flat, he opened his overcoat and found blood flowing from a wound." The article announced that, although the results of an examination would not be known until later, SB's condition was "reassuring"; it closed with a summary of SB's writing career ("Dublin Writer Stabbed: Paris Street Scene," 8 January 1938: 10).

Brian Coffey's letter to George Reavey on 9 January 1938 offers more particulars:

> The latest news of Sam, yesterday afternoon was that he was safe, if no complications set in [...] The facts are as follows. Sam was returning about 8:30 from Café Zeyer – Av D'Orleans with Alan & Belinda, when an individual came from behind some fair booths, & tried to talk to Alan, who was walking behind. Alan took no notice so the man became more insistent and started insulting first Alan, then Belinda. Alan gave him a light shove, & then Sam & the man got into a tangle, there was kicking & a blow. Then the man ran away. After some seconds Sam said he was hurt. A & B found blood on his hand. (TxU)

Reports on the time of the incident vary widely.

May, Frank, and Jean Beckett arrived on 9 January 1938 by airplane, according to Joyce's report in his letter to Giorgio and Helen Joyce on 12 January 1938 (Joyce, *Letters of James Joyce*, III, 411). Frank Beckett wrote to McGreevy on Wednesday [12 January 1938]: "Each day I have seen him he seems better & unless any unseen complications occur should be out of the wood very soon. I am waiting here til I know definitely he is out of danger and then will be speeding back to Ireland, perhaps during next week end" (TCD, MS 10402/152).

"Enfin" (Oh well).

2 SB refers to the poem McGreevy had requested: 5 January 1938, n. 1.

3 "Ça va" (Things are all right).

Nancy Cunard had just returned to Paris following three months in Spain (Chisholm, *Nancy Cunard: A Biography*, 242).

4 As witnesses, Alan and Belinda Duncan had to file police reports; the assailant, Robert-Jules Prudent, was apprehended in a hotel at 155 Avenue du Maine under the name of Germain Prudent ("Robert Prudent agresseur de l'écrivain irlandais Beckett est arrêté," *L'Humanité* 11 January 1938: 8).

5 George and Gwynedd Reavey.

For SB's wish to reprint the image of apes playing chess in *Murphy*: 13 November 1936, n. 5.

Reavey had asked SB for names of possible reviewers.

GEORGE REAVEY

LONDON

13/1/38   Hôpital Broussais
                                             Rue Didot, 14me
                                             [Paris]

dear George & Gwynedd

Many thanks for wire & letters. The boet Peckett gave me great pleasure.

It was a new kind of 12th Night certainly.

You will have heard about it from Brian so wont go over it again.[1]

It appears I shall be all right, tho' no proper X Ray can be taken till I can get up & down to X Ray room. They never vouchsafe a confidence to me, just drift in, together & singly, shake hands, look at the chart, ask for 33, give a few disgusted taps like a connoisseur asked to examine fake Meissen & drift out. So I don't know when I'll be let up. The médécin chef nearly assaulted me to-day because I had the window opened. What a system.[2]

You know the kind of people to send the book to. I shall make out a list later. I shall of course want to go over the proofs myself. If they are sent to the hotel they then can always be collected. Or they could be sent to Brian at the C. Universitaire. By all means let the Viking see the book. I much prefer that to giving any of the others the chance to change their mind. But I would not ask Joyce to move in the matter.[3] And I would be very sorry if anyone else did. The reasons are obvious enough. It will be taken in USA now all right, sooner or later, without any special introduction.

Hope Gwynedd well over pleurisy thing, And that both of you are beginning to feel benefit of excesses -

   Love

    Sam

What about apes?[4]

ALS; 1 leaf, 2 sides; pencil; TxU.

1 Reavey's wire and letters have not been found. He did send cuttings from the column "Items from Abroad," *Daily Telegraph* (8 January 1938: n.p., and 11 January 1938: n.p.), both of which correctly spell SB's name. In London newspapers reporting the stabbing incident there is no evidence of an article that refers to the "boet Peckett"; in both *L'Humanité* and *Le Figaro*, however, SB is referred to as M. Samuel Peckett ("En quelques lignes," *Le Figaro* 8 January 1938: 4; "Drame nocturne: Un écrivain irlandais poignardé par un inconnu," *L'Humanité* 8 January 1938: 7A).

2 "Médecin chef" (senior consultant).

3 At the time, SB was staying at the Hôtel Libéria. Coffey's residence: 3 November 1937 [for 3 December 1937], n. 1.

Reavey had proposed to show *Murphy* to Viking. Joyce's New York publisher of *A Portrait of the Artist as a Young Man*, Benjamin W. Huebsch (1876–1964), had merged his firm with Viking in 1925; Viking published *Finnegans Wake* in 1939.

Routledge began sending advance copies to potential reviewers and book dealers on 15 January 1938 (UoR: Routledge).

4 The "apes at chess": 13 November 1936, n. 5.

GEORGE REAVEY

LONDON

17<u>th</u> [January 1938]   Hopital Broussais
                                            [Paris]

dear George

Proofs safely received. Hope to let you have them back towards end of week. The checking of the chess is what will delay me -- Shall have to get Geer up with his board to help me.[1]

I trust the blurb is not going to be part of the book, i.e. will not appear actually between the boards of the book. That is an arrangement that I quite definitely would not consent to. I suppose I can't stop them putting it on wrapper. If I could I would. But I won't have it tacked on to my text.[2]

I suppose also my apes have faded out as a possibility.[3] I am disappointed. Why the rush anyway?

How are Gwynedd & yourself? Any pourparlers with P. G.? And have you had a look at her premises?[4]

Had an XRay this morning. Can't extract from them when I am likely to get away. Have not been up yet.

            Love to you both
            Sam

ALS; 1 leaf, 1 side; pencil; TxU. *Dating*: SB in Broussais following stabbing on 8 January 1938.

1   SB refers to the game of chess between Murphy and Mr. Endon (*Murphy*, 242–245); he wished to verify its moves by playing this game with Geer van Velde.

2 The blurb for *Murphy* appeared preceding the title page in the proof copy (InU):

> *Description.* – A definition has been "defined" as the "enclosing of the wilderness of an idea within the wall of words". To define some things is to kill them; no less this novel. If it has a meaning, it is implicit and symbolic, never concrete. Murphy is a character for whom the unseen is the real and the seen a necessary obstacle to reality. To get beyond that obstacle is his aim in life, and he neglects or despises the criteria of the substantial world. Hence he lives in the lowest strata of society; he lives intermittently with a prostitute and her persuasions cannot move him to better his material prospects. He pretends to look for a job, but so long as he can devote some time each day to exploring the inner life of the mind, that is all he worries about. Ultimately he gets a job in an asylum, where he feels a certain kinship with the inmates.
>
>   But if the theme of the book defies description, not so the writing. The portrayal of the scenes is masterly. There is a diversity of simile which could only proceed from a mind well stocked with many seemingly antagonistic branches of knowledge, and words and phrases reveal an acquaintance with our language and a natural distinction in their use which a Johnson might admire. The style is leavened with a Celtic waywardness which is as attractive as it is elusive and leaves the reader uncertain of the source of his enjoyment.

The blurb appears with substantial revisions and omission of plot summary on the order form for the book (RUL, Routledge), and still more briefly on the inside dust jacket of the novel.

A portion of the blurb appeared in Routledge's announcement of their spring list (T. M. Ragg to George Reavey, 11 January 1938, TxU). On the same day, Reavey wrote to Ragg to ask him to hold the prospectuses for *Murphy* because he wished to consider another idea for them; on 12 January 1938, Ragg confirmed to Reavey that he had done so; and on 26 January 1938, Ragg reminded Reavey of this and asked for his assistance in generating ideas for sales of the book (UoR, RKP, 103/6).

3 Regarding the "apes at chess."

4 "Pourparlers" (talks, negotiations). SB refers to Peggy Guggenheim and her London art gallery Guggenheim Jeune (see 5 January 1938, n. 4).

THOMAS McGREEVY

LONDON

21/1/38   Broussais

                                                                     [Paris]

dear Tom

Your notes & messages and concern were a great help. Your wire also with G & G & then yesterday with Denis.[1] Is he on his way over?

It has gone pretty well, though it still hurts me to breathe. I was up for 1st time avant[-]hier, for a few hours in afternoon. Fontaine came same day & said she thought I could leave to-morrow. I hope she confirms that when she comes to-day. I shall go straight back to Liberia, where apparently they are bringing me down to 1st floor. I know it will take time to get back to average, & I am told I will be the proud possessor of a pleural barometer for years to come. But all things considered, & with my fingers on the pencil, I am well out of it.[2]

Poor Alan & Belinda have been angelic. They had to appear yesterday before the juge d'instruction & were confronted with the wretch, who seems more cretinous than malicious.[3]

Hope you met Mother & Frank in London.[4] He was relieved to be getting back, and she sorry. I felt great gusts of affection & esteem & compassion for her when she was over. What a relationship!

All kinds of people came to see me that I've either forgotten (e.g. Evrard and his wife) or never known (the Cremins, pals of Denis at Irish legation here, she very pretty, he very earnest). The Joyces have been extraordinarily kind, bringing me round everything from a heating lamp to a custard pudding.[5]

Proofs nearly corrected. I changed more than I intended, chiefly for want of something to do. It strikes me now as a very dull work, painstaking, creditable & dull. Alfie Péron wants to translate it for NRF. When I send it back to Reavey I shall ask him to give it to you for a quick run over, for printer[']s errors that I may have missed, or anything else flagrantly incorrect. I know you won't mind. The blurb, printed on the flypage, infuriated me so much that I wrote to Reavey refusing permission to have it appear between the boards of the book & regretting that I could not keep it off the wrapper also. Then afterwards I realized it was probably written by himself or Gwynedd or both! Try & find out for me – And of course my original idea for apes on cover just fades out – How short it looks in page proof.[6]

This was Verlaine's hospital, wasn't it?[7]

Send the Yeats to Liberia anytime now, also anything else you have. I should think there will be a job going with P. Guggenheim eventually, as Mrs Henderson will hardly be a permanency. Write to Laugier & Delbos still at Foreign Affairs.[8]

Cocteau of course is only interesting as morbid psychology. At least it is more of an act than Nijinsky[9][...]

Have begun Goncharov's Oblomov. Pereant qui ante nos nostra dixerunt!

Some of the infirmières are impayables. One especially is a born comedian – Stoops excruciatedly to pick up something & says "Ah, que la terre est basse." Spontaneous hemistich.[10]

Long affectionate letter from Ruddy.[11]

Shall write you properly from Libéria. Thank Raven for his letter & Hester for her good wishes.[12]

  Love ever

  Sam

ALS; 2 leaves, 3 sides; TCD, MS 10402/153.

 1 McGreevy's letters and the telegrams that he had sent with the Reaveys and with Denis Devlin have not been found.

 2 "Avant-hier" (the day before yesterday).

Joyce had arranged for his own physician Dr. Thérèse Bertrand-Fontaine (1895–1987), who was the first female doctor in the Parisian hospital system, to attend Beckett.

3 As witnesses, Alan and Belinda Duncan were required to appear before the examining magistrate in order to identify Beckett's assailant, Prudent.

4 Frank Beckett's letter to McGreevy: 12 January 1938, TCD, MS 10402/152.

5 Henri Evrard (1908–1985) was an Agrégé from the Ecole Normale Supérieure, Professor in Algeria, Marseille, and Paris, and later became Inspecteur Général de l'Instruction Publique. Cornelius Christopher Cremin (1908–1987), First Secretary in the Irish Legation in Paris, and his wife Patricia Josephine Cremin (née O'Mahony, 1913–1971) were friends of Denis Devlin and Thomas McGreevy.

6 Alfred Péron did not translate *Murphy* into French for Gallimard's NRF imprint, although he worked with SB on the translation which was dedicated to him when the novel was published by Bordas (1947).

The blurb and apes for *Murphy*: 17 January 1938, n. 2 and n. 3.

7 Verlaine was in the Hôpital Broussais several times between 1887 and 1895; the hospital figures in his *Mes Hôpitaux* (1891) and "L'Hôpital chez Soi" in *Dernières chroniques de l'hôpital* (1895), (Antoine Adam, *The Art of Paul Verlaine*, tr. Carl Morse [New York: New York University Press, 1963] 48–51); Paul Verlaine, *Oeuvres en prose complètes*, ed. Jacques Borel, Bibliothèque de la Pléiade (Paris: Gallimard, 1972] 1229, 1237).

8 SB refers to McGreevy's essay on Jack B. Yeats which is dated January 1938, although it was published in June 1945 (MacGreevy, *Jack B. Yeats*, 33).

Peggy Guggenheim's assistant at Guggenheim Jeune was Wyn Henderson (1896–1976), who had earlier worked with Nancy Cunard's Hours Press (Jacqueline Bograd Weld, *Peggy: The Wayward Guggenheim* [New York: E. P. Dutton, 1988] 160).

For Laugier and Delbos: SB to Thomas McGreevy, 3 November 1937 [for 3 December 1937], and 31 December 1937, n. 3. SB urged McGreevy to consider Laugier's suggestion of applying for a subvention.

9 Guggenheim Jeune's first exhibition was of Jean Cocteau's work (see 5 January 1938, n. 4). The Polish-Russian dancer and choreographer Vaslav Fomich Nijinsky (1890–1950) was diagnosed with schizophrenia in 1919 (Peter Ostwald, *Vaslav Nijinsky: A Leap into Madness* [New York: Carol Publishing Group, 1991] 178–184).

10 *Oblomov* (1858), by Russian novelist Ivan Goncharov (1812–1891), is about the eponymous character of prodigious sloth who conducts business from bed. "Oblomov" was Peggy Guggenheim's pet name for SB.

"Pereant qui ante nos nostra dixerunt" (Death to those who have spoken our thoughts before us), a sally attributed to Aelius Donatus, fourth-century Roman grammarian and teacher of rhetoric.

"Infirmières" (nurses). "Ah, que la terre est basse" (Oh, how far down the floor is).

11 T. B. Rudmose-Brown.

12 Thomas Holmes Ravenhill. Hester Dowden.

22 January 1938, Reavey

GEORGE REAVEY
LONDON

22/1/38   Liberia
                                                 [Paris]

[no greeting]
    Merci de ton mot. Ça va, sans que je sache exactement où.

    Epreuves suivent ce soir ou demain matin. Il ne me manque plus qu'une phrase, et comment! Il finit par m'emmerder, Murphy O'Blomov. Je passerai le reste de ma vie à regretter les singes.[1]

      Allons hop! / fier se répète
      Sam   / en homme génial

APCS; 1 leaf, 2 sides; *to* George Reavey Esq, 7 Great Ormond Street, LONDON W.C. 1; *pm* 24-1-38, Paris; TxU.

22/1/38   Liberia
                                                 [Paris]

    Thank you for your note. All going well, though I don't know exactly where.

    Proofs follow this evening or tomorrow morning. Only one sentence to go, and how! In the end, he's becoming a bloody bore, Murphy O'Blomov. I'll spend the rest of my life regretting the apes.[1]

      Enough of this: on we go! / proud, repeats himself
      Sam   / like the genius he is

1 "Murphy O'Blomov" is a reflection of the eponymous Oblomov.
"Apes at chess": 13 November 1936, n. 5.

GEORGE REAVEY
LONDON

25/1/38 Liberia
9 Rue de la Gde Chaumière
Paris 6me

dear George

By this post I return proofs. I trust I have not exceeded my allowance. Will you pass them on to Tom for the once over.[1]

Gobbless
Sam

APCS; 1 leaf, 2 sides; *to* George Reavey Esq, 7 Great Ormond Street, LONDON WC1, *pm* 26-1-38, Paris; TxU.

1 SB asked McGreevy to read his corrected proof of *Murphy*.

GEORGE REAVEY
LONDON

27/1/38 Liberia
[Paris]

dear George

I am sorry to be a thorn in the side of the gentle compositor but I don't see how I can correct my corrections. I considered them very carefully and they seemed to me necessary. The insertions at end of section 5 especially so. If they leave me £10 or £20 in somebody's debt I can't help it. My executors will shoulder the burden. Whatever you do don't send back the proofs and have me add more![1]

God love thee G.

Sam

APCS; 1 leaf, 2 sides; *to* George Reavey Esq, 7 Great Ormond Street, LONDON WC 1; *pm* 27-1-38, Paris; TxU, Reavey.

1 Reavey's letter to SB has not been found. The corrected proof copy has not been found; a final typescript of *Murphy* dated 26 June 1936 is at the Harry Ransom Humanities Research Center (TxU). In *Demented Particulars*, C. J. Ackerley has studied the changes between this typescript and the text as published by Routledge.

THOMAS McGREEVY

LONDON

27/1/38 Liberia

[Paris]

dear Tom

Many thanks for all your letters. Forgive delay in replying. I wanted to wait till I saw Fontaine this morning before writing you.[1]

Have been here since Saturday (on arrival an immense bunch of Parma violets from Joyces) and taking it as easy as poss., just slipping out twice, & sometimes only once, a day for meals & coming back immediately, going to bed between 9 & 10 & lying in till midday. In spite of which the pain has been considerably worse. So I rang up Fontaine & had my appointment with her at Broussais changed from to-morrow to to-day.[2]

I am just back now from seeing her. She examined me & said things were proceeding normally and that the pain was only to be expected & that I might make up my mind to its being there for some time. She prescribed some anti-neuralgic dope for me to take. And I have to take my temp every vespers. She had no objection to my going out for meals. She said to return this day week for a further examination & X Ray. Then I was passed on to her assistant Fauvert, who did a Radioscope, said there was still some blood knocking about & more or less repeated Fontaine. Then on to a sister, who clapped 21 cupping glasses (ventouses) on to my chest & back & left me feeling like an Osram advertisement for 15 minutes. The temporary relief was considerable.[3]

So you see I am getting on as well as can be expected & that there is no need to worry. The Duncans have been angelic, coming every day, sometimes twice, and ready to do anything for me.[4]

I had a card from Reavey this morning, full of alarm about my proof corrections. I made the only possible answer by return. I am sorry you have the corvée of giving it the once over.[5]

Do send along your Yeats, I am in a hurry to see it. I have been reading OBlomov, appallingly translated by one Nathalie [*for* Natalie] Duddington.[6]

Péron wants to translate Murphy for NRF. I suppose again it is a question of handling Reavey with kid gloves.[7]

Mother is a marvel. She sat up all the way from Euston to Dun Laoghaire. They had an appalling crossing.[8]

Had a long letter from Ursula & replied to them jointly at equal length.[9]

J. J. was round avant-hier, very worried about L.[ucia], of whom news is bad, and wondering would Geoffrey be over at Easter. He says he is going away to Zurich to rest after his his [sic] birthday. I should not be surprised if I were invited to go with. I wouldn't really mind, he has been so incredibly good all this time, but I won't be well enough. I wont even be able to be at his birthday party this day week.[10]

Poem dictated itself to me night before last:

they come
different and the same
with each it is different & the same
with each the absence of love is different
with each the absence of love is the same

Thought of sending it to Sheehy – then withheld my hand.[11]

The Van Veldes wanted me to go to Fontainebleau this week-end, but rien à faire.

I am sorry you don't feel equal to taking up the Laugier thing. I was talking about you in a general way to Péron. He knows someone to do with the Louvre and is going to make enquiries.[12]

How lovely it is being here. Even with a hole in the side. A sunlit surface yesterday brighter than the whole of Ireland's summer.

Letter from the Manning. Both Harvard & Buffalo possibilities for the summer apparently. And a cheerful letter from Cissie, now on the sea 20 mins. from Cape Town, & leaving for home beginning of April.[13]

God love thee

Ever Sam

ALS; 2 leaves, 3 sides; TCD, MS 10402/154.

1 McGreevy's letters have not been found. For Dr. Fontaine: 21 January 1938, n. 2.

2 SB left the Hôpital Broussais on Saturday, 22 January 1938.

3 Dr. Fontaine's assistant Fauvert has not been identified. SB was treated with the application of ventouses to stimulate blood circulation in the lungs; when first applied, the cups may have looked like lightbulbs; Osram General Electric Company manufactured light bulbs, lamps, and electrical tubes.

4 Alan and Belinda Duncan.

5 Reavey's card to SB has not been found. SB had asked McGreevy to look over the proofs. "Corvée" (chore).

6 SB refers to McGreevy's study of Jack B. Yeats. SB had been reading Ivan Goncharov, *Oblomov*, tr. Natalie A. Duddington (1929). One review found Duddington's translation "a remarkably accomplished and painstaking piece of work ... as good a translation as one could hope for" ("Gontcharov's 'Oblomov,'" *Times Literary Supplement* 14 November 1929: 919).

7 Péron's interest in translating *Murphy*: 21 January 1938, n. 6.

8 May, Frank, and Jean Beckett had returned to Dublin via London, by a train that left from London's Euston station and connected with the ferry to Dun Laoghaire.

9 Ursula and Geoffrey Thompson.

10 "Avant-hier" (the day before yesterday).
Lucia Joyce was in treatment for mental illness; Geoffrey Thompson was a practicing psychiatrist in London.
Joyce's birthday was 2 February. Joyce left for Switzerland c. 6 February, staying in Lausanne on his way to Zurich (Roger Norburn, *A James Joyce Chronology* [New York: Palgrave Macmillan, 2004] 181).

11 SB did send the poem to Edward Sheehy at *Ireland To-Day*, as he wrote to McGreevy on 11 February 1938: "I sent 'they come' (translated by Péron as 'ils viennent'!!) to Ireland To-day, where the great purity of mind & charity of thought will no doubt see orgasms where nothing so innocent or easy is intended, and reject the poem in consequence" (TCD, MS 10402/156).
The poem was first published in English in Peggy Guggenheim's *Out of This Century: The Informal Memoirs of Peggy Guggenheim* ([New York: Dial Press, 1946] 205; rev. as *Out of This Century: Confessions of an Art Addict* [New York: Universe Books, 1979] 175); in this printing, initial letters of each line are capitalized, "and" replaces "&" in line 3, and "life" replaces "love" in line 5. Federman and Fletcher ascribe the substitution of "life" for "love" in line 5 to SB; however, the text of the poem in the present letter indicates that the variant was introduced in Peggy Guggenheim's transcription of the poem (*Samuel Beckett: His Works and His Critics*, 23, 50). As published in French as "elles viennent" in "Poèmes 38–39," *Les Temps Modernes* 2.14 (November 1946) 288, the poem has no initial capitalization, and line 5 reads: "avec chacune l'absence d'amour est pareille" ("with each the absence of love is the same").

12 Geer and Elizabeth (née Jokl, known as Lisl, b. 1908) van Velde. "Rien à faire" (nothing doing).
Henri Laugier proposal: 10 December 1937 to McGreevy. Alfred Péron.

13 Mary Manning Howe's letter to SB has not been found. Her husband taught at the University of Buffalo, and he had family connections at Harvard.
Cissie Sinclair was visiting her son Morris in Graaff Reinet, near Cape Town, South Africa: 5 June 1936 [*for* 1937], n. 6.

THOMAS McGREEVY
LONDON

31/1/38   Liberia
                                 9 Rue de la Gde. Chaumière
                                 Paris 6

Dear Tom

Many thanks for Yeats essay and letter. I am sorry you haff bin haffing such trouble with the finances of it. Was it necessary to drag in the Authors' Assoc. or whatever it is?[1] Could it not have been a private arrangement between you and him more fair to you?

I have read the essay twice and think you have every reason to be very pleased with it. Certainly in the first 18 pages I do not think there is a syllable that needs touching. The point about the association and spartness [*for* apartness] of figures and landscape is most beautifully established.[2] And the dangers of over-analogy admirably negotiated. On p. 7 the name of Douanier Rousseau suggested itself to me to follow Le Nain, Chardin, Millet and Courbet, but perhaps the idea is too wide for what you want.[3] You develop the Watteau indication very differently from the way it was in my mind, less philosophically and emphatically and probably more justly, certainly in a way that is justified by what leads up to and away from it as my idea of "inorganic juxtaposition" and "non-anthropomorphised humanity" would not have been.[4]

The rest of the essay, though I do not find it quite as self-evident as the beginning, holds together perfectly. It is more "construit" perhaps, more Catena. I understand your anxiety to clarify his pre and post 1916 painting politically and socially, and especially in what concerns the last pictures I think you have provided a clue that will be of great help to a lot of people, to the kind of people who in the phrase of Bergson can't be happy till they have "solidified the flowing", i.e. to most people. I am inclined personally to think that the turning away from the local, not merely in his painting but in his writing (he has just sent me The Charmed Life), even if only in intention, results not so much from the break down of the local, of the local human anyway, as from a very characteristic and very general psychological mechanism, operative in young artists as a naiveté (or an instinct) and in old artists as a wisdom (or an instinct).[5] I am sure I could illustrate this for you if I had the culture. You will always, as an historian, give more credit to circumstance than I, with my less than suilline interest and belief in the fable convenue, ever shall be able to. However you say it yourself on p. 34.[6]

One of the criticisms that I should like to make about the second half and that I should think will certainly be made by the pros, is that for an essay of such brevity the political and social analyses are rather on the long side. I received almost the impression for example, as the essay proceeded, that your interest was passing from the man himself to the forces that formed him – and not only him – and that you returned to him from them with something like reluctance. But perhaps that also is the fault of my mood and of my chronic inability to understand as member of any proposition a phrase like "the Irish people", or to imagine that it ever gave a fart in its corduroys for any form of art whatsoever, whether before the Union or after, or that it was ever capable of any thought or act other than the rudimentary thoughts and acts belted into it by the priests and by the demagogues in service of the priests, or that it will ever care, if it ever knows, any more than the Bog of Allen will ever care or know, that there was once a painter in Ireland called Jack Butler Yeats.[7] This is not a criticism of a criticism that allows as a sentient subject what I can only think of as a nameless and hideous mass, whether in Ireland or in Finland, but only to say that I, as a clot of prejudices, prefer the first half of your work, with its real and radiant individuals, to the second, with our national scene. Et voilà.[8]

I am much better the last few days – less pain. I go back to Broussais this week for exam. & X Ray and no doubt more ventouses. Dr Paul the French Spilsbury has benn [*for* been] commanding me to his presence in the morning at 9.15 and I replying patiently and politely that my condition does not allow me to get up before midday.[9] Soon they will be arresting me. There are all kinds of reasons que je me porte partie civile, and all kinds for my not doing so. There appears to be a remote possibility of my receiving compensation from the Ville de Paris, but if it involves me with lawyers I should prefer to do without it. The police still have my clothes. But whatever I do and however it goes there are going to be plenty of unpleasantness[es] before it can be called an affaire classée.[10]

Joyce's birthday spree next Wednesday at the Jolasses-Molasses. I have accepted en principe. Broadcast first from Athlone[.][11]

Don't you think one of us ought to write to Laugier, since after all he has been kind, to say that you don't see your way to taking the thing up? I shall do it with pleasure if you don't want to.[12]

If you see Denis please thank him for his letter and tell him I am writing[.][13]

God love thee, Tom, and don't be minding me. I can't think of Ireland the way you do.

Ever
s/ Sam

TLS; 1 leaf, 2 sides; TCD, MS 10402/155. *Note*: "Ascension," "La Mouche," and "Prière" are included with MS 10402/155 although it is doubtful that they were enclosed with that letter because the folds on the poems do not match those of the letter. However, the folds and the burn/water damage on left margin do match those on MS 10402/163.

1 McGreevy had sent his manuscript on Jack B. Yeats to the artist, who replied on 6 January 1938: "Later on, if we get an offer, I would of course, automatically consult the Society of Authors" (TCD, MS 10831/151). Yeats wrote to McGreevy on 26 January 1938 enclosing contractual terms suggested by the Society of Authors, and he encouraged McGreevy to consider joining: "I would be lost myself without them. I ask them about all agreements, though I often accept terms a little less than they advise" (TCD, MS 10831/154).

2 The pagination refers to the manuscript of McGreevy's essay: TCD, MS 7991/2. On the relationship between figures and landscape in Yeats's work: MacGreevy, *Jack B. Yeats*, 11–13.

3 SB suggests to McGreevy that the Le Nain family of painters (Antoine Le Nain [c. 1600–1648], Louis Le Nain [c. 1600–1648], and Mathieu Le Nain [c. 1607–1677]), Jean-Siméon Chardin (1699–1779), Jean-François Millet (1814–1875), and Courbet might be seen as forerunners of Jack B. Yeats in their depictions of what MacGreevy calls the "petit peuple" (ordinary people): MacGreevy, *Jack B. Yeats*, 9. To this series, SB suggests adding Henri Rousseau (also known as Le Douanier Rousseau, 1844–1910).

4 SB made observations on Watteau in two earlier letters to McGreevy: [before 23 July 1937] and 14 August 1937; SB's own development of these ideas is further evident in his letter to Cissie Sinclair, 14 [August 1937], in which he uses the terms that he quotes here (see also n. 5 below, and MacGreevy, *Jack B. Yeats*, 14–17).

5 "Construit" (deliberately constructed).
"Catena," a chain or connected series, is generally not capitalized. Although SB may be referring to Italian painter Vincenzo Catena (c. 1470–1531), the point of this reference is not clear.
On McGreevy's positioning of Yeats's work in the context of Irish political realities: MacGreevy, *Jack B. Yeats*, 17–25. For his discussion of the later paintings that move away from the particular and reflect "the subjective tendency" of imagination: pp. 27–33, particularly his analysis of *California* (Pyle 501, private collection) and *In Memory of Boucicault and Bianconi* (Pyle 498, NGI 4206).
No direct source has been found for SB's statement about Bergson, but in *Creative Evolution* Bergson adopts the analogy of a swimmer who "cling[s] to ... solidity" when learning to "struggle against the fluidity" of water. "So of our thought, when it has decided to make the leap" (tr. Arthur Mitchell [London: Macmillan, 1920] 203–204; *L'Evolution créatrice* [Paris: Félix Alcan, 1907] 210–211).
Routledge had just published Jack B. Yeats's novel *The Charmed Life* (1938).

6 "Fable convenue" (received wisdom).

7 In the published book, McGreevy issues a caveat against generalization: "It goes without saying that all Irish people are not like that any more than all French people are like the figures in Watteau's pictures." Yet in the section dealing with political

backgrounds he says, "When Jack Yeats was a small boy the mind of the Irish people was centred on politics ..." (*Jack B. Yeats*, 16–17).
The Bog of Allen is a large peat bog, a wetland from which the River Boyne rises in Co. Kildare.

8 "Et voilà" (That's it).

9 Dr. Charles Paul (1879–?), a "médecin légiste" (forensic doctor), is compared to the British forensic medical expert Dr. Bernard Spilsbury (1877–1947).

10 "Que je me porte partie civile" (why I should sue). "Affaire classée" (closed case).

11 SB did attend the birthday celebration which was staged in two parts: at the Joyces' flat, listening to a birthday broadcast from Radio Éireann, followed by a dinner party at Eugene and Maria Jolas's home. Constantine Curran presented a "Personal Sketch" of Joyce as part of the radio broadcast (Joyce and Léon, *The James Joyce – Paul Léon Papers*, 92); his daughter Elizabeth Curran attended the party in Paris with Beckett, as described in a letter she sent to her father on 3 February 1938 (C. P. Curran, *James Joyce Remembered* [London: Oxford University Press, 1968] 90–91; see also Guggenheim, *Out of This Century: Confessions of an Art Addict*, 168). As SB wrote to McGreevy on 11 February 1938:

> There were 15 at dinner, and Sullivan & Mrs Jolas bawled their heads off afterwards. Philippe Soupault turned up late in the evening. I was glad to see him again. He was asking for you. Nino Franch [*for* Frank] was also there. He may put me in touch with film people here, if by any chance I ever feel like being in touch with anything again. I felt none the worse for the evening. Joyce danced in the old style. (TCD, MS 10402/156)

SB refers to Irish tenor John Sullivan (né John O'Sullivan, 1877–1955), whose musical career Joyce encouraged. The Italian-born film critic Nino Frank (1904–1988) had translated "Anna Livia Plurabelle" into Italian with Joyce.

12 Having acted on McGreevy's behalf with Laugier, SB felt obliged to thank Laugier for his trouble, especially if McGreevy should choose not to accept.

13 Denis Devlin.

GEORGE REAVEY

LONDON

7/2/38   Hotel Liberia

[Paris]

Dear George

Tom seemed nervous about Wynn's. But I can't change the whole topography. So stet.[1]

Will you let me know exact date of pub. as soon as it is known.

Expect to be here for some time yet, with the occasional Katzensprung to Broussais. Na ja.[2]

Love to Gwynedd.

> Yours
>
> s/ Sam

TPCS; 1 leaf, 2 sides; AN AH, *pencil, upper left margin* "re Murphy"; T *to* George Reavey Esq, 7 Great Ormond Street, London W.C.1; *pm* 7-2-38, Paris; TxU.

1 Wynn's Hotel, 35–36 Lower Abbey Street, Dublin (Beckett, *Murphy*, 54–56). As SB wrote to McGreevy on 11 February 1938: "I don't think there is anything to worry about in the Wynn[']s Hotel reference. But thank you for drawing my attention to it" (TCD, MS 10402/156).

2 "Katzensprung" (literally cat's spring); "Na ja" (well now).

GEORGE REAVEY

LONDON

[c. 8 to 19 February 1938]   Liberia

[Paris]

Dear G.

> Sorry.

It has occurred to me that 8/6 is far too dear for a book of only 75000 words. Would you not suggest 5/- to Ragg.[1]

> Yrs
>
> Sam

APCS; 1 leaf, 1 side; AN AH, *pencil* "re Murphy"; TxU.

1 The price of *Murphy* had been set at 8/6; however, the price given on the prospectus was 7/6.

GEORGE REAVEY
LONDON

20/2/38   Liberia
                                                    [Paris]

Dear George

N.C.'s address is c/o Lloyds, 43 Bd. des Capucines, Paris.[1]

Glad to hear Geer is shoved off till May. Haven't seen much of him lately. They want me to go with them to Holland in April. Ne demande pas mieux but shn't have the price. How did you like the Kandinsky?[2]

I shall want 6 copies of M., miserable wretch that I am, in addition to the free ones. Also send me a copy of Ford's poems. And tell me what cheque I am to send you for lot.[3]

I wish very much you were here to advise me about a translation (of Sade[']s 120 Days for Jack Kahane). I should like very much to do it, & the terms are moderately satisfactory, but don't know what effect it wd. have on my lit. situation in England or how it might prejudice future publications of my own there. The surface is of an unheard of obscenity & not 1 in 100 will find literature in the pornography, or beneath the pornography, let alone one of the capital works of the 18th century, which it is for me. I don't mind the obloquy, on the contrary it will get more of me into a certain room. But I don't want to be spiked as a writer, I mean as a publicist in the airiest sense. Of course as an Obelisk book, no attempt would be made to circulate it in England or USA, no official attempt, though I understand Kent ordered 8 copies of Harris's Life & Loves. And I wouldn't do it without putting my name to it. He wants a decision immediately. If I thought you were to be here next week I would hold him off till I had talked it over with you. But I suppose there is no chance of that. Anyhow it can't be a rational decision, the consequences are unforeseeable, though it strikes me you would see a lot that I don't. 150,000 words at 150 francs per 1000 is better than a poem by AE, but doesn't really enter as an element into the problem.[4]

I saw the Sieur Prudent in the Bordel de Justice. He said "Excusez-moi, Monsieur." I said "Je vous en prie, Monsieur." I had my first sneeze yesterday, i.e. I am cured.[5]

Love to Gwynedd. Ora pro me.[6]

s/ Sam

TLS; 1 leaf, 1 side; TxU.

1 Nancy Cunard's address.

2 The exhibition of Geer van Velde's work at Guggenheim Jeune was to be held in May; the Kandinsky Exhibition had opened on 18 February: 5 January 1938, n. 4.
"Ne demande pas mieux" (Couldn't ask for anything nicer).

3 SB ordered personal copies of *Murphy* and the poems of American writer Charles Henri Ford (1913–2002), *The Garden of Disorder and Other Poems* (London: Europa Press, 1938).

4 SB wrote to McGreevy on 11 February 1938: "I said it was unlikely but that I would go & talk it over. I went & said I was interested en principe at 150 francs per 1000. [...] Though I am interested in Sade & have been for a long time, and want the money badly, I would really rather not" (TCD, MS 10402/156).
Following his brief partnership (1930–1931) with French publisher of fine editions Henry Babou (n.d.), British journalist Jack Kahane (1887–1939) founded Obelisk Press in Paris in 1931 and published many books refused by other publishers who feared censorship. Among these were *The Young and Evil* (1933) by American writers Charles Henri Ford and Parker Tyler (1904–1974); *My Life and Loves* (1933) by Irish-American writer Frank Harris (né James Thomas Harris, 1856–1931); *Tropic of Cancer* (1934), *Aller retour New York* (1935), *Black Spring* (1936), *Max and the White Phagocytes* (1938), and *Tropic of Capricorn* (1939) by American writer Henry Miller (1891–1980); *House of Incest* (1936) and *Winter of Artifice* (1939) by French writer Anaïs Nin (née Angela Anaïs Nin y Culmell, 1903–1977); and *The Black Book* (1938) by English writer Lawrence Durrell (1912–1990). To "finance the serious books," he also published works of pornography (John de St Jorre, *Venus Bound: The Erotic Voyage of the Olympia Press and Its Writers* [New York: Random House, 1994] 12).
Marquis de Sade, *Les 120 Journées de Sodome, ou l'école du libertinage* (*The 120 Days of Sodom; or, the Romance of the School for Libertinage*) (written in 1785, published 1904, ed.

Eugène Dühren [Paris: Club des bibliophiles, 1904]); it appeared in a three-volume critical edition edited by Maurice Heine (Paris: Stendhal et Compagnie, aux dépens des bibliophiles souscripteurs, 1931–1935). There was no English translation at this time.

Although Obelisk Press did not officially circulate its books abroad, it did sell to individuals; Kent has not been identified.

SB compares the offer of payment per word to that which he imagines could be commanded by Irish poet AE.

5 SB attended the preliminary hearing of his assailant, Robert-Jules Prudent, on 14 February 1938, as he wrote to McGreevy on 11 February 1938: "Next Monday I have to wait on the juge d'instruction & I suppose be confronted with Prudent. Perhaps I may persuade them to give me back my clothes" (TCD, MS 10402/156). "Juge d'instruction" (examining magistrate).

"Sieur Prudent" (the Prudent gentleman); "Bordel" (literally, brothel) for Palais de Justice. "Excusez-moi, Monsieur" (I'm sorry); "Je vous en prie, Monsieur" (Not at all).

6 "Ora pro me" (pray for me).

THOMAS McGREEVY

LONDON

21/2/38   Liberia

[Paris]

dear Tom

Many thanks for your 2 letters.[1] Forgive my delay in replying.

I like when you write about pictures as much as I do when you talk about them and I envy you a concern with them that has no intermissions. I haven't been to the Louvre since I came to Paris! Nor sacrificed going to anything else. It is the kind of life that filled Dr Johnson with horror. Nothing but the days passing over. It suits me all right.[2]

I have started again to look for a room and have combed most of the 14me. There is hardly anything to be had. A few studios at prices I can't afford, one lovely one looking on to the Parc Montsouris, 12000 francs!, and worth every centime of it. There is a new house in the Rue [de l']Amiral Mouchez with rooms with hot & cold & heating for 2000. A low locality but nevertheless. I shall look at a room there next Tuesday and if it is at all possible shall move to there provisionally. And even if it is not I shall leave the Liberia, because it is too dear & there is no light. I saw a hotel room at the corner of Boulevard Auguste Blanqui & Rue de la Glacière, high up on the angle, with 2 windows, full of light, 440 including service. Whereas at the Liberia I have just got a bill for the last month, 785 fr including breakfast. They have been very decent, but I simply can't afford such prices.[3]

I saw Jack Kahane this morning. He agreed to the following conditions: 1. That I should write the preface. 2. That I should be paid 150 fr per 1000 words irrespective of state of £. 3. That I should receive half on signing of contrac[t] & half on delivery of MS. 4. That there should be no time limit. I then said I would give him a definite answer this day week. He intends to publish in 3 vols. (not simultaneously) of approx. 50,000 words each. I should be paid per vol. I should get my translator's copy (1500 fr) & 6 free copies of translation (3 vols. at 150 francs each). I have read 1st & 3rd vols. of French edition. The obscenity of surface is indescribable. Nothing could be less pornographical. It fills me with a kind of metaphysical ecstasy. The composition is extraordinary, as rigorous as Dante's. If the dispassionate statement of 600 "passions" is Puritan and a complete absence of satire juvenalesque, then it is, as you say, puritanical & juvenalesque.[4] You would loathe it whether or no. I don't know if I shall do it. I think probably I shall. It would be in a limited ed. of 1000 copies. No attempt wd. be made to distribute in England or USA. But of course it would be known that I was the translator. I would not do it without signing my name to it. I know all about the obloquy. What I don't know about is the practical effect on my own future freedom of literary action in England & USA. Would the fact of my being known as the translator, & the very literal translation, of "the most utter filth" tend to spike me as a writer myself? Could I be banned & muzzled retrospectively? The preface is important, because it enables me to make my attitude clear. Alan Belinda & Nick are all against my doing it. Brian simply says he would not himself undertake it. It appears a lot of people are after the job, including Peggy Guggenheim's ex-husband Lawrence [*for* Laurence] Vail.[5]

I wish I had been in London for the Kandinsky. How did you like it?[6]

I go back to Broussais on Thursday and hope that may be the last time. I was confronted with Prudent in the Palais de Justice this day week & we exchanged amiabilities. The trial should come on now soon, when I shall have the pleasure of recovering my sorely missed clothes, and perhaps even receive a franc damages.[7] Talking of which I hear Gogarty gave an oyster party in the Bail[e]y to celebrate my premature demise, and has sold his premises in Ely Place to the Royal Hibernian Academy, which means that Harry will perhaps get some money after all, & I my return fare from Paris.[8]

      Love ever

      Sam

ALS; 2 leaves, 3 sides; *on letterhead:* LA COUPOLE, 102 BD DU MONTPARNASSE; TCD, MS 10402/157.

1 McGreevy's letters to SB have not been found.

2 Samuel Johnson listed as his first purpose "To avoid idleness" (Easter Eve 1761); SB cites from Johnson's *Miscellanies Prayers and Meditations*, Easter Day 7 April 1765): "I know not how the days pass over me" (Johnson, *Diaries, Prayers, and Annals*, 92; BIF, UoR, MS 2461/1, f. 1R).

3 SB had been staying at the Hôtel Libéria since the end of November 1937. He looked for a room in the 14th arrondissement.

According to the Cost-of-living / Consumer Prices Index in 1938, France had the highest increase in costs since 1929 (115 as compared to 99 in Ireland) (B. R. Mitchell, *International Historical Statistics: Europe 1750–1988*, 3rd edn. [New York: Stockton Press, 1992] 848.

4 SB refers to the three-volume edition of Sade's *Les 120 Journées de Sodome* by Maurice Heine (see 20 February 1938, n. 4).

Juvenal (né Decimus Junius Juvenalis c. 55–140), whose satires attacked the vices of Rome.

5 Alan and Belinda Duncan, Nick Balachef, Brian Coffey.

French-born writer and artist Laurence Vail (1891–1968) was married to Peggy Guggenheim from 1922 to 1929.

6 The Kandinsky Exhibition at Guggenheim Jeune: 5 January 1938, n. 4.

7 The Hôpital Broussais, where SB had been taken following the stabbing and to which he returned for check-ups. SB's exchanges with Prudent: 20 February 1938, n. 5.

8 Oliver St. John Gogarty, who lost the libel suit brought against him by Harry Sinclair at which SB had testified for the plaintiff, "celebrated" at The Bailey, Dublin tavern and restaurant, then at 2–3 Duke Street.

The proposed sale of Gogarty's home on Ely Place: 6 October 1937, n. 8.

Harry Sinclair had been awarded damages, which were as yet unpaid; as a consequence, SB's fare to Dublin/Paris had not yet been reimbursed.

GEORGE REAVEY

LONDON

8/3/38 Hôtel Liberia
9 Rue de la Grande Chaumière
Paris 6me

Dear George

Many thanks for card. And for 3 Murphys, in batches of 1 & 2. The appearance is very satisfactory and the effort to make an Irishman of me touching.[1] No mistakes in text that I can see.

I should like Routledge to send copies to the following:

Jack Yeats (whose address they have).

Arland Ussher, Esq., Cappagh House, Cappagh, Co. Waterford, Ireland.

Dr Geoffrey Thompson, 71 Harley Street, London W.1.

Tom McGreevy.

Laz Aaronson Esq., 26 Westbourne Terrace Road, London W.2.

Herr Axel Kaun, Greiffenberg, Uckermark, Germany.

Denis Devlin (whose address you have).[2]

No doubt I shall be fool enough to think of others later.

I have accepted the Sade translation at 150 francs per 1000. He wants to postpone for 3 or 4 months. I have written saying that I can't guarantee being of the same mind then, or having the time to spare. No contract therefore yet.[3]

Prudent got off with 2 months, to my relief. He was ably defended, the plea of blind drunkenness skilfully advanced and I represented as the aggressor.[4]

Alfred Péron, 69 Rue de la Tombe-Issoire, Paris 14me, is anxious to translate Murphy into French. He is a close friend of mine, an expert translator and I should be very glad for him to do it. He has contacts and so have friends of his, notably with the NRF & Dénoël et Steele.[5] Will you make overtures in the matter, or would you prefer us to do so? Perhaps it would be better to leave it till you are over. When is that?

I haven't had a word to throw to a dog, let alone van Velde, so have seen little of him. I haven't done the foreword and wonder if I ever shall. The Sterns introduced me last night in the Flore to one Brian Howard, at his request. He wanted to pump me about modern German art apropos of a big rétrospective planned for London in the summer (Read & Borenius). He was drunk and with Nancy Cunard, whose bottom she said was better and left eye black. She said that the fact of her having been the first to publish him and me should set up a bond between us. It did not. Stern has a novel with Secker in the autumn.[6]

Physically I am quite well again. Yesterday I played 7 sets of
tennis at Mirabeau without collapsing.[7]

Love to Gwynedd

Ever

s/ Sam

TLS; 1 leaf, 1 side; AH *ink checkmark before the names of* Yeats, Ussher, Thompson, and
Kaun; TxU.

1   Reavey's card to SB has not been found.
Murphy was published on 7 March 1938. SB wrote to McGreevy, 8 March 1938: "I got
some advance copies of Murphy. All green white & yellow. In honour of Celia? They do
their best, and not merely with the blurbs, to turn me into an Irishman" (TCD, MS
10402/158). The jacket copy noted: "The reader is carried along on the wave of an
abundant creative imagination expressing itself in scene after scene of superlative
comedy, ironic situations that only the Irish genius could conceive."

2   From SB's list for presentation copies, markings indicate that copies were sent to
Yeats, Ussher, Thompson, and Kaun. SB's presentation copy to "Laz and Dorothy"
(Aaronson) is dated May 1938 (InU).

3   A translation of Sade's *Les 120 Journées de Sodome* was published under the imprint
of Jack Kahane's son Maurice Girodias in 1954 (Marquis de Sade, *The 120 Days of Sodom;
or, The Romance of the School for Libertinage*, tr. Pieralessandro Casavini [pseud. of Austryn
Wainhouse] [Paris: Olympia Press, 1954]).

4   As SB wrote to McGreevy on 8 March 1938: "The Prudent affaire [sic] came on last
Monday. I was there with Alan. We did not press it, he was ably defended, I became
the provocateur in the end, he was sentenced to 2 months imprisonment" (TCD, MS
10402/158). SB wrote to Arland Ussher on 27 March 1938: "The desperado got off with
2 months. Not bad for a 5th conviction. I am still without my clothes, taken away from
me at the time as pièces de conviction & never produced. I have now to prove that they
ever belonged to me. But mentally I am speechless" (TxU). "Pièces à conviction"
(exhibits in evidence).

5   Alfred Péron, who had worked with SB on the preliminary translation of Joyce's
"Anna Livia Plurabelle," encouraged SB to arrange a translation of *Murphy*; Péron had
contacts with the *Nouvelle Revue Française*.
The Paris publishing firm Denoël et Steele was founded in 1930 by Bernard Steele
(1902–1979) and Robert Denoël (1902–1945), but when Steele returned to the United
States at the end of 1936, the firm became Les Editions Denoël.

6   SB had been asked to write a note for the catalogue of the Geer van Velde
Exhibition at Guggenheim Jeune.
Anglo-Irish writer and translator James Andrew Stern (1904–1993) and his wife
Tania Stern (née Kurella, 1904–1995) collaborated on translations from the German;
SB wrote to McGreevy on 8 March 1938, "I met them at Xmas with Aaronson, very
nice. He is Irish and writes. Published I think by Secker" (TCD, MS 10402/158). James

Stern's *Something Wrong: A Collection of Twelve Stories* was published by Secker and Warburg in 1938.

Brian Howard (1905-1958) was a member of the organizing committee, headed by Herbert Read, of the "Exhibition of Twentieth-Century German Art" held in July 1938 at the New Burlington Galleries, London. The exhibition drew on work in private collections so it would not compromise any artist still residing in Germany: [Herbert Read], *Exhibition of Twentieth Century German Art: July, 1938* (London: New Burlington Galleries, 1938) 5-7. The Finnish-born art historian and Editor of *Burlington Magazine* from 1940 to 1945 Tancred Borenius (1885-1948) was a patron of the exhibition.

Nancy Cunard had burned herself on a heater (SB to McGreevy, 11 February 1938, TCD, MS 10402/156). Cunard published Brian Howard's *God Save the King* (Paris: Hours Press, 1930).

7 Tennis couverts Mirabeau (covered tennis courts) were located at 1 Rue Rémusat, Paris 16, near the Mirabeau métro station.

GEORGE REAVEY

LONDON

23/3 [1938]   Liberia

[Paris]

[no greeting]

Thanks for cuttings. It is gratifying to have my <u>intention</u> revealed to me after all this time.[1] Nothing new here. Painting still began with Cézanne.

     Sam

APCS; 1 leaf, 1 side; Baldovinetti, "La Vierge et l'Enfant"; *to* George Reavey Esq, 7 Great Ormond Street, LONDON WC1; *pm* 23-3-38, Paris; TxU.

1 By this date the reviews of *Murphy* were: Anon., "*Murphy*. By Samuel Beckett," *Times Literary Supplement* 12 March 1938: 172; Dilys Powell, "Flight from Reality," *Sunday Times* 13 March 1938: 8; Edwin Muir, "New Novels," *The Listener* 19.479 (16 March 1938) 597; Dylan Thomas, "Recent Novels," *The New English Weekly* 12.23 (17 March 1938) 454-455; and Frank Swinnerton, "People and Puppets," *The Observer* 20 March 1938: 6.

Dylan Thomas wrote of *Murphy*: "It is not rightly what it should be, that is what Mr. Beckett intended it to be: a story about the conflict between the inside and the outsides of certain curious people. It fails in its purpose because the minds and the bodies of these characters are almost utterly without relations to each other" (454).

THOMAS McGREEVY
LONDON

3/4/38   Liberia
                                                               [Paris]

Dear Tom

Thanks for your letter. No, the reviews did not surprise me. No[t] even those of Messrs. Muir & Thomas. Church was friendly in John O'Londons, as I understand so was Kate O'Brien in the last Spectator but one, which I have not seen.[1] Reavey tells me that Routledge are satisfied with sales. Nothing from Ireland so far that I know of. Brian had a long article to appear in this month's Ireland To-Day, but the paper expired just in time. My Bookman experience over again.[2] By the way I told Reavey to give you a copy and hope you got it. I have sent no copies out from here, life is laborious enough without making parcels of books & bringing them to the P.O. And you know how pleased I shall be to write in the book when we meet. Jack Yeats wrote very nicely about it, so did Aaronson & Geoffrey.[3]

I have seen very little of the Joyces since they returned from Zurich. He was very poorly with an eye & then some kind of intestinal flu.[4] [...]

A French translation by Péron of my Alba appeared in Soutes. Not one of his best efforts.[5] He is in good form & I lunch with him every Tuesday & play tennis afterwards. I hope to arrange for him to translate Murphy. He is anxious to do so. I sent a copy to Raymond Queneau, who has just been appointed reader to Gallimard & whom I met in the Volontés galère. But Dénoël & Steele or the Mercure are more likely.[6]

613

I was at the Flore last night to arrange with Alan to go out & see his mother who is installed now in some home outside the Porte d'Orléans. Laugier came in with his woman, but we did not disturb one another.[7]

I wrote a short poem in French but otherwise nothing.[8] I have the feeling that any poems there may happen to be in the future will be in French.

A note from Pelorson this morning, commanding me to his presence next Saturday afternoon for a reading of Caligula (his play). I have seen nothing of them at all lately, I suppose because I am so little interested in the turn his writing has taken. I think I told you about my having been so indiscrete [sic] as to say to Marcelle at the Joyce birthday party, when she invited my opinion, that the review might with more justice be called Nolontés. Also Jolas, Henry Miller, Guégen [for Guéguen], & Cie., all of them leading lights, are not enticing.[9]

I had a few minutes with Nancy Cunard the other evening, the eve of her departure for south of France, to see the exiled Douglas. I also saw Howard again for a moment, very convulsed & aloof.[10]

Had a lovely afternoon yesterday in the Louvre, just strolling around without working. The topography is all changed, for the worse I think, though I suppose it is only provisional. For ex. to get from the Salle des 7 Mètres to the Grande Galerie one has to make a long détour through the French rooms. Half the Grande Galerie is closed. I had forgotten the little Fabritius. A very slapdash attribution. More like a Flinck. The Baldovinetti (?) & Verocchio [for Verrocchio] Virgins & Childs were lovely & the Mantegnas all of a sudden extraordinarily disappointing, except the Sebastian.[11]

News from home good. Mother still very busy spending money on her little house at Greystones harbour, turning down offers for Cooldrinagh, and obviously very lonely. Jean apparently incredibly enormous 2 months before her time, & Frank as usual up to his eyes in work.[12]

I shall probably be in London early in May for the van Velde Exhibition, & expect to stay with Geoffrey. They may be here for a week-end before then.[13] So far I have found nothing in the way of a room here, and am very very tired of hotel life and the lack of my books, and know I shall never do any work until I find a place of my own.

Do you remember the Courbet self-portrait? Airily dismissed in my little book as a pleasant imitation of Titian's Homme au gant![14]

Write soon. God's blessing.

Sam

ALS; 2 leaves, 5 sides; *letterhead*: LA ROTONDE EN MONTPARNASSE, 105 BD DU MONTPARNASSE, PARIS; TCD, MS 10402/159.

1 Dylan Thomas's review was critical of *Murphy*, but Edwin Muir commented positively on SB's wit, and concluded, "there are very amusing episodes ... and if this book does not completely bore or exasperate the reader, it will probably give him more than ordinary amusement" (Muir, "New Novels," 597). Richard Church called *Murphy* "a riot of highbrow fun," and Kate O'Brien (1897–1974) wrote, "Rarely, indeed, have I been so entertained by a book, so tempted to superlatives and perhaps hyperboles of praise. It truly is magnificent and a treasure ... For the right readers it is a book in a hundred thousand" (Richard Church, "Samuel Beckett gives us 'a riot of highbrow fun,'"*John O'London's Weekly* 39.990 (1 April 1938) 23; Kate O'Brien, "Fiction," *The Spectator* 25 March 1938: 546).

2 By 31 March 1938, regular sales of *Murphy* accounted for 240 copies (UoR, Routledge).

No reviews had appeared in Ireland. Brian Coffey's review of *Murphy*, dated "Paris. March, 1938," was written for *Ireland To-Day*, which discontinued publication with the March 1938 issue (3.3) (DeU, Coffey, AMS of review; TxU, Coffey, TMS of review). SB is reminded of his essay "Censorship in the Saorstat" that was commissioned by *The Bookman* but not published because the journal ceased publication in December 1934 (see 8 September 1934, n. 9).

3 The letters from Jack Yeats, Laz Aaronson, and Geoffrey Thompson to SB have not been found.

4 The Joyces left Paris for Switzerland on 6 February and planned to be gone about three weeks, according to SB's letter to McGreevy of 11 February 1938 (TCD, MS 10402/156); Joyce returned to Paris early in March 1938 (Norburn, *A James Joyce Chronology*, 181). Joyce wrote to Carola Giedion-Welcker from Paris on 28 March 1938 that he had been unwell since his return (Joyce, *Letters of James Joyce*, III, 418). As Joyce wrote to Helen Joyce, SB had dinner with them on 6 April at the Gormans' (419).

5 Samuel Beckett, "Alba," tr. A. R. Péron, *Soutes* 9 (1938) 41.

6 French writer and editor Raymond Queneau (1903–1976) was co-founder of *Volontés* (December 1937–1939) with Georges Pelorson, Eugene Jolas, Pierre Guéguen (1889–1965), Henry Miller, Frédéric Joliot-Curie (né Jean-Frédéric Joliot, 1900–1958), and Camille Schuwer (1888–1981); SB calls them the "galère" (crew) (for further information on the group: Vincent Giroud, "Transition to Vichy: The Case of Georges Pelorson," *Modernism/Modernity* 7.2 [2000] 221–248).

The French publishing house Mercure de France was founded in 1894.

7 Alan Duncan's mother was Ellen Duncan (née Douglas, known as Ellie, c. 1850–1939), a founder of the United Arts Club in Dublin, and first Curator of the Municipal Gallery of Modern Art, Dublin.

SB may have seen Henri Laugier with his companion Marie Cuttoli (1879–1973), who, with Laugier, built an important collection of contemporary art (see *Collection Marie Cuttoli – Henri Laugier, Paris* [Basel: Galerie Beyeler, 1970]).

8 This poem may have been one of the twelve published as "Poèmes 38–39," *Les Temps Modernes*, 288–293.

9 Pelorson's play *Caligula*, based on the life of Gaius Caesar Augustus Germanicus (AD 12–41), Emperor of Rome from AD 37 to 41, was partially published in three issues of *Volontés*: "Caligula – Prologue," *Volontés* 1 (January 1938) 18–27; "Caligula – Acte III," *Volontés* 3 (March 1938) 41–59; "Caligula – Acte IV," *Volontés* 8 (August 1938) 30–35.

According to Eugene Jolas's notes for an autobiography, "Pelorson was writing plays with a fascist tendency then and he would invite his friends to listen to his reading of them" (CtY, Eugene and Maria Jolas Papers, GEN MS 108/Boxes 5–12 [Drafts of Man from Babel]; not included in Jolas, *Man from Babel*).

SB had written to McGreevy on 11 February 1938: "I told Marcelle Pelorson bluntly at the Joyce party that I found Georges' editorials negative & far too angry & that a better title for the review, to judge by its appearances to date, would be <u>Nolontés</u>" (TCD, MS 10402/156). "Volontés" (acts of will), a noun ultimately derived from the Latin verb "velle" (to want); SB invents an antonym similarly derived from the Latin verb "nolle" (not to want): "Nolontés."

"Cie." (Co.).

10 Nancy Cunard left to see Norman Douglas, who had been an expatriate in Florence for many years, but who left Italy hurriedly in June 1937 on account of legal difficulties that were unresolved until January 1938, whereupon he decided he would remain in France (see Mark Holloway, *Norman Douglas: A Biography* [London: Secker and Warburg, 1976] 430–438).

Brian Howard.

11 The Louvre's Salle des 7 Mètres, off the Staircase Daru, normally would have led directly into the Grande Galerie de Peinture; however, the adjacent portion of the

Grande Galerie was closed, leaving access through the French rooms (at that time the Salle Daru, the Salle Denon, and the Salle des États, or possibly even a further detour through the Salle Mollien and the small galleries facing the Cour Lefuel).

It is not known to which painting by Carel Fabritius SB refers. *Head of an Elderly Man* (Louvre, R. F. 3834) is a relatively small portrait (24×20.7 cm); it was acquired by the Louvre in 1934 and is attributed to Carel Fabritius, but this attribution is considered doubtful by Christopher Brown (*Carel Fabritius: Complete Edition with a Catalogue Raisonné* [Ithaca, NY: Cornell University Press, 1981] 129). The Louvre did not own a painting by Carel's brother Barent Fabritius (1624–1673) at this time. Dutch painter Govaert Flinck (1615–1660).

The image of *Virgin and Child* (Louvre, R. F. 1112) by Florentine painter Alesso Baldovinetti (c. 1425–1499) was on the card SB had sent to George Reavey on 23 March 1938.

Florentine sculptor and painter Andrea del Verrocchio (Andrea di Michele di Francesco Cioni, 1435 – c. 1488) was a pupil of Baldovinetti, whose workshop also included Leonardo da Vinci, Lorenzo di Credi (c. 1456–1536), Perugino, and Domenico Ghirlandaio. There are few paintings ascribed to Verrocchio and none in the Louvre; however, the association of his workshop may have been mentioned in the many depictions of "Virgin and Child" by da Vinci and his other pupils; Ghirlandaio's *Virgin and Child* (Louvre, R. F. 1266) is described by the Louvre as influenced by Verrocchio.

Andrea Mantegna's *St. Sebastian* (Louvre, R. F. 1766).

12 Greystones is on the coast in Co. Wicklow. Frank and Jean Beckett were expecting their first child.

13 The Geer van Velde Exhibition at Guggenheim Jeune: 5 January 1938, n. 4. Geoffrey and Ursula Thompson.

14 The self-portrait by Gustave Courbet to which SB refers is *Man with the Leather Belt* (Louvre R. F. 339, now in the Musée d'Orsay); Titian's *Portrait of a Man* is also known as *Man with the Glove* (Louvre, inv. 757).

GEORGE REAVEY

LONDON

<u>22 Avril</u> [1938]   6 Rue des Favorites

[Paris] 15me

Dear George

Thanks for letter & article, which I liked very much indeed, though I find him less quietist than you suggest. However it is a good line for the public. The Fabritius street-corner by the way in the National is very Japanese.[1]

I hope some American mug takes <u>Murphy</u> soon. I want money very badly at the moment.[2] Keep the 50 fr till we meet.

I have been camping in the new place for the past week & am slowly getting installed. I like it. It is bright & there is a staircase to stagger up at night. I hope next time you come you will stay with me.[3]

I had a letter from Peggy very worried about the triage of pictures & anxious for the "Picassos" to be excluded as far as possible. I replied telling her not to worry, that Geer's most Picasso was about as Picasso as Dawson's ex-surrealist's arse. She informs me further that she is using my note after all. And my name. Tant pis pour tout le monde.[4]

I am not sure when I shall arrive in London. In time for the vernissage is all I can say for certain. There is a possibility of my getting a free ride <u>par les airs</u>.[5]

Must I see Routledge & Co? With nothing in my hand?[6]

I wrote another French poem. Will the ELB publish <u>Poems in French & English</u>?[7]

Love to you both
Sam

ALS; 2 leaves, 2 sides; *letterhead:* LA ROYALE, 25, RUE ROYALE; TxU.

1 SB refers to George Reavey's introduction for the Geer van Velde Exhibition at the Guggenheim Jeune ("Geer van Velde," *London Bulletin* 2 [May 1938] 16). Reavey writes: "In the case of Geer van Velde, the motive of desire is already dead because life has been lived unsparingly. In its place there is a timeless nostalgia, a sort of disembodied all-pervading harmony more akin to Chinese than to western European philosophy."
   SB refers to Carel Fabritius's painting *A View of Delft with Musical Instrument Seller's Stall* in the National Gallery, London (NGL 3714).

2 Reavey was sending *Murphy* to American publishers.

3 SB writes from his new apartment, 6 Rue des Favorites, Paris 15. It was on the top floor and had inside stairs to a sleeping loft (see Knowlson, *Damned to Fame*, 265–266).

4 Peggy Guggenheim wanted to exclude those paintings by Geer van Velde that she felt were derived from Picasso's style; this may have prompted the final lines of SB's

note introducing Geer van Velde's work: "Believes painting should mind its own business, *i.e.* colour. *I.e.* no more say Picasso than Fabritius, Vermeer. Or inversely" ("Geer van Velde," *London Bulletin* 2 [May 1938] 15; rpt. Beckett, *Disjecta*, 117). SB's note on Geer van Velde is signed. "Tant pis pour tout le monde" (Too bad for everyone). The catalogue for the van Velde Exhibition appeared in the May issue of *London Bulletin*, which published the catalogues of three adjacent galleries on Cork Street (the London, the Major, and Guggenheim Jeune) ("Art: Popular Front," *Cavalcade* [21 May 1938] n.p.).

Peter Norman Dawson (1902–1960), English surrealist painter, graphic artist and ceramicist, a member of the "London Group," and at this time Deputy Principal of the Camberwell School of Arts and Crafts, London; his work was included in the Contemporary Painting and Sculpture exhibition at Guggenheim Jeune, 21 June to 2 July 1938.

5 The "vernissage" (private view) of the Geer van Velde Exhibition was held on 5 May 1938.

"Par les airs" (borne through the airs). On 28 April 1938, SB wrote to Reavey: "As there is no news of the flying-machine it is hard for me to say definitely when I arrive. But unless I am offered a free seat for Wednesday the 4th I shall be in London evening of Tuesday 3rd" (TxU). And to McGreevy, 1 May 1938: "Will you reserve me a room at 49 [Harrington Road] for Tuesday evening, if there is one to spare. I expect to arrive London about 6 p.m via Dieppe-Newhaven" (TCD, MS 10402/165).

6 Routledge was the publisher of *Murphy*. T. M. Ragg, having dealt exclusively with Reavey, had not met SB.

7 The French poem just written by SB has not been identified, but it is one of those published in the group "Poèmes 38–39," *Les Temps Modernes* 288–293. Reavey's agency in London was the European Literary Bureau; its Europa Press had published SB's first collection of poems, *Echo's Bones and Other Precipitates*. SB may be asking if Reavey, now that he is based in London, would publish work that was in both French and English.

THOMAS McGREEVY

LONDON

22 Avril [1938]   6 Rue des Favorites
                                                     Paris 15$^{\underline{\text{me}}}$

Dear Tom

Herewith my new address. I have been camping there for the past week. People have been good with presents to get me started, but it is a terribly expensive business. I like the place, it is bright & comfortable, & I like the quarter, well away from the stage artists. I hope you will very soon come & stay with me.[1]

I have been living very quietly, seeing the Joyces a little, & Brian a little, and one or two French people, & that is all. A couple of poems in French in the last fortnight are the extent of my work since coming to Paris. Péron's Soutes is publishing one, & perhaps Volontés the other.[2] I was round at the Pelorsons['] one afternoon to hear Georges read his play Caligula – 4 acts & a prologue.[3] Very accomplished & very dull. He feels my lack of interest in his present work & we meet very seldom.

[...]

I shall be in London for the van Velde exhibition, staying probably with Geoffrey. I would prefer to be independent at Harrington Road, but I am lamentably broke.[4] I don't expect I shall be able to afford more than a few days, which means I suppose my being rude to people I have no wish to be rude to.

Leventhal was over at Easter, also Aaronson, also Harry Johnson [...] It is a great relief to be out of hotel, & in light & air (7th floor, lift day & night).

Frank was ill but is all right again.[5] Mother melancholy.

Write soon

     Love ever

        Sam

ALS; 3 leaves, 3 sides; *letterhead*: LA ROYALE, 25, RUE ROYALE, Paris; TCD, MS 10402/160. *Dating*: from address.

1 6 Rue des Favorites, near the Vaugirard métro station and off Rue de Vaugirard.

2 Brian Coffey.
None of SB's poems in French was published in either *Soutes* or *Volontés*.

3 Georges Pelorson and his wife Marcelle. *Caligula*: 3 April 1938, n. 9.

4 Originally, SB had planned to stay with Geoffrey and Ursula Thompson in London, but by 28 April he wrote to Reavey that he would probably stay at Harrington Road where McGreevy had a room (TxU).

5 Harry Johnson may refer to Henry John Johnson (n.d.) who was an External Auditor at Trinity College Dublin from 1931, and received an MA *jure officii* in 1940 from TCD; Johnson was Head Cashier of the Bank of Ireland (John Luce, 31 August 1993, 12 November 1993).
Frank Beckett.

ARLAND USSHER

12/5/38   6 Rue des Favorites
                                               Paris 15me

Dear Arland

Thanks for letter and MS, which I liked. The image of the long drop and the garters was the best I have seen for a long time, much better than Herriot's "obsolete vitamins of romanticism". I gave them to my agent, without any great hope of his being able to place them, though the metaphysico-political is exactly his line.[1]

I have just returned from a week in London, where I went for the opening of my Dutch-Paris friend Geer van Velde his exhibition of hand-paintings.[2] At the opening was the Koenigs, who said that her best energies in Berlin at one period were expended on deciphering my postcards to you.[3] The same evening at the Café Royal I ran into Morrison, green-foaming at the commissures after dinner of the TCD association. I saw him the next day at lunch in De Hems oyster paradise, fresh from a successful collaboration in the sterilisation of the wife of a colleague. He quoted the opening of a work on which he is engaged, a version of the Pentateuch in heroic couplets free in every sense rather anti-semitic in tone. This no doubt for the delectation of Aaronson and Voigt, who were present. Uncertain what sandwich to eat with his brandy, and being asked by the waitress did he not care for salmon, he said: "No, nor Gluckstein either." He attributed the word Erse to Chaucer and declared that it was in this language that Moses received the decalogue, from those parts of Jehovah that alone were visible, i.e. the hinder. And so on.[4] A Mr Brown, I think Hilton Brown, a Scottish novelist, left early.[5] So did I. Voigt remained, to drink and enlargen his experience. I thought he was a pleasant man, and the more so a night or two later when he was good enough to incorporate one of my humble and stammering ideas in a wireless address. He quoted the opening of the Midnight Court in what was good enough for me.[6]

I also ran into Harry Sinclair, complete with Norman Reddin, English lawyer and English-Israelite backer. Cissie and family expect to arrive in London in about a week. They met Fleck in Cape Town where apparently he is having some success.[7]

Con was in Paris at Easter, as was Aaronson. He is being mentioned as the rising Provost. He hopes to place an article by me on the divine marquise [*for* divin marquis] in Hermathena of all places, where by the way Miss MacCarthy has suddenly begun to translate from Stefan Georg[e].[8]

I spoke to Voigt of your essays and he became anxious to see them. Why not send him others? I can arrange of course with Reavey to pass on to him those he has.[9]

I read nothing and write nothing, unless it is Kant (de nobis ipsis silemus) and French anacreontics.[10]

Ew. Wohlgeb.

ergebenster Diener[11]

s/ Sam

TLS; 1 leaf, 1 side; pencil signature; TxU.

1 Arland Ussher had sent SB the manuscript of his essay "The Age of Shadows" which addressed the transition from the eighteenth century to the twentieth:

> In the eighteenth century the static world of antiquity had broken thread after thread that suspended it from the arch of heaven, until it hung by a single gossamer; now the last thread has snapped … Then came a first collision, the Great War; and since then we have become a little still, a little frightened. Yet most are drunken with the intoxication of speed, though a few are trying to attach the careering world to some subjective absolute of the Beautiful or the Useful (which is like hoping to break one's fall by pulling at one's own garters). (Arland Ussher, "Three Essays," *Nineteenth Century and After* 124.742 [December 1938] 736–737)

SB compares Ussher's images to those of French politician and writer Edouard Herriot (1872–1957), who studied at the Ecole Normale Supérieure. The source of the phrase "obsolete vitamins of romanticism" is not known. SB gave Ussher's essays to George Reavey.

2 Geer van Velde's exhibition at Guggenheim Jeune; it is not known what SB intends by "hand-paintings."

3 Mrs. Koenig, who knew Ussher in Berlin, has not been identified.

4 Edward Morrison (1897–1968), a physician trained at Trinity College Dublin and practicing at this time in London; his anti-Semitic attitude is evident in a letter to Ussher written on 7 January 1939 (TCD, MS 9037/2597), decrying Ussher's intention to house Jewish refugees in Ireland.

De Hems Pub, 11 Macclesfield Street, Soho, London, called attention to its specialty with oyster shells on its walls.

Morrison's authorship of a version of the Pentateuch is SB's invention.

Lazarus Aaronson, who was Jewish.

Frederick Augustus Voigt (1892–1957), Editor of *Nineteenth Century and After* from 1936 to 1946 and a regular commentator on the BBC. Voigt's anti-Nazi stance was articulated in his book *Unto Caesar: On Political Tendencies in Modern Europe* (1938).

The London catering firm of J. Lyons and Co. was begun by the Salmon and Gluckstein families (Isador Gluckstein, 1851–1920; Montague Gluckstein, 1854–1922; Barney Salmon, 1829–1897; Alfred Salmon, 1868–1928); they collaborated with Joseph Lyons (1847–1917) whose name was adopted for the company.

"Erse" (the Irish language) is linked by Morrison to the spelling of "arse" used by Geoffrey Chaucer.

5 Scottish novelist Charles Hilton Brown (1890–1961), whose short stories were frequently broadcast by the BBC.

6 Frederick Voigt's World Affairs talk on the BBC on 9 May 1938, "The Rome Talks," was the first that followed SB's meeting with him on 5 May. It is not known what he may have incorporated in it from SB's conversation, and there is no quotation of the comic poem in Gaelic by Brian Merriman (c. 1745–1805). Voight must have declaimed the opening of *The Midnight Court* (*Cuirt an Mheadhon Oidhche*, 1780) that evening, for it was not part of his radio talk.

7 Gerard Norman Reddin (1896–1942), a lawyer and playwright, active with the Irish Theatre in Dublin and a founding Director of the Gate Theatre.

Cissie Sinclair and her two youngest daughters were returning from South Africa via London to Dublin. German artist Otto Julius Carl Fleck (1902–1960) studied at the Kassel Academy under Ewald Dülberg and knew the Sinclairs when they lived in Kassel; he later worked as an art restorer with several major collections in Cape Town and Johannesburg, and had an exhibition of his work in 1938 in Johannesburg.

8 There is no evidence that Leventhal was a candidate for Provost at Trinity College Dublin at this time, although he was working editorially with the TCD review *Hermathena*.

SB's interest in Sade makes this a likely subject; however, *Hermathena* did not publish an essay by SB. The Marquis de Sade has sometimes been referred to as "le divin marquis," although here SB, inexplicably, uses the feminine form.

Ethna MacCarthy published the translation of an untitled poem from the German by Stefan George that begins "Wir schreiten auf und ab im reichen flitter . . ." ("Under the beech trees we patrolled . . ."), within the section of poetry entitled "Kottabistae" (*Hermathena*, 51 [May 1938] 152–153).

9 Voight later published three essays by Ussher in *Nineteenth Century and After* (see n. 1 above).

10 SB's set of the complete works of Kant: 5 January 1938, n. 13. "De nobis ipsis silemus" (Of ourselves we are silent). SB quotes from the epigraph to Kant's *First Critique of Reason* (Immanuel Kant, *Immanuel Kants Werke* III, *Kritik der Reinen Vernunft*, ed. Albert Görland [Berlin: Bruno Cassirer, 1922] [unpaginated]).

11 "Ew. Wohlgeb." ([Ehrwürden Wohlgeboren], most noble sir), "ergebenster Diener" (most humble servant).

THOMAS McGREEVY
LONDON

26$^{\underline{th}}$ May [1938]   6 Rue des Favorites
                                                Paris 15$^{\underline{me}}$

Dear Tom

Forgive my not writing before. It has been people, people, people, until I wonder what horrible thing has happened to me that I have so little peace any more. Peggy turned up & had a lot to say about some contract with van Velde. Then he turned up, with his account. You know how interested I am in such things. I told Peggy what you thought of the Reavey contretemps. She seems to have cooled off on the matter. Van Velde does not seem to realise what she has done for him and I must say, after having heard both sides of the business, that he seems to have been rather unwarrantedly avaricious. He is naïf enough to think that his market value in London is now considerable & that people like Mesens & Zwemmer have a real interest in his painting. I understand that he wants security to work undisturbed for a year, but to press for 250 guineas instead of 250 pounds is a pettiness that doesn't fit in at all with the rest of him. Anyhow I am tired of the whole thing.[1]

I had rather shocking news from Frank about mother. Apparently she was reading in bed by candle-light (it is so pathetic to think of her going back to the candle for no reason that I can imagine except that that was how she read in bed 30 years ago), fell asleep over the book & woke up to find the sheets on fire. She succeeded in putting it out but seems to have burnt her hands badly. Of course she kept it from me. I feel sorry for her often to the point of tears. That is the part that was not analysed away, I suppose.

Jean is due in 5 weeks.[2] Frank writes rapturously of lying about in the garden in the sun among the sweet pea & the roses. Happy youth.

Have seen practically nothing of Brian. The last occasion, about a week ago, I had an appointment to meet him at the Rond Point & found him instead in the bar of the Coupole with McCalmon [*for* McAlmon] & Co., excitedly loquacious. He remarked to me when at last I got him away that he found those people "very important", the amalgam of emotion & intelligence "very important", & appeared not to like it when I said

I could find no trace of either emotion or intelligence. On Tuesday he went down to the Vallée de Chevreuse to stay with McCalmon. I am sorry to see him moving in that direction. His conversation is derogating to the kind of thing one said at 17, – if I'm not dead in 2 years I'll join the foreign legion, etc. I have forgotten the answers.[3]

I have not seen the Duncans at all & never go near the Flore or Zeyer. I suppose I must have them to tea.[4] Helen, Giorgio & Peggy were round to see the place yesterday & we dined at Villa Scheffer & went out afterwards. I haven't seen the parents for over a week. The last time was at a party given by Helen, the usual crowd plus Nino Frank, who declaimed the Italian translation of Anna Livia. Then all the old songs & the old stupors. Quel ennui. Helen & Giorgio have not spoken much of you. Last night he was recalling with brandy melancholy the times in 1928–9 when you were so often round at Rue Huysmanns [*for* Huysmans].[5]

A terrible wireless has started next door. They turn it on when they get up, keep it on till they go out, & turn it on again when they come in. One morning it waked me at 7 a.m. I must put up with it.

I am very tired & have been feeling the left side a little. Nothing to worry about but rather discouraging. Nothing in the way of work but a long poem in French that you would not like I fear.[6] Gallimard rejected Murphy.[7]

I have read Sartre's Nausée & find it extraordinarily good.[8] But you would not agree with me.

I enjoyed our afternoon very much indeed, and have often thought since of the Saliba & the Toulouse-Lautrecs.[9] By myself I have not the energy to get to these places.

I wrote about a fortnight ago to Pelorson putting off an engagement & asking him to name any other day. Since then I have heard nothing from him, except the 5th no. of <u>Volontés</u>, considerably more ignominious than any of the former ones.[10]

God love thee. Remember if you are coming to Paris, & if it can be managed without offence to the Lurçats, there is a welcome for you here.[11]

Love to Hester & Dilly.[12]

Ever

Sam

ALS; 4 leaves, 4 sides; *torn left edge*, 1938 *added in* AH; TCD, MS 10402/162. *Dating*: from birth of Frank Beckett's daughter Caroline on 26 June 1938.

1 Because of her interest in SB, Guggenheim agreed to show Geer van Velde's work. The good sales of the paintings in the exhibition were probably due to her generosity: his "paintings were bought up by Peggy under assumed names" (Weld, *Peggy*, 161).

The contretemps between Reavey and Peggy Guggenheim is undocumented.

Belgian artist, writer, and gallery director Edouard Léon Theódore Mesens (1903–1971) was Director of the London Gallery, 28 Cork Street, from 1938 to 1940; he had been among the organizers of the 1936 Surrealist Exhibition in London, and he edited *London Bulletin* (1938–1940). Dutch-born art dealer Anton Zwemmer (1892–1979) was the owner of the fine art bookstore and gallery Zwemmer's; Zwemmer's became "the rendez-vous of painters, poets, novelists" (Geoffrey Grigson, *Anton Zwemmer: Tributes from Some of his Friends on the Occasion of his 70th Birthday* [London: privately printed, 1962] 7–8; rpt. Geoffrey Grigson, *Recollections: Mainly of Writers & Artists* [London: Chatto and Windus / Hogarth Press, 1984] 39).

Geer van Velde's expectation that he would be paid in guineas rather than in pounds meant a difference of 250 shillings; possibly the gallery listed prices for his paintings in guineas, producing this misunderstanding. At that time it was customary in auctions for a bidder to pay in guineas and for the vendor to be paid in pounds (with the auctioneer or the dealer retaining the difference).

2 Jean and Frank Beckett's daughter Caroline was born on 26 June 1938.

3 The Café du Rond Point is connected with the theatre of the same name (on what is now Avenue Franklin Roosevelt). Possibly SB meant Café de La Rotonde, 105 Boulevard du Montparnasse, which is just across the street from the Coupole, 102 Boulevard du Montparnasse.

Robert McAlmon's companions have not been identified; at that time McAlmon lived in Dampierre in the Vallée de Chevreuse, which was then in the department of Seine-et-Oise; since 1974 it is in the department of Yvelines.

4 Alan and Belinda Duncan, who were with SB when he was stabbed while walking from the Café Zeyer, were also habitués of the Café de Flore.

5 Helen and Giorgio Joyce, together with Peggy Guggenheim, visited SB's new apartment. The Joyces' home was on Villa Scheffer.

Nino Frank and Joyce had done the Italian translation of "Anna Livia Plurabelle" from *Finnegans Wake*, the section for which SB and Péron had drafted a French translation. "Quel ennui" (What a bore).

Giorgio Joyce had occupied an apartment in the Rue Huysmans.

6 It is not known to which of the "Poèmes 38–39" SB refers, or if he refers to another that was unpublished.

7 SB's news of Gallimard's rejection of *Murphy* had been received indirectly: a letter from Routledge to George Reavey on 9 May 1938 indicated that Gallimard had sent a letter to SB c/o Routledge in London, which was received on 9 May 1938, opened by mistake, and then sent on to George Reavey (UoR, Routledge 1733). The Gallimard rejection letter has not been found, and it is not known if SB actually saw it.

8 *La Nausée* (1938; *Nausea*) by Jean-Paul Sartre (1905–1980).

9 SB may refer to the topics raised in conversation with McGreevy during the period when he was in London for the opening of the Geer van Velde Exhibition (early May 1938).

There had been a Toulouse-Lautrec Loan Exhibition of Paintings and Drawings from the Albi Museum at the Knoedler Gallery, London, from 19 January to 10 February 1938; McGreevy reviewed it in "Shows in Short," *The Studio* 115.541 (April 1938) 223. Although it is not known if McGreevy had been in Paris, an exhibition of French painting from Corot to Toulouse-Lautrec, La Peinture française en Suisse, opened on 18 May 1938 at the Gazette des Beaux-Arts gallery.

McGreevy's interest in the Sicilian painters Antonio de Saliba (c. 1466 – c. 1535) and Pietro de Saliba (fl. 1497–1530) is not documented. The brothers were part of the workshop of their uncle Antonello da Messina and often copied his work. (Gioacchino Barbera, "The Life and Works of Antonello da Messina" in *Antonello da Messina: Sicily's Renaissance Master*, ed. Gioacchino Barbera [New York: Metropolitan Museum of Art, 2006] 30). One of the few documented works of Pietro de Saliba is *Christ at the Column* (Budapest, Szépművészeti Muzeum, 1156); it is a copy of the painting by Antonello da Messina in the Louvre (R.F. 1992–10).

10 *Volontés* 5 (May 1938) published: Pierre Guéguen, "Interim"; Paul Ibos, "Cribles"; Eugene Jolas, "Télétype"; Henry Miller, "L'Oeil cosmologique"; Georges Pelorson, "Le Théâtre et les moeurs"; Raymond Queneau, "De Jean Coste et l'expérience poétique" and "Paisan qui va-t-en ville"; Camille Schuwer, "Sujets de poèmes impossibles"; and Dr. Madeleine Violet, "Lumière et santé: un dispensaire d'hygiène infantile à Ménilmontant."

11 McGreevy often stayed with his friend Jean Lurçat when he visited Paris.

12 Hester Dowden and her friend Geraldine Cummins (Dilly).

THOMAS McGREEVY
LONDON

15/6/38   6 Rue des Favorites
                                           Paris 15me

Dear Tom

Thanks for your letter and Inquirer.[1]

Nothing of note here. Aaronson & his girl passed through, on their way back from Dijon, where he says there are Konrad Witzes. I always regret not having seen the Museum when I had the chance, but I was with Frank, who refused to go to Albi from Toulouse another time! I ate with them near St. Lazare. He was stupefied by futilities of Wireless Jennings [*for* Jenkins], whose article in the last Bulletin was in the best traditionalist tradition.[2]

My books arrived, 3 crates, and I had a tedious afternoon passing the customs at the Gare des Batignolles.[3] No duty. So far I have no shelves to receive them. The one estimate from a carpenter I got was so high that I couldn't think of giving him the work, & I shall have to try & rig up something myself.

Peggy Guggenheim is here with car but I have not been seeing her. Nor the van Veldes for that matter. Nor the Joyces. The last time I dined with the parents, about a fortnight ago, they had a dreadful Swiss woman, proprietress of the Fouquets of Zürich, & her son. Il y a des limites.[4]

[...]

After not having seen Brian for some time I dined with him last Monday. He has turned to Gouaches, for which he appears to have some talent. He had had a cheerful letter from Denis. He is giving a cocktail party next Friday in one of the

Americans' flats; I tried to get out of it but fear in the end I shall have to go. He is leaving here at end of month.[5]

I went to Otto Freundlich's exhibition at Jeanne Bucher[']s. A subscription list has been opened to buy a picture & present it to the Jeu de Paume. I noticed that Laugier & Lurçat had both subscribed. The picture in question is a very fine one, far & away the best in the show. There is also a very beautiful sculpture in the little garden in front of the gallery. I met him once a couple of months ago & found him very sympathetic.[6] I wrote to Mother offering to go over from mid-July to mid-August & this time suits her. She has let Cooldrinagh from beginning of September for 4 months & will spend that time I suppose in her little house at Greystones harbour.[7] On the way back I shall bring my bike, take boat to St. Malo and ride across the peninsula and the Loire to St. Brévin where Péron is spending his holidays.[8] As you can imagine I am not anxious to go to Ireland, but as long as mother lives I shall go every year.

I continue to be comfortable here, though the noises – babies & wireless – break my heart some times.

I enclose the last few poems in French. When I have enough I thought of taking them to Eluard.[9]

Not a word from Geoffrey. My cousin Sheila wrote not at all offended at my not having contrived to see her.[10] I told her I rang up in vain! She will also be in Ireland with her daughters in August.

Love ever
Sam

Ascension

à travers la mince cloison
ce jour où un enfant

prodigue à sa façon
rentra dans sa famille
j'entends la voix
elle est émue elle commente
la coupe du monde de football

toujours trop jeune

en même temps par la fenêtre ouverte
par les airs tout court
sourdement
la houle des fidèles

son sang gicla avec abondance
sur les draps sur les pois de senteur sur son mec
de ses doigts infects il ferma les paupières
sur les grands yeux verts étonnés

en reçoit-il une colombe
aussi souvent que moi

La Mouche

entre le monde et moi
la vitre
vide sauf elle

ventre à terre
sanglée dans ses boyaux noirs
antennes affolées ailes liées
pattes crochues bouche suçant à vide
sabrant l'azur s'écrasant contre l'invisible
sous mon pouce impuissant elle fait chavirer
la mer et le ciel serein

Prière

musique de l'indifférence
coeur temps air feu sable
du silence éboulement d'amours
couvre leurs voix
et que je ne m'entende plus
me taire

ALS; 2 leaves, 5 sides; TCD, MS 10402/163. *Note*: although "Ascension," "La Mouche," and "Prière" are included with MS 10402/155, it is unlikely that they were originally enclosed with /155 because the folds on the poems do not match those of the letter. However, the folds and the burn/water damage on left margin of the enclosure do match those on the present MS 10402/163.

1 McGreevy's letter and its enclosure have not been found.

2 Lazarus Aaronson's companion was Dorothy Lewin (n.d.) who became his second wife.

The paintings in the collection of the Musée des Beaux-Arts in Dijon by Konrad Witz are a double-sided panel from the *Altarpiece of the Mirror of Salvation* (see 26 March 1937, n. 5): *The Emperor Augustus and the Sibyl of Tibur* (D 161 A) and *Saint Augustin* (D 161B).

In 1931 SB had stopped in Dijon with his brother as they traveled back to Paris from the south of France; he wrote to McGreevy in the first week of August: "We went slowly back to Paris by Digne, Grenoble, Annecy, Dijon, Troyes" (after 2 August 1931 – 8 August 1931, TCD, MS 10402/12). By this point in their travels, as SB indicates with his reference to Albi, which is 47 miles northeast of Toulouse, Frank Beckett was not interested in pursuing SB's interests in art.

SB conflates the monthly newspaper entitled *The Herbert Jenkins' Wireless* [London] with Humphrey Jennings, whose article "The Iron Horse" asserts: "The 'abstract' painter identifies himself or the person in his picture with a machine"; he concludes: "The point of creating pseudomachines was not as an exploitation of machinery but as a 'profanation' of 'Art' parallel to the engineers' 'profanation' of the primitive 'sacred places' of the earth" (*London Bulletin* 3 [June 1938] 22, 27–28).

3 The Gare des Batignolles at Rue de Rome and Rue Cardinet, Paris 17, next to the Gare aux Marchandises, where freight was cleared through Customs.

4 Peggy Guggenheim, Geer and Lisl van Velde, James and Nora Joyce. The Joyces' dinner guests from Zurich have not been identified.
"Il y a des limites." (There are limits.)

5 As Coffey wrote to Gwynedd Reavey, his friend (and later wife) Bridget Rosalind Baynes (1914–1996), a fabric designer, "showed me how to gouache so I did one and to my surprise it is now hanging from a pin in her room" (27 May 1938, TxU).
Denis Devlin's letter to Brian Coffey has not been found. Writing to George Reavey on 27 May 1938, Coffey mentioned plans for "a cocktail party" for his birthday on 8 June, and plans to be in London in July (TxU).

6 The retrospective exhibition of work by German artist Otto Freundlich* (1878-1943) was organized in honor of his sixtieth birthday at the Galerie Jeanne Bucher-Myrbor (then at 9 ter Boulevard du Montparnasse, Paris 6) from 17 June 1938. The subscription was undertaken for Freundlich's 1935 painting *Preparatory Cartoon for the Homage to the Peoples of Color* (Centre d'Art Moderne, Centre Pompidou, AM 1353D; the mosaic triptych based on this painting, *Homage to the Peoples of Color* [1938], is in the Musée de Pontoise, DF 1968.1.41/42/43) (Gerhard Leistner and Thorsten Rodiek, *Otto Freundlich: Ein Webereiter der abstrakten Kunst* [Regensburg: Museum Ostdeutsche Galerie, 1994] 227; Christophe Duvivier, 18 August 2006). The sculpture in the garden was *Ascension* (1929; Pompidou AM 1982-124).

7 Greystones: 3 April 1938, n. 12.

8 St. Malo on the northern coast of Brittany. Alfred Péron and his family were in St. Brévin, at the outlet of the Loire River.

9 The poems enclosed, "Ascension," "La Mouche," and "Prière," were among those published (with variations) as "Poèmes 38-39," *Les Temps Modernes*, 288-293, and later in Samuel Beckett, *Poèmes, suivi de mirlitonnades* (Paris: Les Editions de Minuit, 1978) 10-12.

SB had translated Paul Eluard's poems for *This Quarter*; many were reprinted in Reavey's selection of Eluard's poetry, *Thorns of Thunder*. Eluard was widely published in literary journals such as *Mesures*, *La Nouvelle Revue Française*, *Soutes*, *Minotaure*, *transition*, *Proverbe*, and *L'Humanité* (Violaine Vanoyeke, *Paul Eluard: le poète de la liberté* [Paris: Editions Julliard, 1995] 400-401).

10 Geoffrey Thompson, whom SB had seen in London in early May; Sheila Page, SB's cousin who lived in Surrey.

GEORGE REAVEY

LONDON

20/6/38   6 Rue des Favorites

Paris 15$^{\underline{me}}$

dear Georges

Thanks for letter & 50 fr. Geer had just paid me as it happens. They are none the less welcome.[1]

Please put me down for 3 ordinary copies of 3rd Person. I shall send you a cheque in a few days.[2]

Had a pleasant trip to Chartres with Geer, Lisl & Peggy.[3]

All well here, except no work. Only a few more French poems. When I have enough I thought of sending them to Eluard. Have not submitted Murphy elsewhere since rejection by Gallimard.

A Miss Julie Reman of Editorial Department of Longman Green & Co. N.Y.C. was over here. I did not see her but it appears that Miss Reeder of the American Library spoke to her a lot about More Pricks & Murphy, as a result of which she left a message asking me to send her the books, which I have done. Not that I remember whether Murphy has already been rejected by her firm or not.[4]

No further news of Sade.[5]

Alan Duncan had a very bad haemorrhage about a fortnight ago – but not from lungs it appears.[6] He was in American hospital for X Ray, of which he had not result when I last saw him. In the meantime he is up & about & soaking as usual.

I am going to Dublin to see my mother about the middle of next month & will probably stay a month. Then I may cross to St. Malo with a bike and spend a week or so in Brittany with Péron. Will you be here before going south in September? I hope so.

If this is not too far from Montparnasse and you don't mind the glorious absence of telephone, I hope you will stay with me.[7]

Love to Gwynedd,

Ever

Sam

My poem in transition was all wrong also. Also the article on Dennis [*for* Denis].[8]

ALS; 1 leaf (folded), 3 sides; enclosure, order form for *Third Person*; TxU.

1 Reavey's letter to SB has not been found.

2 Brian Coffey, *Third Person*, Europa Poets 7 (London: Europa Press, 1938). SB's enclosed order form for Coffey's collection of poems is dated 21 June 1938.

3 Geer and Lisl van Velde, Peggy Guggenheim, and SB took a midnight drive to Chartres to see the Cathedral by moonlight (see Knowlson, *Damned to Fame*, 264, 674).

4 Julie Reman (n.d.) was with New York publisher Longman, Green and Company. *Murphy* had not been submitted to the firm previously.

Dorothy M. Reeder (n.d.), who had worked with the American Library in Paris since 1929, was its Director from 1937 through May 1941; Brian Coffey mentions to George Reavey that she was being helpful in suggesting outlets for his book:

> Miss Reeder says that I should send order forms to all the smaller american [sic] libraries and has promised to let me have the list of them [...] Miss Reeder will herself place a lot of copies once she sees the book. She has read the MS and loves it. But she wants to place the book in the Library and she would place any other Europa books there you cared to send her. Or rather let me, say, give them to her from you (if you do not know her) and I'll ask her to put them on her shelves. (23 June 1938, TxU)

5 After SB's provisional acceptance of Jack Kahane's proposal to translate Sade's *Les 120 Journées de Sodome*, there had been no further word from Kahane (see 8 March 1938, n. 3).

6 Alan Duncan suffered from the effects of gassing in World War I.

7 SB refers to his new apartment at 6 Rue des Favorites.

8 SB refers to "Ooftish," which was originally entitled "Whiting" (see 14 [August 1937] to Cissie Sinclair and 14 August 1937 to Thomas McGreevy); it was published in *transition* 27 (April–May 1938) 33.

No manuscript of SB's review "Denis Devlin" has been found to compare with that published in *transition*.

THOMAS McGREEVY

LONDON

Thursday [4 August 1938]   Cooldrinagh
                                  [Foxrock, Co. Dublin]

Dear Tom

Many thanks for your letter. It seems a long time since I wrote to you.

I got your message all right in Paris, but only about 15 mins. before your train was due to leave. I'm glad you had a lively time of sorts down south & hope you are feeling the benefit now of the change.[1]

I found everything as usual here. Mother very nervous, but no more so than usual. She has let Cooldrinagh from September to December and will spend those months in the little house she has at Greystones. Then if she finds that she does not miss Cooldrinagh too much she will probably sell it.

Frank Jean & infant all well. I spend [for spent] the last week-end with them in South Donegal, a place called Rosbeg on the Atlantic, and enjoyed the walking & bathing.[2] Jean is very heavy after the birth and not feeding the baby herself doesn't help to get back to normal.

Brian is over & I was speaking to him to-day on the phone. He announces he is spending 2 months in Ireland – "to work". The thin edge of the axe. I lunch with him to-morrow at the Bail[e]y.[3]

I called on the Yeatses this afternoon & saw them both. He has a magnificent new picture – "Helen" – launching the ships, with a kneeling figure superbly drawn that made me associate at once with Bassano, not that the figure resembles any of his particularly, but because of same extraordinary tenderness & distinction of handling. The sky and sea & ships are really ter-rific, Delacroix plus substance, depth and a courage more than of conviction, of certainty, absolutely natural & unrhetorical. I was really knocked all of a heap.[4] He is anxious for an exhibi-tion in England and was interested when I mentioned the Guggenheim Gallery. He spoke very warmly of your essay, as something that stood on its own feet as a piece of aesthetics and required no profuse illustration from him. I was sorry to hear that Routledge had not taken it up.[5] Going out together to buy the evening paper & taking leave of me on the step he said "It must be 6 or 7 years since I first walked out of the house with you to buy the evening paper and 6 or 7 years should mean a lot to me, but they don't seem to & it doesn't matter."

I shall be leaving for home in a fortnight or 3 weeks. My idea originally was to take the bicycle with me & join Péron in Brittany, taking boat from Southampton to St. Malo, but I don't expect to have either the money or the energy. I haven't even a return ticket to London. In any case I shall pause there a couple of days on the way through.[6]

I seem to have read nothing for months but Vigny's Journal in the bowdlerized Larousse edition, which bored me, and Tristram Shandy, which irritated me in spite of its qualities. Dr Johnson is back in my consciousness & I hope to settle down to it when I get back to Paris. It appears Seumas O'Sullivan is collaborating with Gogarty on a biography of Goldsmith.[7]

Cissie & family are back. She rather worse than when she left, Sonny apparently well & working resentfully for Little Go.[8][...]

I shall be glad to get back to . . unclenchedness. Sinclair is not here & there have been no repercussions of the case so far, but it is the old toxins & the old day soil.[9]

Mary Manning is here on holiday, grown tedious & precious, rather like the learned Swan of Streatham I imagine, with a novel coming from Houghton Mifflin in the autumn entitled Mt. Venus.[10] All the old people & the old places, they make me feel like an amphibian detained forcibly on dry land, very very dry land.

Mother brought me to-day from the Horse Show the Abbey Theatre's festival pamphlet with Introduction by Lennox R. and Lafayettes of all the heroes from W. B. to A. E. Malone. Or do these remain the correct limiting terms? I cannot easily believe there is nothing lower than A. E. Malone. Series of excursions and lectures are announced, the valley of the Boyne & Higgins on Yeats etc.[11]

I had lunch with Geoffrey & Ursula on the way through. He is working from 8 a.m. to 10 p.m., with short intervals to snatch food, and complains of poverty. He & Bion take piano lessons.[12]

I am very sorry to hear about Raven's sister. Give him my
love, & to Hester & to Dilly.[13]

God's blessing

Ever

Sam

ALS; 2 leaves, 6 sides; TCD MS 10402/166. *Dating*: dated in AH as "5-8-38," but Thursday
was 4 August 1938. In SB to George Reavey, 5 August 1938, SB reports that he is
"lunching with Brian to-day," that he saw Jack [Yeats] the day before, and that he
hopes to attend the first night of Yeats's *Purgatory* at the Abbey on the next Wednesday
(TxU). *Purgatory* opened Wednesday, 10 August 1938; the Abbey Festival program lists
an excursion to the Boyne Valley on 7 August 1938; the Horse Show was held from
2 to 6 August 1938.

1 SB had planned to leave Paris on 19 July, stopping in London on his way to Dublin;
McGreevy may have passed through Paris before SB left (SB to McGreevy, 13 July 1938,
TCD, MS 10402/164). On 20 July 1938, McGreevy sent a postcard to George Reavey from
Cavalière, Var (TxU).

2 SB accompanied Frank and Jean Beckett, whose daughter Caroline was born on
26 June 1938, on a weekend in Rosbeg, Co. Donegal, a resort on Dawros Bay.

3 Brian Coffey spent August and September in Ireland prior to his wedding in
London in October; in a letter to George Reavey on 2 August 1938, Coffey presented
plans to circulate his book among patrons and booksellers (TxU). The Bailey:
21 February 1938, n. 8.

4 Jack Yeats and his wife Cottie. In Yeats's painting *Helen* (Pyle 499; Tel Aviv Museum
2372), Helen stands on a quay as if launching a ship, while "a figure kneeling beside
her writes on a wax tablet placed on the ground" (Pyle, *Jack B. Yeats: Catalogue Raisonné of
the Oil Paintings*, I, 455). SB compares *Helen* to paintings by Jacopo Bassano and by
Eugène Delacroix (né Ferdinand-Eugène-Victor Delacroix, 1798–1863).

5 Peggy Guggenheim's memoir gives the impression that SB had already suggested
an exhibition of Yeats's painting at Guggenheim Jeune, but that Yeats did not think his
work was appropriate for her gallery (Guggenheim, *Out of this Century: Confessions of an
Art Addict*, 163–164).
McGreevy's *Jack B. Yeats* had not been accepted by Routledge.

6 With regard to these plans: 15 June 1938, n. 8.

7 Alfred de Vigny, *Journal d'un poète*, ed. Léon-Adolphe Gauthier-Ferrières (Paris:
Bibliothèque Larousse, 1913; rpt. 1919, 1920); the *Journal* was composed of extracts
from the personal papers of Comte Alfred de Vigny (1797–1863) originally published
by Louis Ratisbonne (1867).
Laurence Sterne, *The Life and Opinions of Tristram Shandy, Gentleman* (1760–1767).
SB's long-considered play on Samuel Johnson, extant only as the fragment "Human
Wishes."

Although there are notes in the Seumas O'Sullivan papers on the subject of Oliver Goldsmith, no such biography was published (TCD, MS 4056, 4260–4299, 4630–4649).

8 Cissie Sinclair had returned from South Africa in June. Morris Sinclair was resuming his studies at Trinity College Dublin. "Little Go" was the unofficial name of the Final Freshman examination at TCD.

9 SB refers to Harry Sinclair, in whose libel suit against Gogarty SB testified in November 1937.

10 Poet, biographer, and critic Anna Seward was a member of Lichfield's intellectual circle and known as the "Swan of Lichfield" (Norma Clarke, "Anna Seward: Swan, Duckling or Goose?" *New Rambler* E.7 [2003/2004] 54). SB transfers the appellation to Hester Thrale, whose home was in Streatham, and thence to Mary Manning Howe, whose novel *Mount Venus* was published in autumn 1938.

11 The annual Dublin Horse Show is a major social event of early August. The Abbey Theatre Festival (6 to 20 August 1938) included a lecture on 8 August by drama critic and journalist Andrew E. Malone (né Laurence Patrick Byrne, 1888–1939) on the early history of the Abbey Theatre, a lecture on 11 August by F. R. Higgins on W. B. Yeats, as well as productions of several plays by Yeats: *Cathleen ni Houlihan*, *Purgatory*, and *On Baile's Strand*. The photographic studio Lafayette, 32 Westmoreland Street, Dublin, was credited with several portraits in the program, for which Lennox Robinson wrote the introduction ("Abbey Theatre Festival Souvenir" [1938]). The excursion scheduled for 7 August 1937 was to Tara and the Boyne Valley.

12 Geoffrey and Ursula Thompson with whom SB had lunch in London on his way from Paris to Dublin. W. R. Bion, with whom SB had been in psychotherapy, was a colleague of Geoffrey Thompson; both took piano lessons for relaxation.

13 Thomas Holmes Ravenhill, whose sister's circumstance is unknown. Hester Dowden, Geraldine Cummins.

GEORGE REAVEY

LONDON

5ᵗʰ Aug 1938   6 Clare Street

Dublin

dear George

Many thanks for information.

No, no news from Longman Green & Co. Nor of Sweeney.[1]

I am lunching with Brian to-day. He says he is staying two months here, the better to work …

I expect to be here about another fortnight. Then I don't know whether I shall go to Brittany to join up with Péron or straight back to Paris.[2]

I hope to be here for the first night of Yeats's new play Purgatory next Wednesday week at the Abbey. I saw Jack yesterday. He has some magnificent new pictures.[3]

You might send me a couple of copies of Murphy. No review appeared in Dublin Magazine. Austin Clarke had it for review, having taken it from Sheehy who had it before that, but withheld his hand. He has published another book of verse.[4]

Hope Gwynedd had a pleasant time in the country. Give her my love & à bientôt.[5]

> Yours ever
>
> Sam

ALS; 1 leaf, 2 sides; TxU.

1 Julie Reman at Longman Green and Company in New York had asked to read *More Pricks Than Kicks* and *Murphy* for possible publication in the United States.

American art critic James Johnson Sweeney (1900–1986) worked with Eugene Jolas on numbers 24–27 of *transition* (1936–1938) in the United States; Sweeney was Curator of the Museum of Modern Art in New York from 1935 to 1946, and later Director of the Guggenheim Museum in New York from 1952 to 1960. He was in Dublin in early August 1938 (Sweeney to George Reavey, 22 August 1937, TxU).

2 Brian Coffey. Alfred Péron.

3 The opening night of W. B. Yeats's play *Purgatory* as part of the Abbey Theatre Festival took place on 10 August 1938. The new paintings by Jack B. Yeats have not been identified.

4 An unsigned review of *Murphy* appeared later in *Dublin Magazine* 14.2 (April–June 1939) 98: "*Murphy* comes in the guise of a novel. But it is more a study in words and phrases, the characters being secondary affairs ... The whole thing is a bizarre fantasy, with a nasty twist about it that its self-evident cleverness and scholarship cannot redeem ... And the one really human character in the book is Celia, the lady of loose morals."

Neither Edward Sheehy, an editor of *Ireland To-Day*, nor Austin Clarke wrote a signed review *Murphy*. Austin Clarke had recently published *Night and Morning: Poems* (Dublin: Orwell Press, 1938).

5 "A bientôt" (till soon).

GEORGE REAVEY
LONDON

Friday 38 [19 August 1938]   6 Clare St.

[Dublin]

dear George

I was hoping to receive two copies of <u>Murphy</u> from you. Or did you not get my letter? Anyway don't bother about them now as I expect to be in London early next week.[1]

If any letters come for me in the meantime will you keep them?

I am not yet quite sure whether I shall return directly to Paris or go first to Brittany to visit Péron. Ussher also is in St Malo. In any case I shall not be more than a night in London.

I had a letter from Geer & Lisl. They seem to be enjoying themselves in Cagnes.[2] They have conferred my name on a cat.

I enclose the usual from Julie Reman.[3]

Love to Gwynedd

Ever

Sam

ALS; 1 leaf, 2 sides; *letterhead* <THE DAWROS BAY HOTELS, ROSBEG, GLENTIES, CO. DONEGAL>; enclosure not extant; TxU. *Dating*: SB wrote "38" on the date line of the letterhead; in 5 August 1938 SB had indicated that he planned to be in Dublin for about another fortnight; 19 August was a Friday in 1938.

1 SB's letter of 5 August 1938.

2 Geer and Lisl van Velde had moved to Cagnes-sur-Mer on the Côte d'Azur.

3 Julie Reman wrote on behalf of Longman Green and Company in New York, rejecting *More Pricks Than Kicks* and *Murphy*.

GEORGE REAVEY
LONDON

27$\underline{^{th}}$ Sept 1938   6 Rue des Favorites
                                                                   Paris 15

Dear George

Thanks for letter & poem, which I like very much indeed.[1]

I heard Adolf the Peacemaker on the wireless last night. And thought I heard the air escaping – a slow puncture. But no matter how things go I shall stay on here, on the 7$\underline{^{th}}$ floor with my handful of sand.[2] All I have to lose is legs, arms, balls[,] etc., and I owe them no particular debt of gratitude as far as I know. The streets are full of khaki-cum-civils departing shabbily in requisitioned trade vans – and at night horrible curfew lighting, like that through which Proust stumbled to the Temple of Delights. I have promised Péron, in event of mobilisation, to evacuate in his car his children, his mother-in-law, his aunt-in-law.[3]

I have been running into Gore, flaxenly unshaven & wanly constructive, wondering is he on his way through from Athens to . . Cork. Says art answers questions.[4]

Adler calls for me this afternoon, to take me by the hand to Otto Freundlich's ostentatious miseries. The last time I was there I left behind me a pair of soiled drawers and Sartre's Nausée. These at least I hope to recover. Adler has no news of Geer, but talks of going down there & getting together. His latest painting is distressing. I have no news of Geer either, except that I hear the sister-in-law (not the Prague one, back in Prague) is with them.[5]

I had a good time in Normandy & Brittany before returning to Paris.[6]

No work. I read an average of an hour a day, after an hour the illusion of comprehension ceases, Kant, Descartes, Johnson, Renard and a kindergarten manual of science: "L'air est partout", "Le plomb est un métal lourd et tendre".[7]

Brian sent me an invitation to his wedding, which I could not accept. I suppose now more than ever it will come off on the 8th. Here there is great afflux of tenderness, even in the commune of Vaugirard.[8]

I went to bed one night lately in even more than usual the ordinary way, all the higher centres on the pillow, & woke up greatly refreshed to find my feet there. The perfect suicide: to somnambulate through the window. But would one wake up on the way down?

> Love to Gwynedd
>
> > yrs ever
> >
> > > Sam

ALS; 2 leaves, 2 sides; TxU.

1 Reavey's letter has not been found. The poem enclosed with it has not been identified.

2 Hitler had "ordered an 'historic manifestation' to the nation on the subject of Czechoslovakia" in the Berlin Sportspalast on 26 September 1938, and "the whole German people had been ordered to listen to a broadcast of his address" ("All Reich Rallied: 'Historic Manifestation' Tonight will Reply to a Czech Broadcast," *The New York Times* 26 September 1938: 1; also on this page is a summary of Hitler's memorandum of 23 September 1938 to British Prime Minister Neville Chamberlain [1869–1940] and a map of the Sudetenland; for full text: *The New York Times*, 27 September 1938: 17).

SB refers to his apartment at 6 Rue des Favorites.

3 In *Le Temps retrouvé* Marcel during World War I walks through the darkened streets of Paris and unwittingly enters a male brothel seeking a drink and a place to rest; he leaves during a bombardment which plunges the streets into total blackness (*Le Temps retrouvé* in *A la recherche du temps perdu*, IV, 388–412); *Time Regained* in *In Search of Lost Time*, VI, 173–207).

Alfred Péron's family included his wife, Mania, their twin sons Michel and Alexis (b. 1932), Mania's mother Maria Lézine (née Spiridonof, n.d.), and her mother's sister Elizabeth Spiridonof (n.d.).

4 Gore has not been identified.

5 Polish-born artist Jankel Adler (1895–1949) had been working in Germany, where he had been involved in the Rheinische Sezession and the Union of Progressive International Artists (1922); in 1933 his work was declared "entartet," and in 1934 he moved to Paris. There he was involved in 1937 with the studio of Stanley William Hayter (1901–1988), Atelier 17 (Jankel Adler, *Jankel Adler*, intro. Stanley William Hayter [London: Nicholson and Watson, 1948] viii).

Otto Freundlich, who had been a friend of Adler's since the 1920s in Berlin: 15 June 1938, n. 6.

Geer and Lisl van Velde were living in Cagnes-sur-Mer. Lisl's sister from Berlin was Anna Marie Jokl (known as Moidi, 1911–2001); she and their sister from Prague (not identified) had visited the van Veldes in the summer of 1938.

6 According to a letter from Peggy Guggenheim to American writer Emily Coleman (née Holmes, 1899–1974), Guggenheim had lent SB her car to drive to Brittany (DeU: Coleman, [23 September 1939]; Knowlson, *Damned to Fame*, 265, 674).

7 The specific books SB was reading by Immanuel Kant, René Descartes, Samuel Johnson, Jules Renard, as well as the basic science text, have not been identified. "L'air est partout" (air is everywhere); "Le plomb est un métal lourd et tendre" (lead is a soft heavy metal).

8 The wedding of Brian Coffey and Bridget Baynes took place on 8 October 1938, St. Patrick's Church, Soho Square, London.

Vaugirard was the nearest métro station to SB's apartment.

GEORGE REAVEY

LONDON

[after 24 October 1938]   6 Rue des Favorites
                                           Paris 15

dear George

Many thanks for letter & order form. Put me down for 3 copies at 3/6, for which I enclose cheque for 11/9. It is very good of you to reserve me a special copy. Wish I was in a position to do as much for you.[1]

Nothing new here. It is just possible I may have to go to Dublin for a couple of weeks at Xmas. I would not stop in London on the way through, but might on the way back, if Father Xmas was kind. I hope not to have to go at all.[2]

Adler has left for Cagnes in a Simca. He lent me 3 pictures to keep during his absence. I fear he thinks I spend my time entertaining rich English & Yanks. They have something, the beginnings of a delectatio morosa.[3]

I am halfway through a modified version in French of Love & Lethe. I don't know if it is better than the English version or merely as bad. I have 10 Poems in French also, mostly short. When I have a few more I shall send them to Eluard. Or get Duchamp to do so.[4]

I see Brian & Bridget occasionally. They are smelling after a flat at the Porte de Versailles.[5]

I had a highly coloured card from Geer & Lisl, saying the oranges were orange and the gnats gnats, & that he was working with both.

Poor Barlach is dead. Dans la misère.[6]

Freundlich gave me a large aesthetic essay to read, all about the absolute & the pananthropod.[7]

Love to Gwynedd. I hope she is well again.

Ever

Sam

ALS; 1 leaf, 1 side; TxU. Dating: when SB wrote to Reavey on 27 September 1938, Adler was planning to go to Cagnes-sur-Mer to visit Geer van Velde; Ernst Barlach died on 24 October 1938.

1 SB ordered copies of Reavey's *Quixotic Perquisitions*, formally published in January 1939; he received his copies by 27 January 1939 (SB to George Reavey, 27 January 1939, TxU).

2 SB went to Dublin for Christmas and New Year; he wrote from Greystones to Brian and Bridget Coffey on 30 December 1938 that he expected to return to Paris at the end of the following week (DeU, MS 382, Brian Coffey Papers Supplement).

3 Jankel Adler had planned to visit Geer and Lisl van Velde in Cagnes-sur-Mer. The three pictures lent to SB have not been identified. "Delectatio morosa" (morose delight). Adler's return to Paris is noted in SB to Reavey, 27 January 1939 (TxU).

4 "Love and Lethe" in *More Pricks Than Kicks*, 85–100; SB's French translation of this story was unpublished.

SB refers to ten of the twelve poems published as "Poèmes 38–39," *Les Temps Modernes*, 288–293. SB often played chess with French artist Henri-Robert-Marcel Duchamp (1887–1968), also a friend of Eluard.

5 Brian and Bridget Coffey.

6 German sculptor Ernst Barlach died on 24 October 1938. "Dans la misère" (in poverty).

7 SB read a draft of Freundlich's essay "Der bildhafte Raum" (The Imaginable Space) which formulates a social and aesthetic theory that announces abstraction as a universal language (Dr. Joachim Heusinger von Waldegg, Staatliche Akademie der Bildenden Künste Karlsruhe, 16 February 1995). Observing that religions and mythologies no longer filled the creative spaces between man and the universe, Freundlich proposed that art could respond to the intellectual crisis of modernity and could bring together two dynamics – man's instinct to form and cosmic formlessness – to make visible "the process of becoming rather than being." The Fonds Otto Freundlich/ Archives IMEC has about half (pages 41–89) of Freundlich's draft of this essay dated 1 March 1938; there is also a carbon copy of what may be the full text, possibly prepared by another hand. A summary of those pages and other works written by Freundlich is published in Otto Freundlich, *Otto Freundlich – Schriften: Ein Wegbereiter der gegenstandslosen Kunst*, ed. Uli Bohnen (Cologne: DuMont Buchverlag, 1982) 211–220.

SB shared his own essay "Les Deux Besoins" with Freundlich (NhD, Lawrence Harvey Papers, MS 661[2]: 27). SB wrote to John Fletcher on 3 June 1966 that it "was not on the van Veldes. It must have been written 1938 or early 1939 at latest. I remember showing it to the painter & sculptor Otto Freundlich since disappeared in the 'tourmente'" (TxU; TMS of "Les Deux Besoins," NhD, Beckett collection; Beckett, *Disjecta*, 55–57; see Freundlich's Profile in the Appendix; Alain Bonfand, Christophe Duvivier, Edda Maillet, Jérôme Serri, and Guy Tosatto, *Otto Freundlich* [Rochechouart: Musée Départemental de Rochechouart, 1988] 82).

OTTO FREUNDLICH

PARIS

SB's errors of German in this letter have not been corrected.

[autumn 1938]   [Paris]

Lieber Herr Freundlich

Ich bedaure sehr, heute morgen war ich nicht frei.

Samstag nachmittag zwischen 2 u. 4. werden Sie mich bei mir finden, wenn Sie Lust haben,

dabei zu kommen -
    Ihr
    Sam Beckett

ALS; 1 leaf, 1 side; Fonds Otto Freundlich / Archives IMEC. *Dating*: the year ascribed to this letter is consistent with evidence of a growing acquaintance between SB and Freundlich in 1938. In view of the deepening relationship, it seems more likely that this note was written in the autumn of 1938, rather than earlier in that year.

[autumn 1938]   [Paris]

Dear Mr Freundlich
    I am very sorry, I was not available this morning.
    You will find me at home on Saturday afternoon between 2 and 4, if you feel like coming by.
        Yours
            Sam Beckett

ARLAND USSHER
[?CAPPAGH, CO. WATERFORD]

28/12/38   Greystones

Dear Arland
    Thanks for papers. Glad to sea [sic] you are bursting into print again. The "suspender" essay I always liked very much, and more than ever in such sad company.[1]
    Do not imagine I am returned to the land of my unsuccessful abortion. It is only to keep my mother company during the season of that other. And I hope soon to return to the people where the little operation is cheap, safe, legal & popular. "Curetage".[2]

My mother has been wintering on this côte de misère since September. What does not face north faces east. She is the worse for it. But from the window she can see the cemetery where my father is "at rest".[3]

I have seen nobody except the Sinclairs and shall continue steadfastly in this course.[4]

It is a long time since we had nothing to say to one another, and if your progress has been anything like mine I should think we could now be united in a silence even more substantial – or as some would say, thick – than heretofore.

It is hardly an exaggeration to say that you will always be welcome in 6 rue des Favorites (formerly Impasse des Favorites, not far from the still existing Impasse de L'Enfant Jésus) should your Schicksal at any time allow you so much license.[5]

I have begun a Primer of higher French syntax. It takes the form of Xenian. Here is one

Ci-gît qui y échappa tant

Qu'il n'en échappe que maintenant.[6]

      Porte-toi bien[7]

        Sam

ALS; 1 leaf, 2 sides; TxU.

1 SB refers to Ussher's essay "The Age of Shadows," in *Nineteenth Century and After*: 12 May 1938, n. 1.

2 "Curetage" (curettage).

3 May Beckett moved to Greystones in September. Her view included the Redford cemetery, where William Beckett was buried. "Côte de misère" (Misery Coast).

4 Cissie Sinclair and her family.

5 SB's apartment on Rue des Favorites was off the Rue de Vaugirard, along which was the Impasse de l'Enfant Jésus. "Schicksal" (fate).

6 SB's "Primer of higher French syntax" is for Ussher's amusement. *Xenien* (1796) was a collection of satirical epigrams, written by Goethe and Schiller. Modeled on the epigrams of Martial, "each epigram is a classical distich, composed of hexameter and

pentameter" (Henry Garland and Mary Garland, *The Oxford Companion to German Literature* [Oxford: Oxford University Press, 1986] 1006).

SB's example becomes a part of his story "Premier Amour" (AMS, TxU, begun 28 October 1946, completed 12 November 1946): "Ci-gît qui y échappa tant / Qu'il n'en échappe que maintenant" ("Hereunder lies the above who up below / So hourly died that he survived till now") (*Premier Amour* [Paris: Les Editions de Minuit, 1970] 10; tr. by Samuel Beckett, "First Love" in *First Love and Other Shorts* [New York: Grove Press, 1974] 12).

7 "Porte-toi bien" (Look after yourself).

CHRONOLOGY 1939

1939 January	SB returns to Paris via London.
27 January	Asks Stanley Hayter to engrave a stone from the Liffey, a gift for James Joyce's 57th birthday.
28 February	Writing another "Petit Sot" poem in French, which he will send with other French poems to George Reavey when finished.
Early March	Ill with flu for two weeks. Writes to Joyce from 12 Square Port Royal, 5 March; possibly staying with Suzanne Deschevaux-Dumesnil.
1 April	End of Spanish Civil War.
By 18 April	May Beckett sells Cooldrinagh with plan to build a smaller house nearby. First mention of Suzanne Deschevaux-Dumesnil to Thomas McGreevy. Meets Alfred Péron every week to work on French translation of *Murphy*.
By 6 June	Sends a four-line poem to Blanaid Salkeld, following her request for a contribution to the Dublin Poets and Artists series of Gayfield Press.
14 June	Asks Reavey to return his only copy of "Petit Sot"; asks again on 16 June.
15 June	Visits Brian Coffey in Dampierre.
By 7 July	Reavey returns "Petit Sot."
August	SB in Dublin.
24 August	The Treaty of Non-Aggression is signed by Germany and the USSR.
1 September	Germany invades Poland.

3 September	France as well as Britain, Australia, and New Zealand declare war on Germany. Ireland remains neutral.
4 September	SB returns to France.
By 26 September	Applies to serve France.
By 6 December	Expects to be called to active service as a volunteer, but only receives acknowledgment of his willingness to serve. Has translated all but four chapters of *Murphy* into French.

GEORGE REAVEY
LONDON

28/2/39   6 Rue des Favorites
                                 [Paris] 15$^{\underline{me}}$

dear George
  Thanks for letter & Bulletin.[1]
  I am doing a second Petit Sot & shall send them, when it is finished, with the shorter poems.[2]
  Hope you have good news of Perquisitions.[3]
  Nothing doing here as far as I can see that couldn't be done as well in Beggar's Bush or the 7 Dials.[4]
  Saw the Buckland[-]Wrights one evening chez eux.[5]
  Sartre gave the nouvelle to Paulhan. But no news of it yet.[6]
  How is Gwynedd? When does she expect to go south? Give her my love.[7]
        Yours ever
        Sam

ALS; 1 leaf, 1 side; TxU.

1 Reavey sent SB the most recent issue of *London Bulletin* in which was published SB's translation of André Breton's essay "Wolfgang Paalen" (*London Bulletin* 10 [February 1939] 16–17).

2 SB's first poem entitled "Petit Sot" is included in a series of twenty brief unpublished poems in TMS (Putnam); for further details see Knowlson, *Damned to Fame*, 270–271. Regarding the short poems in French, see [after 24 October 1938], n. 4.

    Le Petit Sot

      je suis le petit sot
      il faut
      être grand pour être malin

653

et se tenir bien
et faire comme eux
et devenir heureux

SB may refer to an untitled and unpublished 24-line poem in French that begins "les joues rouges"; it includes a reference to "Petit Sot" (BIF, UoR, MS 2912, line 18).

3 Reavey, *Quixotic Perquisitions.*

4 Beggar's Bush is an old section of Dublin, as well as the name of a pub that has been located there for approximately 200 years, at 115 Haddington Road, Ballsbridge.

The Seven Dials, London WC2, an area adjacent to Covent Garden and Soho, where seven streets radiate from a central Doric Pillar which was originally topped by a clock with seven faces (Ben Weinreb and Christopher Hibbert, eds., *The London Encyclopaedia* [London: Papermac, Macmillan, 1987] 779).

5 Through George Reavey, SB had met the New-Zealand-born engraver and printmaker John Buckland-Wright (1897–1954), who had illustrated Brian Coffey's *Third Person* as well as Reavey's *Quixotic Perquisitions* in the Europa Poets series. Buckland-Wright joined Stanley William Hayter's Atelier 17 in Paris in 1933 and was appointed its Director in 1936.

"Chez eux" (at their home), the home of John and Mary Buckland-Wright (née Anderson, 1907–1976).

6 The author of the "nouvelle" (story) in question is not clear.

SB would not refer to *Murphy* in this way, and it is not apparent that he himself had written any new French fiction. SB mentions to Reavey that he is "halfway through a translation of *Love and Lethe*" (after 24 October 1938), but no evidence has been found that SB had given this story to Sartre.

Jean Paulhan (1884–1968) was editor of *La Nouvelle Revue Française* from 1925 to 1940, and from 1946 to 1968.

7 When Gwynedd Reavey passed through Paris on her way to see the Geer van Veldes in Cagnes-sur-Mer, SB met her at St. Lazare station with John Buckland-Wright; on 5 March 1939, SB wrote to Reavey: "I was glad to see Gwynedd on her way through and was sorry she was not in better form. I had a note from her from Cagnes, where she seems to be getting rapidly back to her old form" (TxU).

Here SB spells "Gwynedd" correctly.

THOMAS McGREEVY

LONDON

April 11ᵗʰ 1939   6 Rue des Favorites
                                                                             Paris 15ᵐᵉ

Dear Tom

I am sorry that we seem to have lost touch with one another & ceased to correspond.[1] I feel the poorer for it, though that is not what prompts me to write to you again now. I do not think there is any reason for an estrangement, certainly I do not know of any. I do not even feel that there is any question of an estrangement. But I am insensitive to many things, and I may have done something to alienate you without my knowing what it is. If I have I ask your forgiveness.

I know that on my side there is indolence & despondency & the stupid pride that curls up, and that these are things with which it is difficult for grown-up people to have patience. I know also that you have enough troubles without that of calling on your reserves of indulgence. But if our friendship means as much to you as it always has done to me, even when I may have appeared to neglect it, you will agree with me that it would be a great pity for perhaps a small thing to interrupt it.

So let us clear it up, if you will, whatever it is.

> Yours affectionately
> Sam

ALS; 1 leaf, 1 side; TCD, MS 10402/167.

1 The gap in SB's correspondence with McGreevy may have been as long as eight months; the previous extant letter to McGreevy was dated [4 August 1938].

THOMAS McGREEVY

LONDON

April 18ᵗʰ 1939   6 Rue des Favorites

                                       Paris 15me

dear Tom

I was very glad to hear from you again. I am sorry I gave you that impression in London, & that it has remained so long uncorrected.[1] I did not feel at all that way where you were concerned. But I have had a lot of things in the last year, good and bad, and I am not sorry that is over. I was 33 this week & wonder if the second half of the bottle will be any better than the first half. In the sense only I suppose that one has got used to the taste.

Lately I have not been well. [...] I shall not be sorry I think this year to get to Ireland & the sea for a month or a month & a half. If there is a war, as I fear there must be soon, I shall place myself at the disposition of this country.[2]

News from home is good. Mother has sold Cooldrinagh and has bought a field nearby where she is going to build herself a small bungalow. It is on the other side of the road and has a very beautiful view, uninterrupted, across fields to the mountains. It will hardly be ready before Xmas, if so soon. In the meantime she is living in a little shanty on the harbour at Greystones, to which she seems to have become very attached, chiefly I think because she can see Redford cemetery from the sitting-room window, on the slopes of Bray Head across the water. She is of course lonely, but sees Frank & Jean fairly often. They are both well and the infant flourishing apparently. Already when I saw him last he was bothering about the possibility of war and wondering what he would do.[3]

You heard of course about Nick. I had not seen him for some time before, being laid up just then. But he had been looking more & more poorly. I hardly ever seen [*for* see] the Duncans.[4]

Brian has disappeared with Bridget to the tame wilds of Dampierre in the Vallée de Chevreuse and the pleasures of the company of Mr McCalmon [*for* McAlmon], and never manifests.[5]

I see the Joyces now & then. I go every week to Ivry to visit Lucia, who I think gets slowly worse. She sees nobody but her father & myself. Helen also has been ill with a "nervous breakdown" for almost the past two months and shows no signs of pulling out of it. Giorgio is having a bad time.[6] The parents half [sic] left their flat and are in the Hotel d'Iéna for a few days while the flat they have taken in Passy is being made ready. They are as well as can be expected. He is worried about the non-appearance of <u>Finnegans Wake</u>. Hubsch [*for* Huebsch] in New York seems to be doing the dirty.[7]

I have no work to show beyond a few poems in French, of which I think you have already seen some. There are two very long ones that do not belong at all to the series, being quite straightforward descriptive poems (in French) of episodes in the life of a child. I do not know what they are worth. The few people I have shown them to liked them, but they are friends.[8]

I have a queer lot of pictures here now. A German surrealist called Paalen gave me some kind of "automatic" affair that amuses me, and I have started paying for a picture by a Polish Jew called Adler that I like very much.[9] The flat continues to be very satisfactory. Is there no chance of you coming to stay with me for a while?

I lunch every Tuesday with Péron, and am very glad to have him.[10]

There is a French girl also whom I am fond of, dispassionately, and who is very good to me.[11] The hand will not be overbid. As we both know that it will come to an end there is no knowing how long it may last.

And there are a few of my odds & ends. Maybe the wine is not so bad as I feared.

Remember me to Hester. Is she cross with me?[12]

Write again soon.

      Affectionately

        Sam

I liked the Antonello very much.[13]

ALS; 4 leaves, 4 sides; TCD, MS 10402/168.

1 McGreevy's letter to SB has not been found.

2 SB planned to visit his mother in Ireland at the end of July 1939; he would leave Ireland for France on 4 September 1939, the day after France and England declared war against Germany (Knowlson, *Damned to Fame*, 273).

3 SB refers to "New Place" in Foxrock. William Beckett is buried in Redford cemetery near Greystones. Frank and Jean Beckett and their daughter Caroline lived in Killiney, 8 miles north of Greystones.

4 Nick Balachef, whom SB had met through Alan and Belinda Duncan.

5 Brian and Bridget Coffey had moved to the village of Dampierre in the Vallée de Chevreuse, where Robert McAlmon lived.

6 Lucia Joyce was in a maison de santé in the Paris suburb of Ivry. As Paul Léon wrote to Harriet Weaver on 2 April 1939: "Mr. Joyce continues his visits on Sundays [...] Mr. Becket[t] has also been visiting her weekly but these are the only two persons who see her at all" (Joyce and Léon, *The James Joyce – Paul Léon Papers*, 76). For Helen Joyce's illness and its effect on her family, see this letter as well as Joyce, *Letters of James Joyce*, III, 438, 465; Guggenheim, *Out of This Century: Confessions of an Art Addict*, 207–208.

7 James and Nora Joyce moved from 7 Rue Edmond Valentin to 34 Rue des Vignes on 15 April (see Ellmann, *James Joyce*, 721). The Hôtel d'Iéna, 28 Avenue d'Iéna, Paris 16.
Finnegans Wake was not published until 4 May 1939 although its projected publication date had been Joyce's birthday, 2 February 1939. Benjamin Huebsch was Joyce's editor at Viking Press, New York. Joyce wrote to Mary Colum (née Mary Catherine Gunning Maguire, 1887–1957) on 29 March 1939:

> There is no use now in going into the matter of the American publication of my book. So far it has been a hopeless bungle. As for the date every week we hear something different. The book, printed and bound, has been lying on my table for the past two months but the sheets for Mr. Huebsch's limited edition have not yet left England. (Joyce, *Letters of James Joyce*, III, 438)

8 The series of twenty short poems is known only in TMS (private collection); the two longer poems may be "les joues rouges" and/or one or two from those published as "Poèmes 38–39" (see 28 February 1939, n. 2; Knowlson, *Damned to Fame*, 270).

9 Austrian-born artist Wolfgang Paalen (1905–1959), whose work had been exhibited at Guggenheim Jeune (15 February to 11 March 1939), had given SB one of his "fumage" paintings (oil, candle burns and soot on canvas) (for an example: Paalen's *Fumage* in William S. Rubin, *Dada, Surrealism, and their Heritage* [New York: Museum of Modern Art, 1968] 140, no. 207).
The Jankel Adler painting purchased by SB is untitled (private collection).

10 Alfred Péron.

11 Suzanne Deschevaux-Dumesnil* (1900–1989), later SB's wife.

12 Hester Dowden.

13 McGreevy may have enclosed a reproduction of a painting by Antonello da Messina.

THOMAS McGREEVY
LONDON

June 6th 1939   6 Rue des Favorites
                                        Paris 15me

dear Tom

Thanks for your letter and card, which arrived simultaneously.[1]

I gave the papers to Joyce. He was pleased with the Tristan quotation. Shaw doesn't change front very skilfully.[2]

Remember me to Junger [*for* Junyer].[3] I hope you have succeeded in recovering all the stuff you left in Paris.

[...]

I have lost touch altogether with Geoffrey.[4] But if I was in the kind of trouble that he deals in I would go to him and, I know, be helped as before. He may think I stay in London on my ways through & don't look him up, which has never been the case.

I am sorry Harrington Road has become so uncomfortable for you. You talked once of going to stay with the waiter in the joint he was starting.[5]

I saw Péron to-day. He is doing a quarter of an hour's broadcast on the 29th on Finnegans Wake.[6]

Can a citizen of Eire accept a Knighthood? It would indeed be a pity if Bodkin was able to plead immunity. O'Sullivan was over here (the RHA) a short time ago and said he thought Charlemont House would so[o]n be vacant again.[7]

Blanaid Salkeld wrote to me for a poem for a series of broadsheets of Dublin poets that she is bringing out, illustrated – "not exactly illustrated" – by Cecil. I sent her one of 4 lines, the only one I had, which will leave plenty of room for Cecil.[8]

I should like very much to get to Geneva to see the Prado pictures but I fear it is impossible. I have not heard how long the Exhibition is to last. I suppose Franco is howling for that along with the rest.[9]

Longford is a long melancholy hank of amiable misery who has done everything from medicine in Trinity & College of Surgeons to driving a lorry in Yorkshire and finished nothing. He is at present – or was last Xmas – running with some woman well known in Dublin whose name I forget a miniature gallery in Nassau Street called I think New Pictures. I met him years ago in the Mannings' house, where he was lodging.[10] I liked him for his caring for things so little cared for in Dublin & for his ineffectualness. He was interested also in morbid psychology, of which he was – & I think still is – a victim. So shallow called to shallow. The Euston Road group sounds friendly.[11] But all groups are horrible.

Massine & Co. are here at the new Trocadero. I did not know he had done the 7th Symphony. Cocteau is reported to be making a ballet of Britannicus. With Harpo Marx as Junie I suppose.[12]

I drowse through the days & do nothing. I try now & then to get started, but it comes to nothing. If it is to be like that, let it be like that.

I have lost all touch also with Coffey. He is said to be at Dampierre, close to McCalmon [*for* McAlmon], with Mrs Coffey.

At home they seem well. Mother[']s new cottage was begun last week. I shall go over towards the end of July.

How is Hester? Remember me to her. And to Dilly.[13]

Love ever

Sam

Did you see Aldington's bad tempered review of Finnegan? Some Yankee paper. He was scandalised by the morose delectation!!![14]

ALS; 3 leaves, 3 sides; PS written in upper left margin of side 1, perpendicularly to the text; TCD, MS 10402/169.

1 McGreevy's letter and card have not been found.

2 McGreevy may have sent SB London papers with reviews of *Finnegans Wake*. SB's reference to the Tristan quotation, possibly supplied by McGreevy, or mentioned in a review, has not been identified.

George Bernard Shaw wrote a letter to the Editor of *Picture Post* on 3 June 1939 responding to the suggestion in an article on 13 May 1939 by English critic Geoffrey Grigson (1905–1985) that he had been so disgusted by *Ulysses* that he had burned his copy: "'I did not burn it; and I was not disgusted'" (Joyce, *Letters of James Joyce*, III, 444–445).

3 Catalan painter Joan Junyer.

4 Geoffrey Thompson.

5 McGreevy's alternative lodgings have not been identified.

6 On 16 June 1939, Joyce told the French historian and critic Louis Gillet (1876–1943) that the broadcast would be on 22 June; in a letter to Harriet Shaw Weaver on 19 June 1939, Joyce indicated that Alfred Péron would give a short broadcast on *Finnegans Wake* in the following week on Paris PTT (Louis Gillet, *Claybook for James Joyce*, tr. Georges Markow-Totevy [New York: Abelard-Schuman, 1958] 21; Joyce, *Letters of James Joyce*, III, 447). No listing has been found of the broadcast that would confirm either the date given by Joyce or that given by SB. According to correspondence from Paul Léon and James Joyce to Monroe Saw and Co., London, "Samuel Beckett would be willing to do the broadcast for the B.B.C." (Joyce and Léon, *The James Joyce–Paul Léon Papers*, 137).

7 Thomas Bodkin, former Director of The National Gallery of Ireland and from 1935 to 1952 Barber Professor of Fine Arts and Director of the Barber Institute at the University of Birmingham. Queen Mary (Mary of Teck, 1867–1953, consort of George V [1865–1936]) opened the Barber Institute of Fine Arts on 26 July 1939; however, Bodkin was not knighted (Alan Denson, comp., *Thomas Bodkin: A Bio-Bibliographical Survey with a Bibliographical Survey of His Family* [Dublin: The Bodkin Trustees, 1966] 7).

Seán O'Sullivan, a member of the Royal Hibernian Academy, had been in Paris, as SB wrote to Reavey on 5 March 1939: "Sean O'Sullivan, the Irish Sargent, has taken Adler's studio for 2 months" (TxU). SB refers to American portrait painter John Singer Sargent (1856–1925).

Charlemont House was the site of the Municipal Gallery of Modern Art.

8 Blanaid and Cecil Salkeld had initiated Dublin Poets and Artists, a series of twenty-five broadsheets, published by their Gayfield Press from 1941 to 1943; each published a poem (or occasionally two) by a Dublin writer with an illustration by a Dublin artist, and most were hand-printed by Blanaid Salkeld. Beckett's poem has not been found in any of the extant broadsheets, the largest collection of which is in the New York Public Library Rare Books Department (numbers 2–7, 9–10, 21, 25).

SB mentions the poem he sent to Blanaid Salkeld in his letter to Mary Manning Howe of 6 June 1939: "I sent her one of 4 lines, being the second of the two torn from my palpitating sensorium by years of adversity, the first (of five lines) having disappeared" (TxU). SB's poem "Dieppe" was written first in French in 1937 (later translated into English by SB and published in *The Irish Times* 9 June 1945: 2; Federman and Fletcher, *Samuel Beckett: His Works and His Critics*, 75). SB may refer to "they come" as the five-line poem that had disappeared; this was written in English (see SB to Thomas McGreevy, 27 January 1938).

9 With agreement of both Loyalists and Republicans, masterworks from Spanish collections, including from the Prado Museum in Madrid, were removed to Geneva in February 1939 and housed for safekeeping in the Palace of the League of Nations until the end of the Spanish Civil War. A selection of them was exhibited at the Musée d'Art et d'Histoire in Geneva from 1 July to 31 August 1939, prior to their return to Franco's regime in Spain ([Howard Devree], "News and Comments: Spain's Art Treasures at Geneva," *Magazine of Art* 32.7 [July 1939] 425–426; Thomas McGreevy, "Spanish Masterpieces: A Selection Based on the Exhibition of Paintings from the Prado at Geneva," *The Studio* 18 [September 1939] 90–107).

General Francisco Franco (1892–1975).

10 John Manning Longford (known as Jack, 1911–1944) studied medicine at Trinity College Dublin; in 1939 he joined Deirdre McDonagh (née Moira Pilkington, 1897–1970) in running the Contemporary Picture Galleries, then at 5 South Leinster Street, which she had founded in 1938 (S. B. Kennedy, 8 March 2006). Art critic Stephen Rynne observed:

> Longford was a fine connoisseur and a picture vendor – head and should-
> ers above all his kind in Ireland at that time. No one did more for con-
> temporary art or showed a better appreciation of good Irish artists than
> gentle Longford. The old man [Jack B. Yeats] and the young Longford were
> warm friends; there was something of a father and son affinity between
> them. ("Tea with Jack B. Yeats 1940," *Éire-Ireland* 7.2 [1972] 106)

11 The School of Drawing and Painting, 314/316 Euston Road, was founded by William Coldstream (1908–1987) in 1937; he, Claude Rogers (1907–1979), and Victor Pasmore (1908–1998), with about thirty others, were known as the Euston Road School. The School was active from 1937 to 1941.

12 The Palais du Trocadéro had been demolished to be replaced by the Palais de Chaillot, erected for the Exposition Internationale of 1937. Léonide Massine's newly reconstituted Ballets de Monte-Carlo announced two programs at the Théâtre de Chaillot from 5 to 8 June 1939: *Lac des Cygnes*, *L'Etrange Farandole*, and *Tricorne*; *Les Elfes*, *Petrouchka*, and *Noble Vision* (*Le Temps*, 6 June 1939: 5 and 6; *Le Temps*, 7 June 1939: 5).

Seventh Symphony was Massine's symphonic ballet based on Beethoven's Seventh Symphony in A major, op. 92; it premiered in Monte Carlo on 5 May 1938. Massine describes its evolution in *My Life in Ballet*, ed. Phyllis Hartnoll and Robert Rubens (London: Macmillan St. Martin's Press, 1968) 206–207.

Cocteau did not create a ballet of Racine's play *Britannicus* (1669). He had created roles for his companion, actor Jean Marais (1913–1998), who directed, designed, and acted in a production of the play in 1941. In *Britannicus*, Junie is to marry Britannicus, but his half-brother Nero objects; SB imagines Harpo Marx (né Adolph Arthur Marx, 1888–1964) in this female role.

13 Hester Dowden, Geraldine Cummins.

14 Richard Aldington wrote of *Finnegans Wake*:

> The problem of what Mr. Joyce has to say in *Finnegans Wake* may be left
> to those who have time and energy to waste...This heavy compost

is frequently infected with that lecherous suggestiveness of which Mr. Joyce is a master, which was defended in *Ulysses* as germane to the characters, but which here seems to have no purpose more interesting than the author's morose delectations. ("James Joyce," *The Atlantic* 163 (June 1939), unpaginated supplement: "The Bookshelf" [17, 19, 21])

GEORGE REAVEY

LONDON

14/6/39   6 Rue des Favorites
                                                           Paris 15me

dear George

Will you please send me back my <u>Petit Sot</u>.[1] I have no other copy[.]

Ever

Sam

APCS; 1 leaf, 1 side; Vlaminck, "Paysage en Beauce"; *to* George Reavey Esq, 7 Great Ormond Street, London W.C. 1; *pm* 15-[6]-39, Paris; TxU.

1 See 28 February 1939 and n. 2 to that letter, in which SB indicates that he is writing another "Petit Sot," which he intended to send to Reavey with his shorter poems in French.

ARLAND USSHER

[? DUBLIN OR CAPPAGH, CO. WATERFORD]

June 14th [1939]   6 Rue des Favorites
                                                           Paris 15me

dear Arland

If you want a big name I think Piazzetta or Tiepolo are the most likely, & the latter better than the former, though the picture seems rather too maniéré & doubtfully drawn to be of any possible chance by either. The rhythm is Tiepolesque, the format also, the bearded gent above the Maries like a bad copy of a Tiepolo motif (cf. The Almighty in the Dublin Litany of the Virgin for the real thing. There are as few Tiepolos without the beard as Wouwermanns [*for* Wouwermans] without the white horse.), and the stooping John in the foreground, here as far as I can judge hardly a success, is the kind of difficulty that gave him none. The Maries are very curious, the right hand of the topmost seems very good, and the lowest I seem to have seen somewhere in a Cranach, which however if it were so would not invalidate the Tiepolo suggestion, who worked so long in Würzburg. Another possible line obviously would be the Spanish – Neapolitan, but the work seems to be neither sufficiently devout nor sufficiently dramatic to satisfy that mixture in any of its dosages. As a decorative statement of weights & tensions it seems to me to lack only technique & bravura to pair up with the easel recreations of Gianbattista [*for* Giambattista] Tiepolo & Sons.[1]

If you like I shall send it to Tom McGreevy, who is very much better qualified than I am.[2] Can you not obtain a less nebulous reproduction?

Thank you for your essay. When the period represents an end point of meditation your rather dogmatic tone is no doubt the right one.[3] You feel a law, you lay it down. Theology has given philosophy a good paper, clean, honest & obliging, now who will take it up? The State.

Nächstens mehr.[4]

I was glad to meet Jacqueline and hope another time to have again the pleasure. Thank you for your bounteous hospitality which I was unable to reverberate.[5]

I have been reading Hölderlin. It is a depressing thought that perhaps Hyperion was necessary to the Freie Rythmen &

the terrific fragments of the Spätzeit.[6] I obtained someone's agreement last night in a dream that he (Hölderlin) must have been for a long time homosexual.

Did you know that the spider had 2 penes.[7] And that there is plenty of room for both if he does not prefer to prolong his pleasure. And they talk still of evolution.

yrs ever

Sam

Looking at the right hand again it is horribly Rembrandtesque. But T. was one of the great eclectics.[8]

ALS; 2 leaves, 2 sides; TxU. *Dating:* Brian Coffey's letter to Robert MacAlmon on 20 June 1939: n. 7 below, and 16 June 1939.

1 At an auction Ussher had purchased a painting of the crucifixion for £5; later it was sold in an auction at Cappagh for £12. His daughter Henrietta Ussher Staples recalled that it was approximately 24 in. × 30 in. and quite brown, in "terrible condition"; it has not been further identified.

SB refers to the Italian painter and draftsman Giovanni Battista Piazzetta. He compares Ussher's picture to Giovanni Battista (also known as Giambattista) Tiepolo's *An Allegory of the Incarnation* (also called *Litany of the Virgin*, NGI 353) which depicts God with a full beard (*National Gallery of Ireland: Catalogue of the Oil Pictures in the General Collection* [1932], 127; for an image, see *National Gallery of Ireland: Illustrated Summary Catalogue of Paintings* [1981], 162).

Dutch painter Philips Wouwerman (1619–1668) frequently included a white horse in his pictures.

SB is reminded of an unnamed painting by Lucas Cranach; Cranach worked in Wittenberg (not Würzburg) from 1505 to 1550, and both his sons, Hans and Lucas II, were born there.

2 McGreevy's specialty was Italian art; he wrote for the London art journal *The Studio* at this time.

3 It is not known which essay Ussher had sent to SB. During 1939, Ussher frequently published essays in *The New English Weekly and the New Age*: his essay "Works and Faith" (14.23 [16 March 1939] 346–347) discussed philosophy and the Catholic Church; Kant was his starting point for the essay "New Metaphysic and Old Spook" (15.5 [18 May 1939] 80–81).

4 "Nächstens mehr" (More soon).

5 Ussher had met Jacqueline de la Châtre (n.d.) in France. She was a friend of both Ussher and Georges Bleu (b. 1914); on Ussher's behalf, Bleu had attempted to

visit SB at the Hôpital Broussais, only to find that SB had already been released (Georges Bleu to Arland Ussher, 9 February 1938, TCD, MSS 9031/134). SB wrote to Mary Manning Howe about Ussher's hospitality to him: Arland "stood me more food & refreshment in one week than during the whole previous course of our acquaintance" (6 June 1939, TxU).

6 SB had purchased the collected works of the German poet Johann Christian Friedrich Hölderlin (1770–1843) on 24 December 1937, according to the date in SB's edition (BIF, UoR: Friedrich Hölderlin, *Sämtliche Werke* [Leipzig: Insel-Verlag, (1926)]). This edition includes Hölderlin's two-volume novel *Hyperion oder Der Eremit in Griechenland* (*Hyperion, or the Hermit in Greece*, 425–586), his translations of *Antigone* (876–916), and those few poems that were published during his lifetime. SB here refers to two groups of poems: *Freie Rhythmen* (Free Rhythms, 202–241) and *Gedicht der Spätzeit* (*Last Poems*, 1002–1009). SB's poem "Dieppe" was based on a portion of Hölderlin's "Der Spaziergang" ("The Walk," 1005–1006), from *Gedicht der Spätzeit* (see Harvey, *Samuel Beckett*, 218).

7 SB's "information" about the spider is repeated by Brian Coffey in a letter to Robert McAlmon: "Beckett was here on Thursday and had to communicate that when the spider went aloving it filled up two penes with juice and then set off to be ready for instant action, followed by immediate getaway. Otherwise the future of writing was in new technical methods" (20 June 1939; CtY: MSS Survey Za McAlmon).

8 Tiepolo.

GEORGE REAVEY

LONDON

16/6/39   Paris

dear George

Thanks for 200 fr.

Let me have P.S. back when you can.

Il me tarde de le mettre en morceaux.[1]

Had a walk yesterday with Brian round about Dampierre & Lemay. And learned that sin was a form of non being.[2]

Sam

APCS; 1 leaf, 1 side; ink smudged; "Langeais – La Maison de Rabelais"; *to* George Reavey, 7 Great Ormond Street, LONDON, W.C. 1; *pm* 16-6-39, Paris; TxU.

1 SB refers to his poem, or poems, "Petit Sot," sent to Reavey after 28 February 1939; SB indicates that he had received the manuscript of "Petit Sot" in his letter to Reavey written before 7 July 1939 (TxU).

"Il me tarde de le mettre en morceaux" (I can't wait to tear it to pieces).

2 Brian Coffey reported their conversation to Robert McAlmon (see 14 June 1939, n. 7).

GEORGE AND GWYNEDD REAVEY
LONDON

26/9/39   6 Rue des Favorites
                                                 Paris 15

dear George & Gwynedd

I saw Eva Tone yesterday evening and gave her your message as well as I could remember it. She seemed to be au courant. She had been in Calvados with friends (including the wife of the Doctor with Italian name), hoping to stay there during the altercations, but they were all packed back to Paris.[1]

Geer passed through Paris about 3 weeks ago, from the Hague back to rejoin Lisl at Cagnes, where they both are at present. Apparently things did not turn out in Holland as he had hoped, & the Colonial patron did the dirty. Adler is also still at Cagnes, apparently, but I don't think he can remain there much longer.[2]

A few days ago I ran into Peggy Guggenheim at the Dome, with a brand new car & drinking Pernod. She is staying with some Mrs ? Berg at Meudon, and is driving to Mégève to fix up about her children before returning to England. She seemed to think she would be shortly back in France. She was able to tell me about various people I had lost track of, including the Joyces, who are at La Baule.[3]

The Duncans are at Paramé near St. Malo.

Péron is with his regiment at Lorient. I had a card from him. He feeds the horses.[4]

I have no news of my application – God knows when I leave. I am thinking of going to see Cremin at the Irish Legation, though I don't suppose he can do anything.[5]

I see Nizan has resigned from the party & Rolland has come down & Giono has been apprehended. I wonder where Sartre is.[6]

Djuna Barnes apparently is still here. But I haven't been St. Germainising.

The Freundlichs also apparently are still here.[7]

> Love
>
> Sam

ALS; 3 leaves, 3 sides; *env to* Mr & Mrs George Reavey, 19 St. James's Gardens, LONDON W. 11; TxU.

1 Neither Eva Tone nor the wife of the doctor with the Italian name has been identified. France and Great Britain declared war against Germany on 3 September 1939; SB had returned to France, although not without difficulty, the next day (see Knowlson, *Damned to Fame*, 273).

2 Geer van Velde had sought continuing patronage from collector Pierre Regnault (see 5 January 1938, n. 11).

Germany had invaded Poland on 1 September 1939. Adler remained in Cagnes-sur-Mer until 1940 when he joined the Polish Army of the West (Jürgen Harten, Marc Scheps, and Ryszard Stanislawski, eds., *Jankel Adler: 1895–1949* [Cologne: DuMont Buchverlag, 1985] 34).

3 Peggy Guggenheim stayed for some time with Petronella von Doesburg (née van Moorsel, known as Nelly, 1899–1975) at her home in Meudon, near Paris; Guggenheim's children Sindbad (né Michael Cedric Sindbad Vail, 1923–1986) and Pegeen Vail (m. Rumney, 1925–1967) were living with their father Laurence Vail in Megève in the French Alps (Weld, *Peggy*, 188–192).

James and Nora Joyce had gone to La Baule, France, on 28 August 1939 because Lucia was to be evacuated there with other patients of Dr. Delmas from the Ivry Maison de Santé (Joyce, *Letters of James Joyce*, III, 454–456; Ellmann, *James Joyce*, 726–728). "Maison de santé" (private hospital).

4 Alfred Péron had been called up for military service. Lorient, a seaport in Brittany.

5 The exact nature of SB's application to serve France is unknown. Cornelius Cremin was First Secretary of the Irish Legation in France (see 21 January 1938, n. 5).

6 French novelist Paul Nizan (1905–1940), Principal Editor of *La Revue Marxiste*, resigned from the Communist Party on 25 September 1939 ("Les Communistes de la C.G.T. et le pacte germano-soviétique," *Paris Soir* 26 September 1939: 3).

French writer Romain Rolland (1866–1944) left the public arena and made his home in Vézelay; "overcoming the Nazis remained the focus of his intellectual politics from 1939" (David James Fisher, *Romain Rolland and the Politics of Intellectual Engagement* [Berkeley: University of California Press, 1988] 290–292).

French writer Jean Giono (1895–1970), a pacifist, was mobilized on 5 September 1939, arrested on 14 September 1939 as a "défaitiste"(defeatist), and interned in Marseille (Pierre Citron, *Giono: 1895–1970* [Paris: Editions du Seuil, 1990], 318; Jean Giono and Jean Guéhenno, *Correspondance 1928–1969*, ed. Pierre Citron [Paris: Seghers, 1991] 196).

Jean-Paul Sartre was called up in the general mobilization of 2 September 1939 (Annie Cohen-Solal, *Sartre: A Life* (New York: Pantheon Books, 1987] 133; Simone de Beauvoir, *Letters to Sartre*, ed. and tr. Quintin Hoare [New York: Arcade, 1992] 57).

7 American writer Djuna Barnes (1892–1982) was still in Paris at this time and left France only on 12 October 1939 (Phillip F. Herring, *Djuna: The Life and Work of Djuna Barnes* [New York: Viking Penguin, 1995] 247). St. Germainising: frequenting the cafés of the Saint-Germain-des-Prés district of Paris and the intellectual circles associated with it.

Otto Freundlich was interned in a French detention camp in 1939 because he was a German citizen.

GEORGE AND GWYNEDD REAVEY

LONDON

6/12/39   6 Rue de Favorites

                                            Paris 15

Dear George et Gwynedd[1]

Thanks for your note. Sorry the spirits are low. There is nothing left but to work. But long ago it was so also.

I have had no news of my démarche. What I really wanted was their receipt – & they gave me that.[2]

Here I am heated & hot watered as usual & rarely go out. I have been working hard at Murphy & only 4 chapters remain to translate. Another month should see it finished & then I think it will be Johnson at last.[3]

Rivoallan sent me his <u>Littérature Irlandaise Contemporaine</u>, where there is a certain amount about Tom & <u>Intercessions</u> & the <u>Bones</u> & <u>Murphy</u>. Published by Hachette.[4]

I see Brian had a son in Dublin on Armistice Day.[5] I never hear from him.

I met Kandinsky the other day. Sympathetic old Siberian.[6]

I had a note from Lisl some time ago & a prose poem from Geer to the effect that <u>In tristitia hilaris</u> etc. Adler seemed to be still there.[7]

Duncan came up from Paramé for 2 days, looking comparatively well under a <u>casquette de cha[r]cutier</u>.[8]

Péron writes. He was with the British Field Ambulance, now transferred to Etat major.[9]

   Love to you both & to Tom.

   Sam

ALS; 1 leaf, 2 sides; TxU.

1 Here, and hereafter, SB spells "Gwynedd" correctly.

2 SB had applied to serve France in the War effort (see 26 September 1939); "my démarche" (the approach I made).

3 SB may have begun the French translation of *Murphy* with Alfred Péron, but he continued on his own. SB refers to his projected play about Samuel Johnson.

4 French specialist in Irish Literature at the Sorbonne Anatole Rivoallan (1886–1976) edited *Littérature irlandaise contemporaine* (Paris: Hachette, 1939). In his chapter "La Poésie depuis 1916" (Poetry since 1916), poems by McGreevy and Beckett, as well as Devlin's *Intercessions*, are discussed (124–127); in the chapter "Le Roman et la nouvelle" (The Novel and the Short Story), SB's *Murphy* is discussed (143 and *passim*).

5 The son of Brian and Bridget Coffey, John Martin Michael, was born on 11 November 1939 in Dublin (Coffey to Robert McAlmon, 28 November 1939; CtY, MSS survey Za McAlmon).

6 While his father had been born in Siberia, Wassily Kandinsky was born in Moscow. He was seventy-three years old when SB met him.

7 Lisl van Velde's letter and its enclosure have not been found.

"In tristitia hilaris" is the epigraph of Giordano Bruno's play *Il Candelaio* (1582; *The Candle Bearer*): "In tristitia hilaris, in hilaritate tristis" (in sorrow, gaiety; in gaiety, sorrow) (Giordano Bruno and Tommaso Campanella, *Opere di Giordano Bruno e di*

Tommaso Campanella, ed. Augusto Guzzo and Romano Amerio, La Letteratura italiana; storia e testi [Milan: Riccardo Ricciardi, 1956] [35]; tr. Anthony Cuda).

Jankel Adler was in Cagnes-sur-Mer with Geer and Lisl van Velde.

8   Alan Duncan was living in Paramé, near St. Malo. "Casquette de charcutier" (pork butcher's cap).

9   Péron was at this time a liaison agent with the British Expeditionary Force, attached to the staff of the British Field Ambulance; "Etat major" (General Staff).

CHRONOLOGY 1940

1940 13 January   Lacking "safe-conduct" papers, SB cannot visit the Joyces in St. Gérand-le-Puy, Allier. Joyce has enlisted Rivoallan to review SB's French translation of *Murphy*, but SB needs to make a clean copy before sending to Rivoallan.

11 February   Joyce expects Giorgio Joyce and SB to come to St. Gérand-le-Puy for Stephen Joyce's birthday on 15 February.

24–29 March   SB spends Easter with Maria Jolas and the Joyces in La Chapelle, St. Gérand-le-Puy.

9 April   Germany invades Norway and Denmark.

10 May   Germany invades the Netherlands, Belgium, and Luxembourg.

12 May   Germany invades France.

By 21 May   SB applies to serve as an ambulance driver. Rivoallan's revision of SB's French translation of *Murphy* for submission to Jean Paulhan is deferred. SB writes "part of the first act of Johnson." His "sketch" for *Paris Mondial* is canceled. Buys paintings by Bram van Velde and encourages Peggy Guggenheim's interest in his work.

10 June   Arranges to meet Bram van Velde and Marthe Arnaud on 14 June, "provided that we are staying on in Paris." Italy declares war on France and Britain.

12 June   Leaves Paris with Suzanne Deschevaux-Dumesnil.

14 June   German troops enter and occupy Paris.

18 June   Charles de Gaulle calls on the French to stand against the Germans.

JAMES JOYCE
ST. GÉRAND-LE-PUY, ALLIER, FRANCE

13/1/40   6 Rue des Favorites
                                            Paris XV

dear Mr Joyce

I have given up all hope of getting down for the moment. To-day again the safe-conduct is not in. Every day for the past week I have been going up or trotting round to the place in the Champs Elyseés. By the time it comes in, if they don't decide finally to refuse it to me, Giorgio will be starting back. So I have decided to put off the trip to Easter. I am very disappointed, as I was looking forward to seeing you both.[1]

I saw Nino Frank – got from him the various papers. About the scenario, he said it would not be possible to publish it in Pour Vous & seemed to think the best plan would be to have it published in a French translation in the N.R.F. or some other review of the kind. As a scenario, he seemed to think it well arranged.[2] The typescript of the Italian Anna Livia was not ready. He will send you a copy as soon as it is. The new editor of Panorama was apparently enthusiastic, but no doubt he spoke to you of that. He was glad to keep Finnegan a little longer.[3] I shall give him a ring again one of these days & arrange for an evening with him.

I am not quite sure what items "former" & "latter" refer to in your postcard, and whether you wanted Panorama & New Directions or the former only. I am sending the former only, & will send the latter on after if you wish.[4]

I am sending also the list of Censored Publications received from my brother. I asked for the most recent list, but it doesn't seem very recent.[5]

I had a card to-day from Rivoallan. It was kind of you to write him about <u>Murphy</u>. He offers very kindly to read the translation & to "introduce" me to the French public. I have only one copy of the translation, and it is in an awful mess, but if ever I have a clean copy I shall send it to him. In the meantime I am writing to thank him.[6]

My kindest regards to M<u>rs</u> Joyce.

Yours very sincerely

Sam Beckett

ALS; 2 leaves, 2 sides; Zurich James Joyce Foundation.

1 Just before Christmas 1939 the Joyces left Paris for St. Gérand-le-Puy in the Allier, where their grandson Stephen Joyce was enrolled in the bilingual school of Maria Jolas which had evacuated there.

As a resident foreigner, SB was required to have a laissez-passer in order to leave Paris, where he was registered. The *carte d'identité* could be obtained at the Maison de France, 101 Avenue des Champs-Elysées, and it is possible that SB also applied there for the travel document that was required. The Archives du Ministère des Affaires Etrangères indicates that immigration records were lost when the Germans occupied Paris.

2 Nino Frank had been Editor of the Paris film weekly *Pour Vous*, published from 22 November 1928 to 5 June 1940.

The specific scenario, by Joyce or adapted from his work, has not been identified with certainty; none was published in *La Nouvelle Revue Française*. SB may refer to Stuart Gilbert's "Sketch of a Scenario of Anna Livia Plurabelle," written in English in 1935, which incorporated Joyce's suggestions (CtY: Eugene and Maria Jolas Papers, GEN MS 108, series XV, 64/1499); this was later published in Maria Jolas, ed., *A James Joyce Yearbook*, 10–20.

3 The Italian translation of "Anna Livia Plurabelle" was undertaken by Nino Frank and Joyce; however, when published as "Anna Livia Plurabella" in *Prospettive* [Rome] 4.2 (15 February 1940) 13–15, Ettore Settanni and James Joyce were indicated as co-translators. Nino Frank's name was suppressed because of his "antifascist activity," as Joyce wrote to Nino Frank on 13 March 1940: "Il Settanni mi scrive che il Suo nome non appare per ragioni che Lei capirà sul momento. Ma non sarà sempre celato, spero!" ("Settanni writes me that your name does not appear for reasons you will understand at once. But it will not always be kept hidden, I trust!") (Joyce, *Letters of James Joyce*, III, 469).

The published text differed from the translation sanctioned by Joyce. In a card to Nino Frank on 9 April 1940, Joyce wrote: "les pronoms de la 3ième personne singuliere [*for* du … singulier] ont été changés en des pr[é]noms de la 2ième pluriel! [*for* du … pluriel]" (Third person singular pronouns have been changed to second person plural pronouns!); Joyce's letter to Settanni to protest against this and other changes was published as "Una Lettera di Joyce," *Prospettive* 4.4 (15 April 1940) 11. Ellmann explains, writing of direct address: "The use of the second person plural pronoun *voi* instead of [the third person singular pronoun] *Lei* was made obligatory under Fascism" (Joyce, *Letters of James Joyce*, III, 475; for other changes: Eric Bulson, "Getting Noticed: James Joyce's Italian Translations," *Joyce Studies Annual* 12 [Summer 2001] 33–36).

Finnegans Wake was reviewed by Salvatore Rosati, "Il nuovo libro di James Joyce," *Panorama* [Rome] 18 (12 November 1939) 246–247; the Editors of *Panorama* were Raffaele Contu (1895–1953) and Gianni Mazzocchi (1906–1984) (Joyce to Jacques Mercanton on 9 January 1940, to James Laughlin on 21 February 1940, and to Mercanton on 14 March 1940; in Joyce, *Letters of James Joyce*, III, 463, 468, and 470–471).

4 Joyce wrote to James Laughlin on 21 February 1940, thanking him for *New Directions in Prose and Poetry* [4], ed. James Laughlin (Norfolk, CT: New Directions, 1939), which included an article by Harry Levin, "On First Looking into *Finnegans Wake*" (253–287) (Joyce, *Letters of James Joyce*, III, 468, 471).

5 Following every meeting, the Irish Board of Censorship published lists of prohibited books in the *Iris Oifigúil* (Ireland's official State gazette); *The Irish Times* also carried these periodic reports as "an Order made by the Minister for Justice under the Censorship of Publications Act" ("Banned Publications," *The Irish Times* 20 December 1939: 3). The latest *Register of Prohibited Publications* prior to January 1940 was published on 31 March 1938, and updated with a supplement, the *List of the Books Prohibited During the Half-year from the 1st April 1938, to the 30th September 1938*. The next issue of the Register to be published would be that of 31 March 1940 (John Goodwillie, Official Publications Librarian, Trinity College Dublin, 2 August 2006; Peggy Garvey, Office of Censorship of Publications, Dublin, 2 August 2006).

6 The card from Anatole Rivoallan to SB has not been found.

MARIA JOLAS

LA CHAPELLE, ST. GÉRAND-LE-PUY, FRANCE

1/4/40   6 Rue des Favorites
                                              Paris XV

Chère Madame Jolas
    Rien qu'un mot pour vous remercier, bleu-noir sur blanchâtre, de votre profuse hospitalité.[1]

    Ici on chante:
    Au fin fond du blanc Bourbonnais,

> Loin des offensives de paix,
> Madame Maria Jolas
> Donne des lits à pleines mains
> Et du bon vin de St. Pourçain
> Aux scélérats de guerre lasse.[2]

J'espère qu'il me sera encore donné d'en abuser.
> Votre dévoué
> Sam Beckett

ALS; 1 leaf, 1 side; CtY, Gen Mss 108, series VII, 28/535.

1/4/40   6 Rue des Favorites
                                      Paris XV

Dear Madame Jolas,

Just a brief note to thank you, blue-black on off-white, for your profuse hospitality.[1]

Here our song goes:

> Away in the heart of the white Bourbonnais,
> Far from the peace offensives,
> Madame Maria Jolas
> Offers beds galore
> And good St. Pourçain wine
> To war-weary villains.[2]

I hope that I shall have another chance to guzzle it.
> Your devoted
> Sam Beckett

1   SB had joined the Jolases and the Joyces for the holidays; Maria Jolas wrote to Eugene Jolas on 29 March 1940:
> Our Easter house party here is coming to an end. Beckett and Giorgio left this morning for Paris. [...]

In the evenings we sang or played "polite" games, such as portraits, etc. Beckett had a game where you had to choose the name of a city and then make sentences with its initials [...] Some good laughs.

Beckett, by the way is vastly improved and was extremely agreeable and nice about everything. (CtY, Gen Mss 108, series 1, 2/33c)

2 Blanc Bourbonnais refers to the area to which the Ecole bilingue de Neuilly of Maria Jolas had evacuated, 8 miles NE of Vichy. St. Pourçain here refers to wines of this area of the Allier.

GEORGE AND GWYNEDD REAVEY

MADRID, SPAIN

21/5/40   6 Rue des Favorites
                                                     Paris 15me

Dear George & Gwynedd

I am still here and all right. I have no news of Geer. As far as I know he is still at Cagnes with the others. I have been seeing something of Bram & Marthe. They are having a bad time. I am buying a picture from Bram on the stuttering system.[1] I tried to get Peggy to do something for him. She arranged a day to go to his studio and said she would probably take a picture, but at the last moment she sidestepped me. In the meantime she accumulates Braques, Gris, Brancusis, Dalis and other painters in want. I expect to hear any day that she has acquired a Kisling or a Van Dongen.[2] It's not my business. Bram is réformé, Geer not, but I don't think he will be called on.[3]

I never had a reply to the application I made in September. I have offered myself now to drive an ambulance. If they take me they will take me soon. [4]

I have been working a lot. Rivoallan was doing an article on At Swim Two Birds & Murphy for the Mercure, in the place of the one projected by the late Maurice Denhof. He was also going to revise my translation for submission to Paulhan with recommendation from Adrienne Monnier. All that is down the drain for the moment.[5] I did a sketch for Paris Mondial that was cancelled because of recent events. And I wrote half of a first act of Johnson.[6] At Easter I went into the Bourbonnais for a week to see the Joyces, who are still there.[7] McCalmon [*for* McAlmon] tells me he had a letter recently from Brian who is living somewhere outside Dublin with Bridget & Babe, reading 8th century pseudo-sceptics. I have no news of Tom. He had an article in the Irish Times on the poems of one Milne, published at the Gayfield press. Duncan was up for a couple of days.[8] Your successor in the Bureau payed me a visit some months ago. He was very upset that he hadn't been able to find Slonim.[9]

An American friend of mine, Maurice English, poet and journalist, has just gone to Madrid from Paris. He is at the Palace Hotel and would very much like to make your acquaintance [sic]. He is an extremely nice fellow and I think you would get on well together. Look him up. I think it is the Chicago Tribune he works for. If by any chance he has left that hotel you could get him at the American Embassy.[10] I perceive an involuntary metathesis in acquaintance. I shall not correct it.

And how are you getting on yourselves? Write soon.

Love

s/ Sam

I have had several visits from Péron, on leave.[11] He was in good form. But now ... ?

TLS and APS in top margin; 1 leaf, 1 side; TxU.

1 The Battle of France began on 10 May 1940, marking the start of the German advance that culminated with surrender and the Occupation.

George Reavey moved to Madrid in January 1940, where he was working with the British Council. Geer van Velde was still in Cagnes-sur-Mer.

Geer's brother Bram van Velde (né Abraham Gerardus van Velde 1895–1981), also a painter, had moved to Montrouge, a Paris suburb. He had been living in Majorca, but after the death of his wife, the German painter Sophie Caroline Klöker (known as Lilly, 1896–1936), Bram came to Paris; while staying with his brother Geer, Bram met Marthe Arnaud (née Kunst, 1887–1959), a former Protestant missionary in Northern Rhodesia (now Zambia), who became his companion from 1936 until her death (Stoullig and Schoeller, eds., *Bram van Velde*, 146, 155–157; Rainer Michael Mason, ed., *Bram van Velde, 1895–1981: Rétrospective du Centenaire* [Geneva: Musée Rath (Musées d'Art et d'Histoire, 1996)] 305–307).

SB purchased *Sans titre* (Untitled, 1937, Musée National d'Art Moderne, Centre Georges Pompidou, AM 1982-244).

2 With a view to establishing a museum of contemporary art, Guggenheim purchased works by Constantin Brancusi and Catalan painter Salvador Dalí (1904–1989) (see Guggenheim, *Out of This Century: Confessions of an Art Addict*, 210–218; Anton Gill, *Art Lover: A Biography of Peggy Guggenheim* [New York: HarperCollins, 2002] 220). Her collection included works by French artist Georges Braque (1882–1963) and Spanish painter Juan Gris (1887–1927). She did not own work by Polish-born painter Moïse Kisling (1891–1953) or Dutch-born painter Kees van Dongen (1877–1968). (For images and details of the collection see www.guggenheim-venice.it).

3 "Réformé" (judged unfit for military service).

4 SB's application: 6 December 1939, n. 2; also Knowlson, *Damned to Fame*, 275).

5 *Mercure de France* ceased publication following its 1 June 1940 issue and did not resume until 1 December 1946; Anatole Rivoallan did not publish an article in *Mercure de France* on *Murphy* and *At Swim Two Birds* by Flann O'Brien (pseud. of Brian O'Nolan, who also wrote as Myles na gCopaleen, 1911–1966).

Other than its mention in SB's letter to Joyce on 13 January 1940, there is no documentation of Rivoallan's willingness to revise SB's translation of *Murphy* for submission to Jean Paulhan, presumably for publication by the *Nouvelle Revue Française*. Nor is there documentation of Adrienne Monnier's intention to write a covering recommendation.

Publication of the *Nouvelle Revue Française* was suspended in July 1940, but the German ambassador Otto Abetz (1903–1958) was determined to use the review to promote Franco-German collaboration. He approached writer and Nazi-sympathizer Pierre Drieu la Rochelle (1893–1945) to take over its direction, to which the publisher Gaston Gallimard (1881–1975) agreed in October 1940. The first issue under Drieu's editorship appeared in December 1940, "without its Jews" – Julien Benda (1867–1956) most notably. Paulhan refused to collaborate in the review's publication, preferring to lend his talents to the literary resistance as co-founder of *Les Lettres Françaises* (Frédéric Badré, *Paulhan le juste* [Paris: Grasset, 1996] 175–195).

Maurice Denhof (d. ?1939) did not publish a review of *Murphy*. On 28 March 1940, Joyce wrote from St. Gérand-le-Puy asking Adrienne Monnier to see if a review of *Murphy* by Denhof had been published in *Mercure de France* after 1 October 1939. He continued: "Quelques semaines avant sa mort Maurice Denhof m'écrivit qu'il était en train de préparer l'article en question – qui devait faire suite à deux autres articles publiés par lui dans la même revue" (Several weeks before his death, Maurice Denhof wrote to me that he was in the process of preparing the article in question, which was to be a follow-up to two other articles published by him in the same review) (James Joyce [to Adrienne Monnier], "James Joyce," *Mercure de France* 326, "Le Souvenir d'Adrienne Monnier," Special issue [January 1956] 123).

6 No publication bearing the name *Paris Mondial* at this time has been discovered. SB refers to that portion of his projected play on Samuel Johnson later published as "Human Wishes" in *Disjecta*, 155–166.

7 SB and the Joyces: 1 April 1940.

8 Brian Coffey's letter to Robert McAlmon prior to 21 May 1940 has not been found; however, Coffey wrote to him on 9 February 1941, saying only that he, Bridget, and their son John had moved from 2 Mulgrave Terrace to 5 Mulgrave Terrace, Dun Laoghaire, Co. Dublin (CtY, MSS Survey Za McAlmon). Alan Duncan.

McGreevy reviewed *Letter from Ireland* (Dublin: Gayfield Press, 1940) by Ewart Milne (1903–1987) ("New Poetry: 'Letter from Ireland,'" *The Irish Times* 6 April 1940: 5).

9 George Reavey sold the European Literary Bureau to Richard Reginald March (n.d.), who later became involved in the Nicholson and Watson publishing house (George Reavey to Deirdre Bair, 24 October 1974).

George Reavey and Marc Slonim edited and translated *Soviet Literature: An Anthology* (1933).

10 American poet, journalist, translator, and publisher Maurice English* (1909–1983) was Foreign Correspondent for the *Chicago Tribune* until 1941.

11 Alfred Péron was still on active service.

MARTHE ARNAUD, C/O BRAM VAN VELDE

MONTROUGE, FRANCE

lundi [10-6-40]   6 Rue des Favorites

                                                    Paris XV

chère Marthe

Je vous écris chez Bram, n'ayant pas votre adresse.[1]

Les diables sont comme les anges. Priez le vôtre de rester et il partira.

Nous ne sommes pas libres vendredi soir, ni l'un ni l'autre. Mais je pourrais faire un billard avec Bram à 4 heures, Café des Sports, puis passer un petit moment chez vous entre 5 et 6 arranger votre prise. Donc sauf contre-avis de Bram je serai ven-dredi au Café des Sports à 4 heures. Pourquoi ne venez-vous pas assister au match? [2]

Tout ça à condition qu'on reste à Paris. Suzanne a l'air de vouloir partir. Moi non. Où aller et avec quoi?[3]

Sous la vitre bleue le tableau de Bram flambe sombrement. Hier soir j'y voyais Neary au restaurant chinois, "accroupi dans la touffe de ses soucis comme un hibou dans du Lierre"[.][4] Aujourd'hui ce sera autre chose. On croit choisir une chose, et c'est toujours soi qu'on choisit, un soi qu'on ne connaissait pas si on a de la chance. A moins d'être marchand.

> Votre
>
> Sam Beckett

ALS; 1 leaf, 2 sides; *to* Monsieur Bram Van Velde, 777 Avenue Aristide Briand, Montrouge, *pm* 10-6-40, Paris; Collection Putman. *Previously published* (facsimile): *Bram Van Velde* (Paris: Editions du Centre Pompidou, 1989) 160; (facsimile) *Objet: Beckett* (Paris: Centre Pompidou, IMEC Editeur, 2007) illus. 86–87. *Dating*: from pm; 10 June 1940 was a Monday.

Monday [10 June 1940]	6 Rue des Favorites
	Paris XV

Dear Marthe,

Not having your address, I am writing to you at Bram's.[1]

Devils are like angels. Beg yours to stay and he will go away.

We are not free on Friday evening, either of us. But I could have a game of billiards with Bram at 4, at the Café des Sports, and then spend some time at your place between 5 and 6 to make the arrangements for your photo. So, unless I hear from Bram to the contrary, I shall be at the Café des Sports on Friday at 4. Why don't you come and watch the game?[2]

All this provided that we are staying on in Paris. Suzanne seems to want to get away. I don't. Where would we go, and with what?[3]

Under the blue glass Bram's painting gives off a dark flame. Yesterday evening I could see in it Neary at the Chinese restaurant, "huddled in the tod of his troubles like an owl in ivy".[4] Today it will be something different. You think you are choosing something, and it is always yourself that you choose; a self that you did not know, if you are lucky. Unless you are a dealer.

Your

Sam Beckett

1 Bram lived at 777 Avenue Aristide Briand, Montrouge.

2 SB responds to an invitation to himself and Suzanne; this is the first letter in which SB signals that they are a couple.

There was a Café des Sports at the corner of Avenue de la Grande-Armée and Avenue Malakoff (Porte Maillot) at that time (Jean Favier, "Le Café des Sports par M. Aug. Prunier," *La Construction Moderne* 51.45 [23 August 1936] 929–936).

The photo arrangements may have concerned SB's painting by Bram van Velde (see 21 May 1940, n. 1).

3 On the day of the proposed meeting, 14 June 1940, Paris was occupied by the Germans. SB and Suzanne left Paris for Vichy on 12 June, where they were given assistance by Valery Larbaud. They continued, first to Toulouse and then in the direction of Bordeaux as far as Cahors; finally, they were able to find a way to Arcachon on the Atlantic, where they were assisted by Mary Reynolds (née Hubacheck, 1891–1950) and Marcel Duchamp, staying there during the rest of summer 1940 at Villa St. George, 135 Boulevard de la Plage (see Knowlson, *Damned to Fame*, 274–276, 677 n. 8 and n. 9; P. J. O Byrne, Irish Legation in Spain, to George Reavey, 19 August 1940, TxU).

4 In compliance with blackout rules, windows were coated with a solution of blue powder, water, and oil, creating "blue glass." As Simone de Beauvoir describes in her letter to Jean-Paul Sartre on 11 September 1939: "Nos fenêtres sont merveilleusement bleues; nous allons au Dôme à travers de formidables ténèbres, on bute sur les bords des trottoirs" ("Our windows are a wonderful shade of blue. We go through the thick blackout to the Dôme, stumbling against the curb all the way" (*La Force de l'âge* [Paris: Gallimard, 1960) 401; *The Prime of Life*, tr. Peter Green [Cleveland, OH: World Publishing Co., 1962] 310).

SB cites a passage from *Murphy*, 115–116.

APPENDIX

PROFILES

Günter Albrecht (1916-1941) was an apprentice in the bookshop of Kurt Saucke in Hamburg when SB met him in September 1936. During SB's stay in Hamburg, the two struck up a friendship, and SB was introduced to Albrecht's family and friends. Albrecht encouraged SB to meet his friend Axel Kaun in Berlin. As soon as Albrecht had finished his bookdealer's examination in spring 1937, he had to meet his Reichsarbeitsdienst (national service) obligation; immediately afterward, he was conscripted for two years. He had just completed this term and taken a position with the Reclam Verlag in Leipzig when the War broke out and his military service was automatically extended in the Reserves, where he trained as an officer. He was killed in action in the Soviet Union in July 1941.

Richard Aldington (1892-1962), English novelist and poet, lived in France and Italy in the 1930s; he knew SB through his close friendships with James Joyce, Nancy Cunard, Thomas McGreevy, and Charles Prentice. Aldington was Literary Editor of *The Egoist* when it published *A Portrait of the Artist as a Young Man* serially (1914). With Cunard, Aldington provided the prize for the best poem on the subject of time; SB's poem "Whoroscope" won. Aldington suggested that SB add annotations to the poem when it was published by Cunard's Hours Press (1930). Aldington's publisher was Chatto and Windus, whose Editor was Charles Prentice; Aldington put up financial guarantees for their Dolphin Books series. At McGreevy's suggestion, SB wrote *Proust* (1931) which was published in this series. During travels with Frank Beckett in the south of France in 1931, SB visited McGreevy who was staying with Aldington at Le Lavandou. With Prentice, Aldington provided the encouragement and means for McGreevy to concentrate on his writing during 1931-1933. Aldington's kindness was also appreciated by SB: "My first two publications, by Hours Press and Chatto and Windus, I owe in part to his good offices. I think of him with affection and gratitude."[1]

Sylvia Beach (née Nancy Woodbridge Beach, 1887–1962), American bookseller and publisher in Paris, founded Shakespeare and Company in 1919; the Anglo-American bookshop, lending library, and publishing house became a center for both French and expatriate writers during the 1920s and 1930s. In 1922, Shakespeare and Company published the first complete edition of James Joyce's *Ulysses*; Beach continued to act on behalf of Joyce, publishing his *Pomes Penyeach* and *Our Exagmination Round His Factification for Incamination of Work in Progress*. For the latter, SB wrote the essay "Dante... Bruno. Vico. . Joyce." During the Nazi occupation of Paris, Beach closed the bookshop and was interned (1942–1943). Following the war, she continued to represent authors and sell books from her apartment; when Barney Rosset considered adding SB to his list at Grove Press, he consulted Beach. Her memoirs were published as *Shakespeare and Company* (1959). In 1962, SB agreed to contribute to an "Hommage à Sylvia Beach" in *Mercure de France* (August–September 1963), but he later wrote to Maurice Saillet: "Les mots ne sont plus tenables – et avec ça elle m'échappe complètement" (Words elude me – and with that she disappears from me altogether).[2]

Jean Beaufret (1907–1982), called Bowsprit by SB and McGreevy, was a student of Philosophy at the Ecole Normale Supérieure when SB met him in 1930; Beaufret continued his studies on Fichte, Hegel, Marx, and Heidegger in Germany. From a letter sent by Beaufret, SB made note of his "beautiful phrase: 'le diamant du pessimisme.'"[3] Following his 1933 agrégation, Beaufret taught at the Lycée de Montluçon; later he taught in the khâgne, the preparatory class for the entrance examination of the ENS, at the Lycée Louis-le-Grand in Paris. He engaged Heidegger in dialogue about French existentialism and Greek philosophy, publishing *Dialogue avec Heidegger* (in four volumes, 1974–1985) and other studies. In 1982 Beaufret was made Professeur honoraire de philosophie en première supérieure at the Lycée Condorcet in Paris.

---

[1] Alister Kershaw and Frédéric-Jacques Temple, eds., *Richard Aldington: An Intimate Portrait* (Carbondale: Southern Illinois University Press, 1965) 3.
[2] Samuel Beckett to Maurice Saillet, 2 May 1963, TxU Saillet.
[3] Samuel Beckett to Thomas McGreevy, 11 March 1931, TCD, MS 10402/18.

Frank Edward Beckett (1902–1954), elder brother of SB, was educated at Portora Royal School in Northern Ireland and Trinity College Dublin, where he studied Engineering. He worked with his father's firm, Beckett and Medcalf, before joining the Indian Civil Service (1927–1930). SB and Frank traveled together in France during the summer of 1931, and later in the 1930s SB accompanied Frank on business travels to the west and south of Ireland. Following the death of their father in 1933, Frank managed Beckett and Medcalf. He married Jean Violet Wright in 1937, and the couple settled in their home, Shottery, overlooking Killiney Bay, where his children Caroline (b. 1938) and Edward (b. 1943) were raised. SB spent several months there with Frank and his family prior to Frank's death in September 1954.

Maria Jones Beckett (née Roe, known as May, 1871–1950), SB's mother, was raised near Leixlip, Co. Kildare, and educated at the Moravian Mission School in Ballymena. At the age of fifteen, following the death of her father, Samuel Robinson Roe, she became a nurse. She met William Beckett when he was a patient at the Adelaide Hospital in Dublin. They married in 1901 and lived in Cooldrinagh, the home that William Beckett had built in Foxrock, Co. Dublin, where their two sons were born. After their mother's death in 1913, the three children of her brother Edward Roe (Molly, Sheila, and Jack) lived with the Beckett family during their school holidays. A devout Protestant, May regularly attended Tullow Parish Church.

After May Beckett's sudden widowhood in 1933, SB made efforts to accommodate her grieving, including her desire to move house. She paid for SB's psychotherapy with W. R. Bion in London. They traveled together on holiday in England in 1935. SB's definitive break from his mother came in late 1937 and, with it, his move to Paris. When SB was stabbed in January 1938, May, Frank, and Jean Beckett flew to Paris to be with him. From that time, SB traveled to Dublin to visit her for several weeks a year, with the exception of the War years, until her death. SB began *Molloy* in his mother's room in New Place, a bungalow she had had built near Cooldrinagh in Foxrock. SB was with her in Dublin when she died from complications of Parkinson's disease in 1950.

Suzanne Georgette Anna Deschevaux-Dumesnil Beckett (1900–1989) was born in Troyes (Aube). She studied music at the Ecole Normale de Musique in Paris. She first met SB at a tennis party in Paris in the mid-1930s. When he was recovering from the knife attack of January 1938, she visited him in the hospital. In April 1939 SB wrote to McGreevy that there was a French girl of whom he was fond.[4] SB and Suzanne Deschevaux-Dumesnil became companions, and when the Occupation began, in June 1940, they left Paris together for Toulouse, and, later, Arcachon. When they returned to Paris that autumn, SB became involved in Resistance activities. After his réseau was discovered in August 1942, they made their way to Unoccupied France, and remained in Roussillon throughout the Occupation.

After the War, Suzanne Deschevaux-Dumesnil did the rounds of Paris publishers with SB's manuscripts. When finally Les Editions de Minuit took on SB's work, she managed some of his business correspondence with them, as well as attending on his behalf premieres in France and abroad when, as was nearly always the case, he was reluctant to go. SB appreciated her efforts on behalf of his work.[5]

Protective of SB's need for the privacy, rest, and isolation that would allow him to write with the least possible interruption, she arranged retreats from Paris: a period in the Forest of Dreux, near Abondant (Eure-et-Loir), a rental cottage in the Val de Marne, and finally their own cottage in Ussy-sur-Marne (Seine-et-Marne). In later years, she also arranged their holidays in Austria, Italy, Portugal, and Morocco. They married privately in Folkestone, England, on 25 March 1961. Mirroring SB's reaction to the announcement that Beckett had been awarded the Nobel Prize in 1969, she said that it was a "catastrophe."[6]

SB and Suzanne shared enjoyment of music and writing, but differed in their social activities. Whereas SB enjoyed the camaraderie of late evenings with friends and solitary walks after midnight, his wife preferred more regular hours and attended concerts and theatre with her friends. They arranged their Paris apartment with separate entrances that allowed them both independence. Suzanne Beckett died in July 1989, Beckett died the following December.

William Beckett (1871–1933), SB's father, was born to William Frank and Frances Crothers Beckett. He left school at fifteen and worked for

---

[4] SB to Thomas McGreevy, 18 April 1939, TCD, MS 10402/168.
[5] Knowlson, *Damned to Fame*, 340.   [6] Knowlson, *Damned to Fame*, 505.

his father's successful building company in Dublin, later becoming a quantity surveyor. His firm was Beckett and Medcalf. He met Maria Jones Roe when he was a patient at the hospital where she was a nurse; they married in 1901. In 1902, in the Dublin suburb of Foxrock the family home, Cooldrinagh, was built; there Frank and SB were born. Affable, athletic, with a sharp sense of humor, William Beckett enjoyed reading mystery stories, playing golf, and taking long walks in the countryside (often with SB).[7] He asked Joseph Hone if SB had talent as a writer; the answer was affirmative. Although he advised SB to try for a job with the Guinness brewery, William Beckett did not waver in support of his younger son as he traveled his path as a writer.

Wilfred Ruprecht Bion (1897–1979) was SB's psychotherapist in London from 1934 through 1935. Bion graduated from Oxford in History (1921), then studied French Language and Literature at the University of Poitiers (1921–1922). After teaching History and Literature for several years, he studied Medicine at University College London, qualifying as a medical doctor and surgeon in 1930; his interests then turned to Psychiatric Medicine. In 1932 he joined the staff of the Tavistock Clinic, where he was a trainee therapist, "analytically trained" by Dr. J. A. Hadfield. Geoffrey Thompson recommended that SB consult Bion for treatment of his anxiety. Already interested in psychoanalysis, SB read widely in the field during this time; at Bion's invitation, he attended a lecture by Carl Gustav Jung in October 1935. After the War, Bion resumed his work at the Tavistock Clinic until 1948; his later professional publications focused on the psychodynamics of groups, the nature of psychosis, epistemology, and aesthetics.

Jacob Bronowski (1908–1974), Polish-born mathematician, man of letters, and poet, edited the literary magazine *Experiment* with William Empson while a student at Cambridge University; in this capacity he met George Reavey. For *The European Caravan*, the poetry anthology edited by Samuel Putnam and others, Bronowski edited the Irish and English sections and became acquainted with SB. Bronowski dedicated his professional life to scientific inquiry, and in particular to making science accessible, as in his *The Common Sense of Science* (1951) and *Science*

---

[7] Samuel Beckett to Thomas McGreevy, 2 July 1933, TCD, MS 10402/52.

and Human Values (1956). He also wrote on literature, publishing *The Defence of Poetry* in 1939 and *William Blake, A Man Without a Mask* in 1944. Bronowski later became widely known for his work on BBC radio and television, especially for the television series *The Ascent of Man* (1973).

Austin Clarke (né Augustine Joseph Clarke, 1896–1974), Irish poet, dramatist, and novelist, studied at University College Dublin, worked as a reviewer in London, and published several volumes of poetry. His first novel, *The Bright Temptation* (1932), was banned in Ireland for twenty-two years. Writing under the pseudonym of Andrew Belis, SB reviewed Clarke's *Pilgrimage and Other Poems* (1929) in "Recent Irish Poetry" (*The Bookman*, 1934), grouping Clarke with the "antiquarians" or "Celtic twilighters" whom he compared unfavorably with a younger, less insular generation of poets. Clarke also appears in an unflattering light as Austin Ticklepenny in SB's *Murphy*. Clarke was a charter member of the Irish Academy of Letters in 1932. An author of verse drama, Clarke co-founded the Dublin Verse-Speaking Society (1941) and its theatrical counterpart, the Lyric Theatre Company (1944). From 1942 to 1955 he was a broadcaster for Radio Éireann.

Brian Coffey (1905–1995), Irish poet, critic, translator, and teacher, studied Classics as an undergraduate and earned a Master's degree in Chemistry, Physics, and Mathematics (1930) at University College Dublin, where his father Denis Coffey was a professor of Medicine and the University's first President (1908–1940). Coffey pursued postgraduate studies in Paris in Physical Chemistry under Nobel laureate Jean-Baptiste Perrin (1933) and then attended the Institut Catholique de Paris (1934) to study Philosophy with Jacques Maritain; after an interval in London, he returned to Paris in 1937 as an exchange student, to write his doctoral thesis on the idea of order in the work of Thomas Aquinas. Coffey met Denis Devlin when they were both undergraduates at University College Dublin; they published their work jointly as *Poems* (1930). SB met Coffey and Devlin through Thomas McGreevy in Dublin during the summer of 1934; under the pseudonym Andrew Belis, SB's essay "Recent Irish Poetry" (*The Bookman*, 1934) mentioned them as being among the best young poets in Ireland. Coffey encouraged SB to read Geulincx for a possible monograph in a Philosophy series he envisioned. Coffey's collection of poems *Third Person* (1938) was published by the Europa Poets series, which included collections by SB, George Reavey, and Denis Devlin. Coffey taught in England for several years; he received his doctorate in 1947, taught Philosophy at St. Louis University in Missouri, and returned to England in 1952. Coffey published his *Missouri Sequence* (1962), edited *The Complete Poems of Denis Devlin* in a special issue of *University Review* (3.5 [1963]; reissued with additions as *Collected Poems*, 1964), and Devlin's *Heavenly Foreigner* (1967). Coffey founded Advent Press in 1966 to publish books of poetry as well as a poetry series that featured younger writers. Coffey's later collections were *Monster: A Concrete Poem* (1966), *The Big Laugh* (1976), *Death of Hektor* (1979), *Chanterelles: Short Poems 1971–1983* (1985), *Advent* (1986), and translations of Mallarmé. Coffey and SB corresponded often in the later years; SB appreciated his writing and his efforts to make Devlin's poetry available.

Nuala Costello (1907–1984), the daughter of Thomas Costello, Tuam physician and amateur folklorist, and Evelyn Costello (née Drury), who was active in the Irish Language Movement, a judge for Sinn Féin courts during the War of Independence, and Senator in Seanad Éireann. Nuala Costello studied French and History at University College Dublin, and began postgraduate studies at the Sorbonne in 1929. She was a friend of the Joyce family; SB first met her at the home of Giorgio Joyce and his wife, Helen. On one occasion Nuala Costello and her mother accompanied the Joyces and SB to the Paris Opéra to hear tenor John Sullivan. Not a little smitten, SB saw a good deal of Costello in London and Dublin during 1933 and 1934. Nuala Costello settled in Tuam later in the 1930s; she wrote a biography, *John McHale, Archbishop of Tuam* (1939) and edited *Two Diaries of the French Expedition 1798* (1941).

Henry Crowder (1895–1955), American jazz pianist and composer, moved to Paris in 1927 to play with the Eddie South Band and remained to play at the Bateau Ivre in the Place de l'Odéon. Crowder met Nancy Cunard in Venice in 1928. Because he was black, their relationship shocked her upper-class British family, which provoked Cunard to write *Black Man and White Ladyship* (1931). Crowder worked with Cunard at her Hours Press, which produced the first French publication of SB's *Whoroscope* in 1930. Crowder composed *Henry-Music* (1930), a collection of original scores that were improvisations on poetry, including SB's "From the only poet to a shining whore." Crowder's relationship with Cunard inspired her to compile *Negro, Anthology Made by Nancy Cunard, 1931–1933* (1934), which she dedicated to him. Crowder's memoir, *As Wonderful as All That?* (1987), was published posthumously.

Nancy Cunard (1896–1965), English writer, editor, publisher, and activist, was the great-granddaughter of the founder of the Cunard shipping line. She lived in Paris in 1920, where she moved in avant-garde literary, artistic, and political circles. She published three volumes of poetry: *Outlaws* (1921), *Sublunary* (1923), and *Parallax* (1925). From 1928 to 1931 Cunard ran the hand-operated Hours Press with American jazz artist Henry Crowder in La Chapelle-Réanville; the press published small editions of prose and poetry, including SB's *Whoroscope* (1930). Reacting to her family's response to her affair with Henry Crowder, Cunard wrote an essay against racial prejudice, *Black Man and White Ladyship* (1931), and then compiled *Negro, Anthology Made by Nancy Cunard, 1931–1933* (1934) for which SB translated nineteen essays from French. During the Spanish Civil War, Cunard was a correspondent in Spain for the *Manchester Guardian*. She edited *Authors Take Sides On The Spanish Civil War* (1937) to which SB contributed. In the 1950s, SB and Cunard renewed their friendship. Cunard wrote memoirs of Norman Douglas and George Moore, as well as a memoir, *These Were the Hours: Memories of My Hours Press, Réanville and Paris, 1928–1931* (1969).

Denis Devlin (1908–1959), Scots-born to an Irish Catholic family, poet, diplomat, and translator, was a seminarian at Clonliffe College and then studied at University College Dublin where he met Brian Coffey; together they published *Poems* (1930). After study at Munich University and the Sorbonne (1930–1933), Devlin completed his MA on Montaigne at University College Dublin, where he became an Assistant Lecturer in English. Devlin's collection of poems *Intercessions* (1937) was published in the Europa Poets series and reviewed by SB in *transition*. In 1935 Devlin joined the Irish Diplomatic Service; he served in Rome, New York, Washington, and London from 1938 to 1949. He became Minister to Italy (1950) and to Turkey (1951), and Ambassador to Italy (1958). Devlin's international experiences are reflected in his later collections of poetry: *Exile* (1949), *Heavenly Foreigner* (1950), and *Memoirs of a Turcoman*

Diplomat (1959); he also translated works by St.-John Perse, Paul Eluard, René Char, and Paul Valéry. His work was edited by Allen Tate and Robert Penn Warren in *Selected Poems* (1963), by Brian Coffey in *The Complete Poems of Denis Devlin* in a special issue of *University Review* (3.5 1963; reissued with additions as *Collected Poems*, 1964) and *Heavenly Foreigner* (1967), by J. C. C. Mays in *Collected Poems of Denis Devlin* (1989), and by Roger Little, *Translations into English: from French, German, and Italian Poetry: Denis Devlin* (1992).

Hester Dowden (1868–1949) was a daughter of literary critic and Trinity College Dublin Professor of English Edward Dowden; she studied Music in London but returned to Dublin after her mother's death. In 1896 she married Dr. Robert Montgomery Travers-Smith; their daughter was the artist and set-designer Dorothy Travers-Smith (known as Dolly), who married Irish playwright Lennox Robinson. Hester Dowden separated from her husband in 1916, and in 1921 moved to London where she opened her home to lodgers, primarily artists and Dublin acquaintances, including Thomas McGreevy. McGreevy introduced SB to Dowden, who invited SB to musical evenings, played duets with him, and encouraged him to use her piano when he wished. Hester Dowden was also a professional medium and a leading figure in the practice of automatic writing; books written "as dictated" to her as a medium are: *Voices from the Void* (1919), *Psychic Messages from Oscar Wilde* (1923), *The Book of Johannes* (1945) and *Talks with Elizabethans: Revealing the Mystery of William Shakespeare* (1947).

Dublin Magazine (1923–1958), edited by Seumas O'Sullivan, was founded as a non-political, non-partisan publication committed to publishing a variety of literary works. It began as a monthly, but in 1926 it became a quarterly publication. O'Sullivan was interested in SB's writing and asked him for poems to consider, although not all were published, and he occasionally commissioned SB to write reviews. In 1936, O'Sullivan proposed that SB take over the editorship of *Dublin Magazine*, but SB was not interested. O'Sullivan remained Editor until his death in 1958.

Alan George Duncan (1895–1943) was the son of the Dublin art patron Ellen Douglas Duncan, who was a founder of the United Arts Club and the Municipal Gallery of Modern Art. Alan Duncan served in the Royal Welsh Fusiliers during World War I until he was invalided out as a result of having been gassed. When he married Isabel Belinda Atkinson in 1924, Lennox Robinson was his best man. After 1925, the Duncans lived primarily in Paris; they were friends of the Joyce family and of Thomas McGreevy who was godfather to Alan's sister, Betty. Duncan introduced George Reavey to Thomas McGreevy. According to Brian Coffey, Alan Duncan's "only subject" was George Bernard Shaw. When W. B. Yeats made a lecture tour of the United States in 1932, Duncan served as secretary.

SB spent the evening of 7 January 1938 with the Duncans at the Café Zeyer; as the three were returning to the Duncans' apartment, SB was attacked by a stranger and stabbed. The Duncans were very supportive of SB throughout his recovery. By September 1939, the Duncans were living on the western coast of France; just before the invasion by the Nazis in June 1940, they removed to England. Alan Duncan died in Surrey in 1943.

Belinda Duncan (née Isabel Belinda Atkinson, 1893–1964), daughter of a prosperous Dublin china merchant, studied Art and was a friend of painters Jack B. Yeats, Norah McGuinness, and Dolly Travers-Smith. Belinda Atkinson married Alan Duncan in 1924; they settled in Paris where their flat was a place of rendez-vous for many Irish exiles. The Duncans left France for Surrey in June 1940. After Alan Duncan's death in 1943, Belinda Duncan worked in an aircraft factory. Following the war, she returned to Dublin. There she renewed her friendship with SB; both found the relative abundance of food and personal comfort in Ireland a sharp contrast to their war-time experiences. In 1945, Belinda Duncan married Brian Lunn (former husband of Alan Duncan's sister Betty); after several years in England, they lived in Dublin from 1951.

L'Ecole Normale Supérieure, Rue d'Ulm, Paris, founded in 1794, is an elite educational institution; students of the school are among the most brilliant of the French education system. Before taking the fiercely competitive concours d'entrée (entrance examination), Arts candidates prepare, in the two preceding lycée years, for the première supérieure and lettres supérieures (commonly known as hypokhâgne and khâgne).

Once admitted as 'normaliens,' they are expected to prepare for another highly competitive examination, the agrégation. The original purpose of this examination was to ensure high-quality recruits to the teaching profession. As an exchange Lecteur in English from Trinity College Dublin from 1928 to 1930, SB followed Thomas McGreevy in the post, living at the ENS and supervising students in English. Georges Pelorson was his only pupil in 1930. SB also assisted advanced students in their preparations for examinations. Normaliens from the period of the ENS tenures of McGreevy and Beckett (classes of 1924–1930) included Jean-Paul Sartre, Armand Bérard, Paul Nizan, Alfred Péron, Emile Delavenay, Maurice Merleau-Ponty, Jean Beaufret, Georges Pelorson, Jean Rolland, Henri Evrard, and, from the ENS des Jeunes Filles, Simone Weil.

Maurice English (1909–1983), American poet, journalist, translator, and publisher, met SB when he was a foreign correspondent for the *Chicago Tribune* in Paris. English worked with NBC radio news until 1946; later, he edited *Chicago Magazine* (1954–1958). He was Editor of the University of Chicago Press (1961–1969), Temple University Press, Philadelphia (1969–1976), and Director of the University of Pennsylvania Press (1978). English translated the work of Italian poet Eugenio Montale, as did SB, as well as of Greek poet Odysseus Elitis.

The European Caravan: *An Anthology of the New Spirit in European Literature* (1931), planned as a two-volume anthology to introduce "the after-war spirit in European literature," involved SB with editors Samuel Putnam, Jacob Bronowski, and George Reavey. The first volume comprised selections from French, Spanish, English, and Irish literatures; selections from Russian, German, and Italian literatures were prepared for the second volume, which was not published. The English and Irish section, edited by Jacob Bronowski, included SB's poems "Hell Crane to Starling," "Casket of Pralinen for the Daughter of a Dissipated Mandarin," "Text," and "Yoke of Liberty." Samuel Putnam asked SB to suggest and translate some of the selections for the Italian section of the projected second volume.

Otto Freundlich (1878–1943), a German abstract artist of Jewish origin, studied Art in Berlin, was active in Paris avant-garde circles (1910–1914); he then lived and exhibited in Berlin and Cologne

(1914–1924), where he joined the "November Gruppe"; he organized the first Dada Exhibition in Cologne in 1919. He moved between Germany and Paris until 1933, when his work was removed from German museums; his sculpture *The New Man* appeared on the cover of the catalogue of the exhibition of "Degenerate Art" (Munich 1937). Introduced by Polish painter Jankel Adler, who had known Freundlich since the 1920s in Berlin, SB attended the retrospective exhibition of his work at the Galerie Jeanne Bucher (1938). He and Freundlich met several times during that year. SB read a draft of Freundlich's essay on aesthetics "Der bildhafte Raum" and shared his own essay "Les Deux Besoins" with Freundlich. As a German resident in France, Freundlich was interned in 1939; early in 1940, he requested French naturalization and was provisionally released, but was again interned from February to May 1940; on 23 February 1943 he was arrested by the Gestapo and deported to Poland. He died five days later in the Lublin-Majdanek Concentration Camp.

Marguerite Guggenheim (known as Peggy, 1898–1979), American patroness of the arts, moved to Paris in 1920; Guggenheim was married to Laurence Vail, a Dada sculptor and writer, from 1922 to 1930. In 1938 she opened the Guggenheim Jeune gallery in London, exhibiting surrealist and other contemporary art. Her attachment to SB dates from this period, and her autobiographies present her view of their affair. At SB's urging, Guggenheim gave Geer van Velde a one-man show at her gallery in May 1938. SB translated several essays related to the exhibitions of Guggenheim Jeune, published in *London Bulletin*. Guggenheim planned to establish a museum for contemporary art in London and was often in Paris in 1939 and 1940 to amass her collection which included works by Picasso, Ernst, Miró, Magritte, Man Ray, Dalí, Klee, Chagall, and Tunnard. Facing the impending German invasion of France, she asked Maria Jolas to secure her collection until it could be shipped to the United States. In 1941 Guggenheim had moved to New York where she opened the gallery Art of This Century in 1942. She was married to Max Ernst from 1942 to 1946. When the New York gallery closed in 1947, Guggenheim moved to Venice; her villa there, now the Peggy Guggenheim Museum, houses her collection.

Arthur Henry Macnamara Hillis (1905–1997), lawyer and international economist, was a student with SB at Trinity College Dublin;

both were Honours graduates, Hillis in Classics and Law. Hillis was called to the Bar in London in 1931, where SB met him again in 1934–1935; they developed a close friendship through their shared interest in music and literature. Hillis later served the British Government in the Department of the Treasury (from 1941), in the United Nations (1958–1961), and as Comptroller General of the National Debt Office, London (1961–1968). His wife Lillian Mary Hillis (née Francis, 1907–1990) worked with the BBC in the Spanish Section and the South European Service from 1942 to 1967. In later years, SB frequently visited their home in London, often playing four-hand piano duets and listening to music.

Joseph Maunsel Hone (1882–1959), Irish historian, biographer, and writer, was a friend of SB's father William Beckett; although twenty-five years his senior, Hone came to know SB well through shared interests in cricket and literature. Hone was Literary Director of the Dublin publisher Maunsel and Co. and edited the quarterly *Shanachie* (1906–1907) that published writings by John Millington Synge and W. B. Yeats. Hone translated *The Life of Friedrich Nietzsche* (1911), and wrote *Irishmen of To-day* (1915) and *William Butler Yeats* (1916). He collaborated with the Italian scholar of Irish culture Mario Manlio Rossi, translating his *Viaggio in Irlanda* (1932; *Pilgrimage in the West*, 1933) and co-authoring *Bishop Berkeley: His Life, Writings and Philosophy* (1931) and *Swift; or, The Egoist* (1934). Later, he edited George Berkeley's *The Querist* (1936), and wrote *The Life of George Moore* (1936), *The Moores of Moore's Hall* (1939), and an expanded biography, *W. B. Yeats 1865–1939* (1943). He became President of the Irish Academy of Letters in 1957.

Eugene Jolas (1894–1952), American-born poet, writer, and journalist; having been raised both in the United States and in the borderland of Alsace-Lorraine, he was keenly aware of linguistic and cultural divisions. Jolas began his career as a journalist in the United States and became Literary Editor of the Paris edition of the *Chicago Tribune* (1923–1926); his column "Rambles Through Literary Paris" reflected his interest in surrealism and established his reputation among the city's literati. In 1927 Jolas and Elliot Paul founded *transition*, with Maria Jolas as Managing Editor. Having met the Jolases through James Joyce and Thomas McGreevy, SB assisted when *transition* published portions of Joyce's *Work in Progress*.

Jolas saw *Work in Progress* as "the principal text of the avant-garde," an "exemplar of 'the Language of the Night'" at the center of his own poetry.[8] Jolas was also drawn to Jung's work in archetypes as a means to link individual experience with the "collective unconscious." Jolas issued the "Verticalist Manifesto" in 1932 which was "signed" by SB, Georges Pelorson, and Thomas McGreevy, among others. In 1935, Jolas accepted a position in New York with the French news service Havas; with James Johnson Sweeney in the USA and Maria Jolas in France, he continued to publish *transition* irregularly until 1938. Jolas also published *Vertical: A Yearbook for Romantic Mystic Ascensions* (1941, begun but not continued as an annual). In 1941, he worked with the US Office of War Information; after the War he was made Editor of *Deutsche Allgemeine Nachrichten-Agentur* and covered the Nuremberg trials. He lived and worked in Paris, New York, and Germany until 1950, when he joined the *New York Herald Tribune* in Paris. His memoirs have been edited by Andreas Kramer and Rainer Rumold as *Man from Babel* (1998).

Maria Jolas (née MacDonald, 1893–1987) was an American musician who studied voice in Berlin in 1913 and in Paris after World War I, where she met Eugene Jolas. They married in 1926 and together edited the Paris literary journal *transition* (1927–1938); she acted as Managing Editor and translated articles on art and literature, including works by André Breton, Philippe Soupault, and Jean-Paul Sartre. In 1931, she founded the Ecole bilingue de Neuilly; Georges Pelorson and his Irish wife Marcelle (née Graham) were teachers at the school. Jolas evacuated the school to St. Gérand-le-Puy in 1939. Maria Jolas was always a close friend of the Joyce family, joining their celebrations and musical evenings; as war threatened, the Joyces moved from Paris to be near their grandson Stephen who was a student at the school. Maria Jolas joined Eugene in New York in the autumn of 1940 and was active in the "Free France" movement there. After the War, she returned to Paris and advised Georges Duthuit when he became Editor of *Transition*. Maria Jolas remained active as a literary translator, particularly known as a translator of the work of Nathalie Sarraute. Her memoirs have been published as *Maria Jolas, Woman of Action* (2004), edited by Mary Ann Caws.

---

[8] Eugene Jolas, *Man from Babel*, xx–xxi.

Giorgio Joyce (1905–1976), son of James and Nora Joyce, met SB in 1928. At his father's urging, Giorgio began a professional career as a singer; SB attended his public debut in April 1929 with the Joyce parents. Giorgio married Helen Fleischman (née Kastor) in December 1930, and their son, Stephen James Joyce, was born in 1932. The couple lived in New York during the mid-1930s, where Giorgio pursued his singing career. Following their return to France in spring of 1938, Helen suffered a nervous breakdown; the couple eventually separated. SB remained a close friend to Giorgio Joyce and his son; in 1955, SB made an extended visit to Giorgio and his second wife, Dr. Asta Jahnke-Osterwalder, in Zurich.

James Joyce (1882–1941) and **Nora Joyce** (née Barnacle, 1884–1951) met SB in Paris in 1928. Although Harry Sinclair had given SB a letter of introduction, it was Thomas McGreevy who brought SB to meet James Joyce. At Joyce's request, SB wrote "Dante ... Bruno. Vico.. Joyce" for *Our Exagmination Round His Factification for Incamination of Work in Progress*, first published in *transition* (June 1929). Joyce asked SB to prepare a French translation of "Anna Livia Plurabelle"; SB and Alfred Péron finished a first draft in August 1930, which was then revised by a group that included Philippe Soupault, Paul Léon, and Joyce himself. SB, like a number of others, assisted Joyce with research for *Work in Progress*, finding and summarizing books, occasionally taking dictation because of Joyce's failing eyesight, and later correcting proofs. When SB distanced himself from Lucia Joyce's affections in May 1930, the family's fondness for him cooled for a time; but over the years, SB attended Joyce's birthday celebrations, and the two met frequently, often walking together in Paris. SB wrote an acrostic poem to Joyce in 1932, "Home Olga." After SB was stabbed in 1938, Joyce arranged for SB's medical care; in 1940, he promoted SB's work. Although SB's early writing was seen as derivative of Joyce's style and SB vowed to Samuel Putnam that he would "get over J. J. ere I die," SB nonetheless maintained that he had learned artistic integrity from Joyce, saying that what Joyce had achieved was "epic, heroic ... But I realised that I couldn't go down that same road."[9]

---

[9] SB to Samuel Putnam, 28 June 1932, NjP; Knowlson, *Damned to Fame*, 111.

Lucia Joyce (1907–1982) met SB in 1928 at the Joyces' flat in Paris. Lucia Joyce studied dance (1926–1929) with Jacques Dalcroze and Raymond Duncan; SB, who often accompanied the Joyces on family outings, attended her performance on 28 May 1929 at the Bal Bullier with the family and other friends. Her artistic interests also included drawing; Joyce incorporated her designs in *Storiella as She is Syung* (1937). Lucia Joyce, who is widely considered be the model for the Syra-Cusa in SB's *Dream of Fair to Middling Women*, became increasingly infatuated with SB, but in May 1930 SB made it clear that he did not reciprocate her interest. This caused a temporary falling-out with the Joyces. By 1931 she was showing signs of the illness that was later diagnosed as schizophrenia. SB saw Lucia Joyce when she was in London in 1935, and he was a regular visitor after she was institutionalized in Paris. In 1951 Lucia Joyce was moved to Northampton, England, where she remained until her death.

Axel Kaun (1912–1983) was introduced to SB by Günter Albrecht. When they met for the first time at the Nicolaische Buchhandlung in Potsdam in January 1937, Kaun had just taken a position with the Berlin publisher, Rowohlt. Kaun lent SB books by Hans Carossa, Hermann Hesse, and Walter Bauer. After SB returned to Ireland, Kaun asked SB to consider selecting and translating poems by German poet Joachim Ringelnatz for possible publication by Faber and Faber in their Criterion Miscellany series. Although SB began a selection of poems, he refused the commission in a letter to Kaun that has become a touchstone in the understanding of SB's aesthetics. Kaun edited the *Berliner Theater-Almanac* (1942), was a dramaturg for the Württemberg Staatstheater in Stuttgart from 1950, and published *Ballett ohne Pose* (1958). In the 1960s and 1970s Kaun was a literary translator of works by emerging Black writers (John Howard Griffin, James Baldwin, Eldridge Cleaver, and Lee Lockwood), as well as by Christopher Isherwood, Clancy Sigal, Charles Reich, and George Steiner. SB had no contact with Axel Kaun after 1937; when he tried to locate him in the early 1980s, he learned only that Kaun lived in California. Kaun died in San Francisco in 1983.

Henri Laugier (1888–1973) was a Professor of Physiology at the Sorbonne and Director of the Centre National de la Recherche Scientifique (CNRS) from 1938. SB knew Laugier as McGreevy's acquaintance. Laugier and his companion Marie Cuttoli built an important collection of contemporary art, including works by Jean Lurçat, a friend of McGreevy. From 1936 to 1938, Laugier was a member of the Cabinet of the Foreign Affairs Ministry under Yvon Delbos. In 1938, SB offered to pursue with Laugier a subvention that would allow McGreevy to reside in Paris while writing articles for English audiences on French subjects; although SB offered to write the required nomination for Laugier's approval, McGreevy declined the suggestion.

Abraham Jacob Leventhal (known as Con, 1896–1979), Irish and Jewish, critic and scholar, studied Modern Languages at Trinity College Dublin (1920, BA, French and German; 1925, MA; 1933, Ph.D. with a thesis on "Post-War Tendencies in French Literature"). Throughout his career, Leventhal was involved in publishing and teaching; he interrupted his studies to spend a year in Palestine as a secretary with the First Zionist Commission where he helped found *Palestine Weekly* (1919). In 1923 he founded the single-issue literary review *The Klaxon* (Winter 1923/24) to publish his review of Joyce's *Ulysses* (under the pseudonym L. K. Emery), which the printer for *Dublin Magazine* had refused to print. With Francis Stuart, F. R. Higgins, and Cecil Salkeld, Leventhal founded the Dublin review *Tomorrow* in 1924; despite contributions by W. B. Yeats, this lasted only two issues. Leventhal filled the post that SB had resigned as Lecturer in French at TCD (January 1932 through 1933) and served TCD in various administrative positions from 1937; he was Assistant to the Professors of French and German from 1938 to 1939, then (although his title varied) Lecturer in Modern Languages until 1963. Leventhal was a member of the Dublin Drama League, contributed "Dramatic Commentary" (1943–1958) and other writings to *Dublin Magazine*, was a regular broadcaster on Radio Éireann and the BBC, Assistant Editor of *Hermathena* from 1956 to 1963, and reviewed for *The Irish Times*, *Envoy*, and *Irish Art*. After the death of his wife Gertrude (née Zlotover), he married Ethna MacCarthy in 1956. Leventhal frequently visited SB in Paris; following his retirement in 1963, Leventhal moved to Paris and began a bibliography of SB's work and assisted him with correspondence. He remained a close friend until his death. In 1984, SB helped to establish a scholarship at TCD in his name.

Ethna Mary MacCarthy (1903–1959), granddaughter of the Irish poet Denis Florence MacCarthy and daughter of Dublin physician Brendan

MacCarthy, was a poet, linguist, and physician. She studied French and Spanish literature at Trinity College Dublin; like SB, she was a Scholar, and a First Class Moderator (1926). James Knowlson claims that she was the "Alba" of the eponymous poem and of *Dream of Fair to Middling Women*.[10] Although SB had already made plans to travel to Germany by Christmas 1931, he indicated later to Lawrence Harvey that he would not have resigned from TCD had it not been for the automobile accident in which Ethna MacCarthy, his passenger, was badly hurt. When she taught one of Professor Rudmose-Brown's courses in 1936, SB helped her prepare the Provençal lectures. Her poems, stories, translations from Spanish and German poetry, and a short play appeared in *Hermathena*, *Dublin Magazine*, *Ireland To-Day*, and an anthology of *New Irish Poets* (1948). MacCarthy continued her studies, receiving an MA in 1937; from 1939 to 1949 she was "Assistant to the Professor of French" at TCD, and she lectured in Spanish and French even as she studied Medicine (MB, 1941; MD, 1948). MacCarthy practiced medicine in Dublin and then in the East End of London. She married A. J. Leventhal in May 1956. SB remained a close friend to them both, particularly during MacCarthy's illness and death from cancer in 1959.

Thomas McGreevy (after 1943 known as MacGreevy, 1893–1967), Irish poet, critic, translator, art historian, and Director of the National Gallery of Ireland, was born in Tarbert, Co. Kerry. McGreevy worked in Dublin and London with the British Civil Service (1911–1914), served in World War I as an Officer of the Royal Field Artillery, and then studied History and Political Science at Trinity College Dublin (BA, 1920). While an assistant secretary to the Irish Advisory Committee of the Carnegie United Kingdom Trust, McGreevy published articles for *The Leader*, *The Irish Statesman*, and *The Gael*. He moved to London in May 1925, where he joined the editorial staff of *Connoisseur* and wrote criticism for *The Criterion*, the *Times Literary Supplement*, *The Nation and Athenaeum* and the *New Statesman*. In January 1927, he was appointed as Lecteur d'anglais at the Ecole Normale Supérieure in Paris, and when SB took up the same post he and McGreevy became close friends. McGreevy introduced SB to many of his acquaintances in art and

---

[10] Knowlson, *Damned to Fame*, 75.

literary circles in Paris, London, and Dublin, among them James Joyce, Richard Aldington, Jack B. Yeats, Charles Prentice, and Eugene Jolas.

Both men published on Joyce in *transition* and *Our Exagmination Round His Factification for Incamination of Work In Progress*. SB stood in for McGreevy in his role as Secretary of the fine art journal *Formes* when McGreevy had to be away from Paris. In 1931, McGreevy published two monographs in the Chatto and Windus Dolphin Book series: *Thomas Stearns Eliot: A Study* and *Richard Aldington: An Englishman*; SB's *Proust*, also in this series, came about as a result of McGreevy's suggestion. McGreevy stimulated and guided SB's interest in painting. He insisted that SB meet Jack B. Yeats. McGreevy's collection *Poems* was published in 1934. In London, he became chief Art Critic for *The Studio* (1938–1940); returning to Dublin in 1941, he became Art Critic for *The Irish Times* (November 1941 to December 1944). A practicing Catholic all his life, he also wrote for *The Father Matthew Record* and *The Capuchin Annual*. McGreevy's study *Jack B. Yeats* was published in 1945.

McGreevy served as Director of the National Gallery of Ireland from 1950 until his retirement in 1963. He was made Chevalier de l'Ordre de la Légion d'Honneur by the French Government for his services to the arts, made Cavaliere Ufficiale al Merito della Repubblica Italiana by the Italian Government, and awarded the Degree of Doctor of Letters by the National University of Ireland. In the early 1960s, he wrote a critical study on Nicolas Poussin, was made Officier de la Légion d'Honneur, and organized an exhibition of Jack B. Yeats's work for the Venice Biennale.

Mary Manning Howe Adams (1905–1999), playwright, novelist, critic, childhood friend of SB (their mothers were close friends). Mary Manning studied at Alexandra College Dublin and the Abbey Acting School, and joined the Gate Theatre as Publicity Manager, editing the Gate Theatre journal, *Motley*. Her early plays were *Youth's the Season . . . ?* (1931), in which SB had a hand – suggesting a wordless character called Horace Egosmith; *Storm Over Wicklow* (1933); and *Happy Family* (1934). In 1934 Mary Manning moved to Boston and married Harvard law professor Mark DeWolfe Howe, Jr. In the summer of 1936, while visiting Ireland, she had what she later claimed was an affair with SB. The first of her novels *Mount Venus* (1938) was published with Houghton Mifflin, whom she tried to interest in SB's *Murphy*. Director of Drama at

Radcliffe College during World War II, Mary Manning was a founder of The Poets' Theatre in Cambridge, Massachusetts (1950–1968, 1987–), which staged her play *The Voice of Shem* (1955, published 1957), an adaptation of *Finnegans Wake*, as well as a reading of SB's radio play *All That Fall* (1958). After her husband's death in 1967, Mary Manning returned to Dublin where she was Drama Critic for *Hibernia*. Her adaptation of Frank O'Connor's novel *The Saint and Mary Kate* was produced at the Abbey Theatre in 1968, and she wrote a volume of satirical short stories, *The Last Chronicles of Ballyfungus* (1978). In 1980, she married Faneuil Adams (1899–1981), and again lived in Boston. Of her mother's quick and sometimes cutting wit, the poet Susan Howe has written: "She loved to produce and destroy meanings in the same sentence."[11]

Seán O'Sullivan (1906–1964), Irish painter and draftsman, studied at the Metropolitan School of Art in Dublin, the Central School of Arts and Crafts in London, and at the Académie de la Grande Chaumière and the Académie Colarossi in Paris. In 1931, he was the youngest artist to be elected to the Royal Hibernian Academy. Although he painted Irish landscapes, O'Sullivan is best known for portraits, done as drawings and in oils, including ones of such Dublin notables as Douglas Hyde, Éamon De Valera, James Joyce, W. B. Yeats, Maud Gonne MacBride, Jack B. Yeats, SB, and Ethna MacCarthy (see illustrations). He aimed to "record every person of prominence on the Irish scene during his period," and was said to have a story about every person he had painted.[12] O'Sullivan knew McGreevy and Joyce in Paris. Although SB first mentions him in a letter in 1933, the two were most frequently together from 1935 to 1937 in Dublin; in 1939, SB arranged for him to rent Jankel Adler's studio in Paris.

Seumas O'Sullivan (né James Sullivan Starkey, 1879–1958), Irish poet and founding editor of the *Dublin Magazine* (1923–1958), was active in the Irish Literary Revival, appearing in W. B. Yeats's play *On Baile's Strand* at the Abbey Theatre in 1904, and was a supporter of Sinn Féin. A friend of W. B. Yeats, James Joyce, AE, and Oliver St. John Gogarty, O'Sullivan championed young authors, among them Patrick Kavanagh, Padraic

---

[11] Susan Howe, *The Midnight* (New York: New Directions Books, 2003) 64.
[12] Ryan, *Remembering How We Stood*, 46.

Fallon, Mary Lavin, and SB. "Alba" was SB's initial publication in the *Dublin Magazine* (1931), followed by "Gnome" (1934), "Cascando" (1936), and several reviews. O'Sullivan was President of Irish PEN, a founding member of the Irish Academy of Letters, and was given an honorary degree by Trinity College Dublin in 1939. He was married to the painter Estella Solomons.

Georges Pelorson (later known as Georges Belmont, b. 1909), French poet, journalist, editor, and translator, entered the Ecole Normale Supérieure in 1926 and was SB's first student there in 1928. Pelorson came to Trinity College Dublin as part of the exchange with the ENS, beginning in January 1930; in February 1930, he co-authored with SB the dramatic parody *Le Kid* for the Modern Languages Society production at the Peacock Theatre; according to Knowlson, Pelorson figures as Liebert in SB's *Dream of Fair to Middling Women*. Pelorson married Marcelle Graham in Dublin, then returned to Paris in autumn 1931, leaving the ENS with a licence in English, rather than going on to sit for the agrégation; with his wife Marcelle, Pelorson translated Emily Brontë's poems in 1933. He wrote for *Paris-Midi* and *Paris-Soir* (1931–1940), was Director of the Ecole bilingue de Neuilly founded by Maria Jolas, and published in *La Nouvelle Revue Française*, *Mesures*, and *transition*. With Raymond Queneau, Henry Miller, Le Corbusier, and Frédéric Joliot-Curie, Pelorson co-founded *Volontés* (1937–1939); he published *Essai sur une réforme de l'enseignement en France* (1940) and was involved in the literary section of the Jeune France educational movement. A collaborator, Pelorson held positions with the Vichy Government: as Chef de la propagande des jeunes for the Occupied Zone (1941), Secrétaire général adjoint (1942–1943), and Secrétaire général de la jeunesse (1943–1944). Blacklisted after the Liberation by the Comité national des écrivains, briefly imprisoned, and stripped of his civil rights for ten years, Pelorson wrote under the name Georges Belmont. In the early 1950s SB and Belmont resumed their friendship. Belmont worked with Editions Robert Laffont (1952–1953; 1964–1979), as Editor-in-Chief of *Paris Match* (1953–1954), Editor of *Jours de France*, of *Marie Claire*, Review Editor of *Arts* (1953–1964), and as Literary Director for Editions Acropole (1980–1985). As Georges Belmont, he is widely known as the French translator of works by Graham Greene, Evelyn Waugh, Anthony Burgess, Henry James, and Henry Miller.

Alfred Rémy Péron (1904–1945), writer and teacher, was in the class of 1924 at the Ecole Normale Supérieure; Péron came to Trinity College Dublin on the exchange program from the ENS (1926–1928) and first met SB there. As a Lecteur d'anglais at the ENS in 1928, SB helped Péron study for the agrégation. The two worked together on the initial French translation of Joyce's "Anna Livia Plurabelle" in 1930. Péron taught at the Lycée Buffon in Paris. When SB moved to Paris in 1938, Péron encouraged and helped SB to begin the translation of *Murphy* into French; Péron's translation of SB's poem "Alba" was published in *Soutes* (1938). When Péron was mobilized in the French Army, he asked SB to assist his family in the event of evacuation from Paris. Péron served as an agent de liaison for the British Army. He was a member of the Resistance réseaux "Etoile" and "Gloria SMH"; he recruited SB to the latter in September 1941. When Péron was arrested by the Gestapo in August 1942, his wife Maria Péron (known as Mania to SB) warned SB and Suzanne by telegram. Alfred Péron was sent to the concentration camp at Mauthausen; shortly after being freed from the camp, he died on 1 May 1945 in Switzerland, in transit back to France. SB remained supportive of Péron's family. SB enlisted Mania Péron's help with his writings in French, and he helped her as she taught English, translated, and wrote her novel. SB's correspondence with Mania Péron continued into the 1980s.

Charles Prentice (c. 1892–1949) was born in Scotland, studied Classics at Oxford, and was a senior partner in Chatto and Windus when, at Thomas McGreevy's suggestion, SB wrote and submitted *Proust* to the Dolphin Books series. In Prentice SB found a frank yet sympathetic reader. Prentice continued to further SB's writing career, publishing *More Pricks Than Kicks* (1934) despite the reservations of his colleagues at Chatto and Windus. Even when he could not publish SB's work, Prentice reassured SB and suggested other outlets for his writing. Richard Aldington characterized Prentice as a "man utterly without affectations ... of simple dignity and straightforward utterance," considerate, generous, and "full of laughter."[13] Prentice joined Aldington in providing funds so that McGreevy could travel in Italy and have time

[13] Richard Aldington, *Life for Life's Sake: A Book of Reminiscences* (London: Cassell, 1941) 322–323.

to write. Prentice retired from Chatto and Windus in 1935, but he returned to work there during World War II; in retirement he pursued interests in archeology in Italy, Greece, and Africa. He died in Nairobi.

Samuel Putnam (1892–1950), American editor, journalist, and translator, was a feature writer for the *Chicago Tribune* and the *Chicago Evening Post* in the 1920s, and edited *Youth* (1921–1922) and *Prairie* (1923). In 1927, he moved to Paris, where in 1929 he was an editor at *This Quarter* with Edward Titus and then in 1930 founded *The New Review*, which expired with the April 1932 issue. SB published some of his own work as well as translations in both journals. Putnam initiated *The European Caravan: An Anthology of the New Spirit in European Literature* (1931), planned as a two-volume anthology to introduce modern European literature to American and English readers; the editors included Maida Castelhun Darnton, George Reavey, and Jacob Bronowski. Some of SB's poems were published in the Irish section of the first volume; Putnam enlisted SB to help with the selection and translations for the Italian section of a second volume that remained unpublished. He published George Reavey's *Faust's Metamorphoses* (1932). Putnam returned to the United States in 1933, becoming a contributor and editor to several small magazines; in 1947 he published his memoirs, *Paris Was Our Mistress*.

George Reavey (1907–1976), Irish poet, literary agent, publisher, and translator of Russian and French literature, was born and lived in Russia until 1919, when his father was arrested; the family fled to Belfast and moved to London in 1921. From 1926 Reavey studied at Cambridge University, where he knew William Empson, Jacob Bronowski, and Julian Trevelyan through their association with the journal *Experiment*. SB met Reavey in 1929 through Thomas McGreevy in Paris where Reavey was Associate Editor of Samuel Putnam's *The New Review* (1930–1932) as well as of *The European Caravan* (1931); Putnam published his first book of poetry, *Faust's Metamorphoses* (1932). In 1934 Reavey established Europa Press in London and Paris, which published SB's *Echo's Bones and Other Precipitates* (1935) in a series of poetry collections that included his own *Nostradam: A Sequence of Poems* (1935), *Signes d'adieu* (1935), and *Quixotic Perquisitions* (1939); *Intercessions* (1937) by Denis Devlin; and *Third Person* by Brian Coffey (1938). Reavey edited and translated *Soviet Literature: An Anthology* with Marc Slonim (1934), and was a prolific translator from Russian, particularly of the works of Nikolai Berdyaev and Andrei Bely. He edited *Thorns of Thunder* (1936), a collection of selected poems by Paul Eluard translated by SB and others. Having established the European Literary Bureau in Paris, Reavey moved it to London in 1935; the agency represented SB's *Murphy*. Reavey served with the British Institute in Madrid in 1940 and with the British Foreign Office in Russia from 1942 to 1945, where he edited the journal *Britanskii Soyuznik* in Kuibyshev and Moscow. After the War, he published *Soviet Literature Today* (1946), taught at the University of Birmingham, England, and in 1949–1950 was a Rockefeller Fellow at Columbia and Stanford universities; thereafter, he resided primarily in the United States. Reavey continued to write poetry, publishing *Colours of Memory* (1955) and *Seven Seas* (1971), and to translate Russian literature. SB remained a close friend of Reavey; following his death, SB wrote: "Adieu George, to whom I owed so much, with whom shared so much, for whom cared so much."[14]

Gwynedd Cade Reavey (née Clodine Gwynedd Vernon-Jones, 1901–?), Welsh wife of George Reavey, helped Reavey establish the European Literary Bureau in London. During 1938 and 1939, she spent time in Cagnes-sur-Mer with Geer and Lisl van Velde, and she frequently saw SB as she passed through Paris. In 1940 she moved from London to Madrid with her husband, who was then working for the British Institute. In September 1941, she joined the Ministry of Economic Warfare. SB saw her in London as he returned from France to Ireland after the Liberation; she went to Germany with the Control Commission (autumn 1945–1947). After returning to London in 1949, she was employed by the British Iron and Steel Federation; SB lost contact with her after her divorce from George Reavey in 1950.

Lennox Robinson (né Esmé Stuart Lennox Robinson, 1886–1958), Irish playwright, was appointed by W. B. Yeats and Lady Gregory to manage the Abbey Theatre in 1909 and was sent to London to gain theatrical experience with George Bernard Shaw; Robinson resigned

---

[14] Samuel Beckett, "In Memoriam: George Reavey," *Journal of Beckett Studies* 2 (Summer 1977) [1].

from the Abbey in 1914 following a dispute about his decision to keep the theatre open during the mourning period for King Edward VII. In 1919, Robinson returned to the Abbey, where he was a director-producer and served on the theatre's board of directors from 1923 until his death. In 1931 he married the artist and set designer Dorothy Travers Smith, daughter of Hester Dowden. A writer of fiction, biography, autobiography, and essays, Robinson was best known as a playwright. He wrote a history of the Abbey, *Ireland's Abbey Theatre* (1951), and he organized and traveled with the Abbey on lecture tours throughout the world.

Thomas Brown Rudmose-Brown (popularly known as Ruddy, 1878–1942) was Professor of Modern Languages at Trinity College Dublin, and taught SB French and Provençal Literature. Rudmose-Brown studied at the University of Aberdeen and the University of Grenoble and was appointed to TCD in 1909. He had a wide range of scholarly interests, from Pierre de Ronsard and Jean Racine to modern French writers, among them Marcel Proust, Francis Vielé-Griffin, Stuart Merrill, Louis Le Cardonnel, Paul Valéry, Valery Larbaud, and Charles Péguy. He also knew personally many of the poets of the Provençal literary renaissance. TCD awarded him an honorary D.Litt. in 1931. He edited plays by Corneille and Marivaux, published *French Literary Studies* (1917), *French Short Stories* (1925), *Contes du moyen âge* (1926), *A Book of French Verse from Hugo to Larbaud* (1928), *French Town and Country* (1928), and a collection of his own poetry, *Walled Gardens* (1918). Rudmose-Brown nominated SB as Lecteur d'anglais to the Ecole Normale Supérieure in 1927; when this appointment was delayed, he arranged for SB's appointment to Campbell College in Belfast (from January 1928). Following two years at the ENS, SB returned to TCD in 1930–1931 as Rudmose-Brown's Assistant in French. Although he later regretted it, SB portrayed Rudmose-Brown as the "Polar Bear" in *Dream of Fair to Middling Women*. SB said of his mentor: "Much needed light came to me from 'Ruddy', from his teaching and friendship. I think of him often and always with affection and gratitude."[15]

---

[15] Samuel Beckett to Roger Little, 18 May 1983, cited by Knowlson, *Damned to Fame*, 64.

Frances Beckett Sinclair (known as Fanny and as Cissie, 1880–1951), artist and musician, was the only sister of SB's father William Beckett. She studied painting at the Dublin Metropolitan School of Art and at the Académie Colarossi in Paris in 1904, along with her good friends Estella Solomons and Beatrice Elvery (later Lady Glenavy). As Fannie Beckett, she exhibited her paintings in the Royal Hibernian Academy (1897, 1901–1908). In 1908, she married William Abraham (Boss) Sinclair, an art and antiques dealer; their home in Baily, Howth, Co. Dublin was a gathering-place for writers and artists. The Sinclairs moved to Kassel, Germany, in the early 1920s, where SB frequently visited them, sharing in their family and artistic life. In his Aunt Cissie, SB found a mature confidante with whom he could share interests in literature, art, and music. Cissie Sinclair traveled between Dublin and Kassel in 1931–1932, a time when personal difficulties, economic depression, and growing anti-Semitism were making life increasingly difficult in Germany. After the death of their daughter Ruth Margaret Sinclair (known as Peggy) in May 1933, the family returned to Dublin in June. SB remained close to the Sinclairs, especially during Boss's illness and death in 1937; when Cissie was confined by rheumatoid arthritis and Parkinson's disease in her later years, SB was particularly attentive and visited her whenever he was in Ireland.

Morris Sinclair (known as Sunny or Sonny Sinclair, 1918–2007) was SB's first cousin, the only son of Frances (Cissie) and William (Boss) Sinclair. Despite the twelve-year age difference, the cousins were close. Sinclair and his family moved permanently from Germany to Dublin in 1933. SB helped him prepare for his examinations in Modern Languages (German and French) at Trinity College Dublin. Sinclair was a gifted violinist and studied at the Royal Irish Academy of Music. His father and sister Peggy had died of tuberculosis, so when Sinclair became ill in autumn 1936, it was arranged for him to go to the more favorable climate of South Africa (1937–1938) as a private tutor. He completed his studies at TCD in winter 1940. In 1945, Sinclair received a scholarship to study in Paris; as he hesitated about a thesis subject, SB suggested that he might write on Sartre and the influences of Husserl and Kierkegaard, offering to introduce him to Sartre. From 1948 to 1952, Sinclair worked for UNESCO, first in English translation and editing and then as a writer and producer for radio broadcasts in German. He then moved to Geneva, where he worked in the Public Information Office of the World Health Organization (1952–1971), becoming Director of Public Information (1971–1974). He corresponded with SB and often visited him in Paris.

Ruth Margaret Sinclair (known as Peggy, 1911–1933), daughter of Frances (Cissie) and William (Boss) Sinclair, was SB's first cousin. When her family moved to Kassel in the early 1920s, SB often visited. SB and Peggy were attracted to each other when she visited Dublin in mid-summer of 1928. Peggy studied art, music, and movement at the Schule Hellerau-Laxenburg, near Vienna, where SB visited her in September 1928 before beginning his appointment at the Ecole Normale Supérieure in Paris, but by early 1929 their intimacy had ended. She figures in several of SB's early poems and many of her qualities are reflected in the character of Smeraldina-Rima in *Dream of Fair to Middling Women* and "The Smeraldina's Billet-Doux," first published in *More Pricks Than Kicks*. Peggy Sinclair died of tuberculosis in Germany in May 1933.

William Abraham Sinclair (known as Boss, 1882–1937), Jewish, an art and antiques dealer, SB's uncle by marriage to his aunt Frances (Cissie) Sinclair, was an amateur violinist and a member of the Dublin Musical Society; he had been active in the Republican movement. They lived in Howth, Co. Dublin, before their move in the early 1920s to Kassel, Germany, where he dealt in contemporary German art. Sinclair published *Painting* (1918), contributed art criticism to the *Irish Review*, lectured on art, and taught English. SB grew close to the Sinclairs during his visits to Kassel, appreciating their warmth, their easy ways, and their encouragement of his writing. In the early 1930s, economic depression and anti-Semitism made life in Germany inhospitable; Sinclair returned to Dublin in the summer of 1933 after the death of his daughter Margaret (Peggy) Sinclair. He died from tuberculosis in 1937. Fulfilling a death-bed promise to Boss, his twin brother Henry Sinclair pursued a lawsuit against Oliver St. John Gogarty, who had libeled them and their grandfather in his book *As I Was Going Down Sackville Street*; SB gave testimony in the case in November 1937.

Estella Solomons (1882–1968), Irish painter, was married to Seumas O'Sullivan, but used her maiden name professionally. She was a political activist who became involved in the Easter Rising and the War of Independence. She studied with William Orpen at the Metropolitan School of Art in Dublin, and with Walter Osborne at the Royal Hibernian Academy, and in London. Solomons painted portraits of many Irish literary and artistic figures, including Jack B. Yeats, and showed her work regularly at the Royal Hibernian Academy Exhibitions. She was named an Honorary Royal Hibernian Academician. SB attended the opening of Solomons's exhibition (with her cousin Louise Jacobs and friend Mary Duncan) at the Arlington Gallery in 1935. Having studied Art together, Estella Solomons and Frances (Cissie) Sinclair were close friends. Estella Solomons took an interest in SB and his work, and her sister the singer Sophie Jacobs (née Solomons, 1887–1972) befriended SB in the 1930s in Paris and London. SB occasionally visited the home of Solomons and O'Sullivan, "The Grange," in Rathfarnham, Co. Dublin.

Francis Stuart (né Henry Francis Montgomery Stuart, 1902–2000), Australian-born Irish novelist, poet, and dramatist, converted to Catholicism in 1920, and was married to Iseult MacBride, the daughter of Maud Gonne. With A. J. Leventhal, Cecil Salkeld, and others, he began the short-lived literary magazine *Tomorrow* (1924). SB's letters mention, among Stuart's prolific early writings, the novels *Women and God* (1931), which was dedicated to Thomas McGreevy; *The Coloured Dome* (1932); and *The Great Squire* (1939). In 1939, Stuart gave a series of academic lectures in Germany, and then taught English and Irish Literature in Berlin in 1940. From 1942 to January 1944, Stuart read German radio broadcasts aimed at Ireland. Although Stuart claimed that he wrote to SB in August 1942, and that SB replied, the letter has not been found. After World War II, Stuart lived in Germany, France, and England; he married Gertrude Meissner in 1954, returning to Ireland in 1958. He is perhaps best known for his book *Black List Section H* (1971). Although "men of differing viewpoints," he and SB met occasionally in Paris after World War II.[16]

Jean Thomas (1900–1983), French educator, entered the Ecole Normale Supérieure in 1920, became Agrégé-répétiteur (1926–1932), and Secrétaire général of the ENS (1933). He taught French Language and

---

[16] Elborn, *Francis Stuart*, 8.

Literature at the Sorbonne (1934–1936), French Literature at the University of Poitiers (1936–1938), and Modern Comparative Literature at the University of Lyon (1938–1944). Thomas published studies of Diderot, Musset, and Sainte-Beuve. He was appointed as Directeur du cabinet du Ministre de l'Education Nationale (October 1944) and Chef du service des relations universitaires et artistiques avec l'étranger (1945); having been a member of the French delegation to the constituting conference of UNESCO, he became its Director of Cultural Activities (1947–1954), and then Assistant Director General of UNESCO (1955–1960). In 1932, Thomas wrote a letter of reference for SB, and in his position with UNESCO suggested SB for various translation projects during the 1950s, most notably the English translation of *The Mexican Anthology* edited by Octavio Paz. Thomas's eminence in French public and international education culminated in his appointment as Président de la Commission de la République Française pour l'éducation, la science, et la culture (1972–1980).

Arthur Geoffrey Thompson (known to SB as Geoffrey, 1905–1976) was, with his brother Alan, a childhood friend of SB; they studied together at Portora Royal School and Trinity College Dublin. They shared interests in music, literature, and sports, and, while students at TCD, attended the Abbey Theatre together. Thompson qualified in Medicine at TCD in 1928, then studied Biochemistry in London and Paris as a Rockefeller Research Fellow. Returning to Dublin in 1930, he took up the position of Physician at Baggot St. Hospital. Thompson became increasingly interested in mental illness manifested as physical symptoms, and moved to London in 1934 to train in psychoanalysis, a specialty that could not be pursued in Dublin at that time. He was resident Senior House Physician at Bethlem Royal Hospital and later worked at the Maudsley Hospital and St. Bartholomew's Hospital in London. When SB came to see Thompson, he would also visit long-term patients who otherwise were seldom visited. Thompson has said that SB was "preoccupied with decrepitude, people who could hardly help themselves."[17] It was Thompson who suggested that SB begin psychotherapy with W. R. Bion in 1934. In 1935, Thompson

---

[17] Geoffrey Thomson interviewed by Andy O'Mahoney, RTE, 1976.

took a post in the Tavistock Clinic. In November 1935, SB was best man at Thompson's wedding to Ursula Stenhouse.

After war-time service, Thompson practiced privately and at the Tavistock Clinic, qualifying in psychoanalysis in 1949. He worked with the National Health Service and was a member of the Institute of Marital Studies, retiring from the Tavistock Clinic in 1970. In later years, the Thompsons and SB saw each other from time to time in London and in Paris.

Edward William Titus (1870–1952), Polish-born American bibliophile, translator, and publisher, opened his anglophone bookstore, At the Sign of the Black Manikin, in Paris in 1924. Subsidized by his wife Helena Rubinstein, he published twenty-five books under the Black Manikin imprint from 1926 to 1932: ranging from works by Austrian playwright Arthur Schnitzler to those by British modernist Mary Butts, from Harlem Renaissance poets Claude McKay and Countee Cullen to Anaïs Nin's *An Unprofessional Study of D. H. Lawrence*, and also translations of Rimbaud and Baudelaire. In 1929 he became Editor of *This Quarter* (1925–1932), initiating prizes to attract submissions and encourage young writers. In *This Quarter* SB published translations from Italian of work by Eugenio Montale, Raffaelo Franchi, Giovanni Comisso (1930), as well as his own story "Dante and the Lobster" (1932), and many of his translations from French for the surrealist number (1932) guest-edited by André Breton. In 1932, SB translated Rimbaud's "Le Bateau ivre" (*Drunken Boat*), unpublished until 1976, as a commission from Titus.

transition (1927–1938), an international avant-garde literary magazine, was founded by Eugene Jolas, Maria Jolas, and Elliot Paul to present new European writing to American readers and to create a forum for linguistic experimentation: as Jolas put it, "a laboratory of the word." Eugene Jolas's ideas about language and literature were expressed most concisely in two manifestos, "The Revolution of the Word" (1929) and "Poetry is Vertical" (1932). Among the writers published by *transition* were André Breton, Franz Kafka, Gertrude Stein, William Carlos Williams, Hart Crane, and Dylan Thomas; *transition* may be best known for serially publishing sections of James Joyce's *Work in Progress* (1927–1935), a process in which SB was involved. SB's first published writing, his essay "Dante … Bruno. Vico. . Joyce," appeared in *transition* (June 1929). He also published in *transition* the short stories "Assumption" and "Sedendo et Quiesciendo [sic]," poems ("For Future Reference," "Malacoda," "Enueg II," "Dortmunder," and "Ooftish"), and a review of Denis Devlin's collection of poetry *Intercessions*.

After World War II, the Jolases transferred the publishing licence of *transition* to Georges Duthuit, who capitalized its title and changed the focus of the journal (see profile of *Transition* in Volume II).

Percival Arland Ussher (known as Percy until mid-1937, then as Arland, 1899–1980), essayist, critic, and translator, was born in London and studied at Trinity College Dublin (1917–1919) and St. John's College, Cambridge (1920). He settled on his family's estate in Co. Waterford, where he wrote on the Gaelic language and the way of life of the Déise Gaeltacht. His translation from Irish of Brian Merriman's *The Midnight Court* (1926) was prefaced by W. B. Yeats. SB visited Ussher at Cappagh, and Ussher often sent him his essays on philosophy, history, politics, and art, especially in the late 1930s and again after World War II, when he occasionally visited SB in Paris. Acerbic wit and strong opinions mark his writing, which he called "philosophical belles lettres." He published *Postscript on Existentialism and Other Essays* (1946); *The Twilight of Ideas and Other Essays* (1948); *The Face and Mind of Ireland* (1949); a study of Jewish culture and an analysis of anti-Semitism, *The Magic People* (1949); a study of Shaw, Yeats, and Joyce, *Three Great Irishmen* (1952); a book on existentialism with reference to Kierkegaard, Heidegger, and Sartre, *Journey Through Dread* (1955); *Sages and Schoolmen* (1967); and *Eros and Psyche* (1976). His interest in folklore and divination is reflected in his study *Twenty Two Keys to the Tarot* (1957). Edited selections from Ussher's diary (1943–1977) were published as *From a Dead Lantern* (1978) and *The Journal of Arland Ussher* (1980).

Jack Butler Yeats (1871–1957), Irish painter, illustrator, novelist, and playwright, the son of John Butler Yeats and younger brother to the poet William Butler Yeats, was born in London, but spent his boyhood in County Sligo with his maternal grandparents. In 1887, he returned to London where he studied Art and established himself as an illustrator; in 1894 he married Mary Cottenham White (known as Cottie), a fellow-student at the Chiswick Art School. Although he visited Ireland frequently, Jack Yeats did not settle there until 1910. In 1912 he published a book of paintings and drawings, *Life in the West of Ireland*, and began to work in oils. SB met Yeats through Thomas McGreevy in November 1930; over time, Yeats became a trusted older friend to SB. In the 1930s, SB occasionally attended Yeats's "at-homes" in Fitzwilliam Square, but much preferred to visit the painter in his studio. SB greatly admired Yeats's paintings and saw a correlation between them and his own work. SB owned several of Yeats's works, including the painting *A Morning* ("a setting out without the coming home"), which he bought on what he called the "stuttering system." Yeats was also an accomplished writer, and in 1936 SB reviewed his novel *The Amaranthers* in the *Dublin Magazine*. In 1938, Yeats wrote to Routledge, his own London publisher, on behalf of Beckett's *Murphy*. At the time of Yeats's 1954 Paris exhibition, SB wrote "Hommage à Jack B. Yeats" and elicited tributes about Yeats's work from Pierre Schneider and Jacques Putman for *Les Lettres Nouvelles* (April 1954). SB was deeply disappointed that he was unable to return to Dublin for Yeats's funeral in April 1957.

BIBLIOGRAPHY OF WORKS CITED

Abbot, Vivienne. "How It Was: Egan and Beckett." *Desmond Egan: The Poet and His Work.* Ed. Hugh Kenner. Orono, ME: Northern Lights, 1990. 45–53.

Ackerley, C. J. *Demented Particulars: The Annotated Murphy.* 2nd rev. edn. Tallahassee, FL: Journal of Beckett Studies Books, 2004.

Ackerley, C. J., and S. E. Gontarski. *The Grove Companion to Samuel Beckett: A Reader's Guide to His Works, Life, and Thought.* New York: Grove Press, 2004.

Adam, Antoine. *The Art of Paul Verlaine.* Tr. Carl Morse. New York: New York University Press, 1963.

Adler, Alfred. *The Neurotic Constitution: Outlines of a Comparative Individualistic Psychology and Psychotherapy.* Tr. Bernard Glueck and John E. Lind. New York: Moffat, 1916. Rpt. London: Kegan Paul, 1921.

Adler, Jankel. *Jankel Adler.* Intro. Stanley William Hayter. London: Nicholson and Watson, 1948.

Aldington, Richard. *The Complete Poems of Richard Aldington.* London: Allan Wingate, 1948.

"James Joyce." Rev. of *Finnegans Wake,* by James Joyce. *The Atlantic* 163 (June 1939) [supplement] "The Bookshelf" [17, 19, 21].

Life for Life's Sake: A Book of Reminiscences. London: Cassell, 1941.

Alphant, Marianne, and Nathalie Léger, eds. *Objet: Beckett.* Paris: Centre Pompidou, IMEC-Editeur, 2007.

André Lhote, 1885–1962: Cubism. New York: Leonard Hutton Galleries, 1976.

Andrews, Keith. *Adam Elsheimer: Paintings – Drawings – Prints.* New York: Rizzoli, 1977.

Annuaire diplomatique et consulaire de la République Française. Nouvelle série. Vol. 49. Paris: Imprimerie Nationale, 1938.

Anon. "Gontcharov's [sic] 'Oblomov.'" Rev. of *Oblomov,* by Ivan Goncharov. *Times Literary Supplement* (14 November 1929) 919.

"*Murphy.* By Samuel Beckett." Rev. of *Murphy,* by Samuel Beckett. *Times Literary Supplement* (12 March 1938) 172.

Rev. of *James Joyce's "Ulysses,"* by Stuart Gilbert. *Dublin Magazine* 6.2 (April–June 1931) 64–65.

Rev. of *Murphy,* by Samuel Beckett. *Dublin Magazine* 14.2 (April–June 1939) 98.

Arnheim, Rudolf. *Film*. Tr. L. M. Sieveking and Ian F. D. Morrow. London: Faber and Faber, 1933.

Association amicale des anciens élèves de l'Ecole normale supérieure. Paris: Hachette-Université, 1973. *Supplément historique*. Paris: Hachette-Université, 1990.

Atik, Anne. *How It Was: A Memoir of Samuel Beckett*. London: Faber and Faber, 2003.

Augustine. *Confessions*. Tr. E. B. Pusey. Everyman's Library. London: Dent, 1907.

Baedeker, Karl. *Das Deutsche Reich und einige Grenzgebiete, Reisehandbuch für Bahn und Auto*. Leipzig: Karl Baedeker, 1936.

Bair, Deirdre. *Samuel Beckett: A Biography*. New York: Harcourt Brace Jovanovich, 1978.

Bald, Wambly. *On the Left Bank, 1929–1933*. Ed. Benjamin Franklin, V. Athens: Ohio University Press, 1987.

Barbera, Gioacchino. "The Life and Works of Antonello da Messina." *Antonello da Messina: Sicily's Renaissance Master*. Ed. Gioacchino Barbera. New York: Metropolitan Museum of Art, 2006. 17–30.

Barnett, Vivian Endicott. *Kandinsky Watercolours: Catalogue Raisonné*. Ithaca, NY: Cornell University Press, 1992–1994. 2 vols.

Barron, Stephanie, ed. *"Degenerate Art": The Fate of the Avant-Garde in Nazi Germany*. Los Angeles: Los Angeles County Museum of Art, 1991.

Bate, W. Jackson. *Samuel Johnson*. New York: Harcourt Brace Jovanovich, 1975.

Baudelaire, Charles. *Les Fleurs du mal, The Flowers of Evil*. Tr. Richard Howard. Boston: David R. Godine, 1982.

 Oeuvres complètes. Ed. Claude Pichois and Jean Ziegler. Bibliothèque de la Pléiade. Paris: Gallimard, 1975–1976. 2 vols.

Beach, Sylvia, ed. *Our Exagmination Round His Factification for Incamination of Work in Progress*. Paris: Shakespeare and Company, 1929. Rpt. London: Faber and Faber, 1936.

Beauvoir, Simone de. *La Force de l'âge*. Paris: Gallimard, 1960.

 Letters to Sartre. Ed. and tr. Quintin Hoare. New York: Arcade, 1992.

 The Prime of Life. Tr. Peter Green. Cleveland, OH: World Publishing Co., 1962.

Beckett, Samuel. "Alba." *Dublin Magazine* 6.4 (October–December 1931) 4. "Alba." Tr. A[lfred] R. Péron. *Soutes* 9 (1938) 41.

 Alles kommt auf so viel an: Das Hamburg-Kapitel aus den "German Diaries" 2. Oktober–4. Dezember 1936. Transcribed by Erika Tophoven. Schenefeld: Raamin-Press, 2003.

 "Assumption." *transition* 16–17 (June 1929) 268–271.

 "Beckett's Letters on 'Endgame': Extracts from His Correspondence with Director Alan Schneider." *The Village Voice* 19 March 1958: 8, 15.

"Cascando." *Dublin Magazine* 11.4 (October–December 1936) 3–4.

"Dante ... Bruno. Vico .. Joyce." *Our Exagmination Round His Factification for Incamination of Work in Progress*. Paris: Shakespeare and Company, 1929. 1–22.

"Dante ... Bruno. Vico .. Joyce." *transition* 16–17 (June 1929) 242–253.

"Dante and the Lobster." *This Quarter* 5.2 (December 1932) 222–236.

"Denis Devlin." Rev. of *Intercessions*, by Denis Devlin. *transition* 27 (April–May 1938) 289–294.

Disjecta: Miscellaneous Writings and a Dramatic Fragment. Ed. Ruby Cohn. New York: Grove Press, 1984.

"Dortmunder." *transition* 24 (June 1936) 10.

Dream of Fair to Middling Women. Ed. Eoin O'Brien and Edith Fournier. London: Calder, 1992. Rpt. New York: Arcade Publishing in association with Riverrun Press, 1993.

Drunken Boat. Ed. James Knowlson and Felix Leakey. Reading: Whiteknights Press, 1976.

Echo's Bones and Other Precipitates. Europa Poets 3. Paris: Europa Press, 1935.

"Enueg 2." *transition* 24 (June 1936) 9.

First Love and Other Shorts. New York: Grove Press, 1974.

"From the Only Poet to a Shining Whore: for Henry Crowder to Sing." *Henry-Music*. Paris: Hours Press, 1930. [6, 12–14.]

"Geer van Velde." *London Bulletin* 2 (May 1938) 15.

"German Letter of 1937." *Disjecta: Miscellaneous Writings and a Dramatic Fragment*. Ed. Ruby Cohn. Tr. Martin Esslin. New York: Grove Press, 1984. German text, 51–54; English text, 170–173.

"Home Olga." *Contempo* 3.13 (February 1934) 3.

"An Imaginative Work!" Rev. of *The Amaranthers*, by Jack B. Yeats. *Dublin Magazine* 11.3 (July–September 1936) 80–81.

"In Memoriam: George Reavey." *Journal of Beckett Studies* 2 (Summer 1977).

"Le Concentrisme." *Disjecta: Miscellaneous Writings and a Dramatic Fragment*. Ed. Ruby Cohn. New York: Grove Press, 1984. 35–42.

"Letters to Barney Rosset." *The Review of Contemporary Fiction* 10.3 (Fall 1990) 64–71.

"Malacoda." *transition* 24 (June 1936) 8.

More Pricks Than Kicks. London: Chatto and Windus, 1934.

More Pricks Than Kicks. New York: Grove Press, 1972.

Murphy. London: Routledge, 1938. Rpt. New York: Grove Press, 1957.

No Author Better Served: The Correspondence of Samuel Beckett and Alan Schneider. Ed. Maurice Harmon. Cambridge, MA: Harvard University Press, 1998.

"Ooftish." *transition* 27 (April–May 1938) 33.

"Poèmes 38–39." *Les Temps Modernes* 2.14 (November 1946) 288–293.

Poèmes, suivi de mirlitonnades. Paris: Les Editions de Minuit, 1978.

Poems 1930–1989. London: Calder Publications, 2002.

Premier Amour. Paris: Les Editions de Minuit, 1970.

Proust. The Dolphin Books. London: Chatto and Windus, 1931. Rpt. New York: Grove Press, 1957.

"Return to the Vestry." *The New Review* 1.3 (August–September–October 1931) 98–99.

"Sedendo et Quiesciendo [*for* Quiescendo]." *transition* 21 (March 1932) 13–20.

"Three Dialogues with Georges Duthuit." *Disjecta: Miscellaneous Writings and a Dramatic Fragment*. Ed. Ruby Cohn. New York: Grove Press, 1984. 138–145.

Whoroscope. Paris: Hours Press, 1930.

[Beckett, Samuel.] Andrew Belis, pseud. "Recent Irish Poetry." *The Bookman* 86.515 (August 1934) 235–236.

Beckett, Samuel, and Erich Franzen. "Correspondence on Translating MOLLOY." *Babel* 3 (Spring 1984) 21–35.

Beckett, Samuel, and Barney Rosset. "The Godot Letters: A Lasting Effect" (Letters of Samuel Beckett and Barney Rosset). *The New Theater Review* [now *Lincoln Center Theater Review*] 12 (Spring 1995) 10–13.

Bell, J. Bowyer. "Waiting for Mario: The Espositos, Joyce, and Beckett." *Éire-Ireland* 30.2 (1995) 7–26.

Belmont, Georges. *Souvenirs d'outre-monde: Histoire d'une naissance*. Paris: Calmann-Lévy, 2001.

Bénézit, Emmanuel, ed. *Dictionnaire critique et documentaire des Peintres, Sculpteurs, Dessinateurs et Graveurs de tous les temps et de tous les pays*. 3rd edn. Paris: Gründ, 1976.

Bentley, Edmund. *Far Horizon: A Biography of Hester Dowden, Medium and Psychic Investigator*. London: Rider and Company, 1951.

Bergson, Henri. *Creative Evolution*. Tr. Arthur Mitchell. London: Macmillan, 1920.

L'Evolution créatrice. Paris: Félix Alcan, 1907.

"Introduction à la métaphysique." *Revue de Métaphysique et de Morale* 11 (1903) 1–36.

Berkeley, George. *Berkeley's Commonplace Book*. Ed. G. A. Johnston. London: Faber and Faber, 1931.

Bessy, Maurice, and Jean-Louis Chardans. *Dictionnaire du cinéma et de la télévision*. Paris: Pauvert, 1967–1971. 4 vols.

Bidwell, Bruce, and Linda Heffer. *The Joycean Way*. Baltimore: Johns Hopkins University Press, 1981.

Biermann, Georg. *Heinrich Campendonk. Junge Kunst*. Leipzig: Verlag von Klinkhardt und Biermann, 1921.

Bock, Henning, Irene Geismeier, Rainald Grosshans, *et al.*, eds. *Gemäldegalerie Berlin: Gesamtverzeichnis*. Berlin: Staatliche Museen zu Berlin, Preussischer Kulturbesitz, 1996.

Boetzkes, Ottilie G. *Salvator Rosa: Seventeenth-Century Painter, Poet and Patriot*. New York: Vantage Press, 1960.

Bonfand, Alain, Christophe Duvivier, Edda Maillet, Jérôme Serri, and Guy Tosatto. *Otto Freundlich*. Rochechouart: Musée Départemental de Rochechouart, 1988.

The Book of Common Prayer . . . The Church of Ireland. Dublin: Association for Promoting Christian Knowledge, Church of Ireland, 1927.

"Books and Authors." *Everyman* 75 (3 July 1930) 728.

Boswell, James. *Boswell's Life of Johnson, Together with Boswell's Journal of a Tour to the Hebrides and Johnson's Diary of a Journey into North Wales*. Ed. George Birkbeck Hill. Rev. and enlarged. L. F. Powell. Oxford: Clarendon Press, 1934. 6 vols.

Boussinot, Roger, ed. *L'Encyclopédie du cinéma*. Paris: Bordas, 1967.

Bowe, Nicola Gordon. *The Life and Work of Harry Clarke*. Dublin: Irish Academic Press, 1989.

Boylan, Patricia. *All Cultivated People: A History of the United Arts Club, Dublin*. Gerrards Cross, Bucks., UK: Colin Smythe, 1988.

Bredsdorff, Elias. *Hans Christian Andersen: The Story of His Life and Work, 1805–75*. London: Phaidon Press, 1975.

Breton, André. "Wolfgang Paalen." Tr. Samuel Beckett. *London Bulletin* 10 (February 1939) 16–17.

Brewer, Ebenezer Cobham. *Brewer's Dictionary of Phrase and Fable*. Rev. Adrian Room. 16th edn. New York: HarperResource-HarperCollins, 1999.

Briggs, John. *The Collector's Beethoven*. Westport, CT: Greenwood Press, 1978.

Brown, Beverly Louise, and Paola Marini. *Jacopo Bassano, c. 1510–1592*. Fort Worth, TX: Kimbell Art Museum, 1993.

Brown, Christopher. *Carel Fabritius: Complete Edition with a Catalogue Raisonné*. Ithaca, NY: Cornell University Press, 1981.

Brown, Jonathan, and Richard G. Mann. *Spanish Paintings of the Fifteenth through Nineteenth Centuries*. The Collections of the National Gallery of Art Systematic Catalogue. Washington, DC: National Gallery of Art; Cambridge: Cambridge University Press, 1990.

Bruhns, Maike. *Kunst in der Krise: Hamburger Kunst im "Dritten Reich."* Hamburg: Dölling und Galitz Verlag, 2001.

Bruni, Leonardo. *Le vite di Dante e del Petrarca*. Ed. Antonio Lanza. Rome: Archivio Guido Izzi, 1987.

Bruno, Giordano, and Tommaso Campanella. *Opere di Giordano Bruno e di Tommaso Campanella*. Ed. Augusto Guzzo and Romano Amerio. La Letteratura italiana; storia e testi. Milan: Riccardo Ricciardi, 1956.

723

Bryden, Mary, Julian Garforth, and Peter Mills, eds. *Beckett at Reading: Catalogue of the Beckett Manuscript Collection at the University of Reading.* Reading: Whiteknights Press and the Beckett International Foundation, 1998.

Budde, Rainer. *Deutsche romanische Skulptur, 1050–1250.* Munich: Hirmer Verlag, 1979.

Bulson, Eric. "Getting Noticed: James Joyce's Italian Translations." *Joyce Studies Annual* 12 (Summer 2001) 10–37.

Camesasca, Ettore. *The Complete Paintings of Watteau.* New York: Harry N. Abrams, 1968.

Carossa, Hans, and Eva Kampmann-Carossa. *Gedichte: Die Veröffentlichungen zu Lebzeiten und Gedichte aus dem Nachlass.* Frankfurt: Insel, 1995.

Cartwright, David E. *Historical Dictionary of Schopenhauer's Philosophy.* Lanham, MD: The Scarecrow Press, 2005.

Caselli, Daniela. "The 'Florentia Edition in the Ignoble Salani Collection': A Textual Comparison." *Journal of Beckett Studies* 9.2 (2001) 1–20.

"The Promise of Dante in the Beckett Manuscripts." *Notes Diverse Holo.* Special issue, *Samuel Beckett Today/Aujourd'hui* 16 (2006) 237–257.

Champion, Pierre. *Marcel Schwob et son temps.* Paris: Bernard Grasset, 1927.

Chisholm, Anne. *Nancy Cunard: A Biography.* New York: Alfred A. Knopf, 1979.

Christiansen, Keith. "Some Observations on the Brancacci Frescoes after their Cleaning." *Burlington Magazine* 133.1054 (January 1991) 5–20.

Church, Richard. "Samuel Beckett Gives us 'a riot of highbrow fun.'" Rev. of *Murphy*, by Samuel Beckett. *John O'London's Weekly* 39.990 (1 April 1938) 23.

Churchill, Charles. *The Ghost.* London: William Flexney, 1762.

Citerne, Georges, and Francis Jourdain. "French Imperialism at Work in Madagascar." Tr. Samuel Beckett. *Negro, Anthology Made by Nancy Cunard, 1931–1933.* Ed. Nancy Cunard. London: Published by Nancy Cunard at Wishart and Co., 1934. 801–802.

Citron, Pierre. *Giono: 1895–1970.* Paris: Editions du Seuil, 1990.

Clark, Kenneth. *Rembrandt and the Italian Renaissance.* London: John Murray, 1966.

Clarke, Norma. "Anna Seward: Swan, Duckling or Goose?" *New Rambler* E.7 (2003/2004) 54–67.

Cocteau, Jean. *Cocteau's World: An Anthology of Writings by Jean Cocteau.* Ed. and tr. Margaret Crosland. London: Peter Owen, 1972.

Coffey, Brian. Rev. of "*Sainte-Beuve, Les Meilleurs Textes.* Introduction by André Thérive." *The Criterion* 16.64 (April 1937) 716–721.

Third Person. Europa Poets 7. London: Europa Press, 1938.

Cohen-Solal, Annie. *Sartre: A Life*. New York: Pantheon Books, 1987.

Cohn, Ruby. *A Beckett Canon*. Theater: Theory/Text/Performance. Ann Arbor: University of Michigan Press, 2001.

Collection Marie Cuttoli – Henri Laugier, Paris. Basel: Galerie Beyeler, 1970.

Colum, Mary. *Life and the Dream*. Garden City, NY: Doubleday and Co., 1947.

Colum, Padraic. "From a Work in Progress." Rev. of "Haveth Childers Everywhere," by James Joyce. *Dublin Magazine* 6.3 (July–September 1931) 33–37.

Comisso, Giovanni. "The Home-Coming." Tr. Samuel Beckett. *This Quarter* 2.4 (April–May–June 1930) 675–683.

Conrad, Lore. *Die romanische Schottenkirche in Regensburg und ihre Bildsymbolsprache: Darstellung einer systematischen Deutung sakraler Kunst aus dem Europa des 12. Jahrhunderts*. 5th edn. Regensburg: Lore Conrad, 1987.

Conway, Martin. *Giorgione: A New Study of His Art as a Landscape Painter*. London: Ernest Benn, 1929.

Copleston, Frederick. *A History of Philosophy*. Westminster, MD: The Newman Press, 1955. 8 vols.

Corcoran, John. "The Rev. Robert Martin Hilliard (1904–1937)." *Kerry Archaeological and Historical Society Journal*. 2nd series, 5 (2005) 207–219.

Croke, Fionnuala, ed. *Samuel Beckett: A Passion for Paintings*. Dublin: National Gallery of Ireland, 2006.

Cronon, E. David, ed. *Marcus Garvey*. Great Lives Observed. Englewood Cliffs, NJ: Prentice-Hall, 1973.

Crowder, Henry. *Henry-Music*. Paris: Hours Press, 1930.

Crowder, Henry, and Hugo Speck. *As Wonderful as All That?: Henry Crowder's Memoir of His Affair with Nancy Cunard 1928–1935*. Ed. Robert L. Allen. Navarro, CA: Wild Trees Press, 1987.

Cunard, Nancy. *Parallax*. London: Hogarth Press, 1925.

These Were the Hours: Memories of My Hours Press, Réanville and Paris, 1928–1931. Ed. Hugh Ford. Carbondale: Southern Illinois University Press; London: Feffer and Simons, 1969.

Cunard, Nancy, ed. *Authors Take Sides on the Spanish War*. London: Left Review, [1937].

ed. *Negro, Anthology Made by Nancy Cunard, 1931–1933*. London: Published by Nancy Cunard at Wishart and Co., 1934.

Curran, C. P. *James Joyce Remembered*. London: Oxford University Press, 1968.

Curran, Elizabeth. "The National Gallery Revisited." *The Bell* 2.5 (August 1941) 65–72.

D'Annunzio, Gabriele. "Dell'arte di Giorgio Barbarelli." *Prose scelte*. Milan: Fratelli Treves, Editori, 1924. 17–22.

The Flame of Life: The Romances of the Pomegranate. Tr. Kassandra Vivaria. Boston: L. C. Page and Company, 1900.

Prose di romanzi. Ed. Ezio Raimondi, Annamaria Andreoli, and Niva Lorenzini. Milan: Arnaldo Mondadori Editore, 1989. 2 vols.

D. C. S.-T. Rev. of *Echo's Bones and Other Precipitates*, by Samuel Beckett. *Dublin Magazine* 11.2 (April–June 1936) 77–80.

D. H. V. "Reviews." Rev. of *Thomas Stearns Eliot: A Study*, by Thomas McGreevy. *T.C.D.: A College Miscellany* (21 May 1931) 162.

Dallapiccola, Luigi. *Italian Songs of the 17th and 18th Centuries, for Voice and Piano*. New York: International Music, 1961. 2 vols.

Dante. *La Divina Commedia*. Comment by Enrico Bianchi. Florence: Adriano Salani, 1927.

The Divine Comedy of Dante Alighieri. Tr. and comment John D. Sinclair. London: John Lane The Bodley Head, 1939–1948, rev. 1948. 3 vols.

Darwin, Charles. *On the Origin of Species: A Facsimile of the First Edition*. Cambridge, MA: Harvard University Press, 1964.

Davies, Martin. *National Gallery Catalogues: The Earlier Italian Schools*. London: National Gallery, 1986.

De Sanctis, Francesco. *Storia della letteratura italiana*. Vol. II. Ed. Niccolò Gallo. Turin: Giulio Einaudi Editore, 1958. 2 vols.

Degenhart, Bernhard, and Annegrit Schmitt. *Corpus der Italienischen Zeichnungen, 1300–1450*. Berlin: Gebr. Mann Verlag, 1968. 8 vols.

Delaney, John J. *Dictionary of Saints*. 2nd edn. New York: Image-Doubleday, 2004.

Delaporte, Louis-Joseph. "Chronicle of Archaeology." Tr. [Samuel Beckett]. *Formes* 4 (April 1930) [2], 25.

Delavenay, Emile. *Témoignage: d'un village savoyard au village mondial, 1905–1991*. La Calade: Diffusion EDISUD, 1992.

Denson, Alan, comp. *Thomas Bodkin: A Bio-Bibliographical Survey with a Bibliographical Survey of His Family*. Dublin: The Bodkin Trustees, 1966.

Devlin, Denis. "Another Irish Poet." Rev. of *Three Old Brothers*, by Frank O'Connor. *Ireland To-Day* 1.2 (July 1936) 77–79.

Collected Poems of Denis Devlin. Ed. J. C. C. Mays. Dublin: Dedalus Press, 1989.

"The Investiture of D'Artagnan." *Dublin Magazine* 11.3 (July–September 1936) 4.

[Devree, Howard]. "News and Comments: Spain's Art Treasures at Geneva." *Magazine of Art* 32.7 (July 1939) 425–426.

Dewald, Ernst T. *Italian Painting 1200–1600*. New York: Holt, Rinehart and Winston, 1961.

Diderot, Denis. *Dorval, or the Test of Virtue: A Comedy*. Tr. unattributed. London: privately printed, 1767.

Le Fils naturel et les Entretiens sur "Le Fils naturel." Ed. Jean-Pol Caput. Paris: Librairie Larousse, 1970.

Donaghy, John Lyle. *Into the Light, and Other Poems.* Dublin: The Cuala Press, 1934.

Donald, David Herbert. *Look Homeward: A Life of Thomas Wolfe.* Boston: Little, Brown and Co., 1987.

Dostoevsky, Fyodor. *Les Possédés.* Tr. Victor Derély. Paris: Editions Plon-Nourrit, 1886. 2 vols.

Dowling, John. "Art: Advice and Estimates Free." *Ireland To-Day* 2.10 (October 1937) 63, 77.

"Art: The Academy." *Ireland To-Day* 1.1 (June 1936) 60–61.

"The National College of Art." *Ireland To-Day* 1.4 (September 1936) 54–55.

Doyle, Charles. *Richard Aldington: A Biography.* Carbondale: Southern Illinois University Press, 1989.

Dryden, John. *All for Love* and *The Spanish Fryar.* Ed. William Strunk, Jr. Boston: D. C. Heath and Company, 1911.

Duffy, Maureen. *A Thousand Capricious Chances: A History of the Methuen List, 1889–1989.* London: Methuen, 1989.

Eckardt, Götz. *Die Gemälde in der Bildergalerie von Sanssouci.* Potsdam: Sanssouci, 1975.

Eggum, Arne. *Edvard Munch: Portretter.* Oslo: Munch-Musette / Labyrinth Press, 1994.

Eisenstein, Sergei. "Cinematography with Tears!: The Way of Learning." *Close Up* 10 (March 1933) 3–17.

"Detective Work in the GIK." *Close Up* 9 (December 1932) 287–294.

"The Dinamic Square." *Close Up* 8 (March 1931) 2–16.

"The Dinamic Square (Conclusion)." *Close Up* 8 (June 1931) 91–95.

"Filmic Art and Training (in an interview with Mark Segal)." *Close Up* 6 (March 1930) 195–197.

"The Fourth Dimension in the Kino." *Close Up* 6 (March 1930) 184–194.

"The Fourth Dimension in the Kino: Part II." *Close Up* 6 (April 1930) 253–268.

"The New Language of Cinematography." *Close Up* 4 (May 1929) 10–13.

"The Principles of Film Form." *Close Up* 8 (September 1931) 167–181.

Eisenstein, S[ergei] M., W. I. Pudowkin, and G. V. Alexandroff. "The Sound Film: A Statement from U.S.S.R." *Close Up* 3 (October 1928) 10–13.

Elborn, Geoffrey. *Francis Stuart: A Life.* Dublin: Raven Arts Press, 1990.

Eliot, T. S. *Complete Poems and Plays: 1909–1950.* New York: Harcourt, Brace and World, 1962.

Ellmann, Richard. *James Joyce: New and Revised Edition.* Oxford: Oxford University Press, [paperback with corrections], 1983.

Eluard, Paul. "All-Proof: Universe-Solitude." Tr. Samuel Beckett. *This Quarter* 5.1 (September 1932) 94–95.

Capitale de la douleur. Paris: Gallimard, 1964.

"Confections." Tr. Samuel Beckett. *This Quarter* 5.1 (September 1932) 96–98.

"Definition." Tr. Samuel Beckett. *This Quarter* 5.1 (September 1932) 89.

"Do Thou Sleep." Tr. Samuel Beckett. *This Quarter* 5.1 (September 1932) 90–91.

"The Invention." Tr. Samuel Beckett. *This Quarter* 5.1 (September 1932) 87–88.

"Lady Love." Tr. Samuel Beckett. *This Quarter* 5.1 (September 1932) 86.

"A Life Uncovered or The Human Pyramid." Tr. Samuel Beckett. *This Quarter* 5.1 (September 1932) 89.

Oeuvres complètes. Ed. Marcelle Dumas and Lucien Scheler. Bibliothèque de la Pléiade. Paris: Gallimard, 1968. 2 vols.

"Out of Sight in the Direction of My Body." Tr. Samuel Beckett. *This Quarter* 5.1 (September 1932) 86–87.

"The Queen of Diamonds." Tr. Samuel Beckett. *This Quarter* 5.1 (September 1932) 89–90.

"Scarcely Disfigured." Tr. Samuel Beckett. *This Quarter* 5.1 (September 1932) 87.

"Scene." Tr. Samuel Beckett. *This Quarter* 5.1 (September 1932) 92–93.

"Second Nature." Tr. Samuel Beckett. *This Quarter* 5.1 (September 1932) 92.

Thorns of Thunder: Selected Poems. Ed. George Reavey. Tr. Samuel Beckett, Denis Devlin, David Gascoyne, *et al.* London: Europa Press and Stanley Nott, 1936.

Ember, Ildikó, Annamária Gosztola, and Zsuzsa Urbach. *Old Masters' Gallery: Summary Catalogue, Museum of Fine Arts, Budapest*, Vol. II, *Early Netherlandish, Dutch and Flemish Paintings.* Budapest: Szépművészeti Múzeum, 2000.

Engelberts, Matthijs, Everett Frost, and Jane Maxwell, eds. *Notes Diverse Holo: Catalogues of Beckett's Reading Notes and Other Manuscripts at Trinity College Dublin with Supporting Essays.* Special issue, *Samuel Beckett Today/ Aujourd'hui* 16 (2006).

Engelen, Cor. *Le Mythe du Moyen Age: premiers éléments d'une remise en question du style moyenâgeux.* Tr. Benoît Boëlens van Waesberghe. Leuven: C. Engelen, 1999.

Epstein, M., ed. *The Annual Register: A Review of Public Events at Home and Abroad for the Year 1931.* London: Longmans, Green and Co., 1932.

Euripides. *Alcestis.* Tr. Richard Aldington. The Dolphin Books. London: Chatto and Windus, 1930.

Farrar, Frederic William. *Eric, or Little by Little: The Story of Roslyn School.* Edinburgh: Adam and Charles Black, 1858.

Favier, Jean. "Le Café des Sports par M. Aug. Prunier." *La Construction Moderne* 51.45 (23 August 1936) 929–936.

Federman, Raymond, and John Fletcher. *Samuel Beckett: His Works and His Critics, An Essay in Bibliography.* Berkeley: University of California Press, 1970.

Feldman, Matthew. *Beckett's Books: A Cultural History of Samuel Beckett's 'Interwar Notes.'* New York: Continuum, 2006.

Ferrières, Gauthier, ed. *Parnasse Royal: Poèmes choisis des monarques françois et autres personnages royaux.* Paris: Chez Sansot, Libraire, 1909.

Fielding, Henry. *Joseph Andrews.* Ed. Martin C. Battestin. Middletown, CT: Wesleyan University Press, 1967.

Fisher, David James. *Romain Rolland and the Politics of Intellectual Engagement.* Berkeley: University of California Press, 1988.

Fleming, Lionel. *Head or Harp.* London: Barrie and Rockliff, 1965.

Franchi, Raffaelo. "Landscape." Tr. Samuel Beckett. *This Quarter* 2.4 (April–May–June 1930) 672.

Piazza natia. Turin: Fratelli Buratti Editori, 1929.

Freundlich, Otto. *Otto Freundlich – Schriften: Ein Wegbereiter der gegenstandslosen Kunst.* Ed. Uli Bohnen. Cologne: DuMont Buchverlag, 1982.

Frost, Everett, and Jane Maxwell. "TCD MS 10962: Niccolò Machiavelli and Ludovico Ariosto." *Notes Diverse Holo.* Special issue, *Samuel Beckett Today/ Aujourd'hui* 16 (2006) 29–37.

"TCD MS 10967: History of Western Philosophy." *Notes Diverse Holo.* Special issue, *Samuel Beckett Today/Aujourd'hui* 16 (2006) 67–89.

"TCD MS 10968: Augustine of Hippo and Porphyry on Plotinus." *Notes Diverse Holo.* Special issue, *Samuel Beckett Today/Aujourd'hui* 16 (2006) 91–93.

"TCD MS 10969: Germany, Europe, and the French Revolution. Rabelais." *Notes Diverse Holo.* Special issue, *Samuel Beckett Today/Aujourd'hui* 16 (2006) 95–103.

"MS 10971/1: German Literature." *Notes Diverse Holo.* Special issue, *Samuel Beckett Today/Aujourd'hui* 16 (2006) 113–123.

"TCD MS 10971/2: Irish History." *Notes Diverse Holo.* Special issue, *Samuel Beckett Today/Aujourd'hui* 16 (2006) 125–128.

"TCD MS 10971/4: Frédéric Mistral and the Félibrige Poets." *Notes Diverse Holo.* Special issue, *Samuel Beckett Today/Aujourd'hui* 16 (2006) 133–136.

"TCD MS 10971/6: Latin excerpts from Arnoldus Geulincx and R. P. Gredt." *Notes Diverse Holo.* Special issue, *Samuel Beckett Today/Aujourd'hui* 16 (2006) 141–155.

Führer durch das Tell Halaf-Museum, Berlin. Berlin: Max Freiherr von Oppenheim-Stiftung, 1934.

Garland, Henry, and Mary Garland. *The Oxford Companion to German Literature.* Oxford: Oxford University Press, 1986.

Gateau, Jean-Charles. *Paul Eluard, ou, le Frère voyant, 1895–1952.* Paris: Editions Robert Laffont, 1988.

Geese, Uwe. "Romanesque Sculpture." *Romanesque: Architecture, Sculpture, Painting.* Ed. Rolf Toman. Cologne: Könemann, 1997. 256–323, 328–375.

George, Stefan. "Wir schreiten auf und ab im reichen flitter" [in poetry section entitled "Kottabistae"]. Tr. Ethna MacCarthy. *Hermathena* 51 (May 1938) 152–153.

George, Waldemar. "The Passion of Picasso." *Formes* 4 (April 1930) [2], 8–9.

Germanisches Nationalmuseum. *Die Gemälde des 13. bis 16. Jahrhunderts.* Ed. Eberhard Lutze and Eberhard Wiegand. Leipzig: K. F. Koehlers Antiquarium, 1937. 2 vols.

Geulincx, Arnold. *Arnoldi Geulincx antverpiensis Opera Philosophica. Sumptibus providerunt Sortis spinozianae curatores.* Ed. Jan Pieter Nicolaas Land. The Hague: apud Martinum Nijhoff, 1891–1893. 3 vols.

Gide, André. *The Counterfeiters.* Tr. Dorothy Bussy. New York: Alfred A. Knopf, 1927.

Oeuvres complètes d'André Gide. Ed. Louis Martin-Chauffier. Paris: Nouvelle Revue Française, 1932–1939. 15 vols.

Romans: récits et soties, oeuvres lyriques. Ed. Yvonne Davet, and Jean-Jacques Thierry. Bibliothèque de la Pléiade. Paris: Gallimard, 1958.

Gilbert, Stuart. "Sketch of a Scenario of Anna Livia Plurabelle." *A James Joyce Yearbook.* Ed. Maria Jolas. Paris: Transition Press, 1949. 10–20.

Gill, Anton. *Art Lover: A Biography of Peggy Guggenheim.* New York: HarperCollins, 2002.

Gillet, Louis. *Claybook for James Joyce.* Tr. Georges Markow-Totevy. New York: Abelard-Schuman, 1958.

Giono, Jean, and Jean Guéhenno. *Correspondance 1928–1969.* Ed. Pierre Citron. Paris: Seghers, 1991.

Giroud, Vincent. "Transition to Vichy: The Case of Georges Pelorson." *Modernism/Modernity* 7.2 (2000) 221–248.

Glendinning, Victoria. *Jonathan Swift: A Portrait.* New York: Henry Holt and Co., 1999.

Goethe, Johann Wolfgang von. *Elective Affinities.* Tr. David Constantine. The World's Classics. Oxford: Oxford University Press, 1994.

Faust. London: G. G. Harrap, 1925.

Die Leiden des jungen Werthers, Die Wahlverwandtschaften, Kleine Prosa, Epen. Ed. Waltraud Wiethölter and Christoph Brecht. Frankfurt: Deutscher Klassiker Verlag, 1994. Vol. VIII of *Sämtliche Werke: Briefe, Tagebücher und Gespräche.* Ed. Friedmar Apel, Hendrik Birus, and Dieter Borchmeyer. 39 vols. 1985– .

Die Leiden des jungen Werthers, Synoptischer Druck der beiden Fassungen 1774 und 1787. Ed. Annika Lorenz and Helmut Schmiedt. Paderborn: Igel Verlag Literatur, 1997.

The Sorrows of Young Werther, Goethe's Collected Works. Ed. David E. Wellbery. Tr. Victor Lange and Judith Ryan. Vol. XI. New York: Suhrkamp Publishers, 1988. 12 vols. 1983–1989.

Gogarty, Oliver St. John. *As I Was Going Down Sackville Street, A Phantasy in Fact*. New York: Reynal and Hitchcock, 1937; *As I Was Going Down Sackville Street: A Phantasy in Fact*. London: Rich and Cowan, 1937.

Gorman, Michael M. "Mario Esposito (1887–1975) and the Study of the Latin Literature of Medieval Ireland." *Studies in Hiberno-Latin Literature*. By Mario Esposito. Ed. Michael M. Gorman. Variorum Collected Studies Series. Aldershot, UK: Ashgate/Variorum, 2006. 299–322.

Granzotto, Gianni. *Christopher Columbus*. Tr. Stephen Sartarelli. Norman: University of Oklahoma Press, 1985.

Grasselli, Margaret Morgan, and Pierre Rosenberg. *Watteau, 1684–1721*. Washington, DC: National Gallery of Art, 1984.

Green, F[rederick] C[harles]. *Minuet: A Critical Survey of French and English Literary Ideas in the Eighteenth Century*. London: J. M. Dent, 1935.

Green, John Richard. *A Short History of the English People*. New York and London: Harper and Brothers Publishers, 1898.

Greene, Robert. *Groatsworth of witte, bought with a million of repentance; The repentance of Robert Greene, 1592*. Ed. G. B. Harrison. London: Bodley Head, 1923.

Plays and Poems of Robert Greene. Ed. J. Churton Collins. Oxford: Clarendon, 1905. 2 vols.

Grigson, Geoffrey. *Anton Zwemmer: Tributes from Some of his Friends on the Occasion of his 70th Birthday*. London: privately printed, 1962. Rpt. Geoffrey Grigson, *Recollections: Mainly of Writers and Artists*. London: Chatto and Windus / Hogarth Press, 1984. 38–40.

Grohmann, Will, ed. *Die Sammlung Ida Bienert, Dresden*. Privatsammlungen neuer Kunst. Potsdam: Müller und I. Kiepenheuer, 1933.

Grossmann, G. Ulrich, und die Sammlungsleiter, eds. *Germanisches Nationalmuseum: Führer durch die Sammlungen*. Nuremberg: Verlag des Germanischen Nationalmuseums, 2001.

Guggenheim, Peggy. *Out of This Century: Confessions of an Art Addict*. [Rev. of *Out of This Century: The Informal Memoirs of Peggy Guggenheim*.] New York: Universe Books, 1979.

Out of This Century: The Informal Memoirs of Peggy Guggenheim. New York: Dial Press, 1946.

Guicciardini, Francesco. *Storie fiorentine dal 1378 al 1509*. Bari: G. Laterza and Figli, 1931.

H. F. "T. S. Eliot." Rev. of *Thomas Stearns Eliot: A Study*, by Thomas McGreevy. *Time and Tide* 12.6 (7 February 1931) 165.

Hackett, Francis. *Queen Anne Boleyn, a novel*. New York: Doubleday Doran, 1939.

Hamilton, Nigel. *The Brothers Mann: The Lives of Heinrich and Thomas Mann, 1871–1950 and 1875–1955*. London: Secker and Warburg, 1978.

Hart-Davis, Duff. *Peter Fleming: A Biography*. London: Jonathan Cape, 1974.

Harten, Jürgen, Marc Scheps, and Ryszard Stanislawski, eds. *Jankel Adler: 1895–1949*. Cologne: DuMont Buchverlag, 1985.

Hartt, Frederick. *History of Italian Renaissance Art: Painting, Sculpture, Architecture*. 3rd edn. New York: Harry N. Abrams, 1987.

Harvey, Lawrence E. *Samuel Beckett: Poet and Critic*. Princeton: Princeton University Press, 1970.

Hecht, Josef, Konstanz. "Der Aufenthalt des Konrad Witz in Konstanz: Ein Problem und seine Lösung Neue Forschungen zur Lebensgeschichte des Meisters." *Zeitschrift für Kunstgeschichte* 6.5/6 (1937) 353–370.

Henry, Tom, and Laurence Kanter. *Luca Signorelli: The Complete Paintings*. New York: Rizzoli, 2002.

Herring, Phillip F. *Djuna: The Life and Work of Djuna Barnes*. New York: Viking Penguin, 1995.

Hess, Hans. *Lyonel Feininger*. New York: Harry N. Abrams, 1961.

Hewitt, John. "Obituary: R. N. D. Wilson (1899–1953)." *Dublin Magazine* 28.2 (April–June 1952) 54–55.

Hibbard, Howard. *Michelangelo*. 2nd edn. Cambridge, MA: Harper and Row, 1985.

Higgins, F. R. *Arable Holdings: Poems*. Dublin: The Cuala Press, 1933.

Hildebrandt, Dieter. *Lessing: Biographie einer Emanzipation*. Munich: Carl Hanser Verlag, 1979.

Hippocrates. "Aphorisms" in *Hippocrates, Heraclitus*. Ed. T. E. Page, E. Capps, and W. H. D. Rouse. Tr. W. H. S. Jones, Vol. IV. The Loeb Classical Library. London: William Heinemann; New York: G. P. Putnam's Sons, 1931. 97–222.

Hoberg, Annegret, and Isabelle Jansen. *Franz Marc: The Complete Works*. London: Philip Wilson, 2004. 2 vols.

Hoffman, Hilmar. *Ohne Auftrag: zur Geschichte des Kunsthandels*. Ed. Rupert Walser and Bernhard Wittenbrink. Munich: Walser und Wittenbrink, 1989.

Hölderlin, Friedrich. *Sämtliche Werke*. Leipzig: Insel-Verlag, [?1926].

Holloway, Joseph. *Joseph Holloway's Irish Theatre*. Ed. Robert Hogan and Michael J. O'Neill. Dixon, CA: Proscenium Press, 1968–1970. 3 vols.

Holloway, Mark. *Norman Douglas: A Biography*. London: Secker and Warburg, 1976.

Homer. *L'Odyssée*. Tr. Victor Bérard. Paris: Société d'édition "Les Belles lettres," 1924.

Hone, Joseph Maunsel. *The Life of Henry Tonks*. London: William Heinemann, 1939.

Horace. *Oeuvres complètes d'Horace*. . . French tr. Jean-Baptiste Monfalcon, Spanish tr. Javier de Burgos, Italian tr. Tommaso Gargallo, English tr. Philip Francis, German tr. Christoph Martin Wieland and Johann Henrich Voss. Polyglotte edn. [Latin text with translations into French, Spanish, Italian, English, and German]. Paris and Lyon: Cormon et Blanc, 1834.

Hoult, Norah. "New Fiction." Rev. of *The Fires of Beltane*, by Geraldine Cummins. *Dublin Magazine* 11.4 (October–December 1936) 94–96.

Houvet, Etienne. *An Illustrated Monograph of Chartres Cathedral*. Chartres Cathedral: E. Houvet, 1938.

Howard, Michael. *Jonathan Cape, Publisher: Herbert Jonathan Cape, G. Wren Howard*. London: Jonathan Cape, 1971.

Howe, Susan. *The Midnight*. New York: New Directions Books, 2003.

Hugnet, Georges, ed. *Petite anthologie poétique du surréalisme*. Paris: Editions Jeanne Bucher, 1934.

Hulle, Dirk van. "Samuel Beckett's *Faust* Notes." *Notes Diverse Holo*. Special issue, *Samuel Beckett Today/Aujourd'hui* 16 (2006) 283–297.

Hüneke, Andreas. *Die faschistische Aktion "Entartete Kunst" 1937 in Halle*. Schriftenreihe zur Geschichte der Staatlichen Galerie Moritzburg Halle. Halle: Staatliche Galerie Moritzburg, 1987.

Hutchins, Patricia. *James Joyce's World*. London: Methuen and Co., 1957.

Huxley, Aldous. *Eyeless in Gaza*. London: Chatto and Windus, 1936.

    Point Counter Point. Garden City, NJ: Doubleday, Doran and Co., 1928.

Index général de la revue "Cahiers d'art," 1926–1960. Paris: Editions Cahiers d'art, 1981.

"The International Surrealist Exhibition." *International Surrealist Bulletin* 4 (September 1936) 1–18.

Jacob, Sabine, and Susanne König-Lein. *Herzog Anton Ulrich-Museum Braunschweig: Die italienischen Gemälde des 16. bis 18. Jahrhunderts*. Munich: Hirmer, 2004.

Jaffé, Aniela. *From the Life and Work of C. G. Jung*. Tr. R. F. C. Hull and Murray Stein. Einsiedeln, Switzerland: Daimon Verlag, 1989.

Jarrell, Mackie L. "'Jack and the Dane': Swift Traditions in Ireland." *Journal of American Folklore* 77.304 (April–June 1964) 99–117.

Jeannin, Pierre. *Deux siècles à Normale Sup: Petite histoire d'une Grande Ecole*. Paris: Larousse, 1994.

Jennings, Humphrey. "The Iron Horse." *London Bulletin* 3 (June 1938) 22, 27–28.

Johnson, Samuel. *Diaries, Prayers, and Annals.* Ed. E. L. McAdam, Jr., with
Donald Hyde and Mary Hyde. Vol. I. The Yale Edition of the Works
of Samuel Johnson. New Haven: Yale University Press 1958. 18 vols.
1958– .

Letters of Samuel Johnson LL.D. Col. and ed. George Birkbeck Hill. New York:
Harper and Brothers, 1892. 2 vols.

Jolas, Eugene. *Man from Babel.* Ed. Andreas Kramer and Rainer Rumod. Henry
McBride Series in Modernism and Modernity. New Haven: Yale
University Press, 1998.

Jorre, John de St. *Venus Bound: The Erotic Voyage of the Olympia Press and Its
Writers.* New York: Random House, 1994.

Joyce, James. "Anna Livia Plurabella." Tr. James Joyce, Ettore Settanni, [and
Nino Frank]. *Prospettive* [Rome] 4.2 (15 February 1940) 13–15.

Anna Livia Plurabelle. New York: Crosby Gaige, 1928.

"Anna Livie Plurabelle." Tr. Samuel Beckett, Alfred Perron [*for* Péron], Ivan
Goll, Eugène [*for* Eugene] Jolas, Paul L. Léon, Adrienne Monnier, and
Philippe Soupault in collaboration with the author. *La Nouvelle Revue
Française* 36.212 (1 May 1931) 637–646.

The Critical Writings of James Joyce. Ed. Ellsworth Mason and Richard
Ellmann. Ithaca, NY: Cornell University Press, 1959.

Finnegans Wake. New York: Viking Press, 1959.

Haveth Childers Everywhere: Fragment from Work in Progress. Criterion
Miscellany. London: Faber and Faber, 1931.

"James Joyce." *Mercure de France* 326 (January 1956) Special issue: *Le
Souvenir d'Adrienne Monnier,* 122–124.

Letters of James Joyce, Vol. I. Ed. Stuart Gilbert. New York: Viking Press,
1957.

Letters of James Joyce, Vols. II and III. Ed. Richard Ellmann. New York: Viking
Press, 1966.

A Portrait of the Artist as a Young Man. Ed. Chester G. Anderson. New York:
Viking Press, 1964.

Ulysses. Paris: Shakespeare and Company, 1922.

"Ulysses: Episode III." *The Little Review* 5.1 (May 1918) 31–45.

"Una Lettera di Joyce." *Prospettive* [Rome] 4.4 (15 April 1940) 11.

Joyce, James, and Paul Léon. *The James Joyce – Paul Léon Papers in the National
Library of Ireland: A Catalogue.* Comp. Catherine Fahy. Dublin: National
Library of Ireland, 1992.

Jung, C. G. *Analytical Psychology: Its Theory and Practice, The Tavistock Lectures.*
London: Routledge and Kegan Paul, 1968.

C. G. Jung: Letters. Ed. Gerhard Adler and Aniela Jaffé. Tr. R. F. C. Hull.
Princeton: Princeton University Press, 1973–1975. 2 vols.

Junge, Heinrike. "Vom Neuen begeistert – Die Sammlerin Ida Bienert." *Avantgarde und Publikum: zur Rezeption avantgardistischer Kunst in Deutschland 1905–1933*. Ed. Heinrike Junge. Cologne: Böhlau, 1992. 29–37.

Kahsnitz, Rainer, ed. *Veit Stoss in Nürnberg: Werke des Meisters und seiner Schule in Nürnberg und Umgebung*. Munich: Deutscher Kunstverlag, 1983.

Kant, Immanuel. *Immanuel Kants Werke*. Ed. Ernst Cassirer, Hermann Cohen, Arthur Buchenau, *et al.* Berlin: Bruno Cassirer, 1921–1923. 11 vols.

Kritik der Reinen Vernunft. Ed. Albert Görland. Vol. III of *Immanuel Kants Werke*. Berlin: Bruno Cassirer, 1922.

Karmitz, Marin. *Comédie*. Paris: Les Editions du Regard, 2001.

Keats, John. *The Poems of John Keats*. Ed. Jack Stillinger. Cambridge, MA: Belknap-Harvard University Press, 1978.

Kennedy, S. B. "An Incisive Aesthetic." *Irish Arts Review* 21.2 (Summer 2004) 90–95.

Kenner, Hugh. *The Pound Era*. Berkeley: University of California Press, 1971. Rpt. London: Pimlico, 1991.

Kershaw, Alister, and Frédéric-Jacques Temple, eds. *Richard Aldington: An Intimate Portrait*. Carbondale: Southern Illinois University Press, 1965.

Klinge, Margret. *David Teniers the Younger: Paintings – Drawings*. Antwerp: Koninklijk Museum Voor Schoene Kunsten, 11 May–1 September 1991. Ghent: Snoeck-Ducaju and Zoon, 1991.

Knowlson, James. "Beckett in Kassel: Erste Begegnungen mit dem deutschen Expressionismus." *Der unbekannte Beckett: Samuel Beckett und die deutsche Kultur*. Ed. Therese Fischer-Seidel and Marion Fries-Dieckmann. Tr. Marion Fries-Dieckmann. Frankfurt: Suhrkamp, 2005. 64–94.

Damned to Fame: The Life of Samuel Beckett. New York: Grove Press, 2004.

Knuttel, Gerard. *Adriaen Brouwer: The Master and His Work*. Tr. J. G. Talma-Schilthuis and Robert Wheaton. The Hague: L. J. C. Bancher, 1962.

Kreul, Andreas. *Oskar Kokoschka: Pariser Oper*. Kunsthalle Bremen 30 June – 30 August 1992. Berlin: Kulturstiftung der Länder and Kunstverein Bremen, 1992.

Labande, Léon-Honoré. *Les Primitifs français: Peintres et peintres-verriers de la Provence occidentale*. Marseille: Librairie Tacussel, 1932.

Laforgue, Jules. *Poems of Jules Laforgue*. Tr. Patricia Terry. Berkeley: University of California Press, 1958.

Poésies complètes. Ed. Pascal Pia. Paris: Gallimard, 1979. 2 vols.

Lake, Carlton, ed., with the assistance of Linda Eichhorn and Sally Leach. *No Symbols Where None Intended: A Catalogue of Books, Manuscripts, and Other Material Relating to Samuel Beckett in the Collections of the Humanities Research Center*. Austin: Humanities Research Center, The University of Texas at Austin, 1984.

Bibliography of works cited

Laughlin, James, ed. *New Directions in Prose and Poetry*. [4]. Norfolk, CT: New Directions, 1939.

Laurence, Dan H. *Bernard Shaw: A Bibliography*. Oxford: Clarendon Press, 1983. 2 vols.

Lavachery, Henri. "Essay on Styles in the Statuary of the Congo." Tr. Samuel Beckett. *Negro, Anthology Made by Nancy Cunard, 1931–1933*. Ed. Nancy Cunard. London: Published by Nancy Cunard at Wishart and Co., 1934. 687–693.

Laveissière, Sylvain. *Le Classicisme français: Masterpieces of Seventeenth Century Painting, a loan exhibition from the Louvre and French regional museums at the National Gallery of Ireland, 30 April – 9 June 1985*. Tr. Kim-Mai Mooney and Raymond Keaveney. Dublin: The Gallery, 1985.

Lawrence, D. H. *Apocalypse*. Ed. Richard Aldington. Florence: G. Orioli, 1931. Rpt. New York: Viking Press, 1931; London: Secker, 1932.

Le Roux, Benoît. *André Thérive et ses amis en 14–18*. Saint-Brieuc: B. Le Roux, 1987.

Lehmann, John. *Autobiography*. London: Longmans, Green and Co., 1955. 3 vols.

Leistner, Gerhard, and Thorsten Rodiek. *Otto Freundlich: Ein Wegbereiter der abstrakten Kunst*. Regensburg: Museum Ostdeutsche Galerie, 1994.

Leventhal, A. J. "Surrealism or Literary Psycho-Therapy." *Dublin Magazine* 11.4 (October–December 1936) 66–73.

Leventhal, A. J., ed. "Extracts from the Unpublished Memoirs of the Late T. B. Rudmose-Brown." *Dublin Magazine* 31.1 (January–March 1956) 30–51.

Levey, Michael. "The Real Theme of Watteau's *Embarkation for Cythera*." *Burlington Magazine* 103.698 (May 1961) 180–185.

Levin, Harry. "On First Looking into *Finnegans Wake*." *New Directions in Prose and Poetry*. [4]. Ed. James Laughlin. Norfolk, CT: New Directions, 1939. 253–287.

Lewis, Wyndham. *The Apes of God*. London: Arthur Press, 1930. Rpt. Santa Barbara, CA: Black Sparrow Press, 1981.

Leyda, Jay, ed. *Eisenstein 2: A Premature Celebration of Eisenstein's Centenary*. Tr. Alan Y. Upchurch, N. Lary, Zina Voynow, and Samuel Brody. Calcutta: Seagull Books, 1985. Rpt. London: Methuen, 1988.

Lidderdale, Jane, and Mary Nicholson. *Dear Miss Weaver: Harriet Shaw Weaver 1876–1961*. London: Faber and Faber, 1970.

Little, Roger. "Beckett's Mentor, Rudmose-Brown: Sketch for a Portrait." *Irish University Review* 14 (Spring 1984) 34–41.

Lucke, Mechthild, Erich Heckel, and Andreas Hüneke. *Erich Heckel, Lebensstufen: die Wandbilder im Angermuseum zu Erfurt*. Dresden: Verlag der Kunst, 1992.

MacCarthy, Desmond. *Memories*. Foreword Cyril Connolly. London: MacGibbon and Kee, 1953.

McDowell, R. B., and D. A. Webb. *Trinity College Dublin, 1592–1952: An Academic History*. Cambridge: Cambridge University Press, 1982.

McGreevy, Thomas. "New Dublin Poetry." Rev. of *Intercessions*, by Denis Devlin. *Ireland To-Day* 2.10 (October 1937) 81–82.

Richard Aldington: An Englishman. The Dolphin Books. London: Chatto and Windus, 1931.

"Shows in Short." *The Studio* 115.541 (April 1938) 223.

"Spanish Masterpieces: A Selection Based on the Exhibition of Paintings from the Prado at Geneva." *The Studio* 18 (September 1939) 90–107.

Thomas Stearns Eliot: A Study. The Dolphin Books. London: Chatto and Windus, 1931.

[McGreevy, Thomas] L. St. Senan, pseud. "Nocturne of the Self-Evident Presence." *The Irish Statesman* 7.3 (25 September 1926) 57. Rpt. in *Collected Poems of Thomas MacGreevy: An Annotated Edition*. Ed. Susan Schreibman. Dublin: Anna Livia Press; Washington, DC: The Catholic University of America Press, 1991. 42–43.

MacGreevy, Thomas. *Collected Poems of Thomas MacGreevy: An Annotated Edition*. Ed. Susan Schreibman. Dublin: Anna Livia Press; Washington, DC: The Catholic University of America Press, 1991.

Jack B. Yeats: An Appreciation and an Interpretation. Dublin: Victor Waddington Publications, 1945.

Nicolas Poussin. Dublin: The Dolmen Press, 1960.

Pictures in the Irish National Gallery. London: B. T. Batsford, 1945.

Machiavelli, Niccolò. *The Literary Works of Machiavelli*. J. R. Hale. London: Oxford University Press, 1961.

Tutte le opere di Niccolò Machiavelli. Ed. Francesco Flora and Carlo Cordiè. I Classici Mondadori. Milan: A. Mondadori; 1949–1950. 2 vols.

McHugh, Roland. *Annotations to Finnegans Wake*. Rev. edn. Baltimore: Johns Hopkins University Press, 1991.

MacLaren, Neil. *The Dutch School, 1600–1900*. Rev. Christopher Brown. London: National Gallery, 1991. 2 vols.

McMillan, Dougald, and Martha Fehsenfeld. *Beckett in the Theatre: The Author as Practical Playwright and Director, From "Waiting for Godot" to "Krapp's Last Tape."* London: John Calder; New York: Riverrun Press, 1988.

MacThomáis, Éamonn. *Me Jewel and Darlin' Dublin*. Dublin: O'Brien Press, 1974.

Maddox, Brenda. *Nora: The Real Life of Molly Bloom*. Boston: Houghton Mifflin Co., 1988.

Maîtres et élèves, célébrités et savants: l'Ecole Normale Supérieure, 1794–1994. Paris: Archives Nationales, 1994.

Mallarmé, Stéphane. *New and Collected Poems*. Tr. Roger Fry, with commentaries by Charles Mauron. The New Classics Series. New York: New Directions Books, 1951.
Oeuvres complètes. Ed. Bertrand Marchal. Bibliothèque de la Pléiade. Paris: Gallimard, 1998. 2 vols.

Malraux, André. *Man's Fate*. Tr. Haakon M. Chevalier. New York: Random House, 1961.
Romans. Bibliothèque de la Pléiade. Paris: Gallimard, 1947.

Manteuffel, Kurt Zoege von. *Adriaen Brouwer: acht farbige Wiedergaben seiner Werke*. Künstlermappen. Leipzig: E. A. Seeman, 1936.

Marani, Pietro C. *Il genio e le passioni, Leonardo da Vinci e il Cenacolo: precedenti, innovazioni, riflessi di un capolavoro*. Milan: Skira, 2001.

Martial. *Epigrams*. Tr. Walter C. A. Ker. Cambridge, MA: Harvard University Press; London: Heinemann, 1968. 2 vols.

Martin, Claude. *Gide*. Paris: Editions du Seuil, 1963 and 1995.

Martin, Gregory. *The Flemish School, circa 1600–circa 1900*. London: National Gallery, 1970.

Mason, Rainer Michael, ed. *Bram van Velde, 1895–1981: Rétrospective du Centenaire*. Geneva: Musée Rath (Musée d'Art et d'Histoire), 1996.

Massine, Léonide. *My Life in Ballet*. Ed. Phyllis Hartnoll and Robert Rubens. London: Macmillan St. Martin's Press, 1968.

Mather, Frank Jewett, Jr. *The Portraits of Dante: Compared with the Measurements of his Skull and Reclassified*. Princeton: Princeton University Press, 1921.

Mayes, Elizabeth, and Paula Murphy, eds. *Images and Insights*. Dublin: Hugh Lane Municipal Gallery of Modern Art, 1993.

Menz, Henner. *The Dresden Gallery*. New York: Harry N. Abrams, 1962.

Mercanton, Jacques. "Finnegans Wake." *La Nouvelle Revue Française* 52.308 (May 1939) 858–864.

"A Meteorologist's Tour from Walton to London." *Gentleman's Magazine and Historical* 63.1 (July 1793) 619–621. Continued 63.2 (August 1793) 720–721.

Mitchell, B. R. *International Historical Statistics: Europe 1750–1988*. 3rd edn. New York: Stockton Press, 1992.

Möhle, Hans. "Eine bisher unbekannte Landschaftsgouache von Adam Elsheimer." *Zeitschrift des Deutschen Vereins für Kunstwissenschaft* 19.34 (1965) 192–196.

Monnier, Adrienne. *The Very Rich Hours of Adrienne Monnier*. New York: Scribner, 1976.

Montagu, Ivor. "Romance and Reality." Rev. of *Man of Aran*, dir. Robert Flaherty. *New Statesman and Nation* (28 April 1934) 638.

Montale, Eugenio. "Delta." Tr. Samuel Beckett. *This Quarter* 2.4
(April–May–June 1930) 630.
Moore, Maurice George. *An Irish Gentleman, George Henry Moore: His Travel,
His Racing, His Politics.* London: T. W. Laurie, 1913.
Mrusek, Hans-Joachim. *Drei sächsische Kathedralen: Merseburg, Naumburg,
Meissen.* Dresden: Verlag der Kunst, 1976.
Mühling, Matthias. *Mit Samuel Beckett in der Hamburger Kunsthalle.* Hamburg:
Hamburger Kunsthalle, 2003.
Muir, Edwin. "New Novels." Rev. of *Murphy*, by Samuel Beckett. *The Listener*
19.479 (16 March 1938) 597.
  "New Short Stories." Rev. of *More Pricks than Kicks*, by Samuel Beckett. *The
Listener* 12.268 (4 July 1934) 42.
Muirhead, Findlay. *London and its Environs.* The Blue Guides. 2nd edn. London:
Macmillan, 1922.
  ed. *Short Guide to London.* London: Ernest Benn, 1933.
Murray, Peter, and Linda Murray, eds. *Penguin Dictionary of Art and Artists.*
London: Penguin, 1993.
Musée de Valence. *André Lhote, 1885–1962.* Paris: Réunion des musées
nationaux, 2003.
Nadeau, Maurice. *Grâces leur soient rendues.* Paris: Albin Michel, 1990.
National Gallery Illustrations: Continental Schools (excluding Italian). London:
Printed for the Trustees, 1937.
National Gallery of Ireland: Catalogue of Pictures of the Italian Schools. Dublin:
The Stationery Office, [1956].
National Gallery of Ireland: Catalogue of Oil Pictures in the General Collection.
Dublin: The Stationery Office, 1932.
National Gallery of Ireland: Illustrated Summary Catalogue of Paintings. Intro.
Homan Potterton. Dublin: Gill and Macmillan, 1981.
Nerdinger, Winfried. *Gottfried von Neureuther, Architekt der Neorenaissance in
Bayern, 1811–1887.* Munich: K. M. Lipp, 1978.
Nersoyan, H[agop] J. *André Gide: The Theism of an Atheist.* Syracuse: Syracuse
University Press, 1969.
Neuhaus, Robert. *Bildnismalerei des Leibl-Kreises: Untersuchungen zur Geschichte
und Technik der Malerei der zweiten Hälfte des 19. Jahrhunderts.* Marburg:
Verlag des Kunstgeschichtlichen Seminars, 1953.
  Unsuspected Genius: The Art and Life of Frank Duveneck. San Francisco: Bedford,
1987.
Nixon, Mark. "Chronik der Deutschlandreise Samuel Becketts 1936/37."
Der unbekannte Beckett: Samuel Beckett und die deutsche Kultur. Ed. Therese
Fischer-Seidel and Marion Fries-Dieckmann. Frankfurt: Suhrkamp,
2005. 34–63.

"'Scraps of German': Samuel Beckett reading German Literature." *Notes Diverse Holo*. Special issue, *Samuel Beckett Today/Aujourd'hui* 16 (2006) 259–282.

Norburn, Roger. *A James Joyce Chronology*. New York: Palgrave Macmillan, 2004.

Nordau, Max Simon. *Degeneration*. London: William Heinemann, 1895.

Nostradamus. *The Complete Prophecies of Nostradamus*. Ed. and tr. Henry C. Roberts. New York: Crown, 1947.

Nowell, Elizabeth. *Thomas Wolfe: A Biography*. Garden City, NY: Doubleday and Co., 1960.

O'Brien, Eoin. *The Beckett Country: Samuel Beckett's Ireland*. Photography, David H. Davison. Foreword, James Knowlson. Illustrations, Robert Ballagh. Dublin: The Black Cat Press in association with Faber and Faber, 1986.

O'Brien, Kate. "Fiction." *The Spectator* (25 March 1938) 546.

O'Connor, Ulick. *Oliver St. John Gogarty: A Poet and His Times*. London: Jonathan Cape, 1964.

O'Dwyer, Frederick. *Lost Dublin*. Dublin: Gill and Macmillan, 1981.

O'Dwyer, Patrick. "Letters from Paris." *The Great Tuam Annual* (1991) 73, 75.

O'Faolain, Sean. "Fiction." Rev. of *Fires of Beltane*, by Geraldine Cummins. *Ireland To-Day* 1.2 (July 1936) 70–72.

O'H., P. S. Rev. of *A History of Ireland*, by Edmund Curtis. *Dublin Magazine* 11.3 (July–September 1936) 60–62.

O'Sullivan, Vincent. *Fifteen Letters to Seumas O'Sullivan*. Edinburgh: Tragara Press, 1979.

  Selected Letters. Ed. Alan Anderson. Loanhead, Scotland: Tragara Press, 1993.

Oppenheim, Lois. "A Preoccupation with Object-Representation: the Beckett-Bion Case Revisited." *International Journal of Psycho-Analysis* 82.4 (2001) 767–784.

Oppenheim, Max Freiherr von. *Die Bildwerke*. Ed. Dietrich Opitz and Anton Moortgat. Berlin: Walter de Gruyter and Co., 1955. Vol. III of *Tell Halaf*. 4 vols. 1943–1962.

Oram, Hugh. *The Newspaper Book: A History of Newspapers in Ireland, 1649–1983*. Dublin: MO Books, 1983.

Ostwald, Peter. *Vaslav Nijinsky: A Leap into Madness*. New York: Carol Publishing Group, 1991.

Osuna, Rafael. *Pablo Neruda y Nancy Cunard: les poètes du monde défendent le peuple espagnol*. Madrid: Editorial Orígenes, 1987.

Overbeck, Lois More, and Martha Dow Fehsenfeld. "In Defense of the Integral Text." *Notes Diverse Holo*. Special issue, *Samuel Beckett Today/ Aujourd'hui* 16 (2006) 347–372.

Pakenham, Thomas, and Valerie Pakenham, eds. *Dublin: A Travellers' Companion*. New York: Atheneum, 1988.

Paret, Peter. *An Artist Against the Third Reich: Ernst Barlach, 1933-1938*.
Cambridge: Cambridge University Press, 2003.

Paris, Gaston. *Penseurs et Poètes*. Ed. Calmann Lévy. Paris: Ancienne Maison,
Michel Lévy Frères, 1896.

Pelorson, Georges. "Caligula – Acte III." *Volontés* 3 (March 1938) 41-59.

"Caligula – Acte IV." *Volontés* 8 (August 1938) 30-35.

"Caligula – Prologue." *Volontés* 1 (January 1938) 18-27.

"Plans." *transition* 21 (March 1932) 182-183.

Péret, Benjamin. "Black and White in Brazil." Tr. Samuel Beckett. *Negro,
Anthology Made by Nancy Cunard, 1931-1933*. Ed. Nancy Cunard. London:
Published by Nancy Cunard at Wishart and Co., 1934. 510-514.

Pilling, John. *Beckett Before Godot*. Cambridge: Cambridge University Press, 1997.

A Companion to "Dream of Fair to Middling Women." Tallahassee, FL: Journal of
Beckett Studies Books, 2004.

"'For Interpolation': Beckett and English Literature." *Notes Diverse Holo*.
Special issue, *Samuel Beckett Today/Aujourd'hui* 16 (2006) 203-235.

A Samuel Beckett Chronology. Houndsmill, Basingstoke, Hampshire: Palgrave
Macmillan, 2006.

Pilling, John, ed. *Beckett's Dream Notebook*. Reading: Beckett International
Foundation, 1999.

Pine, Richard, and Charles Acton, eds. *To Talent Alone: The Royal Irish Academy
of Music, 1848-1998*. Dublin: Gill and Macmillan, 1998.

Poe, Edgar Allan. *Tales of Mystery and Imagination*. London: G. G. Harrap, 1919.

Posse, Hans. "Die Rekonstruktion der Venus mit dem Cupido von
Giorgione." *Jahrbuch der Preussischen Kunstsammlungen*. Vol. LII. Berlin:
G. Grote, 1931. 29-35.

Pourtalès, Guy de. *Chopin; ou, le Poète*. Paris: Gallimard, 1926.

Frederick Chopin: A Man of Solitude. Tr. Charles Bayly Jr. London:
T. Butterworth, 1927.

Powys, Llewelyn. "Dr. Johnson – Idler, Rambler and Straggler." *Dublin
Magazine* 12.2 (April-June 1937) 9-15.

Prévost, Jean. "Les oeuvres d'André Gide (Tomes I, II, et III)." *Notre Temps* (6
April 1933) 121.

Proust, Marcel. *In Search of Lost Time*. Tr. C. K. Scott Moncrieff and Terence
Kilmartin (Vols. I-V); Andreas Mayor and Terence Kilmartin (Vol. VI).
Rev. D. J. Enright. New York: Modern Library, 1992-1993. 6 vols.

A la recherche du temps perdu. Ed. Jean-Yves Tadié. Bibliothèque de la Pléiade.
Paris: Gallimard, 1987-1989. 4 vols.

A la recherche du temps perdu. Editions de la Nouvelle Revue Française. Vol.
VI rev. Robert Proust and Jacques Rivière. Paris: Librairie Gallimard,
1925-1933. 8 vols.

Pudovkin, Vsevolod. *Film Acting: A Course of Lectures delivered at the State Institute of Cinematography, Moscow.* Tr. Ivor Montagu. London: G. Newnes, 1935.

On Film Technique. Tr. Ivor Montagu. London: V. Gollancz, 1929.

Putnam, Samuel, Maida Castelhun Darnton, George Reavey, and J[acob] Bronowski, eds. *The European Caravan: An Anthology of the New Spirit in European Literature.* New York: Brewer, Warren, and Putnam, 1931.

Pyle, Hilary. *Jack B. Yeats: A Biography.* London: Routledge and Kegan Paul, 1970.

Jack B. Yeats: A Catalogue Raisonné of the Oil Paintings. London: Andre Deutsch, 1992. 3 vols.

Jack B. Yeats: His Watercolours, Drawings and Pastels. Dublin: Irish Academic Press, 1993.

Quadflieg, Roswitha. *Beckett was here: Hamburg im Tagebuch Samuel Becketts von 1936.* Hamburg: Hoffman und Campe, 2006.

Rabéarivelo, Jean-Jacques. "A Short Historical Survey of Madagascar." Tr. Samuel Beckett. *Negro, Anthology Made by Nancy Cunard, 1931–1933.* Ed. Nancy Cunard. London: Published by Nancy Cunard at Wishart and Co., 1934. 618–622.

Racine, Jean. *Andromaque.* Ed. T. B. Rudmose-Brown. Oxford: Clarendon Press, 1917.

Bajazet. Paris: Editions du Seuil, 1947.

Complete Plays. Tr. Samuel Solomon. New York: Modern Library, 1969. 2 vols.

Radcliffe, Philip. *Beethoven's String Quartets.* 2nd edn. Cambridge: Cambridge University Press, 1978.

Read, Herbert. *Art Now: An Introduction to the Theory of Modern Painting and Sculpture.* New York: Harcourt, Brace and Co., 1933.

[Read, Herbert]. *Exhibition of Twentieth Century German Art: July, 1938.* London: New Burlington Galleries, 1938.

Reavey, George. *Faust's Metamorphoses: Poems.* Fontenay-Aux-Roses, Seine, France: The New Review Editions, 1932.

"Geer van Velde." *London Bulletin* 2 (May 1938) 16.

"Letter to Richard Thoma." *The New Review* 1.4 (Winter 1931–1932) 397.

Nostradam: A Sequence of Poems. Europa Poets 1. Paris: Europa Press, 1935.

Quixotic Perquisitions: First Series. London: Europa Press, 1939.

Signes d'adieu (Frailty of Love). Tr. Pierre Charnay. Paris: Editions Europa, 1935.

Reavey, George, and Marc Slonim, eds. *Anthologie de la littérature soviétique, 1918–1934.* Paris: Gallimard, 1935.

eds. and tr. *Soviet Literature: An Anthology.* London: Wishart and Co., 1933.

Reich, Wolfgang. "Die Chaconne g-Moll – von Vitali?" *Beiträge zur Musikwissenschaft* 2 (1965) 149–152.

Reid, Thomas. *The Works of Thomas Reid*. Edinburgh: Bell and Bradfute, 1803.

Renard, Jules. *Le Journal, 1887–1910*. Paris: F. Bernouard, 1927. 4 vols.

Oeuvres. Ed. Léon Guichard. Bibliothèque de la Pléiade. Paris: Gallimard, 1970–1971. 2 vols.

Rimbaud, Arthur. *Complete Works*. Tr. Paul Schmidt. New York: Harper and Row, 1975.

Oeuvres complètes. Ed. Antoine Adam. Bibliothèque de la Pléiade. Paris: Gallimard, 1972.

Ringelnatz, Joachim. "Ein männlicher Briefmark erlebt." *Die Schnupftabaksdose: Stumpfsinn in Versen und Bildern*. Ed. Hans Bötticher and Richard J. M. Seewald. Munich: R. Piper, 1912.

Rivoallan, Anatole, ed. *Littérature irlandaise contemporaine*. Paris: Hachette, 1939.

Roethel, Hans K., and Jean K. Benjamin. *Kandinsky, Catalogue Raisonné of the Oil Paintings*. Ithaca, NY: Cornell University Press, 1982–1984. 2 vols.

Rogers, Pat. *Henry Fielding: A Biography*. London: Paul Elk, 1979.

Romains, Jules. "Aristide Maillol." *Formes* 4 (April 1930) [2], 5–7.

Ronsard, Pierre de. *Oeuvres complètes*. Ed. Jean Céard, Daniel Ménager, and Michel Simonin. Bibliothèque de la Pléiade. Paris: Gallimard, 1993. 2 vols.

Roose, Julia. "Backlash against Prostitutes' Rights: Origins and Dynamics of Nazi Prostitution Policy." *Journal of the History of Sexuality* 11.1–2 (2002) 67–94.

Rosati, Salvatore. "Il nuovo libro di James Joyce." *Panorama* [Rome] 18 (12 November 1939) 246–247.

Rose, Danis. *The Textual Diaries of James Joyce*. Dublin: Lilliput Press, 1995.

Rossi, M[ario] M. *Viaggio in Irlanda*. Milan: Doxa Editrice, 1932.

Pilgrimage in the West. Tr. J. M. Hone. Dublin: Cuala Press, 1933.

Roughton, Roger. "Eyewash, Do You?" *Contemporary Poetry and Prose* 7 (November 1936) 137–138.

Rousseau, Jean-Jacques. *Confessions*. Tr. Angela Scholar. Oxford: Oxford University Press, 2000.

Oeuvres complètes. Ed. Bernard Gagnebin and Marcel Raymond. Bibliothèque de la Pléiade. Paris: Gallimard, 1959. 5 vols.

Rubin, William S. *Dada, Surrealism, and their Heritage*. New York: Museum of Modern Art, 1968.

Rudmose-Brown, Thomas. "Extracts from the Unpublished Memoirs of the Late T. B. Rudmose-Brown." Ed. A. J. Leventhal. *Dublin Magazine* 31.1 (January–March 1956) 30–51.

"Grace Withheld from Jean Racine." *The European Caravan: An Anthology of the New Spirit in European Literature*. Ed. Samuel Putnam, Maida Castelhun Darnton, George Reavey, *et al*. New York: Brewer, Warren, and Putnam, 1931. 558–564.

Rev. of "Beitrage zur De Tabley Forschung," by Erna Low. *Dublin Magazine* 12.2 (April–June 1937) 72–74.

Rutter, Frank. "Manet's 'Bar aux Folies-Bergère.'" *Apollo* 19.113 (May 1934) 244–247.

Ryan, John. *Remembering How We Stood: Bohemian Dublin at the Mid-Century*. Dublin: Gill and Macmillan, 1975.

Rynne, Stephen. "Tea with Jack B. Yeats 1940." *Éire-Ireland* 7.2 (1972) 106.

Saddlemyer, Ann. *Becoming George: The Life of Mrs. W. B. Yeats*. Oxford: Oxford University Press, 2002.

Sade, Marquis de. *Oeuvres complètes du Marquis de Sade*. Ed. Annie Le Brun and Jean-Jacques Pauvert. Paris: Pauvert, 1986–1991. 15 vols.

Salkeld, Blanaid. Rev. of *Out of the Picture*, by Louis MacNeice. *Dublin Magazine* 12.4 (October–December 1937) 67–68.

Sarton, May. *A World of Light: Portraits and Celebrations*. New York: W. W. Norton, 1976.

Scheja, Georg. *The Isenheim Altarpiece*. Tr. Robert Erich Wolf. New York: H. N. Abrams, 1969.

Schönzeler, Hans-Hubert. *Furtwängler*. London: Gerald Duckworth, 1990.

Schopenhauer, Arthur. *Essays and Aphorisms*. Ed. and tr. R. J. Hollingdale. London: Penguin, 1970.

On Human Nature: Essays (partly Posthumous) in Ethics and Politics. Selected and tr. Thomas Bailey Saunders. London: George Allen and Unwin, 1897. Rpt. 1926.

Parerga et Paralipomena. Tr. J.-A. Cantacuzène. Paris: Félix Alcan, 1914.

Parerga and Paralipomena: Short Philosophical Essays. Tr. E. F. J. Payne. Oxford: Clarendon Press, 1974. 2 vols.

The World as Will and Representation. Tr. E. F. J. Payne. Indian Hills, CO: The Falcon's Wing Press, 1958. 2 vols.

Schwob, Marcel. "L'Etoile de bois." *Cosmopolis* 8 (22 October 1897) 95–110. Rpt. in *L'Etoile de bois*. Paris: Editions du Boucher, 2003. 3–19.

"Scripted by Beckett." *Rolling Stock* 7 (1984) 4.

Shakespeare, William. *The Riverside Shakespeare: The Complete Works*. General and textual ed. G. Blakemore Evans, assisted by J. J. M. Tobin. 2nd edn. Boston: Houghton Mifflin, 1997.

Shaw, George Bernard. *The Complete Prefaces, Bernard Shaw*. Ed. Dan H. Laurence and Daniel J. Leary. London: The Penguin Press, 1993–1997. 3 vols.

Shloss, Carol Loeb. *Lucia Joyce: To Dance in the Wake*. New York: Farrar, Straus and Giroux, 2003.

Skeffington, F. J. C., and James Joyce. *Two Essays: A Forgotten Aspect of the University Question, and The Day of the Rabblement*. Dublin: Gerrard Brothers, 1901. "The Day of the Rabblement" rpt. in *The Critical Writings of James Joyce*. Ed. Ellsworth Mason and Richard Ellmann. Ithaca, NY: Cornell University Press, 1959.

Slide, Anthony. *The International Film Industry*. New York: Greenwood, 1989.

Slive, Seymour. *Jacob van Ruisdael: A Complete Catalogue of His Paintings, Drawings and Etchings*. New Haven: Yale University Press, 2001.

Smith, James M. "The Politics of Sexual Knowledge: The Origins of Ireland's Containment Culture and 'The Carrigan Report' (1931)." *Journal of the History of Sexuality* 13.2 (April 2004) 208–233.

Smith, James Robinson. *The Earliest Lives of Dante: Translated from the Italian of Giovanni Boccaccio and Leonardo Bruni Aretino*. Yale Studies in English. New York: Holt, 1901. Rpt. New York: Russell and Russell, 1968.

Solomons, Bethel. *One Doctor in His Time*. London: C. Johnson, 1956.

Sonntag, Dina. "Bibliographie Will Grohmann." *In Memoriam Will Grohmann, 1887–1968: Wegbereiter der Moderne*. Stuttgart: Staatsgalerie Stuttgart, 1987. 58–64.

Soupault, Philippe. "A propos de la traduction d'Anna Livia Plurabelle." *La Nouvelle Revue Française* 36.212 (1 May 1931) 633–636.

Souvenirs de James Joyce. Algiers: Editions Fontaine, 1943.

"Traduttore … Traditore?" *A James Joyce Yearbook*. Ed. Maria Jolas. Paris: Transition Press, 1949. 171–178.

Spinoza, Benedictus de. *Ethique, démontrée suivant l'ordre géométrique et divisée en cinq parties, Texte latin soigneusement revu*. Tr. Ch. Appuhn. Classiques Garnier. Paris: Garnier Frères, 1908. Rpt. 1934.

Staatliche Museen Berlin. *Die Gemäldegalerie*. Berlin: Paul Cassirer Verlag, 1929–1933. 5 vols.

Staay, Elizabeth van der. *Le Monologue intérieur dans l'oeuvre de Valéry Larbaud*. Paris: Champion-Slatkine, 1987.

Starkie, Walter. *Scholars and Gypsies: An Autobiography*. London: John Murray, 1963.

The Waveless Plain: An Italian Autobiography. New York: E. P. Dutton and Co., 1938.

Steinitz, Kate Trauman. "The Leonardo Drawings at Weimar." *Raccolta Vinciana* 20 (1964) 339–349.

Stendhal. *Le Rouge et le noir: Chronique du XIXe siècle*. Paris: Librairie Garnier Frères, 1925. Rpt. 1928.

Red and Black. Ed. and tr. Robert M. Adams. Norton Critical Editions. New York: W. W. Norton and Co., 1969.

Stephen, Leslie. *Samuel Johnson*. English Men of Letters. New York: Harper and Brothers, 1879.

Stephens, James. *Letters of James Stephens*. Ed. Richard J. Finneran. London: Macmillan, 1974.

Sterling, Charles. *La Peinture flamande: Rubens et son temps*. Paris: Librairie des Arts Décoratifs, 1936.

Stewart, Gerald Pakenham. *The Rough and the Smooth: An Autobiography*. Walkanae: Heritage, 1994.

Stocker, Mona. *Die Schottenkirche St. Jakob in Regensburg: Skulptur und stilistisches Umfeld*. Regensburger Studien und Quellen zur Kulturgeschichte. Regensburg: Universitätsverlag Regensburg, 2001.

Stoullig, Claire, and Nathalie Schoeller, eds. *Bram van Velde*. Paris: Musée National d'Art Moderne, Centre Georges Pompidou, 1989.

The Surrealist Group in Paris [André Breton, Roger Caillois, René Char, *et al.*]. "Murderous Humanitarianism." Tr. Samuel Beckett. *Negro, Anthology Made by Nancy Cunard, 1931–1933*. Ed. Nancy Cunard. London: Published by Nancy Cunard at Wishart and Co., 1934. 574–575.

Swedenborg, Emanuel. *Heaven and Its Wonders and Hell: Drawn from Things Heard and Seen*. Tr. George F. Dole. With notes by George F. Dole, Robert H. Kirven, and Jonathan Rose. The New Century Edition of the Works of Emanuel Swedenborg. Ed. Jonathan Rose. West Chester, PA: Swedenborg Foundation, 2000.

Synge, J. M. *Collected Works*. Ed. Robin Skelton. London: Oxford University Press, 1962. 4 vols.

Taylor, John. *A Letter to Samuel Johnson, LL.D. on the Subject of a Future State [With some letters of Dr. Johnson and possibly in part written by him]*. London: T. Cadell, 1787.

Tennyson, Alfred. *Tennyson: A Selected Edition, Incorporating the Trinity College Manuscripts*. Ed. Christopher Ricks. Berkeley: University of California Press, 1989.

Thom's Directory of Ireland for the Year 1936. Dublin: Alex. Thom and Co., 1936.

Thoma, Richard. "Island Without Serpents." Rev. of *Thomas Stearns Eliot: A Study*, by Thomas McGreevy. *The New Review* 1.3 (August–September–October 1931) 119–121.

Thomas à Kempis. *De imitatione Christi*. Ed. J. K. Ingram. Early English Text Society Extra Series. London: Kegan Paul, Trench, Turner and Co., 1893.

  De imitatione Christi libri quatuor: sacrae scripturae textuum adnotatione et variis rerum indicibus locupletata. New edn. Mechliniae, Belgium: H. Dessain, 1921.

The Imitation of Christ. Ed. Ernest Rhys. Everyman's Library. London: J. M. Dent; New York: E. P. Dutton, 1910.

Thomas, Donald. *Henry Fielding*. London: Weidenfeld and Nicolson, 1990.

Thomas, Dylan. "Recent Novels." Rev. of *Murphy*, by Samuel Beckett. *The New English Weekly* 12.23 (17 March 1938) 454–455.

Titus, Edward. "Editorially: By the Way of Introducing This Surrealist Number." *This Quarter* 5 (September 1932) 3–6.

Tophoven, Erika. *Becketts Berlin*. Berlin: Nicolai Verlag, 2005.

Ussher, Arland. "New Metaphysic and Old Spook." *The New English Weekly and the New Age* 15.5 (18 May 1939) 80–81.

"Three Essays." *Nineteenth Century and After* 124.742 (December 1938) 733–737.

"Works and Faith." *The New English Weekly and the New Age* 14.23 (16 March 1939) 346–347.

Vanoyeke, Violaine. *Paul Eluard: le poète de la liberté*. Paris: Editions Julliard, 1995.

Verlaine, Paul. *Oeuvres en prose complètes*. Ed. Jacques Borel. Bibliothèque de la Pléiade. Paris: Gallimard, 1972.

Villani, Giovanni, Filippo Villani, Giovanni Boccaccio, Leonardo Aretino, and Giannozzo Manetti. *Le vite di Dante*. Intro. and notes by G[iuseppe] L[ando] Passerini. Florence: G. C. Sansoni, 1917.

Vrancken, Charles, ed. *Exposition Picasso: 16 juin–30 juillet 1932*. Paris: Galeries Georges Petit, 1932.

Vulliamy, C[olwayn] E[dward]. *Mrs. Thrale of Streatham, Her Place in the Life of Dr. Samuel Johnson and in the Society of her Time, her Character and Family Affairs*. London: Heinemann, 1936.

W. J. K. M. "Reviews." Rev. of *Proust*, by Samuel Beckett. *T. C. D.: A College Miscellany* (28 May 1931) 177.

Waiboer, Adriaan. *Northern Nocturnes: Nightscapes in the Age of Rembrandt*. Dublin: National Gallery of Ireland, 2005.

Waugh, Evelyn. *The Diaries of Evelyn Waugh*. Ed. Michael Davie. London: Weidenfeld and Nicolson, 1976.

Weinreb, Ben, and Christopher Hibbert, eds. *The London Encyclopaedia*. London: Papermac, Macmillan, 1987.

Weir, Anthony. *Early Ireland: A Field Guide*. Belfast: Blackstaff Press, 1980.

Weld, Jacqueline Bograd. *Peggy: The Wayward Guggenheim*. New York: E. P. Dutton, 1988.

Wesch, Petra, with Rosemarie Heise-Schirdewan and Bärbel Stranka. *Sanssouci: The Summer Residence of Frederick the Great*. Munich: Prestel, 2003.

West, J. B. "T. H. Ravenhill and His Contributions to Mountain Sickness." *Journal of Applied Physiology* 80.3 (March 1996) 715–724.

White, James, ed. *National Gallery of Ireland: Catalogue of the Paintings*. Dublin: National Gallery of Ireland, 1971.

Wietek, Gerhard. "Rosa Schapire." *Jahrbuch der Hamburger Kunstsammlungen*, Vol. IX. Hamburg: Dr. Ernst Hauswedell and Co. Verlag, 1964. 114–160.

Wigoder, Geoffrey, ed. *The New Standard Jewish Encyclopedia*. 7th edn. New York: Facts on File, 1992.

Wilde, Oscar. *Lord Arthur Savile's Crime, The Canterville Ghost, Poems in Prose*. London: James R. Osgood, McIlvaine, 1891.

Woermann, K. *Catalogue of the Pictures in the Royal Gallery at Dresden*. 7th edn. Dresden: Kunstanstalt Wilhelm Hoffmann, 1908.

Wolfe, Thomas. *The Letters of Thomas Wolfe*. Ed. Elizabeth Nowell. New York: C. Scribner's Sons, 1961.

Wölfel, Kurt, ed. *Lessings Leben und Werk in Daten und Bildern*. Frankfurt: Insel Verlag, 1967.

Wollman, Maurice, ed. *Poems of Twenty Years: An Anthology, 1918–1938*. London: Macmillan and Co., 1938.

Woolf, Leonard. *Downhill All the Way: An Autobiography of the Years 1919–1939*. London: Hogarth Press, 1967.

Wright, Christopher. *Poussin Paintings: A Catalogue Raisonné*. London: Jupiter Books, 1984.

Yeats, Jack B. *The Amaranthers*. London: Heinemann, 1936.

Yeats, W. B. *The Collected Plays of W. B. Yeats*. 2nd edn. New York: Macmillan and Co., 1952.

"The Words Upon the Window Pane: A Commentary." *Dublin Magazine* 6.4 (October–December 1931) 5–19.

Yeats, W. B., ed. *The Oxford Book of Modern Verse: 1892–1935*. Oxford: Oxford University Press, 1936.

ELECTRONIC WORKS CITED

Berkelli, Carlo, Whitney Chadwick, Jessica Rawson, *et al. Grove Art Online*. 14 May 2007. www.groveart.com.

"Mainfränkisches Museum, Würzburg." 30 January 2006. www. mainfraenkischesmuseum.de.

"Peggy Guggenheim Collection." 12 April 2007. www.guggenheim-venice.it.

Quadflieg, Roswitha, Fritz-Renzo Heinze, and Clemens-Tobias Lange. "Beckett in Hamburg 1936." 11 November 2007. www.beckett-in-hamburg-1936.de/.

Robertson, Struan. "A History of the Jews in Hamburg: Three Jewish Women Hamburg Secessionists." 27 October 2006. www1.uni-hamburg.de/ rz3a035//secession.html.

Seemann, Ernest A. "Humorous Poems by Joachim Ringelnatz." 25 May 2006. www.beilharz.com/poetas/ringelnatz.

Thrale, David. "Anchor Brewery." 15 June 2006. www.thrale.com/history/ english/hester_and_henry/brewery/index.php.

"Victoria and Albert Museum." 12 April 2007. www.vam.ac.uk.

"The Victoria Palace: Shows." Victoria Palace Theatre. 24 July 2005. www. victoriapalacetheatre.co.uk.

Whelan, Willie. *Waterford County Museum*. 14 June 2006. www. waterfordcountymuseum.org.

INDEX OF RECIPIENTS

GENERAL INDEX

Persons and publications with Profiles are marked with an asterisk. The letters 'SB' refer to the entry for 'Beckett, Samuel Barclay'. Except in the case of SB, references to literary, artistic and musical works are listed under the name of the author, artist or composer.

Works (*for citations, see individual titles, in
original language*): "Alba," "Alba"
(originally a second "Alba": "give
us a wipe"; renamed "Enueg, 2"),
"Assumption," "Cascando"
(poem), "A Case in a Thousand,"
"Casket of Pralinen for the
Daughter of a Dissipated
Mandarin," "Ce n'est pas au
pélican," "Che Sciagura," "Le
Concentrisme," "Dante and the
Lobster," "Dante...Bruno. Vico..
Joyce," "Da Tagte Es," "Les Deux
Besoins," "Dieppe," "Ding-Dong,"
"Dortmunder," *Dream of Fair to
Middling Women* (stories in, "A
Wet Night," "The Smeraldina's
Billet Doux" "They Go Out for
the Evening"), "Echo's Bones"
(poem), "Echo's Bones" (story),
*Echo's Bones and Other Precipitates,
Eleutheria*, "Enueg 1," "Enueg 2"
(originally a second "Alba": "give
us a wipe"), "Enueg 2" (renamed
as "Serena 1"), "Fingal," "For
Future Reference," "From the
Only Poet to a Shining Whore: for
Henry Crowder to Sing," "Geer
van Velde," "Gnome," "Hell Crane
to Starling," "Home Olga,"
"Hommage à Jack B. Yeats,"
Human Wishes, "Les joues rouges,"
"Lightning Calculation," "Love
and lethe" ("Mort plus
précieuse"), "Malacoda" (initial
title "Undertaker's Man"), "Moly"
see "Yoke of Liberty"), *More Pricks
Than Kicks* (initial title *Draff*)
(stories in *Draff*, "Echo's Bones,"
"Fingal," "Love and Lethe," "The
Smeraldina's Billet Doux,"
"Walking Out," "A Wet Night,"
"What a Misfortune," "Yellow"),
Murphy, "Ooftish" (initial title
"Whiting"), "La Peinture des Van
Velde ou le Monde et le
Pantalon," "Petit Sot," "Poèmes
38-39" ("Ascension," "La
Mouche," "Prière"), "The
Possessed," "Premier Amour,"

Proust, "Recent Irish Poetry"
(pseud. Andrew Belis), "Return to
the Vestry," "Sanies 1" (initial
title "Weg du Einzige!"), "Sanies
2" (initial title "There was a
Happy Land"), "Sedendo et
Quiescendo," "Serena 1" "Serena
2," "Serena 3," "Sonnet" ("At last
I find . . ."), "Spring Song," "Text,"
"They come," [?] "True-born
Jackeen," Untitled ode on public
lavatory, "UPTHEREPUBLIC,"
"The Vulture," "Yoke of Liberty"
(initial title "Moly")
Beckett, Suzanne Georgette Anna
Deschevaux-Dumesnil,* 578, 658,
689–690, 708
attended premieres of SB's plays, 690
death of, 690
first mention of to McGreevy, 651, 657
leaves Paris with SB, 673, 682, 683,
684
marriage to SB, 690
wrote business letters on behalf
of SB, 690
Beckett, William Frank,* 84, 90, 92, 99,
111, 112, 118, 154, 158–159, 338,
504, 507, 689, 690–691, 699
death of, 147, 164–165, 168, 171, 338,
339, 347, 348
photo of, Plate, 1
Beckett and Medcalf, Quantity
Surveyors, 115, 120, 143, 165, 302,
324, 325, 330, 366, 368, 689, 691
Becky Sharp (film), 311–312, 314–315
Beecham, Thomas, Sir, 313, 316
Beethoven, Ludwig van, 68, 70, 172,
173, 179, 193, 194, 197,199–200,
248, 260, 263, 359, 428, 437,
468, 430, 436, 514, 518–519, 521,
660, 662
Beeton, Isabella Mary, 376, 378
Belis, Andrew (pseud. of SB, see "Recent
Irish Poetry")
Belloc, Hilaire, 509, 511
Bellotto, Bernardo (signed as Canaletto),
444, 448, 479, 482, 496, 499
Belmont, Georges *see* Pelorson Georges
Bérard, Armand-Max-Jean-Victor, 90–92,
572, 575, 697